The
INTERNATIONAL CRITICAL COMMENTARY
on the Holy Scriptures of the Old and New Testaments

J. A. EMERTON, F.B.A.

Fellow of St. John's College
Emeritus Regius Professor of Hebrew in the University of Cambridge
Honorary Canon of St George's Cathedral, Jerusalem

C. E. B. CRANFIELD, F.B.A.

Emeritus Professor of Theology in the University of Durham

AND

G. N. STANTON

Lady Margaret's
Professor of Divinity in the University of Cambridge

FORMERLY UNDER THE EDITORSHIP OF

S. R. DRIVER
A. PLUMMER
C. A. BRIGGS

THE ACTS OF THE APOSTLES

Volume II

A CRITICAL AND EXEGETICAL COMMENTARY

ON

THE ACTS OF THE APOSTLES

BY

C. K. BARRETT

Emeritus Professor of Divinity in Durham University

IN TWO VOLUMES

VOLUME II

Introduction and Commentary on Acts XV–XXVIII

T&T CLARK
EDINBURGH

T&T CLARK LTD
59 GEORGE STREET
EDINBURGH EH2 2LQ
SCOTLAND

Copyright © T&T Clark Ltd, 1998

First published 1998

ISBN 0 567 08542 2

British Library Cataloguing-in-Publication Data
A catalogue record for this book is available from the British Library

Typeset by Fakenham Photosetting Limited
Printed and bound in Great Britain by Bookcraft Ltd, Avon

PREFACE

I have little to add to the Preface that I wrote for Volume I of this commentary. What I wrote then, especially by way of thanks to a number of people who in various ways have helped me, is still true. Some things are perhaps better arranged in this volume than in the first; one learns from one's mistakes. This volume contains a more or less conventional 'Introduction'. It will, I think, be clear why I could not write it until I had cleared my mind on a number of questions that arise in Acts 15–28.

Since Volume I was completed, the 27th edition of Nestle-Aland's *Novum Testamentum Graece* has appeared. After some thought I have decided in favour of consistency, and have retained the text and apparatus of NA[26]. Some day, perhaps, the commentary may be revised and the sigla of the later edition used throughout.

C. K. BARRETT

CONTENTS OF VOLUME II

Preface   vii
Additions to Bibliographies and Abbreviations   xi
Map   xvi

INTRODUCTION   xix
   I   TEXT   xix
  II   SOURCES   xxiv
 III   ACTS AS A HISTORICAL DOCUMENT   xxxiii
 IV   ACTS IN HISTORY   lxiii
  V   THE THEOLOGY OF ACTS   lxxxii
 VI   CONCLUSION   cxi

ACTS 15–28: CONTENTS   cxix

COMMENTARY
   X   THE COUNCIL IN JERUSALEM (15.1–35)   695
  XI   PAUL'S MISSION BREAKS NEW GROUND (15.36–18.23)   751
 XII   THE MISSION BASED ON EPHESUS (18.24–20.38)   883
XIII   PAUL RETURNS TO JERUSALEM (21.1–22.29)   985
 XIV   PAUL AND THE JEWS (22.30–23.35)   1052
  XV   PAUL AND THE ROMANS (24.1–26.32)   1089
 XVI   PAUL REACHES ROME (27.1–28.28)   1175
XVII   CONCLUSION (28.(29)–31)   1248

INDEX   1255

ADDITIONS TO BIBLIOGRAPHIES AND ABBREVIATIONS

Commentaries referred to by the Author's Name only

Johnson, L. T. *The Acts of the Apostles*, Sacra Pagina 5, Collegeville, Minnesota, 1992.

Overbeck, F. C. *Kurze Erklärung der Apostelgeschichte von Dr. W. M. L. de Wette, vierte Auflage bearbeitet und stark erweitert von F. Overbeck*, Leipzig, 1870.

Taylor, J. *Les Actes des deux Apôtres*. V *Commentaire Historique (Act. 9.1—18.22)*, Études Bibliques, Nouvelle Série 23, Paris, 1992; VI *(Act. 18.23—28.31)*, Études Bibliques, Nouvelle Série 30, Paris, 1996.

Wikenhauser, A. *Die Apostelgeschichte*, Regensburger NT, 4th edn 1961.

Monographs on (Luke-)Acts

Boismard and Lamouille: M. É. Boismard and A. Lamouille, *Les Actes des deux Apôtres*, I—III, Études Bibliques, Nouvelle Série 12, 13, 14, Paris, 1990.

Book of Acts 1, 2, 3: *The Book of Acts in its First Century Setting*, ed. B. W. Winter.
    I Ancient Literary Setting, ed. B. W. Winter and A. D. Clarke, Grand Rapids/Carlisle, 1993.
    II Graeco-Roman Setting, ed. D. W. J. Gill and C. Gempf, Grand Rapids/Carlisle, 1994.
    III Paul in Roman Custody, by B. Rapske, Grand Rapids/Carlisle, 1994.

Cadbury, *History*: H. J. Cadbury, *The Book of Acts in History*, London, 1955.

Cadbury, *Style*: H. J. Cadbury, *The Style and Literary Method of Luke*, Cambridge, Mass., 1920.

Cassidy and Sharper, *Political Issues*: R. J. Cassidy and P. J. Sharper (eds.), *Political Issues in Luke-Acts*, Maryknoll, 1983.

Ehrhardt, *Acts*: A. Ehrhardt, *The Acts of the Apostles*, Manchester, 1969.

Filson: F. V. Filson, *Three Crucial Decades*, London, 1964.

Parsons and Pervo: M. C. Parsons and R. I. Pervo, *Rethinking the Unity of Luke and Acts*, Minneapolis, 1993.

Ramsay, *Luke*: W. M. Ramsay, *Luke the Physician and other Studies in the History of Religion*, London, 1908.

Tajra: H. W. Tajra, *The Trial of St. Paul. A Juridical Exegesis of the Second Half of Acts*, Tübingen, 1989.

Talbert: C. H. Talbert (ed.), *Perspectives on Luke-Acts*, Edinburgh, 1978.

Thornton: C.-J. Thornton, *Der Zeuge des Zeugen. Lukas als Historiker der Paulusreisen*, Tübingen, 1991.

van Unnik: W. C. van Unnik, *Tarsus of Jeruzalem, De Stad van Paulus' Jeugd*. Mededelingen der koninklijk Nederlandse Akademie van Weten-schappen, Afd. Letterkunde, Nieuwe Reeks, 15.5, Amsterdam, 1952.

Other works referred to by abbreviations

Bacher, *Terminologie*: W. Bacher, *Die exegetische Terminologie der jüdischen Traditionsliteratur*, Leipzig, 1899, 1905; reprint Hildesheim, 1965.

Bammel-Moule: E. Bammel and C. F. D. Moule (eds.), *Jesus and the Politics of His Day*, Cambridge, 1984.

Bauer, *Rechtgläubigkeit*: W. Bauer, *Rechtgläubigkeit und Ketzerei im ältesten Christentum*, BhTh 10, Tübingen, 1934.

Benoit 1, 2, 3, 4: P. Benoit, *Exégèse et Théologie*, Vol. I, Paris, 1961; Vol. II, 1961; Vol. III, 1968; Vol. IV, 1982.

Bornkamm 1, 2, 3, 4: G. Bornkamm, *Gesammelte Aufsätze*, Band I, München, 1966; Band II, 1970; Band III, 1968; Band IV, 1971.

Bousset, *RJ*: W. Bousset, *Die Religion des Judentums*, HNT 21, 3rd edn ed. H. Gressmann, Tübingen, 1926.

Brandon, *Fall*: S. G. F. Brandon, *The Fall of Jerusalem and the Christian Church*, London, 1951.

Calvin, *Institutes*: J. Calvin, *Institutes of the Christian Religion*, tr. H. Beveridge, Vol. I, Edinburgh, 1845; Vol. II, 1845; Vol. III, 1846.

von Campenhausen, *Amt*: H. von Campenhausen, *Kirchliches Amt und geistliche Vollmacht in den ersten drei Jahrhunderten*, Tübingen, 1953.

Cerfaux, *Rec.* 2: *Recueil L. Cerfaux*, Vol. II, Gembloux, 1954.

Clarke, *NT Problems*: W. K. L. Clarke, *New Testament Problems*, London, 1929.

Cranfield, *Romans*: C. E. B. Cranfield, *The Epistle to the Romans*, ICC, Edinburgh, Vol. I, 1975; Vol. II, 1979.

Danby: H. Danby, *The Mishnah*, London, 1933.

Dodd, *AS*: C. H. Dodd, *According to the Scriptures*, London, 1952.

Dunn, *Romans:* J. D. G. Dunn, *Romans 1–8*, Word Biblical Commentary 38A, Dallas, 1988; *Romans 9–16*, WBC 38B, 1988.

Freedom and Obligation: C. K. Barrett, *Freedom and Obligation, A Study of the Epistle to the Galatians*, London, 1985.

Gerhardsson, *Memory and Manuscript*: B. Gerhardsson, *Memory and Manuscript*, Acta Seminarii Neotestamentici Upsaliensis 22, Uppsala, 1961.

Goulder, *Two Missions*: M. Goulder, *A Tale of Two Missions*, London, 1994.

Juster: J. Juster, *Les Juifs dans l'Empire romain*, 2 vols., Paris, 1914.

Käsemann, *EVB* 1, 2: E. Käsemann, *Exegetische Versuche und Besinnungen*, 1. Band, Göttingen 1960; 2. Band 1964.

Kümmel, *Einleitung*: W. G. Kümmel, *Einleitung in das Neue Testament*, 19th edn, Heidelberg, 1978.

Lightfoot, *Ignatius*: J. B. Lightfoot, *The Apostolic Fathers, Part II*, S. Ignatius, S. Polycarp. 3 vols., London, 1885.

MPG: J. P. Migne, *Patrologia Graeca*.

Mommsen, *Provinces*: Th. Mommsen, *The Provinces of the Roman Empire*, ET, 2 vols., London, 1886.

Nock, *Essays*: A. D. Nock, *Essays on Religion and the Ancient World*, ed. Zeph Stewart, 2 vols., Oxford, 1972.

Partsch, *Kephallenia*: J. Partsch, Kephallenia und Ithaka, in Ergänzungsheft 98 zu Petermanns *Mitteilungen*, Gotha, 1890.

Pastorals: C. K. Barrett, *The Pastoral Epistles*, NCB, Oxford, 1963.

Pratscher, *Jakobus*: W. Pratscher, *Der Herrenbruder Jakobus und die Jakobustradition*, FRLANT 139, Göttingen, 1987.

Safrai-Stern: S. Safraï and M. Stern (eds.), *The Jewish People in the First Century*, Vol. I, Assen, 1974.

Sherwin-White: A. N. Sherwin-White, *Roman Society and Roman Law in the New Testament*, Oxford, 1963.

Stendahl, *Scrolls*: K. Stendahl (ed.), *The Scrolls and the New Testament*, London, 1958.

Trebilco: P. R. Trebilco, *Jewish Communities in Asia Minor*, SNTSMS 69, Cambridge, 1991.

Turner, *Insights*: N. Turner, *Grammatical Insights into the New Testament*, Edinburgh, 1965.

Festschrifts (FS) with abbreviated titles

Bammel: *Templum Amicitiae*, Essays on the Second Temple presented to E. Bammel. Ed. W. Horbury. JSNTSS 48. Sheffield, 1991.

Barrett: *Paul and Paulinism*. Essays in honour of C. K. Barrett. Ed. M. D. Hooker and S. G. Wilson. London, 1982.

Beasley-Murray: *Eschatology and the New Testament*. Essays in Honor of G. R. Beasley-Murray. Ed. W. H. Gloer. Peabody, Mass., 1988.

Black (1969): *Neotestamentica et Semitica*. Studies in Honour of M. Black. Ed. E. E. Ellis and M. Wilcox. Edinburgh, 1969.

Bruce (1980): *Pauline Studies*. Essays presented to F. F. Bruce on his 70th birthday. Ed. D. A. Hagner and M. J. Harris. Exeter, 1980.

Bultmann (1964): *Zeit und Geschichte*. Dankesgabe an R. Bultmann zum 80. Geburtstag. Ed. E. Dinkler. Tübingen, 1964.

Corsani: *Protestantesimo* 48.3 (1994). I metodi dell'indagine sul Nuevo Testamento. Omaggio per B. Corsani. Ed. S. Rostagno. Rome, 1994.

Farmer: *Jesus, the Gospels, and the Church*. Ed. E. P. Sanders. Macon, 1987.

Furnish: *Theology and Ethics in Paul and his Interpreters*. Essays in honor of V. P. Furnish. Ed. E. H. Lovering, Jr, and J. L. Samney. Nashville, 1996.

Goulder: *Crossing the Boundaries*. Essays in Biblical Interpretation in Honour of M. D. Goulder. Ed. S. E. Porter, P. Joyce, and D. E. Orton. Leiden, 1994.

Hengel: *Geschichte–Tradition–Reflexion*. Festschrift für Martin Hengel zum 70, Geburtstag. Ed. H. Cancik, H. Lichtenberger, P. Schäfer. Tübingen, 1996.

Hofius: *Christus als die Mitte der Schrift*. [Festschrift für] O. Hofius. Ed. H. Lichtenberger, H.-J. Eckstein, and C. Landmesser. [Tübingen], 1997.

Jaeger: *Unio Christianorum*. Festschrift für Erzbischof L. Jaeger, Paderborn.

Jeremias: *Judentum- Urchristentum- Kirche*. Festschrift für J. Jeremias. Ed. W. Eltester. BZNW 26. Berlin, 1960.

Jervell. *Mighty Minorities?* Essays in honour of J. Jervell on his 70th birthday. Ed. D. Hellholm, H. Moxnes, and T. K. Seim. Oslo/Copenhagen/Stockholm/Boston, 1995.

Kee: *The Social World of Formative Christianity and Judaism*. Essays in Tribute to H. C. Kee. Ed. J. Neusner, E. S. Frerichs, P. Borgen, and R. Horsley. Philadelphia, 1989.

Kuhn: *Tradition und Glaube. Das frühe Christentum in seiner Umwelt*. Festgabe für K. G. Kuhn zum 65. Geburtstag. Ed. G. Jeremias, H.-W. Kuhn, H. Stegemann. Göttingen, 1971.

Mitton: *ExpT* 78.1 (1976). In honour of C. L. Mitton. Edinburgh, 1976.
Mowinckel: *Interpretationes ad Vetus Testamentum pertinentes S. Mowinckel Septuagenario missae.* Norsk teologisk tidsskrift 56. Oslo, 1955.
Neirynck: *The Four Gospels 1992.* Festschrift F. Neirynck. 3 vols. Ed. F. Van Segbroeck, C. M. Tuckett, G. Van Belle, and J. Verheyden. BEThL 100. Leuven, 1992.
Osborn: *ABR* 35 (1987. Special Issue in Honour of E. Osborn. Ed. I. Breward. Melbourne, 1987.
Ramsay: *Anatolian Studies presented to Sir W. M. Ramsay.* Manchester, 1923.
Schnackenburg: *Neues Testament und Kirche.* Für R. Schnackenburg. Ed. J. Gnilka. Freiburg/Basel/Wien, 1974.
Schneider: *Der Treue Gottestrauen.* Ed. C. Bussmann and W. Radl. Freiburg/Basel/Wien, 1991.
Schweizer: *Die Mitte des Neuen Testaments. Einheit und Vielfalt Neutestamentlicher Theologie.* Festschrift für E. Schweizer zum 70. Geburtstag. Ed. U. Luz and H. Weder. Göttingen, 1983.
Smit Sibinga: *NovT* 38.2 (1996). Special number in honour of J. Smit Sibinga. Ed. P. Borgen and others. Leiden, 1996.
Zimmermann: *Begegnung mit dem Wort* Festschrift H. Zimmermann. Ed. J. Zmijewski and E. Nellessen. Bonn, 1979.
de Zwaan: *Studia Paulina* in honorem J. de Zwaan Septuagenarii. Ed. J. N. Sevenster and W. C. van Unnik. Haarlem, 1953.

Works of reference

Altaner: B. Altaner, A. Stuiber, *Patrologie.* 7th edn Freiburg/Basel/Wien, 1966.
A Dictionary of the Bible, ed. J. Hastings, Edinburgh, 1906.
Digest: Digesta Iustiniani, ed. Th. Mommson, Leipzig, 1866, 1870.
Hort: F. J. A. Hort, *The Apocalypse of St John I–III*, London, 1908.
KP: K. Ziegler and W. Sontheimer (eds.), *Der kleine Pauly* 5 vols., Stuttgart 1964ff.
LCL: Loeb Classical Library.
Lobeck: C. A. Lobeck, *Phrynichi Eclogae*, Leipzig, 1820 (repr. 1965).
LS Supp: LS, Revised Supplement, ed. P. G. W. Glare and A. H. Thompson, Oxford, 1996.
M. 4: *A Grammar of New Testament Greek*, by J. H. Moulton, Vol. IV, Style, by N. Turner, Edinburgh, 1976.
ND 6, 7: *New Documents illustrating Early Christianity*, Vol. VI and Vol. VII, by S. R. Llewelyn and R. A. Kearsley, Macquarie University, 1992, 1994.
Quasten: J. Quasten, *Patrology*, 4 vols, I Utrecht, Brussels 1950; II Utrecht, Antwerp 1953; III, IV, Westminster, Maryland, 1986.
RGG: *Die Religion in Geschichte und Gegenwart*, ed. K. Galling, 3rd edn, 6 vols., Tübingen, 1957ff.
Robertson: A. T. Robertson, *A Grammar of the Greek New Testament in the Light of Historical Research*, 3rd edn, London, 1919.
Rutherford, *Gram.*: W. G. Rutherford, *First Greek Grammar*, London, 1907.

SOE: The Shorter Oxford English Dictionary, ed. C. T. Onions, Oxford, ³1955.

Simonson: G. Simonson, *A Greek Grammar: Syntax*, London and New York, 1911.

Swete: H. B. Swete, *The Apocalypse of St John*, London, 1906.

TWAT: Theologisches Wörterbuch zum Alten Testament, ed. G. J. Botterweck and H. Ringgren, Stuttgart, Berlin, Köln, Mainz, 1970–.

Winer-Moulton: *A Treatise on the Grammar of New Testament Greek*, by G. B. Winer, tr. and ed. by W. F. Moulton, 3rd edn, Edinburgh, 1882.

Winer-Schmiedel: G. B. Winer, *Grammatik des neutestamentlichen Sprachidioms*, 8th edn, ed. by P. W. Schmiedel, 1. Teil, Göttingen, 1894.

Periodicals and Series

AbThANT: Abhandlungen zur Theologie des Alten und Neuen Testaments
AnBib: Analecta Biblica
ANRW: Aufstieg und Niedergang der römischen Welt
AThR: Anglican Theological Review
BBB: Bonner biblische Beiträge
BHTh: Beiträge zur historischen Theologie
BiK: Bibel und Kirche
BZ: Biblische Zeitschrift
BZNW: Beihefte zur ZNW
Coniect. Neot.: Coniectanea Neotestamentica
FRLANT: Forschungen zur Literatur des Alten und Neuen Testaments
HNT: Handbuch zum Neuen Testament
JAC: Jahrbuch für Antike und Christentum
JJS: Journal of Jewish Studies
JQR: Jewish Quarterly Review
NGG: Nachrichten der Gesellschaft der Wissenschaften zu Göttingen
NCB: New Century Bible
OCT: Oxford Classical Texts
PEQ: Palestine Exploration Quarterly
REJ: Revue des Études Juives
RHR: Revue d'Histoire des Religions
RScPhTh: Revue des Sciences Philosophiques et Théologiques
RScR: Revue de Science Religieuse
RTR: Reformed Theological Review
SB: Stuttgarter Bibelstudien
SBLDiss: Society of Biblical Literature Dissertation Series
SEÅ: Svensk Exegetisk Årsbok
StANT: Studien zum Alten und Neuen Testament
ThQu: Theologische Quartalschrift
ThR: Theologische Rundschau
ThZ: Theologische Zeitschrift
WMANT: Wissenschaftliche Monographien zum Alten und Neuen Testament
WUNT: Wissenschaftliche Untersuchungen zum Neuen Testament
ZKG: Zeitschrift für Kirchengeschichte
ZKTh: Zeitschrift für katholische Theologie
ZThK: Zeitschrift für Theologie und Kirche

INTRODUCTION

I. TEXT

It is unnecessary here to repeat the information, given in I.2–20, concerning the Greek and other manuscript sources on which the text of Acts is based,[1] or to do more than restate in outline the problem which those sources present; for this problem see I.20–29. It exaggerates only slightly to say that the authorities for the text fall into two blocks: that which in this commentary is described as the Old Uncial text and is represented best by the MSS B and ℵ, and that which is known as Western—a term which, it must be repeated, is geographically misleading but so well established that it scarcely needs the inverted commas with which the adjective is often provided. So far as this simple statement is exaggerated the exaggeration is twofold: there is a third, later, conflate form of text (possibly also a Caesarean text, but this is doubtful); and the Western text, though for many purposes it may reasonably be treated as a unity, manifests a good deal of variety in detail. The view taken in this commentary has already been made clear. It is that the Old Uncial text gives on the whole a trustworthy account of what Luke wrote, though the Western text, which is undoubtedly old, may occasionally point back to the original wording. This view is not taken *a priori* but as the result of the discussion of many passages; if it is adopted, even if it is right, the textual critic's task is not ended. What is the original form (or, what are the earliest forms) of the Western text? And, how, when, and where did the Western text come into being? These are the most pressing, interesting, and divisive, but not the only questions that confront the textual critic.

It seems right to return to the most notable attempt in recent years to vindicate the originality and authority of the Western text, that of M. E. Boismard and A. Lamouille,[2] though serious discussion of it

---

[1] I should however add references to D. C. Parker, *Codex Bezae: An Early Christian Manuscript and its Text*, Cambridge, 1992, and K. Aland, *Text und Textwert der griechischen Handschriften des Neuen Testaments, III Die Apostelgeschichte*, Berlin and New York, 1993, neither of which was published when Volume I was completed and given to the press. Parker thinks that D was written about AD 400, in Berytus. See also K. E. Panten, *A history of research on Codex Bezae, with special reference to the Acts of the Apostles*, unpublished Ph.D dissertation, Murdoch University, Australia, 1995.

[2] M. E. Boismard and A. Lamouille, *Texte Occidental des Actes des Apôtres*, two volumes, Paris, 1984. See 1.24f.

would double the size of this Introduction, and perhaps of the commentary. Boismard and Lamouille attempt to establish the original form of TO (*Texte occidental*, Western text). This is by no means a matter of simply reprinting the text of the MS D, which, they maintain, is an edited Western text. This points at once to a basic difficulty of which of course Boismard and Lamouille are well aware. The other main authorities for the Western text are not in Greek, but in Latin, Syriac, and Coptic, from which an original Greek has to be reconstructed by retroversion. This can be done; it is well done by Boismard and Lamouille; but inevitably a measure of uncertainty remains. The next step is, on the basis of the reconstructed authorities, to establish TO. TO thus established, Boismard and Lamouille investigate its language and style. Drawing up lists of characteristic idioms they argue that it is Lucan; it must have been written by Luke himself, by the author who was responsible for the TA (*Texte alexandrien*, the Old Uncial text). Thus both forms of the text go back to the same author. The Western text is a partly modified form of Luke's original text; the Old Uncial text is his own revision. That is, both texts are Lucan; the Western text, so far as we can recover it, is the older.

The facts are essentially as Boismard and Lamouille have stated them;[3] their lists of Lucan vocabulary and idiom demonstrate a good measure of Lucanism in the Western text. The question is whether this observation can prove their conclusion. Probably it cannot and does not. The alternative view is that the Western text is a revision (or, the various forms of the Western text are revisions) of the earlier, Lucan, Old Uncial text. It seems almost inevitable that a revision, unless an extremely radical one, will continue to show characteristics of the original text. Many will simply slip through into the new text, and even where a new form of words is chosen the reviser, working constantly on a specific, in this case Lucan, base, will tend to adopt the Lucan manner – he may even do so deliberately, in order that his revision may have the appearance though not the substance of authenticity.[4]

The point to which we may return is that of the variety and the

[3]See however the review by J. N. Birdsall, *JTS* 39 (1988), 571–7.

[4]See M. Wilcox, 'Luke and the Bezan Text of Acts' (Kremer, *Actes*, 447–55), who recognizes the text of D as Lucan, and thus offers some support to my essay in *FS* Black (1979), 15–27, and in a different way to Boismard and Lamouille, though he does not refer to my paper and their book was not published when he wrote. See also C. Martini, 'La tradition textuelle des Actes des Apôtres et les tendences de l'Église ancienne' (Kremer, *Actes*, 21–35), with the double conclusion: there is no evidence of clear doctrinal tendencies, but there is a distance from the original context and from Judaism, with concern for fidelity to tradition and freedom with regard to the letter of the text.

characteristics of the Western readings. Some examples have already been given,[5] a few more examples follow.

There are familiar and frequently discussed places where the Western text offers a different view of the matter in hand from that of the Old Uncials. The best example is 15.20, 29; cf. 21.25, where the Apostolic Decree is given in a different form and with (at least) a different emphasis. Other examples are 17.15, where, according to D, Paul passes by Thessaly because he is forbidden to preach the word; 18.7, where the Western text suggests that Paul left the house (or the business?) of Aquila; 18.17, where it asserts that the *Greeks* seized and beat Sosthenes; 19.1, 2, where D and others add that Paul wished to go to Jerusalem but was sent by the Spirit to Asia; at 20.3 there is a similar spiritual direction; at 21.16 the Western text gives a different account of the last stages of Paul's journey to Jerusalem. Variants such as these could all be the work of a single reviser who had his own notions of what happened and what it signified. But another class of variants is significant because of their insignificance. Examples are frequently pointed out in the notes; here the following may represent many.

16.25: τὸ μεσονύκτιον] μέσον τῆς νυκτός D*

16.35: ἀπέστειλεν οἱ στρατηγοί] συνῆλθον οἱ στρατηγοὶ ἐπὶ τὸ αὐτὸ εἰς τὴν ἀγορὰν καὶ ἀναμνησθέντες τὸν σεισμὸν τὸν γεγονότα ἐφοβήθησαν καὶ ἀπέστειλαν D sy[hmg]

17.8: τὸν ὄχλον καὶ τοὺς πολιτάρχας] τοὺς πολιτάρχας καὶ τὸν ὄχλον D gig sy[p]

19.9: ὡς δέ τινες] τινὲς μὲν οὖν αὐτῶν D

22.29: εὐθέως οὖν] τότε D

28.18: οἵτινες] + πολλά 614 pc sy[h**] [D is not extant at this point.]

Variants such as these (and they are many) suggest nothing more (and nothing less) than an intention on the copyist's part to reproduce the content of the text before him, which is evidently judged to be of some value, but a lack of concern with its precise wording: any words will do provided that they represent the sense of the text with reasonable accuracy; if they express that sense with greater vividness and give the narrative a greater connectedness, so much the better. This is very different from the traditional regard for a sacred text, which must be preserved intact, and points to what may probably be regarded as the origin of the Western text, or rather texts, all characterized by a free and therefore not identical paraphrasing of the original. It will appear[6] that there was a period when Acts was in circulation but was not regarded as a canonical text; it is for this

---

[5]See I.5, 16f., 19.
[6]See p. lxviii.

reason that there is a far greater range of textual variation in Acts than occurs in the gospels and in the Pauline letters. This account of the origin of the Western text does not in fact differ as much from that of Prof. B. Aland[7] as may at first sight appear, but it does omit the hypothesis of something like a Western text, in which many 'wild' variants were edited into a unified edition which subsequently split up into the variant forms known to us today in D, the Old Latin, some Syriac versions, and a few other sources. We have no good ground for positing a standard Western text. This observation of course bears also on the work of Boismard and Lamouille. It leaves open the probability that the Western text will have not infrequently preserved the original text, most frequently of course when, as often, it is in agreement with the Old Uncial text and occasionally when the two are in disagreement.[8]

In practical terms, this means that the critic will pursue the 'eclectic' method, for the original wording may turn up anywhere (though it does turn up most frequently in the Old Uncial MSS). Textual divergence was probably at its greatest in the earliest period, and this means that the divergent texts (as known to us) will (whatever the dates of the codices in which they are contained) be early texts, and sometimes their readings will be original when the Old Uncial texts have been revised under the influence of classical rules and good literary taste.[9] It is important that several lines of study concur to establish the picture of Acts as a relatively early work that achieved canonical status late; see also IV: ACTS IN HISTORY.

Bibliography

B. Aland, *EThL* 62 (1986), 5–65.

K. Aland, 'Alter und Entstehung des D-Textes im Neuen Testament', in S. Jeneras (ed.), *Miscellania Papirologica*, Barcelona 1987.

K. Aland, *Text und Textwert der griechischen Handschriften des Neuen Testaments, III Die Apostelgeschichte*, Berlin and New York 1993.

C. K. Barrett, *FS* Black (1979), 15–27.

J. N. Birdsall, *FS* Klijn, 39–45.

M. E. Boismard and A. Lamouille, *Texte Occidental des Actes des Apôtres*, Paris 1984.

[7]'Entstehung, Charakter und Herkunft des sog. westlichen Textes untersucht an der Apostelgeschichte', *EThL* 62 (1986), 5–65. See I.25–29.

[8]See also Ropes on the origin of the Western text, *Begs.* 3.ccxc–ccxcvii.

[9]See here especially the work of G. D. Kilpatrick, notably in the posthumous publication of his textual essays: *The Principles and Practice of New Testament Textual Criticism. Collected Essays of G. D. Kilpatrick*, ed. by J. K. Elliott, BEThL 96, Leuven, 1990.

J. W. Childers, *NTS* 42 (1996), 55–74.

A. C. Clark, *The Acts of the Apostles*, Oxford 1933.

J. K. Elliott, *NTS* 34 (1988), 250–58.

E. J. Epp, *The Theological Tendency of Codex Bezae Cantabrigiensis in Acts*, SNTSMS 3, Cambridge 1966.

T. C. Geer, *Bib* 69 (1988), 27–46.

T. C. Geer, *NovT* 31 (1989), 39–47.

T. C. Geer, *JSNT* 39 (1990), 59–76.

E. Haenchen and P. Weigandt, *NTS* 14 (1968), 469–81.

R. P. C. Hanson, *NTS* 14 (1968), 282–6.

R. F. Hull, *JBL* 107 (1986), 695–707.

A. Jousseu, *Die koptischen Versionen der Apostelgeschichte*, BBB 34, Bonn 1969.

Ad. Jülicher, *ZNW* 15 (1914), 163–88.

R. S. Mackenzie, *JSNT* 6 (1980), 522–76.

R. S. Mackenzie, *JBL* 104 (1985), 637–50.

C. Martini, Kremer, *Actes* 21–35.

C. D. Osburn, *JSNT* 44 (1991), 39–55.

D. C. Parker, *JSNT* 15 (1982), 97–112.

D. C. Parker, *Codex Bezae: An Early Christian Manuscript and its Text*, Cambridge 1992.

T. Petersen, *CBQ* 26 (1964), 225–41.

J. H. Petzer, *NTS* 39 (1993), 227–45.

W. A. Strange, *The Problem of the Text in Acts*, SNTSMS 71, Cambridge 1993.

B. H. Streeter, *JTS* 34 (1933), 232–41.

M. Wilcox, Kremer *Actes* 447–55.

B. Witherington, *JBL* 103 (1989), 282–4.

II. SOURCES

The question what sources were used by Luke in Acts 1–14 is considered in I.49–56.[1] There are now few who think that it is possible, by the detection of doublets, to find in chs. 2–5 a pair of written sources.[2] The apparent doublets can be otherwise explained, and it is improbable that the church of the earliest years kept written records of its activities suitable for literary editing. Luke drew on such oral traditions as were available; he may occasionally have found something in writing (see e.g. 1.15, with the note). More can be said about chs. 6–14, though here too it is well to be cautious with regard to written sources. Whoever the author of Acts may have been he had at his disposal a quantity of information about Paul, and this may well have begun with an account of Paul's conversion (9.1–19). The author's apparent contact (not necessarily at first hand) with Philip the Evangelist (21.8) may have provided information not only about Philip's own activities (8.5–13, 26–40) but also about early Caesarean traditions. There was probably a cycle of stories about Peter (9.32–43; perhaps 10.1–11.18; perhaps 12.3–17; earlier stories such as 3.1–10 may have been included). More important however as we move into the later chapters, is the Antiochene tradition, which runs back from the foundation of the church in Antioch (11.19–26) as far as the story of the Hellenist widows (6.1)[3]—with a great deal of material, some from other traditions, mentioned above, interpolated into it. Antiochene material runs forward also. 11.27–30 manifests the Antiochene church's independence, in that it is able to minister to its mother, and (see I.54f.) the story in chs. 13, 14 of the appointment of Barnabas and Saul, and of their mission in Cyprus and Asia Minor, is told from an Antiochene standpoint. The first question to be considered here is whether the Antiochene tradition continues into ch. 15.

This seems probable.[4] The Jerusalem Council is precipitated by events in Antioch, where, according to the narratives in Acts, there

---

[1]It is important now to add a reference to J. Taylor, *Les Actes des deux Apôtres* (Études Bibliques, Nouvelle Série 23), Paris, 1994; also (p. xxxii) a further volume.

[2]The best statement of this now largely abandoned view is that of A. Harnack, *The Acts of the Apostles*, ET London, 1906, pp. 172–86.

[3]Though this verse and the use of the word Hellenist are probably Luke's own; see the note on the verse, I.305–9.

[4]See below, pp. 696f., 710f.; and the detailed notes on many of the verses in ch. 15.

had been a mixed church including both Jews and Gentiles since
11.20f. Acts 15 begins in Antioch and ends in Antioch (15.30–41),
but it does not seem probable that the whole of the intervening
account was derived from Antioch. According to Acts 15.1–5 the
leading Antiochene representatives were Paul and Barnabas; this is
confirmed in the parallel account[5] in Gal. 2.1–10 where Paul himself
gives a record of the Council which differs in some ways from that in
Acts; the latter probably incorporates Jerusalem memories as well as
Luke's own editing. For further discussion of the sources of ch. 15
see pp. 710f.

With ch. 16 we encounter a new phenomenon.[6] In a number of
passages the narrative is set in the first person plural, which *prima
facie* suggests that the story is being told by one who was present.
The verses in which the significant pronoun or verb form occurs are
the following:[7] 16.10–(14)–17; 20.5–8, 13–15; 21.1–8, 11, 12, 14–
18; 27.1–8, 15, 16, 18, 20, 27, 29, 37; 28.1, 2, 7, 10–16. Between
these verses the narrative is sometimes carried forward in a way that
shows that a story in the first person is being continued, though this is
not always so. The most natural interpretation of these passages is
that in them the story is being told by one who was present and took
part (though possibly only a reporter's part) in the events described.
How this interpretation should be understood, and whether it is in
fact correct, will be considered below (see pp. xxvii–xxx). Our first
task must be to survey the materials. 'We' appears first at 16.10,[8]
when Paul, in Troas, is summoned by a dream vision to extend his
mission to Macedonia. Accordingly, *we* sought to leave for Macedonia. The person, real or fictional, who says this, is in Paul's
company; it is reasonable to think that he joined Paul if not at Troas
itself at least in that area. It seems unreasonable to think (though it
has been suggested) that he himself was the man of Macedonia, in his
narrative transforming himself into a vision. He accompanies Paul to
Macedonia, reaching Philippi at v. 12. The first person continues up
to v. 17 (its absence from 16.14 is insignificant), the point at which
Paul exorcises the Python spirit, and with Silas is thrown into prison.
We appears no more in the chapter. This could mean that the person
responsible for it had left Paul's circle, but a much more probable
cause is that whereas, up to this point, all the party have been
involved in the events described, henceforth the story is focused
upon Paul and Silas, who are arrested, beaten, imprisoned, delivered

---

[5]Some find the parallel to Gal. 2.1–10 not in Acts 15 but in Acts 11.30, or
elsewhere. This is not probable; see pp. lxf., and elsewhere in the notes on ch. 15.

[6]See however the reading of D (p w mae) at 11.28 and Bultmann's conjecture at
13.2; I.564, 604.

[7]In addition at 16.8 the Latin version of Irenaeus has *nos venimus* (for
κατέβησαν).

[8]But see notes 6 and 7 above.

by the earthquake, cared for by the converted gaoler, and as Roman citizens are set free by the apologetic magistrates. The 'first person' was out of the story and was therefore not mentioned. Did he, when Paul moved on, remain in Philippi? The question is proper whether we are thinking in terms of history or of fiction. He does not appear in the rest of Paul's Macedonian ministry (17.1–12), or in his mission to Athens (17.13–34). Throughout ch. 18 the story is told in the third person (the work in Corinth, the journey to the east, and the return to the west), and so it is in ch. 19 (Ephesus). *We* returns at 20.5. Sopater and others waited for *us* in Troas; *we* sailed away from Philippi and joined them at Troas. Had the 'first person' been in Philippi all this time? It may be so; it may be that the author wishes us to think so; it may be that as a writer of fiction he thinks that variety would be pleasant and reintroduces his alternative reporting style. *We* continues up to the Christian supper in v. 8, drops out in the story of Eutychus, and is resumed when the voyage is taken up again in v. 13. Does this mean that the miracle story of the raising of Eutychus was drawn from a different source, perhaps not an eye-witness source, a less trustworthy source? It may be so. *We* continues in vv. 13–15; then stops. This may mean that not only the speech of 20.18–35 but the whole Miletus episode is from a different source. This again seems quite probable, though it cannot be proved.

The journey is resumed in 21.1, and *we* returns, found in every verse up to v. 8. Its absence from v. 9, which simply tells objectively of Philip's four daughters (who could well be there because they were known to *us*), is not significant (though the contact between *us* and Philip may be). In the absence of a pronoun it is implied in v. 10 (made explicit in $\aleph^c$ E $\mathfrak{M}$ gig sy^{hmg}, which have ἡμῶν, explicitly absent in $\aleph^*$ 1175, which have αὐτῶν), and continues up to v. 18, where Paul meets James and the elders, with an unimportant omission in v. 13. *We* thus sees Paul through to his destination; it then disappears. Did the 'first person' leave Jerusalem, so that information about Paul's adventures there and in Caesarea had to be drawn from another source? This could well be so, but we remember 16.19–40, where the Philippian troubles are described in the third person, perhaps for no other reason than that they concerned only Paul and Silas.

We returns in ch. 27, in the account of the voyage and shipwreck, again with possibly significant intermissions. It runs without a break up to v. 8, the arrival of the ship at Fair Havens. It is not resumed till after the breaking of the storm in v. 15. The intervening passage recounts the disagreement between Paul and the nautical authorities on the propriety of continuing the voyage; was this interpolated into narrative that did not originally contain it? or does the absence of the first person simply mean that this part of the story is about Paul and not about *us*? *We* continues from v. 15 to v. 18. Its absence from

vv. 19, 20 does not seem to be significant, but vv. 21–26 are a possibly independent story about Paul, comparable with vv. 9–14. *We* occurs in vv. 27, 29, but after that virtually disappears, since the count of the ship's company in v. 37 could stand on its own.

In ch. 28 *we* is found in vv. 1, 2, 7, 10, that is, in the bare account of the residence in Malta; it is not found in the stories of Paul's snake bite and his cure of the father of Publius. These could be drawn from a different source. Verses 11–16 bring Paul to Rome, and from this point the story is focused on him, and the first person plural disappears.

What is to be made of these We-passages? As was said above, the *prima facie* inference to be drawn from them is that the person who wrote them was present at the events he describes; this however may be, and has been, understood in different ways.

(1) The traditional understanding of them, which goes back as far as the Muratorianum,[9] is that the author of Acts as a whole was an eyewitness of the events concerned, breaking into first person narration at those points at which he was himself a member of Paul's party.

(2) A second view is that the author of Acts is to be distinguished from the person responsible for a source that he was using; it was this latter person who used the 'we' and was present; his first person narration was retained by the author of the book though it was no longer strictly appropriate.

(3) The third possibility is that the 'We' is fictitious, included in the text for some editorial purpose, perhaps simply in order to add to the verisimilitude of the narrative.

An admirable account of the debate between those who have maintained these opinions has been given by C.-J. Thornton,[10] and there is no need to retell the story here. It is impossible also to follow Thornton's careful and thorough examination of the Ich-Erzählung in ancient literature. It must suffice to quote the conclusion that he reaches on the basis of this examination. 'Die Wir-Erzählungen der Apostelgeschichte enthalten nichts, was antike Leser nicht für völlig realistisch gehalten hätten. Sie konnten darin nur einen Bericht über die wirklichen Erlebnisse des Autors erblicken. Hätte der Autor die in Wir-Form geschilderten Reisen gar nicht mitgemacht, so wären seine Erzählungen darüber—auch nach antikem Verständnis—Lügen' (p. 141). So far Thornton's conclusion seems to be fully justified by the evidence cited. He has however a good deal more to say. The writer of the We-passages may—should—be accepted as one of Paul's travelling party. It does not follow that we are dealing

---

[9]Lines 35–37: Lucas optimo Theofilo comprendit quae sub praesentia eius singula gerebantur ... See I.44.

[10]*Der Zeuge des Zeugen*, Tübingen, 1991.

throughout with 'reinen Tatsachenberichten'. There is in fact a 'Skala von Fingiertheitsgraden', and it has many steps. We can accept the author's participation in Paul's journey to Rome 'ohne damit automatisch die Autentizität der Paulusreden an Bord oder der Schlangenbiss Episode auf Melite in Kauf zu nehmen' (p. 142). Here it seems better to take up the observation made earlier. The first person, used three times (ἐπέγνωμεν, ἡμῖν, ἡμᾶς) in 28.1, 2, drops out entirely in vv. 3–6, the story about the snake; it is resumed in v. 7. Similarly, some (see above) though not all of the speeches attributed to Paul in ch. 27 are in the setting of third person narrative. It is a more plausible view that there are places (even within the account of the journey to Rome) which did not come to the author of the book as the words of an eyewitness. This leads to a further point. If 28.1, 2 and 28.3–6 came to the author of Acts along different channels we are dealing not with various degrees of credibility within an Ich-Erzählung but with the combination of different sources, of which only one was a We-source. This immediately suggests the question of the relation of the author-editor of Acts to the author of the We-source. Thornton maintains their identity, but the arguments by which this conclusion is reached are less impress- ive. They are bound up with the attribution of the work to Luke, the companion of Paul (Col. 4.14; Phm. 24). This is a matter that will be considered below (see pp. xxixf.); Thornton lays great stress on the witness of Irenaeus, which he traces back to the beginning of the second century, and, taking the date of Acts to be in the time of Titus or the early years of Domitian, points out that at this time not only the historical Luke but others such as Timothy must still have been alive, so that pseudonymity can hardly have been possible, while in a book with a dedication anonymity would have been out of the question. Ascription to Luke implies a special relation to the history and thus to the eye-witness. All this is interesting and, more important, may be true, but it is not fully convincing. In particular it runs into the difficulty of supposing that the author of Acts *as a whole* was familiar with Paul. On this difficulty see below, pp. xlivf. and elsewhere, where it is argued that the author, though he greatly admired Paul, did not fully understand him and at some points misunderstood him. Thornton recognizes the difficulty, and deliber- ately excludes it from consideration. 'Die Frage nach dem Verhältnis von lukanischer und paulinischer Theologie etwa muss ich ganz ausklammern; das müsste Gegenstand einer eigener Studie sein, die im Licht der folgenden Untersuchungen zu wesentlich anderen—und methodisch gesicherteren – Ergebnissen führen würde, als sie heute zumindest in der deutschen Forschung weithin akzeptiert werden' (p. 200). Such a study might however lead to confirmation of a fairly widely accepted view, and to no more than qualified acceptance of Thornton's opinion. That Acts as a whole was written by one of

Paul's immediate circle is very difficult to believe; that the author, whoever he may have been, was able to draw on one or two sources derived from that circle—the We-passages and perhaps some others—is probable.

On this view we are left with the difficult problem of explaining why the final author saw fit to leave the first person in the passages taken from the presumed source. So far as one can tell he did not in general treat his sources with such wooden rigidity as might lead him to retain the precise wording of this one. If it was a source of such exceptional authority that he felt that he must transcribe it word for word one would have expected him to say what the authority was. It may be that it was the only source available to him that came directly from the Pauline party; this would make it distinctive and he might have supposed that the distinctive mode of expression would make this clear. In the end however we have to balance against each other a factual problem (the misrepresentation of Paul's thought and action) and a verbal problem (the retention of 'We' passages in the midst of 'He/they' passages); and it seems reasonable to give the factual problem priority. It is perhaps best to suppose that the We-source was little more than an itinerary, a list of places visited, with some notes on lodging and means of transport. This applies well to most of the passages listed above (pp. xxv–xxvii). Thus: 'They waited for us in Troas; we sailed from Philippi to Troas, a five-day journey; we sailed to Assos to pick up Paul, who went by land; then Mitylene, Chios, Samos, Miletus;' and so on. When he could do so, the author of Acts supplemented this outline with stories that he collected in the places mentioned. This suggestion works least well with the opening verses which give some details of 'our' stay in Philippi (cf. other more personal notes at 20.36–38; 21.5, 6, 10–14). But the author of the We-source was not compiling a Mediterranean shipping timetable, or even a guidebook.

Between 21.28 and 27.1 there is no first-person narrative. This long passage includes Paul's visit to the Temple with the four vow-makers; the attack on him by the crowd and the intervention of the Romans; his speech to the crowd, renewed violence, and further intervention by the Romans, who learn that Paul himself is a citizen; Paul's appearance before the Sanhedrin, the plot to kill him, and his transference by the tribune to Caesarea; his accusation by the Jews before the Governor, who leaves him in custody for his successor to deal with; Paul's appeal to Caesar and his statement in the presence of Agrippa as well as Festus. There is a great deal of information here, most of which cannot be traced to any specific source or historically checked. One may wonder whether the eye-witness who composed the 'We' passages remained in Jerusalem between 21.18 and 27.1, where he reappears to accompany Paul on the voyage to Rome. This is not impossible. There is no reason to think that he was no longer in Philippi after 16.17: he simply ceased to write in the first person because he was describing what happened to Paul and Silas when they were not in his presence but in prison and dealing with officials. He may have remained in Jerusalem and picked up what information about Paul's affairs he could get. As (presumably) a Gentile he would not be admitted to the Temple; what happened there he could describe only in the third person.[11] Thereafter Paul was in Roman hands and probably for the most part inaccessible, though on the whole his captivity does not seem to have been strict (23.16; 24.23; 26.31, 32) and a friend might have been able to gather information about events at which he was not himself present. The speeches he would no doubt compose himself. All this is no more than a possibility. It must however be added that if it is not accepted, we have no means of investigating the origin of the material concerned; we can say only that if it is not fiction it[12] must be Pauline tradition, going back to some member or members of the Pauline circle, and (in part) to Paul himself. If it is accepted, the problem arising out of Thornton's work on the 'We' passages is to some extent at least alleviated, and we may suppose that Luke (if we accept the name, but here too Thornton is not so easy to follow) was the author of a considerable part of Acts, indeed of most of the second part of the book. The person responsible for Acts 16–28 must in any case be thought of as a traveller, sufficiently familiar with Corinth and Ephesus, probably with other cities also, to have picked up local traditions and memories of Paul and his missions. Much or all of the contents of chs. 17, 18, 19 will be accounted for in this way, as well as some of the paragraphs inserted into the 'We' passages in chs. 27, 28.

ADDITIONAL NOTES

The Acts of the Two Apostles See note 1.

The work of M. E. Boismard and A. Lamouille on the text of Acts was considered in I.24f. and above, pp. xixf. It was followed by three volumes by the same authors on the sources of Acts (*Les Actes des deux Apôtres*). These were published in 1990; I was not yet aware of

[11]Was he right about the vow? Would Paul have taken part in this Jewish ceremony? See pp. 1000f. and the notes on 21.21, 24, 25. He might perhaps have done so. He was prepared to become a Jew to the Jews (1 Cor. 9.20), and this was, or might have seemed to be, a private act which he could perform without committing Gentile Christians to anything, whereas the Decree (15.29) committed them, if they would be saved, to minimal legal observance. On the other hand, it is doubtful whether Paul would have voluntarily undertaken a legal obligation in order to prove what was certainly not the whole truth.

[12]Or some of it; it is to some extent possible to distinguish between tradition and redaction.

their existence when I finished the manuscript of Volume I in January 1991. They are to be followed by a historical commentary, of which J. Taylor has now published the part that deals with Acts 9.1–18.22 (Paris, 1994) and a further volume (p. xxxii). In his Avant-Propos he outlines the thesis of Boismard and Lamouille, on which his own commentary is based. What is offered here is a summary of his outline. The textual work referred to above is presupposed in this account of sources.

The reconstituted Western text of Acts is the nearest approach we have to the original text of Acts, the work of Luke himself. The Alexandrian text is a revision of the original text made by another hand. There are thus two editions of Acts. They contain also many non-Lucan revisions, additions, and redactions. Luke had not only a reviser but a precursor, a document which already had the form of a life, passion, and resurrection of Jesus followed by the story of the earliest church. This Boismard and Lamouille call Act I; Act II is the work of Luke himself; Act III is the work of the Lucan reviser. But Act I also made use of a yet more ancient work, already of the same pattern, and centred on the work of Peter. This is DocP (= Document Pétrinien). What we have here is not so much a theory of sources as of several levels of composition. It is possible to go further still and to distinguish a Journal de Voyage (JV), comprising most of the We-passages, and a Document Johannique, emanating from a group of disciples of John the Baptist who took John to be the Messiah.

The present writer can only say that he finds this elaborate hypothesis not incredible, for it is quite possible, but incapable of proof or of disproof, and therefore beyond serious discussion. There is of course much that is independent of the hypothesis, and of historical and exegetical value, in Taylor's commentary.

Which was the Fourth Gospel? JSNT 54 (1994), 3–28.

In this article R. C. Morgan argues that Jn was known to and used by Luke. This relates much less to Acts than to the Third Gospel (if the term may be allowed), but there are a few points, such as the Ascension, in which it is profitable at least to consider the matter from the stand-point of Johannine priority. Even here, however, we are dealing with theological rather than literary relations.

Bibliography

M. E. Boismard and A. Lamouille, *Les Actes des deux Apôtres*, Paris 1990.

H. J. Cadbury, *NTS* 3 (1957), 128–32.

L. Cerfaux, *Rec.* 2.63–91.

J. Dupont, *The Sources of Acts*, ET London 1964.

J. A. Emerton, *JSS* 13 (1968), 282–97.

A. Harnack, *The Acts of the Apostles*, ET London 1906.

C. J. Hemer, *Tyndale Bulletin* 36 (1985), 79–109.

J. Jeremias, *ZNW* 36 (1937), 205–21.

R. A. Martin, *NTS* 11 (1965), 38–59.

S. E. Parker, 'The "We-Passages"'', in *The Book of Acts* 2.545–74.

S. M. Praeder, *NovT* 29 (1987), 193–218.

J. Taylor, *Les Actes des deux Apôtres* (Actes 9.1–18.22), Paris 1994.

J. Taylor, *Les Actes des deux Apôtres* (Actes 18.23–28.31), Paris 1996.

C.-J. Thornton, *Der Zeuge des Zeugen*, Tübingen 1991.

J. Wehnert, *Die Wir-Passagen in der Apostelgeschichte*, Göttingen 1989.

M. Wilcox, *The Semitisms of Acts*, Oxford 1965.

III. ACTS AS A HISTORICAL DOCUMENT

Read on the surface, as generations of Christians have read it, Acts presents the history of the Christian mission in its first three decades.[1] It is right to say 'of the Christian mission' rather than 'of the Christian church', for Acts shows little interest (it would be wrong to say, no interest) in the structure and development of the church as an institution. The history is only a sketch; its author probably intended to confine himself to one roll of papyrus, matching his earlier volume on the story of Jesus, which in turn matched other works on the same theme. The outline of the sketch is familiar. Everything turned on the fact that the crucified Jesus was raised from death by God, reassembled his disciples, and fulfilled his promise of sending to them the gift of the Holy Spirit. His parting from them is narrated, and the descent of the Spirit on the Day of Pentecost leads immediately to the beginning of the mission in Jerusalem (cf. Lk. 24.47). There follows not a next-day event but what is obviously intended as a specimen of early Christian activity: there is a miracle of healing, a crowd assembles, and the Christian message is proclaimed once more. Another event, doubtless again a representative rather than a unique event, follows: the unauthorized, and unwelcome, preachers are arrested and brought before the Jewish Council. They are warned not to repeat their offence, a warning which they evidently have no intention of heeding. What Luke tells us at this stage about the primitive community is not that it had such-and-such an organization, but that its members prayed and took their meals together, sold their property and shared the proceeds; this leads to the shameful discovery that a couple have lied about the price obtained for their property. Their fate occasions fear of divine retribution but not fear of the religious and civil authorities. Preaching continues; there are further arrests and a beating; and evident intention to continue the mission.

This closes the first part of the story (chs. 1–5). The next begins with a second regrettable discovery: the charitable distribution of supplies proves to be inequitable. The apostles have enough to do without giving time to this task and seven others are appointed. One of them, going far beyond this appointment, preaches and engages in controversy to such effect that he too is arrested and brought before the Sanhedrin. His long speech is followed by his martyrdom, and

[1]F. V. Filson, *Three Crucial Decades*, London, 1964.

the outbreak of general persecution, which has the effect of pushing the mission out beyond Jerusalem, as the Christians escape from their persecutors. Further preaching and miracle working lead to the conversion of Samaritans and of an Ethiopian on his way back from Jerusalem to his own country. The arch-persecutor also leaves Jerusalem in order to deal with Christians in Damascus, but on the way, encountering Christ himself, he becomes a Christian and returns to Jerusalem, where, not without difficulty, he is united with the main body of Christians and works as a mission preacher till opposition enforces his withdrawal from the city (6.1–9.30).

A third phase (9.31–12.25) begins when Peter also leaves Jerusalem and after performing miracles on the way reaches Caesarea where he is led into contact with a Roman centurion. The mission preaching is repeated and the centurion, Gentile though he is, unbaptized as he is, becomes a Christian and receives the Spirit. Peter returns to Jerusalem, receives the inevitable criticism from those who thought it right to maintain the old barriers between Jews and Gentiles, and overcomes it by telling the story. The mission to the Gentiles receives a fresh, independent beginning in Antioch, where the church is founded and develops in independence, manifested in a gift to the mother church in Jerusalem. The third phase is wound up in Jerusalem, where persecution initiated by King (Herod) Agrippa I is ended by the discomfiture of the tyrant.

The scene shifts to Antioch (13.1), where the mixed Jewish-Gentile church commissions Paul and Barnabas to take the mission further. They travel to Cyprus and to central southern Asia Minor, preaching, working miracles, making disciples, establishing churches, eventually returning to their base and reporting to the church. At this point a vital problem appears. It is undoubtedly true that Gentiles have been converted by the preaching of the Gospel of Jesus. What next? There are some who take the view that these converts, if they are to be saved members of the people of God, must be circumcised and thereafter observe the law of Moses. Others think that this is not necessary but imposes an uncalled-for burden upon the Gentiles. This was too big an issue to be settled in Antioch; it must be discussed and decided in Jerusalem. After some debate the decision is reached: Gentile converts do not have to be circumcised and keep the whole Law; they must however observe a few regulations. This has the effect of setting Paul (and no doubt others) free to pursue the mission without restriction; and, with companions and assistants, he does so (chs. 13–15).

The rest of the book contains the record of Paul's work throughout the north-eastern quadrant of the Mediterranean. He repeatedly meets opposition but everywhere there are converts and churches are established in such places as Philippi, Thessalonica, Corinth, Ephesus. Eventually he returns to Jerusalem, where his arrival creates renewed difficulty. Jewish Christians have been given the impression that Paul in his travels throughout the Diaspora has been teaching Jews not to circumcise their children, not to keep the Law, has been, in fact, practising and preaching apostasy from Moses. The Christian authorities are sure that this report is not true, but Paul must somehow demonstrate its falsehood. The suggestion is made that he should accompany and pay the expenses of four men who were due to be released from a vow. Paul accepts the suggestion, but the plan misfires. He is accused not only of attacking the Law but of profaning the Temple by bringing Gentiles into it. He is rescued from an angry mob by Roman soldiers, and from this point to the end of the book is in Roman hands. The Romans do not release but they do protect him. At length he appeals to Caesar and is sent to Rome. It is a stormy and dangerous passage, but in the end he arrives, and the Gospel is preached in the capital of the Empire, and even if Jews close their ears the Gentiles will listen (chs. 16–28).

'Read on the surface' this is a plain tale. It is history, of a popular kind. That means that it is biographical, focusing on a few out-standing characters, episodic in style,[2] highly coloured with wonder-ful and exciting incidents, and not given to philosophizing about the nature and meaning of history or about the theological content of the message. Luke's interest in the spread of the Gospel into the non-Jewish world is plain, and so is his sense of achievement when he can narrate the great missionary's arrival at Rome—a goal probably in his mind as early as 1.8 ('... up to the end of the earth'). More searching inquiry, however, and a reading that digs beneath the surface, unearth problems which the reader cannot ignore. In reading 5.1–11, for example, he will ask whether Ananias and Sapphira were in fact guilty of nothing more than money-grubbing deceit; does there not perhaps lie behind their action a divergent view of the way in which the church should handle its corporate finances? In ch. 6 we seem at first sight to have a simple problem in the field of social concern, speedily resolved by administrative adjustment. Was it so simple? Who were Hellenists and Hebrews, and how did they differ? The word Hellenist is used twice more, in 9.29 and 11.20, each time with a different meaning. Can the difference between the two groups have been purely linguistic? How was it that when *all* the Christians were obliged to leave Jerusalem, the apostles (who would, one would have thought, be regarded as ring-leaders) were excepted (8.1)? Perhaps, notwithstanding the Temple disturbances of chs. 4 and 5, they were less obnoxious to the authorities. The conversion and baptism of an Ethiopian eunuch (who could not have been a proselyte) might seem, as an example, to settle the question whether

[2]See especially E. Plümacher, *Lukas als hellenistischer Schriftsteller* (Göttingen, 1972); 'Die Apostelgeschichte als historische Monographie', in Kremer, *Actes*, 457–66. See also W. C. van Unnik in Kremer, *Actes*, 37–60.

Gentiles might become Christians without circumcision; but Peter's visit to Cornelius is described as an unprecedented step. It leads to the conclusion, 'To the Gentiles also God has granted that repentance that leads to life' (11.18); if this was agreed why was another conference necessary to discuss the question whether Gentile converts should be circumcised (15.1, 5)? This introduces Paul, who, in the Acts narrative, is present at the conference and assents to and helps to disseminate a decree to which in his extant letters he never refers, a decree which it is very difficult to harmonize with the theology of those letters. Apart from this the account of Paul's work to which Acts proceeds raises few serious problems, though some of the speeches attributed to him, especially the Areopagus address (17.22–31), are scarcely consistent with his thought as otherwise known.

These problems, and others, are discussed at appropriate points in the Commentary. What must be attempted here is not a repetition of what is done elsewhere but an integrated statement which may lead to a general evaluation of the book before us. If this is to be done there can be no doubt that we should begin with the problems that are created by the account of the Council in ch. 15. This is not only because these problems are of unusual importance but because they lead, in many cases, to problems in other parts of the book, and because the Council has often, and rightly, been described as the centre of Acts. It is this in itself, and also (as is pointed out on pp. 709f.) as the prime and determining example of a pattern of narration that occurs frequently. It is one of Luke's ways of expressing the victory of the Gospel. A difficulty arises; it is addressed by the Christian community; a solution is found which not merely solves the difficulty but leads to a further expansion of the Christian movement. Acts 15 provides a crucial example of this pattern which may be said without exaggeration to constitute the pattern of the whole book. In the early chapters, having provided a basic statement of Christian faith and life in the primitive Jerusalem context, Luke collects such examples as he can find of the way in which the Gospel spread out of its original setting into the non-Jewish world.[3] There now arises the supreme difficulty, in the assertion that the mission to the Gentiles can be legitimate only if it is a Jewish mission; that is, converts to Christianity must be circumcised. They can become Christians only if they also become Jews, members of the people to whom the promises were spoken and the Messiah came. If this conviction had been upheld the world-wide mission would have come to an end and the distinctive Christian message would have ceased to exist. This supreme difficulty is solved in the Council, but the result is not confined to the relief of the church in Antioch

---

[3]See I.50–52.

(15.31); the result runs through the rest of the book which describes the increasing success of the mission to the Gentiles and reaches its climax when Paul proclaims the Gospel unhindered in Rome.

The difficulties in the account of the Council arise partly within Acts itself, and partly when Acts is compared with the Pauline letters, especially Galatians, where also a Jerusalem Council is described. The internal difficulties may be briefly outlined as follows. See further detail in Sections 38, 39.

1. Verses 1 and 5 prepare the reader for a violent debate, but with the exception of v. 7 and its reference to πολλὴ ζήτησις there is no debate. All the participants are in agreement; there is no opposition.
2. In view of 11.18 it is not clear why there should be a Council; in this verse it seems to be agreed that God is willing to grant to Gentiles as they are, that is, without circumcision, the repentance that leads to life. The issue is already settled.
3. When Peter speaks he seems to claim too much. That he should refer back to the conversion of Cornelius in ch. 10 is natural enough;[4] but with what right can Peter describe the Law as an intolerable burden which neither he nor his Jewish ancestors have been able to bear?
4. It is surprising that Paul and Barnabas, appointed (according to 15.2) its representatives by the church in Antioch, should have virtually nothing to say. They report (15.12) the signs and portents done by God through them, but they bring no theological argument to bear on the question whether circumcision should or should not be demanded of Gentile converts. Has 15.12 been inserted into a source that did not originally contain it? What interest does Luke think that these two represent?[5]
5. When James speaks he agrees with Peter that circumcision should not be required, pointing out that Peter is supported by the words of the prophets; when however he quotes Amos to this effect he uses a passage which in the LXX text (which he uses) makes his point, but in the Hebrew text has a quite different meaning. This use of the LXX is, to say the least, surprising.
6. The issue of the Council is a decree, suggested by James in v. 20 and incorporated (v. 29) in a letter (vv. 23–29).[6] The interpretation of this decree, and the grounds on which it rests, are themselves disputed. The letter, including the decree, is addressed τοῖς κατὰ τὴν Ἀντιόχειαν καὶ Συρίαν καὶ Κιλικίαν ἀδελφοῖς τοῖς ἐξ ἐθνῶν; it is however conveyed by Paul, Barnabas, and

---

[4]Though this story itself is not without some serious problems; see I.491–8.

[5]A related question is whether Luke did or could regard Paul and Barnabas as apostles; see pp. xlivf., lxxxix and I.101, 644, 666f.

[6]On the textual problems that arise here see pp. 735f.; they need not be discussed at this point.

others to Antioch (v. 30), then to Derbe, Lystra, and other cities of that area (16.1, 4); nothing is said of Syria and Cilicia, but it is assumed that the decree is of wider application than the letter itself suggests.

7. Finally, it is not clear exactly what was discussed at the Council. In vv. 1, 5 it seems plain that the issue is that of salvation: without circumcision, οὐ δύνασθε σωθῆναι. It is however often maintained[7] that the decree itself deals with a different matter. It does not present conditions on which Gentiles may receive salvation but lays down procedures that will facilitate fellowship, and especially fellowship at table, between Jewish Christians and Gentile Christians. The latter must (the word ἐπάναγκες in v. 28 is not always noticed and given due weight) observe certain regulations regarding food and other practices. Does the Council—at least in Luke's account of it—change course part way through?

The questions that arise when Acts 15 is compared with the Pauline literature may now be considered.

1. It must first be observed that Paul also describes a Council in Jerusalem, in Gal. 2.1–10. It is hard to doubt[8] that Paul and Luke are describing the same event. Paul, Barnabas, James, and Peter are present in both; according to Paul, Titus and John were there too. Luke does not mention them but does not say that they were not there. There was, according to Galatians, a strong move to bring Paul and his Gentile Christians into bondage (to the Law); this Paul resisted. The 'Pillars' recognized his mission, but there was an agreement that he should go to the Gentiles, they to the Jews, and a request that he and his colleagues should remember the poor. Neither this agreement nor this request is contained in Acts.

2. The Acts Council results in a Decree; there is no reference to this in Galatians, or indeed in the Pauline corpus. The Decree rejects idolatry and fornication; so does Paul, but without reference to the Decree and its authority. The Decree explicitly forbids the use of εἰδωλόθυτα; Paul explicitly permits it (so long as it does not result in unloving treatment of others). Whether the Decree is compatible with Pauline theology at large need not be discussed at this point; it is enough to note that he seems to be unaware of it and on at least one point to contradict it.

3. The Acts Council arises out of a visit of Judaean Christians to Antioch. The Council in Galatians is followed by a visit to Antioch of certain people who came from James and were

---

[7]See pp. 695–7.
[8]Though some do; see for example those mentioned in Kümmel, *Einleitung* 263.

responsible for the separation of Peter, Barnabas, and other Jewish Christians from the Gentile Christians of Antioch.[9]

4. When the two narratives are taken together, each considered in its own context, that of Acts and that of the Pauline corpus respectively, the question of Paul's status and the roots of his theology is acutely raised. For Paul's apostleship in Acts see p. lxxxix; in only two verses (14.4, 14) is he described as an apostle; he is not so described in ch. 15. Too much should not be made of this; neither is Peter. Paul himself insists most strongly on his apostleship (e.g. 1 Cor. 9.1f.), and in Gal. 2.6 he affirms that the men of repute 'added nothing to him' (οὐδὲν προσανέθεντο)—gave him no additional authority, or added nothing to his Gospel. They recognized that he had been entrusted with the 'Gospel of the uncircumcision' as Peter with that 'of the circumcision', and perceived the grace that had been given to him. It is however striking that in v. 8 the word ἀποστολή is used with reference to Peter, not with reference to Paul (though it may be held that it is implied). It seems that in the Galatians narrative Paul's status, though at least partially affirmed, is one of the questions under discussion.[10] Acts 15 is silent about this.

It will be shown below (pp. 709–11) that, as far as the structure of Acts 15 is concerned, the upshot of these observations is that Luke has himself produced the apparently well told story of the Council, though he has not created it out of nothing. He knew (correctly) that there had been a gathering in Jerusalem in which Peter, James, Paul, and Barnabas had taken part. He knew that there had emerged from Jerusalem a decree which regulated the place of Gentile Christians in the people of God. He knew that men who were or claimed to be envoys of the Jerusalem church caused trouble in Antioch, and perhaps elsewhere, by stressing the claims of the old religion. He knew a number of arguments[11] by which the mission to the Gentiles might be justified and Gentiles admitted without the full requirement of the Law. These did not include the great Pauline theological argument, but they were not unworthy of consideration. He believed—wrongly—that the Law in its fullness must be a burden intolerable even to Jews. He knew (and had recounted the fact) that Gentiles had received, in the gift of the Spirit, precisely the same experience of salvation as Jewish Christians. Who could refuse to such believers the water of baptism? He knew that as the mission to the Gentiles had been pursued miracles had taken place. Would God have granted such tokens of his power and favour if he had disapproved of the proceedings? And finally Luke believed that

[9]Some think that in this Paul is not following a chronological order; the events of Gal. 2.11–14 preceded those of 2.1–10. This is unlikely.

[10]Cf. the Western text of Acts 15.2 (see p. 701).

[11]Not (as Haenchen 121 says) only one—the signs and wonders.

Scripture itself made it clear that it was God's intention to include in his saved people 'the rest of men' (Amos 9.12, LXX), that is, the Gentiles. These arguments Luke distributed among the participants in the Council, as he thought, suitably.

The distribution of arguments, however, is sufficient to show that the centrality of the Council in Acts (like the narrative itself) is Luke's own work. The mission to the Gentiles is his chief concern, and he wishes to show that it received the backing of all elements within the church. The few who dissented were speedily silenced or convinced. It was not so in Paul's lifetime. There was (as Galatians shows) a measure of agreement between Paul and the Jerusalem apostles, but it was by no means complete agreement. F. C. Baur[12] rightly pointed out that if the Jerusalem apostles had fully accepted Paul's Gentile mission they would have joined it rather than dissociating it from their own mission (Gal. 2.9). The very existence of Galatians proves that the Council did not put an end to conflict. The welcome Paul receives in 21.18–25 is, even in Luke's narrative, lukewarm, and from that point onwards there is not a word to suggest that the church in Jerusalem and the church in Caesarea had any interest in Paul's fate. Luke associates Paul with Stephen (cf. 22.20), that is, he was a legitimate, harmless, missioner to the Gentiles. But Paul was not a Hellenist;[13] he was a Hebrew. Luke did not write as he did with the intention of conveying a false impression of the church in its first age. He wrote as he did because his understanding was coloured by the period in which he lived. It was a period in which consensus had at last been reached.[14] The strife of the first three decades, often, as the Pauline epistles show, bitter and unrelenting, had worked itself out and a period of peace ensued. In addition to the fact that, badly as some of them failed, the Christians acknowledged a common loyalty to Jesus and acceptance of his authority, which not only gave them a common axis by which to orient their lives but also laid upon them some sort of obligation to love one another, there were several particular factors that contributed to the overcoming of dissent and the establishing of consensus. By the end of the 60s Paul, Peter, and James had all, it seems, died as martyrs.[15] This removed two highly contentious figures and one who, though possibly not contentious in himself, could easily be used as a standard-bearer for a third Christian group; it also made possible, perhaps inevitable, a different evaluation of them. That they had once disagreed over weighty matters now seemed less important than that they had unitedly borne witness to Christ with their blood. They were united in death; it was hard to believe that they had ever been separated in

[12]*Paulus*, [1]125; [2]142f.
[13]On this term see I.308, 309; also *FS* Borgen, 20–25.
[14]It was a Hellenist consensus; see *FS* Jervell 9f.
[15]1 Clement 5.3–7; Eusebius, *HE* 2.23.4–18 (Hegesippus); Josephus, *Ant.* 20.200.

life. Again, Jerusalem, once the scene of dispute and the centre from which Judaizing missions bore down upon the Pauline churches, had virtually ceased to exist as a Jewish and Christian religious centre. Sacrificial worship probably did persist in the Temple between AD 70 and 135,[16] but this did not alter the fact that the Christians had left the city, taking refuge in Pella.[17] The anti-Pauline missions that had emanated from Jerusalem had lost their base of operations; in any case, they (but this is a comprehensive term, calling for differentiation) had defeated Paul,[18] whose radical theology and missionary principles were no longer understood and practised even by those who admired him, such as Luke (who could take the Decree as the core of his faith) and the author, or authors, of the Pastorals. The Gentile mission and the Gentile church were fully accepted, and no one who counted demanded circumcision. The Gentiles for their part were willing to accept the Decree that had been drawn up many years previously, and they continued to observe it for centuries to come.[19]

This was the situation in which Luke lived and wrote. He took it for granted. This makes much better sense than to suppose that he invented a fictitious story designed to conceal the horrid truth about the church's past. If Luke was practising concealment he was an incompetent practitioner: traces of division, of which he was himself perhaps hardly conscious, show through his narrative. These traces are much better explained if we think of Luke as writing honest history but writing it in an atmosphere different from that of the period that he described. It is not merely that contemporary written records were few, perhaps even as some would say non-existent, and that memories, then as now, could be fallible. Any narrative needs an appropriate frame of reference if it is to be intelligible and to give an accurate impression of events. To enter with controlled imagination into a past frame of reference is the historian's hardest task; Luke did not achieve it with complete success. He was describing contentious events within a framework provided by a period of consensus. This was his problem, and, in a different sense, it is ours, as we attempt to understand and assess his work. Varying his language only a little, one learns from F. C. Baur to recognize tendency and tension, the one masking the other. Baur was fundamentally right to see in

---

[16]See K. W. Clark, *NTS* 6 (1960), 269–80.

[17]Eusebius, *HE* 3.5.3, probably drawing on Hegesippus. S. G. F. Brandon, *The Fall of Jerusalem and the Christian Church* (London, 1951), 168–73 thinks that they took refuge not in Pella but in Egypt.

[18]In this (but in little else) I disagree with M. D. Goulder's *A Tale of Two Missions* (London, 1994). He thinks that Paul won.

[19]For a somewhat different, and very important point of view, see J. Jervell, *Luke and the People of God* (Minneapolis 1972) and *The Unknown Paul* (Minneapolis, 1984). In *FS* Jervell 1–10 I have given some indication of points at which, with great respect, I differ from him.

primitive Christianity tension: division and conflict. No one agreed with him more firmly than J. B. Lightfoot.[20] And there was in Acts a contrary force which had the effect of throwing a smoke screen over the battlefield. For Baur's insight one cannot be too grateful. His error was not in perceiving tension and tendency; it lay rather in chronology and in the evaluation of the tendency. Conflicts which Baur placed in the second century, with the books that displayed them, belonged in fact to the first; and the tendency that shrouded the conflicts was not wilful concealment but the—mainly uncon-scious—effect of an environment marked by consensus rather than dispute.

We shall return to this theme (see pp. cxii–cxviii); for the present we have a cue for turning aside to themes that have a conventional, and proper, place in an Introduction. Who wrote our book, and when, and where? These questions are relegated to a relatively subordinate place for the good reason that there is little that can be said about them.

Traces of the knowledge and use of Acts were listed in I.34–38. Acts cannot be proved by quotation to have existed before the second half of the second century. It may have been known to Justin; it was rather more probably known to the author of the *Epistula Aposto-lorum*. It is tempting to see traces of it within the NT itself, in Mk. 16.9–20 and 2 Tim. 3.11, but these passages are adequately explained as due to the use of parallel traditions. External evidence will not take us to a date earlier than c. AD 150, but the lack of earlier evidence does not mean that the book was not written before that date. It seems (see above) to have been written at a time of both inward and outward peace, and there is evidence in remarks about Roman provincial administration and provincial officers[21] that sug-gests a date within the first century. The period of consensus within which Acts appears to have been written (see above, pp. xlf.) was ended by the development of gnosticism, of which signs appear already in the NT, and indeed in Acts (see 20.20, 27, 29, 30), and the last years of Domitian (AD 81–96) were marked by some oppressive measures. Luke's first volume, the Third Gospel, dependent as it is on Mark, can hardly have been written before 80; quite possibly some years later. So far it may seem probable (though anything but certain) that Acts was written in the late 80s or early 90s. This dating is complicated by several factors.

---

[20]See e.g. his *Galatians* p. 374, and the comment by W. G. Kümmel in *Das Neue Testament im 20. Jahrhundert* (Stuttgarter B-S 50; Stuttgart, 1970), 73. Lightfoot corrected Baur's dates but did not wholly disagree with his understanding of early Christian history. M. D. Goulder (see n. 18) makes a welcome restatement of the fundamental points.

[21]See e.g. the notes on 17.6f.; 19.31; and much more in chs. 21–28.

One is constituted by the 'We' passages; it will be better to consider these under the heading of authorship rather than date; see above, pp. xxvii–xxx, and below, pp. xliv–xlix. If the author was one of Paul's travelling companions he cannot have been writing much later than the 80s. Another arises out of the fact that Acts comes to an end at the close of Paul's two year ministry in Rome (28.30, 31). Why does Luke take the story no further? Why in particular does he not finish the story of Paul by taking it up to his death—his martyrdom, if Clement of Rome and later writers are to be believed? The simplest answer to these questions is that Luke has brought the story up to date. He tells no more because there is no more to tell. This is an attractive view. Luke was without doubt an admirer of Paul; he loved a good story, and the account of a martyrdom that would have matched Stephen's is the sort of thing he would have liked to write. It is an attractive view, but it is not convincing. It runs into an insuperable obstacle in the fact that Acts presupposes Lk., and Lk. presupposes Mk., which was not written till about 70. Lk. moreover implies the fall of Jerusalem in AD 70 (Lk. 21.20–24). The later date of Acts is not dependent on our being able to explain why the book ends where it does, but explanations may be suggested. It is fair to observe that the promise and commission of 1.8 are fulfilled by Paul's preaching in Rome; they would not be more completely fulfilled by his death. Again, Luke was writing a work of edification; Paul's death may not have been an edifying story. He may have been deserted, even betrayed, by those who should have stood by him. 2 Tim. 4.16 (πάντες με ἐγκατέλιπον) may or may not be historical, but it is more likely to rest on tradition than on fancy; the story of desertion might have been repeated (or this might have been Paul's only defence). Perhaps there was no dramatic scene; the Romans locked him up and left him to rot.

It is sometimes argued that the confusion over the dates of Judas and Theudas (5.36, 37) arose through a misreading of Josephus, *Ant.* 20.102 (see I.293–295—in line 18 of p. 295 correcting *nothing* to *noting*). This would make Acts later than the publication of the *Antiquities* in AD 93. The argument has little weight.

A more serious matter is Luke's failure to use or to make any reference to Paul's letters, some of which are referred to in 1 Clement (usually dated c. AD 96). Is it conceivable that Luke, if writing about AD 90, would not know them? at least have heard of them? It is a difficult question (see *FS* Mitton, 2–5), but hardly determinative for the dating of Acts.

As to the place of writing almost any guess will do. Rome has been suggested, mainly because the author of the 'We' passages accompanies Paul to Rome; also because this would furnish an explanation of the book's ending—there was no need to write more because the readers already knew the story from Paul's arrival to his death. Luke himself is said to have been an Antiochene;[22] this may or may not be true but in any case tells us nothing about where he wrote. Ephesus, or a Pauline community in Macedonia, Achaea, or Asia Minor have been suggested.[23] But Kümmel's judgement is correct: 'Wo der Verf. schrieb ... lässt sich nicht mehr feststellen.'

The author, who writes prefaces to both gospel (Lk. 1.1–4) and Acts (1.1),[24] reveals himself as a person, and it will be possible on the basis of these prefaces and the two works as wholes, to make certain observations about him, but his name is not mentioned. The earliest sources to name him (Irenaeus, the Anti-Marcionite Prologue, the Muratorian Canon) call him Luke, and it is clear that they think of him as the member of the Pauline circle who is referred to at Col. 4.14 (the beloved physician); Philemon 24; 2 Tim. 4.11. If Thornton is right in his claim, for which there is much to be said, that the author of the book must be also the author of the source expressed in the first person plural,[25] we must conclude that the author of the book was one of the Pauline circle, and it would be reasonable to follow Thornton (see p. xxviii) in the opinion that Luke wrote Acts (and the Third Gospel). Against this conclusion the only substantial argument consists in the errors found in the Acts account of Paul. These must not be exaggerated. The epistles that come from his own hand represent Paul as precisely the kind of person who appears in Acts: a constant traveller, a fearless and effective preacher, a founder and pastor of churches, a Jew who had the gift of ready access to Gentiles. The geographical and chronological details provided by Acts fit reasonably well with the data provided by the letters (see Dates and Places, below). But the differences and problems referred to above are more than sufficient to cast doubt on the identification of our author with a Pauline travelling companion. Did such a companion never see Paul at work writing 'weighty and strong' letters, and observe their effect on the recipients? Was he unaware of the turbulent and complicated relation between Paul and Corinth? Did he understand Pauline theology so ill that he could picture Paul not only helping to compose but distributing a decree which told Gentiles that if they would be saved they need not indeed be circumcised but must

[22]Jerome, *Comm. in Matthaeum*, Praefatio 26–39: Tertius Lucas medicus natione Syrus Antiochensis; Anti-Marcionite Prologue to Luke: Ἔστιν ὁ ἅγιος Λουκᾶς Ἀντιοχεύς Σύρος τῷ γένει, ἰατρὸς τὴν τέχνην.

[23]Kümmel, *Einleitung* 154.

[24]Cadbury's commentary on Lk. 1.1–4 (*Begs.* 2.488–510) is a classic and still worthy of careful study. See also, in addition to commentaries, L. Alexander, *The Preface to Luke's Gospel* (SNTSMS 78, Cambridge, 1993), with a valuable bibliography (and index).

[25]The same conclusion was reached by Harnack, *Luke the Physician* (ET London, 1911); *The Acts of the Apostles* (ET London, 1909).

abstain from εἰδωλόθυτα and food that did not satisfy the *kashrut* regulations? It is certainly true that in every Christian generation there have been those who found Paul's thought difficult and were misled by their misunderstanding of it (2 Peter 3.16), but this is not an adequate explanation. It must have been clear even to the dimmest theologian that Paul was engaged in a running battle with (e.g.) the Galatian and Corinthian disturbers of the peace. The argument, based on his vocabulary, that the author was a medical doctor, which would support the reference to Col. 4.14, was disproved by Cadbury.[26] It is not that Paul does not use terms that are used by Greek medical writers; he does from time to time do so. It is rather that these terms are used by other non-medical writers also; they did not constitute a special technical language, understood and used only within the profession. Luke's use of technical vocabulary suggests, if anything, that he was not a doctor but a sailor. Apart from this, his varied style shows him to be a competent writer but does little or nothing to identify him. That he was capable of writing good idiomatic Greek is shown by his preface to his first volume (Lk. 1.1–4) and by a number of passages in the second, especially in places where he puts words on the lips of educated men. Such are for example the speech of the town clerk in Ephesus (19.35–40), that of Tertullus (24.2–8) and Paul's reply (24.10–21), Festus's words to Agrippa (25.24–27); compare the letter of the tribune Claudius Lysias (23.26–30). The question of Semitism in his style has been much discussed. The view that he was in the first half of Acts translating a continuous Aramaic source had been generally if not universally abandoned. There are however a few passages where the hypothesis of mistranslation of Aramaic is plausible, possibly even convincing, but these have more to do with Luke's sources than with his own background and ability.[27] Anyone may make a mistake in translating Aramaic, or perhaps misread the text he is translating; more relevant to an assessment of Luke as an author is the mildly Semitic atmosphere that can be detected in many parts of the earlier chapters. This could be due to the translation of Semitic documents, but is much better explained as due to the influence of environment and of the Greek of the LXX. This may have been partly subconscious but was probably to a great extent conscious; Luke thought it suitable to write of Palestinian events in a way that evoked the Palestinian background and, more important, to continue the record of God's dealings with his people in language and in a manner that suggested his relation with the elect people of earlier times.

This appears in the Septuagintalisms which are a not uncommon

---

[26]See Cadbury, *Style* 39–72; also *JBL* 45 (1926), 190–209.
[27]See e.g. 1.15, 22; 2.47; 3.16; 4.25; 7.35; 9.28; 10.14, 36f., 40; 12.3.

feature especially of the earlier chapters of Acts.[28] These are not so much a phenomenon of translation as of appropriate, 'biblical' style. It will be necessary here to list only some of the most important turns of phrase and vocabulary that bear witness to Luke's awareness of the OT and of the relation to it of his own work. It is seldom that he allows himself to write intolerable Greek, but some of his idioms attest their origin, though often only by relative frequency.

Καὶ ἐγένετο (or ἐγένετο δὲ) suggests the familiar Hebrew ויהי; the verb with the waw consecutive that would follow in Hebrew is represented in various ways. Thus:

4.5: ἐγένετο δέ with accusative and infinitive, συναχθῆναι τοὺς ἄρχοντας ...

9.3: ἐγένετο with accusative and infinitive, αὐτὸν ἐγγίζειν

9.32: ἐγένετο δέ with accusative and infinitive, Πέτρον κατελθεῖν

9.43: ἐγένετο δέ with the infinitive, μεῖναι

10.25: ὡς δὲ ἐγένετο with accusative and the genitive of the infinitive, τοῦ εἰσελθεῖν τὸν Πέτρον

11.26: ἐγένετο with dative, καί, and infinitive, αὐτοῖς καὶ συναχθῆναι

14.1: ἐγένετο δέ with accusative and infinitive, εἰσελθεῖν αὐτούς

16.16: ἐγένετο δέ with accusative and infinitive, παιδισκὴν ὑπαντῆσαι

19.1: ἐγένετο δέ with accusative and infinitive, Παῦλον κατελθεῖν (and ἐν τῷ with accusative and infinitive)

21.1: ὡς δὲ ἐγένετο with accusative and infinitive, ἀναχθῆναι ἡμᾶς

21.5: ὅτε δὲ ἐγένετο with accusative and infinitive, ἡμᾶς ἐξαρτίσαι

28.8: ἐγένετο δέ with accusative and infinitive, τὸν πατέρα κατακεῖσθαι

Hebrew idiom, reflected in the LXX, is recalled by the use of verbs, often as participles, which are unnecessary to the sense. So for example ἀναστάς (– ἀντες) at 1.15 (ἀναστὰς Πέτρος); 5.6, 17, 34; 8.27; 9.18, 39; 10.13, 20, 23; 11.7, 28; 13.16; 14.20; 15.7; 22.10, 16; 23.9.[29] ἀποκριθείς (– θέντες) is used similarly, reflecting the use of ענה, which sometimes means no more than *he spoke up, intervened*

---

[28]See Wilcox; W. K. L. Clarke in *Begs*. 2.66–105; J. de Zwaan in *Begs*. 2.30–65; H. F. D. Sparks in *JTS* 1 (1950), 16–28; Moulton in M. 1.18; Howard in M. 2.411–485; Turner in M. 4.45–63; BDR § 4 ('Für einen feierlichen und würdevollen Stil erschien die Sprache der LXX als sehr passend.').

[29]In some of these passages it may be argued with some force that the participle plays a significant narrative role and does not necessarily suggest a Semitic background.

in conversation. Thus 4.19; 5.29; 8.24, 34; 9.13; 19.15; 25.9.[30] Another word that sometimes seems superfluous is ἄρχεσθαι, especially the aorist participle: 1.1; 2.4; 11.4 (ἀρξάμενος), 15?; 18.26; 27.35.[31]

(καὶ) ἰδού, recalling the Hebrew הנה(ו), is used more frequently than is usual in Greek: 1.10; 2.7 (οὐχ ἰδού[sic]); 5.9, 25, 28; 7.56; 8.27, 36; 9.10, 11; 10.17, 19, 21, 30; 11.11; 12.7; 13.11 (καὶ νῦν ἰ.), 25, 46; 16.1; 20.22 (καὶ νῦν ἰ.), 25 (καὶ νῦν ἰ.); 27.24.

The use of periphrastic tenses is not un-Greek, but there are more such forms in Acts than would be expected in a piece of ordinary Greek prose. Howard (M. 2.452) lists occurrences of the imperfect of εἰμί with the present participle as follows: 1.10, 13, 14; 2.2, 5, 42; 8.1, 13, 28; 9.9, 28; 10.24, 30; 11.5; 12.5, 6, 20; 14.7; 16.9, 12; 18.7; 21.3; 22.19, 20. It will be noticed that occurrences disappear with the Jewish element in the story; from ch. 22 onwards Paul's dealings are mostly with Romans.

The use of ἐν τῷ with the infinitive in a temporal sense probably reflects the LXX rendering of ב with the Hebrew infinitive. Howard (M. 2.450f.) lists the following passages: 2.1; 8.6; 9.3; 11.15; 19.1, rightly excepting 3.26; 4.30, where the meaning is not temporal and the use can be regarded as classical.[32]

Causal use of ἀπό occurs at least three times in Acts: 11.19; 12.14; 22.11. This recalls the LXX use of ἀπό to render causal מן.

In non-biblical Greek verbs of speaking are normally followed by a dative of the person addressed. In Hebrew prepositions (אל, ל) are used, and these are represented in the LXX by πρός. In Acts, cf. 1.7; 2.29, 37, 38; 3.12, (25); 4.1, 8, 19, 23, 24; 5.8, 9, 35; 7.3; 8.20, 26; 9.10, 11, 15; 10.28; 11.14, 20; 12.8, 15; 13.15; 15.7, 36; 16.36, 37; 17.15; 18.6, 14; 19.2(bis), (3𝔐), (25D); 21.37, 39; 22.8, 10, 21, 25; 23.3, (30); 25.16, 22; 26.1, 14, 28, 31; 28.4.21, 25.[33] This is a feature of Luke's style maintained in the later chapters. It may be due ultimately to the influence of the LXX but can hardly be said to be a conscious attempt to affect a biblical style where the context makes that style suitable.

Emphasis on the action of a finite verb is often expressed in Hebrew by the addition of the infinitive absolute of the same verb. The LXX translators sometimes represented this by the use (with the finite verb) of a participle of the same, or a kindred, verb or by the use of the dative of a cognate noun. The former construction occurs

---

[30]As well as the participle the finite verb is sometimes similarly used; sometimes the verb has, or may be held to have, narrative significance.

[31]1.22; 8.35; 10.37; 24.2 may be taken as part of the narrative.

[32]Howard (M. 2.451) quotes Sophocles, *Ajax* 554, ἐν τῷ φρονεῖν γὰρ μηδὲν ἥδιστος βίος, to show that 'the temporal use of ἐν τῷ c. inf. is not impossible Greek.' There is certainly a temporal element in the thought here.

[33]The list is provided by Turner in M. 4.54. He does notice that the reading in 19.3 is insecure.

in the NT only in actual quotations of the LXX; the latter occurs in Acts 2.30; (4.17 in many MSS); 5.28; 23.14. See M. 2.443f.; also Moule (*IB* 177f., with the quotation of Plato, *Symposium* 195b, φεύγων φυγῇ).

Another Hebrew characteristic is the use of a noun in the genitive instead of an adjective; in Acts see (6.11, ℵ* D 614 lat); 8.23; 9.15.

For further detailed discussion see M. 1.18, and references under Hebraism and Septuagint; M. 2.411–485; M. 4.45–63; Wilcox: H. F. D. Sparks, *JThS* 1 (1950), 16–28; BDR §4.[34] The strongest impression is given by some examples that occur very infrequently. Thus 12.3, προσέθετο συλλαβεῖν τὸν Πέτρον, clearly represents the Hebrew idiom ל הוסיף; 10.14, οὐδέποτε ἔφαγον πᾶν κοινόν recalls the Hebrew לא ... כל; 7.20, ἀστεῖος τῷ θεῷ is probably a Hebrew form of superlative; cardinal for ordinal numeral at 20.7 is a Septuagintal Hebraism; predicative εἰς (if such it is) at 19.27 recalls (though the context is wholly Greek) predicative ל; the use of εἰ in indirect questions (1.6; 7.1; 19.2; 21.37; 22.25) may be of Semitic origin mediated through the LXX.

Luke was a competent writer who, if he was not himself a Jew,[35] had made himself familiar with the OT in its Greek form, and was able, when it suited his purpose, to write in a style that suggested the continuity of his theme with the OT. In telling the unit stories, or episodes, of which his book is composed, he had great skill; Peter's visit to Cornelius (10.1–48), for example, and Paul's conversion (9.1–19), are complicated stories but they are told not only with clarity and effectiveness but with compelling interest. He shows less skill in planning the whole, but here allowance must be made for the fact that he was dependent on sources, often a matter of distant and imprecise recollection. It is probable that he wrote by the light of nature rather than under the control of accepted rhetorical principles—if indeed there were such principles for the writing of history.[36] He gave picture after picture of things he had discovered to have happened in the generation before his own until he came to the ministry of Paul which he was able to tell as a connected whole, though here too the story is constructed in the form of a series of

[34]See fn. 28.

[35]That Luke was a Gentile is widely believed, partly on the ground of his traditional identification with the Gentile physician of Col. 4.14; see however E. E. Ellis, *The Gospel of Luke*, NCB, London, 1966.

[36]Cadbury (*Making* 224) refers to Cicero, *De Oratore* 2.15 (61–63): Videtisne, quantum munus sit oratoris historia? haud scio, an flumine orationis, et varietate maximum, neque tamen eam reperio usquam separatim instructam rhetorum praeceptis. sita sunt enim ante oculos. Namquis nescit, primam esse historiae legem, ne quid falsi dicere audeat? deinde ne quid veri non audeat? ne qua suspicio gratiae sit in scribendo? ne qua simultatis? Haec scilicet fundamenta, nota sunt omnibus. The 'rules' referred to by W. C. van Unnik in the very important paper ('Luke's Second Book and the Rules of Hellenistic Historiography', in Kremer, *Actes* 37–60) relate much more to the substance than to the forms of history.

vivid scenes, and we move from one city to another, and then from one court room to another, and it is seldom that the connecting links are given in much detail.

If we ask why Luke wrote, secular motivation is not to be set aside entirely. Luke was born to write this kind of book and it is impossible to doubt that he enjoyed writing it. The enjoyment was partly a Christian enjoyment: it was good to enjoy fellowship with Christians of the past as well as with Christians of the present. But it was only partly a Christian enjoyment—though there is nothing un-Christian in getting pleasure from telling a good story. Or in reading one; and we may suppose that Luke was pleased that readers should enjoy reading his book.[37] That Luke wrote for pleasure, his own and his readers', is a motivation not to be overlooked and not to be ashamed of; but alone it is not adequate as an account of the origin of Acts.

The book has been described as apologetic, and that in various senses. That it is in the most general sense of the word a piece of apologetic is undoubtedly true; in this sense apologetic shades into evangelism, and there can be no question that Luke wished to commend the Christian faith as true, and as truth that all should, for their own good as well as simply because it was true, accept. The reader could not miss the injunction to save himself from the perverse generation by which he was surrounded (2.40), and the instruction, 'Believe in the Lord Jesus and you will be saved' (16.31); nor could he fail to note the repeated assertion that the crucified Jesus had been raised by God from the dead, an assertion which, if true, must constitute the greatest possible claim on his attention and belief. In this general sense, of statement and commendation, the book (following as it does upon an account of the life and teaching of Jesus) may be described as apologetic. Here and there it goes further than this, notably in 14.15–17 and 17.22–31, where Christian belief is set over against the religion of paganism. Polytheism and idolatry are refuted, and the Christian doctrine of God is defended by reference to his forbearance; if his justice is impugned it may be defended in terms of his patience in the past and his intention in the future, and presumably the near future, to carry out a universal judgement.[38] Jewish religion is not treated in the same way as pagan religion,[39] because Judaism, resting as it does on the OT, is true religion. But true Judaism, that is, Judaism as understood by Christians, is defended over against Judaism which so far misunderstands itself as to resist and persecute Christians. Paul repeatedly insists that he is simply a Jew who sees the fulfilment of

---

[37]R. I. Pervo, *Profit with Delight: The Literary Genre of the Acts of the Apostles* (Philadelphia, 1987).

[38]Luke has successors in Justin and other apologists of the second century.

[39]See below, pp. xcviif.

Judaism and the OT in the life, death, and resurrection of Jesus (e.g. 24.14; 26.22f.). It follows that there is both an affirmation of Judaism and an apologetic directed against its abuse and misinterpretation (e.g. 13.45–47).

It is not incorrect to describe Acts as a work of apologetic, but this is not an adequate description. In particular the view, sometimes held, that Acts is an apology addressed to the Roman judiciary and intended to show that Christianity is a movement which right-thinking Roman officials will view with tolerance is unconvincing. It is true that, according to Acts, Roman courts, when correctly informed, show no disposition to persecute Christians: the proconsul in Cyprus, Sergius Paulus, actually becomes a Christian (13.12); the magistrates in Philippi, when they learn that Paul and Silas are Roman citizens, immediately release them (16.38, 39); the proconsul Gallio in Corinth is not interested in the case brought against Paul (18.15); the town clerk in Ephesus defends him (19.37, 38); and from the time when Paul is rescued by Roman soldiers from the Temple mob (21.31, 32) the Roman tribune and the provincial governors treat him decently and protect him from Jewish violence up to the moment when Agrippa and Festus agree, 'He could have been released if he had not appealed to Caesar' (26.32). Luke would no doubt have been pleased to hear that a Christian on trial had been able to use some of these precedents, but the book as a whole is not to be thought of as serving such a purpose; no Roman court could be expected to wade through so much Jewish religious nonsense in order to find half-a-dozen fragments of legally significant material. The same argument proves even more conclusively that the book was not written as a brief for the defence at Paul's trial; what would be the use of chs. 1–12 for such a purpose?

The theme of apologetic has been inverted in the suggestion[40] that Acts was an apology addressed to the church on behalf of the Empire. Christians (such would be its theme) have no need to fear and ought not to oppose the Roman administration. When Roman officials are informed of the facts they will give a fair trial and will not believe calumnies. The church may settle down to live in confidence whatever time is left before the End. Again, there is something to be said for this as a subordinate interest of Luke's, but it will not account for more than a relatively small part of the book.

An important observation to be made here is that Luke had provided his church (wherever that may have been) with its NT. It probably had no more. We cannot suppose that Luke wrote his gospel with the notion that it should be published in one of four parallel columns in a Synopsis. He used Mk and collected what other

[40]See P. W. Walaskay, *And so we came to Rome*, SNTSMS 49 (Cambridge, 1983).

material he could find;[41] he included what he thought should be included and this meant that Mk was no longer needed and could fall out of use. The Third Gospel would provide what Luke's fellow Christians (locally) needed to know about the life and teaching of Jesus. The second volume, Acts, correspondingly contained what the church (in the 80s or early 90s) needed to know about the apostles and their teaching. The disuse of Paul's epistles in Acts is a familiar and often discussed fact. Whether this was due to ignorance or to deliberate omission,[42] Acts was there to serve as Apostle supplementing Gospel. It was what Luke's contemporaries needed to know about the apostles—and Paul. This leads to two observations.

The first was made by W. C. van Unnik,[43] who wrote of Acts as the confirmation of the gospel. The record of the life and expansion of the church confirms that the claims made in the gospel for the person of Jesus and the effect of his work were true. The two books thus form a unit, and the purpose of the second must be viewed in the light of the first.

This presupposes (what Luke no doubt took for granted) that the earliest period of Christianity was an exemplary and classical period; this conviction supplies perhaps the strongest because the most practical reason for the writing of Acts. Luke wished to hold up before his readers a set of Christian ideals which would show them what their own Christian life should be and at the same time supply them with a strong motivation for following the example. He probably wrote primarily for church leaders, who are given especially in Paul's Miletus speech (20.18–35) a clear account of their pastoral responsibilities. The nearly contemporary (perhaps somewhat later) Pastoral Epistles encouraged the ministers to whom they are addressed to preach: Preach the word, keep at it in season, out of season, reprove, rebuke, exhort (2 Tim. 4.2). Christian leaders towards the end of the century might reply to such exhortations, Yes, but what must we say? Luke replies, You will find no better examples, no clearer instruction, than in the sermons of Peter and Paul that I am providing.[44] He might similarly claim that he had provided an outline of the kind of behaviour to be expected of the Christian rank and file: They continued steadfastly in the teaching of the apostles and the fellowship, in the breaking of bread and the prayers (2.42).

Beyond these matters one may inquire whether there were any

---

[41]No one has in the last fifty years pointed out to me any reason why I should abandon the view of Luke's sources I sketched briefly in *ExpT* 54 (1943), 320–23; see *FS* Smit Sibinga, 96.

[42]See *FS* Mitton, 2–5.

[43]*NovT* 4 (1960–1), 26–59, 'The "Book of Acts"'—the Confirmation of the Gospel'; see also my exploration of the converse of this in *FS* Neirynck 1451–66.

[44]Cf. Dibelius 165: 'This is how the gospel is preached and ought to be preached!'.

specific theological truths that Luke wished to communicate. For his theology as a whole and in some detail see below, pp. lxxxii–cx. One theological point merges with a historical; it is not mentioned by Luke, probably because it seemed to him part of the nature of things, but it was fundamental to his work. For the view that Jesus foretold his suffering and that after his suffering he would be vindicated by God, but did not in this vindication differentiate between resurrection and a coming of the Son of man in glory I may refer to *Jesus and the Gospel Tradition* (London, 1967), pp. 77–83. After his crucifixion Jesus appeared to his disciples, raised from death; but there was no coming with the clouds of heaven. One may guess with some probability, but cannot prove, that the disciples, compelled by events to differentiate where Jesus himself had not done so, believed that the second act, which would complete the first, would follow quickly. It did not do so. Had it done so, there would have been no church history. It was the 'delay of the parousia' that made it possible for the church to have a history, and for the church's historian to write it. It does not seem that the delay, though it must have puzzled many, led to a crisis of belief. Luke did not write to assuage apocalyptic enthusiasm, or to comfort those who were disappointed in their hopes. When he wrote, some measure of delay had been accepted, and Luke himself sets out what were probably widely acknowledged terms of acceptance. After the crucifixion, Jesus had been raised up by God; he had ascended into heaven; he had sent to his followers (and continued to send as more followers were added) the gift of the Holy Spirit. Empowered and directed by the Spirit, the believers would act as witnesses to Jesus till their testimony had reached the end of the earth (1.8). This goal Luke probably saw as representatively achieved in the arrival of Paul at Rome, but there is no hint in his writing that the End could now be expected at any moment. He knew that some thirty years had elapsed between Paul's arrival in Rome and the point at which he was writing; and if God could wait thirty years, he could no doubt wait a good deal longer. This was probably the accepted position; there was no need to argue for it. Luke does however (without saying explicitly that he is doing so) show how the various features of Christian truth cohere with one another. This was something that a gospel alone could not do; his two-volume work was needed. There is an end, including a judgement, to look forward to, and not only Areopagites but all must prepare for it by repentance. For those who repent there is forgiveness and the gift of the Spirit, manifested in such gifts as prophecy and speaking with tongues. The believers live in unity and godly love, and bear witness to Jesus.

This is in fact Luke's theology and he does not see fit to expand it, though there are many points that invite expansion. Who was Jesus, who plays such an important part in the history of God's dealings

with men? How did his death effect forgiveness and release from
sin? How is the Holy Spirit related to Father and Son? What is the
proper constitution of the church, and what happens when it
immerses converts in water, and when its members assemble 'to
break bread'? Luke gives only the barest hints towards answers to
these questions. The basic theology of Judaism he accepts but
scarcely develops. He believes as the apostles did, and does not seek
to go beyond their pronouncements. To do so indeed would cut
across his purpose, which is to record what they said and did, not to
point out what they ought to have said and done. On the theology of
Acts see further below, pp. lxxxii–cx.

The lessons Luke presses upon his readers are not speculative but
practical. The Christian faith is the truth, the truth of God: magna est,
et praevalebit. There is therefore no need for Christians to fear, even
though they are attacked on every side as Paul was, even though, like
Stephen and James, they must die for their faith. God does not fail his
servants whether in life or in death, and his ability to preserve them,
even in acute danger, proves that the truth of the Gospel will not be
suppressed but will eventually triumph. But woe to those who, like
Ananias and Sapphira, trifle with truth and are less than sincere in
their adherence to the community and its principles. Their fault is not
so much that they have attempted to deceive the rulers of the
community; they have lied not to men but to God. The apostles do
indeed have their own dignity, but this is rather because they serve as
an indispensable link between Jesus and the consequences that
flowed from his work than because they occupy positions of
authority and must therefore be obeyed. Luke has not forgotten Lk.
22.24–27; and indeed he knows (or at least tells) hardly anything
about the Twelve. It is right that those who are appointed to share
their ministry (as elders) should be unpaid. Let them rather work for
their living and be ministers in their spare time; they will then be
independent and able to minister to the needs of others.[45]

All that has been said here about the characteristics, interests, and
intentions of Luke as an author bear on the question of the historical
value of his book. For details on a number of specific points see the
appended note on Dates and Places. On such matters, Luke, on the
whole does fairly well. He is not unfamiliar with the roads and
shipping routes that he describes; his references to secular history are
usually in reasonably close agreement with the facts as otherwise
known. He comes down badly over Judas and Theudas (5.36, 37),
but is probably not far out in his references to Claudius, Sergius
Paulus, Agrippa I and II, Gallio, Felix, and Festus. Oddly it is on
Christian matters that he is most open to criticism. His account of
Hebrews and Hellenists, of Paul and the Council, is distorted by the

---

[45]On the supposed Frühkatholizismus of Acts see below, pp. xciii–xcvii.

refracting medium of continuing church life through which he views
the past.

Dates and Places

None of the events in Acts can be dated precisely; some can be given
a relative dating and placed in chronological order, and a few can be
given an approximate absolute date. It will be best first to run through
the main events which could be given dates—if we had the necessary
information.[46]

Acts begins with reference to resurrection appearances of Jesus, his
Ascension, and the gift of the Holy Spirit on the Day of Pentecost.
These are represented by Luke as historical events which therefore
had dates, but these are only to be obtained (if obtained at all) by
reckoning forwards from events in the ministry of Jesus or backwards
from events recorded in Acts. There is nothing in the narratives
themselves to suggest a date, but of course Luke thinks of them as
preceding all the other events in the book. In 4.6 Luke refers to Annas
the High Priest and to Caiaphas.[47] In fact Caiaphas was High Priest
from AD 18 to 36, Annas having been deposed in AD 15. We have in
the text no means of fixing a date more precise than 18–36.

At 5.34 Gamaliel is said to intervene in the Sanhedrin's discussion. This was Rabban Gamaliel I, according to Acts 22.3 the teacher
of Paul. He lived in the first half of the first century. No precise date
can be inferred from this reference. Gamaliel however is said in vv.
36, 37 to refer to Theudas and Judas, in that order. It is very probable
that the revolt of Theudas took place in about AD 44, that of Judas in
AD 6. If Luke's account is taken as it stands Gamaliel must have
been speaking after AD 44 (and into the bargain have inverted the
order of the two revolts). It is virtually impossible to believe that
Gamaliel has been reported correctly; no inference can be drawn
regarding the date of the events in Acts 5.

The reference to Simon the Magus (8.9–24) provides no date.
Even if second-century Simonianism originated with the Magus this
does not tell us the time at which his contact with Philip, Peter, and
John took place.

The narrative of Saul's conversion (9.1–19) does not refer to a
date. The only evidence by which the event can be dated is given by
the reference to it in Gal. 1.15, 16.[48] Here the conversion is followed
by a journey into Arabia; how long he stayed in Arabia and, on his
return, in Damascus Paul does not say. Then after three years (from
the conversion, from the return to Damascus?) Paul went up to

---

[46]Details will be found at the appropriate points in the Commentary; no attempt is
made in this Introduction to cite evidence in full.

[47]The name of Annas appears also at 5.17, but only in p mae.

[48]No help can be drawn from 1 Cor. 15 or Phil. 3.

Jerusalem and stayed there only a fortnight before going to Syria and Cilicia. Then after fourteen years (from the conversion, from the previous visit?) he went back to Jerusalem for the so-called Apostolic Council. If we knew the date of the Council we could work back from this,[49] but even so there would be uncertainties. Three plus fourteen is seventeen but years were commonly counted inclusively, so that three might be (part of a year + a year + part of a year); perhaps little more than one and a half years. Similarly fourteen years might be twelve and a half years. And we do not know whether the three must be added to the fourteen or counted within it. The total span might be anywhere between twelve and a half and seventeen. If the Council is to be dated in 47,[50] the conversion cannot be later than c. 35; it might be considerably earlier.

In 11.28 we read of a famine ἐφ' ὅλην τὴν οἰκουμένην which happened ἐπὶ Κλαυδίου. Claudius ruled from 41 to 54; there is reason to think that the famine may have occurred in 47, though Hemer (165) prefers 45–46. The bearing of this date on the chronology of the Christian movement will depend on conclusions reached with regard to the Council in Acts 15. Was there one Council or were there two, one on the question of circumcision, one dealing with the famine? What was the point of Gal. 2.10? 'I was eager to take up this suggestion?' or, 'I had already been keenly pursuing relief work?' There is much to be said for a Council in 46 or 47; see below, p. lxi.

Most of Acts 12 is concerned directly or indirectly with a person described by Luke as King Herod; he was of the Herod family but his name was in fact Julius Agrippa (= Agrippa I). Some details of his career are given in I.573f. There is no means of dating with certainty the death of James or the imprisonment of Peter, but it is to be noted that Peter's escape took place at or before Passover (12.4). Herod's feud with the Tyrians and Sidonians cannot be dated but his death very probably happened in 44, on or near 5 March, possibly on or near 1 August. If he died on 5 March Peter's Passover escape must have happened in 43; if on 1 August, in 44. These events therefore belong to a time before the famine of 11.28; Luke is not writing in chronological order.

The next possible date arises in 13.7 with the reference to the proconsul of Cyprus, Sergius Paulus. Unfortunately though there is epigraphical evidence that may refer to this man the reference is uncertain and dates (apart from the name of the reigning emperor, which may be [Ga]ius or [Claud]ius) are not given. There is no means of dating the 'first missionary journey'; see below on the question whether it preceded or followed the Council.

In Acts the Council follows the journey, in ch. 15. Nothing in this

[49]See p. lxi.
[50]See p. lxi.

chapter supplies a date apart from the words ascribed to Peter, which look back to the Cornelius episode of ch. 10, and the reference made by Barnabas and Saul to the miracles that had accompanied their missionary work. These references would be useful if we could date the events mentioned; this we cannot do. The relative chronology of the Council is of great importance but it cannot be even tentatively established until all possible points of absolute chronology have been considered and some questions of topography considered too. See below, pp. lvii–lxi.

Luke relates Paul's visit to Corinth (18.1–18) with secular events that can be dated with some probability. When Paul reached Corinth he found there the Jewish couple Aquila and Priscilla who had recently arrived because Claudius had expelled the Jews from Rome. The date of this expulsion is discussed on pp. 861f. The view taken in the Commentary is that AD 49 may be accepted with very considerable confidence; this has the advantage of being consistent with another date given by the account of Paul's ministry in Corinth; see below. The alternative date (see p. 862) for the expulsion is 41; if this is accepted we are likely to conclude that Paul visited Corinth first in AD 41 and again in or about AD 50; see Lüdemann (17–20).

In 18.11 Paul is said to have stayed in Corinth one year and six months; in 18.12 there is a reference to Gallio, proconsul of Achaea; in 18.18 Paul is said to have stayed on in Corinth ἡμέρας ἱκανάς. This is vague, and we do not know whether or not these days were included in the eighteen months of v. 11, or how many ἱκανάς means. The date of Gallio's proconsulship can be determined with some accuracy; see p. 871, where, on the basis of an inscription, it is concluded that Gallio 'probably became proconsul of Achaea in 51 (summer), possibly, if, as was less usual, he held office for two years, in 50'. It is further shown to be reasonable, though by no means certain, that the encounter between Paul and Gallio took place towards the end of Paul's stay in Corinth and early in Gallio's proconsulship. Accepting this view (with due reservation), and naming months for simplicity and brevity of statement, we may suggest that Paul was brought before Gallio in September 51, having arrived in Corinth in March 50. This would be consistent with the recent arrival of Aquila and Priscilla after they, as Jews, had been expelled from Rome in 49. These dates are not certain, but they are more nearly certain than anything else in the life of Paul.

The next two references give no clue to absolute chronology and may be simply mentioned without discussion. In 19.8 Paul spends his first three months in Ephesus discoursing in the synagogue. In 19.10, after moving from the synagogue, he teaches for two years in the school of Tyrannus. A total stay of two years and three months is consistent with 20.31 where Paul recalls to the Ephesian elders that he had spent three years (τριετίαν) among them. Using inclusive

reckoning two and a quarter years would cover three years. These
references are followed by another which tells only of extent of time.
Paul spent three months in Greece (20.3). From Greece he went to
Philippi whence he sailed μετὰ τὰς ἡμέρας τῶν ἀζύμων to Troas,
the voyage taking five days (20.6). In Troas the travellers spent seven
days (20.6) and with the local church met 'to break bread' ἐν τῇ μιᾷ
τῶν σαββάτων; Paul was to leave next day (20.7, 13). From these
data and from the (probable) date of Passover it has been argued that
the events fell in AD 57. This would be an interesting contribution to
chronology; for reasons why it should not be accepted see p. 952.

Ananias, referred to as High Priest at 23.2; 24.1, was in office c.
AD 47–59. There is no doubt that the events of these chapters fell
within this period, so that the reference to Ananias provides no more
than confirmatory evidence.

At 24.27 the succession of Festus to Felix is mentioned. The date
of Festus' accession is discussed on pp. 1116–18. The matter is
contentious. The view taken here is that though some would place the
succession as late as AD 60 the balance of probability is that it
occurred much earlier, perhaps as early as 55. This fits well (see
below, p. lxi) with the chronology of Acts (and of Paul) provided that
the two-year period (διετία) is taken to refer not to Paul's imprisonment but to Felix's term of office.

King Agrippa II (son of Julius Agrippa I, 12.1–23), accompanied
by his sister Bernice, appears with Festus in 25.13 – 26.32. He seems
to have become king not immediately upon his father's death but in
AD 52, or a little later. He died probably in AD 92/3 (see *NS*
1.472–83). For a short time (*c*. 64–66) Bernice was married to King
Polemon of Cilicia. These dates cause no problems but add no
precision to the chronology of Acts.

Acts 27.9 refers to the Fast, that is, the Day of Atonement (10
Tishri). This was already past; sailing was therefore dangerous. This
has been held to mean that in the year of Paul's voyage Tishri 10 must
have fallen late; it was late (on 5 October) in AD 59, later than in 57,
58, 60, 61, 62. From this it has been inferred that the voyage took place
in 59. The inference is very insecure; see p. 1188, and on 28.11.

The two verses (27.9; 28.11) when taken together give rise to a
problem. Even if it is assumed that the ship did not leave Fair Havens
till after 5 October one would suppose that Malta was reached by the
end of October; three months bring us to the end of January, a very
unlikely date for resuming the voyage. One can only say that this
note of time makes one view it and all the other notes of time relating
to the voyage with a measure of suspicion.

According to Acts 28.30, Paul, under guard in Rome, spent two
years lodging at his own expense. The *two years* would be chrono-
logically helpful if we knew when they began or ended; we do not.
See further on 28.30, 31.

Before anything further can be said about chronology some of the routes taken by Christians, and especially by Paul, must be considered. Very few of these give rise to any problems.

The first journey in Acts is that undertaken by Philip in ch. 8. See I.402, 423f. There is a textual ambiguity in 8.5, and we do not know where Philip began the journey of 8.26. There is a straightforward road connection from Azotus to Caesarea (8.40).

There is no difficulty in Paul's journey from Jerusalem to Damascus (9.1, 2); Acts does not mention his visit to Arabia (Gal. 1.17); he would naturally retrace his steps when he returned to Jerusalem (9.26). Peter would take Lydda (9.32) on his way to Joppa (9.36); Caesarea lay further north on the coast. Phoenicia, Cyprus, Antioch (11.19) are easily identified on a map; so is Tarsus, in Cilicia (11.25). There are no complications in the route followed by Paul and Barnabas in chs. 13 and 14, or in their visit to Jerusalem for the Council and subsequent return to Antioch.

Paul, accompanied by Silas, returned to Derbe and Lystra of the first journey not by sea but through Syria and Cilicia (15.41; 16.1). It is at this point that a real problem arises, in 16.6–10. This must be for the moment deferred and considered with 18.22, 23. Many other topographical references follow in Acts and little would be gained by adding here a list of place names. For the most part there is no difficulty, and information is given in the notes. There is a problem of text and interpretation at 17.14, sufficiently discussed in the commentary, and the meaning of τὰ ἀνωτερικὰ μέρη (19.1) is disputed. This question will be raised below. Another difficulty arises at 21.15–17; this is discussed in the commentary, as is the identification of the island on which Paul and his companions were wrecked (28.1).

We have to consider 16.6–10; 18.22, 23; 19.1. For many details see the notes. It is important here to take the evidence of Galatians fully into account. The fundamental question is simple to state: What is meant by Galatia (and the Galatians)? In the epistle (Gal. 1.1; cf. 3.1) it seems that the reference is most probably to the territory in north central Asia Minor inhabited since the third century BC by Gallic tribes rather than to the territory added to this when the whole was made in 25 BC into a Roman province.[51] One objection commonly made to this view is that nowhere in Acts is Paul said to have established churches in this northerly area, whereas there is a detailed account of his work in the additional, southern, part of the province. This was visited in the course of the 'first missionary journey' in Acts 14.1–25 and revisited at the beginning of the second, 16.1–5. If 'Galatia' in the epistle is taken to refer to this, southerly, area, the epistle could have been written at any time after ch. 14; if it were written after 16.1–5, Gal, 4.13 could be taken to

---

[51]The matter is disputed; there is a good summary in Kümmel, *Einleitung* 258–65.

refer to the former of two visits.[52] If the epistle was written soon after
ch. 14, *either* Acts 15 cannot be identified with Gal. 2.1–10 *or* the
sequence of chs. 13, 14, 15 is mistaken. The other view of Paul's use
of *Galatia, Galatians*, however, leaves us with the problem of
finding a mission to Galatia, and we must consider Acts 16.6 (τὴν
Φρυγίαν καὶ Γαλατικὴν χώραν; cf. 18.23, τὴν Γαλατικὴν χώραν
καὶ Φρυγίαν). The meaning of these phrases is discussed in the
commentary, together with the meaning of the aorist participle
κωλυθέντες. The first observation—simple but very important—to
make is that before 16.6 is reached Paul has already passed through
southern, provincial Galatia (16.1–5). Galatic territory must be
different from this. Taking κωλυθέντες as the aorist participle it is
one must suppose that Paul passed through Phrygia and Galatic
territory because he had been forbidden to turn westward into the
province of Asia. He must therefore have gone northwards until he
was compelled to travel towards Troas along the frontier between
Bithynia (which he was not allowed to enter[53]) and Mysia, which he
passed through or beside (παρελθόντες). Between southern provincial Galatia and this Bithynian-Mysian stretch lay τὴν Φρυγίαν καὶ
Γαλατικὴν χώραν. It is a vague expression, and probably reflects the
fact that Luke had no first-hand or even second-hand information
about it and what happened there.[54] It cannot be said that because no
missionary work is described in this region, therefore none happened. 18.23 (τὴν Γαλατικὴν χώραν καὶ Φρυγίαν) is important,
first, because the reversed order reinforces the sense of vagueness
and lack of first-hand knowledge, and secondly because it proves that
there had been missionary work in the area, since on his new journey
Paul was ἐπιστηρίζων πάντας τοὺς μαθητάς.[55] The obscure reference in 19.1 to the ἀνωτερικὰ μέρη through which Paul passed on
his way to Ephesus probably explains Paul's lack of personal contact
with the churches of the Lycus valley. The curious route of 16.6–10
may be a rationalization—or spiritualization—of Paul's surprising
failure to make at once for the great city of Ephesus.[56]

We return to chronology in the light of the questions raised in the
last paragraph. Acts 13 and 14 are a block of Antiochene tradition.

[52]But this is not necessarily implied by the words τὸ πρότερον.

[53]οὐκ εἴασεν αὐτοὺς τὸ πνεῦμα Ἰησοῦ. Some think that this means only that
missionary activity was forbidden; the travellers were allowed to make their way
through Bithynia but not to preach. This is not a natural interpretation of
πορευθῆναι.

[54]The We-passages begin at Troas, 16.10.

[55]This is fully consistent with Gal. 1.2; if there were disciples there were
ἐκκλησίαι.

[56]'On peut voir alors que la raison pour laquelle l'itinéraire de Paul est si difficile à
reconstituer provient du fait que Act 16, 6–8 est une composition artificielle de Luc à
partir d'éléments puisés à ses sources et qu'il s'efforce d'harmoniser' (Taylor 234f.).
Details follow on pp. 759–62.

There are probably some inserted pieces but on the whole they present a complete missionary circuit from Antioch back to Antioch, with a strong claim to historicity. This however does not guarantee the point at which the circuit is inserted in the general outline of Acts. Galatians gives an account of two visits to Jerusalem made by Paul, in 1.18f. and in 2.1–10; in the corresponding period in Acts there are three, in 9.26–30, in 11.30 (12.25), and in 15.1–29.[57] In Galatians the peace of the church is disturbed by a visit of envoys from, or purporting to come from, James (of Jerusalem): 2.12. This takes place after the Jerusalem meeting. In Acts the disturbance from Jerusalem takes place before the Council: 15.1, 2, 24.

Two points are hard to doubt: that Paul in Galatians did not omit any of his visits to Jerusalem—to have done so would have been as foolish as dishonest; and that Galatians 2 corresponds to Acts 15—the persons are the same and the question is the same. There is no better explanation than that Luke has made two visits out of one. In Galatians 2 there is a meeting at which Paul's law-free Gospel was confirmed with the proviso that he should 'remember the poor', which, he said, he was and had been eager (ἐσπούδασα) to do. Luke, we may suggest, had a tradition of a Council at which the Gospel without circumcision was confirmed, and another tradition according to which Paul and Barnabas brought relief for the poor. He concluded, wrongly, that two purposes meant two visits, two meetings.

If this suggestion is accepted we ask, When did the one visit take place, at 11.30, 15.1, 2, or at some other time, and what was its relation to the 'first missionary journey'? If the one Jerusalem visit is put at the time of the famine visit (11.30) the first journey followed it. If we choose the alternative date the order is reversed. The epistles do not suggest that the terms of the mission had all been settled before the mission began; the reverse is more probable. Events had thrown up unforeseen problems; what in fact was to be done with Gentile converts who now existed?[58] If the interpretation of the word Galatia given above is correct the epistle was not written till after Acts 16.1–6—perhaps not till some time after, for time must be allowed for the difficulty to arise in Galatia: ἐτρέχετε καλῶς· τίς ὑμᾶς ἐνέκοψεν; (Gal. 5.7). If undue weight is laid upon

[57]It may be that Acts 18.22 also refers to a visit to Jerusalem.

[58]Lake (*Begs.* 5, 203f.) attempts to solve the problem of the relation between Galatians and Acts by means of source criticism; this is not convincing (though his exposition—5.195–212—is a masterpiece of clarity and should never be overlooked). See also Taylor (225): 'Notons enfin qu'il serait futile [in view of the use of sources] d'essayer de dater le 'Concile de Jérusalem' en calculant le temps que Paul aurait mis à faire son premier voyage missionaire, ou son second, et en tenant compte de la date de la famine sous Claude qui l'a précédé, ou du proconsulat de Gallion qui l'a suivi, et ensuite d'essayer de concilier la chronologie ainsi obtenue avec celle donnée par Paul dans les Galates.'

Gal. 4.13 and the verse is taken to refer to a second visit to Galatia, the letter might have been written after 18.23; it has even been suggested that Gal. 2.1–10 will refer to the (supposed) Jerusalem visit of 18.22. The letter however was written at a time when Paul was unable to visit Galatia (Gal. 4.20)—making perhaps his rapid journey east without time even to linger in Ephesus. In the circumstances he may have lost hope of completing his collection in Galatia (1 Cor. 16.1).

If the Council was in 46 or 47 Paul could easily have reached Corinth by March 50 and left in September 51. The next date that can be even argued about[59] is that at which Festus succeeded Felix (see above, p. lvii). If this was 55, and if the διετία refers to Felix's governorship, Paul's movements fit neatly into the interval. He could 'sail, by one of the last boats of the summer, to Syria (Acts 18.21f.). How long he spent in Antioch (Acts 18.23) we do not know; probably he renewed his travels with the return of favourable weather in the spring of the next year—52. His journey through 'the region of Galatia and Phrygia' (Acts 18.23) and through the 'upper country' (Acts 19.1) might well last most of the following summer; he would reach Ephesus (Acts 19.1) in the autumn. The length of his stay there is given by Acts 19.8 (three months) and 19.10 (two years), confirmed by 20.31; the Pentecost therefore that he was anxious to keep in Jerusalem will have been that of 55, and his three months in Greece (Acts 20.5) must have come to an end a few weeks earlier.'[60] He will have left for Rome not long after the arrival of Festus and reached the city early in the next year—in 56, or as many years later as the date of Festus' accession requires.[61]

Bibliography

P. J. Achtemeier, *CBQ* 48 (1986), 1–26.

L. Alexander, *The Preface to Luke's Gospel*, SNTSMS 78, Cambridge 1993.

C. K. Barrett, *FS* Neirynck, 1451–66.

C. K. Barrett, *FS* Jervell, 1–10.

E. Bickermann, *Studies in Jewish and Christian History*, Leiden 1986.

F. F. Bruce, *ANRW* 2.25.3 (1985), 2570–603.

H. J. Cadbury, *JBL* 45 (1926), 190–209.

[59]I exclude the attempt based on 20.7 (above, p. lvii).

[60]*Romans* 4. If a later date is taken for the accession of Festus the διετία may be taken to apply to Paul's imprisonment or some time added to his travels—or both.

[61]For a different chronology see the summary in Taylor (333–5).

H. J. Cadbury, *The Making of Luke-Acts*, London 1958 (New York 1927).

S. Dockx, *NovT* 13 (1971), 261–304.

F. V. Filson, *Three Crucial Decades*, London 1964.

R. M. Grant, *VigCh* 46 (1992), 105–111.

T. Holtz, *ThLZ* 100 (1975), 321–32.

J. Jervell, *Luke and the People of God*, Minneapolis 1972.

J Jervell, *The Unknown Paul*, Minneapolis 1984.

E. Larsson, *NTS* 33 (1987), 205–25.

D. L. Mealand, *ZNW* 82 (1991), 42–66.

J. Murphy-O'Connor, *Paul, a Critical Life*, Oxford 1996.

R. I. Pervo, *Profit with Delight: the Literary Genre of the Acts of the Apostles*, Philadelphia 1983.

E. Plümacher, *Lukas als hellenistischer Schriftsteller*, Göttingen 1972.

E. Plümacher, in Kremer *Actes* 457–66.

P. Pokorny, *ZNW* 64 (1973), 233–44.

W. M. Ramsay, *The Church in the Roman Empire before A.D. 170*, London, New York and Toronto, 10th ed, n.d.

W. M. Ramsay, *The Cities of St Paul*, London 1907.

W. M. Ramsay, *St Paul the Traveller and Roman Citizen*, London [10]1908.

H. F. D. Sparks, *JTS* 1 (1950), 16–28.

W. Stegemann, *Zwischen Synagoge und Obrigkeit. Zur historischen Situation der lukanischen Christen*, FRLANT 152, Göttingen 1992.

A. Suhl, *NTS* 38 (1992), 430–47.

G. Theissen, *NTS* 21 (1975), 23–39.

E. Trocmé, *Le 'Livre des Actes' et l'Histoire*, Paris 1957.

W. C. van Unnik, *NovT* 4 (1961), 25–59.

W. C. van Unnik, in Kremer, *Actes*, 37–60.

P. W. Walaskay, *And so we came to Rome*, SNTSMS 49, Cambridge 1983.

A number of the works mentioned under § IV are relevant here also.

IV. ACTS IN HISTORY

I have described Acts as the history of the church in a time of conflict written in a time of consensus (see pp. xlf.). It was the consensus that provided Luke's frame of reference and it affected the way in which he wrote, making it impossible for him to understand fully, and so to describe accurately, the story of a church almost torn in two by dissension.[1] The Christian ship had sailed out of the storm into calmer waters, and Luke found it easier to picture the storms of the Mediterranean and Adriatic (which he may well have experienced) than the ecclesiastical troubles of the 40s and 50s. Were it not for a few verses one might suppose that Luke and his colleagues had come to believe that peace would last for ever. But there is enough to show that Luke knew better; indeed, the troubles had already begun. Luke knew that the prophecy he had put on Paul's lips was beginning to be fulfilled: 'I know that after my departure grievous wolves will come in among you, not sparing the flock, and out of your own number there will rise up men speaking perverse things so as to draw away after themselves disciples' (20.29f.). This prediction—or *vaticinium post eventum*—corresponds with surprising exactness to events that are described elsewhere in the NT. Faced by the failure of the Christian mission (for 'the world does not listen to us', 1 Jn 4.6) some members of the Johannine community had 'gone out' into the world (1 Jn 2.9); they had learned to speak out of the world's vocabulary (ἐκ τοῦ κόσμου), and accordingly the world paid attention to them (1 Jn 4.5). But this meant, John said, that they were teaching false doctrine (Luke's διεστραμμένα), and they had ceased to practise love (1 Jn 2.22, 23, 26; 3.7–10, 14, 15). Evidently they were drawing disciples after them. It is doubtful whether John the epistolographer very greatly loved these whom he accused of lack of love. He would not pray for them (1 Jn 5.16), and the church was split into mutually exclusive groups: Diotrephes excommunicated the Elder and his church members (3 Jn 9, 10) and the Elder excommunicated Diotrephes and those who thought as he did (2 Jn 9–11).[2] The force, the doctrine, that split the church was gnosticism;

---

[1]Inevitably one refers to F. C. Baur, especially *Die Christuspartei in der korinthischen Gemeinde* (1831); *Über Zweck und Veranlassung des Römerbriefs* (1836); and *Paulus* (¹1845; ²1866); but now see also M. D. Goulder, *A Tale of two Missions* (1994). Lightfoot's Excursus on 'St Paul and the Three' (pp. 292–374 in his *Galatians*) is also important.

[2]See my *Essays on John* (1982); some, notably R. E. Brown (*The Community of the Beloved Disciple*, 1979), have taken this into much more detail. Not all the details are convincing, and in any case there is no point in going into them here.

this is what Johannine Christians went out into the world to learn, and with them it gave rise to docetism, answered by the watchword, 'Jesus Christ in the flesh'.[3] Against this Luke had set his warning on Paul's lips; he probably saw his own consensus environment as part of the good past that he was holding up for imitation, scarcely aware of the bad past with its different conflicts and dangers.

Of the development of this situation we have little contemporary evidence. Clement of Rome is aware of renewed troubles in Corinth, but they appear to be troubles of the old Corinthian kind, arising out of rivalry, lawlessness, and indiscipline, but local. A better source, probably a little later than Acts, is the Pastoral Epistles. Here too, as in Acts 20, Paul is represented as a prophet who foresees coming problems (1 Tim. 4.1; 2 Tim. 3.1; 4.3). These have a gnostic element (note especially the βεβήλους κενοφωνίας καὶ ἀντιθέσεις τῆς ψευδωνύμου γνώσεως of 1 Tim. 6.20) and a Jewish element (1 Tim. 1.7–9); one might say a Jewish-gnostic element (Ti. 1.14, Ἰουδαϊκοῖς μύθοις). Judaism is a problem also in the Ignatian letters, and Ignatius himself was a gnostic of sorts. Serious division lurks behind what can be known of the work of Hegesippus,[4] whose episcopal lists were designed to demonstrate and perpetuate apostolic unity between the principal sees. The continuity of the lists will prove that each see taught in agreement with the apostles; the agreement between the sees will show that each confirms the rest.

Hegesippus, so far as we can tell, did not know Acts;[5] this introduces us to an obscure but interesting period in the history of the book, written not far from AD 90 (see above, pp. xliif.) but dropping out of use in a period in which its steady emphasis on Christian beginnings, marked (as Luke represents them), by harmony and sound teaching, might seem to have been particularly useful. 'Die Apostelgeschichte finden wir vor Irenäus überhaupt nicht bezeugt.'[6] This is probably an overstatement; see I.34–45. But it does not exaggerate greatly. The possible allusion in Polycarp 1.2 and the strange echoes in the *Epistula Apostolorum* do not carry much weight. A more difficult question arises over Justin (see I.41–44). It cannot be proved either that Justin did or that he did not

---

[3] 2 Jn 7—with the untranslatable present participle ἐρχόμενον.

[4] See Eusebius, *HE*, especially 4.22.3. In every succession and in every city (ἐν ἑκάστῃ δὲ διαδοχῇ καὶ ἐν ἑκάστῃ πόλει) so it is, as the Law and the Prophets and the Lord teach. Eusebius preserves and expands the lists.

[5] Parallels have been seen between the account in Acts of the death of Stephen and Hegesippus' account (in Eusebius, *HE* 2.23.4–18) of the death of James the Just. James speaks of Jesus as the Son of man (2.23.13); he is thrown down, and prays for those who stone him (16). But, in Hegesippus, the Son of man sits, not stands, at God's right hand; James is thrown down from the Temple, and his prayer for the forgiveness of those who stone him (ἄφες αὐτοῖς· οὐ γὰρ οἴδασι τί ποιοῦσιν) resembles Lk. 23.34 rather than Acts 7.60. Does Hegesippus belong to the time when Luke's two books were separated and the gospel was better known than Acts?

[6] H. von Campenhausen, *Die Entstehung der christlichen Bibel* (1968), 152.

know Acts. There are indeed parallels of a sort. 'The mission of the
apostles after the ascension of the Lord [Acts 1.8–10, 1 *Apol* 50.12
and Acts 1.9–11, *Trypho* 68.5] is amplified by the fact that they are
ἰδιῶται [Acts 4.13, 1 *Apol* 39.3] and that it is right to obey God, not
man [Acts 5.29, *Trypho* 80.3]. There are references to food which is
common or unclean [Acts 10.14, *Trypho* 20.3] and the designation of
Christ as judge of living and dead [Acts 10.42, *Trypho* 118.1]. The
word is received with joy and glory is given to God [Acts 13.27, 48,
1 *Apol* 49.5]. In both Acts and Justin may be found the widespread
concept of the ἄγνωστος Θεός and the rhetorical plea of sanity, ''I
am not mad, most excellent Festus'' [Acts 26.5, *Trypho* 39.4].'[7] On
the whole, these are commonplaces, which indicate a common habit
of mind. The same goes for what is a Christian commonplace, the use
of the OT. At *Trypho* 87 Justin quotes Joel 2.28, 29, but P. Prigent[8]
rightly observes, 'Le texte de Joël 2.28s. ne dépend pas d'Actes
2.17ss.'. In addition to specific points such as those listed above we
should note also the general cast of Justin's mind. Like Luke, he has
accepted the notion that Christians have something to learn from the
Greek tradition; there were in it 'Christians before Christ', though
their work has to be accommodated to the OT, which constitutes the
word of God, Scripture, as the Greek writings cannot do. This makes
Justin, as Luke was, a moderate and tolerant man. Again, the limits
of his tolerance are much the same as Luke's. Jewish Christians
Justin is more ready to accept than were some of his contemporaries.
True, they must not be allowed 'to compel the faithful Christian
Gentiles to live according to the Law of Moses' (*Trypho* 47, with a
parallel to Acts 15.1, 5). But they may keep the Law themselves; so
long as they do not impose their ways on others, they are to Justin
Christian brothers. Even the Jews (though Justin can describe them,
perhaps with some exaggeration, as cursing Christians in their
synagogues) are not beyond the range of reasonable and temperate, if
not exactly friendly, discussion, as the mere existence of the
Dialogue with Trypho shows. Justin is working within the limits of
the Decree of Acts 15.29; he disapproves of Jewish pressure only if it
goes beyond this. He does not however refer to the Decree.

More striking than Justin's disuse of Acts is the fact that he
ignores Paul either completely, as is probable, or so nearly completely that the odd reference is almost more a disparagement than a
mark of respect. The neglect of Paul is underlined, and perhaps to
some extent explained, by the fact that Justin wrote a book,
unfortunately lost, against Paul's great supporter Marcion. Even
Eusebius seems not to have seen the book, though he refers to it in

[7]E. F. Osborn, *Justin Martyr* (1973), 135; Osborn's footnote references are given in
square brackets.
[8]*Justin et l'Ancien Testament* (1964), 114.

HE 4.11.8. Justin, he says, 'wrote also a treatise against Marcion, in which he mentions that at the time he composed it the man was alive and well known. He speaks thus.' At this point the reader of Eusebius naturally expects a quotation from the book in question, but Eusebius continues (quoting), '... and a certain Marcion of Pontus, who is even now still teaching his followers to believe in some other God greater than the Creator ...'. This passage is to be found in Justin, 1 *Apol.* 26. It is possible that Eusebius mixed up the quotations; it is possible that Justin remembered what he had written in the *Apology* and used it also in the book against Marcion (or vice versa). But it remains true that though Eusebius tells us that Justin wrote a work against Marcion he gives us no information about its contents, or any evidence that confirms his statement. Irenaeus however also refers to Justin's book and in quoting Irenaeus Eusebius (*HE* 4.18.9) quotes Justin. The passage is in *Adv. Haereses* 4.6.2. In the same passage Eusebius also quotes from *Adv. Haereses* 5.26.2, where Irenaeus quotes Justin. In Eusebius's quotation there is nothing anti-marcionite, but Irenaeus's paragraph ends with words that could be an attack on Marcion. It seems probable (though not proved) that Justin wrote against Marcion; the book may have disappeared because the case against Marcion seemed to have been more comprehensively and powerfully made by Irenaeus himself and by Tertullian; there was no need for the earlier work.

Justin's disuse of Paul may be explained by his strong opposition to Marcion. Marcion claimed to have the support of Paul, so that Paul, also dangerously favoured by Valentinus and other gnostics, could only be regarded as a divisive and disturbing force. This does not however explain Justin's strange combination of general parallels with particular disuse of Acts, which must be taken as part of a general disuse in the first half of the second century. It is tempting to draw the conclusion that Acts was written in the middle of the century as a mediating and conciliatory work, or at least, with John Knox,[9] to think that the double work, Luke-Acts, reached its final form at that time and was directed against Marcion. This conclusion however in its simplest form will not stand in view of the earlier discussion (see pp. xliif.) of the date of Acts. But that Acts was rediscovered, or perhaps deliberately revived, in the controversy with Marcion and the search for a new consensus, a new stability, is a very probable view. Itself the monument to an earlier consensus, distinguishable from but not wholly dissimilar to that which was sought and ultimately achieved in the second century, it was admirably suited for this purpose. Marcion did not include Acts in his canon; he may not have known it, but there is at least something to be said for

[9]*Marcion and the New Testament* (1942).

the view that he knew it and rejected it.[10] Evidence is provided by
Tertullian. In *De Praescriptione* 22 Tertullian does not mention
Marcion by name but there can be no doubt whom he has in mind
when he writes, '... it is proved in the Acts of the Apostles that the
Holy Spirit did come down. Now they who do not receive that book
of Scripture (quam Scripturam qui non recipiunt) can neither belong
to the Holy Spirit, seeing that they cannot acknowledge that the Holy
Spirit has been sent as yet to the disciples, nor can they pretend to
claim to be a church themselves ...' In *Adv. Marcionem* 5.2 he
writes, 'Since the Acts of the Apostles thus agree with Paul it
becomes apparent why you [Marcion] reject them (ea [Acta] respuas-
tis). It is because they declare no other God than the Creator; whilst
the promise of the Holy Spirit is shown to have been fulfilled in no
other place than in the book of Acts (quam de instrumento
Actorum).' It is precisely in this sense that Irenaeus (see above) uses
Acts against Marcion: it shows that the apostles proclaimed no other
God than the God of the OT, who was the creator of the world. The
gnosticism and the anti-Judaism of Marcion are answered at one
blow; and at the same time Paul is shown to be in agreement with the
other apostles.

These observations may be taken a stage further. It is known that
Marcion wrote a book called the *Antitheses*. It is unfortunately lost,
but its contents have been partially reconstructed on the basis of
quotations and references, supplied almost exclusively by Marcion's
enemies.[11] It is certain that the *Antitheses* contained much more—a
theological exposition of Marcion's position and material explanatory of passages in Marcion's gospel, Luke, and in the Pauline
epistles—but it is not wrong to describe it, as Harnack does, as
Marcion's response to the rejected Acts. 'Am Anfang der "Antithesen" hat sich M. im Anschluss an Gal. 1.2 über das Verhältnis von
Paulus und den Uraposteln ausgesprochen und die Uraposteln char-
akterisiert sowie "die falschen Brüder".' (81). Some have gone
further and taken the *Antitheses* to have been part of the new
Marcionite Scriptures. This view is based on *Adv. Marcionem* 1.19
where Tertullian speaks of the *Antitheses* as the Marcionite 'sum-
mum instrumentum', and of the Gospel and the Law as 'instru-
menta'. It is however to be rejected.[12] The *Antitheses* is an 'instrumentum quo denique [the Marcionites] initiantur et indicantur [v.1.,
indurantur] in hanc haeresim'; that is the book serves as an introduction to, not part of the text of Scriptures. Harnack adds (155*, 284*) a
further point, which deserves to be taken more seriously than it is by

[10]A. Harnack, *Marcion: das Evangelium vom fremden Gott* (1921), 153*, 'Marcion
hat die Apokalypse und die Acta als falsche, d.h. als Bücher des Judengottes
verworfen.'
[11]Harnack, *Marcion*, 68–135.
[12]With J. Knox, *Marcion*, 6.

Knox (121). About AD 400 the Marcionite church was still active in
Mesopotamia; it may be assumed that it was in possession of its
sacred literature and that the Marcionite NT and the *Antitheses* were
current and were read both by Marcionites and by those who entered
into controversy with them. Among the latter was a local bishop,
Marutha of Maipherkat (Maipheracti, Martyropolis, Tagsit). His
work confirms what is otherwise known of Marcion's NT, and he
adds (Harnack's translation), 'Das Buch der Πράξεις haben sie [the
Marcionites] vollständig aus der Mitte geräumt und statt seiner ein
anderes Buch ... eingeschoben, das sie Sākā = Summa ... nennen,
so dass es sei gemäss ihren Meinungen und Lehren.' On this Harnack
comments (155*f.), 'Auch nach diesen Worten liegt die Annahme
nahe, dass die Ausstossung der Apostelgesch. ausdrücklich begrün-
det war; das Buch aber, welche sie an ihrer Stelle hatten, können nur
doch wohl die 'Antithesen' sein; denn diese haben auch nach Tert.
eine Auseinandersetzung mit den Uraposteln enthalten, ja wahrscheinlich in ihrer Einleitung. Darüber hinaus aber sind die ''Antithesen'' wirklich ein ''Ersatz'' für die Apostelgeschichte; denn mit
dieser begründete die Kirche die Concordanz zwischen dem Alten
und dem Neuen Bund und zwischen den Uraposteln und Paulus; mit
den Antithesen aber begründete M. die Discordanz zwischen diesen
Grössen.' The words Concordanz and Discordanz are to be noted.

If it is correct that Marcion wrote the *Antitheses* in order to
introduce his NT, and if in doing so he conceived himself to be
replacing Acts (and there are powerful though not overwhelming
arguments in favour of both propositions) we have an important
pointer to the position of Acts at this time. It was thought of not as a
part of the NT as this, consisting of gospels and epistles, was
gradually coming into being; it served rather as an introduction to the
new collection. A number of considerations are consistent with, and
thus give support to, this conclusion.

It is suggested above (pp. lf.) that what Luke in his two-volume
work produced was a primitive NT. It contained everything that a NT
should contain. The life and teaching of Jesus were there, together
with an account of his death and resurrection. The work and teaching
of at least some representative apostles and preachers were there,
together with the necessary check on the continuity between Christ
and the church. What more could a church want? The local church
within and for which Luke wrote was probably for a time content, but
it is evident that the church as a whole wanted a good deal more. It
wanted all the gospels it considered orthodox, four not one, even
though the multiplicity of gospels was eventually to prove a theological problem.[13] More influential than theological problems was the

[13]See O. Cullmann, 'Die Pluralität der Evangelien als theologisches Problem im
Altertum', in *V & A* 548–65.

fact that local churches had local gospels and were unwilling to give them up. And some churches had letters written by apostles, or other authorities. 'Our own precious piece of Paul's handwriting is worth more than Luke's stories.' And churches passed on copies of 'their' letters to other churches, Corinth for example to Rome.[14] Luke's 'Shorter New Testament' (but he had nothing with which to compare it) was out-dated and discarded.

Not wholly out-dated, and in the end not discarded. Half of the total work was a gospel, and gospels were of evident authority and one knew what to do with them. They were stamped with the authority of the Lord himself and could not simply be cast aside. So Lk. became part of a developing four-gospel canon. This meant however that it was separated from Acts, and that Acts now stood alone and (unless Lk. was placed last among the four—as in the Curetonian Syriac) lost the connection that gave it its original meaning and raison d'être as the 'confirmation of the gospel'.[15] As soon as this happened gospel and Acts began to have different histories. Acts had in fact very little history; the epistles gave a more direct contact with their authors and, as was pointed out above, began to circulate and to be accorded a measure of authority which the interesting stories of Acts did not have. It was now not apparent what purposes Acts would serve. Did a reader with theological interest desire to sit at Paul's feet? There was a great deal more for him in Romans than in, say, Acts 13 and 17. Did he need guidance in regard to moral problems? He could find them discussed explicitly in 1 Corinthians, whereas they scarcely reached the surface in Acts. Acts moreover was anonymous; how different from, say, Galatians; or, if you lived in Asia, works ascribed to John!

That Acts lacked the authority of other parts of the NT is clearly proved by the textual phenomena.[16] There is no part of the NT in which textual variants are so many and free. The Western text is, as all know, not geographically Western at all. All over the ancient world, not only in areas in which Greek was spoken, but where Latin, Syriac, and Coptic were used, the text of Acts was handled freely. Again and again changes are made with no apparent concern other than that of introducing a measure of variety, or simply because the copyist did not trouble to remember precisely what he had seen in his exemplar. There is a Western text in other NT books but nowhere does it show the same wild variety as it does in Acts—a clear sign that Acts lacked the strict verbal authority that other Christian books possessed.

The fact is that the church of the next two or three generations

[14]See 1 Clement 47.1f.; Ignatius, *Eph*. 12.2; *Rom*. 4.3; Polycarp, *Phil*. 3.2; 11.2 (quoting 1 Corinthians).
[15]See van Unnik's article referred to on p. li.
[16]I.3–29; II.4.

after its composition did not know what to do with Acts. It was not a gospel; it was not an epistle; it did not fit into any known category of Christian literature, of which indeed there was very little in any form. If the notion of a New Testament over against an Old had been established it might have been classed with the historical books, such as Samuel and Kings. But it was part of the unique event that had brought the Christian movement into being. In separation from the gospel it first came into use as an introduction to the new group of books that formed an incipient NT, or perhaps simply as an introduction to the Apostle over against the Gospel section of the NT, showing how the two parts belonged together. It was no good to Marcion, who supplanted it with his *Antitheses*, and thereby gave his orthodox opponents the cue that they needed. If Marcion did not like Acts, Acts must be anti-Marcionite. And so it was, as first Irenaeus and then Tertullian saw. It showed Paul, in unity with the other apostles, engaged in preaching one God and one Gospel, the one God who was both the Creator of the material universe and the Father of the Lord Jesus Christ the Redeemer. Here was the biblical, apostolic, non-Marcionite, non-Valentinian ground on which all Christians might unite. Acts might be part of the NT, standing in its appropriate place to demonstrate that the story of Jesus issued in the church and that the church arose out of the word of Jesus.

And, from the time of Irenaeus and the Muratorian Canon, Acts was part of the NT.[17] It continued however to stand a little apart from the other books. The canon was not thought of as supplying an authorized history of Christian origins; it existed primarily as a basis, and yardstick, for Christian preaching,[18] and there is little to suggest that Acts was frequently preached on. It remained something of a puzzle, neither a gospel, stamped with the authority of the Lord himself, nor an epistle bearing an apostolic signature. And what could a theologian make of stories? The theologians of the early centuries did not see that there might be a positive answer to this question.

There is little material available for writing a history of the use of Acts in the first centuries.[19] What there is has been admirably collected by P. F. Stuehrenberg.[20] His list contains 147 entries, but the number, impressive at first, says more for Dr Stuehrenberg's diligence and scholarship than for the exegetical activity of the pre-Reformation writers. Most of the works listed have never been

[17]See I.30–34, 44–48.
[18]See *FS* Schweizer 5–21.
[19]Though more than W. Gasque, *A History of the Criticism of the Acts of the Apostles* (1975) takes note of.
[20]'The study of Acts before the Reformation. A Bibliographic Introduction', *NovT* 29 (1987), 100–136. See also F. Stegmüller, *Repertorium Biblicum Medii Aevi* (1940–1980).

published and can be consulted only in manuscript. Most of them are known to us only in fragments containing brief notes on a few scattered verses. Many of them are known only through quotations in Catenae, notably in J. A. Cramer, *Catena in Acta S.S. Apostolorum*, Oxford 1838 (Volume III of *Catenae Graecorum Patrum in Novum Testamentum*). Thus from the third century Stuehrenberg is able to cite a comment on Acts 5.4 from Dionysius of Alexandria; this is in Cramer and comes from a commentary not on Acts but (probably) on Ecclesiastes, and from Origen comments on 1.16 (given by Migne) and on 4.33; 7.4, 52; 21.38 (given by Cramer). Origen however is known to have written homilies on Acts; he wrote on almost the whole Bible. From the early centuries the only works of which we can read a continuous text are the Homilies of Chrysostom, of which there is no satisfactory critical Greek text, and the exposition of Bede. Of Chrysostom's Homilies Stuehrenberg (110) writes, 'John Chrysostom's fifty-five sermons on Acts were extremely influential throughout the Middle Ages, frequently serving as the basis upon which subsequent commentaries were constructed. These sermons, composed ca. 400, were "the only complete commentary on Acts that has survived from the first ten centuries" (Quasten, III, pp. 440–441).' There is little that is original in Bede's commentary but it is of considerable value in having preserved material from a number of older writers, notably Jerome, Gregory, and Arator. The last named should probably be given individual mention for his epic poem, *De Actibus Apostolorum*. This is not quite a commentary; whether it is a paraphrase of Acts which draws special attention to baptism or a work on baptism with special reference to Acts is perhaps open to discussion. There is a recent edition of Arator's 2326 hexameter work by R. Hillier.[21]

Chrysostom's Homilies are practical sermons from which we learn as much about life in Antioch in Chrysostom's time as about the times of the apostles, but there is a good deal of plain practical exposition and application of the text. It is notable that the infelicities that trouble modern readers of the Greek text of Acts and lead to hypotheses such as that of an Aramaic original seem to give the Greek orator little or no trouble. Perhaps we are too sensitive. Bede also was a writer of common sense and practical interest—and good at apt quotation.

Luther saw Acts as essentially a reproduction of Pauline theology. It was not simply a piece of history and an example of good works, expressed in the sharing of property and in mutual concern. 'Sondern darauff sol man mercken Das S. Lucas mit diesem Buch die gantze Christenheit leret bis an der Welt ende das rechte Heubtstück Christlicher lere nemlich Wie wir alle müssen gerecht werden allein

---

[21]R. Hillier, *Arator on the Acts of the Apostles. A Baptismal Commentary*, Oxford Early Christian Studies, 1993.

durch den glauben an Jhesu Christo on alles zuthun des Gesetzes oder Hülffe vnser werck.'[22] It is hard to acquit Luther of reading Acts through spectacles more Pauline than Luke himself used. Luke did have an interest in history, and his one reference to justification though put on Paul's lips is not cast in quite the Pauline mould (see on 13.38f.). Luke does however insist on faith as the primary Christian requirement (e.g. 15.9). Calvin with a full dress commentary on Acts,[23] is able to take exegesis more seriously than many subsequent expositors—sometimes more seriously than even Luke himself.[24] He also takes historical questions seriously, and is perhaps the first of modern commentators, occasionally, and surprisingly, anticipating Enlightenment and post-Enlightenment writers.

It is impossible here to give a full account of more recent work on Acts; also unnecessary, since useful accounts are already available. The following should be noted:

W. Gasque, *A History of the Criticism of the Acts of the Apostles*, BGBE 17, Tübingen, 1975.
   'A Fruitful Field', *Interpretation* 42 (1988), 117–31.
E. Grässer, 'Die Apostelgeschichte in der Forschung der Gegenwart', *ThR* 26 (1960), 93–167.
   'Acta-Forschung seit 1960', *ThR* 41 (1976), 141–94; 259–90; 42 (1977) 1–68.
E. Haenchen, 29–63, 124–41.
   RGG 1.507f.
F. Hahn, 'Der gegenwärtige Stand der Erforschung der Apostelgeschichte', *Theologische Revue* 82 (1986), 177–90.
J. W. Hunkin, British Work on the Acts. *Begs.* 2.396–433.
W. G. Kümmel, 'Das Urchristentum, I, II, III, IV', *ThR* 14 (1942), 81–95, 155–73; 17 (1948), 3–50, 103–42.
   Nachträge zu Teil I–III, 18 (1950), 1–53.
   'Das Urchristentum I, II', *ThR* 22 (1954), 138–70, 191–211.
   'Das Urchristentum I, IIa, b, c, d, e', *ThR* 48 (1983) 101–28; 50 (1985), 132–64, 327–63; 51 (1986), 239–68; 52 (1987), 111–54, 268–85.
   'Zwei Gesamtdarstellungen des Urchristentums', *ThR* 52 (1987), 401–9.
A. C. McGiffert, The Historical Criticism of Acts in Germany, *Begs.* 2.363–95.
A. J. and M. B. Mattill, *A Classified Bibliography of Literature on the Acts of the Apostles*, Leiden, 1966.
E. Plümacher, 'Acta-Forschung 1974–1982', *ThR* 48 (1983), 1–56; 49 (1984), 105–69.

[22]Vorrede auff der Apostel Geschichte, in the 1545 edition (Stuttgart, 1989).
[23]See the translation by J. W. Fraser and W. J. G. McDonald, two volumes, 1965 and 1966.
[24]See *FS* Corsani, 312–26.

The reports contained in *Theologische Rundschau* are of very great value; it is as needless as it is impossible to work on the same scale in this Introduction.

Haenchen (29–63) in his survey of 'die historisch-kritische Acta-forschung' divides his account into the following sections: A. Die Epoche der Tendenzkritik; B. Die Epoche der Quellenkritik; C. Die Kritik bis 1945; die Formgeschichte (1. Phase); D. Die Kritik nach 1945; Formgeschichte (2. Phase). In the edition of 1977 a supplementary section was added, Die Arbeit geht weiter. Whether Haenchen's description of the first period, which focuses on F. C. Baur, Schneckenburger, and Overbeck, is most happily described as that of Tendency-criticism is open to question. The description is of course understandable; it was one of Baur's principles that ancient sources must be examined for their tendencies, that is, in English idiom, one must ask what axes their authors had to grind. It is in the light of this that their historical worth must be assessed. This is truly observed; but there is a prior, though related, observation, namely that our sources (alongside Acts must be placed the Pauline epistles) do not tell the same story, and the historian's task is not to harmonize them but to set them over against one another. This is criticism; and it is when the reader observes that the first Christian decades were not a period of universal peace[25] that he begins to ask why Acts gives the impression that they were, and to inquire what tendency led Luke to write as he did. Tendency may prove to be the wrong word, if it suggests an intention to present things as other than they were. Misleading impressions may be given as a result of incomplete knowledge, or of unconscious presupposition. There is ample room here for debate, and 'tendency' makes the debate theological as well as historical. Baur had his own explanation of the phenomenon he observed, an explanation that was already being questioned and modified in the middle years of the nineteenth century. His most important contribution was the observation (anticipated to some extent by Semler and Michaelis)[26] that the phenomenon existed. The Pauline epistles made it clear that there was a conflict between Pauline Christianity and Judaizing Christianity, whether the latter is to be put down to the original apostles or to other Jewish Christians. This is not the point at which to attempt an answer to the question, What actually happened? The first question, which Baur was perhaps the first to see clearly, is, What are we to make of Acts? It is important, and often overlooked or indeed contradicted, that Baur could write as late in his career as 1845[27] that Acts remains 'eine höchst wichtige Quelle für die Geschichte der apostolischen Zeit,' though he adds immediately 'aber auch eine Quelle, aus welcher

[25]See above, note 1.
[26]See W. G. Kümmel, *The New Testament: The History of the Investigation of its Problems* (ET 1973), 120.
[27]*Paulus*, p. 13; reprinted in the second edition (ed. E. Zeller, 1866), p. 17.

erst durch strenge historische Kritik ein wahrhaft geschichtliches Bild der von ihr geschilderten Personen und Verhältnisse gewonnen werden kann.' What Baur found in Acts was neither pure Paulinism (as determined by the epistles) nor pure Judaizing (the requirement that Gentile converts should be circumcised was clearly rejected, for example). It was not unnatural to think that the middle course between the two extremes was a compromise; and this was not incorrect. Baur was mistaken however in thinking that the compromise was devised and was being commended by Luke and his contemporaries in the second century.[28] Luke did not invent the compromise; already in the first century he found it in operation and did not question that it had been intended by all the chief representatives of the preceding decades. It is in something like this sense that a sentence of Overbeck's, quoted by Haenchen (37) is correct: 'Ihr [der Apostelgeschichte] Heidenchristentum ist nicht das paulinische, aber noch weniger ist ihr Judaismus das urapostolische.' Luke confuses the Pauline Gentile mission with another, and ignores the Judaism that he alludes to in 15.1, 5—probably because it had come to an end.

Baur's tendencies were those that must appear as soon as the notion is abandoned that all apostolic and semi-apostolic writings must (if rightly understood) present a harmonious picture of a peaceful and blameless apostolic age. For unfettered historical inquiry applied to Acts (and of course to the rest of early Christian literature) all subsequent students are indebted to him (and to Loisy after him). But estimates of tendency are apt to be subjective, and Haenchen is right in picking out Quellenkritik as the next stage in the study of Acts. A possible answer to the question why some things are not mentioned in Acts may be not that Luke chose to keep quiet about them but that his knowledge was limited by the sources available to him.

Haenchen takes his account of Quellenkritik as far back as Schleiermacher, and indeed further. A more detailed account is given by J. Dupont,[29] and the question of sources has been discussed earlier in this Introduction, and in I.49–56. Luke probably used a considerable number of sources (if that is the proper name for them), collecting information where he could. He was probably himself a well-travelled man, who sought information in the Christian groups he visited; there is no reason why he should not have obtained written information by letter. The only more extensive pieces that may be singled out are the Antiochene traditions—one cannot tell whether they were in written or in oral form—and the We-passages.

Sections C and D of Haenchen's summary of work on Acts are headed Formgeschichte; the first phase deals with die Kleinen Einheiten, the second with die Komposition. With a few deviations

---

[28]On this see the commentary on ch. 15.
[29]J. Dupont, *The Sources of Acts* (ET 1964).

these sections are devoted to the work of Haenchen's great predecessor, M. Dibelius, whose essays on Acts were collected and edited by Heinrich Greeven in a volume, *Aufsätze zur Apostelgeschichte* (1951).[30] The term Formgeschichte is unfortunate because though there is resemblance between Dibelius's work on Acts and the contributions made by him and others to the form criticism of the gospels there is not the same concern with the form of the units that are studied. Dibelius's concern is to distinguish between and to separate out the traditional material used by Luke and his editorial redaction of it—redaction criticism, much used since his time, would in fact be a better term for what Dibelius himself practised. Speeches may indeed be separated from narrative, and it is sometimes possible to see the literary devices by which speeches have been accommodated to the narrative settings in which they have been placed. A good example is found in ch. 3, where a speech which is on fundamentally similar lines to that of ch. 2 is fitted to the story of the healing of the lame man at the Temple gate (vv. 12, 16). A particularly clear (though not in fact convincing—see I.491–8) example of Dibelius's method is provided by his treatment of the conversion of Cornelius in ch. 10. At the root of this episode (according to Dibelius) there was a simple pious story of a conversion; this was taken up and used as an important step in Luke's account of the expansion of the Gospel into the Gentile world. Not only was Peter's short statement of the Gospel added but also the story of Peter's vision, and the setting was constructed so as to bring out the radical step involved in Peter's visit to and, in the end, baptism of a Gentile household. A somewhat more convincing example is provided within this one by the use made of Peter's vision, which seems in itself to refer to the relaxation of food laws but is used in Acts not with reference to Gentile food but to the Gentiles themselves: no man is to be regarded as unclean (10.26).

The total effect of Dibelius's work, which after 70 years (counting from the earliest of his essays) remains of great importance, was to move the historian's use of Acts a stage or two further back. It is impossible to give an immediate general estimate of the whole book, or even to distinguish between more and less trustworthy sources. The contents of the book must be analysed and classified, rather in terms of content than of form: speeches distinguished from narratives (for speeches contained within narratives may have had a completely different origin) and summaries from particular episodes. In regard to each unit the attempt must be made to distinguish between a traditional basis and the editorial use that has been made of the tradition. It must be emphasized that this is a far more problematical process than some have recognized; it goes too far to describe it as in

[30]ET, *Studies in the Acts of the Apostles*, 1956.

itself and necessarily guesswork, but strict control has to be exercised in order to prevent criticism from descending into guessing. In the Third Gospel Luke's work can be detected by a comparison with Mk., less confidently by comparison with Mt. In Acts the only comparative material is provided by the Pauline epistles, and this material is narrowly limited in extent. The necessary control (so far as control is possible) is provided by study of Lucan interests (but may not Luke's interests be based on, derived from, his knowledge of tradition?) and Lucan style (but the variety of styles that Luke could command has often been noted). Also to be noted is the editor's arrangement of his material.

Mention of Dibelius has led, inevitably, to what may be called redaction criticism; to this we shall soon return. The supplementary chapter in Haenchen's 1977 (7th—16th in the Meyer series) edition (pp. 124–41), entitled 'Die Arbeit geht weiter', is not analysed in the same way as the original chapter but surveys the work of a number of authors. The literature on Acts that has appeared since 1977 (roughly the period occupied by the writing of this commentary) has been diverse in range and immense in quantity. The survey articles by Grässer and Plümacher referred to above (p. lxxii) cover some of it as well as earlier material. No claim is made here to have surveyed the whole, and no attempt will be made to present an adequate account, which would remove all balance from the commentary. A few lines of study will be briefly illustrated.

Redaction criticism has already been described, and is practised, though to a limited degree and with a measure of scepticism, in this commentary. Scepticism is necessary because in Acts redaction criticism turns to so great an extent on subjective judgement, as was pointed out above. Perhaps the best representative of the redactional method is G. Lüdemann (see I xiii), whose 'Kommentar', which omits much of the information traditionally found in commentaries, consists in an attempt to distinguish throughout Acts between tradition and redaction, and on this basis to assess its value as a historical source. One of the examples picked out by Lüdemann himself to illustrate, in his Introduction (pp. 17–20), the method he employs is the account in Acts 18 of Paul's visit to Corinth (see below in this Commentary pp. 858–82). Redactional features stand out at once: Paul's Sabbath preaching in the Synagogue and the favourable picture of Gallio. The use of Jews as a point of contact for the Christian preacher and the representation of Roman authorities as tolerant of the Christian movement are frequently recurring themes. These points may indeed be redactional here, but it is worth noting that the synagogue, rightly approached, did afford a ready-made audience, and if some Roman officials (not necessarily of course Gallio) had not shown a fair-minded approach the apologetic stories in Acts would have been worthless. But there is also (Lüdemann thinks) traditional material: Paul's work with Aquila and Priscilla, and their recent arrival in Corinth as a result of Claudius's expulsion of the Jews from Rome; the arrival of Silas and Timothy from Macedonia; Paul's use of the house of Titius Justus; the conversion of the ruler of the synagogue, Crispus; the 'trial' before Gallio; the reference to the ruler of the synagogue, Sosthenes. 'Nicht sprachliche Gründen führen zu der Annahme von Traditionen, wohl aber die *Konkretheit* der obigen Nachrichten und—wichtiger—der ... Befund, dass ein nicht unerträchtlicher Teil der Nachrichten wenigstens z. T. durch die Paulusbriefe bestätigt wird' (p. 18). Not that Lüdemann neglects linguistic considerations. The above quotation is taken from his brief introductory summary. His full treatment (under the heading Redaktion) of 18.1–17 begins (p. 203), 'V.1: Zu *meta tauta* vgl. die luk. Parallelen 7.7 (cit.); 13.20; 15.16 (cit.); Lk 5.27 (diff. Mk); 10.1; 12.4 (diff Mt.); 17.8; 18.4. V.2–3: Die Verse tragen sprachlich-syntaktisch luk. Kolorit: vgl. *onomati, to genei* (vgl. 4.36; 18.24), AcI [= Accusative and infinitive] mit *dia* eingeleitet (bis); *chorizesthai* nimmt *choristheis* (V. 1) auf. Der gehäufte Partizipialstil ist gleichfalls redaktionell.' And much more.[31] Even when a good deal of redactional material is eliminated (though it would be illogical to assume that anything due to Luke's editorial work on a source is unhistorical) Lüdemann is able to maintain (p. 24) that 'Die Apg bleibt neben den Paulusbriefen eine wichtige Quelle für die Geschichte des frühen Christentums.'

From redaction criticism it is natural to move by way of a book described by its author, P. F. Esler,[32] as socio-redaction criticism, to the sociological study of Acts. Sociological study is not unrelated to historical criticism, for historical study if it is to be complete must always include a social element; the best historians have always known that they must inquire into the way in which men and women—not only kings and queens and their ministers but ordinary folk—conducted their lives, and that even power struggles on the largest scale were conducted by means of personal and administrative agencies. It is however undoubtedly true that in recent years greater stress has been laid upon investigation of the personal lives of Christians in NT times and that the methods of sociology have been employed. Esler looked back to pioneering work by G. Theissen,[33] W. A. Meeks,[34] and others, but developed his sociological observations in the light of Lucan theology. Much of his book is social

[31]For the use of linguistic characteristics as marks of Lucan redaction see especially the commentary of Weiser.

[32]*Community and Gospel in Luke-Acts*, SNTSMS 57, 1987; see now also *The First Christians in their Social Worlds*, 1994; J. H. Neyrey, ed., *The Social World of Luke–Acts*, Peabody, Mass., 1991.

[33]*The Social History of Pauline Christianity* (1982), a translation of articles published some years earlier.

[34]*The First Urban Christians* (1983).

history, and his observations on the Law, the Temple, the Poor and the Rich, and Rome are of great value. What calls for attention here is Esler's debate with the ancient historian E. A. Judge (who has also made very valuable contributions to the study of early Christian social history) about the applicability of the methods of sociology in NT history, and indeed to ancient history in general. Unfortunately it is impossible to follow the debate in detail here. 'Reading between the lines of Judge's article,[35] one senses that his real worry with sociological exegesis is that its exponents will attempt to plug holes in first-century data by drawing upon relevant features of the comparative materials they apply to the New Testament text' (Esler, p. 14). Esler and Judge are in fact not so far apart as might at first appear. Esler's reply to Judge's 'worry' is in essence that models and types should be more accurately defined and more carefully used than they are by some sociological practitioners who turn to ancient history, and his own observations in ancient social history as it concerns the NT are, as was noted above, of considerable value. The NT (like e.g. the *Histories* and *Annals* of Tacitus) is an old book, and there are no easy transitions (beyond the basic facts of human nature) between its world, and its forms of society, and our own. Sociological procedures can help to open up and sharpen questions for us, but the answers are to be found in the patient observation and collection of data found in ancient texts, literary and non-literary, and in the results of archaeological exploration, and it must not be expected that answers will be found by sociological analogy, if indeed answers are to be found anywhere.

More recent years have seen the development of methods of literary study, developed first, for the most part, in the realms of secular literature and applied to the NT as a whole. These have more to do with hermeneutics than with history,[36] and find more scope in other parts of the NT than in a matter-of-fact work such as Acts. This is not to say that they are of no value, though the thought of Acts lies on the surface and does not require elaborate hermeneutical arts to draw it out.

Not that there are no literary questions to ask about Acts. One may ask, for example, to what class of literature it belongs. This is a question that was raised above (pp. xlviii–li) and here it must suffice simply to mention a few terms, all of which cover part of the truth, none the whole truth. It looks like history,[37] biographical history, the

---

[35] *Journal of Religious History* 11 (1980), 201–217.

[36] See R. C. Morgan and J. Barton, *Biblical Interpretation* (1988), where they are dealt with in ch. 7 (pp. 203–68). 'Some of the different ways that interpreters read a work of art today may prove more suggestive for theological interpretation than a historical scholarship which is less interested in the aesthetic and moral significance of great literature' (p. 203).

[37] See Plümacher, *Lukas als hellenistischer Schriftsteller.*

historical monograph.[38] It has been described as an apology, and that in several senses, and like a hellenistic romance. Luke had found his own way of communicating the Gospel and bearing witness to Christ; that is perhaps as near as we can get to a characterization of Acts. To say that the book is *sui generis* may seem like running away from a difficult and disputed problem of classification, but it is in fact true. No Christian wrote a book like it; the apocryphal Acts are at best like a Western text run even wilder.[39]

Also to be briefly mentioned here is the literary analysis of narrative, in relation not only to the narrator but also to the reader. It is possible to distinguish between the actual author of a piece of literature and the implied author, between the actual readers and the implied readers. The actual author of the Sherlock Holmes stories is Conan Doyle, a historical figure, about whom a good deal is known (far more than about most ancient authors). The implied author, implied by the form and content of the stories, is Dr Watson, a person known only from the stories themselves, though from them quite well; we know something of his medical training, his military service, his marriage, his loyal though not always highly intelligent assistance to his friend. In some kinds of literature this distinction is illuminating; hardly so in Acts, where the actual author is known, if at all, only by identification with the implied author, who shows his hand only in the We-passages (if indeed there). Of the actual readers of Acts, again, we know little. Some of the evidence has been set out above (I.30–48). There may have been earlier readers, indeed it is highly probable that there were, but we can hardly give a name to one before Irenaeus. There is an excellent discussion of the implied readers in J. B. Tyson, *Images of Judaism in Luke-Acts* (Columbia, South Carolina, 1992). We may infer the characteristics of the implied readership from the extraneous pieces of information[40] which the author thinks it necessary to supply, and from those facts which the author assumes that the reader will know. Tyson's conclusions (pp. 35f.) are worth quoting.

   1. Our reader is generally a well-educated person with a rudimentary knowledge of eastern Mediterranean geography and a familiarity with the larger and more significant Roman provinces.
   2. The implied reader is familiar with some public figures, especially Roman emperors. He has some knowledge about James and his position within the primitive Christian community ...

[38] Again, Plümacher.
[39] *FS* Black (1979), 27.
[40] See S. M. Sheeley, *Narrative Asides in Luke–Acts*, JSNTSupps 72 (1992); R. Tannehill, *The Narrative Unity of Luke–Acts*, Philadelphia, I, 1986, II, 1990.

3. The implied reader is not expected to know any language other than Greek ...

4. The implied reader is knowledgeable about public affairs ...

5. ... has a working knowledge of common Greek and Roman measurements and coinage.

6. ... has a working knowledge of both pagan and Jewish religions, an aversion to some pagan practices, and an attraction to Jewish religious life. But he is probably not Jewish and is not well informed about certain significant aspects of Jewish religious life.

7. ... is familiar with the Hebrew Scriptures in their Greek translation and acknowledges their authoritative status but is not familiar with those methods of interpretation that find the fulfilment of the scriptures in Jesus.

From these observations Tyson infers that the implied reader 'is similar to those characters in Acts that are called "Godfearers" ' (p. 36).[41] The two centurions (of Luke 7 and Acts 10; 11) serve as good examples.

This sort of observation is interesting and helpful in the study of Acts. It is however fairly described as a further development of historical study, an aspect of historical criticism little noticed in the past and now profitably brought to the fore.

The same comment may be made on the use, of which much is now being made, of the rhetorical principles taught and practised in antiquity. The works of the orators are an important part of ancient literature, and instruction in oratory was an important part of ancient education. These facts are not a new discovery, but the focusing of attention on them is new, and has borne a good deal of fruit in the study of the NT. Not so much fruit however in the study of Acts. As we have seen, Luke writes in such a way as to cause his work to be counted along with and judged alongside the work of ancient historians. His history is a very readable work, clear, fascinating, illuminating, and not inaccurate. But this is not because Luke follows the rules of the rhetoricians. On the whole his manner corresponds closely with the words of Shakespeare's Mark Antony: 'I am no orator, as Brutus is ... I only speak right on.' Special attention has been given to the speeches recorded in Acts, e.g. to the speech of Tertullus (24.2–9), which has been described as a masterpiece of forensic oratory, and Paul's reply (24.10–21). These however, like most of the speeches in Acts, are too short to make the rules of rhetoric applicable. Rules that are suitable to (e.g.) Demosthenes' *De*

---

[41]For the problems arising out of this term, which are not discussed by Tyson, see I.499–501.

Corona (112 pages in OCT), cannot be reasonably adapted to speeches, or summaries of speeches, only a few lines in length.

Bibliography

C. K. Barrett, *FS* Corsani, 312–26.

H. W. Bartsch, *ThLZ* (1972), 721–34.

W. Bieder, *Die Apostelgeschichte in der Historie*, ThSt 61, Zürich 1960.

H. J. Cadbury, *The Book of Acts in History*, London 1955.

H. von Campenhausen, *Die Entstehung der christlichen Bibel*, Tübingen 1968.

M. Dibelius, *Studies in the Acts of the Apostles*, ET London 1956.

P. F. Esler, *Community and Gospel in Luke-Acts*, SNTSMS 57, Cambridge 1987.

P. F. Esler, *The First Christians in their Social Worlds*. London and New York 1994.

W. Gasque, *A History of the Criticism of the Acts of the Apostles*, BGBE 17, Tübingen 1975.

W. W. Gasque, *Interpretation* 42 (1988), 117–31.

A. George, *Études sur l'oeuvre de Luc*, Paris 1978.

A. Harnack, *Marcion: das Evangelium vom fremden Gott*, Leipzig 1921, [2]1924.

R. Hillier, *Arator on the Acts of the Apostles*, Oxford 1993.

E. A. Judge, *Journal of Religious History* 11 (1980), 201–217.

R. J. Karris, *CBQ* 41 (1979), 80–97.

A. F. J. Klijn, *NovT* 10 (1968), 305–312.

J. Knox, *Marcion and the New Testament*, Chicago 1942.

W. S. Kurz, *Bib* 68 (1987), 195–220.

A. J. and M. B. Mattill, *A classified bibliography of literature on the Acts of the Apostles*, Leiden 1966.

A. J. Mattill, *FS* Bruce (1970), 108–122.

A. J. Mattill, *CBQ* 40 (1978), 335–50.

W. A. Meeks, *The First Urban Christians*, New Haven and London 1983.

F. Neirynck and F. van Segbroeck, *EThL* 59 (1983), 338–49.

S. M. Sheeley, *Narrative Asides in Luke-Acts*, JSNTSupp 72, Sheffield 1982.

F. Stegmüller, *Repertorium biblicum Medii Aevi*, Madrid 1940–1980.

P. F. Stuehrenberg, *NovT* 29 (1987), 100–136.

C. H. Talbert (ed.), *Luke-Acts, New Perspectives*, New York 1984.

G. Theissen, *The First Followers of Jesus*, ET London 1978.

J. B. Tyson, *Images of Judaism in Luke-Acts*, Columbia (South Carolina) 1992.

A number of the works mentioned under §3 are relevant here also.

V THE THEOLOGY OF ACTS

So far as Acts makes a specific contribution to the theology of the NT this is to be found not so much in the treatment of particular doctrines as in an understanding of the possibility and course of Christian history and especially of the Christian mission. It may nevertheless be worth while to collect some of Luke's views in relation to a number of important themes before attempting to sum up the general convictions that underlie his presentation of Christian origins.[1]

(a) *Eschatology*. To the modern student of theology biblical eschatology is a problem. It was not a problem to Luke; he knew what to make of it and had already established a position which was, at the end of the first century, quite satisfying. It had long been necessary to recognize the existence of an interval between resurrection and parousia. In the beginning this may not have been expected or, when it happened, understood. The crucifixion (it was believed) would be followed by the vindication of Jesus, and this might be expressed in terms of Daniel 7 (a coming with the clouds) or of Daniel 12 (a rising up of those who sleep in the dust). Luke saw a clear distinction; it appears both in the Third Gospel and in Acts. Jesus was raised from death by God; after a period of forty days during which he appeared to various disciples he went up into heaven, his ascent modelled on Daniel's picture of the coming of the Son of man put into reverse; thence at the right moment he would return. All these events might be described as eschatological in the sense that they belonged to the winding up of God's purpose for the world. God himself had determined that the last act of the play should be a complex one, and had already declared this in the OT. The basic text is given a prominent place in the account of the gift of the Spirit on the Day of Pentecost. Altering the text of Joel 3.1–5 (LXX) Luke writes of the last days, which cover all Christian history. They are initiated by the gift of the Spirit, described by Luke before the text is quoted, and their end will be heralded by cosmic phenomena (the darkening of the sun, and so forth) which have manifestly not yet happened; the great and glorious day of the Lord has not yet arrived. The church exists in the intervening period, its

---

[1]For an admirable and very much fuller analysis of Lucan theology see F. Bovon, *Luke the Theologian, Thirty three years of Research (1950–1983)*, ET Allison Park, 1987; J. A. Fitzmyer, *Luke the Theologian: Aspects of his Teaching*, London, 1989; see also the Bibliography.

life determined by what has already happened and by what is still to come. The period is provided by God so that witness may be borne to Jesus (Acts 1.8); Luke describes the record of this witness from Jerusalem as far as Rome, but there is no hint, as his book draws to a close, that the end may be expected soon. That there will be an end, which will include the return of Jesus and judgement carried out by him, is plainly assumed. It is categorically affirmed at the beginning of the book (1.11) and several times repeated, especially in the earlier chapters (2.19–21; 3.20, 21; 10.42; 17.31; (26.6)); it is implied also by some of the passages that refer to salvation, for this is in part salvation from the judgement that will fall upon the sinful human race. The coming of the Messiah waits upon repentance and faith (3.20, 21), which Luke hopes to encourage, but it is clear that his interest is in the present and he makes little use of eschatological threats to encourage response. In this respect Acts is to be contrasted with Luke's gospel; on this see especially Wilson (*Gentiles* 67–80: 'The two strands in Luke's eschatology'). His conclusion is correct. 'In Acts we have a further development of one of the two strands we found in Luke's Gospel to the exclusion of the other. Luke has moved away from belief in an imminent end. One of his methods of doing this is to schematise and objectify the eschatological timetable. Another is to substitute Ascension theology, the present activity of the exalted Lord in his Church, for belief in an imminent end. This is done not so much by dogmatic statement as by the concentration on this element in Acts. The time-scheme of Acts allows for a hiatus between the Resurrection and the Parousia in which the Church can exist and grow' (p. 80). See also the excellent observations of E. Grässer in Kremer, *Actes* 99–127, especially his conclusion on p. 127. Consideration of Luke's eschatology leads immediately to a second theme.

(b) *The Holy Spirit.* According to 2.17, 18 the gift of the Holy Spirit is (after the resurrection and ascension of Jesus) the first part of the fulfilment of the eschatological hope; it initiates the period in which (see above) the church can 'exist and grow'. References to the Spirit are as frequent as references to the parousia are few. Luke writes 'non tam apostolorum, quam Spiritus sancti Acta describens, sicut prior liber Acta Jesu Christi habet' (Bengel, 389). This is already made clear in 1.6–8 (it is not for disciples to know God's eschatological programme but they will be empowered for witness by the gift of the Spirit) and confirmed in 2.1–4 (after a period of waiting the church receives its full active being in the gift of the Spirit at Pentecost). It is not strictly consistent with this definitive, founding gift of the Spirit that from time to time afterwards Christians are said to be, on special occasions, filled with the Spirit— 4.8, 31; 6.3, 5; 7.55; 9.17; 11.24; 13.9, 52. In addition people are said to be baptized with the Holy Spirit; the Holy Spirit comes upon them, or falls upon them. It is only Luke's mode of expression that is open to logical criticism; his thought is clear and consistent. Believers receive the Holy Spirit as the basic constituent of their believing life, and in times of special need they receive special gifts of the Spirit that enable them to speak or act appropriately. The Holy Spirit has already been at work in the OT (e.g. 1.16; 4.25; 7.51; 28.25), but is now (as prophesied by Joel—2.17, 18) given generally, so that the possession of the Spirit by Gentiles is a proof that they are rightly included in the church's mission (10.44, 45, 47; 11.15, 16; 15.8). In other ways also the Spirit directs the mission, directing Philip to meet the Ethiopian (8.29) and subsequently conveying him to Azotus (8.39f.), telling Peter to go with Cornelius's messengers (10.19f.; 11.12), forbidding Paul to speak in Asia and to travel to Bithynia (16.6, 7), and ordering him to return to Asia (19.1—si v.1.). If in 21.4 the Spirit seems to get the directions wrong this is no doubt to be put down to a piece of careless writing by Luke. The Spirit is offered as a gift to those who repent and believe. The offer is explicit on the Day of Pentecost (2.38); cf. 9.17; 13.52. The gift is often but by no means always associated with baptism, sometimes with the laying on of hands; on this see below, pp. xcif. The Spirit, present as a guiding principle in the Christian fellowship, is abused when Christians practise deceit; so Ananias and Sapphira deceive the Holy Spirit and lie to God (5.3, 4); it goes too far to deduce from this text the deity of the Holy Spirit, though it is unlikely that Luke would have wished to deny the proposition had it been made to him. The Spirit is associated with the Father and the Son at 2.33, a verse that is not without ambiguity. Jesus has been exalted to (or by) the right hand of God; he has received the gift of the Holy Spirit; on the precise meaning of this see I.149f. Having received the promise of the Spirit (the promised Spirit?) he pours out (the verb ἐξέχεεν points back to the quotation from Joel in 2.17) the Spirit whose presence you can detect in observable phenomena. The Spirit is at least a third form of divine activity.

What was observed (heard rather than seen) was the miraculous speaking with tongues of 2.4, 5–12; it is not clear whether the phenomena of 2.2, 3 were observable outside the house or room in which the disciples were assembled. Speech is in Acts the characteristic mark of the Spirit's presence, sometimes in glossolalia (2.4; 10.46; 19.6), sometimes in prophecy (2.17, 18; 11.27; 13.1–3; 21.(4), (9), 10, 11), sometimes in proclamation (e.g. 4.31). It is striking that Luke (unlike Paul) does not see the work of the Spirit in the moral renovation of human life. This does not mean that he did not believe in the power of God to change human behaviour; it does however mean that he was impressed by what may be regarded as the shallower and showier aspects of Christian life—mainly no doubt because they were easy to describe and likely to impress the reader as they had impressed him.

(c) *Christology*. As truly as the Third Gospel, though in a different manner, Acts is an account of the works of Jesus the Messiah. The opening verse refers back to the contents of the former treatise as concerned with all that Jesus began to do and to teach. It is a probable though less than certain implication that the new treatise is about all that Jesus continued to do and to teach; even if he did not intend it Luke would not have disagreed. The disciples are to be his witnesses (1.8; for their continuing witness cf. 1.22; 2.32; 3.15; 5.22; 10.39, 41; 13.31; 22.15, 20; 26. 16, for the word μάρτυς) and he is the foundation of their testimony (2.22; 3.13; 4.2, 10, 33; 5.42; 8.12, 35; 9.20, 27; 10.38; 11.20; 13.32f.; 16.31; 17.3, 18; 18.5, 28; 20.21; 24.24; 28.23, 31). He is the agent of miracles (e.g. 3.6; 4.10; 9.34). Sometimes he acts indirectly, through the Spirit (who may be called the Spirit of Jesus, 16.7); angels also play their part (8.26; 12.7; 27.23); but Jesus also speaks and acts in his own person, and on specially notable occasions, confronting Saul (9.5; 22.8; 26.15), and encouraging him (18.9; 23.11). He is a supernatural person, able at will to participate in historical events.

To this it is necessary to add that what he does he does as the agent of God the Father. In the healing of the lame man at the Temple gate it may be the intention of 3.13 to suggest that God has glorified his servant Jesus by using him as the agent of cure; in 4.30 the disciples pray to God that he will stretch out his hand for healing and that signs and portents may be done through the name of his servant Jesus. Jesus is the agent not only of healing (σωτηρία) in a physical sense but of the salvation that means belonging to the elect people who will be brought safely through the perils of the last days (4.12).

Jesus is described by a number of titles, some of them widely used elsewhere in the NT. He is of course the Christ, the Messiah, the Lord's anointed king. Or should we say, he will be the Christ? This question is raised with reference to 3.20; see the notes on this verse in I.204f. It is not likely that the verse refers to an appointment lying still in the future; Luke undoubtedly believed that Jesus was the Christ from his birth onwards; see especially Lk. 2.11. It is not impossible that a source used by Luke took a different view, but it is improbable. It does however seem likely that Acts 2.36 meant originally that Jesus became Christ at the time of his resurrection, though Luke himself must have been able to accommodate the verse to his own view. *Lord* (κύριος), also occurring in 2.36, is a word that interprets χριστός for the Hellenistic world. It is not correct to say that since in the LXX κύριος is the rendering of יהוה the use of the word in Acts (and in the NT generally) in itself implies the divinity of Jesus. At least it does not imply that Jesus is to be identified with, or placed on the same level as, the God of the OT. Luke, quoting Ps. 110.1 (εἶπεν ὁ κύριος τῷ κυρίῳ μου) in 2.34, shows himself to be fully aware that the word κύριος could be used in two senses, and he took Jesus to be the second κύριος to whom the first κύριος speaks. The word is at once an identification of Jesus with the Davidic king and an approach to the Gentile world with its gods many and lords many (1 Cor. 8.5). *Lord* undoubtedly means that Jesus was, and was understood by the Christians to be, one who enjoyed absolute authority, to whom they owed absolute obedience. He himself however stands under the absolute authority of God the Father: it is he who has made Jesus Lord and Christ. There is thus in Acts, as in much of the NT, an element of subordinationism, but it is the subordination of an obedient Son, active in the Father's service. Jesus is the Son (υἱός) of God in only two passages. It may not be a coincidence that it is Paul who proclaims Jesus as the Son of God (9.20) and quotes Ps. 2.7 at 13.33. It would be wrong to read a metaphysical relation into Luke's reporting, whatever Paul himself may have believed. Only in chs. 3 and 4 (3.13, 26; 4.27, 30) is Jesus spoken of as the Servant (παῖς) of God; this may reflect the use by Luke of a source. It is mistaken to suppose that there is a reference here to the Servant of the Lord in Deutero-Isaiah. In 4.25 the word παῖς is applied to David, and in the OT it is used of kings, prophets, and other outstanding figures. There may however be an allusion to Isaiah 52.13 in 3.13—to the glorification rather than the suffering of the Servant. Luke is here using traditional material; when, in 8.32,33 he quotes Isaiah 53 the word 'servant' does not occur.

Other Christological terms occur infrequently. One is ἀρχηγός: 3.15; 5.31. The word may mean prince, leader, author, origin; see the discussion in I.197f., 290. At 5.31 it is coupled with σωτήρ, which occurs again at 13.23; other words of the family (σῴζειν, σωτηρία, σωτήριον) occur also. It is uncertain whether ὁ δίκαιος (3.14, where we have ὁ ἅγιος καὶ δίκαιος; 7.52; 22.14) is a title or a description; see I.195f., 377. Ναζωραῖος (2.22; 3.6; 4.10; 6.14; 22.8; 26.9; cf. 24.5, where it is used in the plural, of Christians) is taken by some to be a title, not related to the place Nazareth; but cf. 10.38, ὁ ἀπὸ Ναζαρέθ, and see I.140. The expression Son of man, so common on the gospels, is used once only, by Stephen, at 7.56. It is impossible to deduce anything about the meaning of the term from this one verse, but it was probably chosen as one suitable to denote a person now in heaven but waiting to come with the clouds at some future time.[2] At 2.22; 17.31 the word ἀνήρ is used unselfconsciously—and of course quite properly—of Jesus; in the latter verse, where the *man* is to be

---

[2]In Stephen's speech see also words that might have been used in Christology but are in fact used of Moses: ἄρχων. δικαστής. λυτρωτής, 7.35. See I.363f.

the judge of mankind, it recalls part of the connotation of Son of man.

There is in Acts no profound Christological thought;[3] yet it is clear that Jesus Christ of Nazareth is the person who initiated and will conclude the whole story and directs the whole course of it. His career, marked by portents, signs, and mighty works, was sufficient to show that God was with him, not merely as he had been with, for example, the prophets, but in a unique (though undefined) sense. He was killed through an ignorant error on the part of the Jews, both rulers and people, who handed him over to the Romans, but God soon put the mistake right by raising him from death, thereby confirming—or creating—his status as Messiah (a term meaningful to Jews) and Lord (which would make sense to Gentiles). The risen Jesus continued long enough on earth to prove that he was truly alive and then ascended to his rightful place at the right hand of God. This proved that he belonged essentially to the same order of being as the Creator, the Lord (יהוה) of the OT, though within that order secondary. The sense in which a second being might be said to share the throne of God would have constituted a problem, and engendered disputes, for some Jews; not, apparently, for Luke. Jesus had now sent the Spirit so as to bring into being a renewed Israel, soon to be enriched by the addition of Gentiles.[4] Jesus, crucified and risen, thus brought salvation to the mixed community: the forgiveness of sins, the inspiring and sanctifying of the Spirit, and the pledge of safety in the eschatological troubles that still lay ahead.

(d) *The Church.* The community just mentioned was an eschatological entity, living within the period of fulfilment initiated by the gift of the Spirit and awaiting its end in the portents described by Joel (Acts 2.17–21). It was also however an historical phenomenon, manifested in a number of groups of believers scattered through various parts of the Mediterranean world. These groups came into being through the preaching of apostles and others. As their hearers accepted the word that they heard they found themselves gathered into believing companies and shared a common life. There was little by way of outward organization to mark this common life;[5] fellowship was constituted by a shared belief that Jesus in truth was what the preachers had declared him to be, offered salvation, and claimed obedience. The Spirit generated speech and no doubt enthusiasm; and Jesus' command of mutual love was expressed in the sharing of goods (2.44, 45; 4.32, 34, 35, 36, 37; 5.1–11; 6.1). How far this practice, which according to Luke resulted in the absence of poverty

---

[3]P. Vielhauer in his essay on the Paulinism of Acts (*FS* Schubert 33–50; original version in *EvTh* 10 (1950–1951) 1–15) took Acts to be pre-Pauline in Christology.

[4]See below, sections (h) and (j).

[5]See however below, sections (e) and (f).

in the community, resembled and was related to similar customs observed at Qumran is disputed; see I.167–9, 263.

At first there was one such community, in Jerusalem. At 5.11; 8.1, 3; 11.22; 12.5; 15.4, 22; and perhaps 18.22, it is denoted by the word ἐκκλησία. As the Gospel was taken out from Jerusalem into the world this word came to be applied to other local Christian groups: to the Christians of Antioch at 11.26; 13.1; 14.27; 15.3; to the Christians of Ephesus at 20.17.[6] The word is used of the groups of converts made in Paul's first missionary journey: 14.23; 16.5; of those in Syria and Cilicia at 15.41. An ἐκκλησία thus appears to be a local group of Christians. There are two passages that may suggest a wider meaning. It is often maintained that this is so at 9.31, which refers to the church through the whole of Judaea and Galilee and Samaria. This may be the beginning of such a use, but the geographical designation may be taken to indicate a 'local' church residing in more than one town (see I.473–5). More significant is the reference (20.28) to the church of God which he acquired by his own blood, a strange expression in that it appears to refer to the blood of God. However it is interpreted the verse speaks of a single body of all Christians which God has redeemed and constituted through the bloody, that is, sacrificial, death of Christ. ἐκκλησία, then, is here the world-wide company of the redeemed, *ecclesia catholica*. It is important that the same word is used for both purposes. Luke may not have seen deeply into the meaning of his own language, but it implies (and this is borne out elsewhere in the NT) that each local group of Christians is not merely related to the total church but in fact is the total church in the place in which it exists. It is also important that the word ἐκκλησία is used in the LXX as a rendering of קהל, the people of God, living (sometimes rebelliously) under his direction. The connection is underlined by the occurrence in 7.38 of τῇ ἐκκλησίᾳ ἐν τῇ ἐρήμῳ, the people of Israel between Egypt and the Promised Land.[7] Luke was familiar with the LXX and there can be no doubt that this use of ἐκκλησία would be in his mind. In the OT the Lord had acquired a people by the mighty acts that he performed in Egypt; he had now acquired a people, racially mixed, by the shedding of Christ's blood. Why the death of Jesus should be regarded as a sacrifice and how the sacrifice could have the effect of constituting a people are questions that Luke did not address. For questions that did concern him see below, especially (h) the Jews and (j) Gentiles and the Gentile Mission. For the constitution and actions of the church see (e), (f), and (g).

(e) *Apostles and Ministers.* Luke's account of the church is given

---

[6]If at 18.22 ἐκκλησία does not refer to the church of Jerusalem it will refer to that of Caesarea.

[7]The use of ἐκκλησία in 19.(32), 39, 41 for the duly constituted town meeting in Ephesus illustrates the common secular meaning of the word.

for the most part in terms not of its rank and file but of its leading members. Continuity between the earthly life of Jesus of Nazareth and the church after the time of the resurrection is provided by twelve men. Eleven of these (1.13) had belonged to the group of twelve chosen by Jesus (Lk. 6.13–16); from this group Judas Iscariot was removed by defection and death (Acts 1.16–20) and Matthias was added to it (1.21–26), the use of the lot being taken to demonstrate that he equally with the rest had been chosen by Jesus (ἀνάδειξον ὃν ἐξελέξω, 1.24). These Twelve are referred to again under that title at 6.2, and the title is implied at 2.14, where Peter stood up 'with the Eleven' (cf. 1.26). They are thus responsible for the initial proclamation of the Christian message and are still regarded in ch. 6 as responsible for it, since they profess the intention to give themselves to prayer and the ministry of the word, leaving the administration of charity to Stephen and his colleagues (6.2–6), whom, on the nomination of the people, they appoint.

The Eleven when they are joined by Matthias are described as apostles, a term that accords with Lk. 6.13 (οὓς καὶ ἀποστόλους ὠνόμασεν) and is used much more frequently than the numeral, though not after 16.4. It is sometimes but not always suggested fairly definitely that the Apostles are identical with the Twelve, and there are only two verses (14.4, 14; on both see the notes, I.666f., 671f., 678f.) where persons not belonging to the Twelve are called apostles. Only in these verses is Paul (and Barnabas with him) called an apostle, and it is clear that Paul (and presumably Barnabas also) did not fulfil the conditions laid down in 1.21, 22 for appointment. The rest of the NT makes it clear that the word ἀπόστολος was used in more senses than one,[8] and it is probably best to suppose that the (Antiochene?) source used by Luke in ch. 14 referred to Paul and Barnabas as apostles, that is, envoys, or missionaries, of the church of Antioch, and that Luke omitted to bring the reference into line with his use elsewhere.

Luke has some notable stories about Peter: his witness on the Day of Pentecost; his healing of the lame man at the Temple gate and the speech that followed; his appearance before the Jewish Council; his working of miracles, told both in general and particular terms; his visit to Samaria; his dealings with Cornelius; his release from Herod's prison; his share in the Apostolic Council. In chs. 3, 4, 8 John accompanies Peter. In ch. 12 we read of the execution of James, John's brother. Luke has nothing else to tell us of the Twelve Apostles and it is clear that for him their main significance as a group is simply that they exist, and by their existence witness to and (so far as this could be done) guarantee the continuity between Jesus and the

[8]See *The Signs of an Apostle* (London, 1970, Carlisle, 1996), with the summary on pp. 71–3.

post-resurrection church. Only Peter (so far as Luke's narrative goes) makes any other contribution to the life of the church. Their function is important (note the contrast in 13.31, 32, and cf. 10.39) but it neither could nor needed to be repeated. There are no more apostles; the word as used in the sense of 2 Cor. 8.23 (and perhaps Acts 14.4, 14) dropped out of use. Paul, der dreizehnte Zeuge,[9] as was noted above, does not meet with the requirements of apostleship as Luke sets them out, yet he was, for Luke and no doubt in fact, the outstanding missionary of the first generation. He also exemplified, for Luke, Luke's understanding of Judaism as the heir of the OT people of God, who nevertheless must now understand both the OT and their own vocation in the light of the Gospel. How is he to be described? Luke has no category for him; he is a σκεῦος ἐκλογῆς (9.15), a tool selected by God for a special purpose, a man who would bear Christ's name before Gentiles and kings and the children of Israel. He is not subordinated to the Twelve; the only passage that suggests this is 13.32, and this is a matter not of subordination but of distinction. His address to the Ephesian elders in 20.18–35 is important both as showing his understanding of pastoral ministry, as exercised by himself and expected of the elders, and as indicating the origin of the elders' ministry. They have been appointed neither by the church in which they ministered nor by Paul but by the Holy Spirit (20.28). No provision for future ministers is suggested here; they will come from the same source. To say this is not to deny human participation in the process; especially in the earliest days Paul must himself have played a leading part in making appointments (14.23), but 13.1–3 pictures as 20.28 does appointment not so much to an office as to a task by the Holy Spirit, working, one may suppose, through the prophets of 13.1. The task of prophets and teachers was to prophesy and to teach, to utter messages communicated by the Holy Spirit and to maintain and apply the basic traditions of the faith. Elders would like Paul himself declare the counsel of God (20.27) and maintain discipline in the community. Working for their own living they would out of their own as well as out of the church's resources aid those who were in need. This task elsewhere is the work of deacons, but the word διάκονος does not occur in Acts. Elders, called ἐπίσκοποι as well as πρεσβύτεροι, perform all the tasks of ministers; Acts 6 is not intended to be an account of the origin of the diaconate as an order of ministers (see I.304).

(f) *Baptism and the Christian Meal.* These twin topics (they seem to us to be twins; it is by no means certain that they would have seemed so to Luke—like other NT writers he had no word *sacrament* to unite them) give rise to a number of puzzles. If one concentrates

[9]The title of a book by C. Burchard (Göttingen, 1970).

on certain parts of Acts (chs. 1, 2, 8, 9–11, 16, 18, 19, 22), or rather on parts of these chapters, baptism seems to be the normal and universal way into the Christian church. What are we to do? ask the crowd on the Day of Pentecost. Repent, and let each of you be baptized, Peter replies (2.37, 38). The converted Samaritans respond in the same way; Cornelius and his friends, the Philippian gaoler and his household, many of the Corinthians, are baptized. If however we turn to the other chapters (and to parts of those listed above) there is silence. The Temple crowd are urged to repent and have their sins blotted out; they are not told to be baptized. There are no baptisms in Luke's account of the 'first missionary journey', though churches are established (14.23). Apart from Lydia and the Philippian gaoler there are no baptisms in Macedonia or in the main account (apart, that is, from 19.5) of Paul's work in Ephesus. No baptisms take place after ch. 19, even in Malta, where Paul made so deep an impression. Again, if we ask, Does the gift of the Spirit precede, accompany, or follow the rite of water-baptism? we get different answers in different parts of Acts. If we ask, Must baptism be complemented by the laying on of hands? there is no consistent answer. What is meant by baptism in (or with) the Spirit? Is it a consequence of water-baptism or is it independent of water-baptism? Who are the proper recipients of water-baptism? Adult believers only, or infants also? None of these questions can be answered with any confidence on the basis of Acts. There is quite enough of baptism in Acts to make it clear that Luke was familiar with the practice; we can hardly fail to conclude that baptism was not, as is commonly supposed, a universal custom in the early church, or at least that some of Luke's sources (such as that based on Antioch) were not interested in baptism.

When baptism is mentioned, and if it is specified (and since a good deal of baptizing was going on in the first century[10] it must have been specified—Our baptism is . . .), it is said to be in the name (ἐπὶ or ἐν τῷ ὀνόματι; εἰς τὸ ὄνομα) of Jesus.[11] Behind this no doubt lies the Hebrew לשם which here would mean 'so as to come under the authority of'. Taken into Greek the expression gains a financial connotation: 'so as to be added to the account of', that is, 'so as to become the property of'. This seems to be the primary thought in Luke's mind. The converts (one may say, whether baptized or not) become Christ's men or women. From this consequences follow. They become members of Christ's people. Christ bestows upon them the gift of the Spirit. Their sins are forgiven. These units form in Luke's mind a single whole and he is not concerned to specify an order in which they occur. At 2.38 it is not quite stated but it is implied that the gift of the Spirit follows upon baptism: Let each of

[10]See J. Thomas, *Le Mouvement Baptiste en Palestine et Syrie (150 av. J.-C.—300 ap. J.-C.)*, Gembloux, 1935.

[11]There is no hint of a Trinitarian formula such as that of Mt. 28.19.

you be baptized ... and you will receive ... The opposite order occurs at 10.44–48. The Spirit fell upon Cornelius and his friends and to this Peter's response was, 'Can we fail to baptize these people who have received the Holy Spirit just as we did?'[12] There is a further complication in ch. 8 (cf. 19.6) when Philip baptizes the Samaritans and it is not said that they received the Holy Spirit; Peter and John arrive, impose their hands and pray, and the Spirit is given. Is the imposition of hands necessary? It is not mentioned in the other stories we have considered. Is it a rite that only an apostle can execute? We do not know the answers to these questions; see the notes on the various passages. We cannot fail to conclude that Luke gives an unclear account of baptism. He had no fixed principles about its practice, or perhaps its meaning. For Paul baptism meant crucifixion and burial with Christ, and he seems to assume that this is a common Christian understanding (Rom. 6.3). In fact, what Luke says about baptism matches his Christology. He knows quite well that Jesus was crucified and that his resurrection implies his previous death. But for him *Christ crucified* is not his central theme, the theme of all themes that it was for Paul (1 Cor. 2.2); therefore the Christ to whom the converts came to belong was not so specifically and exclusively Christ crucified as he was for Paul. Inevitably, crucifixion dropped out of baptism.

Did Luke's church have a eucharist? He does not say so. Acts contains several references to meals taken by Christians. The description of the Christian fellowship that resulted from Peter's preaching on the Day of Pentecost includes 2.42, 'They continued in the teaching of the apostles and the fellowship, in the breaking of bread and the prayers;' 2.46, 'continuing with one accord in the Temple and breaking bread at home they partook of food with gladness and simplicity of heart;' At 20.7 it is said that Paul and his companions with the church at Troas met to break bread; at v. 11, after the incident of the young man who fell out of the window, Paul went up, broke the bread and ate, and continued his address. At 27.34–36 Paul urged his fellow seafarers to partake of food; this would be for their welfare (σωτηρία); when he had said this and taken the loaf he broke it before them all and began to eat; and they all cheered up and themselves partook of food. On all these passages see the notes. It is striking that all of them refer to the breaking of bread; the last is expressed in language that is particularly close to that of Lk. 22.19, 20 (the Last Supper) and 9.16, 17 (the feeding miracle); see also Lk. 24.30, 35. There is however no reference, as there is in the account of the Last Supper (in 1 Cor. 11.23–26 as well as in the gospels), to the drinking of wine. J. Jeremias (see the notes on 2.42) is probably right in taking the *breaking of bread* to be a

---

[12]The question whether the apostles were baptized cannot be answered.

Christian use, describing a specifically Christian meal, wrong in taking Luke's intention to be the concealment from non-Christian readers of a secret Christian rite confined to believers. Luke had already given an account of the meal including explanatory words ('This is my body', etc.) not only for the bread but for the wine; and he goes out of his way in 27.35 to say that what Paul did he did ἐνώπιον πάντων. The four passages in Acts describe a Christian fellowship meal which derived its special significance not from what was eaten and drunk but from the fellowship of Christians who, as they ate and drank, would not forget the Lord who had given himself for them, and in giving himself for them was giving himself to them. If others were present they would get out of the meal what they could—and this might prove, even in the midst of the storm, to be more than physical sustenance. Whether there was wine to drink or not might well depend on circumstances. There is no indication that the meals referred to in Acts were in any way connected with the Passover, at which the drinking of four cups of wine was obligatory. A more difficult problem is raised by the fact that Paul's account of the Christian meal (1 Cor. 10.16, 21 as well as 11.23–26) includes specific reference to wine. It is natural—and correct—to say that there was probably a great deal of variety in Christian observance in the first century, but Luke (whatever we make of the We-passages) was some sort of Paulinist. It is probably best to suppose that though 'the breaking of bread' was not a cypher designed to keep the proceedings secret it had become a formula that pointed to a whole meal and made no attempt to specify all the substances consumed.

It is hardly open to doubt that what was important to Luke was not the symbolic significance of what was done, of what was eaten and drunk, but the shared life that commensality represented. In 2.42 the breaking of bread appears in a context determined by the teaching of the apostles and prayers and by fellowship (κοινωνία) which in part at least receives its definition from the fact that those taking part had their property in common (κοινά), and used their resources for the relief of the poor.

(g) *Frühkatholizismus.* It has been held that the account in Acts of apostles and ministry, of baptism and eucharist, points to the development of the primitive church into the stage of early catholicism. Before this position can be considered it is important to know precisely what is meant by Frühkatholizismus. It is helpful to go back to an early stage in the discussion, the controversy between Harnack and Sohm on the meaning of catholicism.[13] The significance of the

---

[13]Best studied in A. Harnack, *Entstehung und Entwicklung der Kirchenverfassung und der Kirchenrecht in den zwei ersten Jahrhunderten* (Leipzig 1910), especially the criticism of R. Sohm's 'Wesen und Ursprung des Katholizismus', pp. 121–86 (ET 175–258). Sohm's article (in *Abhandlungen der Phil.-Hist. Klasse der K.Sächs. Gesellschaft der Wissenschaften* 27.3 (1909)) is extensively quoted and summarized.

discussion is brought out by Conzelmann[14] as follows. 'Frühkatholizismus liegt noch nicht vor, wo ein Traditionsgedank da ist. Dieser gehört zur Theologie selbst. Der entscheidende Einschnitt liegt da, wo die Tradition institutionell, durch Bindung an ein Amt und an Sukzession in diesem Amt, gesichert wird. Er liegt noch nicht vor, wo eine feste Amtsordnung besteht—mag diese auch bereits eine monarchische Spitz haben—sondern erst da, wo das Amt heilsmittlerische Qualität erhält, wo die Wirkung von Geist und Sakrament an das Amt gebunden ist. Mit *Bultmann* zu sprechen: Der entscheidende Vorgang ist die Verwandlung der regulierenden Bedeutung des Kirchenrechts in eine konstitutive (Bultmann 449f.)' Sohm and Harnack treated Spirit and Office, or law, as opposite alternatives; Bultmann[15] qualifies, almost reverses the opposition. According to Bultmann, Holl showed 'dass das Wort des Charismatikers als autoritatives Wort Ordnung und Tradition schafft'. The truth is better put by von Campenhausen, because put in reciprocal form. 'Entscheidend ist vielmehr die feste Korrelation, in der das Geist vom Anfang an zum Begriff des Wortes oder Zeugnisses steht, die beide auf die Person Jesu zurückführen. Sie sind die entscheidende Wirklichkeit, und machen zusammen eine Verabsolutierung des Geistes gegen die Tradition oder der Tradition gegen den Geist gleichermassen unmöglich.'[16]

The theology is sharpened when it is given a specific historical reference in relation to Acts by E. Käsemann, who says of Frühkatholizismus that it 'nichts anderes als die kirchliche Abwehrbewegung gegenüber der drohenden Gnostisierung ist.'[17] Eschatology is replaced by Heilsgeschichte. Luke's story of the mission is not that of testimony to the proclaimed Christ but the way and work of the world-embracing Christian agency of salvation (Heilsanstalt). 'Das Wort ist nicht mehr das einzige Kriterium der Kirche, sondern die Kirche ist die Legitimation des Wortes, und der apostolische Ursprung des kirchlichen Amtes bietet die Gewähr für eine legitime Verkündigung' (p.21). This is a matter on which Luke is perhaps hardly theologian enough to wish to take sides.

These authors have seized upon an important theological contrast; this does not answer the question whether they have rightly evaluated the historical evidence of Acts: indeed they do not all evaluate it in the same way. The following have been alleged as features of the narrative in Acts that point in the direction of Frühkatholizismus. (1)

---

[14]*Theologie* 318.

[15]He invokes K. Holl, unfortunately without giving a reference, also H. von Soden in *Studium Generale* 4 (1951), 351ff. and H. von Campenhausen in *Kirchliches Amt und Geistliche Vollmacht* (Tübingen, 1953), 324, 325. The whole of this book is in varying degrees relevant.

[16]*Kirchliches Amt* ... (as in n. 15), 325.

[17]*ZThK* 54 (1957), 20; see also 'Sätze Heiligen Rechtes im NT', *NTS* 1 (1955), 248–60.

The emphasis on the importance of the apostles, and (2) the notion of a succession from the apostles as constituting the being of the church and providing its ministry; (3) the notion of a ministry which is essential to the being of the church, and (4) stress on the importance of the sacraments as means by which the ministry nourishes the life of the church.

To some extent these matters have already been discussed. It is true that Luke lays considerable stress on the apostles.[18] They are the first believers and, with certain women, constitute the first body of Christians. Their number is important and, after the death of Judas, they are restored to their original strength. The twelfth apostle is chosen in such a way as to show that the choice is made by Jesus, as when the original Twelve were appointed. It is not clear that they alone received the Spirit on the Day of Pentecost but it was they who, led by Peter, stood up to speak to the assembled crowds. Converts on that day continued steadfastly in the apostles' teaching, and it is clear through chs. 3, 4, and 5 that they, headed by Peter and John, are the leaders of the Christian movement. In ch. 6, denoted by the designation 'the Twelve', they solve the problem of the neglected widows by appointing seven to serve tables while they continue to devote themselves to prayer and to the service of the word. According to 8.1 they alone escaped persecution and remained in Jerusalem, but we hear little more of them. In ch. 9, after initial distrust, they accept Saul, and Peter makes his way to Caesarea, where Cornelius becomes a Christian. This event is discussed in ch. 11, and Barnabas is sent to see what has been happening in Antioch, as Peter and John had been sent to Samaria in ch. 8. In ch. 12 James is killed and Peter escapes, leaving Jerusalem for 'another place'. After this we learn that the apostles were present at the Council of ch. 15, but only Peter speaks. We hear no more of them, and it seems probable that Luke had no further information about them.

They were important because they had accompanied Jesus during his ministry and thus served as a guarantee—or perhaps a symbol—of the fact that the actions of the post-resurrection church were a valid continuation of the work of Jesus. For this they are important, indeed indispensable, but they execute no administrative authority, though Peter rebukes Ananias and Sapphira and the Twelve appoint the Seven. Their importance is unique to themselves; it cannot be transmitted to a succession because they and they alone bridge the cleavage between the time of Jesus and the time of the church, at the same time being witnesses to the resurrection, which meant that the Jesus who was crucified was also the continuing Lord of the church.

Succession is thus in a strict sense impossible; the primary function of the twelve apostles was not transmissible. We have seen

[18]See section (e) above.

(p. xci) that it is impossible to infer from Acts that baptism was universally practised, and language specifically 'sacramental' is not used of the Christians' common meal. The church in Acts has those whom we may call ministers, but of no uniform kind. At Ephesus there are πρεσβύτεροι, also called ἐπίσκοποι, but at Antioch there appear to have been no presbyters, but prophets and teachers (13.1). All probably performed very similar functions. Philip was an evangelist; and there were the great Pauline assistants, such as Barnabas and Silas. The apostles could, as we have seen, have no successors, but their task of bearing witness to the risen Jesus was shared by others, and Luke apparently did not think that any special authorization (beyond recognition as a Christian) was necessary for this fundamental task; Stephen was a pre-eminent witness, but the only commission he received (in Luke's narrative) was to care for Hellenist widows. Luke is undoubtedly concerned for continuity, but this must be distinguished from succession; in 20.28 Paul does not say that he had ordained the presbyter-bishops of Ephesus, but that the Holy Spirit had made them what they were. Nothing here corresponds with Clement's account of the appointment of the post-apostolic ministry (though that is informal enough—1 Clement 40–44) or with Ignatius' insistence upon the indispensable centrality of monepiscopacy and a threefold ministry. There is at least one rite, which later became a sacrament, not (as far as we know) universally practised. These are the main historical phenomena.

It may be said that there are some hints of what may be regarded as elements in a developing 'catholic' structure of the church, but they are not combined in such a way as themselves to constitute a catholic structure. For this something more than a few more or less ambiguous elements is required, though these may point forward to the development of further change in the future. The important word in the quotation from Conzelmann (above, p. xciv) is *institutionell*. Any group of people that persists recognizably through a number of years persists by means of tradition: the older teach the younger what the group stands for, and when they can no longer continue their work find others who will take it over from them. The important question is what is the vital force that keeps the group alive, and how is it maintained and transmitted. In Acts (*pace* Käsemann), the vital principle is the word that is committed by Jesus to those who follow him and the Spirit of God by which this message is received and activated. It is not bound up with a succession and the apostles are not those who are most active in promoting it. From time to time it is said that those who receive the word (a characteristic Acts expression) are baptized into (or, in) the name of the Lord Jesus; it is quite possible that when this is not mentioned it is nevertheless to be understood, but even if this is so the omission is not unimportant. The group of Christian brothers and sisters very naturally share from time to time a fellowship meal. They may (Luke does not tell us so) have recalled and repeated the words of Jesus: 'This is my body, This cup is the new covenant in my blood;' there is no indication that the breaking of the loaf and the uttering of these words were confined to a special sort of person, though it is not surprising that when Paul was present he spoke for a very long time (20.7, 11).

Haenchen (105) concludes 'dass man mit der Charakterisierung "Frühkatholizismus" vorsichtig sein muss'. The matter might be put more strongly.

(h) *The Jews.* Acts begins with the converse of Jesus, a Jew, with his Jewish disciples in the weeks immediately after his resurrection. His ascension follows, and soon afterwards the gift of the Holy Spirit. The disciples preach to a large and mixed company of people, many of whom accept their message. They have come from many lands but they have come to Jerusalem and most if not all of them must be thought of as Jews. The Jewish atmosphere persists through the next chapters, so that in ch. 8 Philip's conversion of Samaritans and of an Ethiopian is presented as a new step into a strange world. So is Peter's visit to Cornelius, and Cornelius's baptism. From this point the movement into Gentile world (see (j) below) gathers speed; it is led by Paul and his colleagues, and at the end of the book Paul quotes Isa. 6.9, 10 to the Roman Jews and adds, 'Be it known to you that this salvation of God has been sent to the Gentiles; they will listen' (28.26–28). A superficial reading of this story suggests that the mission to Jews is now over; Christians are leaving them to their own devices and concentrating on the mission to Gentiles. This inference from Acts is not without plausibility, and the book has been understood to be a substantial contribution to Christian anti-Semitism.

This it certainly is not. A book whose main actors—Peter, Stephen, Paul, James, not to mention Jesus (mainly off stage)—are all Jews cannot easily be judged anti-Jewish (still less anti-Semitic— Acts shows no interest in race as such). Most of the leaders of the church have to be pushed very hard, by argument, by vision, by divine intervention through the Holy Spirit, to accept uncircumcised Gentiles as fellow believers. Surely, salvation is for Jews, to whom it was promised. The verse quoted above (28.28) does not stand alone. There are parallels in 13.46 ('Since you thrust [the word of God] from you and consider yourselves unworthy of eternal life, see! we are turning to the Gentiles') and 18.6 ('Your blood be upon your own head, I am clean; henceforth I shall go to the Gentiles'); and in each case Paul's first step in the next place he visits (14.1; 18.19) is to enter the synagogue and pursue his mission there. There is no reason why 28.28, though it stands at the end of the book, should be read in a completely different way.

This does not mean that there are no questions to be asked. It is clear (and in this there is no reason to doubt the accuracy of Acts) that large numbers of Jews were rejecting the belief that Jesus was their, Jewish, Messiah. Stephen's accusation is hard and bitter (7.51–53). Does it mean that the Jewish people have forfeited their special place in the purpose of God? that they have now been replaced by the multi-racial company of believers in Jesus? The question what role the Jewish people may continue to have in God's plan, and their ultimate hope of salvation, are discussed by Paul at great depth in Romans 9–11. Luke was not capable of this kind of discussion and was probably less aware of the questions than most theologians are today. We may see a pointer, which resembles those that we have seen in 14.1 and 18.19, by returning to the end of Stephen's speech. 'You constantly resist the Holy Spirit; as your fathers did so do you' (7.53). Stephen has described several notable failures on the part of earlier generations of Jews. His brothers sold Joseph into Egypt; his people rejected Moses; they made and worshipped the golden calf; they desired and built a temple, which God did not desire. On each of these occasions God might well have washed his hands of them, but he did not do so. True, Jesus was in a sense his last word, but a misjudgment by the Sanhedrin on a particular occasion could not be regarded as the last word of Israel's reply to God. In comparison with the Romans the Jews come badly out of Luke's account of Paul's suffering, but his first act on reaching Rome is to send for the leading Jews (28.17), and Luke (rightly or wrongly) asserts that his message was nothing but what the prophets and Moses said should happen (26.22), and this he was ready to proclaim τῷ τε λαῷ καὶ τοῖς ἔθνεσιν (26.23).

Here however was the crux of the matter. Did Paul rightly understand what Moses and the prophets had said? Most Jews said no, and that on two fundamental points. According to Paul the Scriptures prophesied the death and resurrection of the Messiah, and this was fulfilled in Jesus. According to Luke they also foretold that God would take out of the Gentiles a people for his name (15.14–18). On this interpretation, Jesus was the Messiah and the church, including uncircumcised Gentiles, was the people of God, with the nation of Israel alongside in an undefined position, waiting till it should return by faith into the divine purpose. This is perhaps not a very satisfactory, or a very clear, position from the point of view of theology, but it was a practical one and probably satisfied Luke and most of his contemporaries. The same must probably be said of the Apostolic Decree (15.29); on this see below and the notes on 15.20, 29. The crucial issue was the Law; see the next section.

(i) *The Law.* 'By three things is the world sustained: by the Law, by the [Temple] service, and by deeds of loving-kindness' (Aboth

1.2 (Danby)). No NT writer, certainly not Luke, raises any objection to גמילות חסדים, the doing of kindnesses. The attitude to the Temple that is revealed in Acts is not simple.[19] The first Christians are represented as continuing to use the Temple. The scene of the Pentecost event (2.1–4) is not specified; it may have been the Temple; see I.113f. In Acts 3 we see Peter and John on their way to the Temple at the time of prayer; they heal a lame man at the Beautiful Gate, the party proceeds into the Temple, and there Peter and John address the assembled crowd. In ch. 5 the apostles are preaching in the Temple when they are arrested. In 6.13, 14 Stephen is accused of threatening the Temple with destruction, and in ch. 7 he launches the most violent attack on the Temple found outside the OT. From this point in Acts the scene begins to shift from Jerusalem, but when Paul returns he accepts the challenge to demonstrate his faithfulness to Judaism by taking part in Temple rites (21.23, 24, 26) and thereby affirms that he accepted its discipline (21.24). This double attitude to the Temple reflects the attitude of Acts to Judaism in general.[20] Judaism is good if it is understood in the Christian way. The Temple is an aid to prayer; and participation in the resolution of a Nazirite vow included sacrifice so that Paul's visit to the Temple in ch. 21 must be understood to be for the purpose of sacrifice as well as prayer. But any attempt to confine God within a dwelling of human construction is to be rejected, so that the very existence of a Temple was a peril to true religion, whether in Jerusalem or in Athens (17.24). This is a different attitude from that of the Qumran sect, which did not disapprove of the Temple on principle but only of the way in which it was being administered and of those who controlled it. See I.338.

It is notable that Stephen, who attacks the Temple with such vehemence, does not attack the Law. Moses received living oracles to give to us (7.38). The Israelites received the Law εἰς διαταγὰς ἀγγέλων (a thought that Paul uses in a different way—Gal. 3.19). That they had a Law was a good thing; their fault was that they did not observe it. It cannot be said on the basis of Acts that Stephen initiated a law-free Gospel. There is indeed no law-free Gospel in Acts but a compromise between those who wanted to keep the whole Law in operation and those who as a condition of salvation wanted no law at all. This compromise is expressed in the Decree of Acts 15.29. The Decree undoubtedly inclines markedly in the law-free direction. Circumcision is not demanded, but Gentile converts are required (ἐπάναγκες in 15.28) to abstain from food offered to idols, from blood, from strangled meat, and from fornication—requirements that combine the moral with the ceremonial.[21] This is

---

[19]See *FS* Bammel, 345–67.
[20]See above section (h).
[21]See the Commentary on ch. 15.

presumably the result of years of controversy between Paul and his allies and various groups of Judaizers. It is essentially a practical rather than a theological compromise, and though it is set forth as containing conditions of salvation its main practical effect, in addition to establishing peace within the church, was probably that it made it possible for Jewish Christians and Gentile Christians to share together in the church's common meal. It was, however, based[22] on those elements of Judaism that a Jew could not give up even in the extremity of persecution—Judaism reduced to an absolute minimum so as to impose as little strain as possible on Gentiles.

Luke's grounds for so far dispensing with the Law are given in ch. 15. The fundamental reasons are put, probably for reasons of policy, in Peter's mouth. First, the pragmatic reason: God called Peter to speak the word to Gentiles; they received it by faith (not by works of Law), and God gave to them the same gift of the Spirit that he had given at the beginning to (Jewish) apostles (15.7f.). The next emphasizes that God made no distinction between the circumcised and the uncircumcised; the latter, unclean Gentiles that they were, were cleansed by God by faith, without any legal device. Finally Peter asserts that Jews themselves were unable to bear the yoke of the Law and should therefore not seek to impose it on Gentiles—an assertion that can hardly be maintained unless observing the Law is understood to include the practice of perfect love to one's neighbours. Barnabas and Paul support the argument by recounting the signs and portents that God had performed in the course of their mission to the Gentiles; these surely he would not have done had he disapproved of what was going on. Finally James points out that Peter's action had been in accordance with Scripture which manifests God's intention to find a people among the Gentiles. James's further, not too clear, point (15.21) may be intended to cut both ways: Moses is so widely read that his Law cannot be simply ignored; but he has enough people to preach him without our joining them.

This is very different from the Pauline argument, not least in the fact that Christ is nowhere mentioned (unless, obscurely, in the reference to the 'tent of David' in 15.16). For it is Christ who is τέλος νόμου (Rom. 10.4). The precise meaning of these words is disputed,[23] but it is beyond dispute that the whole treatment of the subject turns on the figure of Christ. This is perhaps the clearest indication that Luke did not have a profound understanding of Christian—and especially of Pauline—theology. He was a loyal Christian believer but he did not see all the implications of his faith. Nor was he able to bring out of the various sources that he used a consistent view of the Law. Stephen is accused of speaking against

[22]See pp. 734f.
[23]See Cranfield, *Romans* 515–20; *Romans* 184; Dunn, *Romans* 589–91, with many references.

the Law (κατὰ ... τοῦ νόμου) and of saying that Jesus would change (ἀλλάξει) the Mosaic customs (ἔθη; 6.13, 14), In his speech Stephen speaks highly of the Law and alleges that his accusers break it. The Cornelius episode is full of difficulties. In Mk (though not in Lk.) Jesus declares all foods clean, but Peter has to be convinced by a vision that he must not count common what God makes clean. This vision itself seems to have to do with clean and unclean foods, but it is interpreted with regard to human beings and the legitimacy of dealings with Gentiles.[24] Peter further recognizes that there is no respect of persons with God (10.34). The next verse is difficult to interpret precisely. On the surface it seems to mean that anyone who 'does the right thing' is accepted by God, and that this is as possible for Gentiles as for Jews. If however this is true there seems to be little need for the Gospel Peter is about to preach to Cornelius. If it means only that a good man like Cornelius has as much right as a Jew to have the Gospel preached to him it means that the ordinary man needs a moral conversion before he can have a Christian conversion; and indeed the conversion of Cornelius is not the change of life of one who has previously practised evil but the gift of the Spirit which issues in speaking with tongues (10.44–46). The conclusion reached after discussion (11.18), however, is that Gentiles as such may now be admitted to salvation, hitherto understood to be confined to Jews. From this conclusion not only those whose opinion is quoted in 15.1, 5 but the Council and the Decree appear to retreat. There are certain necessary conditions that Gentiles must fulfil. Later we learn that there is a report that Paul is teaching Diaspora Jews not to circumcise their children or to follow the (Jewish) customs—in a word, is teaching apostasy from Moses (21.21); Paul adopts James's suggestion as the means of clearing himself from this charge. Paul himself taught that circumcision must not be forced on Gentiles and that among Jews it was an adiaphoron: Circumcision is nothing and uncircumcision is nothing (Gal. 6.15). According to Acts he observed Jewish feasts (20.16), though in Gal. 4.10 he speaks disparagingly of them. The Roman opinion is that the difference between Paul and other Jews is a matter of the interpretation of their Law (18.15), and though Luke, where the Romans trivialize the matter, sees its importance, he does not wholly disagree with Gallio. As with the OT as a whole, the Christians have understood the Law rightly, the Jews wrongly.

(j) *Gentiles and the Gentile Mission.* This matter has been almost sufficiently dealt with in the sections on the Law and the Jews; also in that on sources (I.50–52), for to a great extent Luke's sources may be regarded as those accounts of the origin and conduct of the mission to the Gentiles that he was able to collect. The chronological

[24]See I.494, 516.

question who first took the Gospel beyond Judaism to the Gentile world cannot be answered for Luke himself probably did not know. In his account of the Council (15.7) he allows priority to Peter, though he has described Philip's work before Peter's, probably because he had said (8.1) that when all other Christians were scattered from Jerusalem the apostles remained in the city. Mission was his theme (see above, p. xxxiii); the mission to the Gentiles was the greatest of missions, and not its originator but its greatest leader was Paul. It is interesting that in Acts Paul does less than Peter and James to justify a mission to the Gentile world, invoking only (in ch. 15) the miracles that happened in the course of his missioning. He does not invoke the figure of Abraham as one who was justified by faith, without circumcision, and received a promise that included all the nations (Gen. 17.5; Gal. 4.17; Gen. 12.3; Gal. 3.9).

The earliest missions that included non-Jews were not (according to Acts) the result of planning by those who undertook them. Philip's mission to Samaria was the result of the persecution that scattered all the Christians (except the apostles) from Jerusalem. His encounter with the Ethiopian was the consequence of direct instructions given in the first instance (8.26) by an angel, subsequently (8.29) by the Spirit. Peter's visit to Cornelius was the result of co-ordinated directions given to the two men; it is made clear in his response to the vision (10.14) that Peter was not disposed to have dealings with Cornelius and that his resistance had to be broken down by divine pressure. When those who like Philip were driven from Jerusalem arrived in Antioch it is clear that their first intention was to preach only to Jews; at a second stage unnamed men from Cyprus and Cyrene included non-Jews in their scope. In view of this, and the resulting mixed church in Antioch, it may be (though it is not stated) that is was intended from the beginning that the mission to which Barnabas and Saul were committed (13.1–3) should include Gentiles. 13.5, however, refers only to preaching in the synagogues of Cyprus, and the meeting (13.6–12) with the proconsul Sergius Paulus seems to have been unpremeditated. It is a possible but quite uncertain conjecture that the success of this encounter (13.12) stimulated concern for the Gentiles. It is a further possible but quite uncertain guess that John Mark left his senior colleagues (13.13) because he disapproved of this unplanned step. From this point (according to Acts) Paul's own purpose was constant, and he usually adopted the method, on reaching any new town, of first visiting the synagogue, making use of hearers already collected to hear religious discourse, and leaving it when, as regularly happened, the Jews rejected his message, in order to concentrate on Gentiles. He never ceased to be concerned for his fellow Jews (e.g. 28.23; also Rom. 9.1–3; 10.1), but recognized in the Gentile mission a special vocation. This indeed is in Acts traced back to his conversion (9.15;

22.21; 26.17); rightly so, for this is confirmed in Gal. 1.16 (... ἵνα εὐαγγελίζωμαι αὐτὸν ἐν τοῖς ἔθνεσιν). The first journey (to use Luke's division of the material) includes a small circuit in Pamphylia and Pisidia; after this Paul moves more widely.

It is very probable that Jesus gave no explicit command to undertake a mission to the Gentiles. J. Jeremias[25] is probably right in the view that he foresaw after his death the eschatological pilgrimage of the nations to Jerusalem. Their joining with the Jews in one people of God would be one aspect of the end of history. After the resurrection the disciples found that there was to be an unexpected tract of history before the end. This extension of time made a mission to the Gentiles possible (see above, pp. lxxxiif.); but the mere extension of time was not sufficient to cause the Gentile mission. For causes we must look further. To some extent it may have been due to what might look like chance. A Gentile heard what the missionary was saying, accepted it, and manifested the spiritual and moral signs of a changed life. The preacher was faced with the question uttered by Peter at 10.47: How can I refuse to baptize one who shows the same marks of Christian existence as I do myself? He must be welcomed into the saved community. There were also hints in the story of Jesus. He undertook no mission outside Israel, but he did devote himself to and gave his life for those who though of Jewish race had wandered outside the religious framework of their people. If he could eat with tax collectors and sinners it is in fact surprising that Peter should hesitate to eat with Cornelius, and that, if Jesus declared all foods clean,[26] Peter should at first refuse to obey the order, 'Kill and eat' (10.14, 28; 11.3). No doubt sporadic conversions took place, but it was Pauline theological development that established work among the Gentiles, especially the recognition that the significant ancestor of Jesus was not David, the king of Israel, but Adam, the father of the race, and that God was not the God of the Jews only but of the Gentiles also (Rom. 3.29)—a God of half humanity would be only half a God.

This theological development is not found in Acts. Paul is called to go to the Gentiles, and he goes. There were other missions to the Gentiles. There were those of whom we learn most from the Pauline epistles but of whom we can see something in Acts: those who declared roundly that Gentiles might be accepted but only if they accepted circumcision and the Law (Acts 15.1, 5); perhaps there were also those whose existence is admitted though their authorization is denied at 15.24. Different groups insisted on various elements in Judaism: some upon all, the Galatian Judaizers on circumcision and the calendar, the Corinthian Judaizers on food laws, those who

[25]*Jesus' Promise to the Nations* (ET 1958), especially 55–73.
[26]Mk 7.19 (not in Lk.).

were responsible for the Decree on food laws, avoidance of idolatry, and chastity. The last may possibly be connected with the Seven of Acts 6.5. These or other Diaspora Jews may have been responsible for Stephen's speech (which opposes the Temple but accepts the Law) and the Areopagus speech attributed to Paul. Both of these speeches suggest an origin[27] in Hellenistic Judaism. It would be natural—and by no means improper—for a Hellenistic Jew who had become a Christian to edit and reuse a synagogue sermon in which he had combined Greek philosophy with OT religion, introducing a reference to Jesus at the end.

At this point should be mentioned also the so-called 'God-fearers'. For their existence, the nomenclature applied to them, and their possible role in Acts, see I.499–501. Here it suffices to state without discussion that there were Gentiles who found Jewish ethics, theology, and worship attractive, but not to the extent of becoming proselytes. Some of them probably had some contact with the local synagogue. Christian preachers offered to them, as they offered to all, a form of Judaism, stripped of its least attractive features, in particular of the rite of circumcision. If there were no evidence at all, it would seem probable that some of these should adopt the Christian way of admission to the people of God, and thus come to form the nucleus of a non-Jewish, uncircumcised element in the newly formed church.

(k) *Ethics.* Acts contains hardly any direct ethical instruction. The mission speeches include the call to repent, and this implies a change in moral behaviour; note especially 26.20, with the demand that hearers should show ἄξια τῆς μετανοίας ἔργα, works, moral acts, that will demonstrate the sincerity of the repentance they profess. Even here however (cf. 2.38; 3.19; 17.30) there is no attempt to specify the works that might have this effect. The only example of specific ethical instruction is in 20.33–35. where Paul, addressing the Ephesian elders (it is of course Christians whom one would expect to receive ethical teaching), speaks of the example he has given and urges them not to depend on charity but to work as he has done so as to help the weak. He invokes a saying attributed (somewhat improbably—see the note) to Jesus: It is more blessed to give than to receive. Cf. 1.21, 22: the twelfth apostle who is to take the place of Judas Iscariot must have accompanied Jesus throughout his ministry; this implies familiarity with the teaching, including the ethical teaching, of Jesus.

It is consistent with this that the Acts narrative is written on a good ethical level. Clearly the healing of the sick is regarded as a proper activity in which Christians, if they have the appropriate gift, ought

[27]See I.338f.; pp. 331, 344–371; also 14.15–17 (I.665, 680–3).

to engage (3.1–10; 4.9—the healing is a εὐεργεσία; 4.30; 5.12–16; 8.6–8; 9.33., 40f.—raising the dead is a particularly notable act; 14.10; 19.11f.; 20.10–12; 28.8, 9), though compassion for the sick is not the only motive—miracles have evidential value. Violent attacks on Christians are clearly not approved, but no special sympathy is shown for Sosthenes (18.17), and the story of the sons of Sceva (19.14–16) is told with a measure of *Schadenfreude*. Lying and deceit are wrong (5.1–11); so are disloyalty (15.38) and cruelty (in an OT story, e.g. 7.19). Herod Agrippa however is struck down not because he beheaded James and imprisoned Peter but for the theological offence of accepting glory due to God alone (12.23). Courage and determination, in facing death (e.g. 21.13) or in a storm at sea (ch. 27), are virtues. Fornication and the shedding of blood (if this is what αἷμα means—see the note) are forbidden in the Decree (15.20, 29; 21.25). The practice of magic is condemned (8.9; 13.6; 19.13–19).

The teaching of the apostles (2.42), we may suppose, would include ethical teaching though, in a Jewish community, there would be little need for it: high ethical principles were already taught and on the whole practised. Paul's teaching to Felix (24.25) was perhaps not unnecessary. If the Western text is followed the Apostolic Decree included the negative form of the Golden Rule, which certainly was familiar in Judaism. The general requirement of kindness and care for those in need is expressed in a number of ways. For the selling of property and sharing of resources (2.44f.; 4.32, 34, 35, 36, 37; 5.1–11; cf. 6.1) see further below. The church of Antioch sent to the needs of their fellow Christians in Jerusalem (11.29, 30; 12.25). Paul, on his last visit to Jerusalem, had come with alms (24.17). Almsgiving was among the virtues of Cornelius (10.2, 4, 31) and Dorcas was full of good works and charities (9.36, 39). Hospitality is a notable good work (16.15, 34; 21.8, 16). Paul took thought for his fellow travellers who had spent too long without food (27.33–38). Stephen's prayer for the pardon of those who stoned him is modelled on that of Jesus (7.60).

It is interesting to observe that virtue and charity are not confined in Luke's narrative to Christians. Cornelius's practice of charity and righteousness has already been noticed (10.2, 4, 31, 35). Paul's friends among the Asiarchs are not said to be Christians but they took thought for him and tried to protect him (19.31). Julius the centurion took steps to save Paul (27.43—as other Roman officials had done), and the barbarians of Malta 'showed us no common kindness' (28.2).

Paul twice claims to keep, or to have done his best to keep, a good conscience (23.1; 24.16). If Paul himself uttered these words he probably added—aloud or under his breath—the words he uses in 1 Cor. 4.4, ἀλλ' οὐκ ἐν τούτῳ δεδικαίωμαι. For Luke they mean quite simply that Paul regularly tries to do what he believes to be the right thing.[28]

At 21.9 Philip is said to have four daughters who were virgins and prophesied. One can only wonder what, if anything, lies behind this. Did their virginity permit them to prophesy? Was it a qualification for mention in the book? Or was Luke simply stating a set of facts: there were four of them; they had remained unmarried; they uttered prophecies?

The special interest in poverty and wealth, in the danger of riches and the importance of the care of the poor, which are frequently noted as characteristic of the Third Gospel, are present but less emphasized in Acts. They most often take the form of the organizing of charity for those in need. Paul's collection (Rom. 15.25–28, and elsewhere), which may be alluded to at Acts 24.17, is not mentioned in Acts 15 (but cf. Gal. 2.10). It is possible that the Antiochene collection (see above) refers to the same gift. Most relevant here, but discussed in I.167–70, 251–60, 310, 312f., are the sale of properties mentioned in 2.44f.; 4.32–37; 5.1–11 and the διακονία of 6.1. We should note also the use of the word κοινωνία and the statement that the Christians had ἅπαντα κοινά (2.44; 4.32). The ministry of 6.1 is comparable with familiar Jewish charities; the common possession of all goods calls to mind Greek proverbs, which no doubt were sometimes expressed in concrete arrangements, but within Judaism it finds a parallel only in the practices of the Qumran sect; see I.167–9. It is not surprising that arrangements of this kind, natural in minority groups, should be found both at Qumran and among the Christians; it does not prove any close relation between them.

Bibliography

General

F. Bovon, *RScR* 69 (1981), 279–300.

F. Bovon, *Luke the Theologian. Thirty three years of research*, ET Allison Park 1987.

H. von Campenhausen, *ZNW* 63 (1972), 210–53.

C. H. Cosgrove, *NovT* 26 (1984), 168–90.

E. Franklin, *Christ the Lord*, London 1975.

B. R. Gaventa, *Interpretation* 42 (1988), 146–57.

J. L. Houlden, *JSNT* 21 (1984), 53–65.

W. G. Kümmel, *EThL* 46 (1970), 265–281 = *ZNW* 63 (1972), 149–65.

B. F. Meyer, *FS* Farmer, 243–63.

J. C. O'Neill, *The Theology of Acts*, London ²1970.

---

[28]For moral ἄσκησις in Deutero-Pauline literature see *FS* Furnish 161–72.

J. Panagopoulos, *NovT* 14 (1972), 137–59.

C. H. Talbert (ed.), *Luke and the Gnostics*, Nashville and New York 1966.

U. Wilckens, *Die Missionsreden der Apostelgeschichte*, WMANT 5, Neu-kirchen-Vluyn 1963.

1. Eschatology
F. F. Bruce, *FS* Beasley-Murray, 51–63.

J. T. Carroll, *Response to the End of History*, SBLDiss 92, Atlanta 1988.

E. Grässer, Kremer, *Actes* 99–127.

K. Haacker, *NTS* 31 (1985), 437–51.

R. H. Hiers, *NTS* 20 (1974), 145–55.

J. D. Kaestli, *L'eschatologie dans l'oeuvre de Luc*, Geneva 1969.

A. J. Mattill, *CBQ* 34 (1972), 276–93.

D. P. Moessner, *NTS* 34 (1988), 96–104.

G. Schneider, *Lukas, Theologe der Heilsgeschichte*, BBB 59, Bonn 1985.

S. G. Wilson, *Gentiles* 67–80.

2. The Holy Spirit
A. George, *RB* 85 (1978), 500–42.

R. P. Menzies, *JSNT* 49 (1993), 11–20.

M. Turner, *NTS* 38 (1992), 66–88.

3. Christology
G. Delling, *NTS* 19 (1973), 373–89.

L. Hartman, see Baptism.

E. Kränkl, *Jesus der Knecht Gottes*, Biblische Untersuchungen 8, Regens-burg 1972.

D. P. Moessner, *NovT* 28 (1986), 220–56.

R. F. O'Toole, *Bib* 62 (1981), 471–98.

E. Schweizer, *FS* Schubert 186–93.

P. Vielhauer, *FS* Schubert 33–50 = *EvTh* 10 (1950–1), 1–15.

G. Voss, *Die Christologie der lukanischen Schriften in Grundzügen*, Paris and Brügge 1965.

J. A. Ziesler, *JSNT* 4 (1979), 28–41.

4. The Church
R. E. Brown, *Proceedings of the Catholic Theological Society of America* 36 (1981), 1–14.

J. Pathrapankal, *Zeitschrift für Missionswissenschaft und Religionswis-senschaft* 70 (1986), 275–87.

B. Reicke, *Glaube und Lehre der Urgemeinde*, AbThANT 32, Zürich 1957.

J. B. Tyson, *Interpretation* 42 (1988), 132–45.

5. Apostles and Ministers
F. H. Agnew, *JBL* 105 (1986), 75–96.

E. Bammel, *Augustinianum* 30 (1990), 63–72.

C. K. Barrett, *The Signs of an Apostle*, London 1970; Carlisle 1997.

C. Burchard, *Der dreizehnte Zeuge*, Göttingen 1970.

A. Campbell, *JTS* 44 (1993), 511–28.

R. A. Campbell, *The Elders: Seniority Within Earliest Christianity*, Edinburgh 1994.

H. von Campenhausen, *Kirchliches Amt und geistliche Vollmacht in den ersten drei Jahrhunderten*, Tübingen 1953.

L. Cerfaux, *Rec.* 2.157–74.

E. Ferguson, *JTS* 26 (1975), 1–12.

B. Gerhardsson, *SEÅ* 27 (1962), 89–131.

K. Haacker, *NovT* 30 (1988), 9–38.

A. E. Harvey, *JTS* 25 (1974), 318–32.

M. Karrer, *NovT* 32 (1990), 152–88.

G. Klein, *Die zwölf Aposteln*, FRLANT 59, Göttingen 1961.

D. Powell, *JTS* 26 (1975), 290–328.

K. H. Rengstorf, *Apostolat und Predigtamt*, Stuttgart 1934 (1954).

K. H. Rengstorf, *TWNT* 1.397–448.

C. H. Roberts, *JTS* 26 (1975), 403–5.

W. Schmithals, *Das kirchliche Apostelamt*, FRLANT 61, Göttingen 1961.

H. Schürmann, *FS* Erfurt (1977), 1–44.

B. E. Thiering, *JBL* 100 (1981), 59–74.

F. M. Young, *JTS* 45 (1994), 142–8.

6. Baptism and the Christian Meal

G. Barth, *ZThK* 70 (1973), 137–61.

S. Brown, *AThR* 59 (1977), 135–51.

E. J. Christiansen, *StTh* 40 (1986). 55–79.

N. A. Dahl, *FS* Mowinckel 36–52.

L. Hartman, *StTh* 28 (1979), 21–48.

T. W. Manson, *JTS* 48 (1947), 25–33.

P. H. Menoud, *RevHPhR* 33 (1953), 21–36.

M. Quesnel, *Baptisés dans l'Esprit*, Lectio Divina 120, Paris 1985.

B. E. Thiering, *NTS* 27 (1981), 615–31.

J. Thomas, *Le Mouvement baptiste en Palestine et Syrie*, Gembloux 1935.

7. Frühkatholizismus

E. Bammel, *Hervormde teologie Studies* 11 (1993), 690–707.

R. Bultmann, *Theologie* 446–70; 446, 464, 621–3, 718–25 for extensive bibliography.

H. von Campenhausen, *Kirchliches Amt und geistliche Vollmacht in den ersten drei Jahrhunderten*, BHTh, Tübingen 1953.

H. Conzelmann, *Theologie* 58–77, 333–7.

A. Harnack, *Entstehung und Entwicklung der Kirchenverfassung und des*

Kirchenrechtes in den zwei ersten Jahrhunderten, Leipzig 1910; ET *The Constitution and Law of Church in the first two Centuries*, London 1910.

E. Käsemann, *EVB* 1. 109–34 (especially 130–3); cf. 135–57; 2. 239–52, 262–67.

E. Käsemann, in *Das Neue Testament als Kanon* (ed. E. Käsemann), Göttingen 1970, 371–78, 399–410.

H. Küng, in *Das NT als Kanon* (see above), 175–204.

J. B. Tyson, *Interpretation* 42 (1988), 132–45.

8. The Jews
R. L. Brawley, *Luke-Acts and the Jews*, SBLMono 33, Atlanta 1987.

V. Fusco, *NovT* 38 (1996), 1–17.

A. George, *RB* 75 (1968), 481–525.

K. Haacker, *NTS* 31 (1985), 437–51.

W. Horbury, *JTS* 33 (1982), 19–61.

L. T. Johnson, *JBL*108 (1989), 419–41.

G. Lohfink, *Die Sammlung Israels*, StANT 33, Munich 1975.

H. Merkel, *NTS* 40 (1994), 371–98.

M. Rese, *FS* Schneider, 61–79.

J. T. Sanders, *The Jews in Luke-Acts*, London 1987.

R. C. Tannehill, *JBL* 104 (1985), 69–85.

J. B. Tyson, *NTS* 41 (1995), 19–38.

A. Vanhoye, *Bib* 72 (1991), 70–89.

L. M. Wills, *JBL* 110 (1991), 631–54.

9. The Law
C. K. Barrett, *FS* Bammel 345–67.

C. L. Blomberg, *JSNT* 22 (1984), 53–80.

D. R. Catchpole, *NTS* 23 (1977), 428–44.

F. G. Downing, *JSNT* 26 (1986), 49–52.

N. J. McEleney, *NTS* 20 (1974), 319–41.

M. A. Seifrid, *JSNT* 30 (1987), 39–57.

A. J. M. Wedderburn, *NovT* 35 (1993), 362–89.

10. The Gentiles and the Gentile Mission
J. M. G. Barclay, *JSNT* 60 (1995), 89–120.

E. E. Ellis, *StEv* IV (= *TU* 102), 390–99.

P. Frederikson, *JTS* 42 (1991), 532–64.

A. T. Kraabel, *Numen* 28 (1981), 113–26.

A. T. Kraabel, *FS* Stendahl, 147–57.

J. M. Lieu, *JTS* 46 (1995), 483–501.

J. M. Lieu, *FS* Goulder, 329–45.

B. F. Meyer, see General section.

J. Murphy-O'Connor, *RB* 99 (1992), 418–24.

J. A. Overman, *JSNT* 32 (1988), 17–26.

J. Reynolds and R. Tannenbaum, *Jews and Godfearers at Aphrodisias*, Cambridge Philological Society Supplementary Volume 12, Cambridge 1987.

E. Richard, *SBL Seminar Papers 1980*, 267–82.

J. T. Sanders, *NTS* 37 (1991), 434–55.

C. H. Talbert, *FS* Schneider 111–26.

J. B. Tyson, *NTS* 33 (1987), 619–31.

M. Wilcox, *JSNT* 13 (1981), 102–22.

S. G. Wilson, *Gentiles.*

11. Ethics

C. K. Barrett, *FS* Furnish 161–72.

P. Borgen, *FS* Kee 126–41.

R. J. Cassidy, *Society and Politics in the Acts of the Apostles*, Maryknoll, New York [1]1987 [2]1988.

F. G. Downing, *NTS* 27 (1981), 544–63.

L. T. Johnson, *The Literary Function of Possessions in Luke-Acts*, SBLDiss 39, Missoula 1977.

A. J. Malherbe, *Social Aspects of Early Christianity*, Philadelphia [2]1983.

D. L. Mealand, *ThZ* 31 (1975), 129–39.

D. L. Mealand, *JTS* 28 (1977), 96–9

CONCLUSION

In the preface to his gospel (Lk. 1.1–4) Luke claims to have associated with persons[1] who may or may not have been able to supply him with accurate historical information about the life and teaching of Jesus but must have been involved in some way in the life of the early church. They are described as eye-witnesses and ministers of the word (αὐτόπται καὶ ὑπηρέται τοῦ λόγου). Such contacts formed the basis of his affirmation, which was evidently important to him, of the continuity between the pre-crucifixion Jesus and the post-resurrection church. They will have been sources for Acts as well as (in a different way) sources for the gospel. They must also have been sources for Luke's own theological and religious thinking. What is to be made of the author and his book? In the following pages, which will necessitate a small amount of repetition of matters already dealt with, this question will be considered.

It will not be wrong to begin with the observation that Luke was a man who liked telling stories and was good at telling them. He was less good at the connections between the episodes he narrated; perhaps he was less interested in them. He had before him a similarly episodic model, Mark. For this he had no little respect; otherwise he would not have used so much of it. But it was capable of improvement, and he set about improving it. He improved the Greek style, shortened passages that were unnecessarily long, and used his economies in space to add a good deal of fresh material. His revisions and additions had the effect of producing a story less starkly theological, more 'human' in interest and feeling. When he had absorbed Mark that work was finished with; it was superseded and could be dispensed with. Fortunately there were Christians who did not agree, and retained it.

One can hardly suppose that pleasure in telling stories would suffice to produce a written work of some size. Interest in story-telling leads to an interest in history; and there were additional reasons for such an interest. Christianity was a religion, an institution, a system of thought—none of these terms is satisfactory, but they may suffice—that could maintain its identity only by recalling its origin, for when it was truly itself it was determined by its origin. Luke wrote at a time when the old sense of an imminent consummation of history had waned. In the early days there had been no need to

---

[1] If πᾶσιν is taken as masculine παρηκολουθηκότι will imply so much.

remember because the future was short and the end immediate. Memories however were now in danger of fading. Someone had to take steps to secure the church's memory not only of Jesus but of the way in which the transition from Jesus to the church had been effected. Mark, and any other gospel there may have been, had not recorded this; Paul, whose letters (which Luke seems not to have known) contained valuable pieces of history, had not recorded it. Luke may not have seen the need as clearly as it has been stated here, but he, and so far as we know no one else, did something to meet it. In addition to the danger of forgetting there was the danger that moral and doctrinal standards might slip. Most societies tend to think of their origins as heroic days, in which members of the society stood firm in faith and morals and stood by one another. A picture of the past, perhaps an idealized past, will inspire and instruct the present. Luke's picture of first generation Christians was intended to do this for his generation. He was, moreover, aware of the dangers that he puts on Paul's lips in 20.29, 30. What was future to Paul in Miletus was still in the main future to Luke, but it was a good deal nearer and no doubt had already appeared on the horizon. There were those who spoke perverse things and drew away disciples into their own schismatic coteries. Let the warning stand and an appropriate example be provided. Example, both in preaching and in morals, is there in Acts, but it has little positive content. There is little ethical teaching in Acts, though it is clear that the Christians are expected to be, and on the whole are, 'good' people. And Luke has no theological doctrines that he wishes to commend beyond basic Christian conviction. He believes in God, conceived on the lines of the OT, though he is aware of a convergence between the OT and the best Greek thought. Jesus Christ is central in his thought, but there is no attempt to think through the problems of the incarnation. He is Son of God (9.20), as all Christians knew, but the term itself carries with it no implication of 'being of one substance with the Father'; he is Lord and Christ, but there is at least one hint that he became Lord and Christ only at his exaltation (2.36); his death was the result of sin and ignorance, speedily put right by God (3.13–18), but only at 20.28 is there a suggestion that it was by his death that he redeemed mankind. Luke undoubtedly believed in the Holy Spirit, and at 5.3f. there is a hint that he is divine, but it is the phenomenology rather than the personality of the Spirit that interests Luke. He accepted the OT as the word of God, and to this extent stood with the Jewish people, but he would have taken the Christian line that the OT must be interpreted in terms of Christ, not Christ in terms of the OT.

Luke does not argue a special theological position but, it seems, takes the line of the majority of Christians in the 80s and 90s of the first century. This however is a proposition that will call for careful examination. It is by no means clear what group of Christians can be reckoned as constituting a majority in the 80s. In the view of J. Jervell Jewish Christians were numerically a minority but exercised an influence out of proportion to their numbers; it was for example their concern for the theological legitimacy of the Gentile mission that is reflected in Acts. This is in many respects an important observation, but it calls for some modification.[2] That the earlier decades of the century were marked by conflict, often bitter and unrelenting, appears without question from the Pauline letters. The church had now emerged into a period of relative calm; this had happened earlier than Baur (see pp. lxxiiif.) thought, and not quite in the way that Goulder (see p. xli, n. 18; p. lxiii, n. 1) maintains. It was not Paul who won, though it may go too far to say that he lost.[3] Paul and James, the extremists of right and left, were both defeated by the centre party, whom we may call if we wish the Hellenists. It is their compromise that appears in the Apostolic Decree. This Decree is clearly accepted by Luke as the basis of the Gentile mission and the guide line on which the mission was to be conducted. It also provided its theology, which appears in a different form in the Areopagus speech (17.22–31)—the doctrine of God on which Jews and pagan theists could unite, with a reference to Jesus attached to it. This is the theology that prevailed in this period of the church's life, taking inevitably variant forms in different places. It originated with Hellenistic Jews and was accepted by very many Gentiles. The reference to Jesus is minimal in Acts 7.52 and 17.31, and Luke himself, as is clear from many passages, when writing on his own would greatly increase it; so did e.g. 1 and 2 Clement and Ignatius; hardly Hermas. The theological substructure lasted till it was attacked by Marcion, who failed in the end to establish his exaggerated reaction. Acts made a substantial contribution to his defeat, and when this was grasped the book emerged from the obscurity into which it had fallen, and served the purpose of showing that the Creator God and the Redeemer God were one and the same, and that Paul was in agreement with the Twelve. Irenaeus and Tertullian were not wrong in seeing that Luke made these points, though making them was not his main intention.

Historically, then, Luke is right when he celebrates a Hellenist victory; Hellenists (if we may use the word) were a centre party and their Decree guided the church through an obscure period and continued to direct it for much longer. Luke was wrong in representing Paul as one of the victorious Hellenists; he describes himself (2 Cor. 11.22; Phil. 3.5) as a Hebrew. This is the central (though by no means the only) point on which any judgement of Luke as a historian and a theologian must be based.

[2] See my 'What Minorities?' in *FS* Jervell 1–10.
[3] See *FS* Jervell 6–9.

There are many features of Acts that must win a favourable verdict on the author as a historian. There are fairly frequent references to contemporary events and institutions and they are on the whole satisfactory. Many examples are given in the commentary; here it may be sufficient to mention the two kings, Agrippa I and Agrippa II (Luke describes the death of the former in substantial agreement with Josephus and knows that the latter's sister was Bernice); the two Roman governors, Felix and Festus (there is behind 24.27 a problem in the date of accession, but it is non-biblical evidence that lacks conclusiveness); the two proconsuls, Sergius Paulus and Gallio (the latter's governorship in Achaea can be dated with some precision and there is probable epigraphic evidence for the former); the Emperor Claudius (there is evidence for food shortages during his reign and Luke cannot be blamed for some uncertainty with regard to the date of his expulsion of the Jews from Rome). To persons may be added places and institutions associated with them: Luke knows Philippi was a *colonia* and that its magistrates were known as στρατηγοί; he knows of the Areopagus court in Athens and of the world-famous goddess of Ephesus, Artemis; of the connection of Ephesus with magic, of its Asiarchs, and of its γραμματεύς; he knows that one might find a centurion of the *Cohors Italica* in Caesarea; that Appii Forum and Tres Tabernae, not in themselves important towns, were stages on the road to Rome; that to lay hands on a Roman citizen was a dangerous thing to do, but that to resist or oppose δόγματα Καίσαρος was equally dangerous, though a citizen might escape at least immediate punishment by an appeal to Caesar. Luke is less successful in his references to Jews and to Jewish affairs. His reference to Annas may perhaps with some difficulty be defended; Gamaliel is rightly named but Luke puts on his lips a historical howler in the mention of Judas and Theudas; it is difficult to accommodate the details of the events that led to the riot in the Temple with the regulations for vows, though Luke is right in representing the introduction of Gentiles into forbidden areas of the Temple as a very serious and provocative offence.

Luke, then, was in general well informed about persons, events, and institutions in the Graeco-Roman world of the first century, probably better informed than most of his contemporaries, than most of his readers. And he was no fool. Where he agrees with other historical sources, his evidence is confirmed; where he disagrees, or where other evidence is lacking, he must at least be taken seriously. These matters however are incidental to his purpose, for he was not writing political, social, economic, military, or institutional history, but Christian history, and it is in this field that he must be judged.

Little can be said about the first twelve chapters of Acts except that in outline they must represent, with many omissions, the sort of thing that must have happened in the early years of Christianity. This is not the place to discuss the historicity of the resurrection; 1 Cor. 15.4–8 is sufficient to prove that the earliest (pre-Pauline) Christians believed that the crucified Jesus had appeared alive to a number of their leaders. This belief is represented in Acts. The rest of the first five chapters is made up of some traditional narratives and of Lucan constructions which are not without historical foundation. Twelve was a significant number for the inner group of disciples; the Christians did believe themselves to be inspired by the Spirit of God; they must have made speeches to communicate their beliefs; there was a traditional group of miracle stories; there was trouble between the Christians and the Jewish authorities. With ch. 6 a new stage of historiography begins. The sources used are discussed at I.54f. Into Antiochene traditions Luke incorporates more Petrine stories, Jerusalem traditions, stories going back to Philip, and the tradition about Paul's earliest contacts with Christianity. This is serious historical material; what it lacks is continuity and chronological coherence. Luke has set down different accounts of how the mission to the Gentiles began. Only one of these, it seems, has a future. This is given at first in the Antioch-based narrative of chs. 13 and 14. It continues in the Pauline missions, of which traditions, some drawn from members of the Pauline circle, some collected locally in Pauline cities, are set out first in a sequence of missionary journeys. These journeys of Paul as a missionary free to travel wherever he was led by the Spirit end in Jerusalem; from ch. 22 onwards Paul is not a free man, and the story of his encounters with Jewish and Roman authorities is very difficult to evaluate historically. Paul was not held incommunicado. Information about the various legal—and illegal— proceedings could have been got out; but in the narrative itself there is no indication that this happened, no mention of a friend who kept in touch with him except at 24.23. Luke makes nothing of this, and in any case it does not cover the events of chs. 25 and 26. From 27.2 Paul is again accompanied by one or more companions and it is possible to guess with some plausibility at passages inserted in traditions derived from them.

So far nothing has been said about ch. 15, and it is here that questionings arise that cannot but affect our judgement of the rest of Acts. The composition of the chapter is discussed in some detail below (pp. 696f., 710f.). It is Luke's work, though it is not without historical foundation. It contains however difficulties in itself, and more appear when it is compared with the direct Pauline evidence, especially that of Galatians. Did Paul help to produce, assent to, and disseminate a Decree to which, even when he deals with its subject-matter, he makes no reference? a Decree which tells his Gentile Christians of Jewish conditions (not indeed including circumcision) which they must fulfil if they are to be members of the people of God? The only possible answer is No.

At this point the question about Luke the historian runs into the question about Luke the theologian. For that Luke deliberately intended to calumniate Paul, ascribing to him views Luke knew that he did not hold, is inconceivable; he admired him far too greatly for this. The only alternative is that he did not truly understand him. That 'a man is justified by faith and not by works of the Law' (Rom. 3.28) is a proposition not covered by the one reference to justification in Acts (13.38, 39). The explanation of the misunderstanding is latent in the sketch of the last few pages. As Luke himself shows, the mission to the Gentile world did not have a single official beginning. It started independently in different places, through different persons, and on different lines. Among those who began it, in their own way, were Hellenistic Jews who had become Christians. They were the founders of the mixed church in Antioch; their way of theological thinking and of preaching is seen in Acts 7 and 17. Their mission continued and prospered; it became (see above, pp. xlff.) the main official line. But the line of development that Luke knew, admired, and described was Paul's; and he confused the two. Paul was connected with Stephen and Antioch (7.58; 8.1; 11.25f.; 12.25; 13.1–3; 14.26–28; 15.2; 22.20); he must have been Stephen's successor and continuator— this was the volte-face of his conversion. He began as an Antioch envoy; he must have continued to be one. So the Hellenistic Jewish compromise Decree was Paul's decree; and Paul not only lost the battle for a radically law-free Gospel, he lost his integrity at the same time: a strange fate for Luke's hero to suffer at Luke's hands.

It was the only point of serious difference between them. Elsewhere it is enough to say that Luke lacks Paul's profundity. Luke believes in Christ, crucified and risen; but does not think about pre-existence or, in any profound sense, deity, and on the whole (except at 20.28) thinks of the cross as an unfortunate error put right by resurrection, which happily sets the cross aside. He believes in the Spirit, who causes ecstatic speech, rather than love, joy, and peace. He believes in the church, but scarcely sees it as the body of Christ. He knows baptism and a Christian meal, but they are not focused on crucifixion, on dying with Christ and proclaiming the Lord's death till he come. All this does not mean that Luke disagreed with Paul; only that he was not so good at theology. And this takes us back to history; how close to Paul and his ministry did Luke stand?

Theology however must have another word. Is Luke's theology true? Or have we disfranchised a book from the NT?

It must not be assumed that omission, especially in Christological matters, implies contradiction; and Luke either tolerates, or perhaps fails to observe, a measure of contradiction. A superficial reader of Acts 2.36 will infer that Luke supposed that Jesus became Messiah and Lord at his resurrection. Luke's source may have meant this, and Luke may have accepted it as he transcribed the source. But Lk. 2.11

states with equal clarity that Jesus was born as Messiah and Lord. The reformulation in Acts reflects the impression made by the resurrection on those who experienced it.[4] No Christology is complete without the notion of pre-existence, but Christology has often lacked it. Luke's Christology lacks it, but this does not mean that Luke would have denied it, or needed to deny it. The same observation can be made with reference to the doctrine of atonement through the death of Christ. That Luke does not assert it (except at 20.28) does not mean that he would have denied it, still less than his readers need deny it.

Comparison of Acts 17.22–31 with Rom. 1.18–25 raises sharply the question of the place in Paul's thought, and thus in Christian thought generally, of natural theology.[5] The speech must be read in the context that Luke has provided for it and as determined less by Stoic speculation than by the OT prophetic denunciation of idolatry. This denunciation Paul shared (so one learns—credibly—from Luke's own story); he was provoked (παρωξύνετο, 17.16) by the sight of a city overgrown with idols. What the Athenians had made of nature was not natural theology (in a proper sense) but natural idolatry. This is not inconsistent with Romans 1, but it lacks the distinctive Pauline analysis and we cannot think that the speech was delivered by Paul; it comes rather from Hellenistic Judaism, adapted for Christian purposes (see pp. 825f.).

It is in regard to the Law that the greatest problem arises. Luke never says anything more positive about the Law than Paul's 'holy, righteous, good, spiritual' (Rom. 7.12, 14); only once does he condemn it as a burden that neither we nor our ancestors have been able to bear (Acts 15.10), and he never describes it as the origin of sinful passions (Rom. 7.5). The Pauline dialectic is missing, and so is the radical rejection of the Law (legalistically conceived) as an agent of salvation. If Gentiles are to be saved they must accept certain legal conditions—a sharply reduced list of conditions but conditions nonetheless. It is not surprising that Paul was obliged to reject the Decree of Acts 15.29, or at least to ignore it. Nor is it surprising that, as the textual phenomena show,[6] the Decree was given different interpretations; it may sometimes have amounted to little more than a request for consideration and courtesy on the part of Gentile Christians taking meals with Jewish Christians.

It is at this point, as have seen, that Luke's lack of penetrating and radical thinking reacts upon the historical worth of his book. Those whose thought was like his own he can represent successfully even

[4]See *Romans* 20–22, on Rom. 1.3, 4.
[5]See my lecture 'Paulus als Missionar und Theologe' in *ZThK* 86 (1989) 18–32; also *Paulus und das antike Judentum*, ed. M. Hengel and U. Heckel, Tübingen, 1991, 1–15; ET in *Jesus and the Word*, 149–62.
[6]See on 15.20, 29 (pp. 735f., 746).

when he lacks precise contemporary sources. The preaching of Peter in the early chapters has, as has often been remarked, a primitive appearance, but it is the kind of primitiveness that belongs to the 80s as well as the 30s, and indeed to countless excellent but unreflecting Christians in every age. It manifests an absolute loyalty to Jesus Christ as a person but little attempt to evaluate him as very man and very God—or even in less orthodox but equally reflective terms. With Paul a new dimension entered Christian life; and it is probably no more than truth to say that Luke (like many others) was unable to see the difference between an approach to the Gentiles that rested upon the discovery that Gentiles might be as good as Jews, and an approach that sprang from the shattering discovery that Jews were sinners just as much as Gentiles, though perhaps in a different way. It is certain that the author of Acts regarded Paul as the outstanding missionary to Jews and Gentiles, and that to find fault with him was no part of his plan. To identify him with the kind of Hellenistic-Jewish-Christian message accepted in his own day was for Luke a natural error; but it was an error, which needs correction from Paul's own letters and must not be allowed to determine our picture of the first Christian century. Both parts of the quotation from F. C. Baur given on pp. lxxiiif. are true. Acts is a most valuable historical source for the history of early Christianity; but it attains its full value only when used with the strictest—historical and theological—criticism.

ACTS 15–28: CONTENTS

It was pointed out in Volume I, p. 57, that it would be 'idle to attempt to draw up a neat, formal, balanced analysis of the contents of Acts 1–14'. The second part of the book is different. The great theme of the first part, the spread of the Gospel into the Gentile world, is continued, but it is now bound up so closely with the work of Paul that it gains a measure of unity and continuity. Its sources are discussed above (pp. xxiv–xxxi). The story, as Luke has composed it, begins with the Council at which the dogmatic and practical conditions of the Gentile mission are established. Accounts follow of straightforward missionary work, which includes both evangelism, by which new Christian societies are established, and pastoral work, by which they are developed and sustained. Relations between Paul and the Jewish authorities explode in a riot in the Temple, and thereafter the fortunes of Paul at the hands of Jews and Romans are described until, after an appeal to Caesar, he finds himself in Rome. This is the climax of the book, a representative fulfilment of the programme and promise of 1.8.

X.   THE COUNCIL IN JERUSALEM: THE BASIS OF PAUL'S GENTILE MISSION IS QUESTIONED IN ANTIOCH, ESTABLISHED IN JERUSALEM, AND REPORTED TO ANTIOCH.
     (38) Dispute in Antioch (15.1–5)
     (39) Council in Jerusalem (15.6–29)
     (40) Paul and Barnabas return to Antioch (15.30–35)

XI. PAUL'S MISSION BREAKS NEW GROUND: AFTER COVERING SOME OF THE GROUND OF THE FIRST MISSION PAUL AND HIS COMPANIONS CROSS OVER INTO MACEDONIA, REACH ATHENS, WHERE THE THEOLOGICAL APPROACH TO GENTILES IS SET OUT, AND MOVE ON TO CORINTH.
     (41) Territory of the First Journey revisited (15.36–16.5)
     (42) Guided by the Spirit to Troas (16.6–10)
     (43) Paul and Silas at Philippi (16.11–40)
     (44) From Philippi to Athens (17.1–15)
     (45) Paul at Athens (17.16–34)
     (46) Paul at Corinth, with return to Palestine (18.1–23)

XII. THE MISSION BASED ON EPHESUS: THE POSITION OF DISCIPLES OF JOHN THE BAPTIST IS REGULARIZED, PAUL EVANGELIZES EPHESUS AND ITS REGION, IS OVERTAKEN BY A RIOT, RETURNS

TO OTHER PARTS OF GREECE, AND GIVES A PASTORAL ADDRESS
AT MILETUS.
(47) Apollos and the Twelve Disciples (18.24–19.7)
(48) Paul's Successful Ministry at Ephesus (19.8–20)
(49) Riot at Ephesus (19.21–40)
(50) Back to Palestine, through Macedonia, Greece, and
Troas (20.1–16)
(51) Paul's Speech at Miletus (20.17–38)

XIII. PAUL RETURNS TO JERUSALEM: PAUL MEETS JAMES, AND A
PLAN FOR HARMONY BETWEEN JEWISH AND GENTILE CHRIS-
TIANS MISFIRES.
(52) Journey to Jerusalem (21.1–14)
(53) Paul and the Church of Jerusalem (21.15–26)
(54) Riot at Jerusalem (21.27–40)
(55) Paul's Temple Speech and the Sequel (22.1–29)

XIV. PAUL AND THE JEWS: PAUL APPEARS BEFORE THE COUNCIL
AND IS SAFELY MOVED TO CAESAREA.
(56) Paul before the Council (22.30–23.11)
(57) The Plot: Paul removed to Caesarea (23.12–35)

XV. PAUL AND THE ROMANS: NEITHER FELIX NOR FESTUS NOR
AGRIPPA CAN FIND ANY FAULT IN PAUL AND HE APPEALS TO
CAESAR.
(58) Paul and Felix (24.1–27)
(59) Paul appeals to Caesar (25.1–12)
(60) Festus and Agrippa (25.13–22)
(61) Festus, Agrippa, and Paul (25.23–26.32)

XVI. PAUL REACHES ROME AFTER A LONG AND DANGEROUS VOYAGE
AND HAS MEETINGS WITH THE LOCAL JEWS.
(62) The Sea Voyage (27.1–44)
(63) From Malta to Rome (28.1–16)
(64) Paul and the Jews in Rome (28.17–28)

XVII. CONCLUSION: PAUL SPENDS TWO YEARS IN ROME.
(65) Conclusion (28.(29)–31)

X

THE COUNCIL IN JERUSALEM
(15.1–35)

38. DISPUTE IN ANTIOCH 15.1–5

(1) Certain people came down from Judaea and began to teach the brothers, 'Unless you are circumcised in accordance with the Mosaic practice you cannot be saved.' (2) Between them and Paul and Barnabas no small measure of contention and discussion arose, and they appointed Paul and Barnabas, and certain others of their number, to go up to the apostles and elders in Jerusalem about this subject of dispute. (3) So, having been sent on their way by the church, they travelled through both Phoenicia and Samaria, recounting the conversion of the Gentiles, and they gave great joy to all the brothers. (4) When they reached Jerusalem they were welcomed by the church and the apostles and the elders and reported the things that God had done by means of them. (5) But there stood up some believers who belonged to the party of the Pharisees, saying, 'It is necessary to circumcise them and command them to observe the Law of Moses.'

Bibliography

E. Bammel, Kremer, *Actes*, 439–46.

C. K. Barrett, *FS* Black (1969), 1–14.

C. K. Barrett, *FS* Black (1979), 15–27.

R. Bauckham, *JSNT* 2 (1979), 61–70.

P. Benoit, *RB* 64 (1957), 35–47.

J. D. G. Dunn, *JSNT* 18 (1983), 3–57.

T. Holtz, *NovT* 16 (1974), 110–48.

J. L. Houlden, *JSNT* 18 (1983), 58–67.

B. Orchard, *CBQ* 7 (1945), 377–97.

B. Reicke, *FS* de Zwaan, 172–87.

E. Richard, in C. H. Talbert, *Luke-Acts* 188–209.

C. H. Talbert, *NovT* 9 (1967), 26–40.

Commentary

Chapters 13 and 14 contain an account of the commissioning of Paul and Barnabas to act as missionary envoys—called apostles, perhaps (14.4, 14)—of the church at Antioch and of their journey through

Cyprus and parts of Asia Minor. At the end of ch. 14 they report to those who sent them out, and with the new paragraph a new stage in the narrative of Acts begins. In the course of the missionary tour Gentiles have been converted to Christianity. This had already happened in Antioch itself (11.20f.) and had been, apparently, accepted without question; it had also been approved by a representative of the church of Jerusalem (11.22–24). Now however the objection is raised by travellers from Judaea that since circumcision and legal observance are the marks of Judaism those who would be members of the people of God must accept these as necessary conditions. Those who maintain this view are opposed by Paul and Barnabas; it is tacitly accepted that the question cannot be settled in Antioch; it must be taken to the apostles and elders in Jerusalem, where Paul and Barnabas, and some others, are to represent the Antiochene point of view. They set out for Jerusalem, and passing through Phoenicia and Samaria report what has been happening, to the approval and joy of all the Christian brothers. In Jerusalem however the demand for legal observance is repeated by Christian Pharisees. The renewed demand sets in motion a debate, the conclusion of which sets the scene for further missionary work and thus opens the way to the rest of the book.

The debate itself (15.6–29) is rightly described as the centre of Acts ('ihr Herzstück'—Beyer 91); see pp. 709f. The present small paragraph is important in that it introduces the debate, setting out clearly the question at issue: Are circumcision and the keeping of the Law necessary for salvation or not? One view is that Luke allows the theme to shift in the course of ch. 15 from this fundamental problem of theology to the practical question of the terms on which Jewish Christians and Gentile Christians might have fellowship, especially at the common Christian meal, within one society; see pp. 700, 705, 717, 720f., 745f. This however is not what Luke says the debate is about (though it may represent one way in which the decree of 15.29 was used).

Luke's hand is clearly to be seen throughout this introductory paragraph. The pair κατέρχεσθαι, ἀναβαίνειν, is Lucan; so is the use of ἔθη for Mosaic commands, σωθῆναι for entering upon the Christian faith, the litotes of οὐκ ὀλίγης, the description of Christian ministers as πρεσβύτεροι, the use of ζήτησις, διέρχεσθαι, ἐκδιηγεῖσθαι, not ἐπιστροφή but ἐπιστρέφειν, παραγίνεσθαι, παραδέχεσθαι, the use of μετά in v. 4, αἵρεσις, and the use of πεπιστευκότες for those who have become Christians. Evidence is given in the notes. It does not seem possible to distinguish sources, though μὲν οὖν might have marked the beginning of a paragraph.

Luke however has not simply invented his material; see e.g. Lüdemann (176–8), with the conclusion that there is in the tradition behind ch. 15 'eine hohe historische Zuverlässigkeit'. This may be too favourable, as Pesch (2.72–74) and Weiser (376) are too precise in distinguishing Antiochene and Jerusalem (or Decree) traditions; see below. But we have the first-rate evidence of Galatians that there was a meeting in Jerusalem, attended on the one side by James, Peter, and John, and on the other by Paul, Barnabas, and at least one other—Titus (Gal. 2.1–10). We know too that certain (unnamed) people went from Judaea (in fact from James in Jerusalem) to Antioch and there caused a separation between Jewish and Gentile Christians (Gal. 2.11–14). The same epistle makes clear that there was an attempt to persuade all Gentile Christians that circumcision was necessary for their salvation. The correspondence is not exact for in Acts the Jerusalem travellers to Antioch appear first, the Council follows; in Galatians the order is reversed. Luke's order has the effect—an intended effect?—of representing the disagreement as only temporary, whereas Galatians shows that it was not ended by the Council, and was intense at the time the letter was written. We may say that Luke knew that there was a meeting in Jerusalem; knew that Jerusalem made trouble for Antioch; he knew that there was a compromise Decree (see § 39); he knew that when he wrote controversy had subsided and the church was at peace. He did not know precisely how these data were to be fitted together, and in making his own composition he had no intention of going out of his way to present a picture of a disorderly and inharmonious church.

For further analysis and consideration of the chronology see the introduction to § 39 and the general Introduction, pp. xxxvi–xl, lvi, lxf.

1. Καί τινες κατελθόντες ἀπὸ τῆς Ἰουδαίας. In the absence of any indication to the contrary it must be assumed that the scene is unchanged; that is, the persons in question came to Antioch (see 14.26–28). There is no immediate reference (but see 15.3, 12) to the missionary activity of chs. 13 and 14; all that is necessarily presupposed is the existence in Antioch (see 11.20) of a mixed church containing (whether this be regarded as proper or improper) uncircumcised Gentiles as well as Jews. This means that the new material could follow directly upon 11.27–30—a fact to be borne in mind when the chronology of Acts, and especially whether the 'First Missionary Journey' should precede or follow the Council, is considered.

The τινες are defined only by their actions (which appear immediately) and by the place from which they come. They were ἀπὸ τῆς Ἰουδαίας, from Judaea. Luke does not say at this point that they came from Jerusalem, though in fact they did so (15.24); Conzelmann (82) and Roloff (228) think that Luke omitted any reference to Jerusalem at this point because he did not wish to suggest that the trouble-makers had had any support from the leaders of the mother church. This may very well be true; but the travellers from Jerusalem are immediately disowned at 15.24 (οἷς οὐ διεστειλάμεθα), and this could have been done equally well at the present point. Judaea may be intended in an ethnic rather than a strictly geographical sense; they came from Jewish territory and may therefore be expected to represent a Jewish point of view. They are defined more explicitly by Ψ 614 *pc* sy^hmg, which, after Ἰουδαίας, add τῶν πεπιστευκότων ἀπὸ τῆς αἱρέσεως τῶν Φαρισαίων; this secondary reading is due to assimilation to v. 5.

κατελθόντες is geographically correct, since Antioch was on, or near, the coast, but ἀνέρχεσθαι, κατέρχεσθαι, and similar compounds were used of pilgrimages to and departures from the capital; see on 11.2. This may hint at an authorized visitation; cf. 8.15 (καταβάντες). Cf. Gal. 2.12, πρὸ τοῦ γὰρ ἐλθεῖν τινας ἀπὸ Ἰακώβου—from James, and therefore presumably from Jerusalem. The two groups can be identified only if the Jerusalem meeting of Gal. 2.1–10 preceded that of Acts 15, or if we suppose that Galatians 2 does not follow but inverts chronological order. Neither of these is probable; it remains possible however that either Paul or Luke has misplaced the Judaizing visitation. The whole question of the reconstruction of the events behind Galatians 2 and Acts 15 is thus already raised. It cannot be settled or even sensibly discussed on the basis of the present verse alone, but it (and Gal. 2.12) must be kept in mind.

ἐδίδασκον is presumably an inceptive imperfect: when they arrived they set about teaching. The visitants taught τοὺς ἀδελφούς. For the use of ἀδελφός see on 1.15; it implies that the persons in question are Christians (since by definition they are not fellow Jews). It thus grants the question under discussion. This means of course only that *to Luke* they are Christians; it was quite clear to him that circumcision was not necessary. The visitants took the opposite view. Without circumcision there is no salvation. Circumcision is a Mosaic requirement: ἐὰν μὴ περιτμηθῆτε τῷ ἔθει τῷ Μωυσέως. The Western text (D (sy^p) sa mae) makes it clear that more than an initiatory rite is required: ἐὰν μὴ περιτμηθῆτε καὶ τῷ ἔθει Μ. περιπατῆτε (note the present—continuous—tense). This is implied though not mentioned by the Old Uncial text; there would be no point in being circumcised and then neglecting to keep the Law. Characteristically the Western text leaves nothing to imagination—or to common sense. ἔθος is not adequately rendered by *custom*: it refers to the practice originated by Moses (though in fact circumcision goes back to Abraham; Gen. 17.10–14), and this has the force of law. Cf. 6.14; 16.21; 21.21; 26.3; 28.17; also 2 Macc. 11.25 (τὰ ἐπὶ τῶν προγόνων αὐτῶν ἔθη); 4 Macc. 18.5; Josephus (e.g. *Ant.* 20.100, τοῖς γὰρ πατρίοις οὐκ ἐνέμεινεν οὗτος ἔθεσιν); Philo (e.g. *Spec. Leg.* 2.148, πάτριον ἔθος). This use of the word seems to have been a Jewish development (not noted in LS); see however Ditten-berger, *Syll.* 2.1073.20f., κατὰ τὸ πάτριον τῶν ἀγώνων ἔθος. This use (with ἔθος) of κατά might have been expected rather than Luke's dative. This is described by M. 3.242 as a dative of cause (... *'because of the law'*). BDR § 196.1, n.1 also classifies the use as *Dativus Causae*, but—surprisingly—translates 'gemäss' (in con-formity with?), and compares PHolm 2.18, τῆτε (legd. τῆδε) τάξει, 'nach diesem Rezept'. This seems to be Luke's meaning: Gentiles must be circumcised in accordance with the Mosaic practice.

The Judaeans do not say: Gentiles cannot be saved at all. They say: You cannot be saved unless you are circumcised. This almost all Jews would have allowed, for though some Jews were more, others less, enthusiastic about making proselytes, it was generally recog-nized that Gentiles, if they complied with the necessary conditions, might enter the Jewish fold. The Judaeans simply affirm the familiar proposition: the Jews are the elect people of God, and male Jews are circumcised—as infants if born into a Jewish family, otherwise upon conversion. Exceptions to this requirement are hard to find. Josephus, *Ant.* 20.38–48 is only a partial exception. Izates, king of Adiabene, wished to become a Jew, and supposed that circumcision (though it would be for the king of a non-Jewish people a perilous act) was essential. The Jew Ananias said that it was not, δυνάμενον δ'αὐτὸν καὶ χωρὶς τῆς περιτομῆς τὸ θεῖον σέβειν, εἴγε πάντως κέκριϰε ζηλοῦν τὰ πάτρια τῶν Ἰουδαίων· τοῦτ' εἶναι κυριώτερον τοῦ περιτέμνεσθαι· συγγνώμην δ' ἕξειν αὐτῷ καὶ τὸν θεόν ... (41). Another Jew, however, Eleazar from Galilee, maintained the con-trary view, and the rite was carried out. Thus Ananias was overruled; moreover he seems to have argued on the principle that a command might be omitted if it was dangerous to life. At *Ant.* 20.139 Azizus, king of Emesa, and at 145 Polemo, king of Cilicia, are circumcised, in each case in order to marry a Jewish woman. At Yebamoth 46ab the dispute is not whether or not circumcision is necessary but whether baptism or circumcision marks the precise moment of conversion.

σωθῆναι. Certainly not here, perhaps nowhere, does Luke define what he means by being saved; see on 4.12. He probably thought the matter too obvious to warrant discussion. We may, in the context, paraphrase it as 'to receive in full the benefits provided by God for his people', without specific reference to particular benefits. It appears that Luke tells us in this opening verse what the argument of the chapter is to be about: it will be about being saved, about being a Christian at all, not about the regulation of relations between Jewish Christians, who wish to retain their Jewishness, and Gentile Chris-tians, who do not wish to become Jews. This appears to be the issue raised in Galatians 2, and answered by implication in 2.3, οὐδὲ Τίτος ... ἠναγκάσθη περιτμηθῆναι. 'The issue in chapter 15 is thus not merely post-conversion behaviour but what constitutes true conversion in the first place' (Wilson, *Law* 72). Whether Luke adheres to this issue throughout the chapter is a question that must be kept in mind. It must also be remembered that the matter seemed to have been settled at 11.18; see the notes. If that verse does not mean that for Gentiles repentance, without circumcision, suffices for life—salvation—it is meaningless. On these questions see further p. 696 and the references there.

2. The variant οὖν (P⁷⁴ A E 𝔐 d l vg syʰ) for δέ (ℵ B C D L Ψ 36 81 453 945 1175 *al* gig p) emphasizes, what is in any case clearly implied, that it was in consequence of the arrival of the Judaeans, and of their stand, that there arose no small (the litotes is characteristic of the later part of Acts—12.18; but 15.2; 19.11, 23, 24; 20.12; 21.39; 26.19, 26; 27.20; 28.2) στάσεως καὶ ζητήσεως (καὶ ζ. is omitted by P⁷⁴ E vg bo). ζήτησις is the word that would be expected; it never quite loses its normal sense of *inquiry* (see LS 756); BA's *Wortgefecht* (686) perhaps suggests controversy too strongly, though this is supported by the context and not least by the companion word στάσις ('... the well-known classical word for an outbreak between the democratic and oligarchical parties in a state'—Page 175). Cf. Mk 15.7, but also Acts 23.7, 10; Luke does not mean to suggest that the conflict ended in murder, but sharp contention (not merely discussion) is clearly indicated. Josephus, *Ant.* 18.374, ἐν στάσει καὶ διχονοίᾳ, resembles Luke's combination, and here the conflict (between Greeks and Syrians at Seleucia—not far from Antioch) was serious enough.

Paul and Barnabas, leaders in the church of Antioch (11.26) and pioneer missionaries on its behalf (13.1–3), are named as leading contenders on the non-circumcision side; cf. Gal. 2.4f.

The opening clause in the verse (γενομένης ... πρὸς αὐτούς) is a genuine genitive absolute; this means that the subject of ἔταξαν cannot be inferred from the context. Hanson (159) thinks it possible that the subject was intentionally left vague, but adds that syntactical usage demands as subject those who came from Jerusalem. This is not certain; προπεμφθέντες in v. 3 suggests rather that it was the members (or possibly the prophets and teachers—Preuschen 93) of the church at Antioch who were the subject of ἔταξαν. τάσσειν with accusative and infinitive means, according to LS (1760; s.v. II 2), to '*appoint* or *order* one to do or be'. In the present passage *appoint* seems suitable, but in a number (not all) of the passages cited by LS the verb is used in parallel with κελεύειν. Nevertheless, Barnabas and Paul were leaders in the church at Antioch, and it is best to render, 'They (the Christians at Antioch) appointed Paul and Barnabas and certain others to go up'—for ἀναβαίνειν cf. κατελθόντες in v. 1.

The companions of Paul and Barnabas (τινας ἄλλους) are not

named; at Gal. 2.1 Titus accompanies them. Galatians does not exclude the possibility that others went too, and the silence of Acts does not mean that Titus was not one of the ἄλλοι—nor does it mean that Titus was Luke's relative, whose name Luke omitted as he omitted his own (see *FS* Black (1969), 2f.). Mission by appointment is however different, at least in emphasis, from Gal. 2.2, ἀνέβην δὲ κατὰ ἀποκάλυψιν. But the two are not irreconcilable, The human arrangement may have been the result of divine guidance; cf. 13.2, which, written from a different angle, could have been expressed, 'The prophets and teachers appointed Paul and Barnabas to . . .'.

It was argued above that the subject of ἔταξαν is the Christians of Antioch, but the nearest antecedent is αὐτούς, the Judaeans, and these are taken to be the authors of the arrangement by the Western text, which instead of ἔταξαν . . . αὐτῶν has ἔλεγεν γὰρ ὁ Παῦλος μένειν οὕτως καθὼς ἐπίστευσαν διισχυριζόμενος. οἱ δὲ ἐληλυθότες ἀπὸ Ἰερουσαλὴμ παρήγγειλαν τῷ Παύλῳ καὶ Βαρναβᾷ καὶ τισὶν ἄλλοις ἀναβαίνειν (D (gig w sy[hmg] mae)) and adds after a second Ἰερουσαλήμ, ὅπως κριθῶσιν ἐπ' αὐτοῖς (D[(c)]; and with varying order 614 *pc* sy[h**]). See also on 15.7. This is one of those passages in Acts (see Introduction, pp. xxif.) where the Old Uncial text and the Western text are said to give fundamentally different views of an event. In the Old Uncial text arrangements are made for a debate on equal terms; in the Western text Paul and Barnabas and other members of the erring church are peremptorily summoned to Jerusalem to stand trial. The difference is less great than is sometimes supposed. Each side of the debate expresses its views more forcefully. If the Judaeans παρήγγειλαν, Paul is represented as διισχυριζόμενος (for the word see 12.15; Lk. 22.59; also PMich 659.14, cited in *ND* 2.81). The Western characteristic that appears here is that of sharpening the picture, making the story more vivid and exciting; see I.22; *FS* Black (1979), 15–27.

Black, *AA* 104 (cf. Wilcox 132) notes that the Western text has αὐτοῖς τῷ Π. καὶ Β., and suggests that αὐτοῖς represents an Aramaic ethic dative; cf. Metzger 428 ('. . . a clear example of the Semitic proleptic pronoun'). If there were strong evidence for a continuous Aramaic source at this point the suggestion might be convincing, but it is more probable that the Western editor wrote at first *ordered them*, and then thought that he had better specify who *they* were.

The Antiochian representatives were to consult with—or be judged by—*the apostles and elders*; cf. 15.4, 6, 22, 23. For *the apostles* see I.94f., and frequently; for *the elders* see on 11.30; 14.23. It is not at this stage clear in what category James (see I.586f.), who plays a notable part in Luke's account of the Council (15.13–21), is to be placed. Cf. 12.17; 21.18. In terms of the requirement of 1.22, 23, he was no more an apostle than Paul, but he certainly stands out beyond the unspecified elders. See Gal. 2.9; also

1.19, which may or may not refer to him as an apostle. Lack of a specific designation may correspond to historical fact: he was undoubtedly an important and influential person, but one who owed his influence to a special relation with Jesus (Gal. 1.19) and to the strength of his character and convictions rather than to any definable office.

The parties are to consult about τοῦ ζητήματος τούτου. The ζήτημα is the specific matter upon which the ζήτησις (see above) centres. Cf. Plato, *Laws* 1.630e–631a: ἡμεῖς δέ φαμεν εἶναι τὸ περὶ νόμους ζήτημα τῶν εὖ ζητούντων.

Bultmann (*Exegetica* 417) notes how easy it would be, here and at 15.3–5, 12, 22f., 25f., to drop the named references to Paul and Barnabas, regarding them as redactional supplements to a source. For this theory see on the verses in question, especially 15.12.

3. μὲν οὖν often marks the beginning of a story (see on 1.6). *Begs.* 4.171 accepts this here. 'What has gone before is structurally rather the end of the previous narrative, though it is surely editorial and is intended to lead up to the following narrative.' If this were so one would expect Luke to use his μὲν οὖν in his introductory editorial note, unless he allowed it to stand where he found it in a source. It is better to compare with 13.4, where μὲν οὖν marks the change from a preparatory situation to the movement of a narrative.

The representatives were seen off, sent on their way (for προπέμπειν cf. 20.38) by the ἐκκλησία (see I.271), and then journeyed by stages to Jerusalem. The farewell is expressed in the aorist tense, the journey by the imperfect (διήρχοντο, ἐποίουν), and arrival again by the aorist (παραγενόμενοι, v. 4); see BDR § 327.1, n. 1, who bring out the force of ἐποίουν by 'überall, jedesmal'. The present participle ἐκδιηγούμενοι (*narrating*) matches the imperfect indicatives.

At least sometimes in Acts (e.g. 13.8) διέρχεσθαι has almost the technical sense of going on a preaching tour. Perhaps Luke means to suggest that so far from being inhibited Paul and Barnabas took the opportunity of the journey to Jerusalem to continue their mission. Luke's main interest, however, if not his only interest, is in the report given by Paul and Barnabas and its reception in the districts through which they passed.

In Acts as it stands the ἐπιστροφὴ τῶν ἐθνῶν will refer mainly to the events of chs. 13 and 14. The reference could however be satisfied by the conversion of the Antiochene Gentiles (11.21; note the verb (ἐπέστρεψεν)) if the chs. 13 and 14 are thought to be misplaced; see Introduction, pp. lxf. This is the only occurrence of ἐπιστροφή in the NT; ἐπιστρέφειν however occurs at 3.19 (see the note); 9, 35, (40); 11.21; 14.15; 15.19, (36); (16.18); 26.18, 20; 28.27. *ND* 2. 72, noting papyrus use, comments, 'Whether the word [ἐπιστροφή] in its only NT occurrence ... need mean as much as "conversion" is at least worth querying.' The use of the cognate verb suggests that the query is unrewarding.

Zerwick (§ 227) probably presses too hard the distinction between the active ποιεῖν and the middle, though causabant gaudium is undoubtedly correct for ἐποίουν χαράν. All the Christians (πᾶσιν τοῖς ἀδελφοῖς) encountered by Paul and Barnabas on their journey approved of and rejoiced in the mission to the Gentiles. Public opinion was on their side, and the battle was over before it was fought. In fact the Council turns out to be a sham fight; no dissenting voice is heard. We know however from the Pauline epistles that there was some very serious fighting indeed—another fact that must be borne in mind when we discuss the tradition available to Luke and his handling of it. Apparently he knew that there was a dispute, but in order to represent it as speedily dealt with had to invent a few ill-disposed and easily beaten trouble-makers in order to account for it. But he is correct in speaking of a mission from Judaea to Antioch, even if he misplaces it.

Phoenicia (see 11.19; 21.2) is not a precise geographical term; it denotes the coastal area of Palestine stretching northwards from Carmel and including Tyre and Sidon. It borders in the south on *Samaria* (see 8.5, 14, 25). Stählin (201) thinks that the churches in Phoenicia had been founded by Hellenist refugees.

At this point the Coptic MS G⁶⁷ ends; see I.13f. The Gentile mission is now accepted by *all the (Christian) brothers*. The book may finish here; the author's goal is already reached.

4. For the tense of παραγενόμενοι see on v. 3. In this verse the textual authorities are fairly evenly divided between the two spellings of Jerusalem; Ἰερουσαλήμ in ℵ C D E 𝔐, Ἱεροσόλυμα in P⁴⁵ P⁷⁴ A B Ψ 81 614 1175 2495 *pc* gig vg. There is little doubt that παρεδέχθησαν is what Luke wrote, though ὑπεδέχ. and ἀπεδέχ. both have some slight support; the adverb μεγάλως is added by C D(*) 6 614 1704 *pc* syʰ** sa—the Western editor, notwithstanding his revision of v. 2, wished to underline the warmth of the welcome accorded to Paul, Barnabas, and their colleagues when they reached Jerusalem. This confirms the view that he is emphasizing what he finds rather than introducing new points of view.

They were welcomed by (Metzger 428 takes the more Semitic ἀπό (B C 36 453 1175 *pc*) to be original rather than ὑπό (P⁷⁴ ℵ A D E Ψ 𝔐)) the church and the apostles and elders. *Church* (ἐκκλησία) here probably refers to those Christians who did not hold office, whether as apostles or elders. For the extent to which (in Luke's view) these members participated in the Council see on 15.6, 12, 22, 23. For the apostles and elders see on v. 2. Wilson (*Gentiles* 182), following Wikenhauser and Stählin, suggests that in the present verse

704 COMMENTARY ON ACTS

we have a preliminary open meeting, whereas in 15.6 there is a meeting of the apostles and elders alone, at which 'the real business was decided'.

ἀνήγγειλαν (the imperfect of the same verb is used at 14.27) is parallel to ἐκδιηγούμενοι in v. 3; *reported*, perhaps, rather than *recounted*. ὅσα ἐποίησεν ὁ θεὸς μετ᾽αὐτῶν means ἡ ἐπιστροφὴ τῶν ἐθνῶν. This too reproduces the language of 14.27. This use of μετά occurs only in Lk. and Acts (Lk. 1.72; 10.37; Acts 14.27; 15.4); Wilcox 84 considers whether it is taken from the LXX or direct Semitic influence. The former is the likelier alternative. The conversion of the Gentiles had been the work of God; Paul and Barnabas had acted as his agents, but it was his doing. This in itself proved that it was right; it needed no further defence.

The present verse reproduces the statements and themes of vv. 2 and 3; Luke wishes to represent the journey to Jerusalem as something like a triumphal progress. The Gentile mission has begun and it is already clear that nothing is going to stop it. This intended emphasis provides a better explanation of the repetition than a theory of parallel sources; but see below.

5. What had been done could not be undone; but it could be maintained that it was right only so far as it went. It was necessary now to complete what had been done by circumcising the converts and instructing them henceforth to obey the Law of Moses. Cf. Gal. 5.2, where Paul's words seem to imply the proposition (inverted by Paul), If you are not circumcised Christ will do you no good. Those who make this demand are described by Luke as *believers* (πεπιστευκότες) and as coming from the *party* (αἵρεσις; for the word see on 5.17) of the Pharisees. According to Kosmala 110f., 'Dies braucht noch nicht zu heissen, dass sie an den Messias Jesus glaubten, denn der Sprachgebrauch des Lukas erfordert das keineswegs. Danach könnten sie ebensogut nur Essener oder Johannesjünger geworden sein, und sie brauchen darum auch gar nicht zu der in xv. 4 genannten jesusgläubigen Gemeinde gehört zu haben.' This is hardly correct. Luke's usage does in fact connect πιστεύειν with acceptance of the Christian message about Jesus; so e.g. 2.44 (οἱ πιστεύοντες); 4.4 (πολλοὶ ... ἐπίστευσαν), 32 (τῶν πιστευσάντων); et al. Earlier references to the Sadducees (4.1; 5.17) have carried the possible implication that the Pharisees (see on 5.34) were more favourably disposed to the new faith; Luke's statement here confirms the implication (at least, as regards his opinion, if not as regards fact). These Pharisees had presumably come to believe that Jesus was the Messiah without changing their views of the Law. It is however probably correct that 'Welche Autorität die Gruppe in Jerusalem hatte, fragt Lukas nicht, da ihm nicht die historischen Zusammenhänge, sondern die systematische Frage am Herzen lag' (Schille

319). But Luke saw theological questions in historical contexts, and no doubt believed that the position described was one that Pharisees would adopt.

These Pharisaic believers *stood up*—and perhaps *stood out*—for their opinion, ἐξανέστησαν (cf. e.g. Xenophon, *Anabasis* 6.1.30, ἐξαναστὰς εἶπε Ξενοφῶν ...); perhaps in order to take part in a discussion, but the word may be metaphorical and simply represent their readiness to put their point of view. If there is any special significance in the compounded ἐξ it will be that they stood out from among their fellow believers, who adopted a more accommodating attitude.

ὅτι introduces direct speech. Now that the scene has shifted to Jerusalem it cannot be certain whether αὐτούς refers to the Gentile Christians in Antioch or to Gentiles (including Titus, Gal. 2.1, 3) whom Paul and Barnabas had brought with them to Jerusalem. Verse 5 repeats v. 1 (with the addition that after circumcision observance of the Law would be required), as v. 4 to some extent repeats v. 3. If Luke is here writing freely in order to introduce the Council he probably adds v. 5 in order to make clear that there really was an issue to debate; if there were those who rejoiced in the success of the mission there were also those who took a hard line, asserting '... sine circumcisione salutem obtineri non posse' (Bengel 448). This is perhaps the best view; alternatively, there may have been two sources, vv. 1, 2 and vv. 3–5, which Luke put together, or one source, vv. 3–5, to which Luke added vv. 1, 2 as an introduction. It is worth noting that v. 3 could be attached directly to 14.28, or even 11.30, though not as satisfactorily as v. 1 (see above). If we set this passage beside Galatians 2 we may note Gal. 2.4: the ψευδάδελφοι creep in to spy out our liberty, ἵνα ἡμᾶς καταδουλώσουσιν. To be saved, men must become Jews. There is no question that at this point this proposition is given as the theme of the Council. It is often held that in the course of the chapter the theme changes, so that the Decree (15.29) answers the question, not 'On what terms may Gentiles be saved?' but 'On what terms may Jewish Christians and Gentile Christians have fellowship, including table-fellowship, in one body?'. Whether this is so will be considered below (p. 745). There appears to be a comparable shift in ch. 11, where the discussion starts from the complaint that Peter had had dealings and had eaten with Gentiles, but ends with the conviction that uncircumcised Gentiles may as such be saved. This may well mean that Luke himself did not make a clear distinction between the two questions.

(6) The apostles and elders gathered together to look into this matter. (7) When much discussion had taken place, Peter stood up and said to them 'Brothers, you know that in days of old God made his choice among you that through my voice the Gentiles should hear the word of the Gospel and believe; (8) and God, who knows the human heart, bore testimony to them when he gave them the Holy Spirit, as he had done to us, (9) and he made no distinction between us and them when he cleansed their hearts by faith. (10) So now why do you put God to the test by laying on the neck of these disciples a yoke which neither our fathers nor we were able to bear? (11) On the contrary, we believe that it is through the grace of the Lord Jesus that[1] we shall be saved, in the same way as they.' (12) The whole company fell silent, and they listened to Barnabas and Paul as they narrated the signs and portents that God had done among the Gentiles through them. (13) When they had ceased speaking, James joined in,[2] saying, 'Brothers, listen to me. (14) Symeon has reported how[3] God at the first took action so as to take out of the Gentiles a people for his name; (15) and with this the words of the prophets agree—as it is written: (16) ''Afterwards I will return, and I will build up again the tent of David that has fallen down, and I will build up again its ruins, and I will raise it up, (17) in order that the rest of mankind may seek the Lord, even all the Gentiles[4] upon whom my name has been named.'' So says the Lord,[5] making these things (18) known from of old. (19) Therefore for my part I give my judgement that we should not make trouble for those who from the Gentiles turn to God, (20) but write to them that they should abstain from the defilements caused by idols, from fornication,[6] from that which has been strangled, and from blood. (21) For Moses from generations of old has in every city those who proclaim him, since he is read out every Sabbath in the synagogues.'

(22) Then the apostles and the elders, along with the whole church, decided to choose men from among themselves to send to Antioch with Paul and Barnabas; [they chose] Judas called Barsabbas and Silas, leading men among the brothers, (23) and wrote for them to deliver [as follows:] 'The apostles and the elders, your brothers, to the brothers in Antioch, Syria, and Cilicia, who come from among the Gentiles: Greeting. (24) Since we had heard that some of us had disturbed you by what they said, unsettling your

---

[1]NEB, We are saved, and so are they; NJB, We are saved in the same way as they are.

[2]NEB, summed up.

[3]NEB, it first happened that God took notice of the Gentiles. NJB, God first arranged to enlist a people for his name out of the Gentiles.

[4]NEB, whom I have claimed for my own.

[5]NEB, whose work it is, made known long ago.

[6]NJB, illicit marriages.

souls,—men to whom we had given no such instructions—(25) we,[7] when we met together, decided to choose and send men to you along with our beloved Barnabas and Paul, (26) men[8] who have devoted their lives to the name[9] of our Lord Jesus Christ. (27) So we have sent Judas and Silas, who will report the same things to you by word of mouth. (28) For the Holy Spirit and ourselves have reached the decision that we should lay upon you no other burden except these necessary things: (29) that you should abstain from things sacrificed to idols, from blood, from things that have been strangled, and from fornication.[10] If you keep yourselves from these things you will be doing right. Farewell.'

Bibliography

E. Bammel, as in (38).

C. K. Barrett, *FS* Osborn, 50–59.

C. K. Barrett, *FS* Hofius, 323–39.

J. B. Bauer, *BZ* 32 (1988), 114–17.

P. Benoit, 3.285–99 (= *Bib* 40 (1959), 778–92).

C. Blomberg, *JSNT* 22 (1984), 53–80.

M. E. Boismard, *EThL* 64 (1988), 433–40.

T. Boman, *NovT* 7 (1964–5), 26–36.

P. Borgen, *FS* Kee, 125–41 [= *Early Christianity and Hellenistic Judaism* (1996), 233–51].

U. Borse, *FS* Zimmermann, 195–212.

F. F. Bruce, *FS* Greeven, 115–24.

R. Bultmann, *FS* T. W. Manson, 68–80 (= *Exegetica* 412–23).

A. Campbell, *JTS* 44 (1993), 511–28.

D. R. Catchpole, *NTS* 23 (1976–7), 428–44.

L. Cerfaux, *Rec.* 2.105–23.

O. Cullmann, *Petrus*.

N. A. Dahl, *NTS* 4 (1958), 319–27.

F. W. Danker, Cassidy and Sharpes, *Political Issues*, 49–58.

W. Dieterich, *Petrusbild*.

J. Dupont, *NTS* 3 (1957), 47–50 (= *Études* 361–5).

J. Dupont, *NTS* 31 (1985), 321–35.

J. Eckert, in J. Ernst (ed.), *Schriftauslegung* (1972), 281–311.

J. Fitzmyer, *Essays* 271–303 (= *FS* Schubert, 233–57).

P. Gaechter, *ZKTh* 85 (1963), 339–54.

B. Gerhardsson, *Memory and Manuscript* (1961), 249–61.

M. D. Goulder, *Two Missions*.

[7]NEB, We have resolved unanimously; NJB, We have decided unanimously.
[8]RSV, men who have risked.
[9]NEB, cause.
[10]NJB, illicit marriages.

R. M. Grant, *HThR* 73 (1980), 299–310.

E. Haenchen, *FS* Jeremias, 153–64.

T. Holtz, as in (38).

P. W. van der Horst, *NovT* 16 (1974), 309.

J. Jensen, *NovT* 20 (1978), 161–84.

G. D. Kilpatrick, Kremer, *Actes* 84–6.

A. F. J. Klijn, *NovT* 10 (1968), 305–12.

M. Klinghardt, *Gesetz und Volk Gottes*, 158–224.

W. G. Kümmel, *Heilsgeschehen und Geschichte* (1965), 278–88.

H. Lietzmann, *FS* Harris, 203–11.

J. I. H. McDonald, *TU* 126 (= *StEv* VII) 327–32.

J. Manek, *Comm. Viatorum* 15 (1972), 151–60.

P. H. Menoud, *SNTS Bulletin* 2 (1951), 22–8.

E. Molland, StTh 9 (1955), 1–39.

J. Murphy-O'Connor, *RB* 99 (1982), 71–91.

J. Nolland, *NTS* 27 (1981), 105–15.

J. L. North, *NTS* 29 (1983), 264–6.

C. Perrot, *RechScR* 69 (1981), 195–208.

R. Pesch, *FS* Zimmermann, 105–22.

W. Pratscher, *Jakobus* (1987).

B. Reicke, as in (38).

B. Reicke, in Stendahl, *Scrolls* 146.

E. Richard, as in (38).

R. Richard, *NovT* 24 (1982), 37–53.

H. Sahlin, *NovT* 24 (1982), 187.

H. van de Sandt, *JSNT* 46 (1992), 73–97.

A. Schmidt, *ZNW* 81 (1990), 122–31.

D. R. Schwartz, *Bib* 67 (1986), 276–81.

M. Simon, *BJRL* 52 (1969–70), 437–60.

E. R. Smothers, *HThR* 46 (1953), 203–15.

A. Strobel, *FS* Zimmermann, 81–104.

C. H. Talbert, *NovT* 9 (1967), 26–40.

J. Taylor, *RB* 99 (1992), 373–8.

Y. Tissot, *RB* 77 (1970), 321–46.

C. H. Turner, *Theology* 20 (1930), 4–14.

A. J. M. Wedderburn, *NovT* 35 (1993), 362–89.

A. Weiser, *BZ* 28 (1984), 145–67.

P. Winter, *EvTh* 17 (1957), 399–406.

E. Zuckschwerdt, *ZNW* 68 (1977), 122–31.

G. Zuntz, *Opuscula Selecta* (1972), 216–51.

Commentary

The meeting planned in the preceding paragraph takes place. It does not take the form of a trial (so that the Western reading in 15.2 does not correspond to Luke's intention) but rather of a general discussion of a question of practice. B. Gerhardsson (*Memory and Manuscript* (1961), 249–61) compares it to a rabbinic discussion of a piece of *halakah*, and thinks it to be an example of the διακονία τοῦ λόγου to which the apostles propose to devote themselves in 6.4. It is the apostles and elders who gather for discussion and evidently assume the authority to make a decision; they write the letter in which the decision is promulgated, though the whole church concurs (v. 22). At the outset there is much debate, which Luke does not report. After this he assigns speeches to Peter, to Barnabas and Paul, who are not separated as speakers, and to James. Peter is firmly in favour of a liberal attitude; the Law, he says, is an intolerable burden even to Jews, and God has clearly shown that he does not require observance from Gentiles. Barnabas and Paul report the miracles they have witnessed among the Gentiles, a demonstration of God's favour to the Gentiles and of his approval of the way in which the evangelists have conducted their mission. James's attitude is less clear, though he agrees with Peter and finds support for his position in the OT; some requirements, however, must be made. The whole company agrees with his conclusion, and a letter is written, disavowing those who have caused confusion in the Antiochene church and stating the decree proposed by James; if this is observed all will be well in the Gentile churches.

This paragraph is rightly described as the centre of Acts. It is the best example of a pattern that occurs several times in Acts and represents the way in which Luke conceived the progress of Christianity. In this pattern a difficulty is encountered; steps are taken to deal with it; not only is the problem solved but a notable advance takes place as a result. Thus for example at 6.1 the problem of the Hellenist widows (which could have ended in schism) arises; steps are taken to deal with it (6.2–6); the result (6.7) is a great increase in the number of disciples. Similarly in 19.9 there is such vehement opposition to Paul's work in Ephesus that he is obliged to leave the synagogue for another building; but the result (19.10) is that all the Jews and Greeks in the province of Asia hear the Lord's word. In ch. 15 the extension of the Gospel to the Gentiles (which is Luke's primary concern) is threatened by those who would compel all Gentile converts to become Jewish proselytes; steps are taken to deal with this problem; the result is not simply an answer to the problem but the further expansion of the church. This appears immediately in 15.35, but is in fact the theme of the rest of the book. Thus Acts 15 supplies the key to the arrangement and movement of the book as a whole. 'Luc place le récit, tel qu'il l'a recomposé, au centre de l'activité missionaire de Paul' (Taylor 5.222).

Haenchen saw the account of the Council as a Lucan composition. It was not indeed pure fiction; Luke wrote on the basis of traditions, which are not further defined. With this view Bultmann disagreed (*Exegetica* 415f. = *FS* T. W. Manson 71f.); Luke made use of written sources. The sharpest point of disagreement was the Decree, together with the letter of which it formed part. Bultmann agrees with Dibelius that the address to Antioch, Syria, and Cilicia is a clear indication of a written source. Luke believed the letter and Decree to apply to all Gentile Christian churches; he would never have made up so limited a statement of its destination. Certainly (in Bultmann's view) Luke edited the written source, or sources, that he possessed; in particular he introduced the references to Barnabas and Paul.

Subsequent writers have taken different views of the composition of the paragraph. According to Hanson (155) 'The "Apostolic Council" is an imaginative reconstruction by Luke'; but from this Hanson excepts the letter and the Decree. Lüdemann 176 thinks that ch. 15 rests on tradition, but is undecided whether this was written or oral. He sees the marks of tradition in the concreteness of the narrative and in its agreements with Galatians 2. Many think that Luke has combined two traditions, based respectively on Jerusalem and Antioch. Sometimes the combination is set out in literary form. Thus Pesch (2.72) believes that Luke has combined a tradition of an Apostolic Council with an account of the Apostolic Decree; more precisely (2.74), he distinguishes Antiochene tradition (of the founding of the church, 11.19–26, and of the delegation to Jerusalem, 11.27–30; 12.25; 15.1–4, 12b) and the origin of the Decree (10.1–11.18; 15.5–12a, 13–33). Weiser (376) finds the story of a Jerusalem meeting in 15.1, 2, 4, 5, 6, 12, 7, 13, 10, 11, 19, and an account of the Antiochene problem and its solution in 15.5, (1), 23, 30, 20, 29, 23, 22, 27, 30, 31, 32. 'Lukas hat die Elemente beider Traditionen miteinander verbunden und so die eindrucksvolle Gesamtszene "Apostelkonzil" gestaltet.' It may be questioned whether such precise delineation of sources is possible; Luke gave himself too free a hand, and believed that the Decree, formulated as the result of a Council in Jerusalem, originated as the solution of the Antiochene problem. That Luke used all the sources he could find, whether written or oral, was argued already in I.49–56; he did so here. Of the Decree Haenchen (454) writes, 'Lukas hat also nicht ... diese vier Forderungen einem alten Dokument entnommen, das er irgendwo gefunden hat, sondern er hat eine lebendige Tradition beschrieben, die man wahrscheinlich schon damals auf die Apostel zurückgeführt hat.' That Luke found the Decree in use, observed by churches, is true; but were his contemporaries so illiterate that they never wrote down basic rules of their community? The paragraph reproduces written material, folk memory, and Luke's own story-telling.

The story invites comparison with Galatians 2. There are such close parallels between the two passages that it is hard to doubt that somewhere behind both lies a single event. In both Paul accompanied by Barnabas goes up to Jerusalem. In Acts 'certain others' go with them; in Galatians Titus goes, and it is not said that he is the only additional traveller. In Galatians James, Cephas, and John take part; in Acts James and Peter take part and there is nothing to suggest that John was not there as one of the unnamed apostles. In Galatians Paul and Barnabas are accepted by the Jerusalem apostles as colleagues; in Acts they take part in the discussion and are described in the letter as 'our beloved Barnabas and Paul'. In Acts the theme discussed in the Council is the proposition that all converts to Christianity must be circumcised; if the Galatians Council did not deal with this theme it was irrelevant to the Galatian situation to which Paul applies it. This is a weighty list of parallels. On the other hand, the Acts Council ends with the issue of a Decree, binding on Christians; in Galatians there is no sign of this Decree, nor is there any sign of it anywhere else in Paul's letters. In Galatians there is some sort of division of apostolic labour (Gal. 2.9); there is no trace of this in Acts. It would be difficult to maintain (though not a few have done so) that Acts and Paul are describing different events; equally difficult to think that Luke had read Galatians.

We may add, and take as a pointer to the unravelling of the historical problem, that both Acts and Galatians speak of the arrival in Antioch of representatives from Jerusalem. In Acts they take a hard line on circumcision and the Law: all must be circumcised and observe the Law. This demand is represented as the immediate occasion of the Council. In Galatians (assuming, as without indica-tion to the contrary one should, that Paul sets out events in chronological order) the visit is of envoys from James, and it follows the Council. As a result of it the church in Antioch is divided: Peter, followed by Barnabas and all the Jewish Christians, withdrew into isolation, refusing to eat with uncircumcised Gentile Christians. Paul maintained his position and stood by the Gentiles, rebuking Peter to his face. Assuming Paul to have been neither stupid nor dishonest, though doubtless like all men fallible in memory, his account, which is first-hand, must be accepted where it differs from Luke's; and the likeliest explanation of the course of events is as follows.

A mission based on Jerusalem was circulating among the Pauline churches (cf. M. D. Goulder, *A Tale of Two Missions*, London, 1994). Circumcision of all was demanded. This, if unchecked, could have ruined Paul's work, and he went up to Jerusalem that he might not run in vain (Gal. 2.2). Apart from an encounter with false brothers (who are distinguished from the apostles) the meeting was not inharmonious. There was agreement that Paul should go to the Gentiles (to evangelize them), the Jerusalem apostles to the Jews. This sounded well but was inadequately thought out and the terms remained undefined. It probably was related to the question whether an attempt should first be made to win the Jews for the Gospel, leaving the Gentile mission as a second-stage operation. It did not take into account what might be done in churches with mixed Jewish and Gentile membership. In Antioch it was at first assumed that since all were Christians all might have table fellowship together. The messengers from James (Gal. 2.12) must have said something like, We agreed that Gentiles might be accepted as Christians without circumcision; we did not say that Jews might so far cease to be Jews as to have unrestricted dealings with Gentiles. The two leaders, James and Paul, dug in their heels, and it was the Hellenistic Jewish Christians who found a way out by proposing the Decree—which Paul did not accept.

The theme of Luke's narrative does not change (see p. 745); the point of contention between Paul and Jerusalem changed. It was accepted that Gentile Christians did not have to be circumcised; it was not accepted by Jerusalem that there might be table fellowship between Jewish Christians and Gentile Christians. It is clear that the mission that required the circumcision, that is, the full proselytization, of Gentiles continued; it was certainly active in Galatia, but it no longer had the full support (though it may have had the implicit encouragement) of Jerusalem.

For the dating of the Council see Introduction, pp. lvi–lxi. Taylor (5.208) holds that the Council took place towards the end of the reign of Agrippa I, since it is clear from both Acts and Galatians that Peter (cf. 12.17) was still in Jerusalem. The argument is fallacious; 12.17 does not necessarily mean that Peter moved out of Jerusalem, and if he did he might easily have returned, especially after the death of Agrippa.

6. The ἐκκλησία of 15.4 now disappears (to reappear in v. 22 and possibly, as τὸ πλῆθος, in v. 12); the serious business of the Council is to be done by *apostles and elders.* 614 *pc* sy[h] add σὺν τῷ πλήθει; it may be that the Western text did not lay quite so much stress on the importance of the apostles as is sometimes supposed. Of the apostles mentioned in ch. 1 only Peter speaks; Barnabas and Paul, apostles only at 14.4, 14, report on their work; James, who seems to be merged with the apostolic group, proposes a solution which is accepted. It is very probable that Luke is here constructing a scene out of a small quantity of material. Elders (presbyters) probably represent the church officers with whom he was himself familiar. At

13.1 the church at Antioch has prophets and teachers; at that point Luke was probably using an Antiochene source. Here he assumes the church order that he knows, adding in the apostles as, while they lived, the highest authority. It may be said that Luke, though he quotes only Peter, regarded them as the real decision makers (cf. Peter, James, and John in Galatians 2); the elders listen and agree.

ἰδεῖν περί is an unusual expression, though it must mean something like *look into*. J. L. North (*NTS* 29 (1983), 264–6) points out that the Latin *videre de* suggests a legal, judicial sense. Is it intended to suggest (cf. 15.2 and especially the Western text) that Paul and Barnabas are on trial? More probably we should think of something like a rabbinic, or Qumran, court settling a matter of *halakah*. Cf. B. Gerhardsson (above, p. 709). It is doubtful whether Luke knew much about such courts, and it must be borne in mind that groups of people, assembled to discuss courses of action, are all likely to behave in similar ways, whatever their backgrounds.

For λόγου, E 614 *pc* gig sy[h] have ζητήματος, by assimilation to 15.2.

7. πολλῆς δὲ ζητήσεως γενομένης. There was much discussion. For ζήτησις see 15.2; it means search (ζητεῖν) for truth through public inquiry and debate, and it will shortly appear that the leading figures are agreed. Such dispute as is implied must (in Luke's view) come from those mentioned in 15.5.

At this point p[45(vid)] makes substantially the same addition to the text as is made by D in 15.2. Of 15.2, P[45] contains only ζητήματος τούτου, so that it is impossible to tell whether it contained the words there also. They are better restored in the apparatus of NA[26] than in F. G. Kenyon's *editio princeps* (1933).

Peter rose up to speak, ἀναστάς; cf. ἐξανέστησεν in 15.5: biblical style rather than a linguistic Semitism. D* (614 sy[hmg]) have ἀνέστησεν τῷ Πνεύματι Πέτρος καί: Peter is inspired; his pronouncement comes from God. Black (*AA* 69) notes the introduction of parataxis (ἀνέστησεν καὶ εἶπεν). Peter appeals to common knowledge: ὑμεῖς ἐπίστασθε—you know for yourselves, without my telling you. This applies to the reader, who will recall the contents of ch. 10, but there is no reason why some of Peter's activities should not have been generally known.

Peter's first sentence contains several obscurities. ἀφ᾽ ἡμερῶν ἀρχαίων should introduce the assertion that something has been going on continuously since an early time; one would expect an imperfect, but we have in fact the aorist ἐξελέξατο, which calls for the definition of a point of time. We must understand the prepositional phrase to mean not *from* but *in ancient days, in days of old*. Hebrew מן can occasionally be taken in this way (Gen. 6.4; Josh. 24.2; Ps. 77.6), but this is of little help. Preuschen (94) takes the expression to be a stronger equivalent to πρότερον. But what are *the days of old*? Cf. v. 14 (πρῶτον); also 11.15 (ἐν ἀρχῇ), and v. 21, though there ἐκ γενεῶν ἀρχαίων introduces a continuous state (ἔχει). The meaning seems to be that from the start (of the Christian movement—in v. 15 the intention will be traced back to the prophets) God's plan included Gentiles. Whether those who were involved in the movement at the beginning were at the time aware of this is doubtful. There can hardly, in view of the dispute that arose, have been a specific instruction on the matter from Jesus, and in the absence of such an instruction those who questioned the step can hardly be blamed for doing so. Peter claims that he was the first to understand what should be done.

ἐν ὑμῖν ἐξελέξατο ὁ θεός (P[74] ℵ A B C 33 36 81 945 1175 1739 *al* bo Ir[lat]) gave the copyists problems. D[c] E Ψ 𝔐 (lat) sy[h] have (with some variations in order) ὁ θεὸς ἐν ἡμῖν ἐξελέξατο; D* 614 *pc* have ἡμῖν ὁ θεὸς ἐξελέξατο; 189 *pc* sy[p] sa have ὁ θεὸς ἐξελέξατο. The text of ℵ B is almost certainly correct, but it is difficult in that ἐξελέξατο has no direct object and that if the reference is to the Cornelius story (as it must be) Peter might have been expected to say that God made his choice (not among *you* but) among *us* (as in the reading of D[c]), since he himself was the one chosen. The difficulty is not to be dealt with by the observation that the Greek ἐξελέξατο could render the Hebrew בחר, whose direct object is often introduced by the preposition ב, sometimes translated in the LXX by ἐν (Bengel ad loc. compares 1 Chron. 28.4, 5). If this were accepted we should have to translate *God chose you*, that is, God chose the early Jewish Christian body (in the event represented by Peter) as his means of reaching the Gentiles. Wilcox (92f.) takes the Greek in this way and remarks on the Semitism (probably Hebrew, possibly Aramaic). There is however no reason to think that Luke is here translating with verbal literalness a Hebrew source; see below on vv. 16–18 where James quotes the LXX in a passage where it differs from the Hebrew. Peter is speaking of the divine choice that gave him a special task, and it is better to take the object of ἐξελέξατο to be the accusative and infinitive clause ἀκοῦσαι τὰ ἔθνη ... καὶ πιστεῦσαι; ἐν ὑμῖν will mean that God chose among you (Christians, or perhaps apostles), that is, to the exclusion of the rest of you, that the Gentiles should hear and believe the Gospel through my mouth. Johnson (261) takes τὰ ἔθνη to be the direct object of ἐξελέξατο: God chose the Gentiles to hear the message ... This is not impossible, and gives an interesting oxymoron: God chose the un-chosen people ... But the order of words makes this seem improbable.

In this sentence the first phrase (in Greek) is emphatic. Peter has a special right to be heard in the debate because, as all are aware, it was through him that the word of the Gospel (for this expression there is no parallel in Acts, or elsewhere in the NT, but cf. Col. 1.5; in Acts εὐαγγέλιον occurs only here and at 20.24) was first communicated to the Gentiles. The reference is evidently to the story of Cornelius, which is regarded as preceding not only the preaching to the Ἑλληνισταί in 11.20 but also Philip's preaching to the Samaritans and to the Ethiopian in ch. 8. It is hard to know whether this claim rests upon Luke's own understanding of the history or is based upon a memory or tradition of what Peter was believed to have said, whether at the Council or on some other occasion. For the editorial processes that underlie Luke's narrative see pp. 710–12.

What had been required of the Gentiles was that they should hear and believe the Gospel, not that they should be circumcised or commit themselves to observance of the Law.

The verse affirms the absolute priority if not the primacy of Peter in the Gentile mission. One might be inclined to suspect an anti-Pauline interest here, were it not that Luke goes on to fill the rest of his book with material that depicts Paul as the leader in this work, whereas Peter, after this assertion of God's choice of him, disappears. It may be that the motive is 'not only but also'; Paul may have been the greatest but Peter was the first. The two must not be set over against each other. This would accord with the eirenic interest of Luke (displayed not least in this chapter), as also perhaps would his silence regarding the rest of Peter's career, of which some aspects, from a Pauline point of view, were scarcely creditable (Gal. 2.11–18). Luke, through Peter, makes clear that the law-free Gentile mission originated within the apostolic tradition (Schmithals 137).

Peter speaks first; it is not so clear as some (e.g. Roloff 230) think that James was now head of the Jerusalem church.

8. For καρδιογνώστης see on 1.24; there the term is applied (probably) to Christ, here to God. Luke would find no difficulty in the double use of the term. God knew what was in the hearts of Cornelius and his friends and bore witness to them. μαρτυρεῖν is used, especially in the passive, as a word describing a person's reputation; cf. e.g. 16.2, Timothy had a good reputation with the brothers. This, in view of the context and the participial clause that follows, though on the right lines will hardly suffice here. If however we ask in respect of what God bore witness to Cornelius the answer is not clear. It might be to the fact that he feared God and practised righteousness, and was thus acceptable to God (10.35); it might be to the fact that he was, though a Gentile, one of the elect; it might be (looking at the matter from the other side) to the fact that he was about to exercise, was already beginning to exercise, faith. The last is probably nearest to Luke's thought. God bore witness to the fact that Cornelius had fulfilled all the conditions (hearing and believing the Word) necessary for being a Christian, and was thus qualified to receive the Holy Spirit.

The participle δούς (C E (Ψ) 𝔐 1 Ir^lat add αὐτοῖς, D adds ἐπ᾽αὐτούς) is adverbial; *God bore witness to them in that he gave ...* The gift was the visible sign of his approval, or rather the audible sign (10.46): Luke regards inspired speech as the sure sign of the work of the Spirit. It was a sign that placed Cornelius and his company on the same level as Peter and his apostolic colleagues. It was the gift of the Spirit that constituted the apostolic body at the beginning (2.4), and it was manifested in speaking with tongues. The Holy Spirit was given to the Gentiles in Caesarea (10.44) and was described as τὴν ἴσην δωρεάν (11.17). God thus treated them exactly as he had treated Peter and the Eleven (καθὼς καὶ ἡμῖν).

Speaking with tongues is not the best sign of the Spirit's presence; so Calvin (2.33): 'It seems that the evidence of election, that the Holy Spirit fell on them, is not altogether convincing (minus firmum).'

9. God gave them the same gift that he gave us (v. 8); that is, οὐθὲν διέκρινεν μεταξὺ ἡμῶν τε καὶ αὐτῶν, he made no distinction between us and them, treating both groups, circumcised Jews and uncircumcised Gentiles, alike. Since evidently God did not see fit to require circumcision before bestowing his gifts it was not for men to demand it.

For διακρίνειν see 11.12 (for διακρίνεσθαι, 10.20). With God as the subject and the verb in the active there can be no doubt about the meaning. P^74, διεκρίναμεν, would have something to commend it were it not that the finite verb is followed by a singular participle, καθαρίσας, which makes the plural impossible.

For οὐθέν (over against οὐδέν) see Thackeray (58–62) and M. 2.111f. (also BDR § 33.2, n. 2 and LS 1269, s.v. οὐθείς). 'First found in an inscription of 378 BC, it [οὐθείς] is practically the only form in use throughout the Greek-speaking world during iii/B.C. and the first half of ii/B.C. In 132 B.C. the δ forms begin again to reassert themselves, and the period from that date to about 100 B.C. appears to have been one of transition, when the δ and θ forms are found side by side in the same documents. For i/B.C. we are in the dark, but in i/A.D. we find that οὐδείς has completely regained its ascendancy' (Thackeray 58). In the NT forms with θ occur at Lk 22.35; 23.14; Acts 15.9; 19.27; 26.26; 27.33 (μηθέν); 1 Cor. 13.2; thus almost always in Luke-Acts, and never without textual variation. According to Moulton (loc. cit.), 'There has been a re-formation οὐδ᾽ εἷς, with δ + h producing θ.' There is an inconclusive note in *ND* 4.16f. There seems to be no specific reason why Luke should have chosen to use this form of the word at this place, though it may mean that he drew Peter's words from a source. It is however impossible to regard all the passages cited above as derived from a single source; they are not connected with one another.

God's decision to make no distinction between Jew and Gentile was expressed in the act (καθαρίσας, aorist) of cleansing their hearts. There is no parallel to this in Acts. The adjective καθαρός occurs at 18.6; 20.26, each time with reference to Paul's innocence in his relations with others—Jews in Corinth, Christians in Ephesus. καθαρίζειν occurs in the Cornelius story (10.15) and its repetition (11.9), in the injunction with which Peter's vision closes: What God has cleansed (ἐκαθάρισεν), do not you count common. Here, though the reference is to the Cornelius story, the meaning appears to be different. In the story (as Luke tells it—for the question whether the vision and the visit to Cornelius originally belonged together see I.493f., 496f.) the cleansing is presumably anterior to Peter's entry into Cornelius's house: 'You must not consider Cornelius and his house unclean; God has cleansed them.' Here in ch. 15 the cleansing takes place in view of the faith generated in Cornelius as he hears the word: τῇ πίστει (though Knowling (319) takes it to refer to the (Christian) faith) in v. 9 must be interpreted in terms of πιστεῦσαι in v. 7. It is by faith (not by circumcision or other legal works) that God's gift of the Spirit and of cleansing is received. The distinction is real but it is doubtful whether it would occur to Luke. Cornelius had been admitted to the cleansed people of God, and without legal requirement; that was all that mattered.

In the story, the mark of Cornelius's acceptance was baptism (10.47f.; cf. 11.17). Baptism was a bath and could therefore be associated with cleansing; cf. 22.16. This is not however an image that Luke regularly uses (for him baptism is primarily a rite of initiation), and the cleansing of the heart probably means for him the forgiveness of sins (cf. 13.38f.) and inward renewal with a view to future obedience. Baptism is not viewed as the Christian replacement of circumcision.

The notion of inward cleansing is known in antiquity, also in circles that are not notably religious; thus Lucretius 6.23, Veridicis igitur purgavit pectora dictis; Xenophon, *Symposium* 1.4, ... ἀνδράσιν ἐκκεκαθαρμένοις τὰς ψυχάς.

10. νῦν οὖν begins to bring the brief speech to its conclusion with a rhetorical question that leads to a *reductio ad absurdum*. *Why do you ...?* means *You ought not to ...* It is absurd to expect Gentiles to put up with what we Jews cannot endure.

τί πειράζετε τὸν θεόν; The thought appears to be that God has already, by his action, made clear that it is his intention to incorporate the Gentiles as they are—without circumcision or any other legal observance—in his people, and that to hinder their reception by legal stipulation is wantonly to provoke him. For this use of πειράζειν cf. e.g. Exod. 17.2, τί λοιδορεῖσθέ μοι, καὶ τί πειράζετε κύριον; Men are seeing 'how far they can go' with God, insisting on that which is plainly contrary to his will. In this case their action would be 'eine Herausforderung Gottes, der durch die in Jerusalem bekannte Offenbarung im Hause des Cornelius die Gesetzesfreiheit der Heidenchristen als seinem Willen entsprechend erwiesen hatte' (H. Seesemann in *TWNT* 6.33). This use of πειράζειν is almost exclusively biblical, but BA (1291), who understand it in a slightly different way, quote Herodotus 6.86.3 (6.86.γ.2 in *OCT*), ἡ δὲ Πυθίη ἔφη τὸ πειρηθῆναι τοῦ θεοῦ καὶ τὸ ποιῆσαι ἴσον δύνασθαι. Cf. Chrysostom (*Homily* 32.1): τί πειράζετε τὸν θεὸν ὡς οὐκ ἰσχύοντα σῶσαι τῇ πίστει; ἄρα ἀπιστίας ἐστὶ τὸ τὸν νόμον εἰσφέρειν.

The construction continues with the infinitive, ἐπιθεῖναι, which Bruce (1.293) describes as epexegetic, and Zerwick (§ 392) explains as equivalent to a gerundive: 'Quid tentatis Deum ἐπιθεῖναι ζυγόν = *imponendo* iugum super cervices . . .'. M. 3.136 follows this; cf. BDR § 391.4, n. 8. The Vulgate, translating literally, has *imponere*. τῶν here retains something of its demonstrative force; these (Gentile) disciples.

Rabbinic literature uses the word *yoke*, עול, but not as it is used here. See e.g. Aboth 3.5, He that takes upon himself the yoke of the Law (עול תורה), from him shall be taken away the yoke of the kingdom (עול מלכות) (that is, oppression by worldly authority). Thus the yoke of the Law, the obligation to obey it, is a blessing and a privilege. Peter takes it otherwise. In other passages of the NT ζυγός has a bad sense. At 1 Tim. 6.1 slaves are described as being ὑπὸ ζυγόν, and the image is used theologically at Gal. 5.1 (μὴ πάλιν ζυγῷ δουλείας ἐνέχεσθε); cf. Barnabas 2.6: the new law (ὁ καινὸς νόμος) of Christ is ἄνευ ζυγοῦ ἀνάγκης; but cf. also 1 Clement 16.17: We have come ὑπὸ τὸν ζυγὸν τῆς χάριτος αὐτοῦ, which recalls Mt. 11.29f.

Peter claims that to require circumcision and legal observance from Gentile converts would be to lay upon their necks a yoke ὃν οὔτε οἱ πατέρες ἡμῶν οὔτε ἡμεῖς ἰσχύσαμεν βαστάσαι, to demand of them something that Jews themselves could neither endure nor achieve. Cf. Mt. 23.4. This does not agree with the attitude to the yoke of Torah quoted above—it was a privilege and joy; and Paul claims to have fulfilled the Law completely (Phil. 3.6). He was also well aware of Jewish Christians who continued to feel and to respond to its attraction. Conzelmann (83), noting these facts, argues that Luke was writing about something that he did not himself know at first hand. The controversy, when he wrote, lay in the past, and he did not fully understand the point at issue. Only a minimum of legal requirement now remained for any Christian, and Luke was unable to believe that there ever were Christians who loved the Law, and some who wished to impose it on Gentiles. If Peter really felt like this about the Law—that it was an intolerable burden—why did not he and his fellow Jewish Christians themselves give it up? Indeed, if Jews in general (οἱ πατέρες ἡμῶν, not only the Christians but earlier generations) found the Law insupportable how did it survive, and why was it painstakingly developed and interpreted in halakah and haggadah? Haenchen (429) similarly thinks that Peter is made to give the views not of his own but of Luke's time and environment; so also e.g. Weiser (381). This conclusion may be correct, but it is certainly an oversimplification. Paul, who had observed the Law, was a Pharisee (Phil. 3.5; cf. Acts 23.6; also 22.3), as were those who have given us the rabbinic literature. We have no reason to think that Peter was a Pharisee; he may well have been an *'am ha-'areṣ*, and was a Galilean into the bargain. Perhaps he was one of those Jews who made no serious attempt to keep the Law. His opinion may reflect also the views of liberal Hellenistic Jews, who, though they are to be distinguished from Paul, contributed to the Gentile mission. According to Schille (320), Peter represents 'die Anschauung der hellenistischen Kirche'. This again does not say all that is to be said. According to 10.14 and 11.8 Peter claimed that he had never touched unclean food (with the probability that one who was scrupulous in this respect would not be negligent in others). It is in agreement with this, or at least not in disagreement, that according to Gal. 2.12 he withdrew himself from table-fellowship with Gentiles. It is impossible to save the historicity of this speech (or at any rate this part of it) and Peter's reaction to the animal vision in ch. 10, even if some variability in Peter's character (attested by Gal. 2.12–15 as well as in the gospels) is taken into account. He is described here as something of a Paulinist, though the Paulinism is not accurately portrayed. That Luke should describe him in this way must cast some doubt on the view that towards the end of the century there was an influential minority of Jewish Christians.

This is the only place in Luke-Acts where βαστάζειν has the meaning *endure, put up with* (see J. L. Nolland in *NTS* 27 (1980–1), 105–115), but ἰσχύειν is a Lucan word: Lk. 8 times; Acts 6, rest of the NT 14.

11. ἀλλά implies, 'No, indeed, we could not do this, but on the contrary . . .'.

The language of the verse is superficially Pauline (see on v. 10) but lacks Paul's precision. 'Paulinische Begriffe werden von Lukas übernommen, aber nicht die paulinische Theologie, welche sich dieser Begriffe bedient' (Haenchen 429). *The grace of the Lord Jesus* (C D Ψ 33 36 453 945 1175 1739 *pc* it sy^p bo^{pt} Ir^{lat} add Χριστοῦ) recalls 2 Cor. 8.9, but receives no definition. The general sense however is clear. Whatever precisely Luke may have understood by χάρις it did not mean works of the Law. And διὰ τῆς χάριτος stands emphatically at the beginning of the sentence, though it is probably to be connected with σωθῆναι rather than with πιστεύομεν (the third time a word of this root appears in this short speech); the latter connection however is not impossible. Cf. 13.48; faith itself is of the Lord's gracious appointment.

It is to be observed (see the note on 15.1 and p. 696) that in this verse the theme of the Council is still (not rules for table fellowship but) salvation and the conditions on which salvation may be received. 'De *Salute* agebatur' (Bengel 449). The tense of σωθῆναι does not determine the time at which salvation is thought to take place. Past, present, and future are all possible: We believe *that we have been saved, that we shall be saved*, or even as a general proposition, We believe *that we are saved*. It is however probable that Luke here uses a construction whereby 'Verbs and expressions signifying *to hope, to expect, to promise*, and the like, after which the Infinitive in indirect discourse would naturally be in the Future ... as representing a Future Indicative of the direct discourse, sometimes take the Aorist (as well as the Present) Infinitive' (Goodwin, *Moods and Tenses* § 23.2). This however, though probable, is not certain, because the construction normally applies only in cases where the main verb itself points clearly to the future, and πιστεύειν does not necessarily do this. See Nolland, as on v. 10.

In καθ' ὃν τρόπον κἀκεῖνοι, ἐκεῖνοι is most naturally taken to refer to those (the Gentile believers) to whom the Holy Spirit has already been said to have been given καθὼς καὶ ἡμῖν. The parallelism between them and us would then be expressed in two ways: the Holy Spirit was given to them as to us; salvation comes to us as to them, by grace through faith. This is probably what Luke intends, but the grammatically nearest antecedent to ἐκεῖνοι is οἱ πατέρες ἡμῶν; if this is regarded as determinative, the point would be that the saints of the OT, prophets and the like, were saved by faith, and we are, or shall be, saved in the same way, apart from legal works. This was the view of Augustine (*Contra duas Epistolas Pelagianorum* 1.21(39), ... ut eadem gratia Jesu Christi salvi facti credantur antiqui), Calvin (2.42), and Bengel (449). On either view the parallel is to be found neither in *believed* nor in *saved* alone but in the combination of the two.

According to Pesch 2.78 this passage shows the fundamental agreement between Peter and Paul (cf. Gal. 2.15f.). It does so only if the opinions expressed here are correctly ascribed to Peter; it is certainly true that Luke makes Peter speak—more or less—like Paul. Bruce (1.295) quotes the opinion of Ramsay (*Paul the Traveller* 164) who looks at the matter from a different angle and uses it to prove that Gal. 2.11f. cannot have happened after the Council because it would make Peter guilty of a 'meaningless tergiversation'. This is quite unconvincing, for (a) tergiversation is precisely the accusation Paul levels against Peter, and (b) whatever the relation between Gal. 2.11f. and the Council the event in Antioch must have happened after the Cornelius episode.

Peter (as represented by Luke) concludes his argument that by his actions God himself has made clear that Gentiles who believe are acceptable to him, and that he is prepared to bestow his gifts upon them without any condition in addition to their faith. If this is so, who are even apostles to impose conditions when God requires none? This is as far as Peter goes; he, and Luke, do not see that it is implied (Roloff 231) that Jewish Christians also have given up the Law as a means of salvation. It is fair to add, with Marshall (250), 'What Peter disputed was thus the need to obey the law in order to *be saved*; whether Jews kept it for other reasons was a secondary matter.'

12. Ἐσίγησεν δὲ πᾶν τὸ πλῆθος. Luke presumably means that Peter's speech silenced the ζήτησις of v. 7. The πλῆθος is probably the mass of the people (cf. the use of ἐκκλησία in 15.4, 22) as distinct from the apostles and elders, rather than the whole company of apostles and elders. The distinction is made clear in the reading of D (1) sy^h**, συγκατατιθεμένων δὲ τῶν πρεσβυτέρων τοῖς ὑπὸ τοῦ Πέτρου εἰρημένοις ἐσίγησεν πᾶν τὸ πλῆθος. Luke could mean simply that the company were silenced, but probably intends to suggest that they were convinced and agreed. See the long quotation from Musonius Rufus given by P. W. van der Horst in *NovT* 16 (1974), 309.

With ἤκουον Luke forgets that he has used the singular ἐσίγησεν with a noun of multitude, πλῆθος; or rather, picturing the occasion, thinks of a general silence, and of listening individuals, each intent on the story that Barnabas and Paul had to tell.

With ἐξηγουμένων cf. ἐκδιηγούμενοι in 15.3. There is no significant difference in meaning. ἐξηγ. is more frequently used in Acts (10.8; 15.12, 14; 21.19, always in the sense of narrating events) than ἐκδιηγ. (13.41, quoting Hab. 1.5; 15.3), and, it seems, in Greek literature generally. In 15.3 Paul and Barnabas recount the conversion of the Gentiles, in the present verse *the signs and portents* that God had done among the Gentiles. Luke is probably thinking of essentially the same account (cf. 14.27), but the occurrence of signs and portents gives it greater probative value since it shows God's approval. No details are given; Luke expects the narrative of chs. 13 and 14 to be in his readers' minds, though these chapters do not contain many signs and portents. σημεῖα καὶ τέρατα is one of Luke's standard phrases (2.19, 22, 43; 4.30; 5.12; 6.8; 7.36; 14.3) and it slips in; he is responsible for the verse in its present form. The point here is that the signs and portents were done ἐν τοῖς ἔθνεσιν. Haenchen (121) makes the point that since Luke lacks Paul's theological justification of the Gentile mission he is obliged to fall back on miracles. In fact, Luke has several ways of justifying the mission—Peter's argument that God has treated Jews and Gentiles alike, and James's argument (see below) from Scripture; it is paradoxical that Paul should be left with miracles. Cf. however Rom. 15.19; 2 Cor. 12.12; Gal. 3.5. Stählin (203) thinks that the miracles were 'eine wichtige Form der Verkündigung'; Luke might have agreed, but it is doubtful whether Paul would have done so. The most that can be said is 'dass Gott zu dem Missionswerke des Paulus sein Ja gesprochen hat' (Bauernfeind 191).

Bultmann (*Exegetica* 417 = *FS* T. W. Manson 72f. + n. 6) thinks that v. 12, like all the other references to Paul in 15.1–35, was inserted into a source that did not originally contain it; Paul and Barnabas were not present at the Jerusalem meeting that issued the Decree of 15.29. On this question see p. 710 and below; there is no difficulty in conjecturing a source that read ἐσίγησεν δὲ πᾶν τὸ πλῆθος, καὶ ἀπεκρίθη Ἰάκωβος. 'Die Sätze, in denen von Paulus und Barnabas die Rede ist, lassen sich leicht herausheben: V. 2 (es würde genügen: ἔταξαν ἀναβαίνειν τινὰς ἐξ αὐτῶν πρὸς κτλ.), 3–5, 12; das σὺν τῷ Παύλῳ καὶ Βαρναβᾷ in V. 22; V. 25f.—Vgl. W. Bousset, *ZNW* 14 (1913), S. 156–162' (Bultmann). On the other hand Pesch (2.79) thinks that the order Barnabas and Paul does not suggest the hand of an interpolator. If Luke did insert the references to Paul and Barnabas this could have been on one or both of two grounds. (a) He knew a tradition which (correctly) recorded that the two had taken part in a conference at Jerusalem (cf. Gal 2.1–10), and (b) he needed in his record of the Council representatives of those whom he describes as Hellenists (6.1; see the note). He seems to have regarded Paul and Barnabas as representatives of the movement that began with, or was notably represented by, Stephen.

13. μετὰ δὲ τὸ σιγῆσαι αὐτούς may be part of an addition made by Luke. For this possibility—it is no more—see on v. 12. ἐσίγησεν had been used in the introduction of Barnabas and Paul; James had now to be introduced, and the verb σιγᾶν was in Luke's mind and reused.

The introduction of James is slightly more formal in D sy[p]: ἀναστὰς (cf. v. 7) Ἰάκωβος εἶπεν. Luke does not tell us who is intended by the name James. Presumably he is the James of 12.17—evidently a person of such consequence that he needs no description; Luke's readers are sure to know who is meant. It is no doubt he who appears again at 21.18, again as a leading figure among the Jerusalem Christians. A James is mentioned among the brothers of Jesus (Mk 6.3), and as a witness of the resurrection (1 Cor 15.7). It is very probably the same James who plays an active role in Galatians: he was the only notable figure, in addition to Peter, seen by Paul on his first visit to Jerusalem (Gal 1.19); he was one of those who bore the title στῦλοι (2.9—with Cephas and John) but made no contribution to Paul's Gospel or his authority (2.6), rather recognizing his commission (2.7, 8). It was persons who came from James

who induced Peter to change his attitude in Antioch (2.12). The only
other material worth taking seriously is provided by the accounts of
the death of the Lord's brother in Josephus, *Ant.* 20.200, and in
Hegesippus, quoted by Eusebius, *HE* 2.23.4–18. The latter especially
suggests that the martyr had a great reputation for Jewish piety.
Whether, and to what extent, we can also use the Epistle of James is a
disputed question. On all this material see W. Pratscher, *Der
Herrenbruder Jakobus und die Jakobustradition* (Göttingen, 1987);
also Benoit (2.289, cf. 254). James seems at this point to be in
agreement with Peter, Paul, and Barnabas. Whether the evidence of
21.18 and of Galatians confirms or contradicts this is a question that
cannot be avoided.

ἄνδρες ἀδελφοί. For this mode of address cf. 1.16. Sometimes it
means Fellow Christians, sometimes Fellow Jews; here it could mean
either—or both.

ἀκούσατέ μου. According to Roloff (231) this address is a mark
of authority; cf. Stählin 203. This is not necessarily so; cf. 2.22; 7.2;
13.16; 22.1. According to W. Dieterich (*Das Petrusbild der lukanischen Schriften* (Stuttgart, 1972), 317), James's is an Erwider-
ungsrede: it was not Peter who initiated the mission but God himself.
This seems however to be what Peter himself says (ἐξελέξατο ὁ
θεός, v. 7).

14. Συμεών. 'Jacobus, Hebraeorum apostolus, Hebraico nomine
Petrum appellat' (Bengel 449). Cf. 2 Pet. 1.1; this form, which recalls
the Hebrew שמעון, was probably intended to give the passage a
Semitic air, regarded as suitable for James. Simon Peter, who had
just spoken, is intended; notwithstanding Fitzmyer (*Essays* 108), it is
mistaken to see here a reference to Symeon Niger (13.1). Cf.
Cullmann (*Petrus* 18). James refers to Peter, not to Barnabas and
Paul; this does not prove but is at least consistent with the suggestion
that the original source did not contain v. 12; see on that verse.

ἐξηγήσατο. Cf. ἐκδιηγούμενοι (15.3), ἐξηγουμένων (v. 12). The
repetition is striking. The word must surely have the same meaning
here as in v. 12 and will therefore mean that Peter recorded an event;
ἐπεσκέψατο will therefore refer to the conversion of Cornelius
(which Peter clearly has in mind in vv. 7–9).

καθώς has here the very unusual (but see Ep. Aristeas 263; 3 Jn 3)
sense, *how*: Symeon has narrated how God ...

With πρῶτον cf. ἀφ' ἡμερῶν ἀρχαίων (v. 7); the event in mind
belongs to the beginnings of the Christian story, and was the first of
its kind. It is not easy to find a good rendering of ἐπεσκέψατο. Page
(177) says that its meaning is not *visit* but *showed regard* or
consideration in taking. *Begs.* 4.175 says that the meaning is *to make
provision for*. There is in fact much to be said for the meaning
not uncommon in the LXX and Lk. (see 1.68, 78; 7.16), *visit*;

unfortunately it is not easy in English to combine this with the following infinitive. One may suggest the English *take action*; cf. Exod. 3.16, where God takes decisive, liberating, action on behalf of the persons concerned. In this case he so acted in order to take (understanding λαβεῖν as an infinitive of purpose) out of the Gentiles a people for his name. In ἐξ ἐθνῶν λαόν the two nouns stand in sharp contrast with each other. Out of those who are by definition not Jews, who are not the people of God, God takes men (in the first instance, Cornelius and his friends—but on this see below) to be a λαός, to be his own people, even though they lack what has hitherto been the necessary qualification for this: they do not belong to the right race and have not been circumcised as proselytes. J. Dupont (*NTS* 3 (1957), 47–50 = *Études* 361–5, here with an additional note referring to the article by N. A. Dahl, mentioned below) draws attention to the fact that James's words recall the language of the LXX, especially of Deut. 14.2 (σὲ ἐξελέξατο κύριος ὁ θεός σου γενέσθαι σε αὐτῷ λαὸν περιούσιον ἀπὸ πάντων τῶν ἐθνῶν; cf. Deut. 7.6; Exod. 19.5; 23.22). In a different context, James could simply be referring to the distant past when God chose Israel to be his special people; as we have seen, he is taking up Peter's reference to the Cornelius story, which his language interprets as parallel to the original call made on an ethnic basis. A further point is that the LXX distinguishes the two nouns λαός and ἔθνη whereas in the Hebrew there is no distinction (להיות לעם סגלה מכל העמים). Thus the dependence on the LXX that will be noted in vv. 16–18 occurs already in v. 14; James speaks throughout as a Hellenistic Jew dependent on the LXX.

The article by Dupont was taken up by N. A. Dahl (*NTS* 4 (1958), 319–27), who pointed out that λαὸς τῷ ὀνόματι αὐτοῦ does not occur in the LXX, but that 'the phrase "people for His (My, the Lord's) name" is a standard idiom in the old Palestinian Targum, where it is regularly used to render the Hebrew לעם (ליהוה לי, ליהוה) לו (321). He considers that the most interesting parallel to Acts 15.14 is Zech. 2.15(11), 'where it is stated that even Gentiles shall become a people of the Lord' (323). It would be unwise to build much on τῷ ὀνόματι αὐτοῦ; it recalls the baptismal phrase εἰς τὸ ὄνομα αὐτοῦ (see 8.16), and like it probably means 'to his account', 'so as to become his property'. Conzelmann (83) may well be right to question the specific biblical allusions; the words may be due to 'lukanischer Bibelstil'. See also Wilson (*Gentiles* 224).

15. This verse shows that though, as Dupont correctly pointed out, the language of v. 14 echoes that of the LXX, it would be mistaken to lay much stress on the OT background of the verse. Verse 14 states a historical fact, in words that hint at a much earlier historical fact: God acted so as to take to himself a people from among the Gentiles; he did this in the conversion and acceptance of Cornelius. Verse 15 makes the further point that what God then did fulfilled what he had through the prophets promised to do. *With this* (τούτῳ will refer to the whole action described in the preceding verse) *the words of the prophets are in agreement.* For συμφωνεῖν cf. 5.9. James refers to the words of the prophets but quotes only Amos 9.11f. (the slight verbal echoes of Jer. 12.15; Isa. 45.21 can hardly count as prophetic sayings that agree or disagree with anything). *Prophets* (plural) may be a reference to the book of the Twelve (minor) Prophets, but this will hardly account for λόγοι unless λόγος is taken as *word* in the most literal sense. It is better to suppose that καθὼς γέγραπται (cf. 7.42 and very frequently in the rest of the NT) is intended to introduce a specimen quotation. G. D. Kilpatrick (Kremer, *Actes* 84–6) punctuates thus: ... τῶν προφητῶν, καθὼς γέγραπται μετὰ ταῦτα. ἀναστρέψω κτλ.

16. The greater part of James's quotation is undoubtedly taken from Amos 9.11f., and it will be well to begin by setting out the LXX text of Amos 9.11, which is reproduced in this verse.

ἐν τῇ ἡμέρᾳ ἐκείνῃ ἀναστήσω τὴν σκηνὴν Δαυὶδ τὴν πεπτωκυῖαν καὶ ἀνοικοδομήσω τὰ πεπτωκότα αὐτῆς καὶ τὰ κατεσκαμμένα αὐτῆς ἀναστήσω καὶ ἀνοικοδομήσω αὐτὴν καθὼς αἱ ἡμέραι τοῦ αἰῶνος.

It appears at once that Luke (James) (1) has changed *that day* to μετὰ ταῦτα (contrast the quotation from Joel in 2.17), (2) may in doing so have recalled, possibly subconsciously, Jer. 12.15 (καὶ ἔσται μετὰ τὸ ἐκβαλεῖν με αὐτοὺς ἐπιστρέψω; in Acts D has ἐπιστρέψω for ἀναστρέψω), (3) has simplified and abbreviated Amos's cumbersome sentence, (4) has introduced the verb ἀνορθώσω (which may reflect 2 Kdms 7.13, 16, 26; 1 Chron. 17.12, 14, 24; 22.10), and (5) has omitted Amos's reference to *the days of old* (כימי עולם)—Acts is concerned with something new, not a renewal of the past though it was foretold in the past.

In Amos, the fallen tent of David is presumably the Davidic royal house, which came to an end with the fall of Jerusalem in 587/6 BC. The last paragraph of the book (whether written by Amos himself or a subsequent editor) promises its restoration. This however would involve also the restoration of the kingdom, that is, of the tribe of Judah (and Benjamin). Luke (James) may have taken this to refer to the Messiah, whether to his appearance in history or specifically to his having been raised up from death (cf. the ambiguity of 13.33); it is also however possible that he understood the prophecy to mean the restoration in the sense of the conversion of Israel. This divergence of interpretation will have an important bearing on our understanding of the passage as a whole. Is James made to say, Now that Christ has been raised from the dead the way is open for the Gentiles to enter at once into the people of God? Or, The conversion of the Gentiles must wait upon the conversion of the Jews; that is, in practical terms, There must be no such wholesale, indiscriminate, and unregulated admission of the Gentiles as would prejudice or hinder the mission to the Jews? See the brief but clear discussion in Wilson (*Gentiles* 224f.). That the latter view was held is supported by Paul's argument to the contrary in Romans 9–11 (see *Romans* 196–210) as well as by other controversial material in the NT (e.g. Mt. 10.5f.). It is however unlikely that Luke, who is clearly an enthusiastic supporter of the Gentile mission, and understood the Council as furthering the mission, took James's quotation to bear this meaning. It is not unlikely that the OT passage was in early years understood in one way but was used by Luke and his contemporaries in another. It is also possible that at first only Amos 9.11 was used, in support of the view that the conversion of the Jews must come first; there is no question here of a difference between the Hebrew and Greek texts (as in v. 17). Each predicts a restitution of Israel under a Davidic king, who could be understood to be the Messiah.

There is some support for this in the fact that Amos 9.11 is quoted in the Qumran MSS (see especially Fitzmyer *Essays* 25, 50f., 88). In CD 7.15, 16 (in the course of an interpretation of Amos 5.26; cf. Acts 7.42f.) the words 'I will raise up the fallen tent of David' are quoted, and it is explained that the books of the Law (ספרי התורה) are the king's tent; the king is the community (7.17: הקהל). In 4QFlor. 1.11–13 the fallen tent, which will be raised up, is צמח דויד, the shoot of David, who will stand up to save Israel (יעמוד להושיע את ישראל), that is, the Messiah. Fitzmyer (51) says, 'There is, however, no similarity in the use of the text in the three places [two in the Qumran MSS, one in Acts],' and adds that 'without any reference to a scion of David he [James] asserts the fulfilment of the verse in the conversion of the Gentiles to the Gospel.' It seems better to see the conversion of the Gentiles in the next verse (not quoted at Qumran; see below); one interpretation (see above) of Amos 9.11 as quoted here does see a reference to the Davidic Messiah. There remains however a marked difference between Acts and the Qumran Florilegium; in the latter it is said that the Shoot of David will be העומד עם דורש התורה, the one who stands with the interpreter of the Law. Acts knows no such second figure beside the Messiah.

This verse is discussed in the light of the Qumran passages by Wilcox (49); it is hard to see why the ἀναστήσω of Acts should be particularly associated with the Massoretic אקים, the LXX's ἀνοικοδομήσω with והקימותי of CD 7.16. The Messianic interpretation of Amos 9.11 reappears in Sanhedrin 96b–97a, where R. Nahman explains to R. Yitzhaq that Bar Naphli is a name of the Messiah, and bases this interpretation (there are others) on Amos 9.11 (where 'that has fallen' is הנופלת, *han-nopheleth*).

For κατεσκαμμένα (P⁷⁴ A C D 𝔐), ℵ (B) Ψ 33 326 *pc* have κατεστραμμένα, and E has ἀνεσκαμμένα. κατεστραμμένα appears also in some MSS of the LXX.

17, 18. Here we may begin with the LXX text of Amos 9.12.

ὅπως ἐκζητήσωσιν οἱ κατάλοιποι τῶν ἀνθρώπων [A adds, τὸν κύριον], καὶ πάντα τὰ ἔθνη, ἐφ᾽ οὓς ἐπικέκληται τὸ ὄνομά μου ἐπ᾽ αὐτούς, λέγει κύριος ὁ θεὸς ὁ ποιῶν ταῦτα.

James (Luke) adds ἄν after ὅπως; this is common in Attic prose and verse but was dropping out of use in the Hellenistic period (though not uncommon in the papyri). It is used also at 3.20; the MS A has it at Amos 9.12, but this is probably a reading back from the NT, as also was τὸν κύριον which provides an object for ἐκζητήσωσιν. James omits ὁ θεός, probably because he understands κύριος to refer to Christ.

ἐπ᾽ αὐτούς, taking up the relative ἐφ᾽ οὕς, crudely represents the construction of the indeclinable Hebrew relative: upon whom my name has been named, that is, with a view to marking them out as my property. The masculine οὕς, αὐτούς, follows the neuter πάντα τὰ ἔθνη *ad sensum*; 'the Gentiles' signifies a multiplicity of individual human beings. πάντα τὰ ἔθνη is explanatory of οἱ κατάλοιποι τῶν ἀνθρώπων, 'the rest of men', those who are not Jews. What is not clear is whether the relative clause is a limiting or an exclusive definition, that is, whether it means, All the Gentiles upon whom my name has been named, to the exclusion of those over whom it has not been named, or All the Gentiles, upon all of whom my name has been named. It is probable that Luke was prepared to let questions of this kind answer themselves. Cf. 13.48; it became clear who were appointed to eternal life when some believed and others did not. In the same way it would become clear which Gentiles bore God's name and which did not.

Luke's (James's) use of his text is thus clear; but his text is based on the LXX, not on the MT, which differs in several respects. It is translated in RSV: That they may possess (יירשו) the remnant of Edom (את שארית אדום) and all the nations who are called by my name (literally, upon whom my name has been called, אשר נקרא שמי עליהם), says the Lord who does this. In this Hebrew sentence Amos predicts the dominion of Israel over all other nations, including what is left of Edom, whom God is claiming as his possession. This is not what James and the LXX say. In place of יירשו, *they shall possess*, they read ידרשו, *they shall seek*. Instead of את (the sign of the direct object), they read יהוה, *the Lord*. Instead of שארית אדום, *the remnant of Edom*, they read, שארית אדם, *the remnant of men, of humanity*. In this way the meaning of the verse is almost reversed.

It is clear that neither James nor Luke invented this convenient form of the text; it already existed in the LXX. But is it likely that James, meeting in Jerusalem with fellow Jews (who happened also to be Christians) would use a form of the text that differed from the Hebrew? The Targum, incidentally, makes it even clearer that the house of Israel (בית ישראל is inserted in the text) will possess (יחסנון; v.l., ירתון) the remnant of Edom and all the nations. Gerhardsson (*Memory and Manuscript* 260) holds that James might have taken up, as the rabbis did, any known textual variant that would serve his purpose, but this would need a good deal more discussion and justification than is provided. One would expect at least a trace of the אל תקרא form of argument, e.g. Read not אדום but אדם, and so on.

It must be concluded, not with certainty but with high probability, that the quotation, and probably therefore the whole speech, cannot be attributed to James. This does not mean that Luke did not find the quotation among OT passages traditionally used in arguments about the Gentile mission, but it was probably used by Christian Jews who habitually used the OT in Greek. This observation has an important bearing on the historicity of the Acts council as a whole; see Introduction, pp. xxxvi–xli. The different ways (see above pp. 725f.) in which the Amos quotation may have been applied to the legitimacy of the Gentile mission are particularly important.

The LXX of Amos 9.12 ends, λέγει κύριος ὁ θεὸς ὁ ποιῶν ταῦτα, which is a reasonable representation of the Hebrew נאם יהוה עושה זאת. Acts 15.17 reproduces this with the omission of ὁ θεός and of ὁ (though ℵ^c A C D^2 E 𝔐 sy^h Cyril have ὁ). In NA^26 v. 18 continues with the words γνωστὰ ἀπ᾽ αἰῶνος. In this reading the editors follow ℵ B C Ψ 33 81 323 (1175) 1739 2495 *al* w. The words have been held to be based on Isa. 45.21, ... ἵνα γνῶσιν ἅμα τίς ἀκουστὰ ἐποίησεν ταῦτα ἀπ᾽ ἀρχῆς, though the resemblance is far from close. James's version makes what appears to be the point more strongly than the LXX (of Isaiah); by the prophetic oracle God made these truths about the inclusion of the Gentiles not only *heard* but *known*; and ἀπ᾽ αἰῶνος says more forcefully than ἀπ᾽ ἀρχῆς that they were part of his eternal plan. But γνωστὰ ἀπ᾽αἰῶνος is probably a simple gloss rather than an additional quotation.

There are variants for γνωστὰ ἀπ᾽ αἰῶνος. P^74 A D E 𝔐 lat (sy) Ir have ταῦτα (+ πάντα E 𝔐) γνωστὸν (γνωστὰ E 𝔐) ἀπ᾽ αἰῶνος ἐστιν (om. P^74 A) τῷ κυρίῳ (θεῷ E 𝔐) τὸ ἔργον (πάντα τὰ ἔργα E 𝔐) αὐτοῦ. 945 *pc* have ταῦτα πάντα ἅ ἐστιν γνωστὰ αὐτῷ ἀπ᾽ αἰῶνος. 2127 has πάντα τὰ ἔργα αὐτοῦ. All these variants except the last make the same point: God has not suddenly thought of the inclusion of the Gentiles; it has always been his intention, and he has long made his intention known. They are wordier variations on the short text, and this should be preferred.

H. Sahlin (*NovT* 24 (1982), 187) conjectures ὡς τὰ ἀπ᾽ αἰῶνος. G. D. Kilpatrick (Kremer, *Actes* 84–6) punctuates: ... λέγει κύριος ὁ

ποιῶν ταῦτα. γνωστὸν ἀπ᾽ αἰῶνος ἐστιν τῷ κυρίῳ τὸ ἔργον
αὐτοῦ.

19. διό presumably looks back to both the historical fact adduced
in v. 14 and to the prophetic word of vv. 16, 17. ἐγώ is pointless if
not emphatic: This is what *I* say. And not merely *say*. κρίνω may
express no more than a private judgement: This is my opinion. But it
may very naturally be taken as the judgement of a judge, who has the
right to declare a final verdict: I give judgement that . . . ; for example,
cf. Homer, *Odyssey* 12.440, κρίνων νείκεα πολλά; Thucydides
1.87.1, κρίνουσι γὰρ βοῇ καὶ οὐ ψήφῳ. Weiser (383) thinks the
word no stronger than *erachten*, and at Thucydides 4.60.1 the
scholiast paraphrases ὡς ἐγὼ κρίνω as ὡς ἐγὼ νομίζω. But there is
no further discussion after James's speech, and though 'I decree'
(*Begs.* 4.177) is too strong and perhaps does not catch the context
correctly James is at least acting as a chairman and expressing in his
own words the sense of the meeting. If Luke is right in the picture at
which he hints James occupies in the assembly a position if not of
pre-eminence at least of great prominence. Gerhardsson (op. cit. 252)
refers to Bacher (*Terminologie* 1.20f.) for the similar expression
הרי אני דן.

The impression of James's prominence gains some support from
the absence of an accusative subject with the infinitive παρενοχλεῖν.
It is not wrong to supply the first person plural, but James does not
express it, and without a pronoun the singular could well be
understood: I am deciding not to trouble . . . (with the implied
assumption that the speaker has it in his power to trouble or to
abstain from troubling). There is little difference between ὀχλεῖν,
ἐνοχλεῖν, and παρενοχλεῖν, though the effect of composition is
usually to reinforce the sense of the simple verb, which means *to
cause trouble* or *annoyance*. This may be material (e.g. Plutarch,
Timoleon 3.1 (237)) or mental, spiritual (e.g. Epictetus 1.9.23, of the
annoyance caused by Socrates in his persistent questioning). In
Hellenistic Greek the verb usually takes not, as here, the dative but
the accusative (MM 493); the accusative may be avoided here
because it could be taken to be the subject of the infinitive. Further
examples of παρενοχλεῖν from early inscriptions are given in *ND*
4.166f.; in them the verb takes the accusative. *Begs.* 4.177 takes the
present infinitive (with μή) to mean *stop annoying*.

τοῖς ἀπὸ τῶν ἐθνῶν ἐπιστρέφουσιν ἐπὶ τὸν θεόν could be said
by a Jew of Gentile converts to Judaism; to a Jewish Christian the
Christian conversion of Gentiles must have had to a considerable
extent the same appearance. Gentiles were turning from whatever
heathen gods they had previously worshipped to the God of the OT,
the God of the Jews. It was this fact that gave strength to the
requirement that they should behave like converts to Judaism, that is,

should be circumcised and thereafter keep the Law. ἐπιστρέφειν (though without ἐπὶ τὸν θεόν) could be used to describe what was required of Jews (3.19).

The Gentile converts must not be pestered; the context makes clear that this means that demands of full legal observance must not be made.

20. This verse, substantially repeated as adopted by the Council in v. 29 (cf. 21.25), calls for particularly careful examination; it contains noteworthy problems both in text (see, in addition to the note below, Metzger 429–34, with bibliography) and interpretation. James proposes not to cause trouble for the converted Gentiles but ἐπιστεῖλαι αὐτοῖς ... The precise force of ἐπιστέλλειν is not easy to assess. It may mean no more than *to send a written message*; so Heb. 13.22, where it appears that the content of the message is παράκλησις. Cf. Thucydides 8.50.2 (κρύφα ἐπιστείλας, having sent a secret message); also 8.38.3; 8.99.1. More frequently however the word conveys the further meaning of *send written instructions*; not simply a message or exhortation is conveyed but *orders* (usually in writing). 'From the usage of the word in official documents the meaning readily passed over into "instruct", "enjoin" ' (MM 245), and passages show that the instructions were normally communicated in writing. That in the present passage ἐπιστέλλειν points to a required course of action is made clear by the infinitive (τοῦ ἀπέχεσθαι) that follows. What cannot be certainly inferred is where the injunction stands on the scale between We write with the suggestion that you might consider abstaining ... and These are our written instructions: You shall abstain ... This question must be considered again when we reach (vv. 23–29) the letter that Luke ascribes to the Council. The impression however at this stage is that James (as represented by Luke) wishes to proceed *suaviter in modo, fortiter in re*. He wishes to make things as easy as possible for the Gentiles, but there are limits ... 'Not to make trouble for them but write to them that they should ...' retains the ambiguous feeling in English.

The content of the request, suggestion, or command is expressed by τοῦ with the infinitive. The τοῦ is pleonastic, but characteristic of Luke; cf. 3.12; (5.31); 10.25; 13.47; 21.12; 23.15, 20; 27.1. The middle ἀπέχεσθαι is used with the meaning *to abstain* from a thing or from a course of action at all stages in Greek literature; there is a good example in a second century AD inscription given in *ND* 1.21 (προστάσσουσι δὲ Δορατῇ τῷ νεωκόρῳ τούτων τῶν μυστηρίων ἀπέχεσθαι). In this inscription and in older Greek generally the verb is used without a preposition (as here, in P⁴⁵ ℵ B D 81 1175 *pc* e p*; ἀπό is supplied by P⁷⁴ A C E Ψ 𝔐 lat).

Four abstentions, described by nouns in the genitive case, are given in the text of NA[26]. These will be considered first before variant texts are discussed. A number of important Jewish parallels will be found in full in StrB 2.729–39.

(1) ἀλισγημάτων τῶν εἰδώλων. ἀλίσγημα is *hapax legomenon* in the Bible and very rare elsewhere. It is derived from ἀλισγεῖν, *to pollute, defile*. This verb occurs four times in the LXX. In Dan. 1.8 it is used in describing Daniel's determination not to allow himself to be defiled by the food and drink served at the table of the king of Babylon. This was food which for a variety of reasons a Jew would be unwilling to touch; it would not have been prepared in the ways required by the Law, it might well consist of the flesh of unclean animals, it was certain that tithe would not have been paid on it. It is not noted in the context that it might have been offered in sacrifice to a pagan god, or idol (and thus an εἰσωλόθυτον, cf. v. 29). In Mal. 1.7 the verb is used twice (three times in the MSS B ℵ* A) of the priests who have profaned (φαυλίζειν; בוזי שמי (1.6)) God's name; they have done this by offering on the altar ἄρτους ἠλισγημένους. The loaves are defiled because the priests defile the altar (τράπεζα κυρίου ἐξουδενωμένη ἐστίν; שלחן יהוה נבזה הוא) and the offering. At Mal. 1.12 the word is used of the altar itself. There is no suggestion that offerings have been made to other gods. Sirach 40.29 is difficult: A man who looks (with envy) on another man's table, his life is not to be reckoned life; he will defile his soul (ἀλισγήσει ψυχὴν αὐτοῦ) with another man's dainties. Again, the context is concerned with food, but not with idolatry; defilement arises because food is the cause of envy and is obtained only by begging (40.28: 'Son, do not live a life of begging; it is better to die than to beg'). That the eating of food sacrificed to idols was a source of defilement was of course a Jewish belief, which no doubt many Jewish Christians continued to hold.

εἰδώλων must be a subjective genitive; the idols cause defilement, but in the word ἀλισγήματα there is nothing that would restrict this defilement to that caused by the eating of food that had been sacrificed to the idols. This however is what ἀλισγήματα becomes in v. 29 and 21.25; it is a possible but not a necessary meaning of the word. Thus at *The Rest of the Words of Baruch* 7.32(37) Jeremiah ἔμεινε διδάσκων αὐτοὺς τοῦ ἀπέχεσθαι ἐκ τῶν ἀλισγημάτων τῶν ἐθνῶν τῆς Βαβυλῶνος. It seems possible that there was an original prohibition of idolatry which (under the influence of such tensions as are apparent in 1 Corinthians 8 and 10) developed into a specific prohibition of εἰδωλόθυτα. Idolatry is forbidden in the OT (e.g. Exod. 20.4, οὐ ποιήσεις σεαυτῷ εἴδωλον), and at Lev. 17.7 it is forbidden to offer sacrifice to idols (οὐ θύσουσιν ἔτι τὰς θυσίας αὐτῶν τοῖς ματαίοις; in view of what follows in Acts it is interesting that the verse continues, οἷς αὐτοὶ ἐκπορνεύουσιν ὀπίσω αὐτῶν).

(2) τῆς πορνείας (omitted by P⁴⁵; see below). The common meaning of the word is prostitution, fornication, uncleanness; this is borne out by the use of related and compound words, such as πόρνη, πόρνος, πορνοβοσκεῖν, πορνοκόπος and the like (see LS 1450). A prohibition of πορνεία in this sense is intelligible and appropriate. It is however to be noted that in 1 Cor. 5.1 Paul uses the word πορνεία to describe the act of one who has taken (ἔχειν) his father's wife. This Paul describes as an exceptionally gross case of sexual irregularity. It is expressly forbidden in Lev. 18.8 (ἀσχημοσύνην γυναικὸς πατρός σου οὐκ ἀποκαλύψεις), which occurs in a passage that deals with forbidden degrees of marriage (Lev. 18.6–18). This passage does not use the word πορνεία but it (together with some other regulations for sexual behaviour) is made to apply not only to the native Israelite but also to ὁ προσγενόμενος προσήλυτος ἐν ὑμῖν (Lev. 18.26, הגר הגר בתוככם). It is sometimes supposed (e.g. Schneider 2.183; Weiser 383) that we have here the proposed extension to Gentile Christians of the marriage laws that were (according to Leviticus) to be observed by aliens resident in Palestine. There is however no convincing reason for thinking that πορνεία was ever understood to refer simply to marriage within the forbidden degrees. In 1 Cor. 5.1 (see above) the word signifies a relation that was not adultery (assuming that the father was not alive) and not in the physical sense incest, if the woman was, as is usually supposed, the fornicator's stepmother.

(3) τοῦ πνικτοῦ (so P⁴⁵ ℵ C E 𝔐 lat sy; the omission of τοῦ, by P⁷⁴ A B Ψ 33 81 pc, is not important; for the omission of the whole by D gig Ir^lat see below), derived from the verb πνίγειν, to choke, strangle, suffocate, is, literally rendered, that which is strangled. H. J. Schoeps (Paulus 60) turns this into a more definite picture with 'Tieren, die auf der Jagd mit Schlingen gefangen und getötet worden sind.' It is however extremely difficult to find evidence in Jewish sources for the specific classification by this or any related word of food that must be rejected. The natural Hebrew and Aramaic equivalent is the root חנק; this does not however seem to be much used of animals, though there is an important passage in Philo, Spec. Leg. 4.122, where Philo attacks men of the type of Sardanapolus who desire novel kinds of pleasure and prepare meat unfit for the altar (ἄθυτα) by strangling and throttling (ἄγχοντες καὶ ἀποπνίγοντες) the animals. The use of the compound verb may perhaps be taken as an indication that the simple πνίγειν was sometimes used in the same way, but we lack direct evidence of this. Moreover, as the context in De Specialibus Legibus shows, and as would in any case be deduced from the picture of a snared and strangled animal, the objection to the use of such an animal as food lay in the fact that its blood had not been drained away. That is to say, if this is what πνικτόν means, along with αἷμα (as αἷμα is often understood; see below) it is superfluous.

According to StrB 2.730, πνικτόν includes both, 'sowohl was das AT נבלה als auch was es טרפה nennt'. These two Hebrew words are conveniently defined in terms of Josephus, *Ant.* 3.260 (κρέως τοῦ τεθνηκότος αὐτομάτως ζῴου τὴν βρῶσιν διεκώλυσεν) and of Exod. 22.30 (בשר בשדה טרפה לא תאכלו). This interpretation of πνικτόν has been widely accepted together with the further points involved in the claim (StrB 2.730–4) that in rabbinic use נבלה came to mean any beast that had not been subjected to the ritually correct slaughtering process (שחיטה), and טרפה a beast which, dead or alive, had a disqualifying blemish. The Greek word πνικτόν may have been regularly used and understood in this way, but evidence to prove this is lacking.

(4) τοῦ αἵματος. In the form of the text that we are at present considering this is usually understood in relation to the OT prohibition of the consumption of blood. This appears in the primeval commandment given to Noah (Gen. 9.4) and is repeated in later codes (Lev. 7.26, 27; 17.10–14; Deut. 12.16, 23). But, since loss of blood means loss of life, αἷμα came also to be used of *bloodshed*, in particular, of *murder*. This appears in general narrative and in idioms, such as ἐφ᾽ αἵματι φεύγειν, 'to avoid trial for *murder* by going into exile' (LS 38; Demosthenes 21.105; Dittenberger, *Syll.* 1.58.2). See also Sophocles, *Oedipus Tyrannus* 101; Euripides, *Orestes* 285. Since αἷμα can thus mean *bloodshed* it is equivalent to the rabbinic שפיכות דמים. It must therefore not be too readily assumed that avoidance of blood means avoidance of blood in food, especially since avoidance of πνικτόν (if this means meat improperly slaughtered) would include avoidance of blood, making the specific τοῦ αἵματος (in this sense) redundant.

The textual variations, which have the effect of producing a somewhat different 'draft Decree', will be considered shortly; it will be convenient first to consider several suggestions that have been made regarding the background and origin of James's proposals (and of the Decree as formulated in v. 29). These suggestions are not mutually exclusive.

(a) It may be that the terms of the Decree were thought of as practical considerations bearing on the situation as it could be seen to be arising out of the Christian mission to the Gentile world. The fundamental requirement of the Gentile convert was that he should abandon the religion that he had previously practised; that is, he must abandon the gods he had worshipped, turning his back on idolatry. He must abstain from the spiritual defilement that comes from idolatry. Verse 20 states this in absolute terms; v. 29 and 21.25 make the assumption that to eat εἰδωλόθυτα is to commit idolatry and is probably for most Gentile Christians the way in which they would be most likely to commit it. Jews had long known that the temptation to idolatry came most often through the butcher's shop and the brothel.

Hence what is in effect the command to use only Jewish butchers, where one could be confident that no εἰδωλόθυτα, πνικτά, or αἷμα would be sold, and the prohibition of πορνεία. It should be noted that such commands, especially the prohibition of idolatry, would be necessary for salvation, and not merely in order to facilitate fellowship between Jewish Christians and Gentile Christians.

(b) The requirements may have been based upon the so-called Noachian precepts, precepts which it was believed were incumbent not only upon Jews but upon all, of whatever race. In their earliest form (Jubilees 7.20) these are 'to observe righteousness, and to cover the shame of their flesh, and to bless their Creator, and honour father and mother, and love their neighbour, and guard their souls from fornication and uncleanness and all iniquity'. These were subsequently developed (evidence is given in full in StrB 3.37f.) into the prohibition of idolatry, blasphemy, murder, incest, stealing, perverting justice, and eating flesh containing blood. Of these the first, third, fourth, and seventh appear (more or less) in James's decree. The parallel is not close, and there is nothing in the text of Acts to call Noah to mind.

(c) A better, and today widely accepted, parallel is to be found in the regulations given in Leviticus 17 and 18 for Gentiles living among Jews. These are directed to 'Any man of the house of Israel, or of the strangers that sojourn among them (מן הגר אשר יגור בתוכם, Lev. 17.8)'. They require that sacrifices must be brought to the door of the tent of meeting (17.8f.); that blood must not be eaten (17.10–14); that what dies of itself or what is torn by beasts (נבלה וטרפה) must not be eaten (17.15f.); the forbidden degrees of marriage must be observed (18.6–30). These commands may be said to cover, in Acts, the prohibition of πορνεία (if that is understood to mean not fornication in the ordinary sense but forbidden family relationships), πνικτόν (if this is interpreted to mean נבלה and טרפה), and αἷμα (if this means blood as a food and not bloodshed). It cannot be said that the connection is close; see however Stählin (205) Schmithals (139); also Wilson (Law 85–102).

(d) A still better background, which fits readily with (a) above, is provided by a group of passages (p. Shebiith 35a. 49f.; p. Sanhedrin 21b. 10f.; b. Pesahim 25ab; b.Sanhedrin 74a) in which it is urged that, though in persecution a Jew was not expected to give his life on any minor issue, there were three matters on which compromise was impossible. These were עבודה זרה, idolatry; שפיכות דמים, the shedding of blood; and גילוי עריות, incest. Here are what Luke calls the defilements of idols, blood, and πορνεία (which includes incest). There is nothing to correspond with the prohibition of πνικτόν; it is hard to supply any motivation for the inclusion of this except the desire to make it easy for Jewish and Gentile Christians to eat together; such food, with εἰδωλόθυτα (readily understood—though not by Paul—as included in the ἀλισγήματα), would be objectionable to Jews and no doubt also to many Jewish Christians. See further Wilson (*Law* 68–102). Johnson (273) combines (c) and (d).

The important textual variants in the verse must now be noted.

(a) καὶ τῆς πορνείας is omitted by P⁴⁵ (not extant at 15.29; 21.25); also (though not noted in the apparatus of NA²⁶) by some Ethiopic MSS, and (we may infer) by Origen in *c. Celsum* 8.29, though here Origen is referring to the letter sent by the Council, that is, to v. 29. He speaks of the decision 'to write a letter to the Gentile believers, demanding that they should abstain only from what they called ''the essentials'' (μόνα (ὡς ὠνόμασαν) ἐπάναγκες). These are things sacrificed to idols, or things strangled, or blood' (Chadwick 472). Little can be built on this passage, for Origen is dealing with food (and might therefore omit πορνεία as irrelevant), and is writing with less than his usual care, for he says that the Council was held at Antioch. It is probably correct to regard the reading of P⁴⁵ not as one important witness to an otherwise unknown (Caesarean) text of Acts but as a simple error. See however G. Zuntz, *Opuscula Selecta* (1972), 227–9. It is unwise to use the omission as an argument for an original two-clause decree (P. H. Menoud, *SNTS Bulletin* 2 (1951), 22–8).

(b) καὶ τοῦ πνικτοῦ is omitted by D gig Ir^lat. The same omission is found in v. 29 and 21.25; there can be no doubt that it represents another form of the text of the Decree. The omission of an element that is purely ritual, with no ethical bearing whatever, undoubtedly alters the balance of the Decree and has often been held to affect the interpretation that must be given to the reference to *blood*. With πνικτοῦ, blood suggests a ritual food law; without it, it may more readily be understood as a reference to bloodshed, murder. This is however a double-edged argument. Knowling (325) thought that πνικτόν was omitted because it was thought to be covered by αἷμα, Clark (360) that it was added 'to make it clear that αἵματος referred to diet as in Leviticus xvii.14, not to homicide'.

(c) After αἵματος the Western text makes a substantial addition: καὶ ὅσα ἂν μὴ θέλωσιν (ὅσα μὴ θέλουσιν, D) αὐτοῖς (ἑαυτοῖς, D) γίνεσθαι ἑτέροις μὴ ποιεῖν (ποιεῖτε, D), D 323 945 1739 1891 *pc* sa Ir^lat. This addition of the negative form of the Golden Rule strongly reinforces the ethical effect of the omission (also by the Western text) of πνικτοῦ.

It has often been maintained that when the Old Uncial text and the Western text are compared we find on the one hand a set of essentially ritual requirements: abstinence from sacrificial food, from fornication (which could be understood to mean forbidden marriages or sacral prostitution), from non-kosher food, and from food containing blood; and on the other hand an ethical code, requiring the rejection of idolatry (which, put positively, means adherence to the exclusive worship of the one true God), avoidance of all unchaste

behaviour, avoidance of murder, and obedience to the fundamental
moral law, expressed in the Golden Rule. With very few exceptions,
textual critics have maintained that the ritual form must be primitive,
and have been transformed (by the omission of πνικτοῦ and the
addition of the Golden Rule) into an ethical code, perhaps in the
second century, certainly at a time when the older code was no longer
understood. There is enough force in this argument to make one
prefer the Old Uncial text as Luke's work. As often expressed,
however, it is an over-simplification. It can be shown (see *FS*
Osborn, 50–59; Taylor 210) not only that the Decree continued for
centuries to be observed (and often to be found to require explanation—or explaining away), but that it was interpreted in different
ways in different circumstances. Just as the circumstances that
evoked it had both ritual and ethical elements, so the Old Uncial
Decree had both ritual and ethical elements, especially in the form in
which James proposes it, which shows that the real concern in the
prohibition of ἀλισγήματα τῶν εἰδώλων (εἰδωλόθυτα) was the
avoidance of idolatry itself (and hence the cultivation of true
worship). πορνεία may have certain specific associations, but it
means fornication, and the Decree forbids the sin of fornication.
πνικτόν does refer to non-kosher food, and this is a non-ethical
element in the Decree, but since the consumption of blood is already
forbidden in the prohibition of πνικτόν it is by no means impossible
that blood means murder, violence. It is not surprising that those who
accepted the authority of this mixed Decree emphasized sometimes
one sometimes the other aspect of it. The Western editor(s) came
down strongly on the ethical side.

The Golden Rule, in its positive form, appears in Mt. 7.12; Lk.
6.31. In the Matthean form there is the appended note, For this is the
law and the prophets. It was already established in Judaism (though
mostly used in the negative form) as a summary of man's moral
obligation; see e.g. Tobit 4.15 (ὃ μισεῖς, μηδενὶ ποιήσῃς); b.
Shabbath 31a (Hillel: What is hateful (סני) to yourself, do not to your
neighbour); Philo, *Hypothetica* 7.6 (in Eusebius, *Praeparatio Evan-
gelica* 8.7.5, ἅ τις παθεῖν ἐχθαίρει, μὴ ποιεῖν αὐτόν). See further
Bousset, *RJ* 138; StrB 1.459f.

For the further history of the Decree see H. J. Schoeps, *Theologie
und Geschichte des Judenchristentums* (1949), 303; *Aus frühchris-
tlicher Zeit* (1950), 78. See further on v. 29 and 21.25; also above.

21. Moses (as not only the author of the Pentateuch but the founder
of the Jewish religion) has (ἔχει, described by Moule (*IB* 8) as a
'present of past action still in progress' and translated by him as
has had) from generations of old (this—cf. מדורות ראשונים, StrB
2. 739f.—goes further back than ἀφ᾽ ἡμερῶν ἀρχαίων in v. 7) in
every city (distributive use of κατά; cf. 2.46, and other passages)

those who proclaim him, τοὺς κηρύσσοντας αὐτόν. James thus uses a verb frequently used of the proclamation of the Christian Gospel, the proclamation of Christ (cf. 8.5; 9.20). That there were those who proclaimed Moses as a cult figure is certainly true; see 7.22 and the notes there and on I.338f. James however explains what he means in the participial clause that follows: Moses is proclaimed in that he is read (aloud) in the synagogues every Sabbath. For the synagogue service see on 13.15. Throughout the Empire, and beyond, wherever there were Jews the words of Moses were heard every week. Cf. Josephus, *Apion* 2.175, ἑκάστης ἑβδομάδος τῶν ἄλλων ἔργων ἀφεμένους ἐπὶ τὴν ἀκρόασιν ἐκέλευσε τοῦ νόμου συλλέγεσθαι καὶ τοῦτον ἀκριβῶς ἐκμανθάνειν; cf. 282. See Bousset (*RJ* 72, 172); Tcherikover (269–332). 'Jewish communities of greater or lesser extent and significance had settled in almost every part of the then civilized world' (*NS* 3.3; for details, 3–86). It may be that the use of κηρύσσειν implies (as it does with Christian preaching) some kind of authority; Moses is not merely read but asserted as an authority, so that what is read (including for example Leviticus 17 and 18) must be obeyed. This inference seems very doubtful.

The sentence begins with *for* (γάρ), and therefore presumably gives the ground for an earlier statement, but it is not clear which statement it supports. (1) It may look back to v. 19: It is not for us to trouble the Gentiles since Moses already has enough preachers to take his part. Gentiles, moreover, who want the Law can go to the synagogue for it (Williams 184). (2) It may look back to v. 20. It is necessary to lay some obligations on the Gentiles, since Moses has everywhere so many followers—so many observant Jews. (3) It may look back to vv. 15–18: We can see that Amos's prophecy is already being fulfilled in the large number of those who preach the Law. Dibelius (92) suggests that v. 21 may be a marginal gloss on the final words of the quotation. There is no serious basis for this suggestion, and as it stands v. 21 is too remote from the quotation for a reference to it to be likely. The general tone of James's speech is favourable to Gentiles and we may therefore accept (1), but the whole passage is so obscure that it may be that Luke intended both (1) and (2): It is not necessary to trouble the Gentiles seriously (by demanding circumcision) but it is necessary to trouble them a little (by the Decree). Alternatively, Luke may be placing traditional material in a new setting and thereby giving it a new meaning. He is no doubt responsible for James's speech as it now lies before us, but it is improbable that he simply invented it—the Decree itself is certainly traditional, though it was not (see p. 712) James's work. If the Decree is omitted the speech would impose no conditions upon Gentiles and connection (1) would then be virtually the only possibility, though it might be combined with Filson's observation, 'It seems clear from Acts 15.21 that [James] expected synagogue worship to go on in every city and that he also expected Jewish Christians to keep the Mosaic Law' (*Decades* 82). Perhaps somewhat less than clear; see the good discussion by Wilson (*Law* 83f.).

Calvin's comment (2.51f.) is worth quoting: 'He warns that it is not possible for the ceremonies to be abolished so quickly, as if at one fell swoop, because the Jews had already been accustomed to the teaching of the Law for many generations, and Moses had his preachers; that agreement therefore must be gained for a short time until the freedom, procured by Christ, should gradually be more clearly understood; in other words, as the common saying goes, that the ceremonies had to be buried with some decency.' In the early church there were those, notably Paul, who were quick to see the theological principle involved in every arrangement, but no doubt there were many more, who may or may not have included James but certainly included Luke, who were happy to proceed on (what seemed to be) common-sense lines.

22. *The apostles and elders* were those who had met to consider the question raised at Antioch (v. 6). Here they meet σὺν ὅλῃ τῇ ἐκκλησίᾳ, the whole body of Christians, that is, of the Jerusalem church; the church of Antioch had sent only a small delegation (15.2), and no other church seems to have been represented. The rank and file Christians have disappeared in the next verse (but see the note there on ἀδελφοί) and are given no share in the writing of the Council's letter. It goes too far to say, 'Clearly only the presence of the congregation gave legal validity to the resolution, although the members of the congregation did not take part in the discussion and did not vote in the decision' (B. Reicke, in Stendahl, *Scrolls* 146). The report of the discussion is extremely scanty and no vote is recorded. Luke is in any case not thinking in terms of legal validity; what was important was the claim (v. 28) that the Holy Spirit had directed the proceedings. For comparison of this 'democratic' element with the structure of the Qumran community see Braun 2.328f. The representation of monarchical, oligarchical, and democratic elements in the NT church needs, as Braun shows, qualification; categorization in such ready-made terms is dangerous.

The assembled company decided (ἔδοξε; the impersonal use of this verb, very common in 'official' Greek, appears in the NT at Lk. 1.3; Acts 15.22, 25, 28, 34; 25.27; Heb. 12.10—a Lucan characteristic) to write to the church at Antioch, sending the message by men whom they chose to accompany Paul and Barnabas. ἄνδρας is made precise by the appositional Ἰούδαν τὸν καλούμενον (cf. e.g. 1.23) Βαρσαββᾶν (the reading of D, Βαραββᾶν, is no more than an unfortunate slip of the pen) καὶ Σιλᾶν. The name Judas occurs several times in Acts, Judas Barsabbas (for this surname, used also of Joseph, see on 1.23) only in the present context, at vv. 22, 27, 32, and

34 (si v.l.). Nothing else is known of him. Silas becomes an important companion for Paul, in succession to Barnabas: see on vv. 22, 27, 32, 34, (si v.l.), 40; 16.19, 25, 29; 17.4, 10, 14, 15; 18.5. He is sometimes identified with the Silvanus (perhaps a latinized form of the Semitic שאילא) of the Pauline epistles (2 Cor. 1.19; 1 Thess. 1.1; 2 Thess. 1.1), also with the Silvanus of 1 Pet. 5.12, though he can hardly be invoked as responsible for the good Greek of that epistle; he was (according to the present verse) a leading member of the Jerusalem church, and there is no more ground for supposing him capable of stylish Greek than Peter himself. The identification with Paul's Silvanus is probable. For the opposite view, a distinction between two men both bearing the name Silas, the identification of one of them with Titus, the identification of Titus with Luke, and some other curiosities, see the article on Silas by P. W. Schmiedel, in *EBib* 4514–21.

For ἐκλεξαμένους, (P⁷⁴) 33 323 614 945 1739 *pc* (syᵖ) have ἐκλεξαμένοις, which agrees with the case of τοῖς ἀποστόλοις καὶ τοῖς πρεσβυτέροις. In such a sentence Greek usage is tolerant of either case; see Zerwick § 394; BDR § 410 n. 2.

ἡγούμενος (present participle of ἡγεῖσθαι) was on the way to becoming a noun; cf. 7.10; 14.12; and see LS 763, s.v. II 3, with many papyrus references; also MM 277. One may guess that Judas and Silas were among the πρεσβύτεροι.

23. γράψαντες is another false concord (cf. ἐκλεξαμένους in v. 22), perhaps better described as anacoluthon; so BDR § 468.2, n. 3, who point out that Luke continues as if he had written οἱ ἀπ. καὶ οἱ πρεσβ. ἐβουλεύσαντο ... πέμψαι ... γράψαντες, and draw attention to a close and interesting parallel in Thucydides 3.36.2 (ἔδοξεν αὐτοῖς ... ἀποκτεῖναι ... ἐπικαλοῦντες ...).

There is considerable textual confusion in the opening words of the verse. διὰ χειρὸς αὐτῶν may be (*Begs.* 4.179) a Semitism (בידם) but it is common in Acts and there is no special reason why the short and simple text of P⁴⁵ᵛⁱᵈ P⁷⁴ ℵ* A B *pc* bo (γράψαντες διὰ χειρὸς αὐτῶν) should have caused offence to copyists. But ℵᶜ E (33) 𝔐 syʰ add τάδε as an object for γράψαντες. (C) D gig w (syᵖ) (sa) have γρ. ἐπιστολὴν διὰ χ. αὐ. περιέχουσαν τάδε. 614 *pc* syʰᵐᵍ have γρ. διὰ χ. αὐ. ἐπιστολὴν καὶ πέμψαντες περιέχουσαν τάδε. Ψ has γρ. ἐπιστολὴν διὰ χ. αὐ. ἔχουσαν τὸν τύπον τοῦτον. It is easy to understand the addition of a simple object for γράψαντες, not easy to understand the elaboration and variety. There seems to be no better explanation than that copyists and editors recognized and wished to emphasize the central importance that the letter of vv. 23–29 has in Acts.

On the use and construction of περιέχειν see in addition to the lexica BDR § 308 n. 5.

The text of the letter follows. The whole ἐκκλησία of v. 22 now disappears and the letter is written in the name of *the apostles and elders*, though they (or at least the elders) are characterized as *brothers*. The brothers do appear as a *tiers état* in אᶜ ΕΨ 𝔐 sy boᵐˢˢ, which have καὶ οἱ ἀδελφοί. At the other extreme ἀδελφοί is omitted by *pc* vgᵐˢ sa Orˡᵃᵗ; but P⁷³ P⁷⁴ א* A B C D 33 81 *pc* lat Irˡᵃᵗ are to be followed with the simple ἀδελφοί (after πρεσβύτεροι): the elders if not the apostles are at the same time members of, brothers within, the local church, and it is as such that they address the members of the other churches—including Gentiles. Bruce (1.302) quotes Torrey to the effect that the opening words are faultless Aramaic idiom (שליחיא וקשישיא אחיא), and that *brothers* applies to both apostles and elders; if we may suppose that there was an Aramaic original this is a valid observation. Bultmann (*Exegetica* 416; so earlier Preuschen 96) thinks that the letter referred to its senders only as ἀδελφοί, (οἱ) ἀπ. καὶ πρεσβ. being a redactional addition by the author. He thinks further that the specific address, to Antioch, Syria, and Cilicia, points to the use of a written source. It is perhaps more probable (see pp. 710f., 741) that Luke wrote the whole paragraph apart from the Decree itself, notwithstanding 'some old features which suggest that it may be pre-Lukan' (Wilson, *Gentiles* 187). The place names indeed are a feature that may be original. Luke himself believed that the letter (or at least the Decree) was of wider relevance and circulation. Paul and Silas (16.4) delivered it more widely, and v. 19 suggests that it would apply to all areas where Jews lived in the Dispersion. Syria and Cilicia suggest more than the hinterland of Antioch, but the omission of Pisidia is inexplicable if it was intended to suggest the mission area of chs. 13 and 14. For Antioch see 11.19; 13.1; 14.28; for Cilicia see on 6.9. Syria, at this time a Roman province, was the large tract of land in northern Palestine. Till AD 72 eastern Cilicia was administered by Syria; Vespasian made all Cilicia a separate province (*CAH* 11.603). This however does not prove (Hemer 179) that Acts was written in the period of the double province. The two names are mentioned as if they referred to two distinct administrative areas. The use of one article (κατὰ τὴν Α. καὶ Σ. καὶ Κ.) groups them together but does not make a unit of them, or exclude reference to other areas.

For the recipients, the letter takes up the use of ἀδελφοί noted as Luke's in 15.1. They are ἐξ ἐθνῶν, but they are nevertheless brothers because they are Christians.

Χαίρειν, an infinitive standing as a kind of imperative (BDR § 389 n. 2), is a common (and not specifically Christian—Paul does not use it) greeting. As BDR show, this epistolary idiom is elliptic: (We wish you) to rejoice.

24. According to BDR § 464 n. 4, vv. 24–26 form the only true period in Acts. Does this mean that Luke found this piece of fine writing in his source and copied it out? or did he rate the importance of the Decree so highly that he thought it worth while to provide it with an ornate frame? The language of these verses suggests the latter alternative, but not strongly. ἐπειδή occurs twice in Lk. (also ἐπειδήπερ), 3 times in Acts, 5 times in Paul. δοκεῖν is used impersonally once in Lk., 4(5) times in Acts, not elsewhere in the NT. ἐκλέγεσθαι occurs 11 times in Lk-Acts, 15 times in the rest of the NT. ὁμοθυμαδόν occurs 10 times in Acts, once in Romans, nowhere else in the NT. ὑπὲρ τοῦ ὀνόματος is used 4 times in Acts, 3 times in the rest of the NT. Luke certainly regarded the Decree as a most important part of the tradition that he received; it is not unreasonable to suppose that he created a fitting setting (including, it may well be, not only the letter but the whole account of the Council) for it. On the other hand, one must ask in what sort of context the Decree itself might be handed down.

The present verse looks back to 15.1; the trouble-makers are emphatically disowned. They had no official backing: οἷς οὐ διεστειλάμεθα. Cf. Mk 7.36; 8.15; the verb means *to give instructions*. This is one of the points at which other NT evidence, and evidence within Acts itself, lead the reader to ask questions that Luke does not answer. If the circumcisers of 15.1, 5 had had no backing, would they have caused so much trouble and precipitated a high-level conference? If they had no backing at the time, had they later, in Galatia and Corinth? Who provided the commendatory letters of 2 Cor. 3.1? These are questions that must be kept in mind in any attempt to write the history of the first decades of Christianity. We must not forget the possibility that men genuinely commissioned may have gone beyond their brief. This is particularly suggested in 2 Corinthians (see *2 Corinthians* 31f.). And in διεστειλάμεθα we must distinguish between, 'We gave no charge at all', and 'We gave no charge to insist on circumcision'.

For ἐτάραξαν cf. Gal. 1.7; 5.10. ἀνασκευάζειν has a variety of meanings; see LS 120. A logician's destruction of his opponent's position is as good a parallel as any; the Antiochenes did not know where they were or what to believe. It is the opposite of κατασκευάζειν. Thus Aristotle, *Rhetoric* 2 24.4 (140lb), τὸ δεινώσει κατασκευάζειν ἢ ἀνασκευάζειν; Quintilian 2.4.18, opus destruendi confirmandique quod ἀνασκευή et κατασκευή vocatur.

The disturbers of Antiochene peace *went out from us*, ἐξ ἡμῶν ἐξελθόντες. It was the fact that they went *from us* that gave them, in the eyes of the Antiochenes, a disturbing authority. ἐξελθόντες is however omitted by ℵ B 1175 *pc*; it is read by P³³ P⁷⁴ A C D E Ψ 𝔐 latt sy (sa) bo It^lat. There is a strong case for omission, because though the MSS that omit are few they are old, and the short text is *lectio difficilior*, for it makes the disowned envoys 'some of us' (rather than 'some sent from us'). There is much to be said for omitting ἐξελθόντες. See Metzger (436).

25. The report of trouble in Antioch led to a decision in Jerusalem: ἔδοξεν ἡμῖν. The impersonal use of ἔδοξεν occurs twice in this letter (also v. 28). It is possible (see above) that Luke found the whole letter extant in this form and borrowed the expression for narrative use in v. 22; perhaps more likely that he himself elected to use it in all these sentences; it was frequently used to introduce decrees. 'Frequently of a public resolution ... especially in decrees and the like' (LS 242, s.v. II 4b, with many illustrations, including Thucydides 4.118.7, ἔδοξε τῷ δήμῳ (see the whole paragraph); Aristophanes, *Thesmophoriazusae* 372 (379), ἔδοξε τῇ βουλῇ). Cf. also Josephus, *Ant.* 16.163. Luke knows and uses the right word for his purpose, which is rather to utter a decree than to express an opinion.

ὁμοθυμαδόν is a Lucan word, often used by Luke (see on 1.14) with more than its usual meaning of unanimity, denoting also physical assembly; here it probably has both meanings. The apostles and elders met and reached a common mind. This means that, according to Luke, even the extremists agreed (Wilson, *Law* 107).

ἐκλεξαμένοις. In a similar sentence in v. 22 the accusative was used, though in each case there is textual variation. Here the dative is read by P[45vid] A B L Ψ 33 81 614 945 1175 1739 *pm*, the accusative by ℵ C D E H P 36 323 1241 2495 *pm*. See Metzger (437), who finds the textual question 'difficult to decide'; it looks as if he, against the majority of his committee, preferred the accusative. Barnabas and Paul (the order may be significant—Barnabas was an early Jerusalem disciple; cf. v. 12) are τοῖς ἀγαπητοῖς B. καὶ Π. ... It is stressed that there is no division between the Jerusalem apostles and the Antiochene missionaries. The reading of D (ὑμῶν, for ἡμῶν) might suggest a different attitude ('Dear to you, not necessarily so to us'), but is probably a simple error. The two pronouns were identical in pronunciation and were often confused. On the relation between Paul and the Jerusalem church see Introduction, pp. xxxix–xli, et al.

26. Further description of Barnabas and Paul follows. They are ἀνθρώποις παραδεδωκόσι τὰς ψυχὰς αὐτῶν. At first glance this might be taken to mean, Men who have given their lives, but this is obviously not the sense intended. Accordingly the suggestion has been made that the meaning is, Men who have hazarded their lives; so LS 1308, but with no other example of this meaning, which is rightly judged by *Begs.* 4.180 to be 'indefensible'. The phrase must mean, They have devoted their lives (so apparently BA 1242, 'Menschen, die ihr Leben für den Namen des Herrn hingegeben haben'); and this, though followed in Greek by ὑπέρ, must in English be followed by, *to the name of our Lord Jesus Christ*. Barnabas and Paul are Christians of unreserved devotion. τὰς ψυχὰς αὐτῶν is used as a reflexive. Cf. Thucydides 5.16.3, τύχῃ αὐτὸν παραδίδωσι, trust oneself to fortune. StrB (2.740) seem to take the expression to mean 'give one's life for', since they equate it with נתן נפשו על, but Mekhilta Exod. 20.6 (75b) which they quote seems rather to mean 'devote': נותנים נפשם על מצות.

At the end of the verse D E 614 *pc* 1 sy^hmg add εἰς πάντα πειρασμόν. This probably reflects the view that the text as it stood implied, They have handed over their lives to death, which needed correction to, They have handed over their lives to every (kind of) trial. Cf. Sirach 2.1.

27. οὖν connects with v. 25: Since it was decided to send men with Barnabas and Paul we have therefore now sent ... The perfect ἀπεστάλκαμεν implies that Judas and Silas (see v. 22) are now on their way, presumably bearing the letter. They are however not merely bearers but will confirm its contents (τὰ αὐτά, the same things that the letter contains, especially the disavowing of the trouble-makers). Haenchen (436) comments: 'Der Leser weiss ja schon, was das Dekret enthalten wird, die Briefempfänger aber noch nicht. Man sieht, dass die Briefkomposition auf Lukas zurückgeht.' The conclusion is probably correct (see above) but it is difficult to follow the logic by which Haenchen reaches it. The hearers will take in the letter as a whole and find that the hearers say the same things.

The construction of the second part of the sentence is obscure. διὰ λόγου, standing in contrast with an implied δι' ἐπιστολῆς, is clear enough; λόγος, though it means much more, can on occasion refer to speech uttered aloud. But καὶ αὐτοὺς ... ἀπαγγέλλοντας is strange Greek, even when taken from the same standpoint as the perfect ἀπεστάλκαμεν. BDR § 339.2a, n. 8 note that the present participle is sometimes used instead of the final future participle, and cite in addition to this verse not only 21.16 (συνῆλθον ... ἄγοντες) but also Thucydides 7.25.7, ἔπεμψαν ... πρέσβεις οἱ Συρακόσιοι ... ἀγγέλλοντας ..., they sent ambassadors to report ... See also Euripides, *Suppliants* 154, ταῦτ' ἐκδικάζων ἦλθον. This use of the present participle is rare, and the sense of purpose seems usually to be more or less qualified, but it may be taken to cover Luke's ἀπαγγέλλοντας. More difficult is καὶ αὐτούς. This is reminiscent of nothing in Greek so much as of the Hebrew circumstantial clause, which can be introduced in this way, the clause being completed often by a participle; see e.g. Gen. 18.8; 24.62. BDR § 442.4b, n. 12 (noting the Vg *qui*) rightly say that καί may be taken in the sense of a relative, but this does not amount to an explanation. We have seen reason to think that the letter Luke gives here is, apart from the Decree, his own composition; otherwise it would be attractive to think that he had retained a trace of the Hebrew in which such a letter would originally have been composed. If not this, we may think that

Luke heard of the letter in a partly Hebrew-speaking environment. If original at all it must have come from such an environment.

28. ἔδοξεν: cf. vv. 22, 25. The apostles and elders are now joined in their decision by the Holy Spirit. In view of the importance of the decision this must be regarded as the outstanding example of Luke's insistence that all developments in the church's life were directed by the Spirit. For participation in a decision by a divine being cf. Dio Chrysostom 80(30).8, ἔδοξε τῷ θεῷ; Appian, *Syria* 58.303, ἐδόκει τοῖς θεοῖς. It is not suggested that a decision made by the church must be a decision of the Holy Spirit; the unanimity of the church bore witness to a decision already reached by the Holy Spirit. Luke does not claim that any of the participants in the discussion was, when he spoke, moved, or filled, by the Holy Spirit. Whether the claim that the Holy Spirit on this occasion spoke through the church is affected by the fact that Paul (it seems) did not accept the decision is a question that should be borne in mind with regard to such ecclesiastical assertions.

It was not decided that no requirements should be laid upon Gentile Christians, only that such requirements should be limited. Certain demands were to be made, but nothing more, μηδὲν πλέον. 'Att. πλέον nur Lk. 3.13; Jn 21.15; Act 15.28 gegenüber 18mal πλεῖον, aber immer πλείων, πλείονος' (BDR § 30.2, n. 3). The word βάρος (a natural one to use; cf. Polybius 1.315, τὸ βάρος τῶν ἐπιταγμάτων, but note ζυγός in v. 10) occurs in a similar clause at Rev. 2.24, οὐ βάλλω (cf. ἐπιτίθεσθαι) ἐφ᾽ ὑμᾶς ἄλλο βάρος. The same letter (to Thyatira) condemns the false prophetess Jezebel, who teaches the Christians πορνεῦσαι καὶ φαγεῖν εἰδωλόθυτα: similarly 2.14. Nothing is said about blood and non-kosher food, but it seems likely that the Decree, or something like it, circulated in these churches and was approved by them, or at least by leading members in them. This is a matter on which commentators on Revelation do not agree. R. H. Charles (1.74) thinks that the prohibition of non-kosher food and blood was deliberately omitted. 'The use of the word ἄλλο in itself points to the exclusion of the two latter. Thus our author had clearly the Apostolic decree in his mind.' On the other hand, Lohmeyer (*HNT, Apokalypse* 29) writes, 'Die formale Uebereinstimmung mit Act 15.29 ... beweist nicht, dass hier auch inhaltlich an das Aposteldekret zu denken sei.' It is interesting to note F. J. A. Hort (31), on βάρος: 'A curious coincidence with Acts 15.28, but probably accidental'; and H. B. Swete (45), 'A scarcely doubtful reference to the Apostolic decree in Acts 15.28 ... the rest of the prohibitions imposed in the years 49–50 ... are not reimposed'. This allusion to the Decree, if such it be, is probably the earliest, antedating the post-biblical references given in *FS* Osborn 55–9.

πλήν is used as an improper preposition, taking the genitive; cf. 8.1; 27.22, *except*.

The exception is denoted by τούτων τῶν ἐπάναγκες. The meaning is clear; the words mean *these necessary (requirements)* and refer to the four abstinences called for in the next verse. But the expression is unusual: the demonstrative pronoun and article, followed by the adverb (the neuter singular of the adjective ἐπανάγκης forming the corresponding adverb). According to Haenchen (436), this is 'ganz ungewöhnlich'; similarly *Begs.* 4.180: the reading 'can hardly be right. ἐπάναγκες is used in Attic Greek as an adverb ... but not with the article'. These statements call for some qualification. It is quite possible in Greek to use an article with an adverb, but this construction seems to be mainly if not exclusively confined to adverbs of time and place; e.g. οἱ τότε, *those who lived at that time*; οἱ ἔξω, *those who are outside*; τὰ κάτω, τὰ ἄνω, *things below, things above*. The possibility of extending this use of article and adverb must always have existed even if it was seldom taken up. Its unnaturalness in the case of ἐπάναγκες is attested not only by modern attempts at explanation and conjecture but also by ancient variants in the text. It is uncertain whether ἐπ᾽ ἀνάγκαις (ℵ A C) is a genuine variant; αι is a not uncommon itacistic equivalent to ε. If it is intended as ἐπί with the dative plural of ἀνάγκη it will mean *these matters which arise out of necessities*. τῶν ἐπάναγκες τούτων (P³³ᵛⁱᵈ e 𝔐) scarcely differs from the text cited above (though Metzger (437) describes it as 'the easier sequence'). If τούτων ἐπάναγκες (omitting τῶν) is read the way is open to repunctuation, with a colon or full stop after τούτων: '... no other burden than these things: it is necessary to abstain from ...'. There is support for this (see *Begs.* 4.180f.) in Clement of Alexandria, *Stromateis* 4.15, where indirect speech is used: ἐμήνυσαν γὰρ ἐπάναγκες ἀπέχεσθαι δεῖν εἰδωλο– θύτων, κτλ. 'Moreover the *Didascalia* seems here to have felt that somehow it ought to read πλὴν τούτων· τὸ ἐπάναγκες ἀπέχεσθαι ...'. The reading τῶν ἐπάναγκες ((P⁷⁴) A 36 453 1241 *pc*) Metzger ascribes to accidental omission of τούτων.

It is probably best to accept the reading of ℵ² B C Ψ 81 614 945 1175 1739 2495 *al* (τούτων τῶν ἐπ.) and the unusual construction that it involves. But however the text is taken and construed it includes the notion of necessity, compulsion (see LS 607; cf. e.g. Josephus, *Ant.* 16.365; Epictetus 2.20.1; and see Wilson, *Law* 82). It is not said, You Gentiles are completely free of legal requirements, but as a matter of courtesy to your Jewish brothers you might be so kind as to abstain from ... This is important for the understanding of the Decree; Luke at any rate understood it as a matter not of courtesy but of compulsion, and therefore presumably as a condition of salvation (cf. 15.1, 5).

Bauernfeind (198) thinks that abstention from πνικτόν and αἷμα will have been a real burden to Gentiles, yet one that Luke will have regarded as compatible with the law-free Gospel.

29. This verse repeats what is given in v. 20 as James's opinion with the following variations: (1) instead of ἀλισγήματα τῶν εἰδώλων we have εἰδωλόθυτα; (2) the order is idolatry, blood, things strangled, fornication, instead of idolatry, fornication, what is strangled, blood; (3) the plural πνικτῶν is used instead of the singular πνικτοῦ; (4) there is a concluding exhortation. There are textual variants similar to those noted in v. 20; see once more Metzger (429–34). This time fornication is omitted only by some Vulgate MSS.

40. PAUL AND BARNABAS RETURN TO ANTIOCH 15.30–35

(30)So they, when they had been dismissed, went down to Antioch, and when they had gathered the company together they delivered the letter. (31) When they had read it they rejoiced at the comfort[1] that it brought. (32) Judas and Silas, who also were prophets, speaking at length, encouraged[2] and strengthened the brothers. (33) After spending some time [in Antioch] they were released[3] by the brothers in peace [to return] to those who had sent them. (35) But Paul and Barnabas stayed on in Antioch, teaching and preaching[4] the word of the Lord along with many others.

Bibliography

E. Delebecque, *RHPhR* 64 (1984), 47–52.

T. Holtz, as in (38).

B. N. Kaye, *NovT* 21 (1979), 13–26.

E. Richard, as in (38).

Commentary

This short paragraph is the necessary complement to the preceding one. The results of the Council had to be communicated to the church in which the problem arose, and its letter delivered. Nothing is said here that could not have been inferred from the letter of 15.23–29 except that Judas and Silas were prophets. Luke may have been dependent on information derived from Antioch, but he is probably rounding off in his own words the important story of the Council and preparing for Paul's change of partners; Silas is introduced as one who is acceptable both to Jerusalem and to Paul.

30. Luke develops his story into a new phase with μὲν οὖν; see on 1.6. *They* (the group mentioned in 15.23) *then having been dismissed*; the sense makes 'those who had been dismissed' impossible. D* (1) add ἐν ἡμέραις ὀλίγαις; it is hard to see what the Western editors gained by inserting these words, or what would have been gained by omitting them if they were original; nor is it clear whether

---

[1]RSV, exhortation; NEB, NJB encouragement.
[2]RSV, exhorted.
[3]NEB, with the good wishes of the brethren.
[4]NJB, proclaimed the good news, the word of the Lord.

they refer to time spent before departure or to time taken on the journey. The point may have been that the messengers did not delay on the journey, not even stopping to preach in the towns through which they passed. The general effect is to speed up the narrative. κατῆλθον: they went down from the (Jewish) capital; cf. ἀναβαίνειν in 15.2, with the note on the customary use of verbs of going up and going down. They came to Antioch whence they, or some of them, had been sent to represent the Antiochene point of view. For the city of Antioch see on 11.19.

They gathered together the πλῆθος, here without doubt (cf. 15.12) the whole company of Christians in Antioch. Nothing is said of any elders in Antioch; contrast Jerusalem (15.6). In 13.1–3 elders are not mentioned; in the present paragraph there is no reference to prophets and teachers (though local prophets may be implied in v. 32). They delivered (ἐπέδωκαν) the letter—the task with which they had been entrusted. ἐπιδιδόναι is frequently used for handing over a letter or other document; see MM 238, BA 252 (with references including Josephus, *Ant.* 15.170, ἐπιδίδωσιν Ἡρώδῃ τὴν ἐπιστολήν, as well as papyri). ἀναδιδόναι was also used for the purpose: 23.33. It had also been expected that the messengers would supplement the letter with oral communication (15.27); see v. 32.

31. The subject of ἐχάρησαν is evidently the Antiochenes, and it is to them also that the participle ἀναγνόντες will apply. It must however be understood to mean that one or more of them read the letter aloud in the hearing of the rest. All rejoiced; that is to say, they felt that they had got what they wanted. παράκλησις has a variety of meanings; it may be exhortation or encouragement (cf. 13.15); here however (as the cause of rejoicing) it probably means *comfort*; they were relieved that the leading Jewish Christians in Jerusalem had not insisted that they should be circumcised. Cf. however the use of the verb παρακαλεῖν in v. 32.

Had they got what they wanted? Had their objection to the demands of the Judaizers (15.1, 5) been simply to the offensive and painful rite of circumcision, with food laws an insignificant factor? Or had they objected to the principle of legal requirements (however slight and pointless) as a condition of their being accepted as Christians, a condition of salvation? Or are 15.1, 5 misleading statements, the real point at issue being not, On what terms may Gentiles be saved? but, On what conditions may Gentile Christians eat with Jewish Christians? Or again, are these historical questions improperly asked? Can we ask more than, How did Luke view the Decree? Here we can answer plainly: he regarded it as a παράκλησις, no doubt in comparison with a demand for circumcision and full observance of the Law. It must be remembered that (according to Luke) Paul was one of the party who conveyed and presumably commended the letter. Luke is claiming that Gentile Christianity is free from the Law and that the unity of the church had been preserved. His view of the matter is certainly the first question into which we must inquire, but since Luke chooses to write as a historian we are free to ask further questions, and are bound to observe the evidence of the Pauline epistles that there were those who did not consider that Gentile Christians were free from the Law, and that the unity of the church was at least gravely imperilled.

32. Judas and Silas (see 15.22) joined in the operation, καὶ αὐτοὶ προφῆται ὄντες; this is another circumstantial clause (cf. 15.27), commented on by Black (*AA* 83). For prophets in Jerusalem see 11.27. καί (if not simply the relic of a Semitic circumstantial clause) must mean *also*; in addition to Paul and Barnabas (who are not usually described as prophets) or in addition to the native Antiochene prophets? D adds πλήρεις πνεύματος ἁγίου (of course, for prophecy is a gift of the Spirit—D underlines a theme already present in Acts) and omits πολλοῦ (with λόγου). This may be no more than a case of *homoeoteleuton*, or D may be affected by 15.27 and wish to bring out the fact of oral addition to the written letter. But Blass 172 rightly observes 'Sed manente quoque πολλοῦ id fieri potest.' διά is of attendant circumstances (Moule, *IB* 57). The speaking is described by the word παρεκάλεσαν. In v. 31 the cognate noun παράκλησις appeared to mean comfort; here *exhorted*, or perhaps *encouraged*, seems a more natural meaning.

They exhorted *the brothers*; for ἀδελφοί as a word for Christians see 1.15; again, as in v. 30, there is nothing to suggest a hierarchy of ruling members in the church. ἐπιστηρίζειν is used again at 15.41; cf. 14.22. The metaphorical use of the verb requires no explanation.

33. For ποιεῖν χρόνον cf. 18.23; 20.3; also Prov. 13.23 (ποιήσουσιν ... ἔτη πολλά). The use is classical (Demosthenes 19.163 (392); Plato, *Philebus* 50d; and cf. the Latin *facere*, Cicero, *Ad Atticum* 5.20 (79)). Hebrew עשה is used similarly (Jastrow 1125). ποιήσαντες χρόνον here means nothing more definite than that the envoys did not simply deliver the letter and return immediately. How long they stayed before the Antiochene Christians *let them go* (ἀπελύθησαν) on their return journey cannot be determined. They left μετ᾽ εἰρήνης; not only on good terms with their hosts but in a general situation of Christian well-being; cf. 9.31. The Christians in Antioch are still, as in v. 32, *brothers*. The messengers returned to those who had sent them, the apostles and elders of 15.22. Solidarity with Jerusalem is affirmed (Davies, *Land* 276).

If this verse is read on its own it suggests that both Judas and Silas, perhaps Paul and Barnabas too, returned at this point to Jerusalem. This is clearly not Luke's intention; in v. 35 he declares that Paul and Barnabas stayed on in Antioch and v. 40 suggests without quite

proving that Silas stayed on too. This means either that the plural in
the present verse is a mistake, or that others, unnamed in 15.22,
accompanied the four who are named. See on v. 34.

Metzger (439) notes a variant not mentioned in NA²⁶. Instead of
πρὸς τοὺς ἀποστείλαντας αὐτούς (P⁷⁴ ℵ A B C D vg sa bo *al*), H L
P S many minuscules syᵖ ʰ bo arm eth Bede have πρὸς τοὺς
ἀποστόλους, '... to bring the apostolate into greater prominence'. It
is just as likely to be a corruption of αποστειλαντασαυτους The
divided witness of the Bohairic version will be observed.

34. This verse is not in the text of NA²⁶; it is omitted by P⁷⁴ℵ A B
E Ψ 𝔐 vgˢᵗ bo. It is probably a Western 'improvement' designed to
explain the presence of Silas in 15.40 after v. 33 had suggested his
departure from Antioch to Jerusalem. It occurs in several forms with
minor differences. All begin ἔδοξε δὲ τῷ Σίλα (or Σιλέα) ἐπιμεῖναι
(so C D 33 36 323 453 614 (945) 1175 1739 1891 *al* gig l w vgᶜˡ
syʰ** sa boᵐˢˢ). Next C has αὐτοῦ (it seemed good to Silas to stay
there; cf. 18.19). Dᶜ gig l w vgᶜˡ have πρὸς αὐτούς, to stay *with them*.
D* has αὐτούς (it seemed good to Silas that *they should stay*—
unless αὐτούς is a mistake for αὐτοῦ (*Begs*. 4.182)). After this D gig
l w vgᶜˡ have μόνος δὲ Ἰούδας ἐπορεύθη, and w vgᶜˡ add further
hierosolyma.

The language of the verse is Lucan. ἔδοξε has been used three
times in the immediate context (15.22, 25, 28; cf. Lk. 1.3); ἐπιμένειν
is a Lucan word (6 times, not counting this verse; 10 times in the rest
of the NT).

35. Paul and Barnabas did stay (διατρίβειν is another Lucan word:
8 times in Acts; twice (but once with the variant μένειν) in Jn;
nowhere else in the NT) in Antioch, joining *with many others*—
unnamed; we think of the prophets and teachers of 13.1, and of those
who first spoke the word in Antioch, 11.19—in *teaching and
preaching* (preaching as good news, εὐαγγελιζόμενοι) *the word of
the Lord*. For teaching the word of the Lord see 18.11; for preaching
the word of the Lord see 8.4; for the word of the Lord see e.g. 8.25;
15.36.

XI

PAUL'S MISSION BREAKS NEW GROUND
(15.36–18.23)

41. TERRITORY OF THE FIRST JOURNEY REVISITED
15.36–16.5

(36) After some days, Paul said to Barnabas, 'Let us return[1] and visit the brothers from city to city, every one of them, in which we proclaimed the word of the Lord, to see how they are faring.' (37) Barnabas wished[2] to take with them also John, called Mark; (38) Paul however took the view that they should not take with them this man who had parted from[3] them in Pamphylia and failed to accompany them to the work. (39) There arose a sharp disagreement so that they separated from each other, and Barnabas took Mark and sailed away to Cyprus, (40) while Paul chose Silas and went off, committed by the brothers to the[4] Lord's grace. (41) He passed through Syria and Cilicia, strengthening the churches.

(1) He now reached Derbe and Lystra; and there was a certain disciple there whose name was Timothy, the son of a Jewish woman who was a believer and of a father who was a Greek.[5] (2) This disciple had a good reputation with the brothers in Lystra and Iconium. (3) Paul wished him to go with him, and took and circumcised him on account of the Jews who were in those parts, for they all knew that his father had been[6] a Greek.[7] (4) As they passed through the cities they delivered to the believers[8] for their observance the decrees that had been decided by the apostles and elders who were in Jerusalem. (5) So the churches were confirmed in faith and increased in number daily.

Bibliography

T. Baarda, *NovT* 34 (1992), 250–56.

P. Borgen, *Paul Preaches Circumcision* (1983), 33–7 (= *FS* Barrett, 37–46).

[1]NEB, Ought we not to go back now.
[2]NJB, suggested taking John Mark.
[3]NEG, NJB; deserted.
[4]NJB, grace of God.
[5]NEB, Gentile.
[6]NEB, was.
[7]NEB, Gentile.
[8]Greek, them, but the word cannot refer to cities.

C. Bryan, *JBL* 107 (1988), 292–4.

S. J. D. Cohen, *JBL* 105 (1986), 251–68.

D. Daube, *Ancient Jewish Law* (1981), 22–32.

E. Delebecque, as in (40).

R. M. Grant, *VigCh* 46 (1992), 105–111.

B. N. Kaye, as in (40).

G. D. Kilpatrick, *JTS* 41 (1990), 98.

Y. Tissot, as in (39).

A. Wainwright, *JSNT* 8 (1980), 66–70.

W. O. Walker, *ExpT* 92 (1981), 231–5.

Commentary

Paul proposes to Barnabas that they should revisit the Christian brothers in all the cities in which they had preached in the journey described in chs. 13 and 14. According to 14.23 elders had been appointed in every church; that is, there were organized Christian communities, brought into being by the initiative of the church in Antioch. It was an elementary Christian duty to make sure of their well-being. Barnabas agreed, but wished to take with them John Mark, who had accompanied them on the earlier journey. Paul disagreed, on the ground that John Mark was not a man to be trusted. The disagreement led to sharp dissension and separation; Barnabas and Mark sailed to Cyprus, Paul chose Silas as his colleague and went off by land through Syria and Cilicia.

Approaching the old mission field in reverse order Paul and Silas came to Derbe and Lystra, where they encountered Timothy, whom Paul wished to add to his team. Since Timothy was of mixed parentage and uncircumcised, Paul, because of the local Jews who knew that Timothy's father was a Greek (that is, a non-Jew), circumcised him. The journey continued, the decrees of the Council were disseminated, and the churches flourished.

The outline of the passage is thus straightforward, but it raises a number of problems, which are stated and discussed in the notes. The sensible intention of revisiting the churches of the first journey is speedily given up; at 16.6 the party is breaking new ground. That Paul and Barnabas should disagree about the wisdom of taking Mark with them is understandable, but in Gal. 2.13 a different ground of dispute is given. That this has no place in Acts must be taken with the fact that Acts provides no hint of the message from James that split the church at Antioch. Was Luke aware of this? Did he deliberately omit it and find himself obliged to produce a different reason for the separation of Barnabas from Paul? The question of the authorship of Acts is thus raised in acute form. It is of course possible for two men to be in dispute on more issues than one; and these two issues may have been related to each other. Why did Mark turn back on the first journey? One possible answer is that the mission was turning increasingly to the Gentiles, and he disapproved; he may have carried Barnabas with him to the extent that in Antioch Barnabas sided with Peter rather than with Paul. This however does not alter the fact that serious questions of authorship are raised not only by Luke's account of the Council itself but also by his story of the subsequent events.

A second serious problem arises in 16.1–3. The Council had decided that it was not necessary for Gentile converts to Christianity to be circumcised. It was a notable victory for Paul's opinion. Very shortly afterwards Paul, who had (according to Gal. 2.3) vigorously resisted the attempt to have Titus circumcised, himself circumcised Timothy. It is just credible that Paul did this, but only just. He might have reasoned: As he is, Timothy is neither Jew nor Gentile; we cannot undo the Jewishness of his mother; we can give him the circumcision that his Gentile father would not permit. Thus all ambiguity is resolved. This is possible; not probable. The same may be said of other suggestions; see below. If it is rejected, if Luke has given us at best a partial account of Paul's break with Barnabas and an incorrect account of his dealings with Timothy, the traditional authorship of Acts by one of Paul's circle is called in question, and the best we can say of this paragraph is that Luke was dependent on popular stories, which he did not, perhaps could not, check with Paul, with Barnabas, with Timothy, or with the church in Antioch.

36. The process of teaching and evangelizing (15.35) lasted some time—τινὰς ἡμέρας; Luke does not know how long but means to suggest a serious operation. Paul now takes the lead (εἶπεν πρὸς Βαρναβᾶν) with a new suggestion: he proposes that they should revisit the areas in which they had preached in chs. 13 and 14. There are ἀδελφοί there; the word is used of Christians at 14.2 (not 13.15, 26, 28), frequently elsewhere in Acts. It will be a good thing to see how they are faring, πῶς ἔχουσιν; for ἔχειν with an adverb (here interrogative) see on 7.1. Nowhere else in the NT does ἐπισκέπτεσθαι, introduce an indirect question, but the word means *visit* in the sense of *review*, and the question follows naturally, though an extra word is needed in English (*to see how . . .*). Haenchen (456) suggests that ἐπισκεψώμεθα will have made Luke's readers think of the word ἐπίσκοπος (20.28); it is doubtful whether the elders (equivalent to bishops in ch. 20) engaged in wide-ranging visitations.

κατά is used distributively (cf. 15.21); πᾶσαν must be emphatic— *from city to city, every one of them.* Paul proposes a comprehensive visitation of every city *in which* (ἐν αἷς, the plural understood *ad sensum,* BDR 296.1, n. 1; D has ἐν οἷς, which must refer to τοὺς

ἀδελφούς, *among whom*) *we proclaimed* (κατηγγείλαμεν: 11 times
in Acts, 7 times in the rest of the NT) *the word of the Lord* (see
15.35).

δή adds some emphasis: *Come, let us return . . .* (*Begs.* 4.183)

There is obvious contact with 14.28 but this does not in itself mean
that the intervening material is simply an episodic addition. From the
literary point of view it may well be so, but it is possible to think of
the second visit as taking place in the light of the Council, and
therefore on a firmer, more established footing than the earlier, more
or less experimental mission. This at least will have been Luke's
view.

There is a sense in which Roloff (236) is right in the view that this
paragraph, with Galatians 2, marks the end of Paul's close association with Antioch. It is probable that there was a change in Paul's
association with Antioch, but the present paragraph does nothing to
suggest it; what it suggests is an effort to maintain contact between
Antioch and the daughter churches.

37. Βαρναβᾶς δὲ ἐβούλετο. Turner (*Insights* 95) stresses the
imperfect tense, which he would translate 'had half a mind to'. But a
half-hearted suggestion of this kind could not have given rise to the
παροξυσμός and separation of v. 39. Rather more convincing, but
still to be accepted only with caution, is the distinction between the
aorist infinitive συμπαραλαβεῖν here (but P⁷⁴ A 1175 *pc* have the
present, συμπαραλαμβάνειν) and the present in v. 38. So M. 1.130:
'Barnabas, with easy forgetfulness of risk, wishes συμπαραλαβεῖν
Mark—Paul refuses συμπαραλαμβάνειν, to have with them day by
day one who had shown himself unreliable.' Zerwick (§ 249) agrees,
referring to Moulton. M. 3.79 looks at the matter in a similar light:
'All Paul may have objected to was παραλαμβάνειν (Mark's being
with them throughout the journey).' This, like Turner's other attempt
to minimize the conflict between Paul and Barnabas, is unconvincing; there is in the story no hint that there might have been an
arrangement by which Mark would turn back half-way round.

καὶ τόν (ℵ B 81 614 *pc*) is probably correct. P⁷⁴ A C E Ψ 36 945
1175 1241 2495 *pm* have only καί; L 424 have only τόν; D 323 1739
1891 *al* 1 omit both words. But καί is natural—Not only me, *John
too*; τόν is anaphoric and is needed to point back to the earlier
references to John.

John is referred to incidentally in 12.12 to identify his mother. He
appears in the company of Barnabas (to whom according to Col. 4.10
he was related) and Paul at 12.25, and again, on the 'First Missionary
Journey', at 13.5. From Perge, however, he returned (not to Antioch
but) to Jerusalem, leaving the two senior partners to continue the
mission without him. See the notes on 13.13; 15.38; see also Col.
4.10; 2 Tim. 4.11; Philemon 24.

38. For John Mark's defection on the earlier journey, and for Pamphylia, see on 13.13.

ἀξιοῦν in the sense of 'to count something, especially a course of action, right' is in the NT peculiar to Acts (15.38; 28.22; contrast Lk. 7.7), but the usage is classical (LS s.v. III 2, p. 172). M. 3.65 thinks that the imperfect tense 'may mean that Paul's suggestion about Mark was only tentative at first'; contrast BA 156, 'er bestand darauf (Ipf), diesen nicht mitzunehmen'. The latter seems the more probable view; there is no hint in the narrative of a progressive hardening of opinion.

ἀποστάντα suggests (as ἀποχωρήσας in 13.13. does not) the blameworthiness of Mark's departure (cf. e.g. Xenophon, *Anabasis* 2.5.7, εἰς ἐχυρὸν χωρίον ἀποσταίη, to withdraw from battle), and this is borne out by the following words: John Mark failed to accompany Paul and Barnabas εἰς τὸ ἔργον, that is, the work of evangelizing the interior of Asia Minor. This showed that he was not to be trusted, and Paul accordingly thought it right μὴ συμπαραλαμβάνειν (cf. v. 37) τοῦτον, the pronoun taking up τὸν ἀποστάντα ... καὶ μὴ συνελθόντα. The pronoun is unnecessary, and was omitted by P⁴⁵ gig vgᶜˡ.

D rewrites the verse without making any significant change: Π. δὲ οὐκ ἐβούλετο λέγων τὸν ἀποστάντα ... καὶ μή συνελθόντα (om. αὐτοῖς) εἰς τὸ ἔργον εἰς ὃ ἐπέμφθησαν (a natural but unnecessary description of the work in question) τοῦτον μὴ εἶναι σὺν αὐτοῖς. The addition of εἰς ὃ ἐπέμφ. is readily explicable in terms of the tendency of D and its allies to pious expansion; the variants at the beginning and end of the verse are not so explicable, and may suggest that Western editors were working on a different base. The additions 'considerably weaken the force of the B-text' (Metzger 439).

For possible significance of the tenses of συμπαραλαμβάνειν see on v. 37.

A different view-point is given in the certainly fictional *Acta Barnabae* 8 (L.-B. 2.2.294): πολλὴ τοίνυν φιλονεικία μεταξὺ αὐτῶν ἐγένετο. Βαρναβᾶς δὲ παρεκάλει κἀμὲ συνακολουθῆσαι αὐτοῖς ... ὁ δὲ Παῦλος κατέκραζεν τοῦ Βαρναβᾶ ...

Pesch (2.93) thinks it possible that Mark may have been responsible for the conflict in Antioch by informing James of what had happened in chs. 13 and 14. This is pure guesswork, but it could be true.

39. The disagreement between Paul and Barnabas was sharp; exactly how sharp it is not easy to say. The only other occurrence of παροξυσμός in the NT has a good connotation: Christians are to provoke one another to love and good works (Heb. 10.24). It is possible however that this good use hints at a bad one: You are in fact provoking one another to anger; enough of this! 'Provoke' one another to something different. The cognate verb παροξύνεσθαι also has different connotations: at 1 Cor. 13.5 Paul says that love οὐ παροξύνεται; at Acts 17.16 it is said that Paul's spirit παρωξύνετο ἐν αὐτῷ at the sight of Athenian idolatry. Here it seems that relations between Paul and Barnabas were embittered; how far the bitterness was expressed in outbursts of anger is not clear. The result was clear; the partnership that is described in chs. 13 and 14 was broken and the two separated (ἀποχωρισθῆναι; in 13.13 John Mark separated, ἀποχωρήσας, from Paul and Barnabas) from each other. BDR § 391.2, n. 6 write, 'In einem Satz wie Apg 15.39 ... würde ein Attiker wegen der mangelnden engen Verknüpfung und wegen des Gewichtes, das auf die eingetretene Folge fällt, eher den Ind. gesetzt haben.' Haenchen (457) would also prefer the indicative. This probably states correctly the Attic distinction between infinitive and indicative (see M. 1.209f.), but Luke's sentence leaves no doubt about the connection between the quarrel and the separation, and the importance of the result. No other cause is given for the separation (but see below), and Luke does nothing to suggest that the outcome of Paul's future missions would have been different if he had been accompanied by Barnabas and Mark rather than by Silas and Timothy.

Barnabas *took* (παραλαμβάνειν; cf. συμπαραλ. in vv. 37, 38) Mark and they sailed away (ἐκπλεῖν occurs again at 18.18; 20.6—there is a good deal of sailing in the second part of Acts) to Cyprus, revisiting this part of the field covered in chs. 13 and 14, and leaving the rest to Paul (v. 41). Barnabas was originally from Cyprus (4.36); it would however be unfair to suggest a less bold and adventurous attitude on his part. Paul made for Cilicia—of which the capital was Tarsus.

A different ground of controversy, also located in Antioch, is given is Gal. 2.13. When Peter withdrew from table fellowship with Gentile Christians in Antioch even Barnabas was carried away by his hypocrisy, and though only Peter is addressed in the words quoted in Gal. 2.14–18(21) they would apply equally to Barnabas. Nothing is said here about Mark. It may be that there were two distinct quarrels between Paul and Barnabas; it may be that there was one quarrel that had two elements; it may be that Paul gives the true ground of the separation (Paul had little to do with Antioch after this point) and that Luke preferred to find a personal rather than a theological ground for the split. If the disagreement about Mark was a pure invention on Luke's part it was very cunningly worked out, the ground being prepared in ch. 13, and to some extent in ch. 12. There is no reason to think that the story about Mark is totally untrue, for there is no reason why it should have been invented. Luke could have remained silent about the trouble described in Galatians 2, simply saying that, after a period of shared ministry (v. 36), Barnabas accompanied by Mark decided to go to Cyprus, and Paul, accompanied by Silas, to go to Syria and Cilicia. 1 Cor. 9.6 shows that Paul continued to recognize Barnabas as a colleague, and Col. 4.10; 2 Tim. 4.11; Philemon 24, whether written by Paul or not, show that at a somewhat later date Mark was understood to be a member of the Pauline circle.

D (gig pᶜ) rewrite part of the verse as follows: τότε Βαρναβᾶς παραλαβὼν τὸν Μᾶρκον ἔπλευσεν. The best explanation of this reading is that a copyist copied τόν τε as τότε, accidentally omitting the ν, and then rewrote the rest of the sentence as economically as possible. One could equally suggest that τότε was erroneously written τόν τε.

40. Paul was now left without a travelling companion, and it would have been foolhardy to set out alone on the kind of journey (to be inferred from the epistles as well as Acts) that he had in mind. He must choose one from those available, and he chose (ἐπιλέγεσθαι is used in a different sense at Jn 5.2) Silas, on whom see the note on 15.22. It is pure conjecture, but it may be correct, that Paul set out on a new mission with a new companion, because he had lost his battle at Antioch (Gal. 2.1–14). This consideration could well have contributed to his change of companion (see above), but Paul needed no additional motivation to continue his work for the Gospel (1 Cor. 9.16, 23). He began his new mission in what might be described as the Antiochene mission field.

Paul set out, commended by the brothers (singular, παραδοθείς, but it is impossible not to think that Silas was included) to the grace of the Lord. Cf. 15.33, and especially 14.26, παραδεδόμενοι τῇ χάριτι τοῦ θεοῦ. In the present passage θεοῦ is read by P⁴⁵ C E Ψ 𝔐 gig w vgᶜˡ sy bo; κυρίου by P⁷⁴ A B D ⁽*⁾ 33 81 *pc* d vgˢᵗ sa. θεοῦ was no doubt introduced through assimilation to 14.26. The parallel is instructive. Luke does not say, 'The Lord (Jesus) is God', but he writes in such a way as to suggest the possibility to his reader, if not to himself.

According to Luke, Paul set out with the warm approval of the church; he does not say so much of Barnabas.

Lüdemann 175 observes that difficulties regarding the movements of Silas are resolved if 15.22, 27, 32f. may be regarded as redactional, v. 40 as traditional. Or (he asks), is there simply negligence on Luke's part? A further possibility is that the negligence belonged to the tradition as Luke collected it, perhaps not all from one source of information. Thirty years on, who could remember precisely the movements of a secondary character?

41. *Paul* (no doubt we should think of him as accompanied by Silas, but the verbs, διήρχετο ... ἐπιστηρίζων, are singular) *passed* *through Syria and Cilicia*. In the city of Antioch Paul was in Syria, and set out northwards. Cilicia may be roughly described as occupying the northeastern angle of the Mediterranean, joining Syria to the south east (and for the most part administratively united with it; see 6.9; 15.23) and stretching to the west perhaps as far as Pamphylia and thus adjoining the territory of Paul's first journey. Syria and Cilicia were thus new territory as far as missionary work recorded in Acts is concerned. In 9.30 Paul went from Jerusalem to Tarsus, and therefore presumably passed through Syria and Cilicia; cf. Gal. 1.21. Whether at that time he preached in Syria and Cilicia we do not know, but according to the present verses ἐκκλησίαι had been established by someone, since they were now *strengthened* (ἐπιστηρίζειν; on this word see 15.32). This is confirmed by the address of the Council's letter, to Antioch, Syria, and Cilicia. This may in fact be the source of the present reference to Syria and Cilicia. Someone had to take the letter there and it might be assumed that Paul did; cf. Conzelmann (88). It is not clear how Preuschen (98) can regard this part of the journey as a duplicate of chs. 13–14.

For διήρχετο as possibly referring to a preaching mission see 13.6. Apart from this nothing is said about Paul's work in Syria and Cilicia beyond the vague and general ἐπιστηρίζων τὰς ἐκκλησίας, so that the contrast (BDR § 327.1, n. 1) between 15.41 (διήρχετο, imperfect) and 16.6 (διῆλθεν, aorist) seems somewhat contrived.

τὴν Συρίαν καὶ τὴν Κιλικίαν is the reading of B D Ψ 36 453 *pc*. ℵ A C E 𝔐 omit the second article; P⁴⁵ has διὰ τῆς Συρίας καὶ τῆς Κιλικίας. The omission of the second article may reflect the time (see on 15.23) when Syria and Cilicia were united as one province. At the end of the verse D (gig w vg^cl sy^hmg) add παραδιδοὺς τὰς ἐντολὰς τῶν πρεσβυτέρων, forgetting the apostles, but otherwise tying in the new journey with the Council and its Decree.

1. The new subparagraph makes a new beginning, probably the beginning of a new source of information. The reference to Syria and Cilicia in v. 41 was probably based on the address of the letter (15.23); if Luke had any further information about the journey through these areas he chose not to give it. Probably he had none. But he not only recalls Derbe and Lystra from the first journey; he has an important new fact. His narrative is more probably based on local information than on a written source.

The Western text, represented by D (gig sy^hmg), connects this verse more closely with the previous one: διελθὼν (borrowed from 16.6?) δὲ τὰ ἔθνη ταῦτα κατήντησεν. Even if διέρχεσθαι has the sense (see 13.6) of conducting a preaching tour, τὰ ἔθνη is a surprising expression. It recalls the use of the word as equivalent to the Latin *provincia* (LS, s.v. 2c, p. 480). This is relatively late (Appian, Herodian, Dio Cassius, Dio Chrysostom are cited, with papyri of similar date—see also MM 181), but possibly relevant if the Western text is a second century revision. In both forms of the text the singular is used; the writer—or his source, information found in Derbe and Lystra—is interested in Paul, not in Silas. After δέ, καί should probably be read, with P⁴⁵A B Ψ 33 453 614 1175 1739 2495 *al* syʰ. *After he had passed through these provinces he reached also ...* For this use of καταντᾶν εἰς cf. 2 Macc 4.21, 24, 44.

Καὶ ἰδού recalls the Hebrew והנה, but Luke is not translating; he is using his 'Semitic', biblical style as he introduces a story reminiscent of the OT.

Timothy is to play an important part in Acts (16.1; 17.14, 15; 18.5; 19.22; 20.4) and in the Pauline letters (Rom. 16.21; 1 Cor. 4.17; 16.10; 2 Cor. 1.1, 19; Phil. 1.1; 2.19; Col. 1.1; 1 Thess. 1.1; 3.2, 6; 2 Thess. 1.1; 1 Tim. 1.2, 18; 6.20; 2 Tim. 1.2; Philemon 1; cf. Heb. 13.23). The name occurs frequently in Greek from the time of Aristophanes. He was a *disciple* (μαθητής, by which Luke seems always to mean *Christian*; see on 6.1; 9.36, 38, here reinforced by ἀδελφοί in v. 2; cf. πιστής, below). Nothing is said of him on the occasion of Paul's first visit to this area (14.8–20, 21); one may guess therefore that he had not been converted by Paul, though Paul evidently thought well of him, and in 1 Cor. 4.17 speaks of him as his child.

Timothy's mother too was a Christian (according to 2 Tim. 1.5 her name was Eunice); his father was not (Ἕλλην here means simply *non-Jew*, not specifically Greek). Kosmala (425) argues that πιστής, *believing*, does not necessarily mean that Eunice was a Christian. The argument is unconvincing. The wording of the present verse suggests that he came from Derbe.

Timothy is described as of mixed parentage. His mother (notwithstanding the Greek name she bears in 2 Tim. 1.5) was a Jewess, his father a Greek. Their marriage therefore was in Jewish law illegal (see StrB 2.741, quoting Jebamoth 45b). The same passage makes the point that, in mixed marriages, the child followed the nationality of the mother. Preuschen (99) quotes as an analogy Cicero, *De Natura Deorum* 3.18(45), ut enim iure civili qui est matre libera liber est. From this it would follow that Timothy would be regarded as an Israelite, and should in accordance with the law have been circumcised on the eighth day after birth. Of course, a Gentile father might very well object to the rite. This understanding of the position, however, was called in question by D. Daube (*Ancient Jewish Law* (Leiden, 1981), 22–32. who showed that the principle of matrilineal descent was not in operation in the first century; it was brought in in the second century (out of concern for Jewish women who bore children as a result of rape by heathen soldiers, who naturally were not present to claim and bring up their children). This conclusion was—rightly—accepted by S. J. D. Cohen (*JBL* 105 (1986),

251–68) and C. Bryan (*JBL* 107 (1988), 292–94); see below on v. 3 for the bearing of this on Paul's circumcision of Timothy.

In the majority of MSS Timothy's mother is described as a Jewess—104 (*pc*) have χήρας Ἰουδαίας, which is probably a conflate reading, and gig p vg^mss have *viduae*. This may be an inference from ὑπῆρχεν (v. 3; see the note), or possibly (*Begs*. 4.184) due to confusion in the Latin texts in question of *iudeae* and *uiduae*. If she was a Gentile widow (reading *uiduae*) the story of Timothy's circumcision takes on a new significance; but this is most improbable.

Silas now disappears from the story till 16.19; Timothy (apart from the next two verses) till 17.14.

2. μαρτυρεῖσθαι in the sense of *having a good reputation with* is common in Acts (6.3; 10.22; 16.2; 22.12). Timothy was well spoken of by *the brothers*, that is, *the Christians* (for ἀδελφοί see on 1.15) in Lystra (presumably in Derbe also, if this was Timothy's home; see v. 1) and Iconium. The three towns were not (in the days of foot travel) very close together; see on 13.51; 14.6. The Christians in each (no doubt relatively few) may however have found it rewarding to keep in touch with one another. Luke is locating the incident regarding Timothy in the area of the 'first journey'.

3. *Paul wished him* [Timothy] *to go with him.* 1 Thess. 1.1; 3.2, 6 are sufficient to show that a man called Timothy accompanied Paul on the 'second missionary journey' and assisted in a mission that included Macedonia. The epistles cannot be said to confirm the statement that Paul selected him for the purpose from among the Christians of Lystra (or Derbe) and wished him to set out with him from there; equally there is nothing to cast doubt on the statement. The existence of the two epistles to Timothy, though these were not written by Paul, shows that Timothy was known to have survived Paul, and if the author of Acts took seriously the task of finding out what he could about Paul's ministry Timothy would have been a useful and probably available source of information. The first seven words of the present verse give rise to no difficulty; the same cannot be said of the rest of the verse.

Paul had just been contending, on behalf of the church of Antioch, for Gentile freedom from the Law, specifically the law of circumcision, and had elicited the decision that circumcision was not required. The epistles make it clear that the contention had been sharper than Acts allows us to see. 'If you are circumcised, Christ will do you no good at all' (Gal. 5.2). 'If anyone was called in a state of circumcision, let him not undo it; if anyone was called in a state of uncircumcision, let him not be circumcised' (1 Cor. 7.18). He had resisted attempts in Jerusalem to have Titus circumcised (Gal. 2.3–5;

for the text and interpretation see *Freedom and Obligation*, p. 112. n. 12). Is it likely that Paul would, apparently without pressure, circumcise his intended companion?

That he did so is stated in Acts with some emphasis: λαβών περιέτεμεν. This is claimed by Black (*AA* 125, following up a suggestion by J. Jeremias; see also Wilcox, 125, and cf. 9.25; 27.35) as a Semitism; in both Hebrew and Aramaic *take* (לקח, נטל; נסב) is used in a superfluous way, doing no more than accompany and perhaps emphasize the action of the significant verb. This is not convincing; Paul took Timothy as an assistant and travelling companion, and circumcised him. This is plain Greek, and it is quite clear; there is no need to conjecture Semitic influence. Paul did this διὰ τοὺς Ἰουδαίους τοὺς ὄντας ἐν τοῖς τόποις ἐκείνοις. These must be the Jews resident in the Derbe-Lystra area, not those in Jerusalem. It is true that the Jerusalem Jews might have made trouble for Paul if they had known that he was travelling with an uncircumcised half-Jew, but only the local Jews would have known the facts about Timothy's parentage (ᾔδεισαν γὰρ ἅπαντες ...). It is argued that though Paul believed that circumcision was not necessary for salvation—and that if treated as if it were necessary would make salvation impossible—he might have circumcised his companion because he was proposing in his mission to make use of Jewish synagogues and places of prayer (16.13; 17.1; etc.) and could not have taken an uncircumcised man with him; this was part of being to the Jews as if he were a Jew (1 Cor. 9.20). But it is rightly pointed out (Schmithals 145) that Paul is not said to have taken Timothy into a synagogue, and that in any case Gentiles, favourable to Judaism but not circumcised as proselytes, seem to have been admitted to synagogues (see on 10.2). Again, it is argued that Gal. 5.11 bears witness to a current opinion that Paul had, in at least one notable case, practised circumcision. P. Borgen (*Paul Preaches Circumcision and Pleases Men* (1983), 33–37) contends that this means that Paul preached ethical circumcision (circumcision of the heart), and his opponents held that this needed physical circumcision to make it complete. Even if this is correct as an explanation of the difficult verse in Galatians (on which see now in addition T. Baarda, in *NovT* 34 (1992), 250–6) it will hardly justify, or make credible, the statement in Acts. It is hard to contradict the judgement of Bornkamm (4.159), 'So wird man die Notiz Apg 16.3 anfechten und aus der zu Genüge bekannten Tendenz des Lukas erklären müssen, die Loyalität des Paulus gegenüber dem Gesetz im Gegensatz zu allen anders lautenden Vorwürfen zu beweisen.'

The reason given for Paul's alleged action would be understandable if it could be assumed (see on v. 1) that Timothy was legally a Jew by descent. Local Jews who knew that Timothy's father had been (ὑπῆρχεν probably implies that he was now dead; had he been alive the verb would have been ὑπάρχει—see Zerwick § 346, n.1; BDR § 330, n. 2) a Gentile would probably suspect if they did not know that circumcision had been omitted on the eighth day, and would certainly—and not unreasonably—make trouble if Paul tried to pass him off as a Jew. The answer to this would be not to treat him or present him as a Jew. This would have been the right kind of tact, not the wrong kind, which Paul carefully avoided in the case of Titus (Gal. 2.3). It does not seem likely that Luke simply invented the incident; he had heard it, possibly guessed it on the basis of Timothy's sympathy with Judaism. And a bare possibility must remain that Luke was right; that Paul, confronted with a companion who was half Gentile and half Jew, decided to 'make an honest Jew of him'; 'neque salutis aeternae causa T. circumciditur, sed utilitatis' (Blass 175). No other explanation of Luke's account is at all convincing, though Bauernfeind's (204) epigram is worth considering: 'Er [Paulus] wollte christliche Juden und nicht entwurzelte Juden.' So is Schneider's quotation (2.200) of Baumgarten, writing in 1889: 'Man vergisst, dass man bei solchem Eifer für die Freiheit Freiheit selber wieder in eine Knechtschaft verwandelt.' Pesch (2.99) writes similarly that Paul's freedom would be limited if he could not in such a way as this accommodate Jews. Lüdemann's suggestion (183), that Acts is right in saying that Timothy was circumcised but wrong in the timing—Timothy was circumcised on conversion, makes matters more rather than less difficult. There was no point in mentioning the nationality of Timothy's mother (v. 1) unless it was thought (by Luke if not by Paul) that this, if it did not determine legal descent, nevertheless so strongly suggested Judaism as to make it desirable to treat Timothy as a Jew. But would Paul have accepted and acted on such a desirability? Bornkamm's negative answer is almost certainly right. As Schille (333) points out, circumcision that had nothing to do with gaining salvation would be senseless in Jewish thought at the time. Luke (not Paul) may have been preparing for 21.21—the charge is disproved before it is brought (Johnson 290).

Weiser (400) reaches the conclusion that 'Lukas in den Versen 1b, 3a, eine Einzelepisode aus der Timotheus-Überlieferung aufgenommen und die Verse 1a, 2, 3bc, 4, 5 redaktionell gebildet hat.' Concluding himself that the circumcision did not happen, Weiser gives on 402 careful lists of those who agree and those who disagree. To those who think that Timothy was circumcised by Paul must now be added Trebilco (23).

The Western text continues its rewriting in this verse, and indeed has some claim to originality. P⁷⁴ ℵ A B C Ψ 33 36 81 945 1175 1739 *al* vg co have ᾔδεισαν γὰρ ἅπαντες ὅτι Ἕλλην ὁ πατὴρ αὐτοῦ ὑπῆρχεν. But P⁴⁵ᵛⁱᵈ D E 𝔐 (gig) sy have ᾔδ. γὰρ ἅπ. τὸν πατέρα αὐτοῦ (614 2495 *pc* have a different order) ὅτι Ἕλλην ὑπ. This anticipation of the subject of ὑπῆρχεν as the object of ᾔδεισαν is Semitic, and could be original.

4. Temporal ὡς is frequent in Lk. and Acts, see BA 1792. With the imperfect διεπορεύοντο it means while *they were passing through*, *as they passed through*. On their way, in town after town, they delivered the decrees. παρεδίδοσαν is the 'correct' third person plural imperfect of (παρα)διδόναι; contrast 27.1, παρεδίδουν; see M. 2.202. φυλάσσειν is an infinitive of purpose, so obvious that it hardly needed to be made explicit. The decrees were for keeping, not for mere interest. They have now been taken outside the area specified in 15.23 to the churches of the first journey. It is clear that, in Luke's view, they were intended to be 'applicable to all Gentile Churches' (Wilson, *Law* 81; cf. Haenchen 445).

δόγματα is the noun that naturally corresponds with the verb ἔδοξε of 15.28 (cf. 15.22, 25). It is used of orders laid down by a duly constituted person or group. Thus δόγματα συγκλήτου (Polybius 6.13.2) are Senatus consulta; cf. τὰ τῶν Ἀμφικτυόνων δόγματα (Demosthenes 5.19(62)). See *ND* 4.146 and cf. Lk. 2.1; Acts 17.7. At 3 Macc. 1.3; Josephus, *Apion* 1.42 (θεοῦ δόγματα) it is used of the Jewish Law. The word does not suggest a request for considerate behaviour, aimed at making possible harmonious common meals at which both Jewish and Gentile Christians might unite, rather ordinances that must be observed by those who wish to be members of the group that ordains them. With this τὰ κεκριμένα (cf. James's ἐγὼ κρίνω, 15.19) agrees. Cf. Epictetus 2.15.7, τοῖς κριθεῖσιν ἐμμένειν δεῖ.

The verse is rewritten by D sy^hmg Ephraim: διερχόμενοι δὲ τὰς πόλεις ἐκήρυσσον (+ καὶ παρεδίδοσαν αὐτοῖς, D) μετὰ πάσης παρρησίας τὸν κύριον Ἰησοῦν ἅμα παραδιδόντες καὶ τὰς ἐντολὰς ἀποστόλων καὶ ... The intention may have been to prepare for v. 5.

Begs. 4.185 comments: 'Whatever may have been the facts Luke obviously wishes to represent Paul as the delegate of the apostles in Jerusalem in a manner which is incompatible with the Epistle to the Galatians.' This seems to be a valid observation.

It was from the apostles and elders that the decrees originated; cf. 15.2, 6, 23. Nothing is said now of the πλῆθος (15.12) or the ἐκκλησία (15.22).

5. This verse is a summary, reminiscent of the summaries that punctuate the earlier parts of Acts (2.42–47; 4.32–35; 5.12–16; 6.7; 9.31). The plural αἱ ἐκκλησίαι, the various local churches, recalls the Western reading at 9.31. That they were strengthened, made firm in [the] faith recalls 14.22, the increase in numbers 6.7 (ἐπληθύνετο ὁ ἀριθμός), and καθ' ἡμέραν 2.47. τῇ πίστει is omitted by D.

This verse should probably be regarded as Luke's conclusion of the paragraph that began at 15.1. As on other occasions (notably ch. 6), we see the emergence of a problem, its speedy and effective solution, and its outcome in greater progress and expansion for the churches. In this way Luke affirms the truth of the Gospel, demonstrated by the fact that God so evidently cares for and furthers its expansion that believers increase in numbers and believe more firmly.

42. GUIDED BY THE SPIRIT TO TROAS 16.6–10

(6) They passed through Phrygia and Galatian territory, having been forbidden[1] by the Holy Spirit to speak the word in Asia; (7) they came opposite Mysia and tried to go into Bithynia, but the Spirit of Jesus did not permit them to do so. (8) They arrived at[2] Mysia and came down to Troas. (9) A vision appeared to Paul in the night: a man of Macedonia was standing, begging him with the words, 'Come across into Macedonia and help us.' (10) When Paul had seen the vision, immediately we sought to leave for[3] Macedonia, concluding that God had called us to evangelize them.

Bibliography

W. P. Bowers, *JTS* 30 (1979), 507–11.

F. F. Bruce, *BJRL* 61 (1978/9), 337–54.

O. Glombitza, *ZNW* 53 (1962), 77–82.

R. M. Grant, as in (41).

C. J. Hemer, *Tyndale Bulletin* 26 (1975), 79–112.

C. J. Hemer, *JTS* 27 (1976), 122–6.

C. J. Hemer, *JTS* 28 (1977), 99–101.

G. M. Lee, *NovT* 9 (1967), 41f.

G. M. Lee, *Bib* 51 (1970), 235–7.

G. M. Lee, *NovT* 17 (1975), 199.

G. Stählin, *FS* Moule, 229–52.

Commentary

The journey begun in 15.41 reaches Troas by the end of v. 8. The course of it as described in vv. 6–8 raises several notoriously difficult questions; these will be considered in the notes and need not be dealt with here. Luke emphasizes that at every stage the travellers receive supernatural guidance. Such guidance is renewed in dramatic form in vv. 9, 10; Paul is directed by a vision to cross over from Troas into Macedonia. Dibelius (129, 148f., 200) is right to point out the stress which the narrative lays on this movement into Greece, but it is

---

[1]NEB, because they were prevented; NJB, because they had been told ... not to.

[2]RSV, passing by; NEB: they skirted (mg. traversed); NJB, they went through.

[3]NEB, set about getting a passage; NJB, lost no time in arranging a passage.

mistaken (as is pointed out in the notes) to make much of a move from Asia into Europe; Paul and his colleagues remained within the one Greco-Roman world.

What must be noted here is the introduction in the narrative of the first person plural, ἐζητήσαμεν (v. 10). The first impression given by this word is that the person who wrote it was present at the events he describes. The first impression is not necessarily correct, and many different views are held about the so-called We-passages. These are discussed in the Introduction, pp. xxv–xxx, in the light of all the evidence. If attention is restricted to the present passage there is no reason to doubt the *prima facie* meaning of the text. A person whose words are reported, whether by himself or an editor, was with Paul in Troas; he was told of a vision seen by Paul and concurred with the conclusion that the vision constituted a divine call to evangelize Macedonia. Even if the scantily attested *nos venimus* is read in v. 8, Troas marks the beginning of the association of the narrator with Paul. The Western reading (συνεστραμμένων δὲ ἡμῶν) at 11.28 gives a 'We' in Antioch. Very few would accept this reading; see however I.564. Nothing that is said in the present passage points to the identity of the fellow traveller implied by the first person plural.

6. The subject changes from that of 16.5 (probably Luke's additional note) and must now be Paul, Silas, and Timothy. These *passed through*, perhaps preaching on the way; for Luke's use of διέρχεσθαι see 13.6. The area through which they passed is described as τὴν Φρυγίαν καὶ Γαλατικὴν χώραν. It is natural at first sight to take this phrase, with its one article (some MSS have τήν before Γαλατικήν, but this reading is to be rejected—Metzger 441), to mean the *Phrygian and Galatian region*—one region defined by two adjectives. Less probable might seem *the Phrygian [region] and the Galatian region*; or, taking Φρυγίαν as a noun, *Phrygia and the Galatian region*. The last finds some support by analogy in Lk. 3.1; so Blass (176) concludes, 'Χώρα ad Γ. tantum pertinet, v. 18.23.' After inconclusive argument the matter seemed to have been settled about as far as settlement of such a question could be expected by Lake, who (*Begs.* 5.231; see the whole note on Paul's route, 5.224–40) observes, 'Φρύγιος, the adjective formed from Φρύξ, was "of three terminations" in earlier Greek, but Lucian uses it as of only two [Harmonides I], and I know of no instance of the nominative with the feminine termination in Greek contemporary with the New Testament … In any case Φρυγία had undoubtedly become a substantive proper name, and the first thought of any reader would be to interpret it so.' This observation and conclusion were however questioned by C. J. Hemer (*JTS* 27 (1976), 122–6; see also *Acts* 112, 277–307; there is a supplementary note in *ND* 4.174). 'I am far from denying that Φρύγιος *may* be two-terminational, but the

alternative certainly exists, and is probably the more usual' (124).
Hemer gives nine examples, ranging from the fourth century BC to
the fourth century AD. Probably the best, as regards date and clarity
is νόθον ἐκ Φρυγίας γυναικός (Apollodorus, *Bibliotheca* 2.4.5).
That Φρυγίαν in Acts 16.6 is an adjective must be accorded a higher
measure of probability than Lake allowed, but the matter is not
closed in view of the occurrence of the similar expression, τὴν
Γαλατικὴν χώραν καὶ Φρυγίαν at 18.23, where the word must be a
noun. This suggests that in 16.6 also Φρυγία is a noun, but cannot
prove it (cf. Schneider 2.205). Luke may be using, in the two verses,
different sources, in which the word was taken in different ways; or
he may be deliberately changing its sense by changing the order of
words. There remains however some probability that Luke intended
in each place to refer to the same area. If, with Hemer, we take
Φρυγίαν as an adjective we are presented with a χώρα that was both
Phrygian and Galatian. This is explained by Ramsay (*Church* 81) as
that part of Phrygia that had in 25 BC been incorporated (with a
number of other districts) in the new province of Galatia. It could be
'idiomatically rendered "the Phrygo-Galatic territory"' (80), by
analogy with Pontus Galaticus, a term used 'to denote a large district
of Pontus which was added to the province of Galatia a few years
B.C.' (ibidem). It must be noted that though there is good evidence
for the name Pontus Galaticus there is none for Phrygia Galatica. It is
perhaps unlikely that we shall ever possess sufficient literary and
epigraphical evidence to settle this question by a simple consideration of names and the way in which they are used. A stronger
consideration, which Lake (*Begs.* 5.235f.) regards as 'perhaps decisive against Ramsay's theory' is 'the fact that if ἡ Φρυγία καὶ
Γαλατικὴ χώρα means the *regio* of the province of Galatia called
Phrygia Galatica, it is impossible that Paul's route through this
district brought him out anywhere near Mysia. Ramsay has to argue
that Paul, after passing through *Phrygia Galatica*, journeyed through
the province of Asia until he came to the neighbourhood of Mysia,
for though the Spirit prevented him from preaching in Asia, it did not
prevent him from travelling through it.' There is a similar geographical argument in Thornton (267f.). Ramsay's explanation is
hardly convincing. But to follow Lake's point it is necessary to go
further in Luke's text.

Phrygia and Galatia were both ancient kingdoms in Asia Minor.
After a varied history of subjection to various races, 'in 116 B.C. the
greater part of [Phrygia] was absorbed in the province of Asia, and in
25 B.C. the remaining eastern portion became a region of the
province Galatia' (W. M. Calder in *OCD* 829). The Roman province
of Galatia was thus formed in 25 BC, based on the ancient kingdom
of Galatia but including also parts of Phrygia, Lycaonia, and Pisidia.
It was later expanded by further additions.

Paul and his companions, then, passed through τὴν Φρυγίαν καὶ Γαλατικὴν χώραν, κωλυθέντες ὑπὸ τοῦ ἁγίου Πνεύματος λαλῆσαι τὸν λόγον ἐν τῇ Ἀσίᾳ. A reader unfamiliar with the geography of the region in question would certainly translate this, 'They passed through the area described, having been forbidden, that is, after they had been forbidden, or because they had been forbidden, to speak the word in Asia,' following the common rule that an aorist participle (κωλυθέντες) refers to action before the time of the main verb (διῆλθον). This suggests that the journey through Phrygian and Galatian territory was an alternative to a journey through Asia, and led to a point over against Mysia whence entry into Bithynia was possible, though it was prevented by a further intervention of the Spirit. A map however will show that a journey through Galatic Phrygia ('South Galatia'—a frequently used but undesirable term) would have led the travellers only up to the frontier of Asia, so that Mysia could have been reached only by passing through Asia. If however they passed through Phrygia and old Galatic territory ('North Galatia', in the corresponding phrase) they would approach both Bithynia and Mysia, and would be able to reach Troas (v. 8). If the Phrygia Galatica view described above is to be maintained it is necessary to take the aorist participle κωλυθέντες to refer to a time after that of the main verb; so for example Ramsay, *Church* 89. They were forbidden to preach the word in Asia, and (then) passed through the Phrygian–Galatian territory. Ramsay's position is summed up by him (*Church* 89) as follows: 'It has been contended that the participle κωλυθέντες gives the reason for the finite verb διῆλθον, and is therefore preliminary to it in the sequence of time. We reply that the participial construction cannot, in this author, be pressed in that way. He is often loose in the framing of his sentences, and in the long sentence in verses 6 and 7 he varies the succession of verbs by making some of them participles. The sequence of verbs is also the sequence of time: (1) they went through the Phrygo-Galatic land; (2) they were forbidden to speak in Asia; (3) they came over against Mysia; (4) they assayed to go into Bithynia; (5) the Spirit suffered them not; (6) they passed through Mysia; (7) they came to Troas.'

Whether this is a possible way of taking the participle is a question on which opinion is divided. It is of course true that the aorist tense describes a kind of action (Aktionsart) rather than the time at which an action takes place, and aorist participles that describe action coincident in time with that of the main verb though not common are sufficiently familiar. M.1.132–4 discusses the question and concludes by agreeing with P. W. Schmiedel (*EBib* 1599), 'It has to be maintained that the participle must contain, if not something antecedent to "they went" (διῆλθον), at least something synchronous with it, in no case a thing subsequent to it, if all the rules of grammar and all sure understanding of language are not to be given up.' Moule

(*IB* 100), considering on the same page Acts 25.13 (see the note), observes Lake's topography and translation (see above) and says that this 'is certainly the natural explanation of the Greek'. M. 3.80 on the other hand writes, 'Even time which is *future* to the main action seems to be denoted by the aor. ptc.', and cites Mt. 10.4; Jn 11.2 [these examples are quite unconvincing]; Acts 16.6; 25.13. Zerwick (§ 265) notes that Ramsay's interpretation means that 'supponendus esset sensus subsequens participii κωλυθέντες (= ἐκωλύθησαν δέ)'. But he evidently regards this as a minority view. G. M. Lee (*NovT* 9 (1967), 41, 42) cites προσφύς in Babrius (*Fable* 143.1–4) as an example of an aorist participle of subsequent action, but it probably does not strain the facts to say that in this passage all the action (a viper's bite) happens so quickly that one could legitimately think of coincident action. The same author returns to the matter in *Bib* 51 (1970), 235, 236. His Latin analogy (*NovT* 17 (1975), 199) is totally unconvincing. G. W. Hansen (in *Book of Acts* 1.378f.) takes the reference to be to 'the Phrygian-Galatian region' but does not deal with the grammatical question. It is hard to escape the conclusion in *Begs*. 4.186: 'It is impossible to translate the passage without doing violence to the Greek, unless we recognize that the phrase means that Paul first contemplated preaching in Asia, and, being prevented from doing this, passed through τὴν Φρυγίαν καὶ Γαλατικὴν χώραν.' It is worthwhile to add that Luke's geographical knowledge, though better than that of many of his contemporaries, was probably a good deal less precise than that of a modern scholar equipped with good modern maps. This would be especially true of more remote regions which he (Luke) had not himself penetrated.

διελθόντες (𝔐 vg) for διῆλθον (P⁷⁴ ℵ A B C D E Ψ 33 81 323 614 945 1175 1739 2495 *al* gig) makes more easily possible a reversal of the order of this verb and κωλυθέντες. The addition (by D) of μηδενί after πνεύματος improves the Greek and underlines the prohibition. τὸν λόγον alone (for the Gospel) is used e.g. at 4.4; the addition (by D gig vgᶜˡ syᵖ bo Speculum) of τοῦ θεοῦ is conventional.

The province of Asia was a wealthy and highly civilized part of Asia Minor, based upon a considerable number of city states, still at least partially independent. 'From 48 B.C. till *c.* A.D. 297 Asia included all the territory from Tyriaion to the sea, with the adjacent islands; it was bounded on the north by Bithynia, on the south by Lycia, and on the east (after 25 B.C.) by Galatia' (W. M. Calder and E. W. Gray, *OCD* 131). See further on other aspects of Asia below, on ch. 19.

It is characteristic of Luke to ascribe the direction of the mission to the Holy Spirit; cf. v. 7. How the Holy Spirit issued the prohibition in question is not explained. Luke possibly thinks of a communication through prophets; cf. 13.1–3.

7. Forbidden to speak the word in Asia the missionaries came κατὰ τὴν Μυσίαν, *opposite*, *over against*, *Mysia* (LS 883, s.v. κατά, B I 3, with numerous illustrations). This presumably means that they came up to the Mysian border but entered Mysia no more than they had Asia, or rather, since Mysia was a (northern) part of the province of Asia (but see on v. 8), having so far avoided Asia they still avoided it when, moving northward, they came to the Mysian part of Asia. Bithynia lay to the east of Mysian Asia, and stretched eastward along the southern coast of the Black Sea. Pompey the Great organized Bithynia as a province in union with Pontus (further east). During the first century AD it was a senatorial province, though its great importance as lying on the route to the east led to an unusual measure of imperial interference, and finally Marcus Aurelius made it an imperial province.

For ἐπείραζον, D syᵖ have ἤθελαν (sic). For the (unusual) *Spirit of Jesus* C* gig boᵐˢˢ have πνεῦμα κυρίου and 𝔐 sa have simply πνεῦμα. Luke means nothing different from what he means by the Holy Spirit in v. 6; why he has a different expression is not known. It is unlikely that he has a new source of information. He may simply have been seeking variety of expression as he makes his unchanging assertion: the Christians did what they did under the instruction and guidance of God, who worked through his Spirit, here more narrowly defined as the Spirit of Jesus.

8. παρελθόντες τὴν Μυσίαν is usually taken to mean, *They passed by Mysia* (see v. 7). This translation, however, though it accords well with the usual meaning of παρέρχεσθαι, and recognizes that Mysia was, as a part of Asia, forbidden country, encounters a geographical difficulty in that Troas was situated in Mysia and could only be approached by traversing Mysia, which Luke may possibly have distinguished from Asia. BA 1265 (followed by Haenchen and Conzelmann) takes the view that in this passage παρερχ. means not *to pass by* but *to pass through*, citing Appian, *Bellum Civile* 5.68 § 288 (... made their way through a crowd), and 1 Macc. 5.48. Some support may be found also in the use of παρερχ. διά in Mt. 8.28; PAmh 154.2 (6th/7th century AD), μὴ παρελθεῖν τινα διὰ τῶν ἐποικείων αὐτοῦ). BA also note, convincingly, that the variant in D, διελθόντες, which Dibelius (92) says 'appears logically justified', can be explained if it is supposed that the Western editor (a) did not know that παρέρχεσθαι could mean *traverse* (but 17.15 D suggests that he did!), and (b) did know that Troas could not be reached without traversing Mysia. Luke may have used παρέρχεσθαι because διέρχεσθαι suggested to him (see 13.6) a preaching tour, whereas on this occasion Paul and his companions travelled without preaching. An alternative explanation, simpler and perhaps better, is that παρέρχεσθαι means simply *to arrive*, as at Acts 24.7 (an observation relevant even if this verse is not an original part of the text of Acts). Thus in v. 7 the travellers came *opposite* Mysia (κατὰ τὴν Μυσίαν, at v. 8 they entered it (Cf. Metzger 442). 'παρελθόντες (‫ א‬etc.) sensui adversatur: non praetereunda, sed transeunda erat Mysia, ut ad Aegaeum mare venirent' (Blass 176). Otherwise Rackham (276); Pesch (2.101).

κατέβησαν, *they came down*, because Troas lay near the coast; κατήντησαν (D) lacks the clear sense of descent (notwithstanding the compounded κατά), but otherwise scarcely differs; but *nos venimus* (Ir^lat) introduces the 'We' material two verses before the point (v. 10) at which the main textual tradition does so. This is not a slip; the context (*Adv. Haereses* 3.14.1) shows that Irenaeus knows what he is doing: '... this Luke was inseparable from Paul ... he says that when Barnabas ... had sailed to Cyprus, we came to Troas'. The person who associates himself with Paul in the first person plural still appears for the first time at Troas, but he arrives there with Paul. See on v. 10.

Troas, in full Ἀλεξάνδρεια ἡ Τρωάς, was founded by Antigonus (323–301 BC). It was a free city; under Augustus it became a colony. See Hemer 112f. In addition to 16.11; 20.5, 6, cf. also 2 Cor. 2.12; 2 Tim. 4.13.

On vv. 6–8 see also Taylor (5.234–9).

9. The route of the missionaries is still (cf. vv. 6, 7) determined by supernatural means, now however by a vision (ὅραμα; cf. 7.31; 9.10, 12; 10.3, 17, 19; 11.5; 12.9; 16.10; 18.9; elsewhere in the NT only Mt. 17.9; the distribution reflects Luke's insistence on the divine control of the early Christian movement). The vision is seen διὰ τῆς (but τῆς is omitted by A B D 6 36 1175 *pc*) νυκτός; Moule, *IB* 56, noting that νυκτός alone would mean *by night*, translates *in the night*; cf. Zerwick (§ 115: spatium temporis, intra quod ...). Luke's handling of cases and prepositions is perhaps not so precise as this distinction would require.

ὤφθη with the dative will mean *appeared to* (rather than *was seen by*; cf. 2.3 and other passages). Wilcox (125) regards ἑστὼς καὶ παρακαλῶν as perhaps an Aramaism; cf. 1.11; 5.25. It has been asked how Paul was able to tell that the man was a Macedonian (ἀνὴρ Μακεδών τις); if there is a historical event behind the story it is enough to say that in a dream one knows this kind of thing; otherwise the urgent appeal to come and help us (ἡμῖν) in Macedonia might justify the implied inference. The man ἦν ἑστώς; this adds vividness; cf. 11.13. The participles are descriptive rather than members of a periphrastic tense: the man was standing and begging and saying. διαβαίνειν implies coming from one side of a barrier (here the Thracian Sea, the northern part of the Aegean) to the other; cf. Lk. 16.26 (χάσμα μέγα); Heb. 11.29 (τὴν ἐρυθρὰν θάλασσαν).

βοηθεῖν is a surprisingly general word (elsewhere in Acts only 21.28, in a different sense; cf. 27.17); one would expect, Come and preach the Gospel to us, or the like. The intention may be to indicate that the Macedonians do not yet know what the Gospel is; they are aware of a need of help, not of the particular help that Paul had to offer.

A vision that appears in the course of the night is probably a dream; for the communication of supernatural instructions by dreams see references in Betz 53f., e.g. Lucian, *De Morte Peregrini* 26 (an intention changed by dreams). 'Dies ist ein fester Topos in den apokryphen Apostelakten' (Bornkamm, 4.185).

According to Davies (*Land* 278), Luke 'had an acute awareness of the point at which the Gospel passed over to Europe from Asia ... the entry upon a new area of the Christian mission is due to vision'. Davies is right in noting Luke's 'sensitivity to geography', but probably overstates the significance of the transition from Asia to Europe. Both Mysia and Macedonia were in the first century AD associations of Hellenistic cities which had become Roman provinces (in the case of Mysia, part of the province of Asia). In Philippi Paul would speak the same Greek that he had spoken all the way from Antioch.

Macedonia had been a province since 146 BC. More details will be given when individual towns are mentioned.

There is in this verse a good deal of minor textual variation which shows nothing more important than Western readiness to handle the text freely, perhaps inviting reflection on the kind of authority it had; see Introduction, pp. xxif.

The omission of τῆς was mentioned above; the following variants may also be noted:

ὅραμα] ἐν ὁράματι D e syᵖ
ἀνήρ] ὡσεὶ ἀνήρ D syᵖ sa
ἦν] om. D* E *pc*
καί] κατὰ πρόσωπον αὐτοῦ D 614 *pc* (syʰ**) sa

Thus the text of D runs: καὶ ἐν ὁράματι διὰ νυκτὸς ὤφθη τῷ Παύλῳ ὡσεὶ ἀνὴρ Μακεδών τις ἑστὼς κατὰ πρόσωπον αὐτοῦ παρακαλῶν καὶ λέγων· Διαβὰς ... The editor (copyist) is not trying to make a point; he is not concerned to reproduce his text with elaborate precision.

10. For temporal ὡς as a characteristic of Lucan style see 16.4; also BDR § 455.2 and BA 1792; also M. 4.70, but ὡς is seldom if ever due to the Aramaic כד.

Paul saw the vision, and εὐθέως (here expressing unhesitating obedience to a divine command) ἐζητήσαμεν, *we sought* ... first person plural. This (unless variants are accepted at 11.28; 16.8; see the notes) is the first occurrence of the first person plural which is a striking characteristic of some of the narratives in the second part of Acts. For a discussion of their interpretation, significance, and bearing on the authorship of Acts see Introduction, pp. xxv–xxx. There is no doubt that the immediate (but not for that reason necessarily correct) impression given by the present passage is that at this point, or shortly before it, Paul, Silas, and Timothy were joined by another person, who proceeds to describe (presumably at least up to the end of the Philippi story, as well as at later points in the book) events as he himself witnessed and recalled them. He may have been the author of the whole book—'Luke', or the author of a source incorporated by the author of the whole book. Or Luke may at this point have switched from third person to first person narrative for some reason of his own—because it suited his theme, because it added greater vividness, or because it gave the untrue suggestion that he was present so that his narrative might be accepted as an eye-witness account of events. These possibilities can be seriously discussed only when all the material has been surveyed. It should however be borne in mind that, if there was an eye-witness, we may have already met him. Schneider (2.204, cf. 1.89–95) points out that the occurrence of 'we' in this verse does not necessarily mean that the writer has only just joined the party. He might be Timothy or Silas. Pesch (e.g. 2.98) thinks the eye-witness material may come from Timothy. Roloff (239), more cautiously, 'Die Wir-Stücke stammen sicher aus dem Umkreis des paulus, aber der Verfasser ist nicht Lukas.' On this question see especially Thornton, passim. Worth mentioning, but not to be accepted, is the suggestion that Luke had come from Philippi with an invitation to Paul, and was himself the 'vision' of v. 9.

συμβιβάζειν is used in a variety of ways; cf. 9.22; 19.33. Here it can hardly mean anything other than *conclude* (cf. Plato, *Hippias Minor* 369d, διαπυνθάνομαι καὶ ἐπανασκοπῶ καὶ συμβιβάζω ...). 'συμβιβάζειν (9.23) hic ut att. *colligere*' (Blass). The conclusion was inevitable. God had called us to evangelize the Macedonians. πρός adds to καλεῖν a sense of specific direction; cf. 13.2. The verb is followed by an infinitive of purpose, on which Radermacher (153) comments, 'Dieser Infinitiv ist überall möglich, wo irgendeine innere Beziehung zwischen Hauptsatz und Absichtssatz vorhanden ist.' For Luke's use of εὐαγγελίζεσθαι see 5.42; 8.4; etc. Schneider (2.207) connects it here with Isa. 61.1f.

Again (cf. v. 9) there is a free Western rewording: διεγερθεὶς οὖν ... διηγήσατο τὸ ὅραμα ἡμῖν (of course, how else could *we* know of it?), καὶ ἐνοήσαμεν ὅτι προσκέκληται ἡμᾶς ὁ κύριος εὐαγγελίσασθαι τοὺς ἐν τῇ Μακεδονίᾳ. In reading κύριος in place of θεός (P⁷⁴ ℵ A B C 33 81 *al*), D is joined by 𝔐 gig sy sa Ir^lat.

43. PAUL AND SILAS AT PHILIPPI 16.11–40

(11) We set sail from Troas and made a straight run to Samothrace, and on the next day to Neapolis, (12) and thence to Philippi, a leading city[1] of[2] the province of Macedonia, a colony. We stayed in the city several days. (13) On the Sabbath day we went outside the [city] gate by a river, where[3] we supposed that there was a place of prayer. We sat down and[4] spoke with the women who had gathered. (14) A woman, Lydia by name, a[5] dealer in purple from the city of Thyatira, who worshipped God, listened; the Lord opened her heart to give attention to the things spoken by Paul. (15) When she and her household were baptized she asked us, 'If you have judged me to be[6] faithful to the Lord, come into my house and stay;' and she constrained us to do so.

(16) It happened that as we were on our way to the place of prayer, a slave girl who[7] had[8] an oracular spirit met us; she made much profit for her owners by[9] giving oracles. (17) She followed Paul and us, crying out, 'These men are slaves of the Most High God; they are proclaiming to you a way of salvation.' (18) She did this for many days. Paul could endure it no longer, turned, and said to the spirit, 'I command you in the name of Jesus Christ to come out of her.' It came out at once. (19) When her owners saw that the hope of their profit had departed, they seized Paul and Silas and dragged them into the[10] Agora before the rulers. (20) Having brought them to the magistrates they said, 'These men, who are Jews, are greatly disturbing our city, (21) and are proclaiming customs which it is not lawful for us, who are Romans, to receive or practise.' (22) The crowd joined in the attack upon them and the magistrates tore off their clothes and commanded[11] [their officers] to beat them. (23) When they had laid many stripes upon them they cast them into prison, ordering the gaoler to guard them securely. (24) He, having received such a command, put them in the inner prison and secured their feet in the stocks. (25) At midnight Paul and Silas in their prayers were singing psalms to God, and the prisoners were listening to them. (26) Suddenly there was a great earthquake so that the foundations of the prison were shaken. Immediately all the doors were opened and the bonds of all [the prisoners] were loosed. (27) The gaoler woke up, and when he saw the doors of the prison standing open he drew his sword and was about to kill himself

[1]NJB, the principal city.
[2]NEB, NJB, that district.
[3]NEB, thought there would be; NJB, this was a customary place for prayer.
[4]NJB, preached to.
[5]NJB, in the purple-dye trade.
[6]NJB, a true believer in.
[7]NJB, was a soothsayer.
[8]RSV, a spirit of divination.
[9]NEB, telling fortunes.
[10]RSV, NJB, market place; NEB, main square.
[11]RSV, gave orders to beat them with rods.

because he supposed that the prisoners had escaped. (28) But Paul called out with a loud cry, 'Do yourself no harm, for we are all here.' (29) [The gaoler] asked for lights and sprang in. He was trembling, and fell down before Paul and Silas. (30) He brought them outside and said, 'Gentlemen, what must I do to be saved?' (31) They said, 'Believe in the Lord Jesus and you will be saved—you and your household.' (32) And they spoke to him the word of the Lord, together with all who were in his house. (33) He took them in that hour of the night and washed them clean from the effect of the blows they had received, and he was baptized, he and all his family, immediately. (34) He brought them up into his house, prepared a meal, and rejoiced with all his household, because he had come to faith in God. (35) When day broke, the magistrates sent the lictors, saying, 'Release those men.' (36) The gaoler reported these words to Paul, saying, 'The magistrates have sent that you should be released; so now depart and travel on in peace.' (37) Paul said to them, 'They have beaten us publicly, uncondemned, men who are Romans; they have put us in prison; and will they now put us out secretly? No, indeed; rather let them come themselves and lead us out.' (38) The lictors reported these things to the magistrates. When they heard that they were Romans they were afraid, (39) came and placated[12] them, and having brought them out asked them to leave the city. (40) When they had come out of the prison they went into Lydia's house, and when they had seen the brothers they encouraged them, and left.

Bibliography

R. Borger, *ThR* 52 (1987), 36–8.

L. Bormann, *Philippi, SuppNovT* 78 (1995).

C. Burchard, *ZNW* 69 (1978), 143–57.

G. Delling, *NovT* 7 (1964–5), 285–311.

M. Hengel, *FS* Kuhn, 157–84.

P. van Minnen, *JSNT* 56 (1994), 43–52.

Th. Mommsen, *ZNW* 2 (1901), 82f.

D. Noy, *JTS* 43 (1992), 188–22.

D. R. Schwartz, *Bib* 65 (1984), 357–63.

W. Stegemann, *ZNW* 78 (1987), 200–29.

P. R. Trebilco, *JSNT* 36 (1989), 51–73.

W. C. van Unnik, *Sparsa Collecta I, SuppNovT* 29 (1973), 374–85.

A. Vögeli, *ThZ* 9 (1953), 415–38.

C. S. de Vos, *NTS* 41 (1995), 292–6.

P. Weigandt, *NovT* 6 (1963), 49–74.

A. Weiser, *FS* Pallottis, 118–33.

M. Wilcox, *JSNT* 13 (1981), 110f.

[12]RSV, NEB, apologized to.

Commentary

The use of the first person plural which begins in 16.10 continues through the earlier part of the new section, which falls into six parts. 16.11, 12: the missionary group makes it way from Troas to Philippi, where it is to remain for some time. 16.13–15: they make contact with a group of women who are evidently in the habit of frequenting a (Jewish) place of prayer; one of them, Lydia, is converted, and takes the missionaries to her home. 16.16–18: Paul exorcises a demon from a girl. 16.19–24: Paul and Silas are brought before the magistrates, flogged and imprisoned. 16.25–34: there is an earthquake, Paul and Silas, and other prisoners, are set free, and the gaoler becomes a Christian. 16.35–40: the magistrates, learning that Paul and Silas are Roman citizens, release them and ask them to leave the city.

Verbs or pronouns in the first person plural occur in vv. 11, 12, 13, 15, 16, 17; that is, the narrator expressly represents himself as present on the journey from Troas to Philippi, as visiting the place of prayer and entertained by Lydia, and as addressed by the prophesying girl. From this point 'We' disappears; this however means, or need mean, no more than that is was only Paul and Silas who were arrested and imprisoned—the narrator no longer played an active part in the story. If we are to think of the author (real or supposed) of a source (or of the book itself) it is reasonable to think that he joined Paul's party at Troas, possible that he had come to Troas from Philippi (or at least from Macedonia), and probable that having reached Philippi he remained there throughout Paul's stay, and after it. See on 20.4, and Introduction, pp. xxv–xxx. Whoever wrote Acts 16 seems to have known Philippi (especially if in v. 13 ἐνομίζομεν is read), and to have been not unfamiliar with its administration (στρατηγοί, v. 20).

Against such realistic features of the narrative must be placed the earthquake (v. 26). There is nothing incredible in an earthquake, but the reader does not expect one to be violent enough to release all the prisoners in the town gaol, yet gentle enough to do them no harm, and sufficiently localized to be, it seems, unnoticed by the town officials. The development of a story within local tradition creates no difficulty; one would think however that the memory of an observer, whose words were recorded in the narrative we have, would have exercised a critical check on such developments. There are two possible ways of escaping this problem. One is to suppose that the eye-witness implied by 'We' was no longer present after v. 17; his narrative ends at that point. We should have to admit that if he was no longer in Philippi we have no idea what became of him until he reappears at 20.5; he would then have the opportunity of adding local tradition to his own recollections. The other would distinguish between the witness implied in 'We' and the author of Acts; the latter used a 'We-document' up to v. 18 and added local tradition to it. As an example of more radical treatment of the chapter Weiser's analysis may be noted. He rates as standing on their own the travel details of vv. 11, 12a; in addition, tradition supplied the raw material for the conversion of Lydia, the exorcism, the accusation of causing disturbance, flogging and imprisonment, release and dismissal, and the conversion of the gaoler. 'Lukas hat diese Einzelnachrichten mit den Mitteln des dramatischen Episodenstils szenisch ausgestaltet und miteinander zum Bericht eines sich steigernden Geschehensablaufs verbunden. Insbesondere stammen von Lukas: der Wir-Stil, die Kennzeichnung Philippis (V 12b), die Angabe der Aufenthaltsdauer (V 12c), die konkreten Ausgestaltungen der Lydia- und Exorzismusgeschichte (VV 13–15, 16–18), die Anklage wegen Geschäftsschädigung (V 19a) und der Verderbnis römischer Sitten (V 21), die Angaben über die Strenge der Haft (VV 23b, 24), die Befreiungswundererzählung mit den Konkretionen des Berichts über die Bekehrung des Gefängniswärters (VV 25–34), die Diskussion über das römische Bürgerrecht und die davon Abhängigen Aussagen (VV 37–39a), die abschliessende Erwähnung der Einkehr im Hause Lydias (V 40)' (431). It need not be questioned that the author has contributed substantially to the narrative as we have it, or that he was elaborating material that he derived from tradition. The important question left is whether the final author of the book was responsible for adding not only a number of lively details but also the 'We-style'. For this general question see Introduction, pp. xxv–xxx. We may well have to distinguish in this chapter, which provides an important introduction to the general question, (a) eye-witness recollection, using the first person plural; (b) local tradition; (c) the elaboration of local tradition; (d) the editorial work of the final author. Cf. Taylor 241: vv. 11–13a, 16b–23a, 35–40 come from the Journal de Voyage; Luke adds vv. 13b–16a and 25–34; Act III introduces various modifications, especially in vv. 23b, 24.

There is an important discussion of *honour* and *shame* as themes of this paragraph in Johnson (303f.); more fully, Rapske *Book of Acts* (3.303f.).

11. ἀναχθέντες: see 13.13. The participle is followed by δέ in P[74] ℵ A E Ψ 6 33 81 326 1175 *pc* vg, by οὖν (linking more closely with what precedes) in B C 𝔐 gig sy[h]. D(*) 614 sy[hmg] rewrite: τῇ δὲ ἐπαύριον ἀναχθέντες.

ἀπὸ Τρῳάδος: see 16.8.

εὐθυδρομεῖν occurs again at 21.1, not elsewhere in the NT. It is used especially of ships: *to sail a straight course*; so Philo, *Legum Allegoriae* 3.223 (but at *De Agricultura* 174 transitively of the wind driving a ship).

Samothrace is an island at the northern extremity of the Aegean,

not far from the coast of Thrace. It had long possessed a notable
sanctuary of the 'Great Gods', of Thracian origin but widely popular
in the Hellenistic age. Many came to be initiated into the two grades
of the mysteries practised at the temple. Paul and his companions
presumably spent the night there though they may not have left the
ship; there was a beach but no harbour.

τῇ δὲ ἐπιούσῃ (sc. ἡμέρᾳ; cf. 7.26), *on the next day* the journey
was continued to Neapolis, the modern Cavallo, the port of Philippi.
At the time of the battle of Philippi (42 BC) Brutus and Cassius used
Neapolis as their naval base; later a colony was established there (cf.
Philippi, v. 12). Ignatius, *Polycarp* 8.1, records that he sailed from
Troas to Neapolis. Acts describes no missionary work at Samothrace
or Neapolis; possibly neither place had a synagogue or place of
(Jewish) prayer; cf. v. 13.

Neapolis appears as Νεάπολιν in C D* E Ψ 𝔐, but the better
text is Νέαν Πόλιν, in P⁷⁴ᵛⁱᵈ ℵ A B Dᶜ 1175 1739 *pc*. This is the
older form (M.2.151, 278); for inscriptions and coins see Hemer 113,
n. 30.

12. κἀκεῖθεν εἰς Φιλίππους: but at Neapolis the travellers must
have left their ship and travelled about 10 miles inland. The battle of
42 BC, in which the Triumvirate defeated the republican forces under
Brutus and Cassius, was fought a little to the west of the town. After
the battle M. Antonius founded the *colonia* (see below), which was
subsequently augmented by his former colleague Octavian (Augustus) who defeated him at Actium (31 BC). The full name of the new
town was Colonia Julia Augusta Philippensium. The description of
the town in the present verse is obscured by textual and other
problems. The main readings are:

(a)	πρώτη	τῆς	μερίδος	τῆς M.	𝔐
(b)	πρώτη	τῆς	μερίδος	M.	P⁷⁴ ℵ A C Ψ 33 36 81 323 945 1175 1891 *pc*
(c)	πρώτη		μερίδος	τῆς M.	B
(d)	πρώτη			τῆς M.	614 1241 1739 2495 *pc* syʰ
(e)	πρώτη		μερὶς	M.	E saᵐˢˢ
(f)	κεφαλὴ			τῆς M.	D syᵖ

(f) is probably a translation variant. πρώτη was taken into Latin as
caput (so d) and into Syriac as רישא, and then came back into Greek
in a literal and unidiomatic rendering. See however Clark (362–5).
When Μακεδονίας is preceded by τῆς the meaning is probably
partitive—that district (part) of Macedonia. When it is not,
Μακεδονίας is probably in apposition—of the district (i.e. province)
Macedonia. τῆς before μερίδος is demonstrative—of that part of M.
(see Moule, *IB* 111). πρῶτος is used of leading or capital cities (e.g.

Thucydides 2.8.1), but if Luke had intended to describe Philippi as the capital of Macedonia he should have written ἡ πρώτη ... πόλις (with the article). The article is wanting, and with the grammatical goes the further difficulty that Philippi was not the capital of Macedonia or of any part (district, μερίς) of it. Macedonia had however been divided into four districts (Livy 45.29: ... deinde in quatuor regiones dividi Macedoniam). Sherwin-White (93), BDR § 164.3, n. 7, and many others (including recently Tajra 5) conjecture as the original text πρώτης μερίδος Μ. πόλις, *a city of the first district of Macedonia*. Livy (loc. cit.) describes the first region as follows: quod agri inter Strymonem et Nessum amnem sit: accessurum huic parti trans Nessum, ad orientem versum, qua Perseus tenuisset vicos, castella, oppida, praeter Aenum, et Maronem, et Addera; trans Strymonem autem vergentia ad occasum, Bisalticam omnem cum Heraclea, quam Sinticen appellant. Philippi is in this area. The Committee whose work is reported in Metzger (444–6) also approved this conjecture, but there is an appended note, signed K. A[land] and B. M. M[etzger]: 'Despite what have been regarded as insuperable difficulties in the commonly received text (πρώτη τῆς μερίδος), it appears ill-advised to abandon the testimony of P⁷⁴ ℵ A C 81 *al*, especially as the phrase can be taken to mean merely that Philippi was "a leading city of the district of Macedonia"; cf. Bauer's *Griechisch-Deutsches Wörterbuch*, 5te Auflage (1958), s.v. μερίς'. BA (successor to the dictionary referred to) 1023f. however takes the view that 'Die Über. *erste Stadt betreffenden Bezirkes von Maz... ist nur schwer erträglich.*' The article does not consider (an equivalent of) 'a leading city ... ', but prefers the NA²⁶ text πρώτη[s] μερίδος τῆς Μ.—the conjecture referred to above. This is surprising, not least in view of the fact that BA 1452 (s.v. πρῶτος 1.c.α.) recognizes the use of πρῶτος in the sense of rank but 'Ohne superl. Wert', citing Eph. 6.2 ('ein bedeutsames Gebot'); Lk. 15.22; 1 Cor. 15.3 ('*unter den ersten* = wichtigsten Stücken'). The word is not infrequently used in the plural (LS 1535), as for example Thucydides 2.8.1 (referred to above, τῶν πρώτων πόλεων). It would be less natural but not impossible to refer to one of such cities as a πρώτη πόλις. See *Begs*. 4.188f., and for an interesting note on the conjectured reading R. Borger in *ThR* 52 (1987), 36–8. See further Hemer (113f.), and for a bolder conjecture Hort (*Introduction, Notes* 96f.): ('It is not impossible that μερίδος should be read as πιερίδος (Μ for Π Ι), for Philippi belonged to the Pieria of Mount Pangaeon, and might well be called "a chief city of Pierian Macedonia"; so Steph. Byz. Κρηνίδος, πόλις Πιερίας (codd. Σικελίας), ἃς Φίλιππος μετωνόμασε Φιλίππους: cf. Herod. vii 212; Thuc. ii.99. The name ἡ Πιερὶς Μακεδονία does not seem however to occur elsewhere, and would more naturally be applied to the more famous Pieria in the S.W. of Macedonia. For the present the reading must remain in doubt.' For Herodotus 7.212 we should no doubt read 7.112. It will be noted that Hort seems to find no difficulty in taking πρώτη πόλις as 'a chief city'. Page (184) somewhat surprisingly approves the suggestion of Erasmus: 'prima occurrit a Neapoli petentibus Macedoniam.'

Philippi was a *colonia*. A *colonia* was originally a settlement of Roman citizens in conquered territory, intended to help to hold down the local population; then a place to which surplus Italian population could be consigned; then (as with Philippi) a place where discharged soldiers were pensioned off with land. *Coloniae* enjoyed *libertas* (autonomous government), *immunitas* (from tribute and taxation), and *Ius Italicum*, which meant, in effect, that they were considered to be a piece of Italian soil, having a Roman form of administration with Roman law and judicial procedure. Marshall (266) suggests that details about Philippi are provided in order to prepare for Paul's first encounter with *Roman* administrators. He had however already encountered a proconsul at 13.7. On Philippi see further L. Bormann, *Philippi: Stadt und Christengemeinde zur Zeit des Paulus*, Supp-NovT 78, Leiden, 1995.

The periphrastic imperfect, with the auxiliary separated from the participle, ἦσαν ... διατρίβοντες, emphasizing the continuous though not protracted stay (ἡμέρας τινάς; cf. 9.19; for a longer stay Luke has ἡμέραι ἱκαναί) over against the events of the next verses.

13. τῇ τε ἡμέρᾳ τῶν σαββάτων; for the expression see 13.14. Paul and his companions (*we*) went out of the city gate παρὰ ποταμόν (τὸν ποτ., D). M. 1.82 quotes but doubts the view of Ramsay that the absence of the article shows familiarity with the locality. The article may have been dropped because the phrase was a common one (cf. 'down town'). The river on which Philippi stood was the Gangites (or Cangites). The party were, it seems, looking for a προσευχή, or *place of prayer* (on the word see below), but there is considerable textual variation.

(a)	ἐνομίζομεν	προσευχὴν	εἶναι	A^c C Ψ 33 81 *pc* bo
(b)	ἐνόμιζεν	προσευχὴν	εἶναι	ℵ
(c)	ἐνομίζομεν	προσευχῇ	εἶναι	B *pc*
(d)	ἐνομίζετο	προσευχῇ	εἶναι	A*^{vid} E
(e)	ἐδόκει	προσευχῇ	εἶναι	D
(f)	ἐνόμιζεν	προσευχὴ	εἶναι	P^{74vid}

(f) is probably a slip and P[74] is often added to the MSS that have (d), (e) probably comes from (d), perhaps by way of the Latin *videbatur* (in d). (c), which must be translated 'Where we were accustomed to pray (to be in prayer)', involves an unusual use of the dative. Ropes (*Begs.* 3.155) prefers (d) with its less usual use of νομίζομαι: 'Where a place of prayer was accustomed to be', that is, 'We went to an area where it was customary to find a place of prayer'. For this (Ropes thinks) (a), which yields a similar sense, was substituted: 'Where we supposed there was a place of prayer'. Luke however elsewhere uses νομίζειν in the active (Lk. 2.44; Acts 7.25; 8.20; 14.19; 16.27; 17.29; 21.29; the only exception is Lk. 3.23, and this is a genuine passive and does not mean 'is accustomed'), and this may tip the scales in favour of (a), which is accepted with some hesitation by Metzger (447), who thinks that ἐνόμιζεν in P⁷⁴ ℵ may testify to an earlier ἐνομίζομεν, and that προσευχή in P⁷⁴ A B may have arisen through the omission of the horizontal stroke in −χῆ (= −χην). For νομίζειν cf. Josephus, *War* 7.128, 155; 2 Macc. 14.4.

Whether (a) or (d) is accepted, it seems to be implied that the visitors expected to find a προσευχή near the river. προσευχή in the NT is usually *prayer*, but it is used also for *place of prayer*, often but not necessarily a building. In what is described in *ND* 3.121 as the 'earliest mention of a synagogue' (*CIJ* 2.1440) the word used is προσευχή. Josephus, *Life* 277 is explicit (συνάγονται πάντες εἰς τὴν προσευχήν, μέγιστον οἴκημα) and the word was borrowed in Latin (Juvenal, *Satire* 3.296, ede ubi consistas, in qua te quaero proseucha?). See Philo, *Legatio* 132, 152, 346, 371; also *NS* 2.424–7. The question whether it was customary to establish places of prayer in the vicinity of water is discussed in *Begs*. 4.191 and *NS* 2.440–42. That this was a universal practice cannot be proved, though Josephus, *Ant.* 14.258 comes near to asserting it when he quotes a decree of Halicarnassus permitting the Jews to make προσευχαὶ πρὸς τῇ θαλάττῃ κατὰ τὸ πάτριον ἔθος. Cf. *Ant.* 12.106, with R. Marcus' note; also Ep. Aristeas 304f.; PTebt 86.16–20. StrB 2.742 note, 'Der Brauch, die Gebetstätten in der Nähe von Gewässern zu errichten, wird in der rabbin. Literatur nicht erwähnt', though Mekhilta on Exod. 12.1 notes that in the OT the word of God was given to prophets in the vicinity of water (Dan. 8.2; 10.4; Ezek. 1.3). I. Elbogen, *Der jüdische Gottesdienst* (1931/1967) 448 concludes, 'Es ist sehr unwahrscheinlich, dass selbst in der Diaspora die Synagogen *überall* am Wasser lagen.' See also Sukenik (*Synagogues* 49f.), who speaks more positively. 'Although official Judaism has preserved no trace of a precept to that effect, there is abundant evidence that Jews in Hellenistic countries built their synagogues by preference in the proximity of water.'

It is not stated by Luke whether the place of prayer in Philippi was a building; it is probable that it was not, since Luke frequently uses συναγωγή for the building and his choice of προσευχή here may be deliberate. The distinction made by Bowker (*Targums* 10) between συναγωγή and προσευχή has to do not with building but with the purpose for which the building or site was used; it is hardly established by the evidence. For identity of the two see M. Hengel,

FS Kuhn 157–84. That the προσευχή was outside the city gate does not prove that it was not a building; Jews were sometimes obliged to practise their rites outside the walls.

The women who gathered (συνελθούσαις) at the place of prayer were presumably Jewish (by birth, or proselytes) or at least Jewish sympathizers, and they had presumably come to pray. 'Man durfte sie [synagogues] nicht einmal betreten, wenn man nicht beten wollte' (Elbogen, 452). Elbogen notes a good many exceptions to this rule, though if the προσευχή was not a building the women will not have come there for shelter 'bei Regenwetter' or 'brennendem Sonnenschein' (449). For Luke's interest in and concern for women, and in the conversion of women to Christianity, see 1.14; 8.3, 12; 9.2; 16.1; 17.4, 12, 34; 18.2, 26; 21.5; 22.4. For the 'prominence of women in Asia Minor' see Trebilco (104–26).

καθίσταντες ἐλαλοῦμεν does not suggest a formal synagogue service (contrast 13.5, 14f.), though sitting was a natural posture for teaching.

14. Among the women was one called Lydia, a fairly common name, used also in Latin (Horace, *Odes* 1.8). It may but need not be significant that Thyatira (see below) was situated in Lydia. For the name see Hemer (114, 231), with the references also to *ND* 2.25–32; 3.54. The ethnic appellation might suit a freedwoman, the name having been given while she was a slave—ἡ Λυδία (the one from Lydia). But as Hemer points out the name can now be shown to have been used by women of higher class. It occurs as a second name, Νεωνὶς ἡ κ[α]ὶ Λυδία (*TAM* 3.661).

Lydia was a dealer in purple from Thyatira. A large group of compound words (LS 1451f.) based on πορφύρα, the purple-fish (*Musca trunculus* or *Purpura haemastoma*), also the purple dye obtained from it, bears witness to the importance of the dyeing industry and of crafts and trades related to it. W. M. Ramsay (in the *HDB* article, 4.757–9, still an excellent account, to be supplemented by *ND* 2.25–32), however, accepts the view that 'the dyeing in Thyatira was performed in ancient times with madder-root, *rubia* ...,' and that 'the purple stuffs which the Thyatiran Lydia sold in Philippi (Acts 16.14) were dyed with what is, in modern times, called ''Turkey red''' (759). It is not clear whether Lydia was a sort of commercial traveller in purple cloth, who visited Philippi frequently enough to know her way to the place of prayer, or had opened a retail establishment there. A fragmentary Latin inscription from Philippi appears to refer to dealers in purple (*CIL* 3.664.1: pu]rpurari[us *or* i]). *ND* 2.27 gives examples from elsewhere. *CIG* 2519 implies the feminine form used here, πορφυρόπωλις, and thus confirms the activity of women in this business; PFlor 71.461, sometimes quoted, appears to read πορφυροπώλου. For another business woman in the NT cf. Chloe

(1 Cor. 1.11). The connection of Macedonia with Thyatira is illustrated by *IG* 10.2.1.291, in which ἡ συνήθεια τῶν πορφυροβάφων, the gild of dyers of purple in Thessalonica, honour Μένιππον Ἀμ(μ)ίου τὸν καὶ Σεβῆρον Θυατείρηνον.

The history of Thyatira is of greater importance for the interpretation of Rev. 2.18–29 than of the present passage. Several local inscriptions refer to gilds of dyers. In πόλεως Θυατείρων the genitive of the place name is in apposition with πόλεως. A woman trader appears as early as Homer, *Iliad* 4.141f.

σεβομένη τὸν θεόν: for this term see the note on 10.2. It may be that she was neither a born Jew (her name is not Jewish) nor a proselyte but an adherent of the synagogue, a Jewish sympathizer. On the other hand, the words do not necessarily mean more than that she feared God; she was a devout woman. Wilcox (*JSNT* 13 (1981), 111) thinks that Paul would have been less likely to stay with her (v. 15) if she had been 'a mere "adherent" and not a full member of the synagogue'. As the informal meeting proceeded, ἤκουεν, she was listening; the imperfect here cannot refer to 'ein häufigeres Hören' (Delling, *Studien* 305); Delling mentions this only as a possibility, and is right in the observation that no significant interval can have intervened between the opening of Lydia's heart and her baptism (v. 15). Lydia hears, but it is the Lord who opens her heart. For the theological issue raised here see 13.48; cf. Stauffer (*Theologie* 163). προσέχειν must in this passage (cf. 8.6) mean more than *pay attention to*; something more like *believe* (*Begs.* 4.192). Cf. Josephus, *Apion* 1.2, where προσέχειν is the counterpart of ἀπιστεῖν.

15. There is no indication that any period of instruction followed Lydia's hearing of the Gospel and preceded her baptism. On baptism in Acts see Introduction, pp. xcif.; there is no reference here to the *name* or to the use of water. When Lydia was baptized so was (πᾶς, D *pc* (gig) w sa^ms bo^mss) ὁ οἶκος αὐτῆς. On the term *household* and its meaning in such contexts as this see on 10.2; the use of οἶκος cannot prove or disprove that small children were baptized. See Delling (*Studien* 288–310) as well as the studies by Jeremias and Aland.

For a woman as head of a household see Delling (*Studien* 302) quoting Philostratus (*Gymnasticus* 23) ἐπὶ μητρὶ δὲ εἶναι τὸν οἶκον—after her husband's death. See also *ND* 5.108.

BDR § 328.2, n. 3 would expect παρεκάλει rather than παρεκάλεσεν (but cf. v. 39). M. 3.65 would translate 'she invited'. This does not seem to be the sense that Luke gives to παρακαλεῖν, but it agrees with παρεβιάσατο at the end of the verse. For the omission of pronouns—παρεκ. (ἡμᾶς) λεγ. (ἡμῖν)—see BDR § 278; it is correct style.

πιστήν seems to contain both a substantive and an adjective: *if you have judged me to be a believer*, and a true, genuine, faithful, believer.

εἰσελθόντες (plural, all the travellers were invited) εἰς τὸν οἶκόν μου. Unless this means, 'Stay in, as members of, my family, my household', the word οἶκος has changed its meaning in the verse. It probably does now mean *dwelling house*. In *ND* 4.93 papyri are used to analyse the cases in which a woman owns the principal house of a family. In some cases the husband has died and left the house to his widow; it is much more frequently left to the children, though the widow may be given the right to occupy the house. Infrequently, a husband is found to reside in a house owned by his wife. The most frequent case is that of divorce in which the agreement is that the divorced wife shall own and occupy the house. 'If the above factors may legitimately be applied generally to the Mediterranean world, it is quite likely that Lydia, Paul's first convert in Europe, who appears to be the head of a household (Acts 16.14, 15, 40), was in fact divorced' (D. C. Barker). This is possible, perhaps unlikely. It may be that we should see here an early stage in the growth of churches (ἐκκλησίαι) that met in people's houses (e.g. Rom. 16.5).

παρεβιάσατο: a Lucan word, Lk. 24.29 and the present verse only in the NT. It may denote physical or moral constraint; here clearly the latter. Cf. Gen. 19.9; 1 Sam. 28.23, 2 Kings 2.17. Luke is interested in the moral consequences of conversion, and in hospitality.

16. ἐγένετο δὲ ... παιδίσκην ... ὑπαντῆσαι. For the construction, and Luke's ways of using his (biblical) (καὶ) ἐγένετο (δέ) see Introduction, p. xlvi.

ἡμῶν ... ἡμῖν. The construction begins as a genitive absolute but runs into the dative; not one of Luke's best sentences. It is natural to interpret the first person pronouns to mean that the narrative is, or is represented as being, reported by one who was present. Alternatively, the pronouns may be proper to the framework of the story (the itinerary) and have been imported from this into the episode, originally an independent piece of tradition inserted by Luke into the itinerary; so Bultmann (*Exegetica* 420). On the 'we-passages' in general see Introduction, pp. xxv–xxx. The enriching of an outline itinerary by incidents discovered in local tradition is a plausible account of Luke's method.

For the προσευχή see on v. 13.

παιδίσκη has various meanings (see I.584 and *John* 526); at Jn 18.17 the word must mean maidservant, or possibly female slave. Here it must mean *slave*, since the girl has κύριοι. *Prostitute*, well attested in earlier Greek, is not impossible, but would be unsuitable for Rhoda, the παιδίσκη of 12.13. The Philippian παιδίσκη is said to have had a πνεῦμα πύθωνα; so P⁷⁴ ℵ A B C* D* 81 326 *pc*. πύθωνος is read by P⁴⁵ C² D¹ E Ψ 𝔐. πύθων was originally the name of the snake, or dragon, that inhabited Delphi (originally, Pythia). This (a symbol or representative of the underworld) was killed by Apollo, who thus acquired the title Pythian Apollo; his priestess, who delivered the oracles at Delphi, was called the Πυθία (sc. ἱέρεια). There may be some connection with πυνθάνεσθαι (verbal stem πυθ-), *to inquire* (e.g. of an oracle). The word came, however, at the beginning of the imperial period (for evidence see especially W. Foerster, *TWNT* 6.917–19), to mean *ventriloquist* (ἐγγαστρίμυθος). A person capable of this act might well be believed (see Plutarch, *De Defectu Oraculorum* 9 (414e)) to be an instrument through whom a god or spirit spoke; indeed, ἐγγαστ. seems to have been used both of the human instrument and of the deity or spiritual being using it. The word ἐγγαστ. sends us further to 1 Sam. 28.7, where it is used of the Witch of Endor (Hebrew, בעלת אוב); ἐγγαστ. becomes in the Vulgate *python* or *spiritus pythonicus*, and the Hebrew בעל אוב is explained (Sanhedrin 7.7 (not 7.2 as in Foerster, who also gives other examples)) as המדבר משחיו דפיתום (פיתום = πύθων). It is best to suppose that Luke is describing such a person, and himself held the popular view (which the girl herself may well have shared) that the strange natural phenomenon was due to possession; he evidently believes (v. 18) that some being was driven out of the girl, and that this being had supernatural knowledge of what Paul and his colleagues were doing (v. 17). The construction remains unclear. The reading with the genitive is probably an attempt to ease it: a spirit of Python. The accusative is probably to be taken as in apposition: a spirit, a python; or, a spirit called Python. Or we may (see BDR § 242 n. 2) take the whole to mean a pythonic spirit. There is little difference between the first and the last of these. For all its prophesying it is not a good spirit; cf. *Clementine Homilies* 9.16: καὶ πύθωνες μαντεύονται, ἀλλ᾽ ὑφ᾽ ἡμῶν ὡς δαίμονες ἐκριζούμενοι φυγαδεύονται.

The possessed girl provided much ἐργασία—business, or profit. The meaning *business* is well supported by papyri (MM 252), but it was no doubt the profit arising from it that interested the girl's κύριοι (who could have been man and woman—M. 3.22), and in a different way Luke, who disapproved of profit made by the abuse of spiritual agencies (see Kremer, *Actes* 287–91). The profit arose through the girl's μαντεύεσθαι, a word used here only in the NT; thus never of OT or Christian prophets. Here, *by giving oracles*. It confirms the interpretation of πνεῦμα πύθωνα given above and reappearing in Suidas, for whom πύθων is δαιμόνιον μαντικόν.

17. κατακολουθοῦσα (P⁴⁵⁽*⁾ P⁷⁴ ℵ B D 36 453 *pc*), present participle, goes better with ἔκραζεν, imperfect (the aorist ἔκραξεν is read by very few MSS), than κατακολουθήσασα (A C E Ψ 𝔐 co). This might make it the textually inferior reading (a copyist's 'improvement'), but the combination of Old Uncial and Western MSS means that it is probably correct and part of a harmonious picture of a repeated event (cf. v. 18). There is no point in the observation that ventriloquists are unable to make loud noises (κράζειν); Luke was not recording decibels, and believed that the girl was genuinely possessed (v. 18), though by an evil spirit. The spirit has supernatural knowledge of the Gospel; cf. the knowledge shown by the demons in the Synoptic Gospels (e.g. Lk. 4.34).

She *followed Paul and us*; Weiser (435) notes that though ἡμῖν is used Paul is the only person who matters. 'Das Wir nur noch angehängt ist.' He infers that in this verse the first person plural comes not from the source but from the author. There is little force in this argument; on any showing Paul was the most important person in the group.

The omission of ἄνθρωποι by the Western text (D* gig Lucifer) gives a more exclusive identification: not 'These men are slaves' but 'These men are the slaves ...'. This was probably not intended by Luke.

ὕψιστος is a designation of God common in the LXX of the Psalms (rendering nearly always עליון) and of Daniel (rendering עליון and עלי); it is also frequent in Sirach. It is also used of Zeus (e.g. Aeschylus, *Eumenides* 28f.: ... καλοῦσα καὶ τέλειον ὕψιστον Δία, ἔπειτα μάντις ἐς θρόνους καθιζάνω—spoken by the Pythian prophetess). It occurs in Philo and Josephus, but its use in the Hellenistic synagogue has been variously assessed. Thus G. Bertram, in *TWNT* 8.616f.: 'Die weite Verbreitung und der populäre Gebrauch des Gottesnamens *der Höchste* im hellenistischen Judentum ergibt sich aus Synagogeninschriften mit der Widmung τῷ ὑψίστῳ θεῷ, zB aus Athribis in Ägypten Dittenberger *OGIS* 1.96.5' (in fact, line 7; Bertram gives the date of the inscription as about AD 200; it may be somewhat later). See also M. Hengel (*Judentum und Hellenismus* (1969), 545f., n. 244): 'Im Gebrauch der Synagoge trat die Verwendung dagegen wegen der Gefahr eines synkretistischen Missverständnisses zurück, so erscheint der Begriff bei den Inschriften in Rom überhaupt nicht.' One may conclude that the word was used sporadically in Hellenistic Judaism. For the interpretation of Greek and Jewish usage and belief see especially C. H. Roberts, T. C. Skeat, and A. D. Nock, 'The Gild of Zeus Hypsistos' in *HThR* 29 (1936), 39–88, with Hemer (231), *ND* 1.25–29, and Trebilco (127–44). A resident in Philippi, with no first-hand knowledge of Judaism, might well identify the one Jewish God with the highest god in his own pantheon. For *slaves* (δοῦλοι) of God see 2.18; 4.29. The word is Pauline (e.g. Rom. 1.1), and goes well with the description of God as exalted in majesty and power.

The servants of God *announce* (καταγγέλλουσιν; for the word cf. 1 Cor. 11.26) *to you* (ὑμῖν: the spirit speaks; ἡμῖν, in A C Ψ 𝔐 e sa is thus a natural but in fact inappropriate 'correction') ὁδὸν σωτηρίας. For ὁδός see on 9.2, for σωτηρία on 4.12. ὁδός here however will refer not to a manner of life but to the way to, that is the way to acquire, salvation. This answers in advance the question of v. 30, τί με δεῖ ποιεῖν ἵνα σωθῶ; implying the reply given by Paul and Silas, πίστευσον ἐπὶ τὸν κύριον Ἰησοῦν, καὶ σωθήσῃ (v. 31). See below.

For καταγγέλλουσιν D(*) (so also the Peshitto, though this is not noted in NA²⁶) has εὐαγγελίζονται. There is no difference in meaning. D has the slightly more common but with ὁδὸν σωτηρίας slightly less suitable word. It is not correct to say (BDR § 309.1, n. 2) that D* attests the active of the verb εὐαγγελίζειν. It is true that this MS has what appears to be the plural of the active participle εὐαγγελίζοντες, but this is probably an attempt to make some sense of εὐαγγελίζοντε, an itacistic error for εὐαγγελίζονται.

18. τοῦτο δὲ ἐποίει (imperfect, cf. ἔκραζε in v. 17), the process was repeated, and for a considerable though undefined period.

διαπονηθείς: cf. 4.2. POxy 4.743.22, ἐγὼ ὅλος διαπονοῦμαι is rendered by the editor 'I am quite upset', but, especially in the aorist, the word suggests 'I have reached the end of my patience'. Paul put up with the girl's behaviour as long as he could but at length could stand it no longer. The suggestion (Kosmala 339) that Paul was angry because the use of ὁδός (v. 17) suggested Essenism rather than Christianity is fanciful and unconvincing; Paul was well aware of the Christian use of *Way* (9.2)—at least, the author of Acts thought that he was. Paul turned to the spirit, that is, to the girl possessed by the spirit; clearly Paul (Luke) understood the ventriloquial phenomenon to be the result of possession.

D (ἐπιστρ. δὲ ὁ Π. τῷ πν. καὶ διαπον.) gives a less logical (and perhaps therefore textually preferable) order, though it would be fair to say that the two aorist participles signify more or less coincident action: he turned impatiently and said ...

παραγγέλλω certainly means 'Here and now I order you', and in this sense may be called an aoristic present: M. 1.119; BDR § 320 n. 2.

For the significance of *the name* see I.198–200; here, *with the authority* of.

ἐξελθεῖν, infinitive following upon a word of commanding (BDR § 392.1d). The progressive disuse of the infinitive is reflected in the reading of D e gig, ἵνα ἐξέλθῃς, M. 1.240.

The response is immediate; the demon, or spirit, went out αὐτῇ τῇ ὥρᾳ. There can be no doubt that Luke means *at once*; D rightly interprets in the variant εὐθέως. Black (*AA* 109–111) sees behind this an Aramaic construction with proleptic pronoun, בה־שעתא. The Greek is discussed by M. 2.432 (noting that here 'Semitic sources are not in question'; it is a 'mannerism'; a 'Lucan idiom'; cf. Wilcox 130) and by Moule (*IB* 93, 122). There seems to be no good reason why we should not translate 'at that very moment'. LS (282 b top) quote Thucydides 2.3.33, αὐτὸ τὸ περίορθρον, at the point of dawn.

The incident is clearly regarded by Luke as an exorcism (cf. e.g. Lk. 4.35); to take it as an example of pre-baptismal exorcism (Richardson, *Theology* 338; cf. 8.7) might be slightly more convincing if Luke went on to describe the baptism of the girl!

19. ἰδόντες δὲ (B has καὶ ἰδ.) οἱ κύριοι αὐτῆς (see v. 16). D avoids the participle and the pronoun, writing ὡς (for temporal ὡς see BDR § 455.2) δὲ εἶδαν οἱ κ. τῆς παιδίσκης.

When the spirit went out the hope of profit also departed (ἐξῆλθεν). Again D has the same sense in different words: ἀπεστερῆσθαι τῆς ἐργασίας αὐτῶν, ἧς εἶχον δι' αὐτῆς. Loss of profit is treated by Luke as the real cause of the action taken by the girl's owners; the charge they bring in v. 21 is thus a falsehood, and Luke intends that it should be seen as such. Cf. the motive of anti-Christian activity in 19.25. For Luke's interest in money and the abuse of money see e.g. I.413.

ἐπιλαμβάνεσθαι is a Lucan word (Lk. 5 times; Acts 9.27; 16.19; 17.19; 18.17; 21.30, 33; 23.19; in the rest of the NT 7 times, used in good senses and bad. It is commonly used with the genitive, and the present verse is not an exception in that the accusative τὸν Π. καὶ τὸν Σ. is the object of εἵλκυσαν; so BDR § 170.2, n. 2 (cf. 9.27; 18.17). For the resulting economy in pronouns see BDR § 278 n. 3. Silas was last mentioned by name at 15.40; presumably he is to be included in the first person plurals at 16.11, 12, 13, 15, 16, 17. There is nothing to suggest that the author of the 'We-source', or Timothy (if he was not that author) was arrested too.

For εἵλκυσαν (cf. Epictetus 1.29.22, ἕλκει μ'εἰς τὴν ἀγοράν) E has ἔσυραν without significant difference of meaning.

For the procedure of the arrest and the charges brought (vv. 20f.), see Sherwin-White (78–83).

εἰς τὴν ἀγοράν: ' "The courthouse" rather than "the market-place" would give the meaning, but the word is better transliterated than translated' (*Begs.* 4.194). The earliest meaning seems to be *assembly*, especially an assembly of the people rather than a council of chiefs (e.g. Homer, *Iliad* 2.93; *Odyssey* 2.69—cited LS 13); thence it became *place of assembly*, but especially *market-place*. The market-place of a Greek city, however, was much more than a place for buying and selling (cf. 17.17, and passages there cited); it was used for all kinds of public purposes, including judicial purposes. So e.g. Demosthenes 44.36(1091), ἐν τῇ τῶν ἀρχόντων ἀγορᾷ; Lucian, *Bis Accusatus* 4, προτίθεμεν αὐτοῖς ἀγορὰν δικῶν ...; 12. Here the ἄρχοντες (cf. Demosthenes, above) were to be found. The word was a general one and perhaps never quite ceased to suggest the present participle of ἄρχειν: the ἄρχων was one who ruled, though the word had particular associations in e.g. Athens. It can be equivalent to *praefectus* (Polybius 6.26.5); here, magistrate. For the question whether the ἄρχοντες are equivalent to the στρατηγοί see on v. 20.

20. *They brought them to the magistrates*, τοῖς στρατηγοῖς. Are the στρατηγοί of this verse identical with the ἄρχοντες of v. 19? See *Begs.* 4.195, with the references to Meyer and especially to Ramsay. στρατηγός is a standard equivalent for the Latin *praetor*, though the original sense of the Greek word was military, of the Latin judicial. Under the Empire the office of *praetor* intervened in the *cursus honorum* between that of *aedile* or plebeian tribune and the consulship, and it was the duty of praetors to preside in the courts and supervise the public treasury. But *praetor* was no longer (see Sherwin-White 92) the term normally in use for the magistrates of colonies; these were *duoviri* (fully *duoviri iuri dicundo*; occasionally *quattuorviri*), though earlier the term *praetor* was sometimes connected with the office; cf. Cicero, *De Lege Agraria contra Rullum* 2.34(93), 'cum ceteris in coloniis duumviri appellentur, hi ac praetores appellari volebant' (the passage refers to Capua). στρατηγός was thus a not unnatural word to use in Greek, especially in view of the fact that it is virtually impossible to find a literal translation of *duumviri*. The question however remains: Does Luke mean (a) they brought Paul and Silas to the rulers, and then (perhaps because told to do so by the rulers) took them on to the magistrates, or (b) they dragged them to the magistrates (described as ἄρχοντες) and in doing so brought them to the magistrates (described with their judicial function more clearly expressed as στρατηγοί)? (a) requires us to find different functions for ἄρχοντες and στρατηγοί, which is not easy; (b) seems a pointless repetition (though *Begs.* loc. cit. affirms that such repetitious variation is a Lucan characteristic; no references are given but we may perhaps think of those who are described in 20.17 as πρεσβύτεροι and in 20.28 as ἐπίσκοποι).

On the whole, since the repetition in the second clause includes the verb (εἵλκυσαν—προσαγαγόντες) as well as the noun, it seems better to accept (a), giving ἄρχοντες some such meaning as 'the leading people'.

The first charge against the Christians is that of causing a disturbance (cf. 17.6, οἱ τὴν οἰκουμένην ἀναστατώσαντες; 24.5, κινοῦντα στάσεις). For ἐκταράσσειν cf. Plutarch, *Coriolanus* 19 (223) ... τόν τε δῆμον αὖθις οὐ παρέξουσιν ἐκταράττειν τοῖς δημαγωγοῖς (tribunes); Aristophanes, *Knights* 863(867) ... σὺ λαμβάνεις, ἢν τὴν πόλιν ταράττῃς. Paul and Silas are described as Jews (and therefore men who might be expected to cause trouble?), but the substance of the charge is given in the next verse.

21. The remainder of the charge 'so far from being anachronistic is positively archaic' (Sherwin-White 82). It implies that it was illegitimate for Romans (members of a *colonia*) to adopt foreign customs, especially Jewish customs (v. 20). This was in accordance with the ancient principle that Roman citizens must practise the state cult, and might in addition practise only those cults that had been sanctioned by the Senate—*religiones licitae*. This principle was however relaxed in practice in the early Empire, and no objection was made to religions that did not offend against public order and public morality. Here however the 'principle of incompatibility' (Sherwin-White 80) is invoked (the dative Ῥωμαίοις οὖσιν is to be taken with ἔξεστιν ἡμῖν rather than with the infinitive: BDR § 410 n. 2). For this revival of a mostly forgotten principle there may have been two reasons (a) 'It is perhaps characteristic that it is in an isolated Roman community in the Greek half of the Roman Empire that the basic principle of Roman "otherness" should be affirmed, whereas in Italy the usual custom prevailed of treating alien cults on their merits' (Sherwin-White 82). (b) The reference to the fact that Paul and Silas were Jews may be significant. Roman policy was to be tolerant towards Jews in the practice of their religion, but there is some ground for thinking that there was at this time a reaction against any kind of proselytization. See A. Momigliano, *Claudius* (ET 1934), 29–35. Sherwin-White (81) is right to question 'whether there was any precise enactment against proselytism'; the evidence is not strong enough to affirm this. But the distinction between a national religion and attempts to turn this into a missionary religion is certainly in line with general imperial policy, and the juxtaposition of Ἰουδαῖοι ὑπάρχοντες (v. 20) and Ῥωμαίοις οὖσιν suggests that Paul and his companions were accused of illicit prosleytizing. See the note on 18.2. This raises the question whether Paul did in fact present his Christian message as a version, the best version, the only true version, of Judaism. Acts sometimes if not always suggests that he did. He and Silas proclaimed ἔθη; on this word see on 15.1. See W. C. van Unnik, *Sparsa Collecta I*, NovTSupp 29 (1973), 374–85.

22. D (καὶ πολὺς ὄχλος συνεπέστησαν κατ᾽ αὐτῶν κράζοντες) makes the scene more vivid, but is not necessarily secondary. The plural verb and participle, though defensible (with a noun of multitude), are not likely to have arisen out of the συνεπέστη of the other MSS. But the editor may have felt that κατ᾽ αὐτῶν required a supplement. συνεφιστάναι does not occur elsewhere in the NT, but ἐφιστάναι (a Lucan word: Lk. 7 times, Acts 11 times, the rest of the NT twice) at 4.1 in a similar sentence takes a simple dative. For the importance of the crowd here see Rapske (*Book of Acts* 3.121–3).

The magistrates react strongly, περιρήξαντες αὐτῶν τὰ ἱμάτια. Whose clothes? *Begs.* 4.195 points out that throughout the sentences αὐτῶν (first occurrence), αὐτοῖς, αὐτούς refer to Paul and Silas, leaving some likelihood that the second αὐτῶν also will do so. Moreover, for judges to tear off their own clothes in horror is a Jewish (e.g. Mk 14.63) rather than a Roman or Greek custom (noticed already by Calvin, 2.82), whereas to tear off an offender's clothes before beating him has many parallels (e.g. Demosthenes 19.197(403): περιρρήξας τὸν χιτωνίσκον ὁ οἰκέτης ξαίνει κατὰ τοῦ νώτου πολλάς; Plutarch, *Publicola* 6(99) ... συλλαβόντες τοὺς νεανίσκους περιερρήγνυον τὰ ἱμάτια, τὰς χεῖρας ἀπῆγον ὀπίσω, ῥάβδοις ἔξαινον τὰ σώματα. On the use of single or double ρ see M. 2.101f. (with a reference to 14.14, διαρρήξαντες), 192f.; BDR § 11.1, n. 2.

ἐκέλευον: the aorist might have been expected. At M. 3.65 Turner notes this; in *Insights* 96f. he says, 'St. Luke carefully avoids saying that they had explicitly and peremptorily ordered the flogging. The tense of his verb represents a mere pretence at command, satisfying the plaintiff commercial interests, and yet not constituting a breach of Roman law. The magistrates possibly hoped that the gaoler might have the good sense not to carry out what they had diplomatically but half-heartedly commanded.' He refers to the Western text of v. 39 (see the note there for his rendering). A more valuable point in v. 39 however is the use there of the aorist παρεκάλεσαν, where the imperfect παρεκάλουν would have been more natural. The simple fact is that Luke was not always as careful about his tenses as he might have been. One cannot do more than note an exception, as do BDR § 328.1, n. 2, 'κελεύειν im Impf. nur Apg 16.22 ἐκέλευον ῥαβδίζειν statt ἐκέλευσαν wie Vg iusserunt.' Turner's suggestion is inconsistent with v. 24 (παραγγελίαν τοιαύτην).

ῥαβδίζειν, active, not passive; the agent and object must be understood: 'they commanded *the officer* to beat *them*.' See BDR § 392.4, n. 14. The present infinitive (taken with the aorist participle ἐπιθέντες in v. 23) may be noted to Luke's credit: the beating went on until many blows had been inflicted. The verb describes a Roman punishment; cf. 2 Cor. 11.24f., where it is distinguished from the Jewish synagogue beating. It should not have been inflicted on Roman citizens; see on v. 37 (and *2 Corinthians* 297, on 2 Cor. 11.25).

23. The sentence, which began to falter a little in v. 22, since the στρατηγοί, though they gave the command (ἐκέλευον), are unlikely themselves to have torn the clothes off the backs of Paul and Barnabas, now causes further difficulty. Only indirectly can ἐπιθέντες refer to the στρατηγοί, ἔβαλον may be either 'the attendants physically put them in prison' or 'the magistrates committed them to prison', but παραγγείλαντες must refer to the magistrates who are giving an order to the δεσμοφύλαξ. The general sense is perfectly clear; so perhaps is the grammar on the legal principle *qui facit per alium facit per se*.

If Turner rightly understood the imperfect ἐκέλευον (v. 22), the attendants certainly misunderstood their orders, for they applied πολλὰς πληγάς. The expected aorists take over with ἐπιθέντες (contrast ῥαβδίζειν, and see on v. 22), ἔβαλον, and παραγγείλαντες.

δεσμοφύλαξ, gaoler; LS's earliest citation (380) is *BGU* 4.1138.12 (1st century BC). BA 352 refer to but do not specify papyri from the 3rd century BC and add further literary references, including Josephus, *Ant.* 2.61. The word occurs in Lucian, *Toxaris* 30; Lucian's story has a few superficial parallels with Luke's.

Beyer (102) observes that it would be possible to pass directly from this point to v. 35, leaving the possibility that Luke might have inserted the supernatural story of the earthquake into a much more matter-of-fact event.

The special instructions to the gaoler are scarcely consistent with any weakening of the force of ἐκέλευον in v. 22. The active infinitive τηρεῖν corresponds to ῥαβδίζειν in v. 22. Did Luke expect the agent and object (τῷ δεσμοφύλακι and αὐτούς) to be read back into the earlier part of the sentence?

24. ὃς παραγγελίαν τοιαύτην λαβών ... To resume a sentence and continue a narrative by means of a relative (ὅς evidently refers to the δεσμοφύλαξ) is characteristic of Luke in Acts. D sa have the more ordinary ὁ δέ in place of ὅς. The gaoler acts in accordance with the command (*such a command*—not such as is suggested by Turner on v. 22!) that he has received. He picks up the ἀσφαλῶς of v. 23. The prisoners are put εἰς τὴν ἐσωτέραν φυλακήν. The use of ἀνάγειν (literally, to bring *up*) in v. 34 is not enough to prove that this was an underground dungeon; the first action of the gaoler (v. 30) is given as προαγαγών, which might suggest bringing the prisoners forth from an inner room. The reference to the *inner prison* both fulfils the magistrates' instruction and prepares for the miraculous earthquake.

The prisoners' feet were secured (the gaoler ἠσφαλίσατο, referring back to ἀσφαλῶς in v. 23) εἰς τὸ ξύλον. It is not certain whether the ξύλον is to be thought of as a means of security or an instrument of torture. In the classical passages often quoted (Herodotus 6.75.2; Aristophanes, *Knights*, 367, 394, 1049(1046)) it is used with δέω, which suggests confinement (though *Knights* 394, and possibly 1049, also suggest torture). Eusebius (*HE* 5.1.27; 8.10.8; possibly 4.16.3) speaks of the ξύλον as a means by which torture was applied to Christian martyrs. The simple explanation is no doubt correct: the same instrument was used for both purposes. In *HE* 5 and 8 Eusebius speaks of a number (5, 4) of holes (cf. the πεντεσύριγγον ξύλον of *Knights* 1049); apparently the victim's legs could be more or less widely extended and discomfort turned thereby into severe pain. Luke does not suggest that Paul and Silas were being tortured; the context stresses security (ἀσφαλῶς ... εἰς τὴν ἐσωτέραν φυλακήν ... ἠσφαλίσατο); and when in v. 37 Paul complains of the treatment that he and his colleague have received he says δείραντες ... ἔβαλον εἰς φυλακήν, but adds no reference to further ill-usage.

The Western text (D *pc*) has ἐν τῷ ξύλῳ, an improvement on εἰς τὸ ξύλον; cf. Aristophanes, *Knights* 394, ἐν ξύλῳ δήσας. gig Lucifer have *in nervo*, but nervus seems to mean *fetter*.

25. Knox (*Hell. El.* 18) follows Rutherford (*Phrynichus* 36) in describing μεσονύκτιον as poetical, and Ionic. Use by Plutarch, Lucian, Vettius Valens, Strabo, as well as in the LXX (see LS 1107) is sufficient background for its appearance in NT prose. Here the article is used; contrast 20.7 (μέχρι μεσονυκτίου; for the omission there see M. 3.179). At 27.27, κατὰ μέσον τῆς νυκτός is used; here also by D.

προσευχόμενοι: a natural recourse for Christians in distress. In 12.5 the church prays for Peter while he sleeps. James 5.13 enjoins prayer upon anyone who κακοπαθεῖ; Paul and Silas in addition ὕμνουν τὸν θεόν (cf. James's ψαλλέτω for the man in good spirits). ὑμνεῖν without object occurs at Mk 14.26 (= Mt. 26.30, the singing of the Hallel Psalms at Passover); a pronominal object replaces God at Heb. 2.12 (quoting Ps. 22(21).23). For ὑμνεῖν τὸν θεόν parallels are given in *ND* 1.71, 72. ὕμνος occurs at Eph. 5.19; Col. 3.16. The non-biblical usage suggests the celebration of some god or hero, but determinative for Acts is the use of ὕμνος along with ψαλμός for the Psalms of David (cf. especially 2 Chron. 7.6, ἐν ὕμνοις Δαυίδ, בהלל דויד). Paul and Silas were singing OT Psalms or new compositions on the same lines (cf. the Qumran הדיות; also 5.41). Singing in prison may be (see *Begs.* 4.196f., quoting Reitzenstein) a literary convention, intended to show the coolness, courage, and faith of the prisoners. See Tertullian, *Ad Martyres* 2, Nihil crus sentit in nervo cum animus in caelo est. But, bearing in mind that ἐπακροᾶσθαι occurs nowhere else in the NT, the best parallel appears to be Testament of Joseph 8.5: καὶ ὡς ἤμην ἐν τοῖς δεσμοῖς ... καὶ ἐπηκροᾶτό μου πῶς ὕμνουν κύριον ... (text β). But the Testament may be dependent on Acts. Bruce (2.317) quotes also Epictetus 2.6.26, ἐσόμεθα ζηλωταὶ Σωκράτους, ὅταν ἐν φυλακῇ δυνώμεθα παιᾶνας γράφειν. But *Begs.* 4.197 rightly goes on to say that this often really happened. Luke is building up a highly dramatic but not unique story. Whatever we make of the earthquake and release it is true that men in prison for their faith have praised God; this is not the point on which the historicity of Luke's story will stand or fall.

ἐπηκρόωντο—because at night all were put into the inner cell? Rapske, *Book of Acts* 3.203f.

26. ἄφνω is a Lucan word: Acts 2.2; 16.26; 28.6 only in the NT.

The sentence σεισμὸς ἐγένετο μέγας occurs also (no doubt by chance) at Mt. 28.2; Rev. 16.18; cf. Rev. 6.12; 11.13. In the eastern Mediterranean earthquakes were as familiar in antiquity as they are today (e.g. Thucydides 3.87.2). Luke does not directly ascribe this one to divine providence, though he will certainly not have thought it fortuitous.

For σαλευθῆναι see on 4.31. τὰ θεμέλια: the word (an adjective— θεμέλιος λίθος) is normally treated as masculine. See M. 2.122 ('... τὰ θεμέλια here shows the collective sense; contrast οἱ θ. in Rev. 21.19'). See also Radermacher (52).

Unlike δεσμοφύλαξ (v. 23), δεσμωτήριον is classical.

παραχρῆμα is a Lucan word (Mt. twice; Lk. 10 times; Acts 6 times); it is probable therefore that its omission by B gig Lucifer is accidental. Stories of the supernatural characteristically emphasize the immediacy of divine action (see 3.7 and the note).

θύραι could refer to only one door, but it is probable that the prison had several and that the plural is a real plural; πᾶσαι makes this virtually certain. See BDR § 141.4, n. 8.

τὰ δεσμά appears as the plural of ὁ δεσμός here and at Lk. 8.29; Acts 20.23. οἱ δεσμοί is used at Phil. 1.13. In other passages the gender is not made clear by case and construction. Cf. the note on τὰ θεμέλια above, and see M. 2.121f. In this case the neuter plural is hardly a collective. There is an important note in Rutherford, *Phrynichus* 353f.

ἀνέθη (א* D* have ἀνελύθη) is probably correct and signifies further supernatural events; we are not to think (with Ramsay, *Paul the Traveller* 221) of staples loosened from cracks in the building, so that prisoners presumably ran out still manacled and fettered though no longer attached to the walls.

Origen (*c. Celsum* 2.34; cf. 8.41f.), prompted by Celsus' allusion, refers to the story of Dionysus in Euripides, *Bacchae*, quoting 498, λύσει μ'ὁ δαίμων αὐτὸς ὅταν ἐγὼ θέλω; see also 443–8, 586–8, especially 447f.: αὐτόματα δ'αὐταῖς δεσμὰ διελύθη ποδῶν κλῇδές τ'ἀνῆκαν θύρετρ' ἄνευ θνητῆς χερός. See also Ovid, *Metamorphoses* 15.669–671. For other possible connections between Acts and Euripides see 21.39; 26.14.

The question, discussed by Knowling (351), why all the prisoners did not immediately run away, is one that would not occur to Luke. There is a more profitable discussion in *Begs.* 4.196f. of the difference and relation between magic and religion. The observation that the earthquake may well have happened—earthquakes do happen—and that prisoners sometimes escaped without understanding the circumstances of their escape is fair enough; to be added to it is Luke's conviction that a special providence protected Paul as the special agent of God's plan for the spread of the Gospel.

2 Cor. 11.24–27, a list of perils from Paul's own hand, contains evidence of enough well-nigh incredible escapes to persuade a first-century Christian to believe in miracles (though Paul does not ascribe his escapes to miracle).

27. ἔξυπνος, *awake*, seems always to be used with γίνεσθαι, so that γενόμενος is not to be regarded as a Lucanism (*Begs*. 4.198). After ὁ δεσμοφύλαξ (v. 23), 614 *pc* add ὁ πιστὸς Στεφανάς, a Western elaboration, recalling the apocryphal acts and having no ulterior motivation. For the name cf. 1 Cor. 16.15, 17.

σπασάμενος, middle, rightly; see BDR § 310.1, n. 1. τήν is omitted by P⁷⁴ ℵ A E Ψ 𝔐, but B C D 81 1175 *pc*, which have it, are right. The gaoler drew the sword, that is, the one that he had, that was part of his equipment.

νομίζων ... Presumably the gaoler would think that punishment for allowing the escape of the prisoners would be an alternative worse than suicide. Cf. 12.19. Again dramatic effect is heightened (and the question of v. 30 prepared for), but whether the detail is a probable one is questioned. *Begs*. 4.198 observes that the gaoler would have had a reasonable chance of catching the prisoners, and that the earthquake would have been regarded by responsible authorities as a reasonable excuse. See *Digest* 48.3. Bauernfeind (210) on the other hand thinks that the gaoler's superiors would not have believed the story about the earthquake. One would have thought however that an earthquake strong enough to put the prison out of commission would hardly have escaped the notice of other residents in the town.

28. ἐφώνησεν μεγάλῃ φωνῇ is not a normal Greek expression for uttering a loud cry (μέγα φωνεῖν would be better). It has an OT ring, though in the OT φωνεῖν with the cognate dative occurs only at Dan. 5.7 LXX, ἐφώνησε φωνῇ μεγάλῃ, where the Aramaic is ... בחיל ... קרא.

With πράξῃς a double accusative rather than accusative and dative (σεαυτῷ) would be expected; but cf. Lk. 6.27. See Radermacher (99 '... in denen sich Lukas keineswegs als Attizist erweist'). Paul's concern for the gaoler's life recalls Stephen's prayer for those who were stoning him (7.60).

How, in the middle of the night and in the midst of an earthquake, Paul knows that all the prisoners are present is a question that Luke does not need to ask. Rapske (*Book of Acts* 3.203f.) (see on v. 25) answers the question by his suggestion that for security all the prisoners had been put for the night in the inner cell. Paul knows that God is ordering all things for good (and does not stop to consider whether others, like himself, might have been falsely imprisoned). This is not quite the same thing as claiming (Schille 347), 'Paulus erscheint wie ein Theios-anēr.' The divine man boasts, 'I can release

myself when I choose;' Paul knows that all things are in the hands of
a God who is other than himself.

There is much textual variation at the beginning over the verse,
and NA²⁶ may be unwise in following the reading of A alone. In
other witnesses we have (for μεγάλη φωνῇ ὁ Παῦλος)

Π. μεγ. φωνῇ	B *pc*
μεγ. φωνῇ Π.	ℵ C* 33 *pc*
φωνῇ μεγ. Π.	P⁷⁴
φωνῇ μεγ. ὁ Π.	C³ D E 𝔐
ὁ Π. φωνῇ μεγ.	36 *pc*

29. The subject changes without notice; no longer Paul but the
gaoler.

Naturally the gaoler calls for *lights*. φῶτα in the sense of
λαμπάδας is a late use. *Begs*. 4.198 raises the question whether
φῶτα should be taken as the accusative singular of φῶς (by analogy
with ἐρῶτα, ἱδρῶτα). LS (s.v. φάος, 1916) and BA 1738f. give no
example of this and the suggestion has little point since there is
evidence for the use of φῶς as *lamp*. The gaoler *sprang in*,
presumably into the dungeon where Paul and Silas were confined.
For εἰσεπήδησει cf. ἐκπηδᾶν in 14.14; (on both verses see C.
Burchard, *ZNW* 69 (1978), 155). He was *trembling*; for ἔντρομος (cf.
Heb. 12.21) γενόμενος cf. ἔξυπνος γενόμενος in v. 27; ὑπάρχων
(C* D Ψ 614 2495 *pc*) may be a better reading, γενόμενος arising by
assimilation.

προσέπεσεν, *he fell down before* Paul and Silas. The Western text
(D* gig sy) heightens the colour by adding πρὸς τοὺς πόδας. For
such respect to apostles and other preachers cf. 10.25; 14.11–13; see
on these passages. Here Paul and Silas make no comment, not
because they wish to be thought θεῖοι ἄνδρες (see on v. 28) but
because Luke is moving swiftly on to what he regards as the real
climax of his story in vv. 30f.

30. προαγαγών ... ἔξω. See on v. 24. We hear no more of the
earthquake, and the conversation between the gaoler and Paul and
Silas takes place outside the prison.

There is no need to take κύριοι as in itself more than polite
address, but Luke undoubtedly intends to portray a man impressed by
supernatural events which he connects with the persons to whom he
is speaking. This does not mean that he views them as θεῖοι ἄνδρες,
though Euripides and the *Bacchae* come once more to mind (see v.
26). If he did so view them he is immediately corrected by Paul and
Silas who (v. 31) point away from themselves to the truly divine
Man.

The gaoler asks, τί με δεῖ ποιεῖν ἵνα σωθῶ; On σώζειν in Acts
see I.227–31. The word could be used by Luke in a purely 'secular'

sense (notably 27.20, 31), and it is possible to understand it in such a sense here. The gaoler, facing the possible escape of all the prisoners committed to him, is in such straits that he intends suicide; what can he do to evade the consequences he fears? It is however impossible that Luke should have used the word without awareness of its specific Christian sense (see the reply in the next verse). Cf. the movement from 4.9, σέσωται, he has been cured, to 4.12, No other name by which δεῖ σωθῆναι ἡμᾶς—we, who are not lame beggars. The form of the question suggests that it may have been a formula, but no real parallel suggests itself. Cf. 2.37. *ND* 3.99 quotes PVindob G 25683, ... τί [...] ποιήσαι ἵνα σωθῶ ὁ ἁμαρτολός This however is a sixth-century papyrus, perhaps dependent on Acts.

The Western text if represented by D[(c)] (sy[p h**]) gives at the beginning of the verse: καὶ προήγαγεν αὐτοὺς ἔξω τοὺς λοιποὺς ἀσφαλισάμενος καὶ εἶπεν αὐτοῖς. This longer reading holds up the action with a wooden and prosaic addition, and is not to be defended by the observation (Black, *AA* 69) that with v. 29 it forms inelegant parataxis: καὶ ... προσέπεσεν ... καὶ προήγαγεν ... καὶ εἶπεν. The editor filled in a gap, without recognizing that he was (on this occasion) taking life and movement out of the story by putting more detail into it.

31. Whatever may be said about the form of the gaoler's question (see on v. 30), Paul and Silas reply in terms that rest upon an accepted formula; cf. Rom. 10.9, also Phil. 2.11. To believe on the Lord Jesus (Ἰησοῦν: so P[74vid] ℵ A B 33 81 *pc* gig vg bo; Western and Antiochian texts, C D E Ψ 0120 𝔐 sy sa, add Χριστόν) means to accept him as κύριος, that is, as supreme authority (see 2.36), and by implication to believe (in the words of Rom. 10) that God raised him from the dead, since otherwise the crucified Jesus could not be κύριος. It is implied that the word κύριος (repeated perhaps with intention from v. 30) would to such a man as the gaoler denote a recognizable category, and this, it may be noted, would not be a category defined in terms of the familiar κύριος—יהוה equivalence of the OT. Jesus is presented as a cult figure, the origin of the ὁδὸς σωτηρίας that Paul and Silas had preached (v. 17). A divine being who would be insulted when his servants were publicly ill-used and was powerful enough to send an earthquake to release them was one to command allegiance. This is a form of Christian belief neither profound nor exalted, but the historian should remember that this is what Christianity must have looked like to many in the first century, whether believers or unbelievers.

σωθήσῃ: see on v. 30.

σὺ καὶ ὁ οἶκός σου. For οἶκος cf. v. 15. It would be difficult to maintain that the word here includes infants, since not only were οἱ αὐτοῦ ἅπαντες baptized (v. 33), all heard the word of the Lord spoken by Paul and Silas (v. 32) and as a result the whole household rejoiced (ἠγαλλιάσατο πανοικεί). On this sequence of terms see Delling (*Studien* 301), though his conclusion lays the stress else-where—the author of Acts intends to include all 'die zu dem Hausstand des Betreffenden gehören'. Here as in vv. 14f. the conversion of the head of the household carries with it the members of the household. For the relation of the salvation of the household to the faith of one member cf. 1 Cor. 7.14–16 (on which see *1 Corinthians* 164–7).

32. ἐλάλησεν αὐτῷ τὸν λόγον τοῦ κυρίου (so P⁴⁵ P⁷⁴ ℵᶜ A C (D) E Ψ 0120 𝔐 lat sy co; ℵ* B *pc* have θεοῦ); speaking the word of God (no difference is intended if *Lord* is read; it goes with the wording of v. 31) is one of Luke's standard terms for preaching the Gospel. The basic proposition of v. 31 is filled out in a way that Luke's readers could develop for themselves—from the book itself if in no other way.

σὺν πᾶσιν (P⁴⁵ has σύμπασι, presumably omitting αὐτῷ—there is a lacuna before λόγον) ... See on v. 31. *All who were in his house* will be synonymous with ὁ οἶκός σου. Luke must mean all those who were capable of both hearing and understanding. He is not thinking of small children.

33. The gaoler's first reaction is to minister to those who are manifestly favoured by providence and have offered him a way of salvation—which presumably he has accepted, since this verse recounts his baptism.

παραλαβών perhaps (with C. Burchard, *ZNW* 69 (1978) 156f.), took them in as his guests; cf. 21.24, 26. ἔλουσεν ἀπὸ τῶν πληγῶν will mean 'washed their wounded bodies, washed off the effect of the blows (πληγαί, v. 23) they had received'. The expression is unusual and not fully explained by the parallels cited by Deissmann (*BS* 227; cf. Dittenberger, *Syll.* 982.5–7). BA 975 gives no further help; ἀπὸ τῶν πληγῶν shows that religious (i.e. cultic) washing is not in mind (though there may well be an intended play on the ἐβαπτίσθη that follows). This was seen by Chrysostom (*Homily* 36.2): ἔλουσεν αὐτοὺς καὶ ἐλούθη· ἐκείνους μὲν ἀπὸ τῶν πληγῶν ἔλουσεν, αὐτὸς δὲ ἀπὸ τῶν ἁμαρτίων.

οἱ αὐτοῦ πάντες (or, with ℵ B 614 1891 2495 *pc*, ἅπαντες) is the reading of the great majority of MSS, and almost certainly correct. P⁴⁵ vgᶜˡ boᵐˢ have ὁ οἶκος αὐτοῦ ὅλος; this is probably an assimilation to v. 31. A alone has οἱ οἰκίοι αὐτοῦ πάντες. There is no difference in meaning between all these readings. They cannot be used to prove that infants were baptized in the NT church. On baptism in Acts see Introduction, pp. xcif. The gaoler acted imme-diately for the relief of his prisoners (ἐν ἐκείνῃ τῇ ὥρᾳ τῆς νυκτός) and his baptism followed at once (παραχρῆμα, a Lucan word; see on

3.7). Whatever be the historical value of this account of events in Philippi it may probably be inferred that Luke and his readers would find nothing incredible, or improper, in a baptism following immediately, without instruction, upon conversion and profession of faith.

34. ἀναγαγών implies nothing about an underground dungeon (see on v. 24). The prisoners have already been brought out of the prison (ἔξω, v. 30); the gaoler now takes them εἰς τὸν οἶκον, to his house, 'up home'. It has been suggested that he had a flat above the prison; this might have fared badly in the earthquake.

παρέθηκεν τράπεζαν, *he prepared a meal* (that is, what was set on the table). The expression is not uncommon: Homer, *Odyssey* 5.92, ὡς ἄρα φωνήσασα θεὰ παρέθηκε τράπεζαν; Herodotus 6.139.3, τράπεζαν ἐπιπλέην ἀγαθῶν πάντων παραθέντες; Thucydides 1.130.2; Josephus, *Ant.* 6.338. The most natural way of taking the text is to suppose that the gaoler generously entertained men who had been wronged, whom he revered, to whom he was indebted; and rejoiced to do so (ἠγαλλιάσατο). Reicke, *DFZ* 217, however, argues that this meal, following upon baptism, will have been a eucharist (cf. 2.46, κλῶντές τε κατ᾽ οἶκον ἄρτον, μετελάμβανον τροφῆς ἐν ἀγαλλιάσει); so also Schille (348), supporting his view by the use of τράπεζα (cf. *Didache* 11.9). This is unlikely. τράπεζα is too common a word to prove anything, and ἀγαλλιᾶσθαι (Mt. 5.12; Lk. 1.47; 10.21; Jn 5.35; 8.56; Acts 2.26; 16.34; 1 Pet. 1.6, 8; 4.13; Rev. 19.70 and ἀγαλλίασις (Lk. 1.14, 44; Acts 2.46; Heb. 1.9; Jude 24) are anything but certain pointers. If Luke had wished to indicate that the meal was a eucharist he would have done this clearly, perhaps using the phrase, *the breaking of bread* (though whether this refers to the eucharist is quite uncertain). Yet there is a sense in which Reicke is right: every Christian fellowship meal was at least potentially a eucharist. On the Christian meal in Acts see Introduction, pp. xciif.

The rejoicing of the gaoler and his family is connected more clearly with his faith than with the meal. πεπιστευκώς is a causal participle, *because he had believed*, or perhaps somewhat less strongly, rejoiced in his new-found faith.

For πανοικεί cf. v. 31; the whole household is involved. ʽπανοικεσίᾳ, Ἀττικῶς· πανοικί, Ἑλληνικῶς' (Moeris); cf. Lobeck (*Phrynichus* 514). But Plato uses πανοικεί (–ί); it is also common in papyri (MM 476f.). See also Josephus, *Ant.* 4.70.

For the last five words of the verse D has ἠγαλλιάσατο σὺν τῷ οἴκῳ αὐτοῦ, πεπιστευκώς ἐπὶ τὸν θεόν. See M. 1.67f., 235. ἐπὶ τὸν θεόν is an improvement; the simple dative suggests (though Luke cannot have meant) that he simply believed what God said.

35. The night meal takes the story on till dawn, when the

στρατηγοί (vv. 20, 22) are again at their business. It is rightly
pointed out (Beyer 102) that the present verse could follow directly
upon v. 23 or v. 24; there would then however be no apparent motive
for the magistrates' change of mind with regard to their prisoners. In
the story as Luke has presented it it is clear that they too have
experienced the earthquake, and connect it with *those men*. Accordingly they send their officers, τοὺς ῥαβδούχους (in the NT only here
and at v. 38). The word denotes one who carries a rod or staff of
office (ῥάβδος). The Vulgate correctly translates *lictores*. In Rome
itself the lictors bore the *fasces* as their badge of office; those
attending for example Consuls and Praetors had, in addition to
ceremonial duties, the task of carrying out arrests and punishments;
those attached to officials in a colony such as Philippi would no
doubt have the same tasks assigned to them—here, unusually, that of
rectifying wrongful arrest and punishment.

After the plural τοὺς ῥαβδούχους the singular verb ἀπόλυσον is
surprising; presumably we must think of the order that the lictors
were charged to transmit to the gaoler.

The text of the verse in D (with varying support from a few other
Western authorities) runs: συνῆλθον οἱ στρατηγοὶ (this suggests,
though it does not require, a special meeting of the bench) ἐπὶ τὸ
αὐτὸ (a Lucan expression; see 2.47) εἰς τὴν ἀγορὰν (see v. 19) καὶ
ἀπομνησθέντες τὸν σεισμὸν τὸν γεγονότα (if it was as described
they would not merely remember it but see its effects about them)
ἐφοβήθησαν (not simply the earthquake itself but the supernatural
forces exhibited on behalf of the prisoners) καὶ ἀπέστειλαν τοὺς
ῥαβδούχους λέγοντες· ἀπόλυσον τοὺς ἀνθρώπους ἐκείνους οὓς
ἐχθὲς παρέλαβες (this, another singular verb, is clearly addressed to
the gaoler). This reading looks like an attempt to make the statement
fuller and clearer, leaving nothing to the imagination or intelli-
gence—another characteristic Western 'glimpse of the obvious' (cf.
8.1 and the note). ἐπὶ τὸ αὐτό is the sort of Lucan expression that an
editor could easily borrow.

Release, like imprisonment, was a matter of the magistrates'
coercitio (Tajra 26).

36. The lictors brought their message to the gaoler, and the gaoler
passed it on to Paul and Silas—or rather, as far as the wording goes,
to Paul, who stands out as the leading partner.

ἀπέσταλκαν (for the correct perfect form, –ασι). See M. 1.52 and
2.221, where Moulton corrected his earlier view. The tendency to
assimilate was strong, the third person plural ending in –ασι was the
only ending in which the perfect active differed from the weak aorist
active, and –αν had every chance of displacing the 'correct' form,
even among reasonably well educated scribes; in this case
ἀπέστειλαν in v. 35 may have affected the copyist's thought. The

fact is noted without comment (except a reference to unspecified inscriptions and papyri) in BDR § 83.1, n. 1.

πορεύεσθε ἐν εἰρήνῃ. D gig omit ἐν εἰρήνῃ, which may perhaps not be original; in any case, whatever be the foundation of the story, Luke is responsible for the wording. ' "Bibelgriechisch" lässt Lukas sogar den neubekehrten Gefängniswärter in Philippi sprechen' (BDR § 4.3, n. 8).

37. Paul did not find this somewhat casual treatment satisfactory. For his (or Luke's) motives see below.

δείραντες: the illegality of beating a Roman citizen is mentioned, with a reference to 2 Cor. 11.25, on v. 22. The Lex Porcia forbade this: Porcia tamen lex sola pro tergo civium lata videtur: quod gravi poena, si quis verberasset necassetve civem romanum, sanxit (Livy 10.9.4). This is eloquently taken up by Cicero, *In Verrem* 2.5.66 (170), Facinus est vinciri [or vincire] civem Romanum, scelus verberari [or verberare], prope parricidium necari [or necare]. Cicero, of course, knew that what ought not to happen sometimes did happen. In the same oration (2.5.62(162)) he writes, Caedabatur virgis in medio foro Mesanae civis Romanus, iudices, cum interea nullus gemitus, nulla vox alia istius miseri, inter dolorem crepitumque plagarum audiebatur nisi haec, 'Civis Romanus sum'. This incident however confirms that the victim knew that to claim citizenship ought to have delivered him from his suffering. Cf. further 2.5.57(147), and see Sherwin-White (58f.).

Paul stresses the enormity of the offence committed by the magistrates by adding δημοσίᾳ (*publicly*; cf. δημοσίᾳ τεθνάναι, to die at the hands of the public executioner, Demosthenes 45.81(1126). They had been publicly insulted and disgraced by the punishment. On the theme of honour and shame see Rapske (*Book of Acts* 3.303f.) They were also ἀκατακρίτους—uncondemned because there had been no trial (*re incognita*). Cf. Rackham (291). This was a further point well understood in Roman law and custom. Tacitus, *Histories* 1.6, condemns the execution by Galba of Congonius Varro and Petronius Turpilianus: 'inauditi atque indefensi tamquam innocentes perierant.' Augustine (*De Civitate Dei* 1.19) bases an argument against suicide on the principle: 'Vos appello, leges iudicesque Romani. Nempe post perpetrata facinora nec quemquam scelestum indemnatum inpune voluistis occidi.' See also Cicero, *In Verrem* 2.1.9(25): 'Causa cognita multi possunt absolvi, incognita quidem condemnari nemo potest.' D (syᵖ) add (before δείραντες) ἀναιτίους, innocent, guiltless; this is not appropriate in the same clause as ἀκατακρίτους.

The most serious point (in the view of the magistrates), however, is that Paul and Silas are Romans; that is, citizens, enjoying by right a considerable measure of immunity and having the power to seek legal redress. For Paul's claim to be a Roman citizen, and for the means by which he acquired the citizenship, see 22.25, 28; in the present passage the same claim is made for Silas. On the citizenship as it relates to Paul in Acts see especially H. J. Cadbury in *Begs.* 5.297–338 and Sherwin-White (55–72, 144–54). It is not easy to answer the question how he could have demonstrated his citizenship, especially after his clothes, with no doubt any pockets they may have contained, had been torn off (v. 22). Whether in any circumstances he would have had a certificate to show is uncertain (Sherwin-White 148f.); he could hardly from the prison in Philippi ask for the register in Tarsus to be consulted. It may be that the bare claim would be enough to frighten the magistrates on the ground that though it might be false it could possibly be true and that if it were they could be involved in expensive legal proceedings with an unfortunate outcome. There is no reference to the citizenship in any extant epistle of Paul's, and we know (2 Cor. 11.23, 25) that he received a Roman flogging three times and was often imprisoned. These facts do not prove that Paul did not possess the citizenship. We know (1 Cor. 9.12) that he was not in the habit of insisting on all his rights and there is nothing improbable in Luke's own suggestion in this chapter that on occasion action was taken in hot blood and too swiftly to permit an appeal to Paul's rights, supposing Paul to have been willing to make one. This suggests a further question. If it be granted that Paul was a citizen yet often waived such rights as he possessed, why does he in Philippi stand on his dignity, not accepting simple release but demanding from the magistrates personal appearance and (virtually) apology? The question in this form is not answerable, since the historicity of the event is open to question and we have in any case no direct access to Paul's motives. We may however say that Luke uses the incident as a warning to magistrates: they would be well advised to give Christians a fair trial and prove their guilt before punishing them. According to Barth (*CD* 3.4.685), Paul was not motivated by pride or rancour, but by the 'desire for a restoration of disrupted order'. This is fair enough, if we accept both the historicity of the story and that Paul's actions were governed (as they doubtless usually were) by theological principles. For relevant principles see Rom. 13.1–7, with *Romans* 224–9.

On λάθρα (from λανθάνειν), Radermacher (168f.), notes the Hellenistic tendency to prefer adverbs to participles.

ἐκβάλλουσιν neatly takes up ἔβαλον (v. 23): 'put us in ... put us out'.

οὐ γάρ: the use of γάρ in the answer to a question is classical (BDR § 452.2, n. 3), and adds emphasis: *No, indeed*. ἀλλά: but, *on the contrary* ...

For Jews as Roman citizens see Josephus, *Ant.* 14.228, 232, 234, 237, 240; also Juster, 2.25–27; Th. Mommsen, *ZNW* 2 (1901), 82f.; *NS* 3.133, 135.

38. The ῥαβδοῦχοι report back to the στρατηγοί; for the reaction of the latter see v. 37, and cf. 22.29. For δέ, ℵ E 104 *pc* have τε. For the effect of the claim to Roman citizenship see Cicero, *In Verrem* 2.5.57(147), Illa vox et imploratio, 'Civis Romanus sum,' quae saepe multis in ultimis terris opem inter barbaros et salutem tulit.

The text of D (which has some Syriac support) in this verse shows some confusion. It runs: ἀπήγγειλαν δὲ αυτοιςοι (sic) στρατηγοῖς οἱ ῥαβδοῦχοι τὰ ῥήματα ταῦτα τὰ ῥηθέντα πρὸς τοὺς στρατηγούς, οἱ δὲ ἀκούσαντες ὅτι Ῥωμαῖοί εἰσιν εφοβήθησαν. It should be noted that D differs again and even more widely from the other MSS in the next verse; see the note there. It seems clear that D has conflated two texts. τὰ ῥήματα and τὰ ῥηθέντα are doublets, and the impossible αυτοιςοι bears witness to αὐτοῖς (possibly αὐτοί) and τοῖς (στρατηγοῖς). The original Western text (cf. Ropes in *Begs.* 3.160; Clark 106f., 365) probably ran, ἀπήγγ. δὲ οἱ ῥαβ. τὰ ῥηθέντα πρὸς τοὺς στρ., οἱ δὲ ἀκ. ὅτι Ῥωμ. εἰσιν ἐφοβ. This is an innocent and indeed pointless variation on the Old Uncial text, and suggests the work of an editor who was at this point copying, but not too attentively or respectfully. See the note on the next verse, and Introduction, pp. xxi, lxix.

39. παρεκάλεσαν, a word of varying meaning in Acts (see on 15.32). Here, *they asked*—perhaps stronger, *urged*, or, *begged*. BDR § 328.2. n. 3 (cf. v. 15) hint that the more natural tense would be παρεκάλουν, the imperfect. This tense in fact appears immediately in ἠρώτων; could it be that παρακαλεῖν here means *to placate*? They placated them and then set about their request.

ἐξαγαγόντες, brought them out—of what? In view of what follows one is inclined to think that they were now brought out of the prison, and then asked to go away *from the city*, ἀπὸ τῆς πόλεως. But already at v. 30 they were ἔξω, and at v. 34 they were eating in the gaoler's house. Possibly we should, in view of ἀπόλυσον (v. 35), ἐξελθόντες (v. 36), and ἐκβάλλουσιν (v. 37), suppose that Paul and Silas had been brought back into the prison. See also v. 40. This is not the general impression given by the story, which says nothing of a return, but the link was not important, and Luke might well omit it, or not think of it. But perhaps the best explanation is that the original form of the story did not contain the account of the earthquake, vv. 25–34.

BDR § 209.1 note that here, exceptionally, ἀπό and ἐκ are not distinguished; by ἀπελθεῖν ἀπὸ τῆς πόλεως Luke means ' "aus der Stadt hinausgehen" (nicht "aus der Nähe der Stadt weggehen")'.

In this verse the reading of D (partially supported by 614 *pc* sy^h**) is so different from that of other MSS as to call for separate commentary. There is nothing intrinsically impossible or indeed difficult in it and it is of some importance as an outstanding example of a place where the Western text presents a different picture from that of the Old Uncials—different, however, not in essentials but in additional detail. Which is to be preferred, and whether it is right to prefer one as more 'original' than the other, are questions that can be answered only as part of a general discussion of the two texts. See I.20–29 and Introduction, pp. xix–xxiii; the view taken here is that the Western text arose at a time and place in which the text was not regarded as having full canonical authority and was therefore open to free modification. The text of D is

καὶ παραγενόμενοι μετὰ φίλων πολλῶν εἰς τὴν φυλακὴν παρεκάλεσαν αὐτοὺς ἐξελθεῖν εἰπόντες· Ἠγνοήσαμεν τὰ καθ᾽ ὑμᾶς ὅτι ἐστὲ ἄνδρες δίκαιοι. καὶ ἐξαγαγόντες παρεκάλεσαν αὐτοὺς λέγοντες· Ἐκ τῆς πόλεως ταύτης ἐξέλθατε μήποτε πάλιν συστραφῶσιν ἡμεῖν ἐπικράζοντες καθ᾽ ὑμῶν.

See Ropes in *Begs*. 3.160f.; Clark 107, 365f.

The στρατηγοί appear at the prison with many friends, who, they presumably hope, will add weight to their request, Their presence certainly adds to the dignity of Paul and Silas. It is here clearly stated (cf. the note above) that the preachers are back in prison. παρεκάλεσαν αὐτούς may be a gloss introduced from the other text, but here it has an explicit complement, whereas ἠρώτων ἀπελθεῖν is wanting. εἰπόντες is an aorist participle of coincident action. Direct speech follows.

Το Ἠγνοήσαμεν τὰ καθ᾽ὑμᾶς ὅτι ἐστὲ ἄνδρες δίκαιοι there is no parallel in the Old Uncial text. Turner (M. 3.15) translates, 'We acted amiss at your trial in court', adding in brackets the word πρᾶγμα, presumably to show that this is how he understands τὰ καθ᾽ὑμᾶς. This is fair enough, though since there was no trial in court *your case* (in a legal sense) would be better (cf. 25.14). But the rendering *we acted amiss* is questionable. It is true that ἀγνοεῖν, used absolutely, can mean 'go wrong, make a false step . . . to be ignorant of what is right, act amiss' (LS 12, s.v. II). But (a) in the NT the word means almost always *not to know, not to understand* (Heb. 5.2; 2 Pet. 2.12 are unlikely and in any case unimportant exceptions); (b) if the word is taken in Turner's way it is not easy to explain the following clause, ὅτι κτλ.; (c) d has *ignoramus*. It is better to translate, We failed to understand, in reference to your affair, that you were innocent (δίκαιοι) men. The next words bring the Western text into line with other authorities, but fresh material follows, again in direct speech, and the magistrates explain why they are anxious that Paul and Silas should leave. It is μήποτε πάλιν συστραφῶσιν ἡμῖν. They are concerned for their own safety as well as that of the prisoners. Those who brought the initial complaint may again gather together, with aggressive intent; cf. the use of the cognate συστροφή at 19.40;

23.12. They would indeed be shouting against Paul and Silas (καθ' ὑμῶν), but aggressively urging the magistrates to take action against them.

40. ἐξελθόντες: unless this is coincident with ἐξαγαγόντες (v. 39) the chronology is confused once more. ἀπὸ τῆς φυλακῆς: ἐκ (P[74] A D E Ψ 0120 𝔐) is a natural improvement, so that there is no need here to think of a distinct Western tradition of events. εἰσῆλθον (ἦλθον, D e gig) πρὸς τὴν Λυδίαν. Cf. v. 15. The narrator has now faded from the scene, because he had already left Philippi, because the first person plural is a literary device, or because interest is naturally focused on the two witness-bearers who have suffered in the cause. εἰση. πρὸς τ. Λ. is short for εἰσελθόντες εἰς τὸν οἶκον τῆς Λ. (v. 15).

παρακαλεῖν is now used in a sense quite different from that of v. 39. Only the conversion of Lydia has been mentioned so far in the chapter, so that we have no evidence to tell us who the ἀδελφοί were. The phrase is a formula Luke uses from habit; he may think of the brothers—an ἐκκλησία—as meeting in Lydia's house. D extends the formula by introducing a report: καὶ ἰδόντες τοὺς ἀδελφοὺς διηγήσαντο ὅσα ἐποίησεν κύριος αὐτοῖς παρακαλέσαντες αὐτούς. E Ψ 𝔐 introduce a second (pronominal) object: ἰδόντες τοὺς ἀδ. παρεκ. αὐτούς.

'The *Duoviri* left themselves open to severe punishment for they could be deprived of office and disqualified from any further government service for having violated the rights of Roman citizens in a Roman colony' (Tajra 29, referring to Dio Cassius 60.24.4). Luke is not interested in the fate of the Duoviri but only in the next moves of Paul and Silas.

44. FROM PHILIPPI TO ATHENS 17.1–15

(1) They followed the road through Amphipolis and Apollonia and came to Thessalonica, where there was a synagogue of the Jews. (2) Paul, in accordance with his custom, went in to them on three Sabbaths[1] and argued with them on the basis of the Scriptures, (3) expounding them and submitting that it was necessary that the Christ should suffer and rise from the dead, and, 'This man is the Christ, Jesus, whom I am proclaiming to you.' (4) Some of them believed and accepted their lot[2] with Paul and Silas, also a large company of the[3] god-fearing Greeks, and not a few of the leading women. (5) The Jews became jealous,[4] took to themselves evil men from among the market-place louts, gathered a crowd, and set the city in an uproar. They sought to bring them out[5] to the people. (6) When they did not find them they dragged Jason and some brothers before the politarchs, shouting, 'These men who have[6] led the whole world into revolt have come here too. (7) Jason has taken them in; and they are all acting contrary to the decrees of Caesar,[7] saying that there is another king, Jesus.' (8) They disturbed the crowd and the politarchs, as they listened to these [charges], (9) and from Jason and the others they took security[8] and dismissed them.

(10) Immediately, in the course of the night,[9] the brothers sent off Paul and Silas to Beroea. When they arrived they went into the synagogue of the Jews. (11) These [Jews] were more liberal[10] than those in Thessalonica; they received the word with all eagerness, searching the Scriptures daily [to see] if these things were so. (12) So many of them became believers; also not a few of the Greek women of good standing, and men. (13) But when the Jews from Thessalonica knew that the word of God had been preached by Paul in Beroea also they came there too stirring up and disturbing the crowds. (14) Immediately, at that very time, the brothers sent Paul away[11] to travel to the sea. But Silas and Timothy remained there [in Beroea]. (15) Those who were accompanying Paul brought him as far as Athens; they left with instructions for Silas and Timothy that they should come to him as quickly as possible.

[1]RSV, for three weeks.
[2]RSV, NEB, joined.
[3]RSV, devout; NJB, god-fearing people and Greeks.
[4]NJB, full of resentment.
[5]NJB, before the People's Assembly.
[6]RSV, turned the world upside down; NEB, made trouble all over the world; NJB, been turning the whole world upside down.
[7]NEB, flout the Emperor's laws.
[8]NEB, they bound over Jason and the others.
[9]NJB, when it was dark.
[10]RSV, noble; NEB, civil; NJB, noble-minded.
[11]RSV, on his way.

Bibliography

K. P. Donfried, *NTS* 31 (1985), 342–6.

E. A. Judge, *RTR* 30 (1971), 1–7.

D. W. Kemmler, *Faith and Human Reason*, *SuppNovT* 40 (1975).

G. D Kilpatrick, *JTS* 11 (1960), 340.

J. Kremer, in Kremer, *Actes* 11–20.

J. Murphy-O'Connor, *RB* 99 (1992), 418–24.

C. Schuler, *Classical Philology* 55 (1960), 90–100.

M. J. Suggs, *NovT* 4 (1960), 60–8.

Commentary

The most significant stop made by Paul and Silas in Macedonia, after leaving Philippi, is at Thessalonica. The mission begins with considerable success (vv. 1–4). Opposition on the part of the Jews, however, leads the politarchs to take relatively mild action against the Christians (vv. 5–9); Paul and Silas are sent off to Beroea, where they receive a more favourable welcome (vv. 10–12). Jews from Thessalonica pursue the missionaries to Beroea. The Beroean Christians send Paul away to the sea and bring him to Athens; Silas and Timothy remain in Beroea, but with instructions to rejoin Paul as soon as possible (vv. 13–15).

All this makes a connected narrative that follows a logical course and gives rise to no serious difficulty. It is probably to be regarded as a continuous composition by Luke himself. A number of words are characteristic of his vocabulary (e.g. διαλέγεσθαι, καταγγέλλειν, σέβεσθαι, σύρειν, οἰκουμένη, ταράσσειν, ἐκπέμπειν, ἐξιέναι). There are features of Lucan style, such as the litotes of v. 4 and the continuation of a sentence by the use of a relative (v. 7). This is of course not to say that Luke made it all up out of his imagination. That the place names—Amphipolis, Apollonia, Thessalonica, Beroea—were derived from an itinerary is a probable hypothesis which is supported by the fact that no incidents are recorded for Amphipolis and Apollonia. This may be due to the fact that Paul and his companions passed through these towns without making any effort to evangelize them (possibly because they had no synagogues?), but it is at least equally probable that all the names stood in a list and that Luke visited Thessalonica and Beroea and acquired information but was unable to reach the other two towns—or if he reached them gained no usable information. The name Jason suggests contact with local tradition; the use of the correct word 'politarch' will suggest either contact or a good knowledge of Roman provincial administration. Weiser (443) ascribes vv. 1a, 10a, 14f. to the itinerary; for different analyses see Roloff (249); Lüdemann (194f.); Taylor (5.265) ('le récit de Act I se lit maintenant en 17.1b–10, 12a, 13–15').

The essence of Paul's preaching is given in a sentence that recurs frequently in varying forms in Acts: τὸν Χριστὸν ἔδει παθεῖν καὶ ἀναστῆναι ἐκ νεκρῶν. The (deliberate?) misunderstanding of Paul's message to mean that Jesus is another king (and thus a rival to Caesar) is one that must have occurred frequently. It was easy to reject, probably not so easy to dispose of.

1. The new paragraph resumes the account of the journey broken off at 16.12 to describe events at Philippi. It is at least possible that the stories of Lydia and the gaoler were inserted in an itinerary that described a journey from Troas through Samothrace, Neapolis, Philippi, Amphipolis, Apollonia, and Thessalonica; see Introduction p. xxvi. Schneider (2.222f.) however goes too far in the belief that 17.1 cannot have followed upon 16.40. For the structure of the new paragraph see above, p. 807.

Διοδεύσαντες: elsewhere in the NT διοδεύειν is used only at Lk. 8.1, where Jesus is said to go preaching and evangelizing in every city and village. Were it not for this one would be inclined to think that Luke had here abandoned his usual διέρχεσθαι (which sometimes at least refers to a preaching mission) because Paul and his companions passed through Amphipolis and Apollonia without stopping to preach there. This may in any case be true. *ND* 1.45 provide a recently published example of the verb, used of men on military service; here it may well (by the compounded ὁδός) point to the fact that the journey followed the Via Egnatia, the main land route from Rome to the East (see Cicero, *De Provinciis Consularibus* 2(4): via illa nostra, quae per Macedoniam est usque ad Hellespontum militaris).

For the somewhat unpredictable use of the article with placenames in Acts see BDR § 261.2, n. 2. Amphipolis and Apollonia lay on the Via Egnatia between Philippi and Thessalonica. According to Livy (45.29; see above on 16.12) Amphipolis was the capital of the first district of Macedonia (Capita regionum, ubi concilia fierent, primae regionis Amphipolim, secundae Thessalonicen, tertiae Pellam, quartae Pelagoniam fecit). It was formerly called Ἐννέα ὁδοί (Thucydides 1.100.3), but became an Athenian colony (4.102.1). It derived its name from the fact that it was surrounded on two sides by the river Strymon (ἐπ' ἀμφότερα περιρρέοντος τοῦ Στρυμόνος, διὰ τὸ περιέχειν αὐτήν), and it was visible (περιφανής) from both sea and land (4.102.2). Apollonia was further inland, a day's journey beyond Amphipolis (id diei iter est, Livy 45.28). Hemer (115) thinks that Amphipolis and Apollonia were 'the places where the travellers spent successive nights, dividing the journey into three stages of about 30, 27 and 35 miles'. To cover these distances each in a single day presupposes the use of horses (*Begs.* 4.202).

In due course they came to Thessalonica, πόλις ... μεγίστη καὶ πολυάνθρωπος (Theodoret, *HE* 5.17.1; cf. Lucian, *Lucius* 46). In Acts ὅπου is used only here and at 20.6 (but here B (Ψ) 𝔐 have οὗ and D has ἐν ᾗ καί). οὗ is used 9 times if 20.6 is included. According to Zerwick (§ 217) ὅπου contains a causal element; Paul and his company halted in Thessalonica because there was a synagogue there (cf. 16.13); it would be implied that they passed by Amphipolis and Apollonia because there was no Jewish colony in these cities. Knowling (357) thinks that ὅπου is not to be distinguished from οὗ but if it is it implies *oppidum tale in quo esset*. Thessalonica was head of the second division of Macedonia (see above) and a free city (civitas libera; Pliny, *Natural History* 4.36)—hence the politarchs mentioned in v. 6. There is no confirmatory evidence for the existence here of a Jewish community as early as Acts, but *CIJ* 693 attests a synagogue or at least a Jewish family in the late second century, or later (Hemer 115). For the significance of the synagogue and its place in Luke's understanding of the Christian mission see on 6.9; 13.5; et al. Taylor (269) quotes an inscription possibly relevant in time (*IG* 10.2.1.72) which contains the words θεῷ ὑψίστῳ κατ᾽ ἐπιταγὴν ουες (?=יהוה).

For τὴν Ἀπ. ἦλθον εἰς Θεσσ., D has κατῆλθον εἰς Ἀπολλωνίδα κἀκεῖθεν εἰς Θεσσ. Metzger (452) points out that this implies a stop in Apollonia, which is in any case probable; there is no great difference in meaning. κατῆλθον is not correct, since Amphipolis is a seaside, Apollonia an inland town. D, with E 𝔐, also has ἡ συναγωγή, in agreement with Apollonius' canon. But here the omission of the article is legitimate; the meaning is that in Thessalonica there was one of the (many) synagogues of the Jews.

2. For κατὰ τὸ εἰωθός with dative of possession cf. Lk. 4.16. According to BDR § 189.1. n. 1. use of the dative emphasizes the thing possessed, of the genitive the possessor. For Paul's habitual use of the synagogue up to this point cf. 13.5, 14; 14.1; (16.13). For τῷ Παύλῳ, D latt syᵖ have ὁ Παῦλος; with this reading τὸ εἰωθός will refer to the general custom of the Jews in resorting to the synagogue. πρὸς αὐτούς is an *ad sensum* construction: Paul went in to those who might be expected to be found in the synagogue—Jews, with perhaps a few interested Gentiles.

ἐπὶ σάββατα τρία. There is an important note on the use of σάββατον (Sabbath, week) in *Begs.* 4.202f. For the use of ἐπί with reference to time cf. Lk. 4.25 (si v.1.); 18.4; Acts 3.1; 4.5; 11.10; 13.31; 16.18; 18.20; 19.8, 10, 34; 27.20. The meaning varies: time when, time how long, number of occasions. The meaning here could be *for three weeks* but is perhaps more probably *on three Sabbaths* (cf. 13.27, 42, 44; 15.21; 18.4). Phil. 4.16 (cf. 4.9) suggests very strongly that Paul stayed in Thessalonica a good deal longer than three weeks; so does 1 Thessalonians.

διελέξατο, *argued, debated*. G. D. Kilpatrick (*JTS* 11 (1960), 340) points out that in Lk. διαλογίζεσθαι is used, in Acts διαλέγεσθαι. He is right in refusing to see here evidence for different authorship, perhaps right in noting in Acts a change in style in the direction of Attic Greek or a more literary *Koine*. Paul's argument turned (as in the synagogue might be expected) on the interpretation of the OT Scriptures. This is true whether ἀπό (D, ἐκ—an improvement) τῶν γραφῶν is connected with διελέξατο or with διανοίγων καὶ παρατιθέμενος (in the next verse). It makes little difference: Paul's argument as a whole is based on Scripture; it is Scripture that he 'opens' (expounds). The more general sense is probably better: he argued on the basis of Scripture, and the argument consisted of exposition and affirmation. For διελέξατο, διελέγετο (imperfect, as in D at 18.19) might have been expected, but the continuous content of the dispute is brought out by the present participles in v. 3, and BDR § 327.1, n. 2 are probably right in taking διελέξατο as a constative aorist.

Schmithals (155) makes the point that Paul will not have been able to enter every fresh synagogue as an unknown; news of him (as a trouble-maker) will have spread through the Jewish communities. News from Philippi may have helped to precipitate the opposition recorded in v. 5.

3. The new verse continues the sentence of v. 2 with an account of the manner and content of Paul's synagogue disputation. διανοίγων: the verb is used in the same sense at Lk. 24.32, but neither LS 405 nor BA 375 is able to cite a parallel earlier than Aeneas Gazaeus (*Theophrastus* 5B (MPG 85.877), ... διανοίγειν ... πειράσομαι τὰ τῶν παλαιῶν ἀπόρρητα), of the 5th–6th century AD. The connection of the word with the Scriptures suggests a Jewish background; it is however doubtful whether this can be found in the verb פתח, which is commonly employed in exegesis with the meaning 'to open a lecture or sermon with a Bible passage'—so e.g. Berakoth 63b (not 63a as in Bacher), cited by W. Bacher, *Die exegetische Terminologie der jüdischen Traditionsliteratur* I (1965 (1899)), 162f. This is presumably the meaning also of Shekalim 5.1 as this is given in the Babylonian Talmud. Mordecai was given the name Pethahiah שהיה פותח בדברים ודורשן: he began his discourses with words (of Scripture) and proceeded to expound them. In the Palestinian Talmud however the preposition ב is wanting and we have simply פותח דברים, and the meaning may be, 'He opened the words (of Scripture) and expounded them.' Danby translates (a 'fusion of the two types' of Mishnah), ' ... because he was able to "open" matters and to expound them'. The additional statement that Mordecai knew seventy languages suggests an interest in verbal explanation. There can be little doubt of Luke's general meaning—a biblically based argument—but it would be hazardous to assert that his language is based on a Jewish model. In the Qumran literature CD 5.3 is scarcely relevant since this refers to the opening of a sealed book; 1QH 18.20 is difficult but might be relevant, לערל אוזן נפתח דבר, to an uncircumcised ear a word was opened.

παρατίθεσθαι is not used elsewhere in the NT with an object clause (but cf. 28.23 A), and this use of the word appears to be late. Cf. however Plato, *Politicus* 275b, τὸν μῦθον παρεθέμεθα, ἵν' ἐνδείξαιτο ... Dodd, *AS* 18, compares this 'opening up' and 'applying' with Romans 9–11.

No attempt is made here to show which passages in the OT are held to prove that the Messiah must suffer and die (suffering must include death in view of the following words; cf. 1.3; 3.18; Lk. 24.26, 46) and rise from the dead. On this fundamental theme of Christian preaching as represented in Acts see Introduction, pp. lxxxv–lxxxvii. The basic proposition, that Scripture foretells the death and resurrection of the Messiah, is followed by the identification of the dying and rising Messiah with Jesus. The second ὅτι, and perhaps the first, introduces direct speech, as καταγγέλλω shows. 'This man is the Messiah (who thus suffers and rises), namely Jesus, whom I am now proclaiming.' For a similar change from indirect speech to direct cf. 1.4. On the assumption that the text of NA[26] is correct one would say that it was the unusual appositional position of ὁ Ἰησοῦς that gave rise to several variant readings: ὁ Χριστὸς ὁ Ἰησοῦς, B; ὁ Χριστὸς Ἰησοῦς, ΨM; Χριστὸς Ἰησοῦς, P[74] A D 33 81 *pc* gig vg[st]; Ἰησοῦς Χριστός ℵ 614 2495 *pc* vg[cl]; Χριστός, E 36 453 *pc*. But there is something to be said for the reading of D or of ℵ.

4. For πείθεσθαι as a positive response to the Gospel cf. 28.24 (Lk. 16.31; Gal. 5.7); elsewhere in Acts it denotes the acceptance of some other teaching or opinion (5.36, 37, 39; 21.14; 23.21; 26.26; 27.11). Some of the Thessalonians (Jews or proselytes, since they were to be found in the synagogue, and others who might have been there are mentioned separately) accepted the propositions that the Messiah must suffer and die, and that Jesus was the Messiah. It is further said that these believers προσεκληρώθησαν τῷ Π. καὶ τῷ Σ. The verb is *hapax legomenon* in the NT. In the passive its normal meaning would be *to be assigned* (possibly by lot); so for example Josephus, *War* 2.567, of various districts assigned to a military ruler. Philo, *Legatio ad Gaium* 68 suggests a more suitable meaning with τῶν μὲν τούτῳ τῶν δὲ ἐκείνῳ προσκληρουμένων, though here the participle could be regarded as middle, whereas Luke's form must be passive. One is tempted to translate freely *they threw in their lot with P. and S.*; but Luke held a predestinarian view of conversion (13.14; 16.14) and may have thought that those who attached themselves to Paul and Silas did so because God had allocated them to this end.

Blass (186) thinks that προσεκληρώθησαν may have been a corruption of προσεκολλήθησαν (7.34) or of προσεκλίθησαν (5.36). The word is omitted (with καί by P⁷⁴, almost certainly by homoeoteleuton (–θησαν ... –θησαν).

The believing Jews and proselytes were joined by a large crowd of pious (σεβομένων) Greeks. For the participle σεβόμενος see 13.43, 50; 16.14; 18.7. Luke would hardly use it of those who were devout in terms of pagan religion, so that it must refer in some sense to the religion of Judaism. On the question of the precise relation of these persons to the synagogue see I.499–501; also now Trebilco (145–66) and an important article by J. Murphy-O'Connor in *RB* 99 (1992), 418–24. The present verse distinguishes them from proselytes and indicates that notwithstanding their piety they count as ῞Ελληνες, not as Jews.

Luke distinguishes a further group as *leading* (literally, *first*) *women*. The word πρῶτος occurs in this sense several times in the later part of Acts: 13.50; 25.2; 28.7.17. Cf. Josephus, *Ant.* 11.141, τοὺς πρώτους τοῦ λαοῦ. *ND* 1.72 notes an inscription from Assos (*IAssos* 16.3–4, in the time of Augustus, before 2 BC) which refers to Lollia Antiochis as πρώτη γυναικῶν, which appears to be an honorific title. Horsley asks, 'Is the phrase used of women at Thessalonike in Acts 17.4 also a title, or merely a descriptive way of referring to leading women?' An alternative translation is, 'Wives of the leading men'; this meaning is required by the Western text, καὶ γυναῖκες τῶν πρώτων (D lat). For Luke's interest in the conversion of women and their share in the church see 1.14; 5.1; 8.3, 12; 9.2; 13.50; 16.1, 13, 14; 17.1, 2, 34; 18.2; 21.5; 22.4; 24.24. For women in Macedonia see W. W. Tarn, *Hellenistic Civilisation* (1930), 89, 90. The use of τε and the litotes (οὐκ ὀλίγαι) are also characteristic of Luke.

The text of the verse is in some confusion. Clark (108, 366) on the basis of D, reconstructs it as follows:

καί τινες ἐξ αὐτῶν ἐπείσθησαν τῇ διδαχῇ,
καὶ προσεκληρώθησαν
τῷ Παύλῳ καὶ τῷ Σιλᾷ
πολλοὶ τῶν σεβομένων
καὶ ῾Ελλήνων πλῆθος πολὺ
καὶ γυναῖκες τῶν πρώτων οὐκ ὀλίγαι.

5. ζηλώσαντες: as at 7.9 (the patriarchs envied Joseph); cf. 5.17; 13.45. (ἐπλήσθησαν ζήλου). The Jews feared that they were losing control of the synagogue and their appeal to religious non-Jews, and objected to the success of the Christian preachers. Accordingly they took to themselves (προσλαβόμενοι, middle) certain evil (πονηρούς) men τῶν ἀγοραίων. There is no serious doubt about the meaning Luke here ascribes to this word (but cf. 19.38), but there are linguistic problems behind it which focus on its accentuation. Thus M. 2.57: 'ἀγόραιος and ἀγοραῖος are differently distinguished by grammarians. Zonaras [12th century] has ἀγοραῖοι for οἱ ἐν ἀγορᾷ ἀναστρεφόμενοι ἄνθρωποι, and ἀγόραιος as ἡ ἡμέρα ἐν ᾗ ἡ ἀγορὰ τελεῖται. If that is correct, we must write ἀγόραιοι in Acts 19.38, and make ἀγοραῖοι the nominative of the noun in 17.5; but Ammonius [1st or 2nd century AD according to LS], who is eight centuries older [ten or eleven centuries on LS's reckoning] than Zonaras, gives an entirely different distinction,' which is not quite correctly given by LS; see Ammonius 11. The distinction given by Ammonius (4(6)) is ἀγόραιος μὲν γάρ ἐστιν ἡ ἡμέρα, ἀγοραῖος δὲ ὁ Ἑρμῆς ὁ ἐπὶ τῆς ἀγορᾶς (Winer-Moulton 61; Winer-Schmiedel 69). LS 13 however write, 'The distn. ἀγόραιος *vulgar*, ἀγοραῖος *public speaker*, drawn by Ammon., etc., is prob. fictitious.' Fortunately there is no doubt that we may here follow the meaning given by Zonaras to ἀγοραῖος. The word was sometimes used in an innocent sense—traders, but it tended to refer to the lower kind of frequenter of market places; cf. Aristophanes, *Frogs* 1015 (1047) (in company with διαδρασιπολῖται, κόβαλοι, and πανοῦργοι); Plato, *Protagoras* 347c (τῶν φαύλων καὶ ἀγοραίων ἀνθρώπων); Theophrastus, *Characters* 6(7).2; Herodotus 2.141.4; Xenophon, *Hellenica* 6.2.23. Luke means, and would be understood to mean, louts of the worst kind, ready to make any amount of trouble for a consideration. BA 22f. refer to Plutarch, *Aemilius Paulus* 38.4 (275) (... ἀνθρώπους ἀγεννεῖς καὶ δεδουλευκότας, ἀγοραίους δὲ καὶ δυναμένους ὄχλον συναγαγεῖν ...), with the suggestion that the ἀγοραῖοι might be professional agitators, but the meaning is not supported and is not needed here. The subject of ὀχλοποιήσαντες ἐθορύβουν must grammatically be οἱ Ἰουδαῖοι, though one suspects that the ἀγοραῖοι may have been intended. They would without difficulty gather a crowd and set the city in an uproar (θορυβεῖν; cf. Mt. 9.23; Mk 5.39; used in a somewhat different sense at Acts 20.10) for which it would be easy to blame the Christians.

They *gathered at*, perhaps *set upon*, the house of Jason. Of this man we know only what the present passage tells us. The name occurs at Rom. 16.21 as that of a helper of Paul's who is also a συγγενής, that is, a fellow Jew; the name Jason might be a Greek substitute for Joshua (see Josephus, *Ant.* 12.239, ὁ μὲν οὖν Ἰησοῦς Ἰάσονα αὐτὸν μετωνόμασεν). It is not unreasonable to identify the two, but the identification is quite uncertain. It would imply that Jason had at some time travelled to join Paul at Cenchreae (Rom. 16.1). One can say no more than that this is not impossible. *Begs.* 4.205 points to v. 6, Ἰάσονα καὶ τοὺς ἀδελφούς. Does the wording imply that Jason was not a *brother*, a Christian? Not necessarily.

The intention of the trouble-makers is to bring *them* (presumably

Paul and Silas) out to the *mob*. Ordinarily δῆμος would deserve a
better translation, but Luke appears to have in mind not an orderly
assembly but a riotous gathering bent on violence, though not (if we
may judge by v. 6) on lynching. This however is disputed. Hanson
(174) distinguishes the δῆμος (parliament) from the ὄχλος (v. 8);
Conzelmann (95) equates them.

In this verse also the text is in some disorder. The text of NA[26] is
probably correct: Ζηλώσαντες δὲ οἱ Ἰουδαῖοι καὶ προσλαβόμενοι
τῶν ἀγοραίων ἄνδρας τινὰς πονηροὺς καὶ ὀχλοποιήσαντες
ἐθορύβουν. This is the reading of P[74] A B 33 81 945 1175 1739 *al* vg
(sy) co. ℵ Ψ share this text, reversing the order of ἀνδρ. τ. 0120 614
1241 2495 add after Ἰουδ., οἱ ἀπειθοῦντες; E adds after πον.,
ἀπειθήσαντες. These MSS have probably been affected by D which
reads οἱ δὲ ἀπειθοῦντες Ἰουδ. συστρέψαντες τιν. ἀνθ. τῶν ἀγ. πον.
ἐθορυβοῦσαν; this has affected 𝔐, which has προσλ. δὲ οἱ Ἰουδ. οἱ
ἀπειθ. τῶν ἀγ, τιν. ἄνδ. πον. κ. ὀχ. ἐθορ.

6. Paul and Silas were not to be found, whether because they were
not in Jason's house or because they were too well hidden. Other
victims, however, would serve equally well to satisfy the desire of
the πονηροί for violence, and almost equally well as a warning
object-lesson for Christians. Ἰάσονα καί τινας ἀδελφούς is very
probably to be taken to mean, Jason and certain *other* Christian
brothers; that is, Jason himself is a Christian. See however the
reference to *Begs*. 4.205 on v. 5. Probably Jason's name was
remembered because he was a member of the Christian group; so e.g.
Weiser (449). Luke evidently thinks it possible that three Sabbaths
might suffice to gather men into the new brotherhood; having been
nurtured in the synagogue they would probably need little instruction
beyond the simple identification of the Messiah with Jesus.

The rioters set about dragging (ἔσυρον, imperfect; the word at 8.3;
14.19) Jason and his fellow Christians ἐπὶ τοὺς πολιτάρχας. Cf.
Lucian, *Lexiphanes* 10, Δεινίαν σύρουσιν ἄγδην ἐπὶ τὴν ἀρχήν,
ἔγκλημα ἐπάγοντες ... πολιτάρχης 'is mainly if not exclusively a
Macedonian title for the non-Roman magistrates of a city. It is found
in inscriptions ranging from the second century B.C. to the third
century A.D.. ... It would appear that the Macedonian cities had
several politarchs, the number varying with their importance.
Amphipolis had five, Pella only two, Thessalonica had five in the
time of Augustus, but afterwards six' (*Begs*. 4.205). See Sherwin-
White (96) with his reference to C. Schuler, *Classical Philology* 55
(1960), 90–100; also Tajra (34) and Hemer (115). There is further
bibliography in Bruce (2.324) and an important note with much fresh
evidence in *ND* 2.34f. There is no doubt that Luke has here used the
correct term; naturally, this does not vindicate the accuracy of his
story as a whole, and we shall see that there are obscurities in it, but it

suggests that someone involved in some way in the report was not unfamiliar with Macedonia.

βοῶντες, a Lucan word; 7 times in Luke-Acts, 6 times in the rest of the NT.

ἀναστατοῦν: the word is used in a different sense at Gal. 5.12, in a fundamentally similar sense at Acts 21.38—the Egyptian rebel led an armed terrorist revolt against Rome. It is of something similar that the Christians are here accused, as the next lines make clear. They are acting (it is alleged) contrary to imperial decrees and attempting to set up a rival emperor (v. 7). The charge is much more dangerous than 'They have upset everyone' or even than 'they have turned the world upside down'. Cf. 24.5. Conzelmann (95) quotes from the *Acta Isidori* (Musurillo 23): ἐνϰ[αλῶ αὐτοῖς] [ὅτι ϰ]αὶ ὅλην τὴν οἰϰουμένην [θέλουσι] [ταράσ]σειν. This charge is brought against the Jews.

οἰϰουμένη is a Lucan word: in Luke-Acts 8 times; in the rest of the NT 7 times (of which 3 are in Revelation). Luke uses it in the accepted sense: the whole civilized world.

πάρεισιν (cf. the cognate noun, παρουσία) is a present tense used (see BDR § 322.2, n. 2) for the perfect of a different verb—better, perhaps, for a perfect and present combined: they have come, and here they are.

After βοῶντες, D gig w unnecessarily add ϰαὶ λέγοντες. D* Ψ gig w change the construction slightly by adding εἰσιν after οὗτοι.

7. Luke characteristically continues the sentence with a relative: οὕς ὑποδέδεκται. ὑποδέχεσθαι (deponent) is used from the time of Homer for 'to welcome into one's house'; examples in BA 1682. Approval of the guests and of their mission is implied; Jason if not fully a Christian is at least a sympathizer.

οὗτοι πάντες: Jason; the brothers (v. 6); Paul and Silas; any other Christian converts. The phrase is vague, but precision is hardly to be looked for in the circumstances. Similarly it is difficult to give a precise meaning to the δόγματα Καίσαρος. In any case, Thessalonica was a *civitas libera*, and the decrees (Vg has *decreta*; contrast Lk. 2.1, where δόγμα is *edictum*) of Caesar were thus not binding on the magistrates; Sherwin-White (96) observes that for this reason 'the city magistrates were not compelled to take serious action'. Ehrhardt (*Acts* 96) asks, 'What decrees were they? The most likely answer is that they were the very ones by which the Jews had been banished from Rome because of their rioting *impulsore Chresto* ... The mob thus regarded the differences between St Paul and the synagogal Jews at Thessalonica as an internal quarrel of the Jews, and was determined to side with that party which was loyal to the Emperor.' It may be possible to do better than this. E. A. Judge saw here 'reference to edicts against predictions, especially of the death or change of rulers, first promulgated by the aged Augustus in AD 11 (Dio 56.25.5–6) and enforced through the local administration of oaths of loyalty' (Hemer 167, summarizing Judge in *RTR* 30 (1971), 1–7). K. P. Donfried (*NTS* 31 (1985), 342–6) asks why the politarchs are appealed to rather than the proconsul; his answer is that it was the politarchs who were responsible for administering the oath of loyalty to the Emperor.

λέγοντες is probably to be taken as explanatory of πράσσουσιν: they act against the decrees of Caesar by proclaiming a rival emperor (βασιλεύς). There may not have been a decree specifically to this effect, but it was action that would hardly be encouraged by the reigning Emperor. The charge was one that could readily be used against Christians; the term βασιλεία τοῦ θεοῦ runs deep into the gospel tradition and must have found its way from time to time into Christian preaching, especially in the synagogue. The preachers could hardly deny that they were proclaiming Jesus as βασιλεύς; Lk. 23.2 shows how dangerous this could be and Jn 18.36 may reflect explanations that Christians found it necessary to give.

Schille (351) finds in vv. 6, 7 two different accusations (causing disturbance and proclaiming a different emperor), and concludes, 'Die Dublette beweist vollends die Bearbeitung eines älteren Textes.' But it would be quite reasonable to allege that the Christians were setting the world in turmoil precisely by making claims for a rival Emperor, and thus inciting civil war.

8. ἐτάραξαν τὸν ὄχλον picks up ὀχλοποιήσαντες rather than δῆμος in v. 5, especially if that verse describes the intention to bring Paul before the δῆμος as a duly constituted court; on this see however the note on v. 5.

The Western text (D gig sy[p]) reverses the order of ὄχλον and πολιτάρχας (for this word see on v. 6), putting the authorities first. The common text makes better sense: the crowd heard the allegation about the proclamation of another Emperor first, and thus it came to the ears of the magistrates. The better sense, however, is not necessarily the better text.

9. λαβόντες τὸ ἱκανόν is a Latinism, *cum satis accepissent*; see M. 1.20; BDR § 5.4; Moule, *IB* 192. The Greeks adopted the legal usage from Rome; 'What is happening to Jason is clear enough: he is giving security for the good behaviour of his guests, and hence hastens to dispatch Paul and Silas out of the way to Beroea, where the jurisdiction of the magistrates of Thessalonica was not valid' (Sherwin-White 95f.). This comment does not quite do justice to καὶ τῶν λοιπῶν. Not only Jason but also the brothers (v. 6) were thus cautioned, and no doubt they were required to give security for their own behaviour as well as that of Paul and Silas before being dismissed (the magistrates ἀπέλυσαν αὐτούς)—indeed it had not been proved that Paul and Silas were guests with Jason (v. 6).

The verse begins οἱ μὲν οὖν πολιτάρχαι in sy^hmg. As Clark (xxxvi) points out, in the text of all other authorities, if it is strictly read, it was the rioters who took security and dismissed the persons charged.

10. For διὰ νυκτός see on 16.9.

οἱ ἀδελφοί are here not the 'certain brothers' of v. 6 but the newly founded Christian community as a whole, who acted in defence and protection of the missionaries; 1 Thessalonians (e.g. 1.4 for ἀδελφοί) is sufficient proof that after a short ministry Paul left a church in Thessalonica; so also is 20.4. They sent Paul and Silas to Beroea, a good place for flight, *oppidum devium* (Cicero, *In Pisonem* 36(89)) in that it lay off the Via Egnatia which Paul had followed as far as Thessalonica. It lay 45 miles WSW of Thessalonica in the district of Bottiaea (not, as sometimes is said, of Emathia—C. M. Danoff, in *KP* 1.869), the first town to give itself up to the Romans after the battle of Pydna. It was μεγάλη καὶ πολυάνθρωπος (Lucian, *Lucius* 34—cf. the reference to *Lucius* 46 on v. 1). The existence of Jews there is confirmed by inscriptions (*NS* 3.67, 68). It is possible that there was only one synagogue (τὴν συναγωγήν), but the definite article can hardly be pressed so far.

ἄπειμι occurs here only in the NT (ἔξειμι only at 13.42; 17.15; 20.7; 27.43; εἶμι not at all, unless, improbably, at Jn 7.34, 36). ἀπῄεσαν is to be taken with εἰς τὴν συναγωγήν: Having arrived (παραγενόμενοι; in the town), they went into the synagogue. The verb does not imply that they went out of the town to a synagogue situated outside the walls (Zerwick § 133).

11. The decision to go at once to the synagogue in Beroea, notwithstanding indifferent success at Thessalonica, was rewarded. In Thessalonica, though some Jews had believed, 'the Jews' were opposed to Paul; in Beroea 'the Jews' were more favourable. They were εὐγενέστεροι (D p*, εὐγενεῖς). εὐγενής (Lk. 19.12; 1 Cor. 1.26) refers originally to noble birth, but it came naturally to be applied to noble behaviour (cf. Josephus, *Ant.* 12.255, οἱ δὲ δοκιμώτατοι καὶ τὰς ψυχὰς εὐγενεῖς οὐκ ἐφρόντισαν αὐτοῦ—the threatening Antiochus Epiphanes; Chrysostom, in Cramer, *Catena* 282, τουτέστιν ἐπιεικέστεροι). See also Philo, *Moses* 1.18. the infant Moses was εὐγενῆ καὶ ἀστεῖον. Luke means that the Beroean Jews allowed no prejudice to prevent them from giving Paul a fair hearing.

Moule (*IB* 124) thinks this one of the passages in Acts (see also 10.47) where οἵτινες may be used not as a simple substitute for οἵ (contrast v. 10). It should perhaps be rendered, '... seeing that they received the word ...'. For receiving the word see 2.41. μετὰ πάσης προθυμίας, with all eagerness; not an uncommon expression. See e.g. Herodotus 7.6.2, πᾶσαν προθυμίην παρεχόμενοι; Philo, *Abraham* 246, μετὰ προθυμίας πάσης.

καθ' ἡμέραν is a common expression in Acts (2.46, 47; 3.2; 16.5; 19.9; cf. 17.17. In none of these passages is τό prefixed, even as a variant; this is in favour of its inclusion here (it is read by B H L P 6 1175 *pm*, omitted by P⁴⁵ P⁷⁵ ℵ D E Ψ 0120 33 81 323 614 945 1739 249k5 *pm*). There is no evident reason why if it was original a copyist should omit it.

Paul's fundamental assertion in Beroea, as in Thessalonica, was understood by Luke to have been (a) that the OT Scriptures affirm the coming of a Messiah who will suffer and rise from the dead, and (b) that Jesus was this Messiah. This was a novel interpretation of the OT and the Beroean Jews wished, before committing themselves to the new faith, to see if it was true. ἀνακρίνειν is nowhere else in the NT used of the study of Scripture; it suggests rather the legal examination of witnesses (or of an accused person)—see Acts 4.9; 12.19; 24.8; 28.18—and this is in fact the sense in which it is used here. Paul has set up the Scriptures as witnesses: does their testimony, when tested, prove his case?

εἰ ἔχοι (D* E (0120) 36 453 2495 *al* have ἔχει) ταῦτα οὕτως is virtually an indirect question (M. 3.127). Cf. Josephus, *Ant.* 12.197, εἰ δύναιτο πρὸς τὸν βασιλέα βαδίσαι ... ἀνέκρινεν. Cf. the direct question of 7.1, εἰ ταῦτα οὕτως ἔχει. After οὕτως, 614 *pc* gig sy^h** add καθὼς Παῦλος ἀπαγγέλλει.

12. For the very frequent use of μὲν οὖν in Acts see on 1.6. It is less common in the middle of a paragraph than at the beginning or the end; it does however sometimes, as here, introduce the result of preaching: 2.41; (8.25); 9.31; 16.5. The result of Paul's work in the synagogue, and of the open-minded study by the Beroeans, was that many believed (ἐπίστευσαν; cf. v. 4, ἐπείσθησαν)—many ἐξ αὐτῶν (the use of a preposition where earlier Greek would have been content with a partitive genitive was growing in the Hellenistic period), that is of the Beroean Jews; also not a few (for the characteristic litotes see v. 4) of the Greek (that is, non-Jewish) women of good standing (εὐσχημόνων; for the word see 13.50), and men. For Luke's frequent references to women converts see v. 4.

The text of this verse appears in a somewhat different form in D and some of its allies. Combining the readings of D*, D, and 614 we obtain as possibly a primitive form of the Western text: τινὲς μὲν οὖν αὐτῶν [without ἐξ] ἐπίστευσαν, τινὲς δὲ ἠπίστησαν, καὶ τῶν Ἑλλήνων καὶ τῶν εὐσχημόνων ἄνδρες καὶ γυναῖκες ἱκανοὶ ἐπίστευσαν. The effect of this is to reduce the response of the Beroean Jews, to distinguish between Greeks and εὐσχημόνες, and slightly to take the emphasis off the women converts—D can scarcely be labelled anti-feminist here (see the reference in Epp, 75, n. 3; also Ramsay (*Church* 161f.), who sees here a mark of 'Catholic' editing), but the women take second rather than a special place. The reading of d is curious: ... et Grecorum et non placentium et viri et mulieris [*sic*—a slip for mulieres] pleres crediderunt.

13. The result of the preaching in Beroea was naturally unpleasing in Thessalonica, and the Jews of that city (ἀπό as at Jn 21.2—place of origin, and in this case of normal residence also) made the journey to Beroea to stir up trouble there.

ὁ λόγος τοῦ θεοῦ is one of Luke's commonest terms for the Christian message as preached by the apostles and others.

The object of the Jews was to stir up trouble among the crowds; if Paul and his colleagues could be represented as the source of unrest and as likely to cause riots they were sure to be turned out even if the magistrates could find no fault with what they actually said.

σαλεύειν is a Lucan word (Lk., 4 times; Acts, 4 times; rest of the NT, 7 times). the word is more often used of literal, physical disturbance (but cf. 2.25 = Ps. 16.8); it was probably felt to double with καὶ ταράσσοντες, which was accordingly omitted by P⁴⁵ E 0120 𝔐. In the Old Uncial text the participles σαλεύοντες, ταράσσοντες, are adverbial to ἦλθον; they are differently constructed by D (cf. syᵖ), which adds οὐ διελίμπανον: they came, and did not cease ...

14. The main cause of the trouble in Beroea was no doubt Paul, and it was therefore important to get him away quickly. τότε is intended to underline εὐθέως: *immediately, at that very time*. The Western text (see below) avoids the conjunction of the two adverbs.

οἱ ἀδελφοί, the Christian brotherhood (cf. v. 10), sent Paul off (ἐξαπέστειλαν in this context means facilitating his departure rather than dismissing him) to go (πορεύεσθαι) in the direction of the sea. This is expressed in the majority of MSS (Ψ 0120 𝔐 syʰ) by the phrase ὡς ἐπὶ τὴν θάλασσαν. This use of ὡς ἐπί is a standard Hellenistic construction meaning *towards*, sometimes *against*. See M. 3.321 and BDR § 453.4, n. 7, but especially Field (79): 'Π. ὡς ἐπί "to go in the direction of" a place, whether the person arrives there or not, is an excellent Greek idiom.' As Field observes, Wettstein gives examples, and Field adds Pausanias 2.11.2, καταβαίνουσι δὲ ὡς ἐπὶ τὸ πεδίον; 3.20.3, ἰοῦσιν εὐθεῖαν ὡς ἐπὶ θάλασσαν; and other passages. ὡς is omitted by the Western text (D 049 *pc* gig syᵖ), and in P⁷⁴ ℵ A B E 33 81 323 945 1175 1739 *al* lat is replaced by ἕως. The short text (ἐπί alone) is quite intelligible: Paul is to go to the sea. But there is no good reason why ὡς ἐπί, if it had stood originally in the text, should have been disturbed, unless, as Field continues, the 'excellent Greek idiom' may not have been familiar to those scribes who changed ὡς into ἕως. Bruce (1.330) thinks that Paul's companions acted 'as if to conduct Paul to the sea'; that is, they were trying to put possible pursuers off the trail. ἕως may be an orthographical variant (or error) for ὡς, but it may be original and mean (in English as awkward as the Greek would be) that Paul was accompanied *as far as to the sea*; that is, his companions saw him on board (cf. 20.38). He would reach the sea probably at Pydna, and sea travel would take him into a different jurisdiction (Hemer 116). The reference to the sea must almost certainly mean (unless we follow Bruce) that Paul, to avoid further trouble in northern Greece, went from Beroea to Athens by ship, avoiding the land journey through Thessaly (though for θάλασσαν Markland conjectures Θεσσαλίαν; see also the textual note on v. 15). Clark (366f.) argues that if Paul went by sea one would expect the port, Methone or Pydna, to be mentioned; and οἱ δὲ καθιστῶντες ... ἤγαγον (v. 15) suggests a land journey. 'There was a Roman road with stations and organized services from Pydna to Athens by way of Dium, Larisa, Demetrias, Opus, Chalcis, Thebes, and Oropus, the total distance being 222 miles.'

The Western text of the opening part of the verse runs: τὸν μὲν οὖν Παῦλον οἱ ἀδελφοὶ ἐξαπέστειλαν ἀπελθεῖν ἐπί ... It is hard to see any motive for the change, apart from a possible distaste for εὐθέως τότε; either we recognize two early recensions of the text, or have an example of the free copying of a text that lacks full canonical authority. See Introduction, pp. xxi, lxviii.

When Paul left Beroea for Athens, Silas and Timothy stayed behind (this is how Luke understands the verb ὑπομένειν; with him it does not mean *to endure*). So far in chs. 16 and 17 we have heard only of the movements of Paul and Silas; Timothy has not been mentioned since 16.1–3, and 1 Thess. 3.2 might suggest that Timothy was not known to the Thessalonians till Paul sent him from Athens. This however is not the necessary meaning of the verse, and, as Haenchen (490) observes. Luke tends not to mention unimportant secondary figures. A *prima facie* reading of Acts 16 and 17 suggests that he had accompanied Paul, perhaps as a subordinate member of the party, from Lystra to Beroea. 1 Thess. 3.2 should perhaps be understood as an assurance that this hitherto slightly regarded assistant was in fact a trusted lieutenant.

15. καθιστάνειν is a late form of καθιστάναι; on the tendency to replace –μι verbs with simpler forms in –ω see M. 1.33, 38, 55f. In meaning the word duplicates ἤγαγον; cf. Thucydides 4.78.5, οἱ δὲ Περαιβοὶ αὐτὸν ... κατέστησαν ἐς Δῖον. The brothers who were seeing Paul on his way brought him as far as Athens (see on v. 16), a considerable journey, whether by land or sea. They returned with instructions (ἐντολήν) that Silas and Timothy, left behind in Beroea (v. 14), were to join Paul as quickly as possible—ὡς τάχιστα, a literary expression; see BDR § 60.2, n. 3; 244.1, n. 2; § 453.4, n. 7.

According to Acts (18.5) they caught up with him at Corinth. 1
Thess. 3.2 suggests that Silas and Timothy, or at least Timothy, had
joined Paul in Athens. 'Das Befehl zum Nachkommen gehört zu den
typisch redaktionellen Massnahmen' (Schille 352). It is not clear
why this should be so. Cf. 1 Thess. 2.14.

With ἐξῇεσαν cf. ἀπῇεσαν, v. 10.

In the first half of the verse the Western text introduces fresh
features: παρῆλθεν δὲ τὴν Θεσσαλίαν ἐκωλύθη γὰρ εἰς αὐτοὺς (the
inhabitants of Thessaly) κηρύξαι τὸν λόγον (D). It is hard to think
that these interesting observations stood in the original text and were
omitted by an editor. Their addition is easier to understand. A reviser
who missed the hint in v. 14 that Paul travelled by sea and noted the
long stretch of Thessaly between Beroea and Attica (Athens) might
well have asked himself why Paul left the area unevangelized. The
example of 16.6f. suggested an answer which it was easy to frame in
Lucan language. The addition after ἐντολήν of παρὰ Παύλου (D) or
ἀπ᾽ αὐτοῦ (E vg sy^p sa) was a natural and no doubt correct, though
scarcely necessary, piece of interpretation. It is however by no means
clear why ὅπως ἐν τάχει should be substituted for ἵνα ὡς τάχιστα. It
is probable that we see again the free rewriting of a text not yet fully
canonical. It seems worthwhile to give the text of D for vv. 14, 15 in
full.

τὸν μὲν οὖν Παῦλον οἱ ἀδελφοὶ ἐξαπέστειλαν ἀπελθεῖν ἐπὶ
τὴν θάλασσαν· ὑπέμεινεν δὲ ὁ Σείλας καὶ ὁ Τιμόθεος ἐκεῖ. οἱ
δὲ καταστάνοντες τὸν Παῦλον ἤγαγον ἕως Ἀθηνῶν,
παρῆλθεν δὲ τὴν Θεσσαλίαν, ἐκωλύθη γὰρ εἰς αὐτοὺς
κηρύξαι τὸν λόγον, λαβόντες δὲ ἐντολὴν παρὰ Παύλου πρὸς
τὸν Σείλαν καὶ Τιμόθεον ὅπως ἐν τάχει ἔλθωσιν πρὸς αὐτὸν
ἐξῇεσαν.

On παρ. δὲ τὴν Θεσσ. Weiser (452) comments, 'Die einfügung lässt
erkennen, dass man den Weg ans Meer als Täuschung verstand ...'.
This understanding would agree with the opinion of Bruce given
above.

45. PAUL AT ATHENS 17.16–34

(16) While Paul in Athens was waiting for Silas and Timothy[1] his spirit was vexed within him as he saw that the city was overgrown with idols. (17) So in the synagogue he disputed with the Jews and the devout persons and in the Agora every day with those he chanced to meet. (18) Some of the Stoic and Epicurean philosophers argued with him, and some said, 'What does this third-rate journalist want to tell us?' Others said, 'He seems to be a preacher of foreign gods.' For he was preaching the message of Jesus and the resurrection. (19) They got hold of him and brought him to the Areopagus, saying, 'May we know what this new teaching, spoken by you, is? (20) For you are bringing strange things to our ears. We should like to know therefore what these things mean.' (21) For all the Athenians and the resident foreigners had leisure for nothing but to say or hear some novelty.

(22) Paul stood up in the midst of the Areopagus, and said, 'Gentlemen of Athens, I see that you make a great display of piety. (23) For as I passed by and looked at your objects and instruments of worship I saw among other things an altar on which was inscribed, To an unknown god. What therefore you worship in ignorance, that I proclaim to you. (24) The God who made the world and all the things that are in it, since he is Lord of heaven and earth does not live in shrines made by human hands, (25) nor is he served by human hands as though he were in need of anything, since he himself gives to all life and breath and all things. (26) He made of one origin every race of men to dwell upon the whole face of the earth, having appointed fore-ordained seasons and the boundaries of their habitation, (27) with a view to their seeking God, though indeed his being is[2] not far from each one of us. (28) For in him we live and move and are; as indeed some of your own poets have said: ''We too are his family.'' (29) Since then we have our being[3] as God's family, we ought not to suppose that the divine being is like gold or silver or stone, an object carved by man's art or imagination. (30) So the times of ignorance God has overlooked, but now he is commanding men that they should all everywhere repent, (31) inasmuch as he has set a day on which he will judge the whole world in righteousness by a man whom he has appointed. Of this appointment he has provided proof in that he raised him from the dead.'

(32) When they heard of the resurrection of the dead some mocked, but others said, 'We will hear you on this topic again.' (33) So Paul went out of their midst. (34) But some men adhered to him and believed, among whom were Dionysius the Areopagite, and a woman, Damaris by name, and others with them.

[1]Greek, them.
[2]RSV, NEB, NJB, he is; Greek perhaps, he exists.
[3]See n. 2.

Bibliography

P. Auffret, *NovT* 20 (1978), 185–202.

T. D. Barnes, *JTS* 20 (1969), 407–19.

C. K. Barrett, *FS* Sawyerr, 69–77.

C. K. Barrett, *ZThK* 86 (1989), 18–32 (ET, *Jesus and the Word* (1995), 149–62).

G. Bornkamm, 2.119–37; 4.149–61.

C. Burchard, *ZNW* 61 (1970), 159f.

F. C. Burkitt, *JTS* 15 (1914), 455–64.

J. Calloud, *RechScR* 69 (1981), 209–48.

P. Colaclides, *VigCh* 27 (1973), 161–4.

H. Conzelmann, *FS* Schubert, 217–30.

F. G. Downing, *NTS* 28 (1982), 546–59.

A. M. Dubarle, *RScPhTh* 57 (1973), 576–610.

J. Dupont, *Études* 157–60.

J. Dupont, *Bib* 60 (1979), 530–46 (= *Nouvelles Études* 380–423).

M. J. Edwards, *ZNW* 83 (1992), 266–9.

W. Eltester, *FS* Bultmann (1954), 202–27.

W. Eltester, *NTS* 3 (1957), 93–114.

B. Gärtner, *The Areopagus Speech and Natural Revelation* (1955).

D. J. Geagan, *ANRW* 2.7.1 (1975), 371–437.

S. Halstead, *FS* Lake (1937), 139–43.

C. J. Hemer, *NTS* 20 (1974), 341–50.

H. Hommel, *ZNW* 46 (1955), 145–78; 48 (1957), 193–200.

P. W. van der Horst, *NovT* 16 (1974), 309.

P. W. van der Horst, in *Knowledge of God in the Graeco-Roman World* ed. R. van den Broek, T. Baarda, J. Mansfield (1988), 19–42.

P. W. van der Horst, *ANRW* 2.18.2 (1989), 1426–56.

H. Külling, *ThZ* 36 (1980), 65–83.

J. C. Lebram, *ZNW* 55 (1964), 221–43.

L. Legrand, in Coppens, BEThL 41 (1976), 337–50.

R. S. Mackenzie, *JBL* 104 (1985), 637–50.

A. J. Mattill, *CBQ* 34 (1972), 276–93.

W. Nauck, *ZThK* 53 (1956), 11–52.

A. D. Nock, *Gnomon* 25 (1953), 506.

E. Norden, *Agnostos Theos* ([4]1956).

R. F. O'Toole, *RB* 89 (1982), 185–97.

H. P. Owen, *NTS* 5 (1959), 133–43.

É. des Places, *Bib* 46 (1965), 219–22.

É. des Places, *Bib* 52 (1971), 526–34.

M. Pohlenz, *ZNW* 42 (1949), 69–104.

K. O. Sandnes, *JSNT* 50 (1993), 13–26.

R. E. Wycherley, *JTS* 19 (1968), 619–20.
D. Zweck, *NTS* 35 (1989), 94–103.

Commentary

Escaping from Beroea, Paul reached Athens alone, where he awaited Silas and Timothy. Shocked by the idolatry of the city he discoursed in the synagogue and the Agora. His reception was mixed; and when he took the opportunity of addressing the Areopagus court the response was again divided. A few disciples however were made.

That Paul visited Athens is confirmed by 1 Thessalonians (see 3.1, and cf. the references to Achaea in 1.7, 8). That Luke's account of the visit is at least incomplete is shown by 1 Thess. 3.2, in which Paul sends Timothy back from Athens to Thessalonica; Timothy's presence in Athens is not mentioned in Acts. There is in this section no use of the first person plural, nothing to suggest that the writer was present—nothing, that is, apart from the content of the narrative, which shows some awareness of what Athens was like: the forest of idols (or, as otherwise expressed, of priceless works of art); the curiosity of the population; the presence of philosophers, notably Epicureans and Stoics; the existence of a court known as the Areopagus (or, much less probably though equally valid as showing acquaintance with the city, of the Areopagus hill); a particular altar, dedicated to an Unknown God; the fact that Paul made a speech; the names of the two converts, Damaris and Dionysius. To these observations may be added a few touches which show some knowledge of the most famous of all Athenian citizens, Socrates. These features may constitute a case for believing that the writer was personally familiar with the city, whether or not he had been there in company with Paul. It is not however a wholly convincing case; there is little in it to prove first-hand knowledge. The notable features of Athens were very widely known and the picture given in this chapter may be derivative (see on v. 21). There is however nothing in vv. 16–21, 34 that is in any way incredible. If we know anything at all about Paul it is that in whatever city he found himself he would use every opportunity—synagogue and market place—to commend the Gospel, and though the writer has probably gone out of his way to hint at an analogy with Socrates, the summary of Paul's teaching in v. 18 (He was preaching as good news Jesus and the resurrection) bears remarkable resemblance to the word of faith quoted by Paul in Rom. 10.9 (If with your mouth you confess Jesus as Lord, and in your heart believe that God raised him from the dead, you will be saved). The speech attributed to Paul (vv. 22–31), however, is a different matter.

Weiser (458f.) rightly says that the preaching in synagogue and agora, and the conversion of Dionysius and Damaris, may be taken from a pre-Lucan itinerary, but the Areopagus scene and speech must be viewed as 'Produkt der luk Gestaltungskunst und nicht als Detailwiedergabe eines historischen Einzelereignisses'. Pesch (2.131) takes vv. 16–20, 22, 23 to come from the pre-Lucan source, v. 21 to be Lucan redaction. Weiser's rhetorical analysis is instructive, though possibly too formal; he takes (457) vv. 22f. as *Captatio benevolentiae*; 24–26 as *Narratio*; 27–29a as *Argumentatio*; 29bc as *Reprehensio*. These terms are suitable for the analysis of a full-length speech, less so for a sketch of a dozen or so lines. Luke has probably given as short a summary as he could of the kind of address to Gentiles that Hellenistic Christians had inherited from Hellenistic Jews. This being so, it is correct to say (again with Weiser, 479), 'Methodisch ist es erforderlich, den Text weder einseitig atl.-biblisch noch einseitig stoisch auszulegen, sondern gemäss des neuen Kontextes.'

Luke no doubt supposed that this kind of address was what Paul would have said to the Areopagus Court; it was '... not what happened but Luke's idealized version of what ought to have happened' (Johnson 318). It might be a little better to say that Luke was not in a position to recount something that he had himself heard but used what had come to be the accepted Christian approach to Gentiles. It is very doubtful whether he was correct in ascribing this approach to Paul. There is an admirable brief summary of the contrast between Acts 17.22–31 and Rom. 1.18–31 in Maddox (83f.); see also (in addition to commentaries and other works listed in the bibliography on pp. 823f.) Wilson (*Gentiles* 196–218). Haenchen (508) explains the difference in terms of the two different lines that may be detected in Jewish-Hellenistic mission propaganda: the mild line, taken for example by Aristobulus (who, like Paul in Acts, quotes Aratus) and the strict line taken in the Sibylline fragments. Of these the Areopagus speech takes the former (as the Pastorals did— Wilson, *Pastorals* 31), Paul (in Romans 1) the latter. This is an observation worth noting, but it is inadequate as an analysis of the difference between the two passages. The same may be said of Schneider (2.234), who emphasizes—questionably—that the Areopagus speech is distinctively Christian. Paul's approach to the Gentile world is essentially Christocentric (cf. e.g. 1 Cor. 2.2), and his criticism of Gentile society, though Jewish in its line of argument, develops the attack on idolatry found in the Wisdom of Solomon in a way that is ultimately Christologically determined. The Areopagus speech lacks this determining Christological factor. It is again not adequate to say that the language of the speech is not Pauline. 'Though the content of the speech is far from incompatible with Paul's ideas, the language is wholly un-Pauline ... The speech was certainly not composed by Paul; it was composed by Luke ... But the doctrine which it conveys is not the product of Luke's fancy, but of the mind of the early church. In as far as this is true, it may represent in content, though not in expression, the sort of message which Paul used to deliver to Gentile audiences' (Hanson 182f.). That Paul sought to turn his Gentile, idolatrous, hearers from their idols to the living and true God is proved by 1 Thess. 1.9, 10; that he could do this by means of his preaching of Christ crucified is shown in *ZThK* 86 (1989), 18–32 (see bibliography). That he sometimes engaged in polemical speech against materialism, idolatry, and polytheism may well be true; these ways of thinking are open to philosophical attack, but, if we may judge from the epistles, such negative themes did not constitute the basis and prime content of his message. The world's monotheistic and noetic wisdom, no less than its idolatrous wisdom, had failed to lead it to the power and wisdom of God, which were uniquely revealed in Christ crucified.

To say this is not to disparage Luke's work or the preaching of his contemporaries. That the chapter was of great importance to him is certain. 'Athen wird durch die Szene (ähnlich wie Jerusalem in Kap. 15 zum ekklesiologischen) zum geistig-kulturellen Mittelpunkt der Gesamtdarstellung' (Schille 354). It had in Luke's time become clear (as it had not in Paul's) that Christianity was to spend some time in a world that had an important 'geistig–kulturell' element, and it was necessary that Christians should be able and willing to converse with those who represented this element (just as it had long been necessary for Jews to do so). There is much truth in an observation of Bauernfeind's (215): 'So wenig Paulus (Rm 9–11) seine Hoffnung auf die endliche Errettung Israels aufgeben kann, so wenig kann deshalb Lk seine Hoffnung auf die Rettung jener unerschöpflich reich beschenkten Welt aufgeben, die der Name Athen umfasst. Gott hat zu viel an Athen getan, um es wieder los zu lassen.' It was however Luke not Paul who perceived this, and Paul would have insisted on what Luke does in fact with some success achieve: the restriction of the use of philosophy to those themes which it shares with the OT. 'Die entscheidende Frage für die Beurteilung der Rede ist, ob darin tatsächlich die nicht-biblischen Gedanken und Wendungen das Übergewicht haben oder aber doch die biblischen' (Stählin 230f.). Johnson's observation (319), that Luke recognizes Greek philosophy 'as a legitimate conversation partner in the approach to God', needs this qualification.

16. Ἐν δὲ ταῖς Ἀθήναις. Athens was no longer as exciting a place as it had been in, say, the days of Pericles; but it was exciting enough, and the chapter shows that Luke was not unaware of this, though he may have known it only second-hand. There is no first person plural here. Sulla, besieging the city in the Mithridatic war and approached by its representatives with appeals based on its distinguished past, replied that he had not come to study history but to put down rebels (οὐ φιλομαθήσων ... ἀλλὰ τοὺς ἀφισταμένους καταστρεψόμενος, Plutarch, *Sulla* 13 (460)); but Rome was aware of the history and respected it as history; Athens was well treated, and continued to be well treated and respected in its role of notable university city. Luke's narrative in this chapter shows that the story of Socrates was not forgotten and that more recent philosophers were still at work. 'Adsunt Athenienses, unde humanitas, doctrina, religio, fruges, jura, leges ortae, atque in omnes terras distributae putantur' (Cicero, *Pro Flacco* 26 (62)).

ἐκδεχομένου αὐτούς: but (as far as Luke informs us) in vain, for Silas and Timothy did not come, only joining Paul later in Corinth (18.5), when they came *from Macedonia*, with no suggestion that they had left Macedonia for Athens and then returned. But 1 Thess. 3.1f. shows that Timothy (at least) joined Paul in Athens. Perhaps he had come but not Silas, since when Paul sent Timothy back to Thessalonica he was left alone. This however is not certain for Paul uses the plural—εὐδοκήσαμεν καταλειφθῆναι ἐν Ἀθήναις μόνοι. This may be a genuine plural (we = Paul and Silas) or an epistolary plural. The fact that Timothy and Silas are not said to have joined Paul in Athens may account for the variants (for αὐτοὺς τοῦ Παύλου: αὐτοῦ, א *; αὐτοῦ τοῦ Παύλου, D*). This verse (but see on v. 17) suggests that at first Paul occupied himself simply in observation of the city in which he found himself and did not immediately begin his mission.

His *spirit* (πνεῦμα—here simply his inward life, thought and feeling) *was vexed*. For παροξύνεσθαι cf. the use of the cognate noun παροξυσμός in 15.39. Paul had not ceased to be a Jew, whose primary theological conviction was that there was but one God, and that he was to be worshipped without the use of images (Exod. 20.2–5; Deut. 5.6–9). He was vexed to find the city a 'veritable forest of idols'. The meaning of κατείδωλος is discussed by R. E. Wycherley (*JTS* 19 (1968), 619f.), who draws attention to the fact that κατά in composition often refers to an abundance of something, but that 'a very large proportion of these words refer to luxuriant vegetation' (619); 'the association with trees and plants is predominant' (620). He draws attention to the Herms, which were particularly numerous. 'We are told of a particularly large and important accumulation which stood (we now know) at the north-west corner of the agora, between the Poikile (Painted) Stoa and the Basileios (Royal) Stoa; in fact the figures so dominated the scene that the place was called simply "the Herms". This was the main approach to the agora, by which Paul would probably enter as he came up from Peiraeus. Moreover, these stoas, and above all the Poikile, were the favourite resort of philosophers, and one need not doubt that Paul frequented them as Socrates, Krates, Zeno, and many others had done before him. The adjacent Herms more than anything else would make him feel that at Athens idols were like trees in a wood' (620). Wycherley probably makes rather too much of this. He himself cites a number of examples of κατά in combination with words that have nothing to do with vegetation. What is important is that Paul was impressed by Athens not as a city of art but as a city of false religion. See two columns of quotation in Wettstein (2.562f.). Contrast Livy 45.27, ... simulacra deorum hominumque, omni genere et materiae et artium insignia.

For θεωροῦντος (אַ A B E 33 81 323 (614) 945 1175 1739 al), D Ψ 0120 𝔐 have θεωροῦντι, assimilating to the immediately preceding αὐτῷ rather than the slightly more remote genitive. It is possible to defend each case, or rather to attack each case; neither is elegant. It would have been better to recast the sentence.

οὖσαν τὴν πόλιν, accusative and participle after a verb of perceiving. Here Luke's style is correct.

17. As in Thessalonica (17.1f.) and Beroea (17.10) Paul visited the synagogue and used it as an opportunity of evangelism. On this occasion, however, the synagogue is dismissed in a sentence. There were many synagogues but there was only one Athens, and the notable scene in Athens was the Agora.

For the synagogue as an institution see on 6.8. For Jewish-Greek inscriptions at Athens see *NS* 3.65 (*CIJ* 712–15). None refers explicitly to a synagogue, though there is evidence that there were Jews in the city from the second century BC, and it is very probable that a long-established community would have a building. μὲν οὖν is a common expression in Acts; see on 1.6. It often introduces a development in the story, here the beginning of Paul's public ministry. Conzelmann (96) takes διελέγετο (17.2; 18.4, 19; 19.8f.; 20.7, 9) to mean *preached*; it is more likely (especially in view of the fact that the one verb controls the whole verse and both scenes of Paul's activity) that it means that in the synagogue Paul discussed and argued with the Jews, also with the σεβόμενοι, who presumably were not Jews either by birth or by proselytization. On the question whether such persons constituted a distinct and recognized class of 'God-fearers' see on 10.2.

Haenchen (496) thinks that Paul used the synagogue on the Sabbath; on other days he was at work elsewhere. διαλέγεσθαι is a word that could be appropriately used of discussion in the synagogue but it was especially suitable to Paul's activity ἐν τῇ ἀγορᾷ. It is used only in the later part of Acts (see above; in the rest of the NT only 3 times). ἀγορά occurs in Acts only here and at 16.19. Both verb and noun recall the archetypal philosophical figure of Socrates, who was always available for discussion in the public places of Athens. In Xenophon, *Memorabilia* 1.1.10, ἀγορά is used in the first instance to denote time: πληθούσης ἀγορᾶς ἐκεῖ φανερὸς ἦν, When the market was in full swing (i.e. in the morning) he (Socrates) was to be seen there (i.e. in the market); cf. the preceding clause, πρωί τε γὰρ εἰς τοὺς περιπάτους καὶ τὰ γυμνάσια ᾔει. For διαλέγεσθαι see e.g. Plato, *Apology* 33a, οὐδὲ χρήματα μὲν λαμβάνων διαλέγομαι; 19d, ἐμοῦ ... ἀκηκόατε διαλεγομένου. Cf. 38a. For the dialectical method (which grew out of market-place arguments), *Republic* 454a, οὐκ ἐρίζειν ἀλλὰ διαλέγεσθαι.

πρὸς τοὺς παρατυγχάνοντας recalls Socrates' readiness to converse with anyone willing to converse with him—ὅτῳ ἂν ἀεὶ ἐντυγχάνω ὑμῶν (Plato, *Apology* 29d). The present participle παρατυγχάνοντας expresses better than the aorist (D*, παρατυχόντος) the fact that this was Paul's habit.

For topography and archaeology see the Princeton publication, *The Athenian Agora*, 1953 onwards.

18. Among the strangers whom Paul chanced to meet were philosophers. Luke mentions Epicureans and Stoics. There are good summary articles, with bibliographies, in *OCD*; see also *NT Background* 65–77, 78–81. It may be asked why these two groups are singled out. Rackham (303) remarks that both were practical rather than speculative philosophers, but the answer may be that their views are alluded to, and indeed used, in the Areopagus speech that follows. It is of course possible to put this differently and say that Paul included Epicurean and Stoic material in his speech because he happened to have met Epicurean and Stoic philosophers. The speech includes a criticism of popular religion: If we are to conceive a god who created the universe (and the Epicureans were not necessarily atheist, though they believed that any gods that existed were, in all senses, too remote to be taken into practical account) then it is ridiculous to bring him a pig or a sheep, as if he were a hungry beggar, or to suppose that he could be localized in a building. This was an Epicurean criticism of popular religion. The Stoics believed that the human race was one, proceeding as it did from a single point of origin, that there was a divine being (note the neuter τὸ θεῖον in v. 29), conceived in pantheistic rather than personal terms (in him we live and move and have our being, v. 28), and that it was man's duty to seek and to live in accordance with this indwelling god. The speech (whatever we make of its origin; see above, pp. 825f.) may from one point of view be looked on as an attempt to see how far a Christian preacher can go in company with Greek philosophy.

The Stoics were a popular group, whose beliefs the Romans found naturally attractive; the Epicureans were not comparably numerous, and the use of Epicurean doctrine in the speech is the best explanation of the reference to them.

The philosophers συνέβαλλον αὐτῷ, *argued with him*; the word is Lucan (3 times in Lk, 4 times in Acts; nowhere else in the NT). Here it means that they argued with him; not all of them politely, though the impolite are made to express themselves in (for the NT) unusually stylish Greek—unless, that is, Page (193) is right in the belief that in καί τινες ἔλεγον the subject is 'probably not the philosophers but generally some of those who heard Paul'. τί ἂν θέλοι . . .; ἂν with the potential optative 'was old-fashioned in the NT age' (M. 3.123). For its infrequency in papyri, LXX, and Apostolic Fathers see BDR § 385.1, n. 1. θέλειν λέγειν recalls the French *vouloir dire, to mean*, but it is not quite so firm an idiom. 'What does he want to say?' Perhaps, 'What is he getting at?' See LS 479, ἐθέλω II 3; e.g. Herodotus 4.131.2, . . . γνῶναι τὸ θέλει τὰ δῶρα λέγειν.

Used of a person present οὗτος is often disparaging; so BDR § 290.1, n. 1, adding Lk. 15.30; 18.11. σπερμολόγος is certainly disparaging. It is used by Demosthenes (18.127(269)) along with περίτριμμ' ἀγορᾶς, ὄλεθρος γραμματεύς. Literally it means *picking up seeds*, and so came to be used of an inferior speaker or writer who picks up and uses as his own ideas that he has found in others. It is again connected with περίτριμμα by Philo (*Legatio ad Gaium* 203), where Colson (*LCL*) translates 'scrap retailer, piece of riff-raff'. BA (1522) have *Schwätzer*, which does not seem quite right; it fails to take up the first cumbersome part of 'one who picks up and retails scraps of knowledge, an idle babbler, gossip' (LS 1627). Hanson (176) has 'an intellectual magpie'. *Begs.* 4.211 gives a long quotation from Eustathius of Thessalonica on *Odyssey* 5.490, suggesting *cock-sparrow*, which does not suggest (to me) the right image. 'Journalist' is an admirable suggestion provided it is understood that an inferior and not a superior journalist is intended. 'What does this third-rate journalist want to tell us?' will perhaps do.

The hints at the figure of Socrates noted in v. 17 now become more definite in what is nearly an explicit quotation. According to Xenophon, *Memorabilia* 1.1.1 the charge against Socrates was (in addition to the corruption of the youth), Ἀδικεῖ Σωκράτης οὗς μὲν ἡ πόλις θεοὺς οὐ νομίζων, ἕτερα δὲ καινὰ δαιμόνια εἰσφέρων. For Athenian objections to strange gods and strange religions see Josephus, *Apion* 2.265–267, and cf. Euripides, *Bacchae* 255f., τόνδ' αὖ θέλεις τὸν δαίμον' ἀνθρώποισιν εἰσφέρων νέον. In the charge δαιμόνιον is of course used in a sense different from that of the gospels (e.g. Mk 1.34); it means a deity, though clearly not in a monotheistic sense; cf. the special δαιμόνιον of Socrates (e.g. Xenophon, *Memorabilia* 1.1.2) and the wording of the charge in Plato, *Apology* 24bc, which includes ἕτερα δὲ δαιμόνια καινά. Of such foreign deities it was alleged that Paul was a καταγγελεύς. The noun does not occur elsewhere in the NT, but καταγγέλλειν is characteristic of Acts (11 times, including 17.3, 13, 23; rest of the NT, 7 times); *preacher*, or *herald* (as at the games). The objection to introducing new deities may have been partly political; Dio Cassius

52.36.1f. records that Maecenas advised Augustus to hate and punish those who bring in new ideas about τὸ θεῖον.

The impression Paul gave was based on the fact that he τὸν Ἰησοῦν καὶ τὴν ἀνάστασιν εὐηγγελίζετο (the verb is a near enough synonym—but a Christian synonym—of καταγγέλλειν). It can be readily understood that Paul's preaching of Jesus could be regarded as the proclamation of a new δαιμόνιον. ἀνάστασις as commonly understood will hardly serve as a second personal deity (the plural ξένων δαιμονίων, taken literally, implies at least two). For this reason it has been suggested (e.g. Bultmann, *Theologie* 80) that Ἀνάστασις was taken to be a female deity corresponding to the male deity Jesus. The suggestion is superficially attractive but could be maintained only if there were reason to think that Paul in his preaching constantly referred in quasi-personal terms to Ἰησοῦς καί ἀνάστασις. This is unlikely; it is much more probable that he used verbs: Χριστὸς ἀπέθανεν ... ὃν ὁ θεὸς ἀνέστησεν (or ἤγειρεν). Luke gives a brief summary of what Paul said, less than perfectly clear; cf. 4.2. The Athenian comment is cast in a form intended to recall the story of Socrates, and means no more than, This is a strange new religion, with all this talk about a man called Jesus and a resurrection. 'Jesus and the resurrection' is Pauline enough, and indeed probably pre-Pauline; see Rom. 10.9 (*Romans* 186f.). But the formulation in Acts is different, and far less clear and trenchant.

The last clause in the verse, ὅτι ... εὐηγγελίζετο, is omitted by D gig, possibly because it did not seem consistent with the plural ξένων δαιμονίων, possibly (Metzger 455) because the writer did not wish to class Jesus among the δαιμόνια.

Taylor (5.304–6) reconstructs the place where the whole incident (vv. 18–34) took place—the Στοὰ βασίλειος, at the NW corner of the Agora.

19. ἐπιλαβόμενοι is an ambiguous word. It may mean an arrest, with or without violence (16.19; 18.17; 21.30, 33) or a well intentioned attachment (9.27; 23.19). It is a Lucan word; in addition to the seven occurrences in Acts there are five in Luke, six in the rest of the NT. The meaning here will depend on the view that is taken of the proceedings as a whole: Was Paul arrested and brought before the Council of the Areios Pagos to be tried by them, or was he conducted to the Areios Pagos hill in order that he might in a convenient place (Haenchen's statement (498) that the hill was too small for a meeting is rightly contradicted by Marshall (285)) address a number of interested inquirers? Or is this statement of alternatives fallacious?

The history of the Areopagus court (ἡ βουλὴ ἡ ἐξ Ἀρείου πάγου, Demosthenes 18.133 (271); ἡ β. ἡ ἐν Ἀρείῳ πάγῳ, 59.80 (1372)) in the first century, indeed in the Roman period generally, is obscure. It has however been shown, especially by T. D. Barnes (*JTS* 20 (1969),

407–19; useful bibliography), that it remained in this period the supreme authority in Athens. 'The Areopagus seems to be the effective government of Roman Athens and its chief court. As such, like the imperial Senate in Rome, it could interfere in any aspect of corporate life—education, philosophical lectures, public morality, foreign cults' (413). It could try crimes of any kind, and probably had authority to inflict capital punishment (412). It is incorrect to say that it no longer met on the Areopagus Hill but only in the Stoa Basileios (409; see however Hemer, *NTS* 20 (1974), 341–50). Barnes concludes, 'The obvious meaning of the words in Acts should be accepted: Paul was taken before the Areopagus, i.e. before the council sitting on the hill' (410). This perhaps goes too far. The words ἐπὶ τὸν Ἄρειον πάγον ἤγαγον may mean, They brought him before the Areopagus council (wherever it met), or They brought him to the Areopagus hill (for whatever purpose). Luke may have meant both, but if he intended to *say* both he should have done so explicitly. According to Schneider (2.237) he is using a 'literarischer Topos'; one may compare the way in which the Areopagus council is brought in by Cicero, *De Natura Deorum* 2.29 (74) (Si quis dicat, Atheniensium rempublicam consilio regi, desit illud, Ariopagi). Weiser (466) notes (1) that there is a change of place from the Agora, (2) that more are present than the members of the council; 'Lukas schwebte eine ideale Szene vor.' Barnes concludes that, as in many other Hellenistic cities, Paul was brought before the local authority, accused of introducing a new religion. He seems to be mistaken in the view that ἐπιλαμβάνεσθαι must imply a violent arrest; see above. *Begs.* 4.213 had already observed that here Luke uses the local name, Areopagus, as he does at Philippi (στρατηγοί), Thessalonica (πολιτάρχαι), and Corinth (ἀνθύπατος)—and gets it right every time.

Ἄρειον πάγον is correctly so written, *divisim*; this is confirmed by many inscriptions. The compound Ἀρειόπαγος 'never had any real existence', though Ἀρεοπαγίτης (v. 34) was formed from it as if it existed; at a late period it came into existence as a back-formation from Ἀρεοπαγίτης (M. 2.151, 277).

δυνάμεθα in this sentence is more like the English 'May we ... ?' than 'Can we ... ?', 'Are we able ... ?'; that is, it looks more like a polite request than a demand for an explanation, such as a court might have made.

In ἡ καινὴ αὕτη ἡ ὑπὸ σοῦ λαλουμένη διδαχή the second article is superfluous (see Robertson 701, 785); not surprisingly it is omitted by B D *pc*. For λαλουμένη, D sy^p have καταγγελλομένη (v. 18) and E 81 have λεγομένη. Instead of τε, and suggesting an adversative element in the sentence, B Ψ 33 36 81 453 1241 *al* have δέ. More interesting than these variants is the fact that D (614 *pc* sy^{h**}) rewrite the beginning of the verse: μετὰ δὲ ἡμέρας τινὰς ἐπιλαβόμενοι αὐτοῦ ἤγαγον αὐτὸν ἐπὶ Ἄριον πάγον, πυνθανόμενοι καὶ λέγοντες. The insertion of *certain days* gives Paul a period of undisturbed activity, and *inquiring* suggests interest rather than an attempt to set in motion a legal process.

20. This verse is a duplicate of vv. 18, 19. The ξένα δαιμόνια have now become simply ξενίζοντα, by which Luke presumably means things (statements, beliefs) that are strange, surprising, though at every other place in Acts where the verb is used it means *to receive as a guest* (or, in the passive, *to lodge*); so 10.6, 18, 23, 32; 21.16; 28.7. Elsewhere in the NT it is used only at Heb. 13.2 (*to entertain*) and 1 Pet. 4.4, 12 (both, passive, *to be surprised*). 'You are bringing into our ears (for ἀκοαί as *ears*, rather than the faculty of hearing, cf. Mk 7.35) surprising things.' For εἰσφέρεις cf. Euripides, *Bacchae* 650, τοὺς λόγους γὰρ ἐσφέρεις καινοὺς ἀεί. Cf. also Sophocles, *Ajax* 148f., τοιούσδε λόγους ψιθύρους πλάσσων εἰς ὦτα φέρει πᾶσιν Ὀδυσσεύς. Instead of εἰσφέρεις, E has ῥήματα εἰσφέρεις, D co have φέρεις ῥήματα, and ℵ* (Ψ) *pc* have εἰσφέρει.

The questioners want to know what these surprising things mean, θέλει εἶναι (cf. the similar but not identical θέλειν λέγειν in v. 18). In τίνα θέλει ταῦτα εἶναι BDR § 299.1, n. 1 take τίνα as neuter plural subject of θέλει, and translate, ... wie es sich damit verhält. Instead of τίνα θέλει (P⁷⁴ ℵ A B Ψ 33 36 81 945 1175 1739 *al*), D E 𝔐 have τί ἂν θέλοι (cf. the optative in v. 18).

The verse suggests nothing more than a desire for information and enlightenment, but the severe attitude reported by Josephus, *Apion* 2.267 (... τιμωρία κατὰ τῶν ξένον εἰσαγόντων θεὸν ὥριστο θάνατος) should be borne in mind.

21. The Athenians have expressed a desire to hear the new message that Paul appears to have brought; Luke adds a note that explains this and at the same time shows an acquaintance with Athenian life and characteristics. This acquaintance is not necessarily first-hand; Athenian curiosity was widely recognized and commented on. So e.g. Demosthenes 4.10(43), ἢ βούλεσθ', εἰπέ μοι, περιίοντες αὐτῶν πυνθάνεσθαι, 'λέγεταί τι καινόν;' γένοιτο γὰρ ἄν τι καινότερον ἢ ... Cf. Thucydides 3.38.4. The proverbial characterization of the Athenians (*inter alia*) led A. D. Nock to the judgement (*Gnomon* 25 (1953), 506), 'brilliant as is the picture of Athens [in Acts 17], it makes on me the impression of being based on literature, which was easy to find, rather than on personal observation'. The fact that others had observed Athenian curiosity does not in itself prove that Luke had not himself observed it; but it makes it more difficult to prove, or to feel confident, that he had.

In this curiosity native Athenians were joined by οἱ ἐπιδημοῦντες ξένοι. For ἐπιδημεῖν cf. 2.10 (and 18.27 P³⁸ᵛⁱᵈ D). For the combination with ξένοι cf. Lysias 12.35, ὅσοι ξένοι ἐπιδημοῦσιν.

Many visitors came to Athens, some as serious students, some as tourists. It is not clear why D should add εἰς αὐτούς after ἐπιδημοῦντες. The preposition may be intended to bring out the fact that the foreigners had entered Athenian society and so had come to share its ways.

For εὐκαιρεῖν cf. Mk 6.31 (with an infinitive, as here); 1 Cor. 16.12. For the use of the infinitive see BDR § 392.3, n. 11.

The Athenians desire ἢ λέγειν τι ἢ ἀκούειν τι καινότερον (the second τι is omitted by D E 𝔐). The comparative adjective is probably used for the positive; so e.g. M. 3.30, adding 'but possibly an Atticistic refinement: *newer*'. It is not clear what this means; possibly 'newer than the last thing we heard'. Zerwick (§ 150) agrees that the positive is the probable meaning, 'nisi quis mavult hunc comparativum sumere pro superlativo: "recentissimum quodque" '. BDR § 244.2 after saying that καινότερον can 'mit dem Positiv wiedergegeben werden' rather surprisingly translate 'etwas ganz Neues = das Allerneuste', which looks more like a superlative.

For the whole picture cf. Demosthenes 11.17 (156), ἡμεῖς δὲ (εἰρήσεται γὰρ τἀληθῆ) οὐδὲν ποιοῦντες ἐνθάδε καθήμεθα, μέλλοντες ἀεὶ καὶ ψηφιζόμενοι καὶ πυνθανόμενοι κατὰ τὴν ἀγορὰν εἴ τι λέγεται νεώτερον.

This verse had probably been read by the author of the Acts of Philip 7(2) (L.-B. 2.2.4), εἰ δέ τι καινότερον ἔχεις, ὦ ξένε, ἐπίδειξον ἡμῖν ἀφθόνως μετὰ παρρησίας· οὐδενὸς γὰρ ἄλλου χρείαν ἔχομεν ἢ μόνον ἀκούειν τι καινότερον. 8(3) ... Ὦ ἄνδρες φιλόσοφοι τῆς Ἑλλάδος, εἰ βούλεσθε καινοτέρου πράγματος ἀκοῦσαι καί ἐστε ποθοῦντές τι καινότερον ...

22. Σταθείς: Paul *stood*. This would be expected in Athens, as it would not in the synagogue at Pisidian Antioch (13.16). He stood ἐν μέσῳ τοῦ Ἀρείου πάγου. For Areopagus see v. 19; ἐν μέσῳ (cf. 1.15; 2.22; 4.7; 27.21) suggests in the midst of a group of people rather than at the mid-point of an area.

Ἄνδρες Ἀθηναῖοι. The form of address is common in Acts (cf. Ἄνδρες Γαλιλαῖοι, 1.11, and 20 other examples), but here, with Ἀθηναῖοι, it adds to the reminiscence of Socrates (e.g. Plato, *Apology* 17a).

The interpretation of this verse has been much discussed: is it an accusation ('unter schwelligen Spott', Schille 356), or a *captatio benevolentiae* (forbidden before the Areopagus court, according to Lucian, *De Gymnasiis* 19)? The answer must to a great extent turn on the interpretation of ὡς δεισιδαιμονεστέρους, discussed below. Luke has however prepared the way for the understanding of the address by recording Paul's observation of the city as κατείδωλον (v. 16). The Athenians practise religion, but their religion is expressed in a profusion of idols. For δεισιδαίμων cf. in Acts itself δεισιδαιμονία at 25.19. Festus uses this word when speaking of Judaism to Agrippa II, whom, as a Jew, he would not deliberately insult by calling his religion a superstition.

LS (375) define δεισιδαιμονέω as *have superstitious fears* ... , rare in good sense, *to be religious*'; δεισιδαιμονία as *'fear of the gods, religious feeling* ... in bad sense, *superstition*'; δεισιδαίμων as *'fearing the gods*, 1. in good sense, *pious, religious* ... 2. in bad sense, *superstitious*'. Examples can be found for both senses. Yet the δεισιδαίμων described by Theophrastus (16(17)) is not an admirable character. 'δεισιδαιμονία is cowardice in face of the supernatural (δειλία πρὸς τὸ δαιμόνιον).' 'The δεισιδαίμων is one who, if anything dirty touches him, will wash his hands, sprinkle himself with water from a holy fountain, and walk about all day with his mouth full of bay leaves.' In *De Superstitione* (= περὶ δεισιδαιμονίας) Plutarch places atheism and δεισιδαιμονία at opposite extremes (1 (164E)). The atheist is unmoved by any thought of the divine (τὸ θεῖον); the δεισιδαίμων is moved, but in a perverse way (2(165BC)). Atheists acknowledge no gods at all; δεισιδαίμονες take the gods to be evil, holding what is kind to be fearful, what is fatherly to be tyrannous, what is gentle to be hurtful, what is kindly to be savage (6 (167DEF)). Neither Theophrastus (4th/3rd century BC) nor Plutarch (1st/2nd century AD) would have been pleased to be described as ὡς δεισιδαιμονέστερος. The word could indeed be used in a good sense; so e.g. Xenophon, *Cyropaedia* 3.3.58 (οἱ δεισιδαίμονες ἧττον τοὺς ἀνθρώπους φοβοῦνται); *Agesilaus* 11.8 (ἀεὶ δὲ δεισιδαίμων ἦν, νομίζων τοὺς μὲν καλῶς ζῶντας οὔπω εὐδαίμονας, τοὺς δ᾽ εὐκλεῶς τετελευτηκότας ἤδη μακαρίους). An inscription describes the person commemorated as φίλος θνητοῖς εἰς τἀθανάτους δεισιδαίμων (*IG* 14.1683). The simple fact is that δεισιδαίμων means *religious*. To the sceptic, this means superstitious; to the religious, judgement depends on whether the religion is one he shares, or at least approves, or is one that he rejects. We shall see that Paul's attitude (as represented in the speech) is not simple; he has however noted with disapproval, one might almost say with arrogance, that the city is full of idols.

The word was discussed by Hatch (*Essays* 43–5), who argued that 'in the first century and a half of the Christian era the words had come to have in ordinary Greek a bad or at least a depreciatory sense' (45). This should perhaps be qualified by the addition of 'especially among Jews'. Hatch quotes Philo, *De Sacrificiis* 15 (... δεισιδαιμονίαν δὲ πρᾶγμα ἀδελφὸν ἀσεβείᾳ ...); *Quod Deus* 164 (the mean between δεισιδαιμονία and ἀσέβεια is εὐσέβεια); *De Gigantibus* 16; *De Plantatione* 107 (δεισιδαιμονία a parasitic growth (παραναπέφυκεν) on true religion); *De Specialibus Legibus* 4.147 (γεννήσει γὰρ ἡ μὲν πρόσθεσις [τὸ εὐσέβεια] δεισιδαιμονίαν, ἡ δ᾽ ἀφαίρεσις ἀσέβειαν); Josephus, *Ant.* 15.227 (but here Marcus and

Wikgren (LCL edition) translate *religious scruples*, though they recognize *superstition* as a possible alternative); and Plutarch, as above. Also Justin, *1 Apology* 2: those addressed are not 'under the dominion of prejudice or a desire to gratify superstitious persons (ἀνθρωπαρεσκείᾳ τῇ δεισιδαιμόνων)'. Conzelmann's argument (97) that δεισ. must be understood *sensu bono* because it occurs in a *captatio benevolentiae* is invalid: Paul's words are to be understood as a *captatio benevolentiae* only if we know that δεισ. is intended *sensu bono*.

ὡς δεισιδαιμονεστέρους. Opinions differ not only in regard to the meaning of the word δεισ. but also in regard to the comparative form of the adjective and the use of ὡς. M. 3.30 comments on the comparative: '... not class. *rather* but probably popular elative *extremely god-fearing* (strengthened by ὡς)'. Similarly Zerwick (§ 148): 'Paulus Athenienses laudat agnoscens eos ὡς δεισιδαιμονεστέρους "superstitiosiores", quod nihil aliud est quam "valde pios" (comparativus pro superlativo "elativo")'. Zerwick has no note on ὡς. It is hard to understand the alternatives in BDR § 224.1, n. 2 '... ist zweideutig: "ungewöhnlich götterfürchtig" (klass.) oder "sehr götterfürchtig"'. Perhaps this corresponds to Robertson (665): '... more religious ... than ordinary or than I had supposed'. A comparative may still be elative even if truly comparative. So far as one may think of δεισιδαιμονεστέρους as standing for a superlative we may perhaps compare the familiar construction of ὡς with a superlative—as ὡς τάχιστα, as quickly as possible. But in the long article on ὡς BA 1789–1793 do not mention Acts 17.22; under δεισιδαίμων (347) they offer the translation, 'ich nehme wahr, dass ihr durch und durch religiöse Leute seid.' It may be that ὡς here has something of the 'as if' sense to be found in Rom. 9.32 (ὡς ἐξ ἔργων); Athens presents a show of (idolatrous) piety, but it is an unreal, uninformed piety directed towards a deity who must remain unknown (v. 23).

BDR § 416.1, n. 3 note the absence of a participle (contrast v. 16). Cf. Radermacher (170).

The piety of Athenians was well known (and need not therefore have been observed at first hand by Luke). The following are among passages often quoted. Pausanias 1.17.1: The Athenians θεούς εὐσεβοῦσιν ἄλλων πλέον. Sophocles, *Oedipus Coloneus* 260: τὰς γ' Ἀθήνας φασὶ θεοσεβεστάτας. Josephus, *Apion* 2.130: ... τοὺς δὲ εὐσεβεστάτους τῶν Ἑλλήνων ἅπαντες λέγουσιν.

The meaning of this in some ways ambiguous verse can be found only in the light of ἀγνώστῳ, ἀγνοοῦντες, in v. 23. See further below.

23. διερχόμενος here does not have the meaning that διέρχεσθαι sometimes (see on 8.4) has in Acts. Paul was simply making his way through the city; as he went, however, he was looking carefully at religious objects. ἀναθεωρεῖν is a stronger word than θεωρεῖν (v. 16); διϊστορεῖν (D*) is stronger still. Idols struck the eye; Paul looked more closely at the σεβάσματα. The word is derived from σέβας, *reverential awe* (LS 1587): something viewed with such awe; broadly, any object related to cultus. At Wisd. 14.20; 15.17; Josephus, *Ant.* 18.344 the word is used of objects of idolatrous worship, and so it is here, though one such object will be found to point to, or rather to suggest, the true God. εὗρον does not necessarily imply that Paul was looking for what he *found*—he *came across*. Among various religious objects, σεβάσματα, a βωμός is almost certainly an altar, though the base of a statue (Homer, *Odyssey* 7.100) is, in the context, not impossible. The statue would be an image of the unknown god. The altar, or base, was *inscribed*. There is no difference between ἐπεγέγραπτο and the periphrastic pluperfect (ἦν γεγραμμένον) of D; the variant, like many other Western variants, points to a time of greater textual flexiblity than obtained later. Luke writes καὶ βωμόν, *also an altar*, that is, in addition to other things, an altar.

The inscription was Ἀγνώστῳ θεῷ; on this see especially *Begs.* 5.240–6; also P. W. van der Horst in *ANRW* II 18.2 (1989), 1426–56 (with bibliography). No such inscription has been uncovered in Athens by archaeologists. This of course does not prove that no such inscription ever existed; countless inscriptions must have perished or become indecipherable. But already Jerome (*Ad Titum* 1.12) wrote, 'Inscriptio autem arae non ita erat, ut Paulus asseruit, "ignoto deo", sed ita, "diis Asiae et Europae et Africae, diis ignotis et peregrinis".' The plural form of the dedication is firmly attested, notably by Pausanias 1.1.4 (βωμοὶ δὲ θεῶν τε ὀνομαζομένων ἀγνώστων καὶ ἡρώων καὶ παίδων τῶν Θησέως καὶ Φαλήρου—these are at Munychaia, a harbour of Athens) and Philostratus, *Apollonius* 6.3 (... Ἀθήνησιν, οὗ καὶ ἀγνώστων δαιμόνων βωμοὶ ἵδρυνται). See also Tertullian, *Ad Nationes* 2.9, Nam et Athenis ara est inscripta: ignotis deis. colit ergo quis quod ignoret? But Tertullian had presumably read Acts. Pausanias's reference to heroes lends some support to the suggestion of R. E. Wycherley (*JTS* 19 (1968), 620f.). In the establishment of the agora and adjacent buildings many earlier burials were disturbed; Athenian δεισιδαιμονία would lead to the foundation of cults to placate the dead. 'A legend and a name might grow and attach itself to the spot, but not necessarily so; the cult might remain truly the cult of an unknown god. Strictly speaking it would be a hero cult, and the shrine a *heröon*, but the distinction is not at all clear, and even an obscure local hero could be called *theos*' (621). This is no more than an interesting possibility. The balance of probability remains with Jerome, but it is by no means impossible that Paul saw what he describes—or that there was in Athens for him and for others to see what Luke says that Paul says that he saw. Van der Horst (op. cit.) and Taylor (290) draw attention to a Pergamene inscription (*Die Arbeiten zu Pergamon 1908–1909, II* (Mitteilungen des kaiserlich deutschen archäologischen Instituts, Athenische Abteilung 35), 1910, pp. 454–7), restored, not certainly but with some probability as θεοῖς ἀγνώστοις. There could have been a similar dedication in Athens, due to anxiety lest any gods should be inadvertently left without due honour. It is worth while to add, though they furnish no more precise information, Diogenes Laertius, *Epimenides* 3 (10), βωμοὺς ἀνωνύμους and Tertullian, *Adversus Marcionem* 1.9, Invenio plane ignotis deis aras prostitutas, sed Attica idololatria est. More important is the use that is made of the alleged inscription. This, even in the singular, implies polytheism; the speaker makes it monotheist.

Surprisingly, the masculine θεός is taken up as if it were neuter: ὃ οὖν ἀγνοοῦντες εὐσεβεῖτε, τοῦτο ἐγὼ καταγγέλλω ὑμῖν. This is the reading of P⁷⁴ ℵ* A* B D (81) 1175 *pc* lat; masculine pronouns (ὃν ... τοῦτον) appear in ℵ Aᶜ E Ψ 𝔐 sy Clement. It is likely that the neuters are original; there was a double reason for changing them, the grammatical reason that the antecedent was θεός, the theological reason that Paul was understood to proclaim a personal, not an impersonal, deity (but cf. τὸ θεῖον in v. 29).

The sentence taken as a whole makes two statements, one about the Athenians and one about Paul. The subjects are different, the verbs are different, but the objects are the same, as the relative construction shows (ὃ ... τοῦτο). The Athenians reverence a certain object, Paul proclaims it. εὐσεβεῖν (often with a preposition, *act piously towards*, rather than an object accusative) denotes the appropriate attitude towards divine beings, the practice of religion. καταγγέλλειν in Greek generally is *to declare* or *proclaim* anything, in the NT *to proclaim* the Gospel (or an aspect of it), or the being whose person and work constitute or determine the Gospel.

On this passage Bultmann (*Theologie* 470) writes: 'Auch insofern ordnet der Verf. der Act das Christentum als Religion in die Weltgeschichte ein, als er in der Areopagrede den Paulus an die heidnische Frömmigkeit anknüpfen lässt durch Bezugnahme auf die athenische Altar-Inschrift und auf den stoischen Gottesglauben (17.23, 28). Dadurch wird "die heidnische Geschichte, Kultur- und Religionswelt als Vorgeschichte des Christentums reklamiert" (Vielhauer), und das entspricht der Auffassung der Act vom Verhältnis des Christentums zum Judentum: die paulinische Gesetzeslehre ist nicht mehr verstanden, und die jüdische Geschichte ist einfach zur Vorgeschichte des Christentums geworden.'

There is much in this that is well said, but it is important not to give too heavy a theological treatment to Paul's (Luke's) sentence; it must be understood as a preacher's ad hoc way of introducing his theme, and it would be unfair to hold him bound to all the theological implications of his illustration. The Athenians (those of them who were religiously rather than sceptically disposed) reverenced a considerable number of gods. The preacher could have made a note of many other σεβάσματα bearing the names of particular gods; he picked out this god, whose name was not given because it was not known, as the one whom, to the exclusion of all the others, he intended to proclaim. The Athenians worshipped ἀγνοοῦντες; this picks up the adjective ἄγνωστος (and perhaps we should add the δυνάμεθα (implying θέλομεν) γνῶναι in v. 19), but it does so in a general rather than a particular way, and must not be used as the basis of inferences about the knowability, or unknowability, of God. Paul declares: You are religious, but your religion is uninstructed (cf.— from a different angle—Rom. 10.2: the Jews have a zeal for God but it is not κατ᾽ ἐπίγνωσιν; Jn 4.22 is more remote); I am now proclaiming what you must know if your religion is to be real. ὅ should be taken rather as the object of ἀγνοοῦωτες than of εὐσεβεῖτε: What in the practice of your religion you do not know (namely, the true God; see 1 Thess. 4.5; Gal. 4.8), that I proclaim.

'Die Welt des Heidentums gilt als in ἄγνοια und πλάνη versunken' (Bultmann, *Theologie* 70). Yet after this beginning Paul goes on to say much that religious Athenians would find familiar, and never reaches what in his Gospel was truly (to the heathen world) unknown. On the other hand, to say that Luke means to show that Paul is not preaching something that 'vollkommen ausserhalb des athenischen Erwartungshorizontes lag' (Weiser 468) is in danger of going too far in the other direction; and to claim that the Gentiles live in a simultaneous Yes and No to the true God (Haenchen 501) makes Luke too much of a theologian. For the language cf. Isa. 45.15: σὺ γὰρ εἶ ὁ θεός, καὶ οὐκ ᾔδειμεν (אל מסתתר).

24. The truth that Paul has to communicate to the ignorant Athenians is the truth about God and his relation to the world and men. The first part of this truth, given as a predicate of the opening words, ὁ θεός, is that God is the creator: ὁ ποιήσας τὸν κόσμον καὶ πάντα τὰ ἐν αὐτῷ. This is a truth frequently asserted in the OT, not only in the creation narratives but in other summary statements which the present statement resembles without actually reproducing any of them. The following may serve as examples. Gen. 1.1, ἐν ἀρχῇ ἐποίησεν ὁ θεὸς τὸν οὐρανὸν καὶ τὴν γῆν; cf. Exod. 20.11. Isa. 42.5, κύριος ὁ θεὸς ὁ ποιήσας τὸν οὐρανὸν ... ὁ στερεώσας τὴν γῆν καὶ τὰ ἐν αὐτῇ; Wisd. 9.1, ὁ ποιήσας τὰ πάντα, 9, ἐποίεις τὸν κόσμον. Cf. 4 Macc. 5.25, and in the same tradition 1 Clement 19.2; Barnabas 21.5. Philo not merely borrowed and re-expressed the language of the OT but wrote περὶ τῆς κατὰ Μωυσέα κοσμοποιίας (*de Opificio Mundi*). Josephus began the *Antiquities* with creation, altering one word in Gen. 1.1, ἐν ἀρχῇ ἔκτισεν ὁ θεός. But the concept of God as the maker of the universe was Greek as well as Jewish. Plato's *Timaeus* is an account of creation very different from that of Genesis except in the notion of divine causation. Cf. Epictetus 4.7.6: ὁ θεὸς πάντα πεποίηκεν τὰ ἐν τῷ κόσμῳ καὶ αὐτὸν τὸν κόσμον. *Corpus Hermeticum* 4.1: τὸν πάντα κόσμον ἐποίησεν ὁ δημιουργός. The word κόσμος was used by Greek philosophers (Schneider 2.239), but, as appears above, it was used by Jewish writers too. 'All the things that are in it' is paralleled also, and in biblical sources; we may add 1QH 1.13–15, Thou hast created the earth by thy power, seas and floods (תהומות) [...] thou hast established in thy wisdom, and all that is in them (וכול אשר בם) thou hast determined by thy counsel. In Acts the theme of God as creator has already appeared at 4.24, where the language is even closer to that of the OT.

God thus described, in terms that would be familiar to both Jews and Greeks, is naturally κύριος of the things that he has made, that is, of heaven and earth, the totality of creation, including of course men. As such a universal creator and lord he is not to be confined within a space circumscribed by human invention and manufacture. Cf. 7.48–50, where again the language is more scriptural than here, though in the present verse χειροποίητος, used in secular Greek (e.g. Herodotus 1.195.1, σκῆπτρον χειροποίητον), cannot fail to recall its frequent use in OT denunciations of idolatry. The question of the Jerusalem Temple is not raised here, as it is in ch. 7. Cf. Isa. 2.18; 16.12; Lev. 26.1 (LXX).

Conzelmann (98) points out that Judaism used such polemic against heathen temples, referring to Josephus, *Ant.* 8.227ff. (which does not seem to make his point) and *Oracula Sibyllina* 4.8–11. But Greeks could say this too. Plutarch (*De Repugnantiis Stoicis* 6 (1034B)) quotes a δόγμα Ζήνωνος as follows: ἱερὰ θεῶν μή οἰκοδομεῖν· ἱερὸν γὰρ μὴ πολλοῦ ἄξιον καὶ ἅγιον οὐκ ἔστιν· οἰκοδόμων δ᾽ἔργον καὶ βαναύσων οὐδέν ἐστι πολλοῦ ἄξιον. *SVF* 1.264 (pp. 61f.) quotes versions of the same saying from Clement of Alexandria, Theodoret, and Epiphanius.

H. P. Owen (*NTS* 5 (1958), 133–43 (cf. Hanson 178)), rightly observes that Luke is not presenting the Hellenistic-Jewish argument that God can be known from creation; he is known only by the word, or Gospel; God's creatorship is known by faith.

25. The form of this verse is parallel to that of v. 24, with διδούς occupying the place of ὑπάρχων (since he is ... since he gives ...). θεραπεύειν is often in the NT (and elsewhere) used of the service done by men to men, especially in the healing of diseases. It is ridiculous to suppose that God needs service by human hands (ὑπὸ χειρῶν ἀνθρωπίνων; cf. χειροποίητος in v. 24). There is an implied contrast between ἀνθρώπινος and θεῖος; cf. an Athenian inscription of AD 174/175 quoted in *ND* 4.83f. (περί τε τὰ θεῖα καὶ τὰ ἀνθρώπινα). He made everything; how can he need anything? He not only created all things in the beginning but continues to give (διδούς, present participle) to all life, breath, and all things, that is, all the things men need for their human existence. It is scarcely possible to distinguish between ζωή and πνοή (take away men's breath and they die), and τὰ πάντα is deliberately imprecise. In Gen. 2.7 when God formed man of the dust of the earth he breathed into his face πνοὴν ζωῆς; as a result man became ψυχὴ ζῶσα. Cf. 2 Macc. 7.22, 23.

For τινος, αὐτὸς διδούς, D(c) has ὅτι οὗτος ὁ δούς, for it is he who gave. The absence of τινος makes no difference to the sense; the use of the aorist participle points to the act of creation.

There are many parallels to this verse, biblical, Jewish, non-Jewish. Isa. 42.5 is close; it is interesting to note the differences. Isaiah's πνεῦμα is omitted, because the Spirit is given not to all but to believers; τῷ λαῷ, which suggests the chosen people, is changed into *all*; *all things* is added. Cf. Ps. 50.12f.; 2 Macc. 14.35; Tobit 7.17; 3 Macc. 2.9; Mt. 11.25 = Lk. 10.21.

Among other Jewish writings: Josephus, *Ant.* 8.111, ἀπροσδεὲς γὰρ τὸ θεῖον ἁπάντων (it is interesting to note the Stoic treatment of Solomon); among non-Jewish texts Calvin notes Persius, *Satire* 2.69–71. See also Euripides, *Hercules Furens* 1345f., δεῖται γὰρ ὁ θεός, εἴπερ ἐστ᾽ ὀρθῶς [? ὄντως] θεός, οὐδενός; Seneca, *Epistle* 95.47, non quaerit ministros deus, quidni? ipse humano generi ministrat . . . ; *Corpus Hermeticum* 5.10, πάντα δὲ ἐν σοί, πάντα ἀπὸ σοῦ, πάντα δίδως καὶ οὐδὲν λαμβάνεις. Cf. *Corpus Hermeticum* 2.16.

It is interesting to note that Luther (perhaps remembering Seneca) takes τινος to be masculine (*ymands*). Chrysostom (*Homily* 38.2) takes up a fresh (and probably unintended) point λέγων δέ, μὴ ὑπὸ χειρῶν ἀνθρωπίνων θεραπεύεσθαι τὸν θεόν, αἰνίττεται ὅτι διανοίᾳ καὶ νῷ θεραπεύεται.

26. ἐποίησεν resumes the ποιήσας of v. 24, a fact which probably determines the way in which the word is to be taken (Haenchen 502). It may be taken either as an equivalent of *created* (as ἐποίησεν translates ברא in Gen 1.1) or understood modally with κατοικεῖν, or with ζητεῖν (v. 27), or with both. The former view is taken by Dibelius (35f.), the latter by Pohlenz (*ZNW* 42 (1949), 84f.); there is a reply by Dibelius (153, n. 37). The occurrence of ἐξ ἑνός as an adverbial description of the circumstances of creation seems decisive in favour of Dibelius' view; κατοικεῖν and ζητεῖν follow epexegetically. God made them *of one* (on this see below), with a view to their dwelling . . . seeking. It must be emphasized that the whole sentence, comprising vv. 26, 27, is a unit of which the various parts belong together; one consequence of this is that the method of making (ἐξ ἑνός) must be seen in relation to the dwelling and seeking.

After ἑνός (P⁷⁴ ℵ A B 33 81 323 1175 1739 pc vg co Clement), αἵματος is added by D E 𝔐 gig sy. It has been maintained that this longer way of expressing the original unity of mankind was changed and αἵματος dropped because it was recalled that God made men not out of blood but out of the dust of the earth (Gen. 2.7; Preuschen 109). More probably the short text was original and referred to the creation of the one man, Adam, the father of all; there was no clear parallel to this in Greek thought and mythology, and blood was added as a different way of expressing the unity of all races. Instead of αἵματος, Ψ has στόματος; if this is not a simple negligent error (homoeoteleuton) it must refer to mankind before the confusion of languages at Babel (Gen. 11.1–9; note in 11.9, ἐπὶ πρόσωπον πάσης τῆς γῆς and the words later in the present verse).

Beginning from unity God made πᾶν ἔθνος ἀνθρώπων. ἑνός and πᾶν are juxtaposed in sharp contrast. Again there is a measure of ambiguity in the Greek: every race of men, or the whole race of men. The absence of an article before πᾶν might suggest the former, but is in fact not decisive; cf. in this verse ἐπὶ πάντος προσώπου τῆς γῆς (on the text see below). The meaning is in fact determined by the words that follow. See Dibelius 29–34, and below; on the grammatical point, Moule (IB 94f.); Zerwick (§ 191).

The infinitive κατοικεῖν is epexegetical rather than strictly purposive, and πάντος προσώπου recalls πᾶν ἔθνος. The human race as a whole (based on its unitary origin) is to occupy the whole earth. Of ἐπὶ προσώπου M. 2.466, noting Jer. 32.12 (LXX; = Hebrew 25.26) rightly says, 'the influence of the Greek of the LXX is unmistakable'. Only in this sense is the expression a Semitism, but it is significant that Luke should (in this Areopagus speech) use the language of the Bible. His criticism of popular polytheism and idolatry is at once philosophical and biblical, and his statement of God's intention in creation also is twofold, though the use of ποιεῖν, of ἐξ ἑνός, and of πρόσωπον is biblical. Instead of πάντος προσώπου, E Ψ 𝔐 have πᾶν τὸ πρόσωπον, either an accidental error, or a correction.

The next clause (cf. Corpus Hermeticum 5.4) is introduced by the aorist participle ὁρίσας. This has been taken (Rackham 184) as an example of an aorist participle of subsequent action, but M. 1.133 rightly observes that the truth is the opposite of this: 'the determination of man's home preceded his creation, in the Divine plan'; similarly Bruce (1.337). God determined προστεταγμένους (D* pc bo have προτεταγμένους, with no significant difference—if the times were appointed at all they were appointed in advance) καιροὺς καὶ τὰς ὁροθεσίας (D* Irˡᵃᵗ have κατὰ τὴν ὁροθεσίαν) τῆς κατοικίας αὐτῶν. The last words simply take up the verb κατοικεῖν, but the meaning of καιρούς and ὁροθεσίας is disputed, with Dibelius and Pohlenz again taking opposite sides. The main possibilities are:

1 (a) God has ordained the various areas in which the races live, and the periods in history of their dominance.
   (b) As 1(a) but the periods are those not of history but of apocalyptic; that is, they belong to the future.
2 The areas are the different zones of the earth, and the καιροί are the seasons of the year.

Pohlenz (87f.), who took πᾶν ἔθνος to refer to the various races of men, takes interpretation 1(a); they have their assigned areas (cf. Deut. 32.8) and God controls their 'zeitliche und räumliche Entwicklung' (87). Dibelius (29–32), who took πᾶν ἔθνος to refer to the whole human race, observes that the readers or hearers of the speech would not have the historical knowledge to appreciate 1(a), and argues that 14.17 points to the meaning *seasons* for καιροί. The ὁροθεσίαι refer to the zones of the earth, of which only two, the temperate zones, were fit for and assigned to human habitation. As for 1(b), Dibelius points out that the passage is not apocalyptic-eschatological.

Passages from the Qumran literature have been invoked on either side. In favour of 1(a), 1QH 1.16f.: In their times (בקציהם) thou hast appointed their service (עבודתם) for all their generations (דוריהם) and judgement for their appointed times (במועדיה, but read במועדיהם). In favour of 2, 1QM 10.12–16: He who created the earth and the laws of its divisions for desert and steppe (ערבה), and all that it brings forth with [...], the circle of the seas and the containers (מקוי) of the rivers and the divisions of the primal floods (תהומות) ... the divisions of the peoples and the dwelling of the tribes (מושב משפחות), and the inheritance of the lands (נחלת ארצות) ... sacred festivals and the cycles of the years and eternal times (ותקופות שנים וקצי עד). See also 1QM 2.6–15; 1QS 1.14, 15. Braun (*ThR* 29 (1963), 171f.) observes that since in Qumran *times* may refer to both Geschichtsabschnitte and Feste it may be a mistake to regard the different interpretations of Acts as mutually exclusive.

The parallel with 14.17 suggests that καιροί refers to seasons of the year, though as Hanson (179f.) emphasizes, the classical word for *seasons* is not καιροί but ὧραι; on this however see Eltester (*NTS* 3 (1957), 100f.) who agrees with Dibelius and sees allusions to Gen. 1.14, 9. *Begs.* 4.216 argues that Lk. 21.24 and Dan. 8.10 [this must be a mistake; it seems possible though not certain that 8.19 is intended] point to *periods* rather than *seasons*, but also notes lines 7–9 of Aratus (quoted in v. 28): 'He telleth it, when the clod is best for oxen and for mattocks; he telleth it when the seasons are favourable.'

Corpus Hermeticum 5.4 may also be cited and Roloff (362) refers to Ps. 74(73).12–17; Jer. 31.35. The parallel with ch. 14 would be important only if both speeches were composed by the same speaker (Luke?). In any case, the point made is that all the affairs of men and nations are in the hand of God.

Schmithals (163) draws attention to similar thoughts expressed at about the same time as Acts: 1 Clement 19.3; 20.6, 9; cf. Slavonic Enoch 19.4; *Apostolic Constitutions* 8.12.

27. The human race was disposed in areas of the earth's surface, and under climatic conditions, calculated to make human life possible; but physical existence was not the final purpose for which men were made. They were intended ζητεῖν τὸν θεόν, *to seek God*, whom (it is implied) they would know only if they sought him; the search itself had value and was willed by God. ζητεῖν τὸν κύριον (E 𝔐, if κύριον refers to Christ, misses the point; Christ is the self-motivated self-revelation of God, which is not yet being considered. Seeking God is a theme of the OT: among many examples the following will suffice. Isa. 51.1, οἱ διώκοντες τὸ δίκαιον καὶ ζητοῦντες τὸν κύριον (מבקשי יהוה); 55.6, ζητήσατε τὸν κύριον (v.1., θεόν) (דרשו יהוה). Dibelius rightly observes (32) that in the OT seeking the Lord is 'a matter of the will', but it is perhaps not so exclusively so as he suggests. As with γινώσκειν (see R. Bultmann, *TWNT* 1.688–719, especially 697; J. Bergmann and G. J. Botterweck, *TWAT* 3.479–512, especially 500–510) there is also an intellectual element, and, under Greek influence, this is brought out in Hellenistic Judaism (as it is here). Thus e.g. Philo, *De Specialibus Legibus* 1.36, ἄμεινον γὰρ οὐδὲν τοῦ ζητεῖν τὸν ἀληθῆ θεόν, κἂν ἡ εὕρεσις αὐτοῦ διαφεύγῃ δύναμιν ἀνθρωπίνην. In Wisd. 13.6 there is an unfavourable view of the Gentile search for God, but the language is strikingly akin to Paul's (Luke's): θεὸν ζητοῦντες καί θέλοντες εὑρεῖν.

Paul (Luke) does not regard the search for God as an impossible one, though he does not represent its successful conclusion as certain. Confidence in the possibility of successful seeking is expressed at the end of the next clause by the use of the verb εὑρίσκειν, uncertainty by the form of the clause, introduced by εἰ ἄρα γε and containing verbs, ψηλαφήσειαν and εὕροιεν, in the optative mood. M. 3.127 writes that 'the other instances [17.27; 27.12] of εἰ c. opt. are not so much real conditions as final clauses', but the very fact that they are expressed in this way shows that the purpose of the final clauses will not be unconditionally achieved. This use of the optative is in the NT peculiar to Acts. The forms of the verbs should be noted. D has in each case the ending –σαν: ψηλαφήσαισαν and εὕροισαν. This form is common the LXX (Thackeray (215) gives many examples); M. 2.196 (cf. 211) thinks that the occurrences in D should probably be linked with those in the LXX, but this does not explain why the form should occur only in D. See also M. 1.56.

As the infinitive is modified by the uncertainty of εἰ and the optative, so the uncertainty is modified by the next clause, where again there is textual variation. καί γε is the reading of B D Ψ 0120 𝔐; καίτοι is read by P⁷⁴ A E 945 1739 1891 pc Clement, καίτοι γε by ℵ 323 pc. καίτοι (γε) followed by the participle ὑπάρχοντα is straightforward: though he is not far ... This is closely parallel to 14.17, in construction and in sense. καί however can equally well be used in a concessive sense, though other meanings could not be excluded. γε adds little (see BDR § 439.2, n. 3); according to Radermacher (29) it was added to avoid the clash between αι and the following ου.

God is near; notwithstanding Philo (above) the search is not hopeless. Cf. Josephus, Ant. 8.108: οὐδὲ ... ἀπολείπεις τοῦ πᾶσιν ἔγγιστα εἶναι. (Solomon). God's nearness is not that intended in Acta Andreae et Matthiae 26 (L.-B. 2.1.103): ἐγὼ γὰρ γινώσκω, κύριε, ὅτι οὐκ εἶ μακρὰν ἀπὸ τῶν σῶν δούλων), which, though the author may have had our verse in mind, refers to God's nearness to his own people who acknowledge and serve him. The present verse refers to God's nearness to men as such, to all men. This was a Stoic belief; cf. e.g. Seneca, Epistle 41.1: prope est a te deus, tecum est, intus est ... 2: in unoquoque virorum bonorum ... habitat deus. The OT is nearer to Andreae et Matthiae; e.g. Ps. 144(145).18, ἐγγὺς κύριος πᾶσιν τοῖς ἐπικαλουμένοις αὐτὸν ... ἐν ἀληθείᾳ; cf. Deut. 4.7.

The primary sense of ψηλαφᾶν is well illustrated by Homer, Odyssey 9.416, where the blinded Cyclops is described as χερσὶ ψηλαφόων, as he tried to lay hands on Odysseus and his men. That he was unsuccessful was due to the ruse employed by his prisoners. Cf. Plato, Phaedo 99b, ὃ δή μοι φαίνονται ψηλαφῶντες οἱ πολλοὶ ὥσπερ ἐν σκότῳ ... This leads to the transferred sense of the word (which does not imply a hopeless quest); see Philo, De Mutatione Nominum 126, an allusion to Moses as ψηλαφῶντος ... καὶ διὰ χειρὸς ἔχοντος ἀεὶ τὰ θεῖα. See Gärtner, 156–61, who however emphasizes too much the difficulty of the quest and the unlikelihood of success. Luke does represent the outcome as uncertain, but (a) God intends that men should seek and, presumably, find, and (b) he is not far from us. The Western text, which at the beginning of the verse had τὸ θεῖον instead of τὸν θεόν, continues with the neuter gender. For αὐτόν, D* (gig) Ir^lat have αὐτό; and for ἀπὸ ἑνὸς ἑκάστου ἡμῶν ὑπάρχοντα, D has ὅν (neuter participle, agreeing with θεῖον) ἀφ' ἑνὸς ἑκάστου ἡμῶν. In the opening clause D has not only τὸ θεῖον but an unwanted ἐστιν. This is probably due to the influence of the Latin, quaerere quod divinum est.

Commentators differ in their understanding of what Luke means by this verse, Calvin, who comes near to rewriting the address, says (2.119), unconvincingly, 'Of course Paul is not speaking here about the ability of men, but he is only warning that they are inexcusable, when they are blind in such a clear light.' Bengel (459) is better: 'Via patet; Deus inveniri paratus est: sed hominem non cogit. Ita liberum eum esse voluit, ut, quum homo Deum quaerit et invenit, id respectu DEI sit quodammodo quasi contingens quiddam.' Modern writers note the difference between seeking and knowing God in the OT and with the philosophers; e.g. Roloff (262f.): in Greek philosophy seeking is rational (Plato, *Apology* 19b; 23b; *Gorgias* 457d); in the OT it is wider and more existential (Amos 8.12, Ps. 14(13).2; 53(52).3; Rom. 3.11; 10.20; et al.). Given the distinction, opinions differ. Thus Stählin 235: The seeking required is not 'ein verstandesmässiges Aufsuchen und wissenschaftliches Untersuchen wie in der Philosophie der neutestamentlichen Zeit, sondern eine Sache des Willens, der Dankbarkeit und der Ehrfurcht, das Verlangen des ganzen Menschen nach Gott ...'. On the other hand, Conzelmann (100): 'Das Suchen ist hier nicht wie im AT (Deut. 4.29; Amos 5.6: Jes. 55.6 usw) Sache des Willens, sondern des Erkennens (Dibelius *Aufs.* 33ff. [= ET 32]); doch fehlt die systematische Reflexion, zB die Unterscheidung der Fragestellung εἰ ἔστι τὸ θεῖον und τί ἐστι κατ᾽ οὐσίαν (Philo, *Spec Leg* 1.32; ähnlich Cicero *De Natura Deorum* 2.4(12)).' This seems not far from being a contradiction. Weiser (472) sees in Luke's words a combination of the two lines of thought: 'Wie schon mehrfach in der Rede, so verbindet Lukas mit dem Wort ''suchen'' (zētein) biblische und griechisch-philosophische Inhalte.' There is something like this, a small rapprochement of two ways of thinking, in Seneca, *Epistle* 95.47, Deum colit, qui novit. Cf. Cicero, *De Natura Deorum* 1.61(153), Cognitio dei, e qua oritur pietas [So Weiser, but Cicero wrote '... cognitionem deorum ...'.].

But we do well to ask whether Luke had seen as clearly as modern students the difference between the biblical and the philosophical search. All used (more or less) the same words; must they not mean the same? To analyse the distinctions too sharply may mean missing Luke's point.

28. This verse is intended to supply the basis (γάρ) for the statement in v. 27, or at least for the last clause in that verse. God is not far from each one of us, for it is in fact in him that we exist. So Chrysostom (Homily 38.3): τί λέγω μακράν; οὕτως ἐγγύς ἐστιν, ὡς χωρὶς αὐτοῦ μὴ ζῆν. ἐν αὐτῷ γὰρ ζῶμεν κτλ.... καὶ οὐκ εἶπε, δι᾽ αὐτοῦ, ἀλλ᾽ ὃ ἐγγύτερον ἦν, ἐν αὐτῷ. This is put in a threefold proposition, using the three verbs, ζῶμεν, κινούμεθα, ἐσμέν. Gärtner's conclusion (195) seems to be correct: 'The triad ... is used to bring out all sides of man's absolute dependence on God for life. It is not a veiled poetic quotation, but a combination that must be ascribed to Paul or Luke.' The positive part of this conclusion rests upon the negative, which excludes other possibilities, and on the observation that though the Stoics connected life with movement (the Prime Mover being God) and movement with being ('κίνησις transforms that which only has ἕξις into οὐσία') they did not put the three together. This is true—as far as we know; but it is somewhat precarious to suggest that no Stoic ever combined the three. We may say that Paul (Luke) was responsible for the use of the triad in the speech, but may have heard it used and borrowed it. Paul omits the preposition ἐν at Rom. 11.36. On it *Begs.* 4.217 says, 'The ἐν is an obvious example of the meaning "in the power of": cf. Sophocles, *Oedipus Coloneus* 1443, ταῦτα δ'ἐν τῷ δαίμονι, and other examples given by Liddell and Scott.' *Begs.* translates, 'By him we live and move and are.' It is true that the reference to the poets may refer backwards rather than (or as well as) forwards, and it has been maintained (see *Begs.* 5.246–51; but see Williams 205; Bruce 2.339, n. 75) that the triad is a quotation from Epimenides. This view however finds its strongest support in a passage of Isho'dad of Merv, and it has been shown by Pohlenz (*ZNW* 42 (1949), 101–4, an appendix to his article 'Paulus und die Stoa') that the passage in Isho'dad is not to be used in this way. H. Hommel (two articles, *ZNW* 46 (1955), 145–78; 48 (1957), 193–200; for this expression especially the latter; also Schneider 2.241) makes Posidonius the starting-point for this sentence, though there is a background in Plato. The conclusion is best summed up in Hommel's own words. 'Also dürfen wir jetzt wohl auch unsere *ZNW* 46.165ff. an Hand zahlreicher Belege auf den platonisierenden Poseidonios zurückgeführte Stelle Act 17.28a ἐν αὐτῷ γὰρ ζῶμεν καὶ κινούμεθα καὶ ἐσμέν, indem wir das dort gefundene Ergebnis abrunden, so erklären, dass in ζῶμεν das physische, in ἐσμέν dagegen das seelische-geistige Leben steckt, während das Dritte, das κινούμεθα, beides ins Kosmische überhöht, d.h. solche leiblich-geistige Existenz als Abbild der himmlischen περίοδοι zu begreifen lehrt. Dass Poseidonios die ersten beiden Glieder—Leben und Bewegung—einfach aus dem "Timaios" zu übernehmen brauchte, ist seinerzeit von uns ausführlich gezeigt worden. Nun sehen wir, dass er aus intimer Kenntnis des ganzen Platon auch noch das im Sinn des geistigen Seins zugefügt hat, was die Reihenfolge der Glieder erklären mag' (198f.).

So far this says more about Posidonius than about Paul and Luke. In Luke's mind, ἐν αὐτῷ must be understood in terms of v. 27c, οὐ μακράν ... God is not remote but accessible, so near as to constitute the environment in which we live, but in a personal sense. In the Greek philosophical background the words will have had a pantheistic meaning, God being hardly anything other than our environment. The change is likely to have been made already in Jewish-Hellenistic use.

The same observation will apply to the quotation that follows. It is ascribed to τινες ... ποιητῶν. This may be a device for concealing ignorance of the actual author, or for suggesting that the words wre used (as in fact they were) by more than one (*Begs.* 4.218). Dibelius 50, 51 (n. 76) contradicts the argument that 'it was not in accordance with literary convention that the word τινες should be used to give a veiled reference to one only'. He cites however only two passages from Philo (*De Specialibus Legibus* 1.48, 74); Pohlenz (104, n. 77) adds Pseudo-Aristotle, *De Mundo* 397b, 16 [? 6]. Three passages hardly amount to a convention (Conzelmann 101 also speaks of a 'literarische Konvention'), but they are enough to indicate a possibility.

καθ' ὑμᾶς is a little more than equivalent to a possessive pronoun (BA 828). In 18.15 νόμου τοῖ καθ' ὑμᾶς is a little more than 'the law you happen to have'; it means the law that you regard as authoritative. Here as a translation 'Your own poets' suffices, with the sense, Poets that you ought to be prepared to listen to. For καθ' ὑμᾶς, P⁷⁴ B 049 326 614 *pc* have καθ' ἡμᾶς, which sets Paul among 'us Greeks'; this is in the context unlikely, even though Aratus was like Paul a Cilician—'us Cilicians'. η and υ were often confused. καθ' ὑμᾶς can hardly be taken as 'poets of your own (Stoic) party' (so Blass 192).

The words quoted are found in Aratus, *Phaenomena* 5, as was already observed by Clement of Alexandria (*Stromateis* 1.19). There is a similar half line in the Hymn to Zeus of Cleanthes: ἐκ σοῦ γὰρ γένος εἶσι (*SVF* 1.537 (line 4), p. 121). It is possible (see above) that more than one source is in mind, but the quotation is definitely from Aratus. For him the words are pantheistic (1.4: πάντη δὲ Διὸς κεχρήμεθα πάντες), and to be distinguished from such passages as Vergil, *Aeneid* 1.250 (Nos, tua progenies), which are mythical. Luke (Paul) uses the quotation, as the context (γένος ὑπάρχοντες, v. 29) shows, in the attack on idolatry which has continued, more or less, from the beginning of the speech. The words are of course in themselves capable of a purely Christian meaning: through the Holy Spirit we are born again as children of God (Jn 3.5). But they lose their point here if they are not used in a sense different from this: Not the regenerate but human beings as such are the children of God— you cannot deny it for we have it on the authority of your own poets.

Between καὶ ἐσμέν and εἰρήκασιν, D (gig) Ir^lat have τὸ καθ' ἡμέραν, ὥσπερ καὶ τῶν καθ' ὑμᾶς τινές. *Daily* adds little to living, moving, and being, and there is little to be said for the suggestion that it is a misplaced marginal note (from v. 11). There seems to be little point in omitting *poets*; D may perhaps be right here. 'It would be difficult to find a more typical example of a gloss than the addition of ποιητῶν᾽ (Clark 367). This however is not the only variation, and it is probably correct to observe that the reading of D reflects a period of freedom in regard to the transmission of the text; the general sense sufficed. For the scansion of the quoted line see BDR § 487.1.

τοῦ is worth noting as the only example in the NT of the use of the article as a demonstrative pronoun (otherwise than with μέν and δέ)—unless in Rev. 19.20 τῆς stands for ταύτης or αὐτῆς (BDR § 249; § 423.4, n. 10).

Here as elsewhere in the speech it is easy to interpret the material one-sidedly. The Greek side is unmistakable; a Greek poet is quoted, and the thought is not only Stoic but pre-Stoic; see e.g. Orphic Fragment 164:

ἔστιν δὴ πάντων ἀρχὴ Ζεύς· ζῆν γὰρ ἔδωκεν
ζῷά τ᾽ ἐγέννησεν, καὶ Ζῆν᾽ αὐτὸν καλέουσιν
καὶ Δία τῇδ᾽, ὅτι δὴ διὰ τοῦτον ἅπαντα τέτυκται.
εἰς δὲ πατὴρ οὗτος πάντων, θηρῶν τε βροτῶν τε.

Stählin (236) takes it that Luke is thinking of the creation of man in the image of God, as in the OT. He continues: 'Die Gottesverwandschaft des Menschen als Geschöpf ist aber etwas anders als die Gotteskindschaft aller Menschen; diese kennt das Neue Testament nicht (ausser vielleicht der Epheserbrief, vgl 4.6; 3.15).' See also Bauernfeind (219): The first part of the speech ends at vv. 28, 29, and the end corresponds with the beginning. 'Dort: In allem Heidentum dennoch die Altarinschrift, die über das Heidentum hinausführen sollte; hier: ein heidnisches Dichterwort (v. 28), dessen Konsequenz im Grunde auch Sprengung der heidnischen Abgötterei ist.'

29. The new sentence follows verbally and argumentatively upon the quotation from Aratus in v. 28: γένος οὖν ὑπάρχοντες—since we are, as has just been stated, God's offspring. The argument runs back from men to God: since we are the thinking and feeling persons that we are, we ought not to suppose that the divine being (τὸ θεῖον, rather than τὸν θεόν; on this see below) is made of metal, even precious metal, or of wood. Luke might have balanced θεῖον with ἀνθρώπειον. If human nature is what we know it to be, and if we who have human nature are God's children, the divine nature will be of no lower order. We deny our own proper being if we identify our progenitor with material objects.

For χρυσῷ, P⁴¹ P⁷⁴ ℵ A E 104 326 *pc* have χρυσίῳ; for ἀργύρῳ, P⁴¹ P⁷⁴ A E 36 104 453 *pc* have ἀργυρίῳ. The forms in –ιον are much more common in the OT.

χάραγμα is a carved object, and the genitives τεχνῆς and ἐνθυμ–ήσεως are subjective, an object carved by man's art and imagination. One would expect imagination, conception, to precede art, the realization of the concept (Bengel 459: *artis* externae, *cogitationis* internae), and this might add weight to the omission of καὶ ἐνθυμ–ήσεως ἀνθρώπου (P⁷⁴), but the attestation is too slight to be credible since there is no serious problem, only at most inappropriateness, in the word order.

Idolatry was condemned by Jews and by Christians, also by some pagan philosophers, though, as Gärtner (224) says, 'The polemic is not often levied direct at the images, since the general opinion obviously was that an identification of the image and the god was too absurd to require treatment.' The prophetic attack on image-worship is sufficiently familiar (Isa. 40.18–20; 41.5–7, 29; 42.17; 44.9–20; 46.1–7; 48.5; 57.13; Jer. 1.16; 2.26–28; 10.2–5, 8, 9); it was echoed in Judaism of all kinds. It suffices to mention the Mishnah tractate Abodah Zarah (though here we have regulations for the avoidance of idolatry rather than polemic against idolatry; see however 3.4). Wisdom takes up the polemic in Greek; see chs. 13 and 14 (especially 13.10–19); so also Philo, *De Vita Contemplativa* 7 (τὰ ξόανα καὶ ἀγάλματα); *De Decalogo* 66 (τῶν ξύλα καὶ λίθους ἀργυρόν τε καὶ χρυσὸν καὶ τὰς παραπλησίους ὕλας μορφωσάντων); *De Specialibus Legibus* 1.21f. Among Gentile writers see for example Seneca, *Epistle* 31.11, 'Finges autem non auro vel argento; non potest ex hac materia imago Deo exprimi similis'; Lucretius 1.63–80; Plutarch, *De Superstitione* 6 (167DEF).

For the neuter τὸ θεῖον (*ND* 3.68 supplements examples in MM 285f.) cf. v. 23 (ὃ ... τοῦτο) and v. 27 (D). Here it is less remarkable. We have just heard of the relation between God and men, so that there is no question of the personality of God; τὸ θεῖον refers to the property of being divine, divinity contrasted with an implicit τὸ ἀνθρώπειον, that which is human, and τὸ ὑλικόν, that which is material.

30. The sentence is introduced by μὲν οὖν; for this characteristic expression see on 1.6. There is no answering δέ; according to Knowling (377) this is because the opening clause has a participle, ὑπεριδών, not a finite verb; we may note also the adversative force of τὰ νῦν.

It is not quite correct to say, as Conzelmann (101) does, that the more specifically Christian material is now introduced into the speech without any transition. Verse 29 complains of the ignorant error of supposing the Divine to be identifiable with material objects. To make this identification—and according to Luke the Athenians were doing it all over the city (v. 16)—was to act in ignorance, ἄγνοια. This takes up the ἀγνοοῦντες of v. 23. This ignorance, which perverts the εὐσέβεια that accompanies it into δεισιδαιμονία, has been going on for a long time; the story of Athens is a record of χρόνοι τῆς ἀγνοίας. From nature the Greeks have evolved not natural theology but natural idolatry. That this should have been permitted was a mark of God's forbearance (cf. 14.16; also and especially Rom. 3.26). God did not will or approve this ignorant idolatrous worship, but he did not suppress it; he overlooked it, ὑπεριδών. ὑπερορᾶν is occasionally used literally (BA 1867 quote Herodotus 7.326.5, ... ἵνα μὴ φοβῆται τὰ ὑποζύγια τὴν θάλασσαν ὑπερορῶντα), more often metaphorically, sometimes in the sense of *looking down upon* a person, *despising* him (Herodotus 5.69.1, ὑπεριδὼν ᾽Ιωνας), sometimes, as here, in the sense of *looking down and not at*, thus *ignoring, overlooking* (e.g. Aeschines, 1 (= *Adv. Timarchum*) 116, τὴν ὕβριν ... ὑπερεώρακε; also Gen. 42.21; Deut. 21.1; Ps. 55.1 (54.2); 78(77).62).

It was not God's intention that men should continue permanently in this ignorance of his true being and worship in ignorant idolatry. *Now* (τὰ νῦν simply = νῦν; so LS (1185), referring to Herodotus 7.104.2; Euripides, *Heraclidae* 641) he is taking steps to end this situation. It is ὁ τῆς μετανοίας καιρός (*Clementine Homilies* 1.7.6). He does this with a command (παραγγέλλει: 14 (15) times in Luke-Acts out of 30 in the whole NT, but the word is too common to be regarded as a Lucan characteristic) that all everywhere should repent. Emphasis is given to the command by the paronomasia of πάντες πανταχοῦ. 21.28 is similar (πάντας πανταχῇ) and there is another example in the next verse (πίστιν παρασχὼν πᾶσιν). These suggest original composition in Greek, with some rhetorical refinement.

The summons to repentance may be regarded as parallel to the demonstration of God's righteousness in Rom. 3.26; in each case there is an implicit charge that God's righteousness is impugned; does he not care what his creatures do? See *Romans* 75f. There is however a marked difference in that in Romans God takes the initiative by revealing his saving righteousness whereas in Acts man must initiate the process by repentance. It is only in this sense that Pesch (2.132) is right in saying that the present verse corresponds to the good news (εὐαγγελίζεσθαι) of Jesus and the resurrection (v. 18). On repentance see on 2.38. Here it is clear that repentance will mean in the first instance turning from the false gods with which Athens abounds. It is also true however that since the call is for repentance the defect of Greek religion is not simply intellectual but existential. Man is guilty of having withdrawn from fellowship with the Creator. Cf. Weiser, who points out (475) 'dass die heidnische Haltung nicht nur als ein *Erkenntnismangel*, sondern auch als eine zum Teil *schuldhafte* Verweigerung und religiöse Verirrung angesehen werden muss'. Cf. also 479f. ' ... die Unkenntnis wird nicht durch Erkenntnis, sondern durch existentielle Umkehr aufgehoben (v. 30)'.

For ὑπεριδών, D[(c)] vg have ταύτης παριδών, which Metzger (458) (against Epp 48–50) regards as an 'innocent heightening'.

Haenchen (505), following Zahn, refers to Sirach 28.7, πάριδε ἄγνοιαν. See also *ND* 1.62.

For παραγγέλλει, in P⁴¹ P⁷⁴ ℵ⁽ᶜ⁾ A D E Ψ 𝔐 syʰ Ath Cyr, ℵ B have ἀπαγγέλλει, a weaker verb.

31. The requirement of repentance is supported by the sanction of judgement. καθότι is a Lucan word (Lk. twice; Acts 4 times; nowhere else in the NT), *inasmuch as* (= καθ' ὅ τι). ἱστάναι is said not to be used for fixing a day for a special purpose (but see Dionysius of Halicarnassus 6.48.3, ἡμέραν ἔστησαν); it is in any case readily understandable and there is no need to seek any other translation. It is however not impossible that, through its association with the *day of judgement*, ἡμέρα had come to bear occasionally (as at 1 Cor. 4.3) the meaning *court, institution for dispensing justice*. God has established an agency of justice. But *day* is better. It is implied that the day is near, otherwise the warning would carry little force.

ἐν ᾗ μέλλει is omitted by D Irˡᵃᵗ Speculum (partly affected by the Latin (*iudicaturus est*); this leaves κρίνειν as a quasi-final infinitive (M. 1.240f.): God has appointed a day for judging. There is little or no difference in meaning; again there seems to be a readiness to vary the wording of the text which suggests something less than a belief in its canonical inspiration.

οἰκουμένη also is Lucan (Lk. 3 times; Acts, 5 times; rest of the NT, 7 times). For God's judging the οἰκουμένη see Ps. 9.9; 95.13; 97.9 (LXX). Nothing different is intended from judging the living and the dead (10.42—also with ὁρίζειν). ἐν δικαιοσύνῃ is equivalent to δικαίως: a sort of instrumental ἐν. Cf. (for Lucan style) 5.23, ἐν πάσῃ ἀσφαλείᾳ, and see LS (552), s.v. ἐν II 3.

Not only has God determined judgement day (ἔστησεν), he has appointed (ὥρισεν, cf. 10.42) the judge. The use of ἐν to introduce the agent of judgement is classical according to BDR § 219.1, n. 1, but this is hardly proved by the third-century Delphi inscription (Dittenberger, *Syll.* 850.8, κριθέντω ἐν ἄνδροις τριοις [sic; this is oddly described as classical!]) alluded to by BDR and quoted by M. 1.107. The only example of ἐν as introducing a personal instrument given by LS (552) is Mt. 9.34. MM 209 cite only the inscription given above (dating it 173–172 BC). BA 525 add Synesius, *Epistle* 91, p. 231B [in MPG the reference appears to be 90,231A]. Bruce 1.340 quotes 1 Cor. 6.2 and Dittenberger, *Syll.* 147.57f. (4th century BC), κρινέσθω ἐν Ἀθην[αίο]ις καὶ τ[οῖς] συμμάχοις.

It is of course clear that the Judge whom Paul (Luke) proclaims, here in what had been the court of the Erinyes (Stählin 238), is Jesus. He is however simply introduced in the words ἐν ἀνδρί. For ἐν ἀνδρί, D Irˡᵃᵗ have ἀνδρὶ Ἰησοῦ. The omission of ἐν is probably accidental; it was thought well to identify the judge explicitly. But if

Ἰησοῦ had been original it would hardly have been so widely omitted. All that the absence of the name means is that, at this stage, the speaker is more interested in the theme of judgement than in the details of the process. The next clause effects the identification—for the reader. Luke has not forgotten that Jesus is the man who is also Lord and Christ. (2.22, 36). *Begs.* 4.219 writes; 'This is "Son of man" eschatology, and if the custom of the gospels had been followed the underlying "bar nasha" would have been rendered by υἱὸς τοῦ ἀνθρώπου instead of by ἀνδρί.' This is important and worthy of consideration, but it is too simple. Where—in Athens— was the underlying Aramaic?

That one who has been a man should be exalted to the role of universal judge is unheard of and needs proof. God provided this by raising him from the dead. It is evidently implied that the man had died, but nothing is said of the manner or significance of his death. The proof was provided for all; for the paronomasia of πίστιν παρασχὼν πᾶσιν see v. 30 and the note. Nowhere else in the NT does πίστις have the meaning *proof*. The meaning appears regularly in Aristotle (where πίστις is distinguished from ἀπόδειξις, a demonstrative proof—*Rhetoric* 3.13 [1414ab]) and elsewhere (e.g. Plato, *Phaedo* 70b), though it is not the most common meaning of the word. At Josephus, *Ant.* 15.260 it is combined as here with παρέχειν. The suggestion that the word does have its usual NT meaning, and that the clause means that, in the resurrection, God was offering to all (the opportunity of) faith, is unconvincing. Bornkamm (4.158) is right therefore to conclude, 'Von einem Zugleich von Anknüpfung und Widerspruch lässt sich hier streng genommen nicht mehr reden, während es für Paulus selbst allerdings zu behaupten ist. Die Areopagrede als solche intendiert vielmehr eine Anknüpfung ohne Widerspruch [dem entspricht die Einführung der Auferstehung Jesu als "Beweis" (πίστιν παρέχειν)]—nämlich an die religiösen Voraussetzungen ihrer Hörer, um gerade so deren faktischen Widerspruch als Verstocktheit erscheinen zu lassen.'

For παρασχών, D gig have according to NA[26] παρεσχειν, according to Ropes (*Begs.* 3.171) παρασχεῖν. This is presumably Ropes's correction, his conjecture of what D meant (so Dibelius 62). WW (3.156) have παρεσχειν for D, exibere (sic) for d gig. The reading of D (as intended) may be taken to suggest the usual, Christian meaning of πίστις.

LS 1338 (s.v. παρέχω B II) give the meaning '*bring forward* witnesses or proofs'. This seems to be the technical usage, but the active means *furnish*, *supply*, in a variety of contexts, and there is no problem in its use here.

Calvin (2.125f.) again wishes to rewrite, or at least expand, the speech. 'There is no doubt that Paul said a good deal more about Christ, so that the Athenians might know that he is the Son of God, by whom salvation had been brought to the world, and to whom all power in heaven and on earth had been given. Otherwise the speech, such as we read it here, would have been powerless to persuade.' This comment, by a theologian, on the theological content of the speech as it stands, is not without interest.

32. The speech is ended. Haenchen (506), following Dibelius, is probably right when he says that it is not to be thought of as a fragment, in need of a supplement; 'sie ist innerlich völlig geschlossen'. Schneider (2.246) understands the framework in too historicistic a way when he says that it was the speaker's intention that the hearers should respond (to v. 31) with the question, Who is this man? Luke represents the resurrection of the dead as more than the Athenians, or some of them, can stand. Cf. v. 18. He knows the Greek belief that the dead do not stand up (ἀνιστάναι). Cf. Homer, *Iliad* 24.551, οὐδέ μιν ἀνστήσεις; Aeschylus, *Eumenides* 647f., ἀνδρὸς δ' ἐπειδὰν αἷμ' ἀνασπάσῃ κόνις ἅπαξ θανόντος, οὔτις ἔστ' ἀνάστασις; *Agamemnon* 1360f.; Sophocles, *Electra* 137–9, οὔτοι τόν γ' ἐξ Ἀΐδα παγκοίνου λίμνας πατέρα θρήνοις οὔτε λιταῖσιν ἀνστάσεις. For Celsus's reaction to (what he understands to be) Christian teaching see Origen, *c. Celsum* 5.14. Since it is clear that Paul is speaking absurdities some of his hearers (οἱ μέν) are content to mock, ἐχλεύαζον. It is often supposed that the words of the second group of hearers (οἱ δέ) come to the same thing—We will hear you again; that is, we will not listen to you now, and we shall be careful not to fix a date for a second session; we say that we will hear you καὶ πάλιν, but we do not really intend to do so. This is probably a mistaken understanding of the text. There is nothing in the narrative as a whole to suggest that Luke wished to represent the mission in Athens as a complete failure; and the use of the οἱ μέν ... οἱ δέ construction seems decisive. It is impossible that Luke should have meant, On the one hand there were those who mocked; on the other hand, there were those who made a mocking reply. Certainly, the latter group did not make the immediate and whole-hearted response that the evangelist would have desired, but it is probably part of Luke's attempt to portray a philosophical scene that they should say, This is interesting; we do not come to decisions quickly, but there is a *prima facie* case and we should like to hear the argument again.

33. οὕτως, *so*, receiving this response. ἐκ μέσου: cf. 23.10, but here the words, with αὐτῶν, correspond to v. 22, ἐν μέσῳ τοῦ Ἀρείου πάγου, and confirm the view (see also v. 34) that the Areopagus is a company of people, not a locality.

Paul has said what he had to say, and there is no more to do. Cf. Lk. 4.30 (διὰ μέσου αὐτῶν) for a comparable event in the story of Jesus; but there is no suggestion of a violent attack on Paul.

34. The general meaning of this verse goes with that of v. 32. The Athenian environment made Paul's work exceptionally difficult, but it was nevertheless not without fruit. Two converts can be named, and there were others.

For κολληθέντες cf. 5.13, where there is a difficulty that does not occur here, where κολληθέντες is linked with ἐπίστευσαν; those in question definitely joined the Christian group. See C. Burchard (*ZNW* 61 (1970), 159f.) There is no mention of baptism. Dionysius the Areopagite is otherwise unknown. According to Dionysius, bishop of Corinth in the second century, he was the first bishop of Athens (Eusebius, *HE* 3.4.10; 4.23.3). He was sometimes confused with Dionysius of Paris (*c.* AD 250) and with the author (Pseudo-Dionysius) of a number of mystical writings (*c.* AD 500). His designation as Ἀρεοπαγίτης is correct; the Council was ἡ ἐξ Ἀρείου πάγου βουλή, but the compound form for an individual member is usual in Athenian inscriptions, e.g. *IG* 3.1.704 (Hemer, 119). The term confirms that, in Luke's view, the Areopagus was a body of men, not a place. As an Areopagite, Dionysius must have served as an archon; a not undistinguished person. It is possible that the traditional name gave rise to the Areopagus story. Damaris also is unknown; Luke's interest in the part played by women is familiar; cf. e.g. 17.4, 12. On the name there is a detailed note in Hemer (232). No other example of it is known, but it may be a variant of Damalis. Lüdemann (202) takes the view that Dionysius and Damaris are historical figures, but cannot have been converted on the occasion of Paul's first preaching in Athens, since Stephanas, Fortunatus, and Achaicus were the 'first fruits of Achaea' (1 Cor. 16.15).

D spoils the sentence by turning the participle κολληθέντες into an indicative, ἐκολλήθησαν, and omits Damaris, adding after Ἀρεοπαγίτης, εὐσχήμων. Ramsay (*Church* 161f.) thinks that the omission of Damaris was due to catholic depreciation of women, but it was probably accidental, because at the end of the verse D retains σὺν αὐτοῖς (plural). E describes Damaris as γυνὴ τιμία ὀνόματι Δ. τιμία may (by way of e's *honesta*) have led to D's εὐσχήμων. ὁ (before Ἀρ.) is omitted by B and is replaced in D by τις.

46. PAUL AT CORINTH, WITH RETURN TO PALESTINE
18.1–23

(1) After these things Paul[1] left Athens and came to Corinth, (2) and found[2] a Jew, Aquila by name, of Pontus in origin, who had recently come from Italy, with Priscilla his wife, because Claudius had issued an edict that all the Jews should leave Rome. Paul[1] approached them,[3] (3) and because they were of the same trade he[4] stayed with them and worked; for by trade they were tentmakers. (4) Every Sabbath he argued in the synagogue[5] and sought to persuade Jews and Greeks; (5) but when Silas and Timothy came down from Macedonia Paul[6] was constrained by the word, testifying to the Jews that[7] the Christ was Jesus. (6) When they opposed him and[8] blasphemed Paul[1] shook out his clothes and said to them, 'Your blood be upon your own heads;[9] I am clean. Henceforth I shall go to the Gentiles.' (7) He moved away from there and entered the house of Titius Justus,[10] one who reverenced God, whose house was adjacent to the synagogue. (8) But Crispus, the Archisynagogue, became a believer in the Lord, with all his household, and many of the Corinthians when they heard this[11] believed and were baptized. (9) In the night the Lord said to Paul in a vision, 'Do not be afraid but continue to speak and do not fall silent; (10) for I am with you and no one will set upon you so as to harm you, for I have a people, a large people, in this city.' (11) He stayed a year and six months teaching[12] the word of God among them.

(12) When Gallio was proconsul of Achaea the Jews with one accord set upon Paul and brought him to the place of judgement, (13) saying, 'This man is persuading people to worship God in a manner contrary to the law.' (14) As Paul was about to open his mouth, Gallio said to the Jews, 'If there had been some matter of[13] injury or wicked deceit, you Jews, I should[14] of course

[1]Greek, he.

[2]NEB, fell in with.

[3]NJB, went to visit them.

[4]NEB, made his home with them.

[5]NJB, synagogues.

[6]RSV, occupied with preaching; NEB, devoted himself entirely to preaching; NJB, devoted all his time to preaching.

[7]NJB, that Jesus was the Christ.

[8]RSV, reviled him; NEB, resorted to abuse; NJB, started to insult him.

[9]NEB, my conscience is clear; NJB, from now on I will go to the Gentiles with a clear conscience.

[10]RSV, NEB, NJB, a worship(p)er of God.

[11]RSV, hearing Paul; NEB, listened; NJB, had heard him. In Greek the verb has no object.

[12]NJB, preaching.

[13]RSV, wrongdoing or vicious crime; NEB, crime or grave misdemeanour; NJB, misdemeanour or a crime.

[14]RSV, have reason to bear with you.

have been forbearing with you; (15) but if they are disputes[15] about talk and words[16] and the law that you observe, you will have to see to it yourselves; I have no wish to be a judge of these things.' (16) And he drove them from the place of judgement. (17) They all took hold of Sosthenes the Archisynagogue and beat him before the place of judgement; and none of these things troubled Gallio.[17]

(18) Paul stayed on a number of days, took his leave, and sailed away to Syria. With him were Priscilla and Aquila. He had shaved his head in Cenchreae, for he had a vow. (19) They reached Ephesus and there he left them; he himself went into the synagogue and argued with the Jews. (20) When they asked him to stay a longer time he did not consent, (21) but took his leave with the words, 'I will come back to you, God willing.' Then he set sail from Ephesus (22) and landed at Caesarea. He went up and greeted the church and came down to Antioch.

(23) Having spent some time there he left, passing through, in order, the Galatian territory and Phrygia, strengthening all the disciples.

Bibliography

S. Benko, *ThZ* 25 (1969), 406–18.

M. Black, in *FS* Nida, 119–31.

E. Dinkler, *Signum Crucis*, 118–33.

E. J. Goodspeed, *JBL* 69 (1950), 382, 383; 110 (1991), 439–49.

K. Haacker, *BZ* 16 (1972), 252–5.

C. J. Hemer, *JTS* 28 (1977), 99–101.

C. J. Hemer, in *FS* Bruce (1980), 3–18.

R. F. Hock, *BL* 97 (1978), 555–64.

R. F. Hock, *CBQ* 41 (1979), 438–50.

G. H. R. Horsley, *NovT* 34 (1992), 105–68.

J. Jeremias, *ZNW* 30 (1931), 299.

P. Lampe, *BZ* 31 (1987), 256–61.

G. Lüdemann, in *FS* Schneider, 289–98.

J. Murphy-O'Connor, *St Paul's Corinth* (1983).

J. Murphy-O'Connor, *JBL* 112 (1993), 315–17.

J. L. North, *NTS* 29 (1983), 264–6.

R. Riesner, *Die Frühzeit des Apostels Paulus*, WUNT 71 (1994), 139–80; 180–89.

J. M. Ross, *NovT* 34 (1992), 247–9.

D. Slingerland, *JBL* 110 (1991), 439–49.

D. Slingerland, *JQR* 83 (1992), 127–44.

D. E. Smith, *HThR* 70 (1977), 201–31.

C. H. Talbert, *NovT* 9 (1967), 26–40.

J. Wiseman, *ANRW* 2.7.1 (1979), 438–548.

[15]NEB, bickering; NJB, quibbles.
[16]NEB, NJB, words and names.
[17]RSV, but Gallio paid no attention to this; NJB, Gallio refused to take any notice at all.

Commentary

This paragraph unites a striking number of Lucan themes. Paul continues his travels and visits two notable cities, Corinth and Ephesus, both of which are to become important centres of early Christianity. He is assisted by colleagues: among those who are named are new ones, and in introducing them Luke finds another opportunity of relating his story to secular history. Paul begins his work in the synagogue, but finds it necessary to move to a different centre, and the Jews (with some exceptions) prove to be opponents rather than allies. Their opposition has the effect of bringing Paul a second time (cf. 16.19–23) before a Roman authority, and the reference to Gallio (v. 12) provides the modern historian with the means of dating the event with fair accuracy and provides Luke with an example of Rome's sense of justice and unwillingness to take action against the Christians. After the encounter with Gallio Luke shows Paul again on his travels and is able to represent him as a good Jew, who takes a vow upon himself (unless v. 18 means that Aquila took the vow). Paul visits Palestine, perhaps Jerusalem (v. 22), then sets out again towards the old mission fields.

All this Luke will have enjoyed writing. Every piece contributed to the picture of Paul that he wished to convey. To infer from this that it was all Luke's own invention would be mistaken. That Paul was acquainted with and assisted by a married couple, Aquila and Priscilla, is confirmed by the epistles (Rom. 16.3–5; 1 Cor. 16.19: cf. 2 Tim. 4.19). Expulsion of the Jews from Rome raises historical problems (see on v. 2) as regards its date but hardly as regards the fact. There is nothing in the NT more certain than that Paul founded a church in Corinth and continued to have a complex and sometimes stormy relation with it; the name of Crispus (v. 8) recurs in 1 Cor. 1.14. Gallio was proconsul of Achaea in the 50s of the first century. The epistles also bear witness to the fact that Paul visited Jerusalem from time to time.

Lüdemann (203–12) finds in vv. 1–17 a mixture of tradition and redaction; Schneider (2.247) agrees with Haenchen (516) that Luke wrote out the whole Corinthian story, not interpolating pieces here and there into a source. It seems probable that both of these views are true and must be combined. Schmithals (166) rightly observes that in the whole section there are too many concrete details, which in themselves show no special Lucan tendency, for the paragraph not to have been drawn from a Paul-source. The name for example of Titius Justus (v. 7) serves no purpose beyond its evident narrative use; Luke would gain nothing by inventing it. But it is equally true that the whole section shows Lucan editorial management. There is no first person plural in it; Luke probably wrote up in his best style pieces of information derived from the Pauline circle and, perhaps, collected in

Corinth itself. Apart from the name Crispus there is nothing to suggest knowledge of the Corinthian epistles; these were not Luke's source of information.

There are two points at which the historicity of Luke's story may be seriously questioned. The first turns on the date of the expulsion of the Roman Jews by Claudius. The question is discussed on v. 2. If the view is taken that the expulsion took place, and resulted in the arrival in Corinth of Aquila and Priscilla, in AD 41, we must suppose that Paul reached Corinth for the first time in that year, or soon after. This throws out the whole of Pauline chronology as this is usually understood, and also means that the order of Acts is distorted; Paul reached Corinth before the famine (11.28) and before the Council (15.6–29). We must of course be prepared, if the facts require it, to review the whole question, but the view taken here is that though Claudius did act against the Jews early in his reign he did not expel them till much later.

More serious questions are raised at the end of the paragraph. According to v. 18 Paul (but Aquila may be intended—see the note) had a vow, usually taken to be a Nazirite vow. Is it credible that Paul would accept so much of Judaism? For this, unlike (for example) keeping the Sabbath, was not an obligatory act; one could be a very good Jew without ever taking a vow. This therefore was not a matter of being to the Jews (as if he were) a Jew (1 Cor. 9.20), though it could be part of Luke's picture of Paul as the good Jew. The vow is mentioned in the account of a journey from Corinth to Syria, perhaps (see the note on v. 22) to Jerusalem. No events are described as taking place in Palestine, and at least since Loisy (704) it has been maintained that we have here a doublet of the journey from Greece (Corinth?) to the east (εἰς τὴν Συρίαν in both 18.18 and 20.3) which introduces the last stage in Paul's career, the legal contests with both Jews and Romans. The suggestion is possible but further questions arise: What purpose can Luke have had in introducing an additional journey to Palestine? And why, if he himself is responsible for it, does he omit to say that Paul reached Jerusalem? The first question can be answered by the existence of the next two pieces, which Luke probably found in existence: the enlistment of Apollos in the Pauline circle (18.24–28) and Paul's treatment of disciples of John the Baptist in Ephesus (19.1–7). The first of these made it necessary to get Paul out of the way (the long journey from Ephesus to Palestine and back would leave Aquila and Priscilla a free hand to conduct affairs in Ephesus), and the brief halt in Ephesus (vv. 19–21) would give Paul a foothold and enable him to solve a problem there. All this it is impossible to disprove, but it is also impossible to disprove that Paul made a hurried journey back to Jerusalem. He had heard of the threatened destruction of his work in Galatia by men who, rightly or wrongly, assumed the support of Jerusalem; did he hurry back to ask his Jerusalem colleagues what they meant, then make haste back to the Galatian territory and Phrygia (v. 23) to set things right? To this the vow could be Luke's counterpoise: Paul was the adversary of Judaizers, but he remained a true Jew.

According to Taylor (5.307f.), vv. 1 (TO), 4a, 5b, 6a (TA), 9, 10a (TO), 12–14a, 15b–17, come from Act I; Act II provides additions and changes in vv. 2–3, 4b, 5a, 7–8, 11, 14b–15a.

1. Μετὰ ταῦτα, after the Athenian episode was over. As a connecting link the phrase is common in the gospels, not in Acts; in addition to this passage 7.7; 13.20; 15.16, all in OT material, quoted or summarized. Paul left (χωρίζεσθαι; 1.4; 18.2) Athens; see on 17.16. ''Αθήναζε, 'Αθήνηθεν, 'Αττικῶς· εἰς 'Αθήνας, ἐξ 'Αθήνων, Ἑλληνικῶς' (Moeris). He came to Corinth; in full, Colonia Laus Julia Corinthiensis. For some account of the city see *1 Corinthians* 1–3, *2 Corinthians* 1, 2; more fully J. Wiseman (*ANRW* II 7.1 (1979), 438–548) and J. Murphy-O'Connor (*St Paul's Corinth: Texts and Archaeology* (1983)). The old city had been wealthy and influential, but 'in 146 BC a sharp line is drawn through the history of Corinth, when Rome brought the Achaean League to an end. After the decisive engagement at Leucopetra, on the isthmus, the consul Lucius Mummius was able to occupy Corinth without a blow. The citizens were killed, or sold into slavery; the city itself was levelled with the ground ... After 100 years of desolation Corinth was refounded by Julius Caesar as a Roman colony' (*1 Corinthians* 1f.). Its natural advantages enabled it to regain its prosperity; it probably did little to shake off the reputation for immorality that the old city had acquired. From Athens Paul would have about 37 miles to travel, by way of Eleusis and Megara.

For μετὰ ταῦτα χωρισθεὶς ἐκ, D (cf. h) has ἀναχωρήσας δὲ ἀπό, without change of meaning, but does not add (as A E Ψ 𝔐 sy⁽ᵖ⁾ boᵐˢ do) ὁ Παῦλος. Metzger (460) is no doubt right in the view that the name was added when the passage was used as an ecclesiastical lection. The earliest MSS do not suggest this use.

2. εὑρών: εὑρίσκειν may mean finding as the result of chance (e.g. 9.33), or finding as the result of search (e.g. 9.2). A combination of the two may be seen here: Paul would look for a fellow Jew with whom he might settle; he would be glad to come across a fellow σκηνοποιός, surprised to find a fellow Christian (if Aquila and Priscilla were already Christians, as seems probable; see below); and he did not know that the person he would find would be Aquila.

'Ιουδαῖον. There was a Jewish community in Corinth; see in addition to Acts itself and the note on v. 1 *NS* 3.64–66; for a fragmentary inscription from a Corinthian synagogue, *Background* 53; also E. Dinkler (*Signum Crucis* 131) for fragments found near the theatre, 'ein Säulenende mit drei Menorot und dazwischen Lulab und Etrog'.

Ἀκύλας. See on 18.18, 26; also Rom. 16.3; 1 Cor. 16.19; 2 Tim. 4.19. It is clear that Aquila and his wife (see below) played an important part in early Christianity. From the passages cited it appears that they entertained Christians in their home; travelled with Paul; instructed others. Aquila came from Pontus (see 2.9; also 1 Pet. 1.1); τῷ γένει would normally mean *by race*, but Aquila has already been described as a Jew (cf. Barnabas, 4.36). His family must have settled in Pontus, which was united with Bithynia (see 16.7) to form a Roman province. He was not a Roman citizen, or he would not have been affected by the decree mentioned in this verse. Christianity spread rapidly in Pontus (Pliny, *Epistles* 10.96.5, 9, 10). This may suggest that there was already a good population of Jews, but of further evidence for this *NS* 3.35f. can supply only a reference to Philo, *Legatio ad Gaium* 281. At some point Aquila had moved to Rome. For interesting, but not really important, references that connected the name Aquila with both Rome and the Pontus region see Hemer (232f.).

Aquila had recently (προσφάτως) come from Italy (ἐληλυθότα). M. 3.85 says that Classical Greek would probably have used the aorist rather than the perfect participle; whether it is true that 'there was a distinct tendency in the Hellenistic period to connect very closely a past action with its present consequences', so that they thought, 'he has been here since coming from Rome recently' is another question. The choice of participle may be no more than a literary fad. Luke will mention in a moment the reason why Aquila had left Italy (Rome).

Aquila is unique in the NT in that whenever he is named his wife is named too. In Acts she is Priscilla; in the epistles she is Prisca. It is hardly open to doubt that the same woman is intended. καὶ Πρίσκιλλαν γυναῖκα αὐτοῦ is somewhat awkwardly attached to the sentence but this is an insufficient reason for regarding the words as an insertion, especially since to omit them here would leave Priscilla's presence in 18.18, 26 unexplained. It is most improbable that she would have been mentioned so frequently by name if she had not been an outstanding person in her own right. The two were in Corinth διὰ τὸ διατεταχέναι Κλαύδιον χωρίζεσθαι πάντας τοὺς Ἰουδαίους ἀπὸ τῆς Ῥώμης. διατάσσειν means to issue a διάταγμα, Latin *edictum*. The simple form, τεταχέναι, read by (ℵ*) D E L P 6 33 104 323 (1175 1241) *pm*, must be understood in the same way. Luke means that the Jews had been banished from Rome by imperial edict. It would make an important contribution to the chronology of Acts if this edict could be dated. Suetonius, *Claudius* 25, writes: Iudaeos, impulsore Chresto assidue tumultuantes, Roma expulit. This act occurs in a series of what may be described as police measures, in regard to one of which the term *edictum* is used: Viatores ne per Italiae oppida, nisi aut pedibus, aut sella, aut lectica transirent, monuit edicto. There is a similar expression in which the word *edictum* is used by Suetonius in *Vitellius* 14: ... edictum suum, quo iubebat intra Kalendas Octobris Urbe Italiaque mathematici excederent. Whether Chrestus is (in *Claudius* 25) the name of a person otherwise unknown, an error for Christus, or a corruption of Christus in the MS tradition, is disputed and cannot be settled with certainty. It is known from Romans (as well as from Acts—28.15) that Christianity had reached Rome before Paul did, and the suggestion is at least plausible that the Jewish community had become intolerably agitated by Christian preaching. Suetonius supplies no evidence for the date of the expulsion. Orosius (5th century), *Historiae contra Paganos* 7.6.15f., says, Anno eiusdem nono expulsos per Claudium urbe Iudaeos Josephus refert. There is no such reference in the works of Josephus as now extant, and the source of Orosius' remark is unknown. It seems quite probable that he had in mind a confused recollection of Josephus, *Ant.* 18.81–84, which tells the story of four Jews who persuaded the proselytess Fulvia to send large gifts to the Jerusalem Temple, which they themselves pocketed. As a result Tiberius (not Claudius) κελεύει πᾶν τὸ Ἰουδαϊκὸν τῆς Ῥώμης ἀπελθεῖν. No reliance can be placed upon Orosius (on whom see e.g. B. Altaner, *Patrologie*, § 59.II.9 (with bibliography)), though in fact he may be right about the date. The ninth year of Claudius corresponds almost exactly with AD 49 (the accession of Claudius took place on 25 January 41). If Paul arrived in Corinth in or just after this year, Aquila and Priscilla having only recently (προσφάτως) come from Rome, the date would harmonize with what may be deduced from the reference in v. 12 (see the note) to Gallio. Claudius' relations with Jews deteriorated after the death of Herod Agrippa I (see I.590–2); see A. Momigliano (*Claudius* (ET 1934), 32).

The date (AD 49) is disputed on the ground of a reference by Cassius Dio to anti-Jewish action taken by Claudius in AD 41. Lüdemann (209) takes this to be the date of the expulsion mentioned by Suetonius and deals with the Pauline chronology on this basis. But Dio (60.6.6) does not speak of an expulsion; his words are οὐκ ἐξήλασε μὲν ... ἐκέλευσε μὴ συναναθροίζεσθαι. This statement may in fact have been intended to point forward to an occasion when Claudius did expel the Jews, described in a later—lost—book of Dio's history. Tajra (52–4), Momigliano (loc. cit.), and Jewett (*Dating Paul's Life* (1979), 36–8) are very probably right in thinking that Claudius twice took steps against the Jews. The date 41 is accepted by Taylor (5.312–14); but see also Hemer (167f.); *NS* 3.77f.; D. Slingerland (*JBL* 109 (1990), 686–90); J. Murphy-O'Connor (*JBL* 112 (1993), 315–17).

The addition after Ῥώμης of οἳ κατῴκησαν εἰς τὴν Ἀχαῖαν (D), and the further addition (h sy^hmg), 'Paulus autem agnitus est Aquilae', may come from tradition of some kind; the substitution of προσῆλθεν αὐτῷ ὁ Παῦλος (D^(c)) for προσῆλθεν αὐτοῖς may possibly represent an (anti-feminist) interest of a Western editor; for the reconstruction of the Western text at this point see Ropes (*Begs.* 3.170f.) and Clark 367f. προσῆλθεν suggests that the initiative was Paul's; whether it was due in the first instance to the necessity of earning a living, to the natural desire to seek the company of fellow Jews, or to evangelistic enterprise cannot be determined; they may all be true.

Brandon (*Fall* 145, 147) suggests that the encounter with Aquila and Priscilla, with the attendant fact that the mixed Roman church had lost its large Jewish element, led to the writing of Romans. The epistle certainly seems to have been written from Corinth or thereabouts.

3. Whether or not Paul sought out Aquila and Priscilla in order to find work he stayed with them (ἔμενεν) because he was ὁμότεχνον; he and Aquila were both σκηνοποιοί. This is probably the right way to take the plural noun; but Taylor (5.315) (cf. *ND* 2.17) thinks it refers to husband and wife. For a short note on the social status of the craft see W. A. Meeks (*The First Urban Christians* (1983), 59). The natural rendering of σκηνοποιός is *tent-maker*, and this should in fact be accepted, though *Begs.* 4.223 (cf. J. Jeremias, *ZNW* 30 (1931), 299) strongly supports *leather-worker*; the strongest evidence for this is that h renders the word *lectarius*, maker of beds, that is presumably of the leather-covered cushions used as mattresses, and that the Peshitto has לולרא, which, according to *Begs.* 4.223 'merely transliterates the Latin *lorarius*, a maker of leather thongs'. It is however at least arguable that *lectarius* arose as the corruption (in Greek) of σκηνοποιός into κλινοποιός, and the meaning of *lulara* is not certain; according to Payne Smith (238) it is *a maker of rough cloth for tents or horsecloths*. In any case, it cannot be assumed that h and pesh understood σκηνοποιός correctly. It is true that Chrysostom (Cramer 3.302) says that Paul ἐπὶ σκηνορραφείου ἑστὼς δέρματα ἔρραπτε, but there is nothing in σκηνοποιός to say of what material the tents were made and skins are as likely as the goat hair that was woven in Cilicia (Tarsus!) into coarse cloth. It is in the highest degree unlikely that the other meaning of σκηνοποιός (LS 1608) should be adopted—the three Jews were not makers of stage properties! Preuschen (111) draws attention to *CIL* III 5183^b, aeditus collegi tabernaclariorum, which shows the existence in Rome of a corporation of tentmakers.

μένειν here approaches the stronger sense of *to lodge*. Cf. Rom. 16.3–5; 1 Cor. 16.19; not only was there a church κατ᾽ οἶκον αὐτῶν, all the Gentile churches had reason to be grateful to Aquila and Priscilla. It is probable that they were wealthy and entertained not only Paul but other Christians too. For παρ' αὐτοῖς, D 36 453 *pc* have πρὸς αὐτούς. There is no difference in meaning; the variant suggests a copyist or editor concerned to give the sense but not unduly careful about word-for-word accuracy. ἠργάζετο (P⁷⁴ ℵ ⁽ᶜ⁾ A D E Ψ 𝔐 lat sy saᵐˢˢ) is more probably original than the plural (ℵ* B⁽²⁾ saᵐˢˢ bo); Paul's readiness to work to support himself was a theme important to Luke (see 20.34), in itself as a record of Paul's manner of life (attested also in the epistles, 1 Cor. 4.12; 2 Cor. 11.7; 1 Thess. 2.9) and also as an example for future generations of ministers (20.35). The importance of this is perhaps underestimated by Barth (*CD* 3.4.472: 'His work is done on the margin of his apostolic existence, and such exhortations are given only on the fringe of his apostolic instruction.'

The clause ἦσαν γὰρ ... τέχνῃ is omitted by D gig (which with other Western MSS will differ more widely from the Old Uncial text in v. 4). If this is not simply a by-product of a wholesale rewriting of the text one must suppose that the Western editor thought tent-making an unworthy occupation for an apostle.

4. διελέγετο: the word is characteristic of Luke's accounts of Paul's work; see e.g. 17.17. ἐν τῇ συναγωγῇ: for the synagogue and its role in the early Christian mission see on the same verse; for a synagogue in Corinth see on v. 2; for a (very dubious) conjectural restoration (including the word ἀρχισυνάγωγος as well as συναγωγή) of a 'very fragmentary' Corinthian inscription (*SEG* 29 (1979 [1982], 300) see *ND* 4.213 (with on the following pages a valuable discussion of the two words). It is not surprising that a wealthy and cosmopolitan city such as Corinth should contain a colony of Jews, or that they should be able to provide themselves with a building (contrast the Jews at Philippi, 16.13).

κατὰ πᾶν σάββατον: the weekly service provided a ready-made congregation; if Paul was not invited to preach (as e.g. at Pisidian Antioch, 13.15) he would at least have the opportunity of conversing with those who attended.

ἔπειθεν: conative use of the imperfect. Paul set about the task of persuading men to become Christians, he endeavoured to persuade them. For the use of πείθειν cf. 17.4. Paul's efforts were directed to both Jews and Greeks; the latter were presumably Gentiles whom he found in the synagogue. He turns decisively to the Gentiles in v. 6.

The whole of this verse is omitted by the Sixtine Vulgate, and by WW. It is contained in some Vulgate and other Latin MSS; for details see WW 3.158. D⁽ᶜ⁾ (to which gig syʰᵐᵍ approximate) has εἰσπορευόμενος δὲ εἰς τὴν συναγωγὴν κατὰ πᾶν σάββατον διελέγετο καὶ ἐντιθεὶς τὸ ὄνομα τοῦ κυρίου Ἰησοῦ καὶ ἔπειθεν δὲ οὐ μόνον Ἰουδαίους ἀλλὰ καὶ Ἕλληνας. See Ropes (*Begs.* 3.172) and Metzger 460f. In his translation Metzger drops without comment the καί before ἐντιθείς and translates the participle *inserting* (so also Bruce 2.348), which seems an odd piece of English; *bringing in*, if slightly colloquial, would be a more natural idiom: Paul explained the OT, bringing the name of Jesus into his interpretation. καὶ ἐντιθείς ... καὶ ἔπειθεν is incorrect; it cannot be explained here as an Aramaism. It is best taken as due to careless paraphrasing and expansion of the Old Uncial text.

5. Temporal ὡς is characteristic of Acts; see on 16.4.

κατῆλθον (but παρεγένοντο δέ in D (h)), down from the mountainous districts in the north to the maritime region of Corinth in northern Peloponnese. Silas and Timothy had been left in Beroea (17.14), and when Paul reached Athens he sent back a message that they were to join him as soon as possible (17.15). In the account of Paul's Athenian mission that follows (17.16–34) there is no reference to Silas and Timothy; it seems however from 1 Thess. 3.2 that Timothy at least joined Paul in Athens, since Paul, anxious about his Thessalonian friends, decided that he could put up with loneliness in Athens and sent Timothy for news. The movements of Paul's colleagues were probably more complicated than Luke knew, or saw fit to describe. He treats Silas and Timothy as a pair; it may be that, for some reason unknown to us, they decided for a time to separate, or were given different instructions by Paul. The meagre evidence at our disposal would be satisfied if (after 17.14)

(1) Paul went to Athens, leaving S. and T. in Beroea.
(2) T. joined Paul in Athens, leaving S. in Beroea (or somewhere in Macedonia).
(3) T. was sent by Paul from Athens to Thessalonica,
(4) T. returned from Thessalonica (1 Thess. 3.6), possibly accompanied by S., since *Silvanus* joins in the writing of 1 Thessalonians (1.1).
(5) This return may have been to Corinth, if 1 Thessalonians was written from Corinth. If it was written from Athens, T. and S. will have made yet another visit to Macedonia, whence they return at 18.5.

'It is perhaps easier to accept the plain statement of 1 Thessalonians and assume that the writer of Acts made a mistake in thinking that Silas and Timothy did not join Paul before he had reached Corinth' (*Begs.* 4.224). It is possible that the words ὅ τε Σιλᾶς καὶ ὁ Τιμόθεος lay some emphasis on *both* Silas *and* Timothy, implying an earlier occasion when only one of the two came down from Macedonia.

συνέχεσθαι is a Lucan word (Lk., 6 times; Acts, 3 times; Mt., once; Paul, twice), and is used frequently in a bad sense (e.g. 28.8, πυρετοῖς καὶ δυσεντερίῳ συνεχόμενον). To this use the main exception is Paul (2 Cor. 5.14; Phil. 1.23). In the present passage there is no difficulty in the reading of the majority of MSS (𝔐 sy^hmg), συνείχετο τῷ πνεύματι: Paul was constrained by the Spirit, who impelled him to concentrate on his mission. This reading, however, because it is easy, should probably be regarded as an alleviation of συνείχετο τῷ λόγῳ (the rest). This must be understood in a similar way. The word of God (conceived as an almost personal force) constrained Paul. Another possibility is, Paul *was confined* (*confined himself*) to the word; that is, though he had previously spent some of his time working as a tent-maker, he now, after the arrival of Silas and Timothy, who were perhaps able to earn enough for three, or had brought money from Macedonia (2 Cor. 11.8f.—so Haenchen 517), concentrated on preaching.

The above interpretation may not do justice to Luke's use of tenses—the aorist κατῆλθον and the imperfect συνείχετο. 'The imperfect clearly expresses that when they arrived "they found Paul wholly occupied with the word"' (Page 199).

For the characteristic διαμαρτυρόμενος cf. 2.40. Paul still addresses Jews and the mission is presumably still based on the synagogue.

εἶναι τὸν χριστὸν Ἰησοῦν. τὸν χριστόν, having the article, will be the subject. Paul's contention was that the Christ (he could assume that his Jewish hearers knew that there would be a Messiah) was Jesus. Cf. 17.3. This was the fundamental and distinctive Christian conviction; cf. 2.36.

Schmithals 168f. finds no problem in 1 Thess. 3.1, 6 since, in his view, these verses deal with events on the third journey.

6. The Western text (D h (sy^hmg)) opens this verse with a vivid account of much talk and biblical discussion (πολλοῦ δὲ λόγου γινομένου καὶ γραφῶν διερμηνευομένων); the main substance of the verse begins with the negative response of the Jews to the testimony of v. 5. The blasphemy (βλασφημούντων—omitted by P^74—could refer to evil speaking against the human bearer of the message, but in the context probably means blasphemy) consists in the denying of Paul's affirmation—Jesus, they say, is not the Christ; they may have reinforced their denial by saying what they thought he really was.

Paul's reaction (see Wilson, *Gentiles* 225f.; for the language *Begs.* 5.274f.) is to shake out his clothes (τὰ ἱμάτια; BDR § 141.5, n. 11 think that the plural may be used for the singular ἱμάτιον, his cloak; in any case we can hardly suppose that Paul stripped completely, and the vague English 'clothes' probably represents what Luke meant). The same verb, ἐκτινάσσειν, is used at 13.51, there more naturally for shaking dust off the feet. It is not clear why Paul should shake out his clothes, though it is clear enough that he means to break off relations with the Jews against whom he performs the symbolic action. The uses of ἐκτινάσσειν in MM 199 all seem to be in various senses literal; BA (496) cite *UPZ* 6.11, where ἐκτ. is 'Gebärde d. Unschuldsbeteuerung'. This would agree with καθαρὸς ἐγώ (below). In *UPZ* however, Wilcken has 'schüttelten (? den Kopf)'.

τὸ αἷμα ὑμῶν ἐπὶ τὴν κεφαλὴν ὑμῶν: supply ἐλθέτω and cf. Mt. 23.35, where the verb is necessarily added. BDR § 480.5, n. 8 cite this parallel, also Mt. 27.25. Neither of these is a perfect parallel since in them it is another person's blood that is to come upon 'you' (equivalent here to 'on your head'); that is, you have shed his blood and you will be held responsible for having done so. In Paul's words, the point is that the Jews will be responsible for their own loss in rejecting the Gospel; Paul is free of responsibility, having faithfully proclaimed it to them. Cf. 20.26; Ezek. 33.4, 5. Ammonius (Cramer 3.303) comments, ἀσαφές ἐστι τὸ ῥητόν; that is, presumably, it was not a Greek idiom. He continues, οἶμαι δὲ αὐτὸ τοῦτο λέγειν· ἕκαστος τῶν ἀπιστούντων Χριστῷ, ὅς ἐστι ζωή, δοκεῖ ἑαυτὸν φονεύειν ... Wilcox (65) thinks that there may be an allusion to 2 Kdms 1.16; it is a Septuagintal expression, though not frequent.

It is not clear whether a stop should be placed after καθαρὸς ἐγώ or these words should be attached to what follows: *either* (a) 'I am clean; henceforth I shall go to the Gentiles', *or* (b) 'Clean, I shall go to the Gentiles'. There is a similar ambiguity in the Western variant, ἀφ᾽ ὑμῶν (D*vid h) for ἀπὸ τοῦ. It is against (a) that it makes the second sentence start without a connecting particle (though it could be said that ἀπὸ τοῦ νῦν has the force of an adversative particle), but against (b) that it yields a sentence that is not characteristically Lucan in form. For Paul's turning to the Gentiles cf. 13.46; 28.28. Luke evidently thinks of it as a frequently repeated pattern rather than as a once-for-all event. So e.g. Blass (196f.) (Hoc est: non amplius in hanc synagogam intrabo, sed alium locum quaeram ubi praedicem, Graecis scil. Ceterum ad eos tantum Iud. qui Corinthi erant hoc pertinere patet ...) and Weiser (492) ('Aus dieser Programmatik folgt für Lukas aber nicht, dass Paulus sich bei der nächsten Gelegenheit nicht doch wieder an Juden wendet').

7. Paul transferred his operations (μεταβάς) from there (ἐκεῖθεν), that is, probably, from the synagogue, though the Western text took the words to mean that Paul separated from Aquila (μεταβὰς δὲ ἀπὸ Ἀκύλα, D*vid h; 614 has ἀπὸ τοῦ Ἀ.). This is an improbable way of taking ἐκεῖθεν (which does not mean *from him*), and is also inconsistent with Paul's references to Aquila in the epistles. It is possible that the Western editor meant only that Paul no longer lived with Aquila, but with Titius Justus; the meaning however seems to be not that Paul lodged with Titius Justus but that he used his house as a preaching centre; cf. 19.9. It is possible that Luke's reticent statement conceals the fact that Paul was expelled from the synagogue (became ἀποσυνάγωγος—Jn 9.22); Wilson (*Law* 116).

The new host is called Titus Justus by ℵ E 36 453 945 1175 1739 1891 *pc* co; Titius Justus by B* D² syʰ; Justus by A B² D* Ψ 𝔐 p; Titus by syᵖ. The most probable form of the name is Titius Justus. Titus and Titus Justus probably arose from a desire to identify the person whose house Paul used with the colleague mentioned frequently in the epistles (2 Cor. 2.13; and elsewhere). Justus may have arisen by the omission of Titus on the ground that the Titus of the epistles was not a Corinthian. It is an interesting but not quite convincing suggestion that Τιτίου and Τίτου Ἰούστου arose from Ἰούστου through repetition of the last letters of ὀνόματι and the first letters of Ἰούστου. Metzger rejects the suggestion because ὀνόματι is omitted by A *pc* h.

'Of all the persons with Latin names only one has two convincing Roman names, Titius Justus in Acts 18.7' (Sherwin-White 158). His praenomen is not given. E. J. Goodspeed, *JBL* 69 (1950), 382–3, on the basis of 1 Cor. 1.14; Rom. 16.23, conjectures that he was Gaius Titius Justus. He was one who reverenced God; see on 10.2. His house was adjacent (συνομορεῖν is a rare and late word; the simplex is more frequent and has the same meaning) to the synagogue. This may have been convenient but would hardly promote good relations.

8. Κρίσπος, probably the Crispus whose baptism (not recorded here unless in the plural at the end of the verse) is mentioned in 1 Cor. 1.14. As ἀρχισυνάγωγος (for this office see 13.15; each Jewish community had a number of synagogue heads, their number depending on the size of the community; for Corinth see on v. 4) he was a notable convert, though evidently not weighty enough to carry with him the Jews as a group, or even his colleagues in office. The aorist ἐπίστευσεν describes his conversion, not the lasting faith he maintained as a Christian. It is here constructed with the dative τῷ κυρίῳ. D h have εἰς τὸν κύριον, though the Western text at the end of the verse has a dative. The usage in Acts varies.

Crispus was accompanied in his move into the Christian body by all his household; for the expression, and the question whether Luke intended the reader to understand that little children and infants were included, see on 16.15, 31–33. It is to be noted that it is not said that all the household (or for that matter Crispus himself) were baptized, but that they believed. They were not the first converts in the locality; this distinction was held by Stephanas and his household (1 Cor. 16.15). Many others followed, described simply as τῶν Κορινθίων; probably we are to think that some were Jews, some Gentiles. The Gentile element is emphasized by the reading of D (h), which add, after ἐβαπτίζοντο, πιστεύοντες τῷ θεῷ (contrast the Western εἰς and accusative above) διὰ τοῦ ὀνόματος τοῦ κυρίου ἡμῶν Ἰησοῦ Χριστοῦ—that is, they came to faith in God only through Christ, not through the Jewish religion. They believed because they heard, ἀκούοντες (but P⁷⁴ L 614 1241 2495 *pm* have ἀκούσαντες). It is not clear whether this means because they heard the word of God preached by Paul or because they heard of the conversion of Crispus. According to Schneider 2.251 if Luke had meant the former he would have included αὐτοῦ in the sentence; this is not a conclusive argument.

The imperfect ἐπίστευον (contrast ἐπίστευσεν, above) could be inceptive—they began to be believers—but the imperfect ἐβαπτίζοντο cannot be explained in this way. Both imperfects reflect their subject, one after another became a believer and was baptized. On baptism in Acts see Introduction, pp. xc–xcii.

9. The divine message of encouragement stands at this point to mark the transition from work in the synagogue to unrestricted mission among the Gentiles (v. 6), and to prepare for the attack of v. 12. Relative (though not complete—v. 8) failure in the synagogue must not hold Paul back; the Jews may be unbelieving but there can yet be many who will enter the people of God.

εἶπεν δὲ ὁ κύριος. For the direct speech of the Lord (Jesus) see 9.4–6, 10–16; 10.13, 15: 11.7, 9: 22.18, 21: 23.11. It comes at notable points in Paul's career.

ἐν νυκτί; cf. 16.9, διὰ νυκτός. No difference is intended between the two prepositional phrases. διά is probably avoided here because δι' ὁράματος follows. This probably refers to a dream. ὅραμα occurs at 7.31; 9.10, 12 (si v.l.); 10.3, 17, 19; 11.5; 12.9; 16.9, 10; elsewhere in the NT only at Mt. 17.9. In 2 Cor. 12.1 Paul refers to visions (here, ὀπτασίαι), but records only one, which had appeared to him 14 years previously. There can be little doubt that Luke was more impressed than Paul by visions and similar phenomena, but it is not necessary to infer from 2 Corinthians 12 that Paul had had no visionary experience for 14 years, still less that he would have disapproved of this one.

μὴ φοβοῦ, that is, Do not fear those who might wish to harm you (v. 10). This means that the parallels adduced by Betz (55) are not true parallels, since they bid the hearer not to fear the supernatural giver of vision or voice. Deut. 31.6; Josh. 1.6, 9; Isa. 41.10; Jer. 1.8 are better parallels.

λαλεῖ, present imperative, and μὴ σιωπήσῃς, aorist subjunctive, fit well together: Go on speaking, as you have done; do not fall silent.

Acts of Thomas 1 (L.-B. 2.2.100) may show knowledge of this passage: ὤφθη αὐτῷ ὁ σωτὴρ διὰ τῆς νυκτός, καὶ λέγει αὐτῷ· Μὴ φοβοῦ, Θωμᾶ, ἄπελθε εἰς τὴν Ἰνδίαν ...

10. Paul is not to fear (v. 9) διότι (3 times in Lk and in no other gospel; 5 times in Acts) ἐγώ εἰμι μετὰ σοῦ. The promise recalls OT passages, e.g. (in addition to those cited on v. 9) Exod. 3.12; Isa. 43.5. ἐπιτίθεσθαι (middle) is used with the dative to mean *to attack* (e.g. Aristophanes, *Wasps* 1029 (1024), ἀνθρώποις ... ἐπιθέσθαι), less frequently with the genitive of the infinitive, as here; so Gen. 43.18 (with both constructions), ... ἐπιθέσθαι ἡμῖν τοῦ λαβεῖν ἡμᾶς ... The infinitive is epexegetic (BDR § 400.8, n. 10). Cf. 7.19.

The general sense of the second διότι clause is clear: Paul is to continue his ministry without fear of opposition, for, as will appear, there are in Corinth many who are, potentially and by predestination (cf. 13.48), the Lord's people, and it is therefore impossible that Paul's work should be in vain. Grammatically the sentence is twofold. Luke could have written λαός ἐστί μοι, there is to me a people, I have a people; he incorporates πολύς in a predicative sense: there is to me a people, and a large one. λαός is here the people of God; and it includes both Jews and Gentiles.

11. ἐκάθισεν δέ (D h (sy^p sy^h**) have καὶ ἐκάθισεν ἐν Κορίνθῳ): elsewhere in Luke-Acts (except at Lk. 24.49) the verb when used intransitively means *to sit*. The meaning *to reside* is uncommon in Greek (see BA 791). Elsewhere this meaning could be due to the ambiguity of the Hebrew ישב, but it is hard to see how Hebrew could have affected the present passage. The aorist ἐκάθισεν is constative, Paul's residence being regarded as a unit (M. 3.72; Zerwick § 253; BDR § 332.1, n. 2). Cf. 28.30.

ἐνιαυτὸν (א sy add ἕνα, unnecessarily) καὶ μῆνας ἕξ. For the dating of Paul's residence in Corinth see above on v. 2 and below on v. 12; it seems to be implied (though it is not explicitly stated) that if not the whole at least the greater part of the 18 months fell before the attempt to bring Paul before Gallio. The ἡμέραι ἱκαναί of v. 18 are probably to be taken as additional. It is unlikely that Luke intended or was in a position to give anything more than an approximation to the dates of Paul's movements.

διδάσκων, as v. 13 shows (but Schneider disagrees), must include mission preaching as well as the instruction of the church. τὸν λόγον τοῦ θεοῦ is one of Luke's usual ways of summarizing the message of the Christian preachers. For ἐν αὐτοῖς D has the second accusative αὐτούς, without any substantial difference in meaning.

12. *Gallio* (... *dulcem* ... *Gallionem*: Statius, *Sylvae* 2.7.32), originally L. Annaeus Novatus, eldest son of Seneca the Orator and thus brother of the famous writer and philosopher Seneca, was adopted by Junius Gallio and became L. Junius Gallio Annaeanus. He had a sufficiently distinguished career (*consul suffectus* between 53 and 55) but eventually committed suicide. The date of his proconsulship in Achaea can be determined with some exactness from an inscription (see *Begs.* 5.460–4; *Background* 51f.) found at

Delphi and dated by a reference to the 26th acclamation of Claudius (as *imperator*). The precise date of this is not known, but it fell probably in the first half of Claudius' twelfth year, between 25 January and 1 August 52, possibly at the close of the eleventh year. This means that Gallio probably became proconsul of Achaea in 51 (summer), possibly, if, as was less usual, he held office for two years, in 50.

ἀνθύπατος was the regular Greek equivalent of proconsul (on *proconsul* see a note in Tajra 46). Achaea had been a Roman province since 27 BC and included central Greece, with the islands, Thessaly, Aetolia, Acarnania, and parts of Epirus, with Corinth, as a colony, its chief town, though Athens and Sparta were also included. As a senatorial province it was administered by a proconsul.

We have seen that the natural (though not the certain) sense of v. 11 is that Paul had already spent 18 months (or nearly so much) in Corinth at the time when the Jews attacked him; only a relatively short period (v. 18) remained. The wording of the present verse does not show at what point in his proconsulship Paul was brought before Gallio, but it is not unreasonable to suggest that Paul's opponents took an early opportunity of bringing their case before the new proconsul in the hope that he would take their side. If this view is correct we may suggest with some probability that Paul appeared before Gallio in the Autumn—say, September—of 51; this would mean, if Acts if trustworthy, that he arrived in the Spring—say, March—of 50; see *Romans* 4f. These dates cannot be regarded as certain (Tajra 55, for example, puts Paul's appearance before Gallio towards the close of the proconsul's term, in Spring 52—Gallio shows that he had had experience in dealing with Graeco-Jewish rivalries), but they are nearer to a fixed point than any other event in Paul's career. They are moreover consistent with v. 2, if we may accept (see the note) 49 as the date of Claudius' edict against the Jews. On the chronology see further D. Slingerland (*JBL* 110 (1991), 439–49); J. Murphy-O'Connor (*JBL* 112 (1993), 315–17).

κατεφιστάναι is *hapax legomenon* in the NT; ὁμοθυμαδόν is a Lucan word; see on 1.14.

The Jews brought Paul ἐπὶ τὸ βῆμα. It has often been supposed that the βῆμα is to be identified with the podium excavated in the market place of ancient Corinth, which recalls the rostra in the Roman forum and was probably a place for the making of public speeches. E. Dinkler, however ('Das Bema zu Korinth', *Signum Crucis* 118–33) has shown that this identification is quite uncertain. The βῆμα denotes the place where the judge holds his court, and is determined by the presence of the judge, not topographically (cf. 25.10, 17). 'Dass man ab und zu auch im Freien eine Rednerbühne als βῆμα benutzte, ist nicht ausgeschlossen, aber keineswegs als üblicher Brauch nachweisbar' (124). 'Wir wissen nicht und können schlechterdings nicht herausfinden, wo der Bericht von Apg lokali-sierbar ist' (129).

The verses that follow are of considerable historical importance, On the legal issues raised see Sherwin-White (99–107). 'The narrative ... agrees very well with the workings of *cognitio extra ordinem*. It is within the competence of the judge to decide whether to accept a novel charge or not' (99f.).

Schmithals writes on vv. 12–17: 'Er [Lukas] stellt damit seiner Zeit, einer Zeit akuter Christenverfolgungen, ein Ideal vor Augen, von dem er hofft, dass es sich wie in der Frühzeit der Kirche auch in seiner Gegenwart verwirklichen wird' (157). Were there such acute persecutions in Luke's time? Weiser, in agreement with Haenchen and Roloff, more cautiously: 'Es hat eine Anklage des Paulus durch Juden vor Gallio stattgefunden. Sie wurde mit einer Unzuständig-keitserklärung abgewiesen. Daraufhin verprügelte die judenfeind-liche Menge den jüdischen Sprecher Sosthenes' (487).

For Rome's attitude to Christianity cf. the attitude to Artemis, illustrated in *ND* 4.77.

The Western text presents a more vivid picture. In place of τῷ Παύλῳ καί, D h (sy^h** sa) have συλλαλήσαντες μεθ' ἑαυτῶν ἐπὶ τὸν Παῦλον καὶ ἐπιθέντες τὰς χεῖρας.

13. D h add, before λέγοντες, καταβοῶντες καί. These words add to the narrative nothing of substance but serve merely to intensify feeling; a characteristic Western addition.

The Jews accuse Paul of persuading men to worship God παρὰ τὸν νόμον (these words, placed at the beginning of the sentence, carry a good deal of emphasis). 'The question is whether Jewish residents at Corinth, who presumably were not citizens of Corinth, could expect the proconsul to enforce their domestic law within the territory of a community that was a Roman colony' (Sherwin-White 100). Sherwin-White has taken νόμος in this sentence to be the Jewish law, noting that Gallio takes it in that way (v. 15, νόμου τοῦ καθ' ὑμᾶς), even though that is not necessarily what the Jews intended. Their best way of attacking Paul would have been to plead that he was commending a religion that Romans could not legally adopt (cf. the charge at Philippi, 16.21; also 17.7), and this may have been the intention of the words in this verse, though, if it was, Gallio either misunderstood or deliberately misinterpreted the charge. It might have been a dangerous though not a legally sound charge, for at this period proselytism and circumcision were not strictly contrary to law and did not become so till the time of Domitian (see Tajra 21–3; *NS* 3.122–3). Circumcision was undoubtedly frowned upon, and it may not have been known to the authorities that Paul did not circumcise Gentile converts. It was known that many Corinthians (v. 8) were being baptized and brought into something that looked like a variety of Judaism; the Jews may have hoped that this would support a charge that Paul was contravening Roman law. If however they were referring to their own law they would, it may be supposed, be invoking the imperial protection of the Jewish religion. For this see Josephus, *Ant.* 19.278–91, and especially 19.290 (καλῶς οὖν ἔχειν καὶ Ἰουδαίους τοὺς ἐν παντὶ τῷ ὑφ' ἡμᾶς κόσμῳ τὰ πάτρια ἔθη ἀνεπικωλύτως φυλάσσειν—an edict of Claudius). Paul, though himself a Jew, was a Jew of doubtful practice and was undoubtedly responsible for a good deal of disturbance in the Jewish community. It is true that the edicts issued by Claudius had been intended to protect Jews against interference by non-Jews rather than from Jewish heretics, but Paul (1 Cor. 9.20) could evidently regard himself as something other than a Jew, and could from the standpoint of orthodoxy be considered a menace. Perhaps the Jews wished to prove that Christianity was so different from Judaism that it could not be regarded as a *religio licita* (Stählin 246).

It may be that if Luke was writing as late as the time of Domitian, when conversion to Judaism was punishable with death or at least confiscation of property (Dio Cassius 67.14.2), he imported into his narrative circumstances that belonged to his day, not Paul's. Perhaps 'there was a deliberate and conscious ambiguity in the accusation which demonstrates a certain cunning, but also the weakness of the plaintiffs' case against Paul' (Tajra 56). According to Calvin (2.137) the law in question was the Law of Moses.

As the next verses show, Gallio understood the proceedings as being *cognitio extra ordinem*; see above, also Sherwin-White (14, 15).

14. ἀνοίγειν τὸ στόμα should be regarded as one of Luke's OT borrowings (e.g. Job 3.1), though the image is so obvious that it is not surprising that it occurs elsewhere (e.g. Aristophanes, *Birds* 1719 (1716)). It proves to be unnecessary for Paul to offer any defence (though he is prepared to do so). Gallio cuts him short and dismisses the case. His conditional sentence (unfulfilled condition, correctly formulated with ἄν in the apodosis) implies that no ἀδίκημα (an intentional but not necessarily premeditated injury committed contrary to law; see especially Aristotle, *Ethica Nicomachea* 1135b (8.8); *Rhetoric* 1.13.16) or ῥᾳδιούργημα πονηρόν (there were many kinds of ῥᾳδιούργημα—Lucian, *Calumniae* 20, μυρία ῥᾳδιουργήματα—but see on 13.10; there may be stress on some kind of deception, or, here, misrepresentation) had been committed. If there had been such an offence, Gallio says, I should of course have been forbearing with you. κατὰ λόγον is probably (*Begs.* 4.227) *of course*, but may be *in accordance with what is right*, or *what is natural*; cf. Thucydides 3.39.4; Josephus, *Ant.* 13.195. Dictionaries and commentaries, referring backwards and forwards to one another, say that ἀνέχεσθαι is a legal and technical term and means *to accept a complaint* or *charge*. Evidence is seldom cited, and the meaning is not recorded in LS 136f., but see Wettstein (2.205) on 2 Cor. 11.1.

On the use of ὦ with the vocative see Zerwick § 35, and on 1.1. Its use in the present verse indicates no warmth or depth of feeling, and accords with Luke's use in general, which follows classical custom (where ὦ is always used unless there is some special reason for omission) rather than Hellenistic (where the custom is to omit, so that ὦ becomes the mark of exceptional feeling).

ἄνδρες Ἰουδαῖοι (D h vg) assimilates to other passages (e.g. 2.14) and is a secondary reading.

There is an interesting survey of the scene in Ehrhardt (*Acts* 77f.): 'Here we have the whole case of Judaism in the Roman Empire in a nutshell; their privileged status which made them approach imperial dignitaries with very little reserve, and reluctance of even a man like Gallio, the brother of Seneca ..., to deal with their internal quarrels, and the open contempt for them on the part of the masses, who took whatever opportunity offered itself to use violence against them.'

15. The new condition is open (not an unfulfilled condition as in v. 14): if in fact ... then ... Gallio makes clear what he takes to be the truth.

ζητήματα, plural, occurs in ℵ A B Dᶜ E 33 323 614 945 1175 1739 2495 *al* lat sy co; it conveys a hint of disparagement not suggested by the singular ζήτημα (in P⁷⁴ D* Ψ 0120 𝔐 e). The word occurs only in Acts in the NT (where also 3/7 of the occurrences of ζήτησις are found), normally in a pejorative sense; see 15.2; 23.29; 25.19; 26.3. Luke suggests that small and insignificant disputes, which sensible people would not consider, are in mind. They are not important enough to concern a Roman court.

ἔχετε (D gig) is an improvement, doubtless secondary, on ἐστιν, which would be easier if ὑμῖν were in the text. This would give the same meaning as ἔχετε. 'If you have disputes ...'.

λόγος is probably *talk* (contrasted with such acts as are referred to in v. 16), and ὀνόματα *words* (cf. Plato, *Apology* 17bc). It is probably correct to say (Haenchen 515) that νόμου τοῦ καθ᾽ ὑμᾶς is equivalent to τοῦ ὑμετέρου νόμου, but it seems to lay some stress on the fact that the law is Jewish—the law that is current among you but not in this (Roman) court.

ὄψεσθε (future) αὐτοί, You will have to see to it yourselves. This may be a Latinism; so, with a query, M. 3.86. 'Magis ea latina consuetudo: *ipse viderit, tu videris*: ad me nihil attinet' (Blass 199). It occurs on the lips of a Roman official at Mt. 27.24 (ὑμεῖς ὄψεσθε); otherwise at Mt. 27.4. BDR § 362.2, n. 3 also treats this as a Latinism, but notes parenthetically Epictetus and Marcus Aurelius, without giving references. Cf. also Vergil, *Eclogue* 3.108, *Non nostrum inter vos tantas componere lites*. See J. L. North as cited on 15.6. The Jews of course did have their own synagogue machinery for trying cases under Jewish law.

Theology and religious practice are matters for Jews, not Gallio, to see to: κριτής (E Ψ 𝔐 sy sa add γάρ, which gives the right sense, but the speech is stronger, more abrupt, without it) ἐγὼ τούτων (looking back to the first part of the verse) οὐ βούλομαι (θέλω (D), *I choose* rather than *I wish* is a classical improvement, but in Hellenistic Greek the two words scarcely differed in meaning) εἶναι.

16. ἀπέλυσεν (D* h) is a much weaker variant of ἀπήλασεν. Gallio had no patience with the Jews; if Luke's account is correct he judged that they were wasting the time of his court; that is, either the charge was purely irrelevant (a matter of Jewish theology), or there was not even *prima facie* evidence to support the belief that Paul constituted a danger to the Empire. Either way, the precedent was a useful one.

For βῆμα see on v. 12.

17. Schille (366) regards this verse as a doublet of v. 16, but all they have in common is Gallio's indifference to the Jewish move against Paul.

Who beat Sosthenes? According to the Western followed by the Byzantine text (D E Ψ 0120 𝔐 gig h sy sa), πάντες οἱ Ἕλληνες. This is probably correct interpretation. Jews were often unpopular; they were for the moment out of favour and it would be safe to attack one of them. Cf. the reference to Crispus in v. 8. Ehrhardt (*Acts* 77f.) remarks on the inadequacy of Gallio's police force. Alternatively πάντες may be determined by the preceding αὐτούς; all the Jews (so explicitly 36 453 *pc*) beat Sosthenes, presumably because he had mismanaged the case against Paul, failing even to secure a hearing. We have not however been told that Sosthenes was in charge of the proceedings. The reading that leaves πάντες undefined (P⁷⁴ ℵ A B *pc* vg bo) is to be preferred; and it may be that the two views mentioned above should be combined: the Jews beat Sosthenes for his inefficiency, the Greeks because he was a Jew and out of favour with the authorities. A Sosthenes is mentioned at 1 Cor. 1.1 as sharing with Paul in the writing of the letter. He may be the former ruler of the synagogue, a Corinthian Jew now become a Christian and travelling with Paul. This identification is by no means certain; Sosthenes is not an uncommon name (see BA 1596); if however it is accepted and Sosthenes' conversion dates from this period both Jews and Greeks might have felt that they had an additional reason for beating him. It is conceivable that he succeeded Crispus, or that the synagogue had more than one ruler.

ἐπιλαμβάνεσθαι (often used of violent aggression; see *ND* 4.104 (A. L. Connolly)) is normally followed by a genitive. It would however be incorrect to take the present sentence as an exception, since Σωσθένην, accusative, takes its case as the object of the finite verb ἔτυπτον; see BDR § 170.2, n. 2, and cf. 9.27; 16.19.

A similar point arises in the last clause. The general meaning is clear: Gallio was not concerned either to persecute Paul or to protect Sosthenes. The disturbance was evidently on a sufficiently small scale to justify the view that public order was not threatened and Gallio considered that it would do no harm if a few angry people vented their wrath on a Jew. But is the verb ἔμελεν impersonal or does it have οὐδέν as its subject? According to BDR § 176.3, n. 4 οὐδέν is the subject with τούτων as a partitive genitive: None of these things troubled Gallio; so classical usage (many examples in Wettstein 2.576), and cf. Hermas, *Similitude* 9.13.6. Radermacher (26) however regards οὐδέν as a strengthened negative, and Moule (*IB* 28) compares 1 Cor. 9.9, 'which makes it just possible that in the Gallio passage also ἔμελεν is impersonal, τούτων is a Genitive of Reference, and οὐδέν is an Accusative of Respect'. The absence of περί, on which Moule remarks, is in fact no problem; see LS, s.v. μέλω Α I 4, p. 1100.

There can be no doubt that Luke found Gallio's attitude a matter of interest and importance; it would serve as a precedent that Christians on trial might cite with advantage. For the apologetic motive in Acts see Introduction, pp. xlixf.

At the end of the verse d (D being erased) has: tunc Gallio fingebat eum non videre. h (so Clark 369) has et Gallio simulabat [se non vid]ere. Ephrem (Clark loc. cit.) comments: factus est (probably a mistranslation of προσεποιεῖτο) quasi non videns.

18. ἔτι προσμείνας suggests the addition of a relatively short stay (ἡμέρας ἱκανάς is a Lucan expression; cf. 9.23, 43; 27.7; and the use of ἱκανός with other nouns) to the 18 months of v. 11. Paul was not driven out of Corinth. ἀποτάσσεσθαι is used only here and at v. 21 (twice in Lk., once in Mk, once in Paul; it is hardly the mark of a source). τοῖς ἀδελφοῖς are the members of the church in Corinth. In Acts as it stands this marks the end of the 'Second Journey' which began at 15.35. Vv. 18–23 have however been taken as a doublet of Paul's last visit to Jerusalem (considered by Williams 213). Weiser (502) thinks that 18.18b, 22a, 22c; 19.1b were taken from the Itinerary, and that the following are Lucan: 18a (stay in Corinth), 18d (haircutting), 19b–21a (work in Ephesus), 22b (to Jerusalem), 23a (stay in Antioch), 23c (strengthening of disciples, possibly 23b (journey). On this basis he concludes (503) that it is wrong to speak of 'Second' and 'Third' Journeys; there is one continuous journey.

ἐξέπλει is 'improved' by D to ἔπλευσεν (Eᶜ has ἐξέπλευσεν), but the imperfect can be understood in the sense of 'began the voyage'. This is very briefly narrated in the following verses, but it is possible that Luke was working with an Itinerary that conveyed even less information, the few details being supplied by Luke. He notes that Priscilla and Aquila (cf. v. 2; Priscilla now takes precedence) accompanied Paul. They travelled widely: from Rome to Corinth, from Corinth to Ephesus, whence they send greetings to Corinth (1 Cor. 16.19). 2 Tim. 4.19 may also point to Ephesus. According to Rom. 16.3 they are back in Rome (unless Romans 16 was directed originally to Ephesus; see *Romans* 11, 257f.).

κειράμενος ... τὴν κεφαλήν. It is not clear whether this statement refers to Paul or to Aquila. Aquila is the nearest noun and is in the appropriate case (nominative), but Paul is the effective subject of the sentence and of the first singular verb in v. 19 (κατέλιπεν); he is moreover the character in whom Luke is supremely interested. Page (201) is confident that Paul is intended; Preuschen (113) and Ehrhardt (100) that it was Aquila who shaved his head (a sign, according to Ehrhardt, that he retained legalistic presuppositions). The man in question shaved his head εἶχεν γὰρ εὐχήν. This is usually taken to have been a Nazirite vow; cf. 21.23f. and see Num. 6.1–21, with StrB (2.747–51). The rule was that the hair was cut off at the end of the period of the vow. *Begs.* 4.230 guesses that it may have been customary to cut the hair at the beginning of the period with a view to not cutting it again till the end, but we have no evidence for such a practice. On Cenchreae cf. Rom. 16.1; it was one of the two seaports of Corinth, situated on the Saronic Gulf; the other, on the Gulf of Corinth, was Lechaeum. Assuming that it was Paul who took the vow, Conzelmann (107) sees it as part of the unhistorical picture of Paul as a good Jew, but if Luke thought of it in this way he threw away his opportunity, for he makes nothing whatever of the incident, using it rather to account (somewhat obscurely) for the movements of the missionaries. Such vows were sometimes taken before a difficult or dangerous undertaking; it is possible that this vow should be connected with the vision of v. 9 and the appearance before Gallio (vv. 12–17). But is this how the Paul of the epistles would have confronted difficulty and danger? Paul 'shaved his head for no other purpose except to accommodate himself to the Jews' (Calvin 2.140). But had he any occasion in these circumstances to become a Jew to the Jews (1 Cor. 9.20)? *ND* 1.24 points out that 'Paul's vow (Acts 18.18) may appear to reflect his Jewish background in view of the decision to cut his hair. But it may be rather a standard Greek cultural reaction to some dream through which came divine guidance.' At *ND* 4.114f. there is a reference to Juvenal, *Satire* 12.81f. where sailors after escape from shipwreck rejoice with shaved head—gaudent ibi vertice raso garrula securi narrare pericula nautae. Taylor (5.329) somewhat similarly thinks that this incident marks the end of a vow taken previously; 'pas de voeu de naziréat évidemment'; Greek rather than Jewish.

Cenchreae was the natural port of embarkation for eastward voyages. This is exemplified by the large number of eastern coins found there (*ND* 3.60; 4.139f.).

19. κατήντησαν is in ℵ A B E 33 *pc* d vg^mss sy^p sa; κατήντησεν, P^74 Ψ 0120 𝔐 lat sy^h; καταντήσας, D h; there would be a natural tendency to focus on Paul and his movements. The verb occurs 9 times in Acts (8 times with reference to journeys), 3 times in Paul, once in Ephesians: an Acts word. They arrived at Ephesus, here mentioned for the first time, missed on the outward journey because the missionaries had been prevented from preaching in Asia (16.6), of which province it was the chief city and the residence of the governor. It lay at the mouth of the Cayster (the ruins are now found inland because of a change in the coastline), and was a city of great size and importance both commercially and culturally. It contained the greatest of the seven wonders of the world, the temple of Artemis. See further on 19.1.

The next words are expanded by the Western text; instead of κἀκείνους, D (614 h sy^h**) have καὶ τῷ ἐπιόντι σαββάτῳ ἐκείνους. The Sabbath was a likely day for Paul to visit the synagogue. The sentence might at first seem to suggest that whereas the whole party arrived in Ephesus only Paul entered the synagogue. αὐτὸς δέ, however, is to be taken as introducing what is contained in vv. 20f. That is, Paul left Priscilla and Aquila in Ephesus (*there*: αὐτοῦ in B Ψ 0120 𝔐, but ἐκεῖ is well supported by P^74vid ℵ A D E 33 104 326 1241 *al* and may be original), where they are still to be found in 18.26, but he himself continued his journey. It is clear from Acts and from other sources that there were Jews in Ephesus, and it would be amazing if they were to be found in many other parts of Asia Minor but not here; yet among the many buildings of ancient Ephesus still remaining no synagogue has been found and the earliest Jewish inscriptions date from the second century. See *NS* 3.22, 23, where the literary and other evidence for Jews in Ephesus is given.

In the synagogue Paul διελέξατο (so P^74 ℵ A B 33 1739 1891 *pc*; D *pc* bo have διελέγετο, E Ψ 0120 𝔐 διελέχθη, without substantial difference in meaning); for the word see 17.2. Paul turned at once to the Jews in the synagogue; 18.6 refers to Corinth, not to general policy.

See Weiser's analysis of this passage, given on v. 18. Many take the view that Luke inserted the reference to Ephesus into the Itinerary or some such source; so e.g. Haenchen (521); Schneider (2.254). Pesch (2.155) thinks that Luke wished to make clear that Paul was the first Christian to preach in Ephesus. This seems a rather feeble reason for an insertion; unless a better can be given Paul's visit must appear fruitless and pointless, and this is against its being a Lucan insertion.

20. The Ephesian Jews were welcoming, at least to the extent of wishing to hear more from Paul. They asked him to stay; D E 𝔐 w sy sa^ms bo add παρ' αὐτοῖς, unnecessarily. This however was contrary to his plans; see below, vv. 21–23. He had, according to Acts, established a foothold and received an invitation he could use in the future (though Acts does not say that he did), and for the present this sufficed.

ἐπί is unnecessary; the accusative of duration of time (πλείονα χρόνον) would suffice, but the use of ἐπί in this sense is old and widespread; see LS 623, s.v. ἐπί C II.

ἐπινεύειν occurs here only in the NT, but is as old as Homer.

21. ἀποταξάμενος, as at v. 18.

πάλιν ἀνακάμψω, pleonastic; see BDR § 484. This reading, of P^74 A B E 33 36 945 1739 1891 *al* vg, is very probably correct; the pleonasm is avoided by D sa bo^pt, which omit πάλιν, not by Ψ 𝔐 gig sy, which have πάλιν δέ. Paul was soon back in Ephesus; 19.1.

τοῦ θεοῦ θέλοντος is a pious formula with pagan as well as Jewish parallels. The thought is Pauline: 1 Cor. 4.19, ἐὰν ὁ κύριος θελήσῃ; 16.7; also Heb. 6.3; Jas 4.15. Josephus is virtually within the biblical tradition: *Ant.* 2.333, τοῦ θεοῦ θελήσοντος; 7.373. Plato (with some emphasis) *Alcibiades I* 135d, ἐὰν θεὸς ἐθέλῃ; Epictetus 1.1.17. *DBS* 252 quotes a papyrus letter (*BGU* 2. 423.18), τῶν θεῶν θελόντων (2nd century AD).

ἀνάγεσθαι (see 13.13) is a regular word for *put out to sea, set sail*, and is naturally answered by κατελθών in v. 22.

The verse contains a major Western addition. After εἰπών, the first hand of D has δεῖ δὲ πάντως τὴν ἑορτὴν τὴν ἡμέραν ἐρχομένην ποιῆσαι εἰς Ἱεροσόλυμα. The corrector changes δέ to με (in agreement with d: oportet me). This reading with με but without ἡμέραν occurs also in Ψ 𝔐 gig w sy. d continues in complete agreement with D: solemnem diem advenientem facere. The words recall 20.16 (see also 19.1), but unlike that verse do not specify the feast in question. If we accept the Western text as original, and as an accurate account of what Paul thought and said, and if further we are right in the view (see v. 12) that Paul left Corinth in or about September, he may have been thinking of the Day of Atonement (though that was not a feast but a fast; cf. 27.9) or of Tabernacles. It is however likely that the Western editor, who is followed here by the greater part of the textual tradition, felt himself called upon to provide a reason for Paul's hurried journey and refusal to stay in Ephesus. It may be possible to suggest a better reason; see on the next verse. It will be necessary to raise at 20.16 the question whether Paul found attendance at the festivals compulsory. Calvin (2.141) thinks that this, like the vow in v. 18, was simply an accommodation to Judaism. J. M. Ross (*NovT* 34 (1992), 247–9) defends the long text of D.

A further textual variant runs over into v. 22; see on that verse.

22. Almost all MSS begin the verse with the simple statement that Paul, having set sail from Ephesus, *landed* (κατελθών) at Caesarea. Instead of this, 614 (sy^p sy^hmg) have τὸν δὲ Ἀκύλαν εἴασεν ἐν Ἐφέσῳ, αὐτὸς δὲ ἀνενεχθεὶς ἦλθεν εἰς Καισάρειαν. This repeats what had been said in v. 19 (though now Priscilla is left out of account) and in v. 21; the reading continues to the same destination as in the other MSS. It is hard to detect any motivation here; the Western text (or part of it) offers a rewording of the narrative.

Luke gives no account of the voyage which begins at Ephesus and ends in Caesarea. It is unlikely that an ancient ship would be able to make so long a voyage without calling at a number of ports to take on supplies; if Luke had any information about what happened at any port of call he suppresses it. It is probable that he had nothing to tell; Paul may not have wished to linger on the way; see below.

For Caesarea see on 8.40. It lay in Judaea, not in Syria (v. 18). Luke may possibly have been confused over this; or Paul may have intended to land at Antioch, where he spent some time (v. 23) on the return journey. Northerly winds may have made it impossible to put in at Antioch. On points such as these nothing better than guesswork is possible, though Conzelmann (107) thinks that had Paul been compelled by unfavourable winds to travel to Caesarea, Luke would have said so; he does not say so, so that Caesarea must have been the intended destination, and a consequent visit to Jerusalem must have been planned. Perhaps.

ἀναβάς is ambiguous. It may mean simply that Paul went up from the docks where the ship had berthed and went up into the town and there greeted (ἀσπασάμενος) the church of Caesarea. Cf. Herodotus 5.100, πλοῖα μὲν κατέλιπον ... αὐτοὶ δὲ ἀνέβαινον ... But ἀναβαίνειν is also used for going up to a capital or holy place (see on 11.2), and it is therefore possible that, though its name is not mentioned, Jerusalem may have been the goal of Paul's journey. ἡ ἐκκλησία was used for the church of Jerusalem 'long after [this] had ceased to correspond with the facts' (C. H. Dodd, *NT Studies* 58). We cannot be certain that a visit to Jerusalem took place at this point; if it did we are left wondering why Luke should have referred to it without mentioning it explicitly. That Jerusalem is not mentioned is of course a reason for taking the view that it was not visited (Clark 369: 'It is incredible that so important an event [as a visit to Jerusalem] could have been recorded so briefly'), but Luke's reticence may have an explanation. It is a reasonable suggestion that Paul, profoundly disturbed by opposition that had already made itself felt in Galatia and may have begun to affect Corinth and other centres also, made his way to Jerusalem to find out how far the Jerusalem authorities were behind the trouble-makers, and if possible to stop the trouble at its source. This might account for the speed of his journey—he was not at this point concerned to visit churches *en route* but to get to his destination as quickly as possible—and also for Luke's silence; he did not wish to dig up old troubles. Roloff (277) thinks that Luke understood the story in this way, but was in error; if such a visit had happened Paul would have mentioned it in Galatians 1 and 2. This however depends on the date of Galatians. Johnson (335) takes a different view. Paul went to Jerusalem 'for one reason only: to assert his continuing fidelity to the original apostolic community'.

κατέβη reinforces the sense that has been suggested for ἀναβάς. 'He went up from the harbour into the town of Caesarea and then went down to Antioch' does not make as good sense as 'He went up to Jerusalem from Caesarea and then went down from Jerusalem to Antioch.'

For Antioch see on 11.19.

23. ποιήσας χρόνον τινα—at Antioch, as he had not done in Jerusalem. It is easy to guess, impossible to prove, that Paul was occupied in straightening out tangled relations with the church; cf. Gal. 2.11–14. For the expression cf. 15.33.

The sequence of finite verb and participles, ἐξῆλθεν, διερχόμενος, στηρίζων, is discussed by BDR § 339.2a; § 421. διερχόμενος has something of future significance and adds descriptive intention to ἐξῆλθεν, as if Luke had written ἐξῆλθεν καὶ διήρχετο—that was why he left. στηρίζων, in asyndetic relation with διερχόμενος, is of less weight, as if Luke had written διήρχετο στηρίζων. Cf. M. 3.80, similarly; but not quite convincingly. The sense requires that purpose, intention, should be seen in στηρίζων rather than in διερχόμενος. On the meaning Luke sometimes gives to διέρχεσθαι see on 13.6.

καθεξῆς is a Lucan word (Lk. 1.3; 8.1; Acts 3.24; 8.4; nowhere else in the NT). It is not easy to see why it should be used here unless either (a) it is intended to emphasize that Paul omitted no group of disciples on his way; but this is already covered by πάντας, or (b) it is intended to emphasize the order in which the areas were covered, first the Galatian territory, then Phrygia. This would conflict with 16.6, where the two districts are mentioned in opposite order, though there too Paul is travelling from East to West. For the two terms see on 16.6. It is hard not to agree with Haenchen (523): 'καθεξῆς zeigt, dass mit ''galatisches Land'' und ''Phrygien'' zwei verschiedene Landschaften gemeint sind (gegen Ramsay).' See however Hemer (120). See also 19.1. If Paul's journey to Ephesus had taken him through the southern part of the Galatian province he would very probably have passed through Colossae and Laodicaea, where however he was not personally known (Col. 2.1—which is valid evidence whether Paul wrote Colossians or not).

At this point what is conventionally known as the Third Missionary Journey begins. Cf. Schille (369): 'Das ist die lukanische Zäsur zwischen zwei Reisen.' On this question, and on Paul's routes, see Introduction, pp. lviiif.

For ἐπιστηρίζων (D E Ψ 0120 𝔐), P[74] ℵ A B 33 1891 pc have στηρίζων, probably rightly, but without difference of meaning. The aim is to make the disciples (μαθητάς here must be, as usual in Acts, Christian disciples, notwithstanding 19.1) strong in their faith. To infer from the absence of the word ἐκκλησία that in this area there were disciples but no churches makes nonsense of Luke's understanding of discipleship.

XII

THE MISSION BASED ON EPHESUS
(18.24–20.38)

47. APOLLOS AND THE TWELVE DISCIPLES 18.24–19.7

(24) A certain Jew, Apollos by name, an Alexandrian in origin, an eloquent man, arrived in Ephesus. He was powerful in the Scriptures. (25) He had been instructed in the way of the Lord and[1] was fervent in the Spirit as he spoke and taught accurately the things concerning Jesus, though he knew only John's baptism. (26) He began to speak boldly in the synagogue. When Priscilla and Aquila heard him they[2] took him in, and expounded the way of God to him more accurately. (27) When he wished to pass on to Achaea the brothers encouraged him and wrote to the disciples that they should welcome him. When he arrived he[3] supported those who through grace had become believers, (28) for he vigorously debated with the Jews, showing publicly through the Scriptures that[4] the Christ was Jesus.

(1) It was while Apollos was in Corinth that Paul[5] passed through[6] the hill country of the hinterland and came down to Ephesus, where he found certain disciples. (2) He said to them, 'Did you receive the Holy Spirit when you became believers?' They said to him, 'We did not hear[7] if there is a Holy Spirit.' (3) He said, 'Into what then[8] were you baptized?' They said, 'Into John's baptism.' (4) Paul said, 'John baptized with a baptism of repentance, telling the people that they should believe in the one who was coming after him, that is, in Jesus.' (5) When they heard this they were baptized into the name of the Lord Jesus, (6) and when Paul laid his hands upon them the Holy Spirit came upon them, and they spoke with tongues and prophesied. (7) The total number of the men was about twelve.

Bibliography

C. K. Barrett, in *FS* Reicke, 29–39.

M. Black, as in (46).

[1]NJB, preached with great spiritual fervour.
[2]NEB, took him in hand; NJB, attached themselves to him.
[3]NJB, was able by God's grace to help the believers considerably.
[4]NJB, Jesus was the Christ.
[5]NJB, made his way overland.
[6]RSV, upper; NEB, inland.
[7]NJB, that there was such a thing as a Holy Spirit.
[8]NEB, Then what baptism were you given? NJB, Then how were you baptized?

C. Burchard, *ZNW* 52 (1961), 73–82.

E. C. Colwell, *JBL* 52 (1933), 12–21.

J. Coppens, Kremer, *Actes* 405–38.

K. Haacker, *NovT* 12 (1970), 70–77.

J. H. A. Hart, *JTS* 7 (1905), 16–28.

G. H. R. Horsley, as in (46).

J. H. Hughes, *NovT* 14 (1972), 214–18.

E. Käsemann, *ZThK* 49 (1952), 144–54 (= *EVB* 1.158–68).

G. D. Kilpatrick, *JBL* 89 (1970), 77.

J. Murphy-O'Connor, *NTS* 36 (1990), 359–74.

J. E. L. Oulton, *ExpT* 66 (1955), 236–40.

J. K. Parratt, *ExpT* 79 (1968), 182f.; 80 (1969), 210–14.

H. Preisker, *ZNW* 30 (1931), 301–4.

E. Schweizer, *EvTh* 15 (1955), 247–54 (= *Beiträge* 71–9).

B. T. D. Smith, *JTS* 16 (1915), 241–6.

W. A. Strange, *NTS* 38 (1992), 145–8.

M. Wolter, *ZNW* 78 (1987), 49–73.

Commentary

It would be easy to make out of what is here treated as a single paragraph two distinct paragraphs, 18.24–28, the story of Apollos, and 19.1–7, the story of (about) twelve disciples; easy, but misleading, for the most difficult problems and the most important observations would be missed. The Apollos story would depict the arrival in Ephesus of a learned Alexandrian, who, richly endowed with the Spirit, preached with great fervour and effect. His preaching showed accurate acquaintance with Christian tradition (the way of the Lord, the truths concerning Jesus). He had not received Christian baptism but he had been baptized as a disciple of John the Baptist, and Paul's colleagues, Priscilla and Aquila, were glad to teach him the little he did not yet know and to accept him as a fellow worker who could be commended to the churches of Achaea. Some eyebrows might be raised over such readiness to dispense with baptism into the name of Jesus (or the Trinity), but the tracts of Acts (such as chs. 13 and 14) that make no mention of baptism will be recalled. The 'Disciples' story also can be retold on its own. Paul himself is now back (18.19–21) in Ephesus and there meets some twelve men who are described as μαθηταί. Unlike Apollos they show no sign of the activity of the Spirit, and on inquiry profess that they have never heard of the Holy Spirit; like Apollos they have been baptized with John the Baptist's baptism. Paul instructs them briefly in the relation between John the Baptist and Jesus, baptizes them in the name of the Lord Jesus, and lays his hands upon them. This done, the Holy Spirit comes upon them and his presence is manifested by the charismatic phenomena of glossolalia and prophecy (cf. 2.4). Read on its own this story assumes that baptism (with the imposition of hands) is the indispensable mode of entry into the Christian life and that it and it alone leads to the operation of the Holy Spirit.

It is however impossible to read either of these stories 'on its own', and it may be assumed that Luke intended each to be read in the light of the other. When they are so read a parallel and a difference immediately stand out. In the first we meet a man who has received John's baptism and no other; he is given some instruction and then is not merely received into the church but continues a preaching activity he has already begun. In the second, there are (about) twelve who are in the same position; they must receive a new baptism and the imposition of hands before they take part in Christian activities. Why, the reader asks, should Apollos be treated differently from the twelve? Is it because he is already ζέων τῷ πνεύματι (18.25)? If so, it seems that the purpose of baptism is simply to generate charismatic phenomena. What was the more accurate instruction about the Way that Priscilla and Aquila imparted to Apollos? Again, in the second story, why are the twelve described as μαθηταί, a word which in Acts nearly if not quite always refers to Christian disciples? Were they Christians, though unbaptized? Or were they disciples of John? How could they have been unaware of the very existence of the Holy Spirit?

The two paragraphs are united by two themes: the work of John the Baptist, and the Holy Spirit, inadequate and adequate marks respectively of the Christian faith. There is good though not overwhelming evidence for the continuing existence of groups of disciples of John the Baptist after their master's death, and the existence of such groups, if they wished to become Christians, must have presented the early church with a problem. What was to be done with them? They were hardly in the ordinary sense members of the church, but it was impossible to treat as enemies the disciples of the one whom Christians accepted as the forerunner of the Christ, men who had received the only baptism that Jesus himself, and no doubt many of his earliest followers, had received. It is probable that different answers to the problem were given, and that the two fundamental ones are reflected in the double pericope with which we are dealing. Some would hold: All that they need is to be instructed more fully in what Christians believe about Christ. Others would take the view that they were essentially like other unbaptized unbelievers and must enter through the only door universally recognized. Many discussions of this question (very notably that of Käsemann and to some extent that of Schweizer—see the bibliography) are vitiated by the assumption that Luke's mind worked within a rigid framework which assumed the absolute necessity of ecclesiastical regulations, including the requirement of baptism. This is not so; the story of

Samaria (8.4–25) so far from manifesting a *frühkatholisch* view of sacramental admission to the church views baptism and the gift of the Spirit with very considerable freedom.

This is not to say that Luke has presented us with two historically verifiable stories, told with objective interest in what really happened. Precise analysis of the stories (e.g. Weiser 509 thinks that in vv. 24, 25a Luke uses traditions about Apollos; in 25b about his Christian preaching in Ephesus; and in 26b the taking of Apollos into their home by Priscilla and Aquila; whereas Luke added 24d (Apollos's arrival in Ephesus), 25c (Apollos baptized by John), 26c (instruction by Priscilla and Aquila), perhaps 27abc, 28) is unconvincing. It is much more probable that Luke wrote both straight out on the basis of common talk in Ephesus. It is not to be thought that Luke put them together in order to inform later historians of the diverse attitudes to disciples of John in the first century. Haenchen (534) is probably right: Luke 'wollte in Kap. 19 ein Gesamtbild von der erfolgreichen Arbeit des Paulus geben. Dafür trug diese Geschichte einen wichtigen Zug bei: Paulus überwindet die Sekte.' Perhaps not 'überwindet', but 'absorbs'.

[I have drawn upon my contribution in *FS* Reicke, 29–39.]

24. A new paragraph is introduced without connection with the preceding narrative. There is no reference to Paul whose story will not be resumed till 19.1, when he is seen in—distant—relation to the man who is the centre of the present story. The new figure is connected not only with Ephesus but with the Christians there, and it must be concluded that there was a pre-pauline church in Ephesus. We hear nothing of any other founder, but Paul's brief visit to the synagogue (18.19f.) would hardly suffice for the foundation of a church. The work of Priscilla and Aquila might have done so in the time that the travels of 18.21–23 would take.

The new figure is a Jew, whose name is variously given in different authorities. The majority of MSS have Ἀπολλῶς ὀνόματι; ℵ* 36 453 1175 *pc* bo have ὀνόματι Ἀπελλῆς; D has ὀνόματι Ἀπολλώνιος. BDR § 29.4, n. 6 surprisingly write, 'Obschon Ἀπελλῆς und Ἀπολλῶς etymologisch verwandt sind, scheint es sich um zwei Personen zu handeln, indem Ἀπολλῶς aus 1 Kor 1.12 usw in Apg eingedrungen ist; auch die Scholien (Cramer Catenen zu Apg p. 309f.) scheinen die Verschiedenheit der Personen für möglich zu halten.' Cramer has in fact one scholion, and it is wrongly taken by BDR. The conclusion seems highly improbable; a baseless assimilation of the name given in Acts to that of the person mentioned in 1 Corinthians is unlikely to have affected very nearly all MSS. We must conclude (not with certainty but with reasonable probability) that the same person is mentioned in both books. They do not throw much light on each other.

Apollos then was a Jew: also Ἀλεξανδρεὺς τῷ γένει (D has γένει Ἀλεξ., another of those variants that can have arisen only out of the belief that the precise wording of the original did not matter so long as the sense was given). As in 18.2 the word γένος cannot refer to race; it must refer to place of origin and thus of political association. Little can be made of the reference to Alexandria, of which Acts tells us nothing except in a variant reading in v. 25. Philo was not a representative Alexandrian Jew, and it should not be assumed that Apollos must have been a philosopher and allegorist. If he was instructed in Christianity in his native city (see v. 25) we can say nothing about the kind of Christianity he must have learnt. Ehrhardt (*Acts* 101, 102) thinks that Alexandria is represented here as heterodox. 'Alexandria had rejected the Jerusalem influence, which the Church at Antioch had accepted.' This view, like every other about Christianity in Alexandria in the first century, is a guess, and has no serious foundation. Luke does state that Apollos was ἀνὴρ λόγιος. The adjective may mean *eloquent* or *learned*; it is fruitless to inquire which is intended, since in the Hellenistic world education was to a great extent training in rhetoric. Phrynichus disapproved of the former rendering (Λόγιος· ὡς οἱ πολλοὶ λέγουσιν ἐπὶ τοῦ δεινοῦ εἰπεῖν … οὐ τιθέασιν οἱ ἀρχαῖοι … (176; Rutherford 284)). But the early translations have *eloquent* (e.g. vg, *eloquens*; d gig, *disertus*). See Foerster (*Weltreich* 102f.).

Apollos was also δυνατὸς ἐν ταῖς γραφαῖς, powerful, presumably, in his understanding of the Scriptures and in his use of them in preaching and debate.

Surprisingly placed between ἀνὴρ λόγιος and δυνατὸς ὢν ἐν ταῖς γραφαῖς is the statement that Apollos reached Ephesus—which Paul had left in 18.21.

The name Apollos is 'virtually unattested outside Egypt' (*ND* 1.88; see also Hemer 233f.) Haenchen (528 n. 4) gives various suggestions about Apollos and Weiser (509) gives a careful analysis of the story. To Lüdemann (216) he was 'urchristlicher Pneumatiker'.

25. The most natural way of understanding the first seven words of this verse is that Apollos had been instructed in the Christian way and was a Christian. In Acts, Christianity is described as the Way, ἡ ὁδός, at 9.2; (16.17); 18.25, 26; 19.9, 23; 22.4; 24.14, 22; see especially the note on 9.2. Here it is natural to take κύριος to refer, as frequently, to the Lord Jesus. ἦν κατηχημένος is a periphrastic pluperfect. For κατηχεῖν in the Lucan writings see Lk. 1.4, where it may possibly refer to some more or less formal instruction on Christian matters, as Acts 21.21 certainly does not—hearsay only, and that inaccurate. In the present verse instruction must be intended. D (gig) substitute the word of the Lord for the way of the Lord, and place the instruction in Apollos's home territory of Alexandria: ὃς ἦν κατηχημένος ἐν τῇ πατρίδι τὸν λόγον τοῦ θεοῦ. This means (if accepted) that the Christian message had already spread as far as Alexandria and had been established there. There is no evidence to support this, but it is by no means impossible. There was a very large Jewish community in Alexandria, and in the constant coming and going between that city and Jerusalem there must have been some Jews who had accepted and were concerned to spread the new faith.

This interpretation is rejected by Kosmala (107, 338), who here (as elsewhere) takes *the way* to be the Essene way. See 1QS 8.13 for an example of the use of the word דרך at Qumran. This is most improbable; see Fitzmyer (*Essays* 282), and above, on 9.2.

Apollos further was ζέων τῷ πνεύματι. This does not in itself necessarily mean that he was a Christian, but the close verbal parallel in Rom. 12.11 (τῷ πνεύματι ζέοντες) makes it seem probable, and it is unlikely that one as interested as Luke in phenomena due to the Spirit would use ζέων τῷ πνεύματι to mean no more than an effervescent, lively human spirit (but cf. Blass (201), 'animo ut 17.16, non spiritu s.'). Moreover, Apollos ἐλάλει (D, ἀπελάλει, without significant difference in meaning—*spoke, spoke forth*) καὶ ἐδίδασκεν ἀκριβῶς τὰ περὶ τοῦ Ἰησοῦ (so P⁴¹ᵛⁱᵈ P⁷⁴ᵛⁱᵈ ℵ A B E Ψ 0120 614 945 1175 1241 1739 2495 *al*; τοῦ κυρίου, 𝔐). This is how Paul spoke in Rome (28.31), and it is impossible to take it as anything other than a description of an inspired and accurate Christian teacher.

Yet that inspired and accurate Christian teacher had not been baptized, or rather, the baptism he had received had been that of John the Baptist; he had not received Christian baptism. Nor (see v. 26) did he now do so. This stands in sharp contrast with 19.1–7, in which Paul baptizes a group of disciples of John the Baptist in Ephesus. ἐπιστάμενος means *being aware of, having experience of*. Weiser (507) finds the choice of this word significant. 'Die behutsame Wahl des Verbums "kennen" ermöglichte ihm, hernach den Mangel durch *Unterweisung* beheben zu lassen.' Whether he had been baptized by John himself in Jordan, or had been a member of one of the groups of disciples of John the Baptist which are believed by some (see J. H. Hughes, *NovT* 14 (1972), 214–18) to have continued to exist after the master's death, is not clear. τὸ βάπτισμα Ἰωάννου is the baptism John preached and practised; it cannot mean the baptism of Jesus by John.

The questions that arise out of the text are clear, and increase as we proceed. Was Apollos a Christian? If he was, how had he escaped baptism? Why was he not baptized now (v. 26)? Weiser's explanation is inadequate; no amount of instruction could *confer* baptism. If he already knew so much, why was he further, ἀκριβέστερον, instructed? Can an earlier form of the story be traced? Many answers have been given. Apollos was a Jewish Christian (Weiser 507). 'Ap. war also gewissermassen jüdischer "Jesus-anhänger" aber noch nicht Christ' (Schneider 2.226; cf. Schmithals 172). Unfavourable details have been added to the picture of Apollos in order to depreciate him (Käsemann). Baptism was introduced by Hellenistic Christians rather than by the original Jerusalem disciples (*Begs.* 4.231). These suggestions should be borne in mind, though none is entirely satisfactory.

26. Thus gifted, Apollos began to preach boldly in the synagogue. For παρρησιάζεσθαι cf. 9.27, 28: Paul had already spoken boldly in synagogues. Could this mean, could it in an earlier form of the story have meant, that he was a Jewish, not a Christian preacher? On ἤρξατο see Wilcox (125–7). It is unlikely that it here represents the Aramaic שׁרא. Having reached Ephesus Apollos *began* to preach there. It is not said, and is unlikely to be intended, that this was the beginning of his preaching ministry; he had preached before he came to Ephesus. παρρησιάζεσθαι corresponds to ζέων τῷ πνεύματι (v. 25).

Priscilla and Aquila, whom Paul had left in Ephesus (18.21), apparently attended the synagogue, and there heard Apollos preach. They were impressed, but, it seems, with his promise rather than his achievement. He needed further instruction, so they took him aside (προσελάβοντο) and set forth to him (ἐξέθεντο; cf. 28.23) the way of God more accurately. If *the way of God* and *the way of the Lord* (v. 25) were reversed in order we might guess that Apollos knew already the (Jewish) way of God (for the expression cf. CD 20.18) and now needed to be taught the (Christian) way of the Lord (Jesus). But this is not what Luke says; moreover he has already said that Apollos taught accurately the things concerning Jesus. ἀκριβῶς and ἀκριβέστερον have an artificial ring and sound contrived. Why did not Priscilla and Aquila baptize Apollos? Was this feature of the story for some reason omitted, and did Luke supply the ἀκριβέστερον instruction, taking up ἀκριβῶς from v. 25 and improving on it? This is a more probable suggestion than Schweizer's (*Beiträge* 78), that ἀκριβέστερον was originally elative (cf. 24.22) but was taken by Luke to be a true comparative, which led him to infer ἀκριβῶς in v. 25.

D Ψ 0120 𝕸 gig sy sa^mss reverse the order of names and have 'Aκ. καὶ Πρ. A mark of anti-feminism in the Western editor?

27. Apollos, at present in Ephesus (v. 24), wished to cross over (διέρχεσθαι can hardly mean more than this here; contrast 13.6) to Achaea. Whether he intended to travel by sea, sailing across the Aegean, or to make the long land journey through Macedonia, is not stated. For *Achaea* see on 18.12. The *brothers* (for this designation of Christians see 1.15 and frequently) *encouraged* him (for this use of the middle of προτρέπειν cf. e.g. Josephus, *Ant.* 12.166, τοῦ πρεσβευτοῦ προτρεψαμένου) and *wrote* to the *disciples* (in Corinth, we may guess, in view of 19.1). This was a commendatory letter, συστατικὴ ἐπιστολή; such letters were known in the NT world; cf. 2 Cor. 3.1; Rom. 16.1; Col. 4.10; and see *ND* 1.64–66. The aorist participle (προτρεψάμενοι may be antecedent to ἔγραψαν, or contemporaneous—they encouraged by writing; see BDR § 339.1, n. 3. In place of the infinitive ἀποδέξασθαι the Western text (see below) has ὅπως with the subjunctive; see BDR § 392.1, n. 5. Marshall (304) writes 'RSV says that they encouraged Apollos to go *to Achaia*, but the text could also mean that they encouraged the disciples at Corinth to welcome Apollos.' This is undoubtedly correct; but encouragement of the newly instructed preacher and the furthering of his plans is perhaps more natural.

Having arrived (again we may guess) at Corinth, though other Achaean towns cannot be excluded, Apollos gave support (for this use of the middle of συμβάλλειν cf. Epictetus 3.22.78, Ὁμήρου πλείονα τῇ κοινωνίᾳ συνεβάλετο Πρίαμος ...) to those who had believed, οἱ πεπιστευκότες, the perfect participle implying that having once come to believe they continued to do so—but Acts also uses the aorist, οἱ πιστεύσαντες, without implying that those so described were no longer believers.

διὰ τῆς χάριτος is used as at 15.11. That they became and continued to be believers was due only to the grace of God. Luke does not develop the theme of grace as Paul does, but makes it quite clear that faith comes through divine not human initiative. It would be possible to take διὰ τῆς χάριτος not with πεπιστευκότες but with συνεβάλετο; Calvin (2.146) does so. But it seems better to take the adverbial phrase with the nearer verb.

The verse appears in a different form in D (with some support from P³⁸ and sy^hmg). It runs: ἐν δὲ τῇ Ἐφέσῳ ἐπιδημοῦντές τινες Κορίνθιοι καὶ ἀκούσαντες αὐτοῦ παρεκάλουν διελθεῖν σὺν αὐτοῖς εἰς τὴν πατρίδα αὐτῶν. συνκατανεύσαντος δὲ αὐτοῦ οἱ Ἐφέσιοι ἔγραψαν τοῖς ἐν Κορίνθῳ μαθηταῖς ὅπως ἀποδέξωνται τὸν ἄνδρα· ὃς ἐπιδημήσας εἰς τὴν Ἀχαίαν πολὺ συνεβάλλετο ἐν ταῖς ἐκκλησίαις.

There is more here than a certain indifference to the exact reproduction of words. The initiative is taken not by Apollos but by Corinthians who happen to be resident in Ephesus and have heard Apollos preaching. They were travelling home to Corinth—on business?—and urged Apollos to travel with them. He agreed (συνκατανεύσαντος; the word occurs nowhere else in the NT), and the Ephesians backed up their Corinthian visitors with a commendatory letter. Apollos took up residence *in Achaea*; this presumably means that though he may have had a base in Corinth he travelled over the province. This is supported by the plural ἐν ταῖς ἐκκλησίαις—not only in the ἐκκλησία of Corinth but in other

Achaean Christian centres too. Or were these the house-churches which seem to have been forming in Corinth (1 Cor. 1.11f.)?

Metzger (467f.) points out difficulties in the Western readings, but does not discuss the question where or how they originated. 'Nowhere else in Acts do we hear of members of one church acting in another church, nor do we ever hear of an invitation to an apostle or evangelist to come to a church (16.9 is not a parallel)' (468). It is probably correct that these things are more likely in the more developed situation of the second century than in the first. 'If Apollos's visit is made on his own initiative, an introductory letter recommending him to the Corinthians is appropriate; if, on the other hand, he goes at the invitation of members of the Corinthian church, why is it necessary that the Ephesians supply such a letter?' The difficulty is not as great as Metzger suggests. Logically, the letter seems unnecessary, but such actions are not always in strict accord with logic; the Corinthians who had taken up temporary residence in Ephesus would probably be only a small proportion of the whole church, and might not be trusted by all—the church at Corinth was notorious for its divisions. Here too, however, it may well be that we see a glimpse of second-century rather than first-century church life. There may also be a connection between the Western editor and Corinth, where traditions about Apollos may still have been current in the second century.

28. εὐτόνως (2 Macc. 12.23; 4 Macc. 7.10; Aristophanes, *Plutus* 1095), elsewhere in the NT only at Lk. 23.10: *vigorously*—often in a physical sense, here determined by the verb διακατηλέγχετο, which occurs here only in the NT. The double compound is quoted by LS (397) only from this passage; 'a very strong word' (Page 203). M. 2.301f. says that it 'might be taken as a sort of double perfective, a combination of διελέγχομαι *confute* and κατελέγχομαι *convict*; but Blass is probably right in classing it with διαλέγομαι'. Of this word (with διαλαλέω, διαλογίζομαι, διερωτάω) Moulton says that it recalls (by means of διά) the 'two parties in a conversation'.

Apollos confuted the Jews energetically and δημοσίᾳ, *publicly*. Cf. 16.37. The confutation naturally took the form of a scriptural demonstration (ἐπιδεικνύς; cf. 9.39, demonstrating in a different sense) that the Christ was Jesus. It is to be expected that the noun with the article should be the subject (see M. 3.182–4; Moule, *IB* 115f., both referring to E. C. Colwell, *JBL* 52 (1933), 12–21; also Zerwick § 172), and this makes good sense. Jews agreed with Christians that there was, or was to be, a figure described by the term Χριστός; what Apollos had to prove from Scripture was that this figure had appeared in the person of Jesus. Luke finds it unnecessary to specify the Scriptures used.

After δημοσίᾳ there are two different Western insertions, bearing clear witness to a stage at which the wording of the text was handled with some freedom while the meaning was retained. D 614 add διαλεγόμενος καὶ (P³⁸ has διαλ. only); this seems unnecessary after διακατηλέγχετο. E adds καὶ κατ᾽ οἶκον, possibly recalling 20.20 rather than picturing private discussions. There is no indication whose οἶκος might be used. At the end of the verse D has τὸν Ἰησοῦν εἶναι χριστόν; P³⁸ᵛⁱᵈ has χριστὸν εἶναι Ἰησοῦν. The former reading requires, the latter permits, the rather more obvious ' . . . that Jesus was (the) Christ'.

Knowledge of this verse may be reflected by *Acts of Thomas* 59(56) (L.-B. 2.2.176), . . . ὑποδεικνύων ὅτι οὗτός ἐστιν Ἰησοῦς ὁ χριστὸς περὶ οὗ αἱ γραφαὶ ἐκήρυξαν; but the thought is too commonplace to constitute proof.

1, 2. For Luke's use of ἐγένετο see Introduction, p. xlvi. Here it is followed by an accusative and infinitives (ἐγένετο . . . Παῦλον . . . ἐλθεῖν . . . καὶ εὐρεῖν . . .), which is by no means an exact reproduction of the Hebrew construction with ויהי. It must be classed as a Septuagintalism, part of Luke's 'biblical' style. See Zerwick (§ 389). Radermacher (149), however, takes the infinitives as subject: 'was passierte, wird durch den Infinitiv ausgedrückt.' We might render crudely, 'Paul's coming to Ephesus happened'. It seems more probable that Luke is telling his story in a way intended to recall the OT.

According to 18.27 Apollos had gone to Achaea; it is not surprising that he should find himself in Achaea's largest city, Corinth (the Western text of 18.27 says explicitly that he went there). For his activity in Corinth see 1 Cor. 1.12; 3.4, 5, 6, 22; 16.12; and *1 Corinthians* 8–11, 43–6, 81–7, 104–8, 391f. Of all this Acts has nothing to tell except his general assistance to the believers and his disputes with the Jews (18.27, 28). As the subject of εἶναι his name appears in the accusative, which is given as Ἀπολλῶ by most authorities, as Ἀπολλῶν by P⁷⁴ Aᶜ L 33 *pc*, and as Ἀπολλῆν by ℵ* 36 453 1175 *pc* bo (for this variant see 18.24). On the declension see M. 2.121.

While (expressed by ἐν τῷ and the present infinitive; see BDR § 404.1, n. 2) Apollos was in Corinth Paul *passed through* (διελθόντα, possibly preaching as he went; see on 13.6) *the upper regions*, τὰ ἀνωτερικὰ μέρη (vg, superioribus partibus). The precise meaning of this phrase is uncertain. The adjective is rare, and is not used elsewhere as a geographical term. So far as we know it is attested only for medical writers, but if this proves anything about Luke it proves that he was not a doctor, for he was not thinking of *medicines delivered by mouth* or of *emetics*. The adjective may be taken in the most literal sense to refer to *hill country* or it may refer to the *hinterland* (of Ephesus). ἄνω is used geographically (e.g. Herodotus

1.177, τὰ μὲν νῦν κάτω τῆς Ἀσίας ... τὰ δὲ ἄνω αὐτῆς.). This suggests with some probability the meaning of τὰ ἀνωτερικὰ μέρη here. Paul was said at 18.23 to be passing through τὴν Γαλατικὴν χώραν καὶ Φρυγίαν; the present verse takes up the same journey and will refer either to the same territory or, more probably, to the country between Phrygia and Ephesus. Paul was unknown to the churches of Colossae and Laodicea (Col. 2.1) and therefore probably did not use the route that follows (more or less) the line of the Meander but a more northerly one. The route through the Cayster valley was shorter and would also make possible the use of ἀνωτερικά in both available senses: the hinterland was elevated. Cf. Hemer (120): 'τὰ ἀνωτερικὰ μέρη are plausibly understood to refer to the traverse of the hill-road reaching Ephesus by the Cayster valley north of Mt. Messogis, and not by the Lycus and Maeander valleys, with which Paul may have been unacquainted.'

The nature of the hinterland makes κατελθεῖν a suitable verb (it is read by P[74vid] א A E Ψ 33 945 1739 1891 *pc*) but does not make ἐλθεῖν (B 𝔐 lat) unsuitable. The compound verb may have been introduced in order to match ἀνωτερικά.

Paul came to Ephesus. When Rome took over the kingdom of Attalus III in 133 BC Ephesus was already a large and notable city and as part of the Empire it continued to expand in wealth and in architectural splendour. It was the residence of the proconsular governor of the province Asia, though not the titular capital. Further details of its government will be mentioned later in this chapter. For its fame as a centre of magic arts see on 19.18f. In Ephesus Paul found τινὰς μαθητάς. The word itself (see on 9.36) strongly suggests Christian disciples, but the content of the narrative has led some (from Chrysostom onwards) to question this. Pesch (2.165) thinks that the fact that the men appear to be separate from the synagogue suggests that they are Christians, but in fact they are not. Kosmala (106f.) and others take them to be disciples of John the Baptist (as the context in part—v. 3—suggests). Schneider (2.263), Bruce (2.363), Blass (203), Beyer (116) think that they are Christians; and there are intermediate views. Marshall (306) (referring to K. Haacker, *NovT* 12 (1970), 70–77) thinks that they cannot be Christians and notes that 'Luke is not saying that the men are disciples but is describing how they appeared to Paul.' Stählin (253) prudently observes that there were 'mancherlei Zwischenstellungen zwischen Täufer- und Jesusgemeinde'; but where is the evidence for these Zwischen-stellungen? and how indeed can they be conceived? Weiser (515) says that the men were not Christians but 'auf der unmittelbaren *Vorstufe* zum christlichen Glauben'. Again, there is some difficulty in defining this Vorstufe. The problem will be considered below.

It is not clear why Paul should immediately ask whether these disciples received the Holy Spirit when they became believers (the aorist participle πιστεύσαντες is to be taken as coincident in time with the finite verb ἐλάβετε; see M. 1.131). Paul does not ask if they *believe*; this he accepts because they are Christians—so Preuschen (115). It may be (in Luke's understanding of the matter) that there were no charismatic manifestations such as speaking with tongues and prophesying; contrast v. 6. Luke (though not Paul) might think of this as a sign that the Holy Spirit was not present. Schmithals (174) thinks that the question is constructed so as to lead to the answer given.

The direct question is introduced by εἰ, which normally introduces indirect questions. Cf. 1.6. 'Der Gebrauch ist unklassisch, findet sich dagegen auch in LXX (Gen 17.17 us), ist also wohl Hebraismus als Übersetzung (neben μή) von hebr. ה, das in der indirekten Frage εἰ entspricht, und אם, das auch direkte Fragen einleitet' (BDR § 440.3, n. 5). See however I.76.

The disciples' reply is surprising: We have not even heard if there is a Holy Spirit. Is it conceivable that Christian disciples should have said this? Is it conceivable that disciples of John the Baptist should have said this? According to Acts itself, Jesus had promised that the disciples would be baptized with the Holy Spirit (1.5; 11.16) and John had foretold this (Lk. 3.16). Readers of the OT must have been aware of the existence of the Holy Spirit. Bengel (463): 'Nam neque Mosen neque Iohannem Baptistam sequi potuissent, quin de Spiritu sancto ipso audissent.' Haenchen (530) comments with an exclamation mark: 'Der heilige Geist der Christen ist ihnen völlig unbekannt!' Marshall (306) quotes Rom. 8.9 and concludes that the disciples cannot be Christians. It must be asked however whether Luke in this passage and Paul in Romans 8 mean precisely the same thing by the Holy Spirit. The variant (instead of ἔστιν), λαμβάνουσίν τινες (P³⁸ P⁴¹ D* sy^hmg sa) was no doubt introduced in order to obviate the difficulty. On the construction (οὐδ' εἰ ... ἠκούσαμεν) see C. Burchard in *ZNW* 52 (1961), 73–82—εἰ is used for *that*. Page (203) explains the substance of the disciples' reply with the suggestion that their words mean, 'We did not *at our baptism* hear whether there is a Holy Spirit'; that is, 'Our baptism (John's baptism) was simply a baptism of repentance and conveyed no promise beyond that of the forgiveness of sins.'

There are further variants to be observed in these verses (see W. A. Strange, *NTS* 38 (1992), 145–8). The opening sentence, ἐγένετο ... Ἔφεσον, is given in P³⁸ᵛⁱᵈ D sy^hmg as follows: θέλοντος Παύλου κατὰ τὴν ἰδίαν βουλὴν πορεύεσθαι εἰς Ἱεροσόλυμα εἶπεν αὐτῷ τὸ πνεῦμα ὑποστρέφειν εἰς τὴν Ἀσίαν, διελθὼν δὲ τὰ ἀνωτερικὰ μέρη ἔρχεται εἰς Ἔφεσον. In addition to a good deal of verbal resemblance there are two major differences: Apollos and his residence in Corinth disappear, and we hear of a change of plan on Paul's part—he wishes to return to Jerusalem (we should probably infer that the writer did not suspect, as we have done, a visit to

Jerusalem at 18.22) but is directed to Asia and comes to Ephesus. The dropping of Apollos is relatively easy to understand. His work in Corinth contributes nothing to the new paragraph apart from the fact that it explains why Paul did not meet him in Ephesus. The account of Paul's overruled plan underlines the fact that Paul's plans are not made κατὰ σάρκα (cf. 2 Cor. 1.17) but under divine direction. Metzger (469) quotes B. Weiss (*Der Codex D*, p. 94, n. 1): 'the whole antithesis between ἰδία βουλή and an order of the Spirit is neither in the character of Paul nor of Luke, who brings expressly into prominence how Paul allows all his decisions to be made by the will of God made known to him through the Spirit.' But this seems to be exactly what happens in the text before us, as it does also e.g. at 16.6, 7: They passed through Phrygia and Galatic territory having been forbidden to speak the word in Asia [as they evidently would otherwise have done] ... they tried to enter Bithynia [this was evidently their intention] but the Spirit of Jesus did not permit them to do so. The Western text seems here to be quite in the spirit of the Lucan narrative, but this of course does not establish its originality; the old Uncial text also is Lucan. The very fact that Lucan thought and language are used in the Western text is in a sense an argument against its authenticity; had the reading stood in the text from the beginning it would have seemed—it would have been—a passage that no one would have wished to remove. G. D. Kilpatrick (*FS* Greeven, 193) thinks that 'we may avoid some of our difficulties by assuming that part of the original text survives in WT [= Western text] and part in GT [= General text]'. He sees further difficulties however and takes the suggestion no further.

A further variant spans vv. 1, 2:

καὶ εὑρεῖν τινας μαθητὰς εἶπέν τε πρὸς αὐτούς: P[74vid] ℵ A B
    33 36 453 945 1175 1739 1891 *al* vg co
καὶ εὑρών τινας μαθητὰς εἶπεν πρ. αὐ. D E Ψ 𝔐 gig sy[h] bo[ms]
καὶ εἶπεν τοῖς μαθηταῖς P[38vid]

The second is the neater sentence; probably to be regarded as an 'improvement' on the first.

3. The surprising reply of the disciples leads to a further question. εἰς τί οὖν ἐβαπτίσθητε; οὖν 'presupposes that if they had been baptized into the name of Jesus, they would have received the Spirit at Baptism' (Knowling 403). What sort of baptism can you have had if you profess ignorance of the Holy Spirit? The answer is, (We were baptized) εἰς τὸ Ἰωάννου βάπτισμα. εἰς τί and εἰς βάπτισμα are unexpected. When εἰς is used with βαπτίζειν it is usually followed by the name of a person, normally in the NT Christ (or some variant or fuller form of the name). It is probable that the expressions used here presuppose the usual baptismal formula and were used because it was impossible (or was thought by Luke to be impossible) to say, We were baptized into (or into the name of) John (Conzelmann 110f.). Zerwick (§ 101) thinks that εἰς is used as if it were instrumental ἐν, but in fact the preposition requires no further definition than that of εἰς and ἐν with ὄνομα and ὀνόματι.

But if these men were Christian disciples, why had they received only John's baptism? According to Wettstein (2.580) they were Christians 'quos Apollos docuerat'—had taught, presumably, before Priscilla and Aquila took him in hand (see vv. 24–8).

Variants in this verse again suggest freedom in copying a text that was respected because of those of whom it told but was not regarded as canonical and sacrosanct. Thus at the beginning of the verse εἶπέν τε is read by B 36 453 614 1175 *pc* d; εἶπέν τε πρὸς αὐτούς by 𝔐 vg^mss (sy^p sa); ὁ δὲ εἶπεν by P^41vid P^74 ℵ A E 33 *pc* bo; εἶπεν δέ by D Ψ 945 1739 1891 (2495) *pc*; ὁ δὲ Παῦλος πρὸς αὐτούς by P^38. The disciples' answer is introduced by εἶπαν in the majority of MSS, by ἔλεγον in P^45 D.

4. One might have expected Paul to reply to the disciples, John's baptism, which you have received, was a baptism with water; the new baptism, which was promised by John and is now given in the name of Jesus Christ, is a baptism with the Holy Spirit (Lk. 3.16; Acts 1.5). This will make good the deficiency implied by your words. In fact nothing more is said about the connection between baptism and the Holy Spirit (though the Spirit is in due course given; v. 6); instead Paul takes up another aspect of John's prediction. John ἐβάπτισεν (one would have expected the imperfect; the aorist is constative and sums up John's ministry) βάπτισμα μετανοίας. This is the only place where the noun βάπτισμα is used as cognate accusative with the active verb (for the passive cf. Mk 10.38, 39; Lk. 7.29; 12.50). Elsewhere in Acts John preaches, proclaims a baptism (10.37; 13.24). John's ministry was a summons to repentance (Lk. 3.3, 8), and this was expressed in baptism. Christian baptism also included repentance and led to the forgiveness of sins (Acts 2.38).

John pointed forward not only to a new baptism with the Holy Spirit but to a Coming One, who would be the agent of the new baptism. So Lk. 3.16: ἔρχεται δὲ ὁ ἰσχυρότερός μου, οὗ οὐκ εἰμὶ ἱκανὸς λῦσαι τὸν ἱμάντα τῶν ὑποδημάτων αὐτοῦ. John continues with the promise that this Stronger One will baptize with the Holy Spirit and fire, but does not expressly require faith in the Stronger One. It may however reasonably be said that this is implied; only those who have faith in him will accept his baptism. The clause in which the requirement of faith ('ἵνα πιστευσ. pro πιστεῦσαι', Blass 203) is made is oddly expressed. The order of words 'is strange, considering how natural and easy it would have been to write λέγων τῷ λαῷ ἵνα πιστεύσωσιν εἰς τὸν …' (Moule, *IB* 169). It is not a

simple matter of the prolepsis of the subject of the subordinate clause
(M. 3.325), which is not uncommon in Greek. It may be that we must
be content to note another example of the lack of revision that
appears in a number of passages in Acts.

The last five words of the verse may be read in different ways,
which illustrate the problem of the passage as a whole. They may be
either: the Coming One—that is, of course, as you, being Christians
though unbaptized know, Jesus; *or*: the Coming One, who, I now
inform you disciples of John, is to be identified with Jesus, to whom
you should now, in accordance with your teacher's word, transfer
your loyalty.

The name *Jesus* was too simple for many copyists, though it is
undoubtedly the best reading (P³⁸ P⁷⁴ ℵ A B E 614 2495 *pc* vg
syʰ saᵐˢˢ bo); D r have Χριστόν; 𝔐 has τὸν Χριστὸν Ἰησοῦν; Ψ 945
1175 1739 1891 *pc* gig syᵖ saᵐˢˢ have τὸν Ἰησοῦν Χριστόν.

5. Paul had not said that the 'disciples' should be rebaptized but
that John had bidden them believe in the one who was to come;
believing in him however could be expressed by being baptized in
his name, and the rite was duly carried out.

After τοῦ κυρίου Ἰησοῦ the Western text (D 614 syʰ**; also P³⁸
but without Χριστοῦ) makes the pious but secondary addition
Χριστοῦ εἰς ἄφεσιν ἁμαρτιῶν. Schille (377) regards this as 'litur-
gisch gerundeter', but it makes little sense since the baptism the men
had already received was εἰς ἄφεσιν ἁμαρτιῶν.

A curious interpretation of the verse is given by Barth (*CD* 4.4.62,
75), who takes the subject of ἀκούσαντες ἐβαπτίσθησαν to be the
crowds who listened to John and were baptized by him. His baptism
was, by anticipation, baptism into the name of Christ. This being so
there was no need for further baptism of the 'disciples', and, their
baptism being now removed from the verse, they no more than
Apollos receive a second baptism. Apart from its general improbabil-
ity this is an impossible way of understanding the sentence. Those
who heard and were baptized were the αὐτοῖς on whom Paul laid his
hands, the αὐτούς on whom the Spirit came (v. 6), the group of men
who numbered about twelve (v. 7). It is unfortunate that Barth's
important discussion of baptism should be marred by this piece of
exegesis.

'Manus imposuit Paulus: actum baptismi aliis reliquit' (Bengel
463). This is a possible but by no means necessary way of
understanding the passive ἐβαπτίσθησαν.

6. Whether Paul or some others deputed by him carried out the
baptism of the disciples (v. 5) is not stated; Paul himself laid hands
on them. For the relation in Acts between baptism, the laying on of
hands, and the gift of the Spirit, see on 8.17. That Luke intended to
affirm and commend as necessary some supplement to the baptismal

rite, or for that matter the rite itself, is excluded by the preceding story. Apollos, who equally knew only the baptism of John (18.25), was not baptized again, nor were hands laid upon him; moreover he was already ζέων τῷ πνεύματι, though without Christian baptism. It is probable (see *FS* Reicke 29–39) that the two stories reflect different ways of receiving disciples of John the Baptist into the church. Some would accept them on the ground of some further instruction; others thought that the new Christian baptism should be given. The laying on of hands was 'oratio super hominem' (see I.606), prayer directed to an indicated intention. Marshall (308) thinks that it incorporated the disciples into the fellowship of the church. ' ... so ist damit aber keineswegs eine Abhängigkeit oder gar Kontrollierung und regulierung des Geistes von Seiten der Menschen oder kirchlicher Amtsträger gemeint; denn Lukas hebt an anderen Stellen das freie, von menschlicher Beeinflussung unabhängige Wirken des Geistes ... und seine Unverfügbarkeit ... deutlich hervor' (Weiser 518). The question whether ἐπιτιθέναι represents סמך or שית is unanswerable, and *for Luke* is probably meaningless. See on 6.6.

The ignorance of v. 2 is immediately ended by the coming of the Spirit. For ἦλθε, P[38vid] D (vg[mss]) have εὐθέως ἐπέπεσεν, a variant that adds at most a little vividness to the narrative. According to Turner (*Insights* 20), the article with πνεῦμα is anaphoric and refers back to v. 2, '*that very* Holy Spirit came upon them'. This is no doubt true, but should not be pressed lest we come to the conclusion that Luke believed that there was a multiplicity of Holy Spirits.

For speaking with tongues and prophesying see 2.4; for Luke this was the clearest indication that the Spirit was at work. Cf. 2.4; 10.46. Whether the Paul who wrote 1 Corinthians would have been satisfied with this outcome of his work is another matter.

The imperfects ἐλάλουν, ἐπροφήτευον, are inceptive: they began and continued to do these things.

Instead of ἐλάλουν δὲ γλώσσαις καί sy[hmg] has et loquebantur linguis aliis et cognoscebant ipsi eas, quas et interpretabantur ipsi sibi; quidam autem etiam prophetabant (Ropes, *Begs.* 3.181).

7. Luke is interested in numbers, and likes to give them. He is also aware that he can as a rule give only an approximation, and indicates this by the use of ὡσεί (as here) or ὡς.

οἱ πάντες ἄνδρες means the whole company of the men, the sum total. So Zerwick (§ 188): 'Attributive positum dicit [πᾶς] rei vel rerum complexum, summam (in oppositione ad partem) e.g. ... "summa virorum erat duodecim" A 19.7 (cf. 27.37).' Similarly Moule, *IB* 94; M. 3.201; BDR § 275.3.

There is no reason to think that Luke saw any special significance in the number twelve; most think that the ὡσεί proves this, but

Williams (220) thinks that the 'about' can be disregarded. 'Does this section point to the existence of a primitive "college" of Twelve at Ephesus, recognized perhaps by Paul, who governed the Church there?'

Kosmala, whose view of the 'disciples' is mentioned above, adds in a footnote (116, n. 27), 'Nach jüdischer (und essenischer) Weise zählten nur die Männer; aber vielleicht waren die ''Jünger'', die striktere Regel befolgend, überhaupt nicht verheiratet.' Vielleicht: but there is no reason to think so; in first-century Ephesus Paul was more likely to encounter a group of men than a mixed group, or a group of women, even though the men might be married.

48. PAUL'S SUCCESSFUL MINISTRY AT EPHESUS 19.8–20

(8) Paul[1] went into the synagogue and[2] spoke boldly, for three months arguing and persuading about the kingdom of God. (9) But when some grew hard and disbelieved, and spoke evil of the Way[3], in the hearing of the[4] populace, he separated from them and withdrew the disciples, arguing daily in the school of Tyrannus. (10) This lasted for two years, with the result that all who lived in the province of Asia[5] heard the word of the Lord, both Jews and Greeks. (11) God performed no common works of power by Paul's hands, (12) so that[6] sweatbands and sweatcloths were carried from contact with his skin to the sick, and their diseases left them and the evil spirits went out.

(13) Some of the[7] itinerant Jewish exorcists[8] set about naming the name of the Lord Jesus over those who had evil spirits, saying, 'I adjure you by Jesus whom Paul preaches.' (14) There were seven sons of a certain Sceva, a Jew, a chief priest, doing this. (15) But the evil spirit answered them, 'I[9] know Jesus and I[10] am acquainted with Paul, but who are you?' (16) and the man in whom the evil spirit was leapt upon them, overpowered them all, and mastered them, so that they fled from the[11] house naked and wounded. (17) This became known to all, both Jews and Greeks, who lived in Ephesus; fear fell upon them all, and the name of the Lord Jesus was magnified. (18) Many of those who had believed would come, confessing [their sins][12] and disclosing their magical practices. (19) A good many of those who practised magic gathered their books together and burned them in the presence of all. They counted up the prices [of the books][13] and found that they came to 50,000 silver [drachmae][14] (20) Thus the word of the Lord grew mightily and prevailed.

Bibliography

C. K. Barrett, *FS* Lohse, 96–110.

K. Berger, *NTS* 20 (1973), 25, n. 95.

[1]Greek; RSV, NJB, he; NEB, During the next three months he attended the synagogue.
[2]RSV, for three months spoke boldly.
[3]NJB, in public
[4]RSV, congregation; NEB, whole congregation.
[5]NJB, were able to hear.
[6]RSV, NJB, handkerchiefs or aprons; NEB, handkerchiefs and scarves.
[7]NEB, strolling.
[8]NEB, tried their hand at using; NJB, tried pronouncing.
[9]NEB, I acknowledge; NJB, I recognize.
[10]RSV, NJB, know; NEB, know about.
[11]Greek, RSV, that.
[12]Greek, RSV, omit.
[13]Greek, omit; RSV, of them; NJB, of these.
[14]Greek, omit; RSV, NEB, NJB, pieces.

E. Delebecque, *RScPhTh* 66 (1982), 225–32.

J. A. Fitzmyer, *FS* Schneider, 299–305.

G. H. R. Horsley, as in (46).

P. W. van der Horst, *ZNW* 69 (1978), 187–202.

P. Lampe, *BZ* 36 (1992), 59–76.

T. J. Leary, *JTS* 41 (1990), 527–9.

G. M. Lee, *Bib* 51 (1970), 237.

B. A. Mastin, *JTS* 27 (1976), 405–12.

B. A. Mastin, *Bib* 59 (1978), 97–9.

F. Miltner, *Ephesos. Stadt der Artemis und des Johannes*, Vienna 1958.

W. A. Strange, *JTS* 38 (1987), 97–106.

B. E. Taylor *ExpT* 57 (1946), 222.

P. Wexler, *REJ* 140 (1981), 123, 124, 133.

Commentary

This section falls into four parts. The first describes in summary form Paul's two-year ministry in Ephesus. It follows the usual pattern. Paul begins in the synagogue and is able to continue there for three months before he is obliged to move to a non-Jewish site, discoursing daily in the school of Tyrannus. The result of his unusually long period of teaching there is the dissemination of his message through the whole of Asia. This plain account could well be the entry under 'Ephesus' in a Pauline itinerary. Verse 8 reproduces words (εἰσελθὼν εἰς τὴν συναγωγήν) used in 18.19; it is quite possible that all the intervening material was introduced by Luke into the itinerary from other sources.

The rest of this section, together with 19.21–40, is probably best understood as consisting of local traditions picked up by Luke in Ephesus. Their historical value is uneven. Ephesus was a great centre of magical practices (see below, especially on v. 19), and it is not surprising that Paul should leave the impression of an opponent of magic; nor is it surprising that his opposition should be expressed in various ways—by his appearance as a more striking wonder-worker than any of his rivals (vv. 11, 12), as one who discomfited the professional exorcists (vv. 13–17), and as one who banished magic from the city (vv. 18, 19). The paragraph is wound up with a Lucan summary. The next incident (19.23–40) is related to pagan religion rather than magic.

Of the opening sub-paragraph (vv. 8–10) Haenchen (536) writes that it 'lässt naturgemäss viele Fragen unbeantwortet, die der Historiker stellen muss'. The questions are in fact not many, and they are not of great weight. How is it that the Jews did not turn against the new faith while Aquila and Priscilla taught in Ephesus (18.26)? Why did they wait until Paul had been teaching for three months? The question assumes that the Apollos episode is rightly placed in the chronology, which is by no means certain, and that after 18.19 Aquila and Priscilla immediately began to teach. We do not know how these two presented the Christian message and what sort of provocation their teaching may have caused. It is true that Paul seems to have left the synagogue at Corinth more quickly (18.6), but he probably spent most of his eighteen months in Corinth before the Jews took serious action against him (18.11,12). And how quickly do people take notice of and react to a new message? At the same rate on every occasion? There are too many unknowns here for rational comment. There are questions that a historian may feel bound to ask, but it is well to recognize that there are some that are not important and many that cannot be answered because the necessary evidence does not exist. The *three months* of 19.8 is probably a guess, or at best an approximation; and it probably never occurred to Luke to wonder how things went before Paul arrived. 'Oder eine andere Frage. Paulus sondert die Jünger ab—hat die christliche Gemeinde dort ... nicht schon vorher ihre Sonderversammlungen gehabt, bei denen sie das Herrenmahl feierte?' (Haenchen 537). Perhaps they had; but we may say with confidence that such meals as they had were church suppers which would naturally be held not in the synagogue but in private houses (cf. Rom. 16.5; 1 Cor. 16.19; Col. 4.15; Phm. 2; and see *1 Corinthians* 263, 325; *Ch., M., S.* 65f.). The school of Tyrannus no more than the synagogue would be suitable and used for such purposes; and Luke probably thought church suppers less important than Paul's preaching and teaching. The question is pointless. 'Oder noch eine Frage: hat Paulus nach einem Wirken von drei Monaten die Gemeinde (die er nicht gegründet hatte!) so souverän beherrscht, dass er ihre Trennung von der Synagogue verfügen konnte?' (Haenchen 537). Another ill-thought-out question. The separation probably received a powerful impulse from the Jewish side; and it would be foolish to underestimate Paul's power of leadership.

Haenchen's questions do nothing to destroy the historical worth of vv. 8–10, but it is equally true that this cannot be demonstrated. Luke probably had before him a reference to a long stay in Ephesus; on this ground he probably felt it safe to extend the period of work in the synagogue (beyond for example the three weeks in Thessalonica, 17.2). And he may have had good reason to know that the word of the Lord had spread pretty widely in Asia, and among both Jews and Greeks.

It was natural to represent Paul in Ephesus as the foe of magic, because of the reputation enjoyed by Ephesus and because Luke was always ready to use an opportunity of expressing one of his favourite antagonisms (see 8.9–25; 13.6–12, with the notes). The stories about Paul's successful healings (vv. 11, 12) and of the marked lack of success of the sons of Sceva were no doubt told with delight—and probably with some exaggeration—by Ephesian Christians, and listened to by Luke with equal pleasure. 19.23–40 is matter of a different kind, though acquired in the same way. 'The present passage [this includes 19.1–7] ... compresses into three vivid scenes the essence of Paul's prophetic ministry as an apostle and serves to "legitimate" him firmly in the reader's eyes as having fulfilled precisely what was predicted of him' (Johnson 344).

8. Εἰσελθὼν δὲ εἰς τὴν συναγωγήν. Cf. 18.19, where the same words are used. The repetition suggests that Luke may here be taking up again a source that he was using at the earlier point and into which he inserted material that took Paul to Palestine and back to Ephesus. There is here no reference back to a previous visit to Ephesus and the synagogue, to Apollos, or to the disciples of 19.1–7. This verse could be describing the beginning of Paul's work in Ephesus. For Jews in Ephesus see *NS* 3.22, 23, 88, 122, 123; also Trebilco, 17, 18, 24f., 167. Cf. Josephus, *Apion* 2.39.

D sy[hmg], adding ἐν δυνάμει μεγάλῃ, underline the power and effectiveness of Paul's preaching. No copyist would have omitted this had it been original. The phrase is constructed adverbially with ἐπαρρησιάζετο; cf. 9.27. This is an Acts word (7 times; once in 1 Thessalonians; once in Ephesians), used of Paul and at 18.26 of Apollos.

ἐπὶ μῆνας τρεῖς. For the use of the preposition cf. 18.20. After these three months Paul remained in Ephesus a further two years (v. 10); the total is summed up at 20.31 as three years (counted inclusively). Three months was a long time for Paul to be tolerated in a synagogue; Pesch (2.167) considers that this synagogue was one that tolerated *Sondergruppen*; they had been prepared to accommodate the disciples of John the Baptist (19.1–7). For the surprising lack of evidence of a synagogue community in Ephesus see on 18.19.

ἐπαρρησιάζετο may suggest (it hardly proves) inspired speech; διαλέγεσθαι (see 17.17) suggests reason: Paul argues and debates. πείθων belongs to the same realm of discourse. This word also is characteristic of Acts, though it is often used in the passive of those who are convinced by Christian argument and believe (e.g. 17.4). For the active cf. 13.43; 18.4. It usually has a personal object, and here one must be understood—those who frequented the synagogue, whom Paul persuaded concerning the kingdom of God, i.e., that it had been manifested in Jesus; but *kingdom of God* is a term Luke uses in Acts as a summary of the Gospel preached by the apostles and others; see e.g. 20.25. The great majority of MSS have τὰ περὶ τῆς β. τ. θ., but B D Ψ 1175 1891ᶜ *pc* are right to omit the article, which other MSS have added in order to conform with 1.3.

9. ὡς δέ τινες ἐσκληρύνοντο (D has τινὲς μὲν οὖν αὐτῶν, introducing a characteristically Lucan μὲν οὖν, but this is probably due to assimilation to other passages); as usual, Paul's preaching in the synagogue brings only limited success and stirs up trouble. ἐσκληρύνοντο is passive in form but probably intransitive in meaning; Luke is not thinking of an extraneous hardening agent. *They grew hard*; possibly (taking the verb as middle), they hardened themselves, hardened their hearts against Paul and his message; so Schneider (2.268). The word is active and transitive at e.g. Exod. 7.3; Rom. 9.18, and we should note 13.48, but Luke will be more inclined to blame the recalcitrant synagogue members than a divine decree. ἀπειθεῖν, for *unbelief*, is used at 14.2; cf. πείθων in v. 8.

Not content with disbelief they also slandered (κακολογεῖν here only in Acts) the Christianity preached by Paul so as to give it a bad name with the public. According to MM 316 the verb 'in the NT seems always to be used in the weaker sense of "speak evil of"'. *ND* 1.28f., but especially 2.88, disagrees, though the papyrus evidence quoted there is not stronger than that given by MM where the editors' translations are 'abused ... in the most unmeasured terms', 'insulted me immoderately'). *ND* shows that the word is often used in litigation. The fact is that κακολογεῖν means *to speak evil*, and only a context can show how evil evil is. Here there is no illuminating context apart from the fact that Paul felt it necessary to take decisive action. For ἡ ὁδός as a term meaning *Christianity* see 9.2. It is not clear how πλῆθος is to be taken. It may refer to (a) the Christians in the synagogue; for πλῆθος as a local community of Christians cf. e.g. 15.30; the effect on them might be to cause them to give up the faith they had accepted; (b) the synagogue community as a whole, who might in consequence expel or punish the Christians; (c) the general public of the city, who would decide not to become Christians and perhaps to persecute those who were. See Fitzmyer, *Essays* 290. The third possibility is perhaps the best. It was adopted by D (E) syᵖ syʰ**, which add τῶν ἐθνῶν. Τότε. See however Ropes (*Begs.* 3.182).

Paul's response was to separate (ἀποστάς) from the Jews and to withdraw the disciples (as usual μαθηταί are Christian disciples) from the synagogue. Cf. 18.7. Instead of teaching there he continued his work ἐν τῇ σχολῇ Τυράννου (D, Τυραννίου). For the name, not uncommon in inscriptions in Ephesus, see Hemer (120f.), who gives a reference also to a building described by the Latin-Greek word αὐδειτώριον. σχολή here can hardly mean anything other than a building, though *ND* 1.129f. think that it may mean not a place but a 'group of people to whom addresses were given during their leisure hours'. The meaning *building* is unusual and late (see *FS* Lohse, 96–110, especially 96f.). It is not clear from their contexts that Josephus, *Apion* 1.53 and Epictetus 1.29.34 (cited BA 1591) refer to places or buildings. *Building* seems to be correct in Plutarch, *De Recta Ratione Audiendi* 8 (42A), where σχολή is used with διδασκαλεῖον; not correct in *De Curiositate* 9 (579F), where the parallels are θεάματα, ἀκούσματα, διατριβαί; not correct in *De Exilio* 14 (605A), with the parallel διατριβαί. Cf. Cicero, *De Oratore* 1.22 (102), ... qui cum in schola assedissent ... For the name Tyrannus see above; he may have been a philosopher, otherwise unknown, who lectured in the class-room, or the owner of the building. The name occurs in Josephus, *Ant.* 16.314; Ephesian inscriptions are given in *ND* 4.186; 5.97. *ND* 5.92, referring to P. Wexler, *REJ* 140 (1981), 123, 124, 133, considers the possibility that σχολή may mean synagogue. This can hardly be the meaning here.

Paul taught here καθ' ἡμέραν. Roloff (283) assumes that in the synagogue the Christians could meet only on the Sabbath, so that the move will have made not only a change of venue but a multiplication of gatherings and of publicity. Roloff also thinks it must be assumed that in addition to the lectures in the lecture-room the Christians also had 'Mahlversammlungen in den Häusern' (as in 2.42–46). It could be so, but these are not in the text. διαλέγεσθαι, as in v. 8.

At the end of the verse D (614 gig sy[h]) add, ἀπὸ ὥρας έ ἕως δεκάτης, that is, from 11 a.m. to 4 p.m. (or with the greater precision provided by J. Carcopino, *La Vie Quotidienne à Rome à l'Apogée de l'Empire* (1939), 178f. from 11.15 to 2.58 in the winter and from 10.44 to 5.2 in the summer—the figures will of course have varied daily so that the calculations are worth little). It is probably a correct observation that these were the siesta hours when the lecture-room would not normally be in use. In quintam [horam] varios extendit labores; Sexta quies lassis (Martial 4.8.3f.).

10. τοῦτο δὲ ἐγένετο ἐπὶ ἔτη δύο. Cf. Plato, *Phaedo* 84bc, σιγὴ οὖν ἐγένετο ... ἐπὶ πολὺν χρόνον. The imperfect rather than the aorist might have been expected (this went on for two years); the effect of the aorist is to treat Paul's activity as a single unit; his ministry *lasted for two years*. Plato's ἐγένετο is similar: Silence fell and lasted ... For ἐπί see v. 8. The two years must be added to the three months already mentioned (v. 8); taken together they justify the τριετία of 20.31. The dates are probably Autumn 52 to Spring 55; see Introduction, pp. lvi–lxi and *Romans* 4f.

The result (ὥστε) was that all who lived in Asia heard the word of the Lord, spreading outward from the chief city of the province. For *Asia* see 16.6; there is no reason to think that anything less than the whole province is intended. The verse does not assert that Paul personally proclaimed the word even in all the major cities of the province (for his own inclusive and representative way of referring to the extent of his missionary activity see Rom. 15.19). According to Col. 1.7; 2.1 Paul had not himself evangelized Colossae; Epaphras had represented him there. Revelation 2 and 3 are sufficient to show that leading cities in Asia had been evangelized at a fairly early date; at the time of writing some at least of the seven churches addressed were in a state of decline. Luke simply affirms widespread evangelistic activity, and the affirmation could be based simply on the fact that Asia as he knew it was one of the most developed Christian mission fields. He takes the opportunity of adding that the Christian groups were mixed, comprising both Jews and Greeks. The seven letters of Revelation probably reflect a later stage when there was trouble between Jews and Gentiles; see Rev. 2.9; 3.9. Of Paul's stay in Ephesus Stählin (255) rightly notes, 'Es war für Paulus nicht nur eine Zeit des Wirkens, sondern auch des Leidens (vgl 20.19; 2 Kor 1.8–11; 1 Kor 15.32).'

The latter part of the verse is given by D* (e sy^p) as follows: ἕως πάντες οἱ κατοικοῦντες τὴν Ἀσίαν ἤκουσαν τοὺς λόγους τοῦ κυρίου, Ἰουδαῖοι καὶ Ἕλληνες. Most of this is simply a moderately free paraphrase which does not change the meaning, but the plural τοὺς λόγους is unusual. It is probably a slip (corrected in the MS itself). Zahn thought the reading original (and indeed it is unusual enough to have been assimilated, if it was original, to the more usual 'word of the Lord'), and inferred from it—correctly from a theological if not from a textual point of view—that the Lord himself spoke in the words of the preacher.

11. The preaching of the word of the Lord (v. 10) was accompanied, as often in Acts (cf. e.g. 4.29f.), by miracles (here δυνάμεις; the words σημεῖον and τέρας are not used in this context, or anywhere after 15.12). God himself performed the mighty works, though διὰ τῶν χειρῶν Π.; this is a Semitism, due not to translation but to Luke's imitation of biblical (i.e. LXX) language. Schille (379) thinks that there may be a magical reference here; in view of what is about to be said about Ephesian magic (vv. 13–19) this seems highly improbable. The mighty works were οὐ τὰς τυχούσας, not any works that might happen to anyone at any time, but special ones, uncommon miracles; cf. a second-century AD inscription from Ephesus, οὐχ ὡς ἔτυχεν, in no ordinary manner (BMI 4.481*.340). Wettstein 2.580f. gives many examples of the use of the participle; e.g. Artemidorus 2.13, κινδύνους οὐ τοὺς τυχόντας; Porphyry, *De Abstinentia* 1.7.1; Herodian 2.3.7. It may have been a late development. Bruce (1.357) notes that it is common in Vettius Valens.

'V.11f. zeichnen das Bild des Paulus so, wie es nach den Forderungen des urchristlichen Pneumatikertums hätte aussehen müssen' (Haenchen 540); over against this, 'Lk setzt natürlich voraus, dass es wirklicher Glaube war, der so handelte, nicht Glaube an den Wundertäter, sondern an seinen Gott' (Bauernfeind 230). Weiser (529) rightly emphasizes that it is *God* who works, but through man. See further on the next verse.

12. Physical contact between the healer and the sick person is a common feature of miracle stories; the wonder is heightened here in that the contact is indirect.

σουδάριον translates the Latin *sudarium*, σιμικίνθιον, *semicinctium*. The precise meaning is not known with certainty; no better suggestion is available than the definition of Ammonius (*Fragmenta in Acta Apostolorum*, ad 19.12; MPG 85, 1576 = Cramer 3.316f.), ἀμφότερα νομίζω λινοειδῆ εἶναι πλὴν τὰ μὲν σουδάρια ἐπὶ τῆς κεφαλῆς ἐπιβάλλεται, τὰ δὲ σιμικίνθια ἐν ταῖς χερσὶν κατέχουσιν, οἱ μὴ δυνάμενοι ὀράρια [= Latin *oraria*, (pocket) handkerchief] φορέσαι. Thus probably both were sweat-rags, σουδάρια worn on the head to prevent the sweat from running into the eyes, σιμικίνθια carried in the hand for general mopping up. An alternative possibility for σιμικίνθιον is *apron*. In each case the important point would be contact (this is against *belt*—T. J. Leary, *JTS* 41 (1990), 527–9) with Paul's skin. χρώς is not common in prose, but is used in the LXX.

The effect of these objects, presumably applied to the sufferers, was that their diseases left them (for ἀπαλλάσσεσθαι cf. Pseudo-Plato, *Eryxias* 401c, εἰ αἱ νόσοι ἀπαλλαγείησαν ἐκ τῶν σωμάτων), and evil spirits went out from those whom they had possessed. It is customary to point out the parallel with the effect of Peter's shadow (5.15f.). The parallel is valid, but it is doubtful whether Luke went out of his way to draw up a precise but varied balance between Peter and Paul. He was probably more concerned to claim that Paul could beat the Ephesian magicians at their own game. It was 'ein typisches Beispiel von Mana-Glauben' (Stählin 255).

Cf. *Acta Johannis* 62 (L.-B. 2.1.181): Μετὰ δὲ ταῦτα γινόμεθα εἰς τὴν Ἔφεσον ... Τῶν ποδῶν αὐτοῦ ἁπτόμενοι, καὶ τὰς χεῖρας αὐτοῦ εἰς τὰ ἴδια πρόσωπα τιθέντες ἐφίλουν αὐτάς, ὡς ὅτι κἂν ἥψαντο τῶν ἐκείνου ἐνδυμάτων.

13. Paul's success as healer and exorcist prompted imitation, and the use by others of the means he had so successfully employed. It is not stated in vv. 11, 12 but implied by v. 13 that the name of Jesus had been invoked when the miracles were performed.

ἐπιχειρεῖν is used by Luke only in the NT (Lk. 1.1; Acts 9.29; 19.13). περιέρχεσθαι (cf. 28.13, si v.l.; Heb. 11.37) means *to go around*, but, as 1 Tim. 5.13 may confirm, could (but does not necessarily) suggest the migration of wandering charlatans. Xenophon, *Cyropaedia* 8.2.16 suggests the behaviour of a wandering beggar; Luke, who had no high opinion of wandering magicians, no doubt thought of itinerant exorcists in this, or a less favourable way. See also Betz (142), 'die wandernden Bettelpriester der Syrischen Göttin'. Cf. Lucian, *Asinus* 37, τὴν χώραν περιῄειμεν. It is here only that Luke uses the word ἐξορκιστής, but he probably thinks of the persons in question as belonging to the same class as Simon (8.9–11) and Elymas (13.6–8). *ND* 2.11 has interesting evidence of the non-inclusion of exorcists in a recognized state health service.

For Jewish exorcists see StrB (4.534f.); *NS* 3.342–79; Hemer (121). Their existence is presupposed in Mt. 12.27 = Lk. 11.19. Josephus, *Ant.* 8.45–49 is good proof of the fact that Solomon's legendary power as an exorcist was believed to have been transmitted, through incantations and formulas, to first-century exorcists. For the use outside orthodox Christian circles of the name of Jesus see Mk 9.38–41. Rabbinic disapproval of the practice (StrB 1.468) shows that it existed. For the use in Acts of ὄνομα see on 3.6; here only (apart from Eph. 1.21; 2 Tim. 2.19, where the usage is different) do we have ὀνομάζειν τὸ ὄμομα—a pointer to the fact that when Luke speaks of the proper use of the name by authentic Christians he is thinking of something different from the incantation of a formula. The story that follows Luke would regard as a clear proof of his own understanding of *the name*: the name itself has anything but the desired effect (so rightly Conzelmann 111). Again, Christians do not, in the NT, use the verb (ἐξ)ορκίζειν. The verb is found in the sense that it has here in magical papyri (LS 1251; BA 1178; MM 457), sometimes, as here (ὁρκίζω ὑμᾶς τὸν Ἰησοῦν), with a double accusative, sometimes with other constructions. The relation of the NT narratives to magic is difficult to assess (according to Lüdemann the story of vv. 13–16 is 'schon aus formgeschichtlichen Gründen unhistorisch', but he does not explain the judgement), but a narrative such as the present suggests that Luke was aware of a resemblance between Christian miracle-working and contemporary magic but at the same time wished to make a fundamental distinction. For the borrowing of names cf. *PGM* 4.3019f. (in Deissmann, *LAE* 252): ὁρκίζω σε κατὰ τοῦ θεοῦ τῶν Ἑβραίων Ἰησοῦ; Origen, *C. Celsum* 1.6; 6.40.

ὁρκίζομεν (𝔐) and ἐξορκίζομεν (36 453 614 945 1739 1891 *pc*) are assimilations to the preceding plurals and to the compound noun ἐξορκιστής.

'No rule will account for' the use of the article with names here and in v. 15 (M. 3.166). ὃν Παῦλος κηρύσσει is simply a means of identification; for the content of Paul's preaching cf. 17.18.

14. The general statement of v. 13 is supported by a particular example. ἦσαν ... ποιοῦντες should not be taken as a periphrastic tense; ποιοῦντες is predicative (there were seven sons ... doing this;

cf. 21.23; Lk. 2.8; and see BDR § 353.2b, though this example is not quoted there). That is, they were saying to demons, ὁρκίζω ὑμᾶς, κτλ. The construction is changed by E Ψ 𝔐, which add οἱ before τοῦτο.

These were the sons of one *Sceva, a Jew, a high priest*. On the name see Hemer (234); add Horace, *Epistle* 1.17.1, Quamvis, Scaeva ... There is no Sceva in the list of Jewish High Priests otherwise known (see Jeremias, *Jerusalem* 377f.). What else could ἀρχιερεύς mean? The word is used in the plural in the gospels and Acts (e.g. 4.1 (v.1. ἱερεῖς, 23) to denote, it seems, members of the Jewish priestly aristocracy, or of the court that determined issues relating to the priests and the Temple (Jeremias, *Jerusalem* 178). On this question see B. A. Mastin, *JTS* 27 (1976), 405–12. Rejecting the views of Haenchen (Luke thought that Sceva really had been high priest—this had the effect of magnifying Paul), Burkitt (*Begs.* 4.241, 'Scaeva, ''a rascally Levantine (real race very uncertain)'', claimed the title ''as an advertisement''''), and B. E. Taylor (Sceva was a renegade Jew who held the office of ἀρχιερεύς in the imperial cult) Mastin refers to Apuleius, *Metamorphoses* 2.28–30, in which Zatchlas (Zachlas), an Egyptian, raises a dead man to life. Zatchlas is described twice as *propheta*, once as *propheta primarius*, once addressed as *sacerdos*. In a similar way, the description of the father of the seven exorcists as a priest, whose sons will have been priests too, is consistent with their work as exorcists, and helps 'to show how true religion triumphed' (409). Cf. K. Berger (*NTS* 20 (1973), 25, n. 95). For pagan ἀρχιερεῖς in Asia see Mommsen (*Provinces*, 1.347f.); cf. the Asiarchs of 19.31. A better parallel however than Mastin's is to be found in Juvenal, *Satire* 6.544, where the fortune-telling Jewess is described as *magna sacerdos*. Luke should have known, and indeed did know, a great deal better than Juvenal what a priest, or chief priest, was in Judaism; that he uses the word here probably means that he found it in the tradition, written or oral, that he was using. The story may not have been connected with Paul (Weiser 524, and others).

For τινός, τινές is read by P⁷⁴ ℵ A Ψ 𝔐 lat syʰ, rightly accordingly to Ropes (*Begs.* 3.182); it is the sons, not their father, who are being introduced. According to this view, seven exorcists were involved; in v. 16 they are collectively referred to in the word ἀμφοτέρων. See on that verse. The suggestion that the number came into the text as a gloss, Σκευᾶ = שבע = ἑπτά, seems very improbable (M. 1.246). For *seven* gig alone has *duo*.

The text appears in a different form in (P³⁸) D w syʰᵐᵍ, as follows: ἐν οἷς καὶ υἱοὶ (+ ἑπτά syʰᵐᵍ) Σκευᾶ (+ Ἰουδαίου) τινος ἱερέως ἠθέλησαν τὸ αὐτὸ ποιῆσαι. ἔθος εἶχαν τοὺς τοιούτους ἐξορκίζειν· καὶ εἰσελθόντες πρὸς τὸν δαιμονιζόμενον ἤρξαντο ἐπικαλεῖσθαι τὸ ὄνομα λέγοντες παραγγέλλομέν σοι ἐν Ἰησοῦ ὃν Παῦλος κηρύσσει ἐξελθεῖν. The basic D form of this reading omits the two problem words, *seven* and *Jew*; in all forms there is *priest*, not *high priest*. See further Clark (370–3); he thinks *priest* original and suggests that the number *seven* may have arisen through a misunderstood marginal ζ (= ζήτει), a critical sign, or a mark of interrogation.

It is interesting to compare Testament of Levi 18.12: the sons of the true high priest will have authority to trample on τὰ πονηρὰ πνεύματα.

15. The variant in D (τότε ἀπεκρίθη ... καὶ εἶπεν) seems to be an arbitrary piece of rewriting; it resembles the Syriac but need not be ascribed either to underlying Aramaic or to a reaction from a Syriac version.

τὸ πνεῦμα τὸ πονηρόν is introduced abruptly. Evil spirits (plural) were mentioned in v. 13; we must suppose that Luke has now moved on to a particular example of the work of the sons of Scaeva (themselves already invoked as a special example of the Jewish exorcists of v. 13), who entered a house (v. 16; cf. v. 14 D) and attempted to exorcise a single spirit from a possessed man. The spirit is not to be so easily overpowered and driven out.

The evidence for the inclusion of μέν (P[41] א[c] B E Ψ 614 2495 *pc*) and the evidence for its omission (P[38] P[74] א* A D 𝔐 latt sa) are evenly balanced. On the whole there is a stronger case for omission. τὸν μὲν Ἰησοῦν ... ὑμεῖς δέ ... makes a pleasing Greek sentence, which copyists would be more likely to create than to destroy. This is confirmed by the fact that the first hand of א did not include the word, whereas a corrector did.

With regard to τὸν Ἰησοῦν ... τὸν Παῦλον there seems to be no explanation of the use of the article; see the reference on v. 13 to M. 3.166. It is probably simply a Hellenistic development; Turner points out that the article is always used with proper names in Modern Greek. If further meaning is sought in the articles the point may be 'The great Jesus ... the great Paul ... but who *in comparison* are you?' Cf. Mk 1.34, the demons ᾔδεισαν αὐτόν (cf. also Acts 16.17). In the present verse the verb is γινώσκειν, but no difference in meaning is to be sought; this is probably true also with regard to ἐπίσταμαι. According to Weiser (524), *for Luke* ἐπιστᾶσθαι always has as object 'historische Faktoren', and it is possible that Luke intends, I recognize Jesus as the one with authority, and I know who Paul is, namely that he, unlike the sons of Sceva, is entitled to use Jesus' name; but it is more probable that Luke is introducing verbal variation.

ὑμεῖς δὲ τίνες ἐστέ; That is, What right have you to invoke the name of Jesus? The point is important for Luke's understanding of *the name* (see on v. 13; cf. Schneider 2.266). ὑμεῖς is emphatic, 'thrown forward contemptuously' (Page 206). Cf. Isaeus, *De Heredi-tate Cironis* 24, σὺ δὲ τίς εἶ; σοὶ δὲ τί προσήκει θάπτειν; οὐ γιγνώσκω σε.

16. In v. 15 the subject of the verb was the evil spirit; here it is the man possessed by the spirit, which is apparently able to speak but can act only through its host. ἐφαλόμενος (aorist participle, P⁷⁴ ℵ* A B 1175 *pc*) is more suitable to the narrative than the present participle (ἐφαλλόμενος, P⁴¹ ℵᶜ E Ψ 𝔐; ἐναλλόμενος, D); this could mean however that the present was original and was improved by copyists. The changed order (ἐπ' (or εἰς) αὐτοὺς ὁ ἄνθρωπος), which brings the antecedent nearer to the relative pronoun, is secondary. The spirit, taking action through the man it controls, suits the deed to the word and the would-be exorcists are discomfited. κατακυριεύσας (against the simple verb, κυριεύσας, ℵᶜ D *pc*) may be accepted, and the καί that precedes it in ℵ* (Ψ) 104 323 453 1241 *al* rejected as introduced by copyists in a wooden attempt to avoid asyndeton between the participles ἐφαλ. and κατακ. 'Die Partizipia folgen sich asyndetisch (ohne καί bzw τε) wenn sie nicht den gleichen Wert im Satzgefüge haben' (BDR § 421). κατακ. is indeed virtually unneces-sary with ἴσχυσεν.

ἀμφοτέρων would normally mean *both*, which is inconsistent with ἑπτά in v. 14. For a variety of conjectures and variant readings see Metzger (471f.). There is an interesting but inconclusive discussion in M. 1.80. There are a few somewhat later papyrus examples of the use of ἀμφότεροι in the sense of *all* (MM 28; BA 93) and it is probably best to suppose that Luke here gives us the earliest known occurrence. See *Begs.* 4.241f., and cf. 23.8. The omission by E and the substitution of αὐτῶν by (Ψ) 𝔐 are certainly secondary.

The possessed man, provoked by the demon, tore the clothes off the would-be exorcists (γυμνούς) and beat them (τετραυματισμένους) so that they fled ἐκ τοῦ οἴκου ἐκείνου. This should refer back to a previously mentioned house; there is none. Ephraim (Ropes, *Begs.* 3.184) gives a fuller picture: et stridit dentibus daemonium ad rectam et sinistram et expulit eos a domo. Roloff (285) concludes from the unexplained reference to a house that Luke is abbreviating tradition. But the whole of vv. 14–16 creates a somewhat unsatisfactory impression, which probably accounts for the rewriting in D. One is inclined to suppose that a fragmentary and unsatisfactory traditional narrative has been incor-porated here; its unsatisfactory state might be held to speak well for Luke's faithfulness to tradition. But he could have tidied it up without unfaithfulness, and it is hard to know why he did not. The alternative possibility, that he himself caused the untidiness by incorporating into his story of Paul an incident that did not belong to it, has much to be said for it. It is surprising that Paul does not in the end drive the spirit out. But the spirit had shown that it was on Paul's side.

We may note once more that 'Die Nennung des Namens Jesu wirkt nicht automatisch' (Weiser 532; cf. Conzelmann 111).

17. τοῦτο δὲ ἐγένετο γνωστόν: cf. 9.42, a Lucan phrase, but not an unnatural one. Ἰουδαίοις τε καὶ Ἕλλησιν also is by way of becoming a formula; cf. 19.10. For Jews in Ephesus see on v. 8, and 18.19. ἐπέπεσεν φόβος ἐπί: cf. 2.42; 5.5, 11.

ἐμεγαλύνετο (cf. 5.13; 10.46; Wilcox 66 for the Septuagintalism) τὸ ὄνομα τοῦ κυρίου Ἰησοῦ. The negative effect of the name as it reacts on those who use it improperly is as impressive as its positive effect. For the significance of *the name* in Acts see on 3.6. The mere pronouncing of the name was not effective; it is a means of access to the person whose name it is; hence in the present verse it is Jesus who is magnified (glorified). The reference to his name is a way of saying this.

Schneider (2.267) sees in vv. 17–20 Paul confronted by syncretism; he refers to G. Klein, *Das Synkretismus* (1967), 59.

18. πεπιστευκότων: D Ψ 614 2495 *pc* have πιστευόντων, E has πιστευσάντων; the perfect, as here, occurs at 15.5; 18.27; 21.20, 25. In a sentence determined by a verb in a past tense (ἤρχοντο, imperfect, describing a sequence of events, many would come, one after another) it will have a pluperfect sense: *those who had believed* (and of course continued to believe; that is, those who had become believers).

The general sense of the next words is clear, but not their precise construction and meaning. (1) Is πράξεις governed only by ἀναγγέλλοντες or by ἐξομολογούμενοι also? Is ἐξομ. used absolutely, without object? (2) Does πράξεις mean actions in general, or does it have its specialized meaning of (magical) *spells*? For this meaning see MM 533; BA 1399 (e.g. *PGM* 4. 1227, πρᾶξις γενναία ἐκβάλλουσα δαίμονας). ἐξομολογεῖσθαι usually has a direct object (e.g. Mk 1.5) but it seems best here to separate it from ἀναγγέλλειν, which otherwise would come near to duplicating it, and take the meaning to be that they confessed (their sins, in general) and disclosed their magical spells (which otherwise would have been kept secret in the books burned in v. 19). For this use of ἐξομολογεῖσθαι cf. 2 Clement 8.3 (οὐκέτι δυνάμεθα ἐκεῖ ἐξομολογήσασθαι ἢ μετανοεῖν ἔτι). The special sense of πράξεις is supported by the use of πράσσειν in v. 19.

19. ἱκανοί, one of Luke's favourite words of quantity, is about as imprecise as 'a good many'. Like πράξεις (v. 18), περίεργα is a semi-technical term for magical practices. The meaning originates with 'things better left alone, not meddled with'; cf. Plato, *Apology*

19b, Σωκράτης ἀδικεῖ καὶ περιεργάζεται ζητῶν τά τε ὑπὸ γῆς καὶ τὰ ἐπουράνια. So too Ecclesiasticus 3.23 (Page 206). Cf. Xenophon, *Memorabilia* 1.3.1. For περίεργα itself see MM 505; BA 1303. πράσσειν derives meaning from its object, but the use (v. 18) of πρᾶξις gives it added force and direction.

τὰς βίβλους, the books in which the spells were written down and thus kept ready for use. They would no doubt resemble the papyri edited and published by K. Preisendanz in *Papyri Graecae Magicae* (1928, 1931). There is an example in *Background* 34–7. See also Betz (154, n. 4, quoting Lucian, *Philopseudes* 12, … ἐπειπὼν ἱερατικά τινα ἐκ βίβλου παλαιᾶς ὀνόματα ἑπτά …). Ephesus was noted for such products, and the term Ἐφέσια γράμματα was current. Thus Plutarch, *Symposium* 7.5.4 (706D), ὥσπερ γὰρ οἱ Μάγοι τοὺς δαιμονιζομένους κελεύουσι τὰ Ἐφέσια γράμματα πρὸς αὐτοὺς καταλέγειν καὶ ὀνομάζειν … ; Clement of Alexandria, *Stromata* 5.8.45.2, τὰ Ἐφέσια καλούμενα γράμματα ἐν πολλοῖς δὴ πολυθρύλητα ὄντα. Magic was officially discouraged (see probably Tabula VIII, Qui malum carmen incantassit …) but almost universally believed in. Only sceptics such as Lucian (not Christians, who disapproved but did not disbelieve) denied its power. For the burning of the books cf. Suetonius, *Octavian* 31, … quicquid fatidicorum librorum Graeci Latinique generis, nullis vel parum idoneis auctoribus, vulgo ferebatur, supra duo millia contracta undique cremavit. But here the owners were not consulted and Augustus's motive was different. Cf. Livy 40.29, Libri in comitio, igne a victimariis facto, in conspectu populi cremati sunt; Diogenes Laertius 9.52; Lucian, *Alexander* 47.

συνεψήφισαν: no subject is expressed, unless we are to think of the owners of the books, who brought them. It may be better to take a subject out of πάντων. The public who witnessed the conflagration were so impressed that they computed the value of the books they saw on the bonfire—no doubt in a rough and ready way. Wilcox (127), comparing the use of the third person plural active instead of a passive and the frequency of this construction in Hebrew and Aramaic, thinks of a Semitism, but in the present context this is most unlikely. An impersonal plural—'they did this or that'—occurs from time to time in many languages.

In the computation of the value of the books that were destroyed no unit of currency is expressed. For the ellipse see M. 3.17, where Turner rightly notes that δραχμῶν must be supplied, and adds that with this ἀργυρίων (rather than ἀργυρίου) would be expected—50,000 silver (pieces). For the omission of the monetary unit cf. Plutarch, *Galba* 17 (πέντε καὶ εἴκοσι μυριάδας ἀργυρίου); Josephus, *Ant.* 17.189 (ἀργυρίου ἐπισήμου μυριάδας πεντήκοντα). Was it customary to use the singular ἀργυρίου when no unit was specified? It might have seemed more natural to give an estimate of the number of books burned (as Suetonius does). That Luke puts a price on them may reflect his strong dislike of the money-making side of magic and his clear rejection of it from the Christian side; cf. his treatment of Simon Magus (8.4–25). The whole episode, with the kind of judgement and attitude it reflects, is important. Luke has a strong dislike of magic and of anything related to it. A miracle-working magus is the last sort of model he would use for an apostle. Cf. Pseudo-Phocylides 149: Make no potions, keep away from magical books.

20. A characteristic concluding summary. For ὁ λόγος ηὔξανεν cf. 6.7 (ὁ λ. τ. θεοῦ) and 12.24. ἰσχύειν is not used elsewhere in this sense, but it is a Lucan word (Lk., 8 times; Acts, 6 times, including 19.16, above; rest of the NT, 14 times). κατὰ κράτος is not used elsewhere in the NT. It may mean *with all one's might* (e.g. Plato, *Laws* 692d), or *by force*, *with violence*, usually in military contexts (e.g. Thucydides, 8.100.5). The latter, taken metaphorically, is the sense here, though the metaphor is living in view of the discomfiture of the sons of Scaeva and the burning of the magical books. An alternative possibility is to take κράτος with the following words, τοῦ κυρίου, 'by the power of the Lord the word grew ...'. This cannot be ruled out but it does not seem probable; one would expect κράτος to have the article.

If this possibility is rejected we have the unusual word order τοῦ κυρίου ὁ λόγος (this is reversed in P⁷⁴ ℵᶜ (E Ψ) 𝔐 lat syʰ) Cf. 4.33, and see Moule (*IB* 169). The text of D* is also strange: ἐνίσχυσεν καὶ ἡ πίστις τοῦ θεοῦ ηὔξανε καὶ ἐπλήθυνε (ἐπληθύνετο, D²). The first verb lacks a subject. It would be easy to conjecture an original from which both forms of the text might have diverged, but impossible to establish it with any certainty. The general sense of the verse is not in doubt.

Luke here brings one incident to a close and is about to embark on a fresh piece of tradition unconnected with the last, except so far as 19.26 refers to the great success of the Christian mission described in 19.11–20.

49. RIOT AT EPHESUS 19.21–40

(21) When these events were done, Paul[1] formed the intention to pass through Macedonia and Achaea and travel to Jerusalem. He said, 'After I have been there I must see Rome too.' (22) He sent[2] into Macedonia two of his assistants, Timothy and Erastus, and himself extended his stay in Asia.

(23) At that time there arose no small disturbance concerning the Way. (24) One Demetrius by name, a silver-smith,[3] by making silver shrines of Artemis[4] provided the craftsmen with[5] no small amount of business. (25) He gathered them and[6] the workmen[7] engaged in this business together, and said, 'Men, you know that our prosperity arises out of this business; (26) and you see and hear that not only in Ephesus but in almost all Asia this fellow Paul[8] has persuaded and led astray a large crowd of people, saying that these that are made with hands are not gods. (27) Not only does this mean for us a risk that this line of business may come into disrepute but also that the temple of the great goddess Artemis[9] may be reckoned as nothing, and she whom all Asia and the inhabited world worship will be cast down from her greatness.'

(28) They listened to this and were filled with rage, and shouted, 'Great is Artemis[9] of the Ephesians.' (29) The city was filled with confusion; they seized Gaius and Aristarchus, Macedonians and travelling companions of Paul's, and rushed with one accord into the theatre. (30) Paul wished to[10] go [into the theatre] to the people, but the disciples would not permit him to do so. (31) And some of the[11] Asiarchs, who were well disposed to him, sent and begged him not to[12] go into the theatre. (32) Some shouted one thing, others another; for the assembly was confused, and the majority did not know why they had come together. (33) Some of the crowd[13] instructed Alexander, and the Jews put him forward. Alexander made a gesture with his hand[14] and wished to make a defence to the people, (34) but when they recognized that he was a Jew there arose one cry from all, who for about two hours shouted, 'Great is Artemis[9] of the Ephesians.'

[1]RSV, resolved in the Spirit.
[2]NJB, sent ahead of him.
[3]RSV, who made; NEB, who made shrines of Diana.
[4]NJB, Diana.
[5]NEB, a great deal of employment.
[6]NJB, others.
[7]RSV, of like occupation; NEB, in allied trades.
[8]NEB, with his propaganda has perverted.
[9]NEB; NJB, Diana.
[10]RSV, to go among the crowd; NEB, to appear before the assembly; NJB, to make an appeal to the people.
[11]NEB, dignitaries of the province.
[12]RSV, to venture; NEB, to take the risk of going.
[13]RSV, prompted; NEB, explained the trouble to; NJB, prevailed upon.
[14]NJB, with the intention of explaining things.

(35) The town clerk stilled the crowd and said, 'Men of Ephesus, what man is there who does not know that the city of the Ephesians is temple warden of the great Artemis[9] and of[15] the stone that fell from heaven? (36) Since these matters are not open to contradiction you must remain quiet and do nothing rash. (37) For you have brought these men [here][16] who are neither guilty of temple profanation nor blasphemers of our goddess. (38) So if Demetrius and the craftsmen associated with him have a suit against anyone, courts are held and there are proconsuls: let them accuse one another. (39) And if you[17] seek anything more than that it will be dealt with in the lawful assembly. (40) For as for this day, we run the risk of being accused of riot, there being no cause for it. We shall not be able to give a reason for this meeting.'[18] With these words he dismissed the assembly.

Bibliography

A. Bammer, *Die Architektur des jüngeren Artemisiums von Ephesos*, Wiesbaden 1972.

S. M. Baugh, *NTS* 36 (1990), 290–4.

W. H. Buckler, *FS* W. M. Ramsay, 27–50.

C. Burchard, *ZNW* 61 (1970), 167f.

H. J. Cadbury, *JBL* 50 (1931), 42–58.

E. Delebecque, *RScPhTh* 66 (1982), 225–32.

G. S. Duncan, *NTS* 3 (1957), 211–18.

E. Fascher, *FS* Bultmann (1954), 247f.

J. A. Fitzmyer, as in (48).

E. L. Hicks, *Expositor* 1 (1890), 401ff.

G. H. R. Horsley, as in (46).

L. J. Kreitzer, *JSNT* 30 (1987), 59–70.

P. Lampe, as in (48).

G. M. Lee, *Bib* 51 (1970), 237.

B. A. Mastin, *JTS* 27 (1976), 405–12.

F. Miltner, as in (48).

C. F. D. Moule, *ExpT* 65 (1945), 221.

R. Oster, *JAC* 19 (1976), 24–44.

R. Oster, *HThR* 77 (1984), 233–7.

F. Sokolowski, *HThR* 58 (1965), 427–31.

R. F. Stoops, *JBL* 108 (1989), 73–91.

W. A. Strange, *JTS* 38 (1987), 97–106.

[15]NJB, her statue.
[16]Greek; RSV, omit.
[17]NJB, want to ask any more questions.
[18]RSV, there being no cause that we can give to justify this commotion; NEB, if the issue is raised, we shall be unable to give any explanation of this uproar; NJB, we can give no justification for this gathering.

Commentary

This paragraph falls into two parts. The second, vv. 23–40, must be based upon information derived by Luke from Ephesus, either on a visit to the city or by inquiry, oral or possibly written, from Ephesian residents. It is full of material that presupposes accurate, or at least reasonably accurate, knowledge of Ephesus. Not only is the great temple of Artemis known—this would prove nothing, since most people in the ancient world had heard of it; there are details about the work and trade of the silversmiths (of whom one is named), appropriate references (the adjective μεγάλη) to Artemis, mention of the Asiarchs, and a part for the town's γραμματεύς. For details see the notes below. Paul's fellow travellers, Gaius and Aristarchus, are involved (and could possibly have provided information). It is most improbable that Luke's account (a page and a half of NA[26]) is complete or that it is correct in all its details, but the objections to its historicity brought by Haenchen (553f.) are superficial and unconvincing. He speaks first of Demetrius, who, in Luke's narrative, appears at first to be in command of the situation. 'Aber dann kommt das Unbegreifliche: er lässt nicht mehr von sich hören. Wie kann ein Mann, der als ein so gut Organisator dargestellt wird, sich gerade dann in Schweigen hüllen, wenn er—vor einem günstigen Publikum—mit einem konkreten Vorschlag herauskommen müsste?' We do not in fact hear a great deal about Demetrius' organizing ability, and why should we hear more? He has raised a mob that threatens to tear Paul in pieces, and secures his immediate (20.1) departure from the city. Nothing *unbegreiflich* here. Again: the Asiarchs. It is hard to see why Paul should not have had friends (Luke does not say converts) among them. 'Diese Asiarchen wohnen doch nicht alle beisammen. Reagieren sie also alle in gleicher Weise? Oder halten sie gerade eine Sitzung ab?' Luke does not say that all the Asiarchs reacted in the same way; he speaks of τινὲς τῶν Ἀσιαρχῶν. And some (many? a few?) of them would hardly need to call a meeting. Finally (Haenchen says *endlich* though he has in fact another point to make) there is the town clerk, who is said to dismiss the complaints too easily, and incredibly frightens the crowd with a threat of the charge of στάσις. But a charge of στάσις could have been a very serious matter for the city; see on v. 40. We cannot tell how far the town clerk's tongue may have been in his cheek when he declared, 'Die Christen lästern die Göttin nicht,' and there was no need for him to add 'sie leugnen nur ihre Gottheit' (554). If 'das hat der Ratschreiber ebenso wie seine Hörer vergessen', one must add that the town clerk would in these circumstances regard it as his business to forget and to cause the crowd to forget. It is of course true that Paul could hardly have been satisfied with what is said in v. 37, but the town clerk was not speaking in order to satisfy Paul but to quell a riot; he may or may not have been sincere in what he (in Luke's narrative) says, but a certain economy of truth has often been practised in a good cause.

In Haenchen's opinion an even greater difficulty arises out of a comparison with 2 Cor. 1.8ff. According to these verses Paul in Asia experienced so severe a θλῖψις, 'dass er den Tod für unausweichlich hielt ... Von diesem Ereignis schweigt Lukas—warum?' Because, Haenchen answers, Paul was obliged to flee for his life from Ephesus. Luke is silent? To have a theatre full of people thirsting for one's blood might well have seemed life-threatening. Moreover, though 2 Cor. 1.8–11 is an obscure passage at least a strong case can be made for seeing in it a reference to illness (see *2 Corinthians* 63f.). It is of course true that the town clerk's speech makes a conclusion that will have pleased Luke more than a description of a hurried flight (and Paul wastes no time in 20.1). The speech forms part of the picture of favourable treatment by unbiased authorities that Luke intends to present. His motivation is undoubtedly visible in the story of the riot—'In dem allen tritt deutlich die apologetische Tendenz als die beherrschende Intention dieser lukanischen Erzäh-lung ans Licht' (Schmithals 181). But it is not a story riddled with improbabilities, and 1 Cor. 15.32 and 2 Cor. 1.8 between them, though they are anything but clear, show that Paul's ministry in Ephesus was a disturbed one.

The first, and much shorter, part of the paragraph (vv. 21, 22) is of a different kind. Paul determines to make a roundabout journey to Jerusalem, travelling by way of Macedonia and Achaea; after visiting Jerusalem he will go to Rome. Two of his assistants, Timothy and Erastus, are sent ahead into Macedonia, whether by land or sea is not stated. Paul is to follow them into Macedonia, and continue into Greece (20.1, 2). For the rest of this journey see 20.3—21.15. In the whole of it a number of place names occur but there are only two incidents, the church meeting in Troas (20.7–12) and the address to the Ephesian elders in Miletus (20.17–38). If any part of Acts may be described as an Itinerary it is this; it is easy to see how the two events, which are best explained as independent Pauline stories collected by Luke, together with the account of the riot, have been inserted into it. That two assistants should have been sent ahead of the main party is quite understandable, especially since (though Luke makes no mention of the matter) this journey to Jerusalem was primarily if not exclusively for the purpose of picking up the sums collected in the various churches for the relief of poverty in Jerusalem and conveying them to their destination. The two assis-tants would tell the members of the churches to complete their preparations: Paul would soon be there. The reader will recall that assistants were sent to Corinth for precisely this purpose; see 2 Corinthians 8. The difficulty arises that Paul mentions three

messengers, of whom the only one named is Titus. Timothy was sent
to Corinth (1 Cor. 4.17; 16.10f.); this however appears to have been
at an earlier date, and no mention is made of a companion. There is
much to be said for the view that v. 22 refers, in mistaken terms, to
the mission of 2 Corinthians 8. Titus is not mentioned in Acts (see *FS
Black* (1969), 2). It may be that Luke in omitting almost all reference
to the collection found it expedient to omit Titus too.

21. Here only in Acts is πληροῦσθαι used of events; cf. Lk. 1.1,
πεπληροφορημένων πραγμάτων. ταῦτα almost certainly means
'these events, just described'; it could refer to ἔτη in 19.10 (*Begs.*
4.244), but this noun is too remote to form a likely antecedent. For
ὡς δὲ ἐπληρώθη ταῦτα, D has τότε. For temporal ὡς cf. e.g. 18.5.

ἔθετο ἐν τῷ πνεύματι, Paul formed the intention. τιθέναι,
τίθεσθαι is used in something like this sense from an early time in
Greek literature (LS 1790, s.v. A II 6); so in Homer, *Odyssey* 4.729
as here with an infinitive (ἐνὶ φρεσὶ θέσθε ... μ' ἀνεγεῖραι). ἔθετο
alone could hardly mean 'purposed', so that τῷ πνεύματι cannot be
taken to refer to the Holy Spirit (as e.g. in RSV, Paul resolved in the
Spirit), though this would accord with other passages in which Paul's
plans are said to be controlled by the Holy Spirit (e.g. 16.6). For the
infinitive πορεύεσθαι, see BDR § 392.3, n. 12, though the reference
there to the influence of Hebrew is doubtful.

Paul's intention is to pass through Macedonia (see 16.9) and
Achaea (see 18.12) and travel to Jerusalem, διελθὼν ... πορεύεσθαι.
D has διελθεῖν ... καὶ πορεύεσθαι, which Black (*AA* 67) regards as
an example of significant parataxis in the Western text, suggesting its
affinity with Aramaic tradition. It is perhaps more likely than he
allows that, though D is joined here by A, the parataxis is due to the
influence of the Latin (d has transire ... et sic ire ...). For διέρχεσθαι
as meaning not merely a journey but a preaching tour see on 13.6; this
is a probable meaning here, since Paul could hardly have avoided
work in the familiar mission field even if he had wished to do so.

It appears to be Luke's understanding of events that the journey
contemplated here was undertaken at 20.1. The riot (v. 23) happened
'at that time' and after the uproar had been quelled (v. 40) Paul set
out for Macedonia, went on to Greece (20.2), spent three months
there (20.3), and then travelled by a circuitous route to Jerusalem.
This account however seems to represent one of Luke's major
omissions. Whether the sending of Timothy (v. 22) is to be identified
with that forecast in 1 Cor. 4.17; 16.10 is not certain; Paul's final visit
to Greece (20.2, 3) seems to follow upon the troubled history to
which 2 Corinthians alludes (see *2 Corinthians* 5–21). This troubled
history is passed over in complete silence. It is difficult to think that
Luke was totally unaware of it; it was not part of the story he wished
to tell. Paul's intention at this time was to travel to Achaea by way of

Macedonia (1 Cor. 16.5); later he changed this plan, and intended to travel to Macedonia by way of Corinth, and then to retrace his steps, giving Corinth the advantage of a double visit (2 Cor. 1.15f.). This plan also was changed (2 Cor. 1.23), a fact which led to unpleasant comments at Corinth. Whether Paul would on the occasion of his projected visit continue to Jerusalem was unsettled (1 Cor. 16.4).

τὴν Μακ. καὶ ʼΑχαῖαν, ℵ B Ψ 𝔐, unites the provinces into one goal. τὴν Μακ. καὶ τὴν ʼΑχ., P⁷⁴ A D E 33 945 1739 pc distinguishes them.

εἰπών must be regarded as contemporaneous with ἔθετο; it is not conversation but the formulation of the purpose as it arose in his mind; the immediate intention to go to Macedonia and Achaea was part of the longer purpose to travel to Jerusalem and Rome.

γενέσθαι με ἐκεῖ looks on the visit to Jerusalem as a unit but it could do so either with reference to arrival (when I have *got* there) or to the stay (when I have *been* there). The difference is real but does not affect the sense. Jerusalem must be visited first, but the more remote objective, Rome, was beginning to fill Paul's mind, according to Acts, and according to Paul himself (Rom. 15.22–29). For Paul, Rome was to be a staging post on the way to Spain. This Luke does not mention (possibly because he knows that Paul did not get so far); Rome is the goal of his story, and if he can show the faith planted, and its great teacher at work, in the capital he will have accomplished his task. If the mission can reach Rome, and within a generation, there is nowhere it cannot go. Rome was probably alluded to at 1.8; Aquila and Priscilla had come from Rome, which probably had already been evangelized (18.2). Acts shows nothing of Paul's diffidence in writing to a church that he himself had not founded. The journey is one that Paul must (δεῖ) make; cf. 23.11; 27.24; and see E. Fascher in *FS* Bultmann (1954), 247f. Stählin (258) points out that the journey was intended (a) to strengthen the churches, (b) to deal with difficulties, and (c) to put together the collection, but Marshall (313) is probably right in commenting that Luke had recognized that Paul's arrest and subsequent story, including the journey to Rome, were in the end more important than the collection.

'Vielleicht haben wir hier [21f.] ein ziemlich unverändertes Stück Itinerar vor uns' (Bauernfeind 232). The Ephesian incidents were inserted into it.

22. Timothy (see 16.1–3) was sent to Corinth (and might well have been sent through Macedonia) at 1 Cor. 16.10 (cf. 4.17). A visit by Timothy to Macedonia (Philippi) is contemplated in Phil. 2.19–23; this may have been from Ephesus, but a more likely place of writing for Philippians is Rome. According to Pesch (2.176) the Macedonian visit of 1 Corinthians 16 belongs to an earlier stage of the Ephesian ministry; it differs in that nothing is said of Erastus. An

Erastus is mentioned at Rom. 16.23 as ὁ οἰκονόμος τῆς πόλεως. The city is not named, but Romans was probably written in or near Corinth, and it is a fair guess that Erastus was city treasurer of Corinth. The name occurs again at 2 Tim. 4.20: Erastus ἔμεινεν ἐν Κορίνθῳ. This would agree with but does not require his being a Corinthian official. We cannot be certain who wrote these words (in 2 Timothy), though even if Paul did not write them they may have been based on sound tradition; we cannot however place in time the residence of Erastus referred to in 2 Timothy. *Begs.* 4.244 refers to a Corinthian inscription that mentions an aedile Erastus; see H. J. Cadbury in *JBL* 50 (1931), 42–58, but also Hemer (235), who (like Cadbury) doubts whether any identification is possible.

Timothy and Erastus are described as two τῶν διακονούντων αὐτῷ. Timothy's role is not defined at 16.3; cf. 13.5, Paul and Barnabas had John as ὑπηρέτης. It is clear from the epistles that Timothy was a trusted and valued colleague (Phil. 2.20), though in 1 Cor. 16.10 (written probably somewhat earlier than Philippians) it seems that Paul has to tell the Corinthians to treat him with proper respect. διακονεῖν suggests a somewhat menial position; cf. Philemon 13 (Onesimus will attend to Paul's needs in prison). The expression 'personal assistant' may cover what is meant, but it is clear that this in fact (whether Luke knew it or not) included pastoral responsibility in the churches.

τὴν Μακεδονίαν: the article is given in P⁷⁴ A B D Ψ 𝔐, omitted by ℵ E 36 323 614 1175 1891 *al.*

When his assistants left for Macedonia Paul stayed in Ephesus; cf. 1 Cor. 16.8 (though it is not clear that the two verses refer to the same occasion). ἐπέχειν is sometimes used with χρόνος (cf. Herodotus 1.132.3, ἐπισχὼν δὲ ὀλίγον χρόνον; D in this verse includes ὀλίγον) for spending an undefined or unspecified time in a place. Luke is making room for one of his best stories.

For the use of εἰς and the accusative when ἐν and the dative would have been expected see 2.5. Here D corrects to ἐν τῇ Ἀσίᾳ. For a number of minor Western variants in vv. 22–37 see Metzger (472f.).

23. A new narrative, complete in itself and free (except in v. 26) from any cross reference to Paul's work in general begins here. This verse is Luke's own introduction to the following narrative (so Lüdemann 224); its basis is not in itself Christian (Lüdemann 226). Though not dependent on it is reasonably consistent with such other knowledge as we possess, and Luke may have heard it told in Ephesus, or by Ephesian Christians elsewhere. Reicke (*DFZ* 313f.) refers to evidence for similar riots in W. H. Buckler (*FS* Ramsay, 27–50) and T. R. S. Broughton (*Roman Asia Minor: An Economic Survey of Ancient Rome*, ed. T. Frank, 4.846ff.)

Ἐγένετο: this is not the Semitic use of this word. A disturbance (τάραχος), and no small one (the litotes is characteristic of Luke; see 12.18), arose—happened. It happened κατὰ τὸν καιρὸν ἐκεῖνον; this means no more than 'during Paul's Ephesian ministry', though Luke (20.1) takes it to have provided the cue for Paul's departure, which is likely enough. The disturbance concerns 'the Way'; on ὁδός as a term for Christianity see on 9.2. In the disturbance, 'Dabei wird deutlich, wie sich Religiosität, Patriotismus und wirtschaftliches Interesse zu einem untrennbaren Ganzen miteinander verbunden haben' (Roloff 291). On the motivation of the story see Schmithals quoted on p. 918.

24. Demetrius: the name occurs at 3 Jn 12, but (though 3 John may well have originated in or in the neighbourhood of Ephesus) it is unlikely that the two should be connected; Der Kleine Pauly 1.1462–71 mentions 33 persons bearing the name. This Demetrius was an ἀργυροκόπος, a silversmith. The participle that follows, ποιῶν, may be either attributive (D, reading ἦν instead of ὀνόματι, makes this certain), ... who made ... , or adverbial, ... by making ... There is no way of deciding with certainty which construction is correct. M. 3.152 notes the ambiguity, and Moule, (IB 105) noting both possibilities, adds 'the latter seems to be the more probable'. Certainly it helps to bind the narrative together. It was by making silver shrines that the silver trade flourished, and it was this activity that was attacked, implicitly or explicitly, by monotheists such as Paul. Hence the τάραχος.

Papyrus examples of the use of ἀργυροκόπος (MM 74; BA 211) have been supplemented by an Ephesian inscription (IEph VI (1980) 2212.4–7, 9; in ND 4.7–10) which mentions 'M. Antonius Hermeias, ἀργυροκόπος, νεοποιός', and also 'τὸ συνέδριον τῶν ἀργυροποίων', the gild of silversmiths. See further Hemer (235f.).

Demetrius made ναοὺς ἀργυροῦς. The adjective is omitted by B gig: possibly by homoeoteleuton, though it is possible that the adjective was not originally in the text and was added on the strength of Demetrius's occupation. ναός usually means a temple, or the most sacred part of a temple, the inner shrine where the image or other sacred object was placed, but it has been conjectured that the word was also used for small portable shrines which were carried in religious processions. Those made by Demetrius were shrines of Artemis (not representations of a deity, so that Lucian, Alexander 18 is not a parallel). On Artemis, the great Ephesian—and Asian—goddess, see especially L. R. Taylor in Begs. 5.251–6, supplemented by ND 4.74–82. As a Greek goddess Artemis was the daughter of Zeus and Leto, and sister of Apollo, worshipped already in Mycenaean times. She was a virgin who helped women in childbirth, a huntress armed with a bow, the goddess of death. The establishment of an Ionian colony at Ephesus, and similar acts of colonization elsewhere in Asia Minor, led to assimilation of the Greek Artemis to deities of oriental origin. Worship of a goddess (perhaps of fertility) seems to have been practised in Ephesus before the arrival of the Greeks, and images (which may once have included the great golden image in the temple at Ephesus) have often been interpreted as many-breasted, suggesting that she was a fertility goddess. An alternative interpretation of the supposed breasts as bull's testicles would suggest fertility even more strongly (see D. W. J. Gill and B. W. Winter in *The Book of Acts* 2.88). The view that Artemis was a fertility goddess is however effectively criticized in the same volume (319f.) by P. A. Trebilco. The Ephesian goddess was probably related to Cybele and to Ma (who had her own temple in Ephesus). The fame and sanctity of the temple of Artemis are widely attested; see below, v. 27, and the note.

There is evidence for the addition, between ποιῶν and ναούς, of the words ἴσως κιβώρια μικρά, *perhaps small cups* (*chalices* might be better, since there is evidence for the liturgical use of κιβώριον). the support for this reading is very slight, but it includes Chrysostom. In view however of the word ἴσως, and of the fact that Chrysostom professes ignorance of the silver shrines, it is probably wise to regard this not as a genuine variant but as a guess at what the ναούς ἀργυροῦς might be.

Another suggestion was made as long ago as 1890 by E. L. Hicks (*Expositor* 1 (1890), 401ff.). Hicks suggested that the text ναούς ποιοῦν was a corruption of the word νεοποιός (there are various spellings, ναοποιός, νεωποιός), the term used in the Roman period for the officials elected by the city tribes to supervise the fabric of the temple of Artemis. For details see most conveniently Sherwin-White (90f.). It is an interesting speculation, and if it is correct it could be used to argue for Luke's knowledge of Ephesus in the first century (though Hicks himself attributed the present text to *Luke's* mis-understanding). But our only ground for it is our ignorance (already in Chrysostom?) of the custom of making silver shrines. Hicks further suggested that the Demetrius of the riot might be identified with a Demetrius referred to in an Ephesian inscription, dating probably (see Sherwin-White 91f.) from the first century, as a νεωποιός (see AGIBM III 578, *Begs.* 5.255). *ND* 4.127–9 quotes a thanksgiving to Lady Artemis, from a νεοποιός αὐθαίρετος (*voluntary*) (IEph 3.961.3).

For descriptions of the great temple of Artemis see Strabo 14.640ff.; Pausanias 2.2.5; 4.31; also A. Bammer, *Die Architektur des jüngeren Artemisiums von Ephesos* (Wiesbaden 1972). The temple measured 120 x 70 m.; it had 128 pillars, 19 m. high.

Demetrius provided (παρείχετο; παρεῖχε A* D E *pc*, without substantial difference in meaning) the craftsmen (τεχνίταις, the skilled workmen who actually produced the shrines, whether in his regular employment or under contract) with a good deal of business, trade (ἐργασίαν), literally, *no little trade*—litotes, as in v. 23.

25. Demetrius gathered together the craftsmen (οὕς, pointing back to v. 24) and the ἐργάτας; the latter seem to be the relatively unskilled workmen. The word is used of farm labourers (Herodotus 5.6.2, ἀργὸν εἶναι κάλλιστον, γῆς δὲ ἐργάτην ἀτιμότατον—admittedly, of the Thracians). The use of περί is classical, 'den Gegenstand des Tuns oder der Bemühung bezeichnend' (BDR § 228.2). 'Alii erant τεχνῖται, *artifices* nobiliores; alii ἐργάται *operarii*' (Bengel 466).

ἄνδρες: in most passages (see 1.16) this address is given a further qualification. Demetrius goes on to appeal to common knowledge, and to natural human instinct. Work, and thereby prosperity, is afforded by the local cult. Anything that threatens the cult therefore threatens also the silver-workers of all grades at a very sensitive point—in their pockets.

For οὕς συναθροίσας καί, D 614 (2495) *pc* gig sy sa have οὗτος συναθροίσας.

For ἐργάτας εἶπεν ἄνδρες, D (sy^p sy^h**) sa have τεχνίτας ἔφη πρὸς αὐτούς ἄνδρες συντεχνῖται. In this reading the ἐργάται disappear.

26. θεωρεῖτε καὶ ἀκούετε. The order is surprising; one would have expected hearing first, then the appeal to first-hand knowledge (sight).

Ἐφέσου: Ἀpg 19.26 οὐ μόνον ... ὄχλον können die Gen. als Gen. des Ortes erklärt werden (Latinismus? = Ephesi ...), möglich aber auch als Gen. von ὄχλον abhängig zu denken (sehr weite Trennung ...); D hat ἕως Ἐφεσίου [sic] ...' (BDR § 186.1, n. 2). M. 1.73 compares Sophocles, *Oedipus Tyrannus* 236f. (γῆς τῆσδε) but thinks that dependence on ὄχλον may be right. 'The gloss ἕως (D), "within", may possibly express the meaning.' It is probably best to take the genitive as a sort of possessive: a crowd of people belonging to Ephesus ...; and to suppose that Ephesus and Asia are placed first for emphasis.

σχεδὸν πάσης τῆς Ἀσίας: cf. 19.10. It must be remembered that Paul had assistants (see 19.22); Col. 1.7 appears to mean that Epaphras acted on Paul's behalf in evangelizing Colossae (and Col. 2.1 suggests that there were Christian groups in Laodicea and elsewhere which Paul had not founded personally though he took responsibility for them). These statements may well reflect local tradition even if Paul did not write the epistle. Demetrius would no doubt be prepared to exaggerate in a good cause, but Luke would equally be prepared to take over the exaggeration in a somewhat different one.

πείσας μετέστησεν: by persuasion he has moved people from one side (idolatry) to another (Christianity). Cf. Xenophon, *Hellenica* 2.2.5, τὰ ἐκεῖ πάντα πρὸς Λακεδαιμονίους μετέστησεν.

The rest of the verse contradicts a somewhat cruder paganism than that contemplated in 17.29. It is no longer a question of deity *resembling* material objects, but whether the material objects were in fact gods. Christians were by no means the only critics to deny this. Jews of course did so; this it is unnecessary to document. There was also a considerable amount of pagan criticism of crude idolatry (see above, pp. 849f., and cf. Betz 40, 43). What the average inhabitant of Ephesus thought about the images he saw on every side of him is not easy to determine; it would certainly be mistaken to credit him with the views of Epicurus or of Lucian. Many if pressed would probably have agreed that the products of human manufacture (οἱ διὰ χειρῶν γινόμενοι) were not themselves θεοί, but would have seen in the symbolic representation of the gods more than bare symbols. 'I think that a man who is altogether burdened in soul and has endured many misfortunes and griefs in his life and does not enjoy sweet sleep, would, if he stood before this image [of Zeus, by Pheidias, at Olympia], forget all the grievous and dreadful things it may befall one to suffer in human life' (Dio of Prusa, quoted by A. D. Nock in *Early Gentile Christianity* (1964), 5). On the whole the philosophical attitude to popular religion grew more tolerant as the Hellenistic age progressed. Thus Zeno (*SVF* 1.264), 'It will not be necessary to build temples, for a temple ought not to be held to be worth much or holy (πολλοῦ ἄξιον καὶ ἅγιον); nothing is worth much or holy which is the work of builders and artisans (οἰκοδόμων ἔργον καὶ βαναύσων)' (in Clement of Alexandria, *Stromata* 5.12.76); also Plutarch, quoted on 17.24. But later see Maximus of Tyre 2.1, 2: 'It is not that the divine Being stands in any need of images or statues. It is poor humanity, because of its weakness and the distance dividing it from God ... which has contrived these things as symbols. People who have an exceptionally strong power of mental realization, who can lift the soul straight away to heaven and come into contact with God—such people, it may be, do not stand in any need of images. But such people are few amongst men.'

The position of Paul, the Jew and the Christian, was more radical, and is not unfairly represented by Demetrius: the objects were not to be identified with gods—indeed, whatever men might think (1 Cor. 8.6), there existed no θεοί with whom they could be identified; there was but one (1 Thess. 1.9f.; Rom. 1.21–3). The question is whether Paul (if rightly represented by Demetrius) was fair in thinking that anyone supposed that the idols actually were gods. It is however clear that Christianity was mounting a major attack on such religions as that of Artemis. Both could not prevail. The town clerk (v. 37) was either more tactful or less intelligent than Demetrius. Cf. Schille (386): 'Demetrius wirkt weitsichtiger als der Stadtschreiber, der die

Dinge v.35 herunterzuspielen versteht.' Demetrius can see the 'weltweite Gefahr'. 'Was Lukas Demetrius in den Mund legt, grenzt an Prophetie.'

Παῦλος οὗτος is a disparaging expression. After it D adds τις τοτε, which must be a mistake for τίς ποτε, *nescio quem* (gig). See Ropes (*Begs.* 3.186f.), and for papyrus parallels (without reference to this passage) BDR § 303, n. 2.

27. οὐ μόνον, repeated from v. 26; a common expression in the later part of Acts (21.13; 26.29; 27.10); characteristic of Jn, and classical. Demetrius puts business considerations first, but adds a religious point.

κινδυνεύει is often used in a weakened sense, 'there is a possibility', but here the context suggests that the basic notion of danger is intended—κινδυνεύει ἡμῖν, there is a risk for us. τοῦτο τὸ μέρος now becomes an accusative subject with the infinitive ἐλθεῖν (otherwise τοῦτο τὸ μέρος would be the subject of κινδυνεύει, *it may come* ...). μέρος is the part played, or enjoyed, by Demetrius and his colleagues; 'line of business' (MM 399) is probably right, though PFlor 1.89.2 (3rd century AD), which MM quote, does not quite prove their point. τὰ μέρη τῆς διοικήσεως are branches of the administration (der Verwaltung) rather than branches of a business, Geschäftszweige (BA 1025). But was Demetrius νεοποιός after all (v. 24), and care for the administration of the temple of Artemis his part in the administration of the city? It is safest to say, Not only is there a risk for us that this line of business may come into disrepute (ἀπελεγμόν, from ἀπελέγχειν) ... Schille (386) takes εἰς ἀπελεγμὸν ἐλθεῖν to be a Latinism, which d and the Vulgate put back as *in redargutionem venire*. See Kilpatrick, *JTS* 10 (1959), 327. The Latin suggests that the word was 'taken to mean something like "reproof, censure, adverse comment, public criticism"'.

Two more infinitives dependent on κινδυνεύει follow, λογισθῆναι and μέλλειν. καθαιρεῖσθαι is dependent on μέλλειν. ℵ* D* have μέλλει (in parallel with κινδυνεύει) instead of μέλλειν. This simplifies the sentence, but is not for that reason necessarily original. There is a danger, a risk ... that the temple of the great goddess Artemis may come to be reckoned as nothing. Artemis is described as θεά. This feminine form is not uncommon, but the masculine form θεός is often used for both genders (e.g. τοῖς θεοῖς εὔχομαι πᾶσι καὶ πάσαις, Demosthenes 18.1 (225), cf. 141 (274); 21.52 (531); M. 3.22 adds inscriptions and papyri). But see especially M. 1.60, 244; and note v. 37, where the town clerk speaks of τὴν θεὸν ἡμῶν. At 1.60 Moulton quotes (abbreviating a little) Blass (209f.): 'Usitate dicitur ἡ θεός (ut 37); verum etiam inscriptio Ephesia Brit. Mus. [= *AGIBM*] nr. 481, v. 324 (cf. 220.278) τῇ μεγίστῃ θεᾷ Ἐφεσίᾳ Ἀρτέμιδι, cum alibi (ibid. 373.375 etc. nr. 482) ἡ θεός eadem dicitur (in illa formula,

v. 13). Itaque formulam sollemnem ἡ μεγάλη θεὰ 'A. mira diligentia L. conservavit.' At 1.244 (Additional note to the second edition), however, Moulton prefers the suggestion of G. Thieme. The town clerk used the technical term; ἡ θεός is used in inscriptions for the great goddess of the city; other people's goddesses were θεαί, and this use determined that of Demetrius. This convinced Moulton, but one would have thought that the silversmith leader would have used the official designation of the goddess whose rights he was defending. There is still much to be said for Blass; also for the view that Luke was not interested in consistency in such a matter. It is worthwhile to note that Xenophon of Ephesus (1.11.5) writes, ... τὴν πάτριον ἡμῖν θεόν, τὴν μεγάλην 'Εφεσίων 'Άρτεμιν.

Notwithstanding Isa. 40.17; Wisdom 3.17; 9.6; Dan. 4.35 (Theodotion) it would be unwise in such a context as this to take λογισθῆναι εἰς as a Semitism (predicative ל represented by εἰς). See M. 2.462, and cf. Xenophon, *Cyropaedia* 3.1.33, χρήματα ... εἰς ἀργύριον λογισθέντα τάλαντα πλείω τῶν τρισχιλίων (not identical in sense, but a pointer to usage).

For οὐθείς (instead of οὐδείς) cf. 15.9 and the note.

And she will be cast down from her greatness; on τῆς μεγαλειότητος see BDR § 180.1, n. 2; a genitive of separation? Page (208) quote Diodorus Siculus 4.8.2, καθαιρεῖν τι τῆς τοῦ θεοῦ δόξης. Some MSS have the accusative, meaning *be deprived of*. Ephesian Artemis was universally recognized and revered; e.g. Pausanias 4.31.8, Ephesian Artemis is the title which all cities recognize, and by which men privately worship her as the greatest of the gods; Xenophon of Ephesus, 1.11.5, quoted above; Livy 1.45.2, iam tum erat inclitum Dianae Ephesiae fanum; id communiter a civitatibus Asiae factum fama ferebat.

The effect of Christianity on pagan religion is shown in Pliny's account of the restoration of paganism when Christianity was repressed: Certo satis constat prope iam desolata templa coepisse celebrari et sacra sollemnia diu intermissa repeti inveniebatur (*Epistles* 10.96.10).

28. Demetrius' speech had its intended effect in rousing his colleagues in opposition to the Christian movement.

The Western variant at the beginning of the verse (ταῦτα δὲ ἀκούσαντες, D (lat) syᵖ) is another example of an insignificant variation which attached no importance to the precise reproduction of wording. πλήρεις is read here by the majority of MSS, and is to be accepted. There is evidence (see MM 519; M. 2.162; BDR § 137.1) for πλήρης as indeclinable; this was a Hellenistic practice which was spreading in the first century AD. It occurs in the NT, but there is no reason to suspect it here.

θυμός has a wide range of meanings, here certainly, *anger, rage*.

The Western text (D (614) sy^hmg) adds that *they ran into the street*, δραμόντες εἰς τὸ ἄμφοδον. This adds nothing to the sense. It could have been removed by an editor motivated by verbal economy but more probably added to brighten the narrative. Ropes (*Begs.* 3.186) however thinks it 'one of the few intrinsically interesting ''Western'' additions'.

μεγάλη ἡ Ἄρτεμις Ἐφεσίων. See the passages quoted on v. 27; many more could be added. For the acclamation cf. Bel and the Dragon 18, 41. ἡ is omitted by D* *pc*, rightly according to Ramsay (*Church* 139–41) on the ground that the article was not used in acclamations. It seems however that there was no uniform practice. The reading with the article violates Apollonius's Canon (that nouns in regimen either both have or both lack the article); but this does happen with proper names and national appellations (Moule, *IB* 115). Cf. vv. 34, 35.

29. Again the Western text begins the verse with what seems to be a pointless paraphrase, for it is hard to see any real difference between ἐπλήσθη (a Lucan word) ἡ πόλις τῆς συγχύσεως (in almost all MSS) and συνεχύθη ὅλη ἡ πόλις (D* (gig sy^p)). D*, it is true, surprisingly adds αἰσχύνης. This however has been plausibly explained as due to the influence of d which (for the Greek συγχύσεως) has *confusionem*. This word was often an equivalent for αἰσχύνη.

ὁρμᾶν is used here and at 7.57, each time of a violent onrush of people; elsewhere in the NT only of the Gadarene swine. ὁμοθυμαδόν occurs 10 times in Acts, elsewhere in the NT only at Rom. 15.6. As usual in Acts it suggests physical association as well as unanimity. Luke appears to be freely writing up the information he had received.

The θέατρον at Ephesus is the only one mentioned in the NT (also at v. 31). The Hellenistic theatre was an imposing building, now fully excavated (see F. Miltner, *Ephesos* (1951(8)), 30–32). Estimates of its capacity vary, but the lowest seems to be 24,000. An inscription cited in Deissmann (*LAE* 113f.) from *Jahreshefte der Österreichischen Archäologischen Instituts* 2 (1899), Supplement 43f., seems to presuppose that meetings of the town ἐκκλησία (vv. 32, 39, 40) were held in the theatre. In AD 103–4, C. Vibius Salutaris presented a silver image of Artemis, together with other statues, ἵνα τέθηνται κατ᾽ ἐκκλησίαν ἐν τῷ (sic) θεάτρῳ (sic) ἐπὶ τῶν βάσεων. The corresponding Latin of the bilingual inscription runs, ... ita ut [om]n[ie]cclesia supra bases ponerentur. Cf. *AGIBM* 3.481.395. Less formal gatherings also took place in theatres. Thus *AGIBM* 4.792.4ff.: ὁ μὲν δᾶμος ἐν οὐ μετρίᾳ συγχύσει γενόμενος ... μετὰ πάσας προθυμίας συνελθὼν εἰς τὸ θέατρον; Cicero, *Pro Flacco* 7 (16): Cum in theatro imperiti homines, rerum omnium rudes ignarique consederant: tum bella inutilia suscipiebant; tum seditiosos homines reipublicae praeficiebant; tum optime meritos cives e civitate ejiciebant.

The rioters seized and dragged along with them (συναρπάσαντες) the two Macedonians Gaius and Aristarchus. The name Gaius recurs at 20.4; for the textual question, on which the question whether the Gaius there can be the Macedonian of this verse depends, see the note. The singular Μακεδόνα (36 453 *pc*), which in the present verse makes only Aristarchus a Macedonian, probably arose through identification of Gaius here with Gaius the Derbaean of 20.4. Aristarchus is mentioned at 20.4 as a Thessalonian and at 27.2 as a Macedonian from Thessalonica; we need not doubt that the same man is in mind in all these passages. An Aristarchus is mentioned at Col. 4.10; Philemon 24. For the movements of Aristarchus and his relation with Paul see on 27.2.

Gaius and Aristarchus were συνέκδημοι of Paul's. The word is used in a similar way at 2 Cor. 8.19, where the person concerned, whose praise in the Gospel circulated in all the churches, had been appointed by the churches (χειροτονηθεὶς ὑπὸ τῶν ἐκκλησιῶν) to be Paul's συνέκδημος in the matter of the collection that Paul was organizing. The word, which in itself means simply fellow-traveller, may thus have acquired a semi-official meaning, 'travelling colleague', or the like. The word has a somewhat similar sense at Josephus, *Life* 79 and Plutarch, *Otho* 5 (1068). In *IG* 12(8).186 line 9 (Samothrace, first century BC) the Doric form συνέγδαμοι is used 'of private persons *accompanying* a public mission' (LS 1706). The word seems very suitable for men who were not simple members of the church but trusted and authorized assistants of Paul. Presumably they were publicly known and thus natural targets for the mob's violence.

30. It was not Paul's intention to avoid dangers to which his subordinates were exposed; he wished εἰσελθεῖν εἰς τὸν δῆμον, that is, to go into the theatre where the people (of the city) were assembled. This however the disciples would not permit; Paul's life was too valuable to be risked in this way. There is no difference in meaning between the Old Uncial and Western texts here, since in the former the negative (οὐκ) and the verb (εἴων) combine to form what is virtually a negative verb (BDR § 433.1), so that οἱ μαθηταὶ ἐκώλυον (D sy^p) is equivalent to the text of the great majority of MSS.

Begs. 4.248 has 'δῆμον is unlikely to mean assembly'; this was a riot. Yet the same company of people becomes in v. 32 ἡ ἐκκλησία.

For the question whether these events are reflected in 1 Cor. 15.32; 16.9; 2 Cor. 1.8 see *1 Corinthians* 365f.; *2 Corinthians* 63f. The answer seems to be, 'Possibly in 1 Cor. 15.32.'

In this sentence Paul appears first in a genitive absolute, then (αὐτόν) as the accusative object of the main verb; Luke is not writing in his best style.

31. It was not only Christian disciples who were concerned for Paul's safety. There were also officials who were ready if not to take his part at least to advise caution. These were some of the Asiarchs. The meaning of this term is disputed, and the question is complicated by the fact that it seems to have changed in the course of time. Literary evidence is meagre; inscriptional and numismatic more plentiful, and there are analogous terms—Galatarchs, Bithyniarchs, Lyciarchs. The main problem lies in the relation (if any) between the office of Asiarch and that of High Priest of the cult of Rome in the league (κοινόν) of Asia. 'My explanation ... is that from the Asiarchs designated in each year as the foremost men of Asia one was chosen to act as high priest of the emperor, and then, as the temples of the league were built, one was selected to serve at the league temple in each city. Thus all Archiereis would have been Asiarchs, but all the Asiarchs would not have acquired the distinction of the highpriesthood. As the number of league temples grew, in time there would have been a priesthood for every Asiarch, and the two terms would thus come to be identical in meaning. It is possible that this was already the case in the time of Paul, or at least in that of Luke' (L. R. Taylor, in *Begs.* 5.261; see the whole admirable discussion, 256–62; also Sherwin-White 88–90). Basic information is given by V. Chapot, *La Province Romaine proconsulaire d'Asie* (1904), 482ff. It is interesting to note *Martyrdom of Polycarp* 12.2 (ἠρώτων τὸν Ἀσιάρχην Φίλιππον, ἵνα ἐπαφῇ τῷ Πολυκάρπῳ λέοντα), but the passage gives no fresh information and may in any case reflect conditions of a later date. Taylor's discussion is too good to be out of date, but some recent work should be noted. There is more recent bibliography in Hemer (121f. and *ND* 1.82), and there is a particularly important discussion (by R. A. Kearsley) in *ND* 4.46–55. Her last sentence is 'All this indicates that the Asiarchy was quite separate from the provincial high-priesthood, at least during the period covered by the evidence considered above' [fifty years after Acts 19].

These Asiarchs were kindly disposed to Paul, ὄντες (D, ὑπάρχοντες; it is hard to see any motive for a change in either direction) αὐτῷ φίλοι (adjective rather than substantive because of the dative: BDR § 190.1, n. 1).

For the construction (πέμψαντες ... παρεκάλουν) cf. Mt. 11.2 (where it is helped out by διὰ τῶν μαθητῶν αὐτοῦ).

δοῦναι ἑαυτὸν εἰς τὸ θέατρον: *Begs.* 4.248 translates 'to venture into the theatre'. This gives a sense appropriate to the context, but the words do not mean more than 'go into ...'. Some have seen in δοῦναι ἑαυτόν an allusion to Mk 10.45 (δοῦναι τὴν ψυχὴν αὐτοῦ). This is most improbable.

Stählin (261) describes the Asiarchs as 'Wächter über die Loyalität'. On the basis of this sort of observation Lüdemann (225) writes, 'Aus diesem Grunde muss die apologetische Erklärung derart ergänzt werden, dass Lukas mit der Freundschaft der Asiarchen die Weltläufigkeit des Christentums betont.' From a different angle, Luke may be said to be pointing out that Christianity in Ephesus already had sympathy in the highest circles (Roloff 293). Differently again, that the Asiarchs were Paul's friends shows that he 'spurned the Pharisaic ideas of ritual purity which would have excluded such a friendship' (Ehrhardt, *Acts* 103).

32. μὲν οὖν: for this frequent construction, often, as here, resumptive, see 1.6; 15.3. After two verses dealing with Paul Luke returns to his description of the crowd.

ἄλλοι ... ἄλλο τι ἔκραζον: some were shouting one thing, others another. For the construction cf. 2.12 and more precisely 21.34; Xenophon, *Anabasis* 2.1.15, οὗτοι ... ἄλλος ἄλλα λέγει.

ἡ ἐκκλησία. For the Christian use of this word see 5.11; Introduction, pp. lxxxviif. In its non-biblical sense it is correctly used at v. 39 (see the note) of the duly constituted assembly of citizens (at Ephesus, held in the theatre; see v. 29); the use in vv. 32, 40 is doubtful, since the assembly seems to be informal, unofficial, and riotous. δῆμος possibly (vv. 30, 33), ὄχλος (vv. 33, 36), and συστροφή (v. 40) are more suitable terms. The use of ἐκκλησία is however understandable; the persons concerned were those who would have been summoned to a lawful assembly even though they were not at the time engaged on lawful business.

συγκεχυμένη; cf. σύγχυσις (v. 29).

οἱ πλείους. It is hard to see more than a free rewriting, in which the editor sometimes wrote from memory without checking his text, in the variant οἱ πλεῖστοι (D). It is true that this superlative is sometimes used for the *best, noblest (people)*, and it is conceivable that the Western editor meant that even the best people in Ephesus did not understand what was going on; but it is doubtful whether so much can be read out of the text.

τίνος ἕνεκα, on account of what, i.e., why. ἕνεκα most often follows its case, but in the NT does so only here and at Lk. 4.18 (in a quotation of Isa. 61.1, LXX).

After ᾔδεισαν the perfect would have had the force of the pluperfect. Thus συνεληλύθεισαν is a case of 'Attraktion des Tempus' (BDR § 345).

For the verse as a whole cf. Charito of Aphrodisias 1.5.3: ἀλλὰ καὶ ὁ δῆμος ἅπας εἰς τὴν ἀγορὰν συνέτρεχεν ἄλλων ἄλλα κεκραγότων.

33. ἐκ δὲ τοῦ ὄχλου. The preposition ἐκ is used in place of a partitive genitive and the phrase serves as subject of the verb: *some of the crowd*. For this ('rather barbarous'—*Begs.* 4.249, but see BDR § 164.2, n. 6) construction cf. 21.16 (without ἐκ); Lk. 21.16; Jn 7.40; 16.17. A not impossible alternative is to take the subject of συνεβίβασαν to be a simple 'they' and ἐκ τοῦ ὄχλου as a qualifying adverbial phrase: They put forward out of the crowd ...

συνεβίβασαν P⁷⁴ ℵ A B E 33 323 945 1739 1891 *pc*

κατεβίβασαν D* lat (detraxerunt; there are some strange Latin equivalents)

προεβίβασαν Dᶜ Ψ 𝔐 vh^{mss} sy^h

Of these words συμβιβάζειν occurs at 9.22 (affirm, allege; teach); 16.10 (conclude); also at 1 Cor. 2.16; Eph. 4.16; Col. 2.2, 19; καταβιβάζειν at Mt. 11.23 (v. 1.) = Lk. 10.15 (v. 1.) (bring down— to Hades); προβιβάζειν at Mt. 14.8 (put forward). The last of these seems at first sight to give the sense required by the passage: some of the crowd put forward Alexander, presumably to act as their spokesman. This however would anticipate προβαλόντων (see below), and it is hard to see why, if προεβίβασαν was the original reading, nearly all the earliest witnesses, Old Uncial and Western, should change it (into συνεβ. and κατεβ.). This argument will carry with it the corollary that συνεβ. does not mean (as many translators have taken it to mean) *put forward*. It is probably best to take the word in the sense (which is that of the LXX—see on 9.22) of *teach*, though here with the quasi-legal connotation of *instruct*; MM (s.v. συνβιβ.; 603) give examples of the legal use of ἐκβιβ. Those authorities that read κατεβίβασαν (detraxerunt) may have taken it with the following clause: When the Jews put forward Alexander some of the crowd brought him down. The general sense, however, seems best served by: Some of the crowd instructed Alexander, and the Jews put him forward. But it remains quite unclear who Alexander was, why he was chosen, and what he was expected to do or to say. See further below.

προβαλόντων αὐτὸν τῶν Ἰουδαίων undoubtedly means that the Jews (for Jews in Ephesus see on 18.19) *put forward* Alexander. In what sense and for what purpose? For the role of the Jews in the whole episode see on v. 40. The next words show that the crowd in general was unfavourably disposed to the Jews, of whom Alexander was one, and we may probably accept the meaning 'to cite in one's defence'; see Isaeus 7.3 (μάρτυρας προὐβαλόμην); Plato, *Laches* 201b; Demosthenes 18.149 (277), though in none of these passages is the verb active. But why else should the Jews have put forward one of their own number? The Jews would be under attack (a) because they were not always differentiated from the Christians, who had provoked the mob, and (b) because in any case they were known to be opposed to idolatry, and were unpopular. See on v. 40.

κατασείσας. The word is characteristic of Acts (12.17; 13.16; 21.40). In all the other passages it is used with the dative, τῇ χειρί, here with the accusative direct object, τὴν χεῖρα. The dative is 'more frequent' (LS 910).

ἀπολογεῖσθαι is in the NT a Lucan word (Acts 24.10; 25.8; 26.1, 2, 24; Lk. 12.11; 21.14; elsewhere in the NT, twice; cf. ἀπολογία, Acts 22.1; 25.16), *to make a defence*. It is implied that the Jews have been attacked (Weiser 547—they felt themselves threatened by the attack on Paul). τῷ δήμῳ. Cf. v. 30.

The name Alexander occurs at 4.6; this cannot be the same man. No identification is offered. The name is found at 1 Tim. 1.20 (Hymenaeus and Alexander have made shipwreck concerning the faith and have been delivered to Satan that they may learn not to blaspheme) and at 2 Tim. 4.14 (Alexander the coppersmith did me much harm; he will get his deserts; Timothy must beware of him). The Pastoral Epistles are probably pseudonymous, but this does not mean that all the names contained in them are purely fictitious. It would however be rash to identify any of these Alexanders; see *Pastorals* 47f., 121. A more plausible suggestion (Klausner, *Jesus* 351) connects the present passage with Mk 15.21 and Rom. 16.13. There was little point in mentioning the names of Simon's sons unless they were known in Christian circles. The suggestion would gain in force if the view were accepted that Romans 16 was addressed not to Rome but to Ephesus; this however is unlikely (*Romans* 257f.). And we do not know that Alexander of Acts 19 was, or became, a Christian. See further on v. 34.

34. ἐπιγνόντες: a sense construction—those who recognized uttered the φωνή (below). This verse still leaves us guessing who Alexander was, why the Jews put him forward, and to what end his defence (ἀπολογεῖσθαι) was directed, but we do learn that he was himself a Jew. The name was borne by Jews (Jastrow 70), notably by an Amora of the third century. The crowd presumably recognized that he was a Jew by the line taken in his defence.

φωνή ἐγένετο μία ἐκ (omitted by D lat) πάντων, one cry arose from them all, that is, from the mass of the mob, who were not Jews. It is not at this point clear why the Jews were brought into the episode; see below. The separation of μία from φωνή stresses the word and thus the unanimity of the crowd—who behave with the irrationality still characteristic of large assemblies.

ὡς, *about, approximately*; see LS, s.v. E, 2039. In Acts this is more often expressed by ὡσεί (see 1.15), which is read here by P⁷⁴ B 33 *pc*.

κράζοντες, read only by ℵ A, should probably be accepted, as *lectio difficilior*; it is easy in view of πάντων to understand the omission of the word by Ψ and the change by all other authorities to κραζόντων (though Ropes (*Begs.* 3.188) thinks that the reverse is what happened). See BDR § 466.4, n. 5. The nominative takes up the case of ἐπιγνόντες, but this does nothing to remove the anacolouthon since the only finite verb in the sentence is ἐγένετο and its subject is φωνή. There is no reason why Luke should not have written (BDR, loc. cit.) ἐπιγνόντες ... ἐβόησαν ὁμοῦ πάντες ... κράζοντες.

μεγάλη ἡ Ἄρτεμις Ἐφεσίων. See v. 28. B repeats the clause. 'Die *Epanadiplosis,* d.h. die nachdrückliche Verdopplung eines gewichtigen Wortes, ist dem NT nicht unbekannt, aber nirgends als rhetorisch zu betrachten, sondern überall als Wiedergabe der wirklichen Rede' (BDR § 493.1).

C. Burchard (*ZNW* 61 (1970), 167f.) quotes T. Benjamin 3.7 (α and β), περιλαβὼν αὐτὸν ἐπὶ δύο ὥρας κατεφίλει, and T. Judah 3.4 (β), πολεμήσας τὸν Ἀχὼρ ἐπὶ ὥρας δύο ἀπέκτεινα αὐτόν, and asks, 'Eine redensart?'

In vv. 33, 34 we have noted some unusual, in some cases also difficult, expressions.

ἐκ τοῦ ὄχλου as subject
Unusual sense of συμβιβάζειν
An otherwise unknown (and unexplained) Alexander
Unexplained action of the Jews
Unexplained defence (against what?) by Alexander
Anacolouthon: ἐπιγνόντες ... φωνὴ ἐγένετο ... κράζοντες (κραζόντων)

We may add the observation that v. 32 could be followed immediately by v. 35, i.e., vv. 33, 34 form a self-contained unit which could be removed without leaving a noticeable gap. It seems worth while at least to raise the question whether these verses contain supplementary information added to a source that gave an outline of the events at Ephesus; possibly Luke supplemented by local inquiry a narrative given him by a travel document (or similar source); or perhaps he had his own reason for making the addition. A probable consequence might be that Alexander either was at the time of the riot, or subsequently became, a Christian.

35. For the connection see the note on v. 34. This verse could be linked directly with v. 32.

καταστέλλειν is used in the NT only here and in v. 36. Cf. Josephus, *War* 2.611, καταστείλας τὸν θόρυβον αὐτῶν; 4.271; *Ant.* 14.156; 20.174; 2 Macc. 4.31. It has the same meaning (*to restrain*) in the papyri, e.g. *BGU* 4.1192.5, τῶν Ἀράβων κατεσταλμένων καὶ πάντων ἐν τῆι μεγίστη[ι] εἰρήναι γεγονότων. The rare occurrence of the word accounts for its replacement by κατασείσας (D E Ψ 614 *pc*), used above in v. 33.

ὁ γραμματεύς. This title of an official at Ephesus (as well as at other Greek cities, including Athens) is confirmed by inscriptions. The noun occurs in Dittenberger, *OGIS* 2.493.11, Λούκιος ... ἀποδε[δει]γμένος γραμματεὺ[ς τοῦ] δήμου, the corresponding verb at 510.11, γραμματεύοντος Ποπλίου Οὐηδίου 'Αντ[ω]νείνου 'Ασιάρχου (cf. v. 31). These inscriptions come from the second century AD, but there is no reason why the office should not have been in existence in the middle of the first. See Sherwin-White (86f.). The word itself was much older; see e.g. Thucydides 7.10. Hanson (197) quotes A. H. M. Jones (*The Greek City* (1940), 181). It seems that some of the wealth of Artemis got into the city treasury and that the town clerk might not have welcomed an inquiry.

ἄνδρες 'Εφέσιοι. For this mode of address see 1.11.

τίς γὰρ ... ; γὰρ is 'inde ab Homero saepe in interrogationibus, fere ut german. *wer denn*' (Blass 212). See BDR § 452.1, n. 2. Either it simply emphasizes the question (cf. Lk. 22.27, and see below on ἀνθρώπων), Why, what man is there ... ?, or it assumes an unexpressed accusation or admonition, You really must restrain yourselves, for who is there ... ? A variant on this might be, I have tried to quieten you, for who ... ? ἀνθρώπων is emphatic: Where can you find anyone in the whole human race who does not know ... ?

The verb of knowing is followed by the accusative and participle (οὖσαν) except in D where the infinitive (εἶναι) is used in place of the participle, possibly through the influence of the Latin of d (*esse*).

As subject of the dependent clause τὴν 'Εφεσίων πόλιν makes good sense, but D has τ. ἡμετέραν πο., which comes perhaps more naturally on the lips of a speaker who is using local patriotism as a means to his end of quietening the crowd. 'Εφεσίων could have been introduced from the end of the preceding verse. The reading of d, *vestram*, plausible in itself, for the town clerk could so address the townspeople, is probably an internal Greek variant, since ὑμετέραν could come from ἡμετέραν even more easily than *vestram* from *nostram*.

The city is νεωκόρον τῆς μεγάλης 'Αρτέμιδος. For Artemis and the adjective *great* see vv. 28, 34. νεωκόρος meant originally *warden of a temple*; the cognate verb is used by Josephus (*War* 5.389, πάλιν τὸν αὐτῶν σύμμαχον ἐνεωκόρουν, they (the Jews after the Exile) re-established the temple worship of their Ally (God)). The noun became a 'title assumed by Asiatic cities in Imperial times, when they had built a temple in honour of their patron-god or the Emperor' (LS 1172), in Ephesus, of Artemis. See Sherwin-White (88f.); Hemer (122). The present seems to be the oldest use that we have. See Dittenberger, *OGIS* 2.481.3; 496.7; BMusInscr 481*.4—all of the second century AD.

Ephesus was thus temple warden of Artemis καὶ τοῦ διοπετοῦς. διοπετής is an adjective but it seems scarcely necessary to speak of the ellipse of a noun (ἄγαλμα), with M. 3.17; LS 433. It is Greek idiom to turn the adjective into a substantive: that which fell down from Zeus. To supply ἄγαλμα is over-precise, though it is used in Euripides, *Iphigenia in Tauris* 977f. (at 87f., 1384f. διοπετής is not used). The object was presumably some kind of meteorite, having perhaps human form. *Begs.* 4.250 makes the point that such objects (also e.g. the Palladium at Troy, the Minerva Polias at Athens, the Cybele at Pessinus) could be used as a counter to Jewish and Christian attacks on paganism as the worship of objects of human manufacture, and quotes Cicero, *In Verrem* 2.5. 72 (187), Simulacrum Cereris ... quod erat tale, ut homines, cum viderent, aut ipsam videre se Cererem, aut effigiem Cereris non humana manu factam sed de caelo lapsam [caelo delapsam] arbitrarentur. See also Herodian, 1.11.1. But the religious evaluation and use of meteorites must have long preceded this polemical interest. For other parallels see Betz (168, n. 2).

D has διοσπετοῦς, which makes clearer that the object not merely fell from the sky (cf. ἄγαλμα διοπ. in *Iph. in T.* 1384f., referred to above) but from Zeus himself. It also probably explains the surprising Vulgate reading, 'iovisque prolis', which WW suggest could be derived from τοῦ Διὸς παιδός (written as πεδός). d has *huius iovis*, hcl mg has *her* διοπετής The words διοπετής, διοσπετής, were probably not well understood.

36. ἀναντιρρήτων, passive: since these matters are not open to contradiction. Contrast 10.29, ἀναντιρρήτως, active: without gainsaying. Presumably Paul and his colleagues would have contradicted if they had been given the opportunity to do so.

κατεσταλμένους. For the word see v. 35. ὑπάρχειν rather than εἶναι, perhaps in order to suggest *remain quiet*.

προπετές. Cf. 2 Tim. 3.4, the only other occurrence in the NT. But the word is not uncommon with the meaning *rash, precipitate*.

37. ἱεροσύλους: classical usage would have had a participle with the predicate; M. 3.159; BDR § 418.6, n. 9. For the cognate verb ἱεροσυλεῖν cf. Rom. 2.22. According to Betz (186 n. 3) the word 'ist oft ein Schimpfwort'; here however it will have its proper sense in view of the charge brought against Paul and his companions, which is virtually that of profaning the temple of Artemis by alleging that she herself was not a deity, and that if she were the worship offered to her was improper. In this sense Paul was a ἱερόσυλος, and he was engaged in speaking evil of (βλασφημοῦντες) the goddess. Thus Chrysostom (Homily 42.2) of the town clerk's words, Ἆρα τὸ πᾶν ψεῦδος, ταῦτα δὲ πρὸς τὸν δῆμον ὥστε κἀκείνους ἐπιεικεστέρους γενέσθαι, φησίν; he is putting the best possible appearance on the matter so as to quieten the crowd. Paul and his colleagues were not profaning or robbing the temple or blaspheming the goddess in a vulgar way. This was the 'correct' Jewish attitude; see *Begs.* 4.251, with reference to Josephus, *Apion* 2.237; *Ant.* 4.207, βλασφημείτω δὲ μηδεὶς θεοὺς οὓς πόλεις ἄλλαι νομίζουσι· μηδὲ συλᾶν ἱερὰ ξενικά. See however *Apion* 1.249, 311. Cf. also Bengel (466): 'Apostoli non collegere multa absurda ex mythologia, sed proposuere veritatem DEI.'

After τούτους, D 614 sy^hmg co add ἐνθάδε, unnecessarily.

For θεόν, D* E^c P 614 1241 2495 *al* have θεάν. On the use of θεός and θεά for female deities see on v. 27.

For ἡμῶν, E* 𝔐 vg sy^h bo have ὑμῶν. Editors and copyists thought it might be well to suggest that the town clerk, who evidently has to be counted as one of the (at least, relatively) good should be distinguished from the wicked and idolatrous Ephesians.

38. Δημήτριος ... τεχνῖται. See on v. 24.

ἔχουσι πρός τινα λόγον, *have a case* (law-suit) *against anyone*, that is, a private suit against individuals, as Demetrius and his colleagues might seem to have against Paul and his. This takes due note of πρός τινα, and of the contrast expressed in the next verse. See Sherwin-White (83). The force of the sentence is not significantly changed if, with D (gig) sa^mss, we read πρὸς αὐτούς τινα λόγον, have any case against them. See v. 39.

For ἀγοραῖοι, ἀγόραιος, see on 17.5. In the present verse it is clear that we must take ἀγοραῖοι as the adjective with ἡμέραι or σύνοδοι understood; it is equivalent to the Latin *fora*, or *conventus, aguntur*. The town clerk points out to Demetrius that there are courts in which private suits may be presented in due form of law and that there is therefore no occasion for riotous assembly. See BDR § 5.4, n. 21; Moule (*IB* 192). 'Ephesus was capital of one of the *conventus*, or assize-districts' (Hemer 123).

Courts are held, and ἀνθύπατοί εἰσιν. 'There are such persons as proconsuls'—before whom such matters may be brought. There was of course only one proconsul of the province of Asia; the plural is *pluralis categoriae* (M. 3.26)—Luke is not to be accused of ignorance of an elementary and universally known fact, nor is it likely that there is a reference to the period after the murder of M. Junius Silanus (Tacitus, *Annals* 13.1; Dio Cassius 61.6) when Helius and Celer (whom Agrippina had employed in the murder) were temporarily in charge in Asia.

39. εἰ δέ τι περαιτέρω ἐπιζητεῖτε. The town clerk now addresses Demetrius and those associated with him directly, in the second person. The sense is correctly given by Sherwin-White: 'If they are after something more than a private lawsuit' (83). τι περαιτέρω is the reading of P^74 B 33 36 453 945 1739 1891 *pc* d gig (*alterius*); ℵ A D (E) Ψ 𝔐 (vg) sy^h co have περὶ ἑτέρων (the Vulgate's '*alterius rei* is an attempt to represent περὶ ἑτέρων without departing too far from the Old Latin rendering' (Ropes, *Begs.* 3.189)). This widely attested reading may have arisen by accident (αι being written, as often in the MSS, ε); it goes too far to say that it does not suit the context (Metzger 473).

Anything beyond a private civil action will be dealt with ἐν τῇ ἐννόμῳ ἐκκλησίᾳ. See v. 32. A similar expression occurs in an inscription (*AGIBM* 3.481.339–40: κατὰ πᾶσαν νόμιμον ἐκκλησίαν. 'According to the latest restoration of the main document (1. 54) there was one monthly meeting called ἱερὰ καὶ νόμιμος ἐκκλησία. Chrysostom in his commentary [Homily 42.2] said that there were three monthly meetings. Presumably there was one regular and two extra meetings a month' (Sherwin-White 87). This otherwise reasonable inference does not take account of the fact that customs may have changed between Luke's time, in the first century, and Chrysostom's, in the fourth. It appears that in any case Demetrius would not have had to wait long for a regular meeting. The present meeting was clearly not ἔννομος. This word can be further documented: Lucian, *Deorum Concilium* 14, ἐκκλησίας ἐννόμου; Dittenberger, *SIG* 2. 672.37, ἐν τᾶι ἐννόμωι ἐκκλησίαι; 2.852.20 (Hemer 123), ἀγομένης ἐκκλησίας ἐννόμου.

For ἐπιζητεῖτε, P⁷⁴ E 36 453 945 1739 1891 *pc* have ζητεῖτε, without difference of meaning.

For τῇ ἐννόμῳ, D* has τῷ νόμῳ, which is meaningless and must be a slip.

40. The syntax of this verse is very confused, and it is not surprising that there are several variants. Hort supposed that there had been a primitive corruption of the text; so also, tentatively, Ropes (*Begs.* 3.189). See Weiser (549) for a good survey of various views of the conclusion of the episode.

The demonstrating artisans, and the whole city with them, *run the risk*, κινδυνεύομεν, of being accused (ἐγκαλεῖν, as in v. 38). Cf. *Begs.* 4.252, ' . . . as though the secretary meant to say the real risk is not in loss of business but trouble with the police for disturbing the peace'. στάσις is a strong word (in the στάσις of Mk 15.7 murder had been committed); *riot*. In classical usage that of which a party was accused was expressed in the accusative, but the genitive case tended in the Hellenistic age to oust the accusative (Radermacher 99). Moule (*IB* 39), however, notes that this would be the only occurrence of this construction in the NT; in 26.6, 29 περί with the genitive is used. He doubts whether the clause can be construed in this way, but offers no alternative. In the present verse περί introduces not the charge but the ground of the charge, in (the events of) this day—περὶ τῆς σήμερον.

μηδενὸς αἰτίου ὑπάρχοντος (D, ὄντος, without substantial difference in meaning). Taken as a unit (genitive absolute) this is intelligible enough: there being no cause (for it, for that which has happened today). Elsewhere αἴτιον may mean *crime* (perhaps as the ground for punishment), but this meaning (negatived by μηδενός) is impossible here. See M. 2.341. Overbeck, referred to by Knowling (419), takes αἰτίου as masculine, 'there being no man guilty'. Cf. the Vulgate, cum nullus obnoxius sit ... This may to some extent avoid the difficulty of the negative.

The next clause contains several difficulties. (1) What is the antecedent of the (masculine or neuter) relative οὗ? It cannot be στάσεως or τῆς σήμερον, both of which are feminine; presumably it is αἰτίου. (2) Taking this to be so, what is meant by saying 'concerning this (ground?), we shall not be able to render account?' Perhaps the town clerk means, 'If we do not at once disperse quietly, we shall not ...' Another possibility is that μηδενὸς αἰτίου ὑπάρχοντος, which was taken above to refer to what precedes, may be taken in close association with what follows: there being no cause (or even crime) concerning which we shall not be able to give an account. This however becomes impossible in view of the next phrase, περὶ τῆς συστροφῆς ταύτης, concerning this concourse (cf. 23.12, the only other use of συστροφή in the NT, where the meaning is *conspiracy*). The omission of περί makes no difference: *an account of* is the same as *an account concerning*. The omission of οὗ (by P⁷⁴ D E 33 36 453 945 1175 1891 *al* gig vg sa bo^mss) does ease the sentence: There being no reason concerning which we shall be able to give an account of this concourse. To this extent the omission must be regarded as *lectio facilior* and unlikely to be correct; but the possibility of accidental dittography or haplography (OYOY) is so strong that no confidence can be felt in either the longer or the shorter reading.

Hort's conjecture of primitive corruption is understandable. 'The difficulty is ... too great to allow acquiescence in any of the transmitted texts as free from error. Probably αἴτιοι ὑπάρχοντες should be read for αἰτίου ὑπάρχοντος, with the construction μηδενὸς αἴτιοι ὑπάρχοντες περὶ οὗ οὐ κ.τ.λ. ("although we are guilty of nothing concerning which" etc.). The usage of the NT admits this use of μή with a participle, and the interchanges of I and Y, E and O, in uncials are of the commonest' (*Introduction: Notes* 97). Unfortunately Hort does not explain how he takes περὶ τῆς συστροφῆς ταύτης. There is very much to be said for C. F. D. Moule's view (*ExpT* 65 (1954), 221) that the author wrote the sentence in several forms, and omitted to delete the rejected words before publication. Even this however will hardly account for the two fundamentally different impressions (not translations) which it is possible to derive from the verse. The town clerk is evidently seeking to achieve the result described in the last words of the verse: he wishes to send everyone home in peace, but he may be arguing: (1) We are running the risk of being accused of riot and insurrection, and there will be no defence, for there is no rational ground or excuse for what has happened; that is, we shall get what we deserve; *or* (2) We are running the risk of being accused of riot and insurrection, even though we have not in fact done anything for which we cannot plead that there was just cause; punishment inflicted by the proconsul will then be undeserved, but this will make it no less unpleasant.

It may be (1) that there has been corruption of the text (Hort); (2) that Luke never revised his original draft (Moule); (3) that Luke was not clear in his own mind how the situation should be viewed; (4) that the town clerk wanted to 'have it both ways' and used ambiguous arguments designed to appeal to different sections of the crowd.

Whichever view we take there is an 'atmosphere of indignant defence of the city's privileges and reputation' (Sherwin-White 84). Sherwin-White compares the description in Acts with the civic speeches of Dion of Prusa [= Dio Chrysostom] (*Orations* 46.14; 48.1–3; 38.38). He adds, 'There is something rather ominous in this tone. This was the last age of civic autonomy in the ancient world. Civic politics in the old pattern of the city-state, with its assemblies and councils, expired in the course of the later second and early third centuries AD. The city councils became closed hereditary oligarchies … The scene belongs unmistakably to an era that did not survive the age of the Antonines … The evidence of Acts not only agrees in general with the civic situation in Asia Minor in the first and early second centuries AD, but falls into place in the earlier rather than the later phase of development' (84f.). These observations are interesting and important but do not greatly affect the dating of Acts; no one would wish to make it later than the age of the Antonines.

An additional aspect of the narrative is suggested by R. F. Stoops in an important article (*JBL* 108 (1989), 73–91). Its main substance may be conveyed by the following paragraph. 'The speech of the town clerk reinforces the apologetic thrust of the passage. This speech identifies opposition to the Way, rather than the Way itself, as the source of trouble and the threat to the established order. The Gentile residents of Ephesus are cautioned against acting the part of a political assembly without being properly constituted. The Way and its local assembly (ἐκκλησία) are not condemned. The silence of the town clerk on this point implies that the ἐκκλησία of believers, unlike Demetrius's mob, can coexist with the legitimate assembly of citizens in Ephesus. The story suggests that the assembly of believers ought to be left alone and allowed to conduct its own affairs. That seemingly small request was an extraordinary privilege in the Roman world, one that had set the Jews apart from other groups' (88f.). Stoops makes the good point that the apologetic element in Acts was not addressed primarily to Roman officials but to Christians. 'Those readers had a concrete need for self-definition and reassurance. Acts is not a handbook of debating points but a presentation of Luke's understanding of the world and the place of the community of believers within that world' (90).

ἀπολύειν is used in a variety of senses in the NT and elsewhere; here *to dismiss*; cf. Josephus, *Ant.* 11.337, ἀπέλυσε τὸ πλῆθος.

50. BACK TO PALESTINE, THROUGH MACEDONIA, GREECE, AND TROAS 20.1–16

(1) After the uproar had ceased Paul sent for the disciples,[1] gave them an exhortation, said farewell, and set out to travel to Macedonia. (2) When he had passed through those parts and[2] exhorted them in much preaching he came into Greece; (3) when he had spent three months [there][3] and a plot was made against him by the Jews as he was about to leave for Syria, he made up his mind to return through Macedonia. (4) There were associated with him Sopater the son of Pyrrhus, a Beroean, of the Thessalonians Aristarchus and Secundus, Gaius[4] of Derbe and Timothy, and the Asians Tychicus and Trophimus. (5) These[5] went on ahead and waited for us in Troas. (6) We sailed from Philippi after the Days of Unleavened Loaves[6] and came to them at Troas after five days; there we stayed[7] seven days.

(7) On the first day of the week,[8] when we had gathered to break bread, Paul, since he was about to leave on the morrow, discoursed with them and prolonged his speech till midnight. (8) There were many lamps[9] in the upper room in which we had met, (9) and a young man, Eutychus by name, sitting[10] by the window, was being gradually overcome by deep sleep[11] as Paul discoursed longer and longer, until having been finally overcome by sleep he fell[12] from the[13] second floor, and was picked up dead. (10) Paul went down,[14] fell on him, embraced him, and said, 'Stop making a disturbance, his life is in him.'[15] (11) He went up, broke bread, and ate; he conversed further until dawn, and so left. (12) They took up the boy alive, and were[16] no little comforted.

(13) We went on ahead to the ship and set sail for Assos, where we were to take up Paul, for so he had[17] given orders, since he himself intended to go by

[1]NEB, after encouraging them; NJB, after speaking words of encouragement to them.
[2]RSV, given them much encouragement; NEB, after speaking words of encouragement; NJB, he said many words of encouragement.
[3]Greek omits.
[4]NEB, the Doberian.
[5]NJB, they all.
[6]NEB, Passover season.
[7]NEB; NJB, a week.
[8]NEB, Saturday night.
[9]RSV, lights.
[10]NEB, on the window-ledge; NJB, on the window-sill.
[11]RSV, sank into a deep sleep.
[12]NJB, to the ground three floors below.
[13]RSV, third story; NEB, third storey.
[14]RSV, bent over him; NEB, threw himself upon him.
[15]NEB; NJB, there is still life in him.
[16]NEB, immensely; NJB, greatly encouraged.
[17]RSV; NJB, arranged; NEB, made this arrangement.

land. (14) When he met us at Assos we took him up and came to Mitylene. (15) Thence we sailed, and on the following day came opposite Chios; on the next day we reached Samos, and[18] the day after that we came to Miletus. (16) For Paul had chosen to sail past Ephesus in order that he might not have to spend time in Asia, for he was making haste so as to be, if possible, in Jerusalem on the Day of Pentecost.

Bibliography

M. Black, as in (46).

H. Conzelmann, *ZNW* 45 (1954), 266.

E. Delebecque, *Bib* 64 (1983), 556–64.

C. J. Hemer, *FS* Bruce (1980), 9–12.

P. W. van der Horst, *NovT* 17 (1975), 158.

B. Lindars, in C. F. D. Moule (ed.), *Miracles*, London 1965, 61–79.

S. M. Praeder, *NovT* 29 (1978), 193–218.

H. Riesenfeld, *FS* T. W. Manson, 210–17.

W. Rordorf, *ZNW* 68 (1977), 138–41.

R. Staats, *ZNW* 66 (1975), 242–63.

G. Zuntz, *Gnomon* 30 (1958), 26.

Commentary

The structure of this section is clear. The first six verses describe the opening stages of Paul's roundabout return from Ephesus to Palestine. When the uproar in Ephesus is over, he leaves for Macedonia, addresses the Christians in those parts, and makes his way to Greece. After spending three months there he determines to sail for Syria; his plan however is changed by a Jewish plot, and he decides to return by the way he came, through Macedonia. In v. 4 we learn the names of men accompanying Paul, but no sooner are they named then they (or some of them) separate from him, go ahead, and wait for *us*—for now the first person plural is re-introduced—in Troas. *We* sailed from Philippi (reached, it seems, though this is not quite definite, by land).

Paul and his companions are thus reunited with one another in Troas. Here there are Christians (not mentioned in v. 6, but the fact becomes evident as the story proceeds), and the travellers join them in the common meal. This becomes the occasion of a miracle. There is nothing in the story of Eutychus to connect the event specifically with this time and place; it could have happened anywhere, and it has no necessary connection with the sequence of events described in the preceding and following verses. It gives the impression of being a

---

[18]NJB adds: after stopping at Trogyllium.

free piece of tradition which Luke had some reason to connect with Troas (perhaps he heard it there) and interpolated into the record of the journey. This is resumed in v. 13. Up to the end of v. 15 there is nothing but geography, as the party, now united and travelling by sea, touch at Assos and Mitylene, sail near Chios, and touch again at Samos and Miletus. This means that Ephesus is by-passed, apparently because Paul had decided (κεκρίκει, v. 16) on this course. Whether Paul as a passenger could decide the ship's route and stopping-places seems questionable; he may well have been glad to find that the ship did not intend to call at Ephesus, though whether the motive for haste that is supplied is convincing raises further questions; see the note on v. 16.

Of the opening sub-paragraph Conzelmann (115) writes, 'Die Liste zeigt, dass Lk altes Material besitzt. Aber die Ereignisse sind wieder vereinfacht.' Conzelmann does not say by whom—by Luke or at some earlier stage in the tradition—they were simplified. Nor is it clear exactly what this means. A writer intent on simplification could have achieved a better result than appears in vv. 1–6, where some points are by no means clear. Conzelmann refers to relevant passages in the Corinthian letters (1 Cor. 16.5; 2. Cor. 2.12ff., 7.6ff.), but here we have not so much simplification as simple omission. *Greece*, an imprecise term, is mentioned, but Corinth is not, and Paul's complicated and often agonized dealings with the church there after the close of his first visit are not mentioned. One must suppose that in the three months of v. 3 the Corinthian problems were solved at least to the extent that Achaea contributed to the collection (Rom. 15.26; see *2 Corinthians* 21, 25–28). Notwithstanding the first person plural in vv. 5, 6, 7, 8, 13, 14, 15, these passages are often distinguished from the other We-passages, and it is at least a plausible suggestion that *We* in vv. 7, 8 has been brought in from the surrounding travel notes. It is rightly observed that in the Eutychus story as a whole interest focuses upon Paul, his companions having no part to play. This is inherent in the form and substance of the story, but it is probably correct to deduce from the absence of *We* and the fact that the Eutychus story interrupts the connection between vv. 6 and 13, that it comes from a different source (probably local tradition; see above). Weiser (557), modifying and developing Conzelmann's view, thinks that behind the travel notices lies 'Überlieferungsgut ... wahrscheinlich in Form eines Itinerars'. It is not easy to see why these first person plurals (except perhaps those in vv. 7 and 8) should be distinguished from those in chs. 16 and 27. 'Auszuschliessen ist auch nicht die Vermutung, dass Titus das Reisetagebuch führte; dieser Vermutung mag man zuneigen wenn man die Differenzen der ''Wir-Berichte'' von der zweiten Missionsreise und der Jerusalemreise entsprechend bewertet' (Pesch 2.187). This is hardly convincing, and it is a striking fact that in vv. 5,

6 the new *We* is taken up at Philippi, where the previous *We* ceased. It is no new suggestion, but there is something to be said for the view that the writer of the Itinerary had remained in Philippi in the interval. For this part of Paul's travels see especially Thornton (146–8, 255–8).

The concluding sub-paragraph (vv. 13–16) sees the party down the west coast of Asia Minor as far as Miletus, Paul, apparently alone and for no given reason, making the first part of the journey by land. For Paul's decision not to visit Ephesus see the note on v. 16. It may be that Luke is concealing the fact that Paul did not dare to show his face in Ephesus, and that the verse is part of the editor's attempt to play down the measure of opposition to Paul's work there, though it is hard to see why he should wish to minimize the perils endured by his hero. It is certainly true that the motive given for by-passing Ephesus—a strong desire to observe the feast of Pentecost in Jerusalem—can hardly fail to evoke scepticism. At least the concluding note (v. 16b) seems clearly to be an editorial supplement to a travel document, which at this point is little more than a list of names.

1. θόρυβος properly denotes sound—not merely *tumult* but *clamour*, and there is no reason why it should not have this meaning here. *After the uproar had ceased* Paul took up again the intention mentioned in 19.21.

μεταπεμψάμενος is the reading of P⁷⁴ ℵ B E 33 36 453 1175 *pc*, προσκαλεσάμενος of A D Ψ 𝔐 latt sy, μεταστειλάμενος of 945 1739 1891 *pc*. The words all have substantially the same meaning. μεταπέμπεσθαι occurs 9 times in Acts, nowhere else in the NT—a Lucan word; μεταστέλλεσθαι occurs here only; προσκαλεῖσθαι occurs 9 times in Acts, 4 times in Lk., but 16 times in the rest of the NT. One is inclined to accept μεταστειλάμενος as inviting assimilation to the more usual words, but the support is very slight. μεταπεμπ. is more likely to have suggested μεταστειλ. than προσκαλ. and should probably be accepted.

παρακαλέσας: see on 2.40 and elsewhere. There was no need for Luke to add a clause explaining what Paul exhorted them *to do*; he gave them a Christian exhortation. D*ᵛⁱᵈ, πολλὰ παρακελεύσας, is probably not more than a slip in writing. d has multo exhortatus, and according to Ropes (*Begs.* 3.191) the first hand of D has παρακελε[ύ]σας; doubt about the υ supports παρακαλέσας as the intended reading.

ἀσπασάμενος must here mean *said Goodbye* (that is, saluted in farewell, as at Euripides, *Trojan Women* 1276, ὡς ἀσπάσωμαι τὴν ταλαίπωρον πόλιν), though the word much more often means a greeting or welcome. The three participles μεταπ ... παρακαλ., ἀσπασ. all precede the finite verb ἐξῆλθεν in time.

πορεύεσθαι is omitted by D E 323 945 1739 2495 *pc* gig bo^[mss]; no doubt it seemed unnecessary to the narrative. There are however two distinct thoughts: he went out of the city of Ephesus, and he set out on the long journey to Macedonia. For Macedonia see 16.9.

2. διελθών. Cf. 19.21.

(πάντα, D) τὰ μέρη ἐκεῖνα. Luke does not indicate what districts he had in mind; presumably those of Macedonia through which Paul would pass on his way to Greece.

παρακαλέσας αὐτοὺς (χρησάμενος, D^[vid]; an unusual word in such a setting in Acts; possibly therefore original?) λόγῳ πολλῷ. If a single occasion in one place were in question, one would say, *with a long speech*; since work in various areas (μέρη) is in mind the sense must be *much speaking, much preaching*.

Moving round the north-western angle of the Aegean, Paul came into Greece, εἰς τὴν Ἑλλάδα. The article is used (contrast Μακεδονίαν, anarthrous, in v. 1) because Ἑλλάς was originally adjectival (supply γῆ or χώρα)—BDR § 261.4. ''Ἑλλάς steht ... volkstümlich für ''Achaia'' '—Pausanias 7.16 (Schneider 2.280).

3. ποιήσας τε μῆνας τρεῖς. For this use of ποιεῖν cf. 15.33; 18.23; also 2 Cor. 11.25; Jas 4.13. It occurs outside the NT, though mostly in later Greek (e.g. Josephus, *Ant.* 6.18 (ποιήσασα ... μῆνας τέσσαρας); also PIand 6 (1934) 97.7, quoted in *ND* 4.63–67). This seems to be the occasion when Paul paid his third visit to Corinth (2 Cor. 12.14; 13.1) and settled the Corinthian problems at least to the extent that Achaea joined in the collection that Paul was organizing (Rom. 15.26). He was now on his way to Jerusalem, bearing, it seems, the proceeds of his appeal. The visit to Corinth seems to have been a difficult one, difficult and stormy even if in the end triumphant. Problems and success are alike passed over in Acts. Because Luke thought them unedifying and suppressed them? Because he was not aware of them? These are questions to which only hesitant answers can be given, and that when all such questions have been collected and reviewed. The silences of Acts are an important factor in any discussion of its authorship.

γενομένης ἐπιβουλῆς ... ὑπὸ τῶν Ἰουδαίων. The participle follows upon the preceding one without connecting particle. Cf. 20.19, ἐν ταῖς ἐπιβουλαῖς τῶν Ἰουδαίων; and other passages— 9.24; 21.27; 23.12. There is no means of knowing what the Jewish plot was. Bornkamm (4.136) thinks that the Jews, probably on pilgrimage to Jerusalem for Passover, were travelling on the ship that Paul was intending to use and that it was for this reason that Paul, changing his plans, decided to travel overland through Macedonia, and eventually picked up a ship in Philippi or Troas (vv. 5f.). This is an ingenious suggestion, possibly correct. Certainly Paul was about to sail to Syria (see 21.3) when ἐγένετο γνώμης ... τοῦ ὑποστρέφειν διὰ Μακεδονίας. For the genitive γνώμης see BDR § 162.7, n. 9: 'att. τῆς αὐτῆς γνώμης ἦσαν udg1.' LS 354 refer to Thucydides 1.113.2 (ὅσοι τῆς αὐτῆς γνώμης ἦσαν); 1.140.1 (τῆς μὲν γνώμης ... ἀεὶ τῆς αὐτῆς ἔχομαι. We may add Plutarch, *Phocion* 23.4 (752), τὴν μὲν πόλιν ἐλπίδος μεγάλης γενομένην; Josephus, *War* 6.287. Paul's change of plan is thus represented as purely rational: consideration of the Jewish plot leads him to travel by a different route from that which he had intended to take. The Western text (D (gig) sy^hmg) emphasizes the supernatural guidance afforded by the Holy Spirit. Instead of μέλλοντι τοῦ it reads ἠθέλησαν ἀναχθῆναι εἰς Συρίαν· εἶπεν δὲ τὸ πνεῦμα αὐτῷ ...

It was at this time that Romans was written (cf. Rom. 15.23–28).

4. This verse is remarkable for a considerable measure of textual confusion; there is an excellent discussion (covering vv. 3–5) by Ropes (*Begs.* 3.190f.).

In the Old Uncial text the verse begins συνείπετο δὲ αὐτῷ, which Ropes rightly translates *there were associated with him*, and understands as a general association of persons who were assembling from various places to share in the journey to Syria, which, according to v. 3, was planned, but changed as far as the immediate future was concerned into a return to Asia by way of Macedonia. The named companions went ahead to Troas; Paul and at least one companion joined them there (v. 6). D however omits συνειπ. δὲ αὐ. and has instead μέλλοντος οὖν ἐξιέναι αὐτοῦ; sy^hmg has this clause but adds συνείποντο αὐτῷ. At this point there is a further addition, by A (D) E Ψ 𝔐 gig vg^mss sy, of ἄχρι (μέχρι) τῆς Ἀσίας. This implies, with some confusion, that the named group accompanied Paul throughout the journey, from Corinth to Syria. It must be added that if the Western editor did not grasp clearly what Luke meant in these verses he was not without excuse.

It is certain that the journey undertaken here had as at least one of its purposes, probably its primary purpose, the conveying to Jerusalem of the proceeds of Paul's collection. That Luke does not mention it is a surprising fact; see Dibelius (211) and many subsequent writers. Luke's only hint at this event, of evident importance to Paul, is in 24.17; reasons for his silence can only be conjectural; see pp. 1001, 1107f. According to 1 Cor. 16.3f., it was Paul's intention that local representatives should convey the money to Jerusalem, perhaps in his company. It is reasonable to infer that those mentioned in this verse (except perhaps Timothy) were such local representatives and not assistant missionaries (so e.g. Roloff 296).

There are textual problems also in the list of names.

Σώπατρος Πύρρου, *Sopater the son of Pyrrhus*. For both names see Hemer (236). Πύρρου is anarthrous, as in classical use: BDR § 162.2, n. 4; M. 3.168. This word is omitted by 𝔐 sy; Ropes (*Begs.*

3.191) thinks that ΠΥΡΡΟΣ arose through confused repetition of the preceding six letters (ΠΑΤΡΟΣ); this does not seem probable, but it is hard to see why Pyrrhus should be omitted if the name stood originally in the text. Neither Sopater nor Pyrrhus appears elsewhere in the NT; Sosipater (whose name appears here in 104 (1175) *pc* gig p^c vg^s co) is mentioned at Rom. 16.21. Hemer identifies the two. Sopater came from Beroea (Βεροιαῖος); Hemer (124) shows that this is the form used in local inscriptions.

There follow two who came from Thessalonica (see 17.1), Aristarchus and Secundus. The former is presumably the Aristarchus mentioned at 19.29 as a Macedonian (see the note on this verse). He reappears at 27.2; see also Col. 4.10; Philemon 24. Secundus (the Greek form of the name is derived from Latin) is not mentioned elsewhere. For the accentuation (Σέκουνδος or Σεκοῦνδος) see BDR § 41.3.

The next pair is Gaius Derbaeus (that is, Gaius of Derbe; see 14.6 and the note) and Timothy. See 16.1; this verse suggests but does not positively affirm that Timothy's home was in Lystra whereas the association with Gaius might suggest that Timothy came from Derbe. Both were Lycaonian towns, though some distance apart. The connection of Gaius with Derbe may however be in error. (1) In 19.29 along with Aristarchus there is mentioned a Gaius who was a Macedonian (see the note on the text of 19.29). (2) In the present verse a variant reading gives instead of Δερβαῖος, Δουβ[έ]ριος (so D* d (doverius) gig). This would refer to a town Doberos (Δοβῆρος in Thucydides 2.98–100) in Paeonia (see *Der kleine Pauly* 2.110), at this time a northern division of Macedonia, and give us a Macedonian Gaius in agreement with 19.29. This variant, however, though accepted by not a few (Williams 229; but see especially Clark xlix, 1, 374–6) is no more convincing than the singular (Μακεδόνα) in 19.29; in each case the more difficult reading must be accepted. As Metzger (475f.) points out in a detailed note, it is easier, in a second-century context, to understand the change from Δερβαῖος to Δούβριος than *vice versa*, and the pairing of the names suggests that Gaius and Timothy came from the same region.

There follow the Asian pair, Tychicus (see Hemer 236) and Trophimus (see Hemer 236f.; also *ND* 3.91–3—the name was common, non-Jewish, and suggests servile status, in the past or in the present). For Ἀσιανοί, D (sy^{hmg} sa) have Ἐφέσιοι, by assimilation to 21.29, Trophimus the Ephesian (cf. 2 Tim. 4.20). The reading is to be rejected, though the statement may be correct; Ephesians were Asians. For Tychicus, D has Eutychus—an odd slip, since there is no reason to think the Eutychus of v. 9 an Ephesian. Tychicus is mentioned at Eph. 6.21; Col. 4.7; 2 Tim. 4.12; Titus 3.12. The references are sufficient to show that both men were companions and colleagues of Paul's.

On this verse Bultmann (*Exegetica* 418) rightly notes that lists such as this are more likely to have been preserved in writing than in oral tradition.

5. οὗτοι, the persons named in v. 4 (though *Begs.* 4.253 thinks that probably only Tychicus and Trophimus are intended) went on ahead and waited for *us* in Troas (see 16.8). It is implied that whoever was responsible, in whatever way, for the We source joined Paul at Philippi (v. 6). 'We', which persists to v. 15, has not been used since ch. 16, and it is possible that we should think of the writer as having remained in Philippi through the whole of the intervening period. It seems that we should think of the group of travellers as collecting in Greece (v. 2) but then splitting up for the first stage of the journey east, five (or two?) sailing direct across the Aegean to Troas and waiting there, while Paul went, perhaps by land, to Philippi and thence sailed to Troas. For opinions on the question who the companion was who drew up the record, see Weiser (559).

This account of events assumes the reading προελθόντες (P⁷⁴ B² D 36 104 323 614 1891 *pm* latt). προσελθόντες is read by ℵ Aᵛⁱᵈ B* E H L P Ψ 945 1175 1241 1739 2495 (*pm*). This makes a less clear story but has been held to harmonize with 1 Tim. 1.3 (cf. 1 Tim. 3.14; 4.13); it may have been introduced for this reason. According to Conzelmann (115), προσ– is better attested, but the sense requires προ-. It is in fact doubtful whether προσ– is better attested; the agreement of B and D is striking.

For ἡμᾶς, D, alone, has αὐτόν. This may have been intended to take up μέλλοντος ... αὐτοῦ in v. 4, but has little to commend it.

6. *We* sailed with Paul from Philippi; it may be presumed—though it is not certain—that the writer joined Paul in Philippi. On the question of a 'We' source see the Introduction, pp. xxv–xxx.

ἐξεπλεύσαμεν: in the NT only at Acts 15.39; 18.18; 20.6. But only Luke has occasion to use the word (apart from a few short trips on Galilee).

τῶν ἀζύμων. Luke still uses the Jewish calendar as a means of dating events; there is no Christian 'Easter' that he can refer to. See *Begs.* 4.254f. for a note on the origin of the Christian festival. Roloff (296) takes it that Paul naturally observed Jewish festivals; Lüdemann (229) says that dating by Jewish festivals is Lucan; his addition to a source? For Philippi see on 16.12.

We joined the rest (see vv. 4f.) *at Troas* (see 16.8) ἄχρι ἡμερῶν πέντε. This must be intended to mean that the journey from Philippi to Troas lasted five days, but the use of ἄχρι seems to be without parallel. We may think of the time up to which the voyage lasted (Page 112). *Begs.* 4.255 cites Plutarch, *Cicero* 6 (863), ἄχρι παντός, continually, and Hermas, *Mandate* 4.1.5, ἄχρι τῆς ἀγνοίας, so far as he is ignorant; but these are not close parallels. Luke uses the word in its normal sense elsewhere, e.g. at v. 11 (ἄχρι αὐγῆς). The strange-ness of the construction is marked by D's elegant πεμπταῖοι, but the reading of P⁷⁴ ℵ A E 33, ἀπὸ ἡμ. π., is hardly an improvement. This journey took five days, the journey in the opposite direction (16.11) only two. Commentators agree that an easterly wind could be responsible for so great a difference; so e.g. Beyer (122).

ἡμέρας ἑπτά. It is often said that the next verse implies that Paul arrived and left on a Monday; it would be better to say that if he left on a Monday he must have arrived on a Tuesday; Tuesday to Monday, counting inclusively, is seven days.

For ὅπου, B (Ψ) 𝔐 have οὗ, D has ἐν ᾗ καί. There is no difference in meaning. διατρίβειν occurs twice (once) in Jn, but in Acts see 12.19; 14.3, 28; 15.35; 16.12; 20.6; 25.6, 14.

7. A new narrative begins which is entirely separable from the context of the journey from Greece to Jerusalem. It is a straightfor-ward miracle story, the intention of which is to show the supernatural power attendant upon the Gospel and manifested in the work of Paul (cf. e.g. Peter in 9.36–42). Attempts to find an allegorical intention in the story (even Weiser's, 564) are unconvincing.

Ἐν δὲ τῇ μίᾳ τῶν σαββάτων. For σάββατα see 17.2 and the note. The cardinal μία is used where the ordinal would be expected; so also at Mt. 28.1; Mk 16.2; Lk. 24.1; 1 Cor. 16.2. 'It is Jewish Greek' (Black, *AA* 124), though not without some analogy in Greek idiom (M. 1.96; 2.174, 439). *Begs.* 4.255 is probably right in taking the reference to be to what we should call Sunday evening; it is however not impossible that Luke means Saturday evening, when by Jewish reckoning the first day of the week began. See H. Riesenfeld in *FS* T. W. Manson, 210–17; also R. Staats in *ZNW* 66 (1975), 242–63, especially 247f. Staats chooses Saturday night.

συνηγμένων ἡμῶν. 'We' joined Paul at v. 6; the first person plural continues. For a general discussion of this see Introduction. Bult-mann (*Exegetica* 420) thinks that the narrative was drawn from a written source (see on v. 8), and that the first person plural was introduced into it when it was incorporated into the itinerary. See above, p. 949.

κλάσαι ἄρτον. See 2.42, 46; 27.35, and the notes. There is no indication in the present passage, unless it is implied by the phrase itself, that the meal was other or more than a church fellowship meal, accompanied by religious discourse (ὁ Παῦλος διελέγετο) and conversation (v. 11). That the event took place in a private house (v. 8) does not in itself prove that it was not an action of the whole church; at this period there were few, perhaps no, special church buildings. Reicke (*DFZ* 75f.), makes a distinction (perhaps without foundation) between eucharistic agape (Gemeindegottesdienst) and private agape, but notes that the eucharistic agape will often have been held in private houses, and that later the private agape was sometimes held in church. Whether the ἐκκλησία ever in fact had anywhere in which to meet except private houses is very doubtful. For a general consideration of eucharist, agape, and the like in Acts, with the recognition that Acts provides little or no basis for such terminology or for any developed set of practices, see Introduction, pp. xciif.

διελέγετο: see 17.2, 17; 18.4, 19; 19.8, 9; 20.7, 9; 24.12, 25; always of Paul; elsewhere in the NT only Mk 9.34; Heb. 12.5; Jude 9. The meaning varies between dialogue, discussion between two or more persons, and discussion in which one person *discusses* a matter, as in a sermon or lecture. Paul had already spent seven days in Troas, and was to depart on the next day; no doubt for this reason, since he could hardly hope to have another opportunity of speaking to these Christians, he extended his sermon till midnight, μέχρι μεσονυκτίου. The omission of the article with a word denoting time is classical (M. 3.179), but cf. 16.25, where the article is used. There is no indication at what hour the gathering had begun; presumably not till after the day's work had ended. The λαμπάδες in v. 8 show that it was dark. Nor is it said at what point in the proceedings the discourse began. Probably the meeting began with supper, but even if this went on for some time Paul must have preached at very much greater length than any of the sermons recorded in Acts; these are of course no more than the barest outlines. The time was early May (if we build on v. 16). Workmen (apart from indoor household servants) should have been free from their work by 7 or 8 p.m.

It was the first day of the week—the Christian Sunday (even if it was Saturday evening), but of course a working day. Observance of the Jewish Sabbath is already abandoned in the NT (Col. 2.16), and early in the second century the two observances were taken to be typical of the Jewish and Christian religions respectively (Ignatius, *Magnesians* 9.1, μηκέτι σαββατίζοντες ἀλλὰ κατὰ κυριακὴν ζῶντες). 1 Cor. 16.2 refers not to a Christian gathering but to Christian action on the first day of the week; Rev. 1.10 refers to the Lord's Day as an occasion when the Seer was in the Spirit. Cf. Pliny, *Epistles* 10.96.7: … quod essent soliti stato die ante lucem convenire. This was a morning gathering. The passage continues: quibus peractis morem sibi discendendi fuisse, rursusque ad capiendum cibum. The latter gathering, for food, corresponds more to what is described as taking place at Troas. It is often supposed, but without good reason, that the morning gathering mentioned by Pliny was a eucharist, the later (evening?) meeting a non-sacramental meal (an agape); so e.g. Lightfoot (*Ignatius* 1.52). For meetings on the Lord's Day see also *Didache* 14.1; Barnabas 15.9.

The theological significance of the replacement of the Sabbath by the 'Lord's Day' is discussed by Barth (*CD* 3.1.228; 2.458f. 4.53)

and by Calvin (*Institutes* 2.8.33f.)—not convincingly. Luke's reference to the first day of the week is made in passing, as a natural
explanation of the fact that the Christians were taking supper
together. It does not appear that he is pressing the observance of the
day as something that he wishes to commend to his readers; rather he
assumes that they will fully understand what is going on. Commentators are apt to add the assumption that Luke understood the contents
of Christian worship in the terms in which it was later practised.
Bengel (467): Itaque credibile est, *fractione panis* hic denotari
convivium discipulorum cum eucharistia conjunctum; Pesch (2.193):
The 'urchristliche Gottesdienst ... findet am Sonntag statt, in einem
Privathaus, mit Wortgottesdienst und eucharistischem Mahl'. These
are relatively cautious statements.

The reference here to the first day of the week has been made the
basis of a conjectural attempt to find a precise date in the chronology
of Paul's life; see especially Hemer in *FS* Bruce (1980), 9–12; also
Hemer (169, 216) and R. Jewett (*Dating Paul's Life* (1979), 47–50).
The argument in outline is that Paul left Troas on Monday (vv. 7,
11); he therefore began his seven-day stay in Troas on Tuesday. He
arrived after a five-day journey (v. 6) from Philippi, which he must
have left on Friday. But he left Philippi after the days of unleavened
bread (v. 6), therefore Passover fell in that year on a Thursday. But
'the Passover of 57, as calculated from the full moon, fell probably
on Thursday 7 April, and the Passover of neighbouring years could
not have fallen on that day of the week' (Hemer 169). It follows that
Paul's journey took place in AD 57. Unfortunately this is by no
means convincing. (1) Lk. 22.7 is sufficient to show Luke's quite
imprecise knowledge, or careless statement, of the relation between
Passover and Unleavened Bread; (2) Passover in fact coincided with
the first of the days of unleavened bread, so that if Unleavened Bread
ended on a Thursday Passover must have been on a Friday; (3) μετὰ
τὰς ἡμέρας τῶν ἀζύμων does not necessarily mean 'on the next day
after the Feast of Unleavened Bread'; (4) the times of full moon in
the first century can be calculated now with greater accuracy than
they could be observed at the time; (5) even if the 'five' and 'seven'
of v. 6 were drawn from the 'We' source, or Itinerary, it is impossible
to place complete confidence in their precise accuracy. And such
questions as, 'Did the last day of the five coincide with the first day
of the seven, or not?' are unanswerable.

8. Instead of λαμπάδες, D (not d, which has *faculae*) has
ὑπολαμπάδες, a very rare word (see LS 1887; MM 658; BA 1684;
also M. 2.328). The best that LS can offer is 'part of a στοά,
possessing ... a roof, and tiles'. The evidence in MM suffices for the
meaning *window*. Moulton also gives *window*, but adds 'apparently a
screen *under* which the light shines'. The most helpful parallel to the

present use is *Joseph and Aseneth* 14.9, ὑπολαμπαδὸς καιομένης, which would make it a synonym of λαμπάς. It may be that the copyist responsible for the word thought of the meaning *window*, the thought being put into his mind by v. 9. G. Zuntz (*Gnomon* 30 (1958), 26) prefers the reading of D (cf. Metzger 477), but it seems unlikely that the original reading would survive in one MS only. The lamps (which Bultmann, *Exegetica* 420, sees as a pointer to the use of a written source) are probably mentioned to account for the drowsiness of Eutychus (though there are some who think that E. fell asleep in spite of the lamps, which were intended to promote wakefulness). It is most unlikely that Luke had any further motive in mentioning them, though they are said by opponents whom Justin answers to be used in lovefeasts (*1 Apology* 26: εἰ δὲ καὶ τὰ δύσφημα ἐκεῖνα μυθολογούμενα ἔργα πράττουσι, λυχνίας μὲν ἀνατροπὴν καὶ τὰς ἀνέδην μίξεις καὶ ἀνθρωπείων σαρκῶν βόρας, οὐ γινώσκομεν). Cf. Minucius Felix 9.9; Tertullian, *Apology* 7. In a meeting that lasted all night (v. 11) lamps would be needed.

ἐν τῷ ὑπερῴῳ. See on 1.13; the word is used also at 9.37, 39. At 1 Clement 12.3 it is used of the flat roof of a house; in earlier Greek (see LS 1871) it described the women's part of a house; in Acts (nowhere else in the NT) it is simply an upper storey (cf. v. 9).

For ἦμεν, 1 *pc* bo have ἦσαν, which must be a slip; copyists had forgotten the first person plural of v. 7—though Conzelmann (115) regards the 'we' in this verse as 'offensichtlich sekundär'. It may well be that this incident has been incorporated into an Itinerary, but this can hardly be said to be obvious.

Rackham (379) mentions Jewish Sabbath lamps, the use of which was known to Gentiles (Persius, *Satire* 5.180–184). There is no reason to suppose that the lamps in this story were other than functional.

9. νεανίας ὀνόματι Εὔτυχος. For the name see Hemer (237); it means Fortunate, and a young man brought back to life might well be thought fortunate. But the name was a not uncommon one (note the story of Augustus and the peasant Eutychus with his ass Nicon, Suetonius, *Augustus* 96.2). The story in Acts may or may not be historical, but there is no need to suspect its historicity simply because of the occurrence of this name.

θυρίς (cf. 2 Cor 11.33) is, unlike ὑπολαμπάς (v. 8) a common word for window.

καταφερόμενος ... κατενεχθείς. The change of tense brings out vividly the gradually increasing drowsiness and its climax at the point where Eutychus finally falls asleep. The only biblical parallel to this use of καταφέρεσθαι appears to be Ps. 75(76).7 (Aquila; LXX ἐνύσταξαν, Hebrew נרדם), but cf. Aristotle, *De Generatione Animalium* 5.1 [779a] (Hatch, *Essays* 25). Though the verb is repeated it is followed in the first use by the dative (ὕπνῳ βαθεῖ), in the second by ἀπό and the genitive (ἀπὸ τοῦ ὕπνου). ἀπό is used for ὑπό (see M. 1.102, 237, 246; BDR § 210.2, n. 2) at 10.33 (v.1.); 15.4; use with the instrument is less usual than with the agent, but there seems to be no other interest here than a desire for variation. There is yet another construction in Lucian, *Dialogi Meretricii* 2, ἐς ὕπνον κατηνέχθην. Page (212) points out that ὕπνῳ βαθεῖ is not deep sleep but strong drowsiness, which ends in sound sleep. P. W. van der Horst (*NovT* 17 (1975), 158) quotes Hierocles the Stoic, p. 25, col. 5,1 ... βαθυτάτῳ πεπιεσμένοι ... ὕπνῳ; p. 27, col. 5,27 βαθέων ὕπνων.

For τῆς θυρίδος, D has τῇ θυρίδι; for καταφερόμενος, κατεχόμενος; for βαθεῖ, βαρεῖ: ἐπὶ τῇ θυρίδι κατεχόμενος ὕπνῳ βαρεῖ. It would be difficult to find different translations for the two readings; one—almost certainly that of D—is due to loose copying.

Some editors connect ἐπὶ πλεῖον not with διαλεγομένου but with κατενεχθείς—wrongly, since the adverbial phrase is more suitable to the present than to the aorist participle.

In the Qumran community falling asleep in the assembly was punishable by exclusion for 30 days (1QS 7.10). There is nothing to suggest that Luke's interest in Eutychus was of a disciplinary kind; Eutychus' accident provides the occasion for a miracle by Paul and serves no other purpose. See Braun (*ThR* 29 (1963), 173).

ἀπὸ τοῦ τριστέγου, from the third storey, that is, in English usage, from the second floor. The adjective τρίστεγος appears to denote a building on three levels (e.g. Josephus, *War* 5.220); τὸ τρίστεγον (sc. οἴκημα) meant the highest of three. The better houses of antiquity seem for the most part to have been one-storey buildings. The dwellings of the poor were apartment houses of several storeys.

καὶ ἤρθη (καὶ ὃς ἤρθη (sic), D*) νεκρός. In view of v. 10 one might expect ὡς νεκρός. Luke however was capable of expressing the thought that observers mistakenly supposed someone to be dead (14.19), and probably means that Eutychus was truly dead. V. 10 must be interpreted accordingly. Luke thinks of a miraculous resurrection (Schneider 2.283). 'Im Vergleich mit anderen Toten-erweckungserzählungen ist leicht zu erkennen, wie wenig schema-tisch und wie sehr konkret hier erzählt ist' (Pesch 2.189). From this concreteness Pesch (2.193) concludes that we have here a tradition of high historical probability. But concreteness, which may be fictional, is not a criterion of probability.

10. Luke uses 'almost technical language in describing miracles' (Knox, *Hell. El.* 8). There may be special allusions to the Elijah and Elisha stories of the OT: 3 Kdms 17.17–24 (... ὑπερῷον ... ἐκάθητο ... ἐπιστραφήτω δὴ ἡ ψυχὴ τοῦ παιδαρίου τούτου εἰς αὐτόν ... ἔδωκεν αὐτὸν τῇ μητρὶ αὐτοῦ ... ζῇ ὁ υἱός σου); 4 Kdms 4.18–37 (ἐκοιμήθη ... καὶ ἀπέθανεν ... τεθνηκός ... διέκαμψεν ἐπ᾽ αὐτόν ... Λάβε τὸν υἱόν σου). Thus ἡ ψυχή αὐτοῦ ἐν αὐτῷ ἐστιν probably means, His life is now, in virtue of my action, within him; this is consistent with the statement of v. 9, strictly understood, that the boy was (not, appeared to be) dead.

μὴ θορυβεῖσθε, present imperative, that is, Stop this disturbance.

The meaning of συμπεριλαβών is unmistakable, but LS 1682 give no other example of the literal meaning, *to embrace*. BA 1555 quotes Xenophon, *Anabasis* 7.4.10, περιλαβὼν τὸν παῖδα. [Editions of Xenophon, giving no MS variation or conjectural note have περι– βαλών, but OCT has –λαβ–.] D has συμπεριλαβὼν καὶ εἶπεν. This un-Greek construction may be an Aramaism (see Black, *AA* 68f., and cf. 4.3; 5.21; 7.4; 8.2; 10.27; 12.16; 13.7; 14.6, 14), but is more probably due either to the influence of d (circumplexit et dixit), or to a mere slip.

Clark (liii, 130f., 377), who thinks the text to have been written originally in sense lines sets out vv. 10–13 as follows:

καταβὰς δὲ ὁ Παῦλος ἔπεσεν ἐπ᾽ αὐτῷ
καὶ συνπεριλαβὼν καὶ εἶπεν μὴ θορυβεῖσθαι
ἡ γὰρ ψυχὴ αὐτοῦ ἐν αὐτῷ ἔστιν
ἀναβὰς δὲ καὶ κλάσας τὸν ἄρτον
5 καὶ γευσάμενος ἐφ᾽ ἱκανὸν δὲ ὁμειλήσας
ἄχρις αὐγῆς οὕτως ἐξῆλθεν
ἀσπαζομένων δὲ αὐτῶν
ἤγαγεν τὸν νεανισκὸν ζῶντα
καὶ παρεκλήθησαν οὐ μετρίως
10 ἡμεῖς δὲ κατελθόντες εἰς τὸ πλοῖον

and thinks that lines 8 and 9 (with ἤγαγεν—singular) should be read after line 3.

11. ἀναβάς—from the street to the second floor.

κλάσας τὸν ἄρτον, the purpose of the gathering, v. 7; see the note there.

Γευσάμενος. γεύεσθαι normally means *to taste*, but in Luke's use it is *to eat, to take a meal* (see Lk. 14.24; Acts 10.10; 23.14; the only exception, Lk. 9.27, is taken directly from Mk and is in any case metaphorical). It would therefore be mistaken to infer that the reference was to a sacramental meal, in which a mere fragment of bread was tasted. Luke means that Paul joined his fellow Christians in eating a meal; their eating is not specifically mentioned because for Luke Paul is the centre of interest. If Luke had meant that Eutychus now ate a meal, thereby proving his complete restoration, he would have been obliged to express himself differently.

Among NT writers only Luke uses the verb ὁμιλεῖν. At Lk. 24.14, 15; Acts 24.26 it means not to address a meeting but to engage in conversation. This is a normal meaning of the word and probably applies here also. No doubt on such occasions Paul did the lion's share of the talking, but it was not an entirely one-sided engagement.

οὕτως sums up the preceding participles—ἀναβάς, κλάσας, γευσάμενος, ὁμιλήσας: a classical use (BDR § 425.6) which occurs in the NT only here and at 27.17; but cf. 20.35. ἐξῆλθεν could mean *he went out* of the house or *he left* Troas, probably the former; but Luke's main intention is to indicate that the incident is now ended as far as Paul is concerned.

αὐγή, daybreak; cf. Isa. 59.9. *Begs.* 4.257 gives 'the daylight before the sunrise' in the note but not in the translation.

12. Dibelius 87, noting that D begins the verse ἀσπαζομένων δὲ αὐτῶν ἤγαγεν τὸν νεανισκὸν ζῶντα, says that D smoothes out the transition. This is correct; but see Clark, on v. 10.

All that remains is to make explicit the happy ending of the story for the Christians in Troas. Presumably they had brought the boy upstairs before Paul restarted the meal and the discourse. He had been dead (v. 9) and was now alive (ζῶντα)—an astounding miracle, which Luke passes over almost as if it were an everyday occurrence. He does not add that the people were astounded, only that παρεκλήθησαν. In Acts this word usually means *to exhort* or *to ask*; here it must mean *they were comforted*. οὐ μετρίως is a characteristic Lucan litotes; cf. 12.18; 19.11; 21.39; 28.2; also e.g. Plutarch, *Titus* 9 (373), τὸν δὲ Τίτον ... οὐ μετρίως παρώξυνε τὰ τοιαῦτα.

The subject of ἤγαγον is not really indefinite (unbestimmt—Haenchen 561); it must be the Christians of Troas who had assembled for their meeting; it could be that they took him to his home, but the interpretation given above seems more probable. D (see above) makes the subject clear; the subject of the singular ἤγαγεν can only be Paul: while they were saying their farewells Paul brought ... For ἀσπάζεσθαι, *to say goodbye*, see v. 1.

13. ἡμεῖς: the 'We' passage continues, but on this occasion Paul is not included; see below. *We* means 'alle Begleiter des Paulus' (Haenchen, 562). The Commentary of Ephraem and the Armenian Catena, which often give old Syriac readings (*Begs.* 3.442f.), have Ego Lucas et qui mecum. This is at any rate correct interpretation (if Luke is the author of the We passages). See further Metzger (477).

προελθόντες is the reading of P⁴¹ᵛⁱᵈ P⁷⁴ ℵ B² C L Ψ 33 36 323 614 945 1739 2495 *al*; A B* E 𝔐 have προσελθόντες; D gig syᵖ have κατελθόντες. The different sense given to the text by these readings, and the reasons for preferring προελθ., will be discussed below.

ἀνήχθημεν, *we set sail*; for this word see 13.13.

ἐπὶ τὴν Ἄσσον, a town on the mainland, founded from Lesbos (Mitylene; see on v. 14) in the eighth century BC. From 133 BC it was under Roman rule, presumably in the province of Asia. Aristotle lived in Assos from 348 to 345 BC.

On this voyage Paul was not with 'us'; he travelled by land (πεζεύειν—not necessarily on foot; cf. Strabo 6.35, τινὰ τῶν φορτίων πεζεύεται ταῖς ἁρμαμάξαις) from Alexandria Troas to Assos. Why Paul chose to travel alone in this way we do not know. The suggestion that he was liable to sea sickness is exegetical despair. There is nothing to suggest that he made an evangelistic tour through the district.

'We' sailed to Assos with the intention (μέλλοντες) of taking up Paul there, οὕτως γὰρ διατεταγμένος ἦν, *for so he had arranged*; but διατάσσεσθαι has often a stronger sense in Acts (see 7.44; 18.2; 23.31; 24.23)—perhaps, *he had given orders to this effect*, μέλλων αὐτὸς πεζεύειν, since he himself was intending to go (was about to go) by land. D has ὡς μέλλων. See BDR § 425.3: ὡς gives the clause a subjective sense, indicating that μέλλων expresses not necessarily the fact, but the mind of the speaker. It is doubtful whether D can be followed here. It should be noted that D reverses the order of the preceding words, reading ἦν διατεταγμένος; ὡς may have originated in the accidental repetition of the last two letters of the participle.

μέλλων αὐτὸς πεζεύειν, with or without ὡς, fits admirably with the reading προελθόντες at the beginning of the verse. The main party sailed on ahead, and picked Paul up at Assos, where he was obliged to take to the sea. κατελθ. has been defended on the ground that it is *lectio difficilior*: in Greek one does not go down to a ship but up to it, so that κατελθ. would invite correction. but it would hardly be changed to προελθ. or προσελθ., and movement *up* is covered by ἀνήχθημεν—one goes down through the town to the harbour, then up to the boat, and on to the high seas. προσελθ. is possible and could have been assimilated to v. 5 (but B* there has προσελθ.!), but προελθ. fits the context so well that it is probably what Luke intended to write, even if he wrote προσελθ. by mistake.

14. *Where he met us* (συνέβαλεν, C D 𝔐, is an improvement on the imperfect συνέβαλλεν, which is therefore probably original, though it is hard to know why Luke wrote it; συνέβαλλον, ℵ, must be a slip). At Assos (see v. 13; εἰς with the accusative for ἐν with the dative; cf. 2.5), *we took him up*, that is, into the ship, though ἀναλαμβάνειν can be used generally (as at 2 Tim. 4.11).

Mitylene. So the MSS of Acts (Μιτυλήνη), though the earlier (before 300 BC) spelling was Μυτιλήνη. M. was the largest town—and a very large one, almost as great in superficial area as Athens—on the island of Lesbos, for centuries an important centre of Greek life, commerce (M. was a notable port), and art (the home of Alcaeus and Sappho, among others). The cult of Augustus (or Augustus and Roma) was established in M. as early as 27 BC (*CAH* 10.486;

Dittenberger, *OGIS* 2.456), and the island enjoyed, on the whole, imperial favour.

15. ἀποπλεύσαντες. The verb occurs in the NT only in Acts (13.4; 14.26; 20.15; 27.1). It is hardly to be distinguished from ἐκπλεῖν (15.39; 18.18; 20.6).

τῇ ἐπιούσῃ. The distance from Mitylene to Samos was too great for one day.

ἄντικρυς occurs here only in the NT. For the distinction between ἄντικρυς and ἀντικρύ see Rutherford (*Phrynichus* 500f.). Luke probably means that they sailed between the island of Chios and the mainland ('right through'). The town Chios was situated on the east coast of the island, and it may be the town rather than the island that is in mind. The island was prosperous (though the words of Hermocrates in Thucydides 8.45.4, οἱ μὲν Χῖοι ... πλουσιώτατοι ὄντες τῶν Ἑλλήνων, were not an unbiased economic estimate), and the town had been made a *civitas libera* by Sulla (86 BC).

τῇ δὲ ἑτέρᾳ (ἑσπέρᾳ in B 36 453 1175 1241 *pc* bo^pt probably goes back to an accidental slip) ... τῇ δὲ ἐχομένῃ (ἐρχομένῃ in D* 614 1175 1891 *al*): Luke chooses variants for τῇ ἐπιούσῃ (above).

Samos, another of the Ionian islands, separated from the mainland by a channel only just over a mile broad. The main harbour lay on the south east coast. Augustus was there in the winter of 31/30 BC (Suetonius, *Augustus* 17) and again in 21/20 BC, when he declared Samos a *civitas libera* (Dio Cassius, 54.9.7), a privilege withdrawn by Vespasian (Suetonius, *Vespasian* 8).

The meaning of παρεβάλομεν (the first person plural returns) is uncertain. It may mean *to pass by*, here more probably *to reach*; cf. Thucydides 3.32.2, ... ἐς Ἰωνίαν παραβαλεῖν; Josephus, *Ant.* 18.161, Ἀγρίππας δὲ εἰς Ποτιόλους παραβαλών. It is probable that Luke used the word in this sense and that the Western editor (followed by the Byzantine text) misunderstood it in its alternative sense, and by adding the words καὶ μείναντες ἐν Τρωγολ(λ) ίῳ (so D (Ψ) 𝔐 gig sy sa, also omitting the following δέ) provided an alternative port of call. An answer is thus provided to the question (Ropes, *Begs.* 3.195; Hanson 202), Why, if these words were not original, were they added? Trogyllium lay on the mainland, approximately opposite the port of Samos. M. 2.362 refers to WH, *Introduction: Notes* 98; for the spelling see WS 47; Ramsay (*Church* 155).

It was between Chios and Samos that the ship sailed past Ephesus (see v. 16).

Miletus was an ancient, prosperous, and influential city; Ioniae caput ... super XC urbium per cuncta maria genetrix (Pliny, *Natural History* 5.112). Here Paul halted; see below. It may not be a matter of coincidence that there is evidence of a Jewish element in the population (see Trebilco, 12, 56. It is here that the well-known theatre inscription occurs: τόπος Εἰουδέων τῶν καὶ θεοσεβίον (sic) (*CIJ* 2.748; Deissmann, *LAE* 446f.; discussed by Trebilco, 159–62). See *NS* 3.24, 25, 167, 168; G. Kleiner, *Das römische Milet* (Sitzungsberichte der Wissenschaftlichen Gesellschaft, Frankfurt/Main, 8.5; 1970).

A journey the reverse of Paul's was made by Herod: Josephus, *Ant.* 16.16–20.

16. κεκρίκει: for the dropping of the augment in the pluperfect see M. 2.190 (though strangely this example is not given along with 4.22; 14.23). Paul *had chosen*; for *choose* as the meaning of κρίνειν see LS s.v. II 1 (996). His choice (of route) was to sail past Ephesus (see on v. 15; and on Ephesus see on 19.1) in order to save time; he did not wish χρονοτριβῆσαι ἐν τῇ Ἀσίᾳ, as no doubt he would have been obliged to do if he had made direct local contact with the church in Ephesus. For χρονοτριβῆσαι, *to waste time, to loiter*, though given by LS 2009, are probably a little strong for this passage; Paul would not have wasted his time in Ephesus—there is no doubt that he could and would have been usefully employed, but he would probably have found it difficult not to spend longer with the church there than suited his plans. This assumes the details of the story as given by Luke in the second part of the verse. It is possible that Paul's plans and motives may have been different; see below. D (gig) vg reword: μήποτε γενηθῇ αὐτῷ κατάσχεσις.

The use of γένηται is unusual, and is probably not to be connected with the Hebrew construction ... ו ... ויהי, which does seem to underlie some of Luke's expressions (though seldom if ever in the later chapters). M. 1.17, considering the question of Hebraism, compares the English idiom, 'It happened I was at home that day'. This is not a precise parallel, but it is relevant to the use of γίνεσθαι meaning *to happen*. Paul did not wish it to happen to him that (infinitive of result) he should spend more time ... Cf. BDR § 409.4.

The reference to time (χρονοτριβῆσαι) makes it probable that ἔσπευδεν has the intransitive meaning, *to make haste*. Paul wished to be in Jerusalem for the Day of Pentecost; this is no doubt what the Greek means, but the translation veils certain difficulties.

εἰς before Ἱεροσόλυμα (so B C D 𝔐 latt; Ἱερουσαλήμ in P[74] ℵ A E Ψ 1704 1739 2495 *pc*) stands for ἐν with the dative (cf. v. 14).

τὴν ἡμέραν (unless we follow D in prefixing εἰς) is an unusual accusative of point of time. On the growing use of this construction in the papyri see M. 1.63 and M. 3.248 (adding also Demosthenes 54.10 (1260), ἐκείνην τὴν ἑσπέραν).

Paul's desire is qualified by εἰ δυνατὸν εἴη αὐτῷ (omitted, accidentally according to Ropes, *Begs.* 3.195, by D*), which introduces a measure of uncertainty; he recognized that he might come too late. See BDR § 385.2, n. 4; Radermacher (131) puts the matter neatly: 'Die Partikel εἰ leitet, parallel unserm "ob" einen Satz ein, der dem erwarteten Erfolg eine Überlegung angibt.'

Whether Paul reached Jerusalem in time for the feast we do not know. According to Conzelmann (116) it was possible, given favourable weather. Stählin (266) thinks that the crowds of 21.27 show that Paul was in Jerusalem at the time of the feast. In any case we hear no more of it. Would Paul have been so keen to attend a Jewish feast (there was as yet no Christian Pentecost)? Gal. 4.10 suggests a disparagement of calendrical observances; cf. Rom. 14.5f. Would he have saved much time by not calling at Ephesus? He went on to Miletus (v. 15); from Miletus he sent to the church of Ephesus and summoned the elders; addressed them, and sent them home. Haenchen (564) estimates the distance as 50 km. (31 miles) as the crow flies and that Paul's messengers will have taken two days, the elders longer (but elders were not necessarily old) to cover it. If these estimates are correct the proceedings will have taken not less than five days, possibly six. Hemer (125) however thinks that two or three days would be sufficient. It is unlikely that Paul would have been obliged to spend more than five or six days in Ephesus. If we think that Paul was not seeking to save time and wish to guess at a different reason for his movements we may suggest that he was (it seems) carrying a considerable sum of money, the product of his collection for the saints in Jerusalem. He might well feel safer in Miletus than in the great city of Ephesus. Conzelmann (116) suggests that Paul had made Ephesus too hot to hold him, a fact that Luke suppresses for apologetic reasons. Bengel (468) observes, 'In festo, magni conventus: magna benefaciendo occasio'; Calvin (2.172) similarly, but at greater length. Tajra (61) thinks that Paul wished to be in Jerusalem for Pentecost (a) to show loyalty to Jewish tradition and practice, (b) to deliver the collection. It is more probable that we should think on other lines. The story is not all fiction; writers do not often voluntarily concoct the sort of problem that we see here. It might have seemed worth while to an imaginative writer to invent a great farewell speech in Ephesus; he would not of his own accord place such a speech in Miletus. If however he found the tradition of a speech in Miletus (and none in Ephesus), he might ferry the Ephesian elders across in order to provide a partly Ephesian audience.

51. PAUL'S SPEECH AT MILETUS 20.17–38

(17) From Miletus Paul sent to Ephesus and summoned the elders of the church. (18) When they reached him he said to them, 'You [elders][1] know how, from the first day I set foot in Asia, I conducted myself towards you for the whole time I was with you, (19) serving the Lord with all humble-mindedness and tears and afflictions that befell me through the plots of the Jews. (20) [You know][2] that I[3] kept back none of the things that were[4] profitable for you, so as not to declare them to you and teach you in public and[5] in private, (21) testifying to both Jews and Greeks repentance towards God and faith in our Lord Jesus. (22) And now behold I am going to Jerusalem,[6] bound in the Spirit, not knowing the things that will befall me there, (23) only that the Holy Spirit in city after city testifies to me that bonds and afflictions await me. (24) But[7] I take my life to be of no account as valuable to myself[8] so that I may finish my course and the ministry that I received from the Lord Jesus—the ministry that consists in[9] testifying the Gospel of the grace of God. (25) And see now, I know that all of you, among whom I went about proclaiming the kingdom, will see my face no more. (26) Therefore I affirm to you this day that I am clear from the blood of all men, (27) for I kept nothing back so as not to proclaim to you the whole counsel of God. (28) [10]Take thought for yourselves and all the flock in which the Holy Spirit has[11] appointed you bishops, to shepherd[12] the church of[13] God, which he[14] saved and acquired through[15] his own blood. (29) I know that after my departure fearsome wolves will come into your company, not sparing the flock, (30) and from among yourselves men will rise up[16] speaking perverse things so as[17] to draw away disciples[18] as their followers. (31) Watch

[1]Elders is not in the Greek.

[2]You know is not in the Greek.

[3]RSV, did not shrink from declaring to you; NJB, I have not hesitated to do anything.

[4]NEB, for your good.

[5]RSV, from house to house; NEB, NJB, in your homes.

[6]NEB, under the constraint of; NJB, in captivity to.

[7]NEB, I set no store by my life, I only want to finish; NJB, I do not place any value on my own life, provided that.

[8]RSV, if only I may.

[9]the ministry that consists in is not in the Greek.

[10]NEB, keep watch over; NJB, be on your guard.

[11]RSV, made you guardians; NEB, given you charge; NJB, the overseers.

[12]RSV, feed.

[13]RSV, NEB, the Lord.

[14]RSV, obtained; NEB, won for himself.

[15]NJB, the blood of his own Son.

[16]NJB, with a travesty of the truth on their lips.

[17]NEB, to induce the disciples to break away and follow them; NJB, to induce the disciples to follow them.

[18]RSV, after them.

therefore, remembering that night and day for three years I did not cease admonishing each one with tears. (32) And now I commit you to God and to the word of his grace,[19] to him who is able to build you up and to give you the inheritance among all those who have been sanctified. (33) I desired no one's[20] silver or gold or clothing. (34) You yourselves know that these hands[21] ministered to my own needs and to those who were with me. (35) In all ways I showed you that it is necessary[22] to work like this and to help the weak,[23] and to remember the words of the Lord Jesus,[24] [to remember] that he himself said, '[25] It is more blessed to give than to receive.'

(36) When he had said these things he knelt down with them all and prayed. (37) A good deal of lamentation arose on the part of all, and they fell on Paul's neck and kissed him, (38) grieving most of all at the prediction he had uttered, that they should see his face no more. They saw him off to the ship.

Bibliography

L. Aejmelaeus, *Die Reception der Paulusbriefe in der Miletrede* (Apg 20.18–35), Helsinki 1987.

C. K. Barrett, *FS* Mitton, 2–5.

C. K. Barrett, *FS* Dahl, 107–21.

C. K. Barrett, *FS* Dupont, 686f.

H. W. Beyer, *TWNT* 2.606f.

F. Bovon, Kremer, *Actes*, 339–58.

H. Braun, *ThR* 29 (1963), 173.

T. L. Budesheim, *HThR* 69 (1976), 9–30.

C. F. Devine, *CBQ* 9 (1947), 381–408.

J. Dupont, *Le Discours de Milet*, Paris 1962.

J. Dupont, *Nouvelles Études*, 424–45.

C. Exum and C. Talbert, *CBQ* 29 (1967), 233–6.

K. N. Giles, *NTS* 31 (1985), 135–42.

M. D. Hooker, *NTS* 35 (1989), 331–42.

P. W. van der Horst, *NovT* 16 (1974), 309.

M. Karrer, *NovT* 32 (1990), 152–88.

J. J. Kilgallen, *JBL* 112 (1993), 312–14.

W. S. Kurz, *JBL* 109 (1985), 251–8.

J. Lambrecht, Kremer, *Actes*, 307–37.

F. Lövestam, *StTh* 41 (1987), 1–10.

[19]RSV, NEB, which is; NJB, that has power.
[20]NEB, NJB, money.
[21]NEB, earned enough for; NJB, earned enough to meet.
[22]RSV, by so toiling; NEB, in this way, by hard work.
[23]RSV, remembering.
[24][to remember] is not in the Greek; RSV, how he said.
[25]NEB, happiness lies more in; NJB, there is more happiness in.

H. J. Michel, *Die Abschiedsrede des Paulus an die Kirche Apg 20.17–35*, München 1973.

C. F. D. Moule, *BJRL* 47 (1965), 430–52.

J. Munck, *FS* Goguel, 155–70.

E. Plümacher, *ZNW* 83 (1992), 270–5.

W. Pratscher, *NTS* 25 (1979), 284–98.

H. Sahlin, *NovT* 24 (1982), 188.

W. Schmithals, *FS* Schneider, 307–22.

H. Schürmann, *FS* Jaeger, 108–16.

H, Seesemann, *TWNT* 6.23–37.

K. Stowers, *NovT* 26 (1984), 59–82.

A. Strobel, *NTS* 15 (1969), 191–210.

B. E. Thiering, *JBL* 100 (1981), 59–74.

F. M. Young, *JTS* 45 (1994), 142–8.

Commentary

A brief introduction (vv. 17, 18a) and a concluding note (vv. 36–38) provide a framework for a long address by Paul. The framework may certainly be considered Luke's own writing. Verse 17 provides a suitable audience for the speech, which (see below) forms an important part of Luke's presentation of the figure of Paul. That Paul (for whatever reason) did not on this journey visit Ephesus was a datum of tradition; that he made a speech in Miletus may have been. In any case, Miletus was the nearest spot touched on in his journey to the great centre of population. Since Paul could not, or did not, go to Ephesus, Ephesus was brought to him, represented by the elders of the church, who could on behalf of the church as a whole hear Paul's farewell and learn what he had to teach about pastoral responsibility. The speech completed, there must be leave-taking, the more serious a matter because Luke makes it clear that this is a final farewell. The matter is repeated in similar (Lucan) language in 21.5, 6. For stylistic details see the notes.

The speech attributed to Paul raises a number of problems. It is analysed by Pesch (2.199) as follows: Rückblick I (18b–21), Vorblick I (22–24b), Rückblick II (24cd), Vorblick II (25ab), Rückblick III (25c), Unschuldsbeteuerung (26), Rückblick IV (27), Mahnung I (28), Vorblick III (29–30), Mahnung II (31a), mit Rückblick V (31b), Verabschiedung (32), Rückblick VI (33–35). What this list means is that the speech is really incapable of analysis. In fact it is not really quite as bad as this; see Dibelius (157) for a simpler and more convincing analysis. It proceeds from point to point, with numerous repetitions, as various ideas occur to the speaker (writer). Its form is that of the farewell address: for the main biblical and some non-biblical parallels to this form see J. Munck in *FS* Goguel

(155–70). Rackham (383) rightly points out that the themes of this address are those of the farewell address of Lk. 21: Take heed; watch. They are however put in an entirely different setting. The eschatological basis and construction of Lk. 21 have virtually disappeared; there is a warning of problems in the church (vv. 29, 30) but none of a coming judgement. And there is apologetic reference to the speaker's example, which is not found in the gospel. Roloff (301) takes the speech to be Luke's work, on the ground of (a) the Lucan style, (b) the fact that the church order presupposed is that of Luke's (rather than Paul's) period, and (c) the perspective from which Paul himself is viewed, which is that of a later age. In particular, v. 25 (cf. vv. 37, 38) shows that at the time of composition Paul was already dead. The origin of the speech is well discussed by Bauernfeind (239). It appears 'dass der Geist dieser Rede der Geist des Paulus ist. Aber nicht der Buchstabe der uns bekannten paulinischen Briefe.' 'Die Vorgeschichte der Rede werden wir uns also nicht anders zu denken haben, als die Vorgeschichte der meisten anderen Reden in der AG: Lk hat sorgsam auf ältere Predigtüberlieferung geachtet und aus dem, was er vorfand, selbständig aufgebaut.' This does not mean that a primitive form of the speech, on which Luke worked, can be found (though one has been suggested in vv. 18b, 19, 21, 24–28, 29, 30, 31, 32).

Two matters call for special attention. Notwithstanding the view quoted above from Bauernfeind, a stronger case for Luke's knowledge of the Pauline epistles, or some of them, can be made here than anywhere else in Acts. A modest list (see further NT parallels in Weiser 571f.) of Pauline passages to which allusions can with some plausibility be found may be given: Rom. 1.1; 15.14; 1 Cor. 1.2; 3.5, 9, 12; 4.12, 14; 10.13; 14.3, 4, 5, 12, 24; 15.9; 2 Cor. 1.1; 2.4; 4.5; 12.14f.; Gal. 1.13; Phil. 1.1; (Col. 1.20; 3.12, 24;) 1 Thess. 2.9, 14; 5.6, 10, 11, 12. This is an impressive list, but on examination it proves to contain nothing that is truly convincing as a literary allusion to the written Pauline corpus. If even here Luke shows no acquaintance with Paul's letters (and he gives nowhere any hint that Paul ever wrote a letter) a considerable problem results. How could a devoted admirer of Paul, writing up to a generation after Paul's death, be unaware of Paul's literary legacy to the church? And if he was aware of it, how is it that he never mentions it? For provisional answers see *FS* Mitton 2–5.

The second matter to be considered is the relation between this speech and the Pastoral Epistles (see the note on v. 17). That Luke (that is, the author of Acts) wrote also the Pastorals is argued in general terms by S. G. Wilson, *Luke and the Pastoral Epistles*, London, 1979), by C. F. D. Moule (in *BJRL* 47 (1965), 430–52—with the view that Luke wrote them during Paul's life and under his supervision), and by A. Strobel (*NTS* 15 (1969), 191–210).

For the general question of the authorship of Acts see Introduction, pp. xliv–liv. The parallels between this passage and the Pastorals are so well summed up by Wilson that his account may be quoted (117f.).

1. Paul looks back on his past career with some confidence, believing that he has fulfilled the tasks designated for him (Acts 20.18–21, 25–6; 2 Tim. 4.6f.). Moreover, the striking metaphor of an athlete finishing his race is used in both Acts 20.24 ... and 2 Tim. 4.7 ... At the same time he is deeply concerned with the fate of the Church in his absence. This is indicated by the whole of Acts 20.17–35 and each of the Pastoral letters.

2. The problem Paul foresees and warns of is heresy, which will assault the Church from within and without (Acts 20.29–30; 1 Tim. 1.3f.; 3.1f.; 6.20f.; 2 Tim. 2.14f.; 3.1f.). The heresy appears to be an early form of gnosticism and its centre is in Ephesus (Acts 20.17f.; 1 Tim. 1.3). Paul urges constant alertness (Acts 20.31; 2 Tim. 4.2f.).

3. The responsibility for resisting the false teaching is placed on the church leaders or on Paul's assistants. The church leaders are, in both cases, elder-bishops (Acts 20.17–28; 1 Tim. 5.17; 2 Tim. 2.2; Tit. 1.5f.), and it is Paul's example and instruction which will be their chief weapon (Acts 20.27, 30–5; 1 Tim. 3.14; 4.11f.; 6.20; 2 Tim. 1.8f., 13–14; 3.10f.; Tit. 1.5).

4. Paul speaks of his own suffering for the sake of the gospel (Acts 20.19–24; 2 Tim. 1.11–12; 2.3; 3.11) and indicates that for him a martyr's death lies ahead (Acts 20.25, 37; 2 Tim. 4.6f.).

5. The ministers whom Paul appoints and exhorts are warned of the dangers of the love of money (Acts 20.33–5; 1 Tim. 6.9–10; Tit. 1.11).

6. Paul commits his successors to the Lord and his grace (Acts 20.32; 2 Tim. 4.22).

The parallels are real and substantial, and there can be little doubt that Acts and the Pastorals were produced in similar circumstances and at times not very remote from one another. In Acts 20.17–34 (unlike some other parts of Acts) the motivation is very similar to that of the Pastorals, and the resemblance is therefore greater than elsewhere. There is however little in the Pastorals to parallel the most explicit theological verse (28) in the speech, and when both works are considered as wholes it must be remembered that the Pastorals treat Paul as the pre-eminent apostle, whereas Acts is very reticent in the use of the word ἀπόστολος to describe him. But it remains true that there is a clear relation between Acts and the Pastorals.

There is a very full account of earlier discussions of this speech, and an important treatment of it, by J. Lambrecht ('Paul's Farewell Address at Miletus (Acts 20.17–38)') in Kremer, *Actes* 307–37.

17. From Miletus (v. 15) Paul sent to Ephesus (v. 16) and *summoned* (μετεκαλέσατο; D has μετεπέμψατο, *sent for*; there is no significant difference in meaning) *the elders* (τοὺς πρεσβυτέρους; see on 14.23) *of the church* (τῆς ἐκκλησίας; see on 5.11, and Introduction pp. lxxxviif.). Stählin (267) thinks that vv. 18, 25 show that elders from other churches also were present; it seems a doubtful inference. At v. 28 the elders are called ἐπίσκοποι; see on that verse. It is probable that we see here the constitution of the church as known to Luke: a community led by a group known indifferently as πρεσβύτεροι and ἐπίσκοποι. Paul never in the epistles uses the word πρεσβύτερος; ἐπίσκοπος occurs once, in Phil. 1.1. Both occur in the Pastoral Epistles—one of many contacts between these epistles and this part of Acts ('Almost every detail of Acts 20.17–33 can be found in the Pastorals'—Wilson, *Pastorals* 117).

There was in the town of Ephesus not only a βουλή (Council) but a γερουσία which might be thought to consist of πρεσβύτεροι (Hicks, *AGIBM*, 3.74–78). This is not important; there were Christian πρεσβύτεροι in many other places; there was no need to model them on a particular form of local government.

18. παραγίνεσθαι is a Lucan word: Mt. 3 times; Mk, once; Lk., 8 times; Jn, twice; Acts 20 times; rest of the NT, 3 times. Only here in Acts is it constructed with πρός; its frequency is of course connected with the number of journeys described in Acts. After πρὸς αὐτόν, P[74] (A) D lat have ὁμόσε ὄντων αὐτῶν, when they were all in one place; a fairly obvious condition for speech-making. ὁμόσε occurs nowhere else in the NT. E 2464 *pc* have ὁμοθυμαδόν, an Acts word.

ὑμεῖς is presumably emphatic (cf. 10.28; 15.7): You elders know, if no one else does. ἐπιστᾶσθαι is characteristic of Acts: 8 times, in the rest of the NT, 5 times. After ἐπίστασθε, D 2464 *pc* sa have ἀδελφοί, evidently feeling that some form of address was called for. It is surprising that we do not have ἄνδρες ἀδελφοί; cf. 1.16. Paul's work in Asia began in Ephesus (18.19; 19.10), and it is likely that many of the elders would have been chosen from among the earliest converts. They had had the opportunity of observing Paul's ministry, which he describes in the following verses, at first hand and from an early time. A very early time: ἀπὸ πρώτης ἡμέρας. There is no article. According to M. 3.179 this is the effect of the preposition. BDR § 256 n. 3 makes a useful distinction. When an ordinal and a word of time occur the article seems to be present only when the reference is to a particular definite time; it would be implied that here *first day* really means *early days*.

ἀφ' ἧς: the preposition is repeated. Contrast 1.22 and the classical use. BDR § 293.3e, n. 14 suggest that repetition is due to the separation of the initial preposition from the relative, but only two words intervene. According to Blass (219) ἀπὸ πρ. ἡμ. ἀφ' ἧς = ἀφ' ἧς ἡμέρας τὸ πρῶτον.

ἐπιβαίνειν is characteristic of the later part of Acts: 20.18; 21.2, 4; 25.1; 27.2; elsewhere in the NT only Mt. 21.5.

For πῶς with γίνεσθαι see BDR § 434.2, n. 5: how I conducted myself. Cf. the reading of D (see below): ποταπῶς ... ἦν.

The accusative τὸν πάντα χρόνον now rightly indicates extent of time (contract 20.16). πάντα preceded by the article means the whole time; see M. 3.201 (all that time); BDR § 275.3, n. 6.

At the end of the verse, instead of πῶς ... ἐγενόμην, D has ὡς τριετίαν ἢ καὶ πλεῖον ποταπῶς μεθ' ὑμῶν ἦν (the only occurrence in the NT of this form of the first person singular; see M. 1.56; M. 2.203; BDR § 98, n. 1) παντὸς χρόνου. The three year period may be derived from 19.8, 10; and see v. 31; the genitive (which usually expresses time within which) is less apt than the accusative.

The speech begins in the manner of a farewell, with a defence of the speaker's conduct; cf. e.g. 1 Sam. 12.2f.

19. This verse contains a striking number of parallels with the Pauline epistles. They are not quotations; they do not prove that Luke had read the epistles (on this question see Introduction, pp. xxviif., xlivf. but they do show contact with the Pauline tradition, so that this verse may be said to depict a man who could have written the letters.

δουλεύειν τῷ κυρίῳ: see especially Rom. 12.11 (unless τῷ καιρῷ is read); also Rom. 16.18; 1 Thess. 1.9; in addition, passages in which Paul describes himself as δοῦλος Ἰησοῦ Χριστοῦ, or the like (e.g. Rom. 1.1; 1 Cor. 7.22; Gal. 1.10; Phil. 1.1).

He serves μετὰ πάσης ταπεινοφροσύνης: cf. Rom. 12.16; 2 Cor. 7.6; 10.1; 11.7; 12.21; Phil. 2.3; 4.12. The use of πᾶς also is Pauline: 2 Cor. 8.7; 12.12.

δακρύων: cf. 2 Cor. 2.4.

πειρασμῶν: for the biblical history of this word, from its primary Greek sense of trying or proving to affliction, disaster, punishment, see Hatch (Essays 71f.); H. Seesemann (TWNT 6.23–37). It is clear that Paul (Luke) is here thinking of afflictions; that these arose mainly through ἐπιβουλαῖς τῶν Ἰουδαίων is attested (possibly with exaggeration) in Acts repeatedly (e.g. 13.45); see also 1 Thess. 2.15. Titus 1.10, 14 are to be put with the evidence of Acts. In the NT ἐπιβουλή is used only in Acts, always in relation to Jewish opposition to Paul (9.24; 20.3, 19; 23.30). Paul speaks of the Jews almost as if he were not one: Bengel (468), 'Gentium apostolus jam quasi de alienis loquitur.' Yet so he does in 1 Cor. 9.20.

20. ὡς is still dependent on ἐπίστασθε (v. 18; in this verse note πῶς). See BDR § 396.1, n. 4.

Here and at v. 27 Paul emphasizes that he has withheld nothing; the elders and indeed the whole church at Ephesus have received from him the whole of Christian truth. ὑποστέλλεσθαι (middle) is taken by BA 1688 to include always the element of fear or cowardice that is certainly present at Heb. 10.38: in the present verse 'feige verschweigen', in v. 27 'sich schauen vor, aus Angst vermeiden oder unterlassen'. This does not seem to be justified; see LS 1895f. There is a good parallel in Plato, *Apology* 24a: οὔτε μέγα οὔτε μικρὸν ἀποκρυψάμενος ἐγὼ λέγω οὐδ' ὑποστειλάμενος. Luke's motive here does not seem to be the desire to point out Paul's courage in speaking unwelcome truths but rather to emphasize the completeness of his Gospel. He probably has in mind the secret teaching of the gnostics and their claim that they possessed a secret tradition from Paul which he had withheld from the church at large. 'Hier endlich entdecken wir geringfügige Spuren der Abwehr einer der späteren Gnosis vergleichbaren Haltung' (Schille 402). So also Conzelmann (117), adding, 'Über die Gnostisierung des paulinischen Missionsgebietes: Bauer, *Rechtgläubigkeit* bes. 235ff.' Against this Luke asserts that the public tradition of such great Christian centres as Ephesus went back to the apostle and contained the whole of his teaching. Cf. Col. 1.28, where the same motivation is to be seen. Paul withheld οὐδὲν τῶν συμφερόντων; it is implied that anything beyond the known and publicly recognized teaching of Paul was not profitable. Paul made his proclamation to you and taught you δημοσίᾳ καὶ κατ' οἴκους, that is, in public gatherings, and in the private meetings that Christians held in their own houses. '... publicly (as at Athens) and privately (as at Troas)' (Hanson 203). For the adverbial use of δημοσίᾳ cf. 16.37; 18.28; perhaps 5.18.

The infinitives ἀναγγεῖλαι and διδάξαι are introduced by τοῦ μή. They have a consecutive sense (M. 3.142) and μή is usual after verbs of negative meaning (as ὑποστέλλεσθαι). In the present verse (cf. also v. 27) μή is omitted by D. The negative is not always used (e.g. Xenophon, *Memorabilia* 1.2.34, δῆλον ὅτι ἀφεκτέον ἂν εἴη τοῦ ὀρθῶς λέγειν) and it must be left open whether the Old Uncial or the Western text was making a stylistic improvement.

ὑμᾶς is also omitted by D syᵖ Lucifer.

21. διαμαρτυρόμενος, a Lucan word (Lk. once; Acts 9 times; the rest of the NT, 5 times), repeated in a similar way at v. 24 (cf. v. 23).

Ἰουδαίοις τε καὶ Ἕλλησιν is a common Pauline thought and formula; see Rom. 1.16; 10.12; 1 Cor. 1.24; 10.32; 12.13; Gal. 3.28; Col. 3.11. In Ephesus Paul had begun his work among Jews (19.8) but had moved beyond the synagogue (19.9).

The content of Paul's testimony (cf. v. 24, where it has a related but different content) is described as τὴν εἰς (Ρ⁷⁴ A D Ψ 𝔐 add τόν) θεὸν μετάνοιαν καὶ πίστιν εἰς τὸν κύριον ἡμῶν Ἰησοῦν. This phrase has only a superficially Pauline sound. Paul very seldom refers to repentance, and for faith in Christ prefers the genitive πίστις Ἰησοῦ Χριστοῦ (but see on this M. D. Hooker, *NTS* 35 (1989), 321–42, and works cited there). Conzelmann (117) thinks that the phrase recalls the first and second articles of the creed; it might be more apt (though not altogether different) to recall Rom. 10.9. Repentance is called for because men have not treated Jesus as Lord; faith is summed up in acceptance of the resurrection. Paul himself prefers the more objective statement; Luke, like the Pastorals, is apt to give a subjectivized version of Paulinism. The two elements in conversion, repentance and faith, are introduced by one article (τήν), which has the effect of binding them closely together. Zerwick § 184: '... subsumptio plurium sub uno articulo eorum aliquam unionem si non identitatem indicat ... Pulchre A 20.21 obiectum praedicationis dicitur esse ''conversio ad Deum et fides in Christum'', sed sub uno articulo, ut fere intellegas ''conversionem ad Deum per fidem in Christum''.' It is interesting in the light of this to note the reading of D. The text quoted above (that of NA[26]) is contained in B H L P Ψ 614 *pm* gig sy[h]; P[74] ℵ A C E 33 36 323 945 1175 1241 1739 2495 *pm* vg sy[p] bo[pt] add Χριστόν (E omitting ἡμῶν); but D has διὰ τοῦ κυρίου Ἰησοῦ Χριστοῦ. One cannot think that the scribe of D was evaluating the single article in the manner of a modern grammarian. If there was a serious motive for the change it will have been the conviction that faith as well as repentance was directed towards God and that Jesus was the mediator rather than the object of faith. More probably the Western editor was simply indulging, as he seems frequently to do, a love of variation for its own sake.

A further suggestion (mentioned but not accepted by Marshall 331) is that the verse is expressed in chiasmus: Jews needed faith in Jesus Christ, Greeks needed to turn to God. Marshall is right to question this: 'Faith was necessary for all converts ... and repentance was also needed in the case of Jews'. For the latter point it would suffice to refer to 2.38.

22. From this point (to which he will return; v. 25) Paul turns to the future and the lot that awaits him. For καὶ νῦν ἰδού cf. 13.11 and the note. It is probably correct to describe the expression as a Septuagintalism; cf. Gen 12.19. Knox, *Hell. El.* 17, observes that in the 'We' passages the phrase καὶ (...) ἰδού occurs only here and at 20.25; 27.24, all on Paul's lips. This need not mean more than that it belongs to spoken style.

The construction and precise meaning of δεδεμένος ἐγὼ τῷ πνεύματι are not clear. In a literal sense Paul was not yet bound (as later he would be); he was however under divine constraint (and the verb can refer to inward constraint and compulsion: Apollonius

Rhodius, *Argonautica* 4.880, τῷ μιν ἀμηχανίη δῆσεν φρένας; other examples in LS 383) to continue on a course that was certain to lead sooner or later to his arrest. Moreover, as the next verse states explicitly, the Holy Spirit was constantly witnessing to him that this would be the result of his actions. τῷ πνεύματι could refer to Paul's own spirit or to the Holy Spirit. Blass (219) thinks (in view of v. 23) that the Holy Spirit cannot be intended; Bauernfeind (239), cf. Weiser (576), is convinced that it is. *Bound in the Spirit* seems a suitable English translation since it too is imprecise, but suggests control by the Spirit (especially if we write Spirit with a capital S) and is at least not inconsistent with spiritual foreshadowing of what is to come.

Paul must go to Jerusalem (19.21), at whatever cost; this (whatever we make of the present verse) is represented as not only Paul's intention but as God's (the Spirit's) will. As he goes he does not know (εἰδώς) what will befall (συναντᾶν, normally as at 10.25, *to meet* (of persons)) him there. That is, he does not know in detail what form imprisonment and affliction (v. 23) will take.

Instead of εἰδώς, P⁴¹ D have γινώσκων. There is no difference in meaning. Behind the variant is simply the freedom an editor felt in changing the text before him. See Introduction, p. xxi, and many notes.

23. πλὴν ὅτι, *except that*, is classical; so Knox (*Hell. El.* 12), also BDR § 449.1, n. 3, who point out that this is the only place in Acts where πλήν is used as a conjunction.

Paul does not know (v. 22) what will happen to him in Jerusalem, only that the Holy Spirit διαμαρτύρεται (in v. 21 Paul uses this word of his testimony to the Gospel) that bonds and affliction await him. The visit to Jerusalem will be a painful one; he must face imprisonment again.

The masculine singular δεσμός takes here a neuter plural in −α. See M. 2.121f.: 'Δεσμός has plural δεσμά in Lk. 8.29; Acts 16.26; 20.23, δεσμοί Phil. 1.13, the rest being ambiguous. Thackeray (p. 154) observes that in LXX as in NT δεσμά is literary. Rutherford (*Gram.* 9) asserts after Cobet, that δεσμά = actual bonds, δεσμοί = bondage. The distinction cannot be pressed for the NT, though it would suit very well: Acts 20.23 gains vividness from it.' For examples of the Spirit's testimony see 21.4 (in Tyre), 10–14 (in Caesarea).

The Holy Spirit bears witness κατὰ πόλιν, in city after city, κατά being used, as frequently, distributively. The addition of πᾶσαν (D gig (vg) sy) adds nothing to the sense. Some editors or copyists took ὅτι to be recitativum, and changed με into σε, thus: ὅτι δ. καὶ θ. σε μένουσιν ἐν Ἰερουσαλήμ (P⁴¹ (D 614 gig vg^cl sy^h**) sa).

Betz (110, 119) remarks that the θεῖος ἀνήρ knows his approaching end. On apostles as θεῖοι ἄνδρες see e.g. 3.12: what is to be observed here is that Paul professes ignorance of exactly what will happen, that he does not know anything in himself but is given limited information by the Holy Spirit, and that the Holy Spirit gives the same information to all who happen to be present at the time.

24. The text and the construction of the opening clause are alike obscure. The text of NA²⁶, οὐδενὸς λόγου ποιοῦμαι τὴν ψυχὴν τιμίαν ἐμαυτῷ, is read by P⁴¹ ℵ* B C 1175 *pc* (gig syᵖ). There are several ways in which it may be construed. We may take the first five words as virtually complete in themselves: I take my life to be of no account. τιμίαν ἐμαυτῷ is then an epexegetical addition: as being of value to myself. Or, τιμίαν may be taken as equivalent to ἀξίαν. We should then have: I take my life to be worth to myself not a single word, that is, to be worth nothing. A further suggestion is that two clauses, each of which could have stood alone, have been combined: οὐδενὸς λόγου ποιοῦμαι, I take no account of anything (i.e. of any danger), and οὐκ ἔχω τιμίαν ἐμαυτῷ τὴν ψυχήν, I do not hold my life precious to myself. The variants similarly divide the clause in two: (a) οὐδενὸς λόγον ἔχω (+ μοι, D) οὐδὲ ποιοῦμαι τὴν ψυχὴν τιμίαν ἐμαυτῷ (P⁷⁴ ℵᶜ A D⁽ᶜ⁾ 33 *pc*) and (b) οὐδενὸς (+ τούτων 1891 *pc*) λόγον ποιοῦμαι οὐδὲ ἔχω τὴν ψυχήν μου τιμίαν ἐμαυτῷ (E Ψ 𝔐 (syʰ)). (a) will be rendered, I take account of nothing nor do I count my life as valuable to myself, (b) I take account of none of these things nor do I hold my life precious to myself. NA²⁶ rightly choose the most difficult of the three texts; and though it is difficult the general sense of the text is clear. Life itself is worth less to Paul than the fulfilment of his apostolic calling. Metzger (479) says that the text approved here is 'awkward, yet idiomatic'; similarly Ropes (*Begs.* 3.196). Field conjectures ἀλλ' οὐδενὸς λόγου ποιοῦμαι οὐδὲ ἡγοῦμαι τὴν ψυχήν μου τιμίαν ἐμαυτῷ.

The next two words are marked by further textual and linguistic problems. ὡς is read by P⁴¹ P⁷⁴ᵛⁱᵈ ℵ* A B* C Ψ 𝔐, but ℵ² B² vg have ἕως; E 33 323 614 945 1739 2495 *al* have ὥστε; D gig Lucifer have τοῦ (*quam*). τελειῶσαι is read by P⁴¹ᵛⁱᵈ A (C) D E Ψ 𝔐 gig Lucifer, but ℵ B *pc* vg have τελειώσω. Among these variants ἕως may be discounted as an easy complement to τελειώσω. ὥστε, with, on the whole, late attestation, should probably be regarded as an easy companion to the infinitive τελειῶσαι though Blass (220) points out that it would be easy for τε to drop out before τελειῶσαι. The comparative contained in the Western text (... than completing ...) is again a relatively easy reading. We are left with ὡς τελειῶσαι and ὡς τελειώσω. Each is unusual, but neither is impossible. If ὡς τελειώσω is read it is, according to M. 3.105, the only final ὡς in the NT. Turner adds that it is rare also in the Koine. [He refers also to a variant ὅπως, but I do not know where this is to be found.] ὡς may also however be read with the infinitive, again in the final sense, and this is presumably intended by NA²⁶. There is a parallel in Lk. 9.52, where ὡς ἑτοιμάσαι is read by P⁴⁵ P⁷⁵ ℵ* B, but ὥστε ἑτ. by all other

MSS. See BDR § 369, n. 1; § 391.1, n. 2; BA 1793 (s.v. ὡς, IV 3). The meaning, whether τελειώσω or τελειῶσαι is read, is, My purpose in discounting the value of my life is that I may ...

For τελειοῦν τὸν δρόμον cf. 2 Tim. 4.7 (τετέλεκα). Paul frequently uses images drawn from the games, including the verb τρέχειν (δραμ–), but never the word δρόμος. Ε Ψ 𝔐 syʰ add μετὰ χαρᾶς.

After the image of the race Paul speaks more directly of the work he is concerned to complete. It is the διακονία ἣν ἔλαβον. P⁴¹ᵛⁱᵈ P⁷⁴ᵛⁱᵈ 614 2495 have ἣν παρέλαβον; D⁽ᶜ⁾ gig vgᶜˡ have τοῦ λόγου ὃν παρέλαβον. The variants make little difference to the sense, unless διακονία is taken to refer (as it does at Rom. 15.31; 2 Cor. 8.4; 9.1, 12, 13) to Paul's collection for the poor in Jerusalem. This is very unlikely in view of the fact that Acts has made no reference to this collection. The διακονία that Paul had received from the Lord Jesus was to testify (διαμαρτύρεσθαι, as at vv. 21, 23) τὸ εὐαγγέλιον τῆς χάριτος τοῦ θεοῦ. τῆς χάριτος must be taken as a genitive of content. The good news was that God was bestowing his unmerited favour upon, was being gracious to, the human race. The addition Ἰουδαίοις τε καὶ Ἕλλησιν (P⁴¹ᵛⁱᵈ D gig saᵐˢˢ) is a secondary assimilation to v. 21, but is clearly in harmony with the speaker's intention. The content of Paul's preaching is given in other allusive summaries in vv. 25, 27, 28, 32. For the Gospel of the grace of God cf. the word of his (the Lord's) grace at 14.3; 20.32.

25. With καὶ νῦν ἰδού (see v. 22) Paul again turns briefly from the past to the future. This is a farewell speech; see above.

οὐκέτι ὄψεσθε τὸ πρόσωπόν μου is clear, and it is surprising that there seem to be few or no parallels to this mode of expression. Cf. Gen. 48.11 (Hebrew: ראה פניך לא פללתי; Greek different). Whether οὐκέτι is translated *no longer* or *no more* it seems clear (cf. v. 38) that Paul is predicting that personal contact is at an end. It is impossible to draw inferences (but see Harnack, *The Acts of the Apostles* 293f.) from this for the date of Acts; we do not know whether Paul was released from a first imprisonment in Rome and returned to the East. Cf. Phil. 1.25, where Paul himself uses οἶδα in forecasting release. But Luke could hardly have written this verse (and v. 38) if he had known that Paul returned to Asia. So also Haenchen (566).

ὑμᾶς is not so much emphatic as intended to take up the link between the second person plural ὄψεσθε and Paul's recollection, in the second part of the verse, of the manner and content of his ministry. Since the πάντες that follows is so closely attached to this ὑμᾶς it cannot be concluded (as it is by Haenchen 566) that it is intended to refer to all the Pauline communities, of whom he now takes leave. The words do indeed have this secondary reference: the speech serves as a farewell to all; but it is only a secondary reference.

For διῆλθον cf. 9.32; if the whole of Asia is in mind (cf. 19.10) there may be a reference to missionary tours. But probably the writer is thinking only of Paul's long residence in Ephesus during which he went about proclaiming the kingdom. This short text (of P⁷⁴ ℵ A B C Ψ 33 36 453 *pc* sy bo^(pt)) is almost certainly correct. Its brevity attracted 'improvements': τὴν βασ. τοῦ (+ κυρίου, gig) Ἰησοῦ (D gig sa Lucifer); τὴν βασ. τοῦ θεοῦ (E 𝔐 vg bo^(pt) Theodoret); τὸ εὐαγγέλιον τοῦ θεοῦ (323 1891 *pc*). For the use of βασιλεία (τοῦ θεοῦ) in Acts see 8.12; 19.8; 28.23, 31. It means in effect the recognized content of Christian preaching, and is so expressed in order to bring out the continuity between the preaching of Jesus and the preaching of the post-resurrection church.

26. Looking back to his ministry in Ephesus (or Asia) Paul affirms in the strongest terms the testimony of his conscience to his blameless behaviour and in particular to his complete openness in declaring the truth about God and his purpose for mankind.

μαρτύρομαι, a strong word: *asseverate*. Cf. 26.22; Gal. 5.3; Eph. 4.17; 1 Thess. 2.12.

ἐν τῇ σήμερον ἡμέρᾳ also is emphatic. σήμερον occurs 21 times in Acts, here only with ἡμέρα (Acts 27.33 is not parallel). Paul uses the combination at Rom. 11.8 (quoting the OT); 2 Cor. 3.14. *This very day*, however, would perhaps be too strong.

At the beginning of the verse D* has ἄχρι οὖν τῆς σήμερον ἡμέρας and C D² H L *al* have διό (instead of διότι; not noticed in NA²⁶). These variants may be due to the fact that διότι (probably original) does not give the required sense. 'διό means *and so* (cf. ἄρα) and διότι means *because, since*. See MM s.vv. [163f.; 164f.]. But in Acts 20.26, where the context certainly requires *and so*, there is considerable MS support for διότι' (Moule, *IB* 164).

For καθαρός cf. 18.6; also, for the sense, Ezek. 3.18–21; 1 Thess. 2.10. The formulation is Lucan rather than Pauline. The construction with ἀπό is not a Hebraism; see Deissmann (*BS* 196), with reference to ten Fayyum papyri as well as Demosthenes 59.78 (1371) (... εἰμί καθαρὰ καὶ ἁγνὴ ἀπό <τε> τῶν ἄλλων ...) and a Pergamum inscription. The meaning is clear: Paul is responsible for no man's (eternal) death through neglecting to preach the Gospel to all and to deliver it in all its fullness. H. Sahlin (*NovT* 24 (1982), 188) proposes instead of τοῦ αἵμ. π., αἰτιώματος παντός. It does not seem a necessary conjecture.

27. For ὑποστέλλεσθαι see v. 20; also on μή (omitted here by D* *pc*). Here ἀναγγέλλειν, at v. 20 left without an object (but see v. 21), has an object: πᾶσαν τὴν βουλήν τοῦ θεοῦ. βουλή is a Lucan, and especially an Acts (2.23; 4.28; 5.38; 13.36; 19.1 (v.l.); 20.27; 27.12, 42), rather than a Pauline (1 Cor. 4.5 only) word. Here it must refer to the saving purpose of God for the human race. Paul has proclaimed this in its entirety. See J. T. Squires, *The Plan of God in Luke-Acts*, SNTSMS 76 (1993).

For Luke's motivation in emphasizing this point see on v. 20. At this point Conzelmann (118) adds a reference to 'die Esoterik der Qumran-Sekte, 1 QpHab 7.1ff.; 1 QS 3.13f.; 11.5ff.'. He continues, 'Zu dieser polemischen Zuspitzung vgl Iren[aeus] Haer[eses] 1.1; Tert[ullian] Praescr[iptione] Haer[eticorum] 22f.; W. Bauer bei Hennecke[2] 139.'

28. This verse is both the practical and the theological centre of the speech; the practical centre, because Paul's primary intention is to urge the Ephesian elders to do their duty effectively—or rather, Luke's primary intention is to convey the same exhortation to his contemporaries, and the theological centre, because here only in Acts is there an attempt to state the significance of the death of Christ and at the same time to bring out the ground of the church's ministry in the work of the Holy Spirit.

προσέχειν (sc. τὸν νοῦν) in itself means *to direct the mind towards, to give thought to*, but this naturally extends along the line of *with a view to the advantage of*, i.e. *take thought for*. Here the elders are bidden in the first instance to take thought for themselves, that is, to maintain the quality and integrity of their own Christian life, and in the second place to take thought for the church in which they hold a responsible position. Their position has so far (v. 17) been described as that of elders; another word will shortly be used, but before that the image of the flock, and therewith by implication that of the shepherd, is introduced. The noun τῷ ποιμνίῳ is taken up in the verb ποιμαίνειν, but this is preceded by another noun, ἐπίσκοπος. The language of shepherding is—perhaps surprisingly— not Pauline, but later the image became common; see Jn 21.15–17 (cf. 10.11, etc.); 1 Pet. 2.25; 5.2–4; Eph. 4.11; Heb. 13.20; Jude 12. It rests upon familiar OT passages; e.g. the story of David; Ps. 23; Jer. 3.15; 23.1–4; Ezek. 34.1–24; but it is also used of rulers and leaders in the non-biblical world. See *St John* 373f. The shepherd directs his sheep, knowing where they ought to go in their own interests, and also protects them, against wild beasts and robbers. The Christian shepherd is one who is able to guide and also to protect against the agencies that mislead and endanger Christians.

It was the Holy Spirit who appointed (τίθεσθαι, middle, not differing in meaning from the active, and taking a double accusative) the elders. As a procedure this does not necessarily differ from 14.23, but throws the process further back. Paul may appoint elders, but only those whom the Holy Spirit has already singled out and has thus himself appointed. The ministry is not appointed from below, nor from above if this means by those already ministers; the Holy Spirit is at work in the church choosing and preparing by his gifts those who are to be ministers. The Holy Spirit appointed them in order that they might shepherd (ποιμαίνειν, infinitive of purpose; Radermacher (153); BDR § 390.2, n. 5) God's flock. In this sense it is true that there is 'im Sinn des Lukas ein gewisses Gegenüber von Amt und Gemeinde' (Weiser 584).

It is clear that the same persons, who act as shepherds, are described both as πρεσβύτεροι (v. 17) and as ἐπίσκοποι (v. 28). That the two terms are applied equally to the same persons does not mean that they are identical in meaning. Thus ' "Bischöfe" bezeichnet hier die Aufgabe der Ältesten' (Conzelmann 119). Similarly Weiser (578) says that ἐπίσκοπος is not an *Amtstitel* but a *Funktionsbezeichnung*. Cf. H. von Campenhausen (*Amt* 87f.). Not quite the same is the view of Schneider (2.296) (and others) that we have here a combination of the 'elder' pattern of church order with the Pauline (Phil. 1.1) pattern of bishops and deacons. This view is not helped by the absence of deacons. Cf. also Roloff (305): Jewish based elders were combined with Hellenistic ἐπίσκοποι. It is broadly speaking true that the one designation describes ministers from a sociological, the other from a theological angle. It seems that up to the time when Acts was written elders were for the most part found among the older members of the church, those at least who had been Christians longest, and that they exercised the kind of leadership that older members may be expected to give, guiding the younger by their experience and accumulated wisdom (cf. 1 Pet. 5.1, 5; and the Pastorals passim). Yet the church is not a school or club, and the noun ἐπίσκοπος is related to the verb ἐπισκέπτεσθαι, which suggests the saving act in which God visited and redeemed his people, and the kind of ministry in which this redeeming visitation is constantly applied and brought before the minds of church members. This is not a simple function of age. Here it is closely connected with the work of a shepherd. Elsewhere in the NT the word ἐπίσκοπος is used at 1 Peter 2.25 (of Christ or God, in parallel with ποιμήν) and at Titus 1.7 (where it is certainly used of elders); 1 Tim. 3.2 (where it is probably used of elders; see *Pastoral Epistles* 32, 58); Phil. 1.1 (along with διάκονοι, and with no reference in the epistle to πρεσβύτεροι). Its general equivalence (but not synonymity) with elder is clear. It is used of officials in various social groups (see evidence in BA 606); it is used by Philo of Moses (*Quis rerum divinarum Haeres*? 30, ὁ ἐπίσκοπος Μωυσῆς, who keeps watch over men and affairs; it is used of the Cynic-Stoic preacher (see H. W. Beyer in *TWNT* 2.606f.). The background of the NT ἐπίσκοπος has also been found in the מבקר of the Qumran community; see especially CD 13.7–9: This is the rule for the overseer of the camp (סרך המבקר למחנה); he shall instruct the Many (הרבים) in the works of God and shall give them understanding of his marvellous acts of power and shall recount before them the eternal events. And he shall have pity on them as a father with his sons and

shall bring them back as a shepherd his flock (כרעה עדרו) (omitting
two unintelligible words). On this see Haenchen (567); but the best
discussion is that of Fitzmyer (*Essays* 293f.). He concludes, 'Grant-
ing then the common etymological meaning of *episkopos* and *mbqr*,
and certain similar functions, it is nevertheless difficult to set up any
direct connection between the Essene ''Overseer'' and the institution
of the early Jewish Christian church in Palestine.' He thinks that
there may possibly have been such a connection outside Palestine; it
is however difficult to envisage this. It is probable that the word was
picked up by Christians from secular institutions but that they were
encouraged to use it by associations which came mainly through the
verb in biblical Greek. See also B. E. Thiering (*JBL* 100 (1981),
59–74, '*Mebaqqer* and *Episkopos* in the Light of the Temple Scroll'.
There is no suggestion of any succession in episcopal office; there is
no need for succession (in the commonly understood sense); the
Holy Spirit will provide ministers as they are required.

The elders or bishops are to act as shepherds for the church of
God, τὴν ἐκκλησίαν (for this word in Acts see 5.11 and Introduction,
pp. lxxxviif.) τοῦ θεοῦ. τοῦ θεοῦ is the reading of ℵ B 614 1175
2495 *al* vg sy bo^{ms} Cyril. Other readings are τοῦ κυρίου (P^{74} A C* D
E Ψ 33 36 453 945 1739 1891 *al* gig p sy^{hmg} co Irenaeus^{lat} Lucifer)
and τοῦ κυρίου καὶ (τοῦ *pm*) θεοῦ (C³ 𝔐). The reading τοῦ θεοῦ
causes so much difficulty when taken with the following words (see
below) that it must be accepted as original, the other two readings
being attempts to ease the difficulty.

τοῦ θεοῦ provides the subject of the relative clause that follows,
ἣν περιεποιήσατο. The verb is often taken to mean simply *to acquire*
(as at 1 Tim. 3.13). *Begs.* 4.261f. argues for the meaning *rescued*.
Its meaning in the OT and NT seems to be prevailingly 'save alive',
or 'rescue from destruction'. This observation is justified; see e.g.
Isa. 31.5, περιποιήσεται καὶ σώσει; 43.21, λαοῦ μου ὃν
περιεποιησάμην; also Luke's own use at Lk. 17.33. Marshall adds
Ps. 74 (73).2, 'which significantly follows a verse in which Israel is
likened to a flock'. The two ideas are very close together: God
acquired a people by saving them.

He did so διὰ τοῦ αἵματος τοῦ ἰδίου; so P^{74} ℵ A B C D E Ψ 33 36
945 1175 1739 1891 *al* Cyril. 𝔐 has διὰ τοῦ ἰδίου αἵματος. The
latter reading can only be translated, *through his own blood*, which is
very difficult theologically unless in the preceding clause we have (as
𝔐 does) κυρίου. Salvation through the blood of the Lord Jesus
Christ raises no special problems, but it is probably incorrect to read
anything other than θεοῦ. The reading of B ℵ etc., which must be
accepted, may, like that of 𝔐, be translated *through his own blood*,
but can also be translated, *through the blood of his Own, his Own*
being taken as a title of Christ, God's own Son. This is rejected by
Turner (*Insights* 14f.) who thinks, mistakenly, that it leads to a denial

of the deity of the Son. In any case, of course, this would not be a reason for rejecting a reading required by grammar. M. 1.90f. is more inclined to defend it, noting that 'in the papyri we find the singular [of ἴδιος] used thus as a term of endearment to near relatives, e.g. ὁ δεῖνα τῷ ἰδίῳ χαίρειν.' Schneider (2.297) similarly thinks that ὁ ἴδιος corresponds to ὁ ἀγαπητός and ὁ μονογενής. *Begs.* 4.262 adopts 'of his own' since 'it is inconceivable that ''his own blood'' is right'. See also Hort, *Introduction: Notes* 98–100 (perhaps υἱοῦ should be inserted); Ropes in *Begs.* 3.197–9. It is very unlikely that a trained theologian would write 'his own blood'; but Luke was not such a theologian, and the natural way of reading the Greek should probably be adopted. It was enough for Luke that when Jesus Christ shed his blood on the cross he was acting as the representative of God; he was God's way of giving life, blood, for the world. Roloff (306) makes the good suggestion that Luke was putting together two formulas: the church of God; Christ has acquired his people by blood (that is, by atoning death). But he was not careful to change the subject. An explanation of this kind is more convincing than Wettstein's long (2.596–9) note on patristic references to blood and Calvin's theological explanation (2.184): '... because ... the two natures are so united in Christ as to constitute one Person, what properly belongs to the one is sometimes improperly transferred to the other. For example in this verse Paul attributes the blood to God, because the man Jesus Christ, who shed His blood for us, was also God. The figure of speech was called the *communicatio idiomatum* by the Fathers, because the property of one nature is applied to the other.' He goes on to warn against the errors of Nestorius and Eutyches. Cf. Rackham (393), with references to Ignatius, *Ephesians* 1.1; Tertullian, *Ad Uxorem* 2.3. *Communicatio idiomatum* will not really serve here because we are dealing not with the two natures of Christ but with two Persons of the Trinity.

How the blood shed on the cross saved a people for God is a question which it would be wrong to pursue at great depth because it probably did not occur to Luke to inquire deeply into it. Derrett (*Law* 403) is right in making a distinction: the blood shed is not a price paid, though the redeemer does acquire rights over the redeemed. And Delling (*Kreuzestod* 94) is right in saying that the shedding of blood does not (or at least does not necessarily) imply the idea of sacrifice. Stephen shed his blood (22.20), but his death was not a sacrifice. Luke nowhere else asserts so plainly that it was the death of Jesus that brought the redeemed people into existence, but the form—and indeed the existence—of his two-volume work, hinging on crucifixion and resurrection, implies so much. And with that Luke seems to be content.

29. Again the speaker turns to the future, this time with definite prophecy of what will happen μετὰ τὴν ἄφιξίν μου. The usual meaning of ἄφιξις is *arrival*, and attempts have been made to give it this meaning here—arrival in Jerusalem, in Rome, or in heaven (after death). These all seem wildly improbable; a simpler and better suggestion, though often overlooked, is that of Bengel (469): 'Sensus igitur est: *primum venit Paulus; deinde venient lupi.*' It seems however that Paul (Luke) must mean *departure*; so already Chrysostom, also e.g. Moule (*IB* 89). Some parallels to this use of the word (probably suggested by the compounded ἀπό) are adduced; not all are quite convincing. BA 254 reduce the unambiguous cases to Demosthenes, *Epistles* 1.2 (1463); 3.39 (1484) (even in these one wonders if ἔνθαδε ἄφιξις might not have been intended to mean *arrival at home*; Aelius Aristides 48.7k = 24p.467D; Josephus, *Ant.* 2.18 (τὴν ἐκεῖσε ἄφιξιν; departure thither (Thackeray)); 4.315 (τῆς πρὸς ἐκείνους ἀφίξεως; departure to them (Thackeray)); 7.247 (τὴν πρὸς τὸν Δανίδην ἄφιξιν; the journey to D. (Thackeray)); PMich 497.12. There seems to be ro example of the use of ἄφιξις in the sense of departure in *death* (cf. Lk. 9.31, ἔξοδος), which may be but is not necessarily intended here. Possibly some ambiguity is intended: 'As soon as I am out of the way.'

Paul's departure will be followed by the entry of λύκοι βαρεῖς, *fearsome wolves*. In D, the adjective is used at 20.9 of heavy sleep; the common idea is oppressiveness. This is the meaning of the word in Josephus, *Ant.* 15.354, where Herod the Great is warned of being βαρὺν ... καὶ τυραννικόν. The adjective is used with ὀργή and χόλος at 3 Macc. 5.1, 30, 47, but it remains somewhat surprising as a description of wolves. *Luporum ... rapacium* (Horace, *Carmina* 4.4.50, cited by Schweizer, *Beiträge* 63) is more natural. G. W. H. Lampe's essay 'Grievous Wolves' (*FS* Moule 253–68), though instructive in regard to early Christian heresy, casts no light on the use of βαρεῖς. βαρύς can also mean *powerful* (e.g. Homer, *Iliad* 1.89; Xenophon, *Agesilaus* 11.12—but this may be an example of βαρύτατος = fiercest) and it may be Luke's point that the heretics are formidable rather than ferocious.

It is the description of the church as a flock (v. 28, repeated in v. 29) that invites the image of wolves. The wolves will not spare the flock; the trouble-makers will pursue their own ends regardless of what becomes of the church. For the imagery, used in various ways in the early church, see *inter alia* Didache 16.3; Ignatius, *Philadelphians* 2.1, 2; 2 Clement 5.2–4; Justin, *1 Apology* 16, 58; *Trypho* 35. For wolves in the OT see Ezek. 22.27; Zeph. 3.3.

The wolves come εἰς ὑμᾶς, that is, they come in from without. They may be Jewish or Gentile teachers, importing their beliefs into the church, or possibly oppressive authorities, though this would fit less well with εἰς, which suggests that the persons in question made their way into the church's fellowship. Contrast v. 30.

For the fulfilment of this verse and of v. 30 see the Pastorals and

Revelation. On the chronological relation between this verse and the Pastorals see Wilson (*Pastorals* 123). For the thought cf. *Acts of Thomas* 67 (L.-B. 2.2.184f.), διατήρησον αὐτὴν ἀπὸ τῶν λύκων τῶν διαρπαζόντων.

At the beginning of the verse some authorities give a closer connection with what precedes: for ἐγὼ οἶδα, C³ E Ψ 𝔐 p syʰ have ἐγὼ γὰρ οἶδα τοῦτο; B alone has ὅτι ἐγὼ οἶδα.

30. In contrast with those who invade the church from without men will rise up ἐξ ὑμῶν αὐτῶν (αὐτῶν is omitted by B, but the emphasis was probably intended), from among yourselves, out of your own number. Heresy and schism will arise from within. Strictly, ὑμεῖς should refer to the Ephesian elders, who are being addressed, but Luke is probably now thinking of the church at large. 'Ambition is the mother of all heresies' (Calvin 2.185); not true, but Luke might have agreed.

Heresy is represented by the διεστραμμένα, the perverse things that are spoken, schism by the desire ἀποσπᾶν, to draw away, disciples. For διαστρέφειν cf. 13.10. For ἀποσπᾶν cf. e.g. Josephus, *Life* 321, βουλόμενος δ' αὐτοὺς ἀποσπάσαι τῶν Τιβεριέων; Lucian, *Lepithae* 26, ... Δίφιλος ... δύο ἤδη μαθητάς μου ἀποσπάσας ... ; Bengel (469): '*abstrahere*, a simplicitate erga Christum et ab unitate corporis.'

There is no evidence in the present passage to suggest in which ways the truth would be perverted or who would attempt to set up rival communities over against what Luke regarded as the true church. It is clear that a time is contemplated when orthodoxy and heresy would be clearly differentiated, and when the church would be an institution with clearly defined boundaries. It did not always appear so simple. Gnostic teachers, for example, emerging within the church would often regard themselves as its most faithful, or at least as its most intelligent and advanced members. See Bultmann (*Theologie* 174); and on the whole question, W. Bauer (*Rechtgläubigkeit und Ketzerei*).

For ἀποσπᾶν, D has ἀποστρέφειν, without difference in meaning. For αὐτῶν (at the end of the verse), ℵ A B have ἑαυτῶν; again there is no difference in meaning.

31. From the future the speaker turns back to the remembered past. The two—past and future—are deliberately mingled in this speech and that which unites them is expressed in the imperative γρηγορεῖτε. The whole is an exhortation to responsible pastoral service, and this is reinforced both by the example given in the past and by warnings of future perils.

γρηγορεῖτε recalls apocalyptic passages in the gospels (especially Mk 13.34, 35, 37, and parallels), in Paul (especially 1 Thess. 5.6), and elsewhere (e.g. Rev. 3.2, 3; 16.15); it is significant that here it refers not to watchful preparedness for the coming of the Son of man at the End but to vigilance in caring for the continuing life of the church. For *Vigilate* as a component in early Christian catechesis see especially E. G. Selwyn, *The First Epistle of Peter* (1946), Essay II, 363–466. Of such watchfulness Paul had given an example in a ministry (in Ephesus) that lasted three years (see 19.8, 10; BDR § 5.3c, n. 17) and was maintained ceaselessly night and day. This claim must be taken with the statement in v. 34 that Paul worked with his hands to supply his own needs and those of others. Unless Luke was very careless and forgetful he meant that Paul was ceaselessly occupied; whenever he was not engaged in working for his living he was working as evangelist and pastor.

It was work over which he shed tears; cf. 2 Cor. 2.4. It included νουθετεῖν (Rom. 15.14; 1 Cor. 4.14; 1 Thess. 5.12, 14; also Col. 1.28; 3.16; 2 Thess. 3.15—found only in these passages: a Pauline word), *admonition* (note also the noun, νουθεσία, 1 Cor. 10.11; Eph. 6.4; Titus 3.10), setting their minds in order, that is, so that they should think, and consequently act, as Christians. He admonished *each one* (ὑμῶν, D E 323 614 945 1739 1891 2495 *al* latt sy, is a thoughtless addition; Paul admonished each member of the church, not only each one of the elders there assembled); cf. Col. 1.28. This may well be an anti-gnostic point: each one, not only the πνευματικοί. Cf. vv. 20f.

32. Paul exhorts his hearers; he also commends them to God, that is, to God's protection and guidance.

For τὰ νῦν cf. 4.29; 17.30 and the notes. For παρατίθεσθαι (middle) cf. Lk. 23.46; Acts 14.23; (17.3 for a different use). Paul has watched over these elders; he now hands over the responsibility to God, as Timothy must hand on the responsibility for Gospel truths to faithful men (2 Tim. 2.2). But 'der lukanische Paulus übergibt bei seinem Abschied den Amtsträgern nicht das Wort als festes Lehrdepositum, er unterstellt sie vielmehr dem Wort als der heilvoll in der Geschichte wirkenden Kraft Gottes' (Roloff 306f.).

παρατ. τῷ θεῷ is the text of P[74] ℵ A C D E Ψ 𝔐 vg sy sa[mss]; B 326 *pc* gig sa[ms] bo have π. τῷ κυρίῳ. This recalls the words of Stephen at 7.59, and is probably due to assimilation. It is doubtful whether Luke would have felt strongly about either reading as against the other.

To God; καὶ τῷ λόγῳ τῆς χάριτος αὐτοῦ. This word is the Gospel; cf. v. 24. This is an example of hendiadyoin; Luke means, 'to God, who is active in the word of grace, which you proclaim and by which you yourselves live'. So Blass (222): ' ... quasi una notio sunt; agit enim Deus per verbum suum'.

If this phrase does in its two parts represent one concept, the grammatical question of the reference of τῷ δυναμένῳ becomes less important. The nearer antecedent is λόγος; θεός (or κύριος, if read) might possibly be thought more appropriate. In fact it is the word of God, God in his word, who is able to build up the elders themselves and the church that they serve. For οἰκοδομεῖν (said of the church) see 9.31; 1 Thess. 5.11 and other Pauline passages. For the church as οἰκοδομή see 1 Cor. 3.9 (and *1 Corinthians* 86–92).

God is able also to give a κληρονομία (another Pauline word, though Paul more frequently has κληρονομεῖν and κληρονόμος). The building up of the church belongs to the present age; the inheritance is probably thought of as received in the age to come. It is an inheritance that God will give and they will receive.

ἐν τοῖς ἡγιασμένοις: ἐν with the dative is not, as it sometimes is, a substitute for the simple dative but means *among*; the Ephesian elders take their place among a larger company (πᾶσιν) of those who have been sanctified (M. 3.264f.). It is not easy to find a reason why the perfect participle passive of ἁγιάζειν should be used (as at 26.18) instead of the adjective ἅγιος. In Acts the adjective is used most frequently of the Holy Spirit, but not exclusively so; see 3.14, 21; 4.27, 30; 6.13; 7.33; 9.13, 32, 41; 10.22; 21.28; 26.10. A number of these passages refer to Christians. The question is discussed in relation to OT passages by Wilcox (35–7), but without adequate ground for suspecting the use of an aberrant LXX text. The OT background of inheritance is of course important; see Deut. 33.3, 4; Ps. 15(16).5; Wisdom 5.5. Also important are some Qumran passages. See 1QS 11.7, 8: To those whom God chose he had given them as an eternal possession, and he has made them to inherit in the lot of the holy ones (וינחילם בגורל קדושים); 1QH 11.11, 12 (בגורל עם קדושיכה).

Polycarp 12.2 (Deus ... aedificet vos ... et det vobis sortem et partem inter sanctos suos) may show knowledge of this verse; see I.37.

At the end of the verse, instead of πᾶσιν, D has τῶν πάντων; after πᾶσιν, 614 *pc* sy^h** add αὐτῷ ἡ δόξα εἰς τοὺς αἰῶνας· ἀμήν. The addition is certainly secondary; it is hard to know what τῶν πάντων means. Ropes (*Begs.* 3.199) says that it 'seems to be a survival of τῶν αἰώνων from' the addition (which he gives in the form αὐτῷ ἡ δ. εἰς τ. αἰῶνας τ. αἰώνων· ἀμήν). This is not very convincing, but may serve till a better guess is made.

Schille (404) writes, 'Übrigens wird nachträglich sichtbar, warum Paulus nicht nach Ephesus gereist ist: weil Lukas nur die Ältesten in die Sukzession des Paulus stellen wollte.' But Luke gave his reason for the omission of Ephesus in 20.16. He may have been wrong; Paul's motive may have been different (see on the verse); but Luke has given his opinion, the opinion he wishes to communicate to his readers, and it is not Schille's.

33. Paul, again looking into the past, justifies his conduct in Ephesus (and, no doubt, Luke means to imply, elsewhere), using language similar to that of Samuel in 1 Sam. 12.3. What he had done he had not done for money (had he been accused of this?), or other material advantage.

For οὐδενός, P⁷⁴ A E have οὐθενός. For this spelling see on 19.27.

ἱματισμός: for additions to the references in MM 304 see *ND* 3.69f.; the meaning of course is not in doubt.

34. Not only did Paul show no desire for other men's property (v. 33); not only did he work for his own living; he worked also for the benefit of his companions.

αὐτοί is correctly used with the second person plural of the verb: *you yourselves know*. It was unnecessary for him to inform them; we might add, But it was useful for Luke to inform his readers. A speaker however will often find it desirable to remind his readers of what they may have forgotten, or be in danger of forgetting.

These hands—the speaker shows them to his hearers. ὑπηρετεῖν, the verb, is used in the NT only in Acts; the cognate noun, ὑπηρέτης, is characteristic of John, but is used at Acts 5.22, 26; 26.16; the use of this word of John Mark at 13.5 may but need not mean that John Mark was engaged in secular paid work in order to maintain Paul and Barnabas. Paul now had no such assistance but worked with his own hands; see 18.3 (cf. 1 Cor 4.12). χρεία has been used to mean *need*, or the *service of need*, at 2.45; 4.35; 6.3; so also 28.10. Here we should expect, after ταῖς χρείαις μου, καὶ ταῖς τῶν ὄντων μετ᾽ ἐμοῦ. But ὑπηρετεῖν is more naturally used with persons than with needs, and with the verb coming into sight Luke takes the opportunity of shortening his sentence by one word. See also *Begs.* 4.263, where the sentence as Luke wrote it is taken as an example of '"comparatio compendiaria" in the old grammars'.

In 1 Corinthians 9 Paul (using a saying of Jesus different from that quoted in v. 35) argues that it is right that preachers of the Gospel should be maintained by those to whom they minister, though he himself chooses to make no use of the principle in relation to the church at Corinth. He did accept gifts from other churches (1 Cor. 9.6–18; 2 Cor. 11.7–11; 12.16–18).

Begs. 4.263 attaches πάντα (v. 35) to this verse: These hands ministered all things (or perhaps, always).

35. In D Speculum the verse begins not with πάντα but with πᾶσιν, an easier, and secondary, text: I showed you all. If πάντα is read it must be taken as an accusative of respect: In all ways, in all respects, I showed you. *Begs.* 4.263 (but see on v. 34) translates, I gave you a thorough example, or I showed you always.

Again 1 Cor. 4.12 is recalled, this time by the word κοπιᾶν, which probably needs a somewhat stronger translation than *working*. When the verb does not simply mean *to be tired* it still carries with it the association of weariness—to wear oneself out with toil. The construction is rightly taken by BDR § 425.6, n. 10, 'nicht etwa "so, nämlich arbeitend", sondern lebhaft mit Gebäude, "seht, so muss man arbeiten und ..."'. There is a reference to Mayser 2.3.73f. for papyrus evidence. One must work, as Paul did, not simply to secure one's independence but also to help the weak (who presumably are not able to work for themselves). Blass (223) takes 'the weak' differently. 'Ut ap. Paul. ἀσθενοῦντες sunt parum firmi, qui facile offensionem capiant; quibus ut parceret, ne suspicionibus de avaritia apostoli laborarent, licita quoque mercede ille abstinuit. Cf. 1 Cor. 9.12, et de re Act. 18.3.' Cf. Eph. 4.28, which is very close to the present passage, except that it is addressed specifically to ὁ κλέπτων.

Just as in 1 Cor. 9.14 Paul clinches his argument that preachers ought to be supported by the congregation by quoting a saying of Jesus, so here he confirms his advice to the elders to support themselves in the same way.

μνημονεύειν is, like ἀντιλαμβάνεσθαι, dependent on δεῖ: You must remember. The formula of remembering (used with λόγοι) is discussed by J. M. Robinson in J. M. Robinson and H. Koester *Trajectories through Early Christianity*, Philadelphia, 1971, 96f.; see not only Lk. 22.61; Jn 15.20 but also 1 Clement 13.1, 2; 46.7, 8; cf. 2.1. The present saying may have been drawn from a collection of such λόγοι. There is no parallel in the canonical gospels. The question of authenticity is left open by Knox (*Hell. El.* 29) and was affirmed by J. Jeremias in the first edition of his *Unknown Sayings of Jesus* (ET, 1957), 77–81. Jeremias notes parallels in Aristotle, *Ethica Nicomachea* 4.1.7 (1120a); Plutarch, *Maxime cum principibus Viris* 3 (778c) Pseudo-Plutarch, *Regum Apophthegmata: Artaxerxes* 1 (173d); Seneca, *Epistles* 81.17; Sirach 4.31; *Didache* 1.5; 4.5; Barnabas 19.9; *Apostolic Constitutions* 7.12.1, but surprisingly does not mention Thucydides 2.97.4, where it is said that the Thracians thought it better λαμβάνειν μᾶλλον ἢ διδόναι, therein being opposite to the Persians (who thus must have thought it better διδόναι μᾶλλον ἢ λαμβάνειν, which is virtually the Lucan saying). It is true, as J. J. Kilgallen points out (*JBL* 112 (1993), 312–14), that Thucydides expresses the matter less clearly than could be desired, but the parallel is valid. See Haenchen (569f.). If the saying is taken, as by Jeremias, in an exclusive sense ('giving is blessed, not receiving'), and even if it is taken comparatively, and if logic is strictly pressed, it is unfair to the weak, who have no choice but to receive. But logic must not be pressed in this way. The saying addresses a single person, for whom giving and receiving are both possibilities; he will do better in giving than in receiving. In later editions Jeremias's view was changed. In the third edition (with O. Hofius as collaborator) we read (37), 'Auch das Apg 20.35 zitierte Agraphon ist wahrscheinlich ein aus der griechisch-römischen Welt stammendes Sprichwort, das Jesus in den Mund gelegt worden ist.' See *FS* Dupont 686f. See further Conzelmann (119): 'μᾶλλον ist nicht semitisierend exklusiv zu fassen ... , sondern ist echt Komparativ ... Vgl den Komparativ von 5.29!' Conzelmann also refers to other passages mentioned above.

D* has the meaningless μακάριος; this comes from Latin—gig has beatus, in error for beatius, an easy mistake. sy^p has μακάριος ὁ διδοὺς μᾶλλον ἢ ὁ λαμβάνων. P. W. van der Horst (*NovT* 16 (1974), 309) adds to the parallels Musonius Rufus VI (56, 10f.L; 27, 14f.H).

36. Weiser (580) argues convincingly that vv. 36–38 are Luke's construction. For the farewell prayer cf. 21.5. For θεὶς τὰ γόνατα see 7.60 and the note.

37. ἱκανός is a Lucan word; see e.g. 18.18. A good deal of lamentation arose on the part of all.

ἐπιπίπτειν ἐπὶ τὸν τράχηλον occurs also at Lk. 15.20. It is frequent in the OT (e.g. Gen. 33.4; 45.14; Tobit 7.6 ‭א‬); also προπίπτειν ἐπὶ τ. τ. It describes an emotional embrace, accompanied by a kiss, κατεφίλουν αὐτόν.

38. ὀδυνᾶσθαι is a Lucan word (Lk., 3 times; Acts, once), used of both physical and mental pain; 'poët., rarius prox. att.' (Blass 224). Nothing grieved them so much as Paul's own prediction that they would never see him again; v. 25. This is a final parting. No difference is intended between ὄψεσθε and μέλλουσιν θεωρεῖν.

For προπέμπειν see 15.3; also 21.5. They saw him off to the ship. The article (τὸ πλοῖον) suggests but does not prove that Paul resumed his journey in the ship that had brought him to Miletus.

Ropes (*Begs.* 3.201): 'In Codex Bezae Blass (*St.Kr.* 1898, p. 542) reads μελλε[τ]αι for μελλει[..]ι [Rope's reading of D.] This recalls *videbitis faciem meam* gig sah, and the omission of αυτου in D leaves the way open for this restoration. Scrivener's conjecture was μελλει[σο]ι.'

XII

PAUL RETURNS TO JERUSALEM
(21.1–22.29)

52. JOURNEY TO JERUSALEM 21.1–14

(1) When we had separated from them and set sail we made a straight course and came to Cos, and on the next day to Rhodes, and thence to Patara. (2) We found a ship crossing to Phoenicia, embarked, and set sail. (3) Having raised Cyprus and left it on our left we sailed to Syria and landed at Tyre, for there the ship was discharging its cargo. (4) We sought out the disciples and stayed there[1] seven days. They told Paul through the Spirit that he should not go to Jerusalem. (5) But it happened that, when we had completed the [seven][2] days, we left and set out on our journey while they all, with their wives and children, saw us off as far as outside the city. We knelt on the beach, prayed, (6) and said farewell to one another. We embarked on the ship, while they returned home.

(7) [3]We continued the voyage from Tyre; we arrived at Ptolemais, greeted the brothers, and stayed with them one day. (8) On the next day we left and came to Caesarea. We entered the house of Philip the evangelist, who was one of the Seven, and stayed with him. (9) He had four daughters, virgins, who prophesied. (10) We stayed on for many days, and there came down from Judaea a prophet, Agabus by name. (11) He came to us, took Paul's belt, bound his own feet and hands, and said, 'Thus speaks the Holy Spirit: So shall the Jews in Jerusalem bind the man whose belt this is, and deliver him into the hands of the Gentiles.' (12) When we heard this, we and the local residents begged [Paul][4] not to go up to Jerusalem. (13) Then answered Paul, 'What[5] are you doing, as you weep and break my heart? for I am ready not only to be bound but even to die in Jerusalem for the name of the Lord Jesus.' (14) Since he would not be persuaded we fell silent, with the words, 'The Lord's will[6] prevail.'

Bibliography

F. Bovon, as in (51).

P. Corssen, *ZNW* 2 (1901), 289–99.

[1]NEB, NJB, a week.
[2]Seven is not in the Greek.
[3]RSV, when we had finished the voyage; NEB, we made the passage; NJB, the end of our voyage from Tyre came.
[4]NEB, begged and implored Paul. Paul is not in the Greek.
[5]NEB, Why are you trying to break my resolution?
[6]RSV, NEB, NJB, be done.

G. Dautzenberg, *BiK* 38 (1983), 153–8.

H. Duensing, *ZNW* 37 (1938), 42–6.

E. E. Ellis, *FS* Bruce (1970), 55–67.

G. D. Kilpatrick, *JTS* 6 (1955), 235–8.

H. Patsch, *ThZ* 28 (1972), 228–32.

H. Sahlin, *NovT* 24 (1982), 188.

Commentary

The journey continues: Miletus, Cos, Patara, Cyprus, Phoenicia, Syria, Tyre, Ptolemais, Caesarea. Compare journeys in Lucan, *Bellum Civile* 8.243–8: Ephesus, Samos, Cos, Gnidus, Rhodes; and Livy 37.16: Miletus, Myndus, Halicarnassus, Cos, Cnidus, Rhodes, Patara. A different kind of parallel is suggested by Ehrhardt (*Acts* 105): In 2 Kings 2.1–12 Elisha accompanies Elijah from place to place, Elijah repeatedly predicting his imminent departure, to the subdued lamentations of the prophets. There is nothing, beyond the narrative itself, to suggest that Luke had the OT story in mind, or that he was thinking of 'S. Paul's temptation' (Rackham 397) as parallel to 'the temptations of Moses and Elijah, and, we may add, of the Lord himself [Num. 20.7–13; 1 Kings 19.4; Lk. 22.40–44]'.

The source of the narrative is disputed. The most natural explanation, especially in view of the first person plural in vv. 1, 2, 3, 4, 5, 6, 7, 8, 11, 12, 14, is that Luke is using the first person plural itinerary used elsewhere in the second part of his book. Conzelmann (120) disagrees; Luke has been following up traces of Paul and on the basis of them constructing a story. Similarly Schille (407): 'Die Stationen sind nicht aus einem Itinerar abgeschrieben.' Lüdemann (241) on the other hand writes: 'Dem Bericht [vv. 1–16] liegt eine Quelle zugrunde, die eine Reise des Paulus von Milet nach Jerualem enthielt.' He adds that there has been a good deal of redaction, shown by the Lucan vocabulary. It is important that Lüdemann (242) takes vv. 8b, 9 to be part of Luke's source and not his own elaboration of it. If this is correct if means that there is at least a second-hand, and conceivably a first-hand, connection between the author of Acts and one of the Seven whose story runs back to ch. 6. It is interesting also that Agabus, previously mentioned at 11.28, now reappears, though introduced, and described as a prophet coming from Judaea, as though he were a new character in the story. This suggests that information about him may have reached Luke along two different channels, Antiochene memories having supplied the reference in ch. 11, Caesarean that in ch. 21. If this is so the present reference must be supposed to have been worked into the Itinerary so completely that the first person plural was introduced into it. It is perhaps more likely that the person responsible for *We* and the itinerary himself encountered Agabus here. The reference to Agabus was important to Luke because it provided him with yet another (cf. 20.37f.; 21.4) fore-shadowing of the trouble that was to befall Paul in Jerusalem.

This paragraph presents a very clear example of what Luke appears to have done throughout the journey narrative which begins at 20.1 (cf. 19.21f.). Three components may be distinguished. There is an itinerary, which gives in simple terms a list of places touched at, probably noting a few additional matters that bear upon the journey, and its route, e.g. the plot of 20.3, the halt in Miletus (20.15f.), and the encounter with disciples at Tyre (21.3f.). To this travel source Luke added incidents which (in all probability) he learned by local inquiry: the miracle at Troas (20.7–12), the farewell at Tyre (21.5f.), perhaps the meeting with Philip (21.8f.), and (but see below) the prophecy of Agabus (21.10–14). The third component consists of theological comment on the meaning of the journey. By far the most important such comment is the speech at Miletus (20.18–35), which shows Paul's pastoral care for the whole church and foretells both his approaching suffering and the perils of heresy and schism which lie ahead. In addition to the speech there are repeated references to Paul's suffering and his determination to face and accept it. Here the most important example is the prophecy of Agabus, with its pro-phetic symbolism (21.10–14), which (if—see above—we may at the same time regard it as a historical reminiscence) is important in that it shows how event and interpretation originated and developed together.

Haenchen (577f.) rightly rejects the objection to the historicity of the narrative that Paul ignores the prophesying of the Christians in Tyre, that we are told that the daughters of Philip prophesied but not what they said, and that Agabus could not have bound his own hands and feet. The story is sufficiently connected and makes sense; Luke is not writing like a professor of history; this he neither was able nor wished to do.

1. ἐγένετο with the infinitive: for Luke's frequent use (in imitation of the LXX?) of this construction see on 4.5.

ἀναχθῆναι: see 20.13. The word recurs in v. 2.

ἀποσπᾶν is used at Mt. 26.51 for drawing a sword from its sheath, but Luke uses it exclusively of persons. At Acts 20.30 it is used in the active of those who draw away disciples; at Lk. 22.41 the passive is used intransitively (ἀπεσπάσθη ἀπ' αὐτῶν); so also here. It suggests a separation made with difficulty; they were loth to part. But 'we tore ourselves away' might be too strong. For ὡς ... ἀποσπασθέντες, D* sa have καὶ ἐπιβάντες ἀνήχθημεν· ἀποσπασθέντων δὲ ἡμῶν. The sense is unchanged; the copyist, or editor, feels free to change the wording.

εὐθυδρομήσαντες: see 16.11. The straight course to Cos implies a north east wind, which was usual.

εἰς τὴν Κῶ. For the declension of Κῶς (cf. Ἀπολλῶς at 19.1) see M. 2.121. After Samos, proceeding southwards, Cos was the next sizeable island. For Cos at approximately the time Paul was there (presumably only for an overnight stay) see Tacitus, *Annals* 12.61. Claudius made it *immunis*; it had fairly consistently taken the Roman side in earlier wars. It was the home of Hippocrates and the site of the medical school founded by him. For Jews on Cos see *NS* 3.69; Trebilco 13, 134f. See also Strabo 14.2; Horace, *Odes* 4.13.13.

τῇ δὲ ἑξῆς, a Lucan term: Lk. 7.11; 9.37; Acts 21.1; 25.17; 27.18. No other NT writer uses it, but it is fairly common elsewhere. Here as in most places ἡμέρα must be supplied (at Lk. 7.11, χρόνῳ). Luke likes to show variety in such words; cf. 20.15.

εἰς τὴν Ῥόδον. The ship was following the chain of inshore Aegean islands, most of which had satisfactory harbours. The same name served for the island and for its chief city, a *civitas libera* through most of the imperial period. 'From Rhodes there is virtually no significant evidence' of Jewish residents (*NS* 3.69). See however 1 Macc. 15.23.

Patara (Herodotus 1.182.2; Horace, *Odes* 3.4.64—an oracle of Apollo) was on the mainland, in Lycia, and the residence of the *legatus Augusti*. The name is a neuter plural. It seems to have been a likelier place for Paul to change ships (v. 2) than Myra, which is introduced here by the Western text. Πάταρα stands alone in ℵ B E Ψ 𝔐 vg sy, Πατέρα in P⁷⁴ A C. καὶ Μύρα is added by P⁴¹ᵛⁱᵈ D (gig vgᵐˢˢ sa). Myra may have been introduced from 27.5, but Clark (377) defends the reading and so does Ropes (*Begs.* 3.201; followed by Hanson 206, 208); both suggest that the second name may have been omitted by homoeoteleuton. 'For deliberate change, either by omission or by addition, no sufficient motive is easy to assign' (Ropes, loc. cit.). Ropes however refers to Paul's presence in Myra according to the *Acts of Paul and Thecla* (§ 40; L.-B. 1.266); it is perhaps somewhat more probable than Ropes thinks that there was a tradition that connected Paul with Myra and this may have affected the text. See Metzger (482).

2. εὑρόντες πλοῖον. A change of ship was necessary; finding in this case (not always) implies search. Stählin (273) says that Paul changed ships 'um rascher voranzukommen'. It may be that the first ship was sailing no further. Another suggestion is that Paul was evading a plot; cf. 20.3.

διαπερῶν, *making the crossing*. The present participle is used to express the future. For other examples in Acts see 14.21f.; 15.27; 18.23; 21.3, 16; 26.17. See the notes; also Zerwick (§ 283); BDR § 339.2. But the idiom is as natural in Greek as in English. The new ship must have been a bigger one, no longer hugging the coast and the islands.

εἰς Φοινίκην. Phoenicia was the strip of coast between Carmel in the south and Nahr-el-Kelb in the north. The Libanus and Anti-Libanus provided a curtain which shut off the interior and meant that the district looked primarily towards the Mediterranean. The chief towns lay on the coast, some of them (e.g. Tyre, v. 3) situated on islands, which gave them great defensive strength.

ἐπιβάντες. Cf. 27.2; the word is synonymous with ἐμβαίνειν. See e.g. Thucydides 1.111.2.

ἀνήχθημεν, as in v. 1; Luke's usual word for putting to sea.

3. ἀναφάναντες (aorist participle active), P⁷⁴ ℵ B* 614 1704 1739 *pc* d; ἀναφανέντες (aorist participle passive), A B² C E Ψ 𝔐. The readings of B and its correctors are uncertain; see Ropes (*Begs.* 3.201). The active participle will have the sense of *cause to become visible*, by coming near; cf. the English idiomatic use of *raise*, 'to come in sight of' (*SOD*, s.v. III 7a). Lucian, *Dialogi Marini* 10.1 (τὴν νῆσον ... ταύτην ... ἀνάφηνον) is not as close a parallel as is sometimes suggested. The passive participle is often said to be meaningless (Ropes: 'yields no good natural sense'), but BDR § 159.4, n. 4 quote Theophanes, *Chronicle* 1.721, ἀναφανέντων αὐτῶν τὴν γῆν, rendering it 'als sie in Sicht des Landes kamen'. At § 309.1, n. 2 they translate ἀναφάναντες τὴν Κύπρον, ' "wir liessen Zypern uns sichtbar werden" ... nämlich durch Herankommen'. Referring again to the passive they add, 'ebenfalls wohl Schifferausdruck wie ἀποκρύπτειν (abscondere) für das Gegenteil'. Cf. Delebecque (101): ἀναφαίνω (ici à l'aoriste 1 actif) est pris dans un sens apparemment nautique: "voir apparaître" (une terre, quand on est en mer).'

Cyprus: see 11.19. They left it on their left, passing to the right, that is, to the south of it, following a direct line from Patara (Myra) to Tyre. Wettstein (2.602), for the expression, compares Lucian, *Navigium* 9, τὴν Κρήτην δεξιὰν λαβόντας ... They continued sailing in this direction (ἐπλέομεν, imperfect) until they arrived (κατήλθομεν, aorist) at their destination. 'Impf. ἐπλέομεν cursum, aor. κατήλθομεν finem denotat' (Blass 224). Similarly M. 3.66; BDR § 327.1, n. 1.

Syria: see 15.23; the word is used here in the sense of Phoenicia. κατήλθομεν (P⁷⁴ ℵ A B E 33 326 1175 *pc* lat sy) is almost certainly correct; κατήχθημεν (C Ψ 𝔐) probably came in by analogy with ἀνήχθημεν (v. 2).

Tyre was the most notable city on the Phoenician coast. It had been destroyed by Alexander the Great in 332 BC (e.g. Arrian, *Anabasis* 2.17–27) but speedily regained prosperity. There were Jews here (Tcherikover 289; *NS* 3.14f.). For the earlier, biblical story of Tyre see 2 Sam. 5.11; 1 Kings 5; Isa. 23; Ezek. 26–28.

For the duration of the voyage there are various estimates. Roloff (309), without supplying evidence, says, with a favourable wind, three days; Xenophon of Ephesus 1.14.6 three days (for Rhodes to Tyre); Chrysostom, *Homily* 43.1, five days (see Bruce 1.385).

ἦν ἀποφορτιζόμενον; as in v. 2, a present participle where a future might have been expected. See Zerwick § 283; BDR § 339.2 β. Again, the idiom is also English: That is where the boat was unloading ... The past tense makes the choice of participle the more natural.

γόμος, *cargo* occurs elsewhere in the NT only at Rev. 18.12f., an oracle based on Ezek. 27, the dirge on Tyre. But this is significant only of the fact that Tyre was a great trading city. Cf. Demosthenes 323.4 (883), τὸν γόμον ... τῆς νεώς.

On this journey Antioch is not included. This may have been simply through failure to catch a convenient boat; it may have been that the church of Antioch was no longer, after the troubles of Gal. 2.11–21, open to Paul. The question is worth asking, though there is no means of answering it.

4. ἀνευρόντες. Cf. v. 2 (εὑρόντες); the compound implies search. Presumably the travellers had reason to think that they would find a group of disciples (τοὺς μαθητάς, with article), and sought them out. Search would be necessary, 'erat enim urbs magna, Christiani pauci' (Blass 225). Roloff (309) thinks that this group of disciples 'auf das Wirken der Hellenisten zurückging (vgl. 11.19; 15.3)'. This is possible; more cannot be said.

ἐπεμείναμεν, constative aorist; the seven days are regarded as a unit. For αὐτοῦ, *there* (cf. 18.19), A L have αὐτοῖς (cf. d, apud eos), we stayed *with them*. For the seven-day stay cf. 20.6. Why did Paul stay here for seven days when he was hurrying (20.16) to get to Jerusalem? Was it because there was no ship available? Preuschen thinks this hardly possible, but it is not clear why. The correct answer is given in *Begs.* 4.265. τὸ πλοῖον (with article) in v. 6 shows that the travellers continued in the same ship; the seven days were therefore spent in unloading and loading the ship.

οἵτινες (equivalent to οἵ); it is characteristic of Acts to continue a narrative with a relative. διὰ τοῦ πνεύματος: presumably, showing the phenomena of inspiration. Luke does not express himself clearly. His words taken strictly would mean either that Paul was deliberately disobedient to the will of God or that the Spirit was mistaken in the guidance given. It is unthinkable that Luke intended either of these. It is probable that what he meant but failed adequately to express was something like what is written in vv. 10–14. The Spirit acting through prophets foretold that the journey to Jerusalem would bring Paul suffering, and his friends acting under the influence not of the Spirit but of human concern sought to dissuade him from going there. So, more or less, Calvin (2.193): 'There are different gifts of the Spirit, so that it is no wonder that those who are strong in the gift of prophecy are sometimes lacking in judgement or courage'; and Bengel (470): 'Spiritus significabat, Paulo imminere vincula: inde rogabant discipuli eum, ne iret.' Weiser (589f.) summarizes at length Bovon's explanation of the contrast with 20.23. 'Lukas folge bei der Gestaltung der Abschiedsszenen (20.36–21.16) dem Muster griechischer Darstellungen des Abschieds berühmter Helden von ihren Familien oder Freunden.' See Bovon in Kremer (*Actes* 339–58).

5. The language of the verse is Lucan. For ἐγένετο and the infinitive see v. 1; for προπέμπειν, 15.3; 20.38; for τιθέναι τὰ γόνατα, 7.60; 9.40; 20.36.

ἐξαρτίσαι of time, where πληρῶσαι might have been expected, 'sonst nicht belegt' (Preuschen 125). LS 587 gives the meaning, but with no other examples (there are examples of finishing buildings and books). BA 553 quote Hippocrates, *Epidemiae* 2.180, ἀπαρτίζειν τὴν ὀκτάμηνον; see 2.7, ὀκταμήνῳ. τὰς ἡμέρας are the seven days of v. 4.

αἰγιαλός 'describes correctly the smooth beach at Tyre, as opposed to ἀκτή, used of a rocky shore' (Hemer 125). Stählin (273) is more precise: the beach to the south of the mole built by Alexander the Great to connect the island of Tyre with the mainland. Hanson (208): '... the beach at Tyre can still be identified. Is not this the vivid touch of an eye-witness?' Possibly; but not necessarily.

6. This verse continues in construction from the previous one— προσευξάμενοι ἀπησπασάμεθα. For the verb ἀπασπάζεσθαι cf. the simple form in 20.1; the combination with ἀπό makes it more suitable for farewells. The leave-taking was mutual—ἀλλήλους. Cf. Plutarch, *De Genio Socratis* 33 (598A), ἀσπασάμενοι ἀλλήλους. The first person plural of ἀπησπασάμεθα is now divided; one group embarks, the other goes home. The textual variations convey no difference in meaning.

ἀνέβημεν P⁷⁴ ℵ* A C 36 453 614 1175 2495 *pc*
ἐνέβημεν ℵᶜ B E (Ψ) 945 1739 1891 *pc*
ἐπέβημεν 𝔐

Bruce (1.386) tends to favour 'the less usual ἀνέβημεν'. But in Acts ἐνεβ. occurs here only and thus may claim to be *in Acts* the less usual.

The travelling party embarked εἰς τὸ πλοῖον, *the* ship, that is, the ship in which they had arrived. See v. 4; the article is anaphoric.

εἰς τὰ ἴδια, to their own places, their own homes. Cf. Jn 16.32; 19.27.

7. τὸν πλοῦν διανύσαντες, *having completed the voyage*. For διανύειν πλοῦν see Bruce (1.386); Conzelmann (121); and Xenophon of Ephesus 1.11.2, 5; 1.14.6. There is no ground for the inference that the voyage was completed in a different ship. It has however been suggested that the sea voyage ended here (though it is difficult to make this agree with v. 7). Page (220) does not take ἀπὸ Τύρου with the participle but with the following verb, and renders, We, having (thereby) completed our voyage, came from Tyre to Ptolemais. See further on v. 8.

κατηντήσαμεν (an 'Acts' word—16.1; 18.19, 24; 20.15; 25.13; 26.7; 27.12; 28.13; so is κατέβημεν, read by P⁷⁴ ℵ² A E) εἰς Πτολεμαΐδα where the sea voyage, as some think, may have ended. Ptolemais was 'einst Haupthafen für Palästina' (Preuschen 125). He cites Josephus, War 1.290, 394; Ant. 14.452; 15.199; 18.155. These do not seem to prove more than that Pt. was *an* important port. It was an ancient town, formerly Acco (Judges 1.13; 4 QpIsᵃ 2.23), renamed after himself by Ptolemy V (285–246 BC). It was an important centre of trade and had a Jewish population (see e.g. Abodah Zarah 3.4—Rabban Gamaliel in the Bath of Aphrodite). It was about 31 miles down the coast from Tyre. Here too were Christians: ἀσπασάμενοι (the simplex; cf. v. 6) τοὺς ἀδελφούς (for this term for Christians see 1.15 and many other passages). The fact that 'we' stayed with them only one day (v. 8), compared with the seven days at Tyre (v. 4) may mean that the company were proceeding to Caesarea by ship and that the ship was staying only one night in Ptolemais. Bauernfeind (241) however suggests that nothing of note happened in Ptolemais and Caesarea because these churches were founded by dependants of the Seven (Acts 6).

8. τῇ δὲ ἐπαύριον corresponds to the ἡμέραν μίαν of v. 7. ἐξελθόντες: out of the city to the harbour or the ship; or, if the travellers went by road, out of the city.

For ἤλθομεν (continuing the 'we' passage) 𝔐 has οἱ περὶ τὸν Παῦλον ἦλθον, Paul and his party went. This text however continues with the first person plural ἐμείναμεν. D is missing at this point; for the means by which the text of d in vv. 7–10 has been reconstructed see in addition to Ropes (*Begs.* 3.201) G. D. Kilpatrick in *JTS* 6 (1955), 235–8. d appears to have read *venimus*, with the Greek ἤλθομεν. One can only guess that the reading of 𝔐 arose because an editor thought it a long time since Paul was last mentioned and that it would be well to make clear to the reader (lest he should have forgotten) that 'we' meant 'Paul and his companions'. Cf. 13.13. From Ptolemais to Caesarea was about 30 miles, 'a suitable day's journey whether this stage was taken by sea or coastal road' (Hemer 125f.) If however the party travelled by land and on foot one would think two days a more likely time.

For Caesarea see 10.1 and the note.

Philip was last heard of at Caesarea (8.40). If the 'we' material is to be thought of as a source it can hardly be insignificant that its author lodged with a Christian whose memories extended as far back as Acts 6, and possibly earlier, since the persons appointed in Acts 6 can hardly have been at that time among the most recent converts. It is unlikely (see I.53f.) that the material in chs. 1–5 depends on written sources, equally unlikely that it is pure fiction. Luke must have made inquiries from those who, he thought, could give him trustworthy information. It seems not impossible that Philip was one such person. See I.51 and Introduction, p. xxiv.

Philip is described as the Evangelist, one of the Seven. The word does not occur elsewhere in Acts (in the NT only at Eph. 4.11; 2 Tim. 4.5), but cf. 8.12, 35, 40, where Philip evangelizes (εὐαγγελίζεσθαι). The article distinguishes this Philip from others of the same name; contrast 10.6 (in this chapter it is the *other* Simon—Peter—who is distinguished) and 21.16 (see BDR § 268.1, though this passage is not mentioned there). It is however the title Evangelist itself that distinguishes this Philip from Philip the Apostle (1.13). The word was little used (see Harnack, *The Mission and Expansion of Christianity in the First Three Centuries*, London ²1908, 1.321, 338, 348f.). Eusebius seems to have regarded it as a term applicable to those who assisted and followed the apostles in the work of mission preaching and founding churches (see especially *HE* 3.37.2, τοὺς ... προκαταβληθέντας ὑπὸ τῶν ἀποστόλων θεμελίους ἐπῳκοδομοῦν ... ἔργον ἐπετέλουν εὐαγγελιστῶν; also 2.3.1; 3.31.2–5; 3.37.4; 3.39.9; 5.10.2; 5.17.3). Bultmann is probably right in saying that the word come into use as the term ἀπόστολος came to be confined to the Twelve, and in adding, 'Als gebräuchlicher Titel hat sich εὐαγγελιστής nicht durchsetzen und halten können, weil allmählich die Gemeindebeamten das Amt der Wortverkündigung übernahmen' (*Theologie* 458). Knowling (444) is probably right with 'a work rather than an order'. Calvin (2.194): 'In my opinion *evangelists* were half-way between apostles and teachers.' This is not really helpful. Roloff (310): 'Eher umschreibt sie [die Bezeichnung εὐαγγ.] hier wie in 2 Tim 4.5 die Funktion des Gemeindeleiters'—a function which in fact we never see Philip exercising. For possible non-christian use of the word see MM 259; and cf. Clement of Alexandria, *Stromateis* 3.52–54.

On the Seven see 6.1–6 and the notes. As Evangelist distinguishes Philip from the Apostles, so 'one of the Seven' distinguishes him from the Twelve. But οἱ ἑπτά seems even less than εὐαγγ. to have remained in use as a technical term. The two Philips are often confused; see Bruce (2.400) for the views of Zahn, Harnack, and Chapman. Hengel (*Between Jesus and Paul* 14) thinks that Philip was originally one of the Twelve and went over to the Seven. This seems to imply more knowledge of the Seven, and of their difference from the Twelve, than we possess.

9. Philip had four virgin daughters who prophesied. Not surprisingly, though writers such as Eusebius (see most of the passages cited on v. 8) refer to this statement, there is little confirmatory evidence for it. At *HE* 3.39.9, however, Eusebius recalls information which Papias claimed to have derived from the daughters of Philip. For prophesying daughters cf. the three daughters of Job in Testament of Job 48–50.

That women should prophesy in Christian gatherings is confirmed by 1 Cor. 11.5 and by the passage from Joel quoted in Acts 2.17; it appears to be denied by 1 Cor. 14.34; 1 Tim. 2.11f. It is hardly to be denied that the practice varied from part to part of the church (though the apparent contradiction within 1 Corinthians is a special problem; see *1 Corinthians* 250f., 330–3), or that the tendency was for attitudes to harden in the direction of the exclusion of women from public participation in Christian meetings. Luke, however, towards the end of the century, must have held that it was legitimate and edifying for women to prophesy, even though he may have wished to see this activity restrained by certain conditions (see below). What Luke understood by prophecy is, at least in part, brought out in the next paragraph, in which Agabus (that he makes the prophecy suggests that the daughters were in the Itinerary—Weiser 591) predicts the sufferings that are to happen to Paul (cf. 11.27–30). In the Pauline epistles prophecy is evidently more than this, and includes what may be called preaching; it is characteristic of Luke's turn of mind that the striking and verifiable predictive element in prophecy should be prominent.

The four prophesying daughters (use of the participle προφητεύουσαι suggests that for Luke prophecy was a function rather than an office) were virgins. It is hard to tell whether Luke relates this as a simple fact or sees a connection between their prophesying and their virginity. If they had not been virgins would they have prophesied? If they had been married would they have been allowed to prophesy? It is noteworthy that in 1 Cor. 14.35, where women (γυναῖκες) are bidden to keep silence in the assemblies, they are told that if they wish to learn anything they must ask their own husbands at home. It is assumed that they are married; is it implied that different regulations would apply to the unmarried? There is nothing else in Acts that bears directly on this subject, but it may be recalled that Priscilla, who taught Apollos (18.26), was married, and that the prophetess Anna (Lk. 2.36) was a widow who had lived with her husband seven years from her virginity. Luke provides no ground for Calvin's observation (2.195), 'One may well believe that they prophesied at home, or in a private place, outside the public meeting.' Bengel (471) is more interesting: 'Philippus evangelista: filiae prophetantes. propheta major est, quam evangelista. Eph. 4.11.'

From Jerome, *Epistles* 108.8 we learn that his correspondent Paula saw in Caesarea the house of Cornelius, now turned into a church, and the house of Philip, with the chamber of the daughters.

10. The genitive absolute participle ἐπιμενόντων must in the context be supplemented by ἡμῶν (see v. 8, ἐμείναμεν, and v. 11, πρὸς ἡμᾶς). Bultmann (*Exegetica* 420; cf. 20.7 and note) thinks that the first person plural has been imported into this narrative (as into that of the supper at Troas) from the Itinerary. Note however the juxtaposition in v. 12 of ἡμεῖς and οἱ ἐντόπιοι. ℵᶜ E 𝔐 gig syʰᵐᵍ add ἡμῶν, ℵ* 1175 αὐτῶν. But the omission of the pronoun in the genitive absolute is classical: Zerwick (§ 50); BDR § 423, n. 3.

τις ... προφήτης ... Ἄγαβος. See 11.28. There is no indication how Agabus has been occupied in the meantime, or whether his prophesying constituted an office or was an occasional act, occurring only when prompted by the Spirit. Marshall (340) observes that Agabus is mentioned as if he were a new character, not previously mentioned, and infers that the reference to him may have been taken over from the 'We' source in which he had not previously appeared; similarly Roloff (310), Bauernfeind (241), Lüdemann (242) (L. argues that vv. 10–14 go back to tradition); otherwise Schille (408). That Agabus is said to have come *from Judaea* suggests to Hemer (126) the Jewish use of Judaea, since the district includes Jerusalem but not Caesarea.

According to Ropes (*Begs.* 3.203) the text of d in this verse (following upon IIII virgines prophetantes) opens with the words *et mansimus aput* (sic) *eam*. It is hardly possible to make sense of this except on the supposition that *eam* is an error for *eum*, and that the Latin is the result of misreading ἐπιμενόντων as ἐπεμένομεν (μετ᾽ αὐτοῦ). Kilpatrick (see on v. 8), however, thinks this part of the reconstruction of the text of d doubtful.

11. Instead of ἑαυτοῦ the mass of late MSS have τε αὐτοῦ, which gives a different picture, according to which Agabus bound (not his own but) Paul's hands and feet. ἑαυτοῦ is certainly correct; Agabus, binding himself hands and feet, performs an acted parable, a prophetic sign comparable with those of the OT prophets (for these Roloff cites 1 Kings 11.29ff.; Isa. 8.1–4; 20.1ff.; Jer. 19.1ff.; 27.2ff.; Ezek. 4–5). His prophecy, so far as Acts records it, is of a predictive kind. Its fulfilment appears in the following chapters. It is not however strictly accurate. The Jews do not themselves bind Paul, nor do they hand him over to the Gentiles. The Jews attack Paul by mob violence; the Romans rescue him and then bind him, subsequently not setting him free but treating him with some respect when they learn that he is a Roman citizen. This lack of complete correspondence between prophecy and fulfilment might be taken to argue for the authenticity of the prophecy, but it would be unwise to take it in this way. Luke is not a writer who notices or is concerned about neat correspondences (witness his three accounts of Paul's conversion) and παραδώσουσιν εἰς χεῖρας ἐθνῶν may well have been formulated so as to recall the arrest and trial of Jesus. So for example Stählin (275); Pesch (2.214); 'Das Leiden Jesu wird als vorbildliches Martyrium gedeutet' (Schmithals 193). See however *Begs.* 4.268, where it is, rightly, pointed out that the Jews must have brought some accusation against Paul or he would not have been kept prisoner so long, or the case represented as 'the Jews v. Paul'.

For καὶ ἐλθών, D* has ἀνελθὼν δέ; for ἐν, P⁷⁴ D have εἰς. For the latter variant is can be argued that εἰς is not the 'correct' preposition; but in Acts it is often used where ἐν would be more suitable.

12. 'We', Paul's travelling companions, continue to be the main subordinate actors, but are here joined by οἱ ἐντόπιοι, the local (Christian) residents. The word is sometimes said to be unusual, but there is plenty of evidence for its use in MM 218, BA 544, LS 577. More is added in *ND* 4.263f. It is used in opposition to ξένοι in *IG* 5.2.491 lines 77, 8 (Megalopolis, ii/iii AD).

παρακαλεῖν is used in several senses in Acts (see e.g. 2.40); here, clearly, *to beg, to entreat*. It is followed (cf. 3.12) by τοῦ and the infinitive, where a simple accusative and infinitive would have sufficed. Pleonastic τοῦ is characteristic of the Lucan writings (Lk., 20 times; Acts, 17 times), but Zerwick (§ 386) notes: 'Ubi subest idea impediendi, abstinendi etc. etiam classice adhibetur τοῦ cum infinitivo (genitivus separationis!), e.g. Lc 4.32; 24.16; A 10.47; R 15.22; 2 C 1.8.' Cf. BDR § 409.5, n. 7.

Betz (118 n. 4) notes with examples how the way of the man of God is beset with friends who warn him of trouble to come. In this context perhaps the best example is that of Peter, Mt. 16.22.

For τοῦ μὴ ἀναβαίνειν, D gig have τὸν Παῦλον τοῦ μη ἐπιβαίνειν. There is no difference in meaning.

13. τότε ἀπεκρίθη is more forceful and solemn than the variants; Then answered Paul ... It was a memorable saying, expressing with special clarity Paul's devotion to the Lord and to his service. The text of NA²⁶ is τότε ἀπεκρίθη ὁ Παῦλος, B(*om. ὁ) C(* + δέ) 36 *pc* bo. The variants are

ἀπεκρίθη δὲ (τε 𝔐) ὁ Π., Ψ 𝔐 syʰ
ἀπεκρίθη δὲ ὁ Π. καὶ εἶπεν, (373) 945 1739 1891 *pc*
εἶπεν δὲ πρὸς ἡμᾶς ὁ Π., D (gig)
τότε ἀπεκρίθη ὁ (om. P⁷⁴) Π. καὶ εἶπεν, P⁷⁴ ℵ A E (33) *pc* vg
syᵖ sa boᵐˢ

It has been suggested with plausibility that the origin of this confusion was the mistake of attaching τότε to the end of the preceding sentence. Fortunately the meaning is unchanged whichever reading is adopted.

The participles κλαίοντες and συνθρύπτοντες appear to modify the verb ποιεῖτε: *What are you doing, as you weep ...?* συνθρυπτ. is a rare word—*to break in pieces, to reduce to powder.* The general but not the precise sense of the transferred use is clear. It must mean *breaking my heart*, but might mean with sorrow or by weakening my resolve. The latter suits the context better. D* gig p have θορυβοῦντες. The question is rhetorical, and the implied sense, grounded in the γάρ that follows, is *either*, You are weeping and persuading in vain, for I am ready ...; *or* Cease to weep and persuade, for I am ready ... For the expression cf. Plato, *Republic* 495de: οὕτω καὶ τὰς ψυχὰς ξυγκεκλασμένοι τε καὶ ἀποτεθρυμμένοι διὰ τὰς βαναυσίας τυγχάνουσιν.

After δεθῆναι D (syᵖ) add βούλομαι, thinking perhaps that ἑτοίμως ἔχω was a long was off. For the infinitives with ἑτοίμως ἔχω see BDR § 393.3, n. 4. Once more, εἰς is used for ἐν. For Paul's determination cf. Josephus, *Ant.*13.6, ὁ Ἰωνάθης φήσας ἑτοίμως ἔχειν ἀποθνήσκειν ὑπὲρ αὐτῶν.

Paul is ready to die ὑπὲρ τοῦ ὀνόματος τοῦ κυρίου Ἰησοῦ. Cf. 9.16; also 5.41; and for the use of ὄνομα in Acts see I.182f. The usage may have originated in the Hebrew לשם (Aramaic לשמא). 'Es fragt sich aber, ob hier nicht schon das Problem des "nomen Christianum" anklingt' (Haenchen 577).

14. Paul is not to be persuaded. It is clear to him that his apostolic duty calls him to Jerusalem (why? not apparently to preach; to convey the proceeds of his collection? to secure the unity of the church? to act as well as speak his testimony to the Crucified?) and nothing will deflect him from it. This is part of Luke's picture of the heroic missionary.

ἡσυχάσαμεν εἰπόντες. For discussion of the time relation of the aorist participle see M. 1.133f.; BDR § 420.3, n. 4; cf. 7.35; 22.24. There is no need to suppose that we have here an aorist participle describing subsequent action; at most the action is coincident. M. 1.134 n. 1 translates, 'we ceased, with the words ...'. But even this is not strong enough. The participle is strictly antecedent: 'When we had said ..., we fell silent'.

τοῦ κυρίου τὸ θέλημα γινέσθω—according to *Begs.* 4.269, 'The Lord's will will prevail;' ... *be done* would be γενέσθω. Cf. Lk. 11.2 (si v.1.), γενηθήτω τὸ θέλημά σου; 22.42, πλὴν μὴ τὸ θέλημά μου ἀλλὰ τὸ σὸν γινέσθω. Since Luke apparently did not have these words in the version of the Lord's Prayer familiar to him, it is probable that, as at v. 11, he was alluding to, and drawing a parallel with, the story of the Lord's passion. His words could be interpreted in a way very unfavourable to the speakers: it was only after they had failed to secure their own will that they were prepared to accept the Lord's. But Luke does not mean this; rather, We are prepared at

length regretfully to recognize that it is the Lord's will that Paul
should suffer; unwelcome as this is, may it nevertheless be done.
Schneider (2.305): 'Das Schlusswort ist nicht Ausdruck von Resig-
nation, sondern bejaht den erkannten Willen Gottes.' Similarly
Schmithals (193); Conzelmann (121) (comparing also *Martyrdom of
Polycarp* 7.1).

After εἰπόντες, D adds, πρὸς ἀλλήλους.

53. PAUL AND THE CHURCH OF JERUSALEM 21.15-26

(15) After these days we[1] packed up and set out on the journey up to Jerusalem. (16) Some of the[2] disciples went with us from Caesarea, bringing[3] us to the man we were to lodge with, Mnason, a Cypriote and an early disciple. (17) When we reached Jerusalem the brothers welcomed us gladly.

(18) On the next day Paul went in with us to James, and all the elders were present. (19) When he had greeted them he related in detail the things that God had done among the Gentiles through his ministry. (20) When they heard it they glorified God and said to him, 'You see, brother, how many tens of thousands there are of those who have believed among the Jews, and they are all zealous for the Law. (21) They have been informed about you that you teach defection from Moses, telling all the Jews who live among the Gentiles that they should not circumcise their children or walk in accordance with the customs. (22) What then? [4]They will certainly hear that you have come. (23) So do this that we tell you. We have four men who have a vow on them. (24) Take these men with you, be purified with them, and pay their expenses that they may shave their heads, and then all will know that there is nothing in the things they have been told about you, but that you yourself also conform, observing the Law. (25) But concerning those Gentiles who have believed we ourselves[5] wrote an injunction with the decision that they should be on their guard against food sacrificed to idols, blood, strangled meat, and fornication.' (26) Then Paul on the next day took the men with him, was purified with them, and entered the Temple, notifying the fulfilment of the days of purification until the offering was offered for each of them.

Bibliography

K. Berger, *NTS* 23 (1977), 180–204.

M. Black, *BJRL* 23 (1939), 201–14.

F. F. Bruce, *BJRL* 67 (1984–85), 641–61.

C. Burchard, as in (43).

H. J. Cadbury, *FS* J. R. Harris, 51–3.

H. von Campenhausen, *ZKG* 63 (1950–51), 133–44.

R. P. Casey, *HThR* 16 (1923), 392–4.

[1]RSV made ready; NJB, made our preparations.
[2]RSV, NEB, NJB, disciples from Caesarea.
[3]NEB, a certain Mnason.
[4]NJB, a crowd is sure to gather, for they.
[5]RSV, sent a letter with our judgement; NEB, sent them our decision; NJB, have written giving them our decision.

H. Duensing, as in (52).

G. Jasper, *Judaica* 19 (1963), 147–62.

J. Jervell, *Luke and the People of God* (1972), 185–207.

G. Kittel, *ZNW* 30 (1931), 145–57.

J. H. Ropes, *HThR* 16 (1923), 162–8.

Commentary

This is a passage of great importance for the understanding and evaluation of Acts, and of equally great difficulty. The opening verses retain the first person plural of the travel narrative: ἀνεβαίνομεν (v. 15); ἡμῖν, ξενισθῶμεν (v. 16); ἡμῶν, ἡμᾶς (v. 17). This may well have brought the We- narrative, or one section of it, to a close. The warm welcome given to 'us' is a suitable conclusion, and after the σὺν ἡμῖν of v. 18 the narrative concentrates on Paul and is written in the third person (vv. 19, 26). In vv. 15–17 there are (see the notes) notable textual obscurities, but there is no reason for thinking the reference to Mnason fictitious, and Paul did arrive in Jerusalem, whether to a warm welcome or not. The story that follows is also not without difficulty, but it is presented as the occasion that leads to all the events in the rest of the book, up to and including Paul's arrival in Rome as a prisoner. It is however important to observe that from 21.27a onwards there is no further reference to the four who needed purification for the due fulfilment on their vows; that is to say, the whole action against Paul, from 21.27b to the end of the book, is totally independent of the proposal made by James in vv. 23, 24. Paul is accused of having brought Greeks into the Temple; and it is certain that the four who had taken (Nazirite) vows were not Greeks but Jews. This observation is important because of the serious doubts that must be raised (see on vv. 21, 24, 25) regarding Paul's alleged action in proof of his alleged obedience to the Law. These doubts are, as they must be, based on theological considerations; but Paul was not only a radical theologian but one who allowed his actions to be dictated by theological motivation. It is true that probably a majority of students take the story to be essentially historical: Paul did act in the way described. It is true also that Paul accepted synagogue discipline to the extent of enduring five fearful beatings (2 Cor. 11.24). The possibility cannot be excluded that in the interests of peace he allowed himself to be persuaded, perhaps against his better judgement, to take part in the legal requirements laid upon those who had taken vows. If so, the outcome must have speedily shown him the error of his decision. Those who wished to misinterpret his action (and, perhaps we should add, were able to perceive the truth behind the sham of James's proposal) were quickly able to do so and to find a ground for accusation.

There is a further possibility, suggested in outline by Haenchen

(586–8), who brings the act of purification into relation with the surprising silence of Luke's narrative (apart from 24.17) regarding the primary purpose of Paul's visit to Jerusalem, which was (Rom. 15.25) to deliver the collection he had made among the Gentile churches for the poor saints in Jerusalem. At what point did Paul hand over the money to the leaders of the Jerusalem church? We do not know, for Luke tells us nothing of the matter. If we are to go further we can only guess. Certainly he would wish to have the money out of his responsibility as soon as possible; did he deliver it as early as v. 17, when ἀσμένως ἀπεδέξαντο ἡμᾶς οἱ ἀδελφοί? A better guess might be vv. 18, 19, partly because this is represented as something like an official reception (by James and πάντες οἱ πρεσβύτεροι). There might even be a hint in the use of the word διακονία: Paul recounts what God has done among the Gentiles διὰ τῆς διακονίας αὐτοῦ—the word that he several times (Rom. 15.31; 2 Cor. 8.4; 9.1, 12, 13) uses to denote his collection. James, having received the money, announced, perhaps with excellent intention, perhaps to Paul's dismay, 'We shall use part of this gift to pay the expenses of our four poor Nazirite brothers, and will do so in your name, so as to still the rumours that you no longer care for the ancestral religion and observe the Law.' If this happened Paul could hardly complain; the gift was presumably given with no strings attached to it, and it was true that he understood the Gospel as the fulfilment of God's promise to his people and was prepared on occasion to act 'as if he were a Jew' (1 Cor. 9.20).

Had James ulterior motives? Did he hope to discredit Paul in the estimation of Gentile Christians? Did he even hope to ensnare him into the Temple and provoke the riot that ensued—in which, as in the whole legal process that followed, there is no indication that the Christians of Jerusalem made any move to aid the apostle of the Gentiles? We have no means of answering these questions, though we cannot avoid asking them, and v. 25 remains ambiguous. It may mean, as many suppose, 'We are keeping faith with the Gentile Christians by adhering to the Decree, which does not require circumcision' (cf. Stählin 278). It may mean, 'This is as far as we will go; no more concessions can be hoped for.' James and his colleagues may have feared for the success of their mission to Jews if Paul should be allowed too much freedom.

Paul's hope to secure the unity of the church by means of his collection failed; it may be that this is why Luke omitted the collection from his story (cf. Haenchen 586f.). According to Roloff (312), 'Nichts deutet darauf hin, dass Jakobus sein früheres grundsätzliches Ja zur gesetzesfreien Heidenmission (15.19; Gal. 2.9) und zur Kirchengemeinschaft mit den Heidenchristen zurückgenommen hätte.' This needs considerable qualification in the light of Gal. 2.12.

15. Μετὰ δὲ τὰς ἡμέρας ταύτας, presumably the days of 21.10, though the expression (perhaps a Hebraism) sometimes means only, After this.

ἐπισκευασάμενοι, here only in the NT; in the middle, as here, *to prepare for one's own benefit or use*, so sometimes *to pack up* in readiness for a journey. So Chrysostom, *Homily* 45.3, τουτέστι, τὰ πρὸς τὴν ὁδοιπορίαν λαβόντες. So also *Begs.* 4.269. At Xenophon, *Hellenica* 5.3.1 the word is used for equipping horses; could it be that Paul was travelling on horseback?

ἀνεβαίνομεν (the first person plural continues; C D E* 36 *pc* have the present, ἀναβαίνομεν) εἰς Ἱεροσόλυμα. The imperfect indicates a process described in terms of its goal (introduced by εἰς). Cf. 21.3, and see BDR § 327.1, n. 1.

Hanson (209) points out, with reference to vv. 15, 16, that from Caesarea to Jerusalem was 67 miles (cf. 23.32). It is unlikely that so great a distance could be covered in one day, even on horseback. See the variant in v. 16.

In vv. 15–18 the text of D has been damaged by three mutilations. For the reconstruction of the text see below and Ropes in *Begs.* 3.202–5; *HThR* 16 (1923), 162–8; and R. P. Casey (*HThR* 16 (1923), 392–4). Clark (377–9) disagrees with Rope's evaluation of the text; see below. The Western text is 'ein Ergebnis exegetischer Überlegung auf der Basis unseres Textes' (Bauernfeind 243). Rope's reconstruction is as follows:

Κεσα[ραίας σὺν ἡμεῖν· οὗτοι δὲ ἤγαγον ἡμᾶς πρὸς οὓς ξενισθῶμεν. καὶ παραγενόμενοι εἴς τινα κώμην ἐγενόμεθα παρὰ Νάσωνί τινι Κυπρίῳ μαθητῇ ἀρχαίῳ. κἀκεῖθεν ἐξιόντες ἤλθομεν εἰς Ἱεροσόλυμα· ὑπεδέξαντο δὲ ἡμᾶς ἀσμένως οἱ ἀδελφοί. τῇ δὲ ἐπιούσῃ εἰσῄει ὁ Παῦλος σὺν ἡμῖν πρὸς Ἰάκωβον]

According to Clark it is doubtful whether ξενισθῶμεν should be preceded by πρὸς οὓς or by παρ' ᾧ.

16. The sense of this verse is on the whole clear, but it contains an unusual number of grammatical uncertainties.

The partitive genitive τῶν μαθητῶν serves as subject of the verb συνῆλθον; see M. 1.73 (also 223 for an interesting papyrus parallel). BDR § 164. 2, n. 6 add that 'hinter μαθητῶν könnte τινες τῶν ausgefallen sein, da man die Wiederholung des Artikels vermisst.' But ἀπὸ Καισαρείας could be taken adverbially with συνῆλθον rather than adjectivally with the subject. Cf. Xenophon, *Anabasis* 3.5.16.

ἄγοντες is taken by grammarians as in place of a future participle, used (in accordance with the familiar idiom) to express purpose. Thus M. 3.80 translates, 'went in with us ... in order to bring us'. So also BDR § 339.2, n. 8, who refer to Thucydides 7.25.7 [correcting their reference], ἔπεμψαν ... πρέσβεις ... ἀγγέλλοντας. It should be noted, however, that the sentence continues, τά τε ἄλλα αὖ δηλώσαντας, ὅτι ...; it seems probable *either* that we should emend to ἀγγελοῦντας, *or* that Thucydides was distinguishing between the present and future participles. The ambassadors handed on the news *as they went*, and also had the purpose of ... In fact it does not seem necessary to find the sense of purpose in Luke's clause; They accompanied us, in doing so taking us to ... Delebecque (103) has a somewhat different explanation, which however does not seem preferable: 'Le participe présent peut être l'équivalent d'un futur après un verbe de mouvement; cf. 15.27.' Cf. also Plato, *Phaedo* 116c, ἦλθον ἀγγέλλων.

In the relative clause (παρ᾽ ᾧ ...) the noun has been attracted into the case of the relative. We must understand πρὸς Μνάσονα, παρ᾽ ᾧ ... So Moule (*IB* 130); and so already Bengel (471); Page (221) (also Delebecque 103). παρὰ Μνάσονα does not differ essentially. The use of the subjunctive however introduces the sense of purpose and the whole is equivalent to a final clause which could be rephrased: ... πρὸς Μνάσονα, ἵνα ξενισθῶμεν παρ᾽ αὐτῷ. Delebecque in the end reaches a similar conclusion: '... chargés de nous mener chez Mnason ... pour être hébergés chez lui'. So Zerwick (§ 343) (cf. § 18); BDR § 378, n. 2; § 294.5, n. 8; M. 3.109. Luke's way of expressing this thought is significant in that it lays some emphasis on the verb ξενισθῶμεν: They brought us to the man we were to lodge with, Mnason ... This corresponds to Luke's interest in travel and lodging; see Cadbury (*Making* 249–53). For παρά see BDR § 238.2, n. 2.

The name Mnason (there is no article; see BDR § 268.1, n. 3) occurs nowhere else in the NT. It was not uncommon in Greek, often in the form Μνήσων (the α appears to be Cypriote—Blass 227); Hemer (237) cites a number of examples. It may however have been a Greek name chosen for use in Greek circles by a Semite bearing some such name as Menahem or Manasseh; see BDR § 53.3, n. 9, and especially H. J. Cadbury in *FS* J. R. Harris, 51–3. The narrative that follows makes it probable that Paul would stay with a Jew rather than with a Gentile; Mnason was probably a Cypriote Jew. For Jews in Cyprus see *NS* 3.68, 69; there were many Phoenicians in the island—in an earlier century Zeno of Citium, whose father bore the similar name Mnaseas). Mnason was also an ἀρχαῖος μαθητής. For the adjective cf. 15.7; here it means that his discipleship, his being a Christian, went back to the earliest days, that is, either the earliest, post-resurrection days of Christianity in Jerusalem, or to the beginnings of Paul's mission in Cyprus (13.4–12)—possibly to neither of these, since Barnabas the Cypriote had been a Christian before Paul's mission. Paul is represented as being in touch with the early days of Christianity (Weiser 596)—if this is indeed what ἀρχαῖος means.

MM 80f. quote an inscription in which an ἀρχαῖος μύστης inscribes an ἀρχαῖος χρησμός; see also *ND* 1.136. The name and description may be fictitious, but it is hard to see what Luke would gain—unless perhaps a measure of verisimilitude—by introducing a fictitious name, and Lüdemann is probably right in thinking that Mnason goes back to tradition. Schille (412f.) however thinks that the description of Mnason as an ἀρχαῖος μαθητής shows only his Zeugnisfähigkeit; but he does not appear in Acts to bear witness to anything. He may have been connected with the Hellenists—the Seven—of Acts 6. So e.g. Stählin (275); Bauernfeind (243).

The Western text in this verse gives a different account of events. It is not of great interest that the name of Paul's host is in D (d) Νάσων and in ℵ gig vg[mss] bo[pt] Ἰάσων. These variations could have arisen accidentally and no known interest or purpose could have occasioned them. The more interesting variation is best given by simply transcribing the text of D. Ropes's reconstruction (*Begs.* 3.203–205) of the broken text is quoted on v. 15. He comments (3.204), 'The "Western" text is inherently highly improbable. Its indefinite reference to the "village" is futile and over-emphasized, especially in view of the extreme interest and importance of the goal of their journey. As their village-host, Mnason is wholly without significance; whereas as a resident of Jerusalem this "old disciple" was of real consequence to the narrative.' Ropes apparently implies that any editor could infer one or more overnight stops on a journey of 67 miles (see on v. 15); this however cuts both ways; Paul and his companions probably did spend one or two nights on the way, and could have stayed with someone called Mnason. The Western text could have preserved a recollection of this. If however this recollection had been embodied in the original text of Acts it is very doubtful whether it would have been removed. The Western text is favoured by Roloff (313), but must probably be rejected. *Begs.* 4.269 may be right in the judgement that both texts are clumsy, and the original may have been clumsier than either.

17. The Western text here connects with its reading in v. 16. In Ropes's restoration of D (see above) we have κἀκεῖθεν (from the village of v. 16) ἐξιόντες ἤλθομεν. d has *et inde exeuntes fuimus*. M. 3.254 regards the Old Uncial text, γενομένων δὲ ἡμῶν εἰς Ἰερουσαλήμ (εἰς for ἐν, as often in Acts, but εἰς may possibly have influenced the Western text), as especially Semitic, along with Lk. 1.44; Acts 20.16; 25.15; Jn 17.23; 1 Jn 5.8. This is probably because ב = both εἰς and ἐν. The genitive absolute (even though incorrect—see BDR § 423.2, n. 8) does not suggest a Semitic source at this point. It is clear that the meaning is, When we reached Jerusalem; perhaps, When we came into Jerusalem.

Luke emphasizes once more (cf. 15.4) that Paul was welcome in

Jerusalem: there were no serious differences between him and the Jerusalem Christians, only false rumours (v. 21). Rom. 15.30, 31 suggest otherwise. So far as Luke's account is correct it may mean that Paul came first into contact with Hellenistic Jewish Christians. See e.g. Beyer (129) ('... ist ... nicht die ganze Gemeinde gemeint, sondern eben der Paulus nahestehende hellenistische Teil'); Marshall (342). The historicity of vv. 17–26(36) has been variously estimated (see further above, pp. 1000f.); thus Dibelius (8): 'The conclusion is best explained if from 21.17 onwards he [Luke] no longer has a guiding "thread"'; Lüdemann (244f.): 'Fragen wir nach der historischen Zuverlässigkeit der obigen Quelle, so muss die Antwort hierauf positiv ausfallen.' Thus James had indeed become head of the Jerusalem church; the charge against Paul (v. 21) is historical; Luke has removed the reference to the collection. Hengel (117) has the interesting comment, 'It becomes particularly clear at this point that he [Luke] knew more than he wanted to say.' Weiser (594) points out that there are Lucan words in the verse (γίνεσθαι, ἀποδέχεσθαι, ἀδελφός), but they are hardly sufficient to prove that Luke is writing independently.

ἀσμένως occurs here only in the NT (except 2.41, E Ψ 𝔐). The adverb is 'common in later Greek' (LS 258); cf. e.g. Demosthenes 18.36 (237).

18. τῇ δὲ (τε, ℵ A E 945 1739 1891 *pc* gig—perhaps rightly) ἐπιούσῃ; cf. 16.11—one of Luke's regular expressions.

εἰσῄει ὁ Παῦλος σὺν ἡμῖν πρὸς Ἰάκωβον. The verb, with πρός, conveys a hint of entering the presence of a great person (Xenophon, *Cyropaedia* 2.4.5, ὁ δ'εἰσῄει πρὸς τὸν Κυαξάρην; Herodotus 1.99.1, εἰσιέναι παρὰ βασιλέα), or of coming into a law court. 'We' are now distinguished from Paul as witnesses of the scene (though it may be—has been—conjectured that 'we' were present to convey the collection to the leaders of the Jerusalem church—Stählin 276). The first person plural does not return till 27.1, but this is because now 'Paulus steht beherrschend im Mitelpunkt der Szene' (Haenchen 582). *James* must be the Lord's brother, as in 15.13 (see the note). There is no mention now of Simon Peter, and James is evidently the leading man in Jerusalem. See H. von Campenhausen, 'Die Nachfolger des Jakobus', *ZKG* 63 (1950/51), 133–44; A. Ehrhardt, *The Apostolic Succession* (1953). He appears in the role of a president accompanied by a group of elders (on πρεσβύτεροι see on 11.30; 14.23; 20.17, 28), or assessors. Easton (75, 130) compares the High Priest, with elders, in the Sanhedrin; see also Ehrhardt (*Acts* 73). For πάντες τε παρεγένοντο οἱ πρεσβύτεροι, D (sa) have ἦσαν δὲ παρ' αὐτῷ οἱ πρεσβύτεροι συνηγμένοι. Delebecque (103) finds this reading 'tentant'. See further on the text of v. 19.

Commentators and others note the absence of any references to

Paul's collection, here and in v. 19. See above. 'Ein Begleiter des Apostels konnte das nicht übersehen' (Preuschen 126); but one must add, unless he had good reason for doing so. Weiser (597), discussing the possibilities, thinks it possible that the fears of Rom. 15.30 may have been realized, but that we cannot know this; Luke omits the collection because he is emphasizing 'den Weg des Paulus als Weg zum Leiden in der Nachfolge Jesu'. It is likely that both motives were operative.

19. καὶ ἀσπασάμενος ... ὧν] οὓς ἀσπασάμενος διηγεῖτο ἓν (D* has ἕνα) ἕκαστον ὡς, D (sa). ἐξηγεῖσθαι is a word of wider meaning than διηγεῖσθαι, but it is impossible here to make a clear distinction between them, since in this context each may—and must—mean *to relate, to describe in detail* (though ἐξηγ. may do more to suggest interpretative comment). Cf. 14.27; 15.4, 12. The use at 15.12 of ἐξηγ. may give some support to διηγ. in the present verse. There is no doubt that Luke does regard the mighty works done by Paul as part of the justification of the Gentile mission (see 15.12); they are not however his only means of supporting it, and it will be noted that the present verse makes no clear reference to miracles at all. The several events referred to comprehensively in καθ' ἓν ἕκαστον consist primarily in the conversion of Gentiles. For καθ' ἕν as the direct object accusative after the verb cf. Demosthenes 54.26 (1265).

διακονία is clearly not yet a technical term (see 6.1, 4); it is simply Paul's service to God that has resulted in the conversion of the Gentiles. It is clear that, in Luke's view, it is what has been going on ἐν τοῖς ἔθνεσιν that is of interest to the Jerusalem church.

20. The tenses in the opening sentence are to be noted: ἀκούσαντες, they heard the news when it was brought to them; ἐδόξαζον, they glorified God, and continued to do so; εἶπον, they said. See BDR § 327.1; M. 3.66. See v. 19, with the note; the Jerusalem authorities are (according to Luke) delighted to hear of the success of the Gentile mission. They address Paul as ἀδελφέ.

πόσαι. In an indirect question the word should be ὅσαι. τῶν πεπιστευκότων goes with μυριάδες ...: how many tens of thousands there are of those who have believed (and continue to believe—perfect participle). These believers are ἐν τοῖς Ἰουδαίοις, not simply among the Jews, as converted Gentiles might be, but drawn from the ranks of the Jews. Baur, Munck, and Nock would like to omit τῶν πεπιστ.—those who complained were not Christians. See Bruce (2.404f.), reporting but not expressing an opinion on this conjecture.

πάντες ζηλωταὶ τοῦ νόμου (cf. Gal. 1.14; also 2 Macc. 4.2). Clarke (*NT Problems* 135), followed by others, has suggested that at this time all the members of the Jerusalem church were zealous for the Law because the Hellenists (6.1; 8.1, πλὴν τῶν ἀποστόλων) had now been driven from the city. This does not appear to be the meaning. (a) Luke's statement that all except the apostles were driven from the city is probably an exaggeration; (b) there had been plenty of time since 6.1 for some Hellenist Christians to return; (c) there had been time for other Jewish Hellenists to become Christians; (d) it is not to be assumed that no Hellenist Jewish Christians were enthusiasts for the Law. Luke is simply making a somewhat exaggerated statement which may nevertheless be a not inaccurate description of the Jerusalem church at the time.

θεόν (P[74] ℵ A B C E L 33 36 323 945 1175 1739 1891 al vg sy[p] bo) is probably better than κύριον (D Ψ 𝔐 gig vg[mss] sy[h] sa). εἶπόν τε (P[74] ℵ A B E L Ψ 36 453 945 al) is better than εἰπόντες (C D 𝔐 sy[h]), which has grown out of it. αὐτῷ is omitted by D. ἐν τοῖς Ἰουδαίοις (A B C E 33 36 945 1175 1739 1891) is awkward and exposed to alteration: P[74] has τοῖς Ἰουδαίοις; Ψ 𝔐 sy[h] have Ἰουδαίων; D gig p sy[p] sa have ἐν τῇ Ἰουδαίᾳ; ℵ pc omit.

Were James and the elders reporting a complaint, or sharing in it? Calvin 2.199: 'Although they [the elders] do not condemn it openly, yet because they distinguish themselves from the attitude of these men, they are tacitly acknowledging them to be wrong.' This is probably the impression that Luke intended to convey. How far this corresponds with the facts cannot be determined with confidence. In the rest of the story James and his party show little concern for Paul.

21. κατηχήθησαν (κατήχησαν, the active, in D* 104 gig, gives a different picture—the Jewish Christians of v. 20 have been spreading the report that Paul is a dissident; see below) is used in a different sense from that of the same verb in 18.25: *they have been informed*. No informers are named; Luke may be thinking of those mentioned in 15.1, 5. Since Luke evidently believed the charge to be false (see below on this) he must be thinking of trouble-makers who spread false reports. But he does not name them; they do not appear on stage. The general picture of a harmonious apostolic age is retained, but it is clear that at most only the surface is smooth. Of the passive verb Page (222) writes, 'The word certainly describes Paul's opponents as acting with deliberate purpose, and suggests that they were in a position of authority and "teachers".' This impression is strengthened if the active (see above) is read, but it is quite possible that two letters, ηθ, dropped out by accident. 'The reader knows this [report] to be a canard, for Paul has from the very start himself shown a commitment to the Jewish *ethos* by circumcising his coworker [Timothy]' (Johnson 290). This is a fair observation as far as Luke's own understanding and intention are concerned.

The report is that Paul teaches ἀποστασίαν ἀπὸ Μωϋσέως.

ἀποστασία (the earlier form was ἀπόστασις) is *revolt, defection*. It is often used in a political sense (e.g. Josephus, *Life* 43, τὴν ἀποστασίαν τὴν ἀπὸ Ῥωμαίων), but also of religious apostasy, especially in the LXX (Josh. 22.22; 2 Chron. 29.19; 1 Macc. 2.15). The revolt is ἀπὸ Μωϋσέως; cf. Plutarch, *Galba* 1 (1053), τὴν ἀπὸ Νέρωνος ἀποστασίαν. Paul is alleged to inculcate the abrogation of loyalty to Moses, that is, to the law of Moses. The allegation is illustrated by, and may even be alluded to in, a saying attributed to R. Eleazar of Modiim (c. AD 120–140) (Aboth 3.12): If a man profanes the Hallowed Things and despises the set feasts ... and makes void the covenant of Abraham our father [i.e., undoes the effect of circumcision], and discloses meanings in the Law which are not according to the *Halakah*, even though a knowledge of the Law and good works are his, he has no share in the world to come. On the truth or falsehood of the report concerning Paul (περὶ σοῦ) see below.

Those who are thus informed (according to the report) are τοὺς κατὰ τὰ ἔθνη πάντας Ἰουδαίους—not Gentiles, but Jews living among (there is a similar though not identical use of κατά at 8.1; 11.1; 13.1; 25.3; 26.13; 27.5) Gentiles, Jews of the Dispersion. The point here thus differs from that of 15.1, 5. No demand is made that Gentiles converted to Christianity should be circumcised and required to keep the Law; the conviction is implied that Jews who become Christians should continue circumcision and other practices of the Jewish Law, and that Paul is, wrongly, contradicting this principle by teaching Christians not to retain their Jewishness. The second πάντες is omitted by P⁷⁴ A E 33 *pc* latt bo. Ropes (*Begs.* 3.205) thinks the word so awkwardly placed that it can hardly be original; Metzger (484) reverses the argument, rightly. For ἔθνη, Dᶜ has ἔθη; if this is not an accidental error it must mean, 'all the Jews who live in accordance with the (Mosaic) customs'. This does not make good sense. But ἔθνος, ἔθος invited scribal confusion. For μηδὲ τοῖς ἔθεσιν, D* has μήτε ἐν τοῖς ἔθνεσιν αὐτοῦ.

As at 15.1, circumcision is mentioned explicitly as the crucial example of legal observance. λέγων takes the accusative αὐτούς and infinitives περιτέμνειν and περιπατεῖν (BDR § 409.2, n. 3 mentions without approving the—unnecessary—conjecture αὐτοῖς). For the use of ἔθος cf. 15.1 and the note; for the dative τοῖς ἔθεσιν cf. 14.16 (ταῖς ὁδοῖς; contrast 8.39, τὴν ὁδόν, accusative).

Did Paul in fact teach Jews to abandon circumcision and other provisions of the Law? 'It was in fact so' (Calvin 2.200). Opinions differ. Blass (229): 'Falsum erat crimen, cf. 1 Cor. 7.18; tamen illi non sine causa metuebant, quia haec ἀδιάφορα esse Christianis ille docebat.' Schmithals (197) argues that Paul would not have taught Jews to abandon the Law because this would have made life intolerable for Christian Jews in Palestine. In successive editions of

NTD: Beyer (129), '... was ja durchaus der Wirklichkeit entspricht'; Stählin 277, 'Dieser Vorwurf ist ungerecht.' Luke appears to assume that Paul did not do what he was alleged to do; the charge was not believed by the elders, it was false, and Paul will proceed by his actions to demonstrate his innocence. It is certain that the epistles contain no explicit instruction that the circumcision of Jewish children should cease, and at 1 Cor. 7.18 Paul tells already circumcised Jews not to undo the marks of their circumcision. If he asserts that circumcision is nothing he asserts equally that uncircumcision is nothing (1 Cor. 7.19; Gal. 6.15). It is clear moreover that there is a great difference between the practice in which devout Jewish parents offer their children to God in circumcision, and the insistence that Gentile converts must be circumcised if they are to be saved. It is hard to believe that Paul *forbade* Jewish parents to circumcise their children, but he probably classed those who insisted on and made much of the rite as 'weak' (Rom. 14; 15; 1 Cor. 8; 10). Here however circumcision is mentioned as the outstanding example of practising the customs generally, and it is undoubtedly true that Paul taught his fellow Jews to sit loose to legal regulations, since he evidently believed (Gal. 2.12–14) that Jewish Christians might, and should, eat with Gentile Christians without any compromise on the part of the latter, and that they could buy and eat meat of any kind without making scrupulous inquiry (1 Cor. 10.25, 27). Luke was probably aware (cf. *Begs.* 4.271) of a body of Jewish Christians who continued to practise Jewish customs without objection from their Gentile brothers (cf. Justin, *Trypho* 47) and assumed that since this state of things existed it must have been not merely tolerated but supported by Paul. Delling (*Studien* 309), thus fails to touch the point when he writes: 'Paulus ist in Apg. 21.21 jedenfalls dann richtig verstanden ... wenn von ihm behauptet wird, nach seiner Unterweisung (διδάσκεις) sei die Beschneidung der Abkömmlinge jüdischer Eltern überflüssig—sofern dieser Satz zumal Kinder christlicher Eltern meint—d.h. für Paulus: nicht heilsnotwendig.' The allegation is not that Paul taught that circumcision was superfluous but that he said that it should not be done. Weiser's statement (598), 'Dadurch aber, dass Lukas den Vorwurf mit dem Begriff "Bräuche" (*ethē*) wiedergibt, deutet er selbst an, dass es sich hier nicht um die Gefährdung der religiösen Identität Israels handelt, sondern um den Bereich kulturbedingter Normen', seems to presuppose an underestimate of the weight of ἔθος.

22. τί οὖν ἐστιν; cf. 1 Cor. 14.15, 16. What then is *to be done*? πάντως ἀκούσονται, *they will certainly hear*. A widely supported variant runs: πάντως δεῖ πλῆθος συνελθεῖν, ἀκούσονται γάρ. This is read not only by Western authorities but by many others also (P⁷⁴ ℵ(*) A (C²) D E Ψ 𝔐 latt), so that if it is in origin a Western expansion it must, as Ropes (*Begs.* 3.205) says, have been 'adopted by the Antiochian revisers'. For the πλῆθος see v. 36. If the long text is original it is not easy to see why B C*ᵛⁱᵈ 36 453 614 1175 1739* 2495 *pc* syᵖ should cut it down.

23. τοῦτο anticipates the relative clause.

BDR § 353.2b rightly point out that εἰσὶν ... ἔχοντες is not a periphrastic tense; cf. 19.14, 24. The existence of the persons concerned and their relation to the speakers (ἡμῖν) are first mentioned, then their religious situation (εὐχήν). εἶναι with the dative denotes possession: We have four men, who ... See BDR § 189.1, n. 1.

The vow (εὐχή) is more like a Nazirite vow (see 18.18 and the note; StrB 2.755–61) than any other, but difficulties arise as the story proceeds; see below. For the use of εὐχή cf. Philo, *de Ebrietate* 2, οἱ τὴν μεγάλην εὐχὴν εὐξάμενοι; the reference in the context to abstinence from strong drink shows that the Nazirite vow is intended.

ℵ B *pc* bo Origen have ἀφ᾽ for ἐφ᾽. The variant is defended by Ropes (*Begs.* 3.206) on the ground that it 'yields good sense ("of their own act," in contrast to Paul's intervention; ...). Especially in view of the infrequency of agreement between B and ℵ in errors peculiar to them, αφ is to be accepted against the testimony of other witnesses to the reading εφ. The latter makes a weak phrase, which, however it originated, would commend itself to the mind of transcribers.' Few agree. Metzger (484) describes ἀφ᾽ as an 'Alexandrian refinement', Haenchen as a Greek substitute for the strange Septuagintal ἐφ᾽; similarly Conzelmann (122).

In Luke's narrative James and his colleagues take the view that only public action on Paul's part will clear his name. 'Als hätte nicht ein Wort der Kirchenleitung selbst genügt!' (Schille 414). Against this, Bruce (2.405), 'It would take more than a merely verbal assurance ...'. It is impossible to pronounce definitely on one side or other of this disagreement without a good deal more knowledge than we possess of the structure of the Jerusalem church, the authority of its leaders, and the extent to which their writ ran in the Diaspora.

24. The structure of the verse is complicated by a variant reading. ξυρήσονται (future indicative) is read by P⁷⁴ ℵ B* Dᶜ E 33 614 1175 1891 2495 *al*; ξυρήσωνται (aorist subjunctive) is read by A B² C D* (so NA²⁶; D* seems in fact to read ξυρῶνται—so e.g. Ropes's text of D in *Begs.* 3.207). All witnesses appear to have as the next verb the future indicative, γνώσονται. If a subjunctive is read in immediate connection with ἵνα it seems natural to separate it from γνώσονται: Pay their expenses in order that they may shave ...; and (then) all will know ... If however both verbs are future it becomes more natural (though by no means necessary) to coordinate them: ...

in order that they may shave ... and that all may know ... The difference in meaning is perhaps not very great. According to BDR § 442.2d the καί (before γνώσονται) may be 'nach Konjunktiv das Futur verbindend zur Bezeichnung des weiteren Ergebnisses'. They add (n. 8) 'Durch καί wird die Folge gewissermassen verselbständigt, ohne dabei aber ein selbständiger Satz zu werden (die Folge gehört in den ἵνα-Satz hinein ...)'. Here undoubtedly *that all should know* is the intention of the proposed action.

The request to Paul is expressed by παραλαβών (see C. Burchard, *ZNW* 69 (1978), 156f.; cf. v. 26; 16.33) and two imperatives, ἁγνίσθητι and δαπάνησον. The meaning of the former imperative is not clear. According to Conzelmann (123) it must mean, 'Tritt mit ihnen in das Gelübde ein!' This however would involve the 30 day period of the Nazirite vow, and it is clear that the proceedings did not last so long (21.27). Marshall (345) points out clearly the possibilities. (1) The four men had incurred some uncleanness during the period of their (Nazirite) vow and thus needed to go through a process of purification (see on v. 26). Luke assumes, incorrectly, that Paul had to share the process with them, although he had not shared the defilement. (2) Paul had been resident outside Palestine and therefore needed purification before he could enter the Temple (Haenchen 586). It was arranged that this should coincide with the end of the four men's Nazirite period. (3) An alternative view is that Paul would not need cleansing in order to enter the Temple but would do so in order to share in the Nazirite vow. He had not yet terminated the vow of 18.18. None of those views is truly satisfactory, and one must conclude that Luke was imperfectly informed about the regulations for vows and uncleanness and the events that were planned. Fortunately the details are less important than the fundamental proposal that Paul should clear his reputation by taking part in the Temple ritual relating to vows, and should do so as a partner with a group of Jewish Christians.

δαπάνησον involves no such problems. Purification required sacrifice and sacrifice required expense. Paul would pay. Was it proposed that the collection he had made, or part of it, should be used for this purpose? Let all see that Gentile funds were going into the Temple? Luke does not say so, but his silence regarding the collection is a major problem, and gives rise to such questions as these.

ἵνα ξυρήσονται τὴν κεφαλήν. It is probable that this refers not only to the shaving of the head and offering of the hair but to the whole process of release from the Nazirite vow. גלח is used in this sense at Nazir 2.5, 6: 'This expression is used throughout for the offering of the he-lamb, ewe-lamb, and ram and their associated Meal-offering (Num 6.14, 15) which the Nazirite brings on the completion of his vow and when he cuts off and burns the "hair of his separation" (Num 6.18)' (Danby, *Mishnah* 282). Cf. Josephus, *Ant.* 19.294, Ναζιραίων ξυρᾶσθαι διέταξε μάλα συχνούς, rightly interpreted by L. H. Feldman (LCL Josephus, 9.353) to mean that 'Agrippa had shouldered the expense for the offerings of poor Nazirites.'

τὴν κεφαλήν. Greek would normally (though not always or necessarily) have the plural. The singular in such cases is possible in Hebrew and normal in Aramaic (cf. Jer. 18.16, LXX (not A)), so that some Semitic influence may be suspected here (BDR § 140, n. 3).

ὧν (the relative is attracted into the case of the antecedent τούτων, which is to be supplied) ... οὐδέν ἐστιν: there is nothing in the things which.

κατήχηνται, See v. 21.

ἀλλά στοιχεῖς. D* has ἀλλ᾽ ὅτι πορεύου, D has πορεύῃ, without significant difference in meaning. The imperative πορεύου (D*) is surprising and yields an awkward sentence requiring a stop after ἐστιν and leaving ὅτι unexplained. It can hardly be other than an accidental error, probably caused by the two preceding imperatives (ἀγν., δαπ.). στοιχεῖν in the sense of *conform (to)* is normally followed by a dative (e.g. Gal. 6.16). LS 1648 quote an absolute use from Dittenberger, *SIG*³ 2.708.5, στοιχεῖν βουλόμενος καὶ τοῖς ἐκείνων ἴχνεσιν ἐπιβαίνειν (cf. BA 1535, citing Dittenberger, *OGIS* 1.308.21; cf. 1.339.51), but in this inscription the context supplies the equivalent of a dative, and this is so also in Acts, in φυλάσσων τὸν νόμον.

φυλάσσων τὸν νόμον. For an extra-biblical example of φυλάσσειν used in this sense see *ND* 4.82. 'Deutlich ist nur, dass sich Paulus durch die vorgeschlagene Handlung als gesetzestreuen Juden ausweisen wird' (Haenchen 584).

Did Paul στοιχεῖν, φυλάσσων τὸν νόμον? Would he have done so even on one special occasion with the intention of proving to Palestinian Jewish Christians that he like them was still a good Jew as well as a Christian? According to Bornkamm (4.160f.) this was no more than an application of the principle stated in 1 Cor. 9.19–24. 'So zeigt Apg 21.10–26 wenigstens an einem historisch gesicherten Beispiel, was Paulus mit seiner 1 Kor 9.19ff. erklärten Bereitschaft, "frei von allem allen zum Knecht" zu werden, gemeint hat. Bekanntlich isr gerade diese letzte Handlung des Paulus im Tempel für ihn zum Verhängnis geworden. Mit anderen Worten: seine Treue zu dem 1 Kor 9.20 formulierten Wort hat ihn in Gefangenschaft und Tod geführt' (161). Davies takes a similar view: 'That the apostle no longer recognized the authority of the Jewish Law did not signify that every legal observance was closed to him when he was among Jews: his very freedom from the Law enabled him to submit to it when he so desired ... He was merely practising in Acts 21.17ff. his policy, or rather strategy, as revealed in 1 Cor. 9.19ff. ... Acts does

not contradict the Epistles on Paul's attitude to the Temple' (192).
(The epistles show no attitude to the Temple!). See also *Begs*. 4.273:
'... in what way was he a Jew to the Jews if not by observing the
Law when he was with them?' So also many others; but the real
question here is not whether on occasion Paul would do what Jews
did: 1 Corinthians 9 proves conclusively that he was prepared to do
this. The question is whether Paul was prepared to use a special
occasion such as the one described in order to suggest something that
was not true, namely that he too (καὶ αὐτός, he just like the ardent
Jews who suspected his loyalty) was regularly observant of the Law
as understood within Judaism. Readiness to do this is not covered by
1 Corinthians 9. The issue is not only a moral one. Paul, one would
think, must have observed that a single action such as that suggested
to him could not prove the point, and that if his motives were
suspected this would enrage the Jews even more than simple
apostasy. Undoubtedly the plan, as described in Acts, misfired. That
is, the demonstration proposed by James was ill adapted to its
purpose—unless indeed we are to suppose (cf. Brandon, *Fall* 135)
that James's real but secret motive was to discredit Paul in the eyes
of the Gentile church. 'Occasional conformity' is an arrangement
that does little credit to the parties on either side of the contract. For
Haenchen's suggestion regarding what took place see above, p.
1000f.

Luke writes in a situation in which it is accepted that Jewish
Christians may and do observe the Law, and it is part of his
conviction that Paul was both a good Jew (this will be frequently
repeated in the ensuing chapters) and a good Christian. Paul was in
fact a Jewish Christian of a kind that could hardly continue to exist
after the first generation—a fact that was not clearly seen by Luke.

The story presupposes that Jewish Christians in Palestine, in
Luke's day and before it, continued to observe the provisions of the
Law. This is brought out by Fitzmyer (*Essays* 280), 'Jewish practices
were still admitted as part of the Christian way of life in Jerusalem as
late as *c.* AD 58, when Paul after a long apostolate among the
Gentiles went through the rite of the Nazirite at James's request
(21.23–26).' Cf. Black (*Scrolls*, 15, 82f.). The point is perhaps more
strongly made if Paul did *not* go through the rite of the Nazirite.

25. περὶ δὲ τῶν πεπιστευκότων. The concern of the Jewish
believers is not with Gentile believers; their behaviour has already
been regulated. It is presupposed here that the Decree of 15.29
applied not to a limited area only but to all Gentile Christians (see
Bruce 1.393). Jewish Christians are not asking that Gentiles should
be made Jews, only that Jews should not be made Gentiles, through
the abandonment of circumcision and other legal requirements. This
concern is clear, and it is easy to see (though not from Acts) how it

would arise. When Paul expected Jews to eat with Gentiles he was asking them to give up some of their Jewishness. This may account sufficiently for the reference here to the Decree though perhaps not for the citation of all the details. It has often been pointed out that, on the surface, it seems that Paul is being informed of the Decree as if he knew nothing about it, although, according to Acts, he was present when it was formulated, approved of it, and was one of its sponsors. The repetition may be introduced in order to inform Paul's companions, or to remind the reader (see Wilson, *Law* 81; cf. *Gentiles* 190); it may be that this is how the Decree was introduced in the 'We'-source; it may be that we have here a trace of a divergent tradition which did not represent Paul as having previously been concerned with the Decree (see Maddox, 60). The last of these possibilities (not incapable of being combined with others) may well be true; but as suggested above Luke's presentation of the matter is not impossible: Here is a new point; the old one (conditions for the admission of Gentiles) was settled long ago.

ἡμεῖς ἐπεστείλαμεν, *We* is emphatic, and if the reader were not familiar with ch. 15 he would probably suppose that it referred to the speaker and his companions—James and the Elders (v. 18). Taking Acts as a whole it must mean 'You Paul and I James'. It is however natural to ask (see above) whether the wording reflects an earlier stage of the tradition, at which James had to inform Paul of the Decree. ἐπεστείλαμεν is *we sent* (or, *wrote*) a message, or injunction. B C* (D) Ψ 049 614 2495 *pc* bo have ἀπεστείλαμεν. This is often (e.g. Metzger 484f.) rejected as the more common word, likely therefore to be substituted for the other; but ἐπιστέλλειν is used at 15.20, and the word that differs from this parallel passage may well be right, especially as B and D join forces in supporting it. Ropes (*Begs.* 3.207) supports ἀπεστ., which is used absolutely in the LXX and may have been changed into the more elegant word of 15.20. κρίναντες, aorist, means *after we had reached the decision*. D* has κρίνοντες (present), *We sent, expressing the judgement that ...* This is unlikely to be right; it may be due to the influence of d (iudicantes). A longer variant occurs in D gig sa, which instead of ἡμεῖς have οὐδὲν ἔχουσι λέγειν πρὸς σέ, ἡμεῖς γάρ. This reinforces the point made above. *They* are the Jewish, law-observing Christians of Jerusalem. They have exhausted their requirements with the Decree, and wish only to make sure that they may continue to be Jews. γάρ is added in order to use the rest of the sentence to make clear why the Jewish Christians are no longer concerned about what may or may not be done by Gentiles but wish only to reserve their own position.

φυλάσσεσθαι is used in the sense of *to be on one's guard against*. At 15.20, 29 ἀπέχεσθαι is used; it is doubtful whether Luke intended, or noticed, any differences in meaning. For the four evils against which Gentile Christians must be on their guard see on 15.20,

29. φυλάσσεσθαι is read by P⁷⁴ ℵ A B 33 1175 *pc* vg syᵖ co. Instead, D 𝔐 gig syʰ have μηδὲν τοιοῦτον τηρεῖν εἰ μὴ φυλ.; and C E Ψ 453 945 1739 1891 2495 *al* have μηδὲν τοιοῦτο τηρεῖν αὐτοὺς εἰ μὴ (ἀλλὰ 945 1739 1891 *pc*) φυλ. Ropes (*Begs.* 3.207) is probably right in describing this as a Western explanatory expansion. τοιοῦτον is the neuter form used in Attic, Epic, and regularly by Herodotus (see LS 1802). The Gentile Christians are to observe no such thing (as e.g. circumcision) but only (or, except) ... καὶ πνικτόν is omitted by D gig; cf. 15.20, 29. The Golden Rule is not added.

Historical questions of great importance focus on this verse. 'One may perhaps infer from Acts 21.25 that Luke knew that Paul himself had not recognized the "apostolic decree": thus James presents it as something new and apparently unknown to him' (Hengel 117). This may be true about Paul but not about Luke. Schneider (2.311) agrees with Conzelmann (123) that this verse is Lucan redaction; this is presumably also the view of Wilson (see above) and of Weiser (599, 'Lukas richtet sich an die Leser'). Those who give a more positive estimate of the historical content of the verse take for the most part the view that James and his party are saying, We are not going back on our pledge to the Gentiles, you therefore may do what we ask so as to deal with the residual problem of Jewish Christians in mixed communities. See Stählin (278); also Knowling (450f.); Roloff (315); Bruce (2.407).

26. Paul assents to the proposal and begins to put it into effect.

On the next day (for ἐχομένῃ, D has ἐπιούσῃ, 2464¹ *pc* e syʰ have ἐρχομένῃ, without differences of meaning) Paul took the men with him (παραλαβών: cf. v. 24; the word suggests and the context implies that Paul was taking charge of the financial arrangements). Having been purified with them he went into (εἰσῄει: D has εἰσῆλθεν) the Temple. εἰσῄει is imperfect; it is not clear that Luke uses the tense with special intent (cf. the aorist in D, but also εἰσῄει in v. 18) unless he is thinking of the four men as purified on different days—but this does not seem probable.

ἁγνισθείς is presumably used in the same way as ἁγνίσθητι in v. 24. For the question whether Paul would need to be purified (possibly on his return from Gentile territory?) see on v. 24; 24.18 (ἡγνισμένον) may simply mean that he was not in a state of impurity. Cf. Num. 6.9; this suggests that the men have not reached the normal completion of their vow (cf. 1 Macc. 3.49, ... τοὺς Ναζιραίους οἳ ἐπλήρωσαν τὰς ἡμέρας) but are renewing if after incurring defilement. σὺν αὐτοῖς: Stählin (279) comments, 'Richtiger wäre wohl: für sie'.

διαγγέλλων ... ἁγνισμοῦ (the process of purification, not the completed act—*Begs.* 4.274). Again this is presumably a reference to Num. 6.9f.: ... he shall shave his head on the day of his cleansing;

on the seventh day he shall shave it. On the eighth day he shall bring two turtle doves ... διαγγέλλειν suggests *proclaim, announce*, but here it perhaps means *notify* (the priest in charge).

ἕως οὗ προσηνέχθη ..., until the offering on behalf of each of them had been brought. This would be consistent with the view (see above—on εἰσῄει) that the offerings for the four men were not all due on the same day. 21.27, however, suggests that the seven day period was the same for all. For ἕως οὗ D has ὅπως; this is regarded by Ropes (*Begs.* 3.207) as a corruption, and so it may well be (d has donec oblata est ...). But a few MSS (323 945 1739 1891 *pc*) have προσενεχθῇ, which is the verb form that ὅπως would require. It is accordingly possible that the original form (or, an original form) of the Western text had ὅπως προσενεχθῇ, a reading that no longer appears in any extant witness.

54. RIOT AT JERUSALEM 21.27–40

(27) When the seven days were almost completed, the Jews from Asia, having seen Paul[1] in the Temple, stirred up the whole crowd and laid their hands upon him, (28) shouting, 'Men of Israel, help! this is the man who teaches all men everywhere against the People and the Law and this place. Moreover, he has also brought Greeks into the Temple and has profaned this holy place.' (29) For they had previously seen Trophimus the Ephesian in the city with him and supposed that Paul had brought him into the Temple. (30) The whole city was excited and there was a tumultuous concourse of the people. They laid hands on Paul and dragged him outside the Temple; and immediately the gates were shut. (31) While they were seeking to kill him word went up to the tribune of the cohort that all Jerusalem was in an uproar. (32) He immediately took soldiers and centurions and ran down upon them. When they saw the tribune and the soldiers they stopped beating Paul. (33) Then the tribune came up, got hold of him, and commanded him to be bound with two chains. He inquired who he might be and what he had done. (34) Some in the crowd called out one thing, others another. Since he was not able to get trustworthy information because of the tumult he ordered him to be brought into the barracks. (35) When he got on the steps he was actually carried by the soldiers because of the violence of the crowd, (36) for the whole multitude of the people were following, shouting, 'Away with him!'

(37) As he was about to enter the barracks Paul said to the tribune, 'May I say something to you?' He said, 'Do you know how to speak Greek? (38) [2]So are you not the Egyptian, who in the past[3] raised and led out into the desert four thousand men of the sicarii?' (39) Paul said, 'Truly I am a Jew, of Tarsus in Cilicia, a citizen of no mean city. I pray you, permit me to speak to the people.' (40) He gave permission; Paul stood on the steps and gestured to the people with his hand. There was dead silence, and Paul called out to them in the Hebrew[4] language:

Bibliography

J. M. Baumgarten, *JJS* 61 (1954), 215–25.

E. J. Bickermann, *JQR* 37 (1947), 387–405.

H. Braun, *ThR* 29 (1963), 174.

J. H. Iliffe, *Quarterly of the Department of Antiquities in Palestine* 6 (1936), 1–3.

S. Légasse, *RechScR* 69 (1981), 249–56.

[1]Greek, him.
[2]NEB, Then you are not; NJB, Aren't you.
[3]Greek, before these days.
[4]Probably Aramaic is intended.

H. Sahlin, *NovT* 24 (1982), 188.
A. A. Trites, *NovT* 16 (1974), 278–84.
L. H. Vincent, *RB* 61 (1954), 87–107.

Commentary

Quickly read, this paragraph gives the impression of a straightforward account of violent events in the Temple, happening at a point determined in relation to the process of purification in which, according to 21.23–26, Paul had agreed to take part. Paul was accused however not of anything amiss in the rite of purification, but of bringing into the part of the Temple from which Gentiles were excluded Trophimus the Ephesian. Trophimus had indeed been in the city with Paul, but not, Luke clearly implies, in the Temple. Paul was beaten, the city was in an uproar; the Roman tribune (Claudius Lysias, we learn from 23.26) intervened at the head of his troops, brought Paul into the barracks, and began to interrogate him, believing him to be an Egyptian trouble-maker. Paul sought and obtained permission to speak to the crowd in the Temple. This appears to be, and is, a plain tale, and whatever its origin every part of it is possibly historical.

There are however points of real or apparent difficulty, real difficulty, for example, in v. 27 in the dating of the event. This appears to be due to Luke's lack of clarity with regard to the rules for the Nazirite vow and other occasions of release from ceremonial impurity. Inaccuracy here of two or three days one way or the other is of no importance to the story. For this question see the note on v. 27 (also on 24.11). Haenchen (591) detects an inconsistency between Paul's being so weak after his beating that he had to be carried up the stairs (v. 35) and his delivering shortly thereafter an energetic speech (ch. 22). There is no problem. Paul was carried not because of physical weakness but διὰ τὴν βίαν τοῦ ὄχλου. Paul was carried to prevent his being torn limb from limb by the mob. We cannot infer that he was gravely weakened; and, if he was, under the pressure of great events sick men have been raised to make powerful speeches.

Paul was not without companions, and it is presumably to them that Luke (who could himself have been one of them, though probably he was not) owes this story and some of those that follow. There is no use of the first person plural, nor could this be expected. The conversation between Paul and the tribune must be based on conjecture. There is little or nothing improbable in it. See the note.

27. αἱ ἑπτὰ ἡμέραι are most naturally understood in terms of Num. 6.9 to mean that the four men who had undertaken (Nazirite) vows had incurred some uncleanness, for removing which a seven-day period was necessary. Alternatively (see e.g. Beyer 132; Pesch

2.224) Paul might have needed to remove uncleanness due to his residence abroad. This would require seven days in view of Num. 19.11–13—a passage which is relevant because uncleanness caused by life outside Palestine was caused 'weil man befürchtete, dass dort überall verunreinigende Gräber auch in verborgenen vorhanden sein möchten' (StrB 2.759). D gig (sy^p) have συντελουμένης δὲ τῆς ἑβδόμης ἡμέρας, the seventh day was coming to its end, which is an alternative expression for the same time, for ὡς δὲ ἔμελλον means *when the seven days were about to be completed* (though Bruce 1.394 thinks that they were about to begin). E. Schwartz, referred to in *Begs.* 4.274, conjectured ἑβδομάδες in place of ἑπτὰ ἡμέραι: the seven *weeks* (between Passover and Pentecost) were about to be completed. This would introduce an otherwise surprisingly absent second reference to the Pentecost of 20.16, but it has no other virtue, and a reference to Pentecost in the midst of a passage dealing with vows would be very odd. H. Sahlin (*NovT* 24 (1982), 188) suggested that the number seven crept into the text from a marginal ζ', intended as a contraction of ζήτει, meaning 'This is doubtful; look it up', and misunderstood as a numeral.

οἱ (+ δέ, D) ἀπὸ τῆς Ἀσίας Ἰουδαῖοι (+ ἐληλυθότες, D), with whom Paul has already had trouble (20.19), saw him in the Temple, where he had of course been for the purpose of purification, if not for other reasons also. On the form of συνέχεον see M. 2.91, 265; also BDR § 73.1, n. 5. These Jews were responsible for trouble in Jerusalem as earlier they had been nearer home. It is they, not Jewish Christians (who stand aloof), who attack Paul.

For ἐπιβάλλειν χεῖρας see 4.3. Instead of the aorist D has the (historic) present ἐπιβάλλουσιν.

Schmithals (198) takes the view that vv. 27–29 are Luke's editorial work. There is little to be said for his opinion that 'Die Paulus–Quelle hat dagegen von einer Verhaftung des Paulus in Jerusalem gar nichts gewusst.' This is part of the theory (199) that Paul in fact travelled to Rome as a free man, the story as we have it being made up to imitate that of Jesus. Roloff (316) on the other hand thinks that Luke had a narrative of Paul in Jerusalem and Caesarea: 21.27–36; 22.24–29; 23.12—24.23, 26f.; 25.1–12.

28. ἄνδρες Ἰσραηλῖται: see 2.22 and the note.

βοηθεῖν in the NT usually means *help*; here it means *come to the rescue* (see LS s.v. 2; p. 320; so e.g. Herodotus 7.158.2, ἤλθετε βοηθήσοντες).

ὁ ἄνθρωπος ὁ ... διδάσκων. The emphasis lies on the participial phrase; BDR § 270.1, n. 2. But the phrase is not consistent with the charge brought in 21.21. There Paul is alleged by Jewish Christians to teach Jews not to observe the Law; here he teaches all men, and this must mean all Gentiles, since he teaches against the people (λαός) as well as against the Law and 'this place' (the Temple). Cf. the charges against Stephen, which include a reference to 'this place' (6.13, 14). In the epistles Paul does not teach against the people (see especially Romans 9–11, though on the other side 1 Thess. 2.14–16); his teaching about the Law is notoriously complex, with positive and negative elements; he does not refer to the Temple. Luke of course does not mean to suggest that the accusations in this verse were justified.

πάντας πανταχῇ. Such paronomasia is classical. BDR § 488.1a, n. 2 does not refer to this passage in Acts but quotes what is a good parallel: Plato, *Menexenus* 247a, διὰ παντὸς πᾶσαν πάντως προθυμίαν πειρᾶσθε ἔχειν. For the spelling of πανταχῇ (with iota subscript) see M. 2.84, and contrast πάντη at 24.3 (where NA²⁶ has the iota but Moulton does not).

῞Ελληνας, plural; in the next verse Trophimus alone is mentioned. *Greeks* may be an inference, wilful exaggeration, or a *pluralis categoriae* (cf. 19.38). See M. 3.26.

Non-Jews were forbidden to enter the Temple beyond the Court of the Gentiles. For the inscription placed on the wall surrounding the inner precincts see Dittenberger, *OGIS* 2.598:

ΜΗΘΕΝΑ ΑΛΛΟΓΕΝΗ ΕΙΣΠΟ
ΡΕΥΕΣΘΑΙ ΕΝΤΟΣ ΤΟΥ ΠΕ
ΡΙ ΤΟ ΙΕΡΟΝ ΤΡΥΦΑΚΤΟΥ ΚΑΙ
ΠΕΡΙΒΟΛΟΥ ΟΣ ΔΑΝ ΛΗ
ΦΘΗ ΕΑΥΤΟΥ ΑΙΤΙΟΣ ΕΣ
ΤΑΙ ΔΙΑ ΤΟ ΕΞΑΚΟΛΟΥ
ΘΕΙΝ ΘΑΝΑΤΟΝ

A further fragment of an inscription was found in 1935; see J. H. Iliffe in *Quarterly of the Department of Antiquities in Palestine* 6 (1936), 1–3. For the prohibition (and some references to the inscription) see Josephus, *Apion* 2.103f.; *War* 5.193f. (an inscription ῾Ελληνικοῖς ... ῾Ρωμαϊκοῖς γράμμασιν); 6.125; *Ant.* 12.145; 15.417 (on the last see the note by R. Marcus and A. Wikgren in LCL Josephus 8.202f.); Philo, *Legatio ad Gaium* 212; Middoth 2.3; Kelim 1.8. Cf Eph. 2.14. On the whole see Sevenster (*Do you know Greek?* 116); *NS* 2.285f. Sherwin-White (38) observes that 'the wording is very curious and suggests lynching rather than execution'.

εἰσήγαγεν ... κεκοίνωκεν, aorist and perfect. 'Die *geschehene* Einführung hat die Befleckung zur dauernden Wirkung gehabt' (BDR § 342.2, n. 5). In 1QpHab 12.6–9 the Wicked Priest defiles the Temple; there is no reference here to Paul.

Tajra (123) emphasizes the importance of the charge of Temple profanation. Only on this could Jews get a death sentence and have it carried out.

29. ἦσαν προεωρακότες, periphrastic pluperfect. The pluperfect forms were not always used in earlier Greek, and were tending to go out of use in the NT period.

Trophimus, from Asia; 20.4. Had the others mentioned in that verse not reached Jerusalem? Or was it by chance that Trophimus had been seen and identified? It was a very common name; see *ND* 3.91–3. Hanson (212): They 'would have known what Trophimus, who came from the capital of their province, looked like.' This seems most unlikely; Ephesus was a large city, Asia a very large province.

ἐνόμιζον, an illogical but perhaps not unnatural supposition. D has ἐνομίσαμεν; it is hardly possible to make sense of this first person plural and it must be regarded as a simple error; Ropes (*Begs.* 3.207) prints ἐνόμισαν as the (intended) text of D, with ἐνομίσαμεν at the foot of the page. d has putaverunt.

ὅν is anticipated from the ὅτι clause = ἐνόμιζον ὅτι Π. εἰσήγαγεν αὐτόν. An accusative and infinitive construction would have been ambiguous here; see BDR § 397.2, n. 5.

30. ἐκινήθη. Cf. Josephus, *Ant.* 3.13, τοῦ πλήθους ... πικρῶς ἐπ'αὐτὸν κεκινημένου. As the context indicates, violent excitement is meant.

συνδρομή, *tumultuous concourse* (LS 1703). Cf. Judith 10.18, with ἐγένετο, as here.

For the sequence of imperfect (εἷλκον) and aorist (ἐκλείσθησαν) see M. 3.66 and especially BDR § 327.1, n. 1. BDR point out that εὐθέως implies ἑλκυσθέντων αὐτῶν (but they must mean ἑλκυσθέντος αὐτοῦ). When the process of dragging Paul out was complete, the doors were shut. Or perhaps, the gate was shut, since θύραι, plural, was used of the folding doors of such a gate as the Temple may be supposed to have had. Presumably once the supposed offender was outside the Temple authorities closed the gate(s) in order to prevent further profanation—by the murder of Paul?

Marshall (348) follows Jeremias (*Jerusalem* 210) in thinking that the gates of the inner courts, not the outer gates of the Temple, were closed.

For ἐπιλαμβάνεσθαι see *ND* 4.104.

31. The subject of ζητούντων (which would be αὐτῶν, the members of the crowd) is not expressed; such omission of the pronoun in a genitive absolute is both classical and Hellenistic: Zerwick § 50; BDR § 423. One would have supposed that a serious attempt to kill Paul would have succeeded long before word could be brought to the tribune. φάσις is not a formal report; nearer to *rumour*. The φάσις ἀνέβη, that is, went up to the official's headquarters in the Antonia; see *NS* 1.361, 362, 366. For the watch over the Temple from the Antonia towers see Josephus, *War* 5.242; there was a view

of the whole area of the Temple. Troops were kept in readiness
during festivals: *War* 5.244; *Ant.* 20.106f.

σπεῖρα is the Latin *cohors*; see 10.1. χιλίαρχος is *tribunus
(militum)*, the commander of a cohort.

The report was that the whole of Jerusalem συγχύννεται (so ℵ* A
B D 33 (1175) *pc* vg; συγκέχυται is read by P⁷⁴ ℵᶜ E Ψ 𝔐 d gig),
was in an uproar. This was the sort of event that could easily get out
of hand; it was the purpose of the Roman garrison to nip such
disturbances in the bud. Metzger (485) notes that syʰᵐᵍ* adds at the
end of the verse, See therefore that they do not make an uprising.

τε is read by ℵ A B E 945 1739 1891 2464 *pc*, δέ by Dᶜ Ψ 𝔐 lat
syʰ; P⁷⁴ (D*) p have neither. After ἀνέβη, P⁷⁴ adds δέ.

32. ὅς ... κατέδραμεν. Continuation of the narrative by means of
a relative clause is characteristic of Acts. ἐξαυτῆς is an Acts word
(10.33; 11.11; 21.32; 23.30; Mk, once, Paul, once). These two
features however could prove at most some Lucan retouching.

BDR § 419.1: Luke uses the participle παραλαβών rather than an
adverbial clause, such as ἐπειδὴ παρέλαβεν, because here the
participle, like the classical λαβών, is virtually equivalent to *with*.
True, but there is in fact nothing unusual in the adverbial use of the
participle. λαβών is read by B (cf. d, sumptis militibus).

ἑκατοντάρχας. For centurions see 10.1. The plural means that at
least two were sent, presumably accompanied by two centuries, with
a paper, but not necessarily an actual, strength of 200 men. This
intervention had the intended effect: the crowd stopped beating
Paul.

33. That the tribune himself led his forces and began the interrogation suggests that the disturbance was taken very seriously.

ἐπιλαμβάνεσθαι: see on v. 30.

Two chains: perhaps attached to two soldiers, one on each side.

ἐπυνθάνετο (imperfect—*began to question*) τίς εἴη καὶ τί ἐστιν
πεποιηκώς. The first dependent verb is optative, the second (periphrastic perfect—cf. v. 29) indicative. If the two dependent questions are to be distinguished, the former indicates uncertainty, the
latter the conviction that the man (whoever he might be) had
certainly committed some crime. So Bruce 1.397; M. 1.199; and
BDR § 386.1, n. 2. But Page (225) thinks it possible that τίς εἴη καὶ τί
εἴη πεπ. may have been avoided as ugly.

From the outset, Paul is in Roman hands.

34. ἄλλοι δὲ ἄλλο τι. For the construction cf. 19.32. There was a
popular move rather than a concerted plan against Paul.

μὴ δυναμένου δὲ αὐτοῦ ... ἐκέλευσεν. The genitive of the
absolute construction becomes the subject of the finite verb, a serious
abuse of the construction. BDR § 473.3, n. 9.

τὸ ἀσφαλές, trustworthy information.

θορυβόν: the sense of *noisy* tumult (cf. 20.1) is evident here.

For ἄγεσθαι, P⁷⁴ has ἀνάγεσθαι, which corresponds with the position of the Antonia, which is no doubt what is intended by τὴν παρεμβολήν. See Josephus, *Ant.* 15.403–409. παρεμβολή meant originally a drawing up of soldiers in battle order, then a company of soldiers, a camp; here, the soldiers' quarters, or barracks. On the origin of the word see Phrynichus (353): παρεμβολὴ δεινῶς Μακεδονικόν· καίτοι ἐνῆν τῷ στρατοπέδῳ χρῆσθαι, πλείστῳ καὶ δοκίμῳ ὄντι.

35. ἐγένετο here is little more than *was*: the sense of *becoming* may be brought out by the colloquial, *When he got on the steps.*

συμβαίνειν (impersonal, *it happened*) was going out of use in post-classical Greek; it was probably used here because the much more common ἐγένετο had already been used in the sentence. *It came about that he was carried.* Cf. M. 2.427 (comparing Tobit 3.7 (א)); BDR § 393.1, n. 2. There is more emphasis than in the simple ἐβαστάσθη: he was actually carried.

τοὺς ἀναβαθμούς. 'At two points, steps (καταβάσεις) led down from the fortress to the Temple-court. This is precisely the situation that emerges from the Acts. For when Paul was taken into custody by the soldiers during the uproar in the courtyard of the temple, and was led away to the barracks (παρεμβολή), he was carried up the steps (ἀναβαθμοί) by the soldiers to protect him from the crowd, and from there, with the permission of the "chiliarch", addressed the people once more (Acts 21.31–40)' (*NS* 1.366). See Josephus, *War* 5.243: καθὰ δὲ συνῆπτε ταῖς τοῦ ἱεροῦ στοαῖς εἰς ἀμφοτέρας εἶχε καταβάσεις, δι᾽ ὧν κατήεσαν οἱ φρουροί. See also Dalman (*SSW* 298).

For ἐπί, D has εἰς—less suitable, and therefore conceivably original. For ὄχλου, D latt syᵖ have λαοῦ—possibly an attempt to pin blame for the riot on the Jewish people. See however v. 36.

Haenchen (591) finds the beating and carrying inconsistent with the speech that follows; on this see p. 1018 above.

36. ἠκολούθει γὰρ explains διὰ τὴν βίαν in v. 35.

κράζοντες may be said to agree with πλῆθος as a noun of multitude.

αἶρε αὐτόν: Cf. Lk. 23.18 (αἶρε τοῦτον); Acts 22.22; Jn 19.15; *Martyrdom of Polycarp* 3.2; 9.2 (αἶρε τοὺς ἀθέους). Luke probably intends to recall the story of Jesus. Cf. also Isa. 53.8, as at 8.33. See Wilcox (67).

τοῦ λαοῦ is omitted by D gig; in its place 614 *pc* syʰ have τοῦ ὄχλου. It cannot be said that the Western text here (cf. v. 30) manifests an anti-semitic (anti-Jewish) tendency; for the Western authorities it is just the crowd, not the crowd of the people (of God), that pressed upon Paul and sought his death. But it is doubtful whether the variants have so much force. At the end of the verse D has ἀναιρεῖσθαι instead of αἶρε αὐτόν. The majority reading is more forceful.

Roloff (318) comments that Jerusalem had now 'seine heils-geschichtliche Stellung verloren'. It is not clear what this means. The Geschichte certainly is moving into a new phase.

37. Μέλλων ... εἰς τὴν παρεμβολήν. Cf. v. 35.

ὁ Παῦλος ... τῷ χιλιάρχῳ: D has τῷ χ. ἀποκριθεὶς εἶπεν. The Old Uncial text makes explicit who is speaking and may well be secondary; there is no evident reason why the name should have been omitted. Equally there seems no reason why εἰπεῖν τε should be replaced by λαλῆσαι (D gig), or vice versa. Some fairly free rewriting has been done. εἰ introduces a direct question (πρὸς σέ); cf. 1.6; 7.1.

The tribune is surprised (for a reason that appears in the next verse) that Paul is able to address him in Greek. 'Do you know how to speak Greek?' 'Not "know" Greek, for γινώσκεις is an ellipse for γινώσκεις λαλῆσαι Ἑλληνιστί' (*Begs.* 4.276). On the general question involved here see S. Lieberman, *Greek in Jewish Palestine* (1965) and J. N. Sevenster, *Do you know Greek?* (1968). Sevenster concludes (188): 'Divers literary and archaeological data from different centuries agree in their testimonial to a knowledge of Greek in broad layers of the Jewish population in Palestine. And they contain not a single manifest indication that this was lacking during certain periods in the first three centuries A.D.' See also *ND* 5.5–40, on bilingualism. Paul is recognized as a 'productive bilingual'.

Of vv. 37–40 Lüdemann (246) writes, 'Der Abschnitt ist in toto redaktionell.' Marshall (350) (cf. the note on v. 33) emphasizes the importance for Luke of Paul's dealings with Romans and his journey to Rome. These will occupy a quarter of the book.

38. οὐκ ἄρα σὺ εἶ ...; It is not easy to be certain of the precise sense of the opening words of the sentence (for which D has οὐ σὺ εἶ). ἄρα is probably used mainly to express surprise (BDR § 440.2, n. 4, 'Die Verwunderung bezeichnend') but it probably includes also an element of inference, missed in the Vulgate's *Nunc tu es ...?* Blass (233) cites as a parallel Aristophanes, *Birds* 280, οὐ σὺ μόνος ἄρ' ἦσθ' ἔποψ ...; The two possibilities are, So you are not the Egyptian? and So are you not the Egyptian? The former alternative is taken by, among others, Haenchen (592): 'Du bist also nicht ...?' But the latter seems better, grammatically and because Egyptians undoubtedly spoke Greek; there was nothing in Paul's use of Greek to show that he was not the Egyptian. It may be that Marshall (352) is somewhat too positive with 'Do you know Greek? Surely, then, you are the Egyptian ...', though in this rendering he is preceded by

Bengel (472): 'Tribunus militum ita colligebat: Paulus Graece loquitur; ergo est Aegyptius.'

ὁ Αἰγύπτιος. Cf. 5.36f. For the Egyptian see Josephus, *War* 2.261–3; *Ant.* 20.169–72. See especially the note by Feldman on the latter passage (LCL Josephus 9.480f.); also Klausner (*Jesus* 21); Knox (*Hell. El.* 26) ('It is at least possible that they [Theudas and the Egyptian] claimed to be Jesus-Joshua returning to fulfil the prophecies of the end (cf. Mk 13.6), hoping to enlist Christian support') *Begs.* 4.277. There is much to be said for the view that the Egyptian is to be identified with the ben Stada of Jewish tradition (T. Sanhedrin 10.11; Sanhedrin 67a; Shabbath 104b). According to Josephus the Egyptian prophet or charlatan proposed to take Jerusalem, either by a conventional attack (*War*) or by causing its walls to fall down (*Ant.*). His forces were put down by Felix, but he himself escaped; the tribune's supposition that Paul was he, renewing his efforts, was thus quite reasonable. The population of Jerusalem had assisted the Romans in repulsing him (*War* 2.263) so that they might well set on him if they saw him again.

ἀναστατώσας (E, ἐξανα.): *unsettled*, but here perhaps *raised* (a mob—or perhaps an army, the 4000). According to Acts he led his men into the desert. According to *War* 2.262 he led them by a circuitous route (περιαγαγών) from the desert (ἐκ τῆς ἐρημίας) to the Mount of Olives. According to *Ant.* 20.169 he counselled the people to go with him to the Mount of Olives. For the significance in this respect of the Mount of Olives see Zech. 14.1–5. For 'messianic' leaders who took the people into the desert see Bammel in E. Bammel and C. F. D. Moule (eds.), *Jesus and the Politics of his Day* (1984), 230. 1QS 8.1–9.11 and 1QM 11.9, though approved by Braun (*ThR* 29 (1963), 174) as evidence for the 'Wüstenzug als Bestandteil der Heilszeit' do not seem to be relevant here. *Begs.* 4.277 makes the suggestion that Luke has here misread Josephus, who says (see above) that the Egyptian led his followers not into but out of the desert (*War* 2.262).

τετρακισχιλίους. According to Josephus, *War* 2.261, 30,000. It is a neat suggestion that the discrepancy may have arisen through confusion of Δ (= 4) and Λ (= 30). Weiser (608) rejects this suggestion because Josephus writes out the number, τρισμύριοι. But how did the number appear in first century MSS of Josephus?

τῶν σικαρίων. Conzelmann (124) thinks that the Egyptian's movement is to be distinguished from the σικάριοι. According to Josephus, *Ant.* 20.169, the Egyptian's followers were simply τὸ δημοτικὸν πλῆθος; in *War* 2.261 they are described as ἠπατημένοι, but were intended to form a bodyguard, δορύφοροι (262). The passage in *Ant.* goes on to speak of λῃσταί. Neither passage refers to σικάριοι, but these are identified with λῃσταί in *Ant.* 20.186. See also *War* 2.254–257. The sicarii carried concealed daggers (ξιφίδια), 'in size resembling the scimitars of the Persians, but curved and more like the weapon called by the Romans *sicae' Ant.* 20.186), and were assassins, according to Josephus committing many secret murders in the time of trouble leading up to the war with Rome. See StrB 2.762f.

If the tribune took Paul to be the leader of such a group, as he may quite reasonably have done, he could hardly be expected to treat him gently. He will learn the truth in two stages, (a) Paul is a Diaspora Jew, (b) he is a Roman citizen. At this stage Paul appears as a 'gebildeter und gesitteter Bürger einer angesehenen Stadt' (Weiser 609).

39. The μέν and δέ in this verse are best taken as independent; the μέν must be taken therefore to add weight to the affirmation (LS 1101, s.v.A I): Of a truth, I am ... Not so Bruce, 1.398 (similarly Page 226): As regards your question to me, I am ... as regards my question to you, I ask ... Paul is Ἰουδαῖος and not the Egyptian.

Ταρσεύς. MM 626 quote only the adjective ταρσικοϋφικός (POxy 14.1705.6); se *ND* 4.173. For Tarsus and its significance in Paul's background see on 9.11; add now M. Hengel (*The Pre-Christian Paul* (1991)). See Strabo 14.5.10–15; Dio Chrysostom 34, referred to with reference to this verse by Sherwin-White (179f.; cf. Lohse, *Umwelt* 88), who emphasizes the importance to Paul and other Diaspora Jews of local citizenship (for Roman citizenship see 22.25). Whether Jews were citizens (in the strict sense of the term) of Hellenistic cities is discussed at length by Tcherikover (309–22), with reference to the views of other writers. His conclusion is: 'Three conclusions may be drawn from all this historical material. 1. The civic status of Diaspora Jews was not uniform, and the extent of their rights depended on when, how, and for what purpose the Jews came to a given country outside Palestine. 2. The organized Jewish community as a whole stood juridically outside the Greek city, and the Jews who lived in it had no civic rights there. 3. Isolated Jews could acquire civic rights individually' (331). These points may be accepted, especially perhaps the first. Most of the evidence available refers to Egypt, and in particular to Alexandria; for Asia, see Trebilco. It would be fallacious to assume that conditions obtaining elsewhere applied also to Tarsus. We have little information about Jews in this city: a Jew of Tarsus was buried at Joppa (*CIJ* 2.925, cited by Safrai and Stern, 1.147, n. 6); an archisynagogue of the province of Cilicia is mentioned by Epiphanius, *Haer.* 30.11. That there was a partly Cilician synagogue in Jerusalem (6.9) suggests a fairly considerable Jewish population, but how many resided in Tarsus is unknown. It may be that Paul (Luke) uses πολίτης in a loose sense: resident in, rather than enrolled citizen of, Tarsus. So Tajra (78–80).

οὐκ ἀσήμου πόλεως, 'a very characteristic Hellenistic addition' which 'touches the theme, with the help of an erudite quotation from the classics, of half the municipal orations of Dio of Prusa' (Sherwin-White 179f.). Sherwin-White is presumably thinking of Euripides, *Ion* 8, ἔστιν γὰρ οὐκ ἄσημος Ἑλλήνων πόλις (cf. *Hercules Furens* 849); but the litotes is not uncharacteristic of Luke (see on 12.18), who could have made it up himself. Hemer (127) accepts the allusion to Euripides. Conzelmann (124) quotes Dittenberger, *OGIS* 2.578.7f., Τάρσος, ἡ πρώτη κ[αὶ μεγίστη] καὶ καλλίστη μ[ητρόπολις]. Paul when speaking to the crowd refers again (22.3) to his Tarsiote origin, but then (see the note) depreciates it in comparison with his connection with Jerusalem. Paul does not refer to his Roman citizenship till 22.25.

For the imperative ἐπίτρεψον, Ψ has the infinitive ἐπιτρέψαι, D gig συγχωρῆσαι; there is no significant difference in meaning. For Ταρσεύς ... πολίτης, D (w syᵖ) have ἐν Ταρσῷ δὲ τῆς Κιλικίας γεγεννημένος, missing the allusion to Euripides and assimilating to 22.3. δέ (after δέομαι) is omitted by P⁷⁴ L 6 *pc*. Bauernfeind (249) analyses Paul's motivation: If he is not to die at the hands of his own people let him at least speak to them; this may be his only chance.

40. The tribune gave permission; ἐπιτρέψαντος δὲ αὐτοῦ takes up ἐπίτρεψον (v. 39). The question must be asked whether, in these circumstances, a responsible Roman officer would have done so. In fact, though Paul was at first heard in silence the upshot was renewed tumult and violence (22.22f.). What could the tribune have hoped for? Would it not have been more sensible to hustle Paul immediately into the Antonia—in the interests of security, supposing Paul to be guilty of some kind of trouble-making, in Paul's own interests, supposing him innocent; in Rome's interests, either way? Against this, one might suggest that the tribune was impressed by Paul's personality; but in 22.24 he proposes to scourge him. Luke needs a speech at this point in order to clarify his view of the situation.

ἐπὶ τῶν ἀναβαθμῶν. See v. 35. 'Er blickt in die Richtung des Tempels' (Schneider 2.319).

κατέσεισεν. Cf. 13.16 and other passages for the orator's gesture, several times referred to in Acts. D has καὶ σείσας, which could easily have arisen as a mechanical error. This Western reading can be reasonably connected, as one of a number of participles (ἑστώς ... σείσας ... γενομένης) with προσεφώνησεν, but the Old Uncial text yields a preferable sentence. For τῷ λαῷ, D syᵖ have πρὸς αὐτούς. For σιγῆς γενομένης, B 945 1739 1891 *pc* have γεν. σιγ.; D has ἡσυχίας γεν. Cf. Xenophon, *Cyropaedia* 7.1.25, πολλὴ σιγή.

τῇ Ἑβραΐδι (ἰδίᾳ, P⁷⁴ A) διαλέκτῳ. Cf. 22.2; 26.14. Probably Aramaic is intended. 'That Aramaic and not Hebrew was really the language of the people is proved by Aramaic proverbs and sentences which occur not only in the Midrashim, but also in the Mishna, and first and foremost by rabbinical Hebrew itself, which is either an aramaicized Hebrew or a hebraicized Aramaic, and so presupposes Aramaic to have been the language of the country' (Dalman, *Jesus-Jeshua* (1929), 16). Cf. also Dalman (*Words of Jesus* (1909), 1–12, especially 6f.). But see M. H. Segal (*A Grammar of Mishnaic Hebrew* (1958), 1–20, especially 5–10); the Dead Sea Scrolls also attest the currency of Hebrew. See also however *NS* 2.20–28: 'The principal language spoken by Jews in the various regions of Palestine during the final centuries of the pre-Christian era was Aramaic' (20, with extensive bibliography). Also important is the discussion of bilingualism in *ND* 5.5–40, especially 23 with the literature referred to there.

55. PAUL'S TEMPLE SPEECH AND THE SEQUEL 22.1-29

(1) 'Brothers! Fathers! Listen to the defence that I now bring to you.' (2) When they heard that he was addressing them in the Hebrew[1] language they gave even greater silence. He went on: (3) 'I am a man, a Jew, born in Tarsus in Cilicia, brought up[2] in this city, educated strictly in the ancestral Law at the feet of Gamaliel, being zealous for God, as are all of you today. (4) And I persecuted this Way to the death, binding and delivering to prison both men and women, (5) as the high priest and all the company of elders bear me witness. From them also I received letters to our [Jewish][3] brothers and journeyed to Damascus, in order that I might bring those [Jewish Christians][4] who were there bound to Jerusalem, for punishment. (6) It happened to me as I travelled and was drawing near to Damascus, about midday, that suddenly there shone round about me from heaven a great light. (7) I fell to the ground and heard a voice saying to me, "Saul, Saul, why are you persecuting me?" (8) I answered, "Who art thou, Lord?" And he said to me, "I am Jesus the Nazoraean, whom you are persecuting." (9) Those who were with me saw the light, but did not hear the voice of him who was speaking to me. (10) I said, "What am I to do, Lord?" The Lord said to me, "Get up and go into Damascus; there you will be told about all the things which it has been appointed for you to do." (11) When I was unable to see because of the glory of that light I was led by the hand by those who were with me and came into Damascus. (12) One Ananias, a pious man according to the Law, who had a good reputation with all the resident Jews, (13) came to me, stood by me and said, "Brother Saul, regain your sight." In that very hour I looked upon him. (14) He said, "The God of our fathers has appointed you to know his will and to see the Righteous One and to hear a voice from his mouth, (15) for you shall be a witness for him to all men of the things you have seen and heard. (16) And now[5] what are you going to do? Get up,[6] get yourself baptized and wash away your sins by calling on his name." (17) And it happened to me when I had returned to Jerusalem and was praying in the Temple, that I fell into an ecstasy (18) and saw him saying to me, "Make haste and depart quickly from Jerusalem because they will not receive your testimony about me." (19) And I said, "Lord, they themselves know that I was engaged in imprisoning and beating from synagogue to synagogue those who believe in thee, (20) and when the blood of Stephen thy witness was shed I was myself standing by and approving and keeping the clothes of those who were killing him." (21) He said to me, "Go, for I shall send you far from here to the Gentiles." '

[1]Probably Aramaic is intended.
[2]NJB, here in this city.
[3]Jewish is not in the Greek.
[4]Jewish Christians is not in the Greek.
[5]RSV, why do you wait? NEB, NJB, why delay?
[6]RSV, NEB, NJB, be baptized.

(22) They listened to him up to this word and [then][7] they lifted up their voices saying, 'Away with such a man from the earth, for it is not fit that he should live.' (23) As they were shouting and flinging off[8] their clothes and throwing dust in the air, (24) the tribune ordered that he should be brought into the barracks, saying that he should be examined with the scourge in order that he [the tribune][9] might know why they were so shouting him down. (25) But when they[10] stretched him out for the lash Paul said to the centurion who was standing there, "Is it lawful for you to scourge a Roman—and one not even tried at that?" (26) When the centurion heard this he approached the tribune and reported the matter, saying, "What are you going to do? This man is a Roman." (27) The tribune approached him and said, "Tell me, are you a Roman?" "Yes" he said. (28) The tribune answered, "I acquired this citizenship at a high price." Paul said, "But I was born a citizen." (29) Immediately those who were about to examine him stood back, and the tribune was afraid when he recognized that [Paul][11] was a Roman, and that he had bound him.

Bibliography

P. W. Barnett, *NTS* 27 (1981), 679–97.

O. Betz, *FS* Stählin, 113–23.

T. L. Budesheim, as in (51).

R. Bultmann, *E & F* 130–2.

C. Burchard, *ZNW* 61 (1970), 168f.

R. H. Connolly, *JTS* 37 (1936), 383f.

J. M. Grintz, *JBL* 79 (1960), 32–47.

K. Haacker, *Das Institutum Judaicum Tübingen* 1971–1972 (1972), 106–20.

P. W. van der Horst, *NovT* 16 (1974), 309.

J. Jeremias, *FS* Black (1969), 94.

S. Légasse, as in (54).

S. Lundgren, as in (23) [= *StTh* 25 (1971), 117–22].

S. Lyonnet, *RechScR* 69 (1981), 149–64.

H. R. Moehring, as in (23) [= *NovT* 3 (1959), 80–99].

Th. Mommsen, *ZNW* 2 (1901), 81–96.

J. Neyrey, in C. H. Talbert, *Luke-Acts* 210–24.

H. P. Rüger, *ZNW* 72 (1981), 257–63.

F. Schulz, *JRS* 32 (1942), 78–91; 33 (1943), 55–64.

O. H. Steck, *ZNW* 67 (1976), 20–28.

W. Stegemann, as in (43).

---

[7]Then is not in the Greek.
[8]RSV, waved; NEB, NJB, waving.
[9]the tribune is not in the Greek.
[10]RSV, tied him up with the thongs; NJB, strapping him down.
[11]Greek, he.

W. C. van Unnik, *Tarsus of Jeruzalem*, 1952.

R. D. Witherup, *JSNT* 48 (1992), 67–86.

See also other works cited in (23) (I.438f.).

Commentary

The staple content of the speech which Paul, with the consent of the tribune, makes to the crowd assembled in the Temple is an account of his conversion. This event is described three times in Acts: in ch. 9, here, and in ch. 26. The event itself, and the three forms in which it is presented, are discussed in the introductory comment on Section 23 (9.1–19a), where the differences between the accounts are analysed. 'The account in ch. 22 is adapted to the Jewish audience to which it is addressed. The High Priest and the council of elders are invoked to testify to Paul's Jewish zeal (22.5); Jesus becomes Ἰησοῦς ὁ Ναζωραῖος (22.8); Ananias is described not as a disciple but as a devout observant of the Law, respected by all the local Jews (22.12), and he speaks not in the name of the Lord Jesus but in that of the God of our fathers (22.14); it is in the Temple that Paul in a vision receives his instructions (22.17); he takes the opportunity of giving his Jewish credentials as a persecutor (22.19, 20); only when he claims to have been sent by God to the Gentiles does he provoke dissent (22.21, 22)' (I.444f.). Further details are given below in the notes on the verses.

This form of the conversion story is undoubtedly suited to a Jewish audience (see pp. 1144f. for the adaptation of virtually the same material to a different audience in ch. 26); whether it was suited to the particular Jewish audience that Paul had before him is not so clear. He is accused (21.28, 29) of teaching all men everywhere against the people, the Law, and the (Holy) Place, and of having brought Greeks into the Temple and thus of profaning it. In the background lurks the report that he teaches all the Jews among the Gentiles apostasy from Moses, saying that they should not circumcise their children or walk in accordance with the (Mosaic) customs (21.21). None of these matters is touched upon, except in the assertion that Paul is a Jew, that he is (or has been) zealous for God, and was educated by the great Pharisee, Gamaliel, also that it was in the Temple that he received the commission to act as a missionary to the Gentiles. The immediate charge that he had brought Greeks into the Temple receives no notice at all. To say this is not to say (as some do) that the speech is irrelevant. On this occasion and throughout the rest of the book Paul insists that he is a Jew, and to make this point as Luke wishes to make it it was necessary to show that the conversion was within and not from Judaism (so e.g. Schmithals 202, arguing further that Luke was concerned to combat the Pauline *Irrlehrer*). In this sense the opening verses were relevant. Relevant also is the conversion itself, told as an event within Judaism: supernatural encounters must be taken seriously. It was no use denying that Paul had lived in the Gentile world and in close relation with Gentile communities, but this was not his choice; he himself had told God that he would be an effective witness to Jews (vv. 19, 20). It was God who had overruled this and sent him to the Gentiles (vv. 18, 21).

At this point the speech breaks off. It is often said that this is an artificial trick of Lucan style. The speech is in fact complete; Luke uses interruption for effect, as he does in 4.1; 7.54, 57; 10.44; 17.32; 19.28; 23.7. This may be true—probably is true in the other cases. It may not be true here. The speaker might well have continued: My mission to the Gentiles was undertaken only on God's command, not at my desire. Obedience to God required contact with Gentiles (whom I was seeking to bring to the Jewish God) which ordinarily a Jew would not have undertaken. I was indeed ready to admit Gentiles to God's people without circumcision or other legal observance, but Jews I never told not to circumcise their children or neglect the divine precepts. Continued in some such way as this, the speech could have been entirely relevant to the situation in which it is placed. One hesitates however to affirm that so much was in Luke's mind, though he no doubt did see that if the course and circumstances of Paul's mission were to be justified at all the justification must include reference to the event which was at once conversion and commission, not because it was psychologically impressive but because it included the presence of Jesus, alive after crucifixion.

The mob violence that follows the interruption of the speech brings the Romans into the story and thus completes the main elements of the dramatic structure of the rest of Acts. The story is told simply; the points of difficulty are dealt with in the detailed notes below. It was the tribune's duty to preserve order, hence to remove one who was evidently provoking disorder. It was conventional to 'examine' him by the use of the lash, the sure method (it was believed) of eliciting truth. It was natural that a Roman citizen should wish to save himself from a possibly fatal flogging by drawing attention to his status and his rights. Whether Paul in fact was a Roman citizen (see 16.37), and how, if he was, he could in the circumstances prove the fact to the tribune, are very difficult questions; see the notes.

Weiser, in a clearly set out paragraph (607), gives nine reasons for rejecting the historicity of the paragraph and seeing it as Lucan redaction. The reasons are by no means of equal value, but to go through them will cover important ground. (1) Paul had been weakened by a severe beating; it is hardly conceivable that he should wish to make a speech, and should make one in unfavourable circumstances. But it is conceivable, and there are parallels; John

Wesley was violently mobbed at Wednesbury, escaped with a torn waistcoat, and spoke with vigour. (2) The tribune would hardly conclude from the fact that he spoke Greek that Paul was not the 'Jew of Egypt'; many Egyptian Jews spoke Greek. This objection may rest upon a misinterpretation of 21.38 (see the note); but it is probably true that the conversation between Paul and the tribune was written by Luke. (3) The silence of 21.40; 22.2 is improbable. A matter of opinion; given a speaker of intense personality it is quite likely. (4) The speech does not deal with the mob's complaints. See above. (5) The account of the conversion is Luke's editing of the story of 9.1–19; true. (6) The Temple vision and the reference to Stephen are probably redactional; probably true. (7) The end of the speech is artificial. The point is dealt with above. (8) The shout αἶρε ... τὸν τοιοῦτον (v. 22) recalls the redactional words of Lk. 23.18; Acts 21.36. There is no force in this observation. (9) References to Roman citizenship are all redactional. Perhaps; but how, without citizenship, would Paul get himself transported to Rome?

These observations do no more than suggest that the material in this chapter has passed through Luke's hands; this is undoubtedly true. He has made and emphasized the point that Paul the Christian was a good Jew, as well as a Christian, a Tarsiote, and a Roman. He was probably aware of the fact that there were those who identified Christians with revolutionaries and trouble-makers, and made an opportunity of showing (to his own satisfaction) that Paul was a quite different kind of person. For the general picture of a tumult, as a result of which the Romans took over Paul's custody from the lynch-minded Jews, there is much to be said. Luke's own redactional statement is made in 28.17, where Paul says that he was handed over to the Romans. The Roman rescue of Paul from fanatical Jews, and their, on the whole, fair-minded treatment of him, which sets in motion the long legal process, is not far from the truth.

1. Ἄνδρες ἀδελφοὶ καὶ πατέρες. Cf. 7.2. The simple address without πατέρες is more common; here Paul is showing proper respect to a gathering which will include his seniors as well as contemporaries and juniors. He asks their attention (ἀκούσατε).

μου stands first after ἀκούσατε, according to BDR § 473.1, n. 2 in agreement with 'die alte Regel, dass unbetonte (enklitische) Prono-mina udgl dem Satzanfang möglichst nahe gerückt werden.' In § 173.1, n. 1 μου is taken as one member of a double (object) genitive, but it may be better to take it as a possessive (the difference in meaning is in the end scarcely perceptible) and as bearing some emphasis: Instead of listening to those who call for my death (21.36), pay attention to what I have to say. Paul may (v. 2; 21.40) have been speaking a Semitic language, but it is not easy to fit μου into one. Delitzsch's Hebrew is interesting: שמעו־נא ואדברה ואצטדק. The

Syriac diverges evern further from the Greek idiom. The Greek is Luke's own.

ἀπολογία is a speech in defence. Haenchen (596) rightly observes that this becomes the theme of the concluding chapters: 24.10; 25.8, 16; 26.1f., 24. So Schille (421): 'Er zielt auf eine Verteidigung der Kirche im Ganzen.' '"Verteidigung" ist das Stichwort für den Schlussteil der Apostelgeschichte.' Roloff (320), also correctly, observes that the speech aims at 'Solidisierung des Paulus mit seinen Gegnern'. See further on v. 3.

2. For τῇ Ἑβραΐδι διαλέκτῳ see on 21.40. προσεφώνει is the reading of ℵ A B 𝔐; P⁷⁴ L 36 614 945 1739 1891 2495 *al* have προσεφώνησεν; D E Ψ 1241 2464 *pc* vg have προσφωνεῖ. Grammatically a case can be made for each of these verbal forms. The use of a Semitic language presumably surprised the crowd, as the use of Greek had surprised the tribune (21.37), though they had not accused him of being a Greek invading the Temple but of bringing Greeks into the Temple (21.28).

παρέσχον ἡσυχίαν is a standard phrase. See Job 34.29; Josephus, *Ant.* 5.235, τοῦ πλήθους ἡσυχίαν αὐτοῦ παρασχόντος; Plutarch, *Coriolanus* 18 (222), παρέσχεν αὐτῷ σιωπὴν καί ἡσυχίαν ὁ δῆμος. Silence naturally implies a measure of attention. D has ἡσύχασαν. The meaning is unchanged; as frequently, the Western text displays freedom with the wording of the text rather any difference in the understanding of its meaning.

With καὶ φησίν the speech proper is introduced.

3. Paul introduces himself as *a man, a Jew*, ἀνὴρ Ἰουδαῖος, coordinating the noun with ἀνήρ (as at 10.28; cf. 21.39); see BDR § 242, n. 1.

γεγεννημένος ἐν Ταρσῷ τῆς Κιλικίας is much the same as Ταρσεὺς ἐκ Κιλικίας in 21.39. For the partitive genitive of the land in which a town is situated see BDR § 164.3 (with the impressive term chorographic genitive!).

At this pricient the question of the punctuation and construction of the sentence must be raised, together with the interpretation of ἐν τῇ πόλει ταύτῃ; does this mean *in Tarsus* or *in Jerusalem*? It has been customary to place a comma after Γαμαλιήλ and another after νόμου. The meaning then is: I was born in Tarsus, brought up in this city (?) at the feet of Gamaliel, instructed strictly in the ancestral law, being zealous for God. This construction was called in question by W. C. van Unnik, *Tarsus of Jeruzalem* (Mededelingen der Konin-klijke Nederlandse Akademie van Wetenschappen, Afd. Letter-kunde, 15:5, 1952: ET 1962), who concluded (169) that the verse means, 'I am a Jewish man, born in Tarsus in Cilicia, but my parental home, where I received my earliest upbringing, was in this city (Jerusalem) and with Gamaliel, well known to you, I received a strict education as a Pharisee, so that I was zealous for God, just as you all are up to this day.' This means punctuating after τῇ πόλει ταύτῃ (though in the translation quoted van Unnik has no stop at this point) and after νόμου. Two main reasons are given for van Unnik's punctuation. (1) The three participles, γεγεννημέος, ἀνατεθραμμένος, πεπαιδευμένος, correspond to the three recognized stages in which the career of a notable person would be sketched (in *Who's Who*, as well as in Hellenistic literature—which to some extent lessens the force of the argument): birth, childhood, education. Haenchen (597) agrees with van Unnik. (2) To this corresponds the fact that, as van Unnik shows, ἀνατρέφειν refers rather to the upbringing of a child than to such training as would be given by a notable rabbinic teacher such as Gamaliel. This argument is referred to by Turner (*Insights* 83f.), who does not take sides over the punctuation, but argues strongly that *this city* must be Tarsus. 'Unless "this city" refers to Tarsus, St. Paul contradicts what he is reported as saying to Claudius Lysias, when he emphasised his origin in the Greek city of Tarsus and on the basis of so respectable an association, political and cultural, he had begged leave to address the crowd (Acts 21.39).' This argument is baseless; the claim to Tarsiote citizenship no more proves long residence in Tarsus than the claim to Roman citizenship means that Paul had resided in Rome; in each case the citizenship was inherited, C. Burchard (*ZNW* 61 (1970), 168f.) agrees with van Unnik, making two refinements. He places a comma not after νόμου but after πεπαιδευμένος, and connects κατὰ ... νόμου with ζηλωτὴς ... θεοῦ:

> I am a Jew,
> > born in Tarsus in Cilicia,
> > brought up in this city,
> > educated at the feet of Gamaliel,
> A zealot for God in accordance with the ancestral law,
> > As all of you are to this day.

For the translation 'bis auf den heutigen Tag' he cites *Joseph and Aseneth* 4.7, ἔστι δὲ οὗτος ... παρθένος ὡς σὺ σήμερον (cf. ed. Philonenko 4.9, ἔστιν Ἰωσήφ ... παρθένος ὡς σὺ σήμερον). There is little point in Burchard's translation; if you are a virgin on this day you have been a virgin up to this day. It is probable that Luke meant that Paul received not only his higher but also his elementary education not in Tarsus but in Jerusalem. This if true would mean that his roots were not in Diaspora but in Palestinian Judaism. This seems to be what Luke is saying; whether or not he is correct is another question, which requires further consideration. J. Jeremias (*FS* Black (1979), 94) writes: 'Die Apostelgeschichte behauptet, Paulus sei Theologe und zwar Schüler des Hilleliten Rabban Gamli'el I gewesen (Ac 22.3). Die Nachprüfung ergibt: der Verfasser der

Paulusbriefe verfügte in der Tat über die theologische Bildung seiner Zeit und gehörte der hillelitischen Schule an.' Cf. K. Haacker, 'War Paulus Hillelit?' in *Das Institutum Judaicum Tübingen 1971–1972* (1972), 106–20. Bultmann (*E & F* 131) thinks that Acts 22.3 cannot be correct since Gal. 1.22 shows that before his conversion Paul 'has not resided for any length of time in Jerusalem'. Gal. 1.22 does not in fact show this; it claims only that Paul was not personally known to the Christian churches in Judaea. And Paul's claim that he advanced in Judaism beyond his contemporaries (Gal. 1.14) almost demands residence in Jerusalem, where Paul's strongest rivals would be found. The same claim refutes the assertion by Schmithals (202) that there is nothing to show that Paul could read Hebrew or speak Aramaic. Betz (107) thinks that this verse proves nothing regarding the historicity of the connection with Gamaliel. It is characteristic of θεῖοι ἄνδρες to provide accounts of their parentage and education. Luke does this on Paul's behalf.

For παρὰ τοὺς πόδας cf. Aboth 1.4, Be in the dust of their feet (i.e. of the חכמים).

κατὰ ἀκρίβειαν = ἀκριβῶς (*Begs.* 4.278). For ἀκρίβεια and cognates in relation to Jewish religion cf. 26.5; Josephus, *Ant.* 17.41; *War* 2.162; Conzelmann (125) adds *Life* 191; also Isocrates 7.40.

For ζηλωτὴς ὑπάρχων cf. Gal. 1.14. See also (for ζηλ. θεοῦ) Num. 25.13; Rom. 10.2; also Epictetus 2.14.13; Musonius Rufus 37.3 (many other references to Musonius are given by P. W. van der Horst, *NovT* 16 (1974), 309).

Roloff (322) comments, 'Das "ich bin Jude" ist gleichsam das Motto, dem alles folgende untersteht.' See on v. 1; and contrast Phil. 3.2–7.

There are in this verse a number of minor textual variants. After ἐγώ (P⁷⁴ᵛⁱᵈ ℵ A B D E 33 36 453 945 1739 1891 *pc*), Ψ 𝔐 60 add μέν. B has Γαμαλιήλον, making the word declinable; see M. 2.144. For πεπαιδευμένος D has παιδευόμενος, an unthinking variation, certainly wrong. ὑπάρχων is omitted by D latt. For τοῦ θεοῦ, 88 vg have τοῦ νόμου, sy^(h**) has τῶν πατρικῶν μου παραδόσεων (cf. Gal. 1.14); Ψ 614 2495 *pc* vg^(mss) have no genitive after ὑπάρχων. For πάντες ὑμεῖς, P⁷⁴ has πάντες, D has ὑμεῖς πάντες. In all these cases the text of NA²⁶ is correct.

4. Practically the whole of this verse appears in 9.2, 3. Cf. 26.10. Christianity is referred to as ἡ ὁδός (9.2); Paul has Christians bound, and that both men and women. Hengel (74) thinks that this verse (ἄχρι θανάτου) exaggerates. At 22.19 (cf. 26.11) Paul inflicts only synagogue punishments. A synagogue beating, however, could kill.

5. Paul in 9.1 makes contact with the High Priest and receives official letters (9.2, to the synagogues). He goes to Damascus with a view to finding Christians and bringing them bound to Jerusalem for punishment. Here πᾶν τὸ πρεσβυτέριον, *the whole body of elders*, is associated with the High Priest, as it naturally would be. For πρεσβυτέριον see Lk. 22.66 (1 Tim. 4.14). *The brothers* are, as at v. 1, Jewish (not Christian) brothers.

ἄξων is a future participle, expressing purpose. ἐκεῖσε (*thither*) is used where ἐκεῖ (*there*) would be expected (but see below). On this (mis)use see Rutherford (*Phrynichus* 114): 'In late Greek the distinction between ποῖ ποῦ, οἷ οὗ, ὅπου ὅποι, ἐκεῖ and ἐκεῖσε, practically disappeared.'

On this verse Delebecque has detailed and important grammatical notes. (1) παρ' ὧν is 'relative complexe' (as at 11.6; 12.4; [15.29]; 17.23; 19.25; [25.18]; 26.7, [12]; [27.17]; 28.8, 15—(passages in square brackets though given by Delebecque seem doubtful or mistaken). 'La phrase équivaut à οἷς, παρ'αὐτῶν ... δεξάμενος ... ἐπορευόμην' (106). καί after ὧν is 'explétif'. (2) πρός cannot mean *pour*; it is *contre*. (3) ἐκεῖσε is used with a double meaning. 'L'expression équivaut à ἄξων ἐκεῖσε (avec mouvement!) τοὺς ἐκεῖ (sans mouvement) ὄντας. De là vient que ἐκεῖσε est pris ici, un peu librement, dans le sens de δεῦρο' (107). The resulting translation is: 'Comme non seulement l'archiprêtre, m'en est témoin mais encore tout le collège des anciens, du fait desquels, pour avoir reçu d'eux des lettres contre des frères, j'étais en train de suivre le chemin de Damas, chargé de mener attachés, ici à Jérusalem, ceux même qui étaient là, afin qu'ils soient châtiés.'

Schneider (2.321) takes the sentence differently: '... mit "Briefen" "an die (jüdischen) Brüder in (den Synagogen von) Damaskus"'. ἀδελφοί are Jews, οἱ ἐκεῖσε (= ἐκεῖ) ὄντες are Christians. Cf. Haenchen (598).

δεδεμένοι, *bound*, is illustrated in *ND* 1.49.

After ἀρχιερεύς, 614 *pc* sy^h** add Ἀνανίας (from 23.2).

6. The construction differs from that of 9.3, but most of the significant words are found in both accounts: πορευομένῳ (πορεύεσθαι); ἐγγίζοντι (ἐγγίζειν); τῇ Δαμασκῷ (identical); ἐξαίφνης (identical); ἐκ τοῦ οὐρανοῦ (identical); περιαστράψαι φῶς (περιήστραψεν φῶς). The present verse adds περὶ μεσημβρίαν, *about noon* (for the meaning of μεσημβρία see on 8.26). The intention may be to stress that this was no dream but an objective occurrence. περὶ ἐμέ is added; this is obvious enough. The construction here is ἐγένετο followed by a dative and an accusative and infinitive. Cf. 20.16, and see BDR § 409.4. One or two details recall Deut. 28.28f., but it is doubtful whether Luke had this passage in mind.

The reading of D is closer to 9.3, and provides a good example of free Western re-writing: ἐγγίζοντι δ[έ μ]οι μεσημβρίας Δαμασκῷ ἐξέφνης ἀ[πὸ] τοῦ οὐρανοῦ περιήστραψέ μ[ε] φῶς ἱκανὸν περὶ ἐμέ.

7. For ἔπεσά (weak aorist ending with strong aorist stem; see M. 2.208; BDR §§ 80, 81) τε, D has καὶ ἔπεσον. Again the construction differs but the significant words are found in 9.5: ἔπεσα (πεσών); ἤκουσα (ἤκουσεν); φωνῆς λεγούσης μοι (φωνὴν—note the case— λέγουσαν αὐτῷ); Σαοὺλ Σαούλ, τί με διώκεις; (identical). The main difference in wording is that here we have εἰς τὸ ἔδαφος; in 9.4, ἐπὶ τὴν γῆν. There is no difference in meaning. In construction the difference is between a main verb and coordinate participle.

In 9.4 E 431 sy[p h**], and in 9.6, 629 it add σκληρόν σοι πρὸς κέντρα λακτίζειν; the same words are added in 22.7 by E gig vg[mss] sy[h]. They are due to assimilation to 26.14; see the note on that verse.

8. This verse substantially reproduces 9.5. The main differences are that in ch. 9 Saul's words are introduced by εἶπεν δέ, here by ἐγὼ δὲ ἀπεκρίθην; Jesus' words by ὁ δέ, here by εἶπέν τε πρὸς ἐμέ; here the name Jesus is followed by ὁ Ναζωραῖος (added in 9.5 by A C E 104 *pc* h p t sy[p h**]. For Ναζωραῖος see on 2.22 and add H. P. Rüger, *ZNW* 72 (1981), 257–63.

9. At this point the narratives diverge, in order and to some extent in substance. The parallel to this verse is found in 9.7.

Here Paul's companions are described as οἱ δὲ σὺν ἐμοὶ ὄντες; in 9.7 they are οἱ δὲ ἄνδρες οἱ συνοδεύοντες αὐτῷ, and it is added that εἱστήκεισαν ἐνεοί. Here it is said that τὸ μὲν φῶς ἐθεάσαντο; there is no parallel in ch. 9, but the companions are described as μηδένα δὲ θεωροῦντες. The most interesting difference is that here in 22.9 the companions τὴν φωνὴν οὐκ ἤκουσαν τοῦ λαλοῦντός μοι, whereas in 9.7 it is said ἀκούοντες μὲν τῆς φωνῆς. Grammarians differ on the possibility of explaining the apparent contradiction by means of the different cases that follow ἀκούειν. Moulton (M. 1.66) seems to have regarded the issue as clear: 'The fact that the maintenance of an old and well-known distinction between the acc. and the gen. with ἀκούω saves the author of Ac 9.7 and 22.9 from a patent self-contradiction, should by itself be enough to make us recognise it for Luke, and for other writers until it is proved wrong.' Turner (M. 3.233) is more cautious: 'There may be something in the difference between the gen. in Ac 9.7 (the men with Paul heard *the sound*) and the accus. in Ac 22.9 (they did not *understand the voice*)', though this does not seem to be quite what Zerwick (§ 69), to whom Turner refers, says: 'Solent quidem distinguere inter "vocem audire" et "vocem intelligere". Physice percipere haberet genitivum, intelligere id quod dicitur, haberet accusativum. Sed haec distinctio est arbitraria et potius facta "ad hoc". Fortasse licet explicare rem potius ita: comites audiunt sonitum (quem Paulus et Lucas sciunt esse Domini et ut talem exhibent: ἡ φωνή) sed sonitum non ut vocem alicuius loquentis cognoscunt.' This however does not explain 9.4,

ἤκουσεν φωνήν, and 22.7, ἤκουσα φωνῆς. It is wise to agree with
Moule (*IB* 36) 'It seems to me (*pace Proleg.* 66 [= M. 1.66])
impossible to find a satisfactory distinction in meaning between the
Gen. and the Acc. in Acts 9.7 ... and 22.9 ...'. BDR § 173.2, n. 5
note the facts and make no attempt to explain them. BA 62 make an
interesting comparison with Maximus of Tyre 9.7.d.f., but do not
claim that this explains the variation in case. See also H. R.
Moehring, in *NovT* 3 (1959), 80–99: 'To insist upon a difference of
meaning in Acts ix.7 and xxii.9 seems, to the present writer at least,
impossible' (98). We must conclude that Luke was writing up a
familiar story freshly, and in each case included what seemed to him
to be impressive details in the most impressive way he could think
of.

After ἐθεάσαντο, D E Ψ 𝔐 gig sy^h sa add καὶ ἔμφοβοι ἐγένοντο.
Cf. 9.7, εἱστήκεισαν ἐνεοί.

10. In ch. 9 there is no parallel to Paul's question, τί ποιήσω,
κύριε; which admirably expresses his readiness to accept obediently
any charge laid upon him. The Lord's words however are closely
parallel in the two accounts. For ἀναστὰς πορεύου, the earlier
narrative has ἀνάστηθι καὶ εἴσελθε; for εἰς Δαμασκόν, it has εἰς τὴν
πόλιν; for κἀκεῖ σοι λαληθήσεται, it has λαληθήσεταί σοι; for περὶ
πάντων ὧν τέτακταί σοι ποιῆσαι, it has (the largest difference) ὅ τί
σε δεῖ ποιεῖν.

For the present imperative πορεύου (where an aorist might have
been expected) see BDR § 336.3, n. 5. πορεύεσθαι is one of a group
of verbs which constitute an exception to the rule: 'Einige Imp. des
Präsens können für bestimmte einmalige Handlungen gebraucht
werden wie ἔγειρε, πορεύου ...'. See however 9.11; 18.26,
πορεύθητι.

The perfect τέτακται shows that the order is already in the thought
of Jesus, having been in the eternal thought of God (Delebecque
107).

11. There are close parallels with 9.8. οὐκ ἐνέβλεπον is parallel to
οὐδὲν ἔβλεπε; χειραγωγούμενος ὑπὸ τῶν συνόντων μοι puts into
the passive the active χειραγωγοῦντες δὲ αὐτόν, which continues
with εἰσήγαγον εἰς Δαμασκόν, for which the present verse has
ἦλθον εἰς Δαμασκόν.

There is no parallel in ch. 22 to ἠγέρθη δὲ Σαῦλος ἀπὸ τῆς γῆς,
unless we follow d (ut autem surrexit non videbam) gig sy^hmg sa;
Clark thinks that the original Western text was, ὡς δὲ ἀνέστην, οὐκ
ἐνέβλεπον. B, with οὐδὲν ἔβλεπον, agrees more closely with ch. 9,
and this reading is preferred by Moule (*IB* 89), apparently because
the role of ἐν in ἐνέβλεπον is far from clear. Probably it is a form of
emphasis, like the English *a thing* in 'I could not see a thing.'
Whereas ch. 9 has ἀνεῳγμένων δὲ τῶν ὀφθαλμῶν αὐτοῦ, ch. 22 has

ἀπὸ τῆς δόξης τοῦ φωτὸς ἐκείνου. M. 2.461 considers that this causal use of ἀπό (cf. 11.19; 12.14) may be due to the causal use of מן, which ἀπό renders in the LXX, but observes that it is also classical.

12. As in ch. 9, the story moves into a second stage with the introduction of Ananias, though here there is nothing of his vision of and conversation with the Lord (9.10–16). Some features of that conversation, however, are taken up in the conversation between Ananias and Saul (vv. 13–16). Ananias is differently described. In 9.10 he is a disciple; here he is εὐλαβὴς κατὰ τὸν νόμον, μαρτυρούμενος ὑπὸ πάντων τῶν κατοικούντων Ἰουδαίων, presumably though not quite certainly a Jew (Cornelius in ch. 10 might have been similarly described). That he should have been a Jew does not mean that he cannot have been also a Christian disciple. He was a pious man, and his piety was determined by the Law. Many MSS substitute εὐσεβής for εὐλαβή͵͂, without significant change of meaning; the adjective is omitted altogether by P⁷⁴ and Augustine. The short text is very difficult; it might be necessary to connect κατὰ τὸν νόμον with μαρτυρούμενος: he was well known to live according to the Law. This however is anything but satisfactory. For the use of μαρτυρεῖσθαι, *to have a good reputation with*, see 6.3; 16.2.

κατοικούντων is used without any indication of where the persons in question lived; no doubt for this reason ἐν (+ τῇ P⁴¹) Δαμασκῷ was added by P⁴¹ Ψ 𝔐 vgᵐˢˢ syʰ sa, ἐκεῖ by gig (syᵖ).

It was important that Paul should be instructed not by a Gentile or by an apostate from the Law (Calvin 2.215). 'Dass Hananias damals schon Glied der christlichen Gemeinde war, weiss ja nur der Leser!' (Roloff 323).

13. The opening words give the sense of 9.17a but that verse adds that Ananias laid his hands on Saul. In both passages Ananias begins with the words Σαοὺλ ἀδελφέ, accepting Paul as already a Christian brother. The simple command, ἀνάβλεψον, summarizes the longer statement (9.17), The Lord has sent me, Jesus who appeared to you on the way by which you were coming, that you may recover your sight and be filled with the Holy Spirit. The cure of Saul's blindness is described with the use of the same word, ἀναβλέπειν, in both passages. In 9.18 there is the narrative third person singular, ἀνέβλεψεν, in 22.13 the first person singular, αὐτῇ τῇ ὥρᾳ ἀνέβλεψα εἰς αὐτόν. For ἀνέβλεψα, 104 1739 1891 *pc* have ἐνέβλεψα, P⁷⁴ A have ἔβλεψα. εἰς αὐτόν is omitted by P⁴¹ *pc* d sa— possibly (Metzger 487) to accommodate both meanings of ἀναβλέπειν (to look up (at); to recover sight).

Saul's recovery of sight took place αὐτῇ τῇ ὥρᾳ. This is one of a number of passages adduced by Moule (*IB* 93, 122) as exceptions to the rule that if αὐτός is to be used as an adjective meaning *same* it must be placed in the position of an attributive adjective; for *at the same hour* one would (according to the rule) expect τῇ αὐτῇ ὥρᾳ. The matter is discussed in M. 1.91 ('In Luke particularly we feel that the pronoun means little more than "that"'); BDR § 288.2, n. 4 (with reference to the Aramaic בה־שעתא); M. 2.432 (using Acts 16.18; 22.13, where 'Semitic sources are not in question', to counter the suggestion of Semitism); Black, *AA* 109–12 (concluding (111) that 'the temporal conjunction (ἐν) αὐτῇ τῇ ὥρᾳ is, therefore, a Lucan Aramaism'); differently Wilcox (128–30). If the expression is an Aramaism it is so in the sense of a Septuagintalism (see Dan. 3.6; 5.5—LXX and Theodotion; 3.15—Theodotion). But it is probably best to treat it as an extension of the usual meaning of αὐτὸς ὁ and translate *that very hour*.

14. Ananias here gives the substance of what is said to him by the Lord in 9.15; the wording is in the main different. He refers first to *the God of our* (thus showing—see v. 12—that he is a Jew and not merely a Jewish sympathizer) *fathers*; he and Saul are servants of the God of the OT; Christianity (it is implied) is the true version of Judaism and Christians are heirs of the OT.

For προχειρίζειν see 3.20 and the note, also 26.16. Material in *ND* 1.28f.; 3.82 adds little. That God has appointed Paul to a special function corresponds with the statement (9.15) that he is a *chosen vessel*. *Begs.* 4.280 emphasizes that the word means *appointed*, not *fore-ordained*, but appointment must logically precede the assumption of the function in question, and in a theological context this verges on fore-ordination. The appointment is in the first instance to conversion and vocation. This is expressed in three clauses: *to know his will, to see the Righteous One*, and *to hear a voice from his mouth*.

It is not clear what sense Luke gives to the first clause: God's will in relation to what? This cannot be simply God's will for Paul's own subsequent service for this is dealt with in v. 15 for the more remote and in v. 16 for the more immediate future. One may guess that Luke's meaning was that, beyond other men, Paul was to understand God's purpose in and his plan for saving mankind, the whole of mankind, including the Gentiles. But this is quite uncertain; the meaning may be simply that Paul will live on exceptionally intimate terms with God.

The Righteous One, τὸν δίκαιον, can hardly be understood otherwise than as a title of Christ; a simple description of him as a just person would not suffice here, though Stählin (285) may be right in the view that as a Messianic title it also has the effect of emphasizing the guilt of the Jews, who condemned one who was righteous. See 3.14 and the note. Bengel (473) connects ὁ δίκαιος with Paul's emphasis on δικαιοσύνη. 'Haec ejus justitia est summa evangelii, cujus testis fit Paulus. Hunc Justum vidit Paulus etiam deinceps.' Paul sees Christ and hears him speak; this, on the present occasion, is the ground and content of his conversion. The vision and audition constitute the ground of what is said in the next verse.

15. This verse corresponds to 9.15b: τοῦ βαστάσαι τὸ ὄνομά μου ἐνώπιον ἐθνῶν τε καὶ βασιλέων υἱῶν τε Ἰσραήλ. *Bearing my name* is equivalent to *being a witness to him*, μάρτυς; for this word and theme see 1.8 and the note. The stress here is on the fact that Paul is to be a witness πρὸς πάντας ἀνθρώπους, that is, not only to Jews but to Gentiles also (cf. 9.15, quoted above; the point is emphasized by Bauernfeind 252). Presumably, in Luke's narrative, the crowd did not see this point, since it is only when the word Gentiles is explicitly used in v. 21 that their anger becomes uncontrollable. Paul as witness will speak of *the things which you have seen and heard.* BDR § 342.1, n. 3 distinguish between the perfect ἑώρακας and the aorist ἤκουσας. The former is more significant; cf. 1 Cor. 9.1. That Paul has seen the Lord 'gibt ihm dauernd die Weihe des Apostels'. This overlooks the fact that Luke has defined the qualification of an apostle to be that he has accompanied Jesus throughout his ministry and has witnessed a (pre-ascension) resurrection appearance (1.21f.), and very seldom (see 14.4, 14, and the notes) refers to Paul as an apostle. It is significant that neither here, nor in ch. 9 or ch. 26, is it said to Paul at his conversion, You are called to be an apostle. This does not invalidate BDR's grammatical observation (of the force of the perfect tense); it would have been easy to write εἶδες καὶ ἤκουσας. But inferences from it must be carefully expressed.

16. This verse is paralleled in narrative form in 9.18b: ἀνέβλεψέν τε καὶ ἀναστὰς ἐβαπτίσθη.

καὶ νῦν τί μέλλεις; *to delay* or *linger* (Haenchen 599) is a relatively infrequent use of μέλλειν, but quite well attested: Aeschylus, *Prometheus Vinctus* 36, τί μέλλεις καὶ κατοικτίζει μάτην; Sophocles, *Antigone* 448, τί δ'οὐκ ἔμελλον; Conzelmann (126) (who compares τί κωλύει, but for this see on 8.37) thinks that it may have been connected with rites of initiation: *Corpus Hermeticum* 1.26, λοιπόν, τί μέλλεις; Marshall (357) suggests, What are you going to do?

βάπτισαι, middle, not *baptize yourself*, but *get yourself baptized*. The middle voice is used here as (according to some MSS) it is at 1 Cor. 10.2 (of baptism into Moses). Cf. 1 Cor. 6.11, where the middle ἀπελούσασθε is used, probably in the intransitive sense, 'you washed', which of course means, 'you washed yourselves'. Ananias does not say (though he may mean), I will baptize you, or Baptize yourself. But it is clear that baptism takes place as the result of a decision made by the baptized person. Thus Zerwick (§ 232), 'Fac ut baptizaris et abluaris'; similarly BDR § 317, n. 1; also Dinkler, *Signum Crucis* 211, 226.

ἀπόλουσαι accompanies βάπτισαι, reinforcing the interpretation of the middle voice given above and also giving an interpretation of baptism: it is for the washing away, that is, for the forgiveness of sins. This is explicit at 2.38; cf. Bultmann (*Theologie* 139). The thought is persistent through the NT; cf. also Barnabas 11.11. It is possible in Paul's case to relate it specifically to his resistance to the Gospel and persecution of Christians, but the words attributed to Ananias are probably formulaic rather than specific.

ἐπικαλούμενος τὸ ὄνομα αὐτοῦ helps to interpret the use of εἰς τὸ ὄνομα, ἐν (ἐπὶ) τῷ ὀνόματι, in other baptismal sayings. See on 3.6. The name is not a magical instrument effecting supernatural results; the name is invoked, that is, it signifies faith and obedience directed towards Christ. Bousset (*Kyrios Christos* (1913), 277), refers to Barnabas 16.8 with the similar formula, ἐλπίσαντες ἐπὶ τὸ ὄνομα.

For καὶ νῦν cf. 3.17; 10.5, and see BDR § 442.8d, n. 26. Like the Hebrew ועתה, which it represents in the LXX, it often introduces commands and questions, but it is not a Semitism.

There is no reference here to the Holy Spirit; contrast 9.17.

17. The construction of this verse is astounding; surprisingly it does not seem to have provoked correction on the part of copyists. Perhaps we are too fastidious. The speaker appears first in the dative case, μοι ὑποστρέψαντι (after ἐγένετο), next in the genitive, προσευχομένου μου (genitive absolute), and finally in the accusative, γενέσθαι με (accusative and infinitive, also dependent on ἐγένετο). Zerwick (§ 49) describes this as 'mira combinatio'. Cf. 15.22. The meaning is undoubtedly clear.

Paul here, omitting 9.19b-25, narrates part of the story of his conversion and commissioning that does not appear at all in ch. 9 (or in ch. 26). After the events near and in Damascus he returned to Jerusalem. The aorist participle ὑποστρέψαντι means that the return journey was completed; ὑποστρέφοντι (P74 33 *pc*) should mean that Paul was on the way back. This does not agree with ἐν τῷ ἱερῷ; it may be that the present participle as the harder reading should be taken as original, but if Luke wrote it he must nevertheless have meant that Paul had reached Jerusalem.

For ἐγένετο with the dative of the person to whom the event happened, followed by an accusative and infinitive describing the event, cf. 20.16; 22.6; and see BDR § 409.4, n. 6.

Having returned to the city Paul was praying in the Temple. Cf. 3.1. In the epistles Paul shows no interest in the Temple; that he should, on the occasion of a visit to Jerusalem, have used it as a place of prayer cannot be regarded as impossible, though Lüdemann (248) thinks that to place the call and the vision in the Temple contradicts

Gal. 1.15 and is therefore unhistorical. Haenchen (600–604) discusses at length the author's intention in giving the Temple episode:
it shows that Paul had been a Jewish ζηλωτής, had wished to be a
witness to his own people, and had gone to the Gentiles only on
direct and repeated command from Jesus.

Prayer turned to ἔκστασις; see 10.10; 11.5 for Peter's ἔκστασις,
with the notes. Paul fell into a trance, outside the ordinary limits of
consciousness.

18. ἰδεῖν continues the infinitives dependent on ἐγένετο: It
happened that I fell ... and saw. ... ℵ 36 453 *pc* d co have εἶδον,
which makes equally good sense.

αὐτόν is of course the Lord, who had appeared on the road. Why
Paul had returned to Jerusalem we do not know; he is now told to
leave the city quickly. This is emphasized by the use of both
σπεῦσον and ἐν τάχει. σπεύδειν is in the NT characteristic of Luke
(Lk., 3 times; Acts 20.16; 22.18; 2 Pet. 3.12) but it is common
enough in Greek of all periods. So is ἐν τάχει, equivalent to the
English *at speed*.

A prolonged stay in Jerusalem would serve no useful purpose. For
παραδέχεσθαι cf. 16.21: They (the—Jewish—inhabitants of Jerusalem) will not accept your testimony. Paul was to be a μάρτυς (v. 15),
but his μαρτυρία would find no credence here.

This story of a visit to Jerusalem is not only wanting in Acts 9.29f.
and Gal. 1.17–19; it can hardly be fitted into them.

19. In this and the next verse Paul appears to argue with the Lord,
asserting that it was in fact probable that the Jews would believe
what he said. They would believe because they knew Paul's past and
would conclude that his position had been changed only by overwhelming considerations.

There is no reason why αὐτοί should not be properly emphatic:
They themselves know. ἐπίστασθαι is a Lucan word: Acts 9 times (8
in chs. 15–28); rest of the NT, 5 times.

ἤμην φυλακίζων may be a periphrastic imperfect (I used to
imprison) or simply descriptive (I was (at work) imprisoning). There
is little difference. See BDR § 353.3, n. 8. See 8.3; 9.2 for Paul's
activity as a persecutor.

20. See 7.58 (the witnesses laid down their clothes at the feet
of a young man called Saul) and 8.1 (Saul was in agreement,
συνευδοκῶν, with his killing, τῇ ἀναιρέσει αὐτοῦ).

Stephen was a μάρτυς; Paul is to be a μάρτυς (v. 15). It seems
probable that Luke understood Paul to have taken Stephen's place,
especially as the leader of a world-wide mission. This was, perhaps,
only superficially true. See Introduction, pp. xcviii, ciiif.

The part of this verse that has no explicit parallel in chs. 7, 8 is ἤμην ἐφεστώς (with συνευδοκῶν and φυλάσσων another periphrastic tense—see v. 19). This was an easy addition; Luke is rewriting traditional material that he has used earlier.

'When Paul in Acts 22.20 calls Stephen the μάρτυς of Jesus, it sounds rather like a title' (Maddox 86 (n. 37)—not quite convincingly).

πρωτομάρτυρος (L 614 945 1739^{v.1.} 1891 2495 *al* sy^h) for μάρτυρος introduces the language of later piety. The addition of τῇ ἀναιρέσει αὐτοῦ by Ψ 𝔐 sy^{(p)} assimilates to 8.1.

At this point the extant part of d ends with the words *adsistens et consentiens*.

21. εἶπεν: the Lord, who had spoken in v. 18, renews his command, knowing that Saul's vocation is to be fulfilled in distant parts.

πορεύου. Moule (*IB* 135) notes that this present imperative is inconsistent with the aorists of v. 18. See however the note on πορεύου in v. 10. If the tense is really significant it may be taken to mean something like, *Be on your way*; possibly, *Start your journey*.

ἐξαποστελῶ, future, is surprising; was not the Lord sending Paul then, in the present? D improves to ἐξαποστέλλω, E to ἀποστέλλω. B has the simple future, ἀποστελῶ. The tense is probably affected by the thought that the fulfilment of the mission belongs to the future.

Whether ἔθνη means Gentiles or simply (far off, μακράν) nations, the meaning is the same. Paul is sent to non-Jews. It is, according to Luke, this that brings the anger of the crowd to a climax.

Knowledge of these words seems to be reflected in apocryphal Acts.

Passio Sanctorum Apostolorum Petri et Pauli 38 (L.-B. 1.153): Vade et ego ero in te Spiritus vitae omnibus credentibus in me; et omnia quaecumque doceris et feceris ego iustificabo.

Acta Petri et Pauli 59 (L.-B. 1.204): Πορεύου, ὅτι ἐγὼ ἔσομαι μετὰ σοῦ, καὶ πάντα ὅσα ἂν εἴπῃς ἢ ποιήσῃς ἐγὼ δικαιώσω.

Schneider (2.322) suggests that Luke could not put this commission in ch. 9 because he was making Peter in ch. 10 the first missionary to the Gentiles. Schmithals (205) notes that the Gentile mission is against Paul's own will. But Luke does not say this, only that Paul thought that the Jews would listen to him. Weiser (612) makes the better point that the evangelizing of the Gentiles is the will of the God of Israel.

22. ἤκουον, imperfect, *they went on listening*; followed by the aorist ἐπῆραν: at that point, *they lifted up* ... In the NT ἐπαίρειν τὴν φωνήν is peculiar to Luke (Lk. 11.27; Acts 2.14; 14.11; 22.22); it is used in the LXX (Judges 21.2 (A); Ruth 1.9,14; 2 Kdms 13.26; Ps. 92(93).3—rendering נשא קול and might seem to be one of Luke's Septuagintalisms if it did not appear also in classical authors

(Demosthenes 18.291 (323), ἐπάρας τὴν φωνήν; Philostratus, *Apollonius* 5.33).

αἶρε ἀπὸ τῆς γῆς recalls 21.36 (see the note), also Lk. 23.18; Jn 19.15; and Isa. 53.8, quoted at Acts 8.33. It is possible that Luke wishes to draw a parallel between the suffering of Jesus and that of Paul. Cf. Wilcox (67, 68). Davies (*Land* 282f.) thinks that γῆ should be understood not as *earth* but as *land*; Paul is unclean and should therefore be driven out of the land of Israel. This is unlikely in view of the next clause, *it is not fit that he should live*. He should therefore be killed, put out of the land of the living. That the mob repeat their cry is 'Zeichen unbelehrbarer Verhärtung' (Weiser 612); perhaps rather of Luke's skill in heightening the dramatic feeling.

On the tense (imperfect though it refers to the present) of καθῆκεν see BDR § 358.2, n. 3: 'Das Impf. enthält dann eine Aufforderung: Apg 22.22 οὐ γὰρ καθῆκεν αὐτὸν ζῆν, "denn er darf nicht am Leben bleiben" (sie fordern zur Tötung auf).'

'Freilich ist dieser von den Hörern erzwungene Abbruch auch hier wieder (vgl. 4.1; 17.32; 23.7) nur literarischer Stilmittel. In Wirklichkeit ist alles, was zu sagen war, gesagt' (Roloff 324f.). See however p. 1032.

23. In addition to shouting, κραυγαζόντων τε (so A B C; P⁷⁴ ℵ D E Ψ 𝔐 have δέ), the crowd find other ways of expressing their feelings.

ῥιπτούντων (from ῥιπτέω; elsewhere in the NT ῥίπτω) τὰ ἱμάτια: this is usually taken to mean *throwing off* their clothes; so e.g. BA 1474. *Begs.* 4.282; 5.275–7 suggests the meaning *waving*. It is perhaps unnecessary to distinguish too nicely. Luke means to describe a frantically excited crowd. Their action is the expression of excitement, not a prophylactic against evil (as Job 2.12; Josephus, *War* 2.322 might suggest). 'Il s'agit de 1a *jactatio togarum*, geste d'une foule excitée' (Delebecque 108). *Acta Isidori* 35ff. might provide a parallel but not as restored by H. A. Musurillo (*The Acts of the Pagan Martyrs* (1954), 137).

κονιορτὸν βαλλόντων εἰς τὸν ἀέρα. Here there is no doubt what is done, and the motive is the same. The dust is not itself a threat that stones will follow, but it is a token of frenzy which will in due course throw anything that comes to hand. Gregory Nazianzen, *Oratio in laudem Basilii* 15 is not a close parallel, nor are those given by Betz (72, 140).

24. The tribune (see 21.31) decided that it was time to put a stop to the riot by removing and dealing with the man who had provoked it. εἰσάγεσθαι passive after a verb of commanding, is not classical (M. 3.138; BDR § 392.4. n. 14), but Luke has already used this construction (21.33) and will do so again (23.3); also in this verse, εἴπας ἀνατάζεσθαι (but D* *pc* have ἀνετάζειν). It is Latin rather than Greek.

Paul is to be brought into the παρεμβολή (see 21.34), the barracks of the Roman troops quartered in Jerusalem. There he will be safe from the mob, but not safe from every kind of injustice: he is to be interrogated with scourges. This is not punishment but the recognized way of 'interviewing' a slave or other lower class and possibly reluctant witness and finding out the truth. ἐξετάζειν (but not ἀνετάζειν) was a technical term for this process. It is the tribune's intention to find out, ἵνα ἐπιγνῷ (γνῷ, P⁷⁴ A 6 33 36 *pc*), the reason why they had so shouted at him. In this indirect question the relative ἥν is used where the interrogative pronoun would have been correct. It has been suggested that the tribune may not have understood the (Hebrew or Aramaic) speech.

It is not easy to know why *Begs.* 4.282 translate ἐπεφώνουν in the text 'they shouted against him' but write the note 'The ἐπι- is not therefore "against" so much as "after", referring to the applause or other demonstration which follows what is said.' It is of course clear that on this occasion the demonstration was not one of applause but of violent rejection. It may be best to render, 'they were shouting him down'. This would be possible with the simple dative, αὐτῷ; there are variants: αὐτοῦ (Ψ 614 *pc*; this goes with the reading κατεφώνουν, contained also in D, which would mean 'to shout down'); περὶ αὐτοῦ (D gig).

For the form εἴπας see BDR § 81.1, n. 1. A more important grammatical question is whether we have here an example of the aorist participle expressing action subsequent to that of the main verb: He ordered him to be brought in … and [then] he said … This is denied by Moulton (M. 1.133, 'Lysias presumably said in one sentence, "Bring him in and examine him"'—aorist participle of coincident action). Turner (M. 3.79f.) seems to allow a few exceptions to the rule (of past action): Mt. 10.4; Jn 11.2; Acts 16.6; 25.13. He does not mention the present case. Nor do BDR § 339.1, n. 4; at § 420.2, n. 3 coordination with a participle of saying (as here) is treated as a special case. See on 16.6 and 25.13; Mt. 10.4 and Jn 11.2 are irrelevant.

μάστιξ represents the Latin *flagrum*.

25. For temporal ὡς see 16.4 and the note.

προτείνειν is *to stretch forward* and is used in a large number of ways. Here the soldiers stretched Paul forward τοῖς ἱμᾶσιν. ἱμάς is a *leather thong*, used for example for a shoe lace (Lk. 3.16; the word is not used at Acts 13.25); but it is also used in the plural for the leather strips that together make a whip (ἱμάντες is used as equivalent to *lora*; Homer, *Iliad* 23.363; POxy 1186.2, τὴν διὰ τῶν ἱμάντων αἰκείαν). The prisoner about to be given a lashing was tied to some sort of frame; it is possible to think of his being stretched out by the leather thongs with which he was fastened, or stretched out for the lash. The latter is probably correct.

There is a centurion in charge and Paul addresses him. For the Lex Porcia and Lex Julia, which (with certain exceptions) forbade the lashing of a Roman citizen, see 16.37, with the notes. Sherwin-White (71) points out with reference to the present passage that 'the narrative of Acts agrees with the lex Julia except that it adds the qualification "uncondemned"'. He proceeds to discuss this addition, which seems to imply that 'the provincial authority might administer a flogging after sentence, presumably in a case in which a Roman citizen had not exercised his right of appeal, or alternately (sic) in a special category of cases at present unknown in which the *lex Julia* did not apply' (71f.). The discussion is probably unnecessary. To ἄνθρωπον Ῥωμαῖον Paul adds καὶ ἀκατάκριτον, and the καί seems to justify the translation 'a Roman—and uncondemned (perhaps *untried—re incognita*) at that'. Cf. Tajra (83f.).

The claim to be a Roman citizen (in circumstances very different from the aftermath of a horrifying earthquake, in ch. 16) must have been ineffectual unless Paul was able to prove it true. A false claim to citizenship might be punishable with death (Suetonius, *Claudius* 25; cf. Epictetus 3.24.41). It is unlikely that Paul was wearing a toga (which only citizens might wear—it was often dispensed with in the East—Sherwin-White 149f.), but he may have been carrying his *diploma*, a small wooden diptych which would attest his registration (and birth) as a citizen. For these *diplomata* see Suetonius, *Nero* 12 (given, conferring citizenship); Sherwin-White (148f.), and especially the articles referred to by him: F. Schulz, *JRS* 32 (1942), 78–91; 33 (1943), 55–64. For Paul's citizenship see further Tajra (81–9); also 27, 74 for ἀκατάκριτος.

Citizenship and lack of trial are separated more sharply in *Begs.* 4.283: 'He claimed immunity from scourging because he was a citizen, if it was an adjunct to examination, and because he was uncondemned, if it was intended as a punishment.'

Why did Paul not disclose his citizenship earlier? 'Adversus vincula v. 29, jus civitatis non allegavit Paulus, nam haec praedicta erant; allegavit adversus verbera, ut corpus vitaque tueretur, evangelium posthac praedicaturus' (Bengel 474). This is not very convincing, a fact that adds weight to Schmithals' (205) opinion that vv. 25–29 are Luke's literary composition, but not to his judgement that it is 'kaum vorstellbar' that a Jew in Tarsus should be born a citizen. See Lüdemann (249f.) for a special note defending Paul's citizenship. Lüdemann thinks that vv. 24–29 show Lucan tendency but are also traditional (217f.).

26. This verse, which carries the narrative forward in a simple way, is marked by a number of Western variants which do not add to or change its meaning. One is an unnecessary expansion; one livens the style a little. They reflect, as many Western variants do, a time at which the wording (not necessarily the sense) of the text could be treated without the respect due to what was regarded as an inspired document.

ἀκούσας δέ] τοῦτο ἀκούσας, D lat. After v. 25 it was scarcely necessary to point out what the centurion heard.

ἑκατοντάρχης] + ὅτι Ῥωμαῖον ἑαυτὸν λέγει, D gig vg^mss— further unnecessary expansion.

λέγων, P⁷⁴ ℵ A B C E Ψ 33 36 614 945* 1739 2495 *al* vg sy bo] + ὅρα D 𝔐 gig p sa—a more numerously attested variant, and one that gives an intelligible, and livelier, sentence: Look out! What are you up to? That the centurion's question is in any case a warning is clear from the context and the γάρ that follows: You had better be careful, *for* the man is a Roman.

27. The centurion had approached the tribune (προσελθών, v. 26); now the tribune approaches Paul. Again D (joined by (sa)) has a somewhat pointless variant: τότε προσελθών ὁ χιλίαρχος ἐπηρώτησεν αὐτόν. He wishes to verify the claim that Paul has made. There is some emphasis on σύ: You, whom at first I took to be the Egyptian rebel (21.38), whom I have heard speaking to the Jews in their own Aramaic and claiming to be one of their race, you who have just escaped with your life from a violent mob—are *you* a Roman?

For ἔφη· ναί, P⁷⁴ has εἶπεν αὐτῷ· ναί, and D gig have εἶπεν, εἰμί.

28. The tribune had grounds for taking Paul's claim with scepticism. He himself had not been born a citizen but had acquired (ἐκτησάμην) the citizenship (πολιτείαν); and it had cost him a large sum, πολλοῦ κεφαλαίου (genitive of price). κεφάλαιον (reflecting its derivation from κεφαλή, *head*) had a variety of meanings; it could mean *principal*, in various senses, including that which the English word also may bear, of *capital sum* (over against *interest* or *income*; so Demosthenes, 27.64 (834)); hence it came to mean *sum* in general, e.g. in the same oration, 27.10 (816): κεφάλαιον τέτταρα τάλαντα καὶ πεντακισχίλιοι. This meaning is well attested in the papyri; see MM 342 (further evidence in *ND* 3.70). Again D(*) has a slightly livelier version, which according to *Begs.* 4.284 makes better sense: καὶ ἀποκριθεὶς ὁ χιλ. εἶπεν· ἐγὼ οἶδα πόσου κεφαλαίου ... The Old Uncial text, however, may be defended by means of an observation by Hemer (170), 'The sale of citizenship was certainly a feature of life under Claudius (Dio Cassius 17.5–7). Dio's statement is placed annalistically in AD 43 (60.17.1) and he says that the privilege, first sold at great cost, became cheapened later under Claudius, an interesting parallel with our present passage. This man, whose name Claudius Lysias (23.26) sufficiently confirms his enfranchisement by Claudius, had presumably gained his rights early in the reign, and had seen his pride reduced by Claudius' later practice, and his remark reflects this.' Bede (in Ropes, *Begs.* 3.215) has the text, Dixit tribunus, tam facile dicis civem romanum esse? ego enim scio quanto pretio civilitatem istam possedi.

Paul had not had to *acquire* the citizenship; he had it by birth, ἐγὼ δὲ καὶ γεγέννημαι. Cf. Cicero, *Ad Familiares* 10.32.3, Civis Romanus natus sum. δὲ καί here as elsewhere (e.g. 1 Cor. 15.15) emphasizes the following word: I was *born* a citizen. 'Zum höheren Ansehen des Altbürgers vgl. Ovid, *Tristitia* 4.10.78f.' (Schneider 2.327). There has been much speculation on the means by which Paul's family, or at least his father, acquired citizenship. If it is true (Jerome, *De Viris Illustribus* 5) that the family came originally from Gischala, they may on account of some services been granted citizenship by Antony. Ramsay (*Cities* 161–3, 198) finds evidence that some Jews became citizens of Tarsus in 171 BC and that some became Roman citizens under Pompey. All this is guesswork, at least as far as Paul is concerned; and it must be remembered that there is in the epistles no hint the writer was a citizen. There is greater probability in the inference (see above) that the tribune received the citizenship under Claudius (41–54).

'Lukas zeichnet Paulus nicht nur als den überzeugenderen Israeliten, sondern auch als den besseren Römer' (Weiser 612).

29. ἀπέστησαν. Cf. 5.38; literally, they stood away from; in English, perhaps, *they stood back*. The word does not in itself mean that they marched away to another place. For ἀνετάζειν cf. v. 24.

καὶ ὁ χιλίαρχος δέ. The position of δέ is unusual. Cf. Mt. 16.12; Jn 8.16; Acts 3.24. BDR § 447.1(d) suggest 'und auch'. Not only the soldiers directly involved but the tribune also was apprehensive. Cf. 16.38.

The aorist participle ἐπιγνούς is in an unusual position, but its meaning is that which is usual for the aorist participle: he perceived the truth (or what might be the truth), and having done so was afraid. The perception preceded the fear, if momentarily.

ἦν δεδεκώς: The periphrastic pluperfect active is uncommon; cf. 8.16; 21.29. It was not illegal for the tribune to arrest a citizen if he thought him a threat to public order. It was not however permitted (Lex Porcia; Lex Julia, quoted at length by Haenchen (606f.); Cicero, *Pro Rabirio* 4.12; Livy, 10.9.4; Paulus, *Sententiae* 5.26.1; see above on v. 25) to inflict on him the disgrace of being led in public bonds (in publica vincula).

At the beginning of the verse D, instead of εὐθέως οὖν, has τότε. At the end of the verse 614 sy^h** sa add καὶ παραχρῆμα ἔλυσεν αὐτόν which at first seems obvious enough, but causes difficulty when taken with a second ἔλυσεν in 22.30. Ropes's note (*Begs.* 3.215) is, 'The "Western" addition in v. 29 ... makes ελυσεν αυτον και in vs. 30 otiose, and that phrase is omitted by sah. The insertion before ελυσεν, vs. 30, of πεμψας 614 1611 minn, "misit" hcl*, suggests that the "Western" text here substituted επεμψεν for ελυσεν.' Cf. Clark (379): 'According to Γ [Clark's symbol for the Western text], which has ἔλυσεν αὐτὸν καί in *v.* 30 before ἐκέλευσεν, Lysias in spite of his fear kept Paul in prison until next day.' There is an excellent note in *Begs.* 4.285: '... confusion has arisen because a superficial reading of v. 30 and an imperfect visualisation of the facts has suggested that in spite of his fear the tribune kept Paul "bound", in an illegal sense, until the next day. But in vs. 30 ἔλυσε surely refers to release, at least temporarily, from custody. Had Paul satisfied the Sanhedrin he would have been free.' It is unlikely that the Sahidic alone contains the original Western text.

For proof of citizenship see on v. 25. Tajra (86–8) argues at length, with reference to Lüdemann and Stegemann, that Paul was in truth a Roman citizen. 'It is quite likely that Paul produced a copy of his birth registration in order to corroborate his claim to Roman citizenship' (85).

Codex Bezae (D), as at present extant, ends with the words τότε ἀπέστησαν ἀπ᾽ αὐτοῦ. For the end of d see on v. 20.

XIV

PAUL AND THE JEWS
(22.30–23.35)

56. PAUL BEFORE THE COUNCIL 22.30–23.11

(30) The next day, wishing to know the truth, that is, what accusation was being brought by the Jews, [the tribune][1] took off his bonds and ordered the chief priests and all the Sanhedrin to assemble. He brought Paul down and caused him to stand before them.

(1) Paul fixed his eyes on the Sanhedrin and said, 'Brothers, up to this day I have conducted myself before God with an entirely good conscience.' (2) The high priest Ananias ordered[2] those who were standing beside him to strike him on the mouth. (3) Then Paul said to him, 'God will strike you, you whitewashed wall. You—do you sit there to judge me according to the Law, and do you contrary to the Law command me to be struck?' (4) Those who were standing there said,[3] 'Do you insult God's high priest?' (5) Paul said, 'I did not know, brothers, that it was the high priest, for it is written, You shall not speak evil of a ruler[4] of your people.' (6) Paul[5] noticed that one part of them was made up of Sadducees, the other of Pharisees, and cried out in the Sanhedrin, 'Brothers, I am a Pharisee, the son of Pharisees; it is for the hope of[6] the resurrection of the dead that I am on trial.' (7) When he had said this there arose a conflict of Pharisees and Sadducees, and the company was divided. (8) For Sadducees say that there is no resurrection, nor angel nor spirit, while the Pharisees confess belief in both.[7] (9) There arose a loud outcry, and some of the scribes on the side of the Pharisees rose up and contended, saying, 'We find no evil in this man; and[8] what if an angel spoke to him, or a spirit?' (10) There was a great conflict, and the tribune became afraid lest Paul should be torn in pieces by them. He ordered the detachment to come down, seize him out of their midst, and take him into the barracks. (11) In the following night the Lord stood by [Paul][9] and said, 'Be of good courage, for as you have testified in Jerusalem to the things concerning me so must you bear witness in Rome too.'

[1]Greek, he.
[2]NEB, his attendants.
[3]RSV, Would you revile; NEB, Would you insult.
[4]NEB, the ruler.
[5]NEB, NJB, was well aware.
[6]RSV, hope and.
[7]RSV, in them all; NEB, them; NJB, all three.
[8]NEB, perhaps an angel; NJB, suppose a spirit.
[9]Greek, him.

Bibliography

B. J. Bamberger, *JBL* 82 (1963), 433–5.

C. K. Barrett, *FS* Furnish 161–72.

C. H. Cosgrove, *NovT* 26 (1984), 168–90.

D. Daube, *JBL* 109 (1990), 493–7.

L. Finkelstein, *HThR* 22 (1929), 239.

K. Haacker, *NTS* 31 (1985), 437–51.

J. Jeremias, as in (55).

S. T. Lachs, *Gratz College Annual of Jewish Studies* 6 (1977), 35–42.

S. Légasse, as in (54).

J. Lührmann, *JSNT* 36 (1989), 75–94.

H. Strathmann, *TWNT* 6.525–8.

G. G. Stroumsa, *RB* 88 (1981), 42–61.

A. A. Trites, as in (54).

B. T. Viviano and J. Taylor, *JBL* 111 (1992), 496–8.

J. A. Ziesler, *NTS* 25 (1979), 146–57.

Commentary

This short paragraph contains a number of historical difficulties, fully, but with some exaggeration, discussed by Haenchen (611–16).

In v. 30 it is said that the tribune loosed, ἔλυσεν, Paul. If already on the previous day (22.29) the thought that he had bound a Roman citizen gave the tribune ground for fear, why did he wait for 24 hours before rectifying his error? There is no serious problem here, nor any reason for elaborate discussion of the question whether the binding referred to (αὐτὸν ἦν δεδεκώς, 22.29) was that of the original arrest or that preparatory to scourging and whether heavy or light bonds were in mind. Luke is not writing a police report; he wishes to indicate that Paul appeared before the Council as a free man; the precise point at which his bonds were removed was of no interest or importance. We note however that Luke is writing his own story; he is not copying out a written source.

The next question invites a similar reply. The tribune ordered (ἐκέλευσεν) the Sanhedrin to meet. Did he, did even the Governor, have the authority to do this? Schneider (2.330) thinks that he had not; evidence one way or the other is hard to come by. It is also very unlikely (Conzelmann 127) that a Roman military officer would simply hand over a Roman citizen to a local, non-Roman, tribunal. It is however by no means unlikely that a Roman officer would require a local body to serve as a fact-finding (and fact-understanding) commission, allowing it to make inquiries and present a report to him. This leads to a further double problem. Would a Roman leave a fellow Roman to stand unprotected before an alien body, obviously moved by strong passions? Would a Roman—undoubtedly unclean—be allowed to be present at a meeting of the Sanhedrin? Verses 30 and 1 certainly suggest a formal meeting of the Sanhedrin, and v. 10 suggests (but does not prove) that Claudius Lysias was present. If however the meeting was an informal one the difficulties are eased. Again: Luke was not a historian of a formal kind; he was introducing a running three-cornered battle, in which the parties were Jewish officialdom, Roman officialdom, and Paul (who was both Jewish and Roman). He knew that this triangular debate took place and put its beginning on a high level, at least as far as Judaism was concerned. In the ensuing verses he will bring out a number of major points which will reappear from time to time in the course of the story. These are more important to him than the technical details. We see what Luke wishes us to see: Paul, Jerusalem, and Rome, standing face to face. And in fact they did so stand.

It is highly inappropriate that, in a trial, the accused should open the proceedings, as Paul does in v. 1. This is a correct observation, but as a complaint against Luke's story it is specious. We have good reason to doubt whether this was a formal trial, or indeed an informal one; and we have no reason to conclude that Paul's words in this verse were the first that were uttered. It is not inconceivable that he was invited to make a statement, and that Luke, who did not have unlimited space, decided to omit what would be no more than a stage direction. He is not writing as a professional historian; but we may at least say that he is not writing like a fool. In this verse he puts on Paul's lips the proposition that he will maintain up to the end of the book: Paul has acted in good faith and good conscience. He is not only a good Christian but a good Jew and a good Roman; of course he has his own understanding (which is in Luke's mind correct) of what being a good Jew and a good Roman means.

The prisoner ought not to have begun the proceedings (but Luke knows that in the whole affair the initiative was his) and the Chief Justice ought not to have initiated a physical attack upon one as yet untried, much less proved guilty of a fault (but Luke knows, or believes, that the official Jewish party was constantly guilty of injustice and violence). Again Luke is describing a scene which will enable the reader to see in advance how the whole story will proceed. This continues in the next verse. Paul is reproved by commentators: Being reviled, we bless, did he say? What Luke wishes us to see (and doubtless he was right) is the courage with which Paul faced official opposition, injustice, and violence. When many a man would cringe, Paul answers back, and points out (this is more important than the curse—if curse is the right word) that the Jewish judge is himself not observing the Law that he is appointed to administer. This is a point that Luke emphasizes throughout his book; his complaint against

Jews is not that they are Jews but that they are not good Jews. The better they are the greater the sympathy they will show to the Christians. This point will shortly reappear in another dress.

The next verse returns to the theme of the relation of Paul to Judaism, viewed from a different angle. Paul's 'I did not know that it was the High Priest' has been variously evaluated. Did he speak ironically? Did he nervously withdraw the aggression he had shown in v. 3? The point seems to be that he will not knowingly violate a rule of Scripture, however strong the provocation. If Exod. 22.27 forbids him to speak evil of the High Priest, however badly the High Priest behaves (and Paul says nothing to moderate his judgement of the High Priest's action), he will abstain from doing so. He is a good Jew, a Christian Jew.

Paul's next contribution to the debate has also evoked condemnation. The historical Paul of course knew (and did not need to observe) that there was in the Sanhedrin a mix of Pharisees and Sadducees. Setting the two parties against each other was a good way of escaping from both. He is a Pharisee, he asserts, and it is the key issue of the resurrection of the dead that is at stake. Historically it was not a very noble piece of self-defence, nor was it one whose effect was likely to last; it would not take the Pharisees long to notice that the resurrection that Paul was proclaiming was not exactly what they had in mind and were prepared to defend. But again Luke has achieved the goal, or goals, that he seeks. He has made clear (a) that Paul was a faithful Jew; (b) that he was a Jew of the Pharisaic kind, so that Pharisees are nearer than Sadducees to Christians and should be encouraged; (c) that the central issue for Christians is resurrection—the resurrection of Jesus; (d) that the Jews are too divided to take effective action. As the story proceeds he shows in v. 10 that Rome is Christians' defence against official Judaism, and in v. 11 that the Lord approves of what Paul has done and guarantees his ultimate arrival in Rome.

The whole passage is certainly Luke's work, but he was probably using a foundation of traditional material as he constructed a narrative that would foreshadow the themes that control the rest of his book.

30. τῇ ἐπαύριον occurs 10 times in Acts (Mt., once; Mk, once; Jn, 5 times); this is no doubt due mainly to the narrative character of the book. Here τῇ ἐπιούσῃ (1241 2495 *pc*; cf. τῇ ἐπιούσῃ ἐπαύριον, 614) may be correct—the less usual word could have been assimilated to that which is more common.

The tribune, it seems, wishes to use the Sanhedrin in an advisory capacity; he wishes γνῶναι τὸ ἀσφαλές. The same words occur in 21.34. ἀσφάλεια and cognates constitute a Lucan group (Luke-Acts 7 times; rest of the NT, 4 times). The indirect question (τί κατηγορεῖται ...), introduced by the article τό (see on 4.21), stands in parallel with τὸ ἀσφαλές. He wished to know the facts, namely, what accusation was being brought ... Page (229) is probably right in taking τί to be nominative and the subject of κατηγορεῖται cf. Thucydides 1.95.2, ἀδικία πολλὴ κατηγορεῖτο; Sophocles, *Oedipus Tyrannus* 529. Alternatively, Why, or of what, he was being accused.

Before ἔλυσεν, 614 *pc* sy[h**] have πέμψας, possibly a relic of a Western substitution of ἔπεμψεν for ἔλυσεν, prompted by ἔλυσεν in 22.29; see on that verse, and see Ropes (*Begs.* 3.215) and Dele-becque (109). After spending the night in custody, in part, perhaps, for his own safety, Paul was a free man. Conzelmann regards it as improbable that the tribune, already alarmed (ἐφοβήθη, 22.29) when he discovers that he has arrested a Roman citizen, should leave him in bonds. Schweizer (*Beiträge* 78) notes the view of Wendt (*Die Apostelgeschichte* (1899), 359) that the whole narrative of 22.30–23.10 may have grown out of ἀκριβέστερον in 23.15.

ἐκέλευσεν can only mean that the tribune ordered the Jewish Council to meet. It is doubtful (see above) whether he would have the authority to do this (Haenchen 612; Schneider, 2.330), but the Romans may well have used the official body as a means of obtaining information about Jewish matters, and in this case the Council would be glad to be called out; it would give them an opportunity to formulate and present a case against an adversary. Wilson (*Law* 67) thinks that the tribune intended to be and was present at the meeting; Luke does not say this, and, though it would be consistent with v. 10, it cannot be regarded as certain. He may have been content to receive a report. The report that reached him in v. 10 was not what he hoped for.

ἀρχιερεῖς: see on 4.5. συνέδριον: see on 4.6. καταγαγών, he brought Paul *down*—from the Antonia (see 21.31). For the Sanhedrin's place of meeting see on 4.5, and note especially StrB 1.997–1001; *NS* 2.223–5.

ἔστησεν εἰς αὐτούς is a pregnant expression: the tribune brought Paul *into* their gathering and caused him to *stand before* them.

1. ἀτενίζειν (Lk., twice; Acts, 6 times with εἰς, 4 times with dative; 2 Corinthians, twice) is a Lucan word. If Knox's observation (*Hell. El.* 16) about the choice of vowels and consonants in Paul's words in this verse and the following two verses (vv. 1–3) is correct the paragraph has been carefully composed, presumably by Luke. Paul's 'opening words have 18 long vowels and the harsh consonants are avoided (χ, 0; π, 3; τ, 5; ξ, 0). But when the High Priest orders the bystanders to strike him on the mouth St. Paul loses his temper and we have only 15 long vowels out of 40 (allowing τύπτειν to be naturally short), and 17 harsh consonants (χ, 7; π, 3; τ, 7).' Without

using this observation Schmithals (206) reaches a similar result: 'Sprache, Stil und Intention sind durchaus lukanisch, so dass 22.30–23.11 ganz der schriftstellerischen Komposition des Lukas entsprungen sein muss.' Schneider (2.329) describes the passage as an Einzelanekdote.

ἀτενίσας, aorist participle: Paul fixed his eyes on the Sanhedrin and said ... ἄνδρες ἀδελφοί. Cf. 1.16. If the address is not purely formal it may mean that Paul regards the members of the Sanhedrin as equals, not as judges or superiors.

πάσῃ συνειδήσει ἀγαθῇ. For συνείδησις (= τὸ συνειδός) see C. Maurer in *TWNT* 7.847–918—for background rather than for Acts itself. Paul claims an entirely good conscience; that is, his conscience is clear in regard to all his behaviour. For Paul's conscience Stählin (288) compares 24.16; 2 Cor. 1.12; 2.17; 4.2. 1 Cor. 4.4 should be added. 'Even his persecution of the church had been carried out with good conscience; it was, as he thought, his bounden duty (cf. 26.9)' (Bruce 2.424). See also Haenchen (609); 'Diese Theologie des "guten Gewissens" wird in der nachapostoloschen Literatur beliebt.' He cites 1 Tim. 1.5, 19; 3.9; 2 Tim. 1.3; 1 Pet. 3.16, 21; Heb. 9.14; 13.18. This is correct as far as it goes, but it is doubtful whether Haenchen does full justice to the present passage. 'Es geht um die bürgerliche Wohlanständigkeit ... nicht um eine "Theologie des 'guten Gewissens' "' (Schille 425). Dr Thrall's article on conscience (*NTS* 14 (1968), 118–25) deals only with the Paul of the letters. Paul (Luke) here means simply, 'I have always done what (at the time) I thought was right.' But see further *FS* Furnish, 165f.

πολιτεύεσθαι meant originally to live as a free citizen of a πόλις, or to take part in the government of a πόλις; it came however to have the more general meaning, *to conduct oneself* (in private as well as in public affairs). This use seems to have been predominantly Jewish and Christian; see H. Strathmann, *TWNT* 6.525–8. This may be illustrated by Phil. 1.27; 2 Macc. 6.1; 11.25; 3 Macc. 3.4; 4 Macc. 2.8, 23; 4.23; 5.16; Philo, *De Virtutibus* 161; Josephus, *Life* 12; Aristeas 31; 1 Clement 6.1; 21.1; also by the synagogue inscription from Stobi (most conveniently in E. L. Sukenik, *Ancient Synagogues in Palestine and Greece* (1934), 79–81), where the father of the synagogue (ὁ πατὴρ τῆς ἐν Στόβοις συναγωγῆς) claims πολειτευσάμενος πᾶσαν πολειτείαν κατὰ τὸν Ἰουδαϊσμόν. The background of this Judaeo-Christian development is well given by Page (229): 'The ideal Jewish state was a state under the direct government of God—a theocracy. Paul says "You accuse me of speaking against the Jews, the Law, etc.; I answer that *in the sight of God*, the ruler and lawgiver of the Jewish nation, *I have acted as a good citizen.*"' Cf. Delebecque (109f.), '... que ma vie, à moi, est celle d'un citoyen de Dieu'. 'Le parfait grec donne toute sa force à cet état de citoyen à la conscience directe en face, non de la Loi, mais de Dieu.' But Delebecque recognizes that πολιτεύεσθαι normally means simply 'to comport oneself'. In the present passage the distinctive feature is the dative τῷ θεῷ. There is a partial parallel in 2 Macc. 6.1, τοῖς τοῦ θεοῦ νόμοις μὴ πολιτεύεσθαι, and a letter in UPZ 144.13f. (cf. 110.78), if this is rightly restored by LS (1434; s.v. VI), πρὸς [τοὺς θεοὺς] ὁσίως καὶ δικαίως (LS do not indicate the place of the verb). This papyrus will also, presumably, show a non-Jewish use of the verb in a religious sense; for this see also Demosthenes 18.4 (226), 8 (227). Paul means that his life has been lived in the sight of God, and in obedience to God. The intention may be to supplement the subjective appeal to conscience with an appeal to the testimony of God himself. Cf. Rom. 9.1.

ἄχρι ταύτης τῆς ἡμέρας implies 'up to and including my becoming and living as a Christian'. Paul was still as a Christian an honest Jew, living as all Jews ought to live.

At the beginning of the verse there are three different forms of the text which do not differ from one another in meaning:

ὁ Παῦλος τῷ συνεδρίῳ   P⁷⁴ Ψ 𝔐
τῷ συνεδρίῳ ὁ Παῦλος   ℵ A C E 33 945 1739 1891 pc latt
Παῦλος τῷ συνεδρίῳ   B 36 453 614 2495 pc

It is not easy to see why NA²⁶ choose the reading which lacks the earliest attestation.

2. Ἀνανίας, Cf. 24.1; appointed by Herod of Chalcis. 'Ananias son of Nedebaeus (c. AD 47–59), Ant. 20.103. Cf. 20.131; War 2.243 ... As a result of his wealth, Ananias remained an influential man even after his deposition, but was unpopular on account of his greed, Ant. 20.206–13. He was murdered by the revolutionaries at the beginning of the war, War 2.429, 441–2' (NS 2.231). See also Jeremias (Jerusalem 378, and the references there); Hemer (170f. with a possible explanation of Paul's failure to recognize him—see below on v. 5). It may be that this account of Ananias is less than fair. According to Josephus, Ant. 20.205 so far from being unpopular he enjoyed the goodwill and esteem of the citizens, ἦν γὰρ χρημάτων ποριστικός. As Feldman (LCL Josephus 9.498f.) points out, all depends on whether ποριστικός refers to the getting or giving of money; the popularity referred to suggests that Feldman is right with 'able to supply them with money'. It is true however that the charge of greed is supported by b. Pesahim 57a. Again, Ant. 20.206 supports a charge of violence only in Ananias' unwillingness, or inability, to control his subordinates, and we are scarcely prepared for the violence used on Paul, except so far as a turbulent society breeds this sort of perversion of justice. This context suggests (but its historical value remains to be assessed) that the High Priest was indignant at Paul's claim to be a conscientious Jew; and so he might well be, for

Paul's conscientiousness would have destroyed Judaism as currently understood. This however is not the impression of the High Priest that Luke wishes to give. An alternative explanation of the High Priest's action is given by Blass (241): 'quia locutus erat [Paulus] non interrogatus'.

τοῖς παρεστῶσιν—probably in a general, non-technical, sense; not 'his assessors'. For the blow and response cf. Jn 18.22f.

For ἐπέταξεν, P⁷⁴ has παρήγγειλεν; C 36 453 945 1739 1891 *pc* have ἐκέλευσεν. This seems to be mere pointless Western verbal variation.

Cf. *Acta Andreae et Matthiae* 26 (L.-B. 2.1.104), ἔλεγεν (the devil) τοῖς ὄχλοις· Τύπτετε αὐτοῦ (Andrew) τὸ στόμα ἵνα μὴ λαλῇ. If there is any dependence here it is clearly on the part of *Acta A. et M.*

3. Paul 'répond par une explosion de gutturals' (Delebecque 110; cf. Knox on v. 1). He answers the assault made upon him: τύπτειν σε μέλλει ὁ θεός. The form of the sentence (with μέλλειν) suggests a statement of (future) fact: At some future time God will smite you. It is apparently so taken by Stauffer (*Theologie* 188); God judges the world in righteousness, and such flagrant unrighteousness is sure to meet with its due reward. Luke may however have in mind the actual fate of Ananias (Josephus, *War* 2.441): ὅ τε ἀρχιερεὺς Ἀνανίας περὶ τὸν τῆς βασιλικῆς αὐλῆς εὔριπον διαλανθάνων ἁλίσκεται καὶ πρὸς τῶν λῃστῶν ἀναιρεῖται). But the intention may be to express an imprecation (= τύπτοι). If this is so, cf. Shebuoth 4.13: [If a man said], 'God smite thee' (יככה אלהים) or 'Thus may God smite thee' (כן יככה אלהים), this is the 'adjuration' that is written in the Law. The Torah reference is given by Danby as Lev. 5.1, by StrB (2.766) as Deut. 28.22. The two interpretations of Paul's words are not incompatible with each other. Beginning from confidence in divine vengeance the speaker may rejoice in and seek to hasten its fulfilment; a curse may be uttered with the conviction that it coincides with God's judgement and is sure to take effect. Opinions differ. 'It is not a curse, as the Greek context makes plain enough, but rather a reproof coupled with the announcement of a punishment' (Calvin 2.227). 'Eine geläufige jüdische Verwünschungsformel' (Schmithals 207). Not unimportant is the observation of Blass (241), 'inde μέλλει, qui fut. erat non τύψω sed πατάξω'. LS 1835f. confirm that 'In Att. and LXX the fut. and aor. are supplied by πατάσσω', but also quote an Attic future τυπτήσω from Aristophanes, Plato, and Demosthenes.

τοῖχε κεκονιαμένε. The precise point of this image is not clear. It is safe to reject Bengel's neat 'Fortasse etiam canos capillos aut albam vestem habuit' (474). It may depend on the image of the white-washed or plastered wall in Ezek. 13, especially 13.14f.: an insecure wall, though covered with whitewash and therefore apparently sound, will easily and quickly fall. Or the whitewashing may suggest hypocrisy, as at Mt. 23.27 (but note that this saying appears in a different form in Lk. 11.44). Bauernfeind (257) refers to the 'Scheingerechtigkeit' of the High Priest; but according to Preuschen (132) the image is 'durch Hinweis auf Mt. 23.27 nicht erklärt'. The Ezekiel image is picked up in CD 8.12: בוני החוץ [החיץ] וטחי התפל, those who build the wall and smear it with plaster. The LXX appears to have taken תפל to be derived from נפל (πεσεῖται).

καὶ σύ. καί in a question expresses indignation or astonishment.

κάθῃ: this second person singular is derived from κάθομαι; the LXX still uses the regular κάθησαι (from κάθημαι). So M. 2.206. The question runs through to the end of the verse: And do *you* sit in judgement on me ..., and do you command ...?

κατὰ τὸν νόμον. The court had been convened by the Roman tribune, but evidently (at least in Luke's mind) considered itself to have met in accordance with the Law to try an Israelite accused of apostasy.

παρανομῶν. See Lev. 19.15 which may be regarded as requiring fair play for the person accused. Sanhedrin and Makkoth go out of their way to emphasize this requirement, though there is no special prohibition of striking the accused. Paul had not at this stage been formally accused of crime, much less found guilty. Demosthenes uses παρανομεῖν, συνείδησις, πολιτεύεσθαι, κονιᾶν: ' ... est-ce un hasard?' asks Delebecque (110). Not exactly chance; Demosthenes, and, at this place, Luke are both concerned with the operation of courts. It is not surprising that their vocabularies overlap.

κελεύεις με τύπτεσθαι. The passive infinitive is used where classical usage would have preferred the active; see M. 3.138. It is unlikely that this is in any direct sense a Latinism, though the construction is Latin rather than Greek. Cf. 22.24.

4. οἱ παρεστῶτες. See v. 2. These words can be punctuated with either a full stop or a question mark. It makes little or no difference to the sense.

According to *Begs.* 4.288, ἀρχιερεύς is used in the LXX only at Lev. 4.3. To this must be added Josh. 22.13, and, according to some MSS, Josh. 24.33; 3 Kdms 1.25; 1 Chron. 15.14. It is frequent in 1 Esdras, 1 and 2 Maccabees, and seven times each in 3 and 4 Maccabees. *Begs.* says also that 'the addition "of God" (Lord) is occasionally found with "priest" (e.g. 1 Kings (= 3 Kdms) 2.27) to denote the high priest'. In the passage cited, τοῦ κυρίου is a rendering of ליהוה. Cf. 1 Kdms 14.3, ἱερεὺς τοῦ θεοῦ, כהן יהוה. See also Gen. 14.18, Melchizedek ἱερεὺς τοῦ θεοῦ τοῦ ὑψίστου, כהן לאל עליון. Probably here in Acts we should recognize ἀρχιερεύς as in the main a post-canonical development and the addition of τοῦ θεοῦ as intended to heighten the offence: it is no common man whom you insult, but the high priest who has been appointed by and thus represents God himself. Schille (426) writes, 'Die Hörer misverstehen die Prophetie als Fluch.' Perhaps they understood it as a curse, and did so correctly. In any case, to tell the High Priest, God will in due course send you to hell, or even, God will have you murdered by terrorists, could hardly be regarded as complimentary. Cf. the reaction to Jesus' reply to the High Priest in Jn 18.22.

Cyprian (*Epistles* 3.2; 59.4; 66.3) quotes the verse in the form, Sic insilis in sacerdotem dei maledicendo? This may represent either a Western, or perhaps Cyprian's own, addition, made in preparation for the quotation that follows in v. 5, Principem plebis non maledices. It was hardly possible to do this with the Greek οὐκ ἐρεῖς κακῶς. Ropes (*Begs.* 3.215) speaks of 'some kind of intensifying expansion'.

Conzelmann (128) says of the incident, 'Zugrunde liegt eine vage Nachricht, nicht ein geschichtstreuer Bericht.' It is however in the next verse that the difficulty becomes acute.

5. οὐκ ᾔδειν ... ὅτι ἐστὶν ἀρχιερεύς—one of the most puzzling sentences in Acts. Apparently Paul withdraws his disrespectful remark; he did not know that the person who had ordered him to be struck was the High Priest. Is this conceivable? In the past (9.1f.) Paul had been a trusted member and agent of the highpriestly party; true, this was some years back and there had been a change of high priest, but Ananias can hardly have been unknown to Paul—though Hemer (171) makes the interesting suggestion that 'Paul's previous, briefly noted visit to Palestine (18.22) was ostensibly in summer 52, likely to have been the very time when Ananias had been sent in chains to Rome.' Who other than the High Priest should have presided over the judicial gathering? *Begs.* 4.288 points out that the Mishnah regulation that the high priest should always preside may be an idealized constitution drawn up after the Sanhedrin and High Priest had ceased to exist. The same passage continues, 'It is also possible that Paul merely meant that he did not know who had given the order'; cf. Blass (241): 'Errat Paulus, putans aliquem ex assessoribus illa locutum esse.' Cf. Chrysostom, *Homily* 48.2, and Knowling (466): 'I wist not that it was the high priest (who spoke).' Those who think that Paul suffered from defective sight have sometimes found evidence for it here: not a convincing explanation. A more widely accepted explanation is that Paul was speaking ironically. So e.g. Calvin (2.229): 'I myself agree with Augustine, and have no doubt that this excuse is ironical.' 'Paul manie l'ironie' (Delebecque 110); also Marshall (364). But Haenchen (610) is probably right in arguing that the address ἀδελφοί (v. 1) and the quotation of Exod. 22.27 show that this is not irony. Bauernfeind (257) finding that irony is improbable concludes that we know too little to be able to explain the text. This may be the right conclusion to draw, but there are other possibilities. Conzelmann (129) observes that Paul withdraws; this is not the moment for final conflict. It would be just possible to translate, I did not know that there was a high priest; that is, that under Roman occupation and restriction it was possible for a high priest to function effectively, that is, to be an effective high priest. This takes no account of the OT quotation. Alternatively again, Paul shows his Gesetzestreue (Pesch 2.243); he shows himself to be a better Jew than the members of the Council (Schmithals 207). This may be held as historically true, or as Luke's non-historical representation of Paul and his insistence on the continuity between Christianity and Judaism (Schweizer, *Beiträge* 75). Finally, it is 'not inconceivable that he remembered his own writing λοιδορούμενοι εὐλογοῦμεν, διωκόμενοι ἀνεχόμεθα (1 Cor 4.12)' (*Begs.* 4.288). And there is Bengel (474): *Nesciebam*, modeste dictum, interpretere, *non veniebat mihi in mentem*.

The multiplicity of explanations shows that the historical question is not an easy one. Paul (in Luke's view—and in his own?) was or is represented as being a good Jew; he believed that his (Christian) version of Judaism was the one that God intended. But there was much more to say, and he would have been careful to present a balanced view on so important an occasion. There is historical material behind this paragraph, but it is deep and remote, and it is wise to recognize with Bauernfeind that there are limits to our power to explain.

That it would be wrong to address the high priest in the manner of v. 3 is proved by the OT. The quotation of Exod. 22.27 agrees exactly with the MS A of the LXX; this however has probably been conformed to the NT, and the better LXX text has ἄρχοντες (plural), and κακῶς ἐρεῖς. The Hebrew has the singular noun (נשיא). Paul could have appealed to an interpretation of the passage that appears in Mekhilta 103a. The Hebrew has נשיא בעמך, and this is explained as follows: 'Was wollen die Worte besagen, "In deinem Volk"? Wenn sie [die Richter und Obersten] die Sitte deines Volkes innehalten [andernfalls geniessen sie den Schutz von Exod 22.27 nicht]' (StrB 2.766f.). Paul could then have argued that a high priest who commanded illegal assault forfeited the protection of the Law. Luke was probably unaware of this interpretation—or perhaps preferred to represent Paul as unquestioningly obedient to the OT.

For κακῶς λέγειν cf. Aristophanes, *Acharnians* 503: ξένων παρόντων τὴν πόλιν κακῶς λέγω.

Robertson (422) finds in ἄρχοντα ... κακῶς an iambic trimeter, but, as BDR § 487.2, n. 6 point out, three of the feet are spondees.

6. γνούς: the aorist participle is a further indication of Lucan composition; Paul would not have to *notice* but would know in advance the mixed membership of the court.

If τὸ ἕν ... τὸ δὲ ἕτερον is a Semitism (Black, *AA* 108) it is a very mild one. Cf. M. 2.438. τὸ ἕν ... τὸ ἕν would correspond more closely to Semitic idiom (אחד ... אחד). Σαδδουκαίων, Φαρισαίων, are predicative partitive genitives (BDR § 164.1c, n. 1): one part *consisted of* S. the other of Ph. On Sadducees see I.219, on Pharisees I.292. There was always (before AD 70) a potential division in the Sanhedrin, which could be exploited by one who was prepared to align himself with one party and to enlist its support.

ἄνδρες ἀδελφοί repeats the address of v. 1.

Paul proclaims himself to be a Pharisee, and a son of Pharisees (Φαρισαίων); E 𝔐 sy^h have Φαρισαίου, an easier reading, referring simply to Paul's father. υἱὸς Φαρισαίων will refer either to a line of ancestors all belonging to the Pharisaic party, or will represent the Semitic use of 'son of', describing essential character: Paul claims to be the quintessential Pharisee, and thus that it was essentially Pharisaism that he was contending for. For Paul as a Hillelite Pharisee see J. Jeremias ('Paulus als Hillelit'), *FS* Black (1969), 88–94; K. Haacker ('War Paulus Hillelit?') (reference on 22.3). Büchsel (*Theologie* 13, 177) notes the consequence that Pharisees were to be found not only in Palestine but also in the Diaspora (see however Rapske, *Book of Acts* 3.95–7). In the Diaspora they would constitute a group determined theologically rather than sociologically (for the sociological setting of Palestinian Pharisaism see the fundamental work of L. Finkelstein, *The Pharisees* (1962); also *NS* 2.381–403, with the excellent bibliography on 381f.). Paul claims that it is as a Pharisee, in the interests of Pharisaic doctrine, that he is standing trial—κρίνομαι. Strictly speaking, Luke's narrative is not an account of a trial; the tribune is trying to ascertain facts (22.30). One can understand however that such an event might seem like a trial; and it suited Luke's purpose to make it seem like one. The charge in the seeming trial is expressed in two terms: περὶ ἐλπίδος καὶ ἀναστάσεως νεκρῶν. Already Bengel (475), followed by many interpreters, saw this as a hendiadys: the two propositions were in fact one. Zerwick (§ 460) renders 'Propter spem in resurrectionem'; cf. BDR § 442.9b. Conzelmann (129) notes that by expressing himself in this way Paul (Luke) avoids a double genitive. Preuschen (133) points out that καί is missing in the Philoxenian Syriac; rightly he thinks. For Paul's assertion see further below. It is certainly true that the resurrection of Jesus was at the heart of his faith (e.g. 1 Cor. 15.13–19), and that if the Sadducees' belief (v. 8) that resurrection did not happen were accepted Paul's Christian belief would be denied; but the Pharisees' belief in resurrection was in general terms, and did not carry with it the specific, and unique, assertion that Paul made about Jesus. The line of argument is not greatly altered if *hope* and *resurrection* are distinguished; thus Haenchen (615): ' ... ich stehe vor Gericht wegen der (messianischen) Hoffnung and der Auferstehung der Toten'.

Of Paul's argument Calvin (2.230) writes, ' ... that was not far from lying'; and has much difficulty in dealing with the problem. Paul's speech 'wirkt wie eine Taktik, die eines Apostels unwürdig ist' (Stählin 288, who goes on to point out (289) that Paul's understanding of resurrection is different from the Jewish). Some have seen in 24.21 a confession of error or fault; this is denied by Bruce 1.411; it is squeamish to blame Paul for his approach. More fully Bengel (475): 'Hic in bonam partem valuit illud: *Divide et impera.* Non usus est Paulus calliditate rationis aut strategemate dialectico; sed ad sui defensionem simpliciter eos invitat, qui propius aberant a veritate.' See also the discussion of 'Christians and Pharisees' in Maddox (40–42). Maddox distinguishes between Luke's rejection of the Pharisees' position with regard to the Law and his acceptance of their doctrine of the resurrection. 'Jervell has rightly seen that the "bond of sympathy"-theme has to be not with the relation of Christians to the Roman state · but with relations between Christians and Jews. It is a doctrinal matter: but the doctrine in question is not the Law, as Jervell supposes, but the resurrection' (41). There is a further pointer in Weiser (617): 'Damit ist nach luk Verständnis die Hoffnung Israels auf die endzeitliche Totenauferstehung (24.15, 21), von der Paulus sagt, dass sie sich als Erfüllung göttlicher Verheissungen (13.32ff.; 26.6) in der Auferstehung Jesu zu verwirklichen begonnen habe.' If the resurrection of Jesus is defined as an anticipatory first stage of the general resurrection at the last day, there is enough agreement between the Pharisees and the Christians to satisfy Luke, and to justify what Schille (426) describes as neither history nor a naive anecdote but a piece written with Lk. 10.3 in mind. (How much better if one could refer to Mt. 10.16!). Whether Paul himself would have been satisfied, would have used the words put in his mouth, is a different matter. Paul refers to his Pharisaic background in a different way in Phil. 3.5f.

In this verse the second ἐγώ is omitted by B gig sa.

7. λαλήσαντος (C Ψ 𝔐) and εἰπόντος (P⁷⁴ ℵ A E 33 323 945 1739 1891 2464 *pc*; and the text of NA²⁶) are both improvements on λαλοῦντος (B *pc*), and are to be rejected; the dissension would naturally arise, as the copyists perceived, after Paul had completed his brief remark rather than while he was making it. B however is surely wrong in supporting ἐπέπεσεν (B*) or ἔπεσεν (B 2138 *pc* sy) against ἐγένετο. A στάσις can hardly be said to fall, even metaphorically; the copyist may have subconsciously remembered 10.44.

στάσις is a strong word; see v. 10. τὸ πλῆθος is the whole company present. The division was of course what Paul intended.

There is truth in both Conzelmann (129), '... die Hoffnungslosigkeit des Judentums ... es ist in sich gespalten' and Haenchen (615),
the truth 'dass zwischen Juden und Christen die Brücken nicht
abgehoben sind'. Pesch (2.245), quoting Roloff (327), goes too far in
the claim that Judaism 'seine innere Identität und äussere Glaubwür-
digkeit verloren hat'. Paul is claiming to be a Pharisee and to believe
what Pharisees believe. Pesch also (2.241f.) notes the repetition of
στάσις in v. 10 and argues that vv. 6–9 are a Lucan insertion in a
source. Lüdemann (252) argues with greater probability that vv. 7–9
are redactional.

8. For the Pharisees see on v. 6; for the Sadducees see R.
Leszynski (*Die Sadduzäer* (1912)) and *NS* 404–14, with the bibliography on 381f. Here Luke concentrates on the matter in hand. The
verse contains two notable problems.

The statement that the Sadducees say that there is no resurrection
is not a problem. It is a widely recognized fact about the Sadducees;
see Mt. 12.18 (and parallels); Josephus, *War* 2.165 (ψυχῆς τε τὴν
διαμονὴν καὶ τὰς καθ' ἄδου τιμωρίας καὶ τιμὰς ἀναιροῦσιν), and
other passages. Cf. Sanhedrin 10.1.

But the statement that the Sadducees do not believe in angels or
spirits, if taken in its most obvious sense, has no parallel, and indeed
can have none, for the Sadducees accepted the authority of the
written Torah, and the Pentateuch contains many references to
angelic and spiritual beings, in whose existence the Sadducees must
have believed. ' ... wirkliche radikal Bestreitung aller Engel- und
Geistermetaphysik liess sich mit dem AT aber doch schlechthin nicht
vereinigen! Es gibt auch kein einziger Zeugnis sonst, das diese
Angabe der AG bestätigte' (Bauernfeind 255). Bauernfeind, assuming that the statement is correct, finds the origin of this scepticism in
Hellenistic free-thinking; cf. StrB (2.767), 'Die Leugnung von
Engeln und Geistern seitens der Sadduzäer lässt sich aus jüdischen
Quellen nicht belegen, entspricht aber ganz ihrer Diesseitigkeitsreli-
gion.' Starting from a different point Conzelmann (129), followed by
Schille (427), puts the matter thus: Luke knows that the Sadducees
do not believe in resurrection but does not know why; he makes them
therefore rationalists, who must in consequence deny also angels and
spirits. Cf. also Roloff (328). A new explanation was given by D.
Daube (*JBL* 109 (1990), 493–7), as follows. The theme that is of
substance to Paul is resurrection, but this is viewed under two
aspects, (1) the final resurrection, and (2) the span between death and
resurrection, 'which, in widespread belief, a good person spends in
the realm or mode of angel or spirit' (493). It is not claimed that the
Sadducees denied outright the existence of spiritual beings—they
could not have done so—only that they denied the existence of an
interim state, in which those who had died existed as angels or

spirits, these being more or less synonymous terms (see 1 Enoch 22.3, 7; 45.4–5; Mt. 22.30: Mk 12.25; Lk. 20.36). Thus in v. 9 the spirit or angel that may have spoken to Paul is Jesus between death and (final) resurrection. Cf. Weiser (617). Daube's article was taken up by B. T. Viviano and J. Taylor (*JBL* 111 (1992), 496–8), who 'take the two nouns ἄγγελον and πνεῦμα as standing in apposition to ἀνάστασιν, and ... translate "the Sadducees say that there is no resurrection either as an angel (i.e. in the form of an angel) or as a spirit (i.e. in the form of a spirit) but the Pharisees acknowledge them both"' (498). Viviano and Taylor refer to an essay by S. T. Lachs in *Gratz College Annual of Jewish Studies* 6 (1977), 35–42 as the origin of their view; but cf. already Bengel (475): '*Spiritus* angelo opposi- tus, dicit hic spiritum hominis defuncti.'

The second problem lies in the words Φαρισαῖοι δὲ ὁμολογοῦσιν τὰ ἀμφότερα. But ἀμφότερα means *both* (of two); and on the usual interpretation three things have been mentioned, resurrection, angel, spirit. The problem was already seen by Chrysostom, *Homilies* 49.1: καὶ μὴν τρία ἐστίν· πῶς οὖν λέγει ἀμφότερα; ἢ ὅτι πνεῦμα καὶ ἄγγελος ἕν ἐστιν, ἢ ὅτι οὐ μόνον ἡ λέξις περὶ δύο, ἀλλὰ καὶ περὶ τριῶν λαμβάνεται, καταχρηστικῶς οὖν οὕτως εἶπεν, καὶ οὐ κυριολογῶν. This points out the problem, and also, on its own terms, the necessary solution: we must simply say that Luke used the word incorrectly—as he appears to have done at 19.16. Parallels (but very few) can be found, e.g. Diodorus Siculus 1.75.1 (so BA 93; but ἀμφότερα here could mean *both*). Alternatively we may say with Blass (242), 'ἄγγελος et πνεῦμα paene pro una notione sunt ... hinc τὰ ἀμφότερα'. Cf. Knowling (468). Blass (242f.) adds, 'Μή ... μήτε ... μήτε ibi locum habet, ubi post primam negationem partitio fit, ut Mt 5.34sq'. If the recent suggestions summarized above are accepted there is of course no problem in ἀμφότερα.

In this verse μέν is omitted by B *pc* latt; this removes the μέν ... δέ construction and may, as stylistically the harder reading, be correct. For the first μήτε, P[74] L 104 323 1241 *pm* have μηδέ. This may have been an attempt to mitigate the difficulty of ἀμφότερα.

9. κραυγή occurs here only in Acts; cf. the verb κραυγάζειν in 22.23; the court behaves like a rioting mob. διαμάχεσθαι, like κραυγή and στάσις, is a strong word—stronger than διαλέγεσθαι (*Begs.* 4.290). The scribes fight for their opinion. For defence of Christians by Pharisaic scribes cf. 5.34, 39 (Gamaliel). μέρος here must look back to and be explained by v. 6, which describes parts of the company assembled in the Sanhedrin, but the word was occasion- ally used for a *party*; see BA 1025, with reference to Josephus, *War* 1.143 (τὸ Ἀριστοβούλου μέρος) and a number of papyri (e.g. POxy 1278.24). For the Pharisee party's view, οὐδὲν κακὸν εὑρίσκομεν ἐν τῷ ἀνθρώπῳ τούτῳ, cf. 23.29; 25.25; also Mt. 27.23, and especially

Lk. 23.4, 14, 22, where there is close verbal similarity. It seems that Luke wished to draw attention to the similarity between the innocent suffering of Paul and that of Jesus.

The verse concludes with a conditional sentence that lacks an apodosis (supplied by 𝔐 sa: μὴ θεομαχῶμεν, which is as effective a supplement as 'was können wir dagegen machen?' (BDR § 482.2, n. 3)). It is best perhaps to supply 'What' and treat the whole as a question (cf. Jn 6.62). Delebecque (111), however, says that this is not aposiopesis; the scribes dare not continue.

The scribes assume that it is at least possible that a spiritual being (πνεῦμα ... ἢ ἄγγελος) has spoken to Paul, making a revelation to him or ordering him to behave in a certain way; better to be safe than sorry. For the words used cf. v. 8 and the note. The story of Paul's conversion and claim to have seen Jesus could easily suggest a manifestation of one between death and resurrection at the last day. This would be against Calvin's view: 'This [the use of πνεῦμα] certainly ought to be taken as applying to the Holy Spirit' (2.235). Cf. *Begs.* 4.290: 'πνεῦμα and ἄγγελος are here tautological. Possibly this is why the Western text found in the African Latin reads *sanctus Spiritus*.' The middle of the verse shows an apparently pointless textual complication.

τινές τῶν γραμματέων τοῦ μέρους τῶν Φαρισαίων: ℵ B C (Ψ) 36 (945) 1175 1739 1891 2495 *al* gig (h) sy sa
οἱ (om. L *al*) γραμματεῖς τ. μ. τ. Φ.: 𝔐
τινὲς τῶν Φ.: P⁷⁴ A E 33 104 *pc* vg bo

10. The present participle γινομένης (ℵ B C 1175 *pc*) gives a better sense than the aorist γενομένης (P⁷⁴ A E Ψ 𝔐); it might be regarded as a scribal improvement but is probably too ancient a reading to be dismissed on this ground. While, and because, the uproar was going on the tribune became afraid (φοβηθείς, aorist). διασπασθῇ, *torn apart*, is probably used literally, as it is at Herodotus 3.13.2 (τοὺς ἄνδρας κρεουργηδὸν διασπάσαντες): something more than a debate was in progress. Cf. Demosthenes 5.5 (58), μόνον οὐ διεσπάσθην. στράτευμα is not here an army but a military detachment—the force available and thought suitable. It is clear that if the tribune was not present in the council (see v. 30) he was near at hand and available to take any necessary steps. For εἰς τὴν παρεμβολήν cf. 22.24.

τε is omitted by B 69. It is needed as a connecting particle and may therefore be a secondary improvement.

Beyer (138) writes, 'Nur aus dem Munde des Paulus selbst ist die offenkundig einseitige Beleuchtung und Verspottung des Bildes jener Vorgänge voll verständlich und erträglich.' He adds that this is confirmed by v. 11, which can have come only from Paul. Neither argument is convincing; this, of course, does not prove the opposite.

11. τῇ δὲ ἐπιούσῃ νυκτί, as in the more common ἐπιούσῃ ἡμέρᾳ, the following night. Paul is comforted by a vision (for presumably he sees the Lord standing by him) and a heavenly voice. Cf. 18.9f.; 27.23f. The Lord himself bids Paul take courage (θαρσεῖ; C³ 𝔐 h vg^mss add Παῦλε, from 27.24). ἐφιστάναι, used in a variety of senses, often of aggressive presence, is a Lucan word (Lk., 7 times; Acts, 11 times; rest of the NT, 3 times). There is a similar use (of a divine presence—Sarapis) in *IG* 10.2.255.3 (*ND* 1.29–32) and *IG* 4².1.123.12 (*ND* 2.21–3). Cf. παριστάναι (of Artemis) in Strabo 4.1.4.

The encouragement constitutes implicit commendation of the past (Paul's bearing witness in Jerusalem is evidently approved) and prediction of the future (he need not fear that he will die in Jerusalem since he will survive to bear witness in Rome). 'Quod Paulus in spiritu sibi proposuerat, 19.21, id nunc maturo tempore confirmat Dominus' (Bengel 476). For διαμαρτύρεσθαι, with a direct object, cf. 20.21, 24 (without direct object, 20.23). Luke's comment on this incident is thus not that Paul has used a clever trick to get out of trouble but that he has borne the witness he was intended to bear and that the Lord has protected him and will continue to do so.

εἰς is twice used for ἐν, as frequently in Acts.

'Sein Weg steht unter dem göttlichen *dei*' (Lüdemann 252). For δεῖ cf. 19.21; also Josephus, *Life* 208f. (... Ῥωμαίοις δεῖ σε πολεμῆσαι).

57. THE PLOT; PAUL REMOVED TO CAESAREA 23.12–35

(12) When day broke the Jews made a plot and bound themselves by oath, saying that they would neither eat nor drink till they had killed Paul. (13) Those who made this conspiracy were more than forty in number. (14) They approached the chief priests and elders and said, 'We have bound ourselves with an oath to eat nothing until we have killed Paul. (15) So do you make a representation to the tribune, with the Sanhedrin, that he may bring him down to you, as though you wanted to make a further inquiry into his case with a view to reaching a decision; but we, before he comes near, will be ready to kill him.' (16) But the son of Paul's sister heard of the ambush, came and entered the barracks, and reported the matter to Paul. (17) Paul called one of the centurions and said, 'Take this young man to the tribune, for he has something to tell him.' (18) So he took him, brought him to the tribune, and said, 'The prisoner Paul called me and asked me to bring this young man to you since he has something to say to you.' (19) The tribune took him by the hand, withdrew privately, and asked, 'What is it that you have to tell me?' (20) He said, 'The Jews have planned to ask you to bring Paul down to the Sanhedrin tomorrow, on the pretext of making some more accurate inquiry about him. (21) Now do not you be persuaded by them; for above forty men of them are lying in wait for him, men who have bound themselves with an oath not to eat or drink until they have killed him, and they are ready now, awaiting your promise.' (22) So the tribune dismissed the young man, with the command not to tell anyone 'that you have given me this information'.

(23) He summoned two of the centurions and said, 'Get ready two hundred soldiers[1] to go to Caesarea, with seventy cavalry and two hundred lancers.[2] [They are to be ready][3] from the third hour of the night, (24) and to provide beasts in order to mount Paul and bring him safely to Felix the governor.' (25) He wrote a letter, as follows: (26) Claudius Lysias to His Excellency the governor Felix: greeting. (27) I came up with the troops and rescued this man, who had been taken by the Jews and was about to be killed by them, when[4] I learned that he was a Roman. (28) Wishing to discover the ground on which they accused him, I brought him down to their Council. (29) I found that he was accused over disputes arising out of their Law but under no charge calling for death or imprisonment. (30) When it was made known to me that there was to be a plot against the man I immediately sent him to you, commanding his accusers also to state the case against him before you.

(31) So the soldiers, in accordance with their instructions, took Paul and brought him by night to Antipatris. (32) On the next day, having let the

[1] NEB, infantry.
[2] RSV, spearmen; NEB, light-armed troops; NJB, auxiliaries.
[3] They are to be ready is not in the Greek.
[4] NEB, because.

cavalry go on[5] with Paul[6] the infantry[7] returned to the barracks. (33) The cavalry entered Caesarea, delivered the letter to the governor, and also presented Paul to him. (34) He read the letter,[8] inquired of what province Paul[9] was, and having found out that he was from Cilicia (35) said, 'I will hear you when your accusers also are present.' And he ordered him to be guarded in Herod's praetorium.

Bibliography

F. F. Bruce, *JSNT* 1 (1978), 33–6.

S. Dav and S. Applebaum, *PEQ* 105 (1973), 91–9.

C. Hemer, *JSNT* 31 (1987), 45–9.

G. D. Kilpatrick, *JTS* 14 (1963), 393f.

S. Légasse, as in (54).

W. Stegemann, as in (43).

Commentary

In chs. 24, 25 and 26 Paul's story is based upon Caesarea, where he is in Roman custody, custody designed not only to prevent him from stirring up trouble but also to protect him from the Jews, whose motives, and the legality of whose actions, were under suspicion. It was thus necessary for Luke, in telling his story, to have Paul removed from Jerusalem to Caesarea, and taken under Roman protection as a Roman citizen who, though he might himself be in the end found guilty of crimes, was entitled meanwhile to protection from illegal attacks. The present paragraph effects these two objects; the question that arises is whether Luke made it up in order to serve these purposes or drew it from some traditional source. If the latter alternative is accepted, the historical value of the tradition must be considered. It is hard to see any theological motive in the paragraph beyond the conviction that Paul is a better Jew—both in theology and in mores—than the official representatives of Judaism, and that the Lord protects his own. Weiser (621) is undoubtedly correct in the view that 'die jetzige Fassung des Textes [vv. 12–35] ist weitgehend von Lukas gestaltet'; he gives many details. Similarly Lüdemann (252f.): the passage is 'sprachlich und inhaltlich von Lukas geprägt'; also Schmithals (209). But opinions on its origin are divided. Probably a majority consider that the story is based on good tradition. Preuschen (133) thinks that since the plot has no outcome and does

[5]Greek, go off.
[6]Greek, with him.
[7]Greek, they.
[8]The letter is not in the Greek.
[9]Greek, he.

not presuppose Paul's appearance before the Council (23.1–10) the story goes back 'auf einen guten Bericht'. Roloff (330) similarly believes that vv. 12–35 'geht sicher auf Tradition zurück', and further that it is part of the Prozessbericht and links with 22.29. Haenchen (621) observes that in this story the Sanhedrin appears to be united whereas in 23.1–10 it is divided: the two scenes are independent and each is self-contained. Schneider (2.336) thinks similarly; Pesch (2.247) disagrees. Marshall (367) comments on Haenchen's observation that in 23.1–10 the Pharisees took Paul's side that in fact only some of them did so (23.9).

The following points must be borne in mind. Luke's strength as a writer lies in the presentation of a single event, not in the logical linking of a sequence of events. The story of the intervention of Paul's nephew and the story of the march to Caesarea are both told with clarity, force, and liveliness. The question whether there was any inconsistency between them and the story of 22.30–23.11, which as we have seen had its own motivation and served its own purposes, is not one that would have troubled him, if indeed he noticed it. In contrast with that paragraph the present one has no directing purpose. Luke's main story would have been adequately served if he had written: The tribune, hearing of a plot against Paul's life, sent him by night and under guard to Caesarea. That Luke did not effect the transference in this way leads to the probable inference that he found in the tradition the story of the nephew and some account of the surprisingly powerful force that escorted Paul to Caesarea. Further, it must be remembered that Paul had friends in Jerusalem, even if only those whom he brought with him (and these could have included the person responsible for the We-passages, who could not now use the first person plural since Paul was alone and the only person who mattered). Again, if it is correct that Paul spent his youth in Jerusalem (22.3) it is not impossible that a married sister lived there. One must not make too much of bare possibilities, but it is at least conceivable that family memories persisted and that someone watched the cavalcade set out (vv. 28f.).

The letter (vv. 26–30) is another matter. It is hard to imagine how Luke could have obtained access to Roman archives whether in Jerusalem or in Caesarea. It makes (with a little variation on the events as described in chs. 21, 22) the points that concern Luke: the trouble was caused not by Paul but by Jews; Paul was a Roman citizen and entitled to protection, especially against plots to assassinate him; the only matter at issue was interpretation of the Jewish Law, and that therefore Paul had committed no offence against the state. The tribune must have written an accompanying letter; must it not have been cast in these terms? So Luke would think.

12. συστροφή in itself need mean no more than at 19.40, where the 'gathering together', though directed against Christians and not, in the opinion of the town clerk, a properly constituted ἐκκλησία, was not for the purpose of secret plotting. The word however is capable of suggesting such a purpose (LS 1736 quote Polybius 4.34.6), and the context shows that this is (*Begs.* 4.290 'may be') the meaning here. Zerwick (§ 227) notes that the active verb ποιήσαντες (contrast v. 13) is used: 'non est simpliciter "convenerunt" sed "instituerunt concursum".'

οἱ Ἰουδαῖοι can hardly mean more than *some* Jews (see the next verse). But they were Jews, and no doubt in Luke's mind represented the Jewish people as the chief enemies of the new faith. It was the impossibility of believing that 'the Jews'—all of them—undertook the vow described that led to the variant τινες τῶν Ἰουδαίων in P⁴⁸ (but for the full reading of this MS see below) 𝔐 lat syᵖ saᵐˢˢ.

The sense of ἀνεθεμάτισαν ἑαυτούς is given by v. 14 where ἀναθέματι is added. Those who thus agreed undertook to accept the ban (חרם) of the synagogue if they failed to accomplish that which they pledged themselves to do. The abstinence from eating and drinking (which if adhered to must in this case have resulted in death) is augmented by the religious sanction. Derrett (*Law* 347) draws attention to Philo, *De Specialibus Legibus* 2.12, 13, where Philo refers to those who excuse their wrong-doing on the ground that they are fulfilling vows. 'There are those who swear at random (ἐὰν τύχῃ, perhaps, as opportunity offers) to commit acts of theft or sacrilege or rape and adultery or assaults and murders or other similar crimes and carry them out without hesitation on the pretext that they must be faithful to their oaths.' Philo properly points out the overriding authority of the prior (implied) oath to observe the law, which forbids such acts. Josephus (*Ant.* 20.163f.; cf. *War* 2.254–6), however, describes the use of hired assassins in Jerusalem for revenge on private and public enemies, though it exaggerates somewhat to describe this (W. Foerster, *Palestinian Judaism in NT Times* (1964, 1967), 105, n. 8) as the assassination of opponents of the Law. Cf. Sanhedrin 9.6. It was possible to be released from certain vows; see Nedarim 3.1–3 ('Four kinds of vows the Sages have declared to be not binding: vows of incitement, vows of exaggeration, vows made in error, and vows [that cannot be fulfilled by reason] of constraint . . .').

For ἀποκτείνωσιν, A *pc* Chrysostom have ἀνέλωσιν, which is probably due to preference for the less usual and obvious word, though it could be original, ἀποκτείνωσιν having been introduced by assimilation to v. 14. The story of a plot going to such lengths is not necessarily to be dismissed as unhistorical because it accords with the picture of the Jews that Luke wishes to paint; we know that Paul sometimes went in danger of his life (2 Cor. 11.24–26).

At this point the fragmentary P⁴⁸ (see I.3) begins, and offers a series of striking and sometimes unique variants. The present verse includes, instead of ποιήσαντες ... Ἰουδαῖοι, βοήθειαν (a force of auxiliaries, as in Xenophon and Thucydides; see LS 320, s.v. II) συστραφέντες τινες τῶν Ἰουδαίων (cf. the reading of 𝔐 lat sy^p sa^mss, above).

For δέ, B Ψ 614 2464 2495 *pc* h have τε. For the first μήτε, P^48 *pc* have μή.

13. For ποιησάμενοι (middle) cf. v. 12 (where the verb is active) and see Zerwick (§ 227). They were *coniurati*, they had made their conspiracy among themselves. For συνωμοσία cf. Plutarch, *Caesar* 7 (710) (Catiline); 64 (738) (Brutus and Cassius). MM 616 cite no papyrus evidence; *ND* 2.99 supplies P.Mil.Vogl. 6.287.9.

14. For chief priests and elders see I.223. Official Jewish collaboration was necessary if Paul was to be placed in a situation in which he could not be defended by Roman swords.

For ἀναθέματι ἀνεθεματίσαμεν cf, v. 12. BDR § 198.6, n. 9 regard this as an imitation of the Hebrew infinitive absolute. M. 2.443f. recognizes the parallel, but in view of classical parallels, adds, with Radermacher, that it is only in the extension of such uses in the NT that we should describe the use as a Semitism. Any Semitic influence behind the examples in Acts is likely to have come through the LXX.

ἑαυτούς is used for the first person plural of the reflexive pronoun (ἡμᾶς αὐτούς). This is very common in the NT and in Hellenistic Greek generally. See Zerwick (§ 209); BDR § 64.1.

γεύσασθαι presumably covers both φαγεῖν and πιεῖν (v. 12). After γεύσασθαι, P^48 gig h Lucifer add τὸ σύνολον—a characteristic Western intensification. For οὗ, P^48 has ὅτου; Ψ 104 1175 2464 *pc* have ἕως ἄν.

StrB (2.767) refer to b. Sanhedrin 82a. The members of the Sanhedrin are not to give counsel to a Zealot in such a case.

15. The conspirators disclose their plot and the part to be played in it by the authorities.

The meaning of ἐμφανίζειν is not clear. At Jn 14.21, 22, with a reflexive pronoun, it means *to manifest*; At Heb. 11.14, introducing a ὅτι clause, it has the same meaning. The passive means *to appear* (Mt. 27.53; Heb. 9.24). At Acts 23.22 the verb means *to disclose*, but at 24.1; 25.2, 15 it appears to have a special legal meaning. At 24.1 (ἐνεφ. τῷ ἡγεμόνι κατὰ τοῦ Π.) it differs little from *to accuse*, or perhaps better, *to lay an information against*; 25.2 has the same construction; at 25.15 the construction is similar (περὶ οὗ ἐνεφ.) and the meaning is probably the same. The only reference given by LS 549 is to the Argument to Aristophanes, *Lysistrata*, but it appears to have developed in Hellenistic usage; so e.g. 2 Macc. 3.7 (other examples in BA 520; also *ND* 2.104; see Josephus, *Ant.* 10.166; 14.213, 226). It is not easy however to fit this meaning into 23.15, which is closely parallel to v. 20 and may mean little more than *ask*. Preuschen (134), quoting Esther 2.22, prefers *mitteilen*; Page (233) is nearer with ' "make a statement" or "declaration to the tribune to induce him (ὅπως) to bring Paul down to you, or the place that you propose ..." '. *Make a representation to* may perhaps suggest the sense of asking with the addition of a legal flavour supplied by a word sometimes used in legal contexts.

σὺν τῷ συνεδρίῳ (on the text see below). With whom is the συνέδριον connected, ὑμεῖς or ὁ χιλίαρχος? Neither alternative is easy. The Sanhedrin was not asked to do anything; only the tribune would *bring Paul down*—and that to the Sanhedrin. Moreover, *you* in effect were the Sanhedrin (ἀρχιερεῖς καὶ πρεσβύτεροι, v. 14). This must probably be regarded as a careless piece of writing; perhaps Luke wished to make it clear that the Sanhedrin would be involved in any mischief that was afoot.

On καταγάγῃ see below. 𝔐 adds αὔριον, a circumstantial touch from v. 20. For εἰς, P[74] C Ψ 𝔐 have πρός, a scribal improvement.

ὡς μέλλοντας, on the pretext that; ὡς suggests deceitfulness that would not be implied by the participle alone.

διαγινώσκειν is a technical term in legal use: *to decide* or *determine* a suit. Cf. 24.22; (and 25.21, διάγνωσις). *Begs.* 4.291 note that the word means something more than inquiry, but find it difficult to get a rendering for its double meaning. One must be prepared to fill out: *to make a further inquiry into his case* (τὰ περὶ αὐτοῦ) *with a view to reaching a decision.*

ἀκριβέστερον may be an elative comparative, *as accurately as possible*; see BDR § 244.2, n. 3. There is some support for this in papyri cited in MM 19. But there is no reason why the word should not be a true comparative: *to find out more accurately than you have so far been able to do.*

Such would be the pretext, and *your* share in the proceeding; but *we* (ἡμεῖς δέ, emphatic) before he comes near (*to you*, ὑμῖν, is added by P[48] vg[mss] sy) ἕτοιμοί ἐσμεν, present for future, giving greater vividness: there we are, all ready ... τοῦ ἀνελεῖν, genitive of purpose, or of the thing aimed at (Page 233). At the end of the sentence 614 h sy[hmg] add ἐὰν δέῃ καὶ ἀποθανεῖν, even if we have to die for it—a characteristic Western sharpening of the narrative.

The principle of the plot is clear; it could hardly be expected that the details should be. καταγάγῃ implies that Paul was to be brought down from the Antonia (see on 21.31) to wherever it was that the Sanhedrin met (see I.223f.); but where the conspirators intended to set upon him, and how they intended to circumvent the Roman guard that would certainly be present, is not explained.

P[48], which must be regarded as an important witness to the

Western text, together with gig h sy^{hmg} sa Lucifer, rewrites the beginning of the verse as follows: παρακαλοῦμεν ὑμᾶς ποιήσατε ἡμῖν τοῦτο, συναγαγόντες τὸ συνέδριον, ἐμφανίσατε τῷ χιλιάρχῳ ὅπως ... This looks like a free improvement, which, among other things, avoids the problem, noted above, of σὺν τῷ συνεδρίῳ. Clark (379), to whom P⁴⁸ was unknown, gives the Latin, Syriac, and Coptic material, reconstructing a Greek text on 149f. See also Ropes, *Begs*. 3.228f.

16. ὁ υἱὸς τῆς ἀδελφῆς. We have no other information about members of Paul's family. 22.3, however, suggests, but does not prove, that some were, or had been, resident in Jerusalem.

τὴν ἐνέδραν. Cf. 25.3; also ἐνεδρεύειν in Lk. 11.54; Acts 23.21. The word could be used for *trickery* or *treachery* of any kind, but its primary sense was *ambush*, and it is clear from v. 15 that something of this kind was included in the plot.

παραγενόμενος καὶ εἰσελθών appears to mean, *having arrived and having entered* the barracks. This is clumsy, and *Begs*. 4.291 suggests that παραγενόμενος should be connected with what precedes: Having heard ... having been present. Paul's nephew heard about the plot because he was present, inadvertently included in the group. As *Begs*. adds, 40 is too many for successful assassination. Paul's nephew has access to him; his residence in the barracks is protective rather than penal, though, if the authorities were favourable, prisoners under charge or even undergoing punishment could be visited (cf. 27.3).

Schmithals (210): this and the following verses show that the Christians 'das Vertrauen der römischen Obrigkeit verdienen und zur Zeit des Paulus auch besassen'. In Luke's time the persecutors did not understand this. 212: 'Das Christentum ist religiös eine Erscheinung des Judentums, politisch ein integrierender Teil der römischen Ökumene.'

17. Again Paul appears to be in a favoured position; he is able to summon a centurion and give him a message for the tribune.

ἄπαγε (‭א‬ B 81 *pc*) is probably original; ἀπάγαγε, the aorist imperative (P⁷⁴ A C E Ψ 𝔐), is the more natural to use and probably an editorial 'improvement'.

18. ὁ δέσμιος. Paul is a prisoner, though favourably treated; that is, the tribune considers that it might be dangerous to let him go.

ἠρώτησεν. As at 10.48, the use of the aorist corresponds to the fact that the request was now fulfilled. See BDR § 328.2, n. 3.

νεανίσκον, P⁷⁴ ‭א‬ A E 33 81 323 453 945 1175 1739 1891 *al*; νεανίαν, B Ψ 𝔐: a textual problem impossible to solve. Has an original νεανίσκον been assimilated to νεανίαν in v. 17, or an original νεανίαν to νεανίσκον in v. 22? Luke evidently regards each word as equally suitable, and uses each several times in Acts.

ἔχοντα, causal: since he has something to say to you.

19. ἐπιλαβόμενος, used correctly with the genitive of the part taken; BDR § 170.2, n. 2.

ἀναχωρήσας κατ᾽ ἰδίαν. The young man will no doubt speak more freely in private.

20. συνέθεντο corresponds to συστροφήν (v. 12) and συνωμοσίαν (v. 13), ἐρωτῆσαι to ἐμφανίσατε (v. 15), without suggesting the semi-technical legal atmosphere of these words. The τοῦ is the genitive of purpose or aim, as in v. 15. μέλλον is probably the reading we should accept, but there is great textual variation.

(a) μέλλον ℵ* 33 1891 *pc*
(b) μέλλων P⁷⁴ A B E 81 453 *pc*
(c) μέλλοντα 𝔐
(d) μέλλοντες 630 *al* lat sy
(e) μέλλοντας 2127 *pc*
(f) μελλόντων ℵ² Ψ 36 614 945 1175 1739 2495 *al*

(a) is the reading that gives the required sense, since, in the terms of the plot, it is the Sanhedrin that wishes to carry out further investigation. *Begs.* 4.292 is prepared to accept this, though as an emendation—the occurrence of the reading in ℵ* is accidental. But since ℵ* is joined by 33 this need not be so. Ropes (*Begs.* 3.219) thinks (b) an orthographical variation of (a). This is possible, since the two words would be pronounced identically, but some scribes at least will have understood μέλλων to be masculine singular nominative, and to refer to the tribune. It is difficult to make sense of (c), though it is widely supported; Ropes describes it as 'particularly unfortunate'. Probably one must refer it back to σε and give it the same meaning as (b) (understanding this as written, masculine nominative). (d), (e), (f) will all, in rather odd ways, give the same sense as (a): They (= the Sanhedrin) with to make a further inquiry.

ἀκριβέστερον. Cf. v. 15.

21. This verse relates matters that we already know, with only small variation in wording.

ἐνεδρεύουσιν. Cf. ἐνέδρα, v. 16.

οἵτινες, men who ...; but in Lucan usage οἵτινες is scarcely distinguishable from οἵ.

ἀνεθεμάτισαν. Cf. v. 14.

Begs. 4.292: 'ἐπαγγελία means most frequently a promise; but its original sense is "a favourable message" and so "consent" or "assent", which is clearly the meaning demanded by this context.' BA 567 similarly gives the meaning *Zusage*, supporting it with references to the *Protevangelium of James* 7.1, where the meaning seems to be *promise*, and Ignatius, *Ephesians* 14.2, where promise and profession are equally suitable—it is not promising or professing to live as a Christian but actually doing so that counts. There is no valid objection to the meaning *promise* here; indeed, *consent* implies *promise*. If the tribune replies, 'Very well, I will bring Paul down tomorrow' he is promising to do so.

22. In the course of the verse the construction changes from indirect to direct speech: μηδενὶ ἐκλαλῆσαι ... ἐνεφάνισας πρὸς ἐμέ. Cf. 1.4; and see BDR § 470.2, n. 3 ('auch bei Klassikern ... nicht ungebräuchlich'). It is interesting that in vv. 23f. the reverse change takes place.

In v. 15 ἐμφανίζειν takes the dative; here πρός and the accusative. This may suggest a small difference in meaning—in v. 15 the legal sense, *lay an information before*, in v. 22 the non-technical, *disclose to*. See on v. 15.

23. δύο τινας (τινας δύο in ℵ B 33 81 *pc*; δύο in P⁷⁴ *pc* lat sy^p) is the reading of A E Ψ 𝔐; copyists felt and exercised considerable freedom over such trifles. The meaning can hardly be *about two* (which is the usual classical sense of τις with a numeral); M. 3.195 and BDR § 301.1, n. 3 suggest *a certain two* or *a pair*. Cf. Thucydides 8.100.5, τινὲς δύο νῆες. The tribune acts through his centurions; normal military practice.

στρατιώτας. The context shows that infantry are in mind. These would naturally determine the speed at which the convoy would proceed. See below. Two hundred men would (on paper) correspond to two centurions.

Καισαρείας, where the governor of the province normally resided. See 10.1 and the note. Jerusalem was no place for the trial of an unpopular Jew who was also a Roman citizen; and no doubt Claudius Lysias would be glad to hand on the explosive package that had been thrust upon him.

ἱππεῖς ἑβδομήκοντα. The garrison at Jerusalem was provided with cavalry (Josephus, *Ant.* 20.171). The Western text (614 1241 2495 *pc* h sy^hmg sa) has ἕκατον as the numeral. It is not easy to see how this variant could have arisen accidentally; at the same time the difference is scarcely great enough to satisfy anyone who wished to heighten the effect of the narrative. The Latin and Syriac texts at this point are unusually free; see Ropes (*Begs.* 3.220f.; Metzger 488f.).

δεξιολάβους (δεξιοβόλους, in A 33, is not attested elsewhere and may be simply a lapsus calami) διακοσίους. The meaning of δεξιολάβος is a notorious problem. The Vulgate here reads *lancearios*, lancers, spearmen; the Syriac has שדיי בימינא, shooters or slingers with the right hand—a wooden imitation of the Greek, though perhaps of δεξιόβολοι rather than of δεξιολάβοι. Until further evidence is found it will probably be wise to follow the Vulgate here—even if Jerome was guessing, his guess is at least as likely to be right as those of modern times. The suggestion of *Begs.* 4.293 should however be noted: led horses. Between Jerusalem and Antipatris (v. 31) the cavalry would need a change of mount; a led horse would be taken by the right hand. See also M. 2.272f.: δεξιολάβοι '... is supposed to mean *taking* (a spear) *in the right hand* (instr. or loc. dependence). In military phraseology the spear was always connected with the right, as the shield with the left. It was certainly not a coined word, but as it does not reappear till vii/ AD we must suppose it a technical term of limited range.' Cf. Schneider (2.339): 'militärischer Fachausdruck'. It may be added that when the word does reappear (see BA 349) it seems to mean light-armed troops (though this may be an inference from a connection with spears). See further below.

The escort comprised 470 men (500 according to the Western text). If the garrison in Jerusalem (which seems to have had only one tribune) was a single cohort, the escort amounted to half the troops in the city, that is, if we assume a *cohors miliaria*; if the tribune commanded only a *cohors quingenaria* he sent virtually his whole force! Using these figures G. D. Kilpatrick (*JTS* 14 (1963), 393f.) argued that the δεξιολάβοι, whatever they were, did not belong to the cohort; only 270 regular soldiers were sent. Who then were the δεξιολάβοι? The later Greek evidence interprets δεξιολάβος as παραφύλαξ, and for this word LS give *gendarme* or *police-officer* (in the Addenda, 2097; in the main text, 1330, *watcher*, *guard*; in the Supplement (1968), 115, 'name of an official, perh. *chief of police*'); so also *Revised Supplement* (1996), 241. Kilpatrick concludes: 'The 200 δεξιολάβοι will be spearmen from the local police and it would be natural for police to be used to help escort a threatened prisoner to a safer area.' Delebecque (112) approves the suggestion. But have we any evidence for local police in Jerusalem in addition to the Temple police (see I.218f.), who would have been most unsuitable as a guard for Paul, and to the Roman military force? The numbers (which prompted Kilpatrick's suggestion) certainly constitute a problem, but the explanation of them is probably that Luke exaggerated them—or guessed on the high side. Hengel (174) however quotes Josephus, *War* 2.540–53 to illustrate dangers on the Palestinian roads, which justify a large military accompaniment. The story as a whole (though of course there is no means of confirming it) need not be fictitious because Luke, who would not have access to official records of troop movements, overestimated the figures. It may be that the infantry did not go all the way to Antipatris.

A similar problem is raised by the distances involved, but this will be considered at v. 31, since though Caesarea (the governor's residence) is mentioned in this verse as the goal of the journey it is not said here when the party is expected to arrive there. Caesarea was about 50 miles from Jerusalem as the crow flies, probably at least 70 by road. See Josephus, *War* 1.79 (600 stadia = 69 miles).

ἀπὸ τρίτης ὥρας must mean that the escort was to be ready from the third hour onwards, that it must be ready to start at any time after that hour. The time would be three hours after sunset (or more precisely 3/12 of the time between sunset and sunrise; according to *Begs.* 4.293, about 9.30 p.m.).

For the Western text at the end of this verse see on v. 24.

Bauernfeind (260), on vv. 23–30; 'Lk hält den Leser bei diesen Bildern fest, nicht aus Freude am Erzählen, auch nicht deshalb, weil Paulus es wert ist, dass man seinem Erleben im grossen und im einzelnen folgt, sondern weil man wissen muss, dass die Korrespondenzen der obrigkeitlichen Dienststellen sowie die Soldaten sämtlicher Waffengattungen alle dem Lauf des Ev dienen müssen, wenn es ein wirklicher Streiter Jesu ist, dem ihr Aufwand gilt.' But was Luke so subtle? And did he not have Freude am Erzählen? See Introduction, pp. xlix, cxi.

24. The text of vv. 23, 24, (25) is in considerable confusion. The text printed in NA[26] (which for convenience if for no other reason will form the basis of the commentary on these verses) is substantially the Old Uncial text. The reconstruction of an alternative (Western?) test is itself a matter of some difficulty, though most of the variations are of no great significance. The Western test as reconstructed by Clark (151, 379f.) is as follows.

Ἑτοιμάσατε στρατιώτας, ὅπως πορευθῶσιν ἕως Καισαρείας, ἱππεῖς ἑκατὸν καὶ δεξιολάβους διακοσίους· καὶ ἀπὸ τρίτης ὥρας τῆς νυκτὸς κελεύει ἑτοίμους εἶναι πορεύεσθαι· καὶ τοῖς ἑκατοντάρχοις παρήγγειλεν κτήνη παραστῆσαι, ἵνα ἐπιβιβάσαντες τὸν Παῦλον διὰ νυκτὸς διασώσωσιν εἰς Καισάρειαν πρὸς Φήλικα τὸν ἡγεμόνα· ἐφοβήθη γὰρ μήποτε ἁρπάσαντες αὐτὸν οἱ Ἰουδαῖοι ἀποκτείνωσιν καὶ αὐτὸς μεταξὺ ἔγκλησιν ἔχῃ ὡς ἀργύριον εἰληφώς, ἔγραψεν δὲ ...

The one substantial addition here supplies an additional motive for the tribune's provision of so large a force to convey a prisoner safely from Jerusalem to Caesarea: he was afraid that if Paul were killed on the way he would be accused of having accepted a bribe to allow this to happen. There is nothing improbable in the suggestion; equally there is nothing in the narrative outside v. 24 to prompt it. The tribune was in any case under obligation to secure the safety of a Roman citizen, as yet not merely uncondemned but untried, and therefore presumed innocent. This is one of the most extensive variations introduced by the Western text; it is noteworthy that it occurs in a passage where there is (unless we follow Bauernfeind—

see on v. 23) no theological interest. This is (apart from one person involved) a secular story, and editors felt no obligation to maintain its wording intact.

κτήνη τε παραστῆσαι. The construction changes from direct speech (imperative, ἑτοιμάσατε, v. 23) to indirect (the infinitive depends on εἶπεν). Contrast v. 22, where the opposite change takes place. It does not seem likely that this should be an example of the use of the infinitive as imperative (see Moule, *IB* 126; also BDR § 470.3). κτῆνος usually means an *ox* or *sheep*, often in the plural, *flocks and herds*. The only examples given by LS 1002 for the meaning *horse* or *mule for riding* are the present passage and Lk. 10.34. It is possible however to add Josephus, *Ant.* 8.241 (λέων ... κατασπάσας αὐτὸν ἀπὸ τοῦ κτήνους ἀπέκτεινεν; the context shows that the animal was an ass, ὄνος) and POxy 17.21253.16, 17, 20.

ἐπιβιβάσαντες is not to be taken as literally as it is by Delebecque (113), who concludes that Paul was perhaps 'un cavalier médiocre'. Paul was mounted on the animal but not necessarily lifted up and seated on it. He was being well treated; not for the first or last time Luke illustrates the favour shown to him by Roman authorities. The tribune, for whatever motive, means to bring him safely through (διασώσωσιν; a Lucan word—5 times in Acts, once in Lk., twice in the rest of the NT) to Felix. κτήνη, plural, may go with the suggestion that the δεξιολάβοι are led horses.

Two Western additions, νυκτός and εἰς Καισάρειαν, are scarcely necessary after v. 23, but perhaps make the story more vivid.

Felix: see *Begs.* 5.286, 465–72; also *NS* 1.459–66. According to Tacitus, *Histories* 5.9, his full name was Antonius Felix, according to Josephus, *Ant.* 20.137, Claudius Felix. This however may be an error. The MSS have πέμπει δὲ καὶ Κλαύδιον Φήλικα, but it is probably right, with the Epitome, to read Κλαύδιος ..., (the Emperor) Claudius sent Felix. He was a brother of the influential freedman Pallas, and was himself a freedman, probably, if we may follow Tacitus in regard to his name, of Antonia, the mother of Claudius. Such an appointment was unusual; provinces such as Judaea were usually entrusted to Roman knights. According to Suetonius, *Claudius* 28, he was married three times, *trium reginarum maritum*. Tacitus, loc. cit., says that he married Drusilla the grand-daughter of Cleopatra and Antony (*Drusilla Cleopatrae et Antonii nepte in matrimonium accepta*), Josephus, *Ant.* 20.141–4, describes how he took Drusilla, the sister of Herod Agrippa II, from her husband Azizus, king of Emesa, and married her. It seems that there may be some confusion here; see Acts 24.24. The dates of Felix's governorship are disputed. *NS* loc. cit. gives as his dates AD 52–60?; *Begs.* 5.465–72 prefers 52 or 53–55. The time of his recall will be discussed at 24.27. Before coming to the appointment of Felix

Josephus narrates the misgovernment of Cumanus and the appearance before Claudius in Rome of rival groups of Samaritans and
Jews. Claudius decided against the Samaritans, whom he put to
death, and Cumanus, whom he exiled, and, at the suggestion of one
of the Jewish party, Jonathan the High Priest (*Ant.* 20.162), appointed Felix. He adds (20.138), 'When he had completed the twelfth
year of his reign, he granted to Agrippa the tetrarchy of Philip
together with Batanaea ...'. The twelfth year of Claudius ended on
24 January 53. Thus if Josephus is maintaining a strict chronological
sequence of events, Felix will have been sent to Judaea in 52
(possibly in January 53). Tacitus's account (in *Annals* 12.54) is
different. Felix had shared in the misdeeds of Cumanus. These were
ended by Ummidius Quadratus, governor of Syria, who, however,
put Cumanus on trial and appointed Felix one of his judges. Felix had
thus been active in Palestine before his appointment as procurator.
This may account for Paul's words in 24.10 (see the note). Felix's
character, and the character of his rule, are described by Tacitus in
the words (*Hist.* 5.9) *per omnem saevitiam ac libidinem ius regium
servili ingenio exercuit*. Most writers accept this judgement; but cf.
Begs. 5.286: 'The appointment of Felix was undoubtedly a bad one,
if we judge it from the state of near anarchy into which he allowed
Judea to sink. Nevertheless in passing judgement upon Claudius's
responsibility for sending him to that country, one should not forget
that the appointment was made at the request of the high priest
Jonathan, and that the procurator's wrongs were acts of omission
rather than commission. One wonders what procurator could have
proved successful in a country where the Zealots had been teaching a
whole generation that relentless opposition to the Roman government was willed by God. The appearance of organized guerrilla
warfare forced Felix to resort to acts which appeared unduly cruel to
the excited populace, and, in turn, increased the fury and influence of
the Zealots.'
   See F. F. Bruce, 'The full name of the Procurator Felix', *JSNT* 1
(1978), 33–6; C. J. Hemer, 'The name of Felix again', *JSNT* 31
(1987), 45–9.
   For ἔγκλημα see Dittenberger, *OGIS* 1.229.41 (*ND* 3.66).

25. The text of this apparently straightforward verse is complicated by many variants, which fortunately make little difference to its
meaning.
   For γράψας

P[48] has ἔγραψε δὲ αὐτοῖς. The participle is replaced by the finite
   verb and a connecting particle (as in the other variants). Unless
   αὐτοῖς means *for them*—for the guard so that they may deliver it
   to the governor—this is a lapse or a misconception; the tribune
   was writing to the governor, not the guard.

614 has ἔγραψε δέ
2147 vg have ἔγραψε δὲ καί
syᵖ has ἔγραψε δὲ καὶ ἔδωκεν αὐτοῖς—a more circumstantial account of the delivery of the message.

For ἔχουσαν τὸν τύπον τοῦτον

A 𝔐 have περιέχουσαν τὸν τύπον τοῦτον
614 (2147) (vg) have περιέχουσαν τάδε
P⁴⁸ has ἐν ᾗ ἐγέγραπτο
syᵖ ʰᵐᵍ have ἐν ᾗ ταῦτα

περιέχειν (for the transitive and intransitive uses see BDR § 308, n. 5) was probably introduced as a more literary way of referring to the contents of a document. See 1 Macc. 15.2, ἦσαν περιέχουσαι τὸν τρόπον τοῦτον; Philo, *De Decalogo* 168, with τύπον. τύπος (like *exemplum*) of the purport or content of a letter: 3 Macc. 3.30; but see E. A. Judge in *ND* 1.77f. (see also 2.75), arguing that the word suggests an exact copy, not merely the drift of a document. 'Such a letter, containing a summary of the facts, when a charge was referred to a superior magistrate, was technically termed *elogium*' (Page 234). Bengel (476), hopefully: 'Hoc sine dubio Latine scriptum et in archivis Romanis servatum Romanos postea de veritate historiae apostolicae, hanc cum legerent, convicit.' Roloff (332), however: 'von Lukas formuliert'. But it is fair to say that the letter contains on the whole the sort of report that the tribune is bound to have made to his superior.

26. For the first time we learn the name of the tribune—Luke's own invention, according to Roloff (332); possibly, but not necessarily so. We know from 22.28 that he had obtained Roman citizenship, and the citizen's nomen, Claudius, has been taken to indicate that he received the citizenship, as many did, under the Emperor Claudius; again, possible but not certain. His letter is addressed in conventional fashion, τῷ κρατίστῳ ἡγεμόνι Φήλικι. κράτιστος corresponds to *egregius* and was an appropriate address. Conzelmann (131) quotes Dittenberger, *OGIS* 2.667.3f. (from the time of Nero): ἐπ<ε>ὶ Ἰουλίου Οὐηστίνου τοῦ κρατίστου ἡγεμόνος. Cf. *I Eph* 1.24.A.6 (quoted in *ND* 4.82). There are several unimportant variants.

Φήλικι τῷ κρατίστῳ ἡγεμόνι P⁴⁸ gig
Κρατίστῳ ἡγεμόνι Φήλικι 614 2495 *pc*
τῷ κρατίστῳ ἡγεμόνι 1838

χαίρειν is the usual greeting in a Greek letter, illustrated many times in the papyri. It appears in the NT at Acts 15.23; Jas 1.1.
'Der griechische Name Lysias macht seine Herkunft aus der

griechisch sprechenden Bevölkerung des Küstengebiets oder Samariens wahrscheinlich, aus der die meisten der in der Provinz Judäa stationisierten Soldaten stammten' (Stählin 292).

27. Claudius Lysias proceeds to give an account of the events leading up to his letter. It does not correspond exactly with the narrative in chs. 21, 22. This may be simply careless writing on Luke's part (cf. his different accounts of Paul's conversion) or an attempt by the tribune to set the story (especially so far as it relates to Paul's citizenship) in a more favourable light than the facts warranted. It would be unwise to exclude either as a contributing factor, though it is hard to see how Luke could have obtained a copy of the official letter. The style however shows a somewhat convoluted officialese (but Luke could write in different styles when he wished—witness Lk. 1; 2), and there are several technical legal terms.

συλληφθέντα, a technical term, *to arrest*, but here rather of seizure by a mob.

σὺν τῷ στρατεύματι: cf. 23.10. Not *with the army*, but *with the military, with a detachment of troops*.

ἐξειλάμην] ἐρυσάμην, P[48].

μαθὼν ὅτι Ῥωμαῖός ἐστιν. It would be difficult to make this mean, 'I rescued him, and subsequently discovered that he was a Roman.' The aorist participle almost certainly refers to action before that of the main verb. 'I rescued him when I discovered, or because I had discovered, that he was a Roman.' If the dialogue of 22.25–29 is derived from Paul's own recollection and is correct one can only suppose that the tribune is improving on the facts for the benefit of his superior (or that Luke wished to attribute this motive to him). If the wording of the letter is correct it is possible that the tribune was speaking the truth and that it was information that Paul was a Roman that led him to take his troops out of the Antonia; why otherwise should he have taken such provocative steps to prevent one insignificant Jew from being beaten by his compatriots? This would do no harm to anyone but the man himself. In this case the narrative of 22.25–29 is in error. It must be remembered that events such as those described in these chapters are seldom clear cut. The situation was no doubt very confused and different people will have retained different impressions of what took place. Schille (430) speaks of Luke's love of variety; Rackham (440) returns to his view of Luke's use of participles; they are to be taken in order, so that we have, 'I rescued ... I learned ...'. Johnson (405) repunctuates, putting a stop after ἐξειλάμην and starting a sentence with μαθών: having learned that ... and wishing ... I brought him down. But surely this would require a particle after μαθών.

P[48vid] gig give a more natural picture, replacing μαθὼν ... ἐστιν by κράζον[τα καὶ λέγοντα ἑαυτὸν] εἶναι Ῥωμαῖον. Neither does this correspond with ch. 22.

The letter as a whole shows: (1) Paul is a Roman citizen and under the Procurator's jurisdiction. (2) His rescue is due to Roman power. (3) No Roman offence was committed. (4) The charge is due to internal Jewish party feeling. So Roloff (332f.). Schneider (2.340) agrees with Haenchen that the variant account in the letter is intended to show Rome's respect for the citizen.

'Perhaps the letter merely meant to say that the tribune intervened in the riot, learned of Paul's citizenship, and examined the case' (*Begs.* 4.294).

28. This verse recalls 22.30. αἰτίαν, *charge*, and ἐνεκάλουν, *accuse* are technical terms.

For τε, 𝔐 e gig sy^h have δέ.

κατήγαγον ... αὐτῶν is omitted by B* 81. Ropes (*Begs.* 3.221) followed by Metzger (489) explains this as due to homoeoteleuton; this could be so (αὐτῷ ... αὐτῶν) if the latter pronoun was written (as frequently) ΑΥΤΩ and the horizontal stroke was missed.

κατήγαγον is left without an object in P^74 ℵ A 33 614 945 1739 1891 2464 *pc*; αὐτόν is added by P^48vid B² E Ψ 𝔐 lat sy.

29. περὶ ζητημάτων τοῦ νόμου αὐτῶν: not a bad summary of 23.6–9, νόμος being the authoritative basis of the Jewish religion. Luke no doubt thought it well that the Romans should think of Christianity as a variety of Judaism, at worst a heretical form of it, at best its supreme expression.

ἔγκλημα, another technical term; cf. v. 25(24), v.l.; 25.16. It is a *complaint*, or more specifically a *charge*. See MM 179f. for papyrus use; add *ND* 3.66. Paul was accused of disputed matters, but there was no accusation calling for (worthy of) death or imprisonment. The charge of bringing Gentiles into the Temple (21.28) appears at this point to have been dropped; but see 24.19f.

The Western text gives more Christian content to the dispute evoked by Paul, adding after αὐτῶν, Μωυσέως καὶ Ἰησοῦ τινός. This could mean 'the Law of Moses and of Jesus', but it more probably means that the dispute concerned their Law, that of Moses, and a certain Jesus. This addition is found in 614 2147 gig sy^hmg; the same MSS add at the end of the verse ἐξήγαγον αὐτὸν μόλις τῇ βίᾳ; a fair account of what is narrated in ch. 21 and heightening the interest at this point.

30. The letter ends with a very stilted sentence. Better than the genitive absolute would have been the accusative absolute μηνυθέν followed by the accusative and infinitive (M. 1.74); alternatively, ἐμηνύθη ἐπιβουλὴ ἔσεσθαι (BDR § 424, n. 2). Preuschen (136) thinks that two constructions are mixed: μηνυθείσης μοι ἐπιβουλῆς ἐσομένης and μηνυθέντος μοι ἐπιβουλὴν μέλλειν ἔσεσθαι. There is a better construction in Thucydides 4.89.2: μηνυθέντος τοῦ ἐπιβουλεύματος ὑπὸ Νικομάχου ... ὃς Λακεδαιμονίοις εἶπεν, ἐκεῖνοι δὲ Βοιωτοῖς. For the latter part of the sentence cf. Herodotus 6.98.1, τοῦτο μέν κου τέρας ἀνθρώποισι τῶν μελλόντων ἔσεσθαι κακῶν ἔφηνε ὁ θεός.

ἔσεσθαι (future infinitive) occurs in the NT only in Acts, and here it 'is in an official letter in stilted style' (M. 2.219); cf. BDR § 350, the future infinitive 'ist der Volkssprache verlorengegangen'.

With these words Claudius Lysias passes on the information brought to him by Paul's nephew, and at the same time passes on his prisoner to the higher authority, adding that he has also ordered the Jews who are accusing Paul to appear before Felix.

ἔσεσθαι ἐξαυτῆς (P⁷⁴ B Ψ 36 453 614 2464 *pc* bo) seems to be the original text, though ἔσεσθαι ἐξ αὐτῶν (𐌀 A E (33) 81 (945) 1175 1739 1891 2495 *pc* (vg) syʰ) has good support and could be right— either of these could give rise to the other; μέλλειν ἔσεσθαι ὑπὸ τῶν Ἰουδαίων, ἐξαυτῆς (𝔐 gig syᵖ) sa) is secondary.

λέγειν πρὸς αὐτόν (B 1175) is surprising, but may be right: the accusers should speak to him, bring their accusations to his face. Instead, 𐌀 A 33 *pc* have λέγειν αὐτούς, he told his accusers to speak themselves, not leaving it to a Roman official to bring a charge in which he had no interest. λέγειν τὰ πρὸς αὐτόν (E Ψ 𝔐 syʰ), to speak with reference to his case, is an attempt to improve an awkward but sufficiently clear phrase.

At the end of the letter 𐌀 E Ψ 𝔐 vgᶜˡ sy add the conventional greeting, ἔρρωσο; P 1241 *pm* have the less likely plural, ἔρρωσθε. See 15.29.

31. μὲν οὖν picks up the narrative after the quotation of the text of the letter. Cf. 15.30.

διά (𝔐 adds τῆς; the whole phrase is omitted by P⁷⁴) νυκτός. Moule, *IB* 56 distinguishes the prepositional phrase from the simple νυκτός: διά ν. means *in the night*, ν. *by night*. Cf. 16.9 (where also many MSS add τῆς); and see Zerwick (§ 115). *In the night* corresponds with τῇ δὲ ἐπαύριον in v. 32. Delebecque (113), 'toute la nuit'.

For Antipatris see *NS* 2.167f. 'A. is to be looked for about eight miles south of Kfar Saba, in a well-watered neighbourhood, whereas Kfar Saba itself stands on arid soil.' This follows Josephus, *Ant.* 16.142 against 13.390. G. A. Smith, *Historical Geography of the Holy Land* (1894, 1968), 124 prefers Ras el-ᶜAin as the site. The city was founded by Herod the Great in honour of his father, Antipater (Josephus, *Ant.* 16.142f.; also *War* 1.417). It was a Hellenistic town; see Sevenster (*Do you know Greek?* SuppNovT 19 (1968), 97) and

Tcherikover (*Hellenistic Civilization* 46–8). It is mentioned at Gittin 7.7 as between Judaea and Galilee. Hemer (128) refers to S. Dar and S. Applebaum, 'The Roman Road from Antipatris to Caesarea', *PEQ* 105 (1973), 91–9, and adds that from Jerusalem to Antipatris (via Lydda) was *c.* 35 miles. Marshall (372) gives 37 miles, 60 km.; Haenchen (620) gives 62 km. (= 38.75) miles), Hanson (223) gives 45 miles (= 72 km.). These surprisingly divergent figures reflect uncertainty about the site (see above) and the existence of alternative routes, by Lydda and by Bethel—see *Begs.* 4.295.

The name bears the article, τὴν Ἀντιπατρίδα, possibly as a well-known station on the route from Jerusalem to Caesarea. See v. 23. It is very unlikely that the cavalry, with Paul mounted, could reach Antipatris in the course of a night, absolutely impossible that the infantry should have done so. Some of the difficulty is removed (also some of the difficulty regarding numbers) if we may suppose that the infantry was intended only to get Paul out of the city, and then to return (cf. Marshall 372); but not the whole of the difficulty. And v. 32 implies (but does not quite state) that it was from Antipatris that the infantry returned. The details of Luke's circumstantial and at first sight convincing narrative tend to crumble, without however destroying the general picture. He has probably written up imaginatively a bare historical outline: 'Paul was transferred to Caesarea.' Luke's knowledge of the geography of Palestine is inexact (Schille 430; Stählin 292f.).

For the whole journey, Jerusalem to Caesarea, see Josephus, *War* 1.79 (600 stadia).

32. τῇ δὲ ἐπαύριον; see on v. 31. This confirms that διὰ νυκτός refers to the activities of a single night. It was (according to Luke) on the day after leaving Jersualem late at night that the party reached Antipatris. For the distance see on v. 31. Knowling's alternative (475), 'Not necessarily the morrow after they left Jerusalem, but the morrow after they arrived at Antipatris', is strained.

ὑπέστρεψαν: the subject must be the infantry, since the cavalry are allowed to go on (ἀπέρχεσθαι, *to go off*, a surprising word, changed by Ψ 𝔐 to the more conventional πορεύεσθαι).

παρεμβολήν: back to the barracks (the Antonia).

ἐάσαντες presumably refers to the subject of ὑπέστρεψαν, that is, the infantry; but Luke must mean the centurions commanding the infantry. Or could ἐάω simply mean, they *left* them?

33. The military escort fulfilled its mission, according to instructions. The journey from Antipatris to Caesarea was about 25 miles.

ἀναδόντες: ἀναδιδόναι is used for delivering letters, e.g. Polybius 29.10(25).7; Diodorus Siculus 11.45.3; cf. *IG* 14.830, line 22 (LS 103). MM 32 quote papyri, including PTebt 2.448.6–11 (ii/iii AD),

τῷ ἀναδιδόντι σοι τὸ ἐπιστόλιον. A different word, παρέστησαν, is
used for handing over the person.

34. ἐπερωτήσας ἐκ ποίας ἐπαρχείας (so B* ℵ A; the rest rather
more correctly, since ἐπαρχεία is strictly the office of a prefect, have
ἐπαρχία, which is *province*) ἐστίν. See the long discussion, correcting Mommsen, by Sherwin-White (28–31). He resumes his argument on p. 55: 'It was argued earlier that the custom of *forum
domicilii* [over against *forum delicti*], that is, of referring an accused
person back to the jurisdiction of his native province, was never more
than optional, and that it was not firmly established in the early
Principate.' So also Tajra (116f.). Sherwin-White adds (ibidem),
'But in the case of a Roman citizen, and of a Jewish imbroglio, the
procurator might well have been glad to avail himself of any such
usage.' Yet he did not. Having ascertained that Paul belonged not to
his own province but to Cilicia he undertook to try the case himself
(v. 35). Why then take the trouble to make the inquiry? Possibly
these were only preliminary inquiries, but Sherwin-White has a
better answer. 'If Cilicia at the time of the incident of Acts xxiv did
not have a separate imperial legate, Felix's decision is explained. The
Legate of Syria was not to be bothered with minor cases from Judaea,
though it was his duty to intervene in times of great crisis, and the
status of Cilicia did not require that its natives should be sent to it for
trial, even if the later usage of *forum domicilii* was in vogue' (56). On
this view, Felix hoped for an answer that would enable him to slip
out of the whole affair, but found that in fact he could not do so. An
alternative explanation is that his inquiry was intended to ascertain
whether Paul came from a Roman province or from one of the client
kingdoms; in the latter case it would have been unwise not to send
Paul back to his place of origin. In view of the changes (see above) in
regard to *forum domicilii* and *forum delicti* Conzelmann's references
(131) to the *Acts of Carpus, Papylus, and Agathonike* 24–27 and to
the *Martyrdom of Justin* 4.7ff lose some relevance; in any case in the
Martyrdom of Justin inquiry is made into the residence of parents
when these are said to have been responsible for making their
children Christians, and thus are themselves liable to a charge.

Cilicia, in the early Principate, was a dependency of the province
of Syria; later, probably in the early years of Nero, it became an
independent province. See Hemer (172, 179, 180, 290f., 381).

ποίας is used for τίνος. Or could it mean, 'What sort of province,
senatorial or imperial?'

The end of this verse and the beginning of the next are rewritten in
direct speech by 614 2147 sy^hmg: ἀναγνοὺς δὲ τὴν ἐπιστ. καὶ
ἐπηρώτησε τὸν Παῦλον· ἐκ ποίας ἐπαρχ. εἶ; ἔφη Κίλιξ. καὶ
πυθόμενος ἔφη· ἀκούσομαί σου ... This Western variant is, as
usual, livelier than that of the Old Uncial text. *ND* 4.173 gives

evidence of the use of the form Κίλιξ, but it was current from Homer onwards. The Western reading is taken up by J. L. North (*JTS* 47 (1996), 439–63) in the light of evidence that Cilicians had a reputation for lying.

35. διακούειν (future deponent διακούσομαι) is used for hearing the various parties in a dispute. See Job 9.33; Plutarch, *Themistocles* 2 (112), Ἀναξαγόρου τε διακοῦσαι τὸν Θεμιστοκλέα φησί: there is much non-literary evidence in MM 150. It also means a *full hearing*; contrast v. 34. Page (235) quotes *Digest* 48.3.6: Qui cum elogio [see on v. 25] mittuntur, ex integro audiendi sunt.

ἔφη. BDR § 465.3, n. 5 say that this is not parenthesis but variation in word-order. Is it not variation that leads to parenthesis?

κελεύσας. M. 1.132f. argues that we cannot take this as an example of subsequent action expressed by an aorist participle. At most it is coincident action: '... "he said ..., meanwhile ordering him ...," which may perfectly well mean that Felix first told his soldiers where they were to take Paul, and then assured the prisoner of an early trial, just before the guards led him away.'

ἐν τῷ πραιτωρίῳ τοῦ (א A E 33 81 453 945 1739 1891 2464 *al*; τῷ, B 1175; omit, P⁷⁴ Ψ 𝔐) Ἡρῴδου, the palace built by Herod the Great and taken over by the Roman administration. We have no archaeological or other information about it (except that it existed) and its site remains unknown. At this point Paul becomes formally a state prisoner (Ehrhardt, *Acts* 113).

XV

PAUL AND THE ROMANS
(24.1–26.32)

58. PAUL AND FELIX 24.1–27

(1) After five days the High Priest Ananias with a number of elders and a barrister Tertullus, came down; these informed the governor against Paul. (2) When he[1] was called, Tertullus began his accusation, saying, 'Since through you we enjoy much peace and since reforms for this nation are coming about through your provident foresight, (3) in all ways and in every place we welcome this, most excellent Felix, with all gratitude. (4) But in order not to weary you further, I ask you in your forbearance to hear us briefly. (5) For we found this man a pest, and one who stirs up riots among all the Jews throughout the world, and a ringleader of the sect of the Nazoraeans. (6) He also tried to profane the Temple, and we seized him.[2] (8) From him you will be able yourself, by examining him, to find out about the things of which we accuse him.' (9) The Jews also joined in this attack, affirming that these things were so.

(10) When the governor motioned to him to speak, Paul answered, 'Since I know that you have been for many years a judge of this nation I cheerfully make my defence, (11) since you can find out that it is not more than twelve days since I came up to Jerusalem to worship. (12) And neither in the Temple nor in the synagogues nor anywhere in the city did they find me arguing with anyone or causing the onset of a crowd, (13) nor can they prove any of those things of which they now accuse me. (14) I do confess this to you, that it is in accordance with the Way, which they call a sect, that I serve our ancestral God, believing all things that are according to the Law and the things that are written in the prophets, (15) having the same hope in God which they also accept, that there will be a resurrection of both the righteous and the unrighteous. (16) And so for my part I too exercise myself so as to have continually a blameless conscience towards both God and men. (17) At the end of many years I arrived [here][3] to bring alms for my nation and offerings. (18) While I was engaged in these sacrifices they found me in the Temple in a state of purity, with no crowd, with no tumult. (19) But some of the Jews from Asia [allege this],[4] who ought to be present before you and bring an accusation, if they have anything against me. (20) Or let these men

---

[1]NEB, the prisoner; NJB, Paul.
[2]For an insertion made here by many MSS see the note on v. 7.
[3]Here is not in the Greek.
[4]Allege this is not in the Greek, where the sentence appears to be incomplete.

themselves say what crime they found in me when I stood before the Sanhedrin, (21) unless it be this one thing that I cried out when I stood among them, I am being judged this day before you concerning the resurrection of the dead.'

(22) Felix[5] adjourned [the hearing][6] since he had an accurate knowledge of the Way, and said, 'When Lysias the tribune comes down I will hear your case and reach a decision.' (23) He charged the centurion that he should be kept[7] safe and have relief from prison regimen, and that he should not prevent any of his friends from doing him service.

(24) After some days Felix arrived with Drusilla his wife, who was a Jewess, and sent for Paul and heard him on faith in Christ [Jesus].[8] (25) As he discoursed on righteousness, self-control, and the judgement to come Felix became afraid, and answered, 'For the present, go your way; when I have an opportunity I will send for you.' (26) At the same time also he hoped that money would be given him by Paul. For this reason also he sent for him pretty often, and conversed with him. (27) When two years were up Felix was succeeded by Porcius Festus. Wishing to curry favour with the Jews Felix left Paul in prison.

Bibliography

C. K. Barrett, *FS* Bammel, 361–7.

C. K. Barrett, *FS* Furnish, 161–72.

K. Berger, *NTS* 23 (1977), 180–204.

M. Black, as in (46).

M. P. Charlesworth, *HThR* 29 (1936), 107–32.

F. Cumont, *RHR* 91 (1925), 1ff.

K. Haacker, as in (56).

J. Jeremias, *ZNW* 27 (1928), 98–103.

G. M. Lee, *NovT* 9 (1967), 41.

S. Légasse, as in (54).

S. Lösch, *ThQu* 112 (1931), 295–319.

A. J. Mattill, *CBQ* 34 (1972), 142.

C. Maurer, *TWNT* 7.897–918.

J. C. O'Neill, *NTS* 35 (1989), 219–28 (224).

G. Schneider, in Bammel-Moule (1984) 403–14.

M. Stern, in Safrai-Stern 1.74–6.

R. D. Sullivan, *ANRW* II.8 (1977), 296–354.

C. H. Turner, *JTS* 3 (1902), 120–3.

W. C. van Unnik, in Kremer, *Actes*, 37–60.

B. Winter, *JTS* 42 (1991), 505–31.

P. Winter, *NTS* 3 (1957), 136–42.

[5]RSV, put them off.
[6]Greek, them.
[7]NEB, under open arrest.
[8]There is textual authority for omitting this word.

Commentary

The paragraph falls into two parts: Paul's appearance in court before Felix (vv. 1–23); Paul's private relations with Felix (vv. 24–27).

In the first part the Sanhedrin, represented by the High Priest and a number of elders, travel to Caesarea in order to present their case against Paul. This assumes a situation that has developed since 22.30, where it seems that Claudius Lysias is making use of the Sanhedrin as a fact-finding and advisory body. The Jews now bring an accusation against Paul in the Governor's court with specific charges (vv. 5, 6), which however it is left to Felix himself to investigate and substantiate. The Jews' advocate, Tertullus, who begins with an admirable *captatio benevolentiae*, must of course be supposed to have made a much longer and more detailed speech. Paul also must be supposed to have spoken at greater length; but between them the two speakers make what Luke wished to be understood as the legal points at issue. Tertullus claims that Paul, as the ringleader of the Nazoraean sect, has been stirring up unrest among Jews all over the world, and that he has attempted to profane the Temple. There is thus at issue a matter of Jewish doctrine (for Paul is leader of a αἵρεσις, with its own understanding of Judaism), but this leads to the Roman crime of *seditio* and to an act which the Romans have agreed shall be forbidden on pain of death. These accusations are repeated, explicitly or implicitly, through the remaining chapters, and Schille (436) is not wrong in describing the present scene as the 'endgültiges Zusammenprall' between Paul and Judaism. To all the charges Paul, on this occasion, replies. (1) Of course it is true that he is a Christian, but what Tertullus calls a αἵρεσις he calls a Way, and the Way consists in the worship of the ancestral Jewish God and believing all the things written in the Law and the Prophets: what Jew could object to that? It includes belief in the resurrection. (2) He has been responsible for no disturbances, in Temple, synagogue, or city. In Jerusalem there has been no time since his arrival; as for the rest of the world, there is— to say no more—no evidence. Jews of Jerusalem cannot supply it, and the Jews of Asia (who, if there were evidence, might have given it) were not present. (3) As for the Temple, he was indeed there because he had come on a charitable mission to his people and was engaged in sacrifice. He was in a state of purity; there was no tumult.

No one is likely to maintain that Luke provides his reader with the very words uttered in Felix's court by Tertullus and by Paul. The question that may reasonably be asked is whether Luke has fairly represented the accusations brought by the Jews and the replies made by Paul. The question whether the Gospel is or is not the fulfilment of the Law and the Prophets runs not only through the whole of Acts but through the whole of the NT. It turns in the end upon a point which is not here specifically mentioned: Was the crucified Jesus now alive or dead? Was he or was he not the Messiah, that is, the person in whom the essence of Judaism was crystallized and fulfilled? On the charge of *seditio* Paul simply utters a denial. This was justified in the sense that he had desired no disturbance; what he desired was that all Jews should peaceably accept his version of Judaism. He had not desired disturbance, but it could be reasonably maintained that he had provoked it by insisting on a version of Judaism which the majority of Jews saw not as the fulfilment but as the destruction of their faith. The theological question and the social or political question were closely related. On the question of Temple profanation Paul was on stronger ground. If the story in Acts is correct, he had not—and scarcely could have—committed it. If the story in Acts is incorrect, this is most likely to be on the ground that Paul would not have entered the Temple to take part in its activities at all.

Thus the Jews seem to be playing down the theological issue; wisely, for it would not interest Romans, who would not be likely to condemn a man simply as an erring theologian. They emphasize the charges that would carry greatest weight in a Roman court. Paul on the other hand emphasizes his Jewishness and responds to the other charges with a flat denial and the challenge, 'Produce your evidence.' There seems to be a reasonable measure of probability on both sides.

'Die Szene ist wohl in toto von Lukas gestaltet' (Lüdemann 256); not however without some foundation in historical tradition and in knowledge of fact and procedure. 'Sherwin-White [48] cites Mommsen's opinion of Paul's trial as "an exemplary account of the provincial procedure *extra ordinem*" '; so Hemer (129), who agrees. It must however be added that there is not much procedure in the narrative. Felix calls Tertullus, Tertullus speaks, Paul speaks, and Felix postpones a decision.

Weiser (627) thinks that vv. 1–23 were built up by Luke on the basis of (1) a Jewish delegation including Tertullus got only a postponement; (2) Paul was accused of desecrating the Temple; (3) he had come to bring alms (this, it is argued, must be traditional because elsewhere Luke shows no knowledge of Paul's collection). We should add the charge of causing *seditio*, of which Luke must have been aware. This means that though the scene is Luke's creation it is based upon and enshrines a historical basis. Cf. Roloff (336) and Preuschen (137).

The second part of the paragraph tells of frequent interviews between Paul and Felix, in which the latter's wife Drusilla also took part. Comparisons with the story of Herod and John the Baptist are worth little. Felix is depicted much more favourably, and so is Drusilla; readiness to take a bribe is of course reprehensible but it is hardly to be compared with rewarding a dance with a severed head. It is somewhat more to the point to say that the judge who did not condemn

Paul must have been (in Luke's view) a good man, whose judgement is therefore to be approved, but not so very good—he hoped for a bribe, and because he did not get one left Paul in prison. Perhaps Luke felt the need to explain why the judge who did not condemn Paul nevertheless failed to release him. Felix's character as depicted by Josephus and Tacitus suggests a readiness to accept bribes; and he had good reason to adopt any means of currying favour with the Jews.

There is something to be said for the view that in v. 27 *two years* originally, in the information used by Luke, referred to the length of Felix's governorship, but was understood by Luke to refer to the length of Paul's imprisonment, which interested him much more. See the note; also Haenchen (632f.); Lüdemann (258–60). The point is important for the chronology of Paul's life.

1. μετὰ δὲ πέντε ἡμέρας looks back to 23.35: Felix waits for Paul's accusers. A has τινὰς ἡμέρας. P[74] reverses the word order: ἡμέρας πέντε. The number *five* either has some traditional basis or is Luke's attempt to add an appearance of first-hand knowledge; probably the former. τινάς or ἱκανάς, rather than a number, would be in accordance with Luke's manner.

κατέβη is geographically correct (from the mountains to the coast), but the word was used as a technical term (cf. ἀναβαίνειν) for a journey from the capital to any other destination; cf. e.g. 8.15.

ὁ ἀρχιερεὺς Ἀνανίας. See 23.2.

πρεσβυτέρων τινῶν; 𝔐 sy[p] have τῶν πρεσβυτέρων, failing to see the impossibility of all the elders' appearing in Felix's court.

ῥήτορος Τερτύλλου τινός. To judge from the papyri the use of a ῥήτωρ, a *barrister* or *advocate* (Latin, causidicus), to represent participants in a suit was a common practice. MM 563f. quote POxy 1.37. col. 1.4f. (AD 49), Ἀριστοκλῆς ῥήτωρ ὑπὲρ Πεσούριος(?); 2.237. col. 7.25 (AD 186), Δίδυμος ῥήτωρ ἀπεκρίνατο μὴ χώρις λόγου τὸν Σεμπρώνιον κεκεινῆσθαι; and refer to other papyri. It should not be assumed that the practice was uniform or that professional advocates could be used in every kind of court or every kind of case (cf. *Begs.* 5.320). Use was not mandatory and probably indicates the importance or complexity of the case. It is interesting that the case referred to in the second quotation above bears some resemblance to the complaint made by the Jews against Paul: it is not (they allege) without ground that they move against him. It is often supposed that Tertullus was himself a Jew, no doubt a Greek-speaking Jew of the Diaspora. Knox (*Hell. El.* 30, n. 2) compares Josephus's journey to Rome (*Life* 13) on behalf of a number of priests whom Felix had sent there λόγον ὑφέξοντας τῷ Καίσαρι. The argument that Tertullus was a Jew rests to a great extent on the first person plural ἐκρατήσαμεν in v. 6. But an advocate would associate himself with his clients, and the reference to 'all the Jews' in v. 5 has been held to show that Tertullus was a Gentile

(Stählin 294). One cannot be certain. If the need for an advocate was linguistic rather than legal it implies that the High Priest and his colleagues could not (or possibly would not) use Greek well enough to use it in court. See Lieberman (*Greek in Jewish Palestine*) and Sevenster (*Do you know Greek?*), neither of whom, however, discusses this passage.

The name Tertullus is derived from Tertius (as Catullus from Catius, Lucullus from Lucius). It occurs in Pliny, *Epistles* 5.15(14).1. The *usus provincialis* was regarded as good training for young lawyers (Cicero, *pro Caelio* 30 (12)).

οἵτινες for οἵ; cf. 23.33.

ἐνεφάνισαν, here with dative and κατά; see 23.15. The plural (rather than the singular, which would refer to Tertullus) is used (a) because the complaint was made by the Jews as a body, and (b) because it would have been made in the first instance in writing.

2. κληθέντος δὲ αὐτοῦ. The pronoun is omitted by B; for the omission of the subject in a genitive absolute cf. 21.31. If the copyist of B took the genitive absolute to be incorrectly used, referring to the subject of the main verb (When Tertullus was called, he began ...), he might have thought that the omission would slightly mend the sentence, or at least make the solecism less evident. But it may be right to take αὐτοῦ to refer to Paul (When Paul was called, Tertullus began ...). We cannot say that Luke would never have used a genitive absolute incorrectly; see e.g. 22.17. But it may be right to give him the benefit of the doubt here. καλεῖν is used as a technical term for the summoning of a witness (Plato, *Laws* 937a: ὁ δ᾽ εἰς μαρτυρίαν κληθείς) or of any other participant in a legal process (Demosthenes 19.211 (406): καλεῖν ἐμ᾽ εἰς τὸ δικαστήριον). The active is used of the judge, the middle of the plaintiff; see LS 866 s.v. I 4a, b. *Begs.* 4.297 quotes POxy 9.1204.13, κληθέντος Πλουτάρχου κρατίστου Ἰσίδωρος (his representative) εἶπ[εν] ...

Tertullus begins his accusation with the customary *captatio benevolentiae*; see Quintilian, *De Institutione Oratoria* 4.1; Cicero, *De Oratore* 2.78, 79 (319–325); Lucian, *Bis Accusatus* 17; for πολύς in such paragraphs, Thucydides 1.80.1; 2.35.1; 3.37.1; Dionysius of Halicarnassus 5.1.4 (Conzelmann 131).

πολλῆς εἰρήνης. It requires some exaggeration, or indeed imagination, to find any peace in Palestine in the time of Felix. It could however be claimed that many bandits had been put down (Josephus, *War* 2.253–263).

διὰ σοῦ. There are parallels in which διά is used, but with the accusative. M. 1.105 quotes PMagdola 16 and 20 where the petitioner asks ἵνα διὰ σὲ βασιλεῦ τοῦ δικαίου τύχω, and comments that 'if the humble petitioner had meant "*through* you", he would have addressed the king as a mere medium of power: referring to a sovereign power, the ordinary meaning "because of you" is more appropriate.' This belongs to the third century BC; the accusative appears also in a close parallel to Acts in POxy 41 (M. 1.106; iii/iv AD), πολλῶν ἀγαθῶν ἀπολαύομεν διὰ σαί [= σέ]. But at the beginning of his speech Tertullus will not have intended to represent Felix as a mere intermediary. In English, however, 'through you' need not imply disparagement.

διορθωμάτων: 𝔐 has κατορθωμάτων. κατορθ. is a Stoic technical term for good actions, the opposite of ἁμαρτήματα. See SVF 4.81 (Index, s.v.) and 3.136 (Frag. 501; Chrysippus, in Stobaeus, Eclogae 2.96.18 (Ed. Heeren, 2.192)), ... κατορθώματα μὲν τὰ τοιαῦτα· φρονεῖν, σωφρονεῖν, δικαιοπράγειν, χαίρειν, εὐεργετεῖν, εὐφραίνεσθαι, φρονίμως περιπατεῖν, πανθ' ὅσα κατὰ τὸν ὀρθὸν λόγον πράττεται· ἁμαρτήματα δ' εἶναι ... Phrynichus 225 somewhat surprisingly rejects κατόρθωμα in favour of ἀνδραγάθημα. διόρθωμα, on the other hand, means setting right, reform, often in connection with laws. Thus Plutarch, Numa 17 (71), τὸ περὶ τὸν νόμον διόρθωμα. It is probable that διόρθωμα was the original reading and reform its meaning, though to what reforms benefiting the ἔθνος (here undoubtedly the Jewish nation; cf. vv. 10, 17; 10.22) Tertullus refers we do not know. Delebecque (114): 'cette nation; le démontratif semble indiquer que Tertullus n'est pas Juif'. See however above.

The participles τυγχάνοντες (since we enjoy; cf. 26.22; 27.3; Lk. 20.35 for this Attic use) and γινομένων (and since there have been) are causal and introduce v. 3.

διὰ τῆς σῆς προνοίας. πρόνοια is prudentia; see 2 Macc. 4.6; Rom. 13.14; (12.17). πρόνοια is one of the standard virtues of the Hellenistic ruler. 'Rühmend von der πρόνοια des Herrschers (nach Dio Chrysostom Oratio 3.43 eine πρόνοια ἀνθρώπων κατὰ νόμον), Feldherrn oder Staatsmannes zu sprechen, wird im Hellenismus stehender Brauch, vgl 2 Makk 4.6 ..., Epistle of Aristeas 30: προνοίας βασιλικῆς οὐ τέτευχε, Diodorus Siculus 29 fragment 19 (von Hannibal) ... PHerm 119B3.3 ...' (J. Behm, in TWNT 4.1006). See also S. Lösch, 'Die Dankesrede des Tertullus', Theol. Quartalschrift 112 (1931), 310ff.; M. P. Charlesworth, 'Providentia et Aeternitas', HThR 29 (1936), 107–32. There is further papyrus evidence in ND 3.143. It is clear that Tertullus (or Luke?) knows the proper style to use.

It is possible to connect πάντῃ τε καὶ πανταχοῦ (v. 3) with this verse, but the sentences seem better balanced if they are joined to what follows. Not so, however, Page (236): great peace and improvements everywhere.

3. πάντῃ (adverbs in –ῃ appear in the NT only here and at 21.28) τε καὶ πανταχοῦ, in every way and in every place. For the spelling

see M. 2.84 and for the paronomasia see BDR § 488.1, n. 2 (quoting Plato, *Menexenus* 247a, διὰ παντὸς πᾶσαν πάντως προθυμίαν πειρᾶσθε ἔχειν, but not referring to this verse). See also as examples Aristotle, *Nicomachean Ethics* 1.10.15 (1101a); Philo, *De Opificio Mundi* 61.

ἀποδεχόμεθα, *we welcome*—the peace and reforms mentioned in v. 2. It is (*Begs.* 4.297) a courteous word, and this is reinforced by εὐχαριστία, for which see I. Assos 7.22, an honorific decree quoted in *ND* 1.83. There is a different Jewish estimate of Felix in Josephus, *Ant.* 20.182. πάσης continues the paronomasia as well as the *captatio benevolentiae*. Cf. 28.31.

κράτιστε: cf. 23.26. Φῆλιξ: so accented by NA[26] in agreement with Blass 251, 'Φῆλιξ scrib., non Φήλιξ, quia ι et υ ante ξ corripiuntur (κῆρῠξ, Φοῖνῐξ).' Against this, and it seems rightly, *Begs.* 4.297: 'Φῆλιξ, not Φήλιξ, *pace* Blass, for Felix is a Latin word in which the last syllable is long (*felīcem*), so that the analogy of κῆρυξ and φοῖνιξ proves nothing.'

4. Tertullus continues the polite, ingratiating, manner of his introduction. Other examples of an orator's self-limitation are collected by Betz, 118, n. 1.

ἐγκόπτω is normally *hinder*. This it can hardly be here, unless in the sense of preventing Felix from attending to other business. The Syriac and Armenian give the meaning *weary*; this is supported by the fact that ἔγκοπος (*Anthologia Palatina* 6.33; but the use is Septuagintal: Job 19.2; Isa. 43.23) means *wearied*. *Begs.* 4.298 translates *detain*. ἐγκόπτω is the reading of ℵ A[c] B E L 𝔐 co; κόπτω is read by P[74] A[*vid] (Ψ) 33 1175 1241 1891 *pc*. κόπτω means *to strike*, in one sense or another; here it could perhaps mean *to annoy*.

τῇ σῇ ἐπιεικείᾳ (B* spells ἐπεικείᾳ; on various questions of spelling in this word see M. 2.89, 314, 348). Moule (*IB* 45) notes but does not explain the unusual dative. Clearly Felix is being asked to listen and to act with ἐπιεικεία—towards the Jews. The word is hard to translate. See H. Preisker (*TWNT* 2.585–7); further parallels in Betz (209, n. 3). It denotes reasonableness, fairness, in general and especially perhaps in a judge, who is prepared not to break the laws but to give them an understanding, non-legalist interpretation. Most significant is the personification of ἐπιεικεία in Plutarch's *Caesar* 57 (734); καὶ τό γε τῆς ἐπιεικείας ἱερὸν οὐκ ἀπὸ τρόπου δοκοῦσι χαριστήριον ἐπὶ τῇ πραότητι ψηφίσασθαι. Note the parallel with πραότης.

5. The logical and grammatical connection implied by γάρ is not immediately clear; the word may in part account for the long interpolation between vv. 6 and 8—see on v. 8. The best explanation of γάρ is that its sentence provides the basis of the appeal for a patient hearing made in v. 4: You should heed our appeal for a careful hearing, for this is a very serious matter of grave concern to the Empire. εὑρόντες looks back to the events of chs. 21, 22, but has in mind also the whole experience of the Jews with the trouble-making prisoner.

λοιμόν properly means *a plague*; it is transferred to human beings both adjectivally (in the LXX especially as the rendering of various combinations of בְּלִיַּעַל, e.g. 1 Kdms 1.16; 2.12) and substantivally (Demosthenes 25.80 (784)), *pestilential, a pest*. Here it could be either a noun or an adjective complement, without significant difference in meaning.

καὶ κινοῦντα: he is a pest, *in that he stirs up*. For καί used to introduce the sense of a preceding word cf. BDR § 442.9b.

στάσεις (𝔐 sy sa have στάσιν): again ch. 22 is chiefly in mind, but (from the Jewish point of view), other events earlier in Paul's career would be relevant, e.g. 17.6. Theological questions (such as resurrection) are now set aside; the issue now is *seditio*, which a Roman court, unconcerned with theology, would be bound to take very seriously. πᾶσιν (om. P[74]) ... κατὰ τὴν οἰκουμένην emphasizes that it is not the Jerusalem incident alone (see v. 6) that is complained of. The Jews had become a universal people, to be found in every part of the Empire, and a disturbance that threatened their peaceful relations with the Roman administration would constitute the basis of a movement that Felix could not ignore. Sherwin-White (51f.) draws attention to this, referring (following F. Cumont, *RHR* 91 (1925), 3–6) to the letter of Claudius to the Alexandrians (see H. I. Bell, *Jews and Christians in Egypt* (1924), 23–6). The relevant passage (lines 98–100) runs: ... εἰ δὲ μή, πάντα τρόπον αὐτοὺς ἐπεξελεύσομαι καθάπερ κοινήν τεινα (*sic*) τῆς οἰκουμένης νόσον ἐξεγείροντας. Luke's λοιμός recalls νόσος in the letter. Sherwin-White comments, 'The similarity is deliberate. It is evident that the narrative of Acts is using contemporary language. The charge was precisely the one to bring against a Jew during the Principate of Claudius or the early years of Nero. The accusers of Paul were putting themselves on the side of the government. The procurator would know at once what the prosecution meant.'

πρωτοστάτην τε. Again, the new clause elucidates the proceedings, indicating the role in which Paul (according to the allegation) had acted as trouble-maker. πρωτοστάτης was originally a military term (a front-line man; so e.g Thucydides 5.71.2, ὁ πρωτοστάτης τοῦ δεξιοῦ κερῶς; Job 15.24, LXX), here in the derived sense of *chief* or *leader*. For αἵρεσις see on 5.17; the accusation makes Paul the head of a dissident and troublesome Jewish party. See Fitzmyer (*Essays* 276, n. 11). Delebecque (115), on πρωτοστάτης '... c'est le soldat du premier rang; il fait partie des troupes de choc (cf. Xénophon, *Cyrop.* 6.3.24). Paul est présenté comme un soldat d'élite, donc dangereux.' Maddox (70) goes further: '... it is precisely as such that Luke himself wants to portray him. He is more important for what he represents than for his own sake.' Papyri using the word are cited in *ND* 4.244, but add nothing relevant.

The party is that τῶν Ναζωραίων. At 2.22; 3.6; 4.10; 6.14; 22.8 (see Rüger as cited on this verse); 26.9. Acts uses the term Ἰησοῦς (Χριστὸς) ὁ Ναζωραῖος; here only do we have the plural describing not Jesus but the Christians. If the evidence of Acts alone is considered it is natural to suppose that the adjective Nazoraean was first applied to Jesus (probably with the meaning 'man coming from the town of Nazareth') and then came to be attached to his followers (cf. 'Christian', 11.26). It is however important to bear in mind also the patristic evidence for the existence of a Jewish sect bearing this or a similar name (see especially Epiphanius, *Panarion* 29.6), Jewish references to הנוצרים, and the possible etymology of the Hebrew word. See, *inter alia*, Black, *Scrolls* 66–74; P. Winter, *NTS* 3 (1957), 136–42; B. Gärtner, *Die Rätselhafte Termini Nazoräer und Iskariot* (Horae Soederblomianae IV; 1957), 5–36; Kosmala (315). As the last named points out, there is an interesting parallel between the words of Acts 24.5 (τῆς τῶν Ναζωραίων αἱρέσεως) and the combination of מינים and נוצרים in the additional 'test' Benediction formulated *c.* AD 85 (see *St John* 127; *Background* 210f.). נוצרים suggests the plural of the Qal participle of נצר, which means *to guard* or *to observe*; it is used with Torah in e.g. the saying of R. Meir (*c.* 150) in Berakoth 17a: נצור תורתי בלבך, Keep my Torah in thy heart. The suggestion thus lies ready to hand that there was a group of Observants, headed perhaps by the Chief Observant. Such a group could have existed independently of the Christian movement, which was subsequently identified with it; or the name could have been given to an early Christian, Jewish Christian, group which reverenced the Law. Later the name may have suggested a connection with Nazareth. Such suggestions are of interest and have the advantage that they may be used to explain Epiphanius's belief that there was a pre-Christian Jewish sect of Nazoraeans. They have the disadvantage that Jesus does not appear to have lived in such a way as to attract to himself the title of Law-keeper in Chief. There is perhaps no better view than that the adjective (also in the form Ναζαρηνός) was first attached to Jesus in view of his connection with Nazareth, and was then passed on to his followers. It is however probable that in the course of time various (false) etymologies were attached to the name. See H. H. Schaeder in *TWNT* 4.879–84; BA 1077.

Schille (432) makes the point that the reference to Nazoraeans is intended to show that all the proceedings described are relevant not only to Paul individually but to all Christians.

For πᾶσιν ... οἰκουμένην, gig has 'non tantum generi nostro sed fere universo orbe terrarum et omnibus Judaeis', 'doubtless the

"Western" rewriting, and wholly in accord with the glossator's method elsewhere' (Ropes, *Begs*. 3.223).

6. ὃς καί adds a further charge. In addition to fomenting trouble throughout the Jewish world Paul had tried to profane the Temple (by bringing Gentiles into it, 21.28—where the word is the more Jewish κοινοῦν).

ὃν καί, anacolouthon. These two words would be better omitted: Having found this man ... we seized him. The author has forgotten εὑρόντες (v. 5), and supposes that he had written ηὕρομεν.

The charge of desecrating the Temple could be brought into a Roman court because the Romans had accepted the provision for maintaining its sanctity (Stählin 295). Disturbances caused by Paul as leader of the Nazoraeans and desecration of the Temple: 'Beide Punkte enthalten religiöse und politische Brisanz.'

On the text of this verse see on v. 7.

7. A number of MSS (E Ψ 33 (323 614) 945 1739 (2495) *pm* gig vg^cl sy^(p)) contain a considerable paraphrase given in some printed copies of the NT as the end of v. 6, v. 7, and the beginning of v. 8. The whole sentence runs as follows.

καὶ κατὰ τὸν ἡμέτερον νόμον ἠθελήσαμεν κρῖναι (κρίνειν, 614 2495 *pc*). παρελθὼν δὲ Λυσίας ὁ χιλίαρχος μετὰ πολλῆς βίας ἐκ τῶν χειρῶν ἡμῶν ἀπήγαγεν, κελεύσας τοὺς κατηγόρους αὐτοῦ ἔρχεσθαι ἐπί (πρός, E 2464 *pc*) σε.

See Clark (xlvii); Ropes (*Begs*. 3.225); Delebecque (115).

This describes the events of 22.22—23.30 from the Jewish point of view and in very compressed form. An editor no doubt thought that some such cross-reference was necessary in order to explain what was taking place. Luke's narrative, written from a non-Jewish, or anti-Jewish, point of view certainly suggests something other than a peaceful Jewish trial according to law—a lynching, rather; and, according to Luke's story, the tribune was not the first to use violence. Is Luke (or his editor) deliberately setting out to represent the Jews as guilty of falsehood? Is he himself guilty of misrepresenting in his narrative Jewish intention fairly set out in Tertullus's speech? Cf. the letter ascribed to Claudius Lysias. Probably neither; he is using traditional material which reflects two points of view. Dibelius (151, n. 32), cautiously suggests that the long text is original.

For μετὰ ... βίας cf. 5.26 and see BDR § 198.4, n. 5 (classical usage would have required βίᾳ, or πρὸς βίαν).

ἐπί σε: cf. 23.30, ἐπὶ σοῦ. These words are contrasted with κατὰ τὸν ἡμέτερον νόμον.

8. The sequence of relatives is continued: ὃς καί ... ὃν καί ...

(v. 6) ... παρ' οὗ ... Tertullus leaves cross-examination to the judge (αὐτὸς ἀνακρίνας). The verb is used as at 4.9; 12.19. 'Il s'agit d'un procès régulier "extra ordinem" devant le procurateur, qui doit entendre accusateurs, accusé, témoins, et faire lui-même son enquêt, avec son pouvoir discrétionnaire' (Delebecque (115), pointing out in the same context that περὶ πάντων τούτων depends on ἀνακρίνας not ἐπιγνῶναι). κατηγορεῖν takes two genitives, as for example in Demosthenes 21.5 (515).

The long Western addition to the text (see on v. 7). has the effect of causing παρ' οὗ to refer not to Paul but to Lysias. This is defended by Clark (xlvii), who observes that 'no evidence could be so cogent as that of the Roman official who had made the arrest, while Paul would be a suspect witness when speaking about himself'. Haenchen (625), on the other hand, thinks that the Western editor thought it so foolish that the truth should be arrived at by the examination of Paul that he made the change that introduces Lysias as witness. Probably both underestimated the power of an examining magistrate to get the truth out of an unco-operative witness. ἀνακρίνειν in fact describes a process that would be applied to Paul rather than to the tribune.

Haenchen (629), Schneider (2.344), Weiser (626), and others, quote the opinion of Lösch that Tertullus's speech is 'ein Meister-stück von ausgesuchter rhetorischer Kleinkunst' (op. cit. (p. 1090), p. 317).

9. συνεπέθεντο, *joined in the attack.* The word is a military term; its use implies that Paul is regarded as a public enemy.

καὶ οἱ Ἰουδαῖοι suggests, but does not prove, that Tertullus was not himself a Jew. Haenchen draws this conclusion, but it is possible to take the sentence as, So said Tertullus, their representative, and so said the Jews themselves. See on v. 1.

ταῦτα οὕτως ἔχειν. For the expression see 7.1; 17.11.

614 2147 sy^h** fill out the picture, having, instead of συνεπ. δέ, εἰπόντος δὲ αὐτοῦ ταῦτα συνεπέθεντο.

10. Paul replies when the governor gives him leave to do so. νεύειν means *to give a signal,* which will be interpreted in accord-ance with the circumstances. Here it is followed by an infinitive, λέγειν; the same construction is used by Euripides, *Hecuba* 545. Homer, *Iliad* 8.246 has accusative and infinitive.

In place of the simple λέγειν, sy^hmg has *defensionem habere pro se statum autem assumens divinum dixit* (כד קומא דין שקל אלהיא אמר). There is no other witness to these words, but Clark (153, 232) takes them to represent the Western text, which he gives in Greek as ἀπολογίαν ἔχειν ὑπὲρ ἑαυτοῦ· ὁ δὲ σχῆμα ἔνθεον ἀναλαβὼν ἔφη. If Clark is right in this, but wrong in thinking the Western text original, the view is confirmed that sees in the Western text some analogies to the development of apocryphal acts; cf. *Acts of Paul and*

Thecla 3 (L.-B.1.237), ποτὲ δὲ ἀγγέλου πρόσωπον εἶχεν. Cf. 26.1 (sy^hmg again); 6.15.

Like Tertullus (v. 2 and note), Paul begins with a *captatio benevolentiae*, not unduly straining the truth. For Felix, see on 23.24. ἐκ πολλῶν ἐτῶν may seem to exaggerate. A two-year term in senatorial provinces was usual, and Hemer (173) draws attention to the relevance of the 'two years' of v. 27, if this is taken to refer to Felix's proconsulship. There is however some ground (see above, pp. 1080f.) for thinking that Felix had been active in Palestine, as a junior colleague of Cumanus, before his appointment as procurator. For any exaggeration cf. Claudius's ἐκ πολλῶν χρόνων in PLond 1912, line 22 (Bell, p. 23); see also Schille (433). That he had been a judge is no exaggerated statement; δίκαιον, inserted after κριτήν by E Ψ 323 614 945 1175 1739 2495 *pm* sy^h, is not an original part of the text. ὄντα σε ... ἐπιστάμενος: accusative and participle are here correctly used, whereas in Hellenistic Greek the participle was often replaced by the infinitive, or a ὅτι clause (M. 1.229). On the tense of ὄντα see Moule, *IB* 101; it is due simply to the paucity of participles of εἶναι.

εὐθύμως, cheerfully; εὐθυμότερον (𝔐) adds a little liveliness to the narrative.

τὰ περὶ ἐμοῦ *my case*, is an accusative of respect: *I make my defence* (for ἀπολογεῖσθαι see 19.33) *in relation to my case*. The argument, according to Conzelmann (132), is not that Christianity and Judaism are essentially the same, but that there is no case to answer. Calvin (2.248) defends Paul's defence. He had no time to expound the Gospel positively and confined himself to answering the false assertions that had been brought against him.

11. δυναμένου σου, causal, *since you are able to perceive ...*

ὅτι is best taken (as in the NA^26 text) to mean *that*, introducing an object clause in dependence on ἐπιγνῶναι. An alternative possibility is to place a stop after ἐπιγνῶναι, which then has no object—you are able to come to a judgement; ὅτι is then *for*.

The construction of the ὅτι clause is obscure, though the general drift is clear. It is not more than twelve days since Paul reached Jerusalem (21.15)—little enough time for the crimes of which he is accused. With πλείους must be understood ἡμέραι: there are not to me (dative of possession: BDR § 189.1, n. 1) more [days] than twelve days. The comparison ought to be expressed either by ἤ with the same case (here nominative) or by the genitive. In fact we have the nominative without ἤ. The error is caused by the emphasis in the writer's mind on the twelve-day period. One might imitate: It is not more than—well, it is (only) twelve days since ... For the omission of ἤ before a numeral Bruce (1.424) compares the Latin omission of *quam*; the parallel though interesting is probably no more than a coincidence. Moule (*IB* 202) notes that it would be possible to take ἡμέραι as subject and understand ἡμερῶν with δώδεκα; possible, but hardly probable. On the calculation of the twelve days, see below.

ἀφ᾽ ἧς stands for ἀπὸ τῆς ἡμέρας ᾗ ...

ἀνέβην, the word of pilgrimage; see on 11.2.

προσκυνήσων, future participle expressing purpose; cf. 8.27. This cannot be said to be a complete statement of Paul's purpose in coming to Jerusalem; he came as the bearer of a gift from the Gentile world (cf. v. 17), and probably with a view to some form of consultation with the leaders of the Jerusalem church.

εἰς Ἰερουσαλήμ may be taken with ἀνέβην: I came up to Jerusalem; more probably, εἰς is used for ἐν, as frequently: ... to worship in Jerusalem. Calvin (2.249) has great difficulty with Paul's intention to worship in the Temple. Luke has none: partly because he is not as systematic and logical a theologian as Calvin, partly because it is his intention to represent Paul the Christian as continuing to be a good Jew. On his attitude to the Temple see *FS* Bammel 361–7.

Others find difficulty in the chronology of the twelve days and their relation to the narrative up to this point. Bauernfeind (263), for example, thinks that the number may come from a source different from that of the preceding narrative. or that it may be the result of adding together the five of v. 1 and the seven of 21.27. Wettstein (2.621) is still worth noting: 'Primus dies is est, quo Hierosolyma venit, secundo Iacobum vidit. IV sequentes circa purificationem fuit occupatus, biduo detentus captivus Hierosolymis, V. postquam Caesaream venisset die, caussam dicit i.e. decimo tertio'—which presumably Wettstein reckons a twelve-day interval. Pesch (2.257) finds the simple 5 + 7 = 12 calculation unsatisfactory and gives the following (Bruce 2.443 is similar):

1.   Arrival in Jerusalem (21.17)
2.   Visit and talk with James (21.18)
3–9. Seven-day purification process (21.27)
9.   Arrest (21.33)
10. Paul before the Sanhedrin (22.30)
11. Plot against Paul (23.12)
12. Arrival in Caesarea (23.32)

It is questionable whether the last three items can be accommodated within three days, and the timetable takes no account of the five days in Caesarea. Further, the question must be considered whether the twelve days refer to time up to the moment of speaking or up to the point at which Paul came under Roman guard (21.33)—the Romans would know very well what crime, if any, he had committed since then. Thus *Begs*. 4.300, 'In spite, therefore, of the εἰσί it is possible that the phrase means "I had not been twelve days in Jerusalem when the trouble arose" '; there is much to be said for this, but it is not clear why *Begs.* continues, 'and the number is merely a literary addition of "seven" in 21.27 and "five" in 24.1.' Surely Luke cannot have failed to see that the five days of 24.1 are placed after 'the trouble arose'. Bauernfeind (see above) may be right in thinking that 'twelve' is derived from another source, or it may be a Lucan approximation.

12. On the sequence οὔτε … οὔτε … οὔτε … οὐδέ (v. 13) see BDR § 445.2, n. 3; the final negative gives the sense 'noch überhaupt'. But the second οὔτε and the third are correlated with οὔτε ἐν τῷ ἱερῷ, and in English it is probably best to put them together: Neither in the Temple, nor in the synagogues, nor in the city did they find me … The reference to *the Temple* is clear. *The synagogue* could refer to the synagogues of the Dispersion, but the reference in v. 11 to the brevity of Paul's stay in Jerusalem, and the reference to the city that follows, suggests that it is Jerusalem synagogues that are in mind. κατὰ τὴν πόλιν is *throughout the city*; with the negative, *nowhere in the city*.

πρός τινα διαλεγόμενον, *arguing with anyone*—the first step towards creating a disturbance.

Zerwick (§ 227) insists upon the full force of the active ποιοῦντα, *provocantem concursum* (the middle would mean simply taking part in such a gathering). For ἐπίστασιν, 𝔐 has ἐπισύστασιν; the former is a word of various and uncertain meaning; followed by ὄχλου it must mean *the collecting* of a crowd, or perhaps a little more—*the onset of a crowd* (see LS 659; BA 607—Andrang, Ansturm). Cf. (also for the variant) 2 Cor. 11.28 (with the note in *2 Corinthians* 301).

13. περὶ ὧν for ταῦτα περὶ ὧν: they cannot prove, substantiate, to you those things concerning which … The accusations are of course those of vv. 5, 6. Paul says nothing about the charge of causing world-wide disturbance (a) because no proof was offered and (b) because Felix could try only crimes committed within the area of his judicial authority. So Pesch (2.257f.).

οὐδέ, in ℵ B 81 *pc.* P⁷⁴ A E Ψ 𝔐 have οὔτε, following the threefold occurrence of that word in v. 12, but missing the point made there (see the reference to BDR).

For νυνί, P⁷⁴ E 𝔐 have νῦν. In Acts νῦν occurs 25 times, νυνί twice (including this verse). Copyists changed the less into the more familiar.

14. ὁμολογῶ, I confess, or admit, more often with an infinitive (e.g. Aristophanes, *Knights* 296, ὁμολογῶ κλέπτειν) than as here with ὅτι. But ὁμολογεῖν here may be not quite *confess*. The ὅτι clause (for details see below) contains a double assertion, one half of which could be regarded as an admission whereas the other protests innocence, or indeed makes an affirmation (cf. 23.8). The word σοι may be significant: *To them* (the Jews) I maintain that I am nothing but a good Jew; *to you* I don't mind admitting that . . .

κατὰ τὴν ὁδὸν . . . τῷ πατρῴῳ θεῷ. The beginning and end of this clause are both emphatic. On the one hand, it is the ancestral Jewish God, the God of the fathers, the God of the OT, that Paul worships, no new deity whom he has discovered or invented for himself. This will be underlined in the following words. On the other hand, he worships the old God in the new way, κατὰ τὴν ὁδόν, that is, in conformity with the (Christian) way. For ὁδός in this sense see 9.2. λατρεύειν is used in the summary of the OT at 7.7, 42; also at 26.7; 27.23. Behind these occurrences is the Jewish עבודה. For τῷ πατρῴῳ θεῷ cf. Sophocles, *Antigone* 838, θεῶν πατρῴων; Vergil, *Aeneid* 9.247, di patrii; cf. Thucydides 2.71.3.

Paul (Luke) accepts the word ὁδός as a description of Christianity. Indeed we see here (so Haenchen 630) why Luke is glad to use the word. 'Dieser Begriff bezeicunet die neue Jesusreligion als eine eigene Grösse und reisst sie trotzdem nicht vom Judentum los: er erinnert ja aufs stärkste an alttestamentliche Wendungen wie "die Wege des Herrn", die das Judentum als die gelobte wahre Religion hinstellen. Dieser Weg hat Paulus nicht aus dem Judentum hinausge-führt . . .' αἵρεσις however is a word that belongs to Jewish opponents: ἣν λέγουσιν αἵρεσιν, used for example by Tertullus (v. 5). The implicit disavowal of αἵρεσις means that Christianity regards itself not as a sect or group within the people of God; it *is* the people of God, and its way is the halakah for all Israel. 'Hanc appelationem Paulus corrigit, non quo tum esset odiosa, sed quod non satis digna' (Bengel 477).

That the God Paul worships is indeed the ancestral, OT, God is proved by the fact that Paul believes πᾶσι τοῖς κατὰ τὸν νόμον καὶ τοῖς ἐν τοῖς προφήταις γεγραμμένοις. The general sense of this clause is clear, but its construction is affected by the omission of ἐν τοῖς by A 𝔐. The shorter text is somewhat simpler; the first τοῖς must be linked with γεγραμμένοις: all the things that are written according to the Law and by (in) the prophets. If the longer text is read it means that a distinction is being made (as well as an association) between *all the things that are according to the Law* and *the things that are written in the prophets* (i.e., in the prophetic books—נביאים as a section of the OT). That Paul should believe what was written in the prophets gives rise to no great difficulty; the next verse gives the outstanding example. Could he have claimed to believe all the things according to the Law? Only if he were allowed to give some of them a new interpretation, to understand circumci-sion, for example, as circumcision of the heart, in spirit not letter (Rom. 2.29). On the representation in Acts of Paul as a faithful and devout Jew see Introduction, pp. xc, ci.

Stauffer (*Theologie* 220) takes this passage with 14.15; 17.23ff.; 22.14 as ground for the proposition, 'Die Herrlichkeit und Allein-herrschaft des Einen Gottes kommt durch das Christusereignis erst voll zur Offenbarung und Durchsetzung.' This is certainly true in the sense that Paul (Luke) never thinks of two Gods, one of the OT and one of the NT, or that the God spoken of in the OT is anything other than the God revealed in the New. But Stauffer (228) goes too far in seeing in this verse a 'Bekenntnis zur Kirche', 'ein Treubekenntinis zum verfolgten Schar Christi', if he means more than that Paul acknowledges that he is a member of the persecuted group.

Again (see on v. 11) Calvin (2.251) is in great difficulty, com-pounded by the fact that he does not see that ὁδός refers to Christianity. Weiser (629) sees Luke's intention clearly: 'Durch diese Argumentation soll deutlich werden, dass der "Weg", d.h. das Christentum, weder eine verengte oder fehlgeleitete und von Israel abgefallene jüdische Sondergruppe ist, sondern wahres Israel.'

15. Not for the first time (cf. 23.6), Paul singles out belief in the resurrection as the central feature of his faith, which it shares with (Pharisaic, not Sadducean) Judaism. It is implied that he ought not to be persecuted for believing what all good Jews believe. There is no reference here to the resurrection of Jesus; it is the general resurrec-tion that is in mind.

The word ἐλπίς has slightly different meanings as it is governed by ἔχων (cf. Thucydides 8.48.1, πολλὰς ἐλπίδας εἶχον), when it means hope itself, the confident expectation that something will happen, or by προσδέχονται, when it means the thing hoped for (id quod speratur—Blass 254); they themselves (the Jews) await, expect, the realization of hope. They and Paul believe that there is to be (μέλλειν ἔσεσθαι, correct use of the future infinitive with μέλλειν; the NT often uses the present infinitive) a resurrection (E Ψ 𝔐 sy unnecessarily add νεκρῶν). On this occasion it is explicitly added that the resurrection will be of both *the righteous and the unright-eous*, that is, for judgement. In many passages of the NT the fate of the unrighteous is left unclear because only the righteous are spoken of and only their resurrection is explicitly affirmed. Cf. Dan. 12.2; Rev. 20.11–15. See also StrB 4.2.1166–1198, the Excursus, Allge-meine oder Teilweise Auferstehung der Toten?—There was a great variety of opinion.

16. ἐν τούτῳ is difficult to interpret precisely. The antecedent of τούτῳ may be the preceding clause, that is (the fact that) there is to be a resurrection of righteous and unrighteous. ἐν is probably causal (*because of this*; see e.g. Xenophon, *Cyropaedia* 1.3.14) though it is hardly necessary to suppose that it is in any direct sense dependent on the use of the Hebrew ב. Cf. Jn 16.30. Many take the phrase this way; thus Bruce (1.425) (= therefore); Schneider (2.348) (darum, aus diesem Grund); Zerwick (§ 119) (propterea, cf. 7.29); BDR § 219.2, n. 2 (deswegen). It may however be better not to give τούτῳ a precise antecedent. Moule (*IB* 79, 132, 197) renders, *and so, that being so* (cf. the use of the similar expression with the relative, ἐν ᾧ; also 26.12, ἐν οἷς).

καὶ αὐτός: ' "I also", as well as my accusers and the Jews whom they represent' (Page 239). ἀσκῶ (*ND* 3.153 refers to H. Dressler, *The Usage of ἀσκέω and its cognates in Greek Documents to 100 AD* (1947); see also *FS* Furnish 161–72) refers in the first instance to the training of the body for various skills and athletic pursuits but was easily adapted for intellectual and moral training; e.g. Xenophon, *Memorabilia* 1.2.19–28: ὁρῶ γὰρ ὥσπερ τὰ τοῦ σώματος ἔργα τοὺς μὴ τὰ σώματα ἀσκοῦντας οὐ δυναμένους ποιεῖν, οὕτω καὶ τὰ τῆς ψυχῆς ἔργα τοὺς μὴ τὴν ψυχὴν ἀσκοῦντας οὐ δυναμένους (19). Neither the verb, nor the noun ἄσκησις (used by Xenophon in the passage referred to), occurs elsewhere in the NT; the thought of 1 Cor. 9.27 is not exactly parallel. Nearer are the passages in which Paul exhorts his readers to imitate him, as he imitates Christ (1 Cor. 4.16; 11.1; 1 Thess. 1.6; cf. 2 Thess. 3.7, 9). Cf. also passages in Paul and elsewhere in which the Christian life is compared to the training, discipline, and effort of the athlete (e.g. 1 Cor. 9.25f., *1 Corinthians* 217f.). The relation between moral discipline and faith is a theme that is not worked out in Acts, or indeed by Paul himself in the certainly genuine letters.

ἀπρόσκοπον συνείδησιν. For Paul's clear conscience cf. 23.1; also 20.20, 27, 33; also however 1 Cor. 4.4, οὐκ ἐν τούτῳ δεδικαίωμαι. ἀπρόσκοπος may mean *not stumbling* or *not causing to stumble*. At 1 Cor. 10.32 the latter meaning is undoubtedly correct (ἀπρόσκοποι ... Ἰουδαίοις ... Ἕλλησιν ... τῇ ἐκκλησίᾳ); at Phil. 1.10 the former is probably though not certainly correct. The present passage is nearer to 1 Cor. 10.32, but that passage does not introduce the word συνείδησις, as this one does. The meaning seems to be that Paul's intention, the aim of his self-training, is that his conscience shall not accuse him of offending against God or man. Since the conscience (see *Romans* 50f.; C. Maurer in *TWNT* 7.897–918) was thought of as an agent that passed judgement on actions already committed this seems to be the probable meaning of ἀπρόσκοπος; alternatively it would be possible to think of a conscience that guided him without stumbling in his relations with God and men. *Begs.* 4.302 refers to papyrus evidence for the meaning *unharmed*; see MM 72, also *ND* 1.55: 'In the papyri ἀπρόσκοπος εἰμί is an idiomatic way of saying, "I'm all right".' Perhaps simply, therefore, a good, or sound, conscience. If ἔχων (𝔐 gig) is read, the balance of sentence and thought changes. For πρὸς τὸν θεὸν καὶ τοὺς ἀνθρώπους, cf. Philo, *Abraham* 208.

διὰ παντός is rather surprisingly added at the end of the sentence;

E 614 1739^v.l. 2495 *pc* gig improve the word order by placing it after ἔχειν. The meaning is clear.

17. Paul resumes his defence. He has pointed out that his beliefs are those of a good Jew and that in practice he keeps his conscience clear. It has been alleged (vv. 5f.) that he is a trouble-maker and has profaned the Temple. What are the facts?

He has been absent from Jerusalem for a long time. On διά in the sense of *after* see Moule, *IB* 56; the meaning is 'common in Greek authors', e.g. Aristophanes, *Plutus* 1045, διὰ πολλοῦ χρόνου. Cf. Mt. 26.61; Gal. 2.1. πλειόνων, comparative, is used in the sense of the superlative, *very many years*. The observation in *Begs.* that in Modern Greek the comparative with the article is used to express the superlative (as in French) is scarcely relevant since here there is no article. No explanation is necessary. 'Used alone, [the comparative degree] often expresses *excess* or *tendency*, and may be rendered by *too, very, rather, somewhat*' (Simonson, § 1340). So e.g. Schneider (2.348), 'im klassischen Sinn, "nach etlichen Jahren"'. It is not clear from what point the 'many years' are calculated. Paul reached Jerusalem at 21.15; his previous visit had been that of ch. 15, or perhaps at 18.22 (if this verse does refer to a visit to Jerusalem; see the note). For the dates of these events see Introduction, pp. liv–lxii; neither interval could be naturally described as covering 'many years', and it may be said that what is in mind is the interval since his conversion, when Paul broke off his earlier relations with official Judaism in Jerusalem. πλειόνων may be an exaggeration; cf. ἐκ πολλῶν ἐτῶν in v. 10. Or it may be a real comparative and refer to this πολλῶν: My last visit to Jerusalem was before you, Felix, took office.

παρεγενόμην, *I arrived*—in Jerusalem.

ἐλεημοσύνας ποιήσων. The future participle expresses purpose; cf. v. 11. ἐλεη. ποι. is not characteristically Greek, but probably reflects both עשה חסד and עשה צדק. In late Hebrew (cf. Aramaic) צדק, צדקה, came more and more to have the meaning of *alms* (see Jastrow 1263f.). ἐλεη. ποι. occurs in Tobit and Sirach; see also Gen. 47.29 (where the Hebrew is עשה חסד). Paul has now visited Jerusalem in order to bring and distribute alms—

εἰς τὸ ἔθνος μου. εἰς (connecting not with ποιήσων but with ἐλεημοσύνην—Delebecque (117); but see also Weiser 629f.) must mean *for the benefit of*; that it should thus replace the *dativus commodi* is discussed by Deissmann (*BS* 117f.) with OT and papyrus parallels (see also MM 186f.) and reference to Mk 8.19f. and—especially important because these deal with Paul's collection—Rom. 15.26; 1 Cor. 16.1; 2 Cor. 8.4; 9.1, 13. See also M. 3.236 and Zerwick (§ 51). In Acts we have heard nothing (since 11.27–30, a mission completed in 12.25) of any intention on Paul's part to give alms to his nation, the Jews, or, for that matter, to anyone. We know however from the epistles (Romans, 1 and 2 Corinthians) that at this point in his ministry he was deeply concerned in a plan to bring relief to the poor saints in Jerusalem, that is, to the Jewish Christians of the mother church. There can be no doubt that this collection (see D. Georgi, *Die Geschichte der Kollekte des Paulus für Jerusalem* (1965); K. F. Nickle, *The Collection* (1966); *Romans* 2f., 255f.; *1 Corinthians* 23, 385–7; *2 Corinthians* 25–8, 216–42) was a matter of the greatest importance to Paul, and it is very surprising that Acts should pass it by in almost complete silence, noticing it only in this inaccurate reference. We must conclude either (1) that Luke was less well informed about Paul's work than one would expect a companion to be, or (2) that he found the collection less interesting than Paul did, or (3) that there was some good reason for suppressing it. Thus Bruce (2.445): 'Luke evidently knew about the collection but, equally evidently, he is very reticent about it. This may have been because the enterprise ended in disaster; another possible reason is that at Paul's trial it was misrepresented as an improper diversion of money that ought to have swelled the Jerusalem temple tax, and Luke judged it wise to refer to it only in the most general terms.' In view of Luke's silence elsewhere Roloff (338) is right to infer that this reference comes from tradition; it is not Luke's invention.

Paul came to Jerusalem with alms and προσφοράς, in the LXX but seldom elsewhere, (*sacrificial*) *offerings*. This is the meaning at 21.26—Paul paid the expenses for the sacrifices due from the men who had taken vows. It is to be noted however that those sacrifices were asked of him by James and his colleagues after he reached Jerusalem; there is nothing to suggest that he came to Jerusalem with the intention of making (ποιήσων) offerings, though silence of course does not in itself prove that he had no such intention. His epistles say nothing to suggest that he would have been likely to plan participation in Temple worship. The words καὶ προσφοράς, at the end of the sentence, look rather like an addition or afterthought; they are however unquestionably part of the text.

18, 19. ἐν αἷς] ἐν οἷς, L 323 326 1241 *pm*. The neuter will refer to the preceding sentence, and the circumstances it describes, in general and is thus the easier reading: 'Meanwhile, they …' αἷς, feminine plural, can only refer to προσφοράς: While I was engaged upon these sacrifices …'.

ἡγνισμένον, not so much 'having been purified' as 'being in a state of purity' (perfect participle). See 21.29 (also 21.24, ἁγνίσθητι σὺν αὐτοῖς).

There was no crowd and no tumult. Cf. v. 12.

'δέ after τινές is opposed to the emphatic οὐ μετὰ ὄχλου οὐδὲ μ. θ.—"I was not creating disturbance, but certain Jews from Asia (brought an accusation to that effect).'' Before stating what the accusation was Paul proceeds parenthetically to comment on the absence of his accusers as indicating the falsity of their charge. Strictly he ought to have gone on to state what the accusation was, instead of doing so however he breaks off, and, turning to the Sanhedrists, says ''*or* let these now say what I was proved guilty of'', the force of ''*or*'' being this—''The absence of my original accusers shows that they had no case, *or*, if this inference is objected to, then let these men *themselves* (though their evidence is only second-hand) say what ...'' '' (Page 239f.). This exposition assumes punctuation (as in NA²⁶) with a full stop at the end of v. 19. This means that the nominative τινὲς Ἰουδαῖοι is left without a verb. A less probable alternative is to place a comma at the end of v. 19 and use the verb εἰπάτωσαν out of v. 20: Let the Jews of Asia speak, or failing them, let those Jews now present themselves speak. Dibelius 92 (cf. Ropes, *Begs.* 3.225) draws attention to the possibility that a few lines may have dropped out at this point. After θορύβου, perp² and some Vulgate MSS add *et apprehenderunt me clamantes et dicentes, tolle inimicum nostrum*, an addition which 'seems to be proved ancient by the reference in Ephrem's commentary' (Ropes). It is however no more ancient than many other Western additions, and the text of all Greek and almost all other authorities should be accepted.

οὓς ἔδει (δεῖ, L 1241 *pm* sa) ἐπὶ σοῦ παρεῖναι. This was a valid point.

The Roman law was very strong against accusers who abandoned their charges. Claudius himself had been busy with legislation aimed at preventing accusers within the system of *ordo* from abandoning their charges. He made a speech about the matter in the Senate, and his proposals were later completed by the SC Turpilianum of AD 61, under Nero. This laid down penalties for the offence which the lawyers call *destitutio* ... Once again, the author of Acts is well informed. But there is more to it than that. The disappearance of one set of accusers may mean the withdrawal of the charge with which they were particularly associated. The Asian Jews had accused Paul of two things: one, teaching everywhere, i.e. throughout the 'world', the *oikoumene*, against the Hebraic law, and two, of bringing Hellenes into the Temple. Charge one was taken over by the Jewish clergy. Charge two, according to Acts, could not be substantiated. 'They had *seen* Trophimus with Paul in the city, and *thought* he had been taken into the Temple.' Hence when the Asian Greeks [*sic* Sherwin-White; but surely he must mean Jews?] withdrew from the case, Paul had a sound technical objection to put forward. (Sherwin-White 52f.)

Luke cannot however report Paul's release. The convincing legal argument may have been Luke's, not Paul's. And could not the Jews of Jerusalem have said, 'Jews are Jews, whether from Asia or Jerusalem; it is Jews who bring charge one, and we are representative Jews'?

On the absence of ἄν in the apodosis Moule (*IB* 149) writes, 'ἄν is usually, if not always, omitted with verbs whose very sense implies *obligation, necessity, possibility*'.

εἴ τι ἔχοιεν. The optative gives, and was doubtless intended to give, the impression of literary effect (Zerwick § 356). It is not however correct; better would have been εἴ τι ἔχουσιν or ἐάν τι ἔχωσιν (BDR §385.2, n. 4). 'En bon grec, εἴ τις est l'équivalent d'une relative exprimant une totalité; mais l'optatif peut surprendre' (Delebecque 118). Similarly Radermacher (132), with the interesting observation, 'Die Reaktion gegen die Volkssprache, die den Optatif aufgibt, hat die Literaten dazu geführt, ihn unter ihre besondere Protektion zu stellen.' Knowling (485), however, takes the optative seriously: 'the optative of *subjective* possibility, representing the subjective view of the agent—if they had anything against me (in their own belief)'.

20. Paul proposes in this verse to introduce (and in the next verse introduces) a new charge that might possibly, but unjustifiably, be brought against him. For the grammatical relation of this verse to the preceding see on v. 19. If the Jews of Asia choose not to appear in order to bring the accusation which only they can bring since they are the supposed witnesses of the supposed offence, let those Jews who are present speak of what happened when I appeared before their own Council. Let them say what offences they found (*in me*, ἐν ἐμοί, is added by C E Ψ (945 1739 1891) 𝔐 lat sy bo—sensible but somewhat superfluous and not easily combined with the genitive that follows) when I stood before (ἐπί, in the presence of) the Sanhedrin. See 22.30–23.10.

For ἤ at the beginning of the verse P⁷⁴ A C *pc* have εἰ, a phonetic itacism.

στάντος: Calvin (2.253) notes the tense, complaining that Erasmus and the Vulgate (*cum stem*) treat it as a present. They should have *cum steti*.

21. This verse recalls 23.6. The Jews have nothing to complain of but one cry (φωνή) that Paul uttered, in which he asserted that the real issue in his trial was that of resurrection; this he affirmed (with no explicit reference to the resurrection of Jesus, though, as 25.19; 26.23 show, this was in fact vital), thereby associating himself with one part of the Sanhedrin (the Pharisees) and setting himself against the other (the Sadducees). True, this produced an uproar in the Sanhedrin; but was that an ἀδίκημα, even though Paul had expressed himself more pointedly than he reports (Φαρισαῖός εἰμι, υἱὸς Φαρισαίων)? If to be a Pharisee was a crime, half the Sanhedrin was guilty.

ἤ after τί = ἀλλ᾽ ἤ; cf. Xenophon, *Oeconomicus* 3.3.

μιᾶς ταύτης φωνῆς: According to BDR § 292.3, n. 5 the absence of the article means that ταύτης is predicative. The words are equivalent to ἡ φωνὴ ἦν μία αὕτη, the cry (that I uttered) was this single one. But M. 3.193 is probably correct in taking the view that though in earlier Greek (except in the epic poets and sometimes in the tragedies) the attributive use of οὗτος would have required the article, we should probably take the use of αὕτη in the present phrase to be attributive. 'The def. art. was being carelessly used, as time went on, in these connections.' Cf. Philo, *De Specialibus Legibus* 3.165: ἢ δι᾽ ἓν τοῦτο μόνον, ὅτι συγγενεῖς εἰσι.

ἐκέκραξα. This form of the aorist occurs here only in the NT (the only other occurrence of the aorist, in Acts 7.60, has ἔκραξεν), but is common in the LXX; see Thackeray, *Grammar* 1.273 (with the reference there to other parts of the book). There are other traces of a reduplicated form of the verb, κεκράγ(ζ)ω, though this form itself apparently does not exist. See LS 988f., s.v. κράζω; 935, where κέκραγμα, κεκραγμός, and κεκράκτης are listed; also BDR § 75, n. 2, 'Neubildung nach dem als Futur umgedeuteten κεκράξομαι; vgl. das präsentische κέκραγα.'

ὑφ᾽ ὑμῶν (ℵ E 𝔐 lat sy[h]) *judged by you*, is the easier reading and certainly a 'correction' of ἐφ᾽ ὑμῶν (A B C Ψ 33 81 104 2464 *pc* s sy[p]), *judged before you*, that is, *in your court*.

'If the Jews speak the truth they must admit that they had no case against him except theological differences, which in the eyes of Felix would be none at all. This was always Paul's position' (*Begs.* 4.304). It would be prudent to add the words, 'as represented by Luke'.

22. ἀναβάλλεσθαι, middle, *to put off*, *to adjourn*, occurs here only in the NT. Felix like other Roman officials, has no intention of being drawn into an internal Jewish dispute, or of doing injustice to a man whose only offence lay in what other Jews regarded as unorthodox theology. He makes use of standard procedure. When a case was put off for fuller hearing in the light of new evidence or prolonged consideration the judge would say 'Amplius'. Thus Cicero, *Brutus* 22 (86), Cum consules, re audita, *amplius* de consilii sententia pronunciavissent ...; cf. *In Verrem* 2.1.29 (74). Knowling (486): ἀνεβάλετο αὐτούς = ampliavit eos. Cf. Plutarch, *Themistocles* 18 (120). MM 30 quotes PTebt 1.22.9, ἀναβαλλόμενος εἰς τὸν φυλακίτην, 'referring the matter to the inspector'.

Felix was, according to Luke, well informed about Christianity (the Way). No other evidence confirms this claim. ἀκριβέστερον: for the use of the comparative cf. 17.22. It is probably elative (cf.

Zerwick § 148, certissime sciens), but it may be a genuine comparative—he had a more accurate knowledge than the Jews had, or perhaps better, a more accurate knowledge than they thought he had. They could not pull wool over his eyes. How did Felix acquire his knowledge? It is sometimes said, Through Drusilla. Bruce (2.446) properly comments, 'But what opportunity had she of knowing about it?'

For ὁδός see on 9.2. τὰ περὶ τῆς ὁδοῦ, the facts relating to Christianity.

εἴπας: the participle refers to time coincident with that of the main verb. *He put them off with the words* ... So M. 1.133 (also for διαταξάμενος, v. 23).

καταβῇ, from Jerusalem to Caesarea; see v. 1.

διαγνώσομαι. See 23.15; cf. 25.21 (διάγνωσις).

The Old Uncial text (in P⁷⁴ ℵ (A) B C E (Ψ 2495) 33 (81) 945 1175 1739 1891 2464 *pc* latt sy bo) begins abruptly with ἀνεβάλετο. The connection is smoothed by 093ᵛⁱᵈ 𝔐 sa, which have ἀκούσας δὲ ταῦτα ὁ Φῆλιξ ἀνεβάλετο αὐτούς. In P⁷⁴ E Ψ 614 (1241) 2495 *pc* Felix's direct speech is introduced by ὅτι.

23. διαταξάμενος. For the tense and time reference see on v. 22. The dismissal of the Jewish accusers was doubly made in the words: I will examine your case ...; Centurion, see that the prisoner is kept ... The various actions (ἀνεβάλετο ... εἴπας ... διαταξάμενος) are all coincident.

On the use of the passive infinitive after a verb of commanding BDR § 392.4 write 'Bei Verben des befehlens steht in mehr lateinischer als klassisch griechischer Weise der AcIPass [= Accusative and passive infinitive] (statt Inf. Akt. mit Akk. Obj.), wenn einer Person etwas geschehen soll, ohne dass der Ausführende genannt ist.' On the present verse they add, 'der Centurio bewacht ihn nicht selbst'. Delebecque (118) says that the passive is used 'pour signifier un ordre impersonnel, que l'on ne discute pas, donné par une autorité officielle'. This passage is the more striking because of the combination of passive (τηρεῖσθαι) with active (ἔχειν, and, with a different subject, κωλύειν). The mixed construction grates somewhat on the ear, but it is in fact perfectly clear: Paul is to be kept; Paul is to have ἄνεσις; the centurion is to prevent no one ...

τηρεῖσθαι may mean simply 'to be kept as a prisoner' and understood *in malam partem*; he will be deprived of his liberty. But it may (and the context suggests this as at least an additional if not an alternative meaning) refer to protective custody. Paul will be kept under Roman guard and not allowed to fall into the hands of the Jews. Cf. 25.4, 21.

ἄνεσις occurs in the NT at 2 Cor. 2.13; 7.5; 8.13; 2 Thess. 1.7;

relief, in this case lightening of the circumstances of his prison régime. It would be *custodia libera*.

οἱ ἴδιοι, *his own people*, would normally suggest his relatives (and these may be included here—see 23.16) and friends (*ND* 3.148 quotes POxy 46.3314.15, true friends); here, fellow Christians. In antiquity, and indeed until modern times, conditions in prison would be made tolerable by the access of friends who brought provisions and comfort. Cf. Lucian, *Peregrinus* 12; Josephus, *Ant.* 18.203f., 235. This corresponds to the fact that for Romans (such as Felix; not for Greeks) imprisonment was not a punishment but a means of keeping people available for trial or for actual punishment. *Digest* 48.19.8,9 (Ulpian): carcer enim ad continendos homines, non ad puniendos haberi debet.

ὑπηρετεῖν will here refer to the services that a man unable to provide for himself would need, especially no doubt food.

24. παραγενόμενος, Felix came—where? It is possible (though Luke does not say so) that he had been absent and returned to Caesarea. Otherwise he came to wherever Paul was. Marshall (381) thinks of the prison. Schneider (2.352) with perhaps greater probability says that παραγεν. 'bezieht sich auf den betreffenden Raum im Prätorium (23.35), in den Felix den Gefangenen rufen liess'.

σὺν Δρουσίλλῃ. See on 23.24. This was not Drusilla the granddaughter of Cleopatra and Antony (Tacitus, *Histories* 5.9) but Drusilla the sister of Herod Agrippa II (Josephus, *Ant.* 20.141–144); this is made clear by the addition of οὔσῃ Ἰουδαίᾳ. Not that the Herods were fully Jewish, though they did maintain at least a façade of Jewishness. Most editors accept the reading of B C² 33 36 81 1175 *pc*, τῇ ἰδίᾳ γυναικί, *his own wife*. Whose wife might be expected to accompany him? It is true that this Drusilla had previously been the wife of Azizus, but Luke shows no interest in this story. C* 093 𝔐 have τῇ γυναικί; P⁷⁴ ℵ*² E Ψ 945 1739 1891 2464 *al* have τῇ γυναικὶ αὐτοῦ; ℵ¹ A *al* have τῇ ἰδίᾳ γυναικὶ αὐτοῦ, which is manifestly conflate. M. 1.88, 90, observing that in the NT ἴδιος though on the way to exhaustion has not yet reached that point, is inclined 'for once to prefer ℵ' to B. A modern textual critic would not write 'for once', with its implication that B is very nearly inerrant. G. M. Lee (*NovT* 9 (1967), 41) defends the reading of B on unconvincing grounds; in his quotation from Babrius (*Fable* 45.12–14) there were excellent metrical reasons why the author should not have written the αὐτῶν which the sense seems to require, but Luke was writing prose, and if he meant ὁ Φῆλιξ αὐτὸς σὺν Δρουσίλλῃ τῇ γυναικί there was no reason at all why he should not have written it. The reading of B is difficult enough to be accepted as the origin of the variants, and not so difficult as to be impossible. There is no doubt that the force of ἴδιος was weakening, and we may conclude that the reading of B is correct, that the present use shows a stage of weakening more advanced than is common in the NT, and that the words should be rendered *his wife*.

After Ἰουδαίᾳ, sy^hmg (bo^ms), possibly representing the Western text, or at least one branch of it, add: quae petebat ut videret Paulum et audiret verbum; volens igitur satisfacere ei. Cf. the variant in v. 27. Both are probably secondary; the editor may have wished (a) simply to 'improve' the story; (b) to supply a reason for v. 24b; (c) to build up a comparison between Drusilla and Herodias; (d) to justify the mention of Drusilla. Clark (155, cf. 381) reconstructs the Western Greek text as: ἥτις ἠρώτησεν ἰδεῖν τὸν Παῦλον καὶ ἀκοῦσαι τὸν λόγον. Θέλων οὖν χαρίζεσθαι αὐτῇ ... Calvin (2.255) dismisses Felix's apparent interest in Paul; he hears him only on account of Drusilla, and she is merely curious.

Luke knows that if Paul is to be heard faith will be one of his themes; cf. 20.21. But if v. 25 is to be regarded as summarizing the content of Paul's discourse on faith it must be said that faith is here understood in a sense different from that of the epistles. See on v. 25.

Ἰησοῦν is omitted by ℵ^c A C^vid H P 614 1241 *pm* sy^p sa^ms. It is hard to see any reason why the name should have been omitted, easy to see why it might have been added. There is much to be said for the short text.

There seems to be no good reason why Felix could not at this point have dismissed the case; cf. Lucian, *Peregrinus* 14.

Pesch (2.260) observes that vv. 26, 27 join up well with v. 23; this suggests that vv. 24, 25 are a Lucan insertion. Weiser (632) thinks that vv. 24–26 were formed by Luke.

25. Paul is of course obliged to obey Felix's summons, no doubt willing to discuss and dispute (διαλέγεσθαι) with him as with others (e.g. 17.17).

Paul's themes (surprisingly under the heading of faith—see v. 24, also below) are δικαιοσύνη, ἐγκράτεια, and κρίμα. δικ. is undoubtedly a major theme is the epistles, but the word seems to be used in a different sense here. See 10.35 and 17.31, which suggest the double meaning of righteous behaviour in men and righteous judgement in God, who will duly reward those who practise righteousness. The only other passage in Acts in which the word is used is 13.10. ἐγκράτεια (see W. Grundmann in *TWNT* 2.338–40) occurs at Gal. 5.23 as part of the fruit of the Spirit, elsewhere in the NT only at 2 Pet. 1.6 (but cf. 1 Cor. 7.9; 9.25, ἐγκρατεύεσθαι; Titus 1.8, ἐγκρατής). In all these passages ethical behaviour is in mind. In itself the word means *mastery over* something or someone, but its sense seems to have been determined by Plato's ἐγκράτεια ἑαυτοῦ (*Republic* 390b) and similar uses. It means mastery over oneself, over one's pleasures and desires (*Republic* 430c); thus discipline, especially *self-discipline*. It is not for man to estimate his own success in righteousness and self-discipline, hence τὸ κρίμα τὸ μέλλον, the judgement to come in which God will make his own estimate. κρίμα occurs nowhere else in Acts, κρίσις only at 8.33, which is clearly not relevant. Of 22 occurrences of the verb κρίνειν, 20 refer to human judgements of one kind or another. The only relevant parallel, but that a close one, is 17.31 (note here also the use of δικαιοσύνη). There is some kinship between these passages in Acts and 1 Thess. 1.9f., where the coming wrath from which Jesus delivers men is certainly the wrath that is the negative aspect of judgement, but neither in Athens nor before Felix does Paul get as far as the deliverance. For these themes cf. *Acts of Paul and Thecla* 5; *Acta Johannis* 84; *Actus Petri cum Simone* 33–35 (L.-B. 1.238; 2.1.192; 1.85–87); also Aristeas 278.

𝔐 is no doubt mistaken (textually, not in sense) in adding ἔσεσθαι after μέλλοντος; C 36 1175 *pc* have μέλλοντος κρίματος.

Felix is frightened (ἔμφοβος, clearly passive in sense, as in Theophrastus, *Characters* 25(26).1; earlier active, e.g. Sophocles, *Oedipus at Colonus* 39), as well he might be, by the thought of judgement. But the words of his response are ambiguous; cf. 17.32. Does he mean that he intends to converse further with Paul, or is he making a polite gesture? V. 26b suggests the former.

In τὸ νῦν ἔχον the last word 'is not very easy to explain' (Moule, *IB* 160). Moule compares Tobit 7.11 (B A), τὸ νῦν ἔχων ἡδέως γίνου, but this is somewhat easier. *Begs.* 4.305 describes the phrase as 'entirely idiomatic in Hellenistic prose', and quotations in Wettstein (2.624; e.g. Lucian, *Cataplus* 13: τὸ δὲ νῦν ἔχον, μὴ διάτριβε) confirm this. Perhaps ἔχον should be taken as an absolute participle and τὸ νῦν as corresponding to an adverb, as in the familiar construction οὕτως ἔχειν, to be thus. 'It being now.'

καιρὸν μεταλαβών, *when I get an opportunity*; similarly with the variants παραλαβών (A), λαβών (093 81), and εὑρών (P⁷⁴). καιρῷ δὲ ἐπιτηδείῳ on a suitable, or convenient, occasion (E latt) is a more commonplace expression (though καιρ. μετ. also is described in *Begs.* as entirely idiomatic and probably a secondary reading).

On faith (v. 24) in this context: it is possible to argue that faith is related to salvation (cf. 16.31) and thus to the forgiveness of sins. It is in the light of judgement that this becomes a serious matter. 'Entsprechend wird in 24.24f. deutlich, dass mit der Verkündigung des "Glaubens an Christus Jesus" vor Heiden die Predigt vom "künftigen Gericht" untrennbar verbunden ist, auch vor einem römischen Prokurator' (Delling, *Kreuzestod* 91).

26. The ambiguity (see v. 25) in the description of Felix's motives reappears in this verse, the first half of which suggests nothing but a corrupt and mercenary interest whereas the second half is open to a more favourable interpretation. Men do have mixed motives, and there is no reason to suppose that Felix could not have kept Paul available to himself for a mixture of good and bad reasons; it seems however unlikely that Luke would have at his disposal information about the governor's inward thoughts; his account will reflect at best the different things that people said about Felix, at worst his own imaginative reconstruction. It is probably true that he did wish to present Felix in a double light: as the 'good' Roman, who recognizes Paul's innocence, and as the 'bad' Roman who does not release him because he hopes for a bribe. But Haenchen's conclusion (634) is not necessarily true: 'Der Mann, der Paulus besucht, um von Jesus zu hören, und der Mann, der Paulus besucht, um Geld zu sehen, ist nicht ein und derselbe.' They might be; not every man is a logically and morally consistent whole.

ἅμα, *at the same time*, that is, at the same time that he was promising to send for Paul and hear what he had to say he was nourishing the thought that the prisoner, who evidently had friends who were interested in his fate (v. 23), might prove a useful source of revenue. 'En bon grec, ἅμα καί, et aussi ἅμα δέ, indique le vrai motif, déguisé sous un prétexte' (Delebecque 119). αὐτῷ is omitted by B p* vg^st; after Παύλου, 𝔐 co add ὅπως λύσῃ αὐτόν, 'unwilling to leave anything to the reader's imagination' (Metzger 492).

The intention ascribed to Felix was of course illegal, specifically proscribed by the *Lex Julia de repetundis* of 59 BC, contained in *Digest* 48.11 (... praecipit ... ne ... quis ob hominem in vincula publica conjiciendum, vinciendum, vincirive jubendum, exve vinculis dimittendum ... aliquid acceperit). The practice was illegal, but it nevertheless existed. For the illegalities of another procurator, Albinus, see Josephus, *War* 2.273; *Ant.* 20.215.

πυκνότερον can hardly be a true comparative, since there is nothing available for comparison; it will be elative, *pretty often*. See M. 3.30; Turner (*Insights* 90). Cf. v. 22.

ὁμιλεῖν with a dative can mean *to speak to*; this is not impossible here, but much more probably is either the general sense *to consort with*, *to hold converse with*, or perhaps even a sense nearer that of Xenophon, *Memorabilia* 1.2.15, 39, where LS's (1222) 'frequent a person's lectures', 'be his pupil' are too strong for Acts but on the right lines. The variant διελέγετο (C 36 453 *pc*) gives the required meaning.

'Sic thesaurum evangelii omisit infelix Felix' (Bengel 478).

27. διάδοχος is usually (LS 393) an adjective, and it should probably be taken here as predicative: Felix received Porcius Festus in succession to himself, as his successor. Little is known of Porcius Festus (it is not logical to assume that this means that he was governor for only a short time). His work as governor is summed up by Josephus in *War* 2.271: 'Festus, who succeeded Felix as procurator, proceeded to attack the principal plague of the country; he captured large numbers of the brigands (λῃστῶν) and put not a few to death.' A few more details are given in *Ant.* 20.182–200. The λῃσταί were called σικάριοι from the weapons, like the Roman *sicae*, that they used. He was reasonably tolerant to the Jews over the wall they built in the Temple with a view to preventing Agrippa from observing the sacrifices. Festus seems to have died in office; he was succeeded by Albinus.

The dates of Festus's governorship are given by the Armenian version of Eusebius's *Chronicle* as 54–60; according to Jerome, whose version of the *Chronicle* is on the whole more trustworthy, they are 56–60. Between Festus and Albinus there was an interregnum during which total confusion reigned. It was at this time that James, the brother of Jesus, was put to death (Josephus, *Ant.* 20.200; cf. Hegesippus in Eusebius, *HE* 2.23.4–18). The martyrdom is usually dated in 62 (rejecting Hegesippus, who seems to think of a date immediately before the outbreak of war in 66). 60–62 makes a long interregnum, but 62 is confirmed by Josephus, *War* 6.300, 305 (Albinus was in office four years before the war) and 308f. (seven years and five months before the last stages of the siege). More important is the question when Festus succeeded Felix. The fullest discussions are to be found in *Begs.* 5.464–7 and in *NS* 1.465f. (note 42), but these come to different conclusions. *Begs.* lays stress on the fact that after his recall Felix was accused by the Jews, and 'he would undoubtedly have paid the penalty for his misdeeds against the Jews had not Nero yielded to the earnest entreaty of Felix's brother Pallas, whom at that time he held in the highest honour (μάλιστα δὴ τότε διὰ τιμῆς ἄγων ἐκεῖνον)' (Josephus, *Ant.* 20.182). But Pallas fell from favour early in Nero's principate, so that 55 or 56 would be the latest possible date for Felix's recall. Moreover (see above) Eusebius's *Chronicle* gives 54 or 56 for the accession of Festus. Thus K. Lake in *Begs. NS*, where the date is 60 is preferred, replies by casting doubt on the trustworthiness of Eusebius' *Chronicle* (and on our knowledge of it), and by pointing out that Pallas had fallen from power at a very early date (by 13 February 55—the 14th birthday of Britannicus—at latest), so that it must be inferred 'that Pallas in spite of his dismissal remained influential—a conclusion which agrees completely with Tacitus' statement' (466). The statement in question occurs in *Annals* 13.14: Nero ... demovet Pallantem cura rerum quis a Claudio impositus velut arbitrum regni agebat; ferebaturque degrediente eo magna prosequentium multitudine, non absurde dixisse ire Pallantem ut eiuraret. For the eventual death of Pallas see Tacitus, *Annals* 14.65. Nero apparently grew tired of waiting for a share of his great wealth. *NS* does not observe that this qualification of the position of Pallas to some extent spoils the case against *Begs*. Pallas's influence is much likelier to have lasted till summer 55, or even 56, than till 60. This is not a matter on which certainty can be attained (unless fresh evidence appears), and to some extent a decision will turn upon the meaning of the next words (διετίας δὲ πληρωθείσης) to be considered. The early date has encountered much criticism but there is still a good deal to be said for it. See in addition to the two works mentioned, E. Schwartz (*NGG* 1907, 263–99, especially 284–7); J. Jeremias (*ZNW* 27 (1928), 98–103); Haenchen (80–84); R. Jewett (*Dating Paul's Life* (1979), 41–4, and the literature there cited); Hemer (173: 'The view of Lake ... is simply unacceptable').

διετίας δὲ πληρωθείσης, when a two-year interval was completed. It is very often supposed that this period refers to Paul's imprisonment in Caesarea; this is assumed, for example, without discussion in *NS* (loc. cit.). Haenchen (632) makes the valid point that Luke 'nur für die Gefangenschaft des Paulus Interesse hat'; cf. Schneider (2.353). On this view, and if Festus was appointed in 55 or even 56, it is impossible to harmonize this date with those arrived at above (p. 871; see also Introduction, pp. lvif.) for Paul's residence in and departure from Corinth: the activities of Acts 18–21 could not be brought to a close by 53 or 54. This would constitute a strong argument in favour of a later date for the supersession of Felix by Festus (though not a date as late as 60). But διετίας πληρωθείσης is a genitive absolute and its connection with the rest of the sentence is an open question. Grammatically it is at least as likely that it refers to Felix's governorship as that it refers to Paul's imprisonment, and though it is correct, as Haenchen observes (see above) that Luke's overall interest is in Paul, at this point he is speaking of the procuratorial succession. And this way of taking the clause suits the chronology admirably (see *Romans* 4f.). The case is further strengthened by the fact that διετία represents the Latin *biennium* (BDR § 5.3; cf. Acts 28.30) and that *biennium* is sometimes (by no means always) used for a two-year period of office (e.g. Cicero, *In Verrem* 2.3.93 (216), Biennium provinciam obtinuit; Suetonius, *Galba* 7, Africam proconsul biennio obtinuit. So H. G. Kippenberg, *Kleine Pauly* 4.1059.

The change of ruler might have seemed a suitable time for Paul's release, but Felix left him in prison (δεδεμένον). According to the majority of MSS Felix's motive was to curry favour with the Jews. χάριτα κατατίθεσθαι is a not uncommon phrase, 'to lay up a store of gratitude or favour' (LS 917, κατατ. II 4); or simply in Hellenistic use 'do a favour' (*Begs*. 4.306). Page (241): καταθέσθαι 'is strictly used of "depositing with a banker"; its metaphorical use is classical'; he cites Thucydides 1.33.1; 1.128.3. Delebecque (119) adds Herodotus 6.41.3; Plato, *Cratylus* 391b; Demosthenes 19.240 (416);

59.21 (1351); Xenophon, *Cyropaedia* 8.3.26. Cf. 25.9, where Festus does the same. The difference between the two passages is that in 25.9 the accusative of χάρις is χάριν (as almost always in the NT), whereas here it is χάριτα (so ℵ* A B C 33 104 1175 *pc*; χάριν in ℵᶜ E L 323 945 1739 1891 2495 *al*; χάριτας, 𝔐). See M. 2.132. In the idiom χαρ. κατατ., χάριτα often appears and this usage was probably in Luke's mind (or possibly in a source). The Western text, represented by 614 2147 syʰᵐᵍ, ascribes to Felix a different reason for leaving Paul in prison: τὸν δὲ Παῦλον εἴασεν ἐν τηρήσει διὰ Δρούσιλλαν. The probable origin of the reading is (a) the desire to find a reason for the reference to Drusilla in v. 24, and (b) the thought that there was a parallel between John the Baptist's suffering at the hands of Herodias and Paul's at the hands of Drusilla.

For κατέλιπε, P⁷⁴ A L 81 104 453 1175 2464 *pc* have κατέλειπε.

For divergent views on this verse see the good account in Weiser (635).

59. PAUL APPEALS TO CAESAR 25.1–12

(1) So Festus arrived in the province and after three days went up to Jerusalem from Caesarea. (2) The chief priests and the leading men of the Jews informed him against Paul and begged him, (3) asking a favour against [Paul],[1] that he would send him to Jerusalem, for they were making an ambush to kill him on the way. (4) Festus answered that Paul was being kept at Caesarea, but that he himself would shortly be[2] going [there]. (5) 'So', he said, 'let the eminent men among you come down with me and, if there is anything wrong in the man, let them accuse him.'

(6) He spent not more than eight or ten days among them, went down to Caesarea, and on the next day sat down in the place of judgement and commanded Paul to be brought. (7) When Paul arrived the Jews who had come down from Jerusalem surrounded him bringing many weighty charges, which they were not able to prove. (8) Paul in his defence said, 'Neither against the Law of the Jews, nor against Caesar, have I done any wrong.' (9) Festus, wishing to curry favour with the Jews, said in response to Paul, 'Are you willing to go up to Jerusalem and be tried concerning these matters there before me?' (10) Paul said, 'I am standing in Caesar's court, where it is right that I should be tried. I have done no wrong to the Jews, as you well know. (11) If then I am a wrongdoer and have done something worthy of death I am not refusing to die, but if there is nothing in the things of which they accuse me no one can make a present of me to them. I appeal to Caesar.' (12) Then Festus spoke with his council and replied, 'You have appealed to Caesar, to Caesar you shall go.'

Bibliography

G. D. Kilpatrick, *EThL* 53 (1977), 107–12.

S. Légasse, as in (54).

H. Sahlin, *NovT* 24 (1982), 188.

Commentary

A new governor has taken office in Judaea. He is a man of energy. Three days are enough for him to settle in Caesarea before setting out for his second capital city, Jerusalem, where not more than eight or ten days are needed for a preliminary survey, which includes a request from the Jews to bring Paul to Jerusalem. The old plot of assassination (23.12) is revived: Paul will be murdered on the way. Whether because he suspects the plot or on general principles Festus

---

[1]Greek, him.
[2]There is not in the Greek; NEB, leaving Jerusalem; NJB, going back there.

refuses. He is going to Caesarea; let the Jews do so too so that there may be a hearing. There is a hearing; and it is inconclusive. Indeed, if Luke's account is followed it is incomplete; witnesses are not called. The Jews present their accusations; Paul affirms his innocence. Instead of reaching a decision Festus asks Paul if he is willing to go to Jerusalem and be tried there. Why does Festus not complete the legal business in Caesarea? The answer given is that he wishes to do the Jews a favour, but this desire is qualified by the question to Paul, which is meaningless if Paul is not free to answer, No, I am not willing to go to Jerusalem. In fact he does so answer, and in doing so demands more than the resumed trial in Caesarea that Festus by implication offers him. Paul had as much to fear from acquittal as from condemnation. Released from custody in Caesarea with no Roman soldiery at hand to protect him he would have been an easy victim to the assassin's knife. By appealing to the Emperor he took the case not merely out of Jerusalem but out of Judea and assured himself (so far as there could be any assurance) of a safe passage to Rome.

The historicity of this narrative has often been assailed. Objections are well summed up by Haenchen (641): 'Bei Lukas bleibt unverständlich: 1. warum nach Abschluss der Verhandlungen kein Urteil erfolgt, sondern eine Verlegung des Prozesses ins Auge verfasst wird, 2. warum Paulus nicht einfach auf Fortführung des Prozesses in Cäsarea besteht, sondern an den Kaiser appelliert, 3. warum Festus einen des crimen laesae maiestatis verdächtigen Mann nicht selbst richten (oder nach Rom senden) will.'

Haenchen's first point may be answered by the observation that, in Luke's narrative, the proceedings had not reached an Abschluss. Each party had made an introductory statement. The second has been answered in the observation that any verdict reached in Caesarea would have been highly dangerous to Paul; to transfer the case to Rome was for him an excellent move. The third is hypothetical: that Paul was accused of causing *seditio* throughout the Empire and thus of the *crimen laesae maiestatis* was true, but it was not unreasonable on Festus' part to wish to form his own judgement on the substance of the charge brought by the Jews. The integrity of Festus has also been called in question. Why should he imperil a man (still presumed innocent) by sending him from Caesarea to a prejudiced trial in Jerusalem? To some extent the force of this complaint rests on the meaning of ἐπ' ἐμοῦ (v. 9; see the note), but in any case the attitude of Festus, as an honourable man, is, given his position, intelligible. He is a new governor with an unusually intractable native population to deal with; of course he would like to do something that would win favour with the Jews. It is to his credit that he is aware that justice demands that he should also bear in mind the rights of his prisoner; hence, 'Are you willing ...?'

The story as Luke tells it hangs together. This does not prove that it is historically true. It might be intelligent fiction. Various views on this question have been held. It is certainly true that the story achieves at least one end that Luke would hope to achieve. 'An dem Weltmissionar Paulus hat der römische Staat als an dem hervorragenden Exempel ein für allemal erkannt und demontriert, dass kein Grund vorliegt, an der politischen Loyalität der Christen zu zweifeln' (Schmithals 217; cf. the less positive estimate in Schille 454). Lüdemann describes vv. 1–5 as a doublet of ch. 24, and vv. 6–12 as even more clearly a doublet (261). Pesch (2.264) on the other hand argues that Luke drew the main features of this paragraph from his Quellenbericht; the tensions in the paragraph are due to his desire to present the Romans in a good light.

Weiser (638) gives ten reasons for the belief that the present paragraph 'sowie die Komposition der Szenen und Reden Kap 25–26 stammen ... erst von Lukas'. Most of these consist of parallels between the 'trial' of Paul and that of Jesus in Lk. 23. They are as follows. (1) The hearing before the Roman Governor is followed by one before the Jewish king. (2) The connection between the two scenes recalls the use of Ps. 2.1f. in Acts 4.27. (3) The combination fulfils the prediction made to Paul in 9.15f. (4) In both hearings leading Jews bring accusations but no condemnation follows. (5) The planned assassination of v. 3 repeats that of 23.12–15. (6) Acts 25.7 repeats 24.5f. as Lk. 23.10 repeats 23.2. (7) Acts 25.7 recalls Lk. 23.14 in that neither accusation is effective. (8) Acts 25.13–23, explaining why Paul appears before Agrippa II, recalls Lk. 23.6f., 11. (9) Paul, after being found innocent before Festus and Agrippa, remains in custody (26.30, 32); so Jesus, though found innocent by Pilate and Herod (Lk. 23.24f.), is not released. (10) Paul's speech in Acts 26 is made up from elements previously used and contained in the narrative.

The last point is not relevant to discussion of the present paragraph (see below, pp. 1144ff.). The points of 1, 4, 6, 7, 8, 9 do bring out a measure of parallelism between the story of Jesus and the story of Paul; it is of course not to be denied that Luke is responsible for both stories in the form in which we read them. He does nothing however to indicate awareness of the parallelism, as he probably would have done had it been important to him, and does not repeat his earlier reference to Ps. 2.1f. It was of central importance to Luke (and he constantly emphasizes the belief) that both Jesus and Paul were innocent of the charges brought against them, and of nearly equal importance that both appeared before both Jews and Romans, of whom the latter were more favourable to them. Luke seems to have had a special interest in, perhaps a special knowledge of, the Herods (see on 13.1). It is not surprising that he should have written up the story of Paul's trials in the way that he does, and a number of details may well be his own contribution; this however does not affect the main outline of events. The essential question we have to ask is whether Paul was a Roman citizen (see on 16.37; 22.25) and used his citizenship as a means of having his case transferred to Rome. Given citizenship, the appeal makes very good sense, and there is little to be said for the argument of Schmithals (219) that Paul travelled to Rome as a free man. The We-narrative returns in ch. 27 with the journey to Rome, and Philippians is best understood (but we must beware of arguing in a circle) as representing a Roman imprisonment consistent with the position of a prisoner on appeal.

1. Little is known of Porcius Festus. For the date of his accession see on 24.27. Josephus records that he had to deal with the *sicarii* (*Ant.* 20.185–187) and with an impostor who led followers into the wilderness (188). He allowed the Jews to send an embassy to Nero about a wall built in the Temple (193, 194); he died in office, and was succeeded by Albinus (197). The precise sense of ἐπιβάς will be determined by the meaning of ἐπαρχείᾳ and the variant ἐπαρχείῳ (both of which have orthographical variants in which ει is replaced by ι). ἐπαρχείᾳ (𝕏ᶜ B C E Ψ 𝔐) will refer to the province, so that ἐπιβὰς τῇ ἐπαρχείᾳ will mean, Having arrived in the province (cf. *Ant.* 20.185, ἀφικομένου δὲ εἰς τὴν Ἰουδαίαν Φήστου …). ἐπαρχείῳ will according to M. 2.157 be short for τῇ ἐπαρχείῳ (the adjective is of two terminations) ἐξουσίᾳ, and the clause will mean, Having entered upon his (provincial) office. This however may be too simple, for it may be right to supply not ἐξουσία but χώρα, so that the meaning would again be, Having arrived in the province. Commentators and others differ in their preference, but *Begs.* 4.306, after a very full note on ἐπαρχείᾳ—ἐπαρχείῳ, rightly concludes, 'There is probably no difference in the meaning of these two phrases.' Festus would enter upon his office as governor of the province when he entered the province. Cf. 23.34. Page (241) points out, 'Strictly Judaea was not a "province", but a department of the province of Syria, but the term is used loosely.' *ND* 2.85 draws attention to a narrower meaning (district) in PMich 659.45, but this belongs to the 6th century AD. Festus may have landed at Caesarea itself, or at Seleucia, completing the journey by land. The procurator usually resided at Caesarea and went up to Jerusalem when occasion required. It would be natural to do so at the beginning of one's term of office and Festus (according to Luke) permitted no delay (*after three days*) in going up to his second capital. ἀνέβη is the pilgrimage word (see 11.2), but here suggests nothing more than actual ascent.

It is not clear what logical force οὖν can have. This is no doubt why, in P⁷⁴ *pc*, it is replaced by δέ.

2. ἐνεφάνισαν: for this word see on 23.15. *ND* 2.104 cites a parallel from an inscription in Beroea. The construction here is identical with that in 24.1 (with dative, and κατά with genitive).

οἱ ἀρχιερεῖς is hardly to be expected and the variant ὁ ἀρχιερεύς (H P 049 189 326 *pm*) is not surprising. But the plural occasions no difficulty; see e.g. 4.23; 5.24 and many passages in the gospels. The High Priest at this time was Ishmael b. Phiabi (Josephus, *Ant.* 20.179).

οἱ πρῶτοι τῶν Ἰουδαίων occurs again at 28.17; cf. 13.50; 28.7. It recalls the use of ראשים for leaders, but is intelligible in itself. It may be right to compare the δυνατοί in v. 5; see on that verse.

In what follows Luke does not use his pronouns with perfect clarity (αὐτῷ ... αὐτόν ... αὐτοῦ ... αὐτόν), but there is little doubt what he means.

The Jewish leaders have a request to make (παρεκάλουν).

3. The request (v. 2) is specified, αἰτούμενοι χάριν κατ᾿ αὐτοῦ χάρις is here used in the concrete sense of *a favour*, somewhat unusually described not as done on behalf of someone (though this is of course a secondary implication) but as done against Paul.

Behind the favour asked for is the same kind of plot as had failed earlier (23.15f.); at 23.21 the verb ἐνεδρεύειν is used. Festus is to send for Paul to Jerusalem, where the Jewish leaders now are; the Jews will make an ambush and kill Paul on the road between Caesarea and Jerusalem. μεταπέμπεσθαι is Lucan: 10.5, 22, 29; 11.13; 20.1; 24.24, 26—and nowhere else in the NT. ἐνέδραν ποιοῦντες: the active is used, not the middle, because the Jewish leaders will cause the ambush to happen but will not themselves take part in it (Zerwick § 227: '... "insidias paraturi", non necessarie "ipsi insidiaturi"'). Contrast Thucydides, 3.90.3, ... δύο φυλαὶ ... ἐνέδραν πεποιημέναι. κατὰ τὴν ὁδόν also is Lucan. 'L'expression est propre à Luc: Lc 10.4; Act 8.36 et 26.13' (Delebecque 120).

There is a variant in this verse not recorded in NA[26]. Ropes (*Begs.* 3.229): 'The Greek translated in the gloss of hcl.*mg* may have run somewhat as follows: οι ευχην ποιησαμενοι οπως επιτυχωσι του γενεσθαι αυτον εν ταις χερσιν αυτων. But the paraphrase probably involved other changes, no longer recoverable, from the B-text, and the Syriac is perhaps not a perfectly literal rendering. No other trace of the gloss is known. The paraphrast seems to have overlooked the lapse of two years since 24.12.' Or perhaps he did not understand the two years of 24.27 to refer to Paul's imprisonment!

4. This is not Luke's characteristic μὲν οὖν; it does not begin a new incident, and there is an answering δέ. So rightly *Begs.* 4.307; Haenchen (636) agrees with *Begs.* that μέν should stand before Παῦλον: ... τὸν μὲν Παῦλον ... ἑαυτὸν δέ ... Festus is not to be hoodwinked but behaves with a proper responsibility towards his prisoner. He is another of Luke's good Roman officials.

τηρεῖσθαι, Paul was (being) kept, and would for the present still be kept.

εἰς Καισάρειαν: 'L'acusatif avec εἰς implique la venue à Césarée: Paul y a été conduit pour y être gardé' (Delebecque 120). But it is more likely that here as frequently εἰς is used for ἐν.

ἑαυτὸν δέ: αὐτός might have been expected, since the pronoun refers to the subject of the verb ἀπεκρίθη; 'att. potius αὐτός ... v. tamen Kühner Gr. II² 595sq.' (Blass 258). M. 3.147: 'Luke may have deviated from class. usage into the accus. because he wished to coordinate the new subject with Παῦλον.' According to BDR § 406.1, n. 1 what Luke does is in fact classical when a contrast is intended, though αὐτός also would be possible.

If the Jews wish to make a case against Paul they must go to Caesarea, where he is; Festus himself is setting out for Caesarea shortly. Festus 'will über Paulus nicht ohne ordentliche Gerichtsverfahren entscheiden' (Schmithals, 217). See also on vv. 5, 16.

For ἐν τάχει see 12.7; 22.18; cf. Lk. 18.8—a Lucan expression.

5. μήτι marks a change from indirect to direct speech; cf. 1.4.

οἱ ἐν ὑμῖν δυνατοί may be taken to be equivalent to the ἀρχιερεῖς and πρῶτοι of v. 2. δυνατοί is not uncommon with the meaning *eminent men* (cf. 1 Cor. 1.26). Thus Thucydides 1.89.3, οἱ δυνατοὶ τῶν Περσῶν; Plutarch, *Romulus* 27 (34), τοὺς ἐν Ῥώμῃ δυνατούς; Philo, *Moses* 1.49; Josephus, *War* 1.242, Ἰουδαίων οἱ δυνατοί. Cf. however Bengel (479): *qui valent*, ad iter faciendum; also Blass (258), qui possunt. But the former meaning is more probable; so Page (242); Schille (441), 'δυνατός ist ein politischer Terminus technicus.' Festus does not intend that the courtroom shall be cluttered with a large number of Jews, and perhaps suspects a violent attempt on Paul's life. For the same reason, probably, he wishes the Jews to accompany him (συγκαταβάντες). Cf. ἀνέβη, v. 1.

The Jews are to accuse Paul εἴ τί ἐστιν ἐν τῷ ἀνδρὶ ἄτοπον. This is straightforward; ἄτοπον is a mild word for crime used either because Festus is showing proper legal caution or because Luke wishes to show Paul in the best possible light. Cf. 28.6. In the text however ἄτοπον is read by ℵ A B C E 33 81 945 1175 (1739 1891) 2464 *al* lat; in place of this τούτῳ is read by 𝔐; τούτῳ ἄτοπον by Ψ 36 453 614 2495 *al* syʰ sa? bo. The majority of (late) MSS thus have an expression εἴ τί ἐστιν ἐν τῷ ἀνδρὶ τούτῳ, to be rendered literally, If there is anything in this man, and evidently meaning, If there is anything evil, criminal, in this man. This does not apper to be a regular Greek idiom, but cf. Jn 14.30, ἐν ἐμοὶ οὐκ ἔχει οὐδέν.

Cf. Schmithals (217) quoted on v. 4.

6. Festus did not stay long among the Jews (ἐν αὐτοῖς, omitted by P⁷⁴) in Jerusalem—in days, οὐ πλείους ὀκτὼ ἢ δέκα. So (P⁷⁴ B ℵ) A C 33 36 81 453 945 1175 1739 1891 *pc* latt bo, probably rightly. But

Ψ 𝔐 have πλείους ὀκτὼ ἢ δέκα; 2147 *pc* have ὀκτὼ ἢ δέκα. There can be little doubt that the text of the old uncials is correct; it gives a natural kind of approximation.

Festus returned to Caesarea, and on the day after his arrival took the matter in hand, ordering Paul to be brought (for the passive infinitive, ἀχθῆναι, after a verb of commanding, see 24.23) to the courthouse. He sat ἐπὶ τοῦ βήματος. For the word βῆμα see on 18.12 (with the reference to Dinkler); see also vv. 10, 17 in this chapter. 'Da eben das Sitzen des Richters zum amtlichen Charakter des Rechtsprechens gehört, so wird mit dem Ausdruck καθίζειν ἐπὶ βήματος nicht nur summarisch das Niederlassen auf dem Richterstuhl, sondern zugleich der Beginn der Amtshandlung ausgedrückt' (Dinkler, *Signum Crucis* 122). Cf. the Latin *sedens pro tribunali*.

τῇ ἐπαύριον. 'Les indications chronologiques sont ici très précises, plus cependant quand il s'agit de Césarée que de Jérusalem' (Delebecque 120).

7. πολλὰ καὶ βαρέα. The καί is classical (BDR § 442.7a), and probably bears witness to an attempt to write in literary style. Blass (258) could write, 'αἰτίωμα pro αἰτίαμα nusquam exstat'. *nusquam* is no longer strictly correct; αἰτίωμα occurs in PFay 111.8. This does not alter the fact that Luke, having just used the classical καί now abandons classical use completely. Whether these many weighty charges included more than had already been brought by the Jews on earlier occasions Luke does not tell us; he is confident that they were incapable of proof.

ἴσχυον] ἴσχυσαν P⁷⁴ ℵ*. The aorist is constative: all they said did not amount to proof. The imperfect suggests continuous but unsuccessful attempts to prove. One might translate, They could not prove, however hard they tried. *ND* 4.86 has an inscription to illustrate the use of ἀποδεῖξαι with the meaning *to prove*.

8. Paul's defence is no more explicit than the Jewish accusations. Luke no doubt feels that he has by now presented the legal material in sufficient detail, and moves rapidly on to the great dramatic dénouement in v. 11. ἀπολογεῖσθαι is the technical term for delivering the defence speech; cf. 22.1.

The three points touched on, but not discussed, do represent the major issues, or rather the major fields in which the issues lay. As regards the Law, Luke maintains that Paul's interpretation, the Christian interpretation, is in fact correct. He has not abandoned the Law, he has not counselled his fellow Jews to abandon the Law; he has revised the conditions for the admission of Gentiles. The Temple offence has been dealt with, both by narrative (which showed Paul engaging in Temple worship in a proper way) and by exposing the slender basis of the charge: Jews of Asia—now unavailable as witnesses—had seen Paul with Gentiles in the city and *thought* he had taken them into the Temple (21.28f.; 24.6, 12, 18). As for the offence against Caesar, he was not the Egyptian, or any other rebel (21.38). He was a Roman citizen, and a loyal one. ἥμαρτον takes on a slightly different sense in each setting—Law, Temple, Caesar.

9. χάριν καταθέσθαι; see 24.27. There χάριτα seems to be the right reading; here it is very scantily attested and χάριν must be original. See M. 2.132; also v. 3. Is Luke following here a different written source from one used in ch. 24? The data are insufficient to warrant such a hypothesis.

Though the Jews, or their most important representatives (v. 5), had accompanied Festus to Caesarea and had brought their charges before his court there, they evidently still wished to try Paul in Jerusalem. No doubt (according to Luke) they would have liked best to conduct the trial on their own, but a trial in Jerusalem with the Procurator in the chair would have been better than nothing, though it is hard to see what they would have gained by thus transferring a Roman trial from Caesarea to Jerusalem unless some form of the plot (v. 3) and an appeal to violence were in mind. This assumes that ἐπ᾽ ἐμοῦ means *before me*, though according to Tajra (141f.) it means only *in my presence*, so that Paul would be in Jewish hands, and Jews would pass sentence on him. But see BDR § 234.2, n. 4; Blass (258f.); 'Apud verbum κρίνεσθαι necessarie iudicem designat, cf. etiam 15.2 [Blass must be referring to the Western text]; 24.21. Sic Chrysost.: ὡσεὶ ἔλεγεν οὐχὶ αὐτοῖς δίδωμί σε, ἀλλ᾽ αὐτὸς κριτὴς ἔσομαι.' See also *Begs.* 4.308: 'The position of ἐπ᾽ ἐμοῦ is emphatic. It seems to imply that Festus undertakes not to give up Paul to Jewish jurisdiction.' See further below.

It does not seem possible to do more than guess at the motivation that lies behind this verse. At one extreme, Calvin (2.262) thinks that Festus may have been motivated by passion for gain and been ready to gratify the Jews for this reason. Hanson (232) recognizes that 'the question why Festus proposed to Paul an adjournment to Jerusalem cannot be answered', but adds (233) that Festus may have been attempting a compromise; Paul may, rightly or wrongly, have thought this. Roloff (343) attacks Festus' integrity. The question that leaves Paul to decide whether or not to go to Jerusalem cloaks dishonesty. If Paul is innocent, he should release him. To hand Paul over to the Jews was to bend the law. Others think differently. Bengel (479): 'Poterat Festus Paulo non rogato decernere: sed conscientia eum retinebat, et res divinitus gubernabatur, ut Paulo daretur causa *appellandi*.' Bengel adds, however, on ἐπ᾽ ἐμοῦ, 'Hoc Festus speciose addit.' Bruce (2.452) takes the view that from Festus's side the suggestion of a trial in Jerusalem but with him as judge was a reasonable enough proposal, and Bauernfeind (265) asks what could be more natural than that the new Governor should seek the answer to a Jewish theological problem in Jerusalem. Knowling, who (492) holds that ἐπ' ἐμοῦ means ' "me praesente", for the Sanhedrists would be the judges; otherwise where would be the favour to the Jews?' adds (493): 'It is possible that Festus may have been quite sincere in his proposal: his words at least showed that in his judgement there was no case against Paul of a political nature, and he may have thought that religious questions could be best decided before the Sanhedrim (sic) in Jerusalem, whilst he would guarantee a safe-conduct for Paul as a Roman citizen.'   ·

These various opinions all rest upon the assumption that we have in this paragraph a factual account and that we ought to be able to find in it, or behind it, the various motives, personal, moral, theological, that made the actors act as they did. This is perhaps a mistaken assumption. The point is made forcibly by Schille in the discussion that begins on p. 441 with the observation that there is no ground in law for Festus's suggestion. Schille takes as the acceptable alternative that Luke is creating a literary motivation for the appeal. It is 'nicht geschichtliche, aber literarische Logik' that determines the story. This is certainly true to the extent that the first question to ask is not, 'What happened?' (though that is a very proper question and should be asked), but, 'What does Luke wish to convey in this paragraph?' Undoubtedly he wishes to show a representative Christian as innocent on all counts and the victim of malice. But when Haenchen (640) states, 'Dann ist aber nicht ersichtlich, warum Festus die Zustimmung des Paulus wünscht' it is quite possible that there is a historical reason, and that it is one that is creditable to the Roman official.

The whole of this discussion would be unnecessary if we could, with 33 *pc*, read ἤ before ἐπ' ἐμοῦ. This makes very good sense in that it presents a clear pair of alternatives ('Would you like to be tried in Jerusalem or before me?'), and does not involve the surprising picture of Festus presiding in a rabbinic court. But the short text is not only the more difficult, which would invite change, but also that of almost all MSS. It must certainly be accepted.

10. Grammarians are agreed that though in Hellenistic Greek the periphrastic perfect is normally a simple equivalent to the ordinary perfect, yet here the periphrastic construction (especially if those MSS are followed that separate ἑστώς from εἰμι—see below) adds 'great emphasis' (M. 3.88). BDR § 352.3, 'Zuweilen dient die Umschreibung dem rhetorisch kräftigeren Ausdruck: Apg 25.10 ...'. Zerwick (§ 360), 'ἑστὼς ἐπὶ τοῦ βήματος Καίσαρός εἰμι (A 25.10) rem multo fortius et magis pictorice exprimit quam simplex ἕστηκα ἐ. τ. β. Καίσαρος.'

The text of Paul's opening words is given in three forms. (1) ἐπὶ τοῦ βήματος Καίσαρος ἑστώς εἰμι, οὗ ... (P⁷⁴ ℵᶜ E Ψ 𝔐); (2) ἑστὼς ἑ. τ. β. Κ. εἰμι, οὗ ... (‭ℵ‬* 453 1175 *pc*). These two forms have the same meaning, I am standing in Caesar's court, where ..., but (2) is more emphatic; see above. (3) ἑστώς ἑ. τ. β. Κ. ἑστώς εἰμι οὗ ... (B only), Standing in Caesar's court I am standing where ... This is more vivid still, and it may be what Luke wrote, copyists regarding one ἑστώς or the other as superfluous. See *Begs.* 4.308, 'I think B ought to be followed.' If the reading of B is rejected it is probably right to accept (1) with its numerous and ancient support. H. Sahlin (*NovT* 24 (1982), 188) considers ἐπὶ τ. β. Κ. 'eine sekundäre Zutat'.

In this sentence βῆμα presumably denotes a place where one may stand (as Dinkler, *Signum Crucis* 122, seems to agree), though there is no reason to suppose that trials would always and necessarily be held in that place. The significance of the place is, however, that trials are held in it; the English *court* seems to have a similar force, meaning both the place and the judicial institution that makes use of the place. Paul, as the context will show, means that only Caesar (or his representative) has the right to pass judgement on him. This is not without difficulty; see Conzelmann (134). Can Paul mean that it is in Caesar's court that the question can be settled whether or not his interpretation of Torah (conditioned by the death and resurrection of Jesus) is correct? Scarcely. Hitherto he has insisted (23.6; 24.21) that the real issue behind his trial is resurrection; in what sense is Caesar a judge of that issue? Caesar may be said to have a right to judge whether Paul has acted as a rebel or rioter or disturber of the peace within a Roman province, but this is only a third of the charge as Paul has stated it in v. 8. The simple fact is that (in Luke's narrative) Paul feels safer with Romans than with Jews and thinks that involvement with the former is a small price to pay for freedom from the latter. The Romans provide a way of escape from the Jews who have made up their minds to have his blood; what is more, pursuit of the Roman process offers a means by which the intended journey to Rome may be achieved (19.21; 23.11). The Jews are his accusers and therefore cannot act as judges of the truth of his claim, Ἰουδαίους οὐδὲν ἠδίκησα (ἠδίκηκα, ‭ℵ‬ B (81)). *Seditio* is the charge that is left, and that means a Roman court, and even if Festus presided in Jerusalem (see v. 9, ἐπ' ἐμοῦ) the court would be Jewish rather than Roman; or so Paul feared. Conzelmann's judgement (134) of Festus ('Festus allein(!) ist schuld daran, dass der Prozes weitergeht. Paulus ist gezwungen, an den Kaiser zu appellieren') is not fair. Paul made use of the privilege of appeal (v. 11) in order (a) to escape the Jews, (b) to make the journey to Rome.

Paul believes that he can even cite Festus as a witness. He knows the facts of the matter well. κάλλιον, comparative, may be used as a superlative; so BDR § 244.2, n. 3 (κάλλιον = ἄριστα). Cf. 1 Tim. 1.18. Not all agree. Wettstein 2.626: 'Multo melius, quam ego possum exponere'; Bengel 479: *melius quam alii*. More to the point is that the verb is ἐπιγινώσκειν (cf. 24.8). Knowling (493) translates, 'As thou also art getting to know better.' He adds that otherwise an 'ungracious and unjust' retort is ascribed to Paul. Delebecque (121) similarly: '… comme tu es en train ‚de le mieux découvrir'. According to *Begs*. 4.308 κάλλιον 'is the "intensive" comparative … it is however possible that κάλλιον ἐπιγινώσκεις … is … the comparative of politely qualified expression'. Cf. 17.22.

11. As in v. 4, μὲν οὖν is not Luke's characteristic formula; there is a δέ (*Begs*. 4.308).

ἀδικῶ is to be compared with ἠδίκησα (or ἠδίκηκα, v. 10) and with πέπραχα (Wettstein 2.626 quotes Moeris: πεπραγώς, Ἀττικῶς· πεπραχώς, Ἑλληνικῶς); the present tense has the effect of summing up the perfects which refer to particular acts of wrongdoing (BDR § 322.1, n. 1). It is in fact a perfective present and can be rendered, *I am a wrongdoer*, or, *I am in the wrong*. ἀδικεῖν is used here as in Xenophon, *Memorabilia* 1.1.1, ἀδικεῖ Σωκράτης … οὐ νομίζων … εἰσφέρων … διαφθείρων, Socrates is guilty … of not believing … of bringing in … of corrupting … The use in Plato's version of the charge against Socrates is somewhat different (*Apology* 19b), Σωκράτης ἀδικεῖ καὶ περιεργάζεται … ζητῶν … ποιῶν …διδάσκων … Socrates does wrong and goes about … seeking … making … teaching … The latter use is more common; cf. Aristotle, *Rhetoric* 1.10.3, Ἔστω δὴ τὸ ἀδικεῖν, τὸ βλάπτειν ἑκόντα παρὰ τὸν νόμον.

παραιτοῦμαι has two meanings, to entreat for something, but also to refuse, to decline, to avert by entreaty (LS 1310f.). It clearly has the latter meaning here. Cf. Plutarch, *Coriolanus* 20 (223), … κολάσεως παραιτεῖσθαι; Euripides, *Heraclidae* 1026, κτεῖν’, οὐ παραιτοῦμαί σε, and especially Josephus, *Life* 141, θανεῖν μὲν εἰ δίκαιόν ἐστιν, οὐ παραιτοῦμαι. If Paul can be found guilty he will not attempt to buy off the appropriate penalty—τὸ ἀποθανεῖν; the article is anaphoric (BDR § 399.1, n. 2) referring back to θάνατος immediately above.

ὧν: assimilation of the relative. If there is nothing in the things of which they accuse me. It is clear that what Paul fears is that his Jewish opponents should be given a free hand. As long as he is in Roman hands he is safe; among Jews his life would be worthless. He knows his rights: οὐδείς με δύναται αὐτοῖς χαρίσασθαι. Cf. v. 16. *Begs*. 4.309 says 'One can hardly say, "make a present of me" '. In the course of 60 years the expression has, I think, become usable. Paul knows his rights and proceeds to make them as secure as possible by appealing over Festus' head to Caesar.

LS 635f. and BA 595f. give no other example of ἐπικαλεῖσθαι Καίσαρα. They quote Plutarch, *Marcellus* 2 (299), τοὺς δημάρχους ἐπικαλούμενος, appealing to the tribunes of the people, and *Tiberius*

Gracchus 16 (832), ἐπικαλεῖσθαι τὸν δῆμον ἀπὸ τῶν δικαστῶν, to appeal from the judges to the people. For Roman law on appealing to the Emperor see Sherwin-White (68–70) (with his reference on 59 to A. H. M. Jones); also Tajra (144–7). At this point in the development of Roman practice the institution was not the later *appellatio*, by which (as in modern English law) a condemned and sentenced person might apply to a higher court to have verdict, or sentence, or both, changed, but *provocatio*, which was an appeal before trial to a higher court which would then take the whole case, trial, verdict, and sentence out of the lower court. It is clearly this procedure that is described in Acts. Attempts of one kind and another have been made to try Paul, but in none has a verdict been reached. Paul knows, or believes, that trial before Jews would be fatal, perhaps thinks that Festus is weakening, and therefore plays his trump card. Cf. Schneider (2.356f.) (against Haenchen): 'Für Lukas ist das genannte Motiv für die Appellation des Paulus mit der Befürchtung verbunden, der Stadthalter könne den Juden weiter entgegenkommen und ihn schliesslich ausliefern.' Henceforward he will appear before the Governor, but only in fact-finding inquiries, designed to provide Festus with material for the report he would be obliged to send.

12. μετὰ τοῦ συμβουλίου. συμβούλιον: LS 1677, s.v. II, give '*a council* of advisors or assessors, PTebt 286.15 (ii AD), Plutarch, *Lucullus* 26 (509); esp. freq. of the *consilium* of a Roman magistrate, governor, etc.'. Numerous examples are given, including inscriptions; interesting as showing the linguistic equivalent is Plutarch, *Romulus* 14 (25), κωνσίλιον γὰρ ἔτι νῦν τὸ συμβούλιον καλοῦσι. Many examples of such *consilia* can be quoted, e.g. Horace, *Carmen* 4.5.4; *Satire* 1.7.23; Cicero, *Pro Sex. Roscio Amerino* 52 (151); *CIL* 10.7852, in consilio fuerunt M. Iulius Romulus leg. Propr., T. Atilius Sabinus, etc. It was established custom that the Governor should (a) consult his council, and (b) make his own decision (Tajra 148f.).

It is not clear what in this case Festus would have to discuss with his council. Assuming that Paul was a Roman citizen (and it was unnecessary for Luke to mention this matter again after 22.25–29) the Governor was bound to grant the request that he made (see Sherwin-White 63f., against Lake in *Begs.* 5.311, 317, 318). He could not disallow the appeal, under the *Lex Iulia de vi publica* (passed in the time of Augustus), of which the relevant part is given in *Digest* 48.6, 7 (Ulpian): Lege Iulia de vi publica tenatur qui cum imperium potestatemve haberet civem Romanum adversus provocationem necaverit verberaverit iusseritve quid fieri aut quid in collum iniecerit ut torqueretur. Another form in the *Sententiae Pauli* 5.26.1, 2 adds, condemnaverit vive publica vincula duci iusserit. Accordingly Festus ἀπεκρίθη: he answered (Paul's appeal). Here however the word probably has the sense of giving an official opinion. The cognate noun ἀπόκριμα is sometimes used with this meaning: so LS 204 ('esp. of the *answers* given by Emperors to *legationes*'); see also Josephus, *Ant.* 14.210 (plural; the Latin version has *responsa*); 2 Cor. 1.9. Festus may have consulted the consilium with a view to his report to the Emperor.

Καίσαρα ... πορεύσῃ: an impressive and justly famous epigram.

Paul preferred a Roman to a Jewish court. In this sense, 'Der Appell an den Kaiser ... symbolisiert ... die Scheidung der entstehenden Kirche vom Judentum' (Pesch 2.267). 'Paulus ist damit endgültig dem jüdischen Bereich entrissen' (Roloff 344); but it is equally true that Paul's first act on reaching Rome was to call together the leaders of the Jewish colony (28.17).

Bruce (1.433) thinks it possible that Paul was appealing to Caesar in the person of his representative; Festus used the words that Paul had spoken as an easy way out of a difficulty, 'If you appeal to Caesar you shall have Caesar himself, not his representative in Judaea.' But Lüdemann's conclusion is probably correct (263): 'Höchst wahrscheinlich hat vor Festus in Cäsarea ein Prozess unter Beteiligung der jüdischen Führung Jerusalems gegen Paulus stattgefunden, in dessen Folge Paulus unter Berufung auf sein römisches Bürgerrecht an den Kaiser appelliert.'

This is a very important point in Luke's book. 'Die *Berufung an den Kaiser*—und damit im Sinn des Lukas: die *Eröffnung des Weges nach Rom*—ist der *Höhepunkt*, auf den alles Bisherige hinzielt' (Weiser 642).

60. FESTUS AND AGRIPPA 25.13–22

(13) When some days had passed King Agrippa and Bernice came to Caesarea and greeted Felix. (14) As they stayed there many days Festus referred Paul's case to the king, saying, 'A man has been left a prisoner by Felix (15) concerning whom, when I was in Jerusalem, the chief priests and elders of the Jews laid information asking for a sentence against him. (16) I answered them that it was not the Romans' custom to hand over any man before the accused has had his accusers face to face and received the opportunity of making a defence against the charge. (17) So they came here with me and I made no delay but on the next day sat in court and commanded the man to be brought. (18) Concerning him his accusers stood and brought no charge of those evil things that I suspected, (19) but they had disputes with him about their own religion[1] and about a certain Jesus who had died and whom Paul alleged to be alive. (20) For myself, I was at a loss over the inquiry about these things and asked if he would be willing to go to Jerusalem to be tried on these matters. (21) But when Paul appealed to be kept for the Emperor's decision I gave orders that he should be kept until I should send him up to Caesar. (22) Agrippa said to Festus, 'I could wish to hear the man myself.' 'Tomorrow', said Festus,[2] 'you shall hear him.'

Bibliography

C. D. Chambers, *JTS* 24 (1923), 183–7.

J. Dupont, *Études*, 527–52 (= *RScR* 49 (1961), 354–85).

W. F. Howard, *JTS* 24 (1923), 403–6.

S. Légasse, as in (54).

Commentary

Weiser (see above, p. 1122) holds that the episode involving King Agrippa was introduced by Luke into the story of the judicial proceedings against Paul in order to create a parallel with the story of Jesus (Lk. 23.6–12). There is much to be said for this view; the historicity of the incident is not easy to defend (see Hemer 348f.). It is however worth while to observe two points of difference. The Agrippa section is far longer than the Herod section: 47 verses (25.13–26.32) against 7. There is far more detail. And in Acts, though she does not contribute to discussion or to the logical

[1]RSV, superstition.
[2]Greek, he.

development of the story, Bernice is on stage all the time and in this sense plays a substantial part. She has no counterpart in Lk. We have reason to think that Agrippa and Bernice did travel together, and made courtesy visits to other rulers. At Josephus, *Life* 49, they went to Berytus to visit (ὑπαντῆσαι) Cestius (Governor of Syria). At *War* 2.309 Agrippa visited Alexander at Alexandria, congratulating him on his appointment in Egypt. The following sections (310–314) do not expressly say that Bernice would have accompanied him if she had not been preoccupied in Jerusalem, but this is an easy inference. There is thus nothing impossible in the statement that the couple visited Festus early in his governorship, and if Luke, hunting in Jerusalem for memories of Paul, discovered the fact, he had at once the basis of his story. Whether he had further information there is no means of judging; he must be himself responsible for the conversation between Festus and Agrippa, which has the effect of presenting Festus as an honourable Roman. 'So hat der kleine Abschnitt viel geleistet: Festus persönlich ist vor dem Leser rehabilitiert' (Haenchen 646). Perhaps on the whole more fairly: '... wollte [Lukas] ... zeigen: so hat ein Römer die Sache des Paulus gesehen' (Stählin 302). This Roman view completely omits the serious Roman charge of *seditio* and *laesa maiestas*; because there was no evidence? Throughout the behaviour of Festus is capable of a better interpretation than is often given to it; but of course we are viewing Festus as Luke intends that we should see him, in contrast with the Jews.

13. Ἡμερῶν ... τινῶν. All one can say of the period is that it seemed more natural to measure it in days than in years (Luke and other biblical writers do not often use weeks and months to express intervals). The story gives the impression that Festus has not made up his mind what to do with the prisoner whom he has just consigned to Rome.

᾽Αγρίππας ὁ βασιλεύς. For the use of the article cf. 12.1 and see BDR § 268.1 (without reference to this passage). This (Herod) Agrippa was the son of the Herod (Agrippa) of 12.1. See *NS* 1.471–483. Claudius would have permitted him to succeed his father when his father died (see I.573f.), but allowed himself to be persuaded not to do so. Agrippa, who had been educated in Rome, remained there at least till the death of his uncle, Herod of Chalcis, in 48. Shortly after this event Claudius conferred on him his uncle's kingdom together with charge of the Temple in Jerusalem and the right to appoint the high priest (Josephus, *Ant.* 20.222, 223). When he entered upon his kingdom is not certainly known; according to *NS* 1.472 it was not till after 52. Later his kingdom was extended to the north. He took the Roman side in the Jewish War, after which he retained no territories west of Jordan. In inscriptions (see *NS* 1.475,

n. 15) he is described as βασιλεὺς μέγας φιλόκαισαρ εὐσεβὴς καὶ φιλορώμαιος. According to Photius, Agrippa II died in AD 100 (the third year of Trajan). The matter is discussed at length in *NS* 1.481–3, with the conclusion that 92 or 93 is a more probable date. Festus and Agrippa seem to have been on good terms (Josephus, *Ant.* 20.189–196). Pesch (2.269, 273) argues against Conzelmann (135) that Luke would not have sought out a pair like Agrippa and Bernice to provide an occasion for an additional appearance of Paul. There must have been a pre-Lucan source which at least alluded to Agrippa. 'Folglich ist unsere Szene wahrscheinlich nicht völlig "frei entworfen".'

Βερνίκη was Agrippa II's sister. See *NS* 1.474–6, 479. She had been married to Herod of Chalcis and bore him two sons. After his death she lived with her brother, and much scandal was talked about the relation between them (Josephus, *Ant.* 20.145, φήμης ἐπισκούσης, ὅτι τἀδελφῷ συνείη; see also Juvenal, *Satire* 5.156–160). She was also said to have been mistress of the Emperor Titus (Suetonius, *Titus* 7: insignem reginae Berenices amorem, cui etiam nuptias pollicitus ferebatur; also Tacitus, *Histories* 2.2; cf. Dio Cassius 65.15.3f.; 66.18.1). To dispel the scandal about her relation with Agrippa she married Polemo, King of Cilicia, but before long returned to her brother (Josephus, *Ant.* 20.146). See a long note in Hemer (173f.); also *Begs.* 4.309. On her name see Hemer (238) and BDR § 42.1. It is more correctly written Βερενίκη (= Attic Φερενίκη); so 1175 *pc* sa; C*vid has Βερηνίκη.

ἀσπασάμενοι. The visit was a courtesy call. The tense of the participle has been much discussed. The future participle (ἀσπασόμενοι) might be expected as a normal manner of expressing purpose, and this is read by Ψ 36 81 323 1739 1891 2495 *pm* lat sy sa. In the versions this may well be a matter of correct interpretation (e.g. Vulgate, ad salutandum Festum), but in Greek texts it must be a 'correction'. C. D. Chambers (*JTS* 24 (1923), 183–7) and W. F. Howard (*JTS* 24 (1923), 403–6) argued that here the aorist participle was used to express purpose; so also Williams (260). It is probably correct to speak of coincident action; so M. 1.132f., observing that some classical precedent can be found for this in Pindar, *Pythians* 4.189 (λέξατο πάντας ἐπαινήσαις), which Bruce (1.435) renders 'mustered and praised them', adding that the phrase in Acts in equivalent to κατήντησαν καὶ ἠσπάσαντο. Cf. Metzger (492), who gives a full bibliography on the grammatical question. Haenchen (643) comments, 'Begrüssung und Besuch fallen zusammen'. Preuschen (143) somewhat differently: 'Die von den meisten Hss gebotene Lesart ἀσπασάμενοι setzt voraus, dass die Begrüssung in Jerusalem stattfand.' See also M. 3.80. Zerwick (§ 264) notes the view that understands 'adventum et salutationem quasi ut actionem unam quae esset "visitatio (adventus) salutaria" (actio coincidens)', but adds (§ 265) that the action may be subsequent. See also Moule (*IB* 100, 202); BDR § 339.1, n. 4 ('wobei sie begrüssten'); § 351.1, n. 2.

Agrippa, Bernice, and the men of 25.23, are like the council of assessors in 25.12. *Begs.* 4.310 compares Josephus, *Ant.* 17.93 (Quinctilius Varus, with Herod the Great and his sister Salome, and others; in *War* 1.620 Salome is not mentioned). Cf. also *Ant.* 16.30.

14. Again, as in v. 13, there is a quite imprecise note of time; with this the imperfect διέτριβον is consistent; cf. 14.28 and see BDR § 332.1, n. 2.

ἀνέθετο is most naturally taken in the technical legal sense of *refer, remit*. Surprisingly LS 123 and MM 38 both prefer *impart, communicate*; the accompanying expression τὰ κατὰ τὸν Παῦλον (see M. 3.15), *Paul's case*, has a definitely legal sound and carries ἀνέθετο with it. Of course the reference here is an informal one. Agrippa and Bernice do not constitute a higher court. The only court to which Paul's case could after his appeal be formally remitted was the Emperor's. But Festus felt himself in need of consultation beyond that which he had had with his συμβούλιον (25.12), and took the opportunity afforded by the neighbourly visit. Festus begins to sum up the case so far as it had gone. With this summing up Ehrhardt (*Acts* 119f.), compares Pliny, *Epistles* 10.74 (the case of Callidromus).

15. γενομένου μου εἰς Ἱεροσόλυμα, when I was in Jerusalem. This use of εἰς (where ἐν would be expected) is described by M. 3.254 as 'especially Semitic'. It cannot be so here, and Turner in the context shows that the distinction between the two prepositions became blurred in Hellenistic Greek. The present is one of many examples in Acts of this blurring.

ἐνεφάνισαν, they laid an information. See on 23.15; 25.2.

οἱ ἀρχιερεῖς καὶ οἱ πρεσβύτεροι. See 4.23; 23.14.

αἰτούμενοι καταδίκην, asking for sentence against him. The variant δίκην (E Ψ 𝔐), in view of κατ᾽ αὐτοῦ, implies no different sense: they were asking for judgement *against him*. Cf. Herodotus 1.2.3, ... πέμψαντα ... κήρυκα αἰτέειν τε δίκας ...

16. Cf. 25.4f. Festus represents himself as having taken a high moral tone with the Jewish accusers. Luke as usual shows Roman officials in a good light; see J. Dupont, 'Aequitas Romana', in *Études* 527–52. Roman custom (on ἔθος as the source of law see Tajra 155) must be observed; but the Roman custom is oddly described in the words χαρίζεσθαί τινα ἄνθρωπον. The meaning of χαρίζεσθαι must be the same as in 25.11, but here there is no dative. To translate, '... to give up anyone' would fail to convey the sense of doing a favour. The lack of a dative was felt by the copyists of C 945 1739 1891 *pc*, who write τινι for τινα; the deficiency was made up differently by 𝔐 gig sy sa, which add εἰς ἀπώλειαν after ἄνθρωπον. The dative must simply be understood: It is not our custom to make a present of any man *to anyone*. An alternative possibility might be to translate χαρίζεσθαι as *to favour*, but for this the verb should be followed by a dative, not an accusative. There is some slight Latin authority for *damnare* (instead of *donare*).

πρὶν ἤ ... ἔχοι ... λάβοι. This construction, as indeed the whole speech, shows Luke's ability to put suitably classical Greek ('kunst-mässig durchgeführte indirekte Rede', Radermacher 131) on the lips of educated men. Cf. Introduction, p. xlv. 'On notera les deux optatifs d'une langue très pure' (Delebecque 122). The optatives replace the subjunctives that would be used in direct speech (cf. Lk. 2.26). See M. 1.169; Moule, *IB* 133; BDR § 386.3, n. 4; Zerwick (§ 346). This is the only example in the NT of this use of the optative. See Schille (444).

Accused and accusers must come face to face. κατὰ πρόσωπον 'used adverbially, as in Acts 25.16; 2 Cor. 10.1; Gal. 2.11, is certainly not Semitic, but the prepositional use in Lk. 2.31; Acts 3.13, though not uncommon in Greek (cf. Xenophon, *Cyropaedia* 6.3.35, τὴν κατὰ πρόσωπον τῆς ἀντίας φάλαγγος τάξιν, "the post imme-diately in front of the enemy's phalanx"), is suggested by the OT idiom', M. 2.466; similarly BDR § 217.1c, n. 3.

The metaphorical use of τόπος (= opportunity) seems to be mainly biblical. At Thucydides 6.54.4, LS 1806 think τρόπῳ a probable conjecture. Preuschen (143) speaks of τόπος as a 'ver-breiteter Latinismus' (= *locus*) but cites only Sirach 4.5 (where *locus* is not used in the Vulgate!); 1 Macc. 9.45; Josephus, *Ant.* 16.258. See however Wettstein 2.628: 'τόπον ... ἀπολογίας λάβοι] ex Latino sermone formata locutio, *locum respondendi*, i.e. facultatem, potesta-tem *accipere*'.

ἀπολογία and ἔγκλημα are both technical forensic terms; see 22.1; 23.29. Properly an ἔγκλημα is a *written* accusation, but there is no need to suppose that Luke had this in mind. MM 139f. quote only papyri; *ND* 3.66 (cf. 4.86) adds Dittenberger, *OGIS* 1.229.41.

For the Roman principle appealed to see *Digest* 48.17.1: et hoc iure utimur, ne absentes damnantur neque enim inaudita causa quemquam damnari aequitatis ratio patitur. Cf. Justin, *1 Apology* 3; Tertullian, *Apology* 1.3; 2.2; Appian, *Bellum Civile* 3.54: ὁ μὲν νόμος, ὦ βουλή, δικαιοῖ τὸν εὐθυνόμενον αὐτὸν ἀκοῦσαί τε τῆς κατηγορίας καὶ ἀπολογησάμενον ὑπὲρ αὐτοῦ κρίνεσθαι; Tacitus, *Histories* 1.6.

'Das sagt Festus, obgleich er sich nicht an den Grundsatz gehalten hatte (siehe VV 9–11)' (Schneider 2.363). This seems unfair; we do not *know* what Festus would have done if Paul had not appealed.

Hanson (235) raises the question whether the Jewish court could have tried Paul in a capital charge and executed him; see Jn 18.31.

17. συνελθόντων: in the great majority of MSS the genitive absolute is completed by the addition of αὐτῶν; only B *pc* omit the pronoun. It is probably correct to omit; it is hard to see why if αὐτῶν originally stood in Luke's text it should have been dropped, whether accidentally or intentionally. And BDR § 423 has (without reference to this verse), 'Der Gen. eines Ptz. kann auch ohne Subst. im Gen. stehen, wenn es sich ohne weiteres ergänzen lässt.' Metzger (492f.) defends the short text. Cf. Lk. 12.36; Acts 21.31.

ἀναβολὴν ... ποιησάμενος, *to make a delay*, as at Thucydides 2.42.3, ... ἀναβολὴν τοῦ δεινοῦ ἐποιήσατο; Plutarch, *Camillus* 35 (147), ... ἔγνω μὴ ποιεῖσθαι τῆς τιμωρίας ἀναβολήν. Luke (like Thucydides and Plutarch, uses the middle of the verb; the active is often used with the same meaning. See 24.22.

ἐπὶ τοῦ βήματος: cf. 25.6, 9, 10. It is usually said that the meaning here must be *on the (judgement-)seat*. This is not necessarily so, since καθίζειν can mean *to sit as judge* (LS, s.v. II 3; 854); e.g. Herodotus 1.97.1; Plato, *Laws* 659b; Philo, *De Ebrietate* 165 (καθίσας οὖν ὁ νοῦς ἐν τῷ ἑαυτοῦ συνεδρίῳ ...). Cf. the English, 'Judge X is sitting at the Old Bailey'.

For the passive infinitive after a verb of commanding see on 22.24.

18. It would be natural to suppose that a man for whom severe punishment was demanded would be accused of serious crime. A Roman official could hardly be expected to understand that to 'deny the root' (כפר בעיקר) of Jewish religion was the most serious crime imaginable—the crime of Esau, for example (Baba Bathra 16b). Luke is emphasizing Paul's innocence from the Roman point of view.

αἰτίαν φέρειν (or ἐπιφέρειν, with 6 104 1241 𝔐) is a standard forensic expression: Herodotus 1.26.3, ἄλλοισι ἄλλας αἰτίας ἐπιφέρων; Thucydides 5.75.2; Philo, *De Josepho* 184, αἰτίαν ἡμῖν ὡς κατασκόποις ἐπέφερεν; Plutarch, *Aratus* 45 (1048).

ὑπενόουν is probably *I supposed*, though *to suspect* is a fairly common meaning of the verb. Sherwin-White interprets differently: ' "The accusers brought no charge against him of any evil act that I could understand", ὧν ἐγὼ ὑπενόουν. The word is pejorative, and at its strongest means "suspect". This phrase may well correspond to the formula "any act of which I was prepared to take cognizance", "de quibus cognoscere volebam".' Hemer (131) is more positive: ὧν ἐγὼ ὑπενόουν, ' "of which I could take cognizance," reflecting the legal formula *de quibus cognoscere volebam*'. But there is nothing in Luke's Greek corresponding to *volebam*. In fact, ὧν ... πονηρῶν, expressed thus by attraction of the relative, is equivalent to τῶν πονηρῶν ἃ ἐγὼ ὑπενόουν (Zerwick § 18), and means 'they brought no accusation of those evil things that I supposed (or suspected).' Copyists may have been confused by the sentence. πονηρῶν is read by ℵᶜ B E 81 104 *pc*; πονηράν by P⁷⁴ A C* Ψ 36 614 945 1175 1739 1891 2495 *al* gig vgʷʷ (sy); πονηρά by ℵ* C² w. The word is omitted by 𝔐 and may be a gloss. The sentence makes sense without it: no charge of those things that I supposed (suspected).

19. Paul was accused not of crime but of heresy, matters of dispute, ζητήματα, concerning their own religion. To Paul the Jew and Christian the religion of Athens was δεισιδαιμονία (17.22); to Festus the religion of Christians and Jews was δεισιδαιμονιά. On this word and its cognates see on 17.22.

So far Paul would have agreed with Festus's assessment; he is reported as claiming (and in the epistles did in fact claim) that Christianity was true Judaism, in the sense that it was the fulfilment of Judaism. He would also have agreed (though in each case he would have expressed the matter differently) with Festus's second point: the dispute between Paul and the Jews turned upon a certain Jesus who had died but was affirmed by Paul to be alive. Cf. Rom. 10.9: Jesus is Lord; God raised him from the dead. 'Nul n'a mieux exprimé l'essence de la religion nouvelle et ce qui sépare doctrinalement Paul des Juifs' (Delebecque 122). More circumspectly, one must recognize that Luke can only have guessed at the contents of any conversation between Agrippa and Festus; but it was a good guess—at least, one creditable to Festus. There is an interesting— but not important—verbal parallel in Lucian, *De Syria Dea* 6: πρῶτα μὲν καταγίζουσι τῷ Ἀδώνιδι, ὅκως ἐόντι νέκυϊ· μετὰ δὲ τῇ ἑτέρῃ ἡμέρῃ, ζώειν τέ μιν μυθολογέουσι. 'Es geht nicht um "Anerkennung des Christentums durch den Staat", sondern um "Ausscheidung aus dem Geschichtsverfahrung"'' (Schneider 2.363).

The construction is changed by P⁷⁴ᵛⁱᵈ sa, which place ἤν after δεισιδαιμονίας.

20. The drift of the verse is clear, but there are several difficult questions of grammar. ἐγώ is clearly emphatic: the Jews (including Paul) thought they knew all about the affair, but *as for me* I was quite at a loss. ἀπορούμενος (middle) is unusually followed by an accusative, rather than by ἐν or περί (εἰς is introduced here by C E L Ψ 33 36 323 614 945 1175 1739 1891 2495 *al*). The active sometimes takes an accusative; here, unless the accusative is treated as one of respect, we have an example of an intransitive verb used transitively. See BDR § 148.2, n. 4; M. 3.244.

ζήτησις is here *(judicial) inquiry*. This is illustrated by an inscription quoted in *ND* 4.86.

ἔλεγον: 'impf. quia condicionem fert, quae res per se est imperfecta, donec accedat alterius consensus, cf. 21.12 παρεκαλοῦμεν al.' (Blass 261).

εἰ βούλοιτο. M. 3.127: 'Other clauses introduced by εἰ and dependent on a verb like ζητεῖν are virtually indirect questions, a class. survival: Acts 17.11; 25.20.' This is well enough in 17.11, where the verb is ἀνακρίνειν; it cannot be so easily applied here, where the verb is λέγειν, which is not like ζητεῖν and seems never to introduce an indirect question. Most modern versions (but contrast Vulgate *dicebam*, Syriac הוית אמרת) translate *ask*, but this is not the meaning of λέγειν. It seems in fact impossible to defend the construction, or to improve on Alford's comment (ad loc.; 2.273), 'There is a mixed construction between "*I said, Wilt thou?*" as in ver. 9, and "*I asked him whether he would ...*"'. It is not the only imperfectly constructed sentence in Acts, or the worst; it is unfortunate that it occurs where Luke is evidently intending (see the optatives in v. 16) to write in a good style. Moule (*IB* 154) gives 'more loosely and idiomatically' the rendering, 'I said, would he like ...?' This loose but idiomatic English represents the Greek well, but the Greek, though loose, is scarcely idiomatic.

Festus does not here, as he does, or may do, or appears to do, in 25.9, say that he himself would preside over a hearing in Jerusalem, but it is evident that Luke is making no attempt to reproduce the original proposal *verbatim*.

For περὶ τούτων, H P 049 323 1241 *pm* have περὶ τούτου.

21. τοῦ δὲ Παύλου ἐπικαλεσαμένου, genitive absolute, though Paul reappears in the accusative case (αὐτόν) later in the sentence, and indeed twice. In the first case the reflexive pronoun might have been expected, or better αὐτός (Delebecque 123). See BDR § 283.1, n. 3.

τηρηθῆναι, τηρεῖσθαι. The passive infinitives are Latin rather than Greek: BDR § 392.4, n. 14. Cf. v. 17. τηρηθῆναι is constative, τηρεῖσθαι describes the process; each leads to a conclusion, εἰς, ἕως.

ὁ Σεβαστός is the usual Greek term for the Emperor (Augustus); contrast Lk. 2.1.

διάγνωσις correponds to the Latin *cognitio*; cf. διαγινώσκειν, 23.15; 24.32. In *IG* 14.1072.4f. the office *a cognitionibus Augusti* is rendered ἐπὶ ... διαγνώσεων τοῦ Σεβαστοῦ. There is papyrus evidence in MM 147; *ND* 1.47; 4.86. Delebecque (123) translates *jusqu'à la décision*; 'la preposition εἰς implique une captivité qui doit durer jusqu'à Rom.'

ἀναπέμψω: many MSS (H L P 049 323 *pm*) have πέμψω, but ἀναπέμπειν is the technical term for the remission of a case to a higher court and is very probably correct.

For ἐπικαλεσαμένου, P⁷⁴ Ψ 1739* *pc* have the less appropriate present participle ἐπικαλουμένου.

The Old Latin MS gig (see Ropes, *Begs*. 3.231) has a different form of the verse: tunc paulus appellavit cesarem et petiit ut reservaretur ad augusti cognitionem; cumque eum non possem judicare jussi eum reservari ut remittam eum cesari.—an example, probably of the sort of rewriting that lies behind the Western text. On this basis Clark (158) reconstructed the Western text thus: τότε ὁ Παῦλος ἐπεκαλέσατο Καίσαρα καὶ ἠτήσατο τηρηθῆναι αὐτὸν εἰς τὴν τοῦ Σεβαστοῦ διάγνωσιν, ἐπειδή τε αὐτὸν οὐκ ἐδυνάμην κρῖναι, ἐκέλευσα ... Metzger (493) expresses no opinion.

22. Ἀγρίππας ... Φῆστον. P⁷⁴ C E Ψ 𝔐 gig vg^{cl} sy add ἔφη, but the short text is no doubt correct. For the ellipse of the verb see BDR § 480.5a, n. 6 (with Hellenistic and papyrus parallels).

ἐβουλόμην, desiderative imperfect, 'possibly a fossilized relic of a conditional clause ... If so, it has lost its ἄν' (Moule, *IB* 151, cf. 9). It takes the place of the older βουλοίμην ἄν (Zerwick § 356), but occurs also 'in der guten Literatursprache' (Radermacher 128, quoting Dionysius of Halicarnassus, *De Demosthene* 1087 (42), ἐβουλόμην ἔτι πλείω παρασχέσθαι παραδείγματα). See also Aristophanes, *Frogs* 866 (890), ἐβουλόμην μὲν οὐκ ἐρίζειν ἐνθάδε. *Begs*. 4.312 translates, I had wished.

αὔριον is 'Vorzugsvokabel des Lukas' (Schneider 2.364).

61. FESTUS, AGRIPPA, AND PAUL 25.23–26.32

(23) On the next day, when Agrippa and Bernice came with great pomp and entered the audience chamber, along with the tribunes and the leading men of the city, and when Festus had given the word of command, Paul was brought. (24) Festus said, 'King Agrippa, and all you gentlemen who are present with us, you behold this man, concerning whom the whole people of the Jews petitioned me, both in Jerusalem and here, shouting out that he ought to live no longer. (25) I however did not see that he had done anything worthy of death, and when he himself appealed to the Emperor I decided to send him. (26) I have nothing definite about him to send in writing to the Emperor;[1] for this reason I have produced him before you, and especially before you, King Agrippa, in order that, when examination has taken place, I may get something that I may write. (27) For it seems to me nonsense to send a prisoner and not at the same time to signify the charges against him.'

(1) Agrippa said to Paul, 'It is permitted you to give an account of yourself.' Then Paul stretched out his hand and began his defence. (2) 'I consider myself fortunate, King Agrippa, that I am today about to make my defence, concerning all the things of which I am accused by the Jews, before you, (3) especially since [I know][2] that you are familiar with all the customs and disputes current among the Jews. So I beg you to hear me patiently. (4) All the Jews know my manner of life from my youth, which was from the beginning within my own nation and in Jerusalem. (5) They have known from of old, if they are willing to testify, that I lived in accordance with the strictest party within our religion, a Pharisee. (6) And now I am standing trial for the hope of the promise made by God to our fathers, (7) [the promise][3] to which our twelve-tribe people, zealously worshipping [God][4] night and day, hope to attain. It is for this hope that I am being accused, O King, by Jews. (8) Why is it judged incredible with you that God raises the dead? (9) I myself thought that I ought to do many things contrary to the name of Jesus the Nazoraean. (10) And this I did in Jerusalem, and I shut up in prison many of the saints, having received authority from the chief priests; and when they were being killed I cast my vote against them. (11) And often in all the synagogues I tried by punishing them to make them blaspheme, and being exceedingly mad against them I persecuted them even to foreign cities. (12) And as I was travelling to Damascus with authority and commission from the chief priests, (13) at midday, on the road, I saw, O King, a light from heaven, beyond the brightness of the sun, shining round me and those who were travelling with me. (14) We all fell to the ground and I heard a voice saying to me in the Hebrew[5] language, "Saul, Saul, why are you persecuting me? It

[1] Greek, the lord (i.e., the Emperor).
[2] I know is not in the Greek.
[3] The promise is not in the Greek.
[4] God is not in the Greek.
[5] Aramaic is probably intended.

is hard for you to kick against the goad.'' (15) I said, ''Who art thou, Lord?'' The Lord said, ''I am Jesus whom you are persecuting. (16) But get up and stand on your feet. For this is why I have appeared to you, to appoint you a minister and witness both of the things that you have seen and of those in which I shall appear to you, (17) rescuing you from the people and from the Gentiles, unto whom I now send you, (18) to open their eyes, so that they may turn from darkness to light and from the authority of Satan to God, so that they may receive forgiveness of sins and a lot among those who have been sanctified by faith in me.'' (19) Consequently, King Agrippa, I did not prove disobedient to the heavenly vision, (20) but first to those in Damascus and in Jerusalem, and in all the land of Judaea and to the Gentiles, I proclaimed that they should repent and turn to God, doing works worthy of repentance. (21) Because of these things Jews seized me when I was in the Temple and tried to make away with me. (22) So, having obtained the help that comes from God, I stand to this day, testifying to small and great, saying nothing but the things which the prophets and Moses said were to happen, (23) that the Christ was to suffer, and that he first would, on the basis of the resurrection of the dead, proclaim light to both the people and the Gentiles.'

(24) While Paul[6] was saying these things in his defence, Festus said with a loud voice. 'Paul, you are mad; your great learning is leading you into madness.' (25) Paul said, 'I am not mad, most excellent Festus, but uttering words of truth and sober-mindedness. (26) For the king, to whom I speak with boldness, knows about these matters, for I am persuaded that none of them escapes him; for this was not done in a corner. (27) King Agrippa, do you believe the prophets? I know that you believe.' (28) Agrippa said to Paul,[7] 'With little trouble you are trying to persuade me to play the Christian.' (29) Paul replied, 'I wish to God that, with[8] little trouble or much, you and all who hear me today would become such as I myself am—apart from these bonds.' (30) The king rose up, and the governor and Bernice and those who were sitting with them. (31) When they had withdrawn they spoke to one another, saying, 'This man is doing nothing worthy of death or imprisonment.' (32) Agrippa said to Festus, 'This man could have been released if he had not appealed to Caesar.'

Bibliography

C. K. Barrett, as in (48).

H. Braun, *ThR* 29 (1963), 175.

H. J. Cadbury, *JBL* 48 (1929), 421f.

J. Dupont, *FS* Schnackenburg, 125–43.

J Dupont, *Nouvelles Études* 446–56 (= *FS* Barrett, 290–9).

A. Fridrichsen, *Coniect. Neot.* 3 (1939), 14f.

K. Haacker, as in (56).

[6]Greek, he.
[7]RSV, In a short time you think to make me a Christian; NEB, You think it will not take much to make me a Christian; NJB, A little more, and your arguments would make a Christian of me.
[8]RSV, whether short or long; NEB, Much or little; NJB, Little or much.

P. Harlé, *NTS* 24 (1977–8), 527–33.

C. J. A. Hickling, Kremer, *Actes* 499–503.

S. Légasse, as in (54).

A. J. Malherbe, *Paul and the Popular Philosophers* (1989), 147–3.

R. F. O'Toole, *The Christological Climax of Paul's Defense*, AnalBib 78 (1978).

J. M. Reynolds, *JRS* 68 (1978), 111–21.

L. Schmid, *TWNT* 3.665–7.

W. Stegemann, as in (43).

A. Vögeli, *ThZ* 9 (1953), 415–38.

R. D. Witherup, as in (55).

See also other works cited in (23) (I.438f.) and in (55) (II.1030f.).

Commentary

For the meeting between Festus and Agrippa see above, in the introduction to Section 60. Such a meeting is not to be dismissed as impossible or even unlikely, but it is hard to see what trustworthy information about it Luke can have found. The new paragraph is somewhat different in that it purports to relate a more public event held in some sort of audience chamber (ἀκροατήριον, v. 23) and attended by the retinues of Festus and of Agrippa and Bernice and a miscellaneous and undefined company of local notables. At least it was not, as represented by Luke, a private conversation. Paul's long speech, which includes the third account of his conversion, is the main feature of the narrative; this will be discussed below. The speech is interrupted by Festus' shout, 'You are mad, Paul'. A brief conversation between Paul and Agrippa follows before the scene is wound up by the explicit affirmation, by both rulers, that Paul is an innocent man. The only historical question that arises and may perhaps have an answer is whether a Christian writer composing freely would introduce into his story the assertion that Paul was mad. The answer is probably, Yes, he might, since as a writer he is evidently able to allow Paul to reply, and even to have the last word. In fact he presents here what he takes to be Paul's reply to a charge brought against Christians in his own (Luke's) time, at the same time constructing a climax in his picture of the heroic Paul. The picture begins with the third account of Paul's conversion (cf. 9.1–19; 22.4–21). The second and third accounts differ from the first partly through Luke's liking for variation but partly also through adaptation to the settings in which they are delivered. The second was addressed to a Jewish crowd in the Temple (see p. 1031). The third is spoken to Gentiles. Thus (for details see the notes below) Paul says that the voice from heaven addressed him as Saul, and adds the explanation that the voice spoke in Hebrew (Aramaic). The voice asks as in the other accounts, 'Why are you persecuting me?' But immediately the Greek proverb is added, 'It is hard for you to kick against the goad'. There will be no need after this for dispute, and the story goes on immediately to Paul's commission to go to the Gentiles, which is not deferred (as in ch. 22) to a later occasion in the Temple. Paul the Jew is to evangelize the Gentiles, and is assured of God's protection as he fulfils his mission. To this vocation Paul had not been untrue; this was why the Jews hated him so bitterly and had tried to kill him, though, as he goes on to point out, his Gospel simply asserts the fulfilment of what had already been written by Moses and the prophets, and was addressed to all (τῷ τε λαῷ καὶ τοῖς ἔθνεσιν, v. 23). Festus's interjection gives him the opportunity of asserting his sober truthfulness and dependence on the prophets, and of uttering as his last word the declaration that makes him, beyond any other, the model of a Christian preacher (v. 29).

Haenchen (662) correctly sums up the effect of the passage. 'Der Leser soll nur den Eindruck mitnehmen: Paulus war ohne alle Schuld, obwohl er nicht frei kam!' This is undoubtedly the effect that Luke intended that the passage should have, and he wrote so as to achieve it. Yet his narrative is not entirely fictional. At the end of the proceedings in Palestine Paul was not free, and the only reason why he was not free was that Roman officials thought that there was at least enough to be said for him to make it worth while to take the case to a higher court. That Paul's Gospel was true was of course for Luke not in question. And the conclusion was one with which Paul himself was probably not displeased. He was as well protected from the Jews as he could hope to be, and would soon be out of reach of Palestinian Judaism, enjoying a free passage to Rome, the place he had made his objective.

23. τῇ οὖν ἐπαύριον takes up αὔριον in 25.22. ἐλθόντος, the singular participle, is followed by the double subject τοῦ Ἀγρίππα καὶ τῆς Βερνίκης; a very natural construction. Bernice is here something of an afterthought; when later in the verse brother and sister are both clearly in mind the plural participle εἰσελθόντων (P[74] *pc* have ἐλθ.) is used.

φαντασία in the sense of *parade, ostentation, show* (as distinct from literary and philosophical meanings) is cited by LS 1916 only from relatively late authors. MM 664 have no papyrus evidence to quote.

ἀκροατήριον is a place designed, or used, for the purpose of hearing; often a lecture room, here perhaps *audience chamber*? For the ending –τήριον see M. 2.342 and BDR § 109.8, n. 10. It is by no means necessarily a law court, and the use of the word suggests, or at least is consistent with, an informal hearing; this indeed it must have been. Once the appeal to the Emperor's court had been made and allowed no lower court had any right to try Paul. The main impression is that of a show put on to gratify Agrippa, though it is doubtless true that Festus would be glad to gain additional information that would help him to write a more adequate account of the case he was sending to Rome. *Begs.* 4.312: 'Festus was merely showing off an interesting prisoner to entertain Agrippa, the chief local dignitaries, and the officers of the Mess.' *Begs.* 4.313: '... to obtain material for a report on a case which puzzled him'.

σύν τε χιλιάρχοις. τε might have been expected to follow the noun χιλ. which is coordinated with ἀνδράσιν, but attraction to follow the preposition is classical (BDR § 444.5, n. 6).

τῆς πόλεως, presumably Caesarea.

κελεύσαντος. The verse is based on a complicated pattern of absolute genitives—ἐλθόντος, εἰσελθόντων, κελεύσαντος. After these the last words, ἤχθη ὁ Παῦλος, stand out with impressive simplicity. This perhaps supports the view of Ehrhardt (*Acts* 120f.), against Cadbury (*History* 43): Luke is not in this elaborate picture indulging in a kind of snobbery.

The Syriac Harclean margin contains (the equivalent of) the words τοῖς καταβεβηκόσιν ἀπὸ τῆς ἐπαρχείας; Ropes (*Begs.* 3.233) observes that it is not clear in the MS (which lacks the usual diacritical marks) whether this is an addition or replaces τοῖς κατ' ἐξοχὴν τῆς πόλεως. Clark (381) disagrees with Ropes's description of the words as a gloss.

Stählin (305): from this point onwards and throughout ch. 26 there is a parallel between Jesus and Paul, with the difference, 'dass Jesus die ganze Szene mit seinem Schweigen, Paulus dagegen mit seiner Rede beherrscht.' It is a quite considerable difference. 'Die Szene vor Agrippa und Bernike ist eine Dublette derjenigen vor Felix und Drusilla' (Lüdemann 262; cf. 25.1, 6). But the counterpart to Felix is Festus.

24. θεωρεῖτε, indicative. So Bengel (480), rightly.

ἐνέτυχον. The plural verb follows properly upon the noun of multitude πλῆθος, but B H Ψ 104 945 *al* thought that the singular (–εν) would be more appropriate. ἐντυγχάνειν means *to approach someone with a request*, often in favour of a person (e.g. Rom. 8.27), hence *to intercede*; here, against.

πλῆθος followed by a national name is often not *multitude*, but '*people* in the official political sense'. So Deissmann (*BS* 232f.), citing 1 Macc. 8.20 and inscriptions (*IMAe* 85.4 and 90.7, both τὸ πλῆθος τὸ Ῥοδίων). It is suggested that the move against Paul was not an occasional riot but a move on the part of the Jewish people as a whole. That (as Deissmann points out) πλῆθος was used also of religious communities is in the light of the nature of Judaism consistent with this. For the position of τε (ἔν τε) see the note on v. 23.

βοῶντες (P⁷⁴ ℵ A B 81 *pc*) is strengthened to ἐπιβ. by C E Ψ 𝔐).

μήκετι at the end of the sentence emphatically doubles the negation.

Ropes (*Begs.* 3.233) translates the Harclean Margin of vv. 24, 25, 26 as follows: et in Hierosolymis et hic, ut traderem eum iis ad tormentum sine defensione. non potui autem tradere eum, propter mandata quae habemus ab Augusto. si autem quis eum accusaturus esset, dicebam ut sequeretur me in Caesaream, ubi custodiebatur: qui quum venissent, clamaverunt ut tolleretur e vita. quum autem hanc et alteram partem audivissem, comperi quod in nullo reus esset mortis. quum autem dixerem: Vis iudicari cum iis in Hierosolyma? Caesarem appelavit. de quo aliquid certum scribere domino meo non habeo. This is given in Greek στίχοι by Clark (381f.).

25. This verse contains the strongest assertion so far of Paul's innocence. The Roman magistrate has found in him nothing worthy of death, which evidently was the penalty that his Jewish accusers sought. μηδὲν ... πεπραχέναι: πράσσειν can be used in a general sense but it is used 'meistens von Handlungen, die nicht löblich sind' (BA 1399f., with many examples from the NT and elsewhere).

Many copyists (ℵ* Ψ 𝔐 gig s sy^h) changed the finite verb κατελαβόμην into the participle καταλαβόμενος and thus produced the neat sentence, I having apprehended ... and he having appealed ... I decided to send ...

For the aorist participle ἐπικαλεσαμένου, P⁷⁴ 2464 *pc* have the present, ἐπικαλουμένου, which makes less good sense, unless the intention is to stress that Paul continued to make his appeal, did not withdraw it; but once the machinery was set in motion he would have little choice about this.

For ἐπικαλεῖσθαι see 25.11; for τὸν Σεβαστόν, 25.21.

26. To decide to send Paul to Rome was one thing; to know what to say in the accompanying report was another. For the duty of sending a report see *Digest* 49.6.1: Post appellationem interpositam litterae dandae sunt ab eo, a quo appellatum est, ad eum, qui de appellatione cogniturus est, sive principem sive alium; quas litteras dimissorias sive apostolos appellant. If Festus was convinced that Paul was innocent he could have released him at once; he may however have recognized that it was in Paul's interests to be packed safely off to Rome. 'Die Sprache (ἀσφαλής, προάγω, ἐφ᾽ὑμῶν, ἀνάκρισις) ist wieder juristisch-technisch' (Conzelmann 137).

τῷ κυρίῳ, for the Emperor; cf. ὁ Σεβαστός in v.25. ' "ὁ κύριος" ist hier der Kaiser. Ein langes Kapitel Religionsgeschichte und ein langes Kapitel Kirchengeschichte klingt an' (Bauernfeind 267).

Bengel (480) is right with 'Nuper orta erat haec *domini* appellatio', but more detail is needed. 'V. 26 enthält den ältesten uns bekannten Beleg für die Anwendung des absolut gebrauchten Titels "Herr" (griech. *kyrios*) auf den Kaiser' (Roloff 350). Yet Luke could use the word without explanation and assume that his reader would know what was meant. For the use of *dominus*/κύριος in the first century see W. Foerster in *TWNT* 4.1053–6; MM 365 ('There is no evidence that this title was applied to the Roman Emperor in the West before the time of Domitian. Indeed it was specifically disclaimed by Augustus and Tiberius as contrary to the Roman conception of the "Principate"'); BA 933 ('Seit Claudius . . . finden wir auch die röm. Kaiser in steigendem Masse so bezeichnet—ganz vereinzelt schon früher'). Among the most important references are Ovid, *Fasti* 2.143 (Tu [Romulus] domini nomen, principis ille [Augustus] tenet); Suetonius, *Augustus* 53 (Domini appelationem, ut maledictum et opprobrium, semper exhorruit); *Tiberius* 27; Tacitus, *Annals* 2.87; POxy 1.37. 1.6; Dittenberger, *OGIS* 2.606.1; *Sylloge* 2.814.30.

προάγειν, though it can be used generally, is a semi-technical term for producing a prisoner in court; so e.g. Josephus, *War* 1.539 (τούς γε μὴν υἱοὺς οὐ προήγαγεν εἰς τὴν δίκην); *Ant.* 16.393; Justin, *1 Apology* 21.3—cited by BA 1406.

ὅπως. The pretext for producing the prisoner was to satisfy Agrippa's curiosity, but Festus does not conceal his intention of using the occasion, and Agrippa's knowledge of Judaism, to help him in writing his report. This is at least as likely as the opposite view, that the report was the pretext for the entertainment of Agrippa. After this point we hear no more of a letter to the Emperor (Weiser 650). Luke knew that one was required but had not seen, and did not need to invent, what Festus wrote.

σχῶ is changed into the more common ἔχω by P⁷⁴ A E Ψ 81 614 945 1891 2495 *al*. The indirect question τί γράψω becomes τί γράψαι in E 𝔐.

27. ἄλογον γάρ μοι δοκεῖ. No doubt it would seem equally unreasonable to the Emperor. After μοι δοκεῖ the dative πέμποντι would have been better that the accusative.

1. ἐπιτρέπεται, an aoristic present (BDR § 320, n. 2; M. 3.64; cf. Acts 9.34): It is hereby permitted you to speak. An impersonal passive, which gives a formal touch to the proceedings.

περί (P⁷⁴ ℵ A C E 33 36 81 453 614 945 1739 1891 2495 *al*) and ὑπέρ (B (Ψ) 𝔐) probably do not differ greatly from each other: *to speak for yourself*. But περί ought strictly to mean *about yourself*, that is, to give an account of your beliefs and behaviour. This may be intended. 'Paulus redet zwar "über sich selbst", kommt dabei aber am Ende auf Jesus Christus zu sprechen' (Schneider 2.370).

ἐκτείνας. Cf. the use of κατασείειν at 12.17; 13.16; 21.40.

ἐκτείνειν is often used for the stretching out of the hand for other purposes (e.g. for healing) but it is not used in the sense of an orator's gesture elsewhere in the NT. LS 521 cites no example, nor does BA 495. BA mentions Quintilian 9.3.84ff. (an error for 11.3.84ff.— Narratio magis prolatam manum, amictum recidentem, gestum distinctum ... postulabit) and Apuleius 2.21: porrigit dexteram, et ad instar oratorum conformat articulum; duobusque infinis conclusis digitis, caeteros eminentes porrigens ...

ἀπελόγειτο. See 19.33. '... although not formally on trial, the word shows that the Apostle was defending himself' (Knowling 500). This, at least, is the way Luke understands the scene. The tense of the verb is an example of the imperfect (a sort of inceptive imperfect) used for a word of speaking that introduces direct speech (especially extended speech).

Here (cf. 25.24–26) the Syriac Harclean margin has, before ἐκτείνας, an addition of its own: 'tunc ipse Paulus, confidens et in spiritu sancto consolatus, extendit manum' (so Ropes, *Begs*. 3.233) another example of the Western tendency to enliven the narrative.

2. περὶ πάντων ὧν ἐγκαλοῦμαι. Various constructions occur with ἐγκαλεῖν; for the use of περί BA 434 compares PHib 96.22, περὶ ὧν ἐνεκάλεσαν ἀλλήλοις. Cf. BDR § 178, n. 2.

Ἰουδαίων, anarthrous; it is customary with Greek orators not to use the article with the names of opponents (BDR § 262.2, n. 5). Delebecque (124) explains differently: 'Paul ne dit pas "par *les Juifs*"; de même au v. 3. Dans le premier cas Paul suggère que tous les Juifs ne l'accusent pas; dans le second il s'incorpore au peuple juif.' Delebecque translates, *par des Juifs, chez des Juifs*. For ὑπό, P⁷⁴ 945 1739 1891 *pc* have παρά: the accusation rose from the Jews.

βασιλεῦ Ἀγρίππα. It is usual for the vocative to stand earlier in the sentence than it does here (BDR § 474. 6a, n. 10). 'Magnam vim habet compellatio in secunda persona, singulari praesertim, et proprio nomine' (Bengel 480).

ἥγημαι, perfect with present sense; this is the classical use (BDR § 341, n. 3), a literary touch (M. 1.148). Contrast Phil. 3.7, where Paul uses the perfect with perfect meaning. It is of course arguable that for an occasion such as this Paul would put on (or attempt to put on— see below and the next verse) a higher style than he would naturally use. Cf. Blass (264), who refers to Herodotus 1.126.6; Plato, *Timaeus* 19e.

After ἐμαυτὸν μακάριον, μέλλων (nominative) is harsh. It is defensible, but would be less harsh if the order of the words were changed: μέλλων ... ἥγημαι ἐμαυτὸν μακάριον ... See Zerwick (§ 15).

ἀπολογεῖσθαι: see v. 1.

3. The attempt at literary style (if such it was) in v. 2 now breaks down completely. The accusative and participle (γνώστην ὄντα σε) has no verb to depend on. (P⁷⁴) ℵᶜ A C 33 (36) 614 945 1891 *al* syᵖ save the situation by adding ἐπιστάμενος after ζητημάτων, but this can hardly (notwithstanding Dibelius 92) be Luke's text. The accusative γνώστην after σου (v. 2) is hard (Bauernfeind 269; Moule, *IB* 37). BDR § 137.3, n. 3 suggest that the accusatives may be dependent on ἥγημαι (v. 2); better is Page (245): 'The acc. is governed by the sense of "thinking" or "considering", which is the main idea of the sentence.' This does not justify the grammar of the defective sentence but explains how the sentence came to be defective in the way it is.

'μάλιστα usually precedes that which it emphasizes' (*Begs.* 4.314). So it is here.

ἐθῶν τε καὶ ζητημάτων. ἐθός is probably used here in the sense of *law*; cf. 15.1. It could have been chosen as less offensive in a court that knew only one (Roman) νόμος. The ζητήματα (cf. 25.19) are the disputes which the Jews were known to have about the interpretation of their laws. So essentially Calvin (2.269).

κατὰ Ἰουδαίους. The use of κατά to suggest a possessive or subjective genitive is 'allgemein hellenistisch' (BDR § 224.1, n. 3). But the genitive equivalent will be different for the two nouns: the customs (laws) *of* the Jews; the disputes current among them, in which they engage.

δέομαι ... ἀκοῦσαι. 'Im Genitiv steht die angeredete Person bei δεῖσθαι "bitten"; dazu tritt der blosse Inf. wenn der Gebetene Subj. des Inf. ist' (BDR § 409.5). Cf. Lk. 9.38. After δέομαι the genitive σου is added by C 𝔐 syᵖ co?.

In vv. 2, 3 Paul is using the customary *captatio benevolentiae*; cf. 24.2f., 10. Beyer (148) misses the point with the observation that Paul is relieved to speak to a Jew after making explanations to ignorant Gentiles; he fared considerably better with Gentiles than with Jews.

4. μὲν οὖν introduces the serious business of the defence.

Rather oddly, βίωσις appears to be, in use, a Jewish word. It is used in Sirach, Prol. 14 (τῆς ἐννόμου βιώσεως), in Symmachus Ps. 38(39).6, and in a Jewish inscription of the first century AD (*IG Rom.* 4.655.12f., διά τε τὴν ἐνάρετον αὐτῶν [βί]ωσιν). BA 283 surprisingly misses the use in Symmachus and adds nothing more. LS 316 add a 6th century AD papyrus. That the word means *manner of life* is clear.

ἐν τῷ ἔθνει μου ἔν τε Ἱεροσολύμοις ... πάντες Ἰουδαῖοι. Turner (*Insights* 84f.) discusses the meaning and construction. Much turns on the meaning here of τε. It is natural at first to suppose that ἔθνος here means what it means on Paul's lips at 24.17; 28.19, that is, the

Jewish nation. Turner argues however that τε means *and*, not *including* or *actually*. Thus life *in my nation* and life *in Jerusalem* are distinguished. Paul 'is referring not to his present position but to the situation of childhood days before he went for his education to Jerusalem. Before that, he would naturally have thought of "his nation" as being the people of the home town of which he was so proud, Tarsus, "no mean city" ' (85). The most obvious difficulty in this view is that it is hard to see how *all the Jews* (even allowing for some rhetorical exaggeration) can have known Paul's manner of life in Tarsus—the Jews of Tarsus, perhaps even the Jews of Cilicia, but in the present scene Paul must be including the Jerusalem Jews who were accusing him. Turner excludes too readily meanings of τε other than the simple *and*; see e.g. Acts 6.7, where the general increase in the number of disciples includes the adherence to the faith of a large number of priests. In the same way it is possible that *in Jerusalem* should be included within the wider *in my nation*. This verse cannot settle the question of the main centre of Paul's education, discussed at 22.3; in any case the question is bound to remain whether 22.3 and 26.4, whatever they mean, are correct. But it would be wrong to conclude that this verse refers to Paul's early youth in Tarsus as well as to his education in Jerusalem. See Bruce (2.462); also Hanson (237). If in fact the reference is to Jerusalem ἐξ ἀρχῆς is significant: his life had been lived if not from birth at least from very early years in Jerusalem. *Begs.* 4.315 takes ἔθνος to be contrasted with Jerusalem, unless possibly it means *province* (i.e. Judaea). Phil. 3.5 shows that Paul's very early life was lived among Jews.

Ἰουδαῖοι, anarthrous, is read by P⁷⁴ B C* E Ψ 33 81 323 614 945 1175 1739 2495 *al.* οἱ is added by ℵ A C² 𝔐. See Delebecque on v. 2. See also M. 3.169 and Metzger (495).

ἴσασι. This seems to be in the NT the only absolutely certain (i.e. unaffected by textual variants) example of the older forms of the perfect (M. 2.221; see also BDR § 99.2, n. 2)—another example of the literary Greek Luke puts into this speech. The third person plural of οἶδα does not occur in the (13) Pauline letters; οἴδατε is common (ἴστε imperative occurs at Eph. 5.5).

In order to explain the real issue Paul must 'von der Geschichte seines Lebens reden. Nur so trifft er den Kern der Sache' (Beyer 149).

5. προ– in προγινώσκοντες and ἄνωθεν virtually reduplicate each other; they have known me in advance, that is, before now; they have known me from of old, from the beginning.

ἀκριβεστάτην is one of the three superlatives in –τατος found in the NT (four if ἁπλούστατος is read with D in Mt. 10.16); see BDR § 60.1, n. 2. It is another mark of literary style in this passage. *ND* 1.37 notes an adverbial use of the superlative in an inscription from

Sagalassos (*JRS* 66 (1976), 106–31. Josephus, *Life* 191, where the Pharisees are said τῶν ἄλλων ἀκριβείᾳ διαφέρειν.

αἵρεσιν. See on 5.17, and *FS* Lohse, 96–110; also Fitzmyer (*Essays* 276), referring to Josephus, *Ant.* 13.171; 20.199; *Life* 10, 12.

θρησκείας. The word occurs seldom in the NT, of the Christian religion only at James 1.27 (contrast 1.26; Col. 2.18). Its most common use suggests the cultic, ritual, and possibly formal side of religion (see 4 Macc. 5.7); hence perhaps the choice of it here, where Judaism and especially Pharisaism are set in an unfavourable light. In addition to the dictionaries see Hatch (*Essays* 55–7); Ropes on James 1.27 (*ICC*, 182f.).

The aorist ἔζησα is constative, looking back on Paul's pre-Christian life and viewing it as a whole: the life I lived up to that point was that of a Pharisee. On the Pharisees and Pharisaism see on 23.6. Cf. Phil. 3.5f. On the sense in which Paul as a Christian continued to be a Pharisee see Schmithals (225).

6. καὶ νῦν, in contrast with my former manner of life as a Pharisee; yet also in continuity with it, for Paul continues to maintain that his Christianity is true Judaism, and that he is maintaining the hope which is the raison d'être of his people's existence.

εἰς is a surprising preposition, not unnaturally 'corrected' by C 𝔐 to πρός. The omission of ἡμῶν by H L P 049 1241 𝔐 seems natural in a Christian speech, but only superficially so: the promise was spoken to the patriarchs, and Christians claimed that they were more truly *our* ancestors than *the Jews'*. This is very characteristic of Luke's thought; Paul also speaks, for example, of Abraham as *our father* (Rom. 4.1).

For ὑπό with an intransitive verb see LS 1873f. (s.v. A II 1).

ἕστηκα κρινόμενος, emphatically, and effectively, at the end of the sentence. For this hope, which you might suppose would win respect and even fame within Judaism, I am standing trial. This pattern—description of the hope, followed by Paul's position as a man on trial—is repeated in the next verse. Strictly speaking Paul was not now on trial, but it must have seemed like it, and it was natural for Luke to describe it so.

7. εἰς ἥν will refer to ἐπαγγελία, not to ἐλπίς, since the Jews *hope* to attain it. When Paul wishes to take up ἐλπίς with a relative he now has to repeat the substantive, περὶ ἧς ἐλπίδος.

τὸ δωδεκάφυλον ἡμῶν, our twelve-tribe unit. For the use of the neuter singular of an adjective as collective noun see BDR § 263.3, n. 6. The adjective is used at *Sibylline Oracles* 2.171; 3.249, the substantivized form at 1 Clement 55.6 (cf. 31.4 for δωδεκάσκηπτρον). At Herodotus 5.66.2 there are the analogous τετράφυλος and δεκάφυλος.

ἐν ἐκτενείᾳ. The moral sense is mainly but not exclusively biblical (Judith 4.9; 2 Macc. 14.38; 3 Macc. 6.41); but see Deissmann *BS* 262 and MM 198 for inscriptions and papyri. Cf. 1 Clement 33.1; 37.1; also Cicero, *Ad Atticum* 10.17.1 (quam in me incredibilem ἐκτενείαν!). Deissmann gives the meaning *endurance* so also BA 495 (Beharrlichkeit). But LS 521, *zeal, assiduousness, 'gush', 'empressement'* seem better.

νύκτα καὶ ἡμέραν, Blass (265) thinks of the *tamid* offering, but the expression simply means *continuously*. With λατρεύειν, τῷ θεῷ must be understood. In classical use ἐλπίζειν sometimes takes the future infinitive; hence the reading of B *pc*, καταντήσειν; but the aorist infinitive is also used, and καταντῆσαι is not wrong by classical standards.

For the end of this verse see v. 6; the same emphasis is repeated. It is concerning this *Jewish* hope that I am accused by *Jews*. There is of course an obvious answer to this complaint. Paul is not being blamed for maintaining the Jewish hope but for holding, falsely in Jewish opinion, that it has been fulfilled by Jesus.

For the position of the vocative βασιλεῦ cf. v. 2, and see BDR § 474.6a, n. 10.

P²⁹ (= POxy 13.1597.1–5) has, using Grenfell's conjectures (*Begs.* 3.235): τὸ δωδεκ[άφυλον ἡμῶν ἐν ἐκτε]νίᾳ νύκτ[α καὶ ἡμέραν λατρεύει ἐν(?)] ἐλπίδι χ[αταντῆσαι· περὶ ἧς νῦν(?)] ἐνκαλοῦ[μαι ὑπὸ Ἰουδαίων· εἰ(?)] ὁ ΘC νεκρ[οὺς ἐγείρει]

On this Clark (382) writes: 'The editors [Grenfell and Hunt] remark that "the omission of a line containing τι ... υμιν is an easy hypothesis. I may point out that the words would form an excellent στίχος).' We must regard this as an example of the freedom—and carelessness—with which Western editors handled the text. 'This papyrus and PMich 1571 raise the question whether the text of Acts in the third century did not vary from any extant authority even more than we had supposed. These two papyri are the oldest extant manuscripts of Acts, they have the "wildest" Western text known, yet they come not from Africa or Edessa but from Egypt' (*Begs.* 4.316).

8. Black (*AA* 59) notes the asyndeton of this verse, but it is not to be ascribed to Semitic influence; there is no grammatical connection with what precedes but there is a connection of thought. The thought of resurrection arises out of the reference to the hope of Israel in v. 7, but it is not in fact the most natural expression of the hope; the hope of the twelve tribes was that they would live unitedly in peace and prosperity in the land promised them. Eb. Nestle suggested that this verse is misplaced and should stand between v. 22 and v. 23; cf. Stählin 306, 307, who thinks that v. 23 should follow v. 8 either at this point or at the end of the speech. The suggestion is attractive linguistically (the word εἰ in v. 23 would follow acceptably after εἰ in this verse) but is not necessary. For Luke (and Paul) the hope was concentrated and fulfilled in resurrection, especially in the resurrection of Jesus; the transition would not be convincing to a Jew, but to Luke and Paul it was. For the connection with what follows see on the next verse. It is of course true (Roloff 351) that the Christian hope of resurrection has a different basis from the Pharisaic.

For ἄπιστον κρίνεται cf. Josephus, *Ant.* 18.76, χρὴ ἄπιστα αὐτὰ κρίνειν; for παρά, 'nach dem Urteil jmds.', BDR § 238.2, n. 3. Cf. Bengel (481): *incredibilia* veteres dixere fabulas poëticas ... sic *incredibile* duxit resurrectionem Festus.

ὑμῖν is surprising here, especially after the singular βασιλεῦ in v. 7. Luke probably thinks of the Christian on trial as addressing Jewish hearers, who might be expected to share Paul's belief in resurrection. If pressed he might have replied that Agrippa was well acquainted with Judaism (v. 3) and that Paul could claim that he believed the prophets (v. 27). For the dative cf. Mk 10.27 and parallels.

For the use of εἰ where ὅτι might have been expected see H. J. Cadbury (*JBL* 48 (1929), 421f.). There may be a little more to say. Thus Delebecque (125): 'Dans le meilleur grec beaucoup de complétives peuvent être introduites par εἰ signifiant la condition, aussi bien que par ὅτι signifiant la cause'; Zerwick (§ 404): εἰ is 'fere aequivalens ὅτι post verba quae exprimunt animi commotionem (admirationem, indignationem), e.g. Mc 15.44 ... A 26.8 'Quid incredibile iudicatur εἰ ὁ Θεὸς νεκροὺς ἐγείρει: Deum mortuos resuscitare.' Haenchen (653) translates 'wenn tatsächlich'.

9. μὲν οὖν (cf. v. 4) takes the speech a stage further. Page (246f.) says, rightly, that it resumes the narrative from v. 5 (vv. 6–8 being a parenthesis). He notes that others take ἐγὼ μ. ο. as answering the question of v. 8, but answers convincingly, (1) such a use of μὲν οὖν requires justification, (2) the words do not answer the question, and (3) the question (of v. 8) is rhetorical and needs no answer. Paul can assert the theme of resurrection in its Christian form (i.e., the beginning of the general resurrection, Christ having been raised as the firstfruits of all who sleep) for two reasons, both of which he is able to cover by means of one narrative, on which he now embarks: (a) he has himself seen the crucified Jesus alive; (b) this event has transformed him from persecutor to apostle. The story of his conversion (cf. 9.1–19; 22.4–21) opens with an account of his enthusiastic resistance to Christianity.

ἔδοξα ἐμαυτῷ is a lapse, though not a serious one, from classical usage, which would have had μοι (BDR § 283.1, n. 3; M. 3.42). See however Aristophanes, *Wasps* 1265 (1257), πολλάκις δὴ 'δοξ' ἐμαυτῷ δεξιὸς πεφυκέναι; Demosthenes 18.255 (312), ὡς ἐμαυτῷ δοκῶ (there is a misprint in Blass 266 and BA 406).

πρὸς τὸ ὄνομα. With ἐναντία the dative would be more usual; e.g. Demosthenes 18.213 (299), ἐναντί᾽ ἐπράξατε Θηβαίοις. For the significance of *the name* in Acts see on 3.6; positively, Christian things are done in the name of Jesus; correspondingly, resistance is offered to his name; 'erst hier wird also wieder (vgl. 4.17f.; 5.28, 40f.; 9.15f.) ganz deutlich, dass es der Name Jesu "des Nazoräers" ... ist, an dem die Wege der Juden und Christen total auseinandergehen' (Stählin 307). 'Der "Name" Jesu umschreibt die Jesus zugehörige Sphäre, d.h. nicht nur ihn selbst, sondern auch die an ihn Glaubenden' (Roloff 352).

For Ναζωραῖος see on 2.22, also Rüger in the note on 22.8.

10. ὃ καὶ ἐποίησα ἐν Ἱεροσολύμοις. See 8.3.

καὶ πολλούς τε. It is impossible to see any purpose that might be served by τε in this sentence; the word has become a mannerism of Luke's (Moule, *IB* 197). For τε, 36 453 *pc* have δέ; B Ψ 𝔐 omit—understandably.

τὴν ἐξουσίαν ... λαβών. See 9.1f., where the authority is expressed in letters and is related to Paul's journey to Damascus.

ἀναιρεῖν is a Lucan word (twice in Lk.; 19 times in Acts; 3 times in the rest of the NT). While the witnesses were actually being killed (ἀναιρουμένων, present participle) voting, one way or the other, would be too late, but one knows what Luke means. Zerwick (§ 274) comments, 'cum ageretur de eis morte plectendis, detuli sententiam'. ψῆφος is a *pebble*, here the pebble used (at Athens and elsewhere)in voting; hence the *vote* itself. ψῆφον φέρειν is *to cast one's vote*; καταφέρειν here means to cast it unfavourably, that is, to vote for the death penalty against Christians. Jeremias (*Jerusalem* 255, n. 34) observes that this statement proves (if we accept its accuracy) that Saul was an 'ordained scribe'. Others express some caution about this. 'Lk würde diesen v. nicht so geprägt haben, wenn er nicht gewusst hätte, dass Paulus Rabbi im eigentlichen Sinne gewesen ist, weitere Folgerungen aber sind kaum statthaft' (Bauernfeind 269). Bruce (1.443) remarks that the statement 'cannot be said to *prove*' anything since the phrase may be used officially or unofficially. Other inferences, interesting if not wholly convincing, are that the Council followed correct legal procedures in acting against Christians (Stählin 307), and that the Sanhedrin had the power to inflict the death penalty; cf. 25.16, and Jn 18.31.

The verse seems to imply that a number of Christians were put to death. Acts has mentioned Stephen and James (with the death of the latter Paul apparently had nothing to do); no more. Doubt has been cast on the implication. 'On the whole, therefore, it seems best to take Paul's statement as being somewhat rhetorical' (Marshall 393). This may be true, but the grounds for such a negative conclusion should be examined. 'Hier wird im Gegensatz zu 8.1 eine Reihe von

Hinrichtungen von Christen behauptet' (Haenchen 654). But 8.1
though it names only one martyr does not say that only one died. Cf.
Jn 16.2; Mt. 24.9; Mk 13.12. Luke was writing many years after
Saul's work as a persecutor, but he probably represents at least folk
memory of that period.

11. κατὰ πάσας τὰς συναγωγάς. There is in chs. 8, 9, 22 no
reference to synagogues in Jerusalem; at 9.2 we have synagogues in
Damascus. It is implied that Christians still frequented synagogues;
that is, they wished to continue to be Jews though now they had
become Christians. This was true also (at a later date) of Paul
himself, who for this reason received five synagogue beatings (2 Cor.
11.24). Such punishment might be implied by τιμωρῶν, *to exact
vengeance from*, hence *to punish* (more frequently in the middle);
e.g. Josephus, *Ant.* 2.107 (τιμωροῦντος αὐτοὺς τοῦ θεοῦ); Sophocles, *Oedipus Rex* 107.

The imperfect ἠνάγκαζον is often (e.g. M. 1.128f.; Turner,
Insights 86f.; Moule, *IB* 9 ('may be')) taken to be conative. BDR §
326, n. 1 are probably right in taking it to be both conative and, like
ἐδίωκον, which cannot be conative, repetitive. Cf. Blass (266). We
have no right to suppose that Saul was never successful in compelling Christians to blaspheme—presumably to utter what would be
blasphemy from a specifically Christian point of view, perhaps
cursing Christ (Roloff 352). Cf 1 Cor. 12.3 (ἀνάθεμα Ἰησοῦ); Pliny,
Epistles 10.96.5 (maledicere Christo). Josephus, *War* 2.152, records
that the Essenes would not yield to torture intended ἵν' ἢ
βλασφημήσωσιν τὸν νομοθετὴν ἢ φάγωσίν τι ἀσυνήθων.

περισσῶς τε ἐμμαινόμενος. There is no difficulty here in τε (=
and); contrast v. 10. περισσῶς according to BDR § 60.3, n. 5 is no
more than 'sehr', but there is no reason why the *extraordinarily,
exceedingly* of LS 1387 should be avoided. ἐμμαίνεσθαι is *to be
furiously (madly) angry* with someone; so Josephus, *Ant.* 17.174,
ἐμμαινομένου πᾶσι τοῦ βασιλέως, where King Herod's rage led him
to plot a frightful massacre. Paul had in the past been mad (with
rage); he was sane now (v. 25).

τὰς ἔξω πόλεις. 9.2; 22.5 mention only Damascus.

12. ἐν οἷς: Moule (*IB* 131, 197) does not decide between *and so*
and *in the course of which activity*. The former is perhaps better. Cf.
9.1; 22.6.

On ἐξουσίας καὶ ἐπιτροπῆς τῆς τῶν ἀρχιερέων M. 3.218 comments that the last three words are (or give the impression of being)
a kind of afterthought; cf. 1.12 (ἀπὸ ὄρους τοῦ καλουμένου
ἐλαιῶνος—article with an attribute after an anarthrous noun). The
singular article probably refers to both ἐξουσίας and ἐπιτροπῆς;
certainly both would be derived from the chief priests as the source
of authority in Jerusalem.

τῆς is omitted by P⁷⁴ᵛⁱᵈ A E 36 1704 *pc*; παρά is inserted before τῶν ἀρχιερέων by C Ψ 𝔐.

According to Kosmala (340) Paul went to Damascus to persecute the people of the (Qumran) Way who had migrated thither; see on 9.2.

On this account of Paul's conversion (vv. 12–18) see Wilson (*Gentiles* 161–7). Details of the earlier accounts have been suppressed so as to make room for more details (vv. 16–18) about Paul's vocation (Hanson 238).

13. ἡμέρας μέσης. Cf. 22.6, περὶ μεσημβρίαν. There is no corresponding note of time in ch. 9. The use of the genitive is not classical (BDR § 186.3; 270.3, n. 5; M. 3.235, noting that there are papyrus parallels). 'Elegantius ἡμ. μεσοῦσα' (Blass 267), but cf. Aeschines, *Epistle* 1 ... περὶ μέσην ἡμέραν κατήχθημεν εἰς Ναρησσὸν τὴν Κείων. Cf. 16.25; 27.27, both with reference to night.

κατὰ τὴν ὁδόν. There is no precise parallel in ch. 9 or in ch. 22, but both narratives note that Paul is travelling—presumably on the road.

βασιλεῦ. For the position of the vocative see on v. 7.

οὐρανόθεν. Both 9.3 and 22.6 have ἐκ τοῦ οὐρανοῦ. Cf. 14.17. The word is omitted by P⁷⁴.

ὑπὲρ ... ἡλίου. In 9.3 simply φῶς, in 22.6 φῶς ἱκανόν. For ὑπέρ with the accusative as a form of comparison see BDR § 230, n. 3.

περιλάμψαν. In 9.3 περιήστραψεν, in 22.6 περιαστράψαι.

καὶ τοὺς ... πορευομένους. In the earlier narratives there is no reference at this point to Paul's fellow travellers.

14. πάντων ... εἰς τὴν γῆν. At 9.4; 22.7 only Paul is said to fall to the ground. It is not however correct to say, 'In 9.4 fällt nur Paulus nieder' (Haenchen 655). There is nothing in the other passages to suggest that others did not fall.

ἤκουσα φωνήν. 9.4, ἤκουσεν φωνήν; 22.7, ἤκουσα φωνῆς. On the case taken by ἀκούειν see I.451f. and BDR §§ 173.2, n. 5; 416.1b, n. 5. In the present account the question whether the remainder of the company heard the voice is not raised (though it is assumed by the addition between γῆν and ἤκουσα of διὰ τὸν φόβον ἐγὼ μόνος, in 614 2147 *pc* (gig syʰᵐᵍ sa boᵐˢˢ)).

The voice is described as λέγουσαν πρός με in P⁷⁴ 𝕏 A B C (E) 048 096 36 81 945 (1175) 1739 1891 *al*; this is certainly the true reading, but H 23 *al* e vg have λαλοῦσαν πρός με, and Ψ 𝔐 (gig) have the conflate λαλοῦσαν πρός με καὶ λέγουσαν.

τῇ Ἑβραΐδι διαλέκτῳ: not in ch. 9 or in ch. 22. 'The introduction of "in the Hebrew tongue" as an apology for the barbarous name "Saul" is more likely, to come from Luke, though it is conceivable that St. Paul would apologize in this way' (Knox, *Hell. El.* 29). Aramaic is probably the language intended; see 21.40.

Σ., Σ., τί με διώκεις; See 9.4; 22.7.

σκληρόν σοι πρὸς κέντρα λακτίζειν. There is no parallel in ch. 9 or in ch. 22 (in the correct text). The proverb is a Greek one (from Pindar and the Tragedians onward) and therefore unlikely to have presented itself to Paul's conscious mind at the time of his conversion; though Knox (ibidem) notes Ps. Sol. 16.4 (ἔνυξέν με ὡς κέντρον ἵππου ἐπὶ τὴν γρηγόρησιν αὐτοῦ) to show that the proverb 'may have been acclimatized in Judaism, and such a proverb might well have found its way into a collection of proverbs available for Jewish students of Greek'. Bultmann rightly says that the phrase does not refer to an inner struggle, but rather is a widespread proverbial expression that means that man cannot withstand the divine (*E&F* 134). It is conflict against the gods that is in mind in the tragic poets; here the proverb takes up the thought that Paul is resisting— persecuting—Jesus by hindering his work. See L. Schmid in *TWNT* 3.665–7; also Dibelius (188–91). Commentators and others cite many parallels; among the most important are the following:

Pindar, *Pythians* 2.94–96: ποτὶ κέντρον δέ τοι λακτίζεμεν τελέθει ὀλισθηρὸς οἶμος.

Euripides, *Bacchae* 795: πρὸς κέντρα λακτίζοιμι θνητὸς ὢν θεῷ. The latter is probably the most important passage. BDR § 487.1, n. 2 point out the metre, but think that there is no literary dependence. See further below; also *Iphigeneia in Tauris* 1395f.; Aeschylus, *Agamemnon* 1624, πρὸς κέντρα μὴ λάκτιζε. In Latin see Terence, *Phormio* 1.2.27f.; Plautus, *Truculentes* 4.741.

Jewish material is hard to find. See Ps. Sol.16.4 (above); Philo, *De Decalogo* 87. Bengel (481) says, 'Syriacum adagium notat Lightfoot' but he seems to have taken a translation into 'Syr' as an illustrative quotation!

Some think that Luke knew the *Bacchae* of Euripides, citing in addition to this passage 5.39 and 16.26. See Bauernfeind (269) and Roloff (352); also A. Vögeli, 'Lukas und Euripides', *ThZ* 9 (1953), 415ff.

15. This verse agrees substantially with 9.5; 22.8. ὁ Ναζωραῖος is added by 048 6 104 614 1175 *pc* gig vg^mss sy^p.h** , assimilating to 22.8.

16. Only in ch. 26 (not in ch. 9 or ch. 22) is the apostolic commission given at the time of the conversion; Stählin 310 notes its resemblance to resurrection narratives in which a commission is given. The question of the provenance of these stories is acutely raised. It cannot be said that the version in this chapter is due solely to abbreviation, for it would have required only a word or two to introduce the commission with 'Later, in the Temple' or some such prefix. Either Luke is deliberately introducing variation, so as to achieve the emphasis that comes from repetition and at the same time avoid the risk of losing his reader, or he is using different traditions. The former alternative is more probable and is supported by a further motivation supplied by Blass (267); 'In hac autem or[atione] tota persona Ananiae sublata est, quippe quae non esset apta apud hos auditores; unde sequebatur ut mandata omnia ut ipsius Iesu effate inducerentur.'

ἀλλά, as at 9.6. 'Sometimes before a command [ἀλλά] is not so much adversative as consecutive, and is best translated as an interjection, Well!' (M. 3.330). There is however an adversative element in the word here. 'I am Jesus, whom you are persecuting. But all this is to change now. Get up and...'.

ἀνάστηθι καὶ στῆθι is a very unpleasing repetition, justified only by the fact that the second verb is virtually a quotation of Ezek. 2.1–3 (στῆθι ἐπὶ τοὺς πόδας σου ... ἤκουον αὐτοῦ ... ἐξαποστέλλω ἐγώ σε ...). This is one of a number of OT passages alluded to here; Hanson (239) collects in addition Jer. 1.7; Isa. 35.5; 42.7, 16; 1 Chron. 16.35.

ὤφθην. Cf. 1 Cor. 15.8, ὤφθη κἀμοί. But note also ὀφθήσομαι at the end of the verse; the word is not confined to resurrection appearances.

προχειρίσασθαι; cf. 3.20. The present verse shows that no temporal significance is to be attached to the προ- in προχειρίζειν; the appearance is for the purpose of appointing. It is not said here that Paul is appointed to be an apostle, and in view of the almost complete silence of Acts regarding Paul's apostleship (see 14.4, 14 and the notes; also Introduction, p. lxxxix) this can hardly be accidental. Paul is to be a ὑπηρέτης; cf. 13.5, also Lk. 1.2, ὑπηρέται τοῦ λόγου. Paul is to be such a ὑπηρέτης, and a witness, of what he has seen and will see. Here there may be a contradiction with 13.31f., where the witnesses of the resurrection, who had followed Jesus from Galilee to Jerusalem, appear to be distinguished from Paul and his colleagues who preach the Gospel.

Paul's testimony will not be confined to a resurrection appearance (this seems to be the primary sense of ὧν τε εἶδές με—με is omitted by P⁷⁴ ℵ A C² E Ψ 096 𝔐 latt bo, perhaps rightly); it extends to ὧν ὀφθήσομαι σοι. This may refer to visions such as 18.9; 23.11. In the epistles Paul displays considerable reluctance to speak about visions (2 Cor. 12.1–5; *2 Corinthians* 34, 250, 305–13); certainly the epistles contain few references to them. It might be possible to assert that, in a sense, the Lord appeared to Paul in his intellectual apprehension of the Gospel, but it is unlikely that this is what Luke had in mind.

ὧν τε ... ὧν τε. This is the only example of co-ordinated τε ... τε in the NT. Zerwick (§ 466) ('in elato stilo oratorio') notes that it appears where Paul is addressing Agrippa—another mark of careful literary composition. See also BDR § 444.1, n. 1. Dibelius however writes, 'Utterly impossible is the text of 26.16 ... The heavenly voice promises Paul not that Christ shall again appear to him but that much shall be shown him. Obviously the clause was corrupted through the influence of the preceding ὤφθη.' The sentence is unusual rather than impossible and corrupt. Page (248) is better: 'ὧν ὀφθ. = ἐκείνων ἃ ὀφθ. where ἃ is acc. plural, such a use being very common with the neuter plural of pronouns even after intransitive verbs, and ἃ ὁρῶμαί σοι = exactly "the visions in which I am seen by you". Cf. Sophocles, *Oedipus Tyrannus* 788 ὧν μὲν ἱκόμην ἄτιμον ἐξέπεμψεν. The passive form of the phrase is due to a desire to bring out the *agency of God*.'

Two of Weiser's comments should be noted. 'Inhalt und Formulierungen sind an atl. Berufungs- und Sendungstexten sowie an jüdisch-hellenistischer und urchristlicher Missionsterminologie orientiert: "die Augen öffnen" (vgl. Jes. 42.7; 61.1); "von der Finsternis zum Licht" vgl Test. der Zwölf Patriarchen 19.1 [Testament of Levi 19.1 is intended]; Josef und Asenet 8.9; Eph. 5.8; Kol. 1.12f.; 1 Pet. 2.9); "sich bekehren zu Gott"...' (653). 'Umkehr versteht Lukas hier vor allem als das Zur-Glaubenseinsicht-Kommen, das durch die Verkündigung ermöglicht wird und das entsprechende Verhaltungsweisen zur Folge haben soll' (654). Another parallel to note is 1QH 11.10–14.

Schille (451) sees in this verse an ordination formula.

17. ἐξαιρούμενος. The exalted style of some of the earlier verses (see the notes) might have suggested the future rather than the present participle, but in fact the present participle takes its time reference from ὀφθήσομαι in v. 16. Page (248) insists that the word must have its classical meaning of *choosing* rather than *delivering* (which he agrees is correct at 7.10, 34; 12.11; 23.27). Bruce (1.445) disagrees, rightly. The determining factor is the probable allusion to the call of Jeremiah (Jer. 1.8, ... μετὰ σοῦ ἐγώ εἰμι τοῦ ἐξαιρεῖσθαί σε). See further Le Déaut (319) on 13.47 for the parallel between Paul and Moses, also between Paul and the Servant of the Lord. Paul too is to be a light of the Gentiles. This is brought out more strongly in v. 18.

εἰς οὓς ἐγὼ ἀποστέλλω σε. See 22.21; there this statement provoked the crowd to frenzy. Naturally there is no such reaction from Agrippa and Festus. The masculine singular λαοῦ (the People, Israel) and the neuter plural ἐθνῶν are taken up—*ad sensum* and quite naturally—in the masculine plural οὕς, which refers to the multiplicity of persons concerned. It is however quite possible that οὕς refers to ἔθνη only; it was important to make the point that the activity that so incensed the Jews was undertaken in obedience to a divine command.

ἀποστέλλω, present, I am here and now sending you, the reading of ℵ A B E 048^vid 𝔐, makes the best sense and is almost certainly correct. Ψ 096 6 81 104 614 945 1241 2495 *al* co have ἀποστελῶ; P⁷⁴ C have ἐξαποστέλλω; 36 323 453 1175 1739 1891 2464 *al* have ἐξαποστελῶ.

18. This is an important verse in that it shows how Paul (according to Luke) understood his mission to the Gentiles (also apparently to the Jews to judge from v. 20; see on that verse as well as the close of v. 17). The language used is based on the OT (see the passages mentioned in the note on v. 16), and had probably already come into existence as 'traditionelle Bekehrungsterminologie' (Schweizer, *Beiträge* 187 n. 19; also 116 n. 10; cf. Kosmala, 172 n. 28). Similar language is found at Qumran; see especially 1QS 11.7f. (note גורל קדושים). The image of light and darkness, and Satan and Belial, also occurs in the Qumran literature; see however Braun, *ThR* 29 (1963), 175.

The language is vividly pictorial; in a sense mythological. 'From darkness to light' is perhaps no more than metaphorical, and it is easy to specify contrasts in the realms of morals and understanding which conversion signifies, though it must be admitted that Acts provides little by way of example. Paul is the only 'bad man' (in the sense of being a persecutor, not otherwise) in Acts who becomes a good one, and there is little in the book that suggests a new intellectual apprehension of the meaning of life. 'From the power of Satan to God' implies that men are held captive by Satan, and by the Gospel are liberated so as to return to God their creator.

ἄφεσιν ἁμαρτιῶν: see on 2.38.

τοὺς ἡγιασμένους are more frequently in Paul the ἅγιοι, but the perfect participle passive is also used (1 Cor. 1.2; in Acts see 20.32, with the note, including the reference to Wilcox 35–7). For κλῆρος in the sense of (allotted) *portion* see Acts 1.17; 8.21; Col. 1.12. There is nothing to indicate whether the *portion* is among the members of the church in the world, or in the age to come; both are intended. The inheritance is (and will be) received by faith in Christ. As at other points in this verse, so here no explanation is given of the relation between faith and the gift received, or indeed between faith and the action of God which is clearly assumed in the opening of men's eyes, and the act of turning them from darkness to light. Cf. 16.14, and see Stauffer, *Theologie* 163 ('Gottes übermächtiger Wille ist ein befreiender Wille').

The structure of the sentence is given by three infinitives, the second and third introduced by τοῦ: ἀνοῖξαι ... τοῦ ἐπιστρέψαι ... τοῦ λαβεῖν. The first is clearly an infinitive of purpose, dependent on ἀποστέλλω (v.17). The second is probably dependent on the first (to open their eyes so that they may turn ...). It is not clear whether the third is dependent on the second or, in parallel with the second, is dependent on the first (to turn ... so that they may receive ..., *or* to open their eyes ... so that they may receive ...). The absence of any connecting particle before τοῦ λαβεῖν suggests but by no means proves the former alternative. It would however be mistaken to read out of this verse a rigid sequence of elements in the process of conversion. Luke is assembling a number of vivid images almost any one of which would, if developed, stand for the whole. Men are unable to see: this inability may be due to inward blindness or to exterior darkness. However it is thought of, the situation is reversed. Light suggests God and darkness Satan; ability to see and inability to see suggest life under the authority of God or of Satan. Turning from Satan to God involves pardon for the old subservience to Satan. Turning to God means joining the ranks of those who are devoted to him. The piling up of images constitutes an impressive, if not perfectly clear, climax. Cf. Isa. 42.7,16; Eph. 6.12; James 1.17; especially Col. 1.12–14. See also 1 Clement 59.2; Wilcox (73f.). thinks of a liturgical background.

Calvin (2.278) insists that πίστει is to be taken not with ἡγιασμένοις but with the whole series of clauses. It is probably correct that Luke adds the reference to faith with the intention that it shall cover all that he is saying. In v. 18b with v. 20b is 'die Summe der biblischen, jüdisch-christlichen Verkündigung, wie Lukas sie versteht' (Schmithals 227).

τυφλῶν for αὐτῶν (E 096 vg^mss) is a not very thoughtful attempt to improve the sentence.

19. An example of Lucan litotes; BDR § 495.2, n. 9 lists as examples 12.18; 15.2; 19.11, 23, 24; 20.12; 21.39; 26.19, 26; 27.20; 28.2. The impression given here is of modesty on Paul's part, but in fact Luke seems use this mode of speech as a form of emphasis. Paul was wholeheartedly obedient.

ὀπτασία is a Lucan word (Lk. 1.32; 24.23); also 2 Cor. 12.1. This Pauline passage is enough to show that Paul was not incapable of speaking of visions that he had received. See also (for the converting and appointing vision) Gal. 1.15f. οὐκ ... ἀπειθής itself implies that the vision included a command. In the present passage this reflects the ἀποστέλλω of v. 17.

οὐράνιος here is an adjective of two terminations; for use elsewhere see BA 1201.

Haenchen (656): 'Die "himmlische Erscheinung" meint hier das himmlische Wesen, das erschienen ist ... Es war für Paulus unmöglich ..., dem himmlischen Befehl zu widerstehen. Damit ist die christliche Mission gerechtfertigt.'

20. In obedience to the divine commission Paul has carried out what is intended to be understood as (at least in outline and in principle) a universal preaching mission. The description of the scope of the mission and of the content of its message is however expressed in a sentence of dubious grammar. The opening phrase is probably intended to refer to Jews; in itself, τοῖς ἐν Δαμασκῷ might include Gentiles (a majority of the city's population; see I.447), but (τοῖς ἐν) Ἱεροσολύμοις must be Jews, and a contrast is needed with τοῖς ἔθνεσιν later in the verse. For Paul's preaching in Damascus (in the synagogues) and in Jerusalem see 9.20–23, 28–30. The first τε would stand better after Δαμασκῷ; it is omitted by the majority of later MSS. See Moule (*IB* 169) and cf. v. 22. There follows a phrase in the accusative, πᾶσάν τε τὴν χώραν τῆς Ἰουδαίας. τε links this with τοῖς ἔθνεσιν; one expects the dative case, and it is by no means clear why χώραν should be in the accusative. E Ψ 𝔐 lat prefix εἰς, which is some improvement (and probably secondary). Ropes (*Begs.* 3.237) writes, 'With so firmly attested a text the theory of a Semitism suggests itself, in view of the strikingly Semitic cast and grammatical difficulties of vv. 16–18. Cf. Deut. 1.19, ἐπορεύθημεν πᾶσαν τὴν ἔρημον τὴν μεγάλην καὶ τὴν φοβεράν.' But the hypothesis of a Semitism requires much clearer support than this. Dibelius (92) suggests that 'the dropping-out of εἰς (after Ἱεροσολύμοις, and thus haplographically identified with the ending -οις) is more credible (see the Antiochian text)' and this suggestion is taken up in BDR § 161.1, n. 1. See also the text of P[29], quoted below. There is probably no better hypothesis available (though it is in the nature of things beyond proof) that Luke began to write πᾶσαν τὴν χώραν τῆς Ἰουδαίας καὶ τὰ ἔθνη εὐηγγελισάμην, and changed course part way through the sentence.

A difficulty of a different kind is that according to Gal. 1.22 Paul remained personally unknown to the churches of Judaea (ταῖς ἐκκλησίαις τῆς Ἰουδαίας). At Rom. 15.19 however he claims to have preached the Gospel from Jerusalem round as far as Illyricum. Paul's preaching is described by the word ἀπαγγέλλειν (16 times in Acts). His hearers are to repent (cf. 2.38) and turn to God (cf. 3.19), and to do works worthy of repentance, that is, they are to prove the sincerity of their repentance by amended lives. The accusative πράσσοντας follows upon the dative τοῖς ἔθνεσιν; πράσσουσιν would have been possible, but a shift of case of this kind is not unknown (see Zerwick § 394 and cf. 15.22). The persons concerned are addressed (which suggests the dative) but they are also the subject of the infinitive (which suggests the accusative). For the requirement cf. Lk. 3.8. The 'whole phrase seems selected to show that Paul's preaching was not other than a Jewish missionary would have used in attempting to convert the heathen (cf. 3.19; 9.35; 14.15; 15.19)' (*Begs.* 4.320).

The second of the two fragments of P²⁹ (on which see on v. 7) occurs at this point. It is said by Hanson (239) to smooth over the difficulty mentioned, but it is probably too fragmentary to have this or any other effect. The text, as reconstituted by Grenfell, runs:

[ἀπειθὴς τῇ οὐρανίῳ ὀπτασίᾳ ἀ]λλὰ τοῖς ἐ[ν Δαμασκῷ πρῶτόν τε καὶ Ἱερο]σολύμοις κα[ὶ τῇ Ἰουδαίᾳ καὶ τοῖς ἔθνεσιν] ἐκήρυξα [... μετανοεῖν καὶ ἐπιστρέφειν ἐ]πὶ τὸν θεόν, [... ἄξια τῆς μετανοίας ἔργα πρ]άοσοντας.

It will be noted that the dative τῇ Ἰουδαίᾳ (which goes much better than the familiar text with the dative τοῖς ἔθνεσιν) is an editorial conjecture; the space available however would, it seems, not permit πᾶσαν τε τὴν χώραν τῆς Ἰουδαίας. See Ropes (*Begs.* 3.235, 237).

21. ἕνεκα τούτων. ἕνεκα (over against ἕνεκεν, εἵνεκεν) is the Attic form, and is 'regarded by Blass [but this is not mentioned in Blass's commentary, or in BDR] as in keeping with a speech in the presence of royalty' (M. 2.67). Cf. however 19.32 and 28.20 (v.l.); there is little weight in this observation. The speech is in any case an odd mixture of style and solecism. τούτων, the things on account of which the Jews seized Paul amount in fact to one thing, his mission to the Gentiles which had the effect of placing Gentiles on the same level as Israelites as potential heirs of salvation. Perhaps one should add, as a second (though closely related) ground of attack, his implicit claim that in doing so he was a better representative of Judaism than his opponents. τούτου (singular) is read by P⁷⁴ *pc*.

συλλαβόμενοι (P⁷⁴ ℵ E Ψ 33 36 81 614 945 1175 1739 1891 2495 *al* latt add ὄντα; A B 048 𝔐 do not): see 21.30f.

ἐπειρῶντο διαχειρίσασθαι. The imperfect means that they were attempting, when prevented by Roman intervention. πειρᾶσθαι with the infinitive occurs here only in the NT; see BDR § 392.1a, n. 2. For διαχειρίζεσθαι see 5.30; it is used in the NT in these two places only.

This verse is a sufficiently accurate summary of what is described at length in chs. 21, 22.

22. Paul now winds up the speech, in which he has described his pre-christian life in Judaism, his conversion, his call to evangelize the Gentiles, and the attack on him which led to his arrest and thus to his present appearance before Festus and Agrippa, by summing up both the religious basis and the theological structure of his Christian life and belief. οὖν brings him back to the main theme (BDR § 451.1, n. 2).

ἐπικουρία occurs here only in the NT; the unusual word may have been chosen on account of the distinction ascribed by Bengel (482) to Ammonius [107]: βοηθεῖ μὲν ὁ συνών· ἐπικουρεῖ δὲ ὁ ἔξωθεν εἰς βοήθειαν ἥκων. Paul's help comes not from within himself but ἀπὸ τοῦ θεοῦ. ἐπικουρία is used by medical writers but also in military contexts; *ND* 3.67f. quotes an inscription from Cyrene (AD 154), re-edited by J. M. Reynolds (*JRS* 68 (1978), 111–21) containing the words κα]θεστῶτες τὴν ἐπικουρίαν παρὰ τῶν Ἑλλή[νων?..., rallying help from the Greeks. τυγχάνειν occurs once in Lk., 5 times in Acts, 8 times in the rest of the NT; on the whole a Lucan characteristic.

ἕστηκα, perfect in form, is commonly used with a present meaning, *I stand*, but in this context the perfect element that underlies the present (I have taken my stand and here I am) is clear: Paul has been standing as he now does ἄχρι τῆς ἡμέρας ταύτης. He stands as one who bears witness to all, of whatever rank.

The content of his testimony is, according to this verse, simply the message of the OT, reinforced by the affirmation that what the OT foretold has now been fulfilled. For this frequent insistence that Paul's Christian message is simply what the OT contains (and therefore ought not to offend Jews but to be accepted by them) see e.g. 24.14; 28.23.

Moule (*IB* 169) notes a second (cf. v. 20) example of the misplacing of τε. One would have expected οἵ τε προφῆται ... καὶ Μωυσῆς. The result is that though τε suggests that some second member of the sentence is to come, καὶ Μωυσῆς gives the impression of being an afterthought, as if Luke intended at first to refer simply to the predictive element in the OT and then reflected that the Gospel is the fulfilment not only of the prophets but of the Law too. For a similar addition cf. Jn 1.45. 'Dass hier Mose an zweiter Stelle genannt wird, hängt wohl damit zusammen, dass er die künftige Totenauferstehung lediglich "angedeutet" hat' (Schneider 2.376).

ἐκτός, meaning *except*, is unclassical (BDR § 216.2, n. 7); but οὐδέν (rather than μηδέν) with a participle is classical (BDR § 430.2, n. 4). The speech retains its mixed character to the end.

For Eb. Nestle's conjecture that v. 8 should be transferred to follow this verse and precede v. 23 see on v. 8.

23. The sentence follows upon μαρτυρόμενος (v. 22); it could follow neatly upon εἰ ὁ θεὸς νεκροὺς ἐγείρει (v. 8), but this is not sufficient ground for a transposition (see above).

Dodd (*AS* 17) writes that 'the main heads of Paul's discussions ... are introduced by the particle εἰ used interrogatively: "*whether* the Messiah is a suffering Messiah ...'" This interrogative form is evidently appropriate to a method of teaching which is described by the verb διαλέγεσθαι, "to discuss". We conclude that in addition to what is called "preaching" (κηρύσσειν), early Christian missionaries also employed the method of discussion, in which certain questions were propounded—questions arising unavoidably out of the *kerygma*—and answers sought by a study of the Old Testament.' It is to be observed that διαλέγεσθαι is not used in this context (it is used at 17.2, which Dodd brings into his argument). Neither this suggestion, nor that of Rendel Harris (*Testimonies*, Part I, 1916; 19f.), that we have before us the headings of sections in a Testimony Book ('The words are headlines of Testimonies, awkwardly incorporated in the text, and are betrayed as such by the previous reference to the prophets and Moses, who are to answer the questions') is called for. εἰ may bear the meaning *that* after a verb of feeling; see BA, s.v. II, 442, with reference to Kühner-Gert 2.369.8 [better, II.2.369.8]; also *Begs.* 4.321, 'εἰ is best rendered by ''that'', but there is in εἰ a stronger implication that the proposition which follows is denied and must be argued out than would be made by the simple ὅτι.' Similarly Blass (269).

παθητός, *liable to suffering* (e.g. Plutarch, *Numa* 8 (65), *Pelopidas* 16 (268)) occurs nowhere else in the NT. It was taken up in the second century (Ignatius, *Ephesians* 7.2; *Polycarp* 3.2; frequently in Justin, e.g. *Trypho* 34, 36) not least in controversy with Jews.

πρῶτος seems to qualify the (unexpressed, though ὁ Χριστός is clearly implied) subject of μέλλει. He, the Messiah, will proclaim light (in this context generally, an image of salvation) to both the people (λαός, the Jews) and the Gentiles. He will be the first to do this, and he will do it ἐξ ἀναστάσεως νεκρῶν. Turner (M. 3.260) and Moule (*IB* 73) are undecided whether to regard ἐξ as instrumental or as (quasi-)local (Moule: 'if he was destined to be the first (to come from) a rising from the dead and announce...'). We may render *on the basis of* (cf. Paul's use of ἐκ πίστεως, ἐξ ἔργων); this is a sort of instrumental use which may also be said to carry the local with it. See however Page (250): '... that he first by a resurrection from the dead ...'; and Bruce (1.447): 'the first that should rise from the dead'.

The Messiah, who suffers and is raised from death, proclaims light to both Jews and Gentiles. Thus the three points are made which, though Paul insists that they are already proclaimed by the prophets and Moses, incense the Jews. It is asserted that these propositions are already contained in the OT, but no passages are cited in support of the assertion. In controversy between Jews and Christians such passages must have been quoted and their interpretation disputed (see the note on v. 24), but this is a debate into which Luke never enters (though a passage such as 17.11 shows that he was aware of it).

24. ἀπολογουμένου. For this word see 19.33; 26.1f. Strictly speaking, Paul was not now making a defence; he was not on trial, since his case had been referred to Rome. He knew however that he was accused by the Jews (v. 2) and that Festus, with the assistance of Agrippa, must have been preparing a dossier that would present the

case before the imperial court. A good impression made upon Festus
would be to his advantage, and to the advantage of his cause.

Festus interrupts at the point at which earlier the Jews had
interrupted, but for a different reason. μεγάλη is predicative: Festus—loud was his voice—said . . . μαίνῃ: the story of a crucified and
risen Messiah is nonsense, (a) because a king would not proceed by
the way of suffering and death, and (b) because dead men do not rise
up (see on 17.32).

Knox (*Hell. El.* 29) writes, 'Festus suggests, whether seriously or
not, that St Paul's studies have driven him mad, implying that he has
been quoting from a number of "writings" . . . But Luke has omitted
the testimonies which alone would explain Festus' interruption.'
Knox is presumably referring to the word γράμματα; for this
however the rendering *learning* is quite possible; BA 330 cite
Xenophon, *Cyropaedia* 1.2.6; Plato, *Apology* 26d; PLond 43.2.γ;
Dan. 1.4; Epistle of Aristeas 121; Testament of Reuben 4.1; of Levi
13.2. A adds (after γράμματα) ἐπίστασθαι—*to know many writings*.
On the position of σε, cf. BDR § 473.1: 'Auch im NT gilt die alte
Regel, dass unbetonte (enklitische) Pronomina udgl dem Satzanfang
möglichst nahe gerückt werden, wodurch oft Zusammengehöriges
getrennt wird.' Bruce (1.448): 'The effect is an added emphasis both
on σε and τὰ πολλά γράμματα.'

For the impression of madness cf. 1 Cor. 14.23 (μαίνεσθε); but it
is learned, not enthusiastic, madness of which Festus accuses Paul.
Cf. ἐμμαινόμενοι in v. 11 (with the note). Thus Bruce (1.448), 'The
remark was not offensive; both μαίνομαι and μανία are cognate with
μάντις, "seer", "inspired person" '; he refers to Plato, *Phaedrus*
245a. Similarly Page (250) speaks of 'the philosophic "madman"',
and quotes *Phaedrus* 249d. StrB 2.770 quote Targum Yerushalmi I
on Num. 22.5: Balaam had become 'irrsinnig' (אישטיש) because of the
greatness of his learning. This rather flattering interpretation of
Paul's 'philosophic' madness is not suitable to the present context. In
the next verse Paul firmly rebuts the suggestion of madness; he is not
what Festus says that he is. This also is against Schille's view (453)
that for Luke the charge is a way of commending Paul's 'Schrift-
gelehrsamkeit'.

For εἰς μανίαν περιτρέπει cf. Lucian, *Abdicatus* 30, ἐς μανίαν
περιέτρεψε (in a discussion of the various causes that lead to μανία).
MM 388 quote an unedited Tebtunis papyrus: φαίνῃ εἰς μανίαν
ἐμπεπτωκέν[α]ι. See also Longinus, *De Sublimitate* 8.4; *Sibylline
Oracles* 1.171f. POxy 1.33. Col. 4.9–15 (. . . νὴ τὴν σὴν τύχην οὔτε
μαίνομαι οὔτε ἀπονενόημαι . . .); Pliny, *Epistles* 10.96.4 (fuerunt
alii similis amentiae—of the Christians' inflexibilis obstinatio).

25. Paul rebuts the charge sharply, οὐ μαίνομαι, but with due
courtesy: κράτιστε Φῆστε. Cf. Lk. 1.3; Acts 23.26; 24.3. κράτιστος

is equivalent to the Latin *egregius*, and is fittingly used of the prefect, as a knight.

ἀλλά, on the contrary.

ἀποφθέγγομαι. Cf. 2.4, 14, where the word is often said to suggest inspired, even ecstatic, speech. This may be true in those verses but is hardly true here, where Paul insists that he is speaking words ἀληθείας καὶ σωφροσύνης. The first of these terms insists that what Paul says (and at the same time its use suggests the contents of the Gospel) is in accordance with the fact; the second claims that his treatment of the facts is in accordance with sober reason. Betz (206, n. 5) notes a number of parallels in Lucian; *Icaromenippus* 30; *De Mercede Conductis* 36; *De Saltatione* 12; *Timon* 55; *Bis Accusatus* 17; *Piscator* 16, 41; *Somnium* 10; *Pro Imaginibus* 11, 20. For a contrast with σωφρονεῖν, *Abdicatus* 1; *De Syria Dea* 22. For this contrast see also Xenophon, *Memorabilia* 1.1.16; also POxy 1.33 (quoted on v. 24; Schille 453); Plato, *Protagoras* 323b; also Lk. 8.35 (Mk 5.15) (Pesch 2.279). These passages illustrate and confirm Roloff's statement (355) about 'das in der hellenistischen Literatur geläufige Gegensatzpaar: Wahnsinn (d.h. Masslosigkeit und Unkontrolliertheit des Denkens)—Vernunft (d.h. besonnen-realitätsbezogenes Denken).'

In ἀληθείας κ. σωφρ. ῥήμ., 'the first gen. is objective, the second subjective' (Page 250). This is correct: the words set forth truth, and they are controlled by sober judgement. The remark by Delebecque (127), 'Luc donne ici au mot ἀλήθεια le sens qu'il a chez Paul, ou il est constant', is not quite so convincing. Still less convincing is Lüdemann's judgement that σωφροσύνη is a thoroughly un-Pauline term. He overlooks Rom. 12.3; 2 Cor. 5.13; not to mention Paul's treatment of glossolalia in Corinth.

26. The king knows about these things. It might at first seem that *these things* were the matters which (according to Paul) were written in the prophets and Moses, that is, that the purpose of Israel was to be fulfilled in the death and resurrection of the Messiah and the extension through him of the light of God's truth and blessing beyond Israel to the Gentile world. The reference however at the end of the verse to something *done* suggests rather the claim that the king was aware of the Christian event, that is, the ministry, death, and resurrection of Jesus. Agrippa II (see on 25.13) was born in AD 27/28, and therefore certainly was not aware of the story of Jesus at first hand; moreover, he lived at Claudius' court till 50 or later, when he was appointed king of Chalcis. He did, however, show considerable concern over Jewish affairs, doing his best to prevent rupture and war with Rome (see e.g. his long speech dissuading the Jews from war, Josephus, *War* 2.344–407); there is no reason why he should not have heard of the origins of Christianity, especially if

Christians were felt to be a disturbing factor in Jewish life. So, more or less, Chrysostom, *Homily* 52.4; Ἐνταῦθα περὶ τοῦ σταυροῦ λέγει τοῦτο, περὶ τῆς ἀναστάσεως, καὶ ὅτι πανταχοῦ τῆς οἰκουμένης γέγονε τὸ δόγμα.

παρρησιαζόμενος λαλῶ. Cf. v. 2. παρρησιάζεσθαι is an Acts word: 9.27, 28; 13.46; 14.3; 18.26; 19.8; elsewhere in the NT only Eph. 6.20; 1 Thess. 2.2. Paul can speak openly and freely.

The transitive use of λανθάνειν (object, αὐτόν) is classical: BDR § 149.1, n. 2. *Begs.* 4.322 notes the present tense: none of these things is escaping him. For the litotes cf. v. 19. The form οὐθέν is much less common in the NT than that with δ; see on 15.9. Moule (*IB* 167f.): 'οὐ belongs not with πείθομαι but, as a double negative, with λανθάνειν.'

καί is omitted by B 104 1175 *pc* h vg^mss. τι is read by P^74 A E sy^p; it is omitted by B Ψ 36 614 1175 2495 *pc* sy^h and replaced by ἐγώ in 945 1739 1891 *pc*. οὐθέν is omitted by P^74 ℵ^c A E 33 81 *al*.

οὐ γάρ ἐστιν ... πεπραγμένον. Moule (*IB* 19) raises the question why the periphrastic perfect should be used here but makes no attempt to answer it. We must probably be content to say only that Luke preferred it to πέπρακται.

'Done in a corner' has become an English idiom, but it was not used in antiquity. Delebecque (127): 'L'expression, qui n'est pas courante, semble prise à Platon, *Gorgias* 485d.' This passage runs: ... μετὰ μειρακίων ἐν γωνίᾳ τριῶν ἢ τεττάρων ψιθυρίζοντα. We may add Epictetus 2.12.17: τὸν γὰρ ποιοῦντα αὐτὸ οὐκ ἐν γωνίᾳ δηλονότι δεήσει ποιεῖν, ἀλλά ...Bruce 1.449 adds Terence, *Adelphi* 4.9.10f. (*or* 5.2.10f.): ... interea in angulum aliquo abeam.

27. Agrippa, like some other members of his family, though in fact a Gentile, could on occasion represent himself as a Jew in spirit, and had certain rights in the Temple and in the appointment of the high priest. Paul appeals to his knowledge of and belief in the OT— knowledge and belief which in some contexts he might have claimed, whether he had them or not. Reference to his belief in the prophets points back to τούτων in v. 26, and, contrary to the suggestion made on v. 26, might suggest that *these things* are the prophetic notions of vv. 22f.—or rather, that there is no great difference between the two interpretations of τούτων. What the prophets foretold is what has happened in the story of Jesus. Belief in the prophets is (for Paul—and Luke) not an end in itself but a step on the way to belief in Christ.

28. Agrippa's words to Paul are perhaps the most disputed, as regards their construction and meaning, in Acts. The text most widely accepted (and printed in NA^26) is: ἐν ὀλίγῳ με πείθεις Χριστιανὸν ποιῆσαι. For πείθεις, A reads πείθῃ. This is often ascribed to accidental error: HI is not unlike EIC. But the two

syllables are not really alike, and πείθῃ would take up πείθομαι in v.
26: You are persuaded that I know all about Christianity; perhaps
you are persuaded that I believe it too. Blass (270): 'tutissimum est A
sequi'. But the connection with v. 26 could cut both ways; πείθεις
might have been changed into πείθῃ in order to make it closer. And it
is perhaps not very safe to follow A alone. For Χριστιανόν, ℵ* has
χρηστιανόν; this is a purely orthographic variant. For ποιῆσαι, E Ψ
𝔐 latt sy, with Cyril of Jerusalem, have γενέσθαι: You are
persuading (seeking to persuade) me to become a Christian. This
makes good sense; it evades a difficulty however and the evidence is
on the whole late, so that it would be unwise to adopt this reading.
Two interrelated questions remain: the meaning of ἐν ὀλίγῳ and of
ποιῆσαι.

With ὀλίγῳ may be understood χρόνῳ or λόγῳ. Calvin (2.283)
says that the phrase may refer to time or degree, but degree is not
easy to support. M. 3.262 similarly: either *in a short time* or *by a
short argument*. It does not seem possible to take the phrase in the
sense *all but a little*, that is, *almost*, though ἐς (εἰς) ὀλ. and παρ' ὀλ.
have this meaning, or something like it (e.g. Thucydides 4.129.5, ἐς
ὀλίγον ἀφίκετο πᾶν τὸ στράτευμα … νικηθῆναι. There is no great
difference between time and argument: a brief argument would
occupy a short time, a short time would not permit a long argument.
Probably the decisive consideration—or the consideration that
comes nearest to being decisive—is the recurrence of ἐν ὀλίγῳ
together with ἐν μεγάλῳ (for a variant see on v. 29) in the next verse.
μεγάλῳ would hardly be used of time. 'It seems best to understand
πόνῳ with ὀλίγῳ, as this noun could fitly stand with both μεγάλῳ
and ὀλίγῳ = with little trouble, with little cost' (Knowling 513). The
same opinion is held by Page (251): 'ἐν ὀλίγῳ is clearly = "with
little (trouble, effort)", ἐν being instrumental, its sense being
determined by the use of the phrase in Paul's reply ἐν ὀλ. καὶ ἐν
μεγάλῳ = "with little or with great (trouble)". It cannot = ἐν ὀλίγῳ
χρόνῳ "quickly" for ἐν μεγάλῳ … could not mean "in much
time".' Similarly Delebecque (128). Cf. Thucydides 2.84.2: αἱ νῆες
ἐν ὀλίγῳ ἤδη οὖσαι … See however on v. 29.

The second question is the meaning of Χριστιανὸν ποιῆσαι. There
are two main possibilities. (a) A. Fridrichsen (*Coniectanea Neotestamentica* 3 (1939), 14f.) drew attention to the parallel in Xenophon,
Memorabilia 1.2.49: πείθων μὲν τοὺς συνόντας ἑαυτῷ
σοφωτέρους ποιεῖν τῶν πατέρων, persuading his companions that
he was making them wiser than their fathers. From this is deduced
and illustrated the rule 'nec subiectum nec obiectum infinitivi
exprimi debet si coincidit cum subiecto obiectove verbi principalis'
(Zerwick § 395). Zerwick and Turner (M. 3.147; at greater length in
Insights 97–100) take this as justifying the rendering *mihi vis
persuadere (te) brevi tempore (me) fecisse Christianum* (Zerwick),

You seek to convince me that you have made me in a moment a Christian (Turner). This has the great advantage of providing a better connection with v. 29, where Paul seeks that Agrippa and his other hearers should become (γενέσθαι) Christians, that is, he desires to make them Christians. On the other hand, *You want to persuade me that you have made me a Christian*, hardly makes sense, even if we allow for a good deal of irony. One who has been made a Christian does not need to be persuaded that he has been made a Christian. (b) The main alternative is based on the use of ποιεῖν in 3 Kdms 20.7 (LXX) where σὺ νῦν οὕτως ποιεῖς βασιλέα ἐπὶ Ἰσραήλ renders the Hebrew (1 Kings 21.7) אתה עתה תעשה מלוכה על־ישראל , and appears to mean 'play the king' (cf. Latin (Christianum) agere; BDR § 5.4, n. 23), so that the meaning of the present passage would be, *You are persuading me to play the Christian*—that is, to act a part for your convenience (by getting me to confess belief in the prophets). This is an attractive suggestion, but one over-literal rendering of a Hebrew verb is not sufficient to establish a Greek idiom. It is 'insufficiently documented' (*Begs.* 4.323). Haenchen adds references to Johannes Climacus and Johannes Malalas; these are too late to give much support, but the Latin parallel, Christianum agere (noted already by P. W. Schmiedel in *EBib* 754) may be worth more than he allows.

Opinions differ. Ropes (*Begs.* 3.239): 'The reading ... of B ..., although difficult, yields an intelligible sense (''play the Christian'') and must be accepted'. But Clark lii: 'That ποιῶ Χριστιανόν can mean ''play the Christian'' is to me incredible. The reading of A πείθῃ = ''thou thinkest (cf. οὐ πείθομαι in v. 26) gives a fair sense. The variant γενέσθαι ... for ποιῆσαι looks like a conjecture.' Bauernfeind (270) thinks that what we have in the text is a combination of two thoughts, In Wenigem überredest du mich, *and* In Wenigem machst du mich zum Christen. Schneider (2.378), mentioning both possibilities, makes the important additional point, 'Auf jeden Fall nimmt Paulus selbst die Aussage des Königs ernst, wie der folgende Vers deutlich macht.' It has usually been assumed that the answer is one of irony on the official side ('''Christian'' in the mouth of Agrippa can only be interpreted as a sneer'—*Begs.* 4.322), serious on Paul's, but this may not be true, and we have to ask what impression Luke wished to convey rather than, in the first instance, what actually happened. Weiser (655) speaks of Agrippa's 'zwischen Ernst und Ironie schwebende Antwort'. He is not speaking of 'playing the Christian' but of being made a Christian; this is confirmed by Paul's answer. It may well be that Bengel (483) rightly caught the impression that Luke wished to suggest: 'Occurrit ergo hic, Festus, sine Christo: Paulus, Christianissimus: Agrippas, in bivio, cum optimo impulsu.'

29. εὐξαίμην ἄν. 'Der Potentialis (Opt. mit ἄν) zur Bezeichnung des lediglich Gedachten ist in der Volssprache ganz abhanden gekommen, im NT nur noch selten und nur in Lk und Apg' (BDR § 385.1); another example of the good style used (intermittently) by Paul on this occasion. Cf. Acts 8.31; 17.18. See M. 3.123. Moule (*IB* 151) points out that the construction is logically that of a conditional sentence with the protasis omitted: if only it were possible, I ...

καὶ ἐν ὀλίγῳ καὶ ἐν μεγάλῳ. See the discussion of ἐν ὀλίγῳ in v. 28. If it was right there to expect the same noun supplement with ὀλίγῳ and with μεγάλῳ, it will be necessary here to take them as *with little trouble, with great trouble*. The difficulty here is that the two phrases are joined not, as might be expected, with ἤ (*or*) but by καί (*and*). This is surprising but not in fact impossible. See BDR § 442.9a (καί alternativum) n. 27 (examples including Acts 10.14, κοινὸν καὶ ἀκάθαρτον, common or unclean). Cf. also Plato, *Apology* 23a, where as in our verse the καί is corrective. 'With little argument, aye, and with much, if needed ...'. The alternatives to this will be either *Begs.* 4.322 (' "in small and great"—meaning "altogether," "wholly"') or the sense of v. 22, μικρῷ τε καὶ μεγάλῳ: Paul's desire to see men become Christians applies to the least and to the greatest, to the king himself. If either of these ways of taking the phrase is accepted the question of ἐν ὀλίγῳ in v. 28 will be reopened. On the whole see P. Harlé, 'Un "Private-Joke" de Paul', *NTS* 24 (1978), 527–33.

σήμερον may be taken either with the preceding participle or the infinitive that follows. There is no way in which this question can be decided with confidence.

τοιούτους ὁποῖος is rightly translated in the Vulgate, tales qualis: of such a kind (of person) as I am. Paul wishes for all his hearers the election, the call, and the commission that he himself has; he does not wish them his bonds. For παρεκτός cf. ἐκτός in v. 22.

'Die Replik des Paulus ist keineswegs von geringerer rhetorische Eleganz' (Roloff 355).

For εὐξαίμην, ℵ* A H L P 049 81 326 1241 *al* have εὐξάμην.

μεγάλῳ is read by P⁷⁴ ℵ A B Ψ 33 81 945* 1739* *pc* latt; instead 𝔐 sy have πολλῷ. For the significance of this see on v. 28. It makes χρόνῳ a possible supplement.

30. ἀνέστη τε. A few MSS (33 945 1739 1891 2495 *al* have δέ instead of τε; there is a major variant, probably of Western origin, in (614) 𝔐 h (syʰ**) sa, καὶ ταῦτα εἰπόντος αὐτοῦ ἀνέστη. This gives a more explicit connection with what precedes and is almost certainly secondary.

ὁ βασιλεὺς καὶ ὁ ἡγεμών. The repeated article makes it clear that two persons are intended.

συγκαθήμενοι: the verb is used specifically of those who sit with others, or another, as assessors in court. So for example Xenophon,

Hellenica 2.4.23, οἱ μὲν τριάκοντα ... ξυνεκάθηντο ἐν τῷ ξυνεδρίῳ. MM 608 have a papyrus example.

'Hier [in this verse and the two following] hat die Apologetik erzählerisch ihren Höhepunkt erreicht' (Lüdemann 265). This is a fair statement; Paul is explicitly pronounced innocent by the highest authorities he has yet encountered. How Luke could be aware of what the king and governor said to each other is not explained.

31. ἀναχωρήσαντες, from the (possibly) public courtroom (25.23, the ἀκροατήριον) into a retiring room. Aorist participle: the conversation took place after they had retired.

πράσσει: BDR § 322.3, n. 3 rightly say that the present tense is 'auf des Paulus ganze Lebensweise und besonders sein Christentum bezogen'.

ὅτι is omitted by P⁷⁴ *pc*. τι is omitted by B 𝔐 it sy; this improves the Greek. With οὐδέν, τι is not required; it is surprising that it is retained (*quid*) in the Vulgate.

Hemer (349) commenting on the lack of any source for the private conversation between Festus and Agrippa, adds 'presumably a verdict in some such terms must in any case have been made known to Paul after the *consilium* of the judges'. But Festus and Agrippa were not acting as judges; Festus was gathering information for his dossier and Agrippa was indulging a curious whim. Of course, if kindly disposed they may have passed on to Paul the essence of the report that would be sent to the higher court.

32. Agrippa (whom Luke may possibly—though inaccurately— have been thinking of as a representative Jew, matching Festus, the representative Roman—see Roloff 348) had been consulted about Paul's case (25.26) and now gives his opinion, which, like v. 31 and other passages to the same effect, must have seemed to Luke and his readers very quotable. The appeal has been made and must go forward; otherwise Paul could have been set free. It seems, however, that continuing custody with a free voyage to Rome will have suited Paul very well. At least he was protected from Jewish assassins. This may have been in mind from early in the proceedings. 'This does not mean that in strict law the governor could not pronounce an acquittal after the act of appeal. It is not a question of law, but of the relation between the emperor and his subordinates, and of the element of non-constitutional power which the Romans called *auctoritas*, "prestige", on which the supremacy of the Princeps so largely depended. No sensible man with hopes of promotion would dream of short-circuiting the appeal to Caesar unless he had specific authority to do so ... Since the charges were *extra ordinem* in large part, the appeal was automatically valid. Festus was naturally only too glad, politically, to rid himself of the prisoner. To have acquitted him despite the appeal would have been to offend both the emperor and the province' (Sherwin-White 65).

The apodosis (ἀπολελύσθαι ἐδύνατο) lacks ἄν (M. 3.91f.). BDR § 358.1, n. 2 point out that the imperfect without ἄν is used to express necessity or possibility where the thing in question did not happen. Similarly Page (251): 'ἄν is often omitted with simple verbs such as ἔδει (24.19), ἔχρην etc. So in Latin *poterat, debebat*, instead of *posset, deberet*.' Cf. Wisdom 11.20. With the pluperfect ἐπεκέκλητο M. 3.91 compares μεμενήκεισαν in 1 Jn 2.19, but this is in the apodosis. The pluperfect is 'significant as implying that this act of Paul had placed him in an irrevocable position' (Hemer 132).

326 2464 omit Ἀγρίππας ... οὗτος, probably by homoeoteleuton (see v. 31). P⁷⁴ has after these words only ἀπολελύσθαι ἐδύνατο; this may be intended abbreviation achieved by combining two favourable statements. At the end of the verse 97 *pc* h w (sy^p sy^hmg) add καὶ οὕτως ἔκρινεν αὐτὸν ὁ ἡγεμὼν ἀναπέμψαι Καίσαρι. This decision had been taken in principle as far back as 25.12; but ἔκρινεν here may refer to a specific decision to send Paul on a specific ship under a specific guard. It is to be noted that h sy^p sy^hmg omit the first nine words of 27.1.

XVI

PAUL REACHES ROME
(27.1–28.28)

62. THE SEA VOYAGE 27.1–44

(1) When it was decided that we should set sail for Italy they handed over Paul and some other prisoners to a centurion called Julius, of the Augustan Cohort. (2) We embarked on a ship of Adramyttium which was about to sail to places on the coast of Asia and put out to sea; the Macedonian Aristarchus, of Thessalonica, was with us. (3) The next day we put in at Sidon and Julius treated Paul in a kindly way, allowing him to go to his friends to receive care. (4) Thence we put out to sea and sailed under the lee of Cyprus because the winds were contrary. (5) We sailed across the open sea off Cilicia and Pamphylia[1] and put in at Myra in Lycia. (6) There the centurion found an Alexandrian ship sailing to Italy and embarked us on it. (7) Sailing slowly for a number of days and barely getting as far as Cnidus, since the wind did not permit us to approach we sailed for refuge under the lee of Crete off Salmone. (8) Coasting along it with difficulty we came to a place called Fair Havens, to which the town of Lasaea is near.

(9) Since a considerable time had now elapsed and sailing was already risky because even the Fast was now already past Paul offered advice, (10) saying to them, 'Men, I see that the voyage is going to be attended by damage and much loss not only of the cargo and the ship but also of our lives.' (11) But the centurion was persuaded by the captain and the owner[2] rather than by Paul's words. (12) Since the harbour was not suitable for wintering the majority formed the plan of putting out from there and getting if they could to Phoenix, a harbour of Crete looking into the south west and north west winds, and wintering there.

(13) When a gentle south wind sprang up they supposed that they had achieved their purpose; they set out and coasted along Crete as close in shore as possible. (14) But before long a tempestuous wind called Euraquilo flung itself down from[3] the island. (15) The boat was seized by the wind and was unable to head into it, so we gave way to it and ran before it. (16) We ran under the lee of a certain small island called Cauda and were scarcely able to gain full control of the dinghy. (17) They hauled it up and[4] made use of auxiliary devices, frapping the ship, and fearing lest they should be cast upon

---

[1] NJB, taking a fortnight to reach.
[2] Or, manager.
[3] Greek, from it; or, upon it (the ship).
[4] NJB, used it to undergird.

the Syrtis they dropped the sea anchor, and so drifted. (18) Since we were severely storm tossed on the next day they[5] jettisoned [some of the cargo]. (19) On the third day they threw out with their own hands the ship's gear. (20) For many days neither sun nor stars were to be seen, no small storm was upon us, and finally all hope of our being saved was disappearing.

(21) [6]Since many were going without food Paul then stood in their midst and said, 'Men, you ought to have listened to me so as not to have left Crete and incur this damage and loss. (22) And now I advise you to take heart, for there will be no loss of life of any of you but only of the ship. (23) For this night there stood by me an angel of the God whose I am and whom I serve, (24) saying, "Fear not, Paul, you must stand before Caesar, and see, God has granted you all those who are sailing with you." (25) So take heart, men; for I believe God that it will be just as it has been told me. (26) But we have to be cast on a certain island.'

(27) When the fourteenth night came and we were[7] being tossed about in Adria, in the middle of the night the sailors thought that land was approaching them. (28) They took soundings, and found twenty fathoms; they moved the boat on a little, sounded again, and found fifteen fathoms. (29) Fearing lest we should fall upon rocky places they threw out four anchors from the stern and wished it were day. (30) The sailors were seeking to escape from the ship and let down the dinghy into the sea, under the pretence that they were going to let out anchors from the bow. (31) Paul said to the centurion and the soldiers, 'Unless these men stay in the ship you cannot be saved.' (32) Then the soldiers cut the ropes of the dinghy and let it fall away.

(33) When it was nearly day Paul exhorted them all to partake of food, saying, 'Today[8] you are looking to the fourteenth day and are continuing without food, having taken nothing. (34) Therefore I urge you to partake of food. For[9] this is for your welfare,[10] for not a hair will be lost from the head of any of you.' (35) When he had said this he took a loaf and gave thanks to God before them all; he broke it and began to eat. (36) They all took heart and themselves also partook of food. (37) We were in all 276 souls in the ship. (38) When they were satisfied with food they set about lightening the ship, casting the[11] food into the sea.

(39) When day broke they did not recognize the land but perceived a bay with a beach on which they planned if possible to run the ship. (40) They detached the anchors and let them slip into the sea, at the same time loosening the fastenings of the rudders and raising the foresail to the breeze they held on to the beach. (41) They[12] ran upon a shoal and ran the ship aground. The bow became fixed and remained firm but the stern began to break up under the violence of the waves. (42) It was the plan of the soldiers

[5]Greek, made a jettisoning.
[6]Greek, literally: Since there was much foodlessness.
[7]RSV, drifting across the sea of; NJB, being driven one way and another.
[8]RSV, you have continued in suspense; NEB, you have lived in suspense; NJB, you have been in suspense.
[9]RSV, it will give you strength; NEB, your lives depend on it; NJB, your safety depends on it.
[10]Welfare; elsewhere the Greek word might be translated salvation.
[11]RSV, wheat; NJB, corn.
[12]NEB, found themselves caught between cross-currents; NJB, the cross-currents carried them into a shoal.

to kill the prisoners, lest any should swim off and escape. (43) But the centurion, wishing to get Paul safely through, put a stop to their intention and commanded those who were able to swim to throw themselves overboard and come first to land (44) and [then][13] the rest, some on planks of wood and some[14] on some of those who came from the ship. And in this way it came about that all got safely to land.

Bibliography

A. Acworth, *JTS* 24 (1973), 190–3.

C. K. Barrett, *FS* A. T. Hanson, 51–64.

J. Behm, *TWNT* 4.928–32.

M. E. Boismard and A. Lamouille, *EThL* 63 (1987), 48–58.

H. J. Cadbury, *JBL* 48 (1929), 419f.

L. Casson, *Ships and Seamanship in the Ancient World* (1971).

D. J. Clark, *BT* 26 (1975), 144–6.

J. M. Gilchrist, *JSNT* 61 (1996), 29–51.

E. Haenchen, *FS* Bultmann (1964), 235–54.

R. P. C. Hanson, *TU* 102 = *StEv* IV 315–18.

C. J. Hemer, *Tyndale Bulletin* 36 (1985), 79–109.

N. Heutger, *BZ* 28 (1984), 86–8.

R. A. Kraft, *JBL* 94 (1975), 256–65.

D. Ladouceur, *HThR* 73 (1980), 435–49.

G. B. Miles and G. Trompf, *HThR* 69 (1976), 259–67.

Eb. Nestle, *ZNW* 8 (1907), 75, 76.

M. Oberwies, *NovT* 30 (1988), 169–83.

R. M. Ogilvie, *JTS* 9 (1958), 308–14.

P. Pokorný, *ZNW* 64 (1973), 233–44.

S. M. Praeder, *CBQ* 46 (1984), 683–706.

B. Reicke, *ThZ* 4 (1948), 401–10.

V. K. Robins, *Biblical Research* (1975), 1–14.

J. Rougé, *VigCh* 14 (1960), 193–203.

J. Rougé, *Recherches sur l'organisation du commerce maritime en Méditerranée sous l'empire romain* (1966).

J. Smith, *The Voyage and Shipwreck of St Paul* (1880/1978).

A. Suhl, *ZThK* 88 (1991), 1–28.

G. W. Trompf, in C. H. Talbert, *Luke-Acts*, 225–39.

J. Wehnert, *ZThK* 87 (1990), 687–99; 88 (1991), 169–80.

W. J. Woodhouse, *Encyclopaedia Biblica*, 3690–92.

W. P. Workman, *ExpT* 11 (1900), 316–19.

[13]Then is not in the Greek.

[14]RSV, on pieces of the ship; NEB, on parts of the ship; NJB, on pieces of wreckage.

Commentary

There can be no doubt that whoever was responsible for the substance of this chapter was familiar with the sea and with seafaring, in particular with conditions and places in the Mediterranean and the Adriatic. On this subject J. Smith, *The Voyage and Shipwreck of St Paul* (Grand Rapids 1978, reprint of the 1880 edition), is still a classical work. It might almost be said that the writer's knowledge of the sea and of sailors is too good for us; he uses what are plainly technical terms, some of which are otherwise unknown so that we can only guess at their meaning (see the detailed notes below). The question that arises is whether all these details, and the events described, belong to a journey actually made by Paul on his way from Caesarea to Rome. The outline of the voyage was taken from life; were the references to Paul, to the things said and done by him on the voyage, an integral part of the story from the beginning, or were they inserted into a narrative of a voyage and shipwreck that did not originally contain them?

The outline of the story is cast in the first person plural (vv. 1, 2, 3, 4, 5, 6, 7, 8, 15, 16, 18, 20, (26), 26, 29, 37). That there are verses where Paul is subject or object and is referred to in the third person singular is no proof that either set of verses was inserted. It would be not only untrue but ridiculous to write in vv. 9f., *We* spoke the following words. If anyone spoke them it was Paul and Paul alone. The same sort of observation covers the use of the third person plural. Thus in v. 12 the majority who ἔθεντο βουλήν ... did not include Paul or Paul's companions—hence *they* is used; v. 13 follows upon this—*they* must include Paul and any who had agreed with him for they were still on the ship and were coasting along by Crete, but παρελέγοντο is used with those in mind who had chosen that course, whereas in v. 15 the first person plural ἐφερόμεθα applies to all who were on board, none of whom wished to be driven by a hurricane. Similar considerations apply throughout. It has to be asked whether the Pauline interventions are credible as parts of the story as a whole.

Weiser (659) counts as Pauline insertions vv. 3b, 9–11, 21–26, 31, 33–36, 43a, and considers that these passages show that 'der Text nicht ein historisch getreuer Geschichtsbericht ist'; similarly Haenchen (678–80), and many others. 'Die eingeschobenen Szenen entsprechen genau dem lukanischen Paulusbild. Paulus steht immer im Mittelpunkt. Er ist nie um Rat verlegen ... Lukas ahnte nicht ... , dass Paulus am Leben verzweifeln konnte (2 Kor 1.8) und gerade so das Wunder des Gottes erfuhr, der die Toten erweckt (2 Kor 1.9f.). Er kennt nur den starken, unerschütterlichen und von Triumph zu Triumph schreitenden Liebling Gottes' (Haenchen 680). There is much truth in this as a general observation, though Paul's triumphal progress (if such it may be called) from Jerusalem to Rome is set within a framework of mob violence, imprisonment, attempted assassination, mocking, and a narrow escape from death by drowning. But there is also a good deal that is thoughtless and out of touch with reality. Of course Paul 'steht immer im Mittelpunkt'; Luke's history has become a biography of Paul and the subject of a biography will not surprisingly occupy the centre of the stage. One could imagine a biography of the centurion Julius, in which Julius, as responsible for the whole voyage, final authority on matters of route, protector of all his charges, stood at the centre; and it would be impossible to find fault with such a biography. Luke admired Paul; this may have been on his part an error of judgement, but it is hardly surprising that it determined his presentation of his material. If he was not mistaken in regarding Paul as an outstanding person this too is a fact that must be taken into account in estimating the historicity of Paul's interventions in the story. 'Die Unwirklichkeit der Szene sieht man am leichtesten bei V. 21–26. Paulus hält auf stampfendem Schiff im heulenden Sturm eine Rede, als stünde er auf dem Areopag' (Haenchen 679). Certainly the scene is Luke's construction and the speech as we read it is Luke's composition; but there is nothing improbable in the influence (not on all 276 on board but on those who mattered) of one man of unshakable faith and imperturbable courage. Parallels are as uncommon as such men are, but they exist. For Haenchen this speech arises out of Paul's earlier warning (v. 10), which he takes to have been based upon the reference in v. 12 to a decision by a majority (οἱ πλείονες) to make for Phoenix. Luke (according to Haenchen) would think of Paul, the centurion, the shipowner, and the captain. If in this group of four a majority was against him Paul must have stood alone. This is a rather mechanical way of estimating the literary form of a historical event, and overlooks a not unimportant point. Paul makes two predictions of the outcome of the voyage (vv. 10; 24–26). They contradict each other; according to the former, lives will be lost; according to the latter there will be no loss of life. Did Luke simply invent these contradictory predictions? It seems unlikely. If he did not, he must have received one or possibly both of them from some kind of tradition of Paul's attitude and actions on the ship. This need not have been much more than, 'In the course of a stormy voyage Paul gave good advice and greatly encouraged and cheered the crew and his fellow passengers.' That the *We* in this chapter is not due to a convention of describing sea voyages in this way is shown in *FS* A. T. Hanson, 52–6; it is part of a source which may have been little more (see Introduction, p. xxix) than an itinerary. Luke has written up such traditions in the light of some acquaintance with the sea and of his estimate of Paul. Neither the acquaintance nor the estimate is to be too readily dismissed.

This is substantially the conclusion reached in *Begs*. 4.324: 'Much the most natural view is that it really represents the actual experience of Paul and his friends, but it is possible [the view taken here is that it is virtually certain] that the narrative has been coloured in a few [a number of] details by traditional accounts of shipwrecks.' There are however few who now hold so high a view of the historical value of Luke's story. Bauernfeind (270–2) thinks it possible to remove 'Pauline supplements' though he believes that these supplements contain some old features. Roloff (358f.) thinks that 27.1–9a, 12–20, 27–30, 32, 38–44; 28.1, 11–13, 14b, 16b come from Aristarchus, but 'die Wir-Form erweist sich an zwei entscheidenden Stellen (V. 1 und V. 6) als sinnwidrig und künstlich.' Luke has put in vv. 9b–11, 21–26, 31, 33–37 to show the centrality of Paul and that nothing can stop God's intention that he should reach Rome. On 27.1–28.15 Schmithals (231) writes, 'Wir haben es anscheinend mit einem von Lukas bearbeiteten Stück seiner Paulus-Quelle zu tun.' Schneider's view is similar to that of Haenchen; he also (2.382) quotes Pokorný 237: 'Die unbestreitbaren Berührungspunkte der Romane mit den Mysterien sind m.E. vor allem dadurch entstanden, dass man im Roman versucht hat, die Grundprobleme und Krisen der menschlichen Existenz (Tod, Trennung der Liebenden, Beraubung, Angst vor den Göttern) durch den Hinweis auf die in den Mysterien gewonnenen Erlebnisse zu lösen.' Lüdemann (266) notes the presence of Paul in vv. 9–11, 21–26, 31, 33–36, 43, and that for the rest he is forgotten. Paul, Lüdemann thinks, was in Malta, but not shipwrecked. This looks like simple invention.

Johnson makes the sound comments: '[Paul] is *not* portrayed as a *theios aner* ... whose will can bend the forces of nature to his own' (458); 'Paul's path is one marked not by thaumaturgy but by faith' (459). If to faith we add courage and hardihood (amply attested by 2 Cor. 11.23–27), some at least of the details of this chapter become credible—more credible than some of the objections that have been quoted above.

1. That Paul should sail to Rome was already implied in the acceptance of his appeal to the emperor (25.12, ἐπὶ Καίσαρα πορεύσῃ). ὡς (the temporal use of ὡς is characteristic of Acts; see 16.4) δὲ ἐκρίθη will refer therefore to a decision with regard to the practical arrangements for the journey. For the (unnecessary) τοῦ before the infinitive see BDR § 400.7, n. 9, where its frequency in Lk. and Acts is said to be due to the influence of the LXX, in which it represents the Hebrew ל. ἡμᾶς means, *prima facie*, that the writer accompanied Paul on the journey; for the origin and significance of the 'We-passages' see Introduction, pp. xxvi–xxx. The first person plural disappears in the reading of P 6 326 2495* *pc*, which instead of ἡμᾶς have τοὺς περὶ τὸν Παῦλον, Paul and his party. These MSS do not consistently remove the first person plural from the narrative, so that there is no attempt to suggest that the author of Acts was not present, and it is not easy to see how the reading originated; perhaps ἡμᾶς was thought to lack clarity and directness. ἀποπλεῖν is (for obvious reasons) used several times in the accounts of Paul's travels; see 13.4; 14.26; 20.15.

παρεδίδουν (for the classical –εδίδοσαν) is Hellenistic; for the tense see on v. 2. The subject is not expressed; in the background lies the authority of the governor Festus, who acts through his officials (hence the plural verb). They handed over both Paul and some other prisoners. The reversal of τόν τε in P⁷⁴ *pc* would lead to *both handed over and ...*—but there is no second verb. We hear of the other prisoners again at v. 42, not however in ch. 28. For ἑκατοντάρχης see on 10.1. Nothing more is known of the Centurion Julius than is contained in the present narrative. σπεῖρα Σεβαστή translates *cohors Augusta*, and there is good epigraphical evidence for the presence of a cohors Augusta I in Syria in the first century (see T. R. S. Broughton in *Begs.* 5.443, quoting H. Dessau, *Inscriptiones Latinae Selectae* I (1892), 2683). Broughton rightly rejects the suggestion that there is a reference to the cohortes Sebastenorum, or cohorts of Samaritans raised in Sebaste (= Samaria). Augusta (Σεβαστή) was an honorary title. On this see also *NS* 1.364. The cohortes Augustae were Syrian auxiliaries, and Broughton expresses surprise that a legionary centurion was not found to carry out the task of conveying an important prisoner to Rome. Perhaps (assuming that the story is not simply fictitious) Julius was the best man available; or was the prisoner not thought as important as Broughton assumes? or (since the appeal was something of a problem) was there a hope that the prisoner might escape on the way?

For the genitive σπείρης (instead of σπείρας) cf. 10.1 and see BDR § 43.1, n. 1.

The first nine words of the verse (ὡς ... Ἰταλίαν) are omitted by h syᵖ syʰᵐᵍ. These MSS have an addition at the end of 26.32; see on that verse.

The use of ἑτέρους implies that there were only two categories of prisoner, Paul and the rest (Delebecque 128).

2. The imperfect παρεδίδουν is brought to a point in the aorists ἐπιβάντες ... ἀνήχθημεν. The process of handing over the prisoners concluded with the actual embarkation, at which point, presumably, Julius assumed full responsibility. ἐπιβ. ἀνήχ. is used at 21.2, with reference to a ship sailing to Phoenicia. For the verb with a dative cf. Thucydides 7.70.5, ἐπειρῶντο ταῖς ἀλλήλων ναυσὶν ἐπιβαίνειν. Here P⁷⁴ places τῷ before πλοίῳ, pointlessly, because we know nothing of this ship until we read the following words; 614 2495 *pc* supply ἐν, needlessly—see e.g. the above quotation from

Thucydides. The ship's home port was Adramyttium, and it was used
no doubt for coastwise traffic round the north-eastern corner of the
Mediterranean. It is described by the adjective Ἀδραμυττηνῷ, for
which there is a respectably attested variant Ἀδραμυντηνῷ (P⁷⁴ᵛⁱᵈ A
B* 33 pc). On the variant spelling see M. 2.106; BDR § 42.3, n. 3
('nasaler ersatz von ττ durch ντ', with a reference for such substitu-
tions to § 39.7, n. 11). It was probably too much to hope to find a ship
sailing direct to Rome; to reach a port in Asia would take the
travellers well on their way and give them a fair chance of finding
another ship that would cover the rest of the journey. Julius cannot
have intended to take his prisoner 'to Adramyttium, and then through
the Troad, across the Hellespont and along the *via Egnatia* to
Dyrrachium, and so by Brundisium to Rome' (Page 252). Cf. Hemer
(133).

εἰς τοὺς ... τόπους. εἰς is omitted by H L P S and the Byzantine
text (Ropes); the omission 'must have been deemed good Greek in
the fourth and following centuries, although only in Greek poetry are
parallels found to this usage' (*Begs.* 3.240).

Paul's only named companion is Aristarchus; see 19.29 (named
with Gaius, both described as Macedonians) and 20.4 (named with
others and Secundus, both described as Thessalonians). Here, for
Aristarchus only, both designations are used. Lightfoot (*Philippians*
35) thought that he left the party at Myra (v. 5), continuing (when the
others changed) in the same ship as far as Adramyttium on his way
home to Thessalonica. Chrysostom (*Homily* 53.1) thought that he
was carrying news of Paul to the churches of Macedonia. He is not
heard of again in Acts and we do not know what happened. It is
impossible to build on Col. 4.10, but the closely parallel reference in
Philemon 24 shows him with Paul at a time of imprisonment; where
and when however are matters of dispute. Conzelmann (141) takes
him as a pointer to the way in which Luke's information reached
him. Secundus is introduced here (from 20.4) by 614 (2147) 2495 *pc*
syʰ.

Begs. 4.325 notes that in this context *Asia* must mean the western,
not the southern, coast of Asia Minor. This is correct, but it is clear
that the ship was putting in at south coast ports too.

Metzger (496f.) quotes the reconstruction made by Clark (163), on
the basis of 97 421 syᵖ syʰᵐᵍ, of the Western text of vv. 1, 2:

οὕτως οὖν ἔκρινεν ὁ ἡγεμὼν ἀναπέμπεσθαι αὐτὸν Καίσαρι.
καὶ τῇ ἐπαύριον προσκαλεσάμενος ἑκατοντάρχην τινὰ
ὀνόματι Ἰούλιον, σπείρης Σεβαστῆς, παρεδίδου αὐτῷ τὸν
Παῦλον σὺν ἑτέροις δεσμώταις. ἀρξάμενοι δὲ τοῦ ἀποπλεῖν
εἰς τὴν Ἰταλίαν ἐπέβημεν πλοίῳ ...

Ropes (*Begs.* 3.240) thinks that this reading was intended to 'relieve
the abruptness of the B-text'.

3. The ship sailed north along the coast, aided by the current due to the outflow from the Nile, and *on the following day* Sidon was reached. With τῇ ἑτέρᾳ, ἡμέρᾳ must be understood, as at Sophocles, *Oedipus Rex* 781f., τὴν μὲν οὖσαν ἡμέραν μόλις κατέσχον, θἀτέρᾳ δέ ... Xenophon, *Cyropaedia* 4.6.10 is somewhat unfortunately chosen by BA (638) as an example, for here the expression follows on αὔριον (as at Acts 20.15 it follows on τῇ ἐπιούσῃ) and accordingly means *on the day after tomorrow, on the third day*. Always however it means on the day after the one last mentioned; here, on the day after leaving Caesarea. According to Marshall the distance was about 69 nautical miles.

κατήχθημεν corresponds to ἀνήχθημεν (v. 2): we put out to sea, we put in to land. Sidon, a Phoenician port, was a hellenized city; in 24 BC Augustus made it part of Ituraea. There is some evidence for the presence of Jews (*NS* 3.14, 15). If τοὺς φίλους refers to Christian friends (see below) it will follow that Sidon had been evangelized and a church established there. We have no other evidence for this at so early a date. Eusebius (*HE* 8.13.3) mentions as a martyr Zenobius, a presbyter of the church at Sidon.

Julius, another of Luke's 'good' centurions (cf. Lk. 7.2; 23.47; Acts 10.1), showed Paul kindness. φιλανθρωπία was a recognized virtue in the ancient world. See Plato, *Euthyphro* 3d; Demosthenes 19.225 (411); Plutarch, *Aemilius Paulus* 39 (276); Iamblichus quoted in Stobaeus 4.5.76 (Gaisford 46[44], 76), ὅτ' ἂν χρηστότητι καὶ φιλανθρωπίᾳ κραθῇ τὸ σεμνὸν καὶ αὐστηρὸν .... For χρῆσθαι cf. Xenophon, *Memorabilia* 1.2.48. The centurion permitted Paul to go πρὸς τοὺς φίλους, *to his friends*, and these would naturally be Christians. It is possible (see *Begs.* 5.379f.) that 'the Friends' was already a term denoting Christians; cf. 3 Jn 15, though here too the word does not necessarily, and indeed does not probably, have a technical sense. See G. Stählin in *TWNT* 9.144–69, especially 159f.

Paul was allowed to go to the friends in order that he might ἐπιμελείας τυχεῖν. ἐπιμέλεια is *care* of all kinds: see Prov. 3.8; 1 Macc. 16.14; 2 Macc. 11.23; 3 Macc. 5.1; Josephus, *Ant.* 2.236, the young Moses was in his upbringing in Egypt πολλῆς ἐπιμελείας τυγχάνων. In the present passage Luke no doubt thinks of what Ignatius (*Polycarp* 1.2) describes as ἐπιμέλεια σαρκική τε καὶ πνευματική. Paul's Christian friends would give him both.

4. How long the ship stayed with its passengers in Sidon Luke does not say. In due course they again put out to sea (ἀναχθέντες; cf. v. 2). ὑπεπλεύσαμεν τὴν Κύπρον, *sailed under (the lee of) Cyprus*. Cf. ὑποδραμεῖν (vv. 7, 16). This is clear, except that it does not tell us which was the lee side of Cyprus. This depends on the direction of the prevailing wind. There is a long note with many nautical and meteorological details in *Begs.* 4.326, but the only consideration that comes near to being decisive is the statement in v. 5 that they sailed through the Cilician and Pamphylian seas to Myra. This can hardly be otherwise interpreted than to mean that they kept to the north of Cyprus. This, unless the ship had trading connections with Salamis and Paphos, would in any case be the more probable course in an age in which shipping hugged the coastline as far as possible.

The winds were contrary (for the expression cf. Mk 6.48 = Mt. 14.24). If they had sailed across in a north-westerly direction they would have had the Etesian winds in their teeth. Nearer the coast of Asia Minor they would have been helped by land winds and a westward-flowing current (Page (252) referring to Smith 67 (better would be 67–9)). See also Hemer (133).

In 21.3 Paul sailed on the other side of Cyprus.

5. πέλαγος (in the NT elsewhere only at Mt. 18.6) is the *high sea*, the *open sea*, in contrast with landward water. Luke means (and this is consistent with his remark about the wind—see v. 4) that instead of keeping to the coast of Cilicia and Pamphylia they sailed straight across the Pamphylian Bight to arrive at Myra (see the Western text of 21.1), here correctly described as belonging to Lycia, the use of the partitive genitive τῆς Λυκίας being also correct (BDR § 164.3, n. 7; M. 3.171). For διαπλεύσαντες cf. Thucydides 4.25.1, ἠναγ–κάσθησαν ὀψὲ τῆς ἡμέρας ναυμαχῆσαι περὶ πλοίου διαπλέοντος; Lucian, *Hermotimus* 28, ... τὸν Αἰγαῖον ἢ τὸν Ἰόνιον διαπλεῦσαι θέλοντας.

κατέρχεσθαι (cf. κατάγεσθαι in v. 3) is the regular term for 'coming down from the high sea' to land.

The Western text (represented by 614 2147 *pc* h vg^mss sy^h**) adds that the voyage lasted δι' ἡμερῶν δεκαπέντε (for διά and the genitive expressing extent of time see BDR § 223.2b, n. 4). This was the time it might have been expected to take; cf. Lucian, *Navigium* 7, ἐκεῖθεν [from Sidon] δὲ χειμῶνι μεγάλῳ δεκάτῃ ἐπὶ Χελιδονέας [on the coast of Lycia] ... ἐλθεῖν. Ten days with a strong wind might easily become fifteen in different conditions. The addition shows knowledge of local conditions. 'Unless in the ''Western'' text the additional words ... are regarded as genuine and accidentally omitted from the B-text, no explanation is at hand' (Ropes, *Begs.* 3.241). Clark (xlvi) observes that the words would form a στίχος. *Begs.* 4.326 accepts them as genuine, because they are so good an estimate. Alternatively, and more probably, they were added by someone who knew the area at a time when the text of Acts could be handled freely, and copyists felt at liberty to add what they knew (or believed) to be true on the basis of their own knowledge.

The port reached at the end of the first stage of the voyage is given in different forms. The apparatus in NA^26 does not distinguish between Μύρ(ρ)α (neuter plural) and Μύρ(ρ)αν (feminine singular).

The neuter plural is more commonly used. Μύρα is read by Ψ 𝔐 h—a not very distinguished group. B 1175 have Μύρραν. In addition 69 has Σμύρναν, P⁷⁴ א lat bo have Λύστραν (and A has Λύστρα). Σμύρνα may be a corruption of Μύρρα. *Begs.* 4.327 points out that Myra was also called Ἀδμυρά, Λάμυρα, and Λιμυρά (or Λιμύρα), and Λύστρα may be derived from one of these. There is no doubt that Myr(r)a is meant. 'Alexandrian corn ships could rarely sail directly to Italy from Egypt, but a west wind, or even one slightly north of west, made it possible to fetch Myra, and thence a north wind would take them to Sicily, from which another shift of wind back to the west would make it possible to reach Pozzuoli, or even Ostia' (*Begs.* 4.327). Cf. Hemer 133f.

6. The Alexandrian ship sailing to Italy would probably belong to the corn fleet (see v. 38). Egypt was an indispensable source of supply for Rome, providing a third of the corn used in the year: Josephus, *War* 2.386 (παρέχει ... τῇ Ῥώμῃ σῖτον μηνῶν τεσσάρων; 383—the remainder came from Africa). Many of the ships were run by private enterprise (Suetonius, *Claudius* 18, 19; cf. Seneca, *Epistle* 77.1f.), but they were used by official travellers as well as by private persons. Thus Titus, returning from Jerusalem to Rome, 'festinans in Italiam, quum Rhegium, deinde Puteolos oneraria nave appulisset, Romam inde contendit expeditissimus' (Suetonius, *Titus* 5). Some ships were large; the ship in Lucian's *Navigium* 5 was 120 cubits (= 180 feet = 54 m.) long, more than 30 cubits (= 45 feet = 13.5 m.) wide, and 29 cubits (= 43.5 feet = 13.05 m.) deep. Alexandrian sailors had a good reputation: Philo, *Flaccus* 26: τάς τε γὰρ ἐκεῖθεν ὁλκάδας ταχυναυτεῖν ἔφασκε καὶ ἐμπειροτάτους εἶναι κυβερνήτας ...

ἐμβιβάζειν is regularly used for the transitive sense of 'to embark', ἐμβαίνειν serving for the intransitive. Cf. Lucian, *Verae Historiae* 2.26, ἐμβιβάσας ὁ Ῥαδάμανθυς πεντήκοντα τῶν ἡρώων εἰς ναῦν ... Cf. Hemer (134).

7, 8. The next stage of the journey is dealt with in a long sentence which runs through the two verses and has a complicated structure. Moule (*IB* 101) notes that the present participle βραδυπλοοῦντες is followed by the aorist indicative ὑπεπλεύσαμεν, and raises the question whether the participle refers to action before that of the main verb or covers the whole episode. In fact the sentence is more complicated than this and it will be necessary to set out its framework as a whole: Present participle (βραδυπλοοῦντες); aorist participle (γενόμενοι); present participle (προσεῶντος); aorist indicative (ὑπεπλεύσαμεν); present participle (παραλεγόμενοι); aorist indicative (ἤλθομεν). When these are considered in the light of a map, it seems to make sense both of the grammar and of the geography to suppose that the first three participles describe the journey as far as Cnidos, ὑπεπλεύσαμεν takes the ship as far as the south coast of Crete, the next participle and finite verb to Fair Havens. The ship could sail only slowly (*Begs.* 4.327 suggests that βραδυπλοεῖν may be a technical term for *beating*, as ἐυθυδρομεῖν (16.11; 21.1) may mean *to run*) in a direct WNW (Etesian) wind from Myra to Cnidus; it then took advantage of the N or NE wind to cross over to Crete with a view to taking the sheltered south side of the island (ὑπεπλεύσαμεν, a sort of inceptive aorist—we took shelter under the lee of Crete). Even so, however, it was with difficulty that they coasted half way along the island and eventually reached (ἤλθομεν) Fair Havens.

ἐν is employed, unusually, to denote the extent of time during which an action takes place. ἱκανός is a favourite word in Acts to denote an interval which Luke either is not able, or has no wish, to give precisely: for a fair number of days.

βραδυπλοεῖν occurs nowhere else in the NT, and is not common in Greek generally. Its broad meaning is not in doubt (see above), and the reason for the slow progress it denotes is clear: the wind did not allow speed, perhaps did not permit the ship to approach Cnidus, but the compounded πρός (in προσεῶντος) may do no more than strengthen the meaning of the verb. For the expression cf. Lucian, *Verae Historiae* 1.29, οὐ μέντοι ἐπέβημεν αὐτῆς, οὐ γὰρ εἴα τὸ πνεῦμα, but (since αὐτῆς refers to Νεφελοκοκκυγία) the sense is somewhat different.

μόλις occurs twice in these two verses; also at 14.18; 27.16; Lk. 9.39 (v. 1. μόγις); elsewhere in the NT only twice—a Lucan word; perhaps one should say a word characteristic of the sources of the present story.

Cnidus is mentioned here only. It lay at the extremity of a peninsula of the mainland, north west of Rhodes. Since 129 BC the town had been a *civitas libera* under Roman rule. See Trebilco (123).

ὑπεπλεύσαμεν was used at v. 4, where it must mean, We sailed under the lee of. Here, after the reference to Cnidus and followed by κατὰ Σαλμώνην, it must mean something like *we took refuge, sailed for refuge* (from the troublesome wind) under the lee of Crete. Twice in these verses (cf. also v. 5) κατά will mean *off*: they did not call at Cnidus, but approached it, and reached Crete off Salmone, the headland at the northeastern extremity of the island. There is some doubt about the spelling of Salmone (several versions are known, though there seems to be no variation in the text of Acts), and also about its precise location; there are two capes, and it is uncertain which is referred to. Crete itself was brought under Roman rule in 67 BC by Q. Metellus; it was united with Cyrenaica and made a senatorial province.

Even the sheltered south side of Crete presented difficulties to the navigators, and it was with difficulty (μόλις) that they coasted (παραλεγόμενοι) as far as a place called Fair Havens. A port bearing this name still exists; it is sheltered on the west, open to the east, and would therefore give protection from northerly and westerly winds. It was about five or six miles from a place that has been identified with (and is said to be still called by local peasants) Lasaea. Apparently the place had little but safety to commend it. For the language cf. Cicero, *Ad Familiares* 14.5 (236a), Athenas venimus, cum sane adversis ventis usi essemus, tardeque et incommode navigassemus.

ἐγγύς is here constructed with the dative, as at 9.38; at 1.12 it is used with the indeclinable Ἰερουσαλήμ. Elsewhere in the NT where the case is determined it is always genitive (notwithstanding the statement in M. 3.216).

According to Titus 1.5 Paul left Titus in Crete; this epistle presupposes the existence of a fairly developed and numerous church in the island. There is no confirmation of these things in the present narrative. However considerately Julius treated Paul he will hardly have permitted him to set about evangelizing the island.

The name of Lasaea is variously given: Λασαία ((ℵ*) Ψ 𝔐); Λασέα (B 33 1175 1739 1891 2464 *al*); Λασία (36 81 453 945 *pc*); Λαίσσα (ℵ²); Ἄλασσα (A sy^hmg sa); Thalassa (lat).

h has the curious reading, devenimus in portum bonum, ubi Anchis ci[vitas er]at. Ropes (*Begs*. 3.243) suggests that Anchis may be a misunderstanding of ἄγχι, which the Western text may have used instead of ἐγγύς. There is no better suggestion.

Hemer (134–6, cf. Smith 75f.) in a long note argues, in dependence on L. Casson (see Bibliography, p. 1177) that it was usual, at least for sailing ships, to take a course to the south of Crete. This may now be taken as established.

It is often held that v. 8 (or v. 9a) connects with v. 12, vv. 9–11 being a Pauline insertion in a non-Pauline account of a voyage. See p. 1191; also Schille (461), who takes the view that vv. 9–11 do not interrupt the sequence of the narrative.

9. In Luke's narrative as it stands it is clear that the continuation of the voyage was under discussion, clear and also understandable. A considerable time (ἱκανοῦ χρόνου; cf. v. 7) had now elapsed (since they left Caesarea? or since they left Myra?), and Fair Havens was not a desirable place in which to spend the winter. Claudius however had taken steps to make even risky winter voyages for the corn fleet profitable (Suetonius, *Claudius* 18). On the other hand the danger of sailing was sufficient to constitute a good case for remaining where they were. In this situation, Paul (according to Luke) intervened. Is it likely that he would be in a position to do so? *Prima facie* one might think not; but it must be remembered that though under guard, and not free, he was in a sense a privileged person, who must be delivered to the Emperor. He had not been found guilty of any crime, and it was the opinion of the governor that he was innocent.

The first two statements in the verse are made in absolute
genitives, the latter expanded by διὰ τό (the use of the article is
characteristic of Acts) and an accusative and infinitive: because the
Fast had now already passed. The Fast is the Day of Atonement, the
only fast in the Jewish calendar. 'On the Day of Atonement, eating,
drinking, washing, anointing, putting on sandals, and marital inter-
course are forbidden' (Yoma 8.1). Many other passages connect the
Day of Atonement with fasting, e.g. Josephus, *Ant.* 17.165: ... μίαν
ἡμέραν, ἣν Ἰουδαῖοι νηστείαν ἄγουσιν; cf. 14.66; Philo, *Moses*
2.23; *De Specialibus Legibus* 1.186; 2.193: μετὰ δὲ τὴν τῶν
σαλπίγγων ἄγεται νηστεία ἑορτή; *Gaius* 306. The Day of Atonement fell on 10 Tishri; Tishri corresponds to the latter part of
September and the former of October. The 10th would fall at the end
of September or the beginning of October. By this time sailing was
unsafe, ἐπισφαλής (here only in the NT, but not an uncommon
word). Cf. Josephus, *Ant.* 16.15: τὸν γὰρ πλοῦν, ἐμβαίνοντος τοῦ
χειμῶνος, οὐκ ἐνόμιζον ἀσφαλῆ. According to Vegetius, *De re
militari* 4.39 sailing became dangerous after 15 September and
ceased after 11 November. The reference to the Fast has been used as
a means of dating the journey. The Fast, τὴν νηστείαν, is introduced
by καί which should mean *The Fast too*, or *even the Fast*. This (see
W. P. Workman, *ExpT* 11 (1900), 316–19 and many commentaries,
e.g. *Begs.* 4.328f.; see also J. Behm in *TWNT* 4.928–32) has been
held to mean that this year the Fast (= 10 Tishri) fell late, later at
least than the autumnal equinox. In AD 59 the date was 5 October; it
was earlier in 57, 58, 60, 61, 62. From this some have inferred that
the date of Paul's journey was AD 59. It is true that problems arise at
28.11 (see the note there); the voyage to Malta must have ended, and
the stay in Malta begun, by about the end of October; the last part of
the voyage, after three months, will therefore have begun at the end
of January, that is, in the period when sailing would be considered
impossibly dangerous. Perhaps in view of Claudius's encouragement
of the corn trade this matters little. But it seems that a great deal is
being made to rest on the word καί, to which there is no need to give
this quasi-superlative force. It was late; even the day usually
considered as marking the end of navigation had gone by. There must
have been an uncertain period; p. Shabbath 2.5b.25 reckons sailing to
be unsafe after the Feast of Tabernacles, 15 Tishri. On this reckoning
the Day of Atonement was late but not impossibly late. See Marshall
(406).

Hanson (245) speculates on where Paul had observed the Day of
Atonement, whether on shipboard or at Lasaea (if there was a
synagogue there). It might be more useful to ask whether he would
have observed it at all; see Gal. 4.10.

In view of the situation, Paul offered advice, παρῄνει. One might
have expected the verb παρακαλεῖν; παραινεῖν is used in the NT

only here and at v. 22. Like μόλις (above) it could be a mark of a special source for this chapter; it is not a word particularly appropriate to a sea voyage—and it does nothing to confirm the view that we have here a Lucan insertion. Since the prediction that follows in v. 10 was proved false we may suppose that Luke (if he thought about the matter) took it to be Paul's human opinion, whereas his later prediction (vv. 22–26) was based on a supernatural communication from an angel.

10. Paul addresses the company. The vocative ἄνδρες is in nearly every other place in Acts accompanied by some other noun (such as ἀδελφοί); here, and at vv. 21, 25, it is alone, probably because there was no other word suitably descriptive of all Paul's fellow travellers.

The sentence that follows the vocative has a mixed construction. It begins θεωρῶ ὅτι; this should be taken up by a finite verb, but in fact the sentence continues with an accusative and infinitive (μέλλειν ἔσεσθαι τὸν πλοῦν), which should have followed upon θεωρῶ without ὅτι. The construction has however been defended. M. 1.213 says that there are classical parallels (from various sources the following may be noted: Xenophon, *Hellenica* 2.2.2, ... εἰδὼς ὅτι ... θᾶττον τῶν ἐπιτηδείων ἔνδειαν ἔσεσθαι; *Cyropaedia* 8.1.25; Thucydides 5.46.3; Plato, *Phaedo* 63c; we may add POxy 2.237.col.5.8, δηλῶν ὅτι εἰ τὰ ἀληθῆ φανείη μηδὲ κρίσεως δεῖσθαι τὸ πρᾶγμα). Blass (274): 'sine ὅτι erat periculum ne coniungerentur θεωρῶ μετὰ κτέ, et idem ὅτι multis interiectis facile e mente elapsum est.' Delebecque (130) calls ὅτι with the infinitive a 'tour classique', which perhaps stretches the evidence somewhat. To Knowling (520) it is 'a vivid dramatic touch'. See also *Begs.* 4.329; H. J. Cadbury in *JBL* 48 (1929), 419f. Cf. Acts 16.19 D.

The future infinitive (found in the NT only in Acts and Hebrews) is rightly used with μέλλειν.

Paul foresees that the voyage if persisted in will be μετὰ ὕβρεως καὶ πολλῆς ζημίας. ὕβρις (also at v. 21) is an unexpected word. LS 1841, in addition to giving the usual meanings of the word (wanton violence, insolence, lust, lewdness, an outrage, especially on the person) have a third division, 'III used of *a loss by sea*' for which they cite only our passage and Pindar, with a cross-reference to ναυσίστανος. Here (LS 1162) ναυσίστανος ὕβρις is rendered 'the *lamentable* loss *of the ships*', with reference to Pindar, *Pythian Odes* 1.72 (ναυσίστανον ὕβριν ἰδὼν τὰν πρὸ Κύμας). Their interpretation may not be correct. B. L. Gildersleeve (*Pindar: the Olympian and Pythian Odes*; 1885) explains the sentence as equivalent to ὅτι ἡ ὕβρις ἡ πρὸ Κύμης ναυσίστονος (sic Gildersleeve) ἐγένετο, and writes (p. 249), 'There is no Pindaric warrant for the use of ὕβρις as "loss", "damage". The reflection that their overweening insolence [ὕβρις] off Cumae had brought groans and lamentation to the ships (cf. P[yth]. 2.28) would silence their savage yell and keep them quiet at home.' Luke's repeated use of the word however suggests that he had reason to think it appropriate, and there is ground for this. See BA 1660, with e.g. *Anthologia Palatina* 7.291.4 (7.29.3f.), δείσασα θαλάττης ὕβριν (a personal outrage inflicted by the sea); Josephus, *Ant.* 3.133, τὴν ἀπὸ τῶν ὄμβρων ὕβριν. ζημία gives rise to no problem: 'damage and much loss not only of the cargo and the ship but also of our lives'. For the last five words contrast v. 24.

Bruce (2.482) counters the argument that it is unlikely that Paul the prisoner would be allowed to attend and address a ship's council with the observation that Paul was on good terms with the centurion and had in the first instance given him his opinion. But Paul's advice is given not to the centurion but to 'ἄνδρες'. For the advice cf. that of Apollonius in Philostratus, 5.18: ἀποβῶμεν, ἔφη, τῆς νεὼς ταύτης, οὐ γὰρ λῷον αὐτῇ ἐς Ἀχαίαν πλεῦσαι. Only Apollonius's friends heeded his warning; the ship sank.

11. Julius's favourable treatment of Paul did not extend to preference for his advice over that of the professionals, who evidently counselled continuation of the voyage as far as Phoenix. Whether it was this short voyage, or the whole journey to Italy, that Paul had in mind in v. 10 is not clear.

The κυβερνήτης was the steersman, and the primary and ultimately responsible steersman was the captain of the ship. The word is used in this sense; so e.g. Plato, *Republic* 341cd, τί δὲ κυβερνήτης; ὁ ὀρθῶς κυβερνήτης ναυτῶν ἄρχων ἐστὶν ἢ ναύτης; ναυτῶν ἄρχων. A special use of the word is for the captain of a Nile-boat (LS 1004). The role of the ναύκληρος is not clear. In some contexts the word denotes the ship-owner (who would certainly even if not travelling be very interested in the possibility of shipwreck). This may well be the meaning here. Many of the ships in the corn fleet were in private ownership (see v. 6); some however were not, and in such a case the ναύκληρος would presumably be the man who represented the 'owner'—that is, the official responsible for the fleet. It may be said that the κυβερνήτης and the ναύκληρος would represent respectively the nautical and the financial interest. If these agreed it would be most unlikely that the centurion would accept the contrary view of Paul. There is an important note on ναύκληρος in MM 422f.; see also BA 1081. A passage in Plutarch, *Praecepta Politica* 13 (807b), is sometimes quoted as if it settled the relation between ναύκληρος and κυβερνήτης: ναύτας μὲν ἐκλέγεται κυβερνήτης καὶ κυβερνήτην ναύκληρος. This is however a very difficult passage. It is introduced by the words δεινὸν γὰρ ὡς ἀληθῶς καὶ σχέτλιον, εἰ ναύτας μὲν ἐκλέγεται, κτλ. See Hemer (138f.).

Conzelmann (141) notes that the κυβ. and the ναυκ. are not mentioned in the account of the wreck and infers that the present verse is an insertion. Stählin (316) thinks that two sources may have been combined, since v. 11 suggests a Führungsgruppe, v. 12 a democratic decision among all (or at least all free) travellers.

The centurion was persuaded by the captain and owner (or manager) rather than by what Paul said; in fact, he did what they said, and did not do what Paul advised. Zerwick (§ 445) notes the use of μᾶλλον ... ἤ in an exclusive sense, and adduces in addition to this passage Jn 3.19; 12.43; Acts 4.19; 5.29; 27.11; 1 Tim. 1.4 (correcting Zerwick's reference); 2 Tim. 3.4; Heb. 11.25. BDR § 246.2a, n. 4 add Acts 20.35, and note the parallel in Plato, *Apology* 29d, πείσομαι δὲ μᾶλλον τῷ θεῷ ἤ ὑμῖν, which means, I will obey God and I will not obey you. It is correct that Luke's interest is in the fact that in face of all opposition Paul is proved right by events (Conzelmann 142).

Opinions of the historicity of this verse and of the whole paragraph of which it is part differ. Some think it impossible that the opinions of a prisoner should even be considered. Haenchen (670) makes much of Paul as a schwerverdächtiger Gefangener; he is not so represented in Acts. Bruce (2.482) quotes Nock (*Essays* 2.823): it is 'an authentic transcript of the recollections of an eyewitness, with the confusion and colouring which so easily attach themselves to recollections'.

12. This verse could be connected with v. 8 or v. 9a; hence the suggestion that vv. 9(b)–11 are an insertion; see above.

The sentence opens with a genitive absolute which states the main fact from which the discussion and disagreement arise. The harbour at Fair Havens was inconvenient (ἀνεύθετος: here only in the NT, but εὔθετος occurs at Lk. 9.62; 14.35; also Heb. 6.7) for wintering (παραχειμασία: here only in the NT; see MM 491; *ND* 4.166). What made it inconvenient is not stated: perhaps insecure anchorage for the ship; perhaps a lack of social amenities for the crew.

This being so the majority (οἱ πλείονες) formed a plan, ἔθεντο βουλήν. For this expression cf. Judges 19.30; Ps. 12(13).3; Plutarch, *Galba* 4 (1054), προὔθηκε βουλὴν τοῖς φίλοις. προτίθεσθαι β. seems to be more common than τίθεσθαι β. Who were the majority? The majority of the whole ship's company? The captain and owner against Paul? See on v. 11. Parallels with the emperor's council, sometimes drawn, are pointless. In a difficult and doubtful situation there is no need for imperial precedent; an intelligent man like Julius knows that it will be wise to call together the interested and knowledgeable parties and find out their views. The majority view is that they should not stay in Fair Havens, equally that they should not attempt the long voyage to Rome, but should make for Phoenix, a little way along the coast.

There was doubt about even this objective; they were to get to Phoenix εἴ πως δύναιντο. M. 3.127 says that such uses of εἰ 'are not so much real conditions as final clauses', and adds Acts 17.27. Others recognize the uncertainty imported into the clause by πως and the optative: Moule (*IB* 154), the optative gives to the indirect question 'a more tentative and cautious tone'; Zerwick (§ 403); Radermacher (131), 'Die Partikel εἰ leitet, parallel unserm "ob", einen Satz ein, der den erwarteten Erfolg einer Ueberlegung angibt.' BDR 375, n. 4 compare Xenophon, *Anabasis* 4.1.21, εἴ πως δυναίμην. Delebecque (130) speaks of the indirect question depending on a verb of action (ἀναχθῆναι) as a '... tour, constant depuis Homère'. εἰ means ' "pour voir si", "au cas où", "dans l'espoir de" '.

The hoped for objective was Phoenix, the precise location of which is disputed. The name, with minor variations in spelling, is found in ancient authors, and the approximate location of the town is known. It was about 50 miles west of Fair Havens (Stählin 316), and it can be deduced from Ptolemy, *Geographia* 3.15 [3.17.3] (see *Begs.* 4.330) that it was about 34 miles east of the western extremity of Crete. It has been customary to identify its harbour with that now known as Loutro (see W. J. Woodhouse in *Ency. Bib.* s.v. Phenice, 3690–92, for a good account of earlier discussion; also Smith (87–93)), which has been described as the best harbour on the relevant part of the southern coast of Crete. Difficulty however arises in the description of the harbour as βλέποντα κατὰ λίβα καὶ κατὰ χῶρον. The meaning of λίψ is clear (though it has other uses, e.g. in the LXX); it means the south west wind. χῶρος is not a native Greek word; it transliterates the Latin Caurus or Corus (e.g. Vergil, *Georgics* 3.356, Semper hiems, semper spirantes frigora Cauri; Caesar, *De Bello Gallico* 5.7, Corus ventus navigationem impediebat). This was a north west wind. βλέπειν κατά is most naturally taken to mean *to look into* a given direction; here to look into the direction of Lips and of Corus, that is, with the sort of approximation inevitable when directions are given with no greater precision than the names of winds afford, to look west. Hence an impasse: the harbour Loutro looks east. No attempt to make βλέπειν κατὰ λίβα καὶ κατὰ χῶρον mean something different can be judged successful. Cf. Caesar's *spectare* in *De Bello Gallico* 7.69 (Sub muro, quae pars collis ad orientem solem spectabat ...). It is hard to believe that βλέπειν κατά means *to look down wind*, hard to believe that βλέπειν implies a sailor's view as he enters harbour—entering an east facing harbour he is looking west. Sailors leave harbour as often as they enter. RV's 'looking NE and SE' means taking either κατὰ λίβα καὶ κατὰ χῶρον rightly but βλέποντα wrongly, or taking κατὰ λ. καὶ κ. χ. wrongly but βλ. rightly (Page 254f.) The right explanation is almost certainly that given by *Begs.* 4.330 (see the sketch map there). The harbour Loutro is formed by a promontory, Muros, projecting south from the coast of Crete. On the other side of the harbour is another harbour whose modern name is Phineha—almost certainly a modification of Φοῖνιξ. Phineha faces west as clearly as Loutro faces east. It has been objected that Phineha offers no suitable anchorage. This objection (with some others) is dealt with in an article by R. M. Ogilvie (*JTS* 9 (1958), 308–14). Astonishingly, he refers to commentaries by Bruce and Haenchen but makes no reference to *Begs.* 4, though he supplies the archaeological and other evidence the authors there desiderated. Since Paul's time there have been notable geological changes in Crete, and there is no difficulty in supposing that in the first century the bay of Phineha could be used by wintering vessels. It may now be regarded as virtually certain that it was the protection of the western harbour that the centurion and his professional advisers sought. It was in the end a north-easterly wind that destroyed the ship (v. 14). On the winds see much detail in *Begs.* 5.338–44; also Hemer (139–41).

Did Luke at this point recall Hesiod, *Works and Days* 618–630 (Delebecque 130)? It seems unlikely.

13. Again a sentence begins with a genitive absolute. ὑποπνεῖν is *to blow gently*. 'ὑπό in composition = "slightly", cf. Homer, *Iliad* 4.423, Ζεφύρου ὑποκινήσαντος' (Page 256; *OCT* prints separatim: ὕπο κινήσαντος). A light south wind was exactly what the seamen wanted; it would enable them to reach Phoenix without difficulty, and they supposed that they had already achieved (κεκρατηκέναι) their intention. κρατεῖν here with an abstract noun does not readily fall in with the 'rule' for the use with it of accusative and genitive (see BDR § 170.2, n. 3; M. 3.232). The voyage seemed as good as complete before it was begun.

ἄραντες: with this verb ἀγκύρας may once have been understood but it had come to mean no more than *to move* (*away*), *depart*. Thus Josephus, *Ant.* 13.86, ἄρας ἀπὸ τῆς Κρήτης κατέπλευσεν εἰς Κιλικίαν; at 7.97 and 9.229 it is used of journeys by land. Page and others add further examples from Thucydides, Plutarch, Lucian, and Philo.

ἆσσον is the comparative of ἄγχι (which does not occur in the NT) and is used as an elative, *as near as possible* (nearer than was usual); see BDR § 244.2, n. 3. It has been conjectured that ἆσσον may be an error for θᾶσσον (comparative of ταχύς), used similarly: *as quickly as possible*. The Latin versions, not recognizing the word, have de Asso(u); for Assos see 20.13.

For παραλέγεσθαι see v. 8.

In this verse h has the first person plural, tulimus … sub-legebamus. The Peshitto has *we sailed*.

14. The calm sea and the prosperous voyage did not last long (οὐ πολύ; cf. 1.5). βάλλειν is nearly always a transitive verb, but here it is intransitive, the wind rushed down upon them (in the background there may lie the thought of a reflexive—the wind hurled itself upon them). M. 3.52 notes parallels in Aeschylus, Euripides, Aeschines, and 1 Enoch 18.6.

κατ᾽ αὐτῆς may mean *against* (the ship; but what would be the antecedent?); more probably it is *down from it* (that is, from Crete). Sudden and violent off-shore winds are known in this area (Page 257). 'There is a noted tendency of a south wind in these climes to back suddenly to a violent north-easter, the well-known *gregale*' (Hemer 141). *Begs.* 4.331 suggests that 'the squall from Mount Ida drove them from the lee of Crete into the steady gale which had passed right over them while they were coasting'. The wind is described as τυφωνικός, translated by BA 1656 as *Wirbelsturm*, but LS 1838 *tempestuous* is better, if it is strong enough. The word (and some would have added, the wind itself) came from Τυφῶν, the father of the winds; see *Begs.* 5.338–44.

As a recognized (and probably not unfamiliar) phenomenon the wind had a name, Εὐρακύλων. Like Χῶρος this is probably a Latinism, at least in part, a compound of Εὖρος, south east wind (Bruce 1.458, east), and Aquila, north wind. For the compound cf. Εὐρόνοτος, a compound of εὖρος and νότος (Aristotle, *Meteorologica* 363b 22 (2.6)). The name Euraquilo suggests a wind blowing somewhat east of north. Εὐρακύλων is the reading of P⁷⁴ ℵ A B* latt (co); Ψ 𝔐 sy have Εὐροκλύδων, a south east wind that stirs up the waves (κλύδωνες). It may have been suggested to copyists by *Etymologicon Magnum* (ed. Gaisford) 772.30, τυφῶν γάρ ἐστιν ἡ τοῦ ἀνέμου σφόδρα πνοή, ὅς καὶ εὐροκλύδων καλεῖται. See further C. J. Hemer, 'Euraquilo and Malta', *JTS* 26 (1975), 100–11.

15. Again the narrative is carried forward by a genitive absolute— a double genitive absolute. The ship was seized (by the wind) and was unable to head into (ἀντοφθαλμεῖν, face up to, used metaphorically at Wisdom 12.14 and in the reading of D *al* at 6.10) it. There was nothing to do but let go and be carried along by it.

Composition with συν–, and the position of the participle, strengthen the sense: '... été saisi d'un coup' (Delebecque 131). Cf. Sophocles, *Electra* 1150f., πάντα γὰρ συναρπάσας θύελλ᾽ ὅπως βέβηκας. This is metaphor. Cf. Thucydides 6.104.3, ἄρας παρέπλει τὴν Ἰταλίαν, καὶ ἁρπασθεὶς ὑπ᾽ ἀνέμου ... ἀποφέρεται ἐς τὸ πέλαγος; Lucian, *Verae Historiae* 1.34, ἁρπασθέντες ἀνέμῳ σφοδρῷ.

ἐπιδόντες stands oddly on its own (see below). According to *ND* 1.49 it needs a reflexive pronoun. BDR § 241.5, n. 7 suggests an ellipse of τῷ ἀνέμῳ but τῷ ἀνέμῳ stands in the text and might be taken with ἐπιδόντες rather than with ἀντοφθαλμεῖν; possibly with both? It would be awkward to repeat it. In such a context as this one thinks of the English 'We let go', with no object, reflexive or other.

Western editors evidently felt the text to be unsatisfactory and added after ἐπιδόντες, τῷ πνέοντι [614 1518 have by a minor slip τῷ πλέοντι] καὶ συστείλαντες τὰ ἱστία (Metzger 497 gives as the authorities for this reading 82 (614) (1518) 2125 sy^(h.*)). It would not be easy to take τῷ πνέοντι as a complement to ἀνέμῳ (*before* ἐπιδόντες); it *might* be a substitute for a noun, ἄνεμος having already been used. The meaning is clear and is no doubt what Luke intended: We gave way to the wind, furled the sails, and ran before it. Marshall (408) notes that the foresail must have been left in place or it would have been impossible to steer. It does not however appear that much steering was being done. For the use of φέρεσθαι and the general picture, cf. Homer, *Odyssey* 5.343f.: σχεδίην ἀνέμοισι φέρεσθαι κάλλιπε.

16. Except that τρέχειν adds the notion of speed, ὑποτρέχειν does not differ in meaning from ὑποπλεῖν (vv. 4, 7): to sail under the lee of—in this case of a certain island. Even in this relatively favourable position we (the writer presumably associates himself with the crew as passengers are apt to do—see *FS* Hanson 53) were scarcely able to gain control of the dinghy, which presumably would in ordinary circumstances would be towed behind the ship but would now (v. 17) be lifted in board lest is should be damaged, or should damage the ship, through a collision caused by the storm.

νησίον is a diminutive, *a little island*; so M. 2.345 (but the whole section, 2.340–47, on Neuter Nouns in –ιον, should be studied; the matter is not a simple one). The island is named, but with considerable textual variation. NA²⁶ has Καῦδα, with P⁷⁴ ℵ² B (Ψ has Γαύδην, an orthographical and declensional variant) 1175 lat sy^p. ℵ* A^(vid) 33 81 614 945 1739 2495 *pc* vg^(mss) sy^h have Κλαῦδα; 𝔐 has Κλαύδην. Whatever the original text, the reference must be to a small island south of Crete, whose modern name is Gaudes (or Γαυδουῆσι, or Guzzo). It is not only in the NT MSS that the spelling of the name varies, and it is impossible to be confident of the original text. The Latin Gaudus (Gaudos) appears in Pliny, *Natural History* 4.61 (12); Pomponius Mela 2.7 (114), Ceudos. See further Hemer (142). Metzger (498) quotes *Begs.* 4.332 (also Haenchen 672) for the suggestion that Κλαῦδα was the Alexandrian, Καῦδα the Latin form of the name.

σκάφη was borrowed into Latin (e.g. Cicero, *De Inventione* 2.51 (154), funiculo qui a puppi religatur scapham annexam trahebat), and tended to drop out of Greek (Hemer 143). It is used in POxy 46.3269.9 (*ND* 3.17).

17. If in v. 13 ἄραντες referred (not simply to setting out but) to pulling up (the anchor), they (third person now, referring to the ship's crew) at this point did the same thing (ἄραντες) with the probably water-logged dinghy (σκάφη, v. 16).

Further steps were necessary. χρῆσθαι with the dative (βοήθειαν, accusative singular in ℵ* gig, and βοηθείας, genitive singular or accusative plural, in 6 36 81 453 614 1241 2464 *pc*, are not to be accepted) means *to make use of*; but in this context the meaning of βοήθεια is not clear. It may mean generally *help*; that is, the sailors made use of unspecified helping devices, designed to reduce danger by increasing their control of the ship and its stability. Or it may have a specific meaning as a nautical technical term. The latter is strongly suggested by a few passages such as Philo, *Joseph* 33, κυβερνήτης ταῖς τῶν πνευμάτων μεταβολαῖς συμμεταβάλλει τὰς πρὸς εὔπλοιαν βοηθείας, εὐθύνων τὸ σκάφος οὐχ ἑνὶ τρόπῳ. Cf. Aristotle, *Rhetoric* 2.5.18. If however the word does refer to specific procedures or instruments we do not know what they were. This does not justify the conjecture (S. A. Naber, *Mnemosyne* 23 (1895), 267–9) of βοείαις, 'ropes of ox-hide', though these might fit with one possible interpretation of ὑποζωννύντες. This word (for the participle in –υς see M. 2.205) occurs here only in the NT; see Polybius 27.3.3. It appears to mean *to provide a ship with* ὑποζώματα. Plato, *Republic* 616c, says that the rainbow holds together τὴν περιφεράν, the circle of the universe, οἷον τὰ ὑποζώματα τῶν τριήρων, '*the ropes* or *braces used to strengthen the hull of a trireme*' (LS 1811). It seems that the sailors perhaps used the recovered dinghy to frap the ship, running ropes round it, presumably at right angles to its axis, in order to prevent it from breaking up under the violence of the waves. The main objection to this interpretation is that the process described does not seem likely to have done anything to prevent what, according to the next words, the sailors feared. That fear, however, was dealt with by what follows.

They feared that they might be cast upon the Syrtis. ἐκπίπτειν serves as the passive of ἐκβάλλειν: BDR § 315, n. 1; M. 3.53. Thus Herodotus 8.13.1, φερόμενοι τῷ πνεύματι καὶ οὐκ εἰδότες τῇ ἐφέροντο ἐξέπιπτον πρὸς τὰς πέτρας; Euripides, *Helena* 409(416): 1211(1227); Xenophon, *Anabasis* 7.5.12. The Greater Syrtis (now the Gulf of Sidra) was the eastern, the Lesser Syrtis (now the Gulf of Gabès) the western, part of the wide stretch of water between Tunisia, Tripolitania, and Cyrenaica. It was reputed to be dangerous to shipping because the water was shallow and the tides caused the sandbanks to shift unpredictably. In 253 BC the Consuls Gnaeus Servilius and Gaius Sempronius had been obliged to jettison their stores in order to escape (Polybius 1.39.2–4). The area was feared and avoided if possible (αἱ φοβεραὶ καὶ τοῖς ἀκούουσιν Σύρτεις, Josephus, *War* 2.381; Sive per Syrtes iter aestuosas..., Horace, *Odes* 1.22). Would the sailors have feared this danger so soon? The Syrtes were about 375 miles from Cauda (Stählin 317). According to Acts they did so fear, and in consequence χαλάσαντες τὸ σκεῦος, οὕτως ἐφέροντο (for φέρεσθαι cf. the passage from Herodotus quoted above). 'Die klass. Freiheit, οὕτως zur Zusammenfassung des Inhalts einer vorangegangenen Partizipialkonstruktion zu verwenden, findet sich im NT nur Apg 20.11 ... und 27.17' (BDR § 425.6; cf. Delebecque 131).

What it was that the crew did we do not know. χαλᾶν means *to loose* or *to let down*; σκεῦος means *gear, equipment* in general, or might refer to a particular piece of equipment as a technical term whose meaning is now lost. BA (1507) think that probably the sea-anchor was meant; to drop this would slow the boat's movement towards the danger they feared. Similarly Preuschen (152), quoting Plutarch, *De Garrulitate* 10 (507A), νεὼς μὲν γὰρ ἁρπαγείσης ὑπὸ πνεύματος ἐπιλαμβάνονται σπείραις καὶ ἀγκύραις τὸ τάχος ἀμβλύνοντες. See also Schneider (2.391). This seems to be the meaning of the reading of g (not given in the apparatus of NA[26]; see *Begs.* 3.243): vas quoddam dimiserunt quod traheret. On the other hand 2495 *pc* s (sy[p]) have (for τὸ σκεῦος) τὰ ἱστία (τὸ ἱστίον); this probably means that the sailors loosed the previously reefed sails, with a view to sailing as close to the wind as they could (though Roloff (362) thinks that reefing of the sails is 'nicht ganz ausgeschlossen'). It will be remembered that the word σκεῦος was used for the sheet (?) of 10.11. These two variant readings (of g and of the Peshitto) represent guesses at the meaning of χαλάσαντες τὸ σκεῦος. They are interesting; one of them might be right; neither is the original text, which remains obscure. Note the occurrence of τὴν σκευήν in v. 19.

For ἐφέροντο, 36 453 *pc* sy[p] bo have ἐφερόμεθα, by assimilation to v. 15. ἐφέροντο is required by ἐχρῶντο. The sailors who handle the tackle are the subject in this verse.

On the verse see Hemer (143f.), and for a very clear statement of various possibilities Marshall (409).

18. The sentence begins with yet another genitive absolute, and the narrative returns briefly to the first person (ἡμῶν), since all those on board were storm-tossed (χειμαζομένων), but it immediately reverts to the third person, for it was the crew who, on the next day (τῇ ἑξῆς; cf. 21.1; 25.17), jettisoned the cargo (cf. Jonah 1.5, οἱ ναυτικοὶ ... ἐκβολὴν ἐποιήσαντο τῶν σκευῶν τῶν ἐν τῷ πλοίῳ; there are classical and Hellenistic parallels too). As in Jonah, the middle of ποιεῖν is correctly used, since ἐκβολήν ποιεῖσθαι is equivalent to a single verb. On the story of Jonah see the long passage of Pirqe R. Eliezer 10, quoted in StrB 1.644–647; also the Targum of Eccles. 3.6; עידן בחיר למשדי עסקא בימא בעידן נחשולא רבא (There is a time for throwing a thing into the sea, namely a time of great tempest). Cf.

Josephus, *War* 1.280, τοῦ φόρτου τὸ πλεῖον ἐκβαλὼν μόλις εἰς Ῥόδον διασῴζεται—a winter voyage.

ἐκβολή is a *throwing out*, presumably of part of the cargo. Some was left at v. 38, which constitutes a difficulty (*Begs.* 4.333) only if we suppose that a full clearance was made at this point. ἐποιοῦντο marks the beginning of the process, completed (as far as this stage was concerned) next day with the aorist ἔρριψαν. Schille thinks that they threw out what was on deck.

For χειμάζεσθαι see Thucydides 2.25.3; 8.99.3; Plato, *Ion* 540b. For ἐκβολή, see Aeschylus, *Seven against Thebes* 769–771; Aristotle, *Nicomachean Ethics* 3.1.5 (1110a); Lucian, *De Mercede Conductis* 1. The meaning of each word is clear and undisputed.

See Hemer (144).

19. On the third day (the next after the day of v. 18) the crew (reading ἔρριψαν, third person, with P⁷⁴ ℵ A B C 33 36 81 323 453 945 1175 1739 1891 *al* latt co; against ἐρρίψαμεν, first person, with Ψ 𝔐 sy) with their own hands (αὐτόχειρες, here only in the NT, but not uncommon elsewhere) threw out the ship's tackle (σκευή; see further below); not all the tackle (if this is what σκευή means)—see vv. 30, 32, (38), 40.

αὐτόχειρες: on the use of the adjective with the value of an adverb Delebecque (131) comments that it is 'très classique', and is almost confined (in the NT) to Luke; see Acts 12.10; 14.10; 20.6 D. He takes σκευή to mean "les agrès": 'les sacrifices sont chaque jour plus graves'.

LS 1607 take σκευή to mean *tackle*; that is, they do not distinguish it from σκεῦος (v. 17). This may well be correct; Luke characteristically varies his vocabulary. There are however other possibilities which, even if they are not convincing, are worthy of consideration. Smith (116), accepting the reading ἐρρίψαμεν (but the editor of the 4th edition corrects this), thinks of the mainyard, an extremely heavy weight, which the crew alone (v. 18) could not deal with, and which was thrown overboard only with the assistance of the passengers. A variant on this is noted by Hemer (145), who refers to the suggestion of D. J. Clark (*BT* 26 (1975), 144–6) that in v. 18 ἐποιοῦντο is conative; they tried by mechanical means to get rid of the mainyard and failed; next day their achieved their object with their own hands. But what other means would have been available? Cf. Jonah 1.5, where σκευων, usually taken to be the genitive plural of σκεῦος could be the genitive plural of σκευή.

At the end of the verse 614 2147 (*pc*) it vg^mss sy^h** sa add εἰς τὴν θάλασσαν. This must probably be regarded as another example of the Western inability to know when to stop.

20. Again the narrative proceeds by means of two absolute genitives. *For many days* (as at 13.31; 21.10, except that these have πλείους) neither sun nor stars were to be seen. Neither noun has the article, and BDR § 253.1, n. 2 suggest that this adds emphasis: '... scheint durch die Auslassung [of the articles] der Sinn "weder etwas von Sonne" verstärkt zu sein'. ἐπιφαίνειν is here intransitive; the English 'neither sun nor stars showed' is similar.

χειμῶνος οὐκ ὀλίγου is characteristic Lucan litotes; see 12.18. τε simply adds a new statement Plutarch, *Timoleon* 28 (250), τοῦ χειμῶνος ἐπικειμένου, is very similar.

λοιπόν, used adverbially in a variety of senses, is here *finally*; see BDR § 160.2, n. 3, with references; also BA 974, with examples. This meaning however is not easily reconciled with BA 1301, where the imperfect περιῃρεῖτο is rendered 'jede Hoffnung entschwand allmählich'. One could perhaps say in English, 'All hope was finally disappearing'. The use of τοῦ with the infinitive is characteristic of Luke. The genitive of the cognate noun could also be used. Cf. Aristophanes, *Thesmophoriazousai* 946 (953), κοὐκ ἔστιν ἔτ᾽ ἐλπὶς οὐδεμία σωτηρίας; Thucydides 1.65.1, ἐλπίδα οὐδεμίαν ἔχων σωτηρίας.

21. A new feature of the situation is introduced by another genitive absolute. People on board were short of food, not because there was nothing to eat (it is not till v. 38 that food is thrown overboard) but because it was not being eaten—through preoccupation, fear, and no doubt seasickness. The Vulgate has *jejunatio*. For πολλῆς ἀσιτίας ὑπαρχούσης cf. 21.40, πολλῆς δὲ σιγῆς γενομένης. With this situation Paul attempts to deal by allaying fear; he seems to have no success till v. 36. 'Wogegen sich Paulus wendet, das ist die Hoffnungslosigkeit' (Bauernfeind 274).

τότε σταθείς: the reference of τότε is not clear. For Paul's standing in the midst of *them* (the ship's company as a whole?) cf. 17.22, σταθεὶς ... ἐν μέσῳ τοῦ Ἀρείου Πάγου. Page (260) recalls also the 'Iustum et tenacem propositi virum ... inquieti ... Hadriae' (Horace, *Odes* 3.3.1,5); an interesting coincidence. One would be inclined to think Paul's 'I-told-you-so' approach unlikely to win him friends (and thus a mark of Lucan fiction?), but Page (260), noting the μέν solitarium (cf. 1.1; 3.21; 28.22; and see BDR § 447.2c, n. 15) comments, 'The words "but you did not listen" are omitted in courtesy.'

For the vocative ἄνδρες cf. v. 10; no further definition would suit them all. The vocative is correctly preceded by ὦ (BDR § 146.3, n. 4; M. 3.33). Paul refers back to the advice he gave at Fair Havens (v. 10). πειθαρχεῖν takes as usual a dative; see MM 500. For ἀνάγεσθαι see v. 2, for ὕβρις and ζημία, v. 10. In the latter part of the verse there is an ambiguity which is best explained in a detailed note in *Begs.* 4.334. There are, for κερδῆσαι ... ζημίαν, two possibilities. (i) The clause means (and there are many parallels in Greek) to gain by

avoiding what is detrimental, that is "to *avoid* this danger and loss";
(ii) to *incur* something disadvantageous. If (ii) is chosen, the μή
negates both ἀνάγεσθαι and κερδῆσαι: If you had listened to me you
would *not* have set out and would *not* have incurred damage and loss;
if (i) is chosen, the μή negatives ἀνάγεσθαι only: ... you would *not*
have set out and would have avoided danger and loss. Both ways of
taking the clause make good—indeed the same—sense.

The verse has three Lucan features: ἔδει, μέν solitarium,
πειθαρχεῖν. Is it then an insertion into a secular sea-story designed
to bring it into the story of Paul? Certainly this verse (and the whole
of vv. 21–26) makes Paul stand out as a commanding character. But
perhaps he was one. See pp. 1178f.

22. Paul is now (τὰ νῦν is perhaps more emphatic than the simple
νῦν would be; cf. e.g. 4.29; 17.30) able to urge his hearers to be of
good cheer. παραινεῖν is followed by an accusative and infinitive; of
this M. 3.138 says, 'the accus. of the object with the infin. after
παραινέω is a mark of literary style'. This is at first sight surprising,
since the usual Attic construction is that the dative should follow
παραινεῖν; so BA 1246, BDR § 152.3, n. 3, and examples in LS
1310; also Blass (278); Radermacher (98). The point presumably is
that Turner wishes to indicate that ὑμᾶς should be taken with the
infinitive rather than with παραινῶ: I urge that you be of good cheer
(not, I urge you to be of good cheer). So perhaps BDR § 392.1,
n. 5.

There will be no throwing away, *loss* (ἀποβολήν) of any human
life; (loss) only of the ship. For πλήν = *only* see BDR § 449.2. This
prediction differs from that of v. 10; it is given on supernatural
authority (vv. 23, 24). For the loss of the ship see v. 41; for the safe
arrival of all the travellers see v. 44.

23. Paul introduces the grounds (γάρ) for the encouragement that
he offers; it derives from an angelic message, delivered ταύτῃ τῇ
νυκτί; the dative expresses 'time when', and, unless Paul is speaking
in the night (which seems *prima facie* unlikely, but see on v. 33),
must mean 'the night just past'—last night. Rapske (*The Book of
Acts* 3.359) quotes Krodel to the effect that Christian readers would
take the angel to be Christ—an 'angel Christology'. In view of what
is said elsewhere in Acts about Christ and about angels this seems
very improbable.

The order of words is striking. According to Haenchen (674) it is
Lucan, but even so it is unusual. παρέστη stands first, though there
seems to be no reason why it should bear the emphasis that this
position would give it. The word itself is common in narratives of
epiphanies, angelic visitations, and the like. Cf. 12.7 (ἐπέστη);
Josephus, *Ant.* 1.341, ὁ θεὸς παραστὰς [Jacob] ἐκέλευσε θαρρεῖν;
Plutarch, *Lysander* 20 (444), ἔνιοι ... φασιν αὐτῷ παραστῆναι τὸν

Ἄμμωνα. It is interesting that in the next verse another semi-technical use of the same verb appears. τοῦ θεοῦ not only precedes ἄγγελος but is separated from it by the relative clause, which thus receives some prominence. This is not unimportant. It has often been pointed out (e.g. Conzelmann 144) that supernatural visitations and supernatural protection are characteristic of the θεῖος ἀνήρ; it is characteristic of Luke, recognizing this, to point out that though in some respects Paul may resemble figures represented as θεῖοι ἄνδρες, he is in fact no such thing. He is the property (οὗ εἰμι) and the servant (ᾧ λατρεύω) of another, who alone can bear the title θεός. See 10.26; 14.15; et al. Elsewhere in Acts λατρεύειν is used for service of the God of Israel (7.7, 42; 26.7); 24.14 (λατρεύω τῷ πατρῴῳ θεῷ) is particularly important. Paul is not speaking here of Christ as θεός. The service implied here is the same as that described in Rom. 1.9 (ᾧ λατρεύω ... ἐν τῷ εὐαγγελίῳ τοῦ υἱοῦ αὐτοῦ). It is the service of preacher and evangelist.

'DEI esse, summa religionis; qua fides, amor, spes comprehenditur. Correlatum, DEO servire' (Bengel 485).

24. The words of the angel are reported. μὴ φοβοῦ is characteristic of such visitations (cf. 18.9; also Lk 1.13, 30; 2.10; 5.10; also Lucian, *Dialogi Deorum* 20.7). Paul is assured that what is (for him) the goal of the journey will be reached: he will stand before Caesar, to whom he has appealed (25.11, 12). παραστῆναι (used in v. 23 of the angel) is used of appearing before a judge, but especially in the (transitive) middle for producing a witness or defendant in court (e.g. Plato, *Republic* 555b, παραστησώμεθ᾿ αὐτὸν εἰς κρίσιν). Cf. also Rom. 14.10.

καὶ ἰδού is not translation Greek, but an imitation of the style of the Greek OT (suitable for angels) where it translates והנה. For Paul to appear before Caesar it is necessary only that he should escape the storm, but as a favour (χάρις) God has granted (κεχάρισται) to him (the lives of) all those who are sailing with him. It is implied, not quite necessarily, that Paul has prayed for his fellow travellers.

25. εὐθυμεῖτε takes up εὐθυμεῖν in v. 22. Paul believes God; that is, not, he trusts in God, but he accepts as true the message that God has sent. God will do what he has said he will do; hence (διό), εὐθυμεῖτε.

καθ᾿ ὃν τρόπον: cf. 15.11. οὕτως is not strictly necessary. Cf. Thucydides 4.92.7, πιστεύσαντες τῷ θεῷ πρὸς ἡμῶν ἔσεσθαι.

26. There is a qualification of the promise of safety in the storm. The ship will be cast (ἐκπίπτειν serves as a passive to ἐκβάλλειν, as at v. 17; see the note there) on a certain island. The angel did not specify the island; it is not identified till 28.1. Schneider (2.394), quoting Wikenhauser, distinguishes the prediction of shipwreck from the angel's message, from which it is an inference.

δεῖ: 'Das Schiff "muss" an einer Insel stranden. Damit ist die Peripetie in der Darstellung der bedrohlichen Irrfahrt vorbereitet und die kommende Rettung vorweg theologisch gedeutet' (Pesch 2.291). This makes too much of δεῖ, but undoubtedly Luke means to represent the whole course of action as leading Paul, under God's providence, to Rome.

27. The time of action of the main clause (ὑπενόουν οἱ ναῦται) is given threefold determination: (a) in a temporal clause introduced by ὡς (temporal ὡς is characteristic of Acts; see v. 1), When the 14th night came (ἐπεγένετο, A 81 *pc* vg, differs little from the simple ἐγένετο); (b) by a genitive absolute, διαφερομένων (for the meaning of this verb see below) ἐν τῷ 'Αδρίᾳ (see below); (c) by the adverbial phrase κατὰ μέσον τῆς νυκτός, about the middle of the night.

Smith (124–8) calculates that 13 or 14 days would be the time required, under the conditions described, for the passage from Cauda to Malta. The converse also applies (128): '... there is no other place [than Malta] agreeing, either in name or description, within the limits to which we are tied down by calculations founded upon the narrative'. On this however see further on 28.1–10.

LS 417 take διαφέρεσθαι to mean *tossed about*; Delebecque (132) agrees with this, rendering *ballottés*, and citing Plutarch, *Galba* 26 (1065); *De his qui sero a Numine puniuntur* 6 (552C). To these passages may be added Philo, *De Migratione Abrahami* 148, ὥσπερ σκάφος ὑπ' ἐναντίων πνευμάτων διαφερόμενον, Bruce (1.462) takes the word to mean *drifting* (not up and down but) *across*, and compares διαπλεύσαντες in v. 5. It should be noted however that διαπλεύσαντες takes an accusative object (τὸ πέλαγος) whereas διαφερομένων is followed by ἐν τῷ 'Αδρίᾳ; it would be hard to translate this 'drifting across Adria'. *Adria* is more than what is now known as the Adriatic Sea. 'At its maximum the Ionian Sea extended all the way West to East from Gibraltar to the Levant, and ... the Adriatic Sea at its maximum stretched North to South from Venice to North Africa. Hence the area between Italy, Sicily, and Epirus sometimes was all Ionian, sometimes all Adria, sometimes Adria in the northern part, Ionian in the southern part' (*Begs.* 4.335). See Ptolemy, *Geography* 3.4.1; 3.15.1; 3.17.1; cf. Josephus, *Life* 15.

μέσον τῆς νυκτός; cf. 16.25, μεσονύκτιον; Xenophon, *Anabasis* 1.8.8, ἦν μέσον ἡμέρας.

At this time the sailors supposed, thought, προσάγειν τινὰ αὐτοῖς χώραν. This is the text of NA[26]; it is read by ℵ[c] A C Ψ 𝔐. This is a strange expression; they thought that a certain land was approaching them. This does in fact make sense as a matter of relative motion, and it is not without precedent. Blass (279) quotes the sixth century commentator on Epictetus, Simplicius 38: δι' ἀπειρίαν [sailors] δοκοῦσιν οὐκ αὐτοὶ προσιέναι τῇ πέτρᾳ, ἀλλὰ τὴν πέτραν κατ' ὀλίγον ἐπ' αὐτοὺς ἰέναι. Cf. Vergil, *Aeneid* 3.72, provehimur portu terraeque urbesque recedunt. There are several variants. προσεγγίζειν (614 2147 2495 (sy)) makes no difference in meaning: a certain land was drawing near to them. προαγαγεῖν (ℵ* (*pc*)) might be taken to mean that land was ahead of them, but it is hard to understand why anyone should express himself in this way. B² has προσανέχειν. It might be just possible to make this mean that land was awaiting them, that is, that it was just ahead. But B* has προσαχεῖν. This could be regarded as a Doric form (α for η) of προσηχεῖν *to resound* or *re-echo* (so LS 1513). What gives this significance is that g has *resonare sibi aliquam regionem*, and s, *resonare sibi quandam regionem*. M. 2.71 describes this as a very attractive reading 'which accounts for the variants'. It 'has the difficulty of being a Doric (etc.) form which disagrees with the common derivatives of the same root: κατηχεῖν and ἦχος are conspicuous in the NT. Could it have been used by sailors from Crete, Cyprus, Lesbos, Corinth, or some other maritime country outside the Ionic-Attic area, appropriated as a t.t.?' See on the other hand M. 3.51, where προσάγειν is assumed without reference to variants. Metzger (498) prefers προσάγειν on the ground that its 'harshness' may have given rise to the other readings, and so does Ropes (*Begs.* 3.245) ('προσάγειν, although itself difficult, is to be preferred'). Clark (385) however prefers προσαχεῖν (= προσηχεῖν = resonare). Hemer (146) takes up the suggestion of Smith (119–22) that the sailors became aware of the breakers on the rocky point of Koura, in the neighbourhood of St Paul's Bay (see on v. 28 and 28.1). The reading must remain doubtful; fortunately the meaning is not. The sailors became aware that they were not far from land.

28. Suspicion that the ship was approaching land naturally led the sailors to take soundings (βολίζειν, a word of very scanty attestation). The result was 20 ὀργυιαί (for the accent see below). The ὄργυια was the combined length of the outstretched arms, about 6 feet, or 1 fathom (1.85 m.); a nautical technical term. The water (at 120 feet) was fairly deep, but it was growing shallower. διαστήσαντες implies τὴν ναῦν as object (BA 393); having moved the boat (the narrative suggests that the wind was in any case moving the boat) a little they sounded again and found a depth of 15 fathoms, 30 feet less water. Blass (279) understands the construction differently: 'βραχὺ διαστησ. = βρ. διάστημα (5.7) ποιήσαντες, quo et de tempore et de loco accipi potest.' The figures seem to be compatible with data derived from St Paul's Bay, Malta.

On ὄργυια LS 1246 have 'Proparox. in nom. and acc. sg.' as used in Homer, 'oxyt. or perispom. in other cases.' More fully Winer-

Schmiedel (72 = § 6.7): 'Zwischen ὄργυιἄ und ὀργυιᾶ (AG 27.28) schwankte die Sprache so, dass die alten Grammatiker ernstlich vorzuschreiben scheinen, die Endung sei theils (sei es im Plural oder auf allen zweifellos langen Vocalen) betont, theils (im Sing. bzw. nur im Nom. Sing. u. pl.) unbetont.' Cf. M. 2.58; BA (1174); Hemer (147).

29. The rapidly shelving seabed meant that it was imperative to halt the ship's motion or at least reduce its speed. φοβούμενοι and ῥίψαντες will go with the third person εὔχοντο and refer to the sailors; the first person ἐκπέσωμεν (81 326 945 1739 1891 *al* have ἐκπέσωσιν) refers in a natural way (see *FS* A. T. Hanson 53) to all who were on board.

τε (A B C 𝔐) gives a better connection than δέ (P⁷⁴ ℵ Ψ 33 81 614 1175 2495 *al* syʰ); φοβούμενοι is positively connected with v. 28 and an adversative particle is not called for. The force of μή (*lest*, becoming *lest perhaps*) is strengthened by the addition of που (for which πῶς and ποτε are more frequently used). As at vv. 17, 26 ἐκπίπτειν is used as the passive of ἐκβάλλειν. The danger was that the ship might be thrown by wind and wave upon τραχεῖς τόπους, rocky (literally rough, jagged) places. τραχύς is a stock epithet of Ithaca (Homer, *Odyssey* 9.27; 10.417). For τραχεῖς, P⁷⁴ 104 2495 *pc* have βραχεῖς. This may be a slip; otherwise it is hard to make a better guess at its meaning than 'auf enge [?] Stellen' (Schneider 2.386). To avoid the danger of running into the rocks the sailors let down (literally, *threw*, ῥίψαντες) four anchors from the stern. It was usual to anchor by the bows (e.g. Vergil, *Aeneid* 3.277, ancora de prora iacitur), but since the ship was driving before the wind (vv. 15, 17) this would be the natural way to check its progress; see however v. 30. What had to be avoded at all costs was allowing the ship to take heavy seas broadside on. See Smith (133).

ηὔχοντο ἡμέραν γενέσθαι, primarily no doubt in order to be able to see and choose the best place at which to beach the ship. Homer, *Odyssey* 9.151, 436 (ἐμείναμεν Ἠῶ δῖαν) is sometimes quoted as a parallel, but in these two lines Odysseus and his men are on shore. See also Longus, *Daphnis and Chloe* 2.8, διὰ τοῦτο θᾶττον εὐχόμεθα γενέσθαι τὴν ἡμέραν.

At the end of the verse g vgᵐˢˢ add ut sciremus an salvi esse possimus (vgᵐˢˢ possemus). This seems to represent τοῦ εἰδέναι εἰ σωθῆναι δυνάμεθα. But the clause may never have existed otherwise than as a Latin Western expansion.

30. Again the narrative is taken forward by means of a genitive absolute, the main indicative verb not appearing till v. 31. Having let down anchors from the stern (v. 29) the sailors prepared to let down more from the bow (πρῴρης, instead of the expected πρῴρας—see

BDR § 43.1, n. 1). It may be supposed that the stern anchors had checked the forward motion of the ship and that the sailors' intention (if it was not that which Luke attributes to them) was to maintain the ship's position in the line of the wind, and so to prevent it from being struck broadside by the heavy seas. This, it seems, would make sense, and whereas the sailors would simply drop anchors over the stern they would need the dinghy to stretch out (ἐκτείνειν) the anchor lines from the bow. For χαλᾶν see v. 17; the dinghy would have to be let down by rope (see v. 32) over the high prow of the ship. For σκάφη see v. 16.

According to Luke, the sailors were deceiving the passengers; it was not their intention to lower anchors but to escape from what they presumably regarded as a doomed ship. Deceit is indicated both by προφάσει, frequently used for *falsely alleged motive* (so LS 1539, s.v. I 2; as e.g. Thucydides 3.86.2, οἱ ᾿Αθηναῖοι ... μὲν ... προφάσει, βουλόμενοι δὲ ...; 6.76.1), and by ὡς, which itself means *under pretence of* (M. 3.158), giving not so much the subjective basis (BDR § 425.3) of an action as the basis suggested, affirmed, by the actor. For ὡς, see 23.15, 20.

Begs. 4.335f. argues strongly that Luke here misrepresents the sailors; they were in fact attempting to do what they said they were doing, would not have attempted to escape in a dark and stormy night in a tiny boat that would hold very few of them, and must have been very sorry to lose the dinghy through the soldiers' precipitate action. The dinghy would have helped them to beach the boat properly and would have assisted passage from the boat to land. It is worth observing that if Luke was making a mistake he was probably making a mistake about something that really happened; one can hardly suppose that he invented an action and invented also, without letting his reader into the secret, a mistaken interpretation of it. Hanson (249) agrees with *Begs.* Schille (466) argues that this observation fails to recognize the literary character of the story; Luke is describing a panic. Conzelmann (145) points out that the flight of the crew is a regular feature in Greek stories; see Achilles Tatius 3.3; Petronius 102, cf. 114.

At the end of the verse (cf v. 29), gig vg^mss add, 'ut tutius navis staret'. This Clark includes as part of the Western text in the form τοῦ ἀσφαλέστερον ... τὸ πλοῖον ἑστάναι.

31. Paul evidently (according to Luke) viewed with dismay what he thought to be the impending departure of the only persons with sailing skills. With them all prospect of safety would disappear. (But could he not as before rely on the divine promise?) It is surprising that he should address the soldiers directly, as well as their commanding officer. And one would have thought that even if some sailors escaped (presumably to the land which the boat seemed to be approaching (v. 28)) enough would have been left, unable to get into the dinghy, to run the ship.

It is worth observing, without prejudice, that what seems improbable as an account of what really happened must also seem improbable in a work of fiction written by an author with any concern for verisimilitude. It may be that Luke's motive was to show (in v. 32) the respect shown to Paul, 'der auch in der Mitternacht wachsam auf Posten ist' (Stählin 319), by the soldiers, who immediately acted on his advice.

32. If the sailors were not to be allowed to escape in the dinghy the simplest, but not necessarily the wisest, course was to get rid of the dinghy. This the soldiers did. It was suspended over the side of the ship (v. 30) and the soldiers simply cut the ropes and permitted (εἴασαν; ἐᾶν occurs 7 times in Acts, twice in Lk., thrice in the rest of the NT) it to fall away. This act was, according to *Begs.* 4.336, responsible for the loss of the ship. 'It was only necessary to wait for the end of the gale, and row ashore in comfort.' It would have been unnecessary to beach the ship and expose it to the violence of the sea (vv. 40, 41).

Delebecque (133) thinks that Luke may have remembered Homer, *Odyssey* 10.27; Xenophon, *Hellenica* 1.6.21. It seems very unlikely.

33. This verse (and the following paragraph) might well have been introduced by v. 21a; see on that verse. It is surprising that the reference to food should come a second time; it may be that Luke took what we read in v. 21 out of the present material and used it to introduce the prediction he ascribes to Paul in vv. 22–26. Conzelmann (145), and others, take vv. 33–36 to be an insertion; see on v. 37.

According to *Begs.* 4.336 (comparing μέχρι at 10.30, and the African rendering—in die quo—of ἄχρι in 1.2), 'ἄχρι gives no good sense if it be rendered ''until'' '. The clause is translated, 'And when it was nearly day'. It is true that this is what the reader would expect, but it is hardly justifiable as a rendering of ἄχρι δὲ οὗ, especially as this is followed by the imperfect παρεκάλει. The imperfect is indeed often used in verbs of requesting, entreating, and the like (these in themselves represent incomplete action; see M. 3.65; BDR § 455.3b, n. 6), but παρεκάλει may well be iterative: Until day was about to break, Paul kept on exhorting ... It may be that this should be connected with v. 23, ταύτῃ τῇ νυκτί, if this means, In this night, which is not yet over (see the note). This could bear on the construction of the chapter, especially if it is thought to include 'Pauline' insertions into an independent sea-voyage story; on this see pp. 1178f.

Paul exhorted them all to partake of food. If ἅπαντας is to be distinguished as a stronger word than πάντας, it will be intended to make the point that Paul had in mind his fellow passengers, the soldiers, and the sailors. This however would be the natural meaning if πάντας were used. It may be no more than a mannerism: ἅπας occurs in Lk. 11 times, in Acts 10 times, in the rest of the NT 11 times. For taking food Paul uses here μεταλαμβάνειν with the genitive; later in the verse, προσλαμβάνεσθαι with the accusative; in v. 34 μεταλαμβάνειν (but H L P Ψ 049 326 1241 2495 have προσλαμβάνεσθαι) and the genitive; in v. 35, ἐσθίειν with no object; in v. 36, προσλαμβάνεσθαι with the genitive. LS 1113 quote only Acts for μεταλαμβάνειν with the meaning *to partake of food*, but it is clear that this meaning was coming into use in the post-classical period; so Josephus, *War* 2.143; PRyl 2.77.19 (BA 1035). For the use of προσλαμβάνεσθαι for taking food MM 549f. offer nothing and BA 1436 only *Clementine Homilies* 3.21 (active). See BDR § 169.2, n. 5.

Paul's exhortation begins with another curious expression of time. (cf. v. 27). BDR § 161.3, n. 6 describe τεσσαρεσκαιδεκάτην σήμερον ἡμέραν προσδοκῶντες as a 'besondere Redensart' (as it is), and translate, 'jetzt schon den 14. Tag wartend'. This can only mean (as *prima facie* the Greek can only mean), 'We are now awaiting the 14th day'. This presumably is to be associated with the 14th night (in v. 27), and the statement at the beginning of the present verse that day was about to break. If nights are counted before days, we have now had almost the whole of the 14th night and are now awaiting the imminent beginning of the 14th day (the omission of the article before τεσσαρεσκαιδεκάτην follows old custom) of flying before the NE wind. We know already from v. 21 that this period had been marked by πολλὴ ἀσιτία. This is now expressed in the words ἄσιτοι διατελεῖτε. Radermacher (169) argues from Phrynichus's (244—he says 277) treatment of τυγχάνειν that 'correct' use would have included the participle (in this verse the plural ὄντες); similarly BDR § 414.1, n. 4. But (if it is in any case legitimate to argue from τυγχάνειν to διατελεῖν) Rutherford's (342) comment should be observed. 'Even in the best age the participle of the substantive verb was sometimes carelessly omitted after τυγχάνω. If the prose instances are set aside as of no importance in such an inquiry, there is a line of Aristophanes to confute such scholars as would correct the texts of prose writers by the dictum of Phrynichus—

καὶ τῶν θεατῶν εἴ τις εὔνους τυγχάνει.

Ecclesiazusae 1141.'

Thus ἄσιτοι διατελεῖτε is You continue without food, or better, You have been (and still are) continuing without food. For the adjective cf. Sophocles, *Ajax* 324, ἄσιτος ἀνήρ, ἄποτος; Galen, *On Phlebotomy* 11.242.

μηθείς occurs here only in the NT; for οὐθείς see 15.9; 19.27; 20.33; 26.26.

'Nachtstunden der äussersten Spannung. Ein Deuteropaulus würde jetzt gewiss gesagt haben: ''Diese Stunden wollen wir in ununterbrochenem Gebet durchleben." Der stattdessen sagte: "Wir wollen endlich etwas essen" ... das ist der historische Paulus gewesen' (Bauernfeind 275). A good remark; but one cannot exclude the possibility that a Deuteropaulus may have learned something from the historische Paulus.

34. The request of v. 33 is now repeated in the first person of direct speech. τοῦτο refers back to the infinitive, μεταλαβεῖν τροφῆς. For μεταλαβεῖν, H L P Ψ 049 326 1241 2495 𝔐 have προσλαβεῖν. ὑπάρχει seems unnecessary; ἐστιν would suffice. πρὸς τῆς ὑμετέρας (A L P 326 614 1241 *pm* w sy^h have ἡμετέρας) σωτηρίας is the only occurrence in the NT of πρός with the genitive. Cf. Thucydides 3.59.1, οὐ πρὸς τῆς ὑμετέρας δόξης ... τάδε; Josephus, *Ant.* 16.313, πρὸς τῆς τοῦ βασιλεύοντος ἐδόκει σωτηρίας. σωτηρία must here refer to physical well-being—a not unimportant consideration.

In the next clause οὐδενός stands first for emphasis: Not one of you will lose a hair ... The promise recalls that of v. 22; the expression is proverbial; cf. 1 Sam. 14.45; 2 Sam. 14.11; 1 Kings 1.52; Lk. 12.7 = Mt. 10.30; Lk. 21.18 is important because it is a Lucan insertion. Luke, we may suppose, liked the image. For ἀπολεῖται, Ψ 𝔐 gig sy^h sa have πεσεῖται. After ὑπάρχει gig adds spero enim in deo meo quia; this MS shows great freedom in handling the wording of the text.

Bruce 1.465 observes that if γάρ is omitted from the sentence οὐδενὸς ... ἀπολεῖται what is left is a perfect hexameter. Interesting; but probably a pure coincidence.

35, 36. To give weight to his words Paul initiates a meal in words and acts that have important parallels; see *FS* A. T. Hanson (60). These may be set out as follows:

λαβὼν ἄρτον: cf. λαβὼν ἄρτον, Lk. 22.19; λαβὼν δὲ τοὺς πέντε ἄρτους, Lk. 9.16

εὐχαρίστησεν τῷ θεῷ; cf. εὐχαριστήσας ... εὐχαριστήσας, Lk. 22.17, 19; εὐλόγησεν, Lk. 9.16

κλάσας: cf. ἔκλασεν, Lk. 22.19; κατέκλασεν, Lk. 9.16

ἤρξατο ἐσθίειν: cf. ἐπιθυμίᾳ ἐπεθύμησα τοῦτο τὸ πάσχα φαγεῖν, Lk. 22.15

ἐπιδιδοὺς καὶ ἡμῖν (614 2147 *pc* sy^h** sa): cf. διαμερίσατε εἰς ἑαυτούς, Lk. 22.17; ἔδωκεν αὐτοῖς, Lk. 22.19; ἐδίδου τοῖς μαθηταῖς, Lk. 9.16

προσελάβοντο τροφῆς: cf. ἔφαγον καὶ ἐχορτάσθησαν πάντες, Lk. 9.17

We may compare also the references to the breaking of bread at Lk. 24.30, 35; Acts 2.42, 46; 20.7, 11. As far as language goes, this is more 'eucharistic' than any other passage in Acts. Here only does the verb εὐχαριστεῖν occur, and here only is the leading figure said to take (λαμβάνειν) the loaf before breaking it. Black, *AA* 125 (cf. Wilcox 125) may be right in describing λαμβάνειν thus used as an auxiliary and seeing its origin in Aramaic usage, but the coincidence in language with that of the Last Supper cannot be missed and can hardly be accidental. At the same time the context demands not a purely symbolic meal but a meal, eaten to overcome the physical hunger of men who for days been too busy and too preoccupied to eat. Paul began to eat and the others—all of them, πάντες— followed his example. The Christians did not withdraw to hold a special, still less a secret, rite of their own. ἐνώπιον πάντων is clear.

Luke's readers can hardly have failed to note the eucharistic allusions; yet these terms and allusions are all such as are rooted in ordinary Jewish practice—a meal began with the blessing of God and the breaking of bread. No explanation of the data is satisfactory that does not include the inference that they belong to a time, probably lasting at least till the date of the composition of Acts, in which the eucharist (understood in the narrow sense of a rite involving the symbolic eating and drinking of bread and wine to which a theological interpretation is attached) was not yet separated from a fellowship meal in which normal quantities of food and drink were consumed. This inference is consistent with the other references in Acts to the breaking of bread (and, it may be added, with Pauline and other NT evidence; see *1 Corinthians* 23 1–5, 26 1–77; *CMS* 60–76).

The question, Is the meal described in this chapter a eucharistic meal or not? has been given diverse answers. Calvin (2.295) makes no reference to the possibility that the eucharist may be in mind. It was not a eucharist but 'einen Akt der Ermutigung und vielleicht auch ... ein Wunder, durch das Paulus die Seekrankheit geheilt hat' (Roloff 364). The meal was a eucharist understood as a φάρμακον ἀθανασίας (Schille 467). 'Lukas deutet dergleichen [a prefiguring of the eucharist] nicht an' (Haenchen 676). It was certainly not 'das christliche Abendmahl' (Schmithals 232). Weiser (664f.) attempts a difficult distinction: 'Auf diese Weise und durch die auffällige Aussage, dass Paulus ''zu essen begann'' und erst ''dann alle Speisen zu sich nahmen'', macht Lukas deutlich, dass zwar nicht alle das eucharistische Brot empfingen, aber doch alle Anteil erhielten an der im eucharistischen Mahl gegenwärtigen Rettungsmahl des auferstandenen erhöhten Herrn.' Pesch (2.292) is somewhat similar: The 'Beschreibung an die Speisungswundererzählungen erinnert, aber nicht auf eine Eucharistiefeier hinweist.' Cf. Rackham (477). Schneider (2.397) goes further: 'Die Mahlzeit hat eine ähnliche Transparenz auf die Eucharistie hin, wie das Stichwort σωτηρία in V.34b auf die Bedeutung ''Heil'' hin offen ist. Der Christ weiss, dass das Herrenmahl als Ausdruck der ''Hoffnung'' (vgl. V.20) dem

"Heil" dient (vgl. V.34b).' Stählin (320) goes farther still. There '... kann kein Zweifel sein, dass er [Luke] ein irgendwie sakramentales Mahl ... skizzieren wollte, wenn auch vielleicht nicht ein eigentliches Herrenmahl'.

All these interpretations, instructive as they are, fail because they assume something like the clear developed distinction between an 'ordinary' meal and a 'sacramental' or 'eucharistic' meal, between bread and eucharistic bread.

For the breaking of bread (κλάσας) see on 2.42; also for the lack of any reference to wine. Of course, the use of wine during a storm at sea would have presented very considerable practical difficulties.

For εὔθυμοι see on vv. 22, 25 (εὐθυμεῖν).

προσελάβοντο, aorist middle, the 'correct' form (see v. 33), is read by B C 𝔐. There are several variants. μετελάμβανον (614 2147 pc) assimilates to μεταλαβεῖν in v. 34, and so (in the use of active rather than middle) do προσέλαβεν (A Ψ 1175 pc) and προσελάμβανον (2495). μεταλαβαν (sic) though read by ℵ as well as 1241, bears witness only to careless inattention.

37. The numbering of those on board the ship follows upon the πάντες of v. 36: Luke will tell his readers what πάντες means. Schneider (2.397) however thinks that the number would link originally with v. 32. The article before πᾶσαι indicates the totality of persons present (M. 3.201—'We were in all ...'; Zerwick § 188; BDR § 275.3, n. 6). Unfortunately the number is textually uncertain. The majority of witnesses have διακόσιαι ἑβδομήκοντα ἕξ, 276; but B (pc) sa have ὡς ἑβδομήκοντα ἕξ, about 76. The textual problem is complicated by the fact that 276, if not written in words, would be written COϚ, and 76 as OϚ. Metzger (499f.) represents a common opinion in the words, The reading of B sa 'probably arose by taking ΠΛΟΙΩCOϚ as ΠΛΟΙΩΩCOϚ. In any case, ὡς with an exact statement of number is inappropriate (despite Luke's penchant for qualifying numbers by using ὡς or ὡσεί, cf. Lk. 3.23; Acts 2.41; 4.4; 5.7, 36; 10.3; 13.18, 20; 19.7, 34).' Metzger notes other variants: A has 275; 69 and Ephraim have 270; bo^mss have 176 or 876; 522 and l^680 have 76; Epiphanius has *about* (ὡς) 70. Metzger (similarly Ropes, *Begs.* 3.247) is probably right but like most commentators does not note the problem of the iota subscript, which in uncials is often though not always written adscript. Thus the two readings discussed might well be not as given above but ΠΛΟΙΩICOϚ and ΠΛΟΙΩΙΩCOϚ. This makes simple confusion less likely. The number 276 is not impossibly large; Josephus (*Life* 15) records his own experience of shipwreck (in Adria), as a result of which about 600 were obliged to swim all night. On the size of ships see Smith (187–90) and Hemer (149f.) A surprising number of commentators repeat the statement that 276 is the sum of the digits from 1 to 24. It is not; it is the sum of the digits from 1 to 23. The fact seems in any case irrelevant; there is no hint of numerical or other symbolism here.

38. When they were *satisfied* (κορεννύναι occurs only here and at 1 Cor. 4.8 in the NT; a literary word—see LS 980) *with food* (τροφῆς, genitive; again, like the verb, a literary touch—BDR § 169.3, n. 7), they *lightened*, perhaps they *set about lightening* (ἐκούφιζον, imperfect, perhaps inceptive) *the ship*. They did this, rashly, one may think, unless they knew that they would soon be on land, by throwing overboard (modal use of the participle ἐκβαλλόμενοι) the supplies of food. It is not clear what may have been thrown overboard at an earlier stage; no doubt it now seemed safe enough to get rid of the food. τὸν σῖτον is not difficult enough to justify the conjecture τὸν ἱστόν, the main mast. See Hemer (150). Cf. Polybius 1.39.4, referred to above on p. 1196.

39. V. 33 describes the ship's company waiting for day. Now it came; they could see land, but not recognize it. It is identified in 28.1; see the note there (also A. Acworth, *JTS* 24 (1973) 190–193; C. J. Hemer, *JTS* 26 (1975) 100–111; also Hemer 150).

M. 1.117 notes that 'durative action is most certainly represented in the present κατανοεῖν, except Acts 27.39'; for this imperfect Moulton tentatively suggests 'noticed one after another'. If one is to make such guesses, the suggestion 'as daylight increased they perceived more and more clearly' might do as well; but it is probably best to suppose that on this occasion Luke did not choose the most suitable tense. What they saw was a bay, with a beach. This offered a way of escape from the storm. Had the dinghy still been available it might have been used for successive trips to the shore; it was not available (v. 32), and the alternative was to run the ship on shore (ἐξῶσαι). ἐξωθεῖν has other meanings, but this is attested in Thucydides 2.90.4; 7.52.2; 8.104.3. B* C *pc* have ἐκσῶσαι, identical in sound (the variant being due to dictation?) but weaker in meaning (M. 2.108; but *Begs.* 4.337 think B C may be right). They did beach the ship, and they did not save it. Their planning (ἐβουλεύοντο) was qualified by the parenthetical (so M. 3.196, 'if possible'; cf. v. 12 and 20.16, but see below) εἰ δύναιντο. On the optative see M. 3.196; also Radermacher (131). Moule (*IB* 151) finds the meaning unclear. We have to choose between Planning *whether* they could … and Planning (*if* they could) to … In the former alternative, *considering* might be a preferable alternative. But it seems better to regard εἰ δύναιντο as parenthetical.

For the manoeuvre cf. Caesar, *De Bello Civile* 3.25, … atque eo naves ejicere possent.

Haenchen (677) considers that this verse connects perfectly with

v. 32. It does not seem to connect less well with v. 38. See Hemer (150).

For δύναιντο (‭א‬ A B Ψ 33 81 323 (614) 945 1175 1739 2495 *al* latt), C 𝔐 co have δυνατόν. 'The gloss οι ναυται, which in 920 is attached to εβουλευοντο, appears in gig vg. *codd.* sah *cod.* P pesh as subject of "knew not" ' (Ropes, *Begs.* 3.247).

40. This verse describes the steps taken by the sailors to achieve the goal planned in v. 39. περιελόντες is a surprising word (it is used at v. 20 and in yet another sense at 28.13); it means *to strip off, to take off*; here it presumably means that the anchors were detached from the ropes that held them and allowed (εἴων) to drop into the sea. At the same time (for ἅμα with participle see BDR § 425.2, n. 2) they (the sailors) let go the fastenings of the rudders. *Fastenings* translates τὰς ζευκτηρίας. According to LS 754 ζευκτηρία is equivalent to ζεύγλη, which (LS 753) means, in addition to a fastening on a yoke for draught animals, the 'cross-bar of the double rudder'. This is the meaning it will have here, used in connection with the steering-paddles, of which Greek ships normally had two. The action described by Luke is reasonably clear: the anchors were let go, the steering apparatus was dismantled. The crew had given up any thought of steering the ship; the wind would drive it where they wished to go.

To accelerate their progress they raised the foresail (τὸν ἀρτέμωνα) to the breeze. τῇ πνεούσῃ is simply *that which was blowing*. Unless with P⁷⁴ we read τῇ πνοῇ, there is probably (see BDR § 241.6, n. 8; M. 3.17) an ellipse of τῇ αὔρᾳ; cf. Arrian, *Epistola ad Traianum* 3.2 (3), ταῖς αὔραις ταῖς ἐκ τῶν ποταμῶν πνεούσαις. αὔρα is a *breeze*, but sometimes in particular an off-sea breeze; this is evidently what was in mind here. With this behind them they held on (κατεῖχον; cf. Herodotus 6.101.1; 7.59.3, ἐς τοῦτον τὸν αἰγιαλὸν κατασχόντες τὰς νέας) to the beach. As appears from the quotation it is necessary to understand τὴν ναῦν as object of κατεῖχον.

Page (262) takes εἴων to mean, They left [the anchors] in the sea. He says that this accounts for the use of εἰς, but it surely does so less well than 'they let them slip into the sea'.

Stählin (321) understands the reference to the rudders in the opposite way: 'man löst die Riemen der zwei während des Ankerns hochgezogenen Steuerruder und macht sie so wieder gebrauchsfertig.'

41. περιπίπτειν is (among other things—for an example see *ND* 3.141)—a nautical term, used of ships falling foul of one another, also of ships being wrecked. Page (262f.) points out its suggestion of the unexpected; they were making for the beach when their course was unexpectedly interrupted, as they fell upon a τόπος διθάλασσος.

The adjective is used of a double sea, that is, a sea divided into two parts (as the Euxine, Strabo 2.5.22). LS 427 give for the present passage, '*between two seas, where two seas meet*, as is often the case off a headland'. This suggests a headland jutting out between two distinguishable stretches of water; Page (263) similarly thinks of a ridge or reef running out to sea. *Begs.* 4.339, though unwilling in translation to commit themselves further than 'of two seas', evidently favour the meaning *shoal*, and this certainly makes good sense of the narrative. If the ship ran on to land it is hard to see why the travellers should need to swim or otherwise take to the water (vv. 42–44). Even if they were at the stern of the ship, this did not break up at once (see below) and they could have made their way to the bow and jumped to the ground (ships often carried a ladder that could have been used). If however the bow was stuck in a shoal and the stern was exposed to the force of the waves all is clear. Everyone would be obliged to swim ashore, or find some other means of getting through the water. The meaning shoal is adopted by BA 392 ('eine dem eigentl. Strand vorgelagerte Sandbank'), but it must be admitted that it rests only upon a consideration of what appears to fit the present context. It is not inconsistent with the etymology of διθάλασσος. There was sea before and behind the ship.

ἐπέκειλαν is a nautical term (ἐπικέλλειν), apparently not used by prose writers: *to run* a ship *on land*. It is used by Homer: *Odyssey* 9.148, πρὶν νῆας ἐϋσσέλμους ἐπικέλσαι; 9.546, νῆα ... ἐκέλσαμεν ἐν ψαμάθοισιν. B² 𝔐 have the prose word, ἐπώκειλαν, used by Herodotus (see LS 675; M.2.243). There is no difference in meaning. Each verb takes τὴν ναῦν as object. This word (ναῦς) was becoming obsolete; did Luke take it from Homer? *Begs.* 4.339 think the suggestion 'very attractive'. 'If Luke was acquainted with Aratus and Epimenides, his knowledge of Homer is easily credible.' Cf. M. 2.9; Bruce (2.474, 493); Hemer (151). BDR § 47.4d are content to describe the sentence as literary.

The bow (πρῷρα) of the ship, striking ground first, stuck fast, became fixed (ἐρείσασα); there it remained, unshaken by what was left of the storm. The stern (πρύμνα; like πρῷρα, sometimes written with –η) was in a different position, exposed to the violence of the waves.

Surprisingly, M. 3.65 describes the imperfect ἐλύετο as conative (or inchoative), and translates 'the surf seemed to be trying to break up the prow'. In the Greek however the subject of the passive verb is πρύμνα (stern), and this was not trying to break up anything, or even to be broken up. The imperfect is clearly durative: bit by bit the stern was being broken up. BDR § 326 also put the verb under the heading 'Imperfekt de conatu' but inconsistently translate, ' "fingen sich zu lösen" oder "löste sich mehr und mehr" '. Blass (282) correctly: 'ἐλύετο dissolvi coepit, cf. [v.] 20, Vergil, *Aeneid* 10.303–305':

namque inflicta vadi dorso dum pendet iniquo
anceps sustentata diu fluctusque fatigat,
solvitur atque viros mediis exponit in undis.

Preuschen (154) adds *Aeneid* 5.206, inlisaque proraque pependit.

The last words appear in various forms. τῆς βίας τῶν κυμάτων is the reading of P⁷⁴ ℵᶜ C 𝔐 sy; ℵ* A B have the first two words only, Ψ 2464 have the third and fourth only; gig vg have vi maris. It was the unessential sort of narrative note with which copyists felt free. 'The curtness of υπο της βιας led to various expansions' (Ropes, *Begs.* 3.249).

Haenchen (677) takes ὑπὸ τῆς βίας to mean 'unter der Gewalt des Rammstosses'. One would have expected this to affect the bow (the point of impact) rather than the stern.

42. The soldiers' plan was sensible enough. They were responsible for the safe custody of the prisoners (v. 1); see on 12.19; 16.27. For them it was better that the prisoners should die than that they should escape. Where they might swim off (ἐκκολυμβᾶν, compound; cf. v. 43) to is not clear, but no doubt some would have felt the risk of drowning to be worth taking. See Hemer (152).

βουλὴ ἐγένετο followed by ἵνα is described by M. 3.139 as a Hebraistic figure of speech; we are not told, and it is not clear, what Hebrew might be responsible for it. To BDR § 393.5 it is a 'freiere Wendung'.

The reading of gig (cf. v. 41) is tunc cogitaverunt milites ut omnes custodios ...

43. The centurion was of another mind. From early in the voyage he had treated Paul with consideration (v. 3), though he had failed to take his advice (v. 11). If διασῶσαι is anything more than a strengthened form of the simple verb it will mean that Julius wished to bring Paul *safely through* the present danger; v. 44; 28.1, 4. There may be a special application (as these verses suggest) to coming safely *through water*; cf. Josephus, *Apion* 1.130, Νῶχος ... διεσώθη. There may also have been a desire to distinguish rescue from shipwreck from being saved in a Christian, religious sense.

ἐκώλυσεν is a perfective aorist (M. 3.72; similarly Zerwick § 252); Julius succeeded in preventing the soldiers from carrying out their intention. For κωλύειν with accusative of the person prevented from doing something or having something done, cf. 8.36; 11.17. He could not however save Paul without saving all, or at least giving all the opportunity of saving themselves. Some could swim (from 2 Cor. 11.25 one guesses that Paul could); they were to throw themselves overboard—ἀπορίπτειν, normally a transitive verb, is here used intransitively, or reflexively (without the reflexive pronoun). They were to begin (πρώτους) the evacuation of the wreck and get to land (ἐπὶ τὴν γῆν; Zerwick § 123 contrasts the use of ἐπί here with the accusative with that in v. 44 where dative and genitive are used).

The reading of gig is: centurio autem prohibuit hoc fieri praecipue propter paulum ut salvum illum faceret. et jussit illos qui possent enatare primos exire ad terram ...

44. The non-swimmers would need help. Two groups are distinguished by οὓς μὲν ... οὓς δὲ ..., where τοὺς μὲν ... τοὺς δὲ ... would have been better. Of Luke's construction BDR § 293.3b, n. 11 say, 'Bei den Attikern kaum belegt (K[ühner]-G[ert] II 228), häufiger in hell. Zeit (Mayser II 1,57).' The first group went ἐπὶ σανίσιν. σανίς is a *plank*, *board*, almost any piece of timber, and ἐπί presumably means *on*. The second group went ἐπί τινων τῶν ἀπὸ τοῦ πλοίου. Here ἐπί is constructed with the genitive, which also would normally mean *on* (it is not clear how Zerwick § 123 is distinguishing between *in tabulis* and *super ea quae de navi erant*). But what were the σανίδες if they were not τὰ ἀπὸ τοῦ πλοίου, broken pieces of timber coming from the ship? This raises the question whether τῶν should be regarded as masculine, οἱ ἀπὸ τοῦ πλοίου. Those who could not swim were assisted by men from the ship who could. M. 3.272 regards ἐπί with the dative and ἐπί with the genitive as here interchangeable; similarly BDR § 235.1, n. 1. It is not however easy to see why Luke should have repeated himself: some on planks or pieces of timber (which must have come from the ship) and others on some of the things that came from the ship (which unless they were pieces of wood would not have been much use as floats). The use of μέν ... δέ indicates a real distinction and this can only have been in the manner of coming ashore. We may add by way of support Hanson (251): τινων without a noun is 'more usually applied to persons than things'; Delebecque (135); 'τῶν (ἀπό) ne peut être un neutre, car l'expression οἱ ἀπό est courante en grec pour désigner des "hommes de", ou "venant de".' Cf. Testament of Naphtali 6.6: ὁ δὲ Ἰωσὴφ ἐπὶ ἀκατίῳ ἐπορεύθη. ἡμεῖς δὲ διεχωρίσθημεν ἐπὶ σανίδων ἐννέα.

However the transit from wreck to shore was made it was safely effected: all came safely (on διασῴζειν see v. 43) to land (ἐπί and the accusative as in v. 43, except in 614, which has ἐπὶ τῆς γῆς). Cf. Thucydides 3.108.3, χαλεπῶς διεσῴζοντο ἐς τὰς Ὄλπας.

63. FROM MALTA TO ROME 28.1–16

(1) Having got safely through we then recognized that the island was called Malta. (2) The local inhabitants showed us no ordinary kindness, for because of the rain that came on and the cold they lit a fire and brought us to it. (3) When Paul gathered a bundle of sticks and put them on the fire a viper came out because of the heat and fastened on his hand. (4) When the inhabitants saw the creature hanging from his hand they said to one another, 'No doubt this man is a murderer; though he escaped from the sea Justice has not permitted him to live.' (5) He however shook off the creature into the fire and suffered no harm. (6) They were expecting that he would swell up or suddenly fall down dead. But as they went on waiting and saw that nothing amiss was happening to him they changed their minds and said that he was a god.

(7) In the neighbourhood of that place there were domains belonging to the chief man of the island, Publius by name, who received and entertained us with kindly hospitality for three days. (8) It happened that Publius' father was sick and confined to bed with fevers and dysentery. Paul went in to him and prayed, laid his hands on him and cured him. (9) When this happened the others in the island who had illnesses approached and were healed. (10) They[1] bestowed upon us many honours, and when we left put on board the things that we needed.

(11) After three months we set sail in a ship that had wintered on the island, a ship of Alexandria, ship's sign, The Dioscuri. (12) We landed at Syracuse and stayed there three days. (13) [2]Casting off from there we reached Rhegium. After one day a south wind arose and we came on the second day to Puteoli. (14) There we found brothers and[3] were invited to stay with them seven days; and[4] in this way we made our journey to Rome. (15) From there the brothers, having heard of our affairs, came to meet us as far as Appius' Market and Three Taverns. When Paul saw them he gave thanks to God and took heart.

(16) When we entered Rome Paul was permitted to stay[5] on his own with the soldier who guarded him.

Bibliography

A. Acworth, as in (62).

H. J. Cadbury, *JBL* 44 (1925), 223–7.

[1]RSV, presented many gifts to us.
[2]RSV, from there we made a circuit; NEB, then we sailed round; NJB, from there we followed the coast.
[3]NIB, had the great encouragement of staying a week.
[4]RSV, so we came to Rome; NEB, and so to Rome.
[5]NJB, in lodgings of his own.

J. Coppens, as in (47).

J. Dupont, in Kremer, *Actes*, 359–404 (= *Nouvelles Études* 457–511).

C. J. Hemer, as in (62).

N. Heutger, as in (62).

W. Kirschschläger, in Kremer, *Actes*, 509–21.

D. Ladouceur, as in (62).

G. B. Miles and G. Trompf, as in (62).

S. M. Praeder, as in (62).

J. Smith, as in (62).

A. Suhl, as in (62).

A. Suhl, *BZ* 36 (1992), 220–6.

G. W. Trompf, as in (62).

H. Warnecke, *Die tatsächliche Romfahrt des Apostels Paulus* (1987).

J. Wehnert, as in (62).

Commentary

The vigorous sea story of ch. 27 winds down quietly into something like domesticity. Paul joins in the necessary task of finding firewood; men are cold and wet and warmth is necessary. In the process he is bitten by a snake. The availability of firewood and of snakes raises the question of the identity of the island on which the travellers have been cast. Can it have been Malta, or was it perhaps Meleda, an island in the Adriatic? A commentary is no place for detailed discussion of winds and tides, flora and fauna, local inhabitants and their rulers. Some essential points are considered in the detailed notes. Here the only point which it is worthwhile to observe is that, whatever the snake population of either island may be, such a story as we have in vv. 3–6 cannot settle the identification. No expert naturalist was at hand to describe the snake and to confirm or dispute the islanders' belief that Paul was in danger of death; moreover, the story is not one of a kind to evoke instant acceptance. If the promise of Mk 16.18 was not drawn from the story in Acts but was traditional it could have given rise to fulfilment narratives.

The paragraph proceeds with the natural reaction to Paul's escape: the ignorant islanders suppose that he is a god, an opinion that Luke does not share (see on v. 6). Paul heals his host's father's sickness and finds himself thronged by sick people who need healing. His response leads to favourable treatment and a generous send-off from the island—at a date earlier than one would have thought desirable (see on v. 11).

Details of the journey from Malta to Rome are given. The seven days' wait in Puteoli is surprising, and so is the double reference to

Rome in vv. 14 and 16. To be confident that there can be no explanation of the seven-day delay is as illogical as to insist on the historicity of any particular explanation. It may have been the author's invention or not; we do not know. The two references to Rome may very well be due to Luke's desire to accommodate the two missions, to Appii Forum and to Three Taverns; these may themselves arise from different sources.

In this paragraph the use of *We*, dropped towards the close of ch. 27, is resumed. It appears in vv. 1, 2, 7, 10, 11, 12, 13, 14, 15, 16, so that it is very natural to think of a travel narrative that identified the island and the host who showed hospitality to Paul (and his friends—but not necessarily to the ship's complement of (2)76 persons) but did not contain the wonders of vv. 2–6, 8, 9. It then took Paul to Rome, but did not contain the references to Appii Forum and Three Taverns. So e.g. Pesch (2.296), who thinks that vv. 1, 2, 10 continue the We-narrative, while vv. 2b–6, 7–9 are Luke's rewriting of tradition (which however was probably from the beginning handed down in this context). Weiser (667) thinks that Luke himself formed the paragraph vv. 1–10 on the basis of two traditional episodes. Roloff (365; cf. Conzelmann 147) thinks that Luke freely created the two miracles, Schille (457) that they were (though not originally) located in Malta, and that this was why Malta was chosen as the place of the shipwreck. Cf. also Kirschschläger in Kremer, *Actes*, 509–21. Schmithals (234) says that the miracles show that Paul 'ist in Wort und Tat ein vollgütiger Zeuge Jesu, aber er ist dies wie die Zwölf Apostel und durch sie'. This is a questionable assessment. The episode of the snake adds nothing to e.g. a miraculous escape from prison by earthquake in Philippi; curing a case of dysentery is poor stuff in comparison with raising up a dead young man in Troas. And there is no reference to the Twelve, *through whom*, according to Schmithals, Paul acts. It is probable that the miracles, whatever we make of their historical trustworthiness, were to be found, and were found by Luke, in the tradition, possibly in local tradition. Luke's supposed θεῖος ἀνήρ motif, made much of by e.g. Haenchen (684) and Conzelmann (147), has already, and rightly, been questioned by Weiser (669), Roloff (367), Pesch (2.299)—not to mention Calvin (2.303).

It is true that Luke is here underlining some features of his description of Paul. He is capable of working miracles; and he comes through all kinds of dangers and opposition to his goal, Rome. It is hardly correct to say (Roloff 368), 'Lukas hat seine Vorlage, die V. 11–13, 14b, 16b umfasste, durch die Hinzufügung von V. 14a, 15, 16a so ausgestaltet, dass aus einem nüchternen Bericht von der letzten Reiseetappe die Schilderung eines feierlichen Triumphzuges wurde', though Schmithals (236) could be right in thinking that these verses originally followed v. 1, and in arguing that since in 28.16–31 we hear no more of the Roman Christians 'Lukas in v. 11–15 eine

Vorlage zugrundelag' (cf. Pesch 2.301). The delegations from Rome are not described by Luke in triumphalist vein; their effect is to cheer Paul and to give him courage for what awaits him.

It would have been easy to omit all reference to the brothers who came out from Rome to meet Paul at Appii Forum and Three Taverns, and this Luke would no doubt have done if it had been his aim to suggest (contrary to fact) that Paul was virtually the founder of the Roman church (so e.g. Haenchen 688). The view may well be correct that we hear little of the Roman Christians because their welcome was not as warm as Luke (and Paul) would have desired; Philippians was probably written from Rome and bears witness to those who preach Christ 'out of envy and strife' (Phil. 1.15, 17). That the word ἐκκλησία is not used is not significant; cf. e.g. 15.36 with 14.23. Luke's silence in 28.17–31 is due to his desire (see pp. 1235, 1237, 1239) finally and decisively to show that Paul is a good and loyal Jew; that Jewish rejection of the Gospel is the fulfilment of prophecy; and that the church is committed to the Gentile mission.

1. Ch. 27 ends with the picture of the seafarers struggling through the water to dry land, which all of them safely reach. Their safe arrival is picked up here by διασωθέντες, for which see 27.43f. The next thing (τότε) was recognition (ἐπιγινώσκειν) of the place in which they found themselves. The island was called Μελίτη. How the stranded travellers were able to recognize the land Luke does not say. The local inhabitants are mentioned in the next verse; perhaps it may be assumed that they had already appeared and been questioned, though if this were so *we learned*, or *we were informed*, would have been more suitable than *we recognized*. It may be, of course, that, once ashore, experienced travellers would know where they were.

It is usually supposed that Μελίτη (in B* lat syʰ bo, Μελιτήνη; see M. 2.359—an adjective agreeing with νῆσος (understood)? or dittography within Μελίτη ἡ νῆσος (Metzger 500)?) refers to the island now known as Malta, where the traditional site of the wreck is known as St Paul's Bay. Early writers seem to have made little or no attempt to identify the scene of the wreck, but in the 8th century Constantinus Porphyrogenitus (*De Administrando Imperio* 36) thought not of Malta but of an island in the Adriatic now known as Meleda, Melite, or Mljet, in antiquity as Cephallenia. This belief, that Paul was shipwrecked in the Adriatic, has been argued at length by H. Warnecke, *Die tatsächliche Romfahrt des Apostels Paulus, SB* 127 (Stuttgart, 1987), on the basis of detailed nautical, topographical, and meteorological observations, which could be pursued here only by throwing the commentary out of proportion and could be assessed only by a commentator with adequate knowledge of the sciences involved. Some relevant facts will be mentioned as they arise in the following verses; here that a gale that threatened to drive the ship on to the Syrtes (27.17) must have been a north easter, and it is hard to see how it could have led to a wreck on the east side of the Adriatic.

Malta had been a Roman island since it was captured from the Carthaginians in 218 BC (Livy 21.51). On its government and some other features see on v. 7 (and the bibliography in Schneider 2.400, n. 1). It has been said that the island was appropriately named, since in Phoenician mĕlēṭā = refuge, escape. There is no indication that Luke was aware of this.

Bauernfeind (276) thinks that ἡ νῆσος (with the article) refers to the island which Paul had foretold (27.26); more probably it is simply the one on which we have just landed.

In the present verse 'we' (ἐπέγνωμεν) is left undefined; as the narrative proceeds it ceases to refer (as it had done on occasion in ch. 27) to the ship's company as a whole and means Paul and his companions.

After the excitement of the voyage the story at this point seems to settle down. Davies (*Land* 282) remarks that there is no urgency in getting to Rome; there is 'almost a "tourist" air about the voyage'. Is this because Luke has here a travel handbook source, different from the theologically motivated source that has at least some relation with Paul?

Weiser (666) quotes Heutger, who, though agreeing that the wreck took place on Malta, disagrees with the traditional location in St Paul's Bay; '... treffe der Ausdruck *dithalassos* viel besser zur nächsten, westlich gelegenen Mellieha-Bucht, wo heute noch ausser der Bai selbst ein zweite See zu sehen sei, der sich jeweils im Winter landeinwärts bildet'.

2. The local inhabitants are described as οἱ βάρβαροι. In Acts the word is used only here and at v. 4; cf. Rom. 1.14; 1 Cor. 14.11; Col. 3.11. Its primary meaning related to language and was presumably onomatopoeic. The βάρβαρος was one who did not speak Greek and whose words therefore sounded (to a Greek) like a meaningless ba-ba-ba. He was someone other than a Greek; the word was used 'specially of the Medes and Persians'; after the Persian war it came to mean 'brutal, rude' (LS 306). This verse suggests that the latter meaning is not in mind; these barbarians were not brutal and rude, but showed courtesy and kindness. The word therefore probably retains its linguistic reference (as it does in 1 Cor. 14.11). This is used by Warnecke (111–18) as an argument in favour of Cephallenia rather than Malta as the scene of the shipwreck. Before the first century AD Malta had been both hellenized and romanized. Inscriptions in both Greek and Latin are found, together with ruins of Roman villas, theatres, and baths. Julius Caesar settled some of his veterans in Malta, and a little later the island received the citizenship, as is confirmed by coins (see also Strabo 7.833). On the other hand, Zahn (842) (quoted by Haenchen 681) wrote that it is proved by inscriptions (details conveniently in Hemer 152) that 'der gemeine Mann, die Fabrikarbeiter und Packträger, die Handelsgärtner und Hundezüchter auf Melita nur ihre punische Muttersprache verstehen, sprechen und lesen konnten.' Similarly Page (264): 'Diod[orus] Sic[ulus] v. 12, ἔστι δὲ ἡ νῆσος αὕτη Φοινίκων ἄποικος. Their language therefore was probably Punic.' Cf. Cicero, *In Verrem* 2.4.46 (103), Itaque in his inscriptum litteris punicis fuit ... It may be assumed that both in Malta and Meleda there were uneducated people who could not, and educated people who could, speak Greek (or Latin or both), and that the former would qualify for the term βαρβαροί.

The barbarians certainly greeted the shipwrecked men in a friendly fashion. For παρεῖχον the middle might have been expected (M. 3.56); for φιλανθρωπία cf. 27.3 (φιλανθρώπως). For οὐ τὴν τυχοῦσαν cf. 19.11; the word is characteristic of the second part of Acts. There is an excellent linguistic parallel (though the meaning reverses that of the present clause) in BGU 1.36 [= 436].9f. (a Fayyum papyrus of the 2nd or 3rd century AD), ὕβριν οὐ τὴν τυχοῦσαν συνετελέσαντο.

Their kindness was shown in that they lit (ἅψαντες; 𝔐 has ἀνάψαντες with no difference in meaning) a fire and welcomed, or received, us all, or simply brought us to it. Action of this kind was desirable because of the rain and the cold. One might have expected a reference to the wetting in the sea that all had experienced. The rain was ἐφεστῶτα; perhaps, that came on suddenly, unexpectedly; cf. 1 Thess. 5.3; also Polybius 18.20.7 (Blass 284), διὰ τὸν ἐφεστῶτα ζόφον. Warnecke (100–2) observes that in Malta the average rainfall in October is 83.3 mm, whereas in Melida, off the Dalmatian coast, the rainfall is heavy. He quotes the geographer Partsch (*Kephallenia* 33f.), '... stärker und anhaltender setzen sie [Gewitter] erst im Oktober ein. Noch pflegt ein kleiner Nachsommer zu folgen ehe der November und Dezember ihre gewaltigen Regenmengen ausschütten. In diesen Monaten rauschen die zahlreichsten und kräftigsten Niederschläge nieder.' As for temperature (Warnecke 102–4), the average minima and maxima are for October 17.2°C and 27.8°C, for November, 12.2 and 23.3. The lowest of these would certainly not strike someone from Northern Europe as cold. Cephallenia is much colder. Two points, perhaps, to Warnecke, but men in wet clothes, with a good breeze blowing, would not be sorry to see a fire.

Kindness to strangers is well illustrated by Betz (94, n. 6) with a quotation from Lucian, *Verae Historiae* 1.29, οὐδὲν ἡμᾶς ἠδίκουν, ἀλλὰ καὶ ἐπὶ ξενίᾳ ἐκάλουν. Cf. *Verae Historiae* 2.46.

For προσελάβοντο, ℵ* Ψ 614 2495 *pc* lat have προσανελάμβανον (reficiebant), *refreshed us*, which Bruce 1.470 regards as the better reading.

3. συστρέφειν is used in a variety of ways: of animals *gathering* themselves to spring; of a man *screwing up* his eyes; of soldiers *rallying, forming* a compact body; it is not easy to find a parallel to what is evidently the meaning here. Paul gathered and twisted together a bundle of twigs with a view to feeding the fire. πλῆθος elsewhere in Acts refers to a company of people, here to a quantity (colloquially in English, *a lot*) of sticks, φρύγανα, for the fire. So Xenophon, *Anabasis* 4.3.11, φρύγανα συλλέγοντες ὡς ἐπὶ πῦρ.

The genitive absolute (συστράψαντος ... τοῦ Παύλου) is combined with another genitive participle, ἐπιθέντος. Paul put the bundle of sticks on the fire. Escaping the heat (ἀπὸ τῆς θέρμης), a snake (ἔχιδνα) came out (ἐξελθοῦσα; H L P Ψ 049 323 614 945 1241 𝔐 have διεξελθοῦσα—came out through the flames, through the sticks?). It appears in the following verses that the snake did Paul no harm. Luke plainly regards this as a miracle, and therefore understood the word ἔχιδνα in its proper sense; he also represents the native inhabitants of the island as sharing his view—a man bitten by one of 'their' snakes should swell up and fall down dead. (v. 6). The occurrence of snakes in Malta and Cephallenia is discussed by Warnecke (108–10). There were, it seems, no poisonous snakes on Malta. 'Auf Malta gibt es weder Sandvipern noch überhaupt eine Vipernart, ja, nicht einmal irgendwelche Giftschlange: "Die drei auf Malta lebenden Schlangenarten sind ungiftig"' (Warnecke 108, quoting H. Egger, *Malta* 159). Cephallenia on the other hand has about twenty kinds of snake, including the *Vipera ammodytus*, that is, the ἔχιδνα. This seems to be a point in favour of Cephallenia as the scene of the incident; alternatively, it means that the story is fictitious (or possibly, belongs to another setting), and was written by one who did not know what kinds of snake were to be found on Malta. A further possibility is that in the first century Malta was richer in snakes than it is now, and possessed poisonous snakes.

The snake fastened on Paul's hand; for καθῆψε, the middle καθήψατο might have been expected. This is read by C 36 453 614 1891 2495 *pm*, but this is plainly copyists' 'improvement'. *Begs.* 4.341 quotes Epictetus 3.20.10, ὁ μὲν τοῦ τραχήλου καθάπτων; this however is in wrestling.

For ἀπὸ τῆς θέρμης cf. Lucian, *Dialogi Marini*, 11.2, ἡ θέρμη δέ, ὡς φῇς, ἀπὸ τοῦ πυρός.

Luke himself would probably be surprised by the comment (Calvin 2.299), 'According to His secret purpose, the Lord directed it [the snake] to bite Paul because He saw that it would be for the glory of His Gospel.'

4. The βάρβαροι (v. 2) saw what was happening; the creature (now τὸ θήριον, used of snakes in a variety of places: BA 733f. cite Diodorus Siculus 20.42 2; Polyaenus 2.3.15; Aretaeus 159.8; 163.2;

Justin, *1 Apology* 60.2; Galen 4.779k) was hanging from his hand. They drew a natural conclusion. Paul has deserved death; having escaped drowning he is to be punished by the snake.

For διασώζειν see on 27.43f. In the NT ἐάν is almost exclusively a Lucan word. In the NT πάντως is used only by Luke and Paul. *Begs.* 4.341 translate it *perhaps*, referring to H. J. Cadbury, *JBL* 44 (1925), 223–7. LS 1301 do not have this meaning; BA 1232 mention Cadbury's interpretation without comment. It is not convincing.

It might be better to spell δίκη with a capital Δ. The word occurs at 2 Thess. 1.9; Jude 7; nowhere else in the NT (unless at Acts 25.15, where E Ψ 𝔐 have δίκην in place of καταδίκην. The barbarians may well have personified Justice as a divine being. Cf. Sophocles, *Antigone* 538f., ἀλλ᾽ οὐκ ἐάσει τοῦτό γ᾽ ἡ δίκη σ᾽, ἐπεὶ οὔτ᾽ ἠθέλησας οὔτ᾽ ἐγὼ ᾽κοινωσάμην; *Oedipus at Colonus* 1381f.; Hesiod, *Theogony* 902; Plutarch, *De Exilio* 5 (601B); *Alexander* 52 (695A), τὴν Δίκην ἔχει πάρεδρον ὁ Ζεὺς καὶ τὴν Θέμιν.

The thought that sins are not left unpunished (and that a snake bite may be used) is illustrated in StrB (2.772) by a long quotation from Sanhedrin 37b.

For a very close parallel to Luke's story see the *Anthologia Palatina* 7.290—a shipwrecked sailor is killed by a viper.

5. ὁ μὲν οὖν: *he, however*. For the adversative use of μὲν οὖν cf. 14.3; 17.17; 25.4 (Moule, *IB* 163).

ἀποτινάξας: Lk. 9.5. ἐκτινάξασθαι: Acts 13.51: 18.6. Cf. Euripides, *Bacchae* 253, οὐκ ἀποτινάξεις κισσόν;

For ἔπαθεν οὐδὲν κακόν cf. Plutarch, *Pericles* 34 (171A), πολλὰ μὲν δρῶντες κακὰ τοὺς Ἀθεναίους, πολλὰ δὲ πάσχοντες ὑπ᾽ ἐκείνων.

For the snake, cf. Lk. 10.19 as well as Mk 16.17f.; in the background of both, Ps. 90 (91).13. In Berakoth 33a there is a fine story of the snake that perished as a result of its attempt to bite R. Hanina b. Dosa (StrB 2.772).

6. The tenses in this verse are to be noted. προσεδόκων (imperfect, they were expecting) that he would begin to swell up (πίμπρασθαι, present) or fall down (καταπίπτειν, present). But while they went on for a long time expecting (προσδοκώντων, present) and observing (θεωρούντων, present) that nothing amiss was happening (γινόμενον, present) to him, they changed their minds (μεταβαλόμενοι, aorist—but ℵ 648 𝔐 have –αλλ–, present) and began to say (ἔλεγον, imperfect) that he was a god. Luke's use of tenses is not always so impressive. Cf. 27.7; see Moule, *IB* 101. For μή with the participle (γινόμενον) in *oratio obliqua* see M. 1.239. For the form ἐμπίπρασθαι, which occurs in ℵ* 323 945 *pc* see BDR § 101, n. 69 (dissimilation). For μέλλειν πίμπρασθαι as a substitute for the future infinitive see BDR § 356.3, n. 4. For the very hard construction in which the genitive in the genitive absolute (αὐτῶν προσδοκώντων) becomes the subject of the main clause see BDR § 423.3, n. 9, but cf. Delebecque (136), 'le génitif absolu peut, en bon grec, se rapporter à un nominatif sujet.'

Neither ἄτοπος nor πίμπρασθαι is to be regarded as a medical term. Doctors are not alone in being aware of accident and illness, and their symptoms. Cf. Josephus, *Ant.* 11.134, μηδὲν κατὰ τὴν ὁδὸν παθεῖν ἄτοπον; 3.271, ... καὶ τὴν γαστέρα πρησθεῖσαν ...; Num. 5.21.

The incident does not support the view that Luke intended to represent Paul as a θεῖος ἀνήρ. Weiser (669) observing that the impression that Paul was a god is not corrected here as it is at 14.15 adds that Luke 'lässt sie als heidnischen Irrtum stehen im Vertrauen darauf, dass die Leser Paulus und der Gott, dem er dient, zu unterscheiden wissen'. One can go further; the erroneous opinion was held by barbarians, whom a Greek could not possibly think to be right. See on v. 2. Luke and his readers would no doubt agree with Calvin (2.301): 'If it was necessary to choose one or the other, it was better to be regarded (sic) a murderer than a god.'

7. It is hardly necessary to ask what noun should be supplied with ἐν δὲ τοῖς. The phrase τὰ περὶ τὸν τόπον ἐκεῖνον means *the neighbourhood of that place* (the place of the wreck). It is possible however that we should think of τοῖς χωρίοις: Among the estates surrounding that place were estates belonging to ... The general meaning is clear. 'Le singulier χωρίον signifie "champ"; le pluriel doit désigner un ensemble de champs, donc une "campagne", où un "domaine", selon l'importance du terrain' (Delebecque 136). Delebecque adds that the meaning here will be *domaine* since the estate is the property of the chief man of the island. See 1.18. for ὑπῆρχεν with the dative as a way of expressing possession cf. 3.6; 4.37; see BDR § 189.1, n. 1. The owner was Publius; the variant spelling Πουπλίῳ (P[74vid] 81 104 945 1739 *pc*) underlines the connection with the Roman name Publius (BDR § 41.1, n. 3). He is described as the πρῶτος τῆς νήσου. The use of this title in Malta is confirmed by epigraphic evidence; see especially *IG* 14.601: Λ. Καστρίκιος Κυρ(είνα) Προύδηνς ἱππεὺς Ῥομ(αίων), πρῶτος Μελιταίων καὶ πάτρων, ἄρξας καὶ ἀμφιπολείσας θεῷ Αὐγούστῳ. Cf. *CIL* 10.7495, municipi Melitensium primus omnium: on this however see Hemer (153). It seems that in this inscription *primus* is not a title but claims that the person named was the first to make certain benefactions. It has often been understood that the inscription(s) referred to the chief Roman administrator of the island, which had long been joined with and governed by the procurator of Sicily. Malta however was separated from Sicily in the early years of Augustus, and *CIL* 10.7494 (proc. insularum Melti. et Gaul.) indicates that Malta and the neighbouring small island of Gaulos (modern Gozo) were governed by a procurator. It is now usual to see in the Protos a local native officer. Cephallenia was a *civitas libera* (Pliny, *Natural History* 4.54), in which Roman interests were looked after by a *legatus* of the governor of Achaea. This office might well have borne the title of *primus*; Warnecke (123) draws attention to one holder of it, at about the time that must be assigned to Paul's journey, whose name was Publius Alf. (= Alfius *or* Alfessus) Primus. This must be taken with the fact, which also has often been observed, that it is unusual for a Roman official to be referred to by his praenomen alone, as Publius. Warnecke suggests that the solution of two problems—the use of the name Publius and the title *primus* (πρῶτος)—may lie here. Luke gives a confused recollection of the name Publius Primus. The suggestion is not convincing. The title πρῶτος was used in Malta, whether of a Roman or a local official. Lüdemann (272) thinks that Publius and πρῶτος were both drawn from tradition.

Publius received and for three days entertained *us* (ἡμᾶς), now in all probability no longer the whole company from the ship but Paul and his companions. There can be no doubt that the statement, correctly or incorrectly, represents the author of the narrative as a close personal associate of Paul's.

φιλοφρόνως, here only in the NT, is not uncommon; e.g. Josephus, *War* 6.115, Καῖσαρ δ'αὐτοὺς τά τε ἀλλὰ φιλοφρόνως ἐδέξατο, with kindly hospitality. It is not said that Publius (or anyone else on the island) became a Christian.

8. For ἐγένετο with accusative and infinitive see Introduction, p. xlvi.

συνέχεσθαι has many meanings; to be afflicted by illness is one (e.g. Lk. 4.38; Josephus, *Ant.* 13.398, τεταρταίῳ πυρετῷ συσχεθείς). κατακεῖσθαι means that Publius' father was laid up in bed (e.g. Herodotus 7.229.1). πυρετός is used in the plural by medical writers; BA 1462 cites Galen, *De Diff. Febr.* 1.1 (7.275) and Alexander of Aphrodisias, *De Febribus Libell.* 31. This proves nothing regarding the identity of the writer; the plural was used also by non-medical writers, e.g. Aristophanes, *Wasps* 1038; Plato, *Timaeus* 86a (dysentery is mentioned in the same context). P⁷⁴ has the singular πυρετῷ. δυσεντέριον is a late form of δυσεντερία (M. 2.125, 342).

Paul went in to the sick man (that is, presumably, into his sick room) and cured him by prayer and the laying on of hands. In πρὸς ὄν ... αὐτῷ Delebecque (136) sees the Hebraism of a relative followed by a pronoun—wrongly. Daube, *NTRJ* 234f., thinks that behind ἐπιθείς there will lie either שׁית or שׂית, but not סמך (see on 6.6). This is not based on the use of ἐπιτιθέναι and faces the formidable contrary evidence of 1QapGen 20.28, 29, one of the rare

Jewish examples of healing by the imposition of hands. The passage runs: I prayed for [...] and laid (סמכת) my hands upon his head; the plague was removed from him ... On this passage see Fitzmyer, *Aramaean* 96f. Cf. James 5.13f.

Hemer (153f.) suggests that 'the cause of fever may well have been that associated with this island, "Malta fever", discovered in 1887 to be caused by an endemic microorganism *Micrococcus Melitensis*, which infected the milk of the Maltese goats'. A point in favour of Malta against Cephallenia, but a small one; there are other causes of fever.

Paul prayed that the cure might be effected. 'By *praying* Paul makes it plain that he is not the one responsible for the miracle, but only the minister, so that God may not be defrauded of His glory' (Calvin 2.303). Later writers make the same observation and relate it to the view that Paul is represented in Acts as a θεῖος ἀνήρ. So Roloff (367); Pesch (2.299); also Weiser (670): 'Darin ist ein wichtiges Korrektiv gegenüber der verbreiteten hellenistischen Auffassung von Wundertätern als "göttlichen Menschen" (*theioi andres*) zu sehen.'

9. The cure of Publius' father naturally kindled hope in other inhabitants of the island who were ill (ἔχοντες ἀσθενείας); these came to Paul for healing and were cured. There is no ground for the suggestion that while Paul (miraculously) cured Publius' father (ἰάσατο) the other inhabitants were given non-miraculous attention (ἐθεραπεύοντο) by Luke and his medical team. Cf. ἐθεραπεύοντο at 5.16.

H, taking τούτου to be masculine and to refer to the sick man, adds ὑγίους. καὶ (before οἱ λοιποί) is omitted by B gig vg^cl.

10. The possibility cannot be excluded that πολλαῖς τιμαῖς ἐτίμησαν means *paid us many fees* (for medical and other services), but it is much more probable that it means *honoured us with* (i.e. bestowed upon us) *many honours*. The expression was current (see BA 1628–1630; e.g. Josephus, *Ant.* 20.68, ταύταις μὲν δὴ ταῖς τιμαῖς ὁ Ἰζάτης ὑπὸ τοῦ τῶν Πάρθων βασιλέως ἐτιμήθη), Luke has not suggested that Paul and his colleagues were working in the ordinary sense as doctors, and material needs are seen to in the next clause. For the alternative interpretation see Sirach 38.1, τίμα ἰατρὸν πρὸς τὰς χρείας τιμαῖς αὐτοῦ.

For ἀνάγεσθαι see on 13.13; 16.11. The grateful inhabitants of the island (in Luke's source, not the whole population but Publius and his household—so Pesch 2.299) saw to it that the Christian travellers should not be in need during the rest of their journey. No conversions are mentioned.

ἐπέθεντο could mean *they bestowed on us* or *they put on board*. sy^h* by adding *in the ship* chooses the latter alternative.

This story seems to be independent of the sea story of ch. 27; that Paul was a prisoner on his way to trial is not hinted at.

11. How many of the (2)76 who had set out on the voyage remained on the island for three months cannot be determined; the first person plural of ἀνήχθημεν (ἤχθημεν in H 049 6 326 1891 2495 *pm*; on the compound verb see v. 10) may refer only to Paul and his companions (including of course the military escort). Ships were commonly laid up during the winter (this had been the intention of all on Paul's ship; the only disagreement had been in the choice of a port to winter in: 27.11f.), and the centurion would probably have little difficulty in finding a ship that had spent the winter (παρακεχειμακότι) in an island port and had room enough to take on the essential passengers.

τρεῖς μῆνας gives rise to some difficulty. As a period of delay on a sea voyage it can be paralleled (Josephus, *War* 2.203, συνέβη χειμασθῆναι τρεῖς μῆνας ἐν τῇ θαλάσσῃ), but Paul's voyage began after the Day of Atonement (27.9) and presumably not very long afterwards or there would have been no point in using the Day as a date; allowing for all the time references given in the narrative, one would suppose that Malta was reached by the end of October. Three months would elapse by the end of January, a very early date for sailing to resume. See the passages cited on 27.9 and cf. Apuleius, *Metamorphoses* 11.5: On the day of Isis (5 March) it could be said sedatis hybernis tempestatibus, et lenitis maris procellosis fluctibus, navigabili jam pelago. *Jam* does not mean that sailing began on this day but it is implied that it had not been in progress long. There were however reasons why a grain ship (see below) might be in a hurry (see Hemer 154), and the crossing to Rhegium was one that might have been made early (Preuschen 156). 'Three months' is in any case to be regarded as an approximation, though Bauernfeind (278) insists that the journey recommenced in January.

The ship was an Alexandrian. Ἀλεξανδρῖνος has a Latin adjectival termination, borrowed into Greek; cf. the use of Ἀλεξανδρεύς (of persons) at 6.9; 18.24 (see BDR § 5.2, n. 11). The ship was in all probability one of the grain fleet, which regularly brought corn from Egypt to Rome. It is unlikely that such a ship should winter in Cephallenia.

The sense of the last two words in the verse is clear but their construction is not. Ships in antiquity often bore an image, or images, of a god, whose name provided the name of the ship (Lucian, *Navigium* 5, ... τὴν ἐπώνυμον τῆς νεὼς θεὸν ἔχουσα τὴν Ἶσιν ...); this one carried and was known by the sign of the Dioscuri. παρασήμῳ and Διοσκούροις are both in the dative case. παρασήμῳ may be an adjective; if so, it would agree with πλοίῳ: a boat marked with, indicated by, the Dioscuri. This, if admissible, makes good

sense; it seems to be preferred by BA 1257. But the adjective
παράσημος seems almost always to have an unfavourable meaning.
The meanings listed in LS 1323 are '*marked amiss* or *falsely,
counterfeit* ... *falsely stamped* ... of words and phrases, *false,
incorrect* ... *eccentricity* of style ... *marked by the side, noted* ...
marked, notorious for ... *remarked as* ... *conspicuousness* ...
indicative'. In nearly all these meanings the effect of the compounded παρά is evident. It seems more probable that Luke is using
the noun παράσημον, for which LS give as a general meaning
distinguishing mark, with examples including *ensign* of a ship, or of
a city, or of patricians and plebeians, *insignia praetoria* (παράσημα
στρατηγικά), *birthmarks* (παράσημα σωματικά), *password*. If this
way of taking παρασήμῳ is adopted one is left with the problem of
the datives. Turner (M. 3.243) thinks that this may be an example of
a dative absolute, mentioning Mt. 14.6 and Mk 9.28 (P⁴⁵) as other NT
examples (of which the latter must be considered very doubtful). He
refers to Moule (*IB* 45), but Moule regards the Matthean and Marcan
passages as the only NT examples and would presumably therefore
not consider Acts 28.11 one. There is a long note in BDR § 198.7, n.
11: 'Als Dat. soz. "mit den Dioskuren als Schiffszeichen" (Ramsay,
Luke 36f. als korrekt nach Inschriftengebrauch); vielfach als Dat.
instr. aufgefasst: "gekennzeichnet durch die Dioskuren" (Bauer sv
παράσημος Haenchen zSt; vgl Plut. mor. 823B [= *Praecepta
Politica* 31] ἐπιφθόνοις παράσημος "durch Gehässigkeiten sich
bemerkbar machend"); vielleicht aber auch nur mechanische Dekli-
nation eines registraturmässigne (πλοῖον) παράσημον Διοσκούροι
"ein Schiff, Schiffszeichen die D." ' The last suggestion is perhaps
the best. Similarly Page (266), quoting an inscription, ... gubernatore
navis parasemo Isopharia. The inscription is given in full in Smith
(269). See also Plutarch, *Septem Sapientium Convivium* 18 (162A);
Mulierum Virtutes 9 (247f.).

Διοσκούροις is the reading of most MSS; P⁷⁴ P* Ψ 81ᶜ 104 326
453 2464 *al* have Διοσκόροις. This is the Attic spelling; –ου– is the
Hellenistic, though it occurs in Plato and Thucydides (BDR § 30.3, n.
6). 'Διόσκουροι, ὀρθότερον Διόσκοροι. γελάσε οὖν τοὺς σὺν τῷ υ
λεγοντας' (Phrynichus 212; see Lobeck quoted in Rutherford, 310f.).
See also M. 2.88. The minuscules that have Διοσκόροις 'are mainly
of the I-groups, and it may well have stood in the "Western" text'
(Ropes, *Begs.* 3.251).

The Dioscuri, Castor and Polydeuces (Latinized as Pollux), were a
natural choice as patrons of the ship; they were called upon by sailors
as helpers in time of need. Epictetus 2.18.29, τοῦ θεοῦ μέμνησο,
ἐκεῖνον ἐπικαλοῦ βοηθὸν καὶ παραστάτην ὡς τοὺς Διοσκόρους
ἐν χειμῶνι οἱ πλέοντες.

12. For κατάγεσθαι (the opposite of ἀνάγεσθαι in v. 11) see 27.3, elsewhere in the NT it is used (in a different sense) only at Rom. 10.6. *We* landed in Syracuse and stayed there three days (ἡμέρας τρεῖς; B has the unexplained dative ἡμέραις τρίσιν). No reason is given for the delay; it was early in the sailing season and an unexpected spell of bad weather is as good a guess as any.

Syracuse, originally (in the 8th century BC) a Corinthian colony, was an old-established Greek city on the east coast of Sicily. It is perhaps twice as far from Cephallenia as from Malta, but neither journey would have been impossible.

13. περιελόντες (ℵ* B Ψ (gig)) is so surprising a reading that the variant περιελθόντες (P⁷⁴ ℵᶜ A 066 𝔐 lat sy) is easily explained. But περιελόντες may be too difficult to be accepted. Its usual meaning is that suggested by its etymology; it means *to take away from round* something. No object is expressed, but BA 1301 (and others) explain it as referring to the raising of anchors. See Hort, *Introduction* 226f. ('the elliptic employment of transitive verbs being common in Greek nautical language as in English'). See 27.40. Metzger (500f.) refers to Hort, but also observes that περιελόντες could easily be derived from περιελθόντες through the simple dropping of Θ before Ο. Given the habit noted by Hort (cf. Delebecque 137) it seems best to take the participle to mean 'weighing anchor', perhaps 'casting off'. It is in any case clear that the ship headed northwards for the strait of Messina and came (καταντᾶν as at 27.12; the word occurs 9 times in Acts, 4 times in the rest of the NT) to Rhegium. After one day, to which no incident is assigned, a south wind arose—exactly what was needed for a voyage up the west coast of Italy. The name of the wind, νότος (it ought perhaps to be printed Νότος; cf. 27.14), has no article; see M. 3.172; BDR § 253.5, n. 7.

With the aid of this wind δευτεραῖοι ἤλθομεν, we came as 'second day' men. See M. 3.225; δευτεραῖοι is an adverbial adjective. This construction became increasingly popular in post-classical Greek, and 'eventually became the regular way of forming adverbs in M[odern] Gr[eek]'. Cf BDR § 243.1. We came to Puteoli (Greek name Δικαιαρχία; modern, Pozzuoli); for the formation of Ποτίολοι from the Latin name see BDR § 41.1, n. 2.

Puteoli was founded by Ionians, taken by the Romans in the Second Punic War, and made a Roman sea colony in 194 BC. Travellers to Rome often landed at Puteoli and made the rest of the journey (about 130 miles) by road (Cicero, *Pro Plancio* 26 (65) ... decidens e provincia, Puteolos forte venisse ...; Josephus, *Ant.* 17.328; 18.248, προσέπλευσαν ἀμφότεροι Δικαιαρχείᾳ). 'Puteoli was the port where passengers were set ashore, though the cargo of grain was taken up to Portus, the new harbour built by Claudius at Ostia, by the mouth of the Tiber (cf. Sen[eca], *Ep. Mor.* 77.1)' (Hemer 154f.). There had been a Jewish colony at Puteoli since at least 4 BC (Josephus, *War* 2.101–110; *Ant.* 17.324–38). See further *NS* 3.81 (and 3.110f. for a Tyrian colony, bearing witness to contact with the east).

14. For the first time since they reached the west the travelling party encountered ἀδελφοί, that is, Christians. The party (in the first person plural) were invited, or encouraged (παρεκλήθημεν; a perfective aorist, *prevailed upon*, according to M. 3.72; cf. Zerwick § 252) to stay seven days. Presumably this suited the ship's programme of unloading and loading (but see below). Haenchen (687) thinks that Luke added this first part of the verse so that news could be brought to Rome and make possible the deputation of v. 15; it does not seem probable that Luke would think of the necessity of making this kind of connection.

For ἐπιμεῖναι H Ψ 049 326 614 2464 2495 have ἐπιμείναντες. If this is read, παρεκλήθημεν must mean *we were encouraged* (or something like this) rather than *we were asked*: We were encouraged, having stayed with them seven days. This alleviates the difficulty of the prisoners' being invited as if they were free men (Metzger 501). This may well have been the origin of the reading. The delay is the more surprising in that the journey was continued by land. Pesch (2.303) comments, 'Auch die Soldaten waren als Schiffsbrüchige in Puteoli angekommen und mussten sich für die Landreise nach Rom neu ausrüsten usw.' They had had three months in Malta to recover, but presumably they had lost much of their equipment in the wreck.

The words οὕτως εἰς τὴν Ῥώμην ἤλθαμεν seem at first sight to constitute the climax of the book; but in fact the travellers did not reach their destination till v. 16. It has been suggested that in v. 14 *Rome* refers to the *Ager Romanus*, but this is inconsistent with κἀκεῖθεν in v. 15. The best way of taking the words is given by Marshall (419) (similarly Delebecque 137): *And in this way we made our journey to Rome.*

There is no confirmatory evidence for the existence of Christians at Puteoli at this time. Herculaneum and Pompeii are not far away; at Herculaneum there are the supposed cross and altar; at Pompeii two examples of the ROTAS-SATOR square. For a properly sceptical discussion (with bibliography) of this highly problematical (and in the end unconvincing) evidence see Hemer (155f.).

15. In the present context the last words of v. 14 (see above) cannot mean that Paul and his companions had entered the city of Rome; but they were well on the way; the final stretch from Puteoli could be covered by a good walker in five days (Schneider 2.407; Stählin 324). They were also now in contact with the city, since the (the article οἱ is omitted by B, perhaps because it suggested that all the Christians of Rome made the journey) brothers (that is, Christians, as in v. 14) came (ἦλθαν; Ψ 𝔐 have ἐξῆλθαν *to meet us*—the first person plural is still in use. They came as far as Appius' Market and Three Taverns; these were distinct places, and we must suppose that two groups came from Rome. This may mean only that one (an advance guard? Pesch 2.303) had more leisure, or could walk better, than the other; it has been suggested that one consisted of Jewish the other of Gentile Christians (Rackham 498), but there is nothing in the text to support this view. They came because they had heard τὰ περὶ ἡμῶν (these words are omitted by gig vg sy^p), *our affairs; about us* would probably serve in English. It is natural to suppose (see above) that they had heard from Puteoli; the seven days of v. 14 might have allowed messengers to reach Rome in time to arrange a deputation. They had presumably had some notice of an intended visit from the Epistle to the Romans, but this would not tell them when to meet the writer. Luke is not interested in the details of such arrangements.

On the two places see Hemer (156). Paul would come first to Appii Forum, 43 Roman miles from Rome: the 43rd milestone is still extant (*CIL* 10.6825). Part of the journey is described by Horace (*Satires* 1.5.1–4):

> Egressum magna me accepit Aricia Roma
> hospitio modico ...
> ... inde Forum Appii,
> differtum nautis cauponibus atque malignis.

It thus took Horace two days to get from Rome to Appii Forum, though the journey should (lines 5, 6) have been done in one—not however on foot. Cf. Cicero, *Ad Atticum* 1.13.

Tres Tabernae (deriving its name probably from the institutions named) was 33 Roman miles from Rome, and thus not far from Appii Forum. It was on the Via Appia, 'probably at the point where the road from Antium crosses it, near the modern Cisterna' (Knowling 545). Cf. Cicero, *Ad Atticum* 2.10, Ab Appii Foro, hora quarta. dederam aliam paulo ante Tribus Tabernis.

How there came to be Christian brothers in Rome we are not informed. It is possible that they were to be found there as early as 18.2; see the note. Romans makes it clear that the church in Rome was not founded by Paul. If it had a special relation with Peter one would expect to find some reference or allusion to this in the epistle; there is none, but the possibility cannot be excluded; see 1 Clement 5.4; Ignatius, *Romans* 4.3. For Peter as a travelling missionary see *FS* Michel (1963), 1–12. Conzelmann (149) (cf. Haenchen 688; Weiser 674) makes the point that Luke wishes at the same time to show that the Roman church already existed and welcomed Paul, and that Paul was a pioneering apostle; hence the speedy disappearance of the Roman Christians. To say (Haenchen 688) that there were Christians but not an organized ἐκκλησία in Rome would be convincing only to one who thought that a specific church order was necessary for full

Christian life. Schille (475f.) thinks that the narrative presupposes an organized community; Paul is given a triumphal entry (ἀπάντησις).

Paul himself (as Luke depicts him) was not distressed by the absence of church order (if indeed it was absent and Luke did not simply leave it out as unimportant). 'Videbat Christum etiam Romae esse' (Bengel 488); and seeing this he gave thanks and took cheer. Beyer (157) may be right in saying, 'Sie hatten seinen Brief richtig verstanden.' For the language cf. Josephus, *Ant.* 9.55: ... πρὸς τὸ λαβεῖν αὐτὸν εὔελπι θάρσος. For the spelling θάρσος (not θάρρος) see BDR § 34.2, n. 7. Cf. 23.11.

For a description of the way see *Acta Petri et Pauli* 13–21 (L.-B. 1.184–88).

16. Verse 16a seems to repeat v. 14b. See the note on v. 14; but the possibility should also be considered that the doublet is due to Luke's use of more than one source, or to the need of an introduction to the final paragraph. Conzelmann (149) thinks v. 14 to be 'redaktionell vorweggenommen'. In contrast with v. 14 Ῥώμην does not have the article. At least this is so in NA²⁶; the article is read by ℵ* L Ψ 048 614 1175 2495 *al*; it is absent from ℵᶜ A B 066 𝔐. The party would enter Rome by the Via Appia through the Porta Copena.

Davies (*Land* 281) notes that as in v. 15 there is no reference to the military escort (why should there have been?) so here there is no reference to the Roman authorities, to whom Paul was being delivered at so much trouble, danger, and expense. The fact is (see further below) that Luke is allowing the legal proceedings against Paul to drop out of his narrative. In any case, Davies' observation needs some qualification. *Paul was permitted* (ἐπετράπη) ... But ἐπετράπη implies someone who ἐπέτρεψε, permitted Paul to take up the relatively free situation described in this verse, and this must have been a Roman authority. Paul was permitted to stay καθ' ἑαυτόν, *on his own*, that is presumably not in a public prison but in private accommodation (cf. 28.30), in *custodia libera*, not *custodia militaris* (see Tajra 179–181). The concession to legal requirements was that he should remain with the soldier who was guarding him. Luke's expression does not contradict the custom that a prisoner was handed over to two soldiers; no doubt they would watch in shifts. If this is correct it must have been at least provisionally decided that Paul was not a threat to public order.

So far the Old Uncial text has been considered. The Western text makes two substantial changes. Where P⁷⁴ᵛⁱᵈ A B Ψ 148ᵛⁱᵈ 066 81 1175 1739 2464 2495 *pc* vg (syᵖ) bo have ἐπετράπη τῷ Παύλῳ (the Antiochian text apparently following the Western), gig p (syʰ**) sa have ὁ ἑκατόνταρχος παρέδωκεν τοὺς δεσμίους τῷ στρατοπεδάρχῳ, τῷ δὲ Παύλῳ ἐπετράπη. And after ἑαυτόν, 614 2147 *pc* it (syʰ**) add ἔξω τῆς παρεμβολῆς.

The στρατοπέδαρχος (some MSS have –άρχης) is the *praefectus castrorum*; so LS 1653; whether this is a correct interpretation of the present passage is disputed. At a later time the official who would most naturally receive prisoners from abroad would be the prefect of the Praetorian Guard; thus Pliny, *Epistles* 10.57.2, where Trajan writes to Pliny that a person who had been banished 'vinctus mitti ad praefectos praetorii mei debet'. The Prefect from AD 51 to 62 was Afranius Burrus; Sherwin-White (108–11) however, thinks it unlikely that Paul would be committed to him. More probable is the view that the prisoners would be handed over to the *princeps peregrinorum*; this may be supported by the association of this *princeps* with the *frumentarii*, the officers responsible for exercising oversight of the corn fleet (to which Paul's ship probably belonged; see v. 11) and receiving and distributing the cargoes of corn. This association however had probably not yet come into being, and a still more probable view is that the prisoners were received and dealt with by the *princeps castrorum*, the chief administrative officer of the Praetorian Guard. It is however to be noted that in this passage gig has *Principi Peregrinorum*. p has *Prefecto*.

ἔξω τῆς παρεμβολῆς (outside the Praetorian camp, or barracks) interprets καθ' ἑαυτοῦ. In the variants we see editors or copyists filling out a rather thin text on the basis of more or less correct and complete knowledge of Roman procedures. In addition to Sherwin-White see a detailed note by Clark (386–8) on the Western text, *princeps peregrinorum*, and *frumentarii*; also Tajra (177–9) and Hemer (157, 199f.).

64. PAUL AND THE JEWS IN ROME 28.17–28

(17) After three days Paul called together the leading men among the Jews. When they assembled he said to them, 'Brothers, although for my part I had done nothing against the people or our ancestral customs I was handed over from Jerusalem into the hands of the Romans as a prisoner. (18) They examined me and wished to release me because they found in me no capital charge. (19) But because the Jews contradicted this I was compelled to appeal to Caesar, though not because I had anything of which to accuse my nation. (20) For this reason therefore I asked to see you and to address you, for it is for the hope of Israel that I wear this chain.' (21) They said to him, 'As for us, we have neither received letters about you from Judaea, nor has any of the brothers who have come here reported or spoken any ill of you. (22) We should therefore like to hear from you what is in your mind, for as for this sect it is known to us that it is everywhere spoken against.'

(23) They appointed him a day and came in large numbers to his lodging. He gave them an exposition, testifying the kingdom of God and persuading them about Jesus on the basis both of the Law of Moses and of the prophets. This he did from early morning till evening, (24) and some believed the things he said, others did not. (25) The gathering broke up without agreement, with Paul saying one thing. 'Well did the Holy Spirit speak to your fathers through Isaiah the prophet, (26) saying, "Go to this people and say: You will hear and hear and not understand, and you will look and look and will not see. (27) The heart of this people has been hardened, and they have heard dully, and they have shut their eyes; lest they should see with their eyes, and hear with their ears, and understand with their heart, and turn, and I should heal them." (28) So let it be known to you that this God-given salvation has been sent to the Gentiles; they will listen.'

Bibliography

C. K. Barrett, *FS* Jervell, 1–10.

F. Bovon, *ZNW* 75 (1984), 226–32.

F. F. Bruce, *BJRL* 46 (1963/64), 326–45; 50 (1967/68), 262–79.

J. Dupont, as in (63).

K. Haacker, as in (56).

H. J. Hauser, *Strukturen der Abschlusserzählung der Apg.*, AnBib 86, (1979).

P. W. van der Horst, *NovT* 17 (1975), 158.

J. Jervell, *The Unknown Paul*, 13–51.

P. Katz, *ThLZ* 61 (1936), 284; 83 (1958), 316.

E. Larsson, *FS* Jervell, 93–105.

D. P. Moessner, *NTS* 34 (1988), 96–104.

G. W. Trompf, as in (62).

W. Wiefel, *Judaica* 26 (1970), 65–88.

Commentary

Apart from the final verses, 28.30, 31, considered below (pp. 1248–53), this is the end of Luke's story. It should be considered first in this light, as a narrative piece which fulfils the goal frequently alluded to in the course of Acts (1.8; 9.15; 19.21; 23.11; 27.24; cf. also Lk. 3.6; 24.47). Paul has now reached Rome, and is (notwithstanding his appeal to the Emperor's court, before which he must in due course appear) in circumstances favourable to the proclamation of the Gospel; Weiser (674) rightly draws attention to the fact that the present paragraph is framed by 28.16 and 28.30f., which depict a hopeful situation. Luke is primarily a narrator, and the end of his book represents the successful achievement of a primary goal, and thereby the victory of the word of God.

As soon, however, as the contents of this final scene in the play are examined questions and difficulties appear. Delegations of Christians had gone out to meet Paul as he approached the city (28.15), but in the final paragraph there is no further hint of their presence; not only are they not mentioned, v. 22 suggests their absence. Had there been Christians in Rome one would have supposed that the Jews of the city would have known something about them. It is an inadequate explanation that Luke wished to suggest (contrary to fact) that Paul was the founder of the church in Rome; had he intended this he must have omitted 28.15. Why is there no further reference to the Roman church, to which Paul had written so notable a letter? Again, what is Luke's authority for the events he narrates? The first person plural appears no more after 28.15. The brothers came out from Rome to meet *us*, so that *we* must surely have been present in Rome. Roloff (371) goes further than this: "Die auffällige Orientierung der Apg auf Rom hin erklärt sich am besten von der Annahme her, für die auch sonst vieles spricht, dass Lukas Glied der römischen Gemeinde war.' For this there is no direct evidence, but it may provide (and would thereby find support in) an explanation of the silence about the local Christians (noted above). Was Paul rejected by the local Christians, or by an influential number of them, when they had had the opportunity of learning more about him than was known at the time of 28.15? When Romans was written there was a majority of Gentiles in the Roman church, but there were also Jews (*Romans* 6, 23). Was one party not pleased by the exposition of the Gospel they had received on paper and now heard from Paul's lips? Roloff (372) goes on to cite 1 Clement 5.5, where Paul is said to have suffered διὰ ζῆλον καὶ ἔριν; Clement does not say this with special reference to

Paul's experiences in Rome, but he was writing in Rome and his statement may be based on memories preserved there. This may be related to a further question, which cannot be fully discussed here (see Introduction, p. xliii). Why does Acts stop at this point? Why does Luke not continue with an account of Paul's trial before the Emperor, culminating in either his release or his martyrdom? Either event would have made a most impressive close for the book. A possible answer to this question is that a true account of the end of Paul's career might have been anything but impressive; it might have had to describe his desertion by those who should have stood by him (cf. 2 Tim. 4.16). For the present we must be content to discuss the ending that we have, without speculating why we do not have what is not there. See pp. 1248–50.

We are on firmer but still difficult ground when we investigate the assertion made by the Jews that they have had no letter about Paul from Judaea, and that no travelling Jew has had any evil to say about him. That the Jews in Rome had heard nothing about Paul from Jerusalem is 'historisch schwer denkbar' (Roloff 373; cf. Stählin 327, but Stählin is assuming on the doubtful basis of 24.27 a long imprisonment of Paul in the East). The combined improbabilities to some extent support the view that 'die Verse [17–28] sind in toto lukanisch' (Lüdemann 273), but this judgement does not necessarily rob them of all historical value. It is not unimportant that Luke describes two meetings of Paul with the Jews. In vv. 17–22 Paul sends for the Jews (he is in custody and cannot come to them). When they arrive he introduces himself as one who had been obliged to appeal to Caesar not because he wished to accuse his own people (v. 19) but simply as a measure of self-defence. He wished to make it clear that his imprisonment was for the sake of the 'hope of Israel' (v. 20). His hearers reply simply that they are ignorant of the whole affair; they have heard nothing, at least nothing evil, of Paul himself. They have heard of Christianity as a (Jewish) sect, and know that it has a bad reputation. This does not predispose them to view it favourably, but they are fair-minded enough to invite Paul to declare his mind to them (v. 22). This leads to a second invitation and appointment. The Jews come to Paul's lodging, as, presumably, they had done in v. 17. Paul now (v. 23) addresses them in terms that recall Luke's customary summaries of the Gospel, and with the customary result: some believe and some do not. Paul then comments on the situation by quoting Isa. 6.9f. and asserting, as in 13.46; 18.6, that the good news of salvation has been sent (he does not say, will now—from this time—be sent) to the Gentiles, who certainly will listen. This double encounter between Paul and the Jews recalls to Weiser (678) the 'Doppelszene am Anfang der ersten Missionsreise (13.14–43, 44–48)'. There seems little point however in an artificial repetition of this double scene; it would have been easy to compress the substance of vv. 17–28 into one event, and there is therefore some probability that there is some distinct traditional recollection of what took place, though the language, especially of vv. 23–28, is undoubtedly Lucan.

What did Luke mean by this encounter between Paul and the Jews, and especially by his use of an OT passage which plays so large a part in the NT (cf. Mt. 13.14f,; Mk 4.12; Lk. 8.10; Jn 12.40: Rom. 11.8)? For different views that have been taken with regard to this question see Introduction, pp. xcviif. Some think that Luke means that the mission to the Jews is now at an end; individual Jews may still, perhaps be converted, but it is recognized, by Luke and by the church at large, that Israel has rejected the Gospel and that henceforth the church will be a Gentile church. A paradoxically opposite view has also been maintained; the mission to the Gentiles has become possible on the basis of the mission to the Jews. For a full discussion of these views see Wilson (*Gentiles* 226–33). Neither of them is convincing; Luke has throughout his book argued that the Christian Gospel is based upon (a true reading of) the OT; it is the true, fulfilled version of Judaism. He has also (and, as we have seen, in this passage) proclaimed the triumph of the Gospel, not its defeat by a recalcitrant people. This he still maintains, using the explicit quotation of Isaiah 6 and the allusion contained in v. 28 (see the notes) to show that even aspects of the completed story that seem less than triumphant are present in fulfilment of Scripture; the whole story is in God's hand. Cf. Dupont, *Nouvelles Études* 510f.

17. For Luke's use of ἐγένετο with the accusative and infinitive see Introduction, p. xlvi. After only three days Paul's first step was to call together (the active and middle of συγκαλεῖν seem to be used indifferently; see BDR § 316.2, n. 3) the leading men among the Jews. From this point we hear no more of the Christians in Rome. Luke offers no explanation of this and no conjecture (see e.g. Lüdemann 273f.) is wholly satisfying. It may well be that the reception of Paul by the Roman Christians was anything but wholehearted. 1 Clement 5.5 ascribes his martyrdom to ζῆλος καὶ ἔρις; these may have been found within the Christian community itself. That Luke wished to make a final clarification of the position of church and Gospel over against Judaism may be true but it is not a sufficient reason for omitting all further reference to the church. πρῶτος is used here as at 25.2. M. 1.228 refers to Ramsay [*Church* 52] as quoting J. A. Robinson to the effect that ὁ ὤν 'introduces some technical phrase, or some term which it marks out as having a technical sense (cf. 5.17; 13.1; 28.17), and is almost equivalent to τοῦ ὀνομαζομένου'. Here it could mean, 'those who bore the title of ...'. The expression recalls the δέκα πρῶτοι of Tiberias (see Josephus, *Life* 69, 168, 296; *War* 2.639; and cf. *NS* 2.180) also the

ראשי כנסת, the heads of a synagogue community. In Rome, the Jews (who have evidently returned after the expulsion of 18.2) were gathered in a number of synagogues. Eleven are known by name (*NS* 3.95–8). For their ἄρχοντες (who might well be styled πρῶτοι) see *NS* 3.98–100. It may be inferred that Paul, as a prisoner, though well treated, was not at liberty to visit the synagogues; if contact was to be made their leaders must come to him.

The next clause is badly constructed; the genitive pronoun in a genitive absolute (συνελθόντων—the result of συγκαλέσασθαι—αὐτῶν) is followed by an accusative (πρὸς αὐτούς).

ἔλεγεν: 'impf. quia expectatur responsum (ut ἠρώτα [3.3] al.)' (Blass 288).

For Paul's address to the Jews, ἄνδρες ἀδελφοί, see e.g. 2.29; 22.1. In good Attic style, the vocative stands close to the beginning of the sentence. Paul continues (unusually in the NT) by using οὐ[δέν] with the participle. The participial clause is concessive: Although I had nothing ... For ἔθεσι πατρῴοις see 15.1; 21.21; 22.3; 26.3. P. W. van der Horst (*NovT* 17 (1975), 158) quotes Hierocles the Stoic 52.9 (= Stobaeus *Florilegium* 3.39.36), τὰ ἔθη φυλακτέον τά γε ὄντως πάτρια. It is not clear whether ἐξ Ἱεροσολύμων is to be connected with δέσμιος or with παρεδόθην. *From Jerusalem* probably represents the 'authority' under which Paul was held before the Romans took charge, but the wording here calls attention to the discrepancy between this brief summary of events and the more detailed account of the preceding chapters. Paul was certainly thought to have acted in a manner contrary to the interests of the People and the Law, though of course he denied this. The first expression of this charge was the mob violence that broke out in the Temple. As a result of this Paul was handed over (παρεδόθην) to the Romans; the Romans took him by force out of the hands of the Jews in order to prevent his being lynched; this at least was the effect of their action. Its initial intention may have been to prevent the development of a dangerous riot. From this point onwards however Paul was in what may equally be described as Roman custody and Roman protection. The Jews would have liked to try him in their own court and, if we may accept Luke's narrative, there can be little doubt that such a trial would have resulted in his death. He refused to be handed over for Jewish trial and the case was transferred to the Governor's court in Caesarea. The Romans could see nothing more serious in the matter than a Jewish theological controversy and the bizarre assertion that a dead man, Jesus, was now alive. Eventually, in order to remain in Roman hands and secure a fair (that is, a non-Jewish) trial—perhaps also in order to win a passage to Rome—Paul used his Roman citizenship in an appeal to Caesar. This summary account is so radically abbreviated by Paul (Luke) as to suggest that Paul's position as a Roman prisoner was due to Jewish legal action. It may be correct to see (with Conzelmann 149) in the expression εἰς τὰς χεῖρας τῶν Ῥωμαίων the influence of the story of Jesus; Conzelmann refers to Lk. 9.22; 24.7; one could add Acts 2.23. The passion of the servant of Christ is described in terms drawn from Christ's own. The conformity with Christ's death that Paul could claim as a theological proposition (most clearly in Phil. 3.10) Luke has expressed in historical—perhaps we should say, quasi-historical—terms.

18. The parallel with the story of Jesus continues. Pilate found Jesus innocent (Lk. 23.4, 15, 22); the Roman court found Paul innocent (23.29; 25.18, 25; 26.31f.).

οἵτινες is here little if anything more than the equivalent of οἵ; perhaps there is a hint of, Fair-minded people like them ... wished to release me. In 614 *pc* sy^h** the relative is followed by πολλά. This is probably used adverbially: The Romans examined (on ἀνακρίνειν see on 24.8) me *strictly*. Metzger (501), however, translates the longer text, 'when they had examined me *concerning many things* [or, after a *long* examination]'.

As a result of their examination the Romans wished to release Paul, because (διά with the articular infinitive and accusative) no charge requiring the death penalty existed in me. For αἰτία see 23.28; 25.18, 27.

19. Paul does not conceal the fact that the Jews took a different view of the loyalty to Judaism that he professed. According to the Old Uncial text they simply denied what he said. In the Western text (represented here by 614 2147 *pc* sy^h**) they went further: καὶ ἐπικραζόντων· αἶρε τὸν ἐχθρὸν ἡμῶν, which, though it recalls 22.22, is not simply a verbal assimilation to that verse. It was their attitude that compelled (ἠναγκάσθην) Paul to appeal to Caesar (25.11). This was (he asserts) simply a matter of self-defence, a step taken in order to secure a fair trial and security till the trial was held. He denies the intention of bringing any accusation against his own race. He has in fact in the preceding sentences accused them of making an unjustified and lethal attack upon himself; it is in Caesar's court that he will not accuse them. Paul's true intention is made explicit in a further Western addition, after κατηγορεῖν (κατηγορῆσαι in Ψ 𝔐): ἀλλ᾽ ἵνα λυτρώσωμαι τὴν ψυχήν μου ἐκ θανάτου (614 2147 *pc* gig p vg^mss sy^h**). Here the Western text is not so much introducing an anti-Jewish element into the text as filling out connections that the shorter text implies but does not state, and at the same time sharpening the narrative. Delebecque (138) accepts the Western reading and defends it at length.

'The Jews' stand over against Paul, who distinguishes himself from them; yet he does not accuse them. The distinction and the lack of accusation are both elements in Luke's attitude to Judaism. See Pesch (2.308).

At first sight it may appear that this verse contains another example (cf. v. 17) of the use of οὐ with a participle; this however may not be so. According to BDR § 430.2, n. 4 οὐχ negatives not the participle but the main verb: I did not appeal because I had ... This however is not quite satisfactory. Paul did in fact appeal. I appealed, but not because I had ..., or, though I did not have ... Cf. BDR § 425.3, n. 3, where οὐχ ὡς is rightly rendered 'nicht, als ob'.

20. διὰ ταύτην τὴν αἰτίαν, *for this reason* (αἰτία not as in v. 18). It is not clear to what reason Paul refers. The phrase may look forward (For this reason, namely because (γάρ) it is for the sake of Israel's hope that I ...), or backward, to Paul's explanation (v. 19) of his appeal to Caesar. The prospective reference scarcely seems adequate, and it is best to give the 'reason' a somewhat wider explanation than the words themselves demand. It is because my appeal to Caesar puts me in an ambiguous position, in which I am at the same time defending myself against an unwarranted attack from the Jewish side while I am in truth maintaining all that is true and valuable in Judaism, that I must seize, or create, an opportunity of making clear to you exactly what the facts are. I have been more than sufficiently misunderstood in Jerusalem, and I hope by seeing you and speaking with you to be understood by you and to be on good terms with you.

M. 2.319 takes παρακαλεῖν to have here its simplest, literal sense, *to call to one*. BDR § 409.5, n. 7 more cautiously allow the two possibilities, *ich habe euch gebeten euch sehen zu dürfen*, and *ich habe euch herbeigerufen, euch zu sehen*. *Call to one* would be a very unusual meaning for παρακαλεῖν in the NT, and there is no reason why the simple meaning *ask* should not be adopted: I have asked to see you and address you. Bruce (1.477) takes ὑμᾶς as the object both of παρεκάλεσα and of ἰδεῖν καὶ προσλαλῆσαι. It is not really needed with παρεκάλεσα (as in English: I asked to see you).

Elsewhere Paul has insisted that the real point at issue between himself and his Jewish adversaries is the resurrection: 23.6; 24.15, and it may be that this is the meaning here of *the hope of Israel*. At 26.6 however (and perhaps at 24.15 also) the meaning of *hope* is different, and it is probable that here the hope of Israel is the realization of the promises God has made to his people, that is, the promise of Messianic salvation. Paul alleges that the hope has been and will be fulfilled in Jesus. For Paul (whether this is true also for Luke is a difficult question) this belief is guaranteed and anticipated by the resurrection of Jesus, but the hope is wider than the personal resurrection of the crucified Messiah. Understood in this way the statement represents fairly enough the issue between Christianity and

Judaism: Jesus was or was not the one in whom the promises were fulfilled. Weiser (680) rightly comments that Luke is concerned with the question of Jewish and Christian identity.

It was this belief that led to Paul's arrest and to his being now in custody. His position is vividly expressed: τὴν ἄλυσιν ταύτην περίκειμαι. This verb is used as a passive of περιτιθέναι (Blass 289: 'Est κεῖσθαι = τιθεῖσθαι'), which takes a dative of the person wearing and accusative of the thing worn. The dative becomes the subject of the passive and the accusative remains. See BDR § 159.4, n. 4. 'Is this metaphorical? If not, what was the force of the *Lex Iulia*?' (*Begs.* 4.346). If Paul was not wearing a chain the metaphor would fall flat. But the wording is due to Luke.

ἕνεκεν stands in NA[26] and no variant is given. In fact, εἵνεκεν is used in a number of MSS, including ℵ* and A (also B, according to Ropes, *Begs.* 3.252). With this variation in mind Blass (289) comments, 'εἵνεκεν forma ionica pro ἕνεκεν (ἕνεκα et εἵνεκα att.) etiam Lc 4.18 ℵ A B al it 2 Cor 3.10.'

21. The Jews in Rome cannot comment on Paul's relations with the Jews in Jerusalem or on the version of 'realized Judaism' that he presents. They are completely uninformed about Paul and have barely heard, and that unfavourably, about Christianity (v. 22). They have received no letters about Paul from Judaea. This 'assumes that there was regular correspondence and personal contact between the Jews in Rome and the Jewish supreme authority in Jerusalem, the Sanhedrin' (J. Jeremias, *Jerusalem* 64). The correspondence had contained no reference to Paul. That is surprising, if the Jewish authorities had in fact determined (as the earlier chapters in Acts suggest) to destroy Paul; even if they thought it unlikely (as indeed it was) that local Jewish opinion could affect the proceedings in the Emperor's court one would expect them to solicit any help that might possibly be available (the Emperor might conceivably wish to sound Jewish opinion) and to put the Roman Jewish communities on their guard against a disruptive and perverting presence.

The latter part of the verse is ambiguous, and its meaning depends on the stress laid upon πονηρόν. It may mean that no report at all concerning Paul and therefore no evil—or good—report had reached Rome, or that those who had spoken of him had had no evil to say. On the whole it seems that the Roman Jews are professing complete ignorance of Paul and are minimizing their knowledge, which they cannot deny altogether, of the Christian movement.

ἀπήγγειλεν ἢ ἐλάλησεν 'reported (officially) or spoken (unofficially)'—Bruce (1.478).

This verse suggests an almost complete cleavage between Jews and Christians in Rome, and between Jews in Rome and Jews in Jerusalem. Neither of these seems probable. The effect is to represent

Paul as not only a pioneer missionary but as the spokesman of Christianity to the Jews. This at least seems to be Luke's intention.

The suggestion that the Jerusalem Jews had decided to withdraw from the prosecution since there was no hope of obtaining a verdict in the Emperor's court and the penalties for accusers who failed to win their case were heavy is dealt with by Sherwin-White (112–19) and Hemer (157f.). It is not strong. 'The possibility that Paul's accusers never intended to pursue their prosecution requires much thought. Roman justice at this period was also severe on default, and A. N. Sherwin-White (112–19) shows that the thrust of contemporary legislation was rather to enforce prosecution than to favour release of the unindicted' (Hemer 157).

22. Having heard nothing about Paul himself and only unfavourable reports of the faith he proclaimed, the Jews desired to hear what he had to say, to know his views, what was in his mind—ἃ φρονεῖς. It was the same desire that was expressed by the Areopagites in 17.19.

Christianity is described as a αἵρεσις; for the word see on 5.17; 24.5, 14. It suggests a party (within Judaism). If pressed, it would mean that the Roman Jews still thought of Christianity as one sect, with its own interpretation of Jewish principles, within Judaism; this indeed is the way in which it is on the whole presented in Acts, though it is presented as a form of Judaism with open access to Gentiles. All that can be said is that it is everywhere (that is, among all Jews) spoken against, rejected and resisted.

μέν (after περί) is omitted by 104 pc, possibly because there is no answering δέ (for μέν solitarium in Acts see 1.1; 3.21; 27.21, and cf. BDR § 447.2c, n. 15). It may be that a δέ clause is to be understood here: We know that this form of religion is everywhere disliked, nevertheless, *or* but for that very reason, we should like to hear what you have to say. This is more or less the suggestion of Blass (289): 'μὲν sine δὲ ut 3.21 al.; supplendum fere ut oppositum idem quod modo praecessit (ἀξιοῦμεν κτέ.).'

The Jews' ignorance of Paul and their knowledge of Christianity only by repute fit badly with the view that the expulsion of the Jews under Claudius (see on 18.2) had been caused by Jewish–Christian riots (impulsore Chresto). This may be explained by the fact that Luke is here writing up material available to him in such a way as to suggest that Paul was virtually the founder of the church in Rome (see above, p. 1235); more probably however Luke wishes to represent Paul as starting a clean sheet in relation with the Roman Jews.

23. The middle ταξάμενος is correctly used (cf. e.g. 2 Macc. 3.14; 14.21) for making an arrangement (cf. 15.2, where the active is used); here for appointing a day for meeting. On the appointed day the Jews came (ἦλθον; but Ψ 𝔐 have ἧκον, and the less common word could be right) to Paul; he, though living καθ' ἑαυτόν (28.16) but with a guard, was not free to go where he chose. The usual meaning of ξενία is *hospitality*, but here 'perh. *lodging*' (LS 1188). *Begs.* 4.346 prefers hospitality, but BA 1109 prefers the concrete sense of the word; so also Haenchen (690). At Philemon 22, the only other occurrence in the NT, it is similarly ambiguous. Cf. the use of μίσθωμα in 28.30. It is not possible to reach a clear decision on this question, and not necessary: if the Jews came to Paul's lodging he was their host (the word ξενία does not necessarily imply elaborate entertainment) and if he entertained them at all it must have been at his lodging.

πλείονες is probably elative, they came in considerable numbers (rather than comparative, more came than on the previous occasion, v. 17). For the form of the word see BDR § 47.2, n. 2. πλείονες is used here and at 27.12, πλείονας at 27.20, but πλείους at 13.31; 19.32; 21.10; 23.13, 21; 24.11; 25.6, 14. This might suggest a special source for chs. 27, 28.

Luke continues the sentence, as often in Acts, with a relative (οἷς). For the use of ἐκτίθεσθαι cf. 11.4; 18.26. It occurs nowhere else in the NT (at 7.21 in a different sense), but the meaning *to set forth* is clear. P[74vid] A*[vid] *pc* have the aorist ἐξέθετο. The imperfect is clearly suitable for a process lasting all day, but the aorist can be understood as constative: on this occasion, viewed as a whole, Paul set forth the Gospel. The setting forth is amplified by the participle διαμαρτυρόμενος (διαμαρτυράμενος, ℵ(*); παρατιθέμενος, A). This fulfils the promise of 23.11. Exactly what testifying the kingdom of God means is not clear, but elsewhere (e.g. 28.31) Luke appears to use the term kingdom of God as a summary of the Christian message (so also Schmithals 239) and it should be so taken here, with the next clause bringing out the Christological content and base of the message. Paul sets out to persuade his hearers about Jesus, namely that he fulfils the meaning and especially the promises of the Law and the prophets. Stählin (327), noting the juxtaposition of kingdom and Jesus, aptly refers to Origen's word, αὐτοβασίλεια. The Law is here understood as a repository of messianic predictions and promises rather than as a body of commandments, though Luke still wishes to present Paul as an observant Jew, in no way an enemy of the Law. Both the Law and the prophets are used: τε stands after the preposition. This is classical; see BDR § 444.5, n. 6. Another classical feature is the omission of the article before a word denoting time (ἕως ἑσπέρας); M. 3.179; BDR § 255.3, n. 5. Paul's interview with the Jewish representatives lasted all day; if in the end any were unbelieving (v. 24) the fault was not his. Of πείθων, Knowling says that the tense is not simply *de conatu*; it refers to the persuasive power of Paul's words but does not claim that they resulted in conviction. But surely the present participle matches ἐξετίθετο, and the imperfect is durative; the process went on all day, ἀπὸ πρωῒ ἕως ἑσπέρας.

Μωϋσέως is omitted by P⁷⁴, either by accident or because it was felt to be unnecessary to specify what law was intended.

24. The outcome was mixed; it is expressed by the use of the classical οἱ μὲν ... οἱ δέ ... construction. cf. 17.32, where a similar consequence of Paul's preaching is described. πείθεσθαι is the opposite of ἀπιστεῖν, that is, it means *to believe*. This is against Bruce's (2.506) rendering of the imperfect, 'were on the way to being persuaded'.

It is important, in view of the following verses, to note that Luke is at pains not to represent all Jews as unbelieving. He refers first to those who were persuaded by Paul's message.

25. The Jews were divided, were in disagreement, ἀσύμφωνοι. The word occurs nowhere else in the NT, but elsewhere is not uncommon in both literal (unharmonious) and metaphorical senses; cf. Plato, *Gorgias* 482c, where ἀσύμφωνοι εἶναι includes ἐναντία λέγειν.

There was no agreement and the gathering broke up, when Paul had fired one Parthian shot (the aorist participle εἰπόντος refers to something said before ἀπελύοντο), quoting a passage (Isa. 6.9f.) used in a number of notable places in the NT (see Mt. 13.14f. = Mk 4.12 = Lk. 8.10; Jn 12.40; Rom. 11.8; cf. Justin, *Trypho* 12.2; 33.1). It was addressed to *your* fathers (ὑμῶν, P⁷⁴ ℵ A B Ψ 049 33 81 323 945 1175 1739 2464 *al* p s syᵖ Cyril of Jerusalem; 𝔐 gig vg have ἡμῶν; syʰ omits); this has the effect of dissociating Paul from his hearers. 'Melius ὑμῶν quam ἡμῶν; neque enim P. sibi partem huius quasi hereditatis vindicat' (Blass 290).

Belief in the inspiration of the OT is plainly expressed. The words were given *through* Isaiah but the actual speaker was the Holy Spirit. Fitzmyer, (*Essays* 301), cites CD 4.13, 14, As God spoke through (literally, by the hand of) Isaiah [דבר אל ביד ישעיה] the prophet, the son of Amoz, saying ...

26. This verse gives the words of Isa. 6.9 substantially as they appear in the LXX. In the opening clause there is variation in order, and where Luke has πρὸς τὸν λαὸν τοῦτον, the LXX has (after εἰπόν) τῷ λαῷ τούτῳ. On the accentuation of ειπον see below. After this the agreement is complete (though there are small variations in the MSS of the LXX).

ειπον is undoubtedly imperative—no other understanding of it (first person singular or third person plural aorist indicative) makes sense, but it may be written εἰπόν (said to be Syracusan Greek) or εἶπον (apparently Attic). The former is used in NA²⁶ and in most printed editions. See M. 2.58; BDR § 81.1, n. 1; also BA 456; P. Katz, *ThLZ* 61 (1936), 284; 83 (1958), 316; earlier, WM 23, 58, 103; WS § 6.7d.

πορεύθητι (aorist) is an emphatic, once-for-all instruction: Go, go now; there is no need to deliberate.

The cognate dative ἀκοῇ represents the Hebrew infinitive absolute, which has the effect of intensifying the meaning of the verb; the participle βλέποντες serves the same purpose. See Zerwick (§ 61); BDR § 198.6, n. 9. In the quotation (and in agreement with the LXX) the future of ἀκούειν has the active form ἀκούσετε; in v. 28, where Luke writes without the constraint of quotation, he uses the classical middle deponent future, ἀκούσονται. See Zerwick (§ 226); BDR § 77.3, n. 2. For details of the quotation see G. J. Steyn, *Septuagint Quotations in the Context of the Petrine and Pauline Speeches of the Acta Apostolorum* (Kampen 1995), 219–29.

The prophet is sent to his people with the message that there is no possibility of their understanding what they hear or seeing what they look at. The built-in failure of the message is the content of it. The unbelief of Israel is not an unhappy accident but part of God's intention. The theme is continued in the next verse; see on that verse and on v. 28 for the use Luke makes of his quotation. Calvin (2.312) draws the lines of interpretation too sharply for Lucan thought: 'This cause, mentioned here [that the reprobate are to blame for their rejection], does not prevent the secret election of God from distinguishing between men, so that those, who have been ordained to life, believe, but the others continue to be senseless.'

27. The quotation of Isaiah 6 continues. In NA[26] there are again small differences. In τοῖς ὠσὶν αὐτῶν Luke drops the unnecessary αὐτῶν. It is worth noting that for ἐπαχύνθη, ℵ* (gig) have ἐβαρύνθη (without LXX parallel); for ἐπιστρέψωσιν, A E Ψ 048 81 *pc* vg^mss have ἐπιστρέψουσιν (in agreement with LXX ℵ), and for ἰάσομαι, E 33 81 2464 *pm* gig vg have ἰάσωμαι (in agreement with LXX V). There would no doubt be a tendency to assimilate the text of Acts to whatever text of Isaiah was known and approved, but the opposite tendency—to assimilate texts of the LXX written and used by Christians to the text of Acts—would also take effect. The word καμμύειν is rejected by Phrynichus (319): δέον ὡς οἱ ἄριστοι τῶν ἀρχαίων καταμύειν.

The verse is probably intended by Luke (and was probably intended by Isaiah) as a description of people who had made up their minds not to understand, not to hear, not to see. The voices of the verbs are probably not significant, unless ἐπαχύνθη is a passive of divine action: God has hardened the hearts of his people. But there is nothing to indicate that this is what Luke intends. βαρέως ἤκουσαν simply states a fact; ἐκάμμυσαν means that the people closed their eyes and were therefore themselves to blame for the fact that they did not see. Like v. 26, this verse states that they did not understand, hear, or see; and that this fact did not stand outside God's purpose. The immediate historical consequence of this fact and of this disclosure of God's purpose was that the Gospel was taken to the Gentiles; Luke is not dealing with the more remote consequence of the ultimate destiny of Israel. He does not see into the situation as acutely as Paul does in Rom. 9–11, and he does not recognize (at least, he does not state) the underlying truth that it is only out of disobedience that men can in faith discover mercy (Rom. 11.30–32).

28. This verse makes explicit the intention that has already been given implicitly in the quotation in vv. 26, 27. As Bornkamm (4.157) points out, there is here a new, Lucan rather than Pauline, basis for the Gentile mission. If the Jews vacate their place, the Gentiles will take it. What the Jews refuse to hear, the Gentiles will listen to (cf. Schmithals 240). For Luke this is not so much a theological proposition as a statement of fact; he could not fail to observe that the Greeks were pressing into the church, the Jews were not. Jewish Christians were becoming a minority, even if, in Jervell's term, a 'mighty minority'. Many take the view that Luke (cf. 13.46; 18.6) considers the mission to the Jewish people as a whole to be at an end; individual Jews may still be converted, but the main direction of the church's work is now towards the Gentiles (see e.g. Roloff 375; Weiser 683). This seems to be too simple an analysis of Acts; this has been shown especially by J. Jervell (especially *The Unknown Paul* (1984), 13–51; cf. *FS* Jervell 1–10; 93–105 (E. Larsson)). It is indeed probable that Luke could see which way things were moving at the time at which he wrote, but the chief Lucan motif which emerges here is one which runs through his work as a whole. Nothing can or will prevent the spread of the Gospel. Preachers may be persecuted, imprisoned, even killed, but the word of God is not bound. The most favoured nation, who of all races should have welcomed the fulfilment of their hope most gladly, may reject God's offer of salvation; others will take it up. You refuse to listen, but they will hear. Luke has his own kind of triumphalism, but it is the proper triumphalism of the word.

γνωστὸν εἶναι (γίνεσθαι) is characteristic of Acts: 1.19; 4.10; 9.42; 13.38; 19.17; 28.22. For the possibility of Semitism see Wilcox 90f., 161f. τοῖς ἔθνεσιν is emphatic in its position, but does not imply that salvation is no longer available to Jews. σωτήριον (neuter of the adjective σωτήριος) is preferred to the noun σωτηρία here only in Acts. See BDR § 263.2, n. 5, and cf. Lk. 2.30; 3.6, remarked on by Dupont (*Nouvelles Études* 509); but the use of σωτήριον may be due to recollection of Ps. 67(66).3, τοῦ γνῶναι ἐν τῇ γῇ τὴν ὁδόν σου, ἐν πᾶσιν ἔθνεσιν τὸ σωτήριόν σου. Stählin (328) points out with reference to this, the end of Paul's mission as recorded in Acts, the way it begins: υἱοὶ γένους ᾿Αβραάμ ... ἡμῖν ὁ λόγος τῆς σωτηρίας ταύτης ἐξαπεστάλη (13.26).

αὐτοὶ καί: For καί used to strengthen the pronoun see BDR § 442.8b, n. 24. Delebecque (140) makes essentially the same point when he says that καί strengthens the verb: 'Eux, oui, ils écouteront.' Luke has just pointed out in his OT quotation the inability or unwillingness of the Jews to hear the message directed to them; *they*, on the other hand, the Gentiles, will hear. ἀκούσονται is the correct middle deponent form of the future; contrast v. 26.

XVII

CONCLUSION
28.(29)–31

65. CONCLUSION 28.(29), 30, 31

(29)[1] When he had said this the Jews went away, holding much debate among themselves. (30) He stayed a full two years[2] in his own hired house, and received all who came to him, (31) preaching the kingdom of God and teaching the truths concerning the Lord Jesus Christ with all boldness and without hindrance.

Bibliography

E. Bammel, in R. P. Bauckham, *The Book of Acts* 4.358–64.

C. K. Barrett, in *FS* Hengel 3.545–55.

F. F. Bruce, as in (64).

O. Cullmann, *RScR* 60 (1972), 55–68.

P. Davies, *ExpT* 94 (1983), 334, 335.

G. Delling, *NovT* 15 (1973), 193–204.

J. Dupont, as in (60), and as in (64).

E. Hansack, *BZ* 19 (1975), 249–53; 21 (1977), 118–21.

H. J. Hauser, as in (64).

D. L. Mealand, *NTS* 36 (1990), 583–97.

F. Saum, *BZ* 20 (1976), 226–9.

G. W. Trompf, as in (62).

Commentary

The contents of these concluding verses are clear enough: the form of custody in which Paul is kept permits him to receive all who wish to visit him, and in this setting he continues to preach with freedom and without restraint. The question that the verses pose is why Luke stops where he does. What happened at the end of the 'two years' (v. 30)?

---

[1]RSV, NEB, NJB omit this verse.
[2]RSV, NEB, at his own expense.

The question has been asked above (p. 1236) but cannot be avoided here. Since we have nothing but conjecture on which to base an answer it is not surprising that many different answers have been given. An admirably clear list is given by Wilson (*Gentiles* 233–6); it may be summarized as follows. 1. Luke was writing at the time to which the verses refer; he wrote no more because nothing more had happened. This view has of course implications for the date of Acts. 2. Luke planned to take the story further in a third volume which either was never written or has been lost. 3. Luke did not record Paul's martyrdom because he wished to avoid parallels both with the acts of the pagan martyrs and with the story of Jesus. 4. Luke did not record Paul's martyrdom because it would not have interested him or his readers; they were concerned with theology, not with biography. 5. It was sufficiently indicated by v. 30 that, after two years had elapsed, Paul would automatically be released. On this suggestion see the note on v. 30. 6. Luke did not recount Paul's death because he did not wish to encourage a piety of martyrdom. Wilson has little difficulty in pointing out objections to all these attempted solutions. He himself makes two points. (a) Luke did not need to recount Paul's trial and its outcome because his readers already knew the facts. This seems to presuppose (though Wilson does not say so) that Acts was written in Rome. (b) 'Acts 28 summarises and rounds off the rest of his narrative' (236). The themes of Jewish obduracy (vv. 26–28) and of the fulfilment of the commission of 1.8 are both brought out. These are important points but even these are open to objection. Was Acts written simply for the Roman church? It cannot be assumed even that it was written in Rome; and if it was Luke would surely hope for a wider readership; he had contacts, personal or on paper, all over the Christian world. Roman Christians may have known what happened, but that would not mean that they had no desire to see the record on paper, and Christians throughout the Empire would be deeply interested in the contact between the church, represented by Paul, and the Emperor. And though Wilson is careful to cite vv. 26–28 as the basis of his reference to the 'obduracy of the Jews' this theme does not occur in the final verses, where Paul welcomes *all* who approach him.

If room remains for conjecture—and there is indeed room for little else—it may be suggested that the end of the story was omitted because it was not edifying. There are two possibilities which may to some extent be combined. One is that after two years Paul's *custodia libera* was changed into more severe imprisonment; in other words he was shut up in a dungeon and left to rot—perhaps to be forgotten; was it part of Luke's purpose to revive the memory of him? The Roman church may have attempted much or little on his behalf; in the end they gave up. The second form of this hypothesis is suggested by 2 Tim. 4.16. The provenance of the apparently autobiographical verses in the Pastorals cannot be discussed here, and it does not matter whether this verse was written by Paul and incorporated in the pseudonymous epistle or came from some other source. Its content is too disreputable for it to be described as pure fiction; there existed a tradition of a desertion of Paul by those who should have stood by him. When this took place we do not know. It could have been at his trial in Rome, perhaps (see A. T. Hanson, *The Pastoral Epistles*, NCB, 1982; p. 160) at the *prima actio*; and it could have been repeated at the later proceedings. One possible explanation (see pp. 1219, 1235) of the curious fact that after 28.15 there is no reference to the Roman church is that the church was divided and lukewarm in its attitude to Paul. If anything like this is true Luke may well have thought that his brief concluding note would do better than a description of what happened when the two years of sustained evangelism ended in discreditable failure on the part of Roman Christians.

The two concluding verses were written by Luke himself. Verse 30 takes up v. 23: ἐν ἰδίῳ μισθώματι takes up εἰς τὴν ξενίαν, εἰσπορευομένους πρὸς αὐτόν takes up ἦλθον πρὸς αὐτόν, κηρύσσων and διδάσκων take up ἐξετίθετο and πείθων, τὴν βασιλείαν τοῦ θεοῦ is repeated, and τὰ περὶ τοῦ κυρίου Ἰησοῦ Χριστοῦ takes up περὶ τοῦ Ἰησοῦ. The circumstances are the same and the message is the same; the only difference is that whereas in vv. 23f. the audience is wholly Jewish v. 30 refers to πάντας, which will certainly include Gentiles but cannot exclude Jews. This is important, because it shows how 28.26–28 are to be understood. These verses mean not that there is no longer to be a mission to the Jews, but that Jewish unbelief is not due to the preacher's failure; it is foretold in Jewish Scripture itself. 'What Luke was defending he has successfully concluded: God's fidelity to his people and to his own word' (Johnson 476). Dupont (*NTS* 6 (1960), 132–55; Kremer, *Actes*, 359–404) agrees with Haenchen that each mission, to Jews and to Gentiles, influences the other. 'L'entrée des Gentiles dans l'histoire du salut devient ainsi un des signes permettant de reconnaître que Jésus est bien le Messie promis à Israël' (404).

29. This verse is added by 𝔐 it vg^cl sy^h**, as follows: καὶ ταῦτα αὐτοῦ εἰπόντος ἀπῆλθον οἱ Ἰουδαῖοι πολλὴν ἔχοντες ἐν ἑαυτοῖς συζήτησιν (ζήτησιν, 104 *pc*). It is clearly of Western origin but has been taken up in the Antiochian text. It was probably felt that the story begun in v. 23 needed some narrative conclusion in addition to Paul's pronouncement in 28.28. 'The addition was probably made because of the abrupt transition from ver. 28 to ver. 30' (Metzger 502). It indicates what Luke probably intended to convey—not the total and final rejection of Judaism but a people divided in their response to the Gospel.

The verse is not contained in P⁷⁴ ℵ A B E Ψ 048 33 81 1175 1739 2464 *pc* s vgˢᵗ syᵖ co.

30. This verse and the next wind up Luke's story. For the questions raised by the fact that Acts ends where and as it does see pp. 1248–50. The verses in themselves are clear and satisfactory; it is not what is said but all that is not said that gives rise to problems.

The aorist ἐνέμεινεν is used to describe a state of affairs that extended over two years; these are viewed as a unit (Moule, *IB* 13; M. 3.72). For διετία (cf. biennium) cf. 24.27; the evidence suggests that the word was coming into use in late Greek (see MM 160f. for inscriptions and papyri; Philo, *In Flaccum* 128; Josephus, *Ant.* 1.302 has ἑπταετία). ὅλην implies that a full period of 24 months is intended; otherwise, using the inclusive method of reckoning common in antiquity, 'two years' (that is, parts of two calendar years) might mean very considerably less. BDR § 332.1 take the aorist (ἐνέμεινεν, above) to imply that at the end of the two-year period the state of things described ended—'dann aber hörte dieser Zustand auf'. This is perhaps a probable rather than a necessary inference from the tense.

In a long note in *Begs.* 5.319–38, Cadbury (quoting Lake at length) argues that the διετία referred to in this verse was significant in view of the Roman legal provision that if the accusers of a prisoner failed to appear within two years the prosecution would lapse and the prisoner be released. A first-century reader would then take the verse to mean that Paul had been released and that even during the time he was kept in custody he was able to preach freely. This suggestion offers what seems in many respects a satisfactory explanation of the end of Acts. It is however radically criticized by Sherwin-White (112–19). The most serious point of criticism is Cadbury's dependence on a Latin papyrus (*BGU* 628 recto), which Cadbury, following L. Mitteis, *Grundzüge und Chrestomathie der Papyruskunde* (1912), 2.1.281, dated in the time of Nero. It seems now to be agreed that this document belongs to a much later period. Sherwin-White writes, 'The rule that Cadbury requires does not make its appearance until AD 529. In texts dated to AD 385 and 409 Theodosius enacts that if an accuser fails to proceed with his case within a fixed period, finally defined as two years, he shall be punished. But that the accused should be acquitted is only laid down in a rule of Justinian dated AD 529' (115, n. 4). In the end however Sherwin-White comes to a conclusion not unlike Cadbury's. 'A more probable technical solution than that of Cadbury lies, as so often, in the nature of *imperium*. Claudius in his edict about absent prosecutors did not establish a law. For that he would have used a decree of the Senate, as was his custom. He simply stated what he himself was going to do ... Nothing prevented the successor of Claudius from taking a similar line [in dismissing prisoners and the like] if he chose ... Perhaps Paul benefited from the clemency of Nero [encouraged by Seneca], and secured a merely casual release' (118f.). Sherwin-White adds, 'But there is no necessity to construe Acts to mean that he was released at all' (119). The reference however to a specific period does suggest termination, whether in release or in death; see above on the aorist ἐνέμεινεν. See also the excellent critical summary in Wilson (*Gentiles* 233–8), and more recently Hemer (383–7, 398); also Dupont (*Études* 544f.), and (still to be studied) *Begs.* 5.319–38 (above). Haenchen's argument (692) that if after two years there had been a favourable verdict its apologetic value would have been too great to be omitted is a strong one. Schmithals (241f.) believes that Paul came to Rome as a free man and survived till Nero's pogrom. See also Schille (479) and Weiser (677, 680).

Paul spent two years ἐν ἰδίῳ μισθώματι. For μίσθωμα LS 1137 give '*that which is let for hire, hired house*', but for this meaning they give no reference in addition to Acts 28.30. BA 1060 agree with reference to this meaning that it is 'anderweitig nicht belegt'. The verb μισθοῦν undoubtedly has to do with letting out for hire, or (in the middle) having let to one, hiring, renting. In the passive it means to be hired for pay, or (of a house) to be let on contract (so LS, loc. cit.). For the latter meaning see e.g. Demosthenes 28.1 (836), ὁ πατὴρ οὐκ ἐβούλετο μισθωθῆναι τὸν οἶκον. The suffix—ωμα is normally passive in sense, so that there seems no good reason why μίσθωμα should not mean *a hired house* (though Hanson (256) declares 'in his own hired lodging' an 'impossible translation'). This would correspond well enough with καθ' ἑαυτόν in 28.16. Schneider (2.408) translates, *in eigener Mietwohnung*. Alternatively, and also in agreement with 28.16, *at his own expense* (Hemer 158)—and thus not dependent 'on the Roman (or any other) Church' (Tajra 192). One wonders, however, who paid the rent.

πάντας τοὺς εἰσπορευομένους (εἰς- would be consistent with a reference (in μίσθωμα) to a dwelling of some kind) would certainly not exclude either Jews or Gentiles. πάντας is important to Luke, and his meaning (though not his text) is rightly given by the Western insertion at the end of the verse of Ἰουδαίους τε καὶ Ἕλληνας (614 2147 *pc* (gig p) vg^mss sy^h**). Before this Clark (171, 388) adds (from gig h) καὶ διελέγετο πρός.

31. As elsewhere (e.g. 28.23) the *kingdom of God* serves as a general summary of the Christian message as preached by the apostles and others; the phrase that follows, τὰ περὶ τοῦ κυρίου Ἰησοῦ Χριστοῦ (the last word is omitted by ℵ* 326 614 2147 2495 *pc* sy^h, probably through assimilation to 28.23), brings out its Christological content. The verse emphasizes '... Jesus Christus als den einen Inhalt der paulinischen Verkündigung' (Stählin 329). 'The

Kingdom of God is founded on, and consists in, the knowledge of the redemption procured by Christ' (Calvin 2.314). κηρύσσων and διδάσκων are here synonyms; Luke does not seem to be distinguishing between two different kinds of communication.

Instead of τοῦ κυρίου, P⁷⁴ has τῆς βασιλείας, putting side by side the two kingdoms, of God and of Christ. This reading is probably due to careless repetition; σωτηρίας in place of παρρησίας is probably another careless error in P⁷⁴. p omits τὰ περὶ τοῦ κυρίου Ἰησοῦ Χριστοῦ and, joined by vg^mss and sy^h, adds after ἀκωλύτως, dicens quia hic est Christus Jesus filius dei per quem incipiet totus mundus iudicari. 'The artistic literary cadence of the concluding phrase of the book of Acts and the powerful note of triumph expressed by ἀκωλύτως are greatly weakened by the pious Western addition after ἀκωλύτως ...' (Metzger 503).

For παρρησία see on 4.13. Here it has its primary sense of freedom of speech, though it is not inconsistent with the exercise of boldness in other ways also. μετὰ (πάσης) π. is an Acts phrase: 4 times, nowhere else in the NT.

ἀκωλύτως, unhindered, that is, with no one venturing or able to hinder or prevent. The word is 'of constant occurrence in legal documents' (MM 20, with many examples; ND 3.17 adds POxy 46.3269.13). For an earlier use see Plato, Cratylus 415d. 'Rome is depicted as showing tolerance towards Paul's ministry and towards the Christian message' (Tajra 193). The word brings out several points that Luke here and elsewhere wishes to make. Nothing, not even imprisonment, was able to put a stop to the spread of the Gospel, and nothing could deter Paul from doing the work of an evangelist, with the result that even in Rome the proclamation of the word was established. 'Paul himself has every right to glory that the Word of God was not bound with his chains (2 Tim 2.9)' (Calvin 2.315). At the end of the verse the word ἀμήν is added by Ψ 36 453 614 1175 2495 al vg^ww sy^h, indicating probably that the copyists took the book to be a liturgical text, read in church services. This is relatively late attestation; contrast Lk. 24.53, where ἀμήν is added by A B C³ Θ Ψ 063 f¹ f¹³ 𝔐 lat sy^p ^h bo^mss. The difference probably bears witness to a time when Lk. was and Acts was not read in church because it was not canonical Scripture.

Bengel (489) ends his commentary with words that would probably have had Luke's approval. 'παρρησίας, *fiducia*) intrinsecus.— ἀκωλύτως, *sine impedimento*) extrinsecus, post superata tot impedimenta. Victoria Verbi Dei. Paulus Romae, apex evangelii, Actorum finis ... Hierosolymis coepit: Romae desinit ... Habes, Ecclesia, formam tuam. tuum est, servare eam, et depositum custodire.'

INDEX

This Index does not include references to the following: any commentaries; Blass, Debrunner, and Rehkopf, *Grammatik des neutestamentlichen Griechisch*; Jackson and Lake (eds), *The Beginnings of Christianity*; Liddell and Scott, *A Greek-English Lexicon*; Moulton, Howard, and Turner, *A Grammar of New Testament Greek*; Wilcox, *The Semitisms of Acts*.

The two volumes are numbered continuously; volume I ends on page 694, the commentary on the text in volume II begins on page 695. Roman numerals refer to the Introduction to volume II.

Abbott, E. 392
Abrahams, I. 340, 605
Achilles Tatius 292, 1205
Achtemeier, P. J. lxi
Acta Andreae et Matthiae 845, 1059
Acta Barnabae 583, 596, 611, 627, 755
Acta Isidori 815, 1046
Acta Joannis 527, 907, 1115
Acta Petri et Andreae 182, 527
Acta Petri et Pauli 450, 1045, 1232
Acts of Carpus, Papylus, and Agathonike 1087
Acts of Paul and Thecla 330, 667, 673, 988, 1100, 1115
Acts of Philip 146, 232, 298, 834
Acts of Thomas 88, 93, 98, 148, 201, 275, 277, 452, 527, 580, 869, 892, 979
Actus Petri cum Simone 413, 1115
Acworth, A. 1177, 1211, 1216
Adam 206
Adamantius 34
Aejmelaeus, L. 962
Aelian 125, 514
Aelius Aristides 978

Aeneas Gazaeus 810
Aeneas Tacticus 635
Aeschines 97, 582, 851, 1157, 1194
Aeschylus 65, 70, 197, 235, 296, 326, 354, 402, 502, 592, 677, 679, 786, 854, 1042, 1158, 1194, 1198
Aesop 676
Aetius 505, 618
Agnew, F. H. 60, cvii
Aḥer (Elisha b. Abuya) 383
Aland, B. 3, 12, 13, 15, 17, 25, 26, 27, 28, xxii, 783; *see also* BA
Aland, K. 2, 9, xix, xxii, 779, 783; *see also* BA
Albright, W. F. 128
Alciphron 82
Alexander Jannaeus 142, 423, 424
Alexander, L. xliv, lxi
Alexander of Aphrodisias 1225
Alexander (Pseudomantis) 591
Alexander the Great 424
Altaner, B. 37, 38, 862
Amaru, B. H. 333
Ambrose 427
Ammonius 73, 813, 867, 907, 1164

Anacreon 125
Ananias (High Priest) 219, 1058
Ananus 219
Annas 224, 225, 282, 286
Anthologia Palatina 1096, 1223
Anti-Marcionite Prologue xliv
Antiochus I 549
Antiochus Epiphanes 508, 591
Antipho 526
Antoninus 449
Apocalypse of Peter 591
Apocryphon of James 70
Apollodorus 767
Apollonius Dyscolus 537
Apollonius (Grammaticus) 138
Apollonius of Tyana 82, 96, 580
Apollonius Rhodius 969
Apollos 886–92
Apostolic Constitutions 506, 844, 983
Appian 156, 322, 326, 499, 744, 758, 770, 1137
Applebaum, S. 1070, 1086
Apuleius 909, 1149, 1227
Aqiba (Akiba) 124, 659
Aquila 618, 953
Aquila (of Corinth) 858–63, 877

Arai, S. 318
Arator lxxi
Aratus 843, 848, 849
Aretaeus 1222
Aretas 460, 466
Argyle, A. W. 128
Aristeas 352, 723, 781, 1057, 1115, 1167
Aristophanes 86, 98, 181, 184, 230, 235, 239, 291, 317, 327, 350, 364, 426, 445, 448, 508, 526, 617, 638, 652, 742, 759, 789, 792, 793, 813, 870, 873, 891, 1024, 1059, 1062, 1073, 1103, 1107, 1141, 1199, 1225
Aristotle 70, 102, 168, 254, 349, 353, 458, 502, 556, 741, 853, 873, 953, 983, 1096, 1130, 1154, 1194, 1196, 1198
Arnold, W. T. 626
Arrian 113, 989, 1212
Artemidorus 67, 618, 906
Artemis 922, 923
Ascension of Isaiah 70
Aseneth 441, 442
Assumption of Moses 193, 365
Athanasius 19, 33, 34
Athenaeus 171
Athenagoras 537
Atomus 407
Attalus II Philadelphus 690
Auffret, P. 823
Augustine 20, 21, 67, 68, 71, 74, 77, 99, 102, 117, 118, 147, 150, 196, 427, 449, 493, 606, 616, 720, 801
Augustus 549, 592, 673
Aune, D. E. 561
BA (W. Bauer, K. and B. Aland) 325, 352, 363, 367, 391, 404, 415, 435, 483, 537, 557, 581, 582, 583, 588, 603, 640, 660, 668, 676, 700, 717, 742, 748, 755, 763, 772, 779,

792, 796, 798, 810, 813, 815, 830, 836, 848, 851, 852, 867, 870, 875, 905, 908, 911, 912, 913, 922, 926, 952, 955, 968, 972, 975, 978, 991, 996, 1012, 1039, 1046, 1066, 1074, 1076, 1078, 1098, 1103, 1130, 1147, 1148, 1149, 1150, 1153, 1154, 1162, 1166, 1167, 1183, 1190, 1194, 1197, 1199, 1200, 1203, 1204, 1207, 1213, 1222, 1223, 1225, 1226, 1228, 1229, 1243, 1245, 1252
Baarda, T. 751, 761
Babrius 1113
Bacher, W. 729, 810
Bagoas 679
Bailey, R. E. 379
Ballance, M. 663, 673
Bamberger, B. J. 1053
Bammel, E. cviii, 695, 707, 1025, 1248
Bammer, A. 916, 923
Barag, D. 216
Barbi, A. 187
Barclay, J. M. G. cix
Bar-Jesus (Elymas) 609, 610, 613, 615, 617, 618
Barker, D. C. 784
Barnabas, Epistle of 36, 37, 39, 70, 173, 194, 229, 300, 354, 374, 514, 718, 839, 861, 951, 983, 1043
Barnard, L. W. 37, 302
Barnard, P. M. 18
Barnes, T. D. 823, 831, 832
Barnett, P. W. 280, 1030
Barnikol, E. 419
Barns, J. W. B. 280, 286
Barrett, C. K. 6, 28, 47, 175, 187, 191, 205, 224, 229, 283, 286, 296, 309, 316, 323, 324, 333, 339, 381, 385, 395, 396, 398, 402, 405, 411, 412, 413, 423, 443, 450, 460, 466,

468, 497, 569, 575, 602, 617, 622, 623, 624, 625, 651, 660, 665, 667, 681, 687, 691, xxii, li, lxi, lxiii, lxxxi, lxxxix, cviii, cix, cx, cxiii, cxvii, 695, 707, 726, 741, 760, 784, 791, 798, 802, 823, 826, 828, 860, 877, 883, 892, 898, 900, 902, 905, 918, 919, 929, 933, 944, 962, 964, 974, 975, 981, 994, 1053, 1090, 1098, 1102, 1103, 1106, 1108, 1118, 1143, 1152, 1159, 1177, 1179, 1195, 1204, 1208, 1209, 1234, 1235, 1248
Barth, G. cviii
Barth, K. 74, 83, 120, 138, 143, 144, 172, 248, 266, 288, 290, 388, 411, 432, 449, 524, 585, 602, 802, 864, 897, 951
Barthes, R. 490
Bartlett, V. 593
Barton, J. lxxviii
Bartsch, H. W. lxxxi
Basil the Great 7
Bates, W. H. 622
Baucis 677
Bauckham, R. 695
Bauer, J. B. 707
Bauer, W. 979; see also BA
Bauernfeind, O. 187, 622
Baugh, S. M. 916
Baumbach, G. 280
Baumgarten, J. M. 1017
Baur, F. C. xl, xli, xlii, lxiii, lxxiii, lxxiv, cxiii, cxviii, 1006
Bavel, T. J. van 106
Beare, F. W. 106, 438, 459, 476, 558
Bede 6, 20, 66, 68, 78, 84, 99, 112, 116, 137, 150, 152, 179, 266, 277, 288, 292, 296, 312, 346, 350, 351, 375, 385, 410, 424, 434, 449, 525, lxxi, 1050

Behm, J. 1095, 1177, 1188
Bell, H. I. 123, 393, 1097
Bengel, J. A. 21
Benko, S. 857
Benoit, P. 55, 60, 91, 98, 147, 158, 160, 165, 170, 213, 251, 272, 273, 535, 558, 568, 577, 587, 594, 695, 707, 723
Bentley, R. 387
Bentzen, A. 208
Berger, K. 187, 900, 909, 999, 1090
Bergmeier, R. 395
Bernice 574, lvii, cxiv, 1135
Bertram, G. 60, 64, 786
Best, E. 60, 128, 598, 600, 601
Betz, H. D. 77, 79, 81, 113, 126, 161, 182, 183, 249, 354, 356, 367, 374, 387, 405, 427, 434, 452, 613, 679, 772, 869, 908, 913, 925, 936, 970, 996, 1036, 1046, 1096, 1168
Betz, O. 106, 1030
Beutler, J. 663
Beyer, H. W. 962, 975
Beyer, K. 377
Beyschlag, K. 395
Beza, T. 5, 323
Bickermann, E. J. 544, lxi, 1017
Bieder, W. 272, lxxxi
Bieler, L. 354, 358
Bietenhard, H. 182
Bihler, J. 333, 379
Billerbeck, P. 622, 628
Bion of Soli 425
Birdsall, J. N. xx, xxii
Bishop, E. F. F. 419, 598
Black, M. 11, 128, 140, 148, 172, 179, 180, 196, 206, 221, 237, 274, 280, 288, 296, 307, 317, 326, 327, 366, 377, 392, 402, 407, 419, 435, 467, 503, 514, 541, 561, 562, 582, 585, 593, 596, 614, 641, 669, 673, 675, 679, 685,

701, 713, 749, 760, 787, 797, 857, 883, 919, 943, 950, 955, 999, 1013, 1041, 1063, 1090, 1098, 1153, 1209; see also NS
Blass, F. 18, 22, 23, 24, 25, 28
Blastus 589
Blinzler, J. 568
Blomberg, C. L. cix, 707
Boers, H. W. 128
Boethus 225, 286
Böhlig, A. 568
Boismard, M. E. 24, 25, 28, 318, 333, 379, xix, xx, xxii, xxx, xxxi, 707, 1177
Boman, T. 707
Boor, C. de 575
Borgen, P. cx, 707, 751, 761
Borger, R. 775, 779
Bormann, L. 775, 780
Bornemann, W. 642
Bornkamm, G. 325, 761, 762, 772, 823, 853, 946, 1012, 1246
Borse, U. 707
Bousset, W. 203, 290, 515, 585, 628, 660, 722, 736, 737, 1043
Bouwmann, G. 60
Bovon, F. 216, 490, 532, lxxxii, cvi, 962, 985, 991, 1234
Bowers, W. P. 765
Bowker, J. W. 128, 350, 622, 624, 781
Bowman, J. 208
Brandon, S. G. F. 80, 87, 103, 497, 574, 575, 578, 586, xli, 863, 1013
Braun, H. 60, 97, 104, 111, 140, 148, 163, 168, 208, 290, 311, 339, 376, 378, 448, 633, 843, 954, 962, 1017, 1025, 1143, 1161
Brawley, R. L. cix
Bréhier, E. 309
Bright, J. 352
Brinkman, J. A. 106

Brock, S. 257, 259
Brodie, T. L. 395, 419
Broughton, T. R. S. 499, 622, 921
Brown, R. E. 89, 95, lxiii, cvii
Brown, S. cviii
Brownlee, W. H. 430
Bruce, F. F. 206, 333, 622, 663, lxi, cvii, 707, 765, 999, 1070, 1081, 1234, 1248
Bryan, C. 752, 760
Buchanan, E. S. 673
Buchanan, G. W. 128
Buckler, W. H. 916, 921
Budesheim, T. L. 962, 1030
Büchsel, F. 194, 1063
Bultmann, R. 53, 55, 76, 78, 118, 135, 141, 151, 169, 170, 207, 231, 250, 307, 314, 396, 400, 552, 564, 594, 597, 599, 600, 604, 682, xxv, xciv, cviii, 702, 707, 710, 722, 740, 784, 831, 838, 839, 949, 950, 953, 979, 993, 995, 1030, 1036, 1043, 1158
Burchard, C. 80, 274, 275, 427, 438, 457, 468, 469, 490, 544, 594, 629, 663, xc, cviii, 775, 796, 798, 823, 855, 883, 894, 916, 934, 999, 1011, 1030, 1035
Burger, J. D. 257
Burkitt, F. C. 10, 158, 172, 199, 608, 615, 823
Burrows, M. 370, 430, 447
Burton, E. de W. 481
Bussler, J. M. 490
Cadbury, H. J. 72, 106, 257, 259, 261, 264, 476, 481, 588, xxxi, xlv, xlviii, lxi, lxii, lxxxi, 916, 921, 999, 1003, 1143, 1146, 1154, 1177, 1189, 1216, 1223

CAH (*Cambridge Ancient History*) 740, 957
Caiaphas 224, 225
Calder, W. M. 767, 769
Caligula (Gaius) 573, 614
Calloud, J. 823
Calvin, J. 400, 498, 952
Cambier, J. 459
Campbell, A. cviii, 707
Campbell, J. Y. 158
Campbell, L. 392
Campbell, R. A. cviii
Campeau, L. 280
Campenhausen, H. von 60, 91, 158, 333, 419, lxiv, lxxxi, xciv, cvi, cviii, 975, 999, 1005
Capper, B. J. 261, 263
Carcopino, J. 905
Carroll, J. T. cvii
Casey, R. P. 999, 1002
Cassidy, R. J. cx
Casson, L. 1177, 1187
Catchpole, D. R. cix, 707
Cato 125
Catullus 98
Causse, A. 106
Cerfaux, L. 60, 106, 257, 395, xxxi, cviii, 707
Chambers, C. D. 593, 596, 1133, 1135
Chapot, V. 930
Charito of Aphrodisias 931
Charles, R. H. 356, 744
Charlesworth, M. P. 1090, 1095
Chase, F. H. 98, 197, 222
Chevallier, M. A. 107, 128
Childers, J. W. xxiii
Christiansen, E. J. 158, cviii
Chrysippus 200
Chrysostom, John 20, 21, 72, 112, 211, 220, 291, 304, 308, 414, 417, 423, 616, 672, 676, lxxi, 718, 798, 817, 841, 846, 863, 923, 936, 938, 978, 990, 1002, 1061, 1066, 1169, 1182

Chuza 570
Cicero 135, 169, 171, 253, 255, 283, 341, 344, 466, 626, 632, 682, xlviii, 749, 759, 789, 801, 803, 808, 817, 827, 832, 846, 905, 928, 936, 1050, 1094, 1111, 1118, 1131, 1153, 1187, 1195, 1221, 1229, 1231
Clark, A. C. 23, 24, 67, 68, 73, 99, 196, 229, 245, 289, 295f., 449f., 523, 537, 564, 581, 615, 642f., 672, xxiii, 735, 778, 803, 804, 820, 910, 955, 1002, 1075, 1079, 1099, 1100, 1141, 1147, 1153, 1182, 1184, 1205
Clark, D. J. 1177, 1198
Clark, K. W. xli
Clarke, W. K. L. 84, 103, 384, 590, 1006
Claudius 527, 556, 559, 563, 564, 573, 574, 614, 661, 673, lv, cxiv, 862
Claudius Lucius Herminianus 591
Cleanthes 848
1 Clement 35, 80, 95, 103, 104, 173, 194, 242, 243, 244, 342, 542, 576, 578, 636, 638, 683, 687, 688, xl, xliii, lxix, xcvi, cxiii, 718, 839, 844, 953, 983, 1057, 1152, 1153, 1162, 1231, 1237
2 Clement 35, 37, 197, 288, 290, cxiii, 912, 978
Clementine literature 72, 192, 208, 234, 292, 336, 347, 362, 405, 406, 417, 445, 785, 851, 1207
Clement of Alexandria 7, 18, 21, 315, 569, 571, 646, 745, 840, 848, 913, 925, 993
Clement of Rome 31, 35, xliii, lxiv, xcvi
Cleopatra 549

Coggins, R. J. 333, 395
Cohen, S. J. D. 752, 759
Colaclides, P. 823
Collins, J. J. 582
Colpe, C. 384
Colwell, E. C. 884, 891
Connolly, A. L. 876
Connolly, R. H. 1030
Constantinus Porphyrogenitus 1219
Conzelmann, H. 141, 413, 672, xciv, xcvi, cviii, 823, 943
Coppens, J. 302, 395, 598, 884, 1217
Corbulo 556
Corpus Hermeticum 840, 841, 842, 1042
Corssen, P. 18, 23, 985
Cosgrove, C. H. cvi, 1053
Cramer, J. A. 676, lxxi
Cranfield, C. E. B. 35, 77, 443
Creed, J. M. 60
Crescens 31
Crito 156
Croesus 633
Cullmann, O. 83, 84, 88, 91, 95, 151, 152, 165, 170, 171, 194, 195, 199, 208, 214, 262, 290, 302, 307, 318, 333, 339, 384, 391, 398, 410, 432, 433, 568, 587, 681, lxviii, 707, 723, 1248
Cumont, F. 107, 1090, 1097
Cyprian 8, 18, 19, 20, 21, 27, 78, 118, 335, 646, 1061
Cyril Lucar, Patriarch 4
Cyril of Alexandria 20, 27, 102
Cyril of Jerusalem 19
Dahl, N. A. 107, 187, 333, 345, cviii, 707, 724
Dalman, G. 66, 75, 85, 86, 99, 100, 140, 148, 159, 180, 191, 224, 259, 430, 1023, 1028
Damasus 9

Danby, H. 810, 1012, 1059
Daniélou, J. 158, 333
Danker, F. W. 707
Danoff, C. M. 817
Dar, S. 1070, 1086
Daube, D. 113, 268, 276, 282, 294, 302, 315, 316, 428, 431, 449, 454, 639, 640, 752, 759, 1053, 1065, 1066, 1225
Dautzenberg, G. 986
Davies, J. G. 107
Davies, P. 1248
Davies, W. D. 72, 75, 76, 80, 101, 333, 339, 342, 345, 413, 426, 457, 473, 525, 529, 535, 749, 772, 1012, 1046, 1220, 1232
Dehandschutter, B. 389, 438
Deissmann, A. 85, 96, 257, 377, 407, 512, 604, 616, 798, 908, 928, 959, 973, 1107, 1146, 1153
De Lacey, D. R. 459
Delebecque, E. 747, 752, 901, 916, 943
Delitzsch, F. J. 508, 606
Delling, G. 69, 121, 128, 142, 155, 158, 171, 197, 213, 244, 245, 248, 289, 290, 388, 405, 429, 490, 501, 528, 622, cvii, 775, 783, 798, 977, 1009, 1115, 1248
Demosthenes 73, 78, 101, 119, 134, 203, 204, 211, 221, 269, 502, 503, 504, 513, 536, 580, 588, 590, 606, 675, 679, lxxx, 733, 749, 763, 788, 791, 801, 830, 831, 833, 834, 926, 932, 959, 973, 978, 990, 1005, 1006, 1046, 1049, 1057, 1059, 1067, 1094, 1097, 1100, 1118, 1154, 1155, 1183, 1252
Demosthenes Ophthalmicus (Aetius) 505
Derrett, J. D. M. 91, 261,

344, 395, 574, 575, 977, 1072
Devine, C. F. 962
Dibelius, M. 69, 101, 109, 156, 168, 240, 245, 270, 293, 298, 304, 321, 323, 337, 382, 386, 397, 436, 486, 491, 496, 511, 571, 585, 587, 589, 609, 625, 640, li, lxxv, lxxvi, lxxxi, 710, 737, 765, 770, 841, 842, 843, 844, 846, 848, 853, 854, 947, 956, 963, 1005, 1099, 1150, 1158, 1160, 1163
Didache 163, 178, 194, 243, 244, 412, 432, 452, 561, 562, 602, 604, 666, 688, 799, 951, 978, 983
Didascalia, Syriac 506
Dieterich, W. 277, 707, 723
Digest 795, 1113, 1116, 1131, 1137, 1147
Dillon, R. J. 128, 187
Dinkler, E. 81, 207, 290, 419, 425, 432, 556, 587, 613, 857, 860, 871, 1043, 1126, 1129
Dio Cassius 123, 308, 424, 425, 564, 611, 758, 805, 830, 862, 873, 937, 958, 1049, 1135
Dio Chrysostom 67, 196, 744, 758, 940, 1026
Diocletian 628
Diodorus Siculus 67, 119, 142, 222, 424, 458, 676, 927, 1066, 1086, 1222
Diogenes Laertius 253, 838, 913
Diognetus, Epistle to 38
Dionysius of Alexandria lxx
Dionysius of Halicarnassus 81, 82, 142, 285, 508, 852, 1094, 1141
Dionysius the Areopagite 855
Dionysus 580

Dio of Prusa 925, 940, 1027
Dioscorides 618
Dittenberger, W. 196, 699, 733, 798, 852, 935, 938, 958, 1012, 1020, 1027, 1081, 1082, 1137, 1148
Doble, P. 379
Dobschütz, E. von 2, 5, 20
Dockx, S. 379, 382, 598, lxii
Dodd, C. H. 70, 130, 207, 212, 234, 390, 657, 811, 880, 1165, 1166
Doignon, J. 438
Dombrowski, B. W. 158
Donaldson, T. L. 333
Donfried, K. P. 89, 95, 807, 816
Dowd, W. A. 158
Downey, G. 549
Downing, F. G. 240, 333, 622, 663, cix, cx, 823
Dressler, H. 1106
Drusilla 574
Dubarle, A. M. 823
Duchesne, L. 606
Duensing, H. 986, 1000
Duncan, G. S. 916
Dunn, J. D. G. 107, 438, c, 695,
Duplacy, J. A. 192
Dupont, J. 53, 60, 91, 107, 128, 149, 158, 187, 216, 238, 240, 251, 272, 280, 302, 333, 377, 438, 459, 490, 532, 558, 568, 593, 596, 598, 622, 663, 689, xxxii, lxxiv, 707, 724, 823, 962, 1133, 1136, 1143, 1217, 1234, 1237, 1246, 1248, 1250, 1252
Easton, B. S. 1005
Eckert, J. 707
Edwards, M. J. 823
Egeria 110
Ehrhardt, A. 586, 815, 874, 875, 877, 887, 931, 986, 1005, 1088, 1136, 1146
Elbogen, I. 781, 782

Elderen, B. van 608, 613, 614, 663, 673
Eleazar 508
Eleazar of Modiim 1008
Electra 70
Eliezer ben Hyrcanus 431
Elijah 206
Elliott, J. K. xxiii
Ellis, E. E. 128, 187, 383, 490, 532, 558, 561, 622, xlviii, cix, 986
Eltester, W. 823, 843
Elymas 262, 609, 613, 615, 908
Emerton, J. A. 60, 91, 107, 128, 158, 187, 216, 240, 333, 361, 622, 636, xxxii
1 Enoch 196, 328, 336, 1066, 1194
2 (Slavonic) Enoch 844
Enslin, M. S. 91
Ephraem Syrus 10, 597
Epictetus 103, 166, 237, 300, 355, 393, 522, 729, 745, 763, 788, 793, 840, 875, 879, 890, 905, 1036, 1048, 1222, 1228
Epimenides 97, 847
Epiphanius 19, 646, 840, 1026, 1098
Epistula Apostolorum 38, 39, 40, 577, xlii, lxiv
Epp, E. J. 6, 14, 28, 60, 102, 187, 514, xxiii, 819
Erasmus 341, 353, 415, 1110
Erman, A. 424
Esler, P. F. lxxvii, lxviii, lxxxi
Etymologicon Magnum 1194
Euler, K. F. 431
Eupolis 153
Euripides 120, 142, 169, 183, 197, 201, 227, 235, 269, 293, 294, 298, 362, 374, 445, 449, 452, 483, 502, 506, 513, 516, 526, 529, 580, 635, 652, 733, 743, 794, 796, 830, 833,

841, 851, 936, 945, 1027, 1100, 1130, 1158, 1194, 1196, 1223
Eusebius 7, 19, 30, 31, 40, 45, 72, 102, 295, 308, 315, 380, 405, 407, 422, 564, 569, 570, 581, 583, 589, 591, 693, xl, xli, lxiv, lxv, lxvi, 723, 736, 792, 855, 993, 994, 1117, 1183
Eustathius of Thessalonica 830
Evans, C. A. 128
Evans, C. F. 128, 187, 490, 622
Exum, C. 962
Ezekiel (tragic poet) 338, 354, 355, 356
4 Ezra 113
Fadus 293
Farmer, W. R. 87
Fascher, E. 438, 561, 916, 919
Feldman, L. H. 615, 1012, 1025, 1058
Felix lvii, cxiv, 1080, 1081,
Fenton, J. C. 663
Ferguson, E. 302, cviii
Festus 236, 445, lvii, cxiv, 835, 1117, 1123
Feuillet, A. 60
Filson, F. V. xxxiii, lxii, 737
Finkelstein, L. 1053, 1063
Finn, T. 490, 501
Fischer, B. 9, 10
Fitzmyer, J. A. 60, 72, 89, 107, 128, 147, 158, 163, 164, 171, 209, 210, 255, 307, 317, 350, 370, 403, 448, 566, lxxxii, 707, 723, 726, 888, 901, 904, 916, 976, 1013, 1097, 1152, 1226, 1244
Flusser, D. 216, 240
Foakes-Jackson, F. J. 334
Foerster, W. 298, 302, 379, 785, 887, 1072, 1148
Fränkel, M. 604

Franklin, E. 60, cvi
Fredriksen, P. 438
Fridrichsen, A. 1143, 1170
Fuller, R. H. 92, 171, 190, 201, 204, 290, 438
Funk, R. W. 558
Fusco, V. cix
Gabinius 424
Gaechter, P. 707
Gärtner, B. 140, 328, 663, 823, 845, 846, 850, 1098
Gager, J. G. 302, 438, 490, 501
Gaius (Caligula) 382, 466, 614
Galazzi, C. 4
Galba 626
Galen 205, 458, 506, 1207, 1223, 1225
Galerius 591
Gallio lvi, cxiv, 858, 870, 871
Gamaliel 292, 293, 294, 296, 297, 308, liv, cxiv
Gapp, K. S. 558
Gasque, W. lxx, lxxii, lxxxi
Gaventa, B. R. cvi
Geagan, D. J. 823
Geer, T. C. xxiii
Geoltrain, P. 302
George, A. 216, 303, lxxxi, cix
Georgi, D. 1108
Georgius Syncellus 351
Gerhardsson, B. 251, 253, 313, cviii, 707, 709, 713, 728, 729
Gerstinger, H. 3
Gert, B. (K.-G.) 525, 542, 1166
Giblin, C. H. 107, 128
Giet, S. 459, 558
Gilchrist, J. M. 1177
Gildersleeve, B. L. 659, 1189
Giles, K. N. 472, 962
Gill, D. W. J. 438, 923
Gilmour, S. M. 107
Glasson, T. F. 208

Glombitza, O. 128, 303, 318, 334, 379, 622, 765
Gog and Magog 245
Goldsmith, D. 622
Goodman, M. *see NS*
Goodwin, W. W. 720
Goodspeed, E. J. 857, 868
Gordon, R. P. 622, 632
Gospel of Peter 482
Goulder, M. D. xli, xlii, lxiii, cxiii, 707, 711
Gourgues, M. 107, 395
Grässer, E. 60, lxxii, lxxvi, lxxxiii, cvii
Grant, R. M. 38, 158, lxii, 708, 752, 765
Grassi, A. 420
Gratus 224
Gray, E. W. 769
Green, H. B. 622
Greeven, H. 598
Gregory, C. R. 4
Gregory Nazianzen 1046
Gregory the Great 384, lxxi
Grelot, P. 622
Gribomont, J. 10
Griesbach, J. J. 21
Grintz, J. M. 1030
Grundmann, W. 303, 395, 544, 557, 1114
Güting, E. 107, 122
Gundry, R. H. 107, 116
Haacker, K. 60, 107, 438, 490, 663, cvii, cviii, cix, 857, 883, 893, 1030, 1036, 1053, 1063, 1090, 1143, 1234
Hadrian 156
Haenchen, E. 14, xxiii, 708, 1177
Hahn, A. 527
Hahn, F. 60, 187, 303, 398, 552, 672, lxxii
Halstead, S. 823
Haltgren, A. J. 438
Ḥama ben Ḥanina, 585
Hamm, D. 174
Hammond, C. E. 583
Hanina b. Dosa 193
Hannas 225

Hansack, E. 1248
Hansen, G. W. 769
Hanson, A. T. 1250
Hanson, R. P. C. xxiii, 1177
Harlé, P. 1144, 1172
Harnack, A. von 53, 54, 55, 98, 187, 281, 473, 547, 560, 564, xxiv, xxxii, xliv, lxvii, lxviii, lxxxi, xciii, xciv, cviii, 972, 993
Harrer, G. A. 608
Harris, J. R. 18, 222, 250, 417, 615, 1166
Harrison, P. N. 37
Harrisville, R. A. 107
Hart, J. H. A. 884
Hartman, L. 128, 158, cviii
Harvey, A. E. cviii
Hatch, E. 89, 297, 342, 358, 835, 953, 967, 1152
Hatch, W. H. P. 11, 13
Haufe, G. 159
Haulotte, E. 490, 532
Hauser, H. J. 1234, 1248
Heckel, U. cxvii
Hedrick, C. W. 438
Hegesippus 380, 693, xl, xli, lxiv, 723, 1117
Heitmüller, W. 199
Helena of Adiabene 563
Heliodorus 441, 635
Hemer, C. J. 62, 102, 122, 124, 180, 197, 296, 324, 402, 453, 466, 483, 498, 503, 556, 563, 584, 603, 614, 615, 628, 672, 676, 678, xxxii, 740, 778, 779, 782, 786, 808, 809, 814, 816, 820, 823, 832, 855, 857, 861, 862, 881, 887, 893, 904, 908, 909, 921, 930, 935, 937, 938, 943, 947, 948, 952, 953, 960, 991, 992, 995, 1003, 1027, 1058, 1061, 1070, 1081, 1087, 1092, 1101, 1118, 1133, 1135,

1138, 1173, 1174, 1177, 1182, 1184, 1185, 1187, 1190, 1193, 1194, 1195, 1198, 1203, 1204, 1210, 1212, 1213, 1214, 1217, 1221, 1224, 1226, 1227, 1229, 1230, 1231, 1233, 1242, 1252
Hengel, M. 87, 118, 142, 187, 280, 303, 459, 468, 469, 470, 473, 487, 566, 568, 622, cxvii, 765, 766, 767, 775, 781, 786, 993, 1005, 1015, 1026, 1036, 1078
Hera 676
Heracleides Ponticus 197
Heracleon 207
Heraclitus 562
Hermas 35, 37, 75, 83, 103, 343, 435, 456, 576, 584, 585, 687, 692, cxiii, 876, 949
Hermes 676, 677
Hermetica 163, 242, 449
Hermippus 382
Herod Agrippa I 262, 564, 569, 570, 571, 572, 573, 574, 575, 576, 577, 579, 582, 588, 589, 590, 591, 592, 593, 595, 603, xxxiv, lv, cxiv
Herod Agrippa II 445, 573, lvii, cxiv, 1134, 1135
Herod (Antipas) 241, 246, 247, 590
Herod (the Great) 146, 246, 436, 446, 573, 591, 604
Herodian 451, 758, 906, 936
Herodotus 82, 125, 140, 142, 182, 227, 230, 260, 278, 298, 301, 311, 356, 359, 371, 373, 402, 426, 505, 515, 536, 582, 603, 619, 633, 667, 668, 677, 678, 718, 780, 792, 799, 813, 818, 830, 840, 851, 880, 892, 921, 924, 988, 1005, 1015, 1019, 1067,

1085, 1118, 1138, 1149, 1152, 1196, 1197, 1212, 1225
Herondas 267
Hesiod 1193, 1223
Hesychius 70, 86, 285, 292, 451, 503, 516, 675
Heutger, N. 1177, 1217
Hickling, C. J. A. 1144
Hicks, E. L. 916, 923, 966
Hierocles the Stoic 954, 1238
Hiers, R. H. cvii
Hill, D. 561
Hillel 211
Hillier, R. lxxi, lxxxi
Hipparchus 505
Hippocrates 267, 618, 991
Hippolytus 406, 416
Hirsch, E. 438
Ḥiyya bar Abba 202
Hock, R. F. 857
Hoehner, H. W. 246
Holl, K. xciv
Holmes, B. T. 568
Holofernes 679
Holtz, T. 334, 438, lxii, 695, 708, 747
Holtzmann, O. 174
Homer 86, 115, 151, 234, 248, 298, 317, 388, 402, 424, 452, 483, 506, 511, 549, 565, 580, 581, 618, 626, 653, 657, 660, 676, 729, 783, 788, 799, 837, 845, 854, 919, 978, 1047, 1100, 1193, 1195, 1203, 1204, 1206, 1213
Hommel, H. 823, 847
Hondius, J. J. E. 264
Honi the Circle-maker 193, 200
Hooker, M. D. 962, 969
Horace 580, 676, 782, 909, 978, 988, 1131, 1196, 1199, 1231
Horbury, W. 92, cix
Horsley, G. H. R. 857, 884, 901, 916
Horsley, R. A. 280
Horst, P. W. van der 60,

92, 107, 128, 159, 174, 187, 216, 240, 251, 272, 357, 438, 708, 721, 823, 837, 901, 943, 954, 962, 984, 1030, 1036, 1234, 1238
Hort, F. J. A. 555, 744
Houlden, J. L. cvi, 695,
Howard, W. F. 593, 596, 1133, 1135
Hughes, J. H. 884, 888
Hull, R. F. xxiii
Hunkin, J. W. 60, 67, 101, 523
Hurd, J. C. 596
Hyrcanus 446
Iamblichus 676, 1183
Ignatius 35, 36, 95, 103, 104, 144, 173, 201, 300, 374, 527, 557, 687, 688, lxiv, lxix, xcvi, cxiii, 778, 951, 977, 978, 1077, 1166, 1183, 1231
Iliffe, J. H. 1017, 1020
Innocent I 400
Irenaeus 7, 15, 16, 17, 26, 27, 45, 46, 47, 70, 97, 184, 196, 244, 304, 315, 422, 433, 450, xliv, lxvi, lxvii, lxx, lxxix, cxiii, 771
Isaeus 227, 911, 932
Ishmael (ben Phiabi) 286, 1124
Isho'dad of Merv 847
Isocrates 65, 255, 1036
Jacob, E. 162
James, M. R. 38, 577
Jasper, G. 1000
Jastrow, M. 99, 234, 259, 267, 424, 749, 933, 1107
Jaubert, A. 92
Jensen, J. 708
Jeremias, J. 54, 55, 60, 146, 147, 155, 164, 170, 174, 180, 201, 218, 219, 222, 223, 225, 230, 238, 259, 260, 262, 266, 267, 281, 310, 324, 351, 355, 401, 402, 430, 431, 484,

486, 547, 558, 560, 563, 564, 566, 583, 604, xxxii, xcii, ciii, 760, 783, 857, 863, 909, 983, 984, 1021, 1030, 1035, 1053, 1058, 1063, 1090, 1118, 1155, 1241
Jerome 8, 9, 20, 21, 27, 32, 34, 36, 51, 78, 152, 268, 351, 406, 564, 616, xliv, lxxi, 837, 994, 1050, 1078, 1117
Jervell, J. 438, 490, xli, lxii, cxiii, 1000, 1234, 1246
Jewett, R. 862, 952, 1118
Joanna 570
Johanan ben Zakkai 431, 520
Johanan b. Gudgeda 260
Johanan the Sandalmaker, 297
John Hyrcanus 146
Johnson, L. T. cix, cx
Johnson, S. E. 263, 317
Johnston, G. 187, 280
Jonathan 65, 225
Jones, A. H. M. 549, 935
Joseph 198, 228
Joseph and Aseneth 330, 953, 1035
Josephus 66, 67, 82, 85, 86, 87, 88, 97, 98, 102, 103, 105, 111, 114, 122, 123, 124, 135, 142, 146, 161, 168, 178, 179, 182, 183, 191, 219, 221, 222, 223, 224, 225, 230, 237, 242, 244, 260, 265, 271, 282, 284, 291, 292, 293, 294, 295, 308, 312, 313, 314, 326, 327, 328, 336, 341, 351, 352, 354, 356, 374, 378, 380, 382, 390, 402, 407, 408, 423, 424, 426, 432, 435, 436, 446, 480, 482, 483, 484, 501, 505, 513, 537, 538, 549, 563, 573, 576, 581, 586, 588, 589, 590, 591, 603, 607, 611, 618, 627, 630,

631, 634, 635, 648, 652, 655, 656, 659, 660, 668, xl, xliii, cxiv, 698, 699, 700, 723, 733, 737, 742, 745, 748, 763, 781, 783, 786, 792, 799, 802, 811, 812, 813, 817, 818, 830, 833, 835, 836, 837, 840, 841, 845, 853, 862, 873, 879, 889, 903, 905, 908, 913, 929, 934, 935, 937, 941, 946, 947, 954, 958, 959, 978, 979, 992, 997, 1008, 1012, 1020, 1021, 1022, 1023, 1025, 1034, 1036, 1046, 1057, 1058, 1059, 1065, 1066, 1068, 1072, 1074, 1077, 1078, 1079, 1080, 1081, 1085, 1086, 1094, 1096, 1113, 1116, 1117, 1123, 1124, 1125, 1130, 1132, 1134, 1135, 1136, 1137, 1148, 1152, 1154, 1156, 1183, 1185, 1188, 1190, 1193, 1196, 1198, 1200, 1202, 1207, 1208, 1210, 1214, 1224, 1225, 1226, 1227, 1229, 1230, 1232, 1237, 1251

Joshua b. Ḥananiah 260
Jousseu, A. xxiii
Jowett, B. 451
Jubilees 111, 351, 356, 734
Judah, R. 575
Judah the Prince, R 211
Judas Galilaeus 294, 295
Judge, E. A. lxxviii, lxxxi, 807, 815, 1082
Jülicher, A. xxiii
Julius Caesar 314, 446, 549, 1192, 1211
Juster, J. 802
Justin Martyr 15, 41, 42, 43, 44, 115, 183, 234, 244, 361, 374, 403, 405, 412, 415, 416, 452, 502, 638, 646, 683, xlii, xlix, lxiv, lxv, lxvi, 836, 953, 978, 1009, 1137, 1148, 1166, 1223, 1244

Justus of Chalcis 102
Juvenal 362, 501, 549, 630, 781, 877, 909, 1135
Käsemann, E. xciv, xcvi, cix, 884, 885, 889
Kaestli, J. D. cvii
Kamith 225
Karrer, M. cviii, 962
Karris, R. J. lxxi
Kathros (Kantheros) 286
Katz, P. 334, 1234, 1245
Kaye, B. N. 747, 752
Kearsley, R. A. 930
Keck, L. E. 303
Kemmler, D. W. 807
Kennard, J. S. 128
Kerigan, A. 128
Kertelge, K. 159
Kilgallen, J. J. 962, 983
Kilpatrick, G. D. 107, 128, 187, 334, 377, 379, 384, 622, 645, 646, 678, 679, xxii, 708, 725, 728, 752, 807, 810, 884, 895, 926, 986, 992, 995, 1070, 1078, 1120
Kippenberg, H. G. 1118
Kirk, J. A. 92
Kirschschläger, W. 1217, 1218
Kittel, G. 1000
Klausner, J. 76, 264, 286, 933, 1025
Klein, G. 75, 102, cviii, 912
Kleiner, G. 959
Klijn, A. F. J. 334, 564, lxxxi, 708
Klinghardt, M. 708
Knauf, E. A. 459
Knibb, M. A. 328
Knopf, R. 243
Knox, J. 47, lxvi, lxvii, lxviii, lxxxi
Knox, W. L. 54, 118, 149, 152, 160, 197, 198, 294, 327, 338, 339, 364, 371, 376, 424, 427, 428, 434, 497, 635, 638, 672, 680, 681, 793, 954, 969, 970, 983, 1025, 1056, 1093, 1158, 1167

Koch, D. A. 395
Kodell, J. 303, 593
Kosmala, H. 118, 383, 392, 448, 479, 480, 482, 484, 704, 759, 787, 888, 893, 899, 1098, 1157, 1161
Kraabel, A. T. 490, 501, cix
Kraeling, C. H. 544
Kränkl, E. cvii
Kraft, R. A. 1177
Kreitzer, L. J. 916
Kremer, J. 110, 111, 116, 785, 807, 1250
Kühner, R. [K.-G.] 525, 542, 1166
Külling, H. 823
Kümmel, W. G. 60, 385, xxxviii, xlii, xliv, lviii, lxxii, lxxiii, cvi, 708
Küng, H. cix
Kurz, W.S. lxxxi, 962
Lachmann, K. 200
Lachs, S. T. 1053, 1066
Lactantius 591
Ladouceur, D. 1177, 1217
Lagercrantz, O. 663
Lagrange, M. J. 24, 285
Lambrecht, J. 962, 966
Lamouille, A. 24, 25, 28, xix, xx, xxii, xxx, xxxi, 1177
Lampe, G. W. H. 107, 400, 978
Lampe, P. 857, 901, 916
Larsson, E. 303, lxii, 1234, 1246
Laud, W. 6, 20
Lawlor, H. J. 31, 591
L.-B. (Lipsius, R. A. and Bonnet, M.) 93, 95, 146, 148, 182, 201, 232, 269, 275, 277, 298, 413, 417, 450, 527, 583, 596, 611, 627, 834, 845, 869, 892, 907, 979, 988, 1045, 1101, 1115, 1232
L. Cornelius Sulla 499
Leary, T. J. 901, 907
Lebram, J. C. 823

Le Déaut, R. 112, 206, 300, 333, 345, 346, 356, 383, 503, 577, 1160
Lee, G. M. 765, 769, 901, 916, 1090, 1113
Leenhardt, F. J. 438
Légasse, S. 1017, 1030, 1053, 1070, 1090, 1120, 1133, 1144
Legrand, L. 823
Le Moyne, J. 219
Lentzen-Deis, F. 379
Lerle, E. 663
Leszynsky, R. 219, 1065
Lewis, N. 123
Libanius 343
Lieberman, S. 1024, 1094
Liechtenhan, R. 459
Lienhard, M. 303
Lietzmann, H. 38, 165, 318, 708
Lieu, J. M. cix
Lifshitz, B. 544
Lightfoot, J. B. 90, 416, 560, 583, xlii, lxiii, 951, 1182
Lilly, J. L. 438
Lindars, B. 149, 943
Lindijer, C. H. 420
Linton, O. 107, 459
Livy 82, 105, 237, 341, 779, 801, 808, 828, 913, 927, 986, 1050, 1220
Lobeck, C. A. 799, 1228
Löning, K. 490
Lösch, S. 420, 1090, 1095, 1100
Lövestam, E. 645, 962
Loewe, R. 9
Lohfink, G. 84, 92, 187, 438, cix
Lohmeyer, E. 80, 473, 744
Lohse, E. 107, 112, 154, 163, 194, 223, 292, 316, 370, 396, 583, 605, 606, 1026
Longenecker, R. N. 196, 204
Longinus 1167
Longus 1204
Lucan 342, 586, 986

Lucian 21, 77, 79, 83, 100, 125, 161, 181, 204, 248, 249, 255, 308, 326, 352, 354, 358, 382, 387, 390, 432, 452, 543, 557, 591, 659, 676, 687, 766, 772, 788, 792, 793, 809, 814, 817, 834, 873, 908, 913, 922, 938, 954, 979, 989, 1094, 1113, 1114, 1115, 1139, 1167, 1168, 1184, 1185, 1186, 1193, 1194, 1198, 1201, 1221, 1222, 1227
Lucifer of Cagliari 8, 19
Lucius Caecilius Metellus 446
Lucius Valerius 446
Lucretius 717, 850
Lüdemann, G. 395, lxxvi, lxxvii, 857
Lührmann, J. 1053
Lundgren, S. 438, 1030
Luther, M. 400, lxxi, lxxii, 841
Lyonnet, S. 159, 438, 1030
Lysanias 573
Lysias 69, 70, 192, 203, 833
4 Maccabees 393, 508, 679, 698, 1152
Mackenzie, R. S. 490, 622, xxiii, 823
Mackinnon, D. M. 159
Maddox, R. 62, 77, 78, 102, 136, 156, 220, 336, 383, 387, 457, 474, 666, 686, 825, 1014, 1045, 1064, 1097
Malherbe, A. J. cx, 1144
Manaen 570
Manek, J. 708
Manson, T. W. 327, 530, cviii
Manson. W. 340
Marcellus 382
Marcion 46, 47 lxv, lxvi, lxvii, lxviii, lxx, cxiii
Marcus Aurelius 166, 635, 875

Mare, W. H. 334
Marin, L. 490, 532
Markland, J. 820
Marshall, I. H. 60, 61, 62, 71, 74, 107, 114, 129, 139, 228, 231, 384
Martial 905
Martin, R. A. xxxii
Martini, C. M. 187, xx, xxiii
Martyrdom of Justin 1087
Martyrdom of Polycarp 930, 998, 1023
Martyrium Andreae Prius 95
Marutha of Maipherkat lxviii
Masson, C. 92, 459
Mastin, B. A. 901, 909, 916
Mattill, A. J. lxxxi, cvii, 823, 1090
Mattill, A. J. and M. B. lxxii, lxxxi
Mattingly, H. B. 544, 556
Maurer, C. 1057, 1090, 1106
Maximus of Tyre 925, 1039
Mayser, E. 283
McCasland, S. V. 438
McDonald, J. I. H. 708
McEleney, N. J. cix
McHugh, J. 90
Mealand, D. L. 60, 159, 169, lxii, cx, 1248
Meecham, H. G. 685
Meeks, W. A. 208, 549, lxxvii, lxxxi, 863
Men 407, 660, 676
Ménard, J. E. 187, 240
Menoud, P. H. 28, 60, 62, 81, 92, 107, 159, 261, 263, 438, 459, 622, cviii, 708, 735
Merkel, H. cix
Metatron 84, 383
Metzger, B. M. 2, 8, 9, 10, 11, 13, 14, 24, 32, 60, 107, 121, 122
Meyer, B. F. cix

Meyer, F. E. 280
Meyer, R. 604
Michaelis, J. D. lxxiii
Michaelis, W. 544
Michel, H. J. 963
Michel, O. 379, 438
Middleton, J. F. 138
Miles, G. B. 1177, 1217
Millar, F. *see NS*
Miltner, F. 901, 916, 928
Minguez, D. 420
Minnen, P. van 775
Minucius Felix 953
Mircea, I. 159
MM (Moulton, J. H. and Milligan, G.) 100, 142, 200, 265, 266, 349, 483, 484, 518, 554, 583, 588, 729, 730, 739, 748, 759, 785, 799, 850, 852, 867, 904, 908, 911, 912, 913, 922, 925, 927, 932, 952, 973, 982, 993, 996, 1026, 1049, 1073, 1074, 1084, 1086, 1088, 1093, 1106, 1107, 1111, 1136, 1137, 1140, 1145, 1148, 1153, 1173, 1190, 1191, 1199, 1207, 1251, 1253
Moehring, H. R. 438, 1030, 1039
Moeris 503, 799, 860, 1130
Moessner, D. P. 187, cvii, 1235
Molland, E. 708
Momigliano, A. 790, 862
Mommsen, T. 33, 549, 775, 802, 909, 1030, 1087, 1092
Morgan, R. C. xxxi, lxxviii
Morgenstern, J. 590
Mosbech, H. 92
Moses 208, 355–67
Moule, C. F. D. 60, 67, 70, 72, 75, 101, 138, 187, 220, 232, 239, 240, 276, 296, 303, 318, 334, 357, 362, 367, 376, 384, 387, 415, 428, 451, 453, 458,

474, 510, 514, 517, 530, 537, 542, 592, 638, 643, 669, 692, xlviii, 736, 749, 768, 771, 778, 788, 816, 817, 842, 876, 891, 896, 898, 914, 916, 922, 928, 937, 938, 939, 940, 963, 964, 973, 978, 1003, 1025, 1039, 1040, 1045, 1080, 1085, 1096, 1101, 1102, 1106, 1107, 1110, 1115, 1136, 1137, 1140, 1141, 1150, 1155, 1156, 1163, 1165, 1166, 1169, 1172, 1185, 1192, 1211, 1223, 1228, 1251
Moule, H. W. 245
Moulton, W. F. 503
Mullins, T. Y. 598
Munck, J. 438, 963, 1006
Mundle, W. 334
Muratorian Canon xxvii, xliv, lxx
Murphy-O'Connor, J. 85, 146, 598, lxii, cix, 708, 807, 812, 857, 860, 862, 871, 884
Musonius Rufus 721, 984, 1036
Mussner, F. 129, 159, 187, 318, 334, 379, 490
Musurillo, H. A. 456, 1046
Myers, J. L. 614
Naber, S. A. 1196
Nairne, A. 593
Nauck, W. 280, 823
ND (Horsley, G. H. R., et al.) 138, 151, 156, 204, 255, 263, 286, 289, 309, 311, 349, 378, 384, 387, 407, 425, 435, 454, 480, 483, 504, 525, 527, 579, 583, 629, 660, 661, 701, 702, 716, 729, 730, 763, 766, 781, 782, 783, 784, 786, 793, 797, 808, 812, 814, 841, 850, 852, 864, 872, 876, 877, 878, 890, 904, 905, 908, 922, 923, 930, 946, 948, 982, 996,

1012, 1021, 1024, 1026, 1028, 1037, 1041, 1049, 1068, 1073, 1074, 1082, 1084, 1087, 1096, 1098, 1106, 1113, 1123, 1126, 1137, 1139, 1140, 1151, 1165, 1191, 1194, 1212, 1253
Neirynck, F. 490, 522, lxxxi
Nellessen, E. 92, 663
Nero 424, 536, 563, 626
Nestle, Eberhard 272, 280, 568, 1153, 1165, 1177
Nestle, Erwin 2, 5, 20
New, S. 182
Neyrey, J. lxxvii, 1030
Nibley, H. 60
Nickle, K. F. 559, 1108
Nicolas of Damascus 424
Nock, A. D. 227, 373, 405, 605, 823, 833, 925, 1006, 1191
Nolland, J. 708, 719, 720
Noorda, S. J. 251, 257, 272
Norden, E. 243, 823
North, J. L. 708, 713, 857, 875, 1088
Noth, M. 352
Noy, D. 775
NS (Schürer, E.; revised by G. Vermes, F. Millar, M. Goodman and M. Black) 218, 219, 223, 224, 260, 292, 323, 324, 325, 382, 402, 407, 423, 435, 436, 446, 447, 454, 482, 515, 549, 550, 566, 573, 592, 626, 628, 781, 802, 817, 828, 860, 861, 872, 878, 903, 908, 959, 988, 989, 1003, 1020, 1021, 1023, 1028, 1056, 1063, 1065, 1080, 1117, 1134, 1135, 1181, 1183, 1230, 1237, 1238
Numenius 446
Oberwies, M. 1177
Odes of Solomon 149
Oepke, A. 205

Ogg, G. 663
Ogilvie, R. M. 1177, 1193
O'Neill, J. C. cvi, 1090
Onias 441
Orchard, B. 695
Oribasius 378
Origen 7, 18, 27, 74, 89,
    147, 198, 207, 234, 356,
    405, 406, 580, 616, lxxi,
    735, 794, 854, 908,
    1243
Orosius 564, 862
Orphic Fragment 849
Osborn, E. F. 41, lxv
Osburn, C. D. xxiii
Oster, R. 107, 916
O'Toole, R. F. 129, 420,
    622, cvii, 823, 1144
Oulton, J. E. L. 31, 395,
    591, 884
Overman, J. A. 490, 501,
    cix
Ovid 114, 249, 387, 580,
    677, 1148
Owen, H. P. 379, 823, 840
Palmer, D. W. 60
Panagopoulos, J. cvii
Panten, K. E. xix
Papias 37, 93, 98, 570, 583
Pappas 676
Papyri
    BGU (= Berliner
        Griechische
        Urkunden) 85, 934,
            1221, 1251
    PAmh (= Amherst
        Papyri) 692, 770
    PBodmer (= Bodmer
        Papyri) 3
    PChester Beatty (=
        Chester Beatty Papyri) 3
    PColl Youtie (= Papyri
        published in Honor
        of H. C. Youtie) 448
    PEg (= Egerton Papyri)
            226
    PFlor (= Florence
        Papyri) 782, 926
    PGM (= Papyri
        Graecae Magicae)
            908, 912, 913

PGenève (= Geneva
    Papyri) 530
PHib (= Hibeh Papyri)
            518
PHolm (= Papyrus
    Graecus Holmiensis)
            699
PIand (= Papyri
    Iandanae) 946
PKöln (= Kölner
    Papyri) 276
PLond (= Papyri in the
    British Museum)1167
PLond medicus (=
    London Medical
    Papyrus) 505
PMacquarie (=
    Macquarie Papyri,
    Australia) 4
PMagdola (= Papyrus
    de Magdola) 1094
PMich (= Michigan
    Papyri) 2, 585, 1153
PMil Vog1 (= Milan
    Papyri) 4, 1073
POxy (= Oxyrhynchus
    Papyri) 2, 142, 204,
    219, 253, 325, 340,
    355, 456, 502, 518,
    527, 577, 661, 787,
    1026, 1047, 1066,
    1080, 1095, 1113,
    1148, 1153, 1167,
        1168, 1189
PStras (= Strasbourg
    Papyri) 525
PTebt (= Tebtunis
    Papyri) 285, 668,
    781, 1086, 1111,
            1131
PVindobG (= Vienna
    Papyri) 3, 102
UPZ (= Urkunden der
    Ptolemäerzeit) 1058
Parker, D. C. xix, xxiii
Parker, P. 60, 460, 545,
    593
Parker, S. E. xxxii
Parratt, J. K. 884
Passio Andreae 269
Passio Apostolorum Petri

et Pauli 413, 417, 450,
    1045
Pathrapankal, J. 438, cvii
Patsch, H. 558, 986
Paullus Fabius Persicus
    613
Paulus 1050
Pausanias 197, 424, 819,
    836, 837, 923, 927,
    946
Payne Smith, J. 274, 863
Perictyone 445
Periplus Maris Erythraei
    86
Perrot, C. 708
Persius 841, 953
Pervo, R. I. xlix, lxii
Pesch, R. 379, 383, 708
Petersen, T. C. 14, 361,
    xxiii
Petersen, W. 577
Peterson, E. 545, 598, 602
Petronius 432, 588, 1205
Petzer, J. H. xxiii
Pfitzner, V. C. 107
Phiabi 225, 286
Philemon 677
Philip (Herod) 573
Philo 65, 67, 82, 98, 104,
    109, 111, 113, 117, 121,
    122, 123, 125, 169, 182,
    197, 205, 207, 208, 242,
    285, 308, 313, 320, 323,
    338, 339, 341, 342, 343,
    350, 354, 355, 356, 374,
    386, 393, 405, 407, 480,
    505, 520, 577, 611, 618,
    626, 628, 629, 656, 698,
    732, 736, 777, 781, 786,
    811, 817, 818, 830, 835,
    839, 844, 845, 848, 850,
    861, 975, 1010, 1020,
    1057, 1072, 1082, 1096,
    1106, 1111, 1125, 1138,
    1158, 1185, 1188, 1193,
    1196, 1202, 1251
Philostratus 82, 134, 322,
    358, 424, 434, 577, 580,
    783, 837, 1046, 1190
Photius 227
Phrynichus 307, 353, 425,

556, 578, 579, 584, 589, 659, 682, 887, 1023, 1095, 1207, 1228, 1245
Pickering, S. 4
Pindar 248, 659, 1135, 1158, 1189
Places, É. des 823
Plato 125, 156, 163, 166, 168, 183, 197, 200, 205, 227, 232, 233, 236, 237, 252, 297, 311, 329, 355, 367, 368, 371, 414, 432, 451, 483, 507, 516, 524, 579, 584, 590, 626, 638, 648, 672, 683, xlviii, 702, 749, 773, 799, 811, 813, 829, 830, 834, 840, 845, 846, 853, 879, 905, 912, 914, 932, 968, 997, 1003, 1020, 1059, 1094, 1096, 1114, 1115, 1118, 1130, 1138, 1149, 1167, 1168, 1172, 1183, 1189, 1190, 1191, 1196, 1198, 1201, 1225, 1228, 1244, 1253
Plautus 393, 1158
Pliny Major 277, 424, 425, 480, 549, 661, 809, 958, 1195
Pliny Minor 171, 557, 588, 861, 927, 951, 1094, 1136, 1156, 1167, 1233
Plümacher, E. 67, 96, 134, 143, 160, 202, 234, 237, 258, 290, 293, 311, 353, 405, 414, 421, 422, 432, 455, 478, 487, 568, 617, 664, xxxv, lxii, lxxii, lxxvi, lxxviii, lxxix, 963
Plutarch 97, 105, 116, 117, 196, 200, 233, 237, 327, 341, 352, 353, 355, 376, 382, 392, 425, 451, 515, 522, 591, 617, 618, 660, 678, 687, 729, 785, 789, 791, 793, 813, 827, 835, 836, 840, 850, 905, 913, 925, 929, 947, 949, 956, 983, 991, 1008, 1034, 1073, 1088, 1095, 1096,

1111, 1125, 1130, 1138, 1166, 1183, 1190, 1191, 1193, 1197, 1199, 1200, 1202, 1223, 1228
Pohlenz, M. 663, 823, 841, 843, 847, 848
Pokorny, P. 129, 159, lxii, 1177, 1180
Polyaenus 1222
Polybius 67, 155, 156, 220, 435, 455, 473, 499, 555, 588, 744, 763, 789, 1072, 1086, 1196, 1211, 1221
Polycarp 11, 36, 37, 87, 98, 144, 325, 330, 456, 542. 687, lxiv, lxix, 981
Polycrates of Ephesus 40
Pomponius Mela 1195
Pontius Pilate 195, 224, 241, 246, 247, 382, 641
Porphyry 906
Posidippus 308
Posidonius 847
Powell, D. cviii
Praeder, S. M. xxxii, 943, 1177, 1217
Pratscher, W. 708, 723, 963
Preisker, H. 884, 1096
Prentice, W. K. 568
Prickard, A. O. 65
Prigent, P. 3, lxv
Priscilla 861
Prometheus 232
Protevangelium of James 1077
Psalms of Solomon 156, 645, 1158
Pseudo-Aristotle 848
Pseudo-Philo 341, 346, 356
Pseudo-Phocylides 914
Pseudo-Plato 907
Pseudo-Plutarch 983
Ptolemy 1192, 1202
Ptolemy VIII 446
Pummer, R. 334, 339, 395
Quasten, J. lxxi

Quesnel, M. 411, cviii
Quintilian 70, 741, 1094, 1149
Quirinius 294, 295
Qumran Sect 104, 163, 164, 167, 168, 252, 263, 271, 307, 311, 338, 447, 480, lxxxviii, xcix, cvi, 738, 793, 954
Qumran Texts
1QS   74, 88, 96, 97, 103, 104, 105, 111, 124, 162, 163, 167, 171, 172, 208, 255, 263, 311, 360, 376, 383, 415, 448, 843, 888, 954, 981, 1025, 1161
Damascus Document (CD)   85, 96, 97, 162, 255, 369, 370, 371, 378, 415, 448, 566, 659, 726, 811, 889, 975, 1060, 1244
1QM   633, 843, 1025
1QSa   96, 97, 171
1QSb   290
4QFlor   147, 245, 290, 726
4QTest   208, 209
1QpHab   376, 653, 1020
Genesis Apocryphon (1QapGen) 341, 1225
1QH   84, 144, 328, 811, 840, 843, 1160
4QPs37   147
4QExod.[4]   350

Rabbinic writings
Mishnah, Tosephta, Talmudim
[M = Mishnah; T = Tosephta; B = Talmud Babli; J = Talmud Yerushalmi]
Berakoth   M 180, 362, 483, 682; T 178, 180; B 178, 180, 202, 245, 646, 659, 810, 1223; J 85
Peah   M 223, 310, 312; T 312
Shebiith   J 734
Shabbath   M 180, 483, 486; B 111, 223, 407, 505, 736, 1025; J 211, 1188
Erubin   B 85
Pesahim   B 111, 211, 286, 486, 505, 734, 1058
Shekalim   M 284; B 810
Yoma   M 104, 285, 1188; T 179; B 179, 223, 635; J 225
Sukkah   T 564
Betzah   J 146
Rosh ha-Shanah   B 124, 223, 659
Taanith   M 193, 200; B 504; J 501
Moed Qatan   M 234, 392, 435; B 264, 616, 659
Hagigah   B 84, 407, 616; J 114, 146, 211

Yebamoth   M 424; B 564, 699, 759
Ketuboth   M 486; B 639
Nedarim   B 616, 1072
Nazir   M 1011
Sotah   M 292, 573, 628; B 292, 616
Gittin   M 616, 1086
Kiddushin   B 486
Baba Qamma   M 212; B 292
Baba Metzia   T 310; B 310
Baba Bathra   M 486; B 86, 310, 312, 520, 1138
Sanhedrin   M 96, 223, 225, 234, 386, 392, 575, 679, 785, 1065, 1072; T 1025; B 203, 223, 726, 734, 1025, 1073, 1223; J 501, 734
Makkoth   B 1060
Shebuoth   B 1059
Eduyoth   M 223, 285; T 564
Abodah Zarah   M 992; B 222, 392, 850
Aboth   M 96, 234, 346, 366, 718, 1008, 1036
Zebahim   M 300
Menahoth   T 286; B 346
Kerithoth   M 210
Tamid   M 104
Middoth   M 179, 191, 223, 286,

1020
Kelim   M 179, 1020
Oholoth   M 516
Niddah   M 424

Targumim
(Fragment) Genesis 435
(Pseudo-Jonathan) Genesis 383
(Onqelos) Genesis 474
(Yerushalmi 1) Exodus 85, Numbers 1167
(Fragment) Numbers 114
1 Samuel 636
(Jonathan) Isaiah 375
Psalms 149
Ecclesiastes 104, 1197
Esther 502
Amos 728

Midrash Rabbah
Bereshith (= Genesis) 350, 383, 501, 585
Exodus 354
Leviticus 265
Numbers 115
Midrash Psalms 145, 509
Midrash Qoheleth 501

Other writings
Mekhilta Exodus 78, 85, 529, 743, 781
Aboth de R. Nathan 431
Tanhuma 137, 501
Derek Eretz Zuta 146
Pesiqta Rabbathi 378
Pirqe R. Eliezer 1197
Rabbula 10, 11
Radermacher, L. 355, 417, 428, 455, 538, 585, 635, 674, 773, 794, 795, 802, 876, 892, 960, 975, 1110, 1137, 1141, 1192, 1200, 1207, 1211
Rahlfs, A. 537

Ramsay, W. M. lxii, 720, 767, 768, 769, 780, 782, 789, 794, 819, 855, 928, 958, 1050, 1237
Rapske, B. 777, 790, 793, 795, 801, 1063, 1200
Rashi 135
Rees, B. R. 185
Reicke, B. 54, 89, 170, 171, 281, 660, cvii, 695, 708, 738, 799, 921, 950, 1177
Rengstorf, K. H. 92, 93, 310, 649, cviii
Renié, J. 92
Rese, M. cix
Reumann, J. 89, 95
Reynolds, J. (M.) 500, cx, 1144, 1165
RGG (Die Religion in Geschichte und Gegenwart) lxxii
Richard, E. 334, cx, 695, 708
Richardson, A. 384, 404, 556, 604, 788
Riesenfeld, H. 490, 522, 943, 950
Riesner, R. 857
Rimaud, R. 240
Roberts, C. H., Skeat, T. C. and Nock, A. D. 373, 786
Robertson, A. T. 593, 832, 836, 1062
Robins, V. K. 1177
Robinson, D. F. 460, 558, 568
Robinson, J. A. T. 187, 190, 202, 204
Robinson, J. M. 542, 983
Rodgers, P. R. 129
Rohde, E. 424
Ropes, J. H. 111, 112, 1000, 1002, 1152
Rordorf, W. 943
Ross, J. M. 689, 857, 880
Rostovtzeff, M. I. 123
Roth, C. 92
Rougé, J. 1177
Rousseau, A. 15

Routh, M. J. 37, 93, 98
Rowland, C. 383
Rudolph, K. 395
Rüger, H. P. 129, 1030, 1038, 1155
Ruphus of Ephesus 377
Russell, D. S. 219
Rutherford, W. G. 556, 578, 584, 660, 682, 793, 794, 887, 958, 970, 1037, 1207
Sabbe, M. 379
Saddok 294
Sahlin, H. 708, 728, 963, 973, 986, 1018, 1019, 1120, 1129
Sallust 80
Sallustius 605
Samuel 210
Sanders, H. A. 2
Sanders, J. T. cix, cx
Sandnes, K. O. 823
Sandt, H. van de 708
Saum, F. 1248
Schaeder, H. H. 140, 1098
Schechter, S. 447
Scheidweiler, F. 261, 267
Schenke, H. M. 13
Schermann, T. 376
Schlatter, A. 101, 229, 307, 381, 467
Schlier, H. 60, 490
Schmid, L. 1144, 1158
Schmidt, A. 708
Schmiedel, P. W. 99, 615, 739, 768, 1171
Schmithals, W. cviii, 963
Schmitt, J. 622
Schnackenburg, R. 490, 689
Schneider, G. 99, cvii, 1090
Schnider, F. 277
Schoeps, H. J. 347, 732, 736
Schrenk, G. 341
Schubert, P. 129
Schürer, E. *see NS*
Schürmann, H. 598, cviii, 963
Schuler, C. 807, 814

Schulz, F. 1030, 1048
Schwartz, D. R. 61, 272, 708, 775
Schwartz, E. 1019, 1118
Schweizer, E. 92, 162, 205, 250, 296, 316, 536, 542, 559, 602, 606, 622, 646, cvii, 884, 888, 1056, 1062, 1161
Schwyzer, E. L. 283
Scobie, C. H. H. 187, 334, 339, 395
Scrivener, F. H. 404, 984
Scroggs, R. 303
Seccombe, D. 159, 303
Seesemann, H. 718, 963, 967
Segal, A. F. 490
Segal, M. H. 1028
Segbroeck, F. van lxxxi
Seifrid, M. A. cix
Seleucus I 549, 610
Selwyn, E. G. 980
Semler, J. S. lxxiii
Seneca 252, 387, 424, 841, 845, 846, 850, 983, 1229
Sententiae Pauli 1131
Sergius Paulus 262, 609, 611, 613, 614, 616, 618, lv, cxiv
Servius 425
Sevenster, J. N. 85, 324, 498, 1020, 1024, 1085, 1094
Sextus Empiricus 308
Sheeley, S. M. lxxix, lxxxi
Sherwin-White, A. N. 779, 788, 789, 790, 801, 802, 814, 815, 816, 868, 872, 873, 923, 930, 935, 937, 938, 940, 1020, 1026, 1027, 1048, 1087, 1092, 1097, 1109, 1131, 1138, 1174, 1233, 1242, 1251, 1252
Sibylline Oracles 208, 840, 1152
Silva, M. 216, 663
Simeon b. Shetah 193
Simon, M. 334, 708

Simonson, G. 1107
Simplicius 1203
Skarsaune, O. 44
Skeat, T. C. 373
Sleeper, C. F. 107
Slingerland, D. 857, 862, 871
Smalley, S. S. 107
Smallwood, E. M. 216, 382
Smith, B. D. T. 884
Smith, D. E. 857
Smith, G. A. 423, 1085
Smith, J. 1177, 1178, 1184, 1187, 1192, 1198, 1202, 1203, 1204, 1210, 1217, 1228
Smit Sibinga, J. 476
Smothers, E. R. 708
Socrates 156, 234, 237, 283, 729, 824, 827, 828, 829, 830, 831, 834
Soden, H. von 8, 18, 408, xciv
Sohm, R. xciii, xciv
Sokolowski, F. 916
Sol Invictus 407
Solon 102
Sophocles 151, 191, 196, 227, 237, 248, 326, 392, 414, 452, 456, 484, 592, 617, 638, xlvii, 733, 833, 836, 847, 854, 924, 1042, 1056, 1104, 1115, 1156, 1160, 1183, 1194, 1207, 1223
Souter, A. 32
Sparks, H. F. D. 10, xlvi, xlviii, lxii
Sperber, D. 303
Spicq, C. 339, 545
Squires, J. T. 974
Staats, R. 943, 950
Stählin, G. 765, 1183
Stanley, D. M. 438
Stanton, G. N. 303, 318, 334, 379
Stauffer, E. 155, 174, 180, 228, 291, 384, 646, 681, 687, 783, 1059, 1105, 1161

Steck, O. H. 438, 1030
Stegemann, W. lxii, 775, 1030, 1051, 1070, 1144
Stegmüller, F. lxx, lxxxi
Stempvoort, P. A. van 61, 81, 82
Stendahl, K. 107, 263, 307, 317, 410, 442
Stenger, W. 107
Stenning, J. F. 375
Stern, M. 1090
Steuernagel, G. 438
Steyn, G. J. 1245
Stobaeus 270, 445, 1238
Stoops, R. F. 916, 940
Stowers, K. 963
Strabo 122, 123, 252, 322, 402, 423, 425, 549, 793, 923, 988, 1026, 1068, 1213, 1221
Strack, H. L. 264
Strange, W. A. xxiii, 884, 894, 901, 916
Strathmann, H. 604, 1053, 1057
Strecker, G. 336, 558, 560, 601, 603
Streeter, B. H. 3, 295, xxiii
Strobel, A. 61, 303, 558, 568, 577, 580, 582, 708, 963, 964
Strom, M. R. 568
Stroumsa, G. G. 1053
Stuehrenberg, P. F. lxx, lxxi, lxxxi
Suetonius 323, 556, 557, 564, 589, 591, 861, 862, 913, 914, 953, 958, 1048, 1080, 1118, 1135, 1148, 1185, 1187
Suggs, M. J. 807
Suhl, A. lxii, 1177, 1217
Sukenik, E. L. 324, 327, 781, 1057
Sulla 591
Sullivan, R. D. 1090
Swete, H. B. 744
Sylva, D. D. 61, 334
Symmachus 298, 553, 565, 618, 1150

Synesius 852
Tacitus 312, 323, 436, 515, 556, 557, 564, 581, 586, 591, lxxviii, 801, 937, 988, 1080, 1081, 1113, 1117, 1135, 1137, 1148
Tajra, H. W. 779, 800, 805, 814, 862, 871, 872, 873, 960, 1020, 1026, 1048, 1051, 1087, 1127, 1131, 1136, 1232, 1233, 1252, 1253
Talbert, C. H. 558, lxxxi, cvii, cx, 695, 708, 857, 962
Tannenbaum, R. 500, cx
Tannehill, R. lxxix, cix
Tarn, W. W. 812
Taylor, B. E. 901
Taylor, J. 708, 1053, 1066
Taylor, R. O. P. 257
Tcherikover, V. 123, 324, 325, 737, 989, 1026, 1086
Terence 112, 417, 1158, 1169
Tertullian 18, 27, 47, 70, 169, 171, 178, 230, 253, 400, 405, 452, 591, 646, lxvi, lxvii, lxx, cxiii, 793, 837, 838, 953, 977, 1137
Testament of Benjamin 934
Testament of Gad 236
Testament of Job 994
Testament of Joseph 793
Testament of Judah 109, 934
Testament of Levi 910, 1167
Testament of Naphtali 1215
Testament of Reuben 351, 1167
Testament of Solomon 230
Testament of Simeon 347
Thackeray, H. St J. 120, 135, 326, 362, 364, 576,

716, 844, 970, 978, 1111
Theissen, G. lxii, lxxvii, lxxxi
Theocritus 244
Theodoret 809, 840
Theodotion 236, 325, 414, 582, 1041
Theodotus 324
Theophanes 989
Theophilus 65
Theophrastus 364, 618, 813, 835, 1115
Theudas 293, 294, 295
Thiede, C. P. 568
Thiele, W. 10, 89
Thieme, G. 927
Thiering, B. E. 159, cviii, 963, 976
Thomas, D. W. 113, 354
Thomas, Gospel of 328
Thomas, J. xci, cviii
Thomas of Harkel 12
Thornton, C.-J. xxvii, xxviii, xxx, xxxii, xliv, 767, 945
Thornton, L. S. 92
Thornton, T. C. G. 61, 334, 375
Throckmorton, B. H. 216
Thucydides 163, 197, 214, 221, 233, 238, 255, 283, 294, 314, 326, 345, 447, 465, 474, 503, 505, 548, 553, 563, 576, 580, 592, 610, 652, 672, 678, 682, 729, 730, 739, 742, 743, 779, 794, 799, 808, 820, 833, 873, 914, 935, 947, 948, 958, 983, 989, 1003, 1056, 1073, 1077, 1085, 1090, 1097, 1104, 1105, 1118, 1124, 1125, 1137, 1138, 1170, 1181, 1184, 1193, 1194, 1199, 1205, 1208, 1211, 1215, 1228
Thyen, H. 129
Tiberius 382
Tiberius Alexander 563
Tiede, D. L. 61

Tischendorf, C. 408
Tissot, Y. 708, 752
Tödt, H. E. 385
Torrey, C. C. 66, 67, 72, 75, 101, 120, 131, 140, 148, 150, 172, 196, 198, 199, 211, 233, 244, 274, 275, 377, 508, 517, 522, 523, 563, 691, 740
Trajan 527
Trebilco, P. R. 762, 775, 782, 786, 812, 903, 923, 959, 988, 1026, 1186
Trites, A. A. 280, 1018, 1053
Trocmé, É. 55, 80, lxii
Troeltsch, E. 168
Trompf, G. 1177, 1217, 1235, 1248
Trygaeus 184
Trypho 43
Turner, C. H. 708, 803, 1090
Turner, N. 220, 266, 408, 754, 791, 792, 898, 910, 976, 1035, 1116, 1150, 1151, 1156
TWAT (Theologisches Wörterbuch zum Alten Testament 844
TWNT (Theologisches Wörterbuch zum Neuen Testament) 162, 182, 430, 604, 785, 962, 963, 967, 975, 1053, 1057, 1106, 1114, 1148, 1177
Tyson, J. B. 490, lxxix, lxxx, lxxxi, cvii, cix, cx
Ullendorf, E. 420
Ulpian 1113, 1131
Unnik, W. C. van 61, 80, 147, 233, 395, 420, 490, 608, xxxv, xlviii, li, lxii, lxix, 775, 790, 1031, 1034, 1035, 1090
Valentinus 46, lxvi
Vanhoye, A. cix
Vaux, R. de 375
Vazakis, A. A. 173
Vegetius 577, 1188

Veitch, W. 227
Vergil 114, 247, 249, 432, 483, 581, 848, 875, 1104, 1192, 1203, 1204, 1213, 1214
Vermes, G. 120, 193, 370, 383; *see also* NS
Vespasian 244, 740
Vettenus 324
Vettius Valens 171, 378, 635, 660, 793, 906
Victor of Rome 40
Vielhauer, P. 132, 321, 650, 651, lxxxvii, cvii
Vincent, L. H. 1018
Vitellius 224
Viviano, B. T. 1053, 1066
Vögeli, A. 280, 568, 775, 1144, 1158
Vögtle, A. 61, 663, 689
Völkel, M. 490
Vööbus, A. 11, 159
Vos, C. S. de 775
Voss, G. cvii
Wainwright, A. W. 460, 752
Waitz, H. 395, 420
Walaskay, P. W. l, lxii
Walker, N. 303
Walker, W. O. 61, 752, 1222
Warnecke, H. 1217, 1219, 1220, 1221, 1225
Weber, R. 10
Wedderburn, A. J. M. cix, 708
Wehnert, J. 1177, 1217
Weigandt, P. 14, xxiii, 775
Weinstock, S. 107
Weiser, A. 490, 708, 775
Weiss, B. 895
Weiss, K. 557
Wendt, H. H. 1056
Wensinck, A. J. 114, 435
Westcott, B. F. 20, 21, 32
Wetter, G. P. 438
Wexler, P. 901, 905
White, H. J. 10
Wiefel, W. 1235

Wikenhauser, A. 81, 438, 490, 703
Wikgren, A. 7
Wilcken, U. 867
Wilckens, U. 129, 133, 141, 152, 187, 207, 216, 280, 438, 490, 521, 523, 622, 637, 641, cvii
Wilcox, M. 25, 92, 97, 280, 490, 491, 501, 654, 659, 669, xx, xxiii, cx, 775, 783
Wilken, R. L. 549
Wilkens, W. 395
Wills, L. M. cix
Wilson, R. McL. 395
Wilson, S. G. 61, 69, 70, 75, 81, 84, 85, 136, 139, 202, 213, 329, 383, 385, 391, 444, 491, 515, 524, 535, 537, 547, 601, 650, 657, 665, 667, lxxxiii, cvii, cx, 700, 703, 724, 726, 734, 735, 738, 740, 742, 745, 763, 825, 866, 868, 964, 966, 979, 1014, 1015, 1056, 1157, 1237, 1249, 1252
Windisch, H. 438
Winer, G. B. 99, 503
Wingren, G. 439
Winter, B. 923, 1090
Winter, P. 280, 708, 1090, 1098
Wiseman, J. 857, 860
Witherington, B. xxiii

Witherup, R. D. 1031, 1144
WM (Winer, G. B. and Moulton, W. F.) 503, 813, 1245
Wolter, M. 884
Wood, H. G. 439
Woodhouse, W. J. 1177, 1192
Wordsworth, J. 10
Workman, W. P. 1177, 1188
WS (Winer, G. B. and Schmiedel, P. W.) 99, 813, 958, 1204, 1245
WW (Wordsworth, J., White, H. J., Sparks, H. F. D. and Adams, A. W.) 9, 10, 89, 595, 853, 864, 936; *see also* White; Wordsworth.
Wycherley, R. E. 191, 824, 827, 828, 837
Xenophon 67, 98, 140, 156, 183, 195, 233, 265, 278, 297, 317, 327, 355, 368, 428, 435, 449, 451, 454, 457, 524, 530, 581, 582, 584, 589, 648, 660, 670, 671, 687, 705, 717, 755, 813, 828, 830, 835, 907, 913, 925, 927, 931, 955, 968, 978, 1002, 1005, 1027, 1073, 1105, 1106, 1116, 1119, 1130, 1137, 1167, 1168,

1170, 1172, 1183, 1189, 1192, 1196, 1202, 1206, 1222
Xenophon of Ephesus 538, 927, 990, 991
Yaure, L. 615
Young, C. M. 81
Young, F. M. 334, cviii, 963
Zahn, T. 15, 22, 23, 24, 28, 583, 906, 1221
Zeller, D. 491
Zeno 925
Zerwick, M. 703, 739, 754, 762, 769, 771, 809, 817, 834, 836, 842, 870, 874, 891, 892, 896, 898, 969, 988, 990, 995, 996, 1003, 1021, 1038, 1042, 1043, 1063, 1073, 1085, 1103, 1106, 1107, 1110, 1135, 1137, 1139, 1141, 1149, 1154, 1155, 1160, 1163, 1170, 1191, 1192, 1210, 1214, 1215, 1230, 1245
Zeus 676, 677, 678, 679
Ziesler, J. A. cvii, 1053
Zimmermann, H. 273, 303
Zonaras 813
Zuckschwerdt, E. 568, 709
Zuntz, G. 709, 735, 943, 953
Zwaan, J. de 172
Zweck, D. 824